EASTERN CHRISTIANITY

This volume brings together in one compass the Orthodox churches of the ecumenical patriarchate – the Russian, Armenian, Ethiopian, Egyptian and Syrian churches. It follows their fortunes from the late Middle Ages until modern times – exactly the period when their history has been most neglected. Inevitably, this emphasises differences in teachings and experience, but it also brings out common threads, most notably the resilience displayed in the face of alien and often hostile political regimes. The central theme of this volume is the survival against the odds of Orthodoxy in its many forms into the modern era. The last phase of Byzantium proves to have been surprisingly important in this survival. It provided Orthodoxy with the intellectual, artistic and spiritual reserves to meet later challenges. The continuing vitality of the Orthodox churches is evident for example in the Sunday School Movement in Egypt and the Zoë brotherhood in Greece.

MICHAEL ANGOLD is a Fellow of the Royal Historical Society and is Professor Emeritus of Byzantine History at the University of Edinburgh. His most recent publications include *The Fourth Crusade: Event and Context* (2003), *Byzantium: The Bridge from Antiquity to the Middle Ages* (2001) and *Church and Society in Byzantium under the Comneni, 1081–1261* (1995).

CHRISTIANITY

The *Cambridge History of Christianity* offers a comprehensive chronological account of the development of Christianity in all its aspects – theological, intellectual, social, political, regional, global – from its beginnings to the present day. Each volume makes a substantial contribution in its own right to the scholarship of its period and the complete *History* constitutes a major work of academic reference. Far from being merely a history of Western European Christianity and its offshoots, the *History* aims to provide a global perspective. Eastern and Coptic Christianity are given full consideration from the early period onwards, and later, African, Far Eastern, New World, South Asian and other non-European developments in Christianity receive proper coverage. The volumes cover popular piety and non-formal expressions of Christian faith and treat the sociology of Christian formation, worship and devotion in a broad cultural context. The question of relations between Christianity and other major faiths is also kept in sight throughout. The *History* will provide an invaluable resource for scholars and students alike.

List of volumes:

Origins to Constantine
EDITED BY MARGARET M. MITCHELL AND
FRANCES M. YOUNG

Constantine to c. 600
EDITED BY AUGUSTINE CASIDAY AND FRED NORRIS

Early Medieval Christianity c. 600–c. 1100
EDITED BY THOMAS NOBLE AND JULIA SMITH

Christianity in Western Europe c. 1100–c. 1500
EDITED BY MIRI RUBIN AND WALTER SIMON

Eastern Christianity
EDITED BY MICHAEL ANGOLD

THE CAMBRIDGE
HISTORY OF
CHRISTIANITY

★

VOLUME 5
Eastern Christianity

★

Edited by
MICHAEL ANGOLD

CAMBRIDGE
UNIVERSITY PRESS

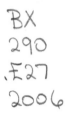

BX
290
.E27
2006

CAMBRIDGE UNIVERSITY PRESS
Cambridge, New York, Melbourne, Madrid, Cape Town, Singapore, São Paulo

Cambridge University Press
The Edinburgh Building, Cambridge CB2 2RU, UK

Published in the United States of America by Cambridge University Press, New York

www.cambridge.org
Information on this title: www.cambridge.org/9780521811132

© Cambridge University Press 2006

First published 2006

Printed in the United Kingdom at the University Press, Cambridge

A catalogue record for this publication is available from the British Library

ISBN-13 978-0-521-81113-2 hardback
ISBN-10 0-521-81113-9 hardback

In Memory of Steven Runciman,
Dimitri Obolensky and Sergei Hackel

Contents

Contents

PART IV

THE MODERN WORLD

Illustrations

Maps

Contributors

MICHAEL ANGOLD is Professor Emeritus of Byzantine History, University of Edinburgh. Among his publications is *Church and society in Byzantium under the Comneni (1081–1261)* (1995).

REVD JOHN BINNS is Vicar of Great St Mary's, Cambridge. Among his publications is *An introduction to the Christian Orthodox churches* (2002).

CANON MICHAEL BOURDEAUX is Founder and President of Keston Institute, Oxford. Among his many publications are *Opium of the people: the Christian religion in the USSR* (1965) and *Gorbachev, Glasnost and the Gospel* (1990).

CHRIS CHULOS is Director of Foundation Relations and Adjunct Professor of History at Roosevelt University, Chicago. He is also a permanent member of the History Faculty at Helsinki University. Among his publications is *Converging worlds: religion and community in peasant Russia, 1861–1917* (2003).

S. PETER COWE holds the Narekatsi Chair of Armenian Studies at UCLA. Among his publications are *Mxit'ar Sasnec'i's theological discourses* (1993); *Catalogue of the Armenian manuscripts in the Cambridge University Library* (1994). He is the editor of *Ani: world architectural heritage of a medieval Armenian capital* (2001).

DONALD CRUMMEY is Professor of African History, University of Illinois at Urbana-Champaign. Among his publications are *Land and society in the Christian Kingdom of Ethiopia from the 13th to the 20th century* (2000) and *African savanna environments: global narratives and local knowledge of environmental change* (with T. J. Bassett, 2003).

ROBERT O. CRUMMEY is Emeritus Professor of Russian History, University of California, Davis. Among his publications are *The Old Believers & the world of Antichrist: the Vyg Community and the Russian state, 1694–1855* (1970) and *Aristocrats and servitors: the Boyar elite in Russia, 1613–1689* (1983).

SIMON DIXON is Professor of Modern History at the University of Leeds. Among his publications are *The modernisation of Russia 1676–1825* (1999) and *Catherine the Great* (2001).

SHARON E. J. GERSTEL is Associate Professor of Byzantine Art and Archaeology, UCLA. Among her publications is *Beholding the sacred mysteries: programs of the Byzantine sanctuary* (1999).

ALEXANDER GRISHIN is Head of Art History, Australian National University. In 2004 he was elected Fellow of the Australian Academy of the Humanities. Among his publications are his two-volume *The art of John Brack* (1990) and *A pilgrim's account of Cyprus: Bars'kyj's travels in Cyprus* (1996).

†ARCHPRIEST SERGEI HACKEL died on 9 February 2005. He combined the work of a parish priest with teaching Russian at the University of Sussex and was a well-known broadcaster. For thirty years he was editor of *Sobornost*, the journal of the Anglican-Orthodox Fellowship of St Sergius. He was the author of *A pearl of great price: the life of Mother Maria Skobstova, 1891–1945* (revised edition 1982).

LINDSEY HUGHES is Professor of Russian History at the School of Slavonic and East European Studies, University of London. Among her publications is *Russia in the age of Peter the Great* (1998).

PASCHALIS M. KITROMILIDES is Professor of Political Science at the University of Athens and Director of the Institute of Neohellenic Research at the National Hellenic Research Foundation. Among his publications are *The Enlightenment as social criticism: Iosipos Moisiodax and Greek culture in the eighteenth century* (1992) and *Enlightenment, nationalism, orthodoxy: studies in the culture and political thought of south-eastern Europe* (1994).

DIRK KRAUSMÜLLER is a Research Fellow at Dumbarton Oaks Research Library and Collection and an Honorary Fellow of Queen's University Belfast. Among his publications is 'Conflicting anthropologies in the Christological discourse at the end of Late Antiquity: the case of Leontius of Jerusalem's Nestorian adversary', *Journal of Theological Studies* 56 (2005).

FRANÇOISE MICHEAU is Professor of Medieval Islamic history at Université Paris I – Panthéon-Sorbonne and director of CNRS (UMR8167): Islam médiéval-éspaces, réseaux et pratiques culturelles. She is the co-translator of the important Christian Arab chronicles of Yahya ibn Sa'id of Antioch and of al-Makin ibn al-'Amid. She has published widely on Arabic medicine and is co-author of *Communautés chrétiennes en pays d'Islam* (1997).

ANTHONY O'MAHONY is Director of Research at the Centre for Christianity and Inter-religious Dialogue, Heythrop College, University of London. Among his publications is *Palestinian Christians: religion, politics and society in the Holy Land* (1999). He is the editor of *Eastern Christianity: studies in modern history, religion and politics* (2004).

ALEXANDRU POPESCU is Research Fellow of Balliol College, Oxford. He is the author of *Petre Ţuţea: between sacrifice and suicide* (2004).

STELLA ROCK was a research fellow at the University of Sussex. She is the co-editor of *Nationalist myths and modern media: contested identities in the age of globalization* (2006). Her *Popular religion in Russia: 'double belief' and the making of an academic myth* will shortly appear.

NANCY ŠEVČENKO is a Vice President of the Association internationale des études byzantines and Associate Editor of the *Oxford Dictionary of Byzantium*. Among her publications are *The life of Saint Nicholas in Byzantine art* (1983) and *Illustrated manuscripts of the Metaphrastian menologion* (1990).

JONATHAN SHEPARD is a former Fellow of Peterhouse, University of Cambridge, and University Lecturer in Russian History. He is the author with Simon Franklin of *The emergence of Rus 750–1200* (1996) and is the editor of the *Cambridge History of Byzantium*.

ALICE-MARY TALBOT is Director of Byzantine Studies, Dumbarton Oaks Research Library and Collection and Executive Editor of the *Oxford dictionary of Byzantium*. She edited *The correspondence of Athanasius I Patriarch of Constantinople* (1975) and is the author of *Faith healing in late Byzantium* (1983) and *Women and religious life in Byzantium* (2001).

ELIZABETH A. ZACHARIADOU is a Fellow of the Institute for Mediterranean Studies, University of Crete. Among her publications are *Trade and crusade: Venetian Crete and the Emirates of Menteshe and Aydin (1300–1415)* (1983) and *Romania and the Turks (c.1300–c.1500)* (1985).

Foreword

by The Archbishop of Canterbury

The average educated westerner is still quite likely to think of Christianity in terms of a basically western Europe-dominated history: the church gradually builds up a centralised system of authority, filling the vacuum left by the fall of the Roman Empire; its ideological monopoly is challenged at the Reformation, and the map of the Christian world is reconfigured; and all the various territories on that map are now engaged in a doubtfully successful struggle with global modernity, except where the newer churches of Africa are mounting a vigorous counter-offensive. Even in some good and sophisticated surveys of world Christianity published in recent years, this remains the dominant picture.

But Christianity is more various than this begins to suggest. The essays in this volume introduce us to a variety of contexts substantially different from what has just been described. The faith of the Byzantine world had nothing to do with the filling of a political gap; the Roman Empire continued, with an educational system and a lay civil service which did not yield to the clergy the kind of cultural closed shop familiar in the mediaeval west. What is intriguing in this particular story is the spread of Byzantine Christianity not as a tool of 'empire' in the crude sense but as the carrier and the ally of a much more subtle process of cultural convergence – the 'Byzantine Commonwealth' over whose character a good deal of controversy continues. The Byzantine Christian heartland continued, even when Byzantium was in steep political decline, to nourish kindred but diverse cultural and intellectual projects, of which Muscovite Russia is probably the most influential (and in many ways the most eccentric). It is a record which does not easily fit into most of the 'faith and culture' typologies familiar in western theological and historical writing.

The 'commonwealth' of Byzantine Christianity was not only about material culture, political rhetoric and artistic style. It was also a commonwealth of spiritual practice – the liturgy, but also, no less importantly, the monastic life. 'Hesychasm', the practice of silent prayer free of ideas and images and grounded in a set of physical disciplines, became, from the fourteenth century to the present day, as clear a sign of the convergent Christian culture of eastern Europe as anything. How far it represented the resurgence and refocusing of a classical spiritual practice and how far it was innovatory and indeed in some ways subversive of such a tradition is a matter of keen debate, and the evidence of this debate can be traced in the pages that follow. In the twentieth century, the hesychast tradition, in ways that might surprise those who know it only through versions of the medieval disputes, has been one of the engines driving intellectual renewal and fresh cultural engagement in historically Orthodox societies like Romania, Greece and Russia.

But the Byzantine world is only part of the story. For most of their history, nearly all those churches that broke with Byzantium for doctrinal reasons or that had always been outside the political reach of the Empire lived as minorities in a Muslim society. It was not always a nakedly hostile environment, but it brought severe pressures to bear in all kinds of ways. Not least, it meant a continuing tradition of intellectual life conducted in the medium of non-European languages; only relatively recently has the world of Christian Arabic begun to receive the attention it merits. And the importance of these Christian communities in mediating classical Europe to the nascent Islamic culture is hard to exaggerate. No 'clash of civilisations' model will do justice to the complex interactions of all these universes of thought. A history of relative isolation and public marginality should not blind us to the substantive role of Christian minorities beyond the Roman and classical frontiers. And the same needs to be said about those churches like the Armenian and Ethiopian that did not live consistently as minorities in a non-Christian environment but experienced something of the same challenge in thinking and expressing their faith in the languages of cultures outside the 'classical' world. Looking at their history helps us make some better sense of the phenomena of marginal Christianities in the west, especially in the Celtic context.

Nor should we be lured into thinking that the schisms of the fifth to the eleventh centuries created hermetically sealed units of Christian discourse. Armenians, Byzantines and Latins participated in the same arguments in the Byzantine court; nearly all the churches of the east at one time or another faced difficult decisions about how far to go in rapprochement with Rome; the choices they made continue to affect relations between the modern churches in acute ways. Whether in the Council of Florence or in the embassy sent from Mongol Iran by Mar Yabh'allaha III to the courts of the west in the thirteenth century, there was always an uncomfortable sense of unfinished business about how to relate with those on the other side of doctrinal and political divisions. Modern ecumenism has roots in a large number of missions and negotiations in the past, and these essays will show something of the variety in that history.

In modern times, eastern Christianity has suffered once again from being the victim of an imposed minority status in many countries; the trauma of communist domination and persecution has indelibly marked the churches of eastern Europe. But at the same time, many of the most creative theological elements in contemporary western theology can trace their origins to eastern sources, thanks partly, though not exclusively, to the Russian diaspora. For both Roman Catholic and Reformed thinkers, the eastern world has opened new pathways which relativise, even if they do not always solve, the historic standoffs between diverse western concerns, and offer a different and often more flexible vocabulary. Throughout the eastern Christian world today, Byzantine and non-Byzantine, there is an upsurge of new thinking, new artistic energy (think of the extraordinary development in the last few decades of Coptic iconography), and *ressourcement* in the monastic life. The final chapter in this volume gives a clear picture of the vitality and the wide impact of this renewal. Despite the unhappy and often violent symbiosis in some contexts between Christian rhetoric and uncritical nationalism, despite the fresh difficulties of Christian minorities that have developed as a result of contemporary geopolitics and a high level of tone-deafness in the west to the needs of these minorities, there is plenty of vigour and sophistication. If it is a cardinal temptation of our time to indulge in crass and destructive stereotyping of both Christian and Muslim worlds, forgetting the variety and wealth of their histories, this book, written out of the most painstaking contemporary scholarship, will be an indispensable aid in resisting that temptation. It is an academic tour de force; but far more than a simple academic exercise.

Rowan Williams, Archbishop of Canterbury

Abbreviations

AA	Archives de l'Athos
AAE	*Akty, sobrannye v bibliotekakh i arkhivakh rossiiskoi imperii arkheograficheskoiu ekspeditsieiu imperatorskoi Akademii nauk*
AI	*Akty istoricheskie, sobrannye i izdannye arkheograficheskoiu komissieiu*
B	*Byzantion*
BF	*Byzantinische Forschungen*
BMGS	*Byzantine and Modern Greek Studies*
Bsl	*Byzantinoslavica*
BZ	*Byzantinische Zeitschrift*
CA	*Cahiers Archéologiques*
CFHB	Corpus fontium historiae byzantinae
ChOIDR	*Chteniia v Obshchestve istorii i drevnostei rossiiskikh pri Moskovskom universitete* (Moscow, 1845–1918)
CNRS	Centre national de la recherche scientifique
CSCO	Corpus scriptorum christianorum orientalium
CSHB	Corpus scriptorum historiae byzantinae
DOP	*Dumbarton Oaks Papers*
DOS	Dumbarton Oaks Studies
DOT	Dumbarton Oaks Texts
DTC	*Dictionnaire de théologie catholique*
JEcclH	*Journal of Ecclesiastical History*
JThSt	*Journal of Theological Studies*
Miklosich and Müller	Miklosich, F. and Müller, J., *Acta patriarchatus constantinopolitani*, 2 vols. (Vienna: Carolus Gerold, 1860–62)
ÖAW	Österreichische Akademie der Wissenschaften
OCA	Orientalia christiana analecta
OCP	*Orientalia Christiana Periodica*
ODB	*Oxford dictionary of Byzantium*, ed. A. P. Kazhdan et al., 3 vols. (Oxford and New York: Oxford University Press, 1991)
PG	Migne, P. G., *Patrologiae cursus completus, Series graeca*
PLDR	*Pamiatniki literatury Drevnei Rusi XIV–seredina XV veka*

PLP	*Prosopographisches Lexikon der Palaiologenzeit*, 13 fasc. (Vienna: ÖAW, 1976–96)
PO	Patrologia orientalis
PSRL	*Polnoe sobranie russkikh letopisei*
PSZRI	*Polnoe sobranie zakonov rossiiskoi imperii*
PVL	*Povest' Vremennykh Let*, ed. V. P. Adrianova-Peretts and D. S. Likhachev, 2nd edn rev. M. B. Sverdlov (St Petersburg: Nauka, 1996)
REB	*Revue des Études Byzantines*
Reg.	*Les regestes des actes du patriarcat de Constantinople*, ed. V. Grumel, V. Laurent and J. Darrouzès, 7 vols. (Paris: Institut français d'études byzantines, 1932–91)
Rhalles and Potles	Rhalles, G. A. and Potles, M., Σύνταγμα τῶν θείων καὶ ἱερῶν κανόνων 6 vols. (Athens, 1852–59)
RIB	*Russkaia Istoricheskaia Biblioteka* (St Petersburg: Imperatorskaia arkheograficheskaia kommissiia, 1880), vi
RPK	*Das Register des Patriarchats von Konstantinopel*
RR	*Russian Review*
Sp	*Speculum*
Thomas and Hero	Thomas, J. and Hero, Angela, *Byzantine monastic foundation documents*, 5 vols. (Washington, DC: Dumbarton Oaks Research Library and Collection, 2000)
TM	*Travaux et Mémoires*

PART I

*

THE ECUMENICAL PATRIARCHATE

The Byzantine Commonwealth
1000–1550

JONATHAN SHEPARD

Introduction

That the rites and remains of the east Roman Empire made an impression on most of the peoples surrounding or settled among them is hardly surprising. Constantinople was purpose-built, a landmark not even the mightiest 'barbarian' warlord could hope to efface. With its numerous market places, massive walls and monuments such as the Golden Gate proclaiming a New Jerusalem and Christian triumph, the 'God-protected city' was a showcase for displays of wealth, social cohesion and military force. These material blessings were attributed by the palace ceremonies, art and orators to the piety of the emperors and their subjects – often termed simply 'the Christians' in the ceremonial acclamations – and to the empire's central role in God's plan for mankind. Constantinople itself was under the special protection of the Mother of God. In the medieval era Mary was venerated ever more dramatically in return for safeguarding her city, wonder-working icons such as the Hodegetria being paraded regularly through the streets in her honour.

Even furthest-flung outsiders could make the connection between Byzantine prosperity, striking-power and religious devotions. From his Orkney vantage point, Arnor the Earl's Poet viewed God as 'ready patron of the Greeks and Garð-folk'.[1] These 'Garð-folk' – Rus – had collectively come under the care of the patriarch of Constantinople, when in or around 988 their ruler, Vladimir, received a Byzantine religious mission and was himself baptised. A prime reason for Vladimir's choice of the Orthodox form of Christianity was probably the divine 'patronage' – in terms of material wealth and social order – which their religion seemed to have secured. Vladimir flagged his personal associations with the senior emperor, by adopting his Christian name, Basil, and by marrying his sister, Anna. By around 1000 the ruling houses of several

---

1 *Þorfinnz-drápa*, in *Corpus poeticum boreale*, ed. and trans. G. Vigfusson and F. York Powell, II (Oxford: Clarendon Press, 1883), 197.

Map 1 The Byzantine Commonwealth

other northern neighbours of Byzantium, such as the Alans, had been baptised
by its priests. They were following a pattern already created in the mid-ninth
century with the conversion of the Bulgarians. The credit for these conversions
was claimed first and foremost for the emperor and in official correspondence
rulers whose forebears had been baptised at Byzantine hands were termed
'spiritual child' of the emperor. In the mid-tenth century, Bulgarian, Alan and –
more tendentiously – Armenian leaders were being addressed in this way.[2]

2 Constantine Porphyrogenitus, *De cerimoniis aulae byzantinae*, ed. I. I. Reiske (Bonn: Ed.
  Weber, 1829), II.48: I, 687–8, 690.

The enamel plaques most probably sent by Michael VII Doukas (1071–78) to the Hungarian ruler Géza make a clear visual statement of the Byzantine version of the correct order of things: Michael and his son are portrayed with nimbuses round their heads; Géza's garb is plainer and he lacks a nimbus. But he wears a crown of sorts, and the object which the plaques adorned was probably itself a crown, perhaps designed for Géza's noble Byzantine-born bride and sent to her in the mid-1070s. Bride, crown and enamelled portraits jointly declared Géza's place among established leaders, and the Greek inscription beside Géza calls him king (κράλης).[3] Such marks of imperial favour also suggested the patronage, which Géza might now be able to dispense to deserving magnates of his own.

These enamels offer a snapshot of Byzantine diplomacy at work. It seems that enamels were only used on crowns designed for external potentates, standing reminders of the superlative craftsmanship of the Byzantines. Yet the fate of Michael Doukas's gift to Géza demonstrates the diversity of uses to which potentates put their associations with the *basileus*: before long, the enamels were forming the lower part of what became known as 'the crown of St Stephen'. What had been intended by Michael as a demonstration of hegemony ended up as the quintessential symbol of an autonomous Hungarian realm. For many potentates, receipt of titles, gifts and emblems from the emperor was compatible with aspirations to control their own dominions; more confident regimes would adapt, if not mimic, symbols, which the *basileus* considered his sole prerogative. Through acts of appropriation and overt references to the imperial court, such potentates were primarily concerned to consolidate their rule over heterogeneous, often inchoate populations. Such unmistakable marks of authority could help transcend local differences and rivalries, providing a visual vocabulary of power that all subjects could understand.

Like Géza, most early medieval potentates sought to demonstrate their right to the throne, whether it was inherited, usurped or still being fashioned. They sought respect, if not obedience, from their kinsmen and other figures of substance in the region, and from those living within their nominal dominions and beyond. The bestowing of offices and concomitant determination of status tended to be viewed as a measure of a ruler's authority. Here, too, Byzantium had much to offer. The notion of the emperor as God's viceroy on earth and

---

3 The doubts of J. Deér as to whether the plaques originally decorated a crown, rather than some other diplomatic gift, are well put, but do not rule out the a priori likelihood that a crown was the enamels' original holder: J. Deér, *Die heilige Krone Ungarns* (ÖAW: Philosoph.-hist. Klasse, Denkschriften 91) (Vienna: Böhlau, 1966), 72–80.

answerable to Him alone flourished, for all the efforts of Byzantine churchmen and monks to qualify it by means of canon law, ritual and denunciations. A commanding role in religious affairs as well as earthly ones appealed to many external potentates, especially those impatient with their senior churchmen. Byzantium offered a working model, dignified yet also efficient, to would-be monarchs without close cultural affinities or traditions of allegiance towards the empire. Some drew unilaterally on Byzantium's stock of visual symbols, seeking neither their bestowal from the emperor nor to efface the old imperial centre. They aimed, rather, at overawing and outshining powerful interest groups in their own realm through borrowed ways of presenting their rule as God-given. For example, Queen Tamara of Georgia reshuffled motifs of Byzantine imagery of monarchy to bolster her unprecedented position as a woman ruling in her own right. Byzantine-derived imagery had long been the means of expressing Georgian kingly power. Tamara modified it in various ways to represent her piety and legitimacy in church portraits of herself, while also highlighting specifically Georgian themes and figures worthy of veneration.[4]

Dimitri Obolensky believed that such borrowings from Byzantium's political culture, religious rites and visual media formed a pattern. In his magisterial work *The Byzantine Commonwealth*, he envisaged constellations of potentates and their subjects acknowledging imperial hegemony – whole societies as well as elites. They were, he maintained, joined together in Orthodox faith, in regard for the laws, which church and emperor jointly upheld, and in respect for the emperor. The centre of their Christian universe was Constantinople, for most of these units had initially received Byzantine missions and came under the patriarch's authority. Obolensky postulated that these peripheral rulers usually accepted the emperor's overlordship of all Orthodox Christians as much from pragmatic desire to unify their own realms as from idealistic devotion to the *basileus*.[5]

Obolensky recognised that motives were mixed: self-interest could impel Orthodox rulers into hostilities against the emperor, and the commonwealth's composition varied over time. He regarded the adherence to Byzantine normative values of most of eastern Europe's Slavonic-speaking regimes at one

---

4 A. Eastmond, *Royal imagery in medieval Georgia* (University Park: Pennsylvania State University Press, 1998), 39, 94, 149–53, 119–23, 181–4; Eastmond, '"Local" saints, art, and regional identity in the Orthodox world after the fourth crusade', *Sp* 78 (2003), 717–24.
5 D. Obolensky, *The Byzantine Commonwealth: eastern Europe 500–1453* (London: Weidenfeld and Nicolson, 1971), 2–3, 203, 206–8, 272–7, 289–90; Obolensky, 'Nationalism in eastern Europe in the middle ages', *Transactions of the Royal Historical Society*, ser. v, 22 (1972), 11–12.

time or another as amounting to membership of an institution, for all their mutability and multiple cultural affinities. Obolensky's theory incurred criticism from some reviewers, who highlighted the difference in circumstances between polities located on the edge of the territorial empire and others further afield. They also questioned why cognate cultures in southern Italy and Caucasia did not qualify for consideration and suggested that the commonwealth was no more than a culturo-religious sphere, lacking any institutional basis or political connotations.[6] In the case of Rus, avowals of allegiance to the tsar, or awareness of Byzantium's claim to be Rome's heir, are singularly sparse.[7] The texts ultimately of Greek origin circulating in pre-Mongol Rus were mostly of religious content, and many had been translated or refashioned among the South Slavs. Several had been translated in the early tenth century at the Bulgarian court, with the aim of furnishing its rulers with guidelines for Orthodox Christian governance. In the process they helped to create a kind of textual community for Slavonic-readers.[8] One might conclude from the study of such texts alone that the Byzantine imperial order provided these rulers with little more than an assembly kit, from which to take what they pleased and set up structures to suit their own preconceptions.

Yet for all the local variations between societies owing their Christianity mainly to Byzantium, certain themes and motifs in their political culture recur. Leaders aspiring to create their own nodes of material patronage, sacral largesse and orderly governance took as a model the offices and honours which Byzantine emperors could confer and retract. This is clearest with thirteenth- and fourteenth-century Bulgarian rulers: most of the names of their senior officials and dignities were translations, or slavicised forms, of Byzantine ones. Serbian leaders, too, borrowed heavily from Byzantine terminology to create court hierarchy. Offices bestowed in sacral settings and determining rank

---

6 A. Kazhdan in *Vizantiiskii Vremennik* 35 (1973), 261–2; G. G. Litavrin in *Voprosy Istorii* no. 5 (1972), 180–5; R. Browning in *English Historical Review* 87 (1972), 812–15.

7 S. Franklin, 'The empire of the *Rhomaioi* as viewed from Kievan Russia: aspects of Byzantino-Russian cultural relations', *B* 53 (1983), 507–37.

8 The issue of which texts were translated by whom, and when, is highly controversial: see F. J. Thomson, 'The Bulgarian contribution of the reception of Byzantine culture in Kievan Rus': the myths and the enigma', *Harvard Ukrainian Studies* 12–13 (1988–89), 239–43; A. A. Turilov and B. N. Floria, 'Khristianskaia literatura u slavian v seredine X-seredine XI v. i mezhslavianskie kul'turnye sviazi', in *Khristianstvo v stranakh vostochnoi, iugo-vostochnoi i tsentral'noi Evropy na poroge vtorogo tysiacheletiia*, ed. B. N. Floria (Moscow: Jazyki slavianskoi kul'tury, 2002), 431–3; S. Franklin, *Writing, society and culture in early Rus, c. 950–1300* (Cambridge: Cambridge University Press, 2002), 101–3, 136–45; A. Nikolov, 'Tsariat bogopodrazhatel. Edin prenebregnat aspekt ot politicheskata kontseptsiia na Simeon I', *Annuaire de l'Université de Sofia 'St Kliment Ohridski'. Centre de Recherches Slavo-Byzantines 'Ivan Dujčev'* 91.10 (2002), 113–17.

appealed to dispenser and recipient alike and texts of Byzantine ceremonies for conferring on individuals such titles as *patrikios* were translated into Slavic. Judging by the quantity of manuscripts found, they seem to have formed the basis for South Slav court practice. There was local adaptation, however: *kouropalates* and *patrikios* were rendered by the more general *kniaz* ('prince' or 'notable').[9] Such allusions to the palace on the Bosporus did not occur in an intellectual vacuum. Stefan Dušan's law-code of 1349 drew heavily on the treatise synthesising secular and church law that Matthew Blastares had composed in Thessalonike some years earlier. Dušan's law-code also adapted novels of fairly recent *basileis*, such as Manuel I Komnenos, as well as *The Farmer's Law* in shortened form. The 'charter' accompanying his code avowed his 'desire to enact certain virtues and truest laws of the Orthodox faith to be adhered to', thus subsuming civil regulation within faith. This scheme of imperial order was supposed to apply to Dušan's Slav and more or less recently acquired Greek subjects alike. The code was intended for practical use: an updated version incorporating Dušan's recent edicts was promulgated in 1354. The divinely inspired nature of the ruler's law making and enforcement was simultaneously propounded through visual media. For example, a prominent theme of the wall paintings in Dušan's church at Lesnovo is the 'holy wisdom' that enlightens the ruler, mystically informing his guidance of his people.[10] Such depictions of Byzantine imperial attributes dovetail with the predilection of Dušan and his predecessors for terms of rank redolent of the imperial court. The distinction between functional and honorific title was not clear-cut, and bestowal of the more senior offices and titles by fourteenth-century Bulgarian and Serb rulers was akin to a religious ordination, as in Byzantium itself.

Neither Byzantine secular law-codes nor the concept of office transforming an individual's status counted for very much among the Rus, for all Prince Semen of Moscow's flattering avowal in 1347 that the empire was 'the fount of all piety and the teacher of law-giving and sanctification'.[11] Yet the Byzantine imperial order, however hazily conceived among the Rus, held out a comprehensive 'package' of concepts, rites and authority-symbols, sealed with the church's blessing. And eventually their leaders took advantage of it. Ivan III of Muscovy had particular reason for making his power-centre redolent of the

---

9 I. Biliarsky, 'Le rite du couronnement des tsars dans les pays slaves et promotion d'autres *axiai*', *OCP* 59 (1993), 94–7, 106–9 (text), 120–2 (trans.); Biliarsky, 'Some observations on the administrative terminology of the second Bulgarian empire (13th–14th centuries)', *BMGS* 25 (2001), 79–80, 83.

10 Z. Gavrilović, 'Divine wisdom as part of Byzantine imperial ideology', in *Studies in Byzantine and Serbian medieval art* (London: Pindar, 2001), 51–3.

11 *RPK* II, no. 168, 478–9.

ancient imperial court, a generation or so after Constantinople fell to the Turks. His build-up of earthly power coincided with eschatological expectations no less intense for being variegated: to churchmen such as Ivan's metropolitan, Zosima, the fall of New Rome in 1453 might herald the present world's end but also God's glorification of 'the new emperor Constantine for the new city of Constantine, Moscow, the sovereign of the whole Rus land and many other lands'.[12] Ivan adopted some of the trappings and ritual of the Byzantine court, laying out the Kremlin as the exemplary centre of newly gathered lands and a new society, poised between this world and the next.[13] The ruler as guardian of souls could be of practical help to whoever believed that a God-willed new age was at hand. What might seem narrowly religious concerns coloured general expectations of a prince's worth, which Ivan built on – in bricks and mortar, and with symbols of Jerusalem such as the liturgical arks donated to one of the Kremlin's churches.[14] The sense of being a New Israel was more clearly articulated and fervently believed among the late fifteenth- and sixteenth-century Rus elite than that of being the New Rome. Yet it was the imperial city on the Bosporus that provided the most recent model of, and familiar pathway towards, the New Jerusalem.

This was not simply a matter of evoking a vanished empire. Ivan's political ambitions gained definition from beliefs about the future that emanated from Orthodox thinking. And, for all their diversity, the eschatological theories took for granted that Byzantium was God's most favoured kingdom on earth: any other Orthodox ruler could only hope to succeed in his own domain by God's will, observing the codes of conduct set out by pious tsars. The ruler's role as overseer of the church, defender of his subjects and caretaker of their souls received fullest articulation in Rus with the coronation of Ivan IV as emperor in 1547. Ivan and his counsellors expressly invoked historical associations with Byzantium. They elaborated upon the tale of the 'crown' sent to one of Ivan's distant forebears by Constantine IX Monomachos and adapted Byzantine rites and texts for the coronation ceremony itself. On murals of the Kremlin's Golden Hall were depicted scenes from the history of Israel and Rus (the New Israel); the God-given quality of the ruler's power was a prominent theme, his 'divine wisdom' being highlighted in the manner of Dušan's at Lesnovo.[15] The

---

12 'Mitropolita Zosimy izveshchenie', *RIB* vi, cols. 798–9.

13 M. S. Flier, 'Till the end of time. The apocalypse in Russian historical experience before 1500', in *Orthodox Russia: belief and practice under the tsars*, ed. V. A. Kivelson and R. H. Greene (University Park: Pennsylvania State University Press, 2003), 135–6.

14 Ibid., 156–8.

15 D. Rowland, 'Two cultures, one throne room. Secular courtiers and orthodox culture in the Golden Hall of the Moscow Kremlin', in *Orthodox Russia*, 41–3, 47–51, 54–5.

symbolism may have been interpreted with varying degrees of subtlety by the courtiers and churchmen who viewed these pictures, but their message was inescapable.

Recourse to Byzantine ideology for this purpose was, in a sense, *faute de mieux*, in default of alternative formulations of imperial dominance consistent with Orthodox doctrine. For justification and demonstration of Moscow's pre-eminent power and piety, the churchmen appropriated Byzantine ideas and motifs about the imperial centre and made express allusions to the old hub of Christian leadership. The sense that Moscow was actually superseding it was conveyed by dubbing the city the 'Third Rome', in succession to the 'Second Rome' on the Bosporus. Describing a new centre of political and religious authority as a 'new Rome', a 'new Tsargrad', had long been a claim made for polities aspiring to create their own self-sufficient centres, especially if adjoining Byzantine territory. From the later thirteenth century, Bulgarian writers were hailing Veliko T'rnovo as a 'new Tsargrad'. More striking is the delay in elaborating upon this claim for Moscow, after somewhat halting experimentation with the epithet in the late fifteenth century. In couching claims for a new centre within the conceptual framework of the old, claiming for their own prince the divine sanction long attributed to the *basileus* in Tsargrad, Muscovite writers could not casually flout his longstanding pre-eminence. They were, for the most part, churchmen themselves and therefore belonged to an organisation whose headquarters remained in his city. There were additional reasons for Moscow's self-restraint from overtly imperial posturing. Tatar khans of the Great Horde, who were, as descendants of Genghis Khan, termed tsars, still collected tribute from north-east Rus until the late fifteenth century and Muscovite princes remained vulnerable to the Crimean Tatars and other Tatar groupings, to whom they paid heavy tribute throughout the sixteenth century.

But a standing caveat to the aspirations of Rus and other rulers was the ecumenical patriarchate's commitment to the idea that Christendom's unity was underpinned by the persistence of a 'Roman' empire in Constantinople. This was given currency by, for example, images woven on the *sakkos* (ceremonial tunic) belonging to Photios, the Moscow-based metropolitan of Kiev and all Rus in the early fifteenth century. Prince Vasilii of Moscow and his wife are depicted facing Emperor John VIII Palaiologos and his bride, who was Vasilii's own daughter. Emperor and Rus-born empress are haloed, unlike the prince of Moscow. The locus of holy rulership and primary authority could scarcely be made plainer.[16] At church services conducted by his head churchman wearing

16 D. Obolensky, 'Some notes concerning a Byzantine portrait of John VIII Palaeologus', *Eastern Churches Review* 4 (1972), 141–6.

the *sakkos*, Vasilii bore witness to the visual message of this gift from Constantinople. He thereby gained status vicariously: his daughter, at least, was now in the nimbus-league. Assent to union with Rome at the council of Florence in 1439 did not inflict lasting damage on the standing among the Slavs of the ecumenical patriarchate. Its reservations about alternative emperors had therefore to be taken into account by any would-be emperor of a New Rome even after Constantinople had fallen to the Turks. Hence the organisers of the coronation of Ivan IV took the precaution of seeking the patriarch's consent, which was eventually given. Even so, at the moment of anointing, the officiating metropolitan, Makarii, pronounced a different form of words from those used in late Byzantine inauguration-rituals. Seemingly, his self-restraint registered awareness that he was no more patriarch of Constantinople than Ivan was emperor of the Romans.[17]

Byzantium was long gone as a territorial empire by the time Makarii performed the coronation in 1547, and paintings in the Golden Hall portrayed Ivan being crowned by angels. Very few other rulers within the Byzantine ambit are shown being crowned, whether by Christ or by heavenly beings. Those few were generally intent on hegemonial status comparable to that of the *basileus*, rather than on his uniquely 'Roman' title. In 1344–45, for example, the Bulgarian Ivan Alexander was depicted in a miniature being crowned by an angel before Christ: Christ is termed 'tsar of tsars and eternal tsar' while Ivan is 'tsar and autocrat of all the Bulgarians and Greeks'.[18] Such outright visual claims to sovereign authority divinely bestowed were rarer even than appropriation of an imperial title.

Such hesitations on the part of potentates suggest awareness of the special status on earth claimed by the *basileus*, whether or not they regarded his polity as the empire of the Romans or merely the land of the Greeks. As a working model of political order underpinned by law, the Byzantine state was of value for leaders seeking to gather the reins of power into their own hands and secure them exclusively for their offspring. With the help of God and His law the *basileus* presided over a hierarchy, which held out a moral for one's own troublesome domestic rivals and subjects in general. There is much to be said for regarding Byzantium as an exemplary centre, conveying in ritualised form the norms of hegemonial leadership. Such rites provided more or less

17 M. Arranz, 'L'aspect rituel de l'onction des empereurs de Constantinople et de Moscou', in *Roma, Costantinopoli, Mosca* [Da Roma alla terza Roma, documenti e studi 1] (Naples: Edizioni scientifiche italiane, 1983), 414–15.
18 C. Walter, 'The iconographical sources for the coronation of Milutin and Simonida at Gračanica', in *Vizantijska umetnost početkom XIV veka*, ed. S. Petković (Belgrade: Filozofski fakultet – Odeljenje za istoriju umetnosti, 1978), 199 and plate 16a.

universally recognisable symbols of authority together with clear intimations of a heaven-sent mandate to rule and they were of practical use as building blocks in the establishment of new structures of hegemony. In so far as a ruler was expressly invoking the Byzantine brand of political culture, he was likely to show at least a measure of deference to its original and principal exponent. The alternative, of seeking to eclipse or to take over the template of Christian authority, was scarcely an option worth considering before 1453.

This rationale can be set out in more or less conventional terms, of self-interest and the profit-and-loss accruing to individual dynasts and would-be monarchs among peoples whose elites, at least, were conscious of the Byzantine Empire. And it is plausible for the period when Byzantium enjoyed overwhelming material wealth and power. However, as Obolensky noted, the heyday of the commonwealth came after Byzantium's politico-military decline and its religion's consequent loss of the aura of success. The work of social anthropologists, such as Mary Helms, on 'superordinate' centres helps to explain this apparent paradox. These are centres, much like the Byzantine capital, which provide outlying leaders and their peoples with the goods, rites and symbols with which to organise and define themselves. They hold out a template to which individuals, political elites or whole communities aspire.[19] A 'superordinate' centre is, in Helms's formulation, 'a geographically distant setting' deemed to be a 'particularly charged point or direction of cosmological contact between various dimensions of the outside. Because of this conjunction it is a place where ritual can bring the gods into contact with humans'.[20] Association with such superhuman forces sets the leaders and elites of outlying lands in positions of advantage over their subjects and all others lacking in such links, and at the same time imbues their existing privileges with further legitimacy.

For their part, those at the centre believe themselves 'charged with the moral obligation to repeat or continue the task of manifesting moral legitimacy and ideological centrality in the face of the non-moral or the less moral on this earth'. These claims to moral superiority over the 'barbarians' take material form in the well-crafted or rare objects, which they bestow on them.[21] It is this ability, rather than just brute force, which ensures a 'superordinate' centre's continuing prestige and goes a long way towards explaining the Byzantine paradox. Long after 1204 Byzantium's imperial-ecclesiastical complex

19 M. W. Helms, *Craft and the kingly ideal: art, trade and power* (Austin: University of Texas Press, 1993).
20 Ibid., 194.
21 Ibid., 180, 181.

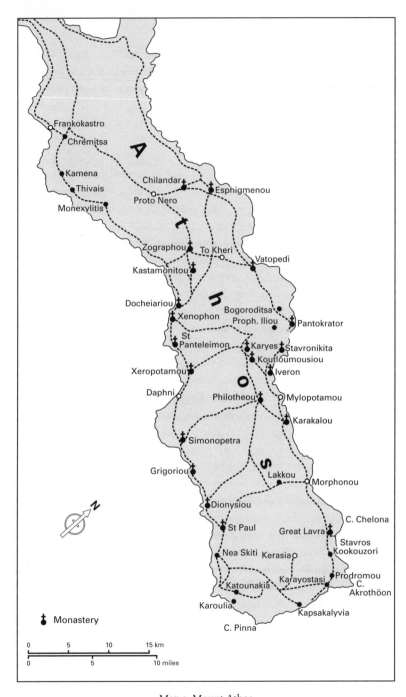

Map 2 Mount Athos

continued to be well equipped to meet the ethical and conceptual as well as material and political requirements of external societies, and its propaganda fostered the idea that the imperial court ceremonial was attuned to the heavenly sphere.

Mount Athos and Serb saints, princes and emperors

The theory of the 'superordinate' centre offers an explanation for the paradox that the standing of the Byzantine Empire remained high, arguably rising further, after 'the God-protected city' succumbed to the Fourth Crusade, losing material wealth and unbroken continuity of sovereignty, as well as sacred relics. The city kept its allure even though it never fully recovered after 1204. But there were other, more specific, reasons why beliefs that the empire was divinely ordained could accommodate such a catastrophe. In Orthodox eyes the fate of the City was intertwined with that of the empire and God's design for mankind. The City's fall to barbarians could herald the End of Time, but it might alternatively warn His people to mend their ways and find spiritual rebirth. Such had been the theme of preachers during barbarian assaults in earlier centuries.[22] The collapse could therefore be interpreted as signalling God's demand for stricter religious observance from His people. The events culminating in the crusaders' seizure of the City seem to have been followed intently by even the most distant Orthodox. A full narrative comes from a Novgorodian chronicle. Probably composed not long afterwards, it apportions blame to the Greek tsars' internecine strife rather than to Latin aggression.[23] The restoration of the capital in 1261 signalled the rehabilitation of Constantinople as a locus of God-blessed authority on earth. The mystique of its rightful incumbents watching over all true-believers appealed to Orthodox rulers not only because the *basileus* was now more malleable and suggestible, but also because of a new-found solidarity in the face of the threat to the Orthodox faith from the Latins.

If the imperial capital provided one conduit to God's kingdom, Byzantine monasteries offered another. The veneration and awe they generated as microcosms of the celestial order had come increasingly since the mid-tenth century to focus on the Holy Mountain of Athos. Imperial patronage ensured

---

22 P. J. Alexander, 'The strength of empire and capital as seen through Byzantine eyes', *Sp* 37 (1962), 343–7; D. M. Nicol, *Church and society in the last centuries of Byzantium* (Cambridge: Cambridge University Press, 1979), 98–9, 104–5.

23 *Novgorodskaia pervaia letopis' starshego i mladshego izvodov*, ed. A. N. Nasonov (Moscow and Leningrad: Akademia nauk SSSR. Institut istorii, 1950; reprinted St Petersburg, 2000), 240–6.

privileged status for its monks. Many individuals were attracted there from out-side the empire, some founding religious communities. Almost from the first there were houses of Iberians (Georgians) and Amalfitans, and from the mid-eleventh century special ties linked Athos with the Kievan cave-monastery, whose founder, Anthony, was tonsured there before being directed back to Rus. His monastery on the Dnieper was thought to have 'originated with the blessing of the Holy Mountain'.[24] Xylourgou, the Rus house on Athos, was the beneficiary of an imperial chrysobull issued in 1169. It granted the abbot's request that the governing body of Athos set aside an additional house, St Pan-teleimon, to accommodate the numerous and well-funded Rus monks, who were expected to restore and fortify it, to serve God and 'pray for our most excellent holy emperor'.[25] By the later twelfth century the hundreds of religious houses and hermits' retreats on Athos exerted at least as great a drawing-power over outsiders as they did over the emperor's subjects. When the seventeen-year-old son of Stefan Nemanja, the Serb ruler, heard the call, he headed for Athos. There he was tonsured and received the monastic name of Sava. A few years later in 1196 his father abdicated and joined him on the Holy Mountain, taking the monastic name of Symeon. The following June the Emperor Alexios III Angelos assigned to Symeon and Sava the monastery of Chilandar, which was to receive 'those of the Serb people choosing the monastic way of life' and was to be 'self-governing and autonomous' like the houses 'of the Iberi-ans and the Amalfitans . . . situated on this mountain'.[26] Chilandar expressly looked to the Byzantine emperor for protection from predatory tax-officials. By ensuring that the emperor rather than the *protos* of Athos confirmed newly elected abbots of the monastery, it also saw the emperor as a counterweight to the *protos*, who exercised a wide-ranging jurisdiction over the monasteries of Athos.[27] A kind of 'triangulation' emerged: non-Greek-speaking communities could secure their place on 'the Holy Mountain' through imperial title-deeds, even while serving as channels for their own people's access to God, each staking its special claim to divine protection.

The gravitation towards Athos of Sava, followed by his father, occurred while Serb political relations with the empire were fraying. Gifts and titles lost something of their allure in a time of imperial indigence and military impotence. The uprising in Bulgaria led by the Asen brothers against Byzantine

24 *PVL*, 69.
25 *Actes de Saint-Pantéléèmôn*, ed. P. Lemerle *et al*. [AA 12] (Paris: P. Lethielleux, 1982), 83 (text); D. Nastase, 'Les débuts de la communauté oecuménique du mont Athos', Σύμμεικτα 6 (1985), 290–2, 294.
26 *Actes de Chilandar*, ed. M. Živojinović *et al*. [AA 20] (Paris: CNRS, 1998), I, 108–9 (text).
27 Ibid., I, 28–9.

rule in 1185–86 was initially directed against excessive taxes. The heterogeneous nature of the insurgents and rivalries between the brothers were handicaps, but the notion of a revived Bulgarian polity began to coalesce around the cults of saints such as Ivan of Rila and Emperor Peter of Bulgaria, aided by texts and folklore concerning past Bulgarian power. The onset of the Fourth Crusade gave the surviving Asen brother, Kalojan, a chance to consolidate his embryonic dominions by turning to the papacy for confirmation of his rule. Together with a crown and sceptre Innocent III bestowed on Kalojan the title of king of the Bulgarians and Vlachs. The Serbs were equally opportunistic. In 1199 the Serb ruler, Sava's brother Stefan, showed his lack of respect for the Byzantine Emperor Alexios III, repudiating the latter's daughter Eudokia and despatching her homewards virtually naked. Stefan eventually received a crown from the legate of Pope Honorius III in 1217, referring to himself in his charters as the 'first-crowned king'. However, these thrusts away from the Byzantine orbit were short-lived and rather superficial. This was partly due to the attachment of local populations, Greek-speaking or Slavonic-speaking, to Orthodox religious rites and imagery.

The aspirations of Serb and Bulgarian rulers to rule over heterogeneous communities scattered across mountainous terrain relied heavily on local cooperation: brute force and intimidation were of only momentary value. Association with the incontestably sacred was a means of gaining such cooperation: thus one of the first moves of the Bulgarian tsar Ivan Asen II upon defeating the 'emperor' of Thessalonike, Theodore Angelos, at Klokotnica in 1230 was to head for Athos and lavish gifts and privileges on the monasteries there. To the family of Stefan Nemanja, association with Athos was especially valuable, highlighting their unique status as well as the sanctity of the monasteries they founded in their own land. In 1206 or 1207 the relics of Stefan Nemanja were borne from Athos to the monastery-church of Studenica he had founded, and soon they were oozing holy oil again. The translation was the work of Sava who, although no longer resident on Athos, was still a frequent visitor. The Serb leadership's commitment to eastern Orthodoxy was further reinforced in 1219 when Sava was ordained 'archbishop of Peć and of all Serbia' by the Orthodox patriarch in Nicaea, his standing being recognised by a synodal decree issued with the emperor's authority.

In this, as in other cases, coterminous ecclesiastical organisation sharpened the territorial definition of still-embryonic polities, while also bringing legitimisation. Sava performed the coronation of Radoslav, the eldest son (by Eudokia) and successor of Stefan 'the first-crowned'. Subsequently, in 1233/4, Sava crowned Radoslav's brother, the usurper Vladislav. Without being precisely formulated, the close involvement of Stefan Nemanja and his descendants with the Holy Mountain was of inestimable value in establishing the dynasty. Sava embedded their piety in his *Life* of his father, in his translation of the *Nomokanon*, and in the monastic rulebook (*Typikon*), which he composed for Chilandar.[28] His work went far towards turning these Serb chieftains not merely into a dynasty, but into a holy family, incomparable in sacred order and law. Through harping on parallels with scriptural figures, literary apologists for the dynasty sought to bring definition and a sense of common purpose to disparate subject-populations, by presenting them as a New Israel with a mission from God. This, in turn, reinforced the dynasty's title to legitimate self-determination. At the same time the ruling house's self-identification with Mount Athos and its patronage of the Serbs' sacral rallying-point on 'the Holy Mountain' wove ties, gossamer-thin yet durable, with the Roman emperors once the latter returned to Constantinople: the *basileus*'s protection and fiscal privileges remained of inestimable value to the monks of Chilandar, as to other Athonite houses.

It was against this background that Stefan Uroš II Milutin (1282–1321) looked to Athos as well as to the patronage of monasteries and churches within the dominions he inherited or acquired. After overrunning Byzantine territories as far south as Prilep and Ohrid and then capturing Durrës (Dyrrakhion), Milutin came to terms, wedding Simonis, the infant daughter of Andronikos II, in 1299. This marked a turning back towards Byzantium and away from the west, which had provided the most lucrative markets for the production of Serbia's silver-mines. Western influence was all too clear in the Romanesque and early Gothic, which had hitherto predominated in Serb church architecture. Milutin now sought to set in stone his hegemony over newly conquered subjects, truculent Serb nobles, and his own disgruntled elder brother and nephew, but he chose to call on the services, not of Latins, but of the most proficient Byzantine-trained architects and craftsmen. Their skills shine out not only from the mausoleums and show-churches built at his expense within his dominions, but also from Chilandar and from monuments in Constantinople, Thessalonike and Jerusalem. These extensive building-projects were recorded among other feats of this new Constantine by his biographer, Danilo.[29] Milutin also made substantial gifts of lands to the monastery of Chilandar, which served as a

---

28 V. Ćorović, *Spisi sv. Save*, in *Zbornik za Istoriju, Jezik i Kniževnost Srpskog Naroda* 17 (1928), 5–13.

29 Danilo II, *Žitije kralja Milutina*, in Archbishop Danilo et al., *Životi kraljeva arhiepiskopa srpskih*, ed. D. Daničić (Zagreb: US. Galca, 1866), 148–51.

kind of seminary for senior churchmen in Serbia.[30] He took care to have these grants confirmed by imperial chrysobulls. On occasion, Andronikos II showed and sought goodwill through his own gifts and privileges. For example, in 1313 to mark the victory of a joint Byzantine–Serbian force over a marauding band of Turks Andronikos provided Milutin, 'my dearest son and son-in-law', with a village with tax-exempt lands on the Strymon, so that he could donate it to Chilandar.[31] Milutin also obtained imperial chrysobulls to confirm the title of monastic possessions within his dominions, for example for the house of St Niketas near Skopje.[32]

Byzantium offered Milutin the richest arsenal for devising a political culture consonant with his aspirations. Direct association with the *basileus* and evocations of his court ceremonial served to legitimise Milutin's gains and to consolidate his monarchical regime. The donor-portrait in Milutin's monastery-church and putative mausoleum at Gračanica shows two angels presenting him and his wife with royal crowns, crowning them on behalf of Christ.[33] Milutin's court decked out with gold and silken trappings was like a stage set, striving for 'imperial and, so far as was possible, even Roman excellence', in the words of a visiting Byzantine ambassador.[34] If he went further than his predecessors in portraying himself and his wife as God-crowned, his audacity owed much to the fact that Simonis was the emperor's daughter, possessing divinely conferred authority in her own right: reportedly, he had dismounted before receiving her 'as a sovereign, not a wife'.[35] He received from the Byzantine empress a crown almost as splendid as the emperor's own.[36] In return for his displays of deference Milutin acquired plausibly quasi-imperial attributes, setting him head and shoulders above his malcontent brother and other members of his family. Not that ancestors were disregarded: near Milutin's donor-portrait in Gračanica, a wall painting depicts his descent from Stefan Nemanja by means of a variant on the Tree of Jesse.

Like his grandfather Milutin, Stefan Dušan was willing to war with the empire when opportunities presented themselves. Exploiting the minority of John V Palaiologos he seized the lands of south-east Macedonia and extended

30 Danilo was its abbot before eventually becoming, in 1324, archbishop of Serbia.
31 *Chilandar*, I, 45, 205–8 (text).
32 Ibid., I, 43, 69–70, 174–5 (text).
33 Walter, 'Iconographical sources', 183–5, 199–200 and fig. 1.
34 Theodore Metochites, Πρεσβευτικός, in K. N. Sathas, Μεσαιωνικὴ Βιβλιοθήκη (Venice: Chronos, 1872), I, 173.
35 George Pachymeres, *Relations historiques*, ed. and trans. A. Failler [CFHB 24/4], IV (Paris: Institut français d'études byzantines, 1999), X.4; 314–15.
36 Nikephoros Gregoras, *Byzantina historia*, ed. L. Schopen and I. Bekker (Bonn: Ed. Weber, 1829), VII.5: 1,242.

his dominions as far as the Strymon and the Chalkidike peninsula. Upon capturing the key town of Serres in September 1345, Stefan was proclaimed emperor and, by the time the newly proclaimed Patriarch Joanikij (formerly archbishop of Peć) crowned him emperor at Skopje on 16 April 1346, he was signalling his territorial acquisitions at Byzantium's expense: in an Athonite charter of January 1346 Stefan styled himself 'emperor and autocrat of Serbia and Romania', thereby alluding to the 'Greek lands' now under his control.[37] In stark contrast to the regimes in Constantinople, Stefan could offer effective protection and order. According to Nikephoros Gregoras, Stefan 'exchanged the barbarian way for the manners of the Romans', wore a crown and robes befitting a Roman emperor, and reserved newly conquered regions 'for himself to rule according to the Romans' custom'.[38]

In keeping with this, Stefan had himself portrayed as receiving, together with his wife and son, crowns directly from Christ. The same wall painting, at Lesnovo, declares his enlightenment by virtue of divine wisdom. In general, Stefan outshone his predecessors in the sophistication with which he harnessed Byzantine iconographical programmes and ideology to his regime's needs. Even so, he appears to have baulked at assailing Constantinople's walls. In so far as Stefan aspired to power in the City, it was through dynastic links: in 1343 he betrothed his infant son-and-heir to the daughter of the late Emperor Andronikos III. He also forbore from styling himself 'emperor of the Romans' in his chrysobulls for Athonite houses, even though their prefaces emphasise that the church and monasteries featured among imperial concerns – in accordance with the *basileus*'s own conventions.

There were several reasons for Stefan's forbearance. He had spent some of his formative years in Constantinople. The emphatic regard he showed for Christian law and church order owed something to his observation of their benefits in a Byzantine setting. Besides, repulse from Constantinople's formidable walls would only confirm that the City was still 'God-protected' against 'the nations', the Serbs included. There was another constraint: the primacy accorded to the 'emperor of the Romans' by the monasteries of Athos. Stefan showed personal devotion to the ways of the monks and belief in the mountain's protective force. Partly to escape the Black Death, he stayed there for eight months in 1347–48 together with his wife and son, visiting several monasteries and venerating their shrines. He restored to many houses properties on the mainland lost during the Byzantine civil wars and made

---

37 *Actes d'Iviron*, IV, *De 1328 au début du XVIe siècle*, ed. J. Lefort *et al.* [AA 19] (Paris: P. Lethielleux, 1995), 114; 116 (text).
38 Nikephoros Gregoras, II, XV.I: II,747.

generous gifts of lands and tax-revenues. For example, he commended himself to the monks of the Rus house of St Panteleimon, hoping their prayers might render Christ merciful for his actions. The monastery of the Iberians – now occupied mostly by Greeks – likewise received land grants and tax-exemptions, as did the houses of Docheiariou and Esphigmenou. Stefan's moves were politic as well as spiritually salutary, but obtaining the monks' prayers came at a price. In 1345 they notified him that despite his generosity they would be praying first for 'the emperor of the Romans' and only then for his 'kingliness' (κραλοτής), a stipulation fraught with connotations of the *basileus*'s superior legitimacy as well as precedence.[39] The prayers or maledictions of Athonite monks were not for Stefan Dušan to decide. General acknowledgement of the *basileus*'s age-old legitimacy was such that in 1351 Stefan even sought confirmation by John V for the charter that he himself had issued for the house of Chilandar.[40] This, in turn, virtually ruled out a hostile bid by Stefan for the throne of John V, an incontestably legitimate emperor of the Romans. Similar constraints weighed with Milutin, who had refrained from styling himself tsar, save on some of his seals.

The Serb rulers stood out from other Orthodox rulers in extending their dominion to Athos: they maintained their overlordship of the mountain for sixteen years after Stefan's death in 1355. But a sacred enclave on the mountain was sought by several other aspiring rulers, Greek-speaking *basileis* among them, perhaps goaded by Stefan's example. In 1374 the emperor of Trebizond, Alexios III, explained his support for the monastery of Dionysiou thus: 'all emperors, kings or rulers of some fame have built monasteries on the Holy Mountain for their eternal memory'. Alexios was therefore adding 'a new foundation in order to survive eternally in the memory of the people'.[41] The princes of Wallachia were no less zealous patrons. The earthly respect and eternal blessings, which the monks' prayers and devotion to the mountain's shrines could earn, spoke to them all.

Such zeal may be dismissed as just another example of how Byzantium's imperial and religious symbols were used as building-materials by external figures for their own political structures. Dušan had to take account of Athonite reverence for the 'emperor of the Romans' in Constantinople, but his practical

---

39 *Grčke povelje srpskih vladara*, ed. A. Solovjev and V. A. Mošin (Belgrade: Srpska kraljevska akademija, 1936; reprinted London: Variorum, 1974), 32–3.

40 Obolensky, *Byzantine Commonwealth*, 256; D. Korać, 'Sveta Gora pod srpskom vlašću (1345–1371)', *Zbornik Radova Vizantiloškog Instituta* 31 (1992), 84–6, 108–11.

41 *Actes de Dionysiou*, ed. N. Oikonomides *et al.* [AA 4] (Paris: P. Lethielleux, 1968), 60 (text).

support for the emperor of the day was clearly determined by self-interest. Besides, the monks of Athos, constantly squabbling over properties and matters of discipline, were far from a united bloc and relatively few saw themselves as cheerleaders for individual emperors. None the less many senior monks and leading holy men on the mountain had strong personal ties with the patriarchate of Constantinople, which assumed formal responsibility for the Holy Mountain in 1312, even if the monasteries continued to look to the emperor as supreme legal authority. Three notable patriarchs of the fourteenth century had spent time on the mountain, Niphon (1310–14), Kallistos (1350–53; 1355–63) and Philotheos Kokkinos (1353–54; 1364–76); so, too, had Isidore I Boucheiras (1347–50). Bitter, heavily documented disputes over religious discipline and hesychasm sometimes divided Athonite monks from the hierarchy in Constantinople, but in an era of spiritual exploration and the high expectations invested in a life of prayer, discord between driven holy men and the ecclesiastical and monastic establishments was more or less inevitable. In fact, the disputatious character of fourteenth-century monasticism made the notion of an overarching custodian of the fundamentals of doctrine and hierarchy all the more desirable to those vested with formal ecclesiastical or monastic authority. This combined with the predisposition of leading Athonites to venerate the 'holy emperor of the Romans' above all others, regarding him as the prime legal guarantor of their estates' tax-exemptions and other privileges.

The arc of Orthodoxy

The Constantinopolitan patriarchs had reasons of their own for insisting on respect for the imperial majesty, now that they played a unique part in the inauguration ritual of emperors. They made themselves indispensable in the early thirteenth century once they began anointing the emperor with chrism, thus providing sacramental confirmation of his fitness to rule with God's grace. By the mid-thirteenth century the patriarch was being described as the spiritual image of Christ and source of the emperor's authority, redoubling claims already made by Photios in the ninth century. The mystique of high ecclesiastical office gained iconographic expression in the fourteenth century, when wall paintings in the Balkans began to depict Christ wearing a patriarchal *sakkos* in liturgical scenes.

In part, this was a reflection of the retreat of effective imperial authority, a consequence of the loss of Constantinople to the Latins in 1204. It was the Patriarch Germanos II (1223–40) who had to confront the new situation. He was repeatedly called upon to intervene and arbitrate between prelates and their flocks in areas lacking imperial governance, for example Latin-dominated Cyprus or Melitene, long under Turkish rule. He found that such recognition of him as arbiter of church discipline and law was of value in dealings with the papacy, as a counterbalance to papal claims to universality. A letter of Germanos addressed to the curia's cardinals in 1232 lists all those peoples who in obedience to their Byzantine mother-church have stayed firm in their Orthodoxy. They range from the Ethiopians and 'all the Syrians' to the Georgians ('Iberians'), Alans, 'the numberless people of the Rus' and the victorious realm of the Bulgarians.[42] That this was more than a rhetorical declaration is evident from Germanos' role in 1228, when called on to determine the jurisdiction of Rus bishops in relation to their princes.[43]

After the restoration in 1261 of the ecumenical patriarchate to Constantinople the pressure on the patriarch to provide guidance to Orthodox communities mounted still further. A happy accident has preserved the patriarchal register for the period from 1315 to the beginning of the fifteenth century. It provides a wealth of detail in comparison with what survives from earlier: copies of letters were quite carefully kept, while the proceedings and judgements recorded display competence in church law and regard for all interested parties. The patriarchate needed to put on record the ways in which it was vindicating its pre-eminence over other Orthodox churches: reorganising sees to take account of new circumstances; answering enquiries from external potentates and churchmen; adjudging disputes; and at least attempting to lay down the law. The patriarchs could, in the process, hope to inspire greater respect from the Greek-speaking congregations and secular authorities on their own doorstep, and this was not the least incentive for them.

A few examples may illustrate the manifold ways in which thirteenth- and fourteenth-century patriarchs of the New Rome provided pastoral care for Orthodox churches and communities. Many sees were instituted, raised in status or merged. While our evidence is seldom specific, the patriarchate seems to have been adapting to new circumstances with alacrity. For the creation of metropolitan sees and transfers of churchmen from one see to another, the emperor's authority was needed. Significantly, a tract dedicated to the subject of transfers underwent two revisions and updates around the turn of the thirteenth and fourteenth centuries, while Andronikos II is said to

---

42 A. L. Tăutu, *Acta Honorii III (1216–1227) et Gregorii IX (1227–1241)* (Rome, 1950), 251–2; *Reg.* no. 1257.
43 *Reg.* no. 1247.

have commissioned a work listing the current ranking-order of sees side by side with a traditional version.[44]

One example of the speed with which the ecclesiastical authorities reacted to the unexpected is the see instituted at the headquarters of the Golden Horde on the Lower Volga. The see of Saraï, named after the encampment that sprang up there, received in 1261 a certain Mitrofan, seemingly its first incumbent. Although Mitrofan himself was apparently Rus-born, appointed by the Rus metropolitan, his immediate successors were Greek-speakers and in close touch with Constantinople. In 1276, for example, Bishop Theognostos attended a meeting of the patriarchal synod and posed questions of canon law and Christian discipline. The synod's answers deal with such questions as what the bishop should do if he wished to celebrate mass and only had priests to hand, rather than (more appropriately) deacons. The responses made allowances for the steppe world in which the bishop was officiating. Masses could be celebrated without deacons, if none were available; consecrated bread could be transported around and former sacred vessels could be restored and reused. However, a priest who had fought in battle must be dismissed from office if he had killed anyone. And the prelates of neighbouring sees were not to visit Saraï and claim the right to look after members of their congregations there,[45] which suggests a predisposition of Orthodox churchmen to frequent the new power centre. Theognostos and his successors served as intermediaries between the khans and the Constantinopolitan authorities, while also brokering the frequent visits of the metropolitans and princes of Rus to the khan's court. In fostering this Christian out-station, the patriarchs of Constantinople acted in close liaison with the emperors, who generally sought amicable relations with the leaders of the Golden Horde, as pillars of stability on their northern approaches and allies against the Turks in Asia Minor. Illegitimate daughters of all three of the first Palaiologan emperors were married to khans, maintaining themselves at Saraï with sizeable entourages. Thus dynastic ties enlivened the Byzantine ecclesiastical presence on the Lower Volga from the turn of the thirteenth century, an example of the way the imperial–ecclesiastical complex extended its reach across the *pax mongolica* in competition with the Latin church.

The patriarchal registers also deal with issues of church order in the eastern Black Sea region. Alania is the subject of several entries. Its metropolitan

---

44 *RPK* II, no. 138, 300–1; *Reg.* no. 2235; *Notitiae episcopatuum*, ed. Darrouzès, 179–81; J. Darrouzès, 'Le traité des transferts. Édition critique et commentaire', *REB* 42 (1984), 169.

45 'Otvety konstantinopol'skogo patriarshogo sobora', in *RIB* VI, *prilozheniia* I, cols. 8–12; *Reg.* no. 1427.

was among those overeager to intervene at Saraï. The main issues seem to have arisen from the proliferation of sees and recalcitrant prelates, rather than lack of revenues or priestly material. Thus around 1344 the ancient coastal see of Soterioupolis was restored to metropolitan status, provoking indignant protests from the metropolitan of Alania, to whose province it had belonged. A subsequent metropolitan of Alania, Symeon, was himself the butt of repeated complaints from clergymen and a monk around the Lower Don: he was accused of infringing their rights, appropriating their revenues, and simony. A further charge levelled against Symeon at the patriarchal synod in 1356 was presuming to consecrate an incumbent for the 'metropolitan see of the Caucasians'.[46]

Resolution of this, as of many other cases, was complicated by the rapid turnover of patriarchs, itself a reflection of the instability of imperial regimes at the time: several judgements concerning distant sees shifted with the vagaries of politics in the City. The synod had simultaneously to cope with continuing changes in local circumstances. Many problems were essentially ones of success: the need, for example, to provide Christian priests for numerous and articulate communities. The appearance of a 'metropolitan see of the Caucasians' in the first half of the fourteenth century implies an expansion in Orthodox populations to the south of Alania; so, too, does Metropolitan Symeon's specious argument that besides this see there now existed a separate 'bishopric of Caucasia' which came under his authority. Symeon's presumption – shown to be fraudulent after the synod consulted 'the canonical books' listing the sees – was probably fuelled by his connections with the Mongol khans: the synod noted that with the aid of his 'bishop of Caucasia' he had also consecrated a new bishop for the see at Saraï.[47]

Symeon was far from unique in being well connected and well funded, or, indeed, in being querulous. Substantial numbers of the Tatar elite became Christians, judging by the names on Greek-language gravestones around Sougdaia and in the mountains of the south-eastern Crimea. The expansion of well-to-do Orthodox households and communities forms the background to a number of disputes involving prelates across an arc of Orthodoxy spanning the north coast of the Black Sea in the first half of the fourteenth century. Thus in 1317 the metropolitan of Sougdaia complained to the synod that patriarchal officials (exarchs) from the metropolitan see of Gotthia were appropriating revenues from churches belonging to his own see. The synod characteristically

---

46 *RPK* III, no. 215, 212–17; *Reg.* no. 2392; Nikephoros Gregoras, xxxvii.6–8: III, 532–3.
47 *RPK* III, no. 215, 218–19; *Reg.* no. 2392.

determined that the case should be investigated on the spot by 'neighbouring metropolitans', in this case of Alania, Vicina and Zichia-Matracha.[48] 'Neighbouring' was no misnomer, seeing how easy – thanks to the Genoese – journeys along the north coast of the Black Sea and between the Crimea and Constantinople had become. The problem in the fore-mentioned case bespeaks rivalries rather than simply uncertainty over diocesan boundaries or insecurity: the issue turned on revenues from newly built churches in the Sougdaian see, and the measures taken by officials acting on behalf of the patriarchate there.

The metropolitan of Alania had a counterpart west of the Black Sea, at Vicina, in the region of the Danube delta. This see was raised to metropolitan status at the behest of Michael VIII Palaiologos, probably during the 1260s. The town soon became an important entrepôt of the Genoese. There are ample signs of trade and Byzantine material culture in the Danube delta of the Palaiologan period.[49] Besides illustrating the adaptability of the imperial–ecclesiastical complex to altered circumstances, the creation of a metropolitan see at Vicina reflected an awareness of its commercial potential, which worked to the benefit of its incumbents, such as Bishop Luke who lent out his church funds for 800 gold pieces annually.[50] The metropolitan's means probably stemmed directly or indirectly from the Genoese merchants' lucrative dealings at Vicina. The metropolitan used his funds to attend to the needs of his spiritual flocks on the fringes of the steppes, as well as carrying out other services for the emperor. Thus in 1301 the metropolitan acted as the intermediary between Andronikos II and several thousand Alan cavalrymen, who were seeking asylum with their families.[51] The patriarchate also maintained a presence at this time in the vicinity of the Danube delta through the possession of a series of strongholds.[52] These initiatives could not, however, ensure lasting security for Vicina. Devastated around 1340 by a Tatar band, the town lost its role as an important emporium for Genoese merchants. Soon afterwards its metropolitans ceased to reside there.[53]

This setback did not, however, put paid to an organised Orthodox presence in the region of the Lower Danube. Alexander was a forceful warlord (*voevoda*)

48 *RPK* I, no. 52, 342–7; *Reg.* no. 2082.
49 On the problem of the precise location of Vicina and on Genoese trading activities there, see P. Ş. Năsturel, 'Mais où donc localiser Vicina?', *BF* 12 (1987); *ODB*, III (sub Vicina). See also V. François, 'Elaborate incised ware: une preuve du rayonnement de la culture byzantine à l'époque paléologue', *Bsl* 61 (2003), 161.
50 Athanasios, *Correspondence*, ed. Talbot, 56–7; *Reg.* no. 1613.
51 George Pachymeres, *Relations historiques*, IV, x.16; 336–9.
52 These are listed in a deed of c.1321: *RPK* I, no. 64, 400–1; *Reg.* no. 2101.
53 *RPK* II, nos. 115, 117, 118; 130–3, 136–45; *Reg.* no. 2184.

based around Curtea de Argeş, who sought Byzantine approval for the creation of an Orthodox see for his territories, as a way of solemnising his secession from the Angevin kingdom of Hungary. For some time he had been hosting at his court the displaced metropolitan of Vicina, Hyakinthos. In 1359 Byzantium acceded to his request that his guest should become the 'legitimate pastor of all Oungrovlachia for the blessing and spiritual direction of himself, his children and all his lordship' and agreed to the creation of a metropolitan see for 'all Oungrovlachia' after Hyakinthos's death. The centre of gravity of Orthodox ecclesiastical organisation in the region thus shifted inland to Alexander's court. In 1370 Alexander obtained permission from the ecumenical patriarchate to create a 'metropolitan see of part of Oungrovlachia', which covered the Banate of Severin, his territories along the Hungarian border. He himself was dubbed 'great *voevoda* and master of all Oungrovlachia'. In return, he provided a written pledge that the patriarch and his synod would appoint all future heads of his church and that all Oungrovlachia should remain under the authority of the Great Church.[54] The emperor and patriarch thereby gained a new out-station of appointees, personal contacts and admirers, north of the Lower Danube. The transfer of Hyakinthos received imperial approval, which was, according to Patriarch Kallistos's letter to Alexander of 1359, 'especially because of your Honour's unblemished good-faith and love towards my most excellent and holy autocrat from God, most sublime emperor of the Romans, the quintessence of all good things'.[55] How far Alexander's 'good-faith' had substance is debatable, but his son and heir Vladislav took a bride who may well have belonged to the imperial court-circle.[56] Around the same time, responding to repeated requests from Mount Athos, Alexander made generous donations to the dilapidated monastery of Koutloumousiou, while his son Vladislav went further still, becoming its 'proprietor and founder', according to his charter for the monastery of 1369.[57]

Young Wallachian monks streamed into the rebuilt house, and their desire to relax some of its disciplines aroused objections from the Greeks remaining there. These were, however, essentially problems of success, exemplifying the attraction exerted by the mountain. An agreement on the degree of asceticism to be practised in Koutloumousiou was eventually reached between its abbot,

---

54 *RPK* III, no. 243, 412–13, 414–17; *Reg.* no. 2411. For the second metropolitanate, see Miklosich and Müller, I, 532–3, 535–6; *Reg.* nos. 2588, 2593.

55 *RPK* III, no. 244, 420–1; *Reg.* no. 2412.

56 S. Andreescu, 'Alliances dynastiques des princes de Valachie (XIV–XVI siècles)', *Revue des Études Sud-Est Européennes* 23 (1985), 359–60.

57 *Actes de Kutlumus*, ed. P. Lemerle [AA 2], new edition (Paris: P. Lethielleux, 1988), 9–11; 104 (text).

Chariton, the Wallachian monks, leading holy men of the mountain, and Vladislav; the latter making generous donations by way of encouragement. In 1372 Chariton was appointed metropolitan of Oungrovlachia in succession to Hyakinthos, supplementing Athos's links with outlying non-grecophone populations of substantial means, while the 'metropolitan of part of Oungrovlachia' was a former senior official of the Great Church, Daniel Kritopoulos, who now took the name of Anthimos. Chariton later added the charge of *protos* of the Holy Mountain to his responsibilities. Thus an intricate web joined Athos and the imperial–ecclesiastical establishment to the Wallachian elite. While many threads were of a personal nature, they often proved durable. At the same time institutional links were forged with other potentates of the region. For example, in 1391 a lesser *voevoda*, Balitza, and his brother presented their monastery of St Michael in Maramureş (near Sighetu Marmatiei) to the patriarchate; as a 'patriarchal monastery', it received direct supervision from Constantinople, while the abbot dispensed ecclesiastical justice locally, serving as patriarchal exarch.[58]

Another important institutional link between Constantinople and a nascent polity north of the Danube delta had been forged by 1386 with the creation of the metropolitan see of 'Maurovlachia' (Moldavia). The local ruler, however, expelled the patriarch's appointee to the new see and imposed his own nominee, a relative named Joseph: a *fait accompli*, which the patriarchate finally accepted in 1401. Meanwhile monasteries were being founded in Moldavia, not least at Suceava, the princely stronghold and metropolitan see. The fact that neighbouring Galicia was now under Catholic rule following the Polish–Lithuanian Union of Krewo in 1385 acted as a stimulus to Byzantine interest in the region. When Joseph died, Emperor Manuel II took it upon himself to appoint his successor in 1416; having made his choice, he pressed the patriarch to issue the new appointee with 'patriarchal letters'. Such was the importance of the see to Manuel, and such was Manuel's capacity for intervening in church affairs.[59]

These developments in the region of the Lower Danube have been recounted at length because they illustrate the adaptability of Byzantine monks and churchmen to circumstances: they turned setbacks to their advantage through their ability to harness the energies and resources of 'upwardly mobile' potentates far beyond the empire's territorial bounds. For most of these men of the cloth, the emperor uniquely symbolised the continuity

---

58 For St Michael's, see Miklosich and Müller, II, 156–7; *Reg.* no. 2892.
59 E. Popescu, *Christianitas Daco-Romana* (Bucharest: Editura Academiei, 1994), 461–3.

of the universal church as part of God's design for mankind. There was no exact counterpart to this in the Latin scheme of things. Beleaguered as they were by Turkish armies, Byzantine emperors could still offer aspiring rulers means of dignifying and legitimising their regimes, not least court ritual. Late fourteenth- and fifteenth-century Wallachian and Moldavian *voevody* conferred Byzantine-style dignities on their notables, like Bulgarian and Serb rulers before them.

Coping with the flux beyond the steppes

Matters stood rather differently in the wider world of the steppes and the northern forest zones. Emperor and patriarch had readily provided for the new power-centres that emerged there after the Tatars' onslaught; early in the fourteenth century, metropolitan sees were created for the Rus principality of Galich (Galicia) and, around 1315, for the polity of the Lithuanian grand dukes. The latter were still practising pagans, but they had drastically extended their dominions to the south and south-east, incorporating large populations of Orthodox Rus. The Orthodox Church seems to have flourished under the pagan regime, and even gained adherents among the ruling family. Sons of Grand Duke Olgerd were Orthodox believers by c. 1347. When three Christians were put to death for refusing the grand duke's orders to eat meat during a fast, the sons reportedly saw to the burial of one of the martyrs. It may well have been the mounting appeal of Orthodoxy to members of Olgerd's court that precipitated persecution.

However, the expansion of Orthodoxy among the Lithuanian elite coincided with further annexations by the grand dukes and confrontation with the princes of Moscow, whose rise to prominence owed much to their acknowledgement of Tatar dominion. Reward for their services as chief tribute-collectors for the Tatar khans came in the form of patents of overlordship (*iarlyki*) over the north-east lands of Rus. A feature of these *iarlyki* was the guarantee they provided of the church's landholdings and jurisdiction in Rus, which bound church and prince still more tightly. From the early 1320s the metropolitan of 'all *Rhosia*' Peter (1308–26) fixed his residence in Moscow, which was to become the permanent abode of his successors. This signalled Byzantine recognition of Moscow's ascendancy, but it also brought the Byzantines face to face with the Lithuanians and their ambition to extend their hegemony over all Rus. By 1352 Grand Duke Olgerd was seeking a metropolitan not, as before, 'of the Lithuanians' but 'of *Rhosia*' in general. What had initially been an expedient means of accommodating a new power within the

Byzantine fold was now re-employed by Olgerd to legitimise the full sweep of his ambitions: disregarding the metropolitan resident in Moscow, Theognostos, he proposed a protégé, Theodoretos, for the post of metropolitan of 'all *Rhosia*'. Olgerd's ambition was not inherently absurd. The metropolitan's close association with Moscow was not only fairly novel, but also unsignalled in the nomenclature of his office: he was still notionally the 'metropolitan of Kiev and all *Rhosia*'. The ancient see of Kiev had been under Lithuanian sway since 1325. None the less, the ecumenical patriarch rejected Olgerd's nomination of Theodoretos.

For Byzantium the choice between this thrusting new power and Moscow was complicated by a series of contingencies. The murder of Khan Berdi-Beg in 1357 followed in quick succession by the death of Prince Ivan of Moscow created a power vacuum in Rus, which the metropolitan Aleksii came to fill. Unlike most of his predecessors, he was not a Greek, but came from a Muscovite boyar family. Before his death Ivan had 'entrusted to [Aleksii] the education and upbringing of his son Dmitrii, so that [the metropolitan] became fully and immediately absorbed by his concern for the prince', as a much later patriarchal synod tersely stated.[60]

Conversant with Byzantine ways and able to read Greek, Aleksii was consecrated as metropolitan 'of Kiev and all *Rhosia*' in 1354, after waiting a year in Constantinople. That he associated his office so closely with the welfare and continuity of the Muscovite princely house need not, in itself, have raised difficulties for Byzantium. But Aleksii's regency in Moscow was a red rag to the Lithuanian grand duke: snubbed by the Constantinopolitan patriarchate, he had promptly turned to the Bulgarian patriarch who consecrated his nominee Theodoretos as metropolitan in 1352. Olgerd and the Muscovite princely court both looked for support in Byzantium, but found a divided ruling elite and an unstable political regime. Olgerd had his sympathisers among the Genoese and other supporters of John V, who regained full power with their help in December 1354. They saw in Olgerd a formidable potential ally and within a few months had arranged for the consecration of his new candidate, Roman, as 'metropolitan of the Lithuanians'. Olgerd was, as the Byzantines well knew, aiming 'to find a means, with Roman's help, of ruling Great Russia', and Roman subsequently showed his hand, by adopting the title of 'metropolitan of Kiev and all *Rhosia*' and going to live in Kiev.[61] Aleksii, in contrast, managed

---

60 Miklosich and Müller, II, 117; *Reg.* no. 2847. See also ibid., II, 12; *Reg.* no. 2705.
61 Miklosich and Müller, II, 12–13; *Reg.* no. 2705; *RPK* III, no. 259, 530–1; *Reg.* no. 2434; J. Meyendorff, *Byzantium and the rise of Russia: a study of Byzantino-Russian relations in the fourteenth century* (Cambridge: Cambridge University Press, 1981), 169–70.

Muscovite affairs during the 1360s, abided by the patriarchal synod's decisions, and was an honoured guest both at Constantinople and at the khan's court. He benefited from the vacancy of the Lithuanian metropolitan see following the death of Roman in 1362. Olgerd finally complained to Constantinople in 1370 that Aleksii never visited the Lithuanian-ruled lands and sided with Dmitrii of Moscow: 'he blesses the Muscovites to commit bloodshed . . . And when someone kisses the cross to me and then escapes to them, the metropolitan frees him from his allegiance [to me].'[62]

The fluctuating power-balances in regions far beyond effective political reach inevitably posed problems for Byzantium. The flexibility earlier shown in accommodating the rise of Lithuanian power was strained once the grand duke aspired to dominance over all Rus. Patriarch Philotheos's response to Olgerd's complaints and demands was, for all its ingenuity, slow to take effect. During Aleksii's lifetime, Philotheos consecrated his own former envoy to Rus, Kiprian, as 'metropolitan of Kiev, Rus and the Lithuanians' and sent him to live temporarily in the lands under Lithuanian dominion; but the synodal act promulgating his appointment in 1375 expressly stated that 'the ancient state of affairs should be restored in the future under one metropolitan'; Kiprian was, after Aleksii's death, to assume jurisdiction over the whole of Rus and be metropolitan 'of all *Rhosia*'.[63]

In the event, after Aleksii's death Prince Dmitrii of Moscow secured the installation as metropolitan of his own candidate, Pimen. Only after the deaths of prince and metropolitan in the same year, 1389, was Kiprian able to take up residence in Moscow. Yet, without downplaying the importance of contingency, both the pagan Olgerd and Moscow's leadership shared the assumption that patriarch and emperor, acting in conjunction, would have the last word in determining the ecclesiastical landscape. Olgerd's complaint to Philotheos about Aleksii's partisanship and plea for his own candidate presupposes a degree of impartiality in Byzantine church discipline not so far removed from Semen's rhetorical-seeming declaration that the empire was 'the teacher of law-giving'.[64] Olgerd's frustration sprang from recognition of the indispensability of Orthodox rites and devotions to most of the Rus inhabitants of his dominions; in light of his subjects' proclivities, the grand duke's bargaining power with the Constantinopolitan patriarchate was limited, for all his martial prowess and intimations of sympathy for Latin churchmen.

---

62 Miklosich and Müller, I, 581; *Reg.* no. 2625; Meyendorff, *Byzantium*, 193–5, 288.
63 Miklosich and Müller, II, 120; *Reg.* no. 2665; Meyendorff, *Byzantium*, 200–1.
64 *RPK* II, no. 168, 478–9.

The issue of the succession to Metropolitan Aleksii reveals the diverse forms of influence still available to Byzantium north of the steppes. The patriarchate showed finesse in choosing Kiprian. Besides being of marked scholastic and administrative ability, he was Bulgarian by birth and so could be expected to communicate easily with the Orthodox Slavonic-speaking inhabitants of Lithuanian-ruled lands and, eventually, throughout Rus. Kiprian, a Bulgarian yet also 'a Roman-friendly man',[65] embodied the talents, upon which the Constantinopolitan patriarchate could still draw, together with the willingness of individuals from peripheral polities to align themselves with the ancient, divinely sanctioned, centre.

The Constantinopolitan patriarch's skilful use of human resources extended to human remains. Olgerd found himself cast as, in effect, a villain in sacred time when the three Lithuanians executed at his behest *c.* 1347 were recognised as martyrs by the ecumenical patriarchate; their relics were brought to the Bosporus by Kiprian upon his return from a mission to Olgerd's court on behalf of Patriarch Philotheos in 1374. There quickly followed an encomium of the martyrs, composed in the milieu of the Great Church, a *Passio* and other liturgical texts honouring them. Their canonisation was an affirmation of moral superiority that hard-bitten potentates ignored at their peril and called to mind events from the earliest era of evangelisation.[66]

The notion of a moral lead set by eastern churchmen involved the emperor as well as the patriarch, given that formal responsibility for instituting external metropolitan sees rested with the former. Moreover the emperor's role as superintendent of the church, static yet salutary, had support from senior churchmen in the patriarchate. They saw in him a kind of unifying focus of allegiance, proof against all alternative church organisations or creeds. Patriarch Anthony IV wrote to Dmitrii of Moscow's son and successor, Vasilii, urging him to let the emperor's 'sacred name' be commemorated in the liturgical diptychs and to show respect: 'it is not possible to have a church and not to have an emperor, for the empire and the church have a great unity and commonality, and it is impossible to separate them'.[67] This was one of a series of attempts by the patriarchate to impress upon external rulers and churchmen their common origins in, and lasting debt to, the 'Roman' imperial order. Byzantine

---

65 Miklosich and Müller, II, 361; *Reg.* no. 3112.
66 The encomium is edited in M. N. Speransky, *Serbskoe zhitie litovskikh muchenikov* (Moscow, 1909), 35–47; D. Baronas, *Trys Vilniaus kankiniai: Gyvenimas ir istorija* [Fontes ecclesiastici historiae lithuaniae 2] (Vilnius: Aidai, 2000), 200–43. See also Meyendorff, *Byzantium*, 187–8; D. Baronas, 'The three martyrs of Vilnius: a fourteenth-century martyrdom and its documentary sources', *Analecta Bollandiana* 122 (2004), 85–7, 90–2.
67 Miklosich and Müller, II, 191; *Reg.* no. 2931.

churchmen were hoping for material repayment of the debt, as witness the letter sent by Patriarch Matthew I in 1400 to Kiprian and other senior church-men in Rus. Matthew represents the raising of funds to aid the city of Con-stantinople as a supreme act of piety: donors will earn more merit with God for this than by performing the liturgy, almsgiving or freeing prisoners, 'for this holy city is the pride, the bulwark, the benediction and the glory of Christians everywhere in the inhabited world'.[68]

It was, in fact, to the Franks in the west and not to the Balkan Slavs or the Rus that Manuel II journeyed in quest of military support, as Matthew's letter acknowledges. The Orthodox potentates' reputed veneration for the 'holy city' did not materialise in a relief force. But this is a reflection of their own military and administrative limitations: it would be rash to underestimate how useful they found the aura of affinity to higher earthly and celestial powers[69] – an aura which still clung to Byzantium. For leaders such as the northern Rus princes, still obliged to render tribute to Tatar khans, the notion of belonging to an alternative order capped by a sacred emperor probably grew more attractive, not less, as the Golden Horde began to fragment and could no longer maintain security against steppe marauders. The prince of Moscow's right to obedience, service and revenues from his subjects relied on a combination of fear, belief and custom. In these circumstances, the imperial Byzantine order brought the prince's stance a certain external validation, best understood through visual renderings of the hierarchy of rulership.

The interrelationship of the Moscow prince and the emperor was solem-nised on the *sakkos*, which Metropolitan Photios wore during liturgies, besides being implied in Photios's testament.[70] On the *sakkos* were depicted, between emperor and prince, the three Lithuanian martyrs whose cult the Byzantines were now furthering: the haloed emperor's mission to spread the faith goes on, but the Rus prince has a place in this scheme of things. The imagery conveys something of what Patriarch Anthony asserted in his letter to Vasilii: that the emperor and the patriarch care for all Christians, irrespective of little local difficulties, and should not be despised because of the empire's material frailties.

The sumptuousness of the vestment carrying the images and the fact that it was a gift from the Byzantine authorities to the head of the church in Rus

---

68 Miklosich and Müller, II, 361; *Reg.* no. 3112.

69 See V. A. Kivelson, 'Merciful father, impersonal state: Russian autocracy in comparative perspective', *Modern Asian Studies* 31 (1997), 648–51.

70 A.-E. N. Tachiaos, 'The testament of Photius Monembasiotes, metropolitan of Russia (1408–31): Byzantine ideology in XVth-century Muscovy', *Cyrillomethodianum* 8–9 (1984–85), 87–8, 106. See also Obolensky, 'Byzantine portrait of John VIII Palaeologus', 141–6.

fit well with the concept of the 'superordinate' centre as formulated by Mary Helms. The blend of ritual, numinous authority and allusion to recent events, the martyrdom of the Lithuanians, focused the Muscovite elite's attention on Constantinople as a 'charged point' 'out-there', offering access to 'up-there'.[71] An institution so graphically presenting claims to be the site of cultural origins could override fluxes in surrounding regimes, actually drawing vitality from their kaleidoscopic shifts.

That many among the political and clerical elite in the late medieval eastern Christian world were amenable to such notions, even if interpreted on their own terms, is likely enough. It may be no accident of survival that Rus travellers' descriptions of Constantinople as a Christian city abounding in holy relics and marvels date mainly from the fourteenth century. This was an era when travel across the Black Sea was relatively commonplace. Large parties of Rus churchmen were not infrequently in town to press their respective candidate's claim to become metropolitan of all Rus; considerable sums of money made their way into patriarchal and other purses in Constantinople in the process. Arriving in 1389 with Metropolitan Pimen was Ignatios of Smolensk, who recorded what he saw during his stay. He was mainly interested in the City's shrines, relics and wonder-working icons. But Ignatios also gives a detailed description of the coronation of Manuel II in 1392 in St Sophia. He was left awe-struck by the sheer beauty of the ceremony.[72] His description may well have been carefully noted for use in inauguration-ritual back in Rus.[73] If the aim of the Muscovite court was to adapt such ritual to the greater glory of their own political order, the arrival in Rus of senior churchmen from Constantinople bearing finely crafted artefacts, including Photios's *sakkos*,[74] served as periodic reminders of Byzantine credentials as a 'superordinate' centre.

Envisaging an imperial order

Some of the envoys sent by the ecumenical patriarchate to the lands of Rus held offices in other eastern churches, for example Michael, archbishop of Bethlehem. They were living testimony to an imperial scheme of things, as was the readiness of eastern Mediterranean churchmen to refer local disputes

71 See Helms, *Craft and the kingly ideal*, 173–80, 192–6.
72 G. Majeska, *Russian travelers to Constantinople in the fourteenth and fifteenth centuries* [DOS 19] (Washington, DC: Dumbarton Oaks Research Library and Collection, 1984), 104–5, 110–11.
73 Ibid., 52, 112–13.
74 T. V. Nikolaeva, *Proizvedeniia russkogo prikladnogo iskusstva s nadpisiami XV – pervoi chetverti XVI v.* (Moscow: Nauka, 1971), 19–20.

or problems to the patriarchal synod. The patriarchate's response was often politic: when invited to nominate a successor to the lately deceased patriarch of Alexandria in 1397, it first checked with the patriarch of Jerusalem whether, as would be quite understandable, the Mamluk sultan had already approved the appointment of a patriarch.[75] Melkite churchmen in the Levant still looked to the patriarch for resolution of disciplinary disputes, while imperial laws remained normative for Christian communities. In the thirteenth century Palestinian scribes were still copying the Melkite Arabic translation of the *Procheiros Nomos*.[76] The emperor's overriding authority was perhaps the more cherished for being remote. It may be to Orthodox employees of the Egyptian sultans that we owe a fairly explicit formulation of the 'Byzantine Commonwealth' in the shape of address-formulae for diplomatic letters sent by the Mamluks to the *basileus*. Thirteenth- and early fourteenth-century salutations of the latter as 'heir of the ancient Caesars, reviving the ways of the philosophers . . . versed in his faith's affairs, equitable in his realms' chime in with conventional imperial attributes. Géza of Hungary and earlier potentates would have recognised in him 'the only sovereign of the faith of Jesus authorised to [distribute] thrones and crowns'. But for almost a hundred years, from the mid-fourteenth century onwards, the *basileus* was addressed in such specific terms as 'head of the communion of the Cross . . . king of Bulgaria and Vlachia, ruler of the great cities of the Rus and the Alans, protector of the faith of the Georgians and Syrians'.[77] While the drafters of this formula may well have found sentiments in similar vein among the diplomatic correspondence received from Constantinople, they would have needed little prompting if, as seems likely, they were themselves Christians linked with the Melkite patriarchate of Alexandria.[78]

To high-placed Christians in Mamluk service, as to the churchmen who formally prayed for the wellbeing of the khan and his family in fourteenth-century Rus, God had sent powers-that-be, which were tolerant of Christians and yet not of their own kind or choosing. Belief in an ancient order transcending these necessary compromises, an ultimate warranty of their faith on earth, offered a certain intellectual coherence, if not solace. The sentiment was seldom articulated at length. Nor could it mobilise armies to relieve Constantinople from the Turks. But the assumption that 'the empire of the Romans' was part of

75 Miklosich and Müller, II, 273–4; *Reg.* no. 3036.
76 J. Pahlitzsch, *Graeci und Suriani im Palästina der Kreuzfahrerzeit* [Berliner historische Studien 33] (Berlin: Duncker und Humbolt, 2001), 213 and n. 475.
77 D. A. Korobeinikov, 'Diplomatic correspondence between Byzantium and the Mamluk Sultanate in the fourteenth century', *Al-Masaq* 16 (2004), 58, 59.
78 Ibid., 66–7.

God's design for mankind, at once fixed point and all-encompassing skein, was widespread among eastern Christians from Egypt to northern Rus. And it was something which Muslim powers had to accommodate within their own spectrum of political thought.

A rather different stance was taken by eastern Christian leaders seeking to acquire the foundations of law and a divinely sanctioned order from the empire and to adapt and enlist its authority-symbols to their particular needs. As has been seen, their aim was to strike out and form their own fulcrums of legitimate authority, while aligned with the creed and most of the church ritual and discipline of the Constantinopolitan church. They sought from Byzantium means of convincing their subjects that they, too, constituted a nation under God, who had allocated a particular dynasty or individual to protect them. Cults venerating members of the ruling family among, for example, the Serbs may have infringed the *basileus*'s claim to be the one true 'Godsend' among earthly rulers, but neither in theory nor in practice could they ignore or belittle the ideal of Christian rulership on display in Byzantium. There was a sense that the true faith overarched local power structures. While this emerges most clearly in relation to patriarchal authority,[79] Byzantium's exquisite symbols of legitimate rule spoke to those in charge of developing political structures. Among the Georgians as among the Rus, the motif of inverted hearts on cloisonné enamels associated ruling houses with Old Testament figures and military saints, as it did in Byzantium. Leaders of and apologists for such houses had an interest in representing their rule as part of cosmic harmony, in key with the *basileus*.

If this holds true of political and social elites and of churchmen, there remains the question of what, if anything, the populations in the regions under review made of a world-emperor residing on the Bosporus: how far did the axioms of written law emanating from the empire impinge on their religious observances and everyday practices? For myriads of rural communities strung across the Balkans and in the forests north of the Black Sea steppes, one's homestead or village was 'the world', and persons or notions from outside tended to evoke suspicion. Few opportunities or encouragements for long-distance travel were available, making pilgrimages to Tsargrad or Jerusalem a minority pursuit. And while Byzantine political culture abounded in visual imagery, beaming out messages of divinely sanctioned hierarchy that even illiterates could grasp, the proportion of rural populations directly exposed to it was finite. But remoteness and a reputation for mystifying yet efficacious

79 Eastmond, '"Local" saints', 746–7.

rites, complex lore and incomparable techniques are characteristics of 'super-ordinate' centres. The patriarchal and imperial establishment acting in virtual unison from 'the reigning City' still met these criteria in the early fifteenth century.

The commonality of Mount Athos and a Slavonic textual community

But to treat the imperial–ecclesiastical complex as sole pillars of a 'common-wealth' would be to disregard 'the Holy Mountain', at once landmark and generator of spiritual movement, and known to fourteenth-century writers as 'the workshop of virtue'.[80] A stay there offered individuals outstanding opportunities for self-improvement and eventual absorption within the god-head. The prospect appealed not only to Byzantines but also to individuals or whole peoples whose ideals of piety were closely aligned with theirs. Athonite monasticism played a key role in the spirituality or political formation of sev-eral of these peoples, whether through directing Anthony to return to Rus and inspiring later generations of monks, or cradling the cult of a sacred dynasty among the Serbs. Fourteenth-century Athos was a hive of spiritual endeavour: it produced innovative ways of staging the liturgy; there were intensive efforts to partake directly of the divine through fasting, prayer and meditation, while Gregory Palamas provided the theological foundations.

The Serb monastery of Chilandar became the scene of intensive copying and the translating of Greek texts into a literary language with South Slav char-acteristics but of sufficient clarity and consistency to be comprehensible to all readers and speakers of Slavonic, including the Rus. A Bulgarian-born monk writing among the Serbs around 1418, Constantine of Kostenets, remarked that there were only two centres producing Slavonic texts that faithfully reproduced the style and content of their Greek originals: one of these was Mount Athos and the other was Veliko T'rnovo.[81] This had been the seat of the Bulgarians' patriarch and tsar, but by the second half of the fourteenth century the over-riding concern of its churchmen seems to have been to improve their religious texts through reference to Greek originals, praising Greek for its inherent ele-gance and precision as a language, and also translating prayers, hymns and other liturgical offices recently composed by Greek-speaking Byzantines.

---

80 *RPK* II, no. 56, 428–9; *Reg.* no. 2309; Nicol, *Church and society*, 19.
81 V. Jagić, *Codex Slovenicus grammaticarum (Rassuzhdeniia iuzhnoslavianskoi i russkoi stariny o tserkovnom-slavianskom iazyke)* (St Petersburg: Weidmann, 1896), 190. Cf. Obolensky, 'Late Byzantine culture', 21 n. 58.

Bulgarian ruling elites had long been trying to secure parity with the realm of the Greeks for their dominions. The encomiasts of Tsar Ivan Alexander proclaimed him 'a new Constantine' and his capital 'a new Tsargrad'. The analogies, like the learned encomia themselves, were a means of exalting Ivan's city as a temple of wisdom, setting it apart from alternative 'God-protected' capitals of rival Bulgarian dynasts, who likewise aspired to imperial status for themselves and their seats of power. Ivan made donations to and fostered cults at long-established monasteries such as Rila and Bachkovo. But high levels of literary culture and religious knowledge still required, in the eyes of Ivan and his entourage, ready access to the Church Fathers in Greek. Bulgarian clergymen showed respect for the copious writings of contemporary Byzantine divines, not least their prayers and the new forms of liturgical offices being composed. The monasteries of Athos contained copies of these texts and, unlike Constantinople's houses, they were more or less continuously accessible, unaffected by the fluctuating relations between *basileus* and tsar. The house of Zographou on Athos was closely associated with the Bulgarians from the thirteenth century onwards. It became an important centre for copying texts and reflective spirituality, even if it did not match Chilandar. Several other monasteries accommodated teachers, copyists and Slavonic translators, notably the Great Lavra. There, a scholar named Ioann and his pupils 'translated into our Bulgarian tongue' and made copies of a formidable corpus of writings, from the Gospels and the Psalter to a monastic *Typikon*, John Klimax's *Ladder of Paradise*, and exegeses of liturgical hymns. Many of these Slavonic texts were sent to Bulgaria, but some ended up in St Catherine's monastery on Sinai, an indication of the keen mutual interest of Orthodox centres in this period.[82]

Another Bulgarian bookman of the Great Lavra, Evtimii, returned apparently of his own accord and founded the Trinity monastery near Veliko T'rnovo in 1371. Ivan Alexander had just died and it was wholly due to Evtimii's ability, piety, and force of personality that his new house became a centre for translating from Greek into Slavonic. According to Evtimii's pupil and encomiast, Gregory Tsamblak, his pupils came 'not only from the Bulgarian peoples . . . but from all the northern peoples as far as the Ocean and from the west as far as Illyricum . . . He became their teacher in piety and they became instructors in their homelands.'[83] In their translation work, Evtimii and his circle showed

82 G. Popov, 'Novootkrito svedenie za prevodacheska deinost na b'lgarski knizhovnitsi ot Sveta Gora prez p'rvata polovina na XIVv.', *B'lgarski Ezik* 28 (1978), 402–10.
83 Gregory Tsamblak, *Pokhvalno slovo za Evtimii*, ed. P. Rusev et al. (Sofia: B'lgarskata akademiia na naukite, 1971), 196–7.

keenest interest in recently composed works, especially prayers, hymns and other texts used for the liturgy. They translated several prayers and sermons of Philotheos, like Evtimii himself, a former hesychast on Athos. Evtimii's concern to align forms of worship with those in Constantinople continued after his appointment as Bulgarian patriarch in 1375. Evtimii treated the texts and forms of worship used in the Great Church as definitive and, in rewriting works on earlier Bulgarian saints such as Ivan of Rila or composing new ones, he underlined the respect that pious emperors had supposedly shown for patriarchs and other senior churchmen. At the same time, he toned down claims made by thirteenth- and earlier fourteenth-century Bulgarian writers that their 'new Tsargrad' was at odds with the old. Evtimii acknowledged that Constantinople was 'the queen of cities' and raised no objection when the important Bulgarian see of Vidin returned to the fold of the ecumenical patriarchate in the 1380s.[84]

The foundation of other Bulgarian monasteries at this time also bears witness to the importance of personal links forged on Athos, a disregard for localised loyalties, and a purposefulness amounting to missionary drive. For example, Feodosii, a Bulgarian by birth, founded a monastery at Kilifarevo in Veliko T'rnovo, which received the support of Tsar Ivan Alexander. The monks' zeal for translation was accompanied by strict insistence on discipline and liturgical practices, to the point where Feodosii and his pupil Roman wrote to the Constantinopolitan patriarch, Kallistos, querying some of the practices of their local – Bulgarian – patriarch. They had reason to expect a sympathetic response, seeing that both Feodosii and Kallistos had the hesychast Gregory of Sinai as a spiritual father. Kallistos went on to write Gregory's *Life*,[85] which was soon translated into Slavonic at the Kilifarevo monastery. The Bulgarian patriarch resented the implied criticism and Feodosii and Roman migrated, with their pupils, to Kallistos in Constantinople. Feodosii and Kallistos had both lived in the monastery, which Gregory of Sinai had founded in the Byzantino-Bulgarian borderlands several years after leaving Athos in the later 1320s. Gregory, too, had received patronage from Ivan Alexander and, renowned for his familiarity with the traditions of the early Fathers, had attracted some seventy disciples, Bulgarian, Serb, but also Greek. Gregory was a mystic, who

84 D. I. Polyviannyi, *Kul'turnoe svoeobrazie srednevekovoi Bolgarii v kontektse vizantiisko-slavianskoi obshchnosti IX–XV vekov* (Ivanovo: Ivanovskii gosudarstvennyi universitet, 2000), 197–8.

85 Patriarch Kallistos, Βίος καὶ πολιτεία τοῦ ἐν ἁγίοις πατρὸς ἡμῶν Γρηγορίου τοῦ Σιναΐτου, ed. I. Pomialovskii, in *Zhitie izhe vo svatykh otsa nashego Grigoriia Sinaita* [Zapiski istoriko-filologicheskogo fakul'teta imperatorskago St.-Peterburgskogo Universiteta 35] (St Petersburg, 1896).

combined disciplined self-denial with meditation and respect for book learning. He laid emphasis on translation into Slavonic of collections of lives of holy men and theological tracts.

It has been argued that while on Athos Gregory gave guidance to his namesake Gregory Palamas.[86] Their adherence to a kind of 'fundamentalism', directing an individual to God via the strictest guidelines, formed part of a chain reaction among reflective souls across the Orthodox world to the shortcomings of earthly institutions and to the intellectual challenge and material wellbeing of Latin churchmen, warriors and traders. This heightened their sense of what they held in common with one another and with the writings of the Fathers. Transcending obstacles of space, language and time was characteristic of these communally aware proponents of individual enlightenment, for whom hesychast is a convenient if 'catch-all' term.

To speak of a 'hesychast movement' is misleading if it implies a hierarchical leadership directing a programme, or card-carrying members with agreed objectives. But the personal bonds of pupil and teacher linked very many of the persons mentioned above.[87] The 'workshop of virtue' on Athos served as a kind of seminary or haven for advocates of the new rigorism; the bonds forged there or in their own foundations transcended existing institutional frameworks. An example of this is the disregard of Feodosii and Roman for their local church leader and the reception they subsequently received from Patriarch Kallistos in Constantinople. Such priorities did not engender unqualified allegiance to any particular emperor. Indeed, these monks' values and frequent journeys across the eastern Christian world might seem on another plane from that of emperors. And yet, the Athonite houses continued to place themselves first and foremost under the protection of the Byzantine emperor, for the empire's existence was interdependent with the fate of mankind in Orthodox eschatology. If there was friction between the patriarchate and the monks of Athos, there was also constant interaction. The patriarchate drew on the networks of monastic rigorists, employing them for its own purposes. This nexus breathed life into the emaciated empire of the 'Romans', even while setting out new coordinates.

Not infrequently monks with affiliations to Athos or kindred houses received assignments from the patriarchate to far-flung sees or gave counsel to churchmen carrying out patriarchal business there. We have already encountered Chariton, the former abbot of Koutloumousiou, who was appointed

86 D. Balfour, 'Was St Gregory Palamas St Gregory the Sinaite's pupil?', *St Vladimir's Theological Quarterly* 28 (1984), 115–30.
87 See Obolensky, 'Late Byzantine culture', 25.

metropolitan of Oungrovlachia. While residing in his Trinity monastery, Evtimii answered questions on monastic discipline put to him by Anthimos, metropolitan 'of part of Oungrovlachia' and by Nikodemos. Nikodemos, himself a product of Athos, assigned by Patriarch Philotheos to Oungrovlachia, proceeded to found important monasteries at Vodita and Tismana. Evtimii also answered questions from a fellow-Bulgarian and former monk of Athos, Kiprian, a future metropolitan of Rus, who spent part of the long interval before taking up this post in scholarly labours in the Stoudios monastery in Constantinople, where he translated the *Ladder* of John Klimax. It is one of several Slavonic translations datable to around the turn of the fourteenth century, which have survived from the Stoudios scriptorium.

Kiprian proved eager to inculcate a combination of accurate book learning and carefully tempered asceticism more deeply and widely among the Rus. He himself translated the prayers and sermons of Philotheos, which became popular in Rus. He paid particular attention to the recently codified and amended texts for the Eucharist and daily offices in use in the Great Church and he saw to their translation, doing some of the work on their detailed rubrics himself. Among them was an updated version of the *Synodikon* of Orthodoxy, wherein the theology of Gregory Palamas was solemnly endorsed. A copy was sent to the clergy of Pskov, as Kiprian noted in a letter in 1395: 'I sent you the correct version of the *Synodikon* of Constantinople, which we also follow here [in Moscow] in commemorating [the Orthodox] and cursing the heretics: you, too, should conform to it.'[88] Thus due performance of the liturgy using accurate texts was indispensable for keeping the faith pure across the land. Kiprian was anxious to maintain worship and belief in common with eastern Christians in Jerusalem and elsewhere, staying true to the Church Fathers. But he looked to the vigorous ecumenical patriarchs of his own day for determination of best liturgical practice and church discipline. Such an attitude entailed acceptance of the imperial order, which the patriarchs propounded. It is probable that Kiprian took the initiative in having the *basileus*'s name entered into Moscow's liturgical diptychs, as in Constantinople.[89]

Just as Kiprian's advocacy of the imperial order as a fitting casement for Orthodoxy has something of the zeal of the convert, so the networks of monkish instructors, patriarchal staff, and metropolitans assigned to remote sees might seem little more than a mutual admiration society. The intensity of their personal relations and their spiritual and physical journeys can be

88 'Gramota mitropolita Kipriana pskovskomu dukhovenstvu', in *RIB* vi, col. 241; Meyendorff, *Byzantium*, 123–4, 260.

89 Meyendorff, *Byzantium*, 253–6.

reconstructed in detail thanks to their almost instant encomia of one another's doings; so much so that it is tempting to dismiss the commonwealth as merely frenetic networking on the part of a handful of individuals, a culturo-political elite whose members' variegated agenda converged partially – and only loosely – around an imperial centre in Constantinople. The hesychasts were mainly concerned with entering the world of the spirit, oblivious to the here-and-now. The materially enfeebled emperor might be regarded as merely a figure of convenience, dignifying this scheme of things. The symbols and imagery adapted by external rulers could be dismissed as efforts to deck out new power-centres in grandest style before an uncomprehending populace to whom the ways of the distant 'Greeks' and their dwindling empire meant little or nothing.

Such salutary caution cannot, however, fully account for the persistence with which would-be masters of their own extensive realms looked to the *basileus's* panoply of symbols and sought to appropriate them to their own pur-poses, sometimes unilaterally but often through negotiations and marriage-ties. It is a puzzle, which benefits from a closer look at Rus, in whose far-flung lands indigenous princely authority was itself tenuous for most of the inhabi-tants.

Commonwealth and a developing society: the case of Rus

A change in settlement-patterns is a salient feature of the forest zones of Rus in the thirteenth and fourteenth centuries. Formerly, populations had tended to congregate in so-called 'compact nests', huge clusters of settlements in the vicinity of lakes or river ways engaged in intensive trading in furs and other primary produce destined for distant markets, while gaining from those markets silver, amphorae containing wine, glass beads and bracelets, metal crosses, locks and keys. The pattern of settlement was uneven, with vast tracts of forest and marshland left virtually uninhabited. From the thirteenth cen-tury onwards the 'compact nests' broke up, longer-distance trading became less common, and settlements began to be dispersed more evenly across the wilderness. These small agrarian communities and homesteads were essen-tially self-sufficient and did not need to barter produce for implements or orna-ments from the outside world.[90] They did not, however, slip out of Orthodox

---

90 N. A. Makarov *et al.*, *Srednevekovoe rasselenie na Belom ozere* (Moscow: Iazyki russkoi kul'tury, 2001), 56, 64–8, 78–94, 216–26; Makarov, 'Rus' v XIII veke: kharakter kul'turnykh

supervision altogether, for monks and monasteries played an important part in opening up the forests, following the trail of new settlements and offering or imposing economic and spiritual management. This marked a change from the pre-Mongol era, when monasteries had largely been confined to towns and 'compact nests'. Many monks probably regarded their forest retreats primarily as opportunities for meditation, uncomplicated by routine secular concerns. But even small communities required continuous funding and consequent organisation. Whatever their original intentions, they tended to draw in additional manpower and rapidly acquired sizeable acreages of cultivable land. They could afford to set rents quite low and impose lighter labour services thanks to the fiscal exemptions issued by their princes and Tatar overlords. Circumstances inevitably varied according to personality and priorities, but monastic complexes emerged as potent economic and social forces in northern Rus, providing pastoral care for the inhabitants of their own lands and beyond. They set the tone for overt displays of spirituality as well as colouring the peasants' view of the world.

Given the extent of the lands belonging to monasteries and to the Rus metropolitan church by the fifteenth century and their sweeping jurisdictional rights over those living on them, the profusion of legal texts of one kind or another compiled or circulating in the monastic and ecclesiastical milieu is unsurprising. An important collection of translated texts of Byzantine church and civil law had been made in the 1260s at the behest of Metropolitan Kirill II, drawing on a recently compiled Serb compendium. Copies of this *Helmsman's Book* (*Kormchaia kniga*) were disseminated across Rus, and regional variants soon appeared, while Kirill himself invoked it in the *Rule* on church discipline that he promulgated. These sets of regulations, dictums and penalties covered a broad range of secular activities, including crimes, and in the fourteenth century a compilation from imperial law-codes in translation known as *Merilo pravednoe* ('Measure of law') was available to senior churchmen. However piecemeal, there were opportunities to apply some of these guidelines among the many communities living under the clerical or monastic wing. The responses of individual peasant households to the monks' material demands, adjudication of disputes and pastoral care are sparsely documented, but there are hints that monastic supervision and example could have an impact for better or for worse on everyday living and manners of dying. So, laymen's testaments witnessed by churchmen start to survive from the late thirteenth

izmenenii', in *Rus' v XIII veke: drevnosti temnogo vremeni*, ed. N. A. Makarov *et al.* (Moscow: Nauka, 2003), 5–11.

century onwards, while funeral rites (including the prayers chanted at the graveside) prescribed for monastic communities became widespread practice in Rus.[91] This may well reflect the frequency with which monks conducted funeral services for laypersons, itself a mark of their involvement with secular society. The wills and funeral rites form a backdrop to the claims of charitable works, miracles, and near-universal veneration made for a number of holy men by their hagiographers from the turn of the fourteenth century.

These holy men were riding waves of socio-economic change that were, as stressed above, peculiar to Rus. They lacked direct experience of monasticism in the eastern Mediterranean world. None the less, three of the most prominent, Sergii of Radonezh, Kirill of Beloozero and Stefan of Perm, looked not only to the Desert Fathers and other early exponents of monasticism but also to contemporary practices on Mount Athos, in Constantinople and in affiliated centres of spiritual excellence. While trusting in their own direct access to God, they sought partly to compensate for instruction by living sages with accurate liturgical texts, recently written manuals of spiritual instruction, and more theoretical works, paying close attention to the 'workshop of virtue' and corresponding with its products. Sergii of Radonezh spent years in a forest 'desert' well to the north of Moscow, founding a house for himself and one brother, but attracting others, reportedly against his will. Eventually he became abbot of the Trinity monastery in Moscow. Anxious to impose discipline as the means to piety, he insisted on ascetic communal living and looked to Byzantium for a model. He repeatedly sought the patriarch's counsel, and obtained an authoritative letter from a patriarch, probably Kallistos, berating those monks who objected to the rigours of cenobitic ways.[92] At the same time Sergii's personal qualities earned him respect from a wide range of persons, including Grand Prince Dmitrii, who sought his blessing before breaking with Muscovite precedent and making a military stand against the Tatars at Kulikovo in 1380. His standing was such that a Byzantine embassy of 1377 successfully sought his good offices with Grand Prince Dmitrii in an attempt to have Kiprian accepted as metropolitan in succession to Aleksii. Among the gifts which the embassy brought him was a small gold cross containing particles of the

---

91 D. H. Kaiser, *The growth of the law in medieval Russia* (Princeton: Princeton University Press, 1980), 153–5; Franklin, *Writing, society and culture*, 181, 184–6; A. A. Musin, *Khristianizatsiia novgorodskoi zemli v IX–XIV vekakh: pogrebal'nyi obriad i khristianskie drevnosti* [Archaeologica Petropolitana Trudy 5] (St Petersburg: Institut istorii material'noi kul'tury, 2002), 75–6.

92 'Poslanie konstantinopol'skogo patriarkha', in *RIB* vi, cols. 187–90; Meyendorff, *Byzantium*, 134 n. 62.

Church Father Athanasios of Alexandria and of the Forty Martyrs, but also of 'the new Lithuanian martyrs', as its inscription terms them.[93] Surviving letters of Kiprian addressed to Sergii presuppose that the patriarch and his synod together with the emperor were joint upholders of order within the church. The imperial–ecclesiastical complex held the key to the newly sacred, as well as to martyrs of old.

Kirill of Beloozero likewise showed enthusiasm for the Desert Fathers and for writings setting out their ways. He filled his monastery's library with a similar array of books to that in Sergii's Trinity monastery, whose holdings bear comparison with those available to monks in well-stocked Byzantine houses.[94] To impart general knowledge about church history and exemplary societies Kirill used textbooks originally intended for Byzantine secondary schools, but glossing them with historical notes, to make them more accessible to his pupils. He himself compiled an encyclopaedia with the aim of providing a manual for right thinking and pure living, for individual contemplation and eventual enlightenment.[95] Kyrill paid particular attention to the '*sketes*' – semi-eremitic houses – of Palestine and Mount Athos, because they offered an ideal spiritual environment. He included in his encyclopaedia the '*skete* rule' (*Skitskoi ustav*), regulations composed earlier in the fourteenth century, whether in Greek or in Slavonic by someone familiar with contemporary Greek. It has been suggested that what appears to be a sketch-map on the encyclopaedia's manuscript is Kirill's attempt to adapt the standard layout of an Athonite *skete* to the lie of the land at Beloozero.[96]

Preoccupation with inner perfection and dedication to a better, invisible, world were compatible with care for the local secular population and also with evangelisation. The most celebrated embodiment of these qualities is Stefan, whose *Life* was composed by a contemporary, Epifanii the Wise, writing in the same mannered 'word-weaving' style that he used for his *Life* of Sergii of Radonezh. Stefan, son of a clergyman in 'the land of midnight', became a monk in Rostov, where the bishop, Parthenios, was apparently a Greek; he learnt Greek and always kept Greek books in his cell. Stefan was ordained a

93 V. A. Kuchkin, 'Sergii Radonezhskii i "Filoveevskii krest"', in *Drevnerusskoe iskusstvo. Sergii Radonezhskii i khudozhestvennaia kul'tura Moskvy XIV–XV vv.*, ed. M. A. Orlova *et al.* (St Petersburg: D. Bulanin, 1998), 16–22; Baronas, 'Three martyrs of Vilnius', 89–90, 120–1.

94 I. Ševčenko, 'Russo-Byzantine relations after the eleventh century', reprinted in his *Byzantium and the Slavs in letters and culture* (Cambridge, MA: Harvard Ukrainian Research Institute 1991), no. 20, 274.

95 *Entsiklopediia russkogo igumena XIV–XV vv.*, ed. G. M. Prokhorov (St Petersburg: Oleg Abyshko, 2003), 149–55 (text); 341 (commentary).

96 Ibid., 19–28 (introduction); 158–65 (text); 345–53 (commentary).

priest and went to Perm near the Urals where he learnt the type of Finnish spoken by the local Zyrian population. He proceeded to create an alphabet and literary language for them. He translated parts of the scriptures and liturgical texts, harnessing the written word to his missionary work. Stefan understood that elevating the Zyrians' tongue to the rank of scriptural language was an effective means of bringing the people around Perm within the wider Christian sphere. But his missionary drive owed much of its urgency to expectations of the end of the world.[97] However loosely understood, he was striving to bring them within a Byzantine commonwealth before it was too late. This sense of belonging to an overarching community emerges, when Epifanii places Stefan's death in 1396: 'During the reign of the Orthodox Greek tsar Manuel, reigning in Tsargrad, under Patriarch Anthony, archbishop of Constantinople, under Patriarchs Dorotheos of Jerusalem, Mark of Alexandria, Neilos of Antioch, under the Orthodox Grand Prince Vasilii Dmitrievich of all Rus.'[98]

This was not merely an empire of the mind, a metaphor akin to the city extolled as a model for well-ordered communities in the works of Sergii of Radonezh and other monastic writers, for membership of the commonwealth had always been quintessentially voluntary and was inevitably so after 1204. Acceptance of the Constantinopolitan patriarch's profession of faith and the Byzantine-authorised forms of worship – virtually the only stable denominators of adherence to the Byzantine order – did not rule out a variety of other cultural identities or political allegiances. The weaker the empire was in material terms, the easier it became for individuals living far beyond its territorial remains, often under uncongenial regimes, to conceive of the emperor's mission as a last best hope for mankind, which might against all rational expectations be fulfilled. Such an attitude among monks and clergy was certainly fostered by the ecumenical patriarchate for the sake of coherence and, ultimately, ecclesiastical and civil discipline among eastern Christians. But the desire for overarching order also arose spontaneously among outsiders in novel situations, whether churchmen objecting to the measures of their local princes or Rus holy men, who found themselves providing social as well as spiritual leadership amidst changing settlement patterns in the fourteenth century. Their prime concern was with regulations for communities of like-minded souls – monasteries – and with correct forms of worship. But in this sphere,

---

97 R. M. Price, 'The holy man and Christianisation from the apocryphal apostles to St Stephen of Perm', in *The cult of saints in late antiquity and the early middle ages: essays on the contribution of Peter Brown*, ed. P. Hayward and J. Howard-Johnston (Oxford: Oxford University Press, 1999), 232–5.

98 Epifanii Premudryi, *Zhitie sviatogo Stefana episkopa Permskogo*, ed. V. G. Druzhinin (St Petersburg: Arkheograficheskaia Kommissiia, 1897), 85; see also ibid., 74.

too, the ideal of a single emperor on earth presiding over a single divinely authorised order of things had its uses.

Horizontal strands in the commonwealth

These considerations go some way to meeting objections that the Byzantine Commonwealth lacked both substance and theoretical formulation. But besides the vertical structures, expressed through hierarchies, horizontal strands served to create a kind of 'force field', replete with positive and negative charges. These circuits were no less important in creating an entity that may be described as a commonwealth. As we have seen, the writings, utterances and itineraries of fourteenth-century Orthodox 'hesychasts' were governed by spiritual preoccupations. They were on occasion prepared to denounce the policies of emperors, as well as one another, and in word and deed they were seldom constrained by earthly boundaries. Yet in envisaging the future, criticising the existing socio-political order or essaying alternative behaviour-patterns, monks and laymen were to a large extent orientated by the range of options deriving from Byzantium.

A few examples may illustrate the workings of this 'force field'. Shared by many senior churchmen in Rus were the expectations of the world's end, which propelled Stefan's endeavours among the Zyrians. Their reckonings about providence and time were likewise in tune with those of other Orthodox communities. The completion of the seventh millennium since the Creation was widely expected to trigger the Second Coming and the end of time. The Byzantine year 7000 from the Creation corresponded to AD 1 September 1492 to 31 August 1493. The leaders of Moscow saw an opening here for their own God-given hegemony, particularly once life on earth continued after that year. South Slav and Greek writers succumbing to Turkish domination were less sanguine, linking up eschatological expectations and calculations with their respective defunct or faltering polities.[99]

Chronological calculations about the end and ideological inferences from them were mostly carried out by the political and clerical elite, but visions of the future, of heaven and hell, circulated, in the form of texts in Slavonic translation, at humbler levels of Orthodox societies, perhaps being read out at

---

99 Polyviannyi, *Kul'turnoe svoeobrazie*, 219–22, 229–31; V. Tăpkova-Zaïmova and A. Miltenova, *Istoriko-apokaliptichnata knizhnina v'v Vizantiia i v srednovekovna B'lgariia* (Sofia: Universitetsko izdatelstvo 'Sv. Kliment Okhridski', 1996), 53–9; G. Podskalsky, *Theologische Literatur des Mittelalters in Bulgarien und Serbien 865–1459* (Munich: Beck, 2000), 472, 482–7.

meetings of confraternities. Accounts of journeys to the other world were very popular among eastern Christians: heaven was envisaged as a superior version of the emperor's hierarchy on earth, while people of this world were punished in hell. Works of Middle Byzantine vision literature, such as the *Apocalypse of Anastasia*, seem to have had negative nuances, criticising the government's harsh corporal punishments and also corrupt officials. However, they did not set out to overturn the imperial order as such or propagate heresy: on the contrary they probably owed their popularity to their effective reinforcing of the Orthodox moral code against proselytising heretics.[100] The *Apocalypse of Anastasia* was translated into Slavonic at an early date, perhaps in twelfth-century Bulgaria, and copies of this *Apocalypse* circulated as far north as Rus. So, too, did copies of Kosmas's treatise against the heretics, a tenth-century Bulgarian text overtly castigating the Bogomils, dualists at odds with the imperial order, as with all ranks and material things. There are several hints, not least the popularity of texts denouncing them, that South Slav or Byzantine dualist proselytisers and writings of one kind or another circulated through the urban centres of Rus. It could even be that the *strigol'niki*, targets of treatises penned by Stefan of Perm as well as by Patriarch Neilos, owed something to dualist notions.[101] These manifestations of dissent inevitably varied according to time and place, but the politico-religious order they denounce is structured along Byzantine hierarchical lines. This 'force field' of beliefs, apprehensions and negations could also take material form in unauthorised but not consciously unorthodox amulets, for example the bronze 'womb' pendants made for the protection of women.

Another instance of the 'force field's' workings comes from the distribution pattern of those whose behaviour flouted conventions of property and propriety in affirmation of otherworldly values, the fools for Christ. They might snatch food from a market-stall, disrupt church services or even berate an emperor. Holy fools were venerated in late antique and earlier medieval Constantinople and the *Lives* of St Andrew the Fool and several other fools had been translated into Slavonic by the twelfth century. Instances of folly for Christ occur in most societies imbued with Byzantine Christianity, for example the Bulgarians and Georgians. Individual monks were acting the fool in Rus by

---

100 J. Baun, 'Middle Byzantine "tours of hell": outsider theodicy?', in *Strangers to themselves: the Byzantine outsider*, ed. D. C. Smythe (Aldershot, 2000), 58–9; Baun, *Tales from another Byzantium: celestial journey and local community in the medieval Greek Apocrypha* (Cambridge: Cambridge University Press, 2006). See also D. Angelov, 'The eschatological views of medieval Bulgaria as reflected in the canonical and apocryphal literature', *Bulgarian Historical Review* 18 (1990), 31–42.
101 Meyendorff, *Byzantium*, 137, 231 and n. 19.

the eleventh century, when Isaac, a monk of the cave-monastery, deliberately made himself an object of ridicule and vilification.[102] Given their lifestyle, holy fools are unlikely to have made the voyage to Rus from Byzantium and the concept was most probably picked up from *Lives* of Byzantine fools available in translation. In this instance, as in others, monks seem to have been the broadcasters of Byzantine notions and practices to the populace at large. Deliberate transgression of social norms for the sake of Christ and literal enactment of His Beatitudes presented, in their way, a kind of living icon. The fool constituted a variant on the icons lodged in many private houses and chapels, which offered their venerators direct access to the holy. During the sixteenth century the theory and practice of holy foolery gained considerable political significance in Rus. Giles Fletcher, an eyewitness of Ivan IV's Muscovy, observed that the fools were regarded 'as prophets and men of great holiness'. Some, such as Basil and Nikolai of Pskov, had freely rebuked Ivan 'for all his cruelty and oppressions, done towards his people'; 'this maketh the people to like very well of them, because they . . . note their great men's faults, that no man else dare speak of'.[103] They were, Fletcher recorded, called 'holy men' by the Rus.

No precise analogies to fools of such persistent political prominence are known from Byzantium, although holy men were not behindhand in speaking out about misdeeds of officials or the emperor himself. Nor do Byzantine emperors offer convincing counterparts to Ivan the Terrible's conduct. Ivan's panoply of ceremonial is understandable in terms of adapting Byzantine rites and concepts of legitimate hegemony to the needs of his own polity, impressing the uniqueness of his authority upon fellow members of his family and truculent boyars, firing them and newly subjugated populations with a sense of divine purpose. That the ideology voiced in Makarii's address at Ivan's coronation should have echoed that of a sixth-century treatise on imperial authority by Deacon Agapetos is likewise unremarkable. More striking is the fact that one of the main responses to Ivan's pretensions to autocracy came from individuals acting in apparent isolation from one another, lacking direct experience of Byzantine precedents. Faced with Ivan's experiment, they reacted by drawing on a cultural idiom and range of behaviour-patterns now

102 *Kievo-Pecherskii paterik*, ed. L. A. Ol'shevskaia in *Biblioteka literatury drevnei Rusi*, ed. D. S. Likhachev, IV (St Petersburg: Nauka, 1997), 478, 480; trans. M. Heppell, *The Paterik of the Kievan Caves Monastery* [Harvard Library of early Ukrainian Literature: English Translations 1] (Cambridge, MA: Ukrainian Research Institute, Harvard University, 1989), 208; S. Ivanov, *Holy Fools*, trans. S. C. Franklin (Oxford: Oxford University Press, 2006).

103 Giles Fletcher, *Of the Russe Commonwealth* (London: Thomas Charde, 1591), reprinted with introduction by R. Pipes (Cambridge, MA: Harvard University Press, 1966), 89v.–91r.

engrained in their own society yet deriving from eastern Christian spirituality, as transmitted via Byzantium. The political holy fools (and occasional martyrs) of Ivan's Muscovy were performing individual variations – if not syncopations – on a Byzantine theme.

These cross-currents of belief and behaviour, not unlike Byzantine vision literature, the teachings of dualists or of other outright heretics, constituted the negative charges in a 'force field' whose principal coordinates had been determined far away. The Greek tsars remained objects of respect among Rus churchmen and some leading laymen, although lacking tangible powers over Rus princes, while Constantinopolitan patriarchs not only provided moral leadership, personnel and authoritative legal rulings but also rallied eastern Christians to the imperial ideal in the fourteenth century. Moreover, 'the workshop of virtue' on Athos still discharged monks, manuscripts and ideas about means of gaining access to God. But by the sixteenth century hierarchical constraints on the rulers of Rus were very faint and the idea of Moscow as the new Tsargrad was gaining ideological coherence. But while the belatedness of the Constantinopolitan patriarch's approval of the imperial coronation of Ivan did not hold back the ceremony, Ivan's sweeping interpretation of God-given autocracy evoked vigorous condemnation from the holy fools. Some 'horizontal' elements of the 'force field', at least, were still active among the urban populace. And, thanks to Athos, the notion of a right-believing empire-out-there, albeit now lost, was still fostered by occasional visiting monks, such as Maksim Grek.[104] His sentiments were pieties: conventional calls for godliness and righteous conduct on the ruler's part, and a denunciation of assumption of imperial rank by the unworthy, who behaved like torturers rather than tsars. The inhibitions of an Orthodox autocrat in a realm far from the empire of the 'Romans' were largely self-imposed. Yet in appropriating the sort of authority symbols that were supposed to have been in the Greek tsar's gift and in drawing upon Agapetos's ideal of imperial hegemony, Ivan and his counsellors remained open to the countercharges and moral constraints which Byzantine imperial ideology could – and sometimes did – generate. We have seen how Metropolitan Makarii showed some compunction at the moment of anointing Ivan in 1547, apparently out of respect for past form and Constantinople's prerogatives.[105]

104 Maksim Grek, *Tvoreniia* (Moscow: Sviato-Troitskaia Sergieva Lavra, 1996), I, 203–6, 211–12; D. Obolensky, *Six Byzantine portraits* (Oxford: Clarendon Press, 1988), 218.
105 See above, p. 11; I. Ševčenko, 'A neglected Byzantine source of Muscovite political ideology', *Harvard Slavic Studies* 2 (1954), 166–73.

The Byzantine 'force field'

If the political culture and behavioural patterns which Byzantium prompted in so-called 'acquiring' societies are almost as notable for their diversity as for common traits, this reflects upon the ambivalence and flexibility of Byzantium's own imperial–ecclesiastical complex. The emperor's aspirations to carry on the divine mandate of Constantine the Great and lead the New Israel in the manner of Old Testament priest-kings remained robust, even after imperial intervention in doctrine and church governance came to grief with iconoclasm. The insistence of court ceremonial and rhetorical declarations on the harmony between emperor and senior churchmen represents the gloss on incessant minor points of friction in everyday affairs and more fundamental differences as to boundaries and values.[106] The emperor's hold over the established church, already uncertain in the twelfth century, was shaken irreparably by the Latin conquest of Constantinople. The subsequent failure of Michael VIII's attempt to dragoon churchmen into union with Rome only served to accentuate the limitations of imperial power in matters of church policy. Throughout the fourteenth century the high calibre and morale of the patriarchate's officials were in marked contrast to the gloom surrounding the imperial apparatus. Moreover, the patriarch's treasury seems to have been in a better state of repair than the emperor's, owing in part to the generous payments which external rulers and churchmen were ready to make in return for decisions to their liking. None the less, the emperor and his associates remained an influential presence in the higher echelons of the patriarchate. Patriarchs tried to impress upon foreign potentates the God-given nature of imperial power and that they were acting in concert with the emperor in caring for Orthodox Christians wherever they were, regardless of the complexion of the local regime. It is probably no accident that patriarchal declarations to this effect became clearest-cut in the second half of the fourteenth century, precisely the time when the material resources and military position of the empire took a turn for the worse. The nearest approach to a formulation of the Byzantine Commonwealth comes from the time when the empire's earthly power was on the ebb and the emperor was least capable of applying duress, enforcing judgements or providing Orthodox communities with physical protection.

It is tempting enough to conclude that the characteristics shared in common by supposedly constituent polities and communities are too faint or banal and

---

106 G. Dagron, *Emperor and priest: the imperial office in Byzantium* (Cambridge: Cambridge University Press, 2003), 2–4, 48–50, 97–114.

their divergences and alternative affinities too pronounced for the concept of a Byzantine Commonwealth as formulated by Obolensky to have force.[107] As we have seen, the prevailing assumption of imperial policy after 1261 was that effective military aid was best had from the west, even at the price of tampering with religious doctrine: Orthodox rulers were generally deemed too remote, indifferent, or barbarous and unruly to be effectual. Alternatively, as in the case of the Serbs, especially Stefan Dušan, they were all too close, and viewed as prospective conquerors. Yet the Serbs also serve as crown witnesses to the operations of some kind of 'force field' for which the term commonwealth is not so *mal à propos*. Members of this ruling elite and pious individuals showed enthusiasm for acquiring texts about, and encountering living exponents of, correct religious doctrine and best practice in church and monastic affairs. In a sense, they were merely joining in the textual community of Orthodox Slavs. Serbian princes appropriated Byzantine political institutions and culture, not merely because they had seized extensive Byzantine territories, but also because they recognised inherent merit in law-codes supposedly issued by pious emperors such as Justinian. A highly ambitious ruler, Stefan Dušan for example, operating from a position of military strength, could have himself crowned 'emperor' by a newly instituted patriarch and expressly place his law-code in the tradition of earlier emperors. But he seems to have baulked at trying to seize Constantinople for himself by force. He had to reckon with the inhibitions of his own churchmen and likely protests from at least some of the monks of Athos whose prayers he valued. But what may have weighed most heavily with him was risk of giving offence to the City's supernatural protectors: he was, as a student of history, well aware of their impressive record to date in shielding the City.

If self-interest counselled caution to Dušan, leaders of Orthodox structures further away from Constantinople also had to handle with care this model of Christian order under ancient imperial tutelage. So long as an unimpeachably Orthodox emperor reigned in Constantinople, no other Orthodox rulers could afford overtly to disengage from, ignore or claim exclusive proprietorship of that ideal, even if the *basileus* had no direct impact on their own regime. Besides, the ideal had support, even within the remoter recesses of their own polities, as the example of Sergii of Radonezh demonstrates. The overlords of extensive territories with undersized administrations needed the cooperation and prayers of such figures, while their populations' predisposition in favour of

---

107 C. Raffensperger, 'Revisiting the idea of the Byzantine Commonwealth', *BF* 28 (2004), 164–8, 172–4.

long-established cults, religious rites and forms of devotion made maintenance of contacts with church authorities in Constantinople a matter of practical prudence, rather than just piety or habit.

The supra-regional entity, which emerges from these considerations, may appear politically passive or negative, a source of inhibitions rather than a focus of active allegiance. We have observed episodes when Serb, Bulgarian and Lithuanian rulers sought to shake off ecclesiastical dependency on Constantinople through creating their own patriarchates or looking elsewhere for consecration of their head churchmen. But we have also seen the tendency of churchmen in even the longest-established Christian polity, Bulgaria, to look back to the Constantinopolitan patriarchate, Athonite spirituality and the Greek language as templates of piety and correct doctrine. And the potency of imperial inauguration-rituals and authority-symbols seems to have become more valued by leaders of Orthodox polities when they were extending their own hegemony over surrounding populations and seeking moral superiority from the artefacts, regalia and imagery emanating from Constantinople, irrespective of its current state, as was the case with the supposed 'crown of Monomachos' with which Ivan IV was crowned in 1547. The dynamics of these polities did not conform to a single set of laws or principles and they operated for the purpose of creating new centres. But access to supernatural powers, religious faith and legitimate hegemonial authority were interwoven in the Byzantine imperial order in an indissoluble and, even after 1204, visually striking, quasi-liturgical web. So long as an emperor worthy of this ancient centre reigned in Constantinople, a particular cosmic order still obtained. It was a matter of political self-interest for leaders of other Orthodox polities not to be seen to flout it. In fact, there was much to be said for abiding by the rites of worship, religious doctrines and ideals of supremely pious conduct that were supposed to prevail in the centre-out-there – Constantinople. In so far as these rites and values commanded general assent, adherence to them was not a matter for the leaders alone to decide. The 'force field', once entered, could be manipulated, but it could not be abandoned or radically reprogrammed to the unequivocal advantage of individual rulers while emperor, patriarch and City still presided on the Bosporus.

2

Byzantium and the west 1204–1453

MICHAEL ANGOLD

One episode presents many of the recurring features of the last phase of Byzantine relations with the west. On 12 December 1452 in the teeth of popular hostility St Sophia witnessed the much-delayed proclamation of the union of Florence. It was the work of the papal legate Isidore of Kiev, whose recent arrival in Constantinople gave new purpose to the unionist cause. He was able to cajole the emperor Constantine XI Palaiologos (1448–53) into staging the proclamation of the union of churches. Isidore understood how little enthusiasm there was among the Greeks of Constantinople for union with Rome. Most preferred to put their trust in their icons rather than in help from the west. Even those who participated in the service of reunion justified their presence in terms of expediency and urged opponents of the union to wait until the present crisis had passed.[1] This incident illustrates the popular opposition to union; the reluctant realism among the ruling elite, which dictated lip service to the union as a way of securing western aid; but also the energy and idealism of a Greek convert to Rome, who saw in the union of churches not only a return to the true faith, but also a path to regeneration. It is the final feature that is the most surprising. Why over two centuries should so many of the ablest and most attractive Byzantines have turned to the Latin West, not in a spirit of expediency, but out of idealism? There is no one answer. But it was part of a growing appreciation by influential members of the Byzantine elite of Latin culture.[2] This was reinforced by a growing sense of despair about the condition of Byzantium and a conviction that salvation could only come from the west.

---

1 *Ducae, Michaelis Ducae Nepotis, Historia Byzantina*, ed. I. Bekker (Bonn: Ed. Weber, 1834), 255–7.
2 F. Tinnefeld, 'Das Niveau der abendländischen Wissenschaft aus der Sicht gebildeter Byzantiner im 13. und 14. Jh.', *BF* 6 (1979), 241–80.

From the fall of Constantinople (1204) to the council of Lyons (1274) and its aftermath

These were not feelings that were widely shared, for a natural consequence of the crusader conquest of Constantinople in 1204 was a vilification of the Latins. The Byzantines remembered the sack of Constantinople as a deliberate insult towards Orthodoxy. This was the theme of a tract compiled soon after 1204 by Constantine Stilbes, bishop of Kyzikos, listing the errors of the Latins.[3] It took this form of polemical literature to its logical conclusion. It provided a rather different image of the Latins from that which prevailed before 1204, when the Byzantines had been inclined to idealise the crusade and crusaders, as opposed to the Latins, who evoked mixed feelings. Stilbes provided an original analysis in which the crusade was presented as part of the apparatus of papal *plenitudo potestatis*. The papacy offered crusaders indulgences which applied not only to past sins, but also to those yet to be committed. Equally, the papacy released them from their oaths. It taught that those dying in battle went directly to paradise. Stilbes's list of Latin errors closes with the crimes committed by the Latins during the sack of Constantinople. These clinched the underlying argument of his tract that addiction to war had perverted Latin Christianity and had turned it into a heresy.

This tract was a key document in the refashioning of the Byzantine identity, which was now defined against the Latins. If the defence of Orthodoxy against the Latin threat became its central feature, the exact nature of that threat was not always clear and produced mixed reactions across the Byzantine population. In the short term, an even greater danger was that the Orthodox Church would split up into a series of autonomous churches, which mirrored the political conditions of the time. That this did not happen was largely the work of the patriarch Germanos II (1223–40). He took his ecumenical duties very seriously, asserting his authority in different ways over the various separated churches, whether in Russia, Georgia, Serbia, Bulgaria, Epiros or Cyprus. He confirmed the Greeks of Constantinople in their faith and exhorted the Cypriots to resist Latin pressure for submission. These actions inevitably brought him into contact with the Latin Church. In the process he rescued five Franciscans, who had fallen into captivity among the Seljuqs of Rum.[4]

3 J. Darrouzès, 'Le mémoire de Constantin Stilbès contre les Latins', *REB* 20 (1962), 61–92. See T. M. Kolbaba, *The Byzantine lists: errors of the Latins* (Urbana and Chicago: University of Illinois Press, 2000), 32–87.

4 M. J. Angold, *Church and society in Byzantium under the Comneni 1081–1261* (Cambridge: Cambridge University Press, 1995), 522–9.

The patriarch's own words betray the immense impression that these friars made on him. They seemed to represent a different and more attractive face of Latin Christianity. Their piety was in tune with the Byzantine ideal. They held out the hope that there might still be a peaceful way of settling the differences that existed between the two churches. The negotiations that ensued over several months in 1234 are among the best documented of any exchange between the two churches.[5] They laid down a pattern that would be repeated over the next two centuries. At its starkest it turned into a series of recriminations, which revealed how far apart Greek and Latin were. It also offered hope that these might be resolved. Dialogue was fruitful because the friars had a good command of Greek and were well versed in Greek patristics. They were able to argue out their case in terms that their Greek counterparts understood. They made some sort of apology for the sack of Constantinople in 1204, insisting that it was done not with the permission of the Roman Church but 'by laymen, sinners, excommunicates presuming on their own authority'.[6]

Among the delegation of friars was a Dominican working at Constantinople, who in 1252 completed the *Contra errores Graecorum*.[7] This tract is notable not only for its rigorous organisation in the best scholastic manner, but also for its use of the Greek Fathers. The author was convinced that the Greeks used their own authorities erroneously in order to support heretical notions. It was his intention to persuade the Greeks on the basis of their own patristic tradition that the Latin position was correct. In this he was building on the works of Hugh Eteriano and his brother Leo Tuscus, who had been in the service of Manuel I Komnenos (1143–80). Their works represented the first systematic attempt by Latin theologians to address the differences between the two churches on the basis of Greek patristics. The Dominican author was familiar with Orthodox practice. Over the question of purgatory he cited wall paintings he had seen in Greek churches, along with extracts from the Greek Fathers, as evidence that the Orthodox had some notion of purgatorial fire.[8] The treatise was translated into Greek and was intended for missionary purposes. The activities of the friars were limited pretty much to Latin Constantinople, but there they met with some success among those of mixed Latin and Greek

5 H. Golubovich (ed.), 'Disputatio Latinorum et Graecorum seu Relatio apocrisariorum Gregorii IX de gestis Nicaea in Bithynia et Nymphaeae in Lydia 1234', *Archivum Franciscanum Historicum* 12 (1919), 418–70; P. Canart, 'Nicéphore Blemmyde et le mémoire adressé aux envoyés de Grégoire IX (Nicée, 1234)', *OCP* 25 (1959), 310–25.

6 Golubovich, 'Disputatio', 451–2.

7 *PG* 140, 487–574; A. Dondaine, '"Contra Graecos". Premiers écrits polémiques des Dominicains d'Orient', *Archivum Fratrum Praedicatorum* 21 (1951), 344–5.

8 *PG* 140, 513B–D.

parentage.[9] At a different level, they seem to have influenced the Byzantine theologian Nikephoros Blemmydes, who was prepared to concede on the basis of Greek patristic texts that the Holy Spirit proceeded from the Father *through* the Son. This represented a shift towards the Latin insistence on the double procession of the Holy Spirit from the Father *and from* the Son (*filioque*).[10] By the end of the period of exile there was, thanks mainly to the friars, a new spirit of reconciliation abroad.

Discussions with the Latins were always intended to bring the recovery of Constantinople closer. But this happened by sheer chance in July 1261, when a small Nicaean force took the City by surprise. It might seem that – with Constantinople recovered – there was no longer a political purpose to dialogue with the Latin Church. However, the new Byzantine emperor Michael VIII Palaiologos (1259/61–82) assessed the situation differently. He reckoned that there was always the danger of western intervention unless the restored empire received papal recognition.[11] To this end – and with Franciscan help – he made contact with the papacy within a year of his triumphal entry into Constantinople. It was a necessary first step to re-establishing his empire on the international stage, but ultimately it proved his undoing, because it led to church union with Rome, which in turn produced the progressive alienation of both church and people.

Why Michael Palaiologos was unable to carry them with him remains a pertinent question. From the outset he encountered opposition to his rule. This was more or less inevitable. He was a usurper and had to face the hostility of those attached to the old Laskarid dynasty. But it went deeper than this. He sought to restore the imperial office as the focus of Byzantine society and identity. This meant reversing developments that occurred during the period of exile. It brought the emperor into conflict with the church, which saw its independence eroded by his autocratic stance. It was this far more than any unionist negotiations that was for much of his reign the real issue: that is, until the emperor's unionist policy came to be seen not only as central to his reassertion of imperial power, but also as a threat to the Orthodox core of the Byzantine identity. At the end of his life Michael Palaiologos wrote two autobiographical pieces. They reveal complete bewilderment at the lack of gratitude for the benefits he had bestowed on his people. Had he not

9 R. L. Wolff, 'The Latin Empire and the Franciscans', *Traditio* 2 (1944), 213–37.

10 J. Munitiz, 'A reappraisal of Blemmydes' First Discussion with the Latins', *BSl* 51 (1990), 20–6, where he shows that Blemmydes changed his position over the procession of the Holy Spirit.

11 D. J. Geanakopolos, *Emperor Michael VIII Palaeologus and the West 1258–82: a study in Byzantino-Latin relations* (Cambridge, MA: Harvard University Press, 1959).

recovered Constantinople; had he not extended the frontiers of the empire and successfully defended them against its enemies? He was especially bitter about opposition from within the church: had he not restored the seat of the patriarchate to Constantinople and rescued it from provincial obscurity?[12]

Michael Palaiologos's overtures to the papacy only became controversial when Pope Gregory X (1271–76) started to take them seriously. Superficially, the emperor's interest in union was as a means of blocking the ambitions of the king of Sicily, Charles of Anjou. But Michael's proposal to link union with a joint crusade suggested something more to the papacy: nothing less than the integration of eastern and western Christendom under papal auspices. The emperor was realistic enough to know that he could not foist union on the church of Constantinople without first obtaining at least token consent from the patriarch, Joseph I (1266–75). The latter was in a weak position. Having inherited bitter divisions within his church he was now caught between the emperor and the anti-unionists, the most prominent of whom was, at this stage, John Bekkos, the *chartophylax* of St Sophia. The patriarch was not entirely convinced by the emperor's assertion that union would mean minimal concessions to the papacy: no more than the commemoration of the pope in the prayers of the Orthodox Church, recognition of papal primacy, and Rome as a final court of appeal. He nevertheless gave his consent to negotiations on condition that Orthodox forms of worship were respected. This enabled Michael Palaiologos to obtain the adhesion of forty-four bishops for negotiations over union. The patriarch knew he was in a false position. His decision taken early in 1274 to retire to a monastery only confirmed how cleverly the emperor had managed the church.[13]

Winning over John Bekkos to the unionist cause was one sign that at this stage it was in the ascendant. Another was the sudden interest taken in Latin texts by Byzantine scholars including the young Maximos Planoudes. His major achievement in this field was the translation of Augustine's *On the Trinity*, which was vital for an informed view of Latin theology.[14] Support for

---

12 A. A. Dmitrievskij, *Opisanie liturgicheskikh rukopisei*, I.i (Kiev: Kievan Academy, 1895), 769–94; H. Grégoire, 'Imperatoris Michael Palaeologi de Vita Sua', *B* 29–30 (1959–60), 447–74.

13 *1274: Année charnière – mutations et continuités* [Colloques internationaux du Centre national de la recherche scientifique 558] (Paris: CNRS, 1977); B. Roberg, *Die Union zwischen der griechischen und der lateinischen Kirche auf dem II. Konzil von Lyon (1274)* (Bonn: Ludwig Röhrscheid Verlag, 1964); B. Roberg, *Das zweite Konzil von Lyon [1274]* (Paderborn: Schöningh, 1990).

14 W. O. Schmitt, 'Lateinische Literatur in Byzanz: die Übersetzungen des Maximos Planudes und die moderne Forschung', *Jahrbuch der Österreichischen Byzantinistik* 17 (1968), 127–47.

union also benefited from the esteem in which the Franciscan John Parastron was held throughout Byzantine society.[15] He was born in Constantinople, then under Latin rule, and knew Greek to perfection. He participated in the Orthodox liturgy and even advocated dropping the *filioque* from the Latin creed as the price of ending the schism between the two churches.

It took time for opposition to the union promulgated at Lyons on 6 July 1274 to gather force. The critical moment came in April 1277 when Michael Palaiologos and his son and heir Andronikos publicly proclaimed their adhesion to the union and recited the creed with the Latin addition of the *filioque*. It was becoming increasingly hard to trust the emperor's assurances that union would bring no substantial changes to Orthodox worship. As alarming were the activities of John Bekkos, whom Michael Palaiologos had made patriarch in May 1275.[16] Imprisonment for his initial opposition to union had given Bekkos the leisure to study the dogmatic differences separating the churches. He discovered more and more support in the Greek Fathers for the compromise position sketched earlier by Nikephoros Blemmydes. This led him to ponder the historical circumstances of the split from the Roman Church. He became convinced that the culprit was the patriarch Photios. He was dismissive of the latter's *Mystagogia*, which provided the theological foundations of Byzantine criticism of Latin teaching on the Trinity. To Bekkos's way of thinking, Photios had allowed his ambition to destroy the harmonious relations that had existed between Rome and Constantinople in an earlier period. Bekkos sought to restore concord. To do so it was essential that the Orthodox Church accepted the patristic view that on the procession of the Holy Spirit there was no essential difference between the two churches.

Bekkos was working within the Orthodox tradition. His knowledge of Latin culture and theology was minimal. He believed that he was recovering the authentic Orthodox teaching on the procession of the Holy Spirit, which had been lost through Photios. He insisted that he was as devoted and loyal to Byzantium as it was possible to be. He could not understand why his opponents treated him as a traitor. This was a line of thought expressed over the years by many Latin sympathisers, along with their dismay at the violence of the popular hatred of the Latins. The union of Lyons set in motion a struggle within Byzantium that was superficially about the Latins but really about

15 Georges Pachymérès, *Relations historiques*, ed. A. Failler (Paris: Belles Lettres, 1984), II, v.xi; 475–6.

16 H. Chadwick, *East and West: the making of a rift in the church: from Apostolic times until the Council of Florence* (Oxford: Oxford University Press, 2003), 246–57; G. Richter, 'Johannes Bekkos und sein Verhältnis zur römischen Kirche', *BF* 15 (1990), 167–217.

the Byzantine identity. Bekkos and his supporters were too high minded to articulate their ideas in a way that had popular appeal. They were formed by a historical perspective, which sought to liquidate four hundred years of increasing friction with the Roman Church and to return to the fraternal relations which had previously existed; to a time when the papacy had so often proved itself the strongest defence of Orthodoxy.

Today Bekkos's revisionism seems very attractive, but at the time it flew in the face of papal intransigence. Michael Palaiologos may have convinced himself that union meant no substantial concessions; John Bekkos may have seen it as the first step towards the restoration of harmonious relations between the two churches, but the papacy viewed it as the reduction of the church of Constantinople to obedience to the mother-church of Rome. To ensure satisfactory implementation the papacy insisted on the presence in Constantinople of a papal legate. Under pressure to prove his commitment to union Palaiologos embarked on the persecution of its opponents. The most vivid testimony to its range and brutality comes from the report submitted in 1278 to the papal legate by the emperor himself.[17] It set out the scale of opposition that the latter faced. It was disturbing how many of the imperial family now opposed union. At their head was the emperor's favourite sister, the nun Eulogia. Palaiologos sent the papal legate on a guided tour of the dungeons of the Great Palace, so that the latter could see for himself how opponents of union were being treated. The emperor also sent back with the legate as a token of his good faith two dissident monks, Meletios and Ignatios.

For his opposition to union Meletios is revered by the Orthodox Church as a confessor.[18] His activities led to exile on the island of Skyros. There as part of a larger work he composed a polemic against the 'Errors of the Latins'. It was written in political verse, which indicates that it was intended for wide circulation. Its purpose was to confirm opponents of the union in their cause and to convince waverers that Latins represented everything repugnant to a good Byzantine. It was, in other words, presenting opposition to union as a patriotic duty. Another product of anti-unionist propaganda was a tract which purported to be a dialogue between an Orthodox bishop and a cardinal.[19] If it turns into the usual list of Latin errors, it begins quite differently. It has one

17 R.-J. Loenertz, 'Mémoire d'Ogier, protonotaire, pour Mario et Marchetto, nonces de Michel VIII Paléologue auprès du Pape Nicholas III. 1278 printemps–été', OCP 31 (1965), 374–408.
18 T. M. Kolbaba, 'Meletios Homologetes On the customs of the Italians', REB 55 (1997), 137–68.
19 D. J. Geanakoplos, Interaction of the 'sibling' Byzantine and Western cultures in the Middle Ages and Italian Renaissance (330–1600) (New Haven and London: Yale University Press, 1976), 156–70.

John – plausibly identified with John Parastron – arriving from Rome leading a mule with an image of the pope on its back. The emperor took the bridle and escorted by twelve cardinals led it into the imperial palace where the pope's name was restored to the diptychs. Now the emperor was assured 'all Christians will partake of communion wafers (azymes)'. It is easy to identify this scene as a travesty of the implementation of the union of Lyons. The tract aimed at discrediting leading unionists, who are named. It catches a moment when much of the elite still supported the emperor over union. It ends by anathematising not only the Latins as heretics, but also the 'azymites', as unionists were called.

This tract illustrates the way the union of Lyons touched a raw nerve at Byzantium. It revived all the rancour that had been created by the fall of Constantinople in 1204, which its recovery some fifty years later temporarily assuaged. The return to Constantinople vindicated the ideology of exile, which saw the Byzantines as the new Israelites. Nicaea was their Babylon. Having atoned for their sins they returned to their Zion – Constantinople. In this scheme of things Latin Christianity was presented as a perversion of the faith, which threatened to pollute Orthodoxy, whether by its espousal of religious warfare, by its use of azymes in the communion service, or by its strange dietary customs. But the return to Constantinople also represented a new beginning:[20] one requiring a greater openness to the west. This was a view shared by many of the imperial elite, as the list of those who were initially sympathetic to unionist negotiations indicates.

Opposition was at first sporadic. It centred on the deposed Patriarch Joseph I. Some of the patriarchal clergy, such as Manuel Holobolos, remained loyal to him, as did the monks of his old monastery of Galesios. The patriarch also had support of members of the aristocracy, who had become convinced – perhaps prompted by their monastic confessors – that union was a betrayal of Orthodoxy and symptomatic of the emperor's misuse of power. These views won more adherents as the actions of the papacy conformed to the stereotype set out in the 'Errors of the Latins' literature. The lack of debate at Lyons underlined that the union was forced, while the emperor's willingness to condone papal demands was humiliating. Many of his erstwhile supporters deserted him, as popular opinion turned against him.

His death in December 1282 allowed his successor Andronikos II (1282–1328) to liquidate the union. John Bekkos was removed from the patriarchate to be

---

20 R. J. Macrides, 'The new Constantine and the new Constantinople – 1261', *BMGS* 6 (1980), 13–41; A.-M. Talbot, 'The restoration of Constantinople under Michael VIII', *DOP* 47 (1993), 243–61.

succeeded in a matter of months by Gregory of Cyprus (1283–89), one of those who had turned from support for union to principled opposition. His choice as patriarch emphasises that ending the union of Lyons was an inside job: the work of men, such as the chief minister Theodore Mouzalon, who had originally favoured the union. They realised that polemical tracts of the 'Errors of the Latins' variety were all very well for the streets of Constantinople, but they still had to win the theological battle against John Bekkos. The latter had given sound reasons for supposing that the Latin position on the procession of the Holy Spirit had strong support in the Greek patristic view that procession entailed God the Father working *through* the Son. It needed somebody of Gregory of Cyprus's intellectual stature to reframe Orthodox teaching on this doctrine.[21]

Gregory was able to vindicate a distinctive Orthodox position. He took as his starting point a detailed examination of the exact meaning ascribed to the phrase *through the Son* by the Greek Fathers. This, he maintained, did not apply to the procession of the Holy Spirit, but to its manifestation both in time and throughout eternity. In other words, it had no relevance to the causation of the Holy Spirit, which was the work of God the Father alone – the Orthodox position. It referred instead to the exercise of divine grace. In this way Gregory of Cyprus was able to discredit Bekkos's insistence that the Greek Fathers provided support for the Latin position on the procession of the Holy Spirit. At the same time Gregory put special emphasis on the working of God's grace, which followed from the contrast he drew between the procession and the manifestation of the Holy Spirit. Implicit in this line of thought was a distinction between the essence and the energies within the Godhead. This provided the point of departure for Gregory Palamas's formulations, which, as we shall see, distinguished Orthodox and Latin teaching on the Trinity still more radically.

Barlaam and Gregory Palamas

The union of Lyons cast its shadow over Orthodox relations with the west.[22] It was remembered as having been imposed by the emperor 'through the use of force and against the general will'.[23] It confirmed the stereotype of the

---

21 A. Papadakis, *Crisis in Byzantium: the filioque controversy in the patriarchate of Gregory II of Cyprus (1283–1289)* (New York: Fordham University Press, 1983).

22 A. E. Laiou, *Constantinople and the Latins: the foreign policy of Andronicus II 1282–1328* (Cambridge, MA: Harvard University Press, 1972).

23 *PG* 151, 1334A.

Latin as the mortal enemy of Byzantium. Under Andronikos II there were no meaningful exchanges with the Latin Church. This isolationism was deliberate policy on the part of Andronikos, but to an extent it was forced on him by a power struggle within the Orthodox Church, as different factions claimed – with little justification – credit for victory over unionism. At the same time, monks were assuming an increasingly dominant role within the Orthodox Church. This was fuelled by a wave of mysticism centring on the vision of the uncreated light, which would take the Orthodox Church even further away from Rome. It was in this period that Mount Athos, which had only had a muted role in the struggle over union, began to come to the forefront of Byzantine ecclesiastical life, as a centre of mysticism or – better – 'hesychasm'.

While Andronikos II reigned, the Orthodox Church was protected from contact with the Latin Church. This changed with his overthrow in January 1328 by his grandson Andronikos III (1328–41), who came to power with ambitious plans to revive Byzantium. Their implementation was largely left to his right-hand man John Kantakouzenos. It was clear that, whereas by itself Byzantium was incapable of holding back the Turkish advance in Asia Minor, with western aid this might still be possible. The price would be talks on the reunion of churches. At the centre of negotiations was a Greek monk from Calabria called Barlaam.[24] Almost nothing is known about his early life and education. In the 1320s when there was increasing pressure on the Greek communities in southern Italy Barlaam moved first to Arta and then to Thessalonike, which had become a major centre of education and scholarship. He soon came to the attention of John Kantakouzenos, who established him as head of a school attached to the Constantinopolitan monastery of St Saviour in Chora. This did not please its previous head, the great scholar Nikephoros Gregoras. He wrote a Platonic dialogue entitled *Phlorentios*, in which he took Barlaam to task for his Latin education and cast of mind.[25] Recent scholarship has dismissed this line of accusation as pure Byzantine prejudice against a Greek from southern Italy. Barlaam's writings at the time underline his sincere attachment to Orthodoxy,

24 J. Meyendorff, 'Un mauvais théologien de l'unité au XIVe siècle: Barlaam le Calabrais', in *1054–1954: l'Église et les églises: neuf siècles de douloureuse séparation entre l'Orient et l'Occident* (Chevetogne: Éditions de Chevetogne, 1954–55), II, 47–64; R. E. Sinkewicz, 'A new interpretation for the first episode in the controversy between Barlaam the Calabrian and Gregory Palamas', *JThSt* n.s. 31 (1980), 489–500; R. E. Sinkewicz, 'The doctrine of Knowledge of God in the early writings of Barlaam the Calabrian', *Mediaeval Studies* 44 (1982), 181–242; T. M. Kolbaba, 'Barlaam the Calabrian. Three treatises on Papal Primacy', *REB* 53 (1995), 41–115.
25 Nikephoros Gregoras, *Fiorenzo o intorno alla sapienza*, ed. P. A. M. Leone [Byzantina e neohellenica napolitana 4] (Naples: Università di Napoli, 1975).

which he vigorously defended against Latin opponents, but in doing so he revealed a quite un-Byzantine grasp of Latin methodology.

Late in 1333 papal emissaries arrived in Constantinople. The ensuing negotiations were accompanied by a theological debate.[26] Invited to present the Orthodox point of view Gregoras declined on the grounds that debate with the Latins was utterly futile. The emperor turned instead to Barlaam, who used his knowledge of scholasticism to make a defence of Orthodoxy in Latin terms. He was the first Orthodox spokesman to demonstrate a proper grasp of the works of Thomas Aquinas, which he consulted in Latin. He offered a general criticism of the Latin use of syllogisms. He contended that they were inappropriate to an understanding of the workings of the Godhead, where scripture interpreted through the Fathers was the only guide. Barlaam's specific criticism of Aquinas was over the use of scripture in such matters. The latter's interpretation was guided not by the Fathers, but by human reason on the mistaken assumption that its rules necessarily applied to the Godhead. Making original use of Pseudo-Dionysios Barlaam then argued against Aquinas that it was necessary to accept the limitations of the human intellect, where the Godhead – and in particular a mystery such as the origins of the Holy Spirit – was concerned. It was a clever and effective defence of Orthodoxy, but delivered by the wrong person.[27]

Barlaam came under attack from the hesychast leader Gregory Palamas, who was acting as a spokesman for a group of Athonite monks.[28] His reaction to Barlaam's defence of Orthodoxy was precipitate and based on little more than hearsay. He grossly misconstrued his adversary's line of thought. His assumption was that this revealed a theologian who was at heart a Latin. He took Barlaam's exposition of the Latin teaching on the procession of the Holy Spirit and of Latin methodology, not as a debating position, but as a statement of belief. Barlaam's attempt to convince Palamas that this was not so only made things worse. He tried to explain his position by reference to the strengths and weaknesses of classical philosophy, always making clear its inferiority to Christian revelation. Palamas took this as an admission of his opponent's adhesion to pagan thought.[29]

26 A. Fyrigos (ed.), *Barlaam Calabro Opere contro i Latini* [Studi e testi 347–8] (Vatican: Biblioteca apostolica vaticana, 1998), I, 211–18.

27 G. Podskalsky, *Theologie und Philosophie in Byzanz: der Streit um die theologische Methodik in der spätbyzantinischen Geistesgeschichte (14/15. Jh.), seine systematischen Grundlagen und seine historische Entwicklung* [Byzantinisches Archiv 15] (Munich: C. H. Beck, 1977).

28 *Barlaam Calabro Opere contro i Latini*, I, 219–33.

29 R. E. Sinkewicz, 'Christian theology and the renewal of philosophical and scientific studies in the early fourteenth century: the *Capita 150* of Gregory Palamas', *Mediaeval Studies* 48 (1986), 334–51.

There were hidden depths to Palamas's stance against Barlaam. After a two-year vacancy the patriarchal throne went to John Kalekas (1334–47), a married man and a member of the imperial clergy. It was a political appointment, which aroused bitter resentment both among the bishops and in monastic circles.[30] Coinciding as this appointment did with the reopening of dialogue with the papacy it could easily be construed as a return to the unionist strategy of Michael Palaiologos. This was an affront to the monks of Mount Athos, where the myth of their brave resistance to his persecution was taking shape. As spokesman in the debate with the Latin cardinal it was easy to cast Barlaam in the role of another Bekkos.

Barlaam objected to criticism, which he judged to be both unfair and ill informed. He also resented the way Palamas was turning friends and acquaintances against him. He expressed his indignation by ridiculing the exercises employed by some hesychasts – navel-gazers, as he called them – to facilitate a vision of the uncreated light. He went further: he accused them of Messalianism or seeking purification through prayer. This was a dangerous charge because of the prominence that repetition of the Jesus Prayer had assumed in hesychast practice. Gregory Palamas had now to defend practices and beliefs that had become central to the monastic ideal. As things stood, only the writings and intuitions of mystics, such as Symeon the New Theologian and Gregory of Sinai, supported a belief that the vision of the uncreated light vouchsafed mystics direct contact with the divine. Gregory Palamas began by making a distinction between the essence and the energies of the Godhead. God in his essence is unknowable, but in His infinite mercy He has manifested Himself in various ways to creation and mankind, most famously at the Transfiguration on Mount Tabor. This Gregory argued was only possible through the exercise of the divine energies. Realising that he would be accused of dividing the Godhead he invoked the analogy of the sun and its rays as proof that there was no necessary division. While Barlaam's agnostic approach threatened to divorce God from humankind, Gregory's theology did the opposite: it celebrated direct contact between God and man, but in such a way as to enhance the role of the mystic. Palamas mobilised support on Mount Athos for his theology, which was then approved by the patriarchal synod meeting on 10 June 1341 under the presidency of the emperor Andronikos III.

---

30 *Ioannis Cantacuzeni eximperatoris Historiarum Libri IV*, ed. L. Schopen (Bonn: Ed. Weber, 1828), I, 432.

Demetrios Kydones and Thomas Aquinas

Barlaam was condemned for his opposition. He left almost immediately for Avignon, where conversion to Catholicism only confirmed existing suspicions. His treatment in Byzantium was symptomatic of the continuing hostility there was from many quarters to any renewal of contacts with the papacy. He has famously been labelled a 'bad theologian',[31] though it was more a case of being wilfully misunderstood. But from a Byzantine point of view his fault was a serious one: he was willing to disturb Byzantine thinking by introducing Latin elements. It might have been a means of defending Orthodoxy, but to use Latin methodology to such an end was to diminish Orthodoxy as the true faith and guarantee of salvation. Barlaam had very little direct influence in his own time, but the value of his work came to be appreciated by Orthodox theologians. Already by the 1360s Neilos Kabasilas was making considerable use of Barlaam's treatises against the Latins, but he could not acknowledge his debt openly.[32]

Barlaam may have laid the foundations for the later appropriation of Latin scholasticism by Byzantine theology, but he was remembered as Gregory Palamas's first opponent and an enemy of Orthodoxy.[33] With his departure the controversy over the uncreated light could be conducted along strictly Byzantine lines. Palamas's opponents recognised his teachings for what they were: a daring innovation, which was difficult to justify either on philosophical grounds or in terms of traditional Byzantine theology. The triumph of the Palamites should not be dismissed as merely a product of the political configurations of the time. Bad theologian that he may well have been, Gregory Palamas was in tune with one of the enduring refrains of Orthodoxy: 'God became man, so that man might become God.' His theology was part of a spiritual revival, which spread via monasteries to all parts of the Orthodox world. It tilted the balance within the Orthodox Church to the monastic order. Effectively, Mount Athos rather than Constantinople became the centre of gravity of Orthodoxy.

Opposition to the triumph of Palamite theology – confirmed at the council of Blakhernai in 1351[34] – came from conservative elements within the Byzantine establishment. Not all opponents of Palamas became Latin sympathisers, let

31 J. Meyendorff, 'Un mauvais théologien'.
32 Podskalsky, *Theologie*, 180–230.
33 J. Gouillard, 'Le Synodikon de l'Orthodoxie', *TM* 2 (1967), 81–5.
34 Ibid., 242–6.

alone converts to Rome, but opposition to Palamas did spawn an influential group of Latin sympathisers. This was the work of Demetrios Kydones, who became chief minister in 1347 following John Kantakouzenos's coup.[35] At this stage, Kydones seems to have been indifferent to the Palamite controversy. This changed when he decided – with the emperor's approval – to learn Latin to help with his diplomatic duties. He made rapid progress; so much so that his tutor – a Spanish Dominican – suggested that he translate Thomas Aquinas's *Contra Gentiles* into Greek. The impact of Aquinas's thought on Kydones was immediate: it had the power of revelation and led very quickly to conversion to Rome.

This was the first major success for the Dominicans, who had been a presence in the Genoese factory of Pera – opposite Constantinople – since the early fourteenth century. But their Pera convent was more a staging post for the mission fields to the north and east of the Black Sea than for work in Constantinople, where their influence was superficial until the mid-fourteenth century, when Demetrios Kydones's enthusiasm for Thomas Aquinas made all the difference.[36] He realised that Aquinas provided what Byzantine theologians had consistently failed to supply: a systematic philosophically based justification of Christian revelation.[37] Aquinas had been dead for nearly eighty years when Kydones began his translation of the *Contra Gentiles*. Byzantine theologians had been able to ignore Aquinas for so long because he was deemed irrelevant to Byzantine needs. However, this was no longer the case once it became clear that at the heart of the Palamite controversy lay the competing claims of mysticism and authority.[38] The traditionalists opposed to Palamas were adamant that mysticism defied rational explanation, but they could no longer appeal to authority because Palamite teaching now had the force of dogma. By way of contrast they found in the rigour of Aquinas's analysis an attractive alternative. By Byzantine standards it was fresh and invigorating, even if in the west its solutions were already being questioned. Furthermore, the translations made by Demetrios Kydones and his brother Prochoros were

35 R.-J. Loenertz, 'Démétrius Cydonès', *OCP* 36 (1970), 47–72; 37 (1971), 5–39; F. Kianka, 'Demetrius Cydones and Thomas Aquinas', *B* 52 (1982), 264–86; F. Kianka, 'Byzantine–papal diplomacy: the role of Demetrius Cydones', *International Historical Review* 7 (1985), 175–213.

36 C. Delacroix-Besnier, 'Conversions constantinopolitaines au XIVe siècle', *Mélanges de l'École Française de Rome* 105 (1993), 715–61; Delacroix-Besnier, *Les Dominicains et la chrétienté grecque aux XIVe et XVe siècles* [Collection de l'École française de Rome 237] (Rome: École française de Rome, 1997).

37 G. Mercati, *Notizie di Procoro e Demetrio Cidone, Manuele Caleca e Teodoro Meliteniota* [Studi e testi 56] (Vatican: Biblioteca apostolica vaticana, 1931), 362–5, 365–6, 391–2.

38 Gouillard, 'Synodikon', 246–51.

outstandingly good, which allowed the power and originality of Aquinas's works to make their impact.

The Latin sympathisers around Demetrios Kydones have been dismissed as men without lasting influence. This may be true of their role within Byzantium, but not of the impact they had on Byzantine relations with the west. In the face of the rapid advance of the Ottomans Demetrios Kydones engineered a rapprochement with the west. He was now the chief minister of John V Palaiologos (1341/54–91), who had secured Constantinople in 1354 with the aid of a Genoese adventurer Francesco Gattelusio, to whom he granted the island of Mytilene. With Kydones by his side the new emperor instituted a Latinophile regime and stubbornly pursued a unionist strategy. He made his intentions clear in a chrysobull of December 1355 addressed to Pope Innocent VI. It contained a request for military aid against an eventual union of churches. The emperor was realistic enough to admit that he was in no position to impose union, when the church was in the hands of the Palamites.[39]

The papacy received these overtures politely, but continued to insist on the old formula of no aid before conversion. And there it might have rested, had not Count Amadaeus of Savoy, a cousin of the emperor, led a crusade to his rescue. In 1366 Amadaeus first recovered the strategic crossing point of Gallipoli from the Ottomans. Next he brought his cousin back from Vidin on the Danube, where the latter had been marooned following an ill-advised journey to Buda to discuss cooperation against the Ottomans with the Hungarian king.[40] At long last, the west had offered the Byzantine emperor solid military aid. He now had to demonstrate his good faith over the union of churches. He promised his cousin that he would travel as soon as conveniently possible to Rome to make his personal submission to the pope. In the meantime, he handed over substantial pledges to his cousin. This was only a start. The union of churches required the establishment of the exact differences separating the two churches. To this end the papal legate Paul of Smyrna debated the issues at an assembly presided over, in the absence of the patriarch, by the ex-emperor John Kantakouzenos, now the monk Joasaph. Kantakouzenos insisted that, whatever the differences, the union of churches must never be forced. It was

39 O. Halecki, *Un empereur de Byzance à Rome: Vingt ans de travail pour l'union des églises et pour la défense de l'Empire d'Orient 1355–1375* [Travaux historiques de la société des sciences et des letters de Varsovie 8] (Warsaw: Société des sciences et des letters de Varsovie, 1930; reprinted London: Variorum, 1972).

40 E. L. Coxe, *The Green Count of Savoy: Amadaeus VI and Transalpine Savoy in the fourteenth century* (Princeton: Princeton University Press, 1967); J. Gill, 'John V Palaeologus at the court of Louis I of Hungary (1366)', *BS* 38 (1977), 31–8.

a way of reminding the emperor and his adviser that union could never be wholly a matter of politics.[41]

At the same time, the gap separating the unionists from the main body of the church was highlighted by the case of Prochoros Kydones, who mounted an attack on Palamite theology. His use of Aquinas was serious enough, but his challenge was even more dangerous because it was launched from Mount Athos, where Prochoros was a monk. Some of the fiercest criticism of Palamism came from monks dissatisfied by the way that the new emphasis on mysticism was displacing the liturgy and the common life as the focus of the monastic ideal. Prochoros was expelled from Athos in 1367 and then brought before the patriarchal synod, which condemned him the next year as an enemy of Orthodoxy. It says much about the divided state of Byzantium that his brother – still the emperor's chief minister – was unable to save him. Bringing Prochoros to trial at this juncture was designed to discredit his brother's unionist strategy.

The condemnation of Prochoros only made an understanding with Rome more essential. Accompanied by Demetrios Kydones the emperor went to Rome where in the winter of 1369/70 he made his personal submission to Pope Urban V. It was all in vain. No tangible help was forthcoming. The emperor finally limped back to Constantinople in October 1371 to discover that the fate of his empire had effectively been decided the previous month at the battle of the Maritsa, where the Ottomans defeated the Serbs. John Palaiologos capitulated and became a tributary of the Ottoman emir Murad I (1362–89). With the collapse of the unionist strategy the influence at court of its architect Demetrios Kydones waned. Other Latin sympathisers either had to temper their opinions or were forced out of Constantinople. Of these some went to Latin courts scattered through the Levant, while others found a home at the papal curia or in the Italian cities, where their scholarship and learning were often admired.

There are parallels between the unionist policies of Michael Palaiologos and of his descendant John V. In both cases, a small but powerful elite around the emperor sought union with Rome against stubborn opposition. There were, however, differences. While Michael was able to bully the ecclesiastical hierarchy into accepting his strategy, John had very little influence over the church. Against this Michael's unionist policies did not create any solid body of Latin sympathisers; rather they instilled into Byzantines of all shades of opinion distaste for things Latin. This changed with Demetrios and Prochoros Kydones. They were intellectual converts to Rome. They believed that

41 J. Meyendorff, 'Projets de concile oecuménique en 1367. Un dialogue inédit entre Jean Cantacuzène et le légat Paul', *DOP* 14 (1960), 147–77.

Aquinas's thought represented an advance in the understanding and elucidation of Christian teaching, of which the Byzantines were now incapable. They introduced Latin methodology into the mainstream of Byzantine thinking. They also established enduring links with the Dominicans, who at last began to exert an influence on members of the Byzantine elite. The Kydones brothers ended the church of Constantinople's insulation from Latin influence, which was a consequence of the reaction against the union of Lyons and was then reinforced by the Palamite victory.

Byzantine scholars and Italy

A complaint made against the Palamites by their opponents was that they condoned the advance of the Turks. Although not strictly true, it caught a new development: the willingness of Greeks, as individuals or as communities, to throw in their lot with the marauding Turks. As often as not this led to assimilation and conversion to Islam. This contrasted with the obstinacy with which the Greeks retained their religion in lands ruled by Latins. The difference is best explained by the conditions of conquest. The Ottoman conquest was a traumatic business, where resistance brought destruction and enslavement, while cooperation offered material benefits. The Latin conquest was far less brutal, but more humiliating, because of the subjection of the mass of the population which was Greek and Orthodox to a ruling class that was Latin and Catholic. The Latin regimes in the Levant were anxious to ensure that this division remained intact, because it was a guarantee of dominance. Equally, it suited the Greeks. It furthered the social dominance of the Orthodox Church and it created an ascendancy, which was able to mediate between the two communities thanks to its access to the Latin ruling class. In Venetian Crete there was interchange on the religious level: Greeks and Latins worshipped in and were patrons of the same churches, and on special occasions participated in the same celebrations. However, Greeks were discouraged from becoming Latin priests and vice versa. The Latin authorities in the Levant were suspicious of union, because it threatened the delicate balance of communities upon which effective rule depended.[42]

42 F. Thiriet, 'La situation religieuse en Crète au début du XVe siècle', B 36 (1966), 201–12; J. Gill, 'Pope Urban V (1362–1370) and the Greeks of Crete', OCP 39 (1973), 461–8; S. McKee, Uncommon dominion: Venetian Crete and the myth of ethnic purity (Philadelphia: University of Pennsylvania Press, 2000), 100–32; M. Georgopoulou, Venice's Mediterranean colonies: architecture and urbanism (Cambridge: Cambridge University Press, 2002), 165–91; J. Richard, 'Culture franque et culture grecque: le royaume de Chypre au XVe siècle', BF 11 (1987), 399–415.

While Greek and Latin were strictly differentiated, at the level of the elite a degree of assimilation and acculturation occurred. Greek increasingly became the language of literature and social intercourse at Levantine courts. At a dynastic level the imperial family of Palaiologos was connected by marriage to the Lusignans of Cyprus and the Gattelusio of Mytilene. In Epiros the Orsini and Tocco were entwined in a bewildering way with local families as well as with the Palaiologoi. The ties of kinship ensured Byzantine aristocrats of a warm welcome at these courts. The best-documented example is that of John Laskaris Kalopheros. Disgraced by John V Palaiologos he sought service with Peter I of Cyprus (1359–69) who rewarded him with a rich Latin heiress. Such favouritism earned the king the hatred of the Cypriot nobles. After his assassination in 1369 their anger turned against his intimates. John Kalopheros was obliged to leave Cyprus, but it was not long before he married another Latin heiress. He also acquired both Genoese and Venetian citizenship. Though he never returned to Constantinople, he maintained his contacts among the Byzantine elite. The ease with which he moved about the Mediterranean reflects the creation of a Levantine society to which many Byzantines gravitated, even if the price was conversion to Rome.[43]

Among these was Demetrios Kydones. Resentful at the failure of his unionist policies he requested that he be allowed to visit Rome to pursue his studies and to perfect his Latin. This was refused, and initially he had to decline Gattelusio hospitality on the island of Mytilene. This did not prevent Kydones devoting his retirement to his studies and to the cultivation of a circle of disciples. Some of the most distinguished of the next generation of Byzantine scholars – Maximos Chrysoberges, Manuel Chrysoloras and Manuel Kalekas – claimed him as their teacher. They followed their master on the path to Rome. There was no question of Kydones having any formal teaching post. His students were at least in their twenties, sometimes older. In typical Byzantine fashion Kydones was regarded as a sage and attracted those interested in the wisdom he offered. That wisdom consisted in initiation into Latin scholasticism through the study of his translations of the works of Thomas Aquinas. Kydones was passionate in his devotion to Aquinas, whom he considered Plato's intellectual equal, but with the advantage that he did not have to express his thought through myths. He jested that, if Plato had had the good fortune to peruse the works of Aquinas, he would have preferred the Christian Church to the Academy. He

---

43 D. Jacoby, 'Jean Lascaris Calophéros, Chypre et la Morée', *REB* 26 (1968), 189–228; A. K. Eszer, *Das abenteuerliche Leben des Johannes Laskaris Kalopheros: Forschungen zur Geschichte des ost-westlichen Beziehungen im 14.Jh.*(Wiesbaden: O. Harrassowitz, 1969); R.-J. Loenertz, 'Pour la biographie de Jean Lascaris Calophéros', *REB* 28 (1970), 129–39.

was, however, completely sincere in his conviction that Aquinas had provided the means by which it was possible to distinguish truth from falsehood.

His devotion to Aquinas was the basis of close relations with the Dominicans. He encouraged his followers to seek refuge with them at Pera when they came under pressure from the Byzantine ecclesiastical authorities to accept Palamite teachings. Maximos Chrysoberges was the first to do so; followed in 1396 by Manuel Kalekas. This was for both of them a decisive step in their conversion to Rome. Kydones also encouraged his followers to do what he had not – to his regret – been able to do: to study in Italy. He congratulated Maximos for enrolling in the University of Padua. He envied his installation in an environment where scholarship was respected, so different from the situation in Constantinople. Kalekas does not seem to have studied at an Italian university, but he stayed in Italy from 1401 to 1403 and attached himself to the circle of émigrés around another of Kydones's followers, Manuel Chrysoloras. In the same way as his master, Kalekas was overwhelmed by the splendour of the Italian cities. He involved himself in translating a wide range of Latin theology, including Anselm's *Cur Deus Homo*. He also cooperated with Maximos Chrysoberges in the creation of a Greco-Roman liturgy, indicative of their hopes of convincing their fellow-countrymen to follow their example. Kalekas returned to Constantinople in 1403 with the emperor Manuel II, but to his surprise his old friends turned on him. He was treated as a traitor and was forced, like Maximos Chrysoberges before him, to seek refuge with the Dominicans of Mytilene, where he died in 1410.[44]

Manuel Chrysoloras[45] accompanied Demetrios Kydones to Italy in 1396 and stayed on after his master's departure the following year for Constantinople.[46] Coluccio Salutati, the chancellor of Florence, recruited Chrysoloras to teach Greek at the city's *Studium*. His brief tenure of the chair of Greek was of immense significance because he used it to lay the foundations of the systematic teaching of Greek in the west. At the core of his teaching was his analytical grammar known as the *Erotemata*. It was much simplified in comparison to earlier Byzantine textbooks of this kind. It also benefited from being translated into Latin by one of Chrysoloras's pupils, Guarino of Verona. Chrysoloras had to cut short his tenure of the Florentine chair because Manuel II Palaiologos

44 R.-J. Loenertz, *Correspondance de Manuel Calécas* [Studi e testi 152] (Vatican: Biblioteca apostolica vaticana, 1950), 16–46.
45 G. Camelli, *Dotti bizantini e le origini dell'Umanesimo I. Manuele Crisolora* (Florence: Centro nazionale di studi sul Rinascimento, 1941); M. Baxandall, 'Guarino, Pisanello and Manuel Chrysoloras', *Journal of the Warburg and Courtauld Institutes* 28 (1965), 185–204.
46 Kydones died *en route* in Crete. It was later believed that on his death bed he sought reconciliation with the Orthodox Church: see Mercati, *Notizie*, 441–50.

(1391–1425) needed him, now that the latter had come to the west in order to seek aid against the Turks. From 1399 Chrysoloras acted as his emissary to a series of western courts. He returned with the emperor in 1403 to Constantinople. Despite imperial support he found life there uncongenial. It hastened his decision to convert to Rome and to make a permanent home in Italy, where he attached himself to the court of Pope John XXIII. He played some role in the negotiations which led to the opening of the council of Constance, where he died in April 1415. He was remembered in the west with deep veneration, while his comparison of the old and new Romes reveals his enthusiasm for the city of Rome. He came to realise that ancient Rome had been an amalgam of Greek and Latin, which he presented to his own times as a paradigm of cooperation between Byzantium and the west.[47]

Chrysoloras was still useful to the emperor Manuel, because his foreign policy remained orientated towards the west. But for all his Latin sympathies, the emperor avoided submission to the papacy. He had his father's fate before him. He also knew from his three years in the west the obstacles there were to the despatch of aid. Perhaps the most serious was the Great Schism, which divided the west into different ecclesiastical obediences. It was in Byzantium's interest to see it ended. Manuel therefore accepted the invitation of the German emperor Sigismund and sent a delegation to the council of Constance, which ensured that the union of churches came quite high on the agenda of the new pope Martin V (1417–31). By 1422 the pope had agreed in principle to debate the differences between the two churches within the framework of a General Council. Credit for the groundwork that eventually led to the council of Ferrara/Florence must therefore go to the emperor Manuel, but how sincere was he? In a famous passage in his *Chronicle* George Sphrantzes claims that Manuel gave the following advice to his son and heir John VIII Palaiologos (1425–48): by all means, use union of the churches as a ploy to discourage the Turks, but on no account ever allow its implementation, because of the divisions that would follow within Byzantium.[48] Even if there is an element of the historian being wise after the event, caution was always Manuel's watchword after his return from exile. He ensured the election of moderates as patriarch of Constantinople. He accepted the ascendancy exercised over the church in Constantinople by the monk Joseph Bryennios. The latter's opposition to union suited the emperor rather well because his main concern was to extract concrete benefits from any engagement with the west. These came

47 G. Dagron, 'Manuel Chrysoloras: Constantinople ou Rome', *BF* 12 (1987), 281–8.
48 Georgios Sphrantzes, *Memorii 1401–1477*, ed. V. Grecu [Scriptores Byzantini V] (Bucharest: Editura Academiei Republicii Socialiste România, 1966), xxiii.5–8; 58–60.

in the shape of a series of prestigious marriages for his children. His eldest son John married Sophia of Montferrat and his second son, Theodore, Cleopa Malatesta, daughter of the despot of Rimini.

The union of Florence (1439) and its aftermath

John succeeded his father in 1425. Why did the new emperor not follow his father's wise example and steer clear of too close an involvement with Rome? It was very largely because temporising over the union of churches became more difficult once a new pope, Eugenius IV (1431–47) – in the face of the challenge from the council of Basel – offered increasingly advantageous terms. Instead of the prospect of a dictated settlement there were guarantees of unfettered discussion of the points at issue between the two churches.[49]

At Byzantium there were fewer objections to negotiations with Rome, as one by one opponents of union died, to be replaced by a more open-minded generation. Prominent among the newcomers were Bessarion, Isidore and Mark Eugenikos,[50] who at a comparatively young age were put at the head of important Constantinopolitan monasteries and then given prestigious sees. They were not Latin sympathisers but neither were they hostile to the west. Their assimilation of scholastic modes of thought meant that they did not dismiss Latin theology out of hand.

The driving force behind negotiations was the emperor John VIII Palaiologos, who emerges as a man of some stature.[51] Like his predecessors, he saw union as the only means of obtaining substantial help from the west. He had already as a young man made two journeys to the west in search of support. He had been entertained at the court of the emperor Sigismund, who admitted that the Orthodox Church had preserved a purer tradition than the Latin Church. And not only that: he anticipated that the Byzantines could help reform the Latin Church, but only if they accepted union. These were sweet words tailored to Byzantine *amour propre*. John made use of them to convince opponents of the union, who at this point included the patriarch Joseph II (1416–39), that a more tolerant spirit existed in the west.[52] The patriarch was won over to union, though his agenda was different from that of the emperor.

---

49 J. Gill, *The Council of Florence* (Cambridge: Cambridge University Press, 1959); G. Alberigo, *Christian unity: the Council of Ferrara-Florence 1438/9–1989* (Leuven: Peeters, 1991).

50 See J. Gill, *Personalities of the Council of Florence and other essays* (Oxford: Basil Blackwell, 1964), 45–78.

51 Ibid., 102–24.

52 *Les 'mémoires' de Sylvestre Syropoulos sur le concile de Florence (1438–1439)*, ed. V. Laurent (Paris: Éditions CNRS, 1971), II.xliv; 148–53.

Joseph was a scion of the imperial house of Bulgaria and a Slavonic-speaker. His background led him to appreciate the importance of the Slav countries to the Orthodox cause. He saw a union council as a stage on which to demonstrate the ecumenical authority of a Byzantine patriarch.[53]

Once the emperor and patriarch arrived at Ferrara in 1438 their hopes of free and open discussion were not disappointed. The Latins invariably accepted their demands about the organisation of debates. Their forbearance offered the possibility of achieving a union of churches which respected Orthodox doctrine; so the Latins conceded that a number of differences, such as over Purgatory, were of secondary importance, and absolute agreement was unnecessary. But on the central issues of the addition of the *filioque* and the procession of the Holy Spirit there had to be agreement. The Byzantine spokesmen were able to hold their own intellectually. In any case, the debates in the end turned on a historical and even codicological analysis.[54] Mark Eugenikos argued the traditional Byzantine line that the unilateral addition of the *filioque* to the creed violated the injunction that there should be no such additions. But he was increasingly isolated as another Byzantine spokesman, Bessarion, argued for a return to the pre-existing harmony between the churches, or 'Concord of the Saints', as it was called.

On arrival in the west Mark Eugenikos was not obviously either more pro- or more anti-Latin than Bessarion.[55] It was the experience of the council that convinced Eugenikos that Latin theology and Orthodox piety were incompatible. He was famed for his mastery of scholastic methodology, but when urged to deploy his expertise he insisted that he preferred to speak as a simple monk. As the debates continued, he came to see the addition of the *filioque* as being opposed to the central dogma of Christianity. He was possibly in competition with Bessarion, but this was less important than the latter's willingness to revive arguments deployed by John Bekkos: to the effect that the patristic view of the Holy Spirit proceeding from the Father *through* the Son was the same as the Latin position represented by the *filioque*. It was on this basis that a compromise was reached with the Latins, who clarified their position by emphasising that behind the procession of the Holy Spirit was a single, not a double, principle. At the end of the debates the Byzantine emperor could be satisfied that he had gained as much as he could have expected. The patriarch had died on

53 Gill, *Personalities*, 15–34.
54 A. Alexakis, 'The Greek patristic *testimonia* presented at the council of Florence (1439) in support of the *Filioque* reconsidered', *REB* 58 (2000), 149–65.
55 C. Tsirpanlis, *Mark Eugenicus and the Council of Florence: a historical reevaluation of his personality* (Thessalonike: Patriarchal Institute, 1974).

10 June 1439, apparently leaving a profession of faith, which accepted that Latin teaching conformed to the Greek. But as the Byzantine delegation prepared to depart it was put under considerable pressure by the papacy to make a number of concessions over important points: demands which fuelled charges that the union was forced. The pope then wanted to have Mark Eugenikos tried by the council. This was a demand too many and the Byzantine emperor stood firm. The council ended on a bad-tempered note. The pope refused any concessions to the Byzantines once the decree of union was signed. They were expected to participate in the Roman liturgy at the close of the council, but were not allowed to celebrate their own liturgy the next day. The emperor's comment revealed a disappointed man: 'We thought that we were correcting many Latin errors. Now I see that those guilty of innovations, who err in so many ways, are correcting us, even though we have changed nothing.'[56] The pope could act in this way because leading figures on the Byzantine side had succumbed to the attractions exercised by Italy. Two, Bessarion and Isidore of Kiev, accepted cardinals' hats. The splendour of the papal curia did not simply dazzle. It also seemed to offer a superior ecclesiastical order. Bessarion found the atmosphere of Florence particularly congenial. The culture of the Florentine humanists was much to his taste with its emphasis on the classical past. He could bask in the reflected glory of his master George Gemistos Plethon,[57] who was added to the Byzantine delegation to give it intellectual muscle. Despite doubts about his commitment to Christianity Plethon made some telling interventions in the debates. At one point he noted an inconsistency in the presentation of the Latin case. Its apparent reliance on logical proof was little more than a debating ploy, since it was historical proof that would be decisive.[58] His advice was highly valued by the Byzantine delegation. He won the confidence of the patriarch, who told him that he was 'an old man and a good one, who puts the truth before everything'.[59] He emerges as something of a traditionalist in ecclesiastical matters. He criticised the emperor for having earlier advocated entering the debate on Purgatory with an open mind. 'What could be worse than that', was his comment, 'for if we have doubts about the faith of our Church, then we do not have to believe in its doctrines.'[60] Along with Mark Eugenikos he had the intellectual self-confidence to stand up to the Latins.

---

56 *Syropoulos*, x.xiv; 500–3.
57 F. Masai, *Pléthon et le platonisme de Mistra* (Paris: Belles Lettres, 1956); C. M. Woodhouse, *Gemistos Plethon: the last of the Hellenes* (Oxford: Clarendon Press, 1986).
58 *Syropoulos*, vi.xxxi; 330–3.
59 Ibid., vii.xvii; 366–9.
60 Ibid., vii.xviii; 368–9.

This is not so much of a surprise as it might seem. Thanks to Ciriaco of Ancona his reputation as a sage, as 'the most learned of the Greeks of our time', had preceded him. What was prized was his knowledge of Plato, now a focus of interest among the Florentine humanists. He was invited to give a series of informal lectures on the differences between Plato and Aristotle. They generated great enthusiasm and were remembered long enough for Cosimo de' Medici to institute a Platonic Academy in his honour. Their success was testimony to the spread of knowledge of Greek among Italian humanists. Leonardo Bruni, the chancellor of Florence – a pupil of Manuel Chrysoloras – will certainly have lent his support, since he translated works of both Plato and Aristotle from the Greek. The reception of Plethon at the council of Florence opened the way for other Byzantine scholars to make their mark on the Italian scene. The transmission of Byzantium's classical heritage to the west was a long-drawn-out process, beginning in the late fourteenth century and continuing into the seventeenth. But the council of Florence was the crux. It gave a further and decisive impetus to the process. The debate over the differences between Plato and Aristotle was largely confined to Byzantine scholars operating in both Byzantium and Italy, but it fuelled Italian interest in Plato, although it took some twenty years before Marsilio Ficino presented Plato in a way that appealed to Italian humanists. However fascinating the Italians found Plethon he remained very much a Byzantine figure. He seems to have understood the gulf that existed between a sage, such as himself, and the Italian humanists he encountered. He refused to accept that the Latins enjoyed any intellectual superiority. It saddened him that so many Byzantine scholars abandoned their traditions on exactly those grounds. Unlike them, he was not seduced by the west.

The majority of the Byzantine delegation found the outcome of the council an anticlimax. Far from triumphantly vindicating Orthodoxy, union seemed to be very largely on Latin terms. In contrast to what happened on the way out, the Byzantines met a hostile reception from the Greeks of the Venetian ports where they stopped. The latter understood union to mean subordination to the Roman Church. This interpretation was not strictly true, but it had a basis of truth. The emperor who had shown such energy and commitment in driving through union was curiously apathetic. He never recovered from the death of his beloved third wife, which occurred a few days before he reached Constantinople. Little was done either to implement the union or to combat its opponents led by Mark Eugenikos, who now emerged as a dominant personality. Bessarion preferred to return to Italy rather than promote the case for union. The emperor could only wait on events. The long-expected aid from the west materialised in the shape of a Hungarian crusade, but in November 1444 it came to grief at the battle of Varna. It does not matter that it was a close run thing. It meant that in practical terms the union of Florence had been in vain. As so often in the past, western aid proved to be a mirage.

On the eve

The aftermath of the council of Florence demonstrated once again the unwillingness of Byzantine society to follow its leaders down the path of union. The career of George Scholarios, the future Patriarch Gennadios, provides testimony of the strength of anti-unionism.[61] Still a layman he was added to the Byzantine delegation to the council. He was selected on the strength of his expertise as a scholastic theologian. He knew Latin well. He had also experienced the hostility that learning Latin provoked at Constantinople. News of his Latin lessons was cause enough for the mob to attack his house. At Florence he was for a long time an advocate of union. He had a very poor opinion of the intellectual level of the Byzantine delegation when compared with the Latins. During the council he cooperated with Bessarion and Isidore, the leaders of unionist opinion, in drafting the Byzantine statement on the procession of the Holy Spirit, but its mixed reception by both Byzantine and Latin was humiliating for Scholarios. This may be part of the explanation for his precipitate withdrawal from the council. He left Florence on 14 June 1439, scarcely a month after drawing up the Byzantine statement, in the company of two anti-unionists: the emperor's brother Demetrios and George Gemistos Plethon. Like them Scholarios was departing early, so as to avoid signing the union decree. How are we to explain this sudden change of heart? The death of the patriarch Joseph was unsettling; working with convinced unionists, such as Bessarion and Isidore, perhaps even more so. It forced him to ponder his loyalties: did his admiration for Thomas Aquinas necessarily point towards conversion to Rome? He decided not, because his purpose in studying scholastic texts was to provide a defence of Orthodoxy that met the requirements of Latin theology. He saluted Demetrios Kydones and Manuel Kalekas for their mastery of scholastic thought, but was bitterly critical of their defection to Rome.[62]

61 Gill, *Personalities*, 79–94; C. J. Turner, 'The career of George-Gennadius Scholarius', *B* 39 (1969), 420–55.
62 C. J. G. Turner, 'George-Gennadius Scholarius and the Union of Florence', *JThSt* 18 (1967), 83–103; Podskalsky, *Theologie*, 222–6.

On his return to Constantinople he was not initially a vociferous opponent of union. Only in 1444 did Mark Eugenikos pick him out as his successor. He was one of the few in the upper ranks of society not tainted by adhesion to the union of Florence. He took on the leadership of the *synaxis*, as the group opposed to union was called, out of a sense of patriotism: to defend Orthodoxy against Latin innovations, which were facilitated, as he saw it, by the ill-judged union of Florence. His actions divided Byzantine society at a critical moment. He had no wish to see Constantinople conquered by the Turks, but it turned out to be a solution of sorts. It ended the schism that the union of Florence had produced. Byzantine society united in condemning the betrayal of Orthodoxy at Florence, as a way of explaining the fall of Constantinople. The conqueror Mehmed II made a shrewd choice when selecting him as the new patriarch of Constantinople. Here was a man willing to cooperate with the new dispensation because he believed that it safeguarded the essentials of Orthodoxy. One of Gennadios's first actions as patriarch was to burn Plethon's *Book of the Laws* on the grounds that it constituted a codification of neoplatonic paganism. His condemnation of Plethon's doctrine owed much to Thomas Aquinas. Under the guidance of Gennadios the ecumenical patriarchate embraced Latin scholasticism, now that the question of union with Rome ceased to matter. At the same time Plethon's autographs became the prized possessions of Italian libraries, confirmation in its way that Byzantium's classical heritage had passed to the west. Here at last was some kind of a resolution to the impasse that faced Byzantine intellectuals in the empire's closing years.

3

The culture of lay piety in medieval Byzantium 1054–1453

SHARON E. J. GERSTEL AND ALICE-MARY TALBOT

Orthodox faith permeated the everyday lives of Byzantine men and women, not just when they attended church services, but at home, in the streets and even at work. The liturgical calendar, which designated certain days of the week for fasting and Sundays for worship, provided a temporal framework for the pious. Each day of the year had a special significance, whether it was a dominical feast day of Christ, a celebration of the Virgin Mary, a saint's day, or a commemoration of key events in the lives of Christ and His Mother. Ecclesiastical rituals sanctified life passages, such as birth, marriage and death. Finally, in addition to their concerns about life on earth, Byzantines focused intensely on the afterlife, with eternal salvation as their foremost goal.

The laity at church

The Byzantine landscape, whether urban or rural, was marked by ecclesiastical structures of varying size, shape and purpose. Within the city, the laity had access to large-scale metropolitan churches, which often retained the architectural form of the venerable basilicas constructed in the early centuries of the empire. Judging from the size of the medieval basilicas that still stand in Berroia, Kalambaka, Servia, Ohrid and Edessa (medieval Vodena), as well as in other large and small Byzantine cities, hundreds of parishioners could have been accommodated within the body of a single church. These buildings provide us the spatial context in which to imagine the powerful sermons of such figures as Gregory Palamas, who, as bishop of Thessalonike (1347–59), brought the city's residents to the heights of religious fervour. In addition, Byzantine cities were marked by dozens of other religious structures, which also provided the laity with access to sacred rite and space. Larger cities would have had a number of parish churches to accommodate weekly services as well as special rites. Around 1405, a Russian pilgrim recorded the names of Thessalonike's parish churches as 'St. Sophia the Metropolis, Acheiropoietos

(Akhironiti), and Holy Asomatoi and many others'.[1] In smaller cities such as Berroia and Kastoria numerous family chapels still stand hidden in residential neighbourhoods as they were in Byzantine times. These modest buildings, intimate in scale and decoration, served the day-to-day devotional needs of the city dweller and were used, in the medieval period, for the burials of members of extended families.

Also present were the enclosures for urban monasteries and for dependencies (*metochia*) of monastic foundations located in more isolated rural settings or on holy mountains. Some members of the laity developed a close relationship with local monasteries, attending services there regularly and consulting the superior as a spiritual mother or father. They might offer various forms of financial support to these institutions and seek burial within their walls. Even if one did not enter within the monastic complex, its very presence conjured up a world of sacred prayer and action, made all the more potent by the icons placed on the outer walls of the monastery, which provided passersby with access to the saints venerated within. While women were not permitted to enter the monastery of the Virgin Kosmosoteira in Pherrai, they could 'if they wished, worship at the mosaic image of the Mother of God above the entrance to the monastic enclosure'.[2] In a similar fashion, the west façade of the *katholikon* of a late Byzantine monastery at Thessalonike (today known as Prophitis Elias) contains tall niches in which holy portraits of Christ, the Virgin holding the Christ child, and St Anne holding the infant Virgin were painted. Supplicants could venerate the all-holy images displayed on the church exterior even when the doors to the church were firmly closed.

A wide range of churches of different form and function also marked the small villages of rural Byzantium. Archaeological and architectural remains demonstrate that a larger church was often located at the proximate centre of the village and that this may have served as the site of weekly liturgical celebration and of other services of importance to the entire community. Smaller churches or chapels were located in discrete neighbourhoods populated by members of extended families. These chapels, which offered liturgical celebration less frequently than the village's central church, were maintained by families for their own devotional purposes and were often dedicated to saints of special import to individual supplicants. The infrequent use of such churches may be inferred from an inscription painted on the south wall near

1 M. Rautman, 'Ignatios of Smolensk and the late Byzantine monasteries of Thessaloniki', *REB* 49 (1991), 145, 146 n. 11.
2 L. Petit, 'Typikon du monastère de la Kosmosotira près d'Aenos (1152)', *Izvestiia Russkago Arkheologicheskago Instituta v Konstantinopole* 13 (1908), 61; Thomas and Hero, II, 836.

the sanctuary of the church of the Virgin at Apeiranthos, Naxos. After naming the donors, Demetrios Maurikas and his wife Maria, the text reads: 'and *if* a priest celebrates the liturgy in this church, may he commemorate us, in the year of the Lord 6789 (=1280/81)'.[3] Many churches in small villages were built by groups of donors, often related by kinship, who provided small sums of money or gifts of land to sustain the church and to support its priest. A number of churches, often situated on the periphery of the village, were surrounded by graveyards and would have accommodated funerary and commemorative rites for families or larger communities. Other shrines, sited at the extremities of villages, may have protected the boundaries of habitation and the cultivated fields through the invocation of saints concerned with the protection of life and livestock.

In addition to these public settings for religious practice private chapels accommodated a more intimate form of worship. The wealthy often included oratories within their homes, as was the case in the imperial palace. Such structures are listed in wills and inventories of the medieval period, which provide information about the furnishings and decoration of private chapels. A property near Miletos, which was given to Andronikos Doukas in 1073, included, for example, 'a church built of mortared masonry, with a dome supported by eight columns . . . a narthex . . . and with a marble floor'.[4] In his will of 1059, Eustathios Boilas bequeathed a set of books and other precious objects to the church on his estate.[5] We might assume that these small chapels housed icons of special significance to individual families. A letter of John Tzetzes provides some insight into the conditions within these structures in Constantinopolitan homes of the twelfth century. Decrying the large number of fraudulent monks wandering the streets of the Byzantine capital, Tzetzes complains that 'leading ladies, and not a few men, of the highest birth consider it a great thing to fit out their private chapels, not with icons of saintly men by the hand of some first-rate artist, but with the leg irons and fetters and chains of these accursed villains'.[6] Such metal implements were standard penitential devices of legitimate holy men, and were often displayed near the tombs of monastic saints and illustrated in holy portraits. Tzetzes condemns those members of the laity who were deceived by false monks. It would seem that the unregulated veneration of false relics rather than the icons of saintly men

---

3 S. Kalopissi-Verti, *Dedicatory inscriptions and donor portraits in thirteenth-century churches of Greece* (Vienna: Verlag ÖAW, 1992), 109.

4 M. Nystazopoulou-Pelekidou, Βυζαντινὰ ἔγγραφα τῆς μονῆς Πάτμου (Athens: Ethnikon Idryma Ereunon, 1980), II, 102–3.

5 P. Lemerle, *Cinq études sur le XIe siècle byzantin* (Paris: CNRS, 1977), 20–9.

6 *Ioannis Tzetzae Epistulae*, ed. P. A. M. Leone (Leipzig: B. G. Teubner, 1972), no. 104.

might have justified concerns of the church hierarchy about the proliferation of private chapels, which fell outside the bounds of church order.

Important, too, in considering the physical accommodation of sacred rite and prayer in terms of lay piety, were the numerous chapels that were embedded in fortifications or associated with other elements of the empire's infrastructure. For example, at Gynaikokastro, a fortified settlement built in the early fourteenth century some 40 miles from Thessalonike, excavations at the tower that crowned the settlement have revealed the existence on its upper floor of a chapel, which was once decorated with frescos.[7] Other towers were built by monasteries to protect their estates and, by extension, the villagers, who lived and worked on their properties. The Athonite monastery of Docheiariou constructed a tall tower near ancient Olynthos in 1373. A chapel occupied the eastern side of the tower's upper floor. Marking the Byzantine landscape, such towers were intended to protect the Byzantine garrison as well as to place the surrounding territory under sacred protection. Images of holy figures and sacred signs such as crosses or apotropaic formulae also branded the walls of urban fortifications and were carried by armies. Byzantine lore is replete with tales of sacred figures interceding to protect cities or to guarantee victory in battle.

Objects and signs associated with Byzantine piety protected ports, bridges and roads as well as the travellers who used them. On a bridge built in Thrace in the twelfth century by Isaac Komnenos 'was set up that stone panel with the image of the Mother of God, as an object of worship for those who are passing across, and as the prayer of my wretched soul'.[8] In the mid-fifteenth century, Raoul Manuel Melikes, a resident of the Morea, repaired a bridge that spanned the River Alpheios at Karytaina. He added a small chapel to the structure's second pier and an inscription, carved in marble, that bore his name and an invocation: 'Learn, O stranger, this bridge was built anew by Raoul Manuel Melikes, a pious man. He who wishes to pass across, let him pray for grace with all his soul lest he look as before into the abyss. In the year 6948 (=1440), the third indiction.'[9] Like bridges, watermills were also marked by Christian signs, for example decorative brick crosses and abbreviated inscriptions, such as the letters ΦΧΦΠ– standing for ΦΩΣ ΧΡΙΣΤΟΥ ΦΑΙΝΕΙ ΠΑΣΙ ('the light of Christ shines on all'). These prominent symbols of Christian faith assured

---

7 A. Tourta, 'Fortifications of Gynaikokastro, Greece', in *Secular medieval architecture in the Balkans, 1300–1500, and its preservation*, ed. S. Ćurčić and E. Hadjitryphonos (Thessalonike: Aimos, Society for the Study of the Medieval Architecture in the Balkans and Its Preservation, 1997), 110–11.

8 Petit, 'Kosmosotira', 51; Thomas and Hero, II, 828.

9 N. Moutsopoulos, Ἀπὸ τὴν Βυζαντινὴ Καρύταινα', *Πελοποννησιακά*, 16 (1985–86), 185.

the laity that the safety of the wayfarer and the bounty of the water supply were under divine protection.

Within the public and private spheres, then, whether in city or countryside, whether in border fortresses or the homes of the elite, the Byzantine laity was confronted with buildings imbued with sacred meaning and infused with holy presence. These structures were powerful reminders of an affiliation to a single church and the unification of the empire under a single rite – factors that assumed political significance in times of internal and external crisis. These constructions helped situate laypeople within a sacred topography that both mandated and guided their adherence to correct faith and encouraged, through the omnipresence of physical reminders, a deep religiosity that was both reflexive and potent.

Parallel to this physical structuring of a religious landscape was a temporal framework that ordered the life of the laity according to church rite and calendar. Attendance at weekly church services was expected in city, town and village. Considering the available sources, however, the degree to which the average Byzantine adhered to such expectations is impossible to gauge. Styliane, the lamented young daughter of Michael Psellos, 'would attend vespers readily, taking part in the doxology, and in the chanting of hymns'. According to her father, she faithfully attended the church liturgy, as well as holy feasts, and chanted matins.[10] Such descriptions of lay piety are counterbalanced by sources suggesting that not everyone attended church with regularity. Although a contemporary panegyric claimed that in Thessalonike the churches were open day and night to facilitate access for services and private devotions,[11] Gregory Palamas complained that the city's churches were deserted for several months of the year as the faithful engaged in agricultural activity outside the city's walls.[12] Images of the Last Judgement in late Byzantine rural churches depict parishioners who spend Sunday in bed – an artistic statement condemning sexual intercourse on holy days, but one that also hints at diminishing church attendance. In the early fourteenth century the patriarch Athanasios I sought to encourage the faithful to go to services by ordering that taverns and baths be closed from mid-afternoon on Saturday to mid-afternoon on Sunday.[13]

10 K. N. Sathas, Μεσαιωνικὴ Βιβλιοθήκη (Paris: Maisonneuve, 1876), v, 67.9–18; M. J. Kyriakis, 'Medieval European society as seen in two eleventh-century texts of Michael Psellos', *Byzantine Studies/Études Byzantines* 3 (1976), 86. Cf. A. Leroy-Molinghen, 'Styliane', *B* 39 (1969), 755–63.

11 *PG* 109, 642C–D.

12 *PG* 151, 333D.

13 *PG* 161, 1066C–D. On further Sunday restrictions, see G. Dagron, 'Jamais le dimanche', in Εὐψυχία: *mélanges offerts à Hélène Ahrweiler*, ed. M. Balard et al. (Paris: Publications de la Sorbonne, 1998), 165–75.

The most common liturgy in the period under discussion was that of St John Chrysostom, a service that could range in length from less than one hour to more than two, depending on the status of the church and number of celebrants. The Liturgy of Basil was used for the Sundays of Lent and for important feast days. As the liturgy unfolded, the faithful were expected to stand and to pay attention, although, judging from the complaints of various churchmen, it was not always easy for the laity to endure the ceremony in quietude and solemnity, or to remain for the duration of the service. A text that is probably of Palaiologan date warns laymen of God's strictures at the Last Judgement for their irregular church attendance and for not paying attention when they did come to services.

> Even if you come to [the churches], you go to them with your feet, but you lag behind with your soul . . . being preoccupied with the worries of daily life you engage each other in conversation, and do not pay attention to the scriptures . . . barely staying until the reading of the Gospel, straightaway you quickly rush out and leave the church as if some force were pushing you out, each person shoving another and trampling upon them as if they were being chased out of there.[14]

Within the body of the church, according to both textual and artistic evidence, laymen and women were segregated, although the manner of division depended on the size and shape of the church as well as on the type of community. Written sources demonstrate that in the great churches of the Byzantine capital women – particularly those of high status – stood in the gallery or in the side aisles. Artistic evidence from the medieval period suggests that in city churches women and men were divided along the north and south sides of the nave, as is the case in contemporary practice. Further afield, as suggested by painted evidence in small rural churches, women and men were divided along the north and south sides of the church, or perhaps even according to perceived levels of sanctity, with men standing closer to the sanctuary and women relegated to the building's west end.

It is widely accepted that communion, in the medieval period, had decreased in frequency compared to early Christian practice. Although in the twelfth century Theodore Balsamon affirms that the laity may receive communion every day (provided that they are properly prepared), most churchgoers appear to

---

14 *Vita* of Basil the Younger, ed. A. N. Veselovskij, 'Razyskanija v oblasti russkogoduchovnogo sticha', *Sbornik Otdelenija Russkago Jazyka i Slovesnosti Imperatorskoj Akademii Nauk* 53 (1891–92), suppl. 172–3. Unpublished English translation by S. McGrath, D. Sullivan and A.-M. Talbot.

have communicated only a few times a year, on the Great Feasts and at Easter.[15] The reception of communion required spiritual preparation and fasting which, according to one thirteenth-century bishop, consisted of a diet of only bread, dried figs, dates and green vegetables.[16]

The infrequency of communion, paired with complaints about church attendance, signals a change in the manner in which laypeople approached sacred rite. By the thirteenth century, in many churches, much of the eucharistic celebration was visually obscured from the faithful by an opaque barrier. This obfuscation of ritual practice in no way diminished the religious experience. In fact, the faithful's spiritual encounter with the sacred may have been heightened by witnessing a series of holy appearances, by being enveloped in incense and by auditory participation in intoned prayers. Moreover, while the priest was celebrating the liturgy the faithful had access to a series of powerful intercessors rendered in paint. Located on the nave side of the sanctuary barrier, on stands and on the interior walls of the church, these large-scale icons presented figures of devotional or doctrinal importance and constituted a complex plan of salvation based on sacred figures of personal, familial or congregational import. The icons structured pietistic exercises through the supplicant's baptismal association with a specific saint, through his or her knowledge of holy biography and the special powers wielded by a specific holy figure, or through the evocation of abstract qualities embodied in the literal understanding of saints' names, such as 'many years' (Polychronia) or 'much fruit' (Polykarpos). Judging from the numerous supplicatory inscriptions affixed to portraits of saints in Byzantium, it was the holy figure that constituted the most immediate intercessor for laypeople, guaranteeing their health, prosperity, safety and salvation. Thus the religious experience of the laity was associated both with the corporate rite and with an intensely private system of prayer.

Feast days and pilgrimage

Churches saw their greatest attendance on important feast days, which were numerous. An edict issued by the emperor Manuel I (who was concerned about the number of days that the law courts were officially closed)

---

15 *PG* 138, 968c. Cf. R. F. Taft, 'The frequency of the eucharist in Byzantine usage: history and practice', *Studi sull' Oriente Cristiano* 4.1 (2000), 103–32.

16 J. B. Pitra, *Analecta sacra Spicilegio Solesmensi parata* (Paris: Roger and Chernowitz, 1891; reprinted Farnborough: Gregg International, 1967), VII (VI), col. 668. The bishop was John of Kitros: see J. Darrouzès, 'Les réponses canoniques de Jean de Kitros', *REB* 31 (1973), 329.

limited the number of festivals to sixty-six full holidays (in addition to Sundays) and twenty-seven half-holidays![17] The celebration of these important feasts extended outside the walls of the church. Many of the traditions today associated with church festivals can be traced to Byzantine practices. The decoration of the church with sweet-smelling bay leaves 'as a symbol of the holy feast' is attested in an eleventh-century poem of Christopher of Mytilene.[18] A reference to cracking eggs at Easter is found in a letter written by John Apokaukos, Metropolitan of Naupaktos, to a suffragan bishop in 1222. In describing a slave boy named John Kleptes, Apokaukos notes: 'at the age when he [Kleptes] was still learning to read and write, he used to watch birds and steal into their nests and remove the eggs, mainly in the fifth week of Lent, which he, according to peasant custom, called Κωφή. Then he would hide the eggs away carefully so that he could crack eggs with the other children at Easter.'[19] Breads made of birds' eggs set in dough were baked at Easter time, and might be offered to the local village priests as a gift.[20] In the fourteenth century Matthew of Ephesos vividly described the joyous celebrations in Constantinople at Easter, 'the mother of feast days', as entire families carrying lanterns assembled in the streets singing hymns and even danced before the church doors on the evening of Holy Saturday.[21]

Epiphany (6 January) constituted an important feast day for the laity. On this day, the priest blessed the waters, either by submerging a cross in a basin or by tossing it directly into the sea to be retrieved. Documentary evidence for the latter ritual is found in a Genoese statute from Kaffa, which describes the outlay of money for a number of feasts, including that of Epiphany:

> The expenses ought to take place yearly on the feast of the epiphany as written below. First of all, the Greeks (*Greci*) who come to the palace and sing the *kalimera* should be given two hundred aspers; likewise for those boys who dive into the sea when the priest blesses the sea water, 75 aspers. For those priests who chant lauds in the palace courtyard 100 aspers. Likewise for the person who sounds the bell six aspers.[22]

The waters blessed during this rite, often bottled and taken home, were considered therapeutic for man, animal and crops.

17 R. Macrides, 'Justice under Manuel I Komnenos', *Fontes Minores* 6 (1984), 140–55.
18 E. Kurtz, *Die Gedichte des Christophoros Mitylenaios* (Leipzig: Neumann, 1903), poem 32.
19 H. Bees-Seferlis, 'Unedierte Schriftstücke aus der Kanzlei des Johannes Apokaukos des Metropolitan von Naupaktos (in Aetolien)', *Byzantinische-Neugriechische Jahrbücher* 21 (1971–74), 151.
20 Rhalles and Potles, II, 355.
21 A. Pignani, *Matteo di Efeso: l'ekphrasis per la Festa di Pasqua* (Naples, [1981]), 29–38; Pignani *Matteo di Efeso. Racconto di una festa popolare* (Naples: M. D'Auria, 1984), 32–5.
22 S. P. Karpov, 'Chto i kak prazdnovali v Kaffe v XV veke', *Srednie Veka* 56 (1993), 226–32.

Saints' feast days fully engaged the Byzantine laity and every city and village participated in the celebration. Annual ceremonies were held at the cult centres of major saints, which attracted pilgrims as well as merchants to fairs held in conjunction with the feast. Numerous descriptions of church festivals survive from the Byzantine period. In Nicaea, for example, the feast of St Tryphon, which took place on 1 February, was associated with the miraculous blossoming of a lily out of season. A mid-thirteenth-century encomium to the saint, written by Theodore Laskaris, describes the crowds assembled for the celebration:

> When the miracle takes place, there is a universal festival – of infants, children, adolescents, men, old men, elders, the aged, women, laymen, soldiers, officials, priests and monks – every kind and age of people sees it and jumps with joy. For what happens does not happen in a corner or some shadowy place, but in the church of God.[23]

At the annual festival of St Demetrios in Thessalonike, visitors came to venerate the saint, but also to participate in the great week-long fair.

Processions of important icons also involved the Byzantine populace. The weekly litany of the Hodegetria icon in Constantinople, sustained by a confraternity whose members carried the heavy icon, attracted large crowds of supplicants and onlookers. The icon, attributed with healing powers, was carried through Constantinople on Tuesdays, when it visited several churches and was then returned to the Hodegon monastery. According to the Russian pilgrim Alexander the Clerk, who travelled to Constantinople in 1394–95 and witnessed the weekly procession of the icon, 'whoever comes with faith receives health'.[24] Eustathios of Thessalonike writes that a similar procession involving an icon of the Virgin Hodegetria took place in his city.[25] Far from the capital in the area of Thebes, members of a lay confraternity transported another icon, the Virgin Naupaktissa, from church to church. The Constantinopolitan procession is represented in a thirteenth-century painting in the narthex of the Blakhernai church near Arta, labelled 'Feast of the All Holy Theotokos the Hodegetria in Constantinople'. In addition to representing the procession of the icon, the scene includes a large number of vendors, suggesting that the display of the icon was as much a commercial event as a sacred one.

23 C. Foss, *Nicaea: a Byzantine capital and its praises* (Brookline, MA: Hellenic College Press, 1996), 105–7.
24 G. Majeska, *Russian travelers to Constantinople in the fourteenth and fifteenth centuries* [DOS 19] (Washington, DC: Dumbarton Oaks Research Library and Collection, 1984), 160.
25 Eustathios of Thessalonike, *The capture of Thessaloniki*, trans. John R. Melville Jones (Canberra: Australian Association for Byzantine Studies, 1988), 142.3–21.

Pilgrimage to holy shrines and to holy men also played an important role in the spiritual life of the Byzantine laity. Although during the middle and late Byzantine eras long-distance pilgrimages to visit the *loca sancta* of the Holy Land were undertaken primarily by monks, a few laymen are known to have made this journey despite the dangers posed by the Muslim occupation of Palestine. While still laymen, Cyril Phileotes and his brother journeyed to the shrines of Rome and Chonai.[26] Far more common were shorter devotional journeys, including trips to a nearby town or city with an important shrine, excursions into the countryside to pray at a rural monastery, or visits to churches within one's own city or neighbourhood. For example, the above-mentioned Cyril used to make weekly journeys from the Thracian village of Philea, some 30 miles distant from Constantinople, to venerate the icon of the Virgin at the church of Blakhernai.[27] Sometimes these pious journeys, especially to the countryside, took on the nature of a holiday. Thus the young Gregory Palamas went once with his entire family by boat up the Bosporus to visit an ascetic at the monastery of St Phokas; *en route* his father caught a fish to present to the holy man.[28] The pleasure derived from natural surroundings permeates a fourteenth-century description of a pilgrimage to the shrine of St Prokopios (near Trebizond), where 'westerly winds come from the so called Mountain of Mithras which rises above, and especially in spring people come there and enjoy the flowers and plants and take great delight in the sight of their bloom and in the thick grass'.[29]

Most pilgrimages, however, had a serious purpose. The faithful visited holy shrines to offer thanksgiving, to pray for salvation, and to seek healing from various diseases and chronic afflictions, such as sterility. In a society with an infant and child mortality rate approaching 50 per cent the principal purpose of marriage was childbearing, and thus barrenness was viewed as a dire misfortune. Byzantine sources are replete with stories of couples who were unable to conceive children and who prayed to a wide variety of saints for assistance. Among female saints, the Virgin Mary and her mother, Anne, were believed to be especially efficacious in granting fertility to barren women. Male saints, too, could be asked for intervention. St Eugenios of Trebizond is

26 É. Sargologos, *La vie de Saint Cyrille le Philéote moine byzantin (1110)* (Brussels: Société des Bollandistes, 1964), §§ 18, 20.

27 Ibid., §14.

28 *Vita* of Gregory Palamas, in D. G. Tsames, *Φιλοθέου Κωνσταντινουπόλεως τοῦ Κοκκίνου ἔργα*, I, *Θεσσαλονικεῖς Ἅγιοι* (Thessalonike: Aristoteleio Panepistemio Thessalonikes, 1985), 433–4.

29 J. O. Rosenqvist, *The hagiographic dossier of St. Eugenios of Trebizond in Codex Athous Dionysiou 154* (Uppsala: Uppsala Universitet, 1996), 268–71.

credited with enabling the sterile wife of the *oikonomos* Magoulas to conceive.[30] For such entreaties, laypeople would have entered the church for assistance, praying to saints whose images graced the walls or whose portraits were found on icons. It was also widely believed that, in the absence of medical assistance, saints could intervene to facilitate the healthy delivery of children or to assist in difficult gynaecological cases.

Ailing pilgrims resorted to various rituals in their search for a miraculous cure: kissing the coffin containing the holy man's remains; prayer or incubation next to the saint's tomb; anointing themselves with perfumed oil that exuded from the saintly relics or with oil from the lamp hanging over the tomb or icon of the saint; or drinking water sanctified through contact with the holy relics. The fourteenth-century account of the posthumous miracles of Athanasios I, patriarch of Constantinople, relates an unusual rite, which verges on sorcery. A certain Maria Phrangopoulina was healed of a long-term uterine disease 'by secretly stealing a tiny piece of the holy ragged garment of the great man; she placed it in a censer over hot coals and inhaled the fumes, and then (praised be the judgments of God) she was delivered from her suffering'.[31] The faithful might also take home with them flasks of holy oil and water or lead and clay tokens imprinted with the image of a saint for their own later use or for distribution to friends and relatives. Preserved examples of such artefacts include the small lead flasks (*koutrouvia*) of the thirteenth and fourteenth centuries bearing the images of Sts Theodora, George, Demetrios and Nestor, all presumably from Thessalonike, and in the eleventh century lead medallions of St Symeon the Stylite the Younger were still being brought from Syria. In gratitude for a miraculous cure, pilgrims would bring to the shrine gifts, ranging from wax and oil to specially commissioned silver-gilt icon frames or liturgical vessels.

Pilgrims might also seek out living holy men, sometimes for healing, but more often to make confession, or to receive a blessing or spiritual advice. A few laymen even made their way to isolated hermitages on Mount Athos to seek counsel, as can be seen in the *Vita* of St Maximos Kausokalybites. The monk Cyril Phileotes, who lived relatively close to Constantinople, received lay visitors from the capital in need of spiritual instruction.[32] Other holy men, such as Gregory Palamas in Thessalonike and the Constantinopolitan patriarch

30 Ibid., 290–1.

31 A.-M. Talbot, *Faith healing in late Byzantium: the posthumous miracles of the patriarch Athanasios I of Constantinople by Theoktistos the Stoudite* (Brookline, MA: Hellenic College Press, 1983), 113.

32 Sargologos, *Cyrille le Philéote*, §§ 34, 35, 46, 47, 50 and 51.

Isidore I Boucheiras, who lived in an urban environment, were more easily accessible to the general public, and could even serve as a spiritual father to fortunate individuals, counselling them on such issues as marriage or a possible monastic vocation.[33]

The domestic sphere

Devotional practices were also incorporated into many aspects of home life, in city and countryside alike. There were blessings upon the house itself, when the foundation stone was laid, or when a family first entered a new home; on such occasions a priest would recite the appropriate prayers and sprinkle the house with holy water.[34] Invocation of divine intercession and prayers of thanksgiving marked the daily routine, such as before and after meals, and at bedtime.[35] There were also prayers appropriate to various stages of the lifecycle, especially at the beginning and end of life, blessings on the birth of a child, the child's first haircut, and his introduction to his letters.[36] Women in labour might seek to receive Holy Communion before giving birth.[37] For adults there were prayers for forgiveness at times of severe illness and impending death.[38]

Other forms of private devotion such as singing of hymns, reading of scripture and other sacred writings, and the veneration of icons all might be carried out in the home. This can be seen at the highest level of society in the household of the emperor Alexios I Komnenos (1081–1118), whose mother, Anna Dalassene, set an example of piety for the rest of the imperial family. We are told by her granddaughter, Anna Komnene, that she spent much of the night in prayerful vigils and singing hymns; she insisted that there be set times for chanting of hymns by the household so that 'the palace assumed the appearance rather of a monastery'.[39] Her daughter-in-law, Irene Doukaina, had to be torn away from her spiritual reading to sit down to meals; among her favourite

33 See, for example, Tsames, *Φιλοθέου Κωνσταντινουπόλεως*, 373–7, 572–4, 579–80.
34 J. Goar, *Εὐχολόγιον seu Rituale Graecorum* (Venice: Bartholomaeus Javarina, 1730; reprinted Graz: Akademische Druck- und Verlagsanstalt, 1960), 483–4. See also *Les regestes des actes du Patriarcat de Constantinople*, ed. J. Darrouzès (Paris: Institut français d'études byzantines, 1971), IV:1777, no. 8.
35 Goar, *Euchologion*, 529, 568–9.
36 Ibid., 261, 264, 306, 572.
37 Cf. V. Grecu, *Ducas: istoria Turco-Bizantina (1341–1462)* ([Bucharest]: Editura Academiei Republicii Populaire Romîne, 1958), 323–5.
38 Goar, *Euchologion*, 543–4, 549–50.
39 Anna Comnène, *Alexiade*, III, viii, 3–4; ed. B. Leib (Paris: Belles Lettres, 1937), I, 125–6; ed. D. R. Reinsch [CFHB 40 (Series Berolinensis)] (Berlin: De Gruyter, 2001), 105–6.

works were the writings of Maximos the Confessor and the lives of saints.[40] A fourteenth-century *Vita* offers a vignette of family life in Thessalonike. The *paterfamilias* used to pray every night in the family chapel which doubled as his children's bedroom. Thus prepared he would then go to the local monastery for morning services.[41]

For families of the middle and upper classes who had access to books, devotional reading in the home was a common pursuit. The psalter was the primer of the Byzantine child; for example, Psellos's daughter Styliane, after learning her letters, 'went on to study the "Psalms of David" and while learning them she was able . . . to form perfect speech'.[42] The future St Symeon the Theologian decided upon his monastic vocation after discovering a copy of the *Spiritual Ladder* of John Klimax in his parents' house and reading it assiduously.[43] The young Alexios, who was destined to become Patriarch Athanasios I of Constantinople, spent his childhood reading the Old and New Testaments, instead of playing games, and was inspired to leave home for his uncle's monastery after reading the *Vita* of St Alypios the Stylite.[44]

Children might also be imbued with sacred lore through the storytelling of their mothers; thus Theodote, the mother of Michael Psellos, lulled him to sleep not with fairytales but with stories about holy children from the Old Testament, such as Isaac's narrow escape from sacrifice by his father Abraham and Isaac's later blessing of his son Jacob.[45] Children may also have learned the stories of saints through sermons and painted images. Representations of the lives of saints were included in church decoration as well as on icons intended for public and private devotion. In a society with a high degree of illiteracy, these visual texts played an important role in transmitting church dogma and biography to the vast majority of the Byzantine populace, whether in towns or in the countryside, and taught the common people the tenets of Orthodoxy. Children might even incorporate elements of Christian ritual into their play, imitating the censing of deacons and the liturgical practice of priests.[46]

40 Ibid., v, ix, 3; ed. Leib, II, 38.2–18; ed. Reinsch, 165–6; ibid., XII, iii, 2; ed. Leib, III, 60.5–12; ed. Reinsch, 364–5.
41 *Vita* of Germanos Maroules, in Tsames, Φιλοθέου Κωνσταντινουπόλεως, 105.
42 Sathas, Μεσαιωνικὴ Βιβλιοθήκη, v, 65.17–21; Kyriakis, 'Medieval society', 85.
43 I. Hausherr and G. Horn, *Un grand mystique byzantin: vie de Syméon le Nouveau Théologien (949–1022) par Nicétas Stéthatos* [OCA 14] (Rome: Pontificium institutum studiorum orientalium, 1928), §6, 12.21–2.
44 A. Papadopoulos-Kerameus, 'Zhitija dvukh' Vselenskikh' patriarkhov XIV v., svv. Afanasiia I i Isidora I', *Zapiski Istoriko-Filologicheskago Fakul'teta Imperatorskago S.-Peterburgskago Universiteta* 76 (1905), 3–4.
45 U. Criscuolo, *Michele Psello. Autobiografia: encomio per la madre* (Naples: M. D'Auria editore, 1989), §8, 101.458–65.
46 Tsames, Φιλοθέου Κωνσταντινουπόλεως, 334.

Families of sufficient means would endeavour to acquire one or more icons, which would be venerated regularly. When the youthful Leontios (future patriarch of Jerusalem 1176–85) stayed in a private home while *en route* to Constantinople, he engaged in private devotions after dinner, singing hymns 'in the place where the divine images were kept' and praying for an uneventful journey.[47] On Cyprus, devotees of St Sabas the Younger had his image painted on wooden boards and venerated these icons in their homes with candles, perfumed oil and incense.[48] Michael Psellos's famous description of the emotional attachment of the empress Zoe to her icon of Christ Antiphonetes gives us some idea of the importance of holy images for private devotions. As he writes, 'I myself have often seen her, in moments of great distress, clasp the sacred object in her hands, contemplate it, talk to it as though it were indeed alive, and address it with one sweet term of endearment after another.'[49] Icons were also viewed as tangible assets and passed down through the generations. They are listed in records of the synodal court, inventories and wills, sometimes with their prices, and an heirloom icon would take pride of place in a dowry contract. Particularly valuable icons, with silver revetments for example, might be stored in a clothes chest, rather than kept on display.[50]

Articles of personal adornment protected the body as well as the spirit. Both men and women wore *enkolpia*, pendants bearing a sacred image and worn on a chain around the neck. The pendants were made of a variety of materials, from enamel and gold to wood; some enclosed relics, thus increasing their value. Finger rings, as well, frequently bore sacred images and abbreviated prayers, such as 'Lord, help thy servant' or 'Bearer of God, help thy servant'. Such rings were made for both men and women, and the quality of the materials reflected the status of the wearer. Cameos and precious stones carved with images of Christ, the Virgin and saints offered spiritual and physical protection and were often inscribed on the reverse side with a second saint or narrative scene, with invocations or with crosses. The material from which the amulet was made was significant; lapidary prescriptions attributed healing powers to

47 D. Tsougarakis, *The Life of Leontios, Patriarch of Jerusalem* [The Medieval Mediterranean 2] (Leiden: E. J. Brill, 1993), §5, 36.1–16.
48 Tsames, *Φιλοθέου Κωνσταντινουπόλεως*, 214.
49 Michel Psellos, *Chronographie*, ed. É. Renauld (Paris: Belles Lettres, 1926; reprinted Paris: Belles Lettres, 1967), I, 149; Michael Psellus. *Fourteen Byzantine rulers*, trans. E. R. A. Sewter (Harmondsworth: Penguin Books, 1966), 188.
50 Miklosich and Müller, I, 538–9, a synodal act from 1370 describing a thief who stole a revetted icon of St John the Baptist from a private house, kept the precious silver covering, and threw away the icon. See N. Oikonomides, 'The Holy Icon as an asset', *DOP* 45 (1991), 35–44.

different types of stones, indicating that in powerful amulets the marriage of physical and spiritual elements could be particularly efficacious.

Hundreds of pendant crosses survive from medieval Byzantium, both hollow, for the insertion of relics, and solid cast. These were manufactured in mass quantities in base metals, as well as in deluxe versions, and must have been affordable for many individuals. Bearing images of the Virgin and Christ or saints and simple narrative scenes, these crosses were linked to church dogma through their imagery. Worn close to the body, the crosses protected the wearer and invited reflection on pietistic prayer through their contemplation and through the perception of their suspended weight around the neck.

Faith and work

Even in the workplace devotional practices were not neglected. Certain festivals, for example, celebrated specific commercial activities within a religious setting. Psellos describes the annual festival of St Agathe, which took place in Constantinople on 12 May.[51] The main actors in the festival were women – spinners, weavers and wool carders (perhaps guild members) – who, in one part of the ceremony, offered ornaments, presumably textiles, to icons. Christopher of Mytilene describes the feast of the Holy Notaries, Saints Martyrios and Markianos. On 25 October, student notaries and their teachers, dressed in a variety of costumes (including women's garments), processed through the streets of the capital to the church of the Hagioi Notarioi, located on a hill in the western part of the capital.[52]

In the village context the church was involved in other extra-liturgical rites that brought daily labour into contact with the sacred. Agricultural workers, for example, might turn to the village priest to bless the fields, pray for the health of silkworms, or to help heal ailing animals. There were special prayers for the cycle of sowing and reaping, prayers over the threshing floor, for planting and harvesting a vineyard, and for good weather.[53] On one occasion, the metropolitan of Thessalonike, Gregory Palamas, himself went to bless and sprinkle holy water at an olive grove whose trees had failed to bear fruit.[54] In these matters, the decoration of the village or rural church often facilitated unmediated prayer to saints who specialised in agricultural activities, such as

---

51 Sathas, Μεσαιωνικὴ Βιβλιοθήκη, v, 527–31. See A. E. Laiou, 'The festival of "Agathe". Comments on the life of Constantinopolitan women', in Byzantium: tribute to Andreas N. Stratos (Athens: [N. A. Stratos], 1986), I, 111–22.
52 Kurtz, Gedichte, 91–8.
53 Goar, Euchologion, 523, 551–2, 609–20, 710.
54 Tsames, Φιλοθέου Κωνσταντινουπόλεως, 471–2.

Mamas, Tryphon and others. Sailors and fishermen could request prayers to bless their fishing nets or the construction of a new boat.

Lifecycle rituals

In addition to lifecycle rituals observed in the home, other rites of passage brought laymen and women into the church and engaged them in pious practices. Children were baptised within the church and were given names that derived primarily from the church calendar, most often names of saints, but occasionally with reference to Christ, the Virgin or feasts. The naming of a child established a close association between the name bearer and the name saint, a fundamental bond that would guide a layperson's devotional prayers throughout his or her lifetime. This bond is demonstrated through inscriptions in church and icon painting as well as in other media. One such example is seen in the church of St Michael, Charouda, in the Mani, dated 1371/72, where the represented donor of the small structure, the humble Michael Karydianos, offers a model of the church to the Archangel Michael.[55]

Among the most important events in the lives of Byzantine families were betrothal and marriage, which the service books of the middle and late Byzantine period include as separate rites. Girls were betrothed at a young age in Byzantium, often before they turned twelve. Depending on family circumstances the actual marriage could take place some years later. Since the rites of both betrothal and marriage took place within the church, the dissolution of these ecclesiastical contracts had to be overseen by church courts. Indeed, a number of cases brought before church courts by women concerned betrothal, marriage, adultery and even divorce.

According to liturgical texts of the late Byzantine period, the betrothed couple stood in the nave of the church directly in front of the sanctuary gates for the duration of the ceremony.[56] In the course of the betrothal rite, preserved in slightly varied forms, the priest asked the prospective groom if he would accept his betrothed before posing the same question to the prospective bride. After swearing in the affirmative, the couple was blessed. Rings were given to the couple, a gold ring to the man and a silver ring to the woman. On occasion, the woman's ring was made of iron or copper. The rings were exchanged three times, the more precious metal ultimately remaining with the man. The priest

---

55 N. B. Drandakes, ''Ο Ταξιάρχης τῆς Χαρούδας καὶ ἡ κτιτορικὴ ἐπιγραφή του', Λακωνικαὶ Σπουδαί, 1 (1972), 287–8.

56 P. N. Trempelas, Μικρὸν Εὐχολόγιον: 1. Αἱ ἀκολουθίαι καὶ τάξεις μνήστρων καὶ γάμου, εὐχελαίου, χειροτονιῶν καὶ βαπτίσματος (Athens: [s.n.], 1950), 7–40.

Figure 3.1 St Anastasia the Poison Curer and Anastasia Saramalyna; St Eirene. Panagia
Phorbiotissa, Asinou, Cyprus.

affirmed to each: 'The servant of God [name] is engaged to the servant of God [name] in the name of the Father and of the Son and of the Holy Spirit.' At the end of the ceremony, the couple took communion, sealing the contract through the blessings of the church.

The ecclesiastical marriage rite, or crowning (στεφάνωμα), followed a ritual that was already in place by the eleventh century. Texts from the period under discussion describe the blessing of the couple in front of the sanctuary portal, the reading of prayers, petitions regarding the propagation of children, the marking of the heads of the couple three times with marriage crowns, and the joining of the couple's hands before they took communion from a common cup.[57] The text of the rite is full of references to Old Testament marriages of renowned strength, such as those of Abraham and Sarah, Isaac and Rebecca, Jacob and Rachel, as well as to New Testament marriages, particularly the Wedding at Cana. At the conclusion of the rite, according to several service books of the period, the couple was escorted from the church to their house.

Funerals, in medieval Byzantium, were held in the church following preparation of the corpse at home. The body of the deceased, if a member of the laity, was placed in the church narthex or nave for the funeral rites. The funeral service offered prayers for the repose of the soul and invited the mourners to approach the body for a final farewell. Wealthy Byzantines were often buried in churches, usually in graves dug below the floor of either the narthex or subsidiary chapels. More humble Christians were laid to rest in cemeteries, which often surrounded burial chapels in which commemorative services could be held. In most cases, the deceased was wrapped in a shroud and placed directly into the earth; only on rare occasions have wooden caskets been documented archaeologically. Corpses were laid in the tomb with their heads at the west end so that their faces would look towards the site of Christ's resurrection in the east; in many cases the heads were propped up by a stone pillow. The hands were crossed over the chest, a pose that is reproduced in numerous funerary portraits on icons and in monumental painting. Graves could be used for multiple burials; this was particularly the case for mothers and children, or for families taken by disease.

Burial was followed by a long period of mourning, punctuated by commemorative services (μνημόσυνα) on the third, ninth and fortieth days after death as well as on the first anniversary. Some Byzantine writers, such as Symeon of Thessalonike, associated these staged memorials with specific days in the life and death of Christ. Thus, the third day was viewed as a ritual *imitatio* of

57 Ibid., 41–96.

Christ's resurrection, and the fortieth his ascension. Commemorations took place in the church and at the tomb or grave, where the family would gather for prayer, bringing offerings to the church of *kollyva*, a dish of boiled wheat mixed with almonds, nuts and raisins.[58]

The search for salvation

In Byzantium, anxiety about salvation was an important factor in developing close links between the laity and monastic institutions. One consequence of this concern was a tendency among the laity to take vows towards the end of their lives in the belief that those consecrated to the monastic life had greater hopes of salvation. They might take this step once their children were grown, or after the death of a spouse, or even on their deathbed. Not only were these elderly monks and nuns assured of housing, food and medical care for the rest of their lives, but, even more important, after death they were guaranteed burial within the monastic complex and commemorative services by the monastic community, whose intercessory prayers were viewed as particularly effective.

Through financial contributions to churches, the faithful were able to build tombs and guarantee commemorative services for the deceased. In order to secure ongoing prayers for their souls, very wealthy laypeople might construct funerary chapels as architectural appendages to important monasteries or guarantee, through donations, their burial within the walls of important ecclesiastical foundations. City dwellers could also seek salvation and commemoration through more modest financial contributions. In Kastoria and Berroia, for example, churches of the middle and late Byzantine period still preserve the colourful portraits of male and female worshippers who were buried in tombs positioned along the buildings' exterior. Elongated funeral icons from Cyprus and monumental portraits on Crete and Rhodes equally record the names and portraits of deceased Christians who were buried within and around Orthodox churches. Burial patterns in villages mirror those from urban contexts, though on a more modest scale. The church of the Holy Anargyroi, in Kepoula, Mani, dated 1265, contains a lengthy inscription enumerating the names of donors and their financial contributions towards the construction and decoration of a small church. The presence of medieval potsherds and human bones in the field surrounding the chapel demonstrates that the building was originally surrounded by a graveyard, most likely housing

58 *PG* 155, 688D–691A; 692B.

the remains of those mentioned in the inscription and their families. The motivation for construction of this modest church, like many of the late period, was to house liturgical celebrations and provide a physical context for private devotions, but also to serve as the nucleus of a family burial plot and the site of perpetual commemoration of the deceased. Written sources confirm, explicitly, that donations were made to churches by the laity in order to ensure that the memory of the deceased be recalled in prayer. In 1457, Constantine Strelitzas and his wife penned crosses on an act of donation to the church of St Kyriake at Mouchli, a hilltop town in the central Peloponnese. According to the brief act, the couple gave a vineyard that they had purchased, 'for the salvation of our souls to the church of St Kyriake for the commemoration of our parents and of ourselves'.[59] Many similar acts of donation in exchange for spiritual benefits (so-called ψυχικά) are found in the acts of Mount Athos. Both men and women eagerly gave property to monasteries on the Holy Mountain in exchange for guarantees of posthumous commemoration (ranging from daily to annual) by the brethren.

The decoration of funeral chapels provides abundant information on their use for burials and for commemorative rites. In a number of chapels, quotations from the funeral service or images evoked in the liturgical text are represented on the walls and vaults. The central representation of all funeral chapels, however, was the scene of the Last Judgement, which was often located on the west wall. This elaborate composition spelled out the process by which the soul would be judged, a process of immediate concern to those who would be buried below the chamber's pavement and those who would view the artistic composition. References to the judgement of the soul are found throughout Byzantine literature. Apocalyptic literature, for example, refers to the interrogation of the soul as it passed through tollgates, whose keepers assessed specific sins and assigned appropriate punishments. Writers of the late Byzantine period draw comparison between judgement by the heavenly court and the corrupt, earthly judiciary. The text of Mazaris's *Journey to Hades or Interviews with Dead Men about Certain Officials of the Imperial Court*, written between January 1414 and October 1415, describes, in highly satirical form, the social and political milieu of the late Byzantine court. The central figure of the text, Mazaris, who finds himself in Hades, asks how a soul is judged in the afterlife. The answer is as follows: 'Justly . . . and impartially, without corruption or favouritism; neither flattery nor bribes can influence

---

59 M. Manoussacas, 'Un acte de donation à l'église Sainte-Kyriakè de Mouchli (1457)', *TM* 8 (1981), 319.

[the judges].'[60] Judging from surviving evidence, representations of sinners within the painted programme of many village churches increased in the late Byzantine period, suggesting that accountability for earthly sins against church and society was an increasing concern of the laity towards the end of the empire when Byzantium was destabilised economically and politically.

But the picture for the afterlife was not exclusively grim. Those who were saved were promised entrance into Paradise, which was envisioned as a garden in Byzantine literature and art. Eulogies and inscriptions of the last Byzantine centuries make frequent reference to Eden or the gardens of Paradise. Deceased laypeople, in the late Byzantine period, are frequently represented in flowering landscapes, expressing their hopes of entering Paradise and manifesting, for the living, the fulfilment of their prayers. This manner of thinking is further expressed in the comparison of the deceased in contemporary texts to all manner of plant life – from cut vines to stalks of wheat ready to be harvested.[61]

While most sources describe Orthodox manifestations of Byzantine piety, we must recall that a large body of written and visual evidence witnesses the survival of deeply held superstitions and certain ceremonies that were the inheritances of Byzantium's antique past or the remnants of folk practices that were never completely expunged from the lives of the empire's citizens. The action of Maria Phrangopoulina, described above, in burning of a piece of the patriarchal robe, fell outside the acceptable boundaries of Orthodox practice. Images of women labelled as witches in wall paintings of the sinners in late Byzantine churches suggest that un-Orthodox practices abounded and were frowned upon by the church. Pagan practices were mingled with Christian ones in a number of rites, and these signal the survival of an ancient belief system that could not be easily suppressed. Calends, the celebration of the New Year on 1 January when gifts were exchanged and costumes worn, was derived from pagan customs and was censured, on occasion, by church authorities. More seriously Niketas, the twelfth-century metropolitan of Thessalonike, confronted the issue of priests slaughtering doves over the tombs of the deceased, a practice redolent of paganism.[62] The Broumalia, a late autumn Dionysiac festival celebrating the production of new wine, is also attested (and criticised by churchmen) well into the late Byzantine era. Several agricultural

---

60 *Mazaris' Journey to Hades or Interviews with Dead Men about Certain Officials of the Imperial Court* (trans.) [Seminar Classics 609] (Buffalo: State University of New York at Buffalo, 1975), 16–19.
61 *Manuelis Philae Carmina. Ex codicibus Escurialensibus, Florentinis, Parisinis et Vaticanis*, ed. E. Miller (Paris: Excusum in Typographeo imperiali, 1855), I, 448–9.
62 Rhalles and Potles, v, 387–8.

festivals, as well, were rooted in celebrations of natural phenomena that derived from antique practices. Although a number of writers condemned these practices, it would seem, as today, that rites responding to superstition and fear were tolerated to some extent and, in some cases, were provided with an Orthodox veneer that made them, at least superficially, acceptable to the church.

In a culture comprised of different economic and social levels, and one in which the population was divided between urban and rural dwellers, lay piety could be manifested in many ways. It would be incorrect to assume that every Byzantine approached his or her religious devotions with equal fervour. Some members of society, particularly those of the upper classes whose education enabled them to read theological texts and to correspond with members of the high clergy, were so pietistic that their worldly lives resembled a monastic existence. An ample number of sources attest to the good works and monastic vocations of upper-class laywomen, who retired to monasteries as they advanced in age. Many of the most stunning works of religious art surviving from the middle and late Byzantine periods were commissioned by extremely pious lay members of the elite: some as personal devotional objects, and others for donation to churches and monasteries. Yet the sermons and encyclical letters of strict churchmen like the patriarch Athanasios I constantly complain of the lax behaviour of the working classes of Constantinople, who are reminded not to work or go to the baths and taverns on Sunday, not to leave church before the service is over, to observe fast days and to avoid magical practices and divination.

Members of the rural population, as we have demonstrated, expressed their piety in a more humble manner. For them, the church was closely linked to agricultural work and to lifecycle rituals. Their manner of worship was affected by their inability to read texts, and their deeply held faith must have sustained them in the absence of high-church rhetoric. Thus the picture of lay piety is a complex one and its study reveals significant differences in the devotional practices of men and women, the elite and the humble, the literate and the unlettered. Thus, while the assumption that the Byzantines were deeply pious is undoubtedly correct, the manifestations of that piety were subtly diverse.

4

The rise of hesychasm

DIRK KRAUSMÜLLER

During the third and fourth decades of the fourteenth century, at a time when the rapidly shrinking Byzantine Empire suffered greatly from internal strife, the Orthodox Church was rocked by an acrimonious controversy. This controversy ultimately led to a redefinition of traditional Trinitarian dogma as it had been formulated in late antiquity: in 1351 a church synod decreed that not only the transcendent being of God was in the true sense divine but also his operations or energies in this world, and it condemned as heretical the alternative belief that these operations were created. The decree of the synod reflects a theological model that the Athonite monk Gregory Palamas had developed in polemical encounters with a string of opponents, among whom the monk Barlaam of Calabria and the *literati* Gregory Akindynos and Nikephoros Gregoras were the most prominent. While these men were excommunicated, Palamas himself was canonised as a saint less than a decade after his death in 1359. Today he is considered one of the authorities of the Orthodox Church and the rediscovery of his writings by theologians of the last century has played a crucial role in the construction of present-day Orthodoxy.[1]

The last stage of the controversy between Palamas and his adversaries was characterised through a high level of abstraction and the extensive use of patristic proof texts. However, its starting point was anything but academic. Palamas formulated his views on the divine operations in order to solve a concrete problem: namely how to reconcile the reality of mystical experiences with traditional theology, which stressed the inaccessibility of God and rejected all claims to visions of God's being. Palamas and his allies were so concerned about this issue because they were followers of the so-called hesychastic method, a set of psychophysical techniques whose *raison d'être* it was to rid the mind of all distracting thoughts and to induce visions of God as light.

---

1 Cf. esp. V. Lossky, *Théologie mystique de l'Église d'Orient* (Paris: Aubier Montaigne, 1944); J. Meyendorff, *St Grégoire Palamas et la mystique orthodoxe* (Paris: Éditions du Seuil, 1959).

First attested in the thirteenth century, this method enjoyed great popularity among Byzantine monks throughout the fourteenth century, in particular on Mount Athos, which after the loss of Asia Minor had become the most important centre of Orthodox monasticism. The proponents of hesychasm saw themselves as the true heirs of the monastic tradition of the Orthodox east and in particular of the school that stressed the need to be on constant guard against sinful thoughts.[2] At the same time they disapproved of other models of monastic life. Two groups of monks in particular attracted their criticism: those who focused on asceticism and psalm singing and those who, like Palamas's adversary Barlaam, stressed the importance of intellectual activity for monks. The hesychasts accused the former group of neglecting the inner man and disparaged the latter as pursuing worldly wisdom, which distracted them from the quest for the divine. The self-portrayal of the hesychasts and their criticism of the two alternative models proved so efficacious that their point of view has become the canonical narrative of late Byzantine spirituality.[3] The following discussion explores the processes that led to the construction of this narrative. It seeks to clarify the link between hesychasm and the Byzantine spiritual tradition and to determine the nature of the debates between hesychasts and non-hesychasts in order to arrive at a more balanced understanding of the rise of the new movement.

Pseudo-Symeon and Nikephoros the Italian

Any discussion of hesychasm must start with the two treatises that set out the specific techniques by which visions might be induced. The first of these treatises, which the manuscripts wrongly attribute to the eleventh-century mystic Symeon the New Theologian, can only tentatively be dated to the late twelfth or early thirteenth century.[4] By comparison, the author of the second treatise is a well-known historical figure, Nikephoros the Italian, who lived as a monk on Mount Athos during the reign of Emperor Michael VIII (1259–82) to whose pro-western religious policy he was fiercely opposed.[5] In the fourteenth century these texts enjoyed enormous success and were widely regarded as

---

2 In the following the terms hesychasm and hesychast are used exclusively to denote the psychophysical method and its practitioners.
3 Cf. especially J. Meyendorff, *Introduction à l'étude de Grégoire Palamas* [Patristica Sorbonensia 3] (Paris: Éditions du Seuil, 1959).
4 I. Hausherr (ed.), *La méthode d'oraison hésychaste* [OCA 9.2] (Rome: Pontificium institutum orientalium studiorum, 1927), 150–72, cf. 111–18 on the identity and date of the anonymous author.
5 Nikephoros the Monk, *On sobriety and the guarding of the heart*, in PG 147, 945–66. Cf. A. Rigo, 'Niceforo l'esicasta (XIII sec.): alcune considerazioni sulla vita e sull'opera', in

authoritative.[6] It is not difficult to see why monks who strove for mystical experiences would be drawn to them: Nikephoros presents his teachings as a 'science' or 'method' for beginners, which is easy, fast, efficacious and free from demonic interference.[7] However, it must also be asked why he and his readers should have regarded such experiences as central to monastic life. The writings of Symeon the New Theologian suggest a possible answer. Symeon criticised the traditional view that visions were the preserve of a few exceptional individuals and maintained that every monk could and should experience the divine.[8] This radical position appears to have become more widespread over time for it resurfaces in later spiritual authors such as the twelfth-century mystic Constantine Chrysomallos.[9] However, Symeon, who was a 'natural' himself, had not set out a specific method to achieve this aim.[10] It is conceivable that Nikephoros refers to this situation when he states that there are spontaneous visionaries but that the multitude needs to be taught.[11] This assessment of the situation defines the rationale of Pseudo-Symeon and Nikephoros: they wished through their teachings to make available such experiences to the average monk.[12]

How does hesychasm work? Both writers promise their readers that they can attain visions in their hearts similar to the apostles' experience of the transfigured Christ on Mount Tabor if they follow a prayer routine that involves a sitting position, control of one's breathing and invocation of the name of Jesus.[13] Despite these similarities, however, the texts are not identical. In Pseudo-Symeon practitioners are advised to look intently at the region around their navel until it becomes suffused with light and transparent, and the transfigured heart becomes visible to the gazer. By comparison, breathing and the Jesus Prayer are only mentioned in passing. Nikephoros, on the other hand, makes no reference to navel-gazing and instead focuses on the other two features. He urges his readers to concentrate on the path that the breath takes from the mouth to the heart and to 'send down' the mind into the heart together with

Amore del bello, studi sulla Filocalia. Atti del Simposio Internazionale sulla Filocalia (Magnano: Edizioni Qiqajon, 1991), 79–119.

6 Cf. e.g. the *Spiritual Century* of Kallistos and Ignatios Xanthopoulos, in PG 147, 677D.

7 Nikephoros, *On sobriety*, in PG 147, 945A–946A, and *passim*.

8 Cf. *Syméon le Nouveau Théologien, Catéchèses*, ed. B. Krivochéine (Paris: Éditions du Cerf, 1964), III, 238–68.

9 Cf. J. Gouillard, 'Quatre procès de mystiques à Byzance (vers 960–1143). Inspiration et autorité', *REB* 36 (1978), 5–81, esp. 31–5.

10 Instead, he recommended tears and contrition. Cf. especially *Catéchèses*, III, 194–222.

11 Nikephoros, *On sobriety*, in PG 147, 962B.

12 This interpretation was first proposed by Hausherr, *Méthode d'oraison*, 127–9.

13 Nikephoros, *On sobriety*, in PG 147, 962A; Hausherr, *Méthode d'oraison*, 160.2–4.

the breath. He claims that by holding their breath they can keep their mind inside their heart and prevent it from roaming and becoming distracted by thoughts. Those who have reached this state are then continuously to invoke the name of Jesus Christ in order to keep the mind occupied and to drown out all 'new' thoughts that might arise. Despite these differences it is evident that Pseudo-Symeon and Nikephoros operate within the same framework: both techniques – navel-gazing and control of breathing – give an important role to sense perception and imagination. Moreover, they are closely linked to the body: concentration on the heart is not merely a device to focus one's mind but is believed to involve and to have an effect on the actual organ.[14]

The success of hesychasm leaves no doubt that these techniques were highly efficacious. However, such efficacy alone does not provide a sufficient explanation for their adoption by monastic communities on Mount Athos and elsewhere. The treatise of Pseudo-Symeon gives an insight into the problems faced by the early hesychasts. It is much more than a simple prayer manual: the description of the 'method' is part of a carefully constructed argument through which the author strives to gain acceptance for it within the monastic discourse of his time. In his preface he announces that he will set out for his readers three different prayer practices so that they can make an informed choice between them. The criteria that he uses are 'attention' (προσοχή) and 'prayer' (προσευχή): effective attention should lead to the detection and seizure of sinful thoughts and effective prayer should then eliminate them.[15] The central role accorded to 'attention' points to a particular tradition within monasticism, which is first attested in the *Heavenly Ladder* of John Klimax and is later elaborated in the *Spiritual Chapters* of Hesychios and Philotheos of Sinai where it becomes the dominant theme.[16] Analysis of Pseudo-Symeon's argument reveals a highly complex relationship between hesychasm and 'Sinaitic' spirituality and sheds light on the context in which the hesychastic method originated.

The disposition of the treatise is straightforward: three chapters present the 'properties' and effects of each practice. The followers of the first practice stand upright and direct their inner and their outer eyes upwards to the sky. They then conjure up in their mind the splendour of heaven until it becomes perceptible to the senses of the body as light, smell and sound.[17] By comparison

---

14 Cf. especially the physiological excursus in Nikephoros, *On sobriety*, in *PG* 147, 963AB.

15 Hausherr, *Méthode d'oraison*, 150.6–18.

16 Cf. ibid., 134–42. John Klimax is also quoted in Nikephoros, *On sobriety*, in *PG* 147, 955A–956A. Cf. J. Kirchmeyer, 'Hésychius le Sinaïte', in *Dictionnaire de spiritualité*, VII (1971), 408–10.

17 Hausherr, *Méthode d'oraison*, 151.17–152.12; 152.20–4.

the second practice requires the mind to keep tight control over the senses and to examine all incoming thoughts for possible demonic interference.[18] Followers of the third practice, which represents the hesychastic method, are told to sit down and direct their inner and their outer eyes to the region of the navel and to search for the place of the heart inside. They are told that they will first experience darkness but that eventually the mind 'sees the air inside the heart and itself as being completely light and full of discretion. And from then on, when a thought arises, the mind expels it and eliminates it through the invocation of Jesus Christ, before it has been completed and shaped into an image.'[19]

The first practice is declared worst: it does not lead to virtue and dispassion and it may result in madness because its followers do not learn to distinguish true visions from demonic illusions. By comparison the second practice is seen in much more positive terms. According to the author it is not so much wrong as incomplete since it focuses on the rebuttal of demonic thoughts coming from the outside and neglects to deal with the thoughts that are already in the heart. As a consequence it remains ineffective and can never rid the monk entirely of his passions. Not surprisingly this is the achievement of the third practice, where according to the author focus on the heart leads to discretion because the practitioner sees all that is in his heart and can therefore easily identify and destroy through prayer all demonic thoughts, not only those coming from the outside but also those that are already inside.

At first, the author's argument seems straightforward enough but a closer look reveals significant anomalies. From his ranking one would expect the hesychastic method to show greater affinity with the second practice. Instead it shows striking similarities with the first: in both cases the author states that the practitioners assume a particular posture, that they direct both their imagination and their bodily senses to the same object, and that they expect mystical experiences. None of these features can be found in the second practice, where the body and sense perception are not given a positive role and where there is no visionary component. As we have seen, the author does create a link between the hesychastic method and the second practice through the common theme of discretion, which then permits him to compare his own position favourably with the first practice. However, the overlaps with the second practice are exclusively found in the latter part of the description of the hesychastic method for which there is no longer a counterpart in the first

18 Ibid., 154.3–16; 157.21–158.5.
19 Ibid., 159.14–160.7; 164.9–165.17.

practice. The author achieves the transition from one framework to the next in the statement that 'the mind sees . . . itself as being completely light *and* full of discretion'. Accordingly discretion is not linked to the examination of one's thoughts as in the second practice but rather is tacked on to a technique that results in visionary experiences. The common criterion of 'attention' thus conceals radical differences in how this aim is achieved. Indeed 'attention' can only have this function because it is given more than one meaning in the text. As we have seen, the author defines it in his preface as the ability to detect all thoughts that are about to enter the heart and to determine their nature and origin. However, the term is then used in this sense only in the discussion of the second practice, which is based on the 'examination of thoughts'. In the first practice, on the other hand, it denotes focus on an object, the sky. Such a use has clearly nothing to do with the way the author defined the term at the beginning. However, it later allows him to collapse the two notions into one: in the third practice 'attention' to the navel results in a vision of the transfigured heart, which at the same time makes visible all demonic thoughts that are present in the heart. He could do so because the 'inward turn' of the hesychastic method, which distinguished it from the first practice, permitted a conflation of the heart as the object of visionary experience with the heart as a metaphor for the 'place' of thoughts.[20]

The author's ingenious exploitation of conceptual and terminological ambiguities has an obvious reason: despite its radically different character he wants his approach to pass muster within the value system that is defined by the advocates of the second practice. Indeed, the treatise may well have been composed as a response to attacks from proponents of this second practice: the author complains that they regarded themselves as 'attentive' (προσεκτικός) and that they criticised others for not being so. There can be no doubt that the second practice with its exclusive focus on incoming thoughts is a caricature of the teachings of the Sinaite authors John Klimax, Philotheos and, in particular, Hesychios.[21] At the same time the description of the third practice contains numerous literal borrowings from Hesychios's *Spiritual Chapters*.[22] In the light of the previous discussion it seems likely that the author inserted these quotations in order to bolster his evidently specious claim to be part of this tradition, which he then merely improves.

20 Cf. ibid., 146.
21 Cf. e.g. Hesychios, *Chapters*, in PG 93, 1496AB, 1497C.
22 Cf. Hausherr, *Méthode d'oraison*, 134–42, who identifies borrowings from Hesychios and also from the *Heavenly Ladder*.

Why did Pseudo-Symeon go to such lengths? Prayer practice in which intense imagination results in sensory experience is attested throughout the Byzantine era. In the ninth-century *Life* of Theophanes the Confessor by Patriarch Methodios, for example, the young saint and his bride 'pursue' Christ by focusing on their sense of smell: they imagine him as fragrance and are eventually rewarded with the miraculous manifestation of 'real' fragrance to their noses.[23] In the hagiographical tradition such experiences are presented as unproblematic and the issue of discretion is hardly ever raised. This unconcern contrasts sharply with the views expressed in late antique and Byzantine spiritual literature.[24] The authors of spiritual texts not only strongly discourage the use of imagination because of the danger of demonic deception but also criticise the exclusive focus on the achievement of visionary experiences and the concomitant lack of interest in moral perfection and the strategies that lead to it.[25] It is evident that with his approach, which focused on visionary experience and had no room for traditional practices of soul-searching, Pseudo-Symeon found himself outside traditional spiritual discourse. With his manipulations he tried to overcome the marginal status of his own position and to make it acceptable within this discourse, represented in his text through the second prayer practice. In order to achieve his aim he pursued a complex strategy. Despite its obvious similarity with the hesychastic method he introduced the first practice as a separate approach. In agreement with the spiritual tradition, he then presented this approach as misguided and dangerous for its practitioners.[26] This allowed the author to show awareness of and pay lip service to the objections against the use of imagination and thus to disguise the fact that his own position was virtually identical to those who made use of imagination in the pursuit of visionary experience.

Pseudo-Symeon's manipulations ensured hesychasm a place in the spiritual mainstream. However, it is evident that the combination of the two traditions remains superficial and is only possible through subversion of the conceptual framework underlying the second practice. Nikephoros in his manual makes it clear that for hesychasts immunity from demonic attacks is not achieved through sifting through thoughts and the exercise of discretion but through

23 Methodios, *Life of Theophanes*, 13–14, ed. V. V. Latyshev, *Methodii Patriarchae Constantinopolitani Vita S. Theophanis Confessoris* [Zapiski rossiiskoi akademii nauk. (po istoriko-filologicheskomu otdeleniiu), ser. viii, 13.4] (Petrograd: Rossiiskaia akademiia nauk, 1918), 9.32–10.20.
24 Cf. G. Dagron, 'Rêver de Dieu et parler de soi. Le rêve et son interprétation d'après les sources byzantines', in *I sogni nel Medioevo* (Seminario internazionale Roma 2–4 ottobre 1983, ed. T. Gregori) [Lessico intellettuale europeo 35] (Rome, 1985), 37–55.
25 Hausherr, *Méthode d'oraison*, 142–4.
26 Ibid., 152.15–153.22.

shutting out such thoughts altogether thanks to the exercise of intense imagination, which takes the place of all other mental activity.[27]

The treatise of Pseudo-Symeon gives us an insight into the earliest stage of the hesychastic movement when it was not yet widespread and had to fight for acceptance. The late thirteenth and early fourteenth centuries saw the rapid expansion of hesychasm on Mount Athos. Nikephoros is said to have attracted numerous disciples, among them Theoleptos of Philadelphia († c. 1325), one of the leading religious authorities of his time.[28] However, the most important figure of the next generation was without doubt Gregory the Sinaite. Caught up in the Turkish conquest of western Asia Minor, Gregory became a monk and then spent several years on Mount Sinai before departing to Mount Athos, where he lived as a hermit. Later he founded a monastery in Thrace, which attracted the patronage of the Bulgarian ruler Ivan Alexander (1331–71). When he died in 1346 he had a great number of disciples, including many Slavs who introduced hesychasm to Bulgaria and Serbia.[29] Gregory propagated the hesychastic method in several prayer manuals, which he addressed to various Athonite monks.[30] In these texts he refers to both earlier treatises but it is clear that his own teachings owe more to Nikephoros than to Pseudo-Symeon: the focus is on breathing and the Jesus Prayer whereas navel-gazing is never mentioned. His own experience is reflected in a strong interest in physical reactions such as trembling and feelings of joy.

Gregory of Sinai

Gregory's prayer manuals are evidence for the spread of hesychasm on Mount Athos and elsewhere. However, they also show that this spread did not take the form of simple imposition but was rather a process of mutual accommodation. There can be no doubt that in its earliest form hesychasm posed great dangers to traditional monastic life. Nikephoros not only sets out techniques that make visions accessible to 'ordinary' monks but also maintains that these techniques can be learnt without the help of a spiritual father.[31] If taken at face value this

---

27 Cf. Nikephoros, *On sobriety*, in *PG* 147, 964B–965A.
28 See however R. E. Sinkewicz, *Theoleptos of Philadelphia, The Monastic Discourses. A critical edition, translation and study* [Studies and Texts 111] (Toronto: Pontifical Institute of Mediaeval Studies, 1992), 2–5.
29 On Gregory's biography cf. A. Rigo, 'Gregorio il Sinaita', *La théologie byzantine*, ed. G. Conticello and V. Conticello (Turnhout: Brepols, 2002), II, 30–130, esp. 35–83. On his influence on Bulgaria cf. G. Podskalsky, *Theologische Literatur des Mittelalters in Bulgarien und Serbien 865–1459* (Munich: C. H. Beck, 2000), 299.
30 See Rigo, 'Gregorio il Sinaita', 106–19.
31 Nikephoros, *On sobriety*, in *PG* 147, 963A.

would have led to a complete erosion of the established process of monastic socialisation, which required novices to subject themselves to the authority of an experienced monk to whom they then gave unquestioning obedience. Such behaviour inculcated the virtue of humility, which would rule out disruption at a later stage when monks might vaunt their achievements. In contrast, Nikephoros claims that reading a few pages of text is sufficient for a beginner and that it can replace a spiritual guide. Gregory of Sinai's writings on the method are of a radically different nature. They limit visionary experiences to those who are advanced and they stress the need for beginners to submit to the discretion of experienced monks.[32] Unsurprisingly Gregory also had an acute sense of the possibility of demonic interference, which made him reject all 'shaped' visions, whereas Nikephoros had shown total unconcern for the dangers incurred by practitioners of the method.[33] From this juxtaposition it is evident that Gregory aimed at domesticating the new movement and at making it compatible with traditional structures of authority.

Through his teachings Gregory of Sinai contributed to the success of the new movement on Mount Athos. Indeed, he appears as an arbiter in matters of visionary experiences in hagiographical texts of the time.[34] However, there can be no doubt that many individuals kept their distance from hesychasm or even felt resentment at its absolutist nature, which is summed up in Pseudo-Symeon's contention that once the Fathers had discovered the method they abandoned everything else.[35] One group of opponents were monks who focused on ascetic practices such as fasting and sleep deprivation and who preferred traditional psalm singing to the hesychastic method. Nikephoros's treatise contains a vicious attack against such monks, while Gregory of Sinai also criticises them repeatedly in his writings.[36] Both authors relied in their arguments on Pseudo-Symeon's equation of the method with Sinaite spirituality: their contention that ascetics neglect the inner dimension is a direct borrowing from the traditional discourse of 'attention'.[37] There

32 Cf. especially Gregory of Sinai, *Opusculum IV*, in PG 150, 1340–1 [= H.-V. Beyer, *Gregorios Sinaïtes, Werke. Einleitung, kritische Textausgabe und Übersetzung* (unpublished Habilitationsschrift, Vienna, 1985), 86].

33 Cf. Gregory of Sinai, *Opusculum II*, in PG 150, 1324A–C [= ed. Beyer, 69–70].

34 F. Halkin, 'Deux vies de S. Maxime le Kausokalybe, ermite au Mont Athos (XIVe s.)', *Analecta Bollandiana* 54 (1936), 38–109, esp. 82–9.

35 Hausherr, *Méthode d'oraison*, 116.22–117.15. For expressions of resentment cf. A. Hero, *Letters of Gregory Akindynos. Greek text and English translation* [DOT 7; CFHB 21] (Washington, DC: Dumbarton Oaks Research Library and Collection, 1983), 208.

36 Nikephoros, *On sobriety*, in PG 147, 947AB; Gregory of Sinai, *Opusculum II*, PG 150, 1317C–1320C [= ed. Beyer, 75–6].

37 Cf. esp. Nikephoros, *On sobriety*, in PG 147, 947B–948A.

are indications that the hesychasts were in turn accused of laxity: Gregory's hagiographer went out of his way to present the saint as an extreme faster at the time when he became first acquainted with the method.[38] On the whole, however, the ascetics do not seem to have posed a serious threat to the new movement.

Barlaam of Calabria

A much more dangerous opponent proved to be the monk Barlaam of Calabria. Around the year 1330 Barlaam had left his homeland and had come to the Byzantine East where he soon gained a reputation for his knowledge of the Orthodox theological tradition and his interests in philosophy and science.[39] In the mid-1330s he met monks in Constantinople and Thessalonike, who acquainted him with the hesychastic method and its effects.[40] Considering the views of the hesychasts at least misguided and at worst heretical, he saw it as his duty to disabuse them of their errors.[41] However, when he set out on his mission he was immediately confronted with vehement opposition, which was led by Gregory Palamas, a member of a Constantinopolitan aristocratic family who had become a monk on Mount Athos.[42] Palamas was no stranger to Barlaam: he had already exchanged with him a series of increasingly polemical letters about the role of logic in the theological discourse.[43] Now he composed a tripartite treatise *In Defence of Those who Live in Quietude in a Sacred Manner*, which offered an arsenal of arguments to the beleaguered hesychasts.[44] It appears that at the same time Barlaam, too, expressed his views in a series of writings. However, once he became aware of Palamas's treatise he withdrew

---

38 I. Pomialovskii, *Zhitie izhe vo svatykh otca nashego Grigorija Sinaita* [Zapiski istoriko-filologicheskago fakul'teta imperatorskago S.-Peterburgskago Universiteta, 35] (St Petersburg, 1896), 8.2–15.

39 Cf. R. E. Sinkewicz, 'The solutions addressed to George Lapithes by Barlaam the Calabrian and their philosophical context', *Mediaeval Studies* 43 (1981), 151–217.

40 For the chronology of the controversy cf. R. E. Sinkewicz, 'A new interpretation for the first episode in the controversy between Barlaam the Calabrian and Gregory Palamas', *JThSt* n.s. 31 (1980), 489–500.

41 Cf. G. Schirò, *Barlaam Calabro. Epistole greche. I primordi episodici e dottrinari delle lotte esicaste* [Testi 1] (Palermo: Istituto siciliano di studi bizantini e neogreci, 1954), 324.127–31.

42 For Gregory's biography see R. E. Sinkewicz, 'Gregory Palamas', in *Théologie byzantine et sa tradition*, II, 131–88, esp. 131–7. For the sake of brevity I will in the following refer to Gregory of Sinai as 'Gregory' and to Gregory Palamas as 'Palamas'.

43 R. E. Sinkewicz, 'The doctrine of the knowledge of God in the early writings of Barlaam the Calabrian', *Mediaeval Studies* 44 (1982), 196–222.

44 Gregory Palamas, *Défense des saints hésychastes*, ed. J. Meyendorff [Spicilegium sacrum lovaniense, Études et documents 30] (Louvain: Spicilegium sacrum lovaniense, 1959), I, 3–223 (triade I).

these texts and revised them in order to address Palamas's criticisms.[45] Palamas responded by composing a second treatise, which had the same disposition as the first but dealt more directly with Barlaam's written statements, which are repeatedly quoted.[46]

What agenda did Barlaam pursue? Unfortunately both redactions of his writings are lost and their content must be reconstructed from other sources. The obvious starting point for such a reconstruction is Palamas's refutation of Barlaam's positions. The last, and longest, parts of Palamas's two treatises deal with Barlaam's claim that the search for God ends with an understanding of his total otherness from all created being: they set out the counterargument that human beings can outstrip their natural faculties, either because the mind possesses the ability to transcend itself or because God becomes accessible to man through the gift of the Holy Spirit.[47] Such a disposition reflects the central importance that this issue had for the hesychasts. However, one must be careful not to see Barlaam exclusively through the hesychastic lens. His own writings appear to have been organised quite differently: it seems that his treatise *On Light* in which he voiced his objections against visionary experiences was the first of his texts on the subject and that it was followed by a treatise with the composite title *On Prayer and on Human Perfection*.[48] This discrepancy suggests that Barlaam had other priorities. Such an interpretation is borne out by his earlier writings, in particular his two *Letters* to the hesychast Ignatios and his second *Letter* to Palamas. These texts show that originally Barlaam was less concerned with the vision of light as such, than with the fact that it did not have the effects on the visionaries, which he considered essential for their spiritual progress. These were the mortification and subjugation of the passionate part of the soul and the vivification of the rational faculty, which enabled human beings to make correct judgements and dispel error and

---

45 This is at least Gregory Palamas's version of the events: Palamas, *Défense*, I, 228–9 (triade II.I.2).

46 Ibid., I, 224–555 (triade II).

47 Ibid., I, 143, 13–18 (triade 1.3.16); I, 209.13–17 (triade 1.3.45), ed. Meyendorff, 143.13–18, 209.13–17. For Barlaam's position see Sinkewicz, 'Knowledge of God', 181–242.

48 These titles can be reconstructed from references in Palamas's second triad (Palamas, *Défense*, I, xxvi); from Gregory Akindynos's *ninth letter* to Barlaam (ed. Hero, *Letters*, 30.25–32.61); from Patriarch John Kalekas's *Explication of the Tome*, in PG 150, 900D; and from the *sixth speech* of Joseph Kalothetos, which was addressed to Kalekas (ed. D. G. Tsames, Ἰωσὴφ Καλοθέτου Συγγράμματα [Θεσσαλονικεῖς Βυζαντινοὶ Συγγραφεῖς 1] (Thessalonike: Centre of Byzantine Studies, 1980), 237.54–238.58). Kalothetos was one of the addressees of Barlaam's letters at the beginning of the controversy. Cf. H. Hunger and O. Kresten, *Studien zum Patriarchatsregister von Konstantinopel* (Vienna: Verlag ÖAW, 1997), II, 71–4. The above-mentioned sequence is suggested by Palamas, *Défense*, I,229.10–23 (triade II.I.2), which appears not only to refer to *On Light*, but also to contain a summary of first *On prayer* and then *On human perfection*.

self-delusion.[49] It is evident that Barlaam had a negative view of both the emotions and the body, which played an important role in the hesychastic experience. Palamas tackles this topic in the second parts of his first and second treatises where he attempts to show that emotions are not necessarily sinful but can be sanctified.[50] However, Barlaam's contempt for feelings must be balanced with his high regard for reason. In the tradition of Christian neoplatonism Barlaam contended that the knowledge about the structure of this world is inscribed in the human soul as common notions, which reproduce at the level of discursive thought the principles of creation inherent in the divine mind.[51] In his lost disquisition *On Human Perfection*, which formed the last part of his *œuvre*, he set out a model of man's ascent to God that corresponded to this framework. He insisted that human beings must first awaken their dormant rationality through exposure of their analytical and logical faculties to all kinds of knowledge before they can transcend the purely human level through a 'folding up' of their thoughts to unitive and intuitive intellection.[52] This model of graded ascent is without doubt the core of Barlaam's teachings.[53] In his refutation Palamas attacked it as an attempt to divert monks from their true vocation, which he identified with the practice of the hesychastic method.[54] He relegated the discussion to the first parts of his two treatises to which he gave the headings: *In what respect and to what extent is the pursuit of letters useful*, and *What is the true salvific knowledge, which should concern the true monks, or against those who say that the knowledge from secular education is truly salvific*.[55] Thus he gave the impression that Barlaam's plea for intellectual activity was completely extraneous to the monastic tradition.

This impression, however, is deceptive. In a letter to his friend Gregory Akindynos, Barlaam defended his treatise *On Prayer and Human Perfection* against criticism by stating that all he did was present an 'exegesis' of the views of the seventh-century monk and spiritual teacher Maximos the Confessor with the intention of confirming the latter's position.[56] This Akindynos was happy to accept, even if he criticised Barlaam for his selective and skewed reading of Maximos. Palamas, on the other hand, subverted Barlaam's purpose by

---

49 See especially Schirò, *Barlaam Calabro*, 302–4, 318.
50 Palamas, *Défense*, I, 70–101 (triade I.2); I, 318–83 (triade II.2).
51 Sinkewicz, 'Knowledge of God', 210, 238–9.
52 Palamas, *Défense*, II, 539 (triade II.3.71). Cf Schirò, *Barlaam Calabro*, 302.566–303.570.
53 The title *On human perfection* is derived from Paul's 'perfect man' in Ephesians 4:13 and refers to the successive stages of growing up from childhood to adulthood.
54 E.g. Palamas, *Défense*, I, 23 (triade I.1.7).
55 Ibid., I, 9 (triade I.1); I, 225 (triade II.1).
56 Akindynos, *Letters*, 42.134–8.

only treating Maximos in passing – and then mainly in the context of prayer.[57] This makes it impossible to reconstruct Barlaam's agenda relying on Palamas alone. It is therefore fortunate that we have at our disposal other contemporary sources, which shed light on the debate. These sources suggest that far from having a secularist agenda Barlaam saw himself as the representative of a genuinely monastic tradition, which he felt to be threatened by the hesychasts.

Gregory of Sinai and the 'wise in the word'

Barlaam was not as isolated a figure as Palamas would have us believe. Already in 1307 Theoleptos of Philadelphia found himself confronted with people who pursued 'profane' wisdom and rejected the hesychastic method.[58] Gregory of Sinai, too, initially faced opposition from the 'more learned' among the Athonite monks who accused him of being an innovator and who attempted to have him expelled from the Holy Mountain.[59] Theoleptos reacted with an outright rejection of his opponents' position, which closely resembles that of Palamas.[60] By comparison, Gregory of Sinai's response was much more nuanced and therefore permits us an insight into the alternative model and into the nature of the debate between the two parties. Gregory dealt with the issue in his treatise *Different words (λόγοι) about commandments, doctrines, threats and promises and also about thoughts and passions and virtues and also about quietude and prayer*, a series of short statements about a variety of spiritual topics, which most likely dates to the year 1327.[61] The *Words* begin with a statement about human nature: 'To be or to become rational (λογικός) according to nature, as we were, is impossible before purity . . . because we have been overwhelmed by the habit of irrationality that is linked to sense perception (αἰσθητική).'[62] In this sentence Gregory sets out an anthropological model according to which human beings are endowed with the faculty of reasoning as well as with sense perception, which in itself is non-rational. The former is distinctive of humans, whereas the latter is shared with animals. Both are linked through a strictly hierarchical relationship: reason controls the senses. This relationship,

---

57 Palamas, *Défense*, I, 355 (triade II.2.16).
58 Sinkewicz, 'Gregory Palamas', 155.
59 *Zhitie . . . Grigoriia Sinaita*, ed. Pomialovskii, 31.25–32.4.
60 Theoleptos, *The monastic discourses*, ed. Sinkewicz, 112–14.
61 Gregory of Sinai, *Words*, in PG 150, 1240–1300 [= ed. Beyer, 38–64]; Gregory's hagiographer mentions a text by Gregory that may well be identical with the *Words*: *Zhitie . . . Grigoriia Sinaita*, ed. Pomialovskii, 36.11–14. If so it can be dated to c.1327. See Rigo, 'Gregorio il Sinaita', 90.
62 Gregory of Sinai, *Words*, in PG 150, 1240A [= ed. Beyer, 38].

however, existed only until the fall, when sense perception came to prevail over reason. As a consequence reason has become inoperative and human beings have been dragged down to the level of non-rational beasts. This defines the task for them: they must return to the state of rational beings that God intended for them at their creation and thus regain their true humanity. As such Gregory's statements are completely traditional.[63] However, for a hesychast the choice of this framework is startling because it makes no provision for the supernatural dimension that is central to the hesychastic experience and it clashes with the positive role that sensation is given in this experience.

There can be no doubt that Gregory's choice of 'rationality' is of great significance: the first chapter and in particular the first word of a collection often introduce the dominant theme.[64] Analysis of the text reveals that Gregory engaged in a controversy with monks who regarded intellectual activity as an integral part of spiritual ascent and who drew on the discourse of 'rationality' to justify their lifestyle. Gregory accepted this discourse as part of the Christian tradition but challenged its appropriation by his opponents and instead claimed it for the hesychasts themselves. In the second chapter he states: 'Only the saints have been seen to be rational beings according to nature because they are pure; for none of the "wise in the word" (τῶν ἐν λόγῳ σόφων) has had pure speech (λόγον... καθαρόν), having from the start [allowed] evil thoughts (λογισμοί) to corrupt their rational faculty (λογικόν). For the material and many-worded spirit of worldly wisdom brings abstract reflections (λόγους) to the more intellectual (γνωστικώτεροι) and evil thoughts (λογισμοί) to the more uncouth, thus denying the cohabitation of the hypostatic wisdom and vision with undivided and uniform knowledge (γνῶσις).'[65] This passage takes up the theme of 'rationality' as the natural state of human beings. Gregory now introduces the 'saints' as a concrete group who have attained this state and juxtaposes them with a second group, 'the wise in the word', who have failed to do so. His argument pivots on the concept of 'purity' that first appeared in the first chapter as the precondition for the preservation of or the return to human rationality. This quality is now attributed to the 'saints' whereas 'the wise in the word' are said to have corrupted their rationality through 'thoughts' or λογισμοί, which in the monastic discourse have connotations

---

63 See E. Hisamatsu, *Gregorios Sinaites als Lehrer des Gebets* [Münsteraner theologische Abhandlungen 34] (Altenberge: Oros, 1994), 201–16.

64 E.g. the theme of 'love' in Maximos's *Chapters on love*, in PG 90, 661A, and that of 'sobriety' in Hesychios's *Chapters on sobriety*, in PG 93, 1480D. Gregory appears to have been the first author of spiritual chapters to opt for this particular topic.

65 Gregory of Sinai, *Words*, in PG 150, 1240A [= ed. Beyer, 39].

of sinfulness and demonic agency.[66] The fight against such thoughts and the struggle for dispassion is traditionally considered the first step on the road to perfection. Gregory implies that the 'wise in the word', who devote themselves to the acquisition of abstract knowledge, have done nothing to control their irrational urges and that they have thus repeated the fall of Adam in their own lives. As a consequence he can present all their subsequent activities as 'non-rational'.

The second part of the chapter shows that Gregory is not content with such a roundabout criticism. There he attributes 'abstract reflections' to the 'wise in the word', who are now referred to as the 'more intellectual', whereas he ascribes 'evil thoughts' to a different group, the 'more uncouth'. At the same time, however, he links the two thought processes by tracing both back to 'the spirit of worldly wisdom', by which he means the devil. The purpose of this configuration is evident: it permits him to reject intellectual pursuits (λόγοι) as a qualification for sanctity. In a further step Gregory then juxtaposes this 'worldly wisdom' with 'hypostatic wisdom', that is the Divine Word. The two forms of wisdom and knowledge are not only different from one another but also mutually exclusive: engagement in the one precludes ascent to the other. In itself such juxtaposition might be considered commonplace in a hesychastic text.[67] However, in the context of the *Words* it is startling because, as an effect of divine grace, visionary experience belongs to the supernatural level and has no place in the chosen framework of 'rationality', which is strictly limited to the sphere of human nature. The oddity becomes even more pronounced in the next chapter, where Gregory draws the conclusion that only the 'sensation (αἴσθησις) of grace' and not 'reflections on thoughts' and 'apodictic proofs of things' can be considered knowledge of truth.[68] The phrase 'sensation of grace' is the first unequivocal reference in the *Words* to the hesychastic experience and thus identifies the 'saints' as hesychasts. By comparison, 'proofs' and syllogistic reasoning are clearly linked to the 'wise in the word'. It is evident that, unlike visions, such pursuits involved the exercise of human reason, which provided the 'wise in the word' with a justification for considering themselves more rational and therefore superior to hesychasts.[69] As a hesychast Gregory had to reject such a conclusion. We have already seen that restoration of rationality is achieved through victory over evil thoughts, which Gregory denies the 'wise

66 Maximos, *Ambigua*, in PG 91, 1124A.
67 A similar criticism is made in Theoleptos, *The monastic discourses*, ed. Sinkewicz, 112.
68 Gregory of Sinai, *Words*, PG 150, 1240A [= ed. Beyer, 39].
69 In the *Chapters* of the twelfth-century author Elias Ekdikos the 'less enlightened' are indeed juxtaposed with the λογικώτεροι, i.e. the 'more rational': PG 127, 1160A.

in the word'. Now it seems that even after this victory is achieved, humans can only preserve their status of 'rational beings' if they desist from syllogistic reasoning and in general from exercising their rational faculty.

That this is indeed the case can be seen from the section in the *Words* that deals with evil 'thoughts'. In chapter 60 Gregory traces these 'thoughts' back to the 'division' of 'simple memory' that resulted from the fall and through which the originally simple human being became 'manifold' and 'composite' in his faculties.[70] In chapter 61 he then states that human beings can bring about a return to the original state 'through the permanent divine memory, which has been firmly entrenched through prayer and which through mixture with the Spirit has been lifted from the natural to the supernatural level'.[71] From this passage it is evident that Gregory conceives of 'simple remembrance of God' in terms of hesychastic prayer practice. In his treatises on prayer he explicitly identifies the 'remembrance of God' with the 'continuous invocation of the name of Jesus',[72] and he warns that one should permit nothing to enter one's heart 'apart from the pure and simple and unshaped memory of Jesus alone'.[73] This practice is now projected back onto the original state of man, which effectively turns Adam into the first hesychastic visionary and the fall into a breakdown of simple memory as the precondition for visionary experience: seduced by the lure of the devil, Adam lets himself be distracted and thus 'forgets' God. This allows the conclusion that, though 'rationality' was part of Adam's natural make-up, it was always transcended. Such a view is already found in earlier authors but Gregory's hesychastic background causes him to draw from it radical consequences.[74] In his framework the more adept human beings are in the exercise of their mental faculties the less 'rational' they become, because the very use of these faculties amounts to their corruption. A return to the original state can only be achieved when thoughts are shut out through hesychastic practice. This is then immediately followed by visionary experience: Gregory makes it clear that the 'natural' state of man is nothing more than a point of transition from which one either regresses to the 'unnatural' or advances to the 'supernatural'.[75]

The reason for this ingenious interpretation is clear: it allows Gregory to sever all links between 'rationality' and intellectual pursuits and thus to integrate the concept of 'rationality' into his own model. Significantly, chapters

70 Gregory of Sinai, *Words*, in *PG* 150, 1256B [= ed. Beyer, 45].
71 Ibid., 1256C [= ed. Beyer, 45].
72 Gregory of Sinai, *Opusculum II*, in *PG* 150, 1308B [= ed. Beyer, 68].
73 Gregory of Sinai, *Opusculum III*, ed. Beyer, 78 (not in *PG*).
74 Cf. Maximos, *Ambigua*, in *PG* 91, 1353D.
75 Gregory of Sinai, *Words*, in *PG* 150, 1257B [= ed. Beyer, 46].

60 and 61 juxtapose 'memory of God' with sinful thoughts and unlike chapter 2 make no mention of intellectual pursuits and learning as a separate category. However, the difference is only apparent since in chapter 2 the two categories – intellectual pursuits and sinful thoughts – are assimilated by being linked back to the same agent. This makes perfect sense in the hesychastic framework where all thoughts are bad in so far as they distract from the Jesus Prayer. It is evident that intellectual pursuits (λόγοι) have no place in such a framework and that they are only introduced because they have had an important role in the model of Gregory's opponents.

Gregory's attempts to define the relationship of the two categories more clearly are obscure and contradictory: at times they are lumped together, as they are in the second chapter where they are both said to originate in the 'material spirit' of this world, whereas elsewhere Gregory appears to distinguish evil thoughts from intellectual pursuits: the former being the work of the devil and the latter being derived from 'matter'.[76] The reason for this ambivalence is that spiritual authors usually make a distinction between 'sensualists' (σαρκικοί) who entertain sinful thoughts and 'intellectuals' (ψυχικοί) who rely exclusively on their human faculties and, according to St Paul, do not accept the spirit and the existence of a supernatural dimension.[77] Gregory himself refers to this concept in chapter 22 where he juxtaposes human knowledge acquired from books to which he applies the Pauline phrase 'wisdom made folly', and supernatural knowledge that comes straight from God.[78] However, in his programmatic statements about the issue Gregory is not prepared to permit the possibility of a 'neutral' human sphere, set apart from the demonic and the divine.

In order to underscore this point Gregory creates binary oppositions: divine simplicity and unity, as reflected in the brief and repetitive Jesus Prayer of the hesychasts, are repeatedly juxtaposed with demonic multiplicity and division (διαίρησις), which are linked to the prolix intellectual pursuits of the 'wise in the word'.[79] However, this neat symmetry is not as self-evident as Gregory would have his readers believe. Close reading of the second chapter shows covert acknowledgement of an alternative framework. The phrase 'cohabitation (συνοίκησις) of the hypostatic wisdom' evokes verse 7:28 of the Wisdom of Solomon: 'for God loves none but him who cohabits (συνοικοῦντα) with wisdom'. This verse is found in a passage where wisdom, traditionally identified

76 Ibid., 1257C–125B [= ed. Beyer, 46–47].
77 E.g. Nicetas Stethatos, *Chapters*, in PG 120, 996BC.
78 Gregory of Sinai, *Words*, in PG 150, 1245C [= ed. Beyer, 41].
79 Ibid., 1273C [= ed. Beyer, 53].

with Christ, appears as the teacher that gives human beings the 'unerring knowledge of beings' together with 'intelligence' and 'scientific knowledge'.[80] This passage not only justifies the intellectual pursuits of Christians but also defines the spirit of wisdom as 'having many parts': a qualification which is reminiscent of the term 'many-worded' that Gregory applied to the demonic 'spirit of the world'. The characterisation of supernatural knowledge, as 'uniform' and 'not broken up in parts', is borrowed from a well-known passage in the Pseudo-Dionysian treatise *On Ecclesiastical Hierarchy*, which explains the Greek term for 'monk' (μοναχός) as signifying that monks lead a 'life that is not broken up in parts and that is uniform, which makes them one in the sacred folding-up of the things that are divided to one God-like monad and God-loving perfection'.[81] This passage is heavily indebted to neoplatonic philosophy, from which it adopts the distinction between discursive thought that takes place in the rational soul and intuition that is a function of the higher faculty of 'intellect' (νοῦς). However, in neoplatonism discursive thought is not seen as an obstacle to reaching the higher level but rather its precondition: through a process of increasing abstraction the human mind ascends from the manifold symbols to the uniform reality behind these symbols.

At the beginning of his *Words* Gregory limits himself to oblique allusions to this concept. A proper discussion only takes place in chapter 127. In this uncommonly long chapter Gregory defines different stages in the spiritual development of monks to which he applies the terms 'grammarian', 'orator' and 'philosopher':

> 'Grammarians' are those who devote themselves to the active life (πρακτικός), in the sense that they are physically (σωματικῶς) engaged in the world of action, while 'divine orators' are those who contemplate nature (φυσικῶς), in the sense that they stand midway between knowledge and reasons for existence (τοὺς λόγους τῶν ὄντων); in the sense too that they apply apodictic logic to the universals in the spirit (τῶν ὅλων ἐν πνεύματι) through the divisive (διαιρετική) power of reason. 'True philosophers' are those who have within themselves the supernatural union with God in a palpable and direct manner.[82]

Here Gregory sets out a tripartite system of spiritual ascent where the struggle against passions and the pursuit of virtue is followed by the search for God

---

80 *Wisdom* 7:21.

81 Pseudo-Dionysius, *De ecclesiastica hierarchia*, 6.1.3: ed. G. Heil and A. M. Ritter, *Corpus Dionysiacum II: De coelesti hierarchia, De ecclesiastica hierarchia, De mystica theologia, Epistolae* (Berlin and New York: Walter de Gruyter, 1991), 116.15–19.

82 Gregory of Sinai, *Words*, in *PG* 150, 1292D [= ed. Beyer, 60–1].

through study of the divine imprint on creation and then through mystical experience of the divine. In itself such a system is, of course, utterly traditional. First defined in late antiquity, it is found in many spiritual texts of the Byzantine period.[83] However, it is evident that it is at odds with the hesychastic model of monastic life where there is no room for an intermediate stage between the achievement of dispassion and mystical experience. This incompatibility becomes even more obvious when we turn to the section of chapter 127 that clarifies the relation between these different stages. The 'philosopher' who represents the highest stage is characterised as a mystic. However, whereas visionary experience was previously presented as a result of the hesychastic method, it is now attributed to those who have previously concluded from their observation of creation that God is the single cause of all beings.[84] The realisation that all creation is derived from one cause establishes unity, but it is a unity that is achieved through intellectual activity and not through prayer alone. This intellectual activity is necessarily 'divisive' because only by classifying all individual beings within the framework of species and genera is it possible to see them as forming a unified whole. Gregory makes that clear in his discussion of the role of the 'orator': 'According to those who are "truly wise in word" an orator is the one who concisely comprehends the beings through general knowledge and who both divides and joins them like one body, thereby showing them as of the same value according to otherness and sameness.' Alternatively, he could be called a 'logician in truth' and 'not one who merely applies apodictic logic'.[85] Here 'distinction' and 'unification' as well as 'otherness' and 'sameness' appear in a dialectical relation instead of being mutually exclusive. There can be no doubt that chapter 127 is intended as a corrective to the first three chapters. Instead of the neat juxtaposition between hesychast 'saints' and depraved 'wise in word' we now find the 'truly wise in word' as a third category. Moreover, whereas before Gregory insinuated that human wisdom is inevitably linked to vainglory and material things, he now juxtaposes love of matter with love of the 'physiological' wisdom of God.[86] Gregory is careful to stress that proper contemplation of nature does not merely involve use of Greek logic but also has a spiritual dimension. However, these qualifications clearly do nothing to make the tripartite system of spiritual ascent more compatible with the hesychastic framework: as we have seen, it

83 E.g. A. and C. Guillaumont, *Évagre le Pontique, Traité pratique ou le moine* (Paris: Éditions du Cerf, 1971), II, 498. Cf. the titles of Nicetas Stethatos, *Centuries*, in PG 120, 852, 900, 953.
84 Gregory of Sinai, *Words*, in PG 150, 1289D [= ed. Beyer, 60].
85 Ibid., 1289CD [= ed. Beyer, 60].
86 Ibid., 1292C [= ed. Beyer, 60].

is intellectual activity as such and not just perverted intellectual activity that is outlawed within hesychasm.

Why then did Gregory feel constrained to incorporate this system into his own model? I have already pointed out that it was an integral part of the monastic tradition. However, his sources can be narrowed down even further. When in chapter 127 he refers to the 'truly wise in word' as authorities for his statements about the 'orator' there can be no doubt that he has in mind the seventh-century spiritual author Maximos the Confessor: his statement that the orator 'divides and joins together the five divided universal and general properties, which the incarnated Word joined together' is a direct adaptation of a famous passage in Maximos's *Ambigua*.[87] The presence in Gregory's *Words* of many terms and concepts borrowed from Maximos has long been noticed, but it has been taken as a sign of a Maximian renaissance among hesychasts.[88] Analysis of the argument suggests a different explanation, namely that Gregory referred to Maximos because he faced opponents who used a Maximian framework to justify their intellectual pursuits. Indeed, Maximos is also one of the main proponents of the view that rationality is an essential part of human beings that needs to be developed if they are to fulfil God's plan for them: only by doing so can human beings lift themselves up from the level of beast and thus become ready for deification.[89]

At this point we can return to Barlaam and his claim to be Maximos's 'exegete'. We have already seen how Barlaam too propagated a graded spiritual ascent with a strong emphasis on 'human perfection' and supported intellectual activity and scientific endeavour. There can therefore be no doubt that he was a proponent of the same model as Gregory's adversaries. What made Maximos so serviceable for them was his use of the philosophical-scientific categories of genera and species that had been developed by Aristotle.[90] In Maximos's writings, of course, contemplation was no longer equated with scientific exploration and the Aristotelian terms had taken on a non-technical quality. However, the very use of these terms left open the possibility of taking the spiritual discourse back to its 'scientific' roots. This permitted Barlaam and other like-minded monks to construct a model of monastic life that accommodated scholarly pursuits.

---

87 Ibid., 1289D [= ed. Beyer, 60]. Cf. Maximos, *Ambigua*, in PG 91, 1304D–1313B.
88 Hisamatsu, *Gregorios Sinaites*, 307.
89 Cf. Maximos, *Ambigua*, in PG 91, 1092B.
90 Ibid., 1225BC, 1312AB.

Gregory's *Words*, and in particular his first chapter and chapter 127, are testimony to the success of such a strategy because they show that Gregory felt constrained to address his opponents' framework even though he was incapable of integrating it into his own version of spiritual ascent.[91] Gregory's *Words* must be seen against the backdrop of a fight for spiritual authority.[92] When he refers to the 'wise in word' he thinks not simply of human rationality but also of man's capacity to use speech. Clearly Gregory chose the term 'orator' because of its connotations: both the 'wise in word' and the 'truly wise in word' articulate and teach their ideas but not all the saints do. Extensive passages in the *Words* where division and classification are applied in a distinctly scholastic manner show that Gregory felt the need to establish his credentials as a 'wise in word'.[93] From the *Words* it is evident that Gregory understood natural contemplation as the symbolic interpretation of natural phenomena: for example, he describes how the Trinity is reflected in the constitution of man.[94] There can be no doubt that his approach was much closer to Maximos's original intentions than that of his opponents.[95] However, this fact plays no role in Gregory's argument. Instead he attempts to contain the impact of his adversaries' model. By insisting that the 'truly wise in word' should focus on 'general science' and the most universal categories, he makes it clear that one should not waste time in the study of particulars and single species.

Palamas and the triumph of hesychasm

When we now turn to Barlaam's direct opponent Palamas, we find that his treatises share many traits with the *Words* of Gregory of Sinai. Palamas, too, cannot accept profane wisdom as morally neutral and instead insinuates that it originates in demons.[96] Furthermore, he claims that those who devote themselves to worldly wisdom are not 'rational' and therefore cannot proceed to the higher stage of intellection because such wisdom 'results in unstable and easily changeable knowledge and thus corrupts the discursive and divisible character of the thought processes (τὸ φρονοῦν) of the soul'.[97] This statement,

---

91 Maximos appears among the authors recommended by Gregory, *Opusculum III*, in PG 150, 1324D [= ed. Beyer, 48].
92 For attacks on hesychasm: e.g. Gregory of Sinai, *Words*, in PG 150, 1289C [= ed. Beyer, 59].
93 Ibid., 1260–1 [= ed. Beyer, 47]. Cf. Maximos, *Ambigua*, in PG 91, 1196C.
94 Gregory of Sinai, *Words*, PG 150, 1262BC [= ed. Beyer, 47–8].
95 E.g. Maximos, *Ambigua*, in PG 91, 1396D.
96 E.g. Palamas, *Défense*, I, 31.7–16 (triade I.1.9).
97 Ibid., I, 243.22–25 (triade II.1.9).

which is directed against Barlaam's belief that one can hone one's rational faculty and attain knowledge through a process of trial and error, closely resembles Gregory of Sinai's view that the human faculty for analytical thought can only be saved if it is never activated. The result is again a subversion of the neoplatonic model of graded spiritual ascent. However, unlike Gregory of Sinai, Palamas refused to engage in a debate about Maximos's spiritual legacy. This allowed him to present Barlaam's ontological framework and the otherwise perfectly acceptable notion of a 'folding-up' of discursive thought as secular in nature and as irreconcilable with monastic spirituality.[98] As a consequence he could reject as ludicrous the conclusion that because of their restored humanity monks with scholarly interests were ready to approach God whereas the hesychasts remained on the level of animals.[99]

Palamas's polemic is certainly more efficacious than that of Gregory of Sinai but this is achieved at the expense of large parts of the Byzantine spiritual tradition.[100] There can be little doubt that contemporaries would have understood Palamas's argument as a rejection not only of Barlaam but also of Maximos himself. Palamas's attitude towards the monastic tradition must be seen against the background of an increasingly heated debate, which made him take ever more radical positions. In many ways these positions hark back to the beginnings of the movement: like Nikephoros, Palamas shows an utter lack of concern for the dangers of mystical experiences whereas Gregory of Sinai had been much more careful.[101] A similar observation can be made when we compare Palamas with Pseudo-Symeon. We saw that Pseudo-Symeon replaced the traditional 'examination of thoughts' with the hesychastic method and thus virtually eliminated the role of discretion in the context of the first stage of a monk's spiritual ascent. Palamas now extends this approach to all its stages. When speaking about the fight against passions he rejects Barlaam's contention that monks need to use their minds in order to distinguish truth from mere semblance of truth. Instead he avers that monks should avoid making independent moral judgements and simply follow the precepts of the fathers,

---

98 Ibid., II, 393.1–5 (triade II.3.3); II, 537.20–539.5 (triade II.3.72). This flatly contradicts Maximos's teachings: e.g. *Mystagogia* 5, in *PG* 90, 681B.

99 Palamas, *Défense*, II, 539.5–17 (triade II.3.72).

100 Palamas displayed the same ruthlessness towards patristic theology: G. Podskalsky, *Theologie und Philosophie in Byzanz: der Streit um die theologische Methodik in der spätbyzantinischen Geistesgeschichte (14.–15. Jh.), seine systematischen Grundlagen und seine historische Entwicklung* [Byzantinisches Archiv 15] (Munich: Beck, 1977), 157–60.

101 E.g. Palamas, *Défense*, I, 213–15 (triade I.3.48–9), with reference to a passage from Mark the Monk. Cf. the radically different interpretation of this passage in Gregory of Sinai in *PG* 150, 1312A.

although this clearly contradicts the teachings of Maximos whom Barlaam without doubt quoted as authority.[102] At the level of natural contemplation Palamas replaces the use of analytical thought with the recommendation that one should look at creation with wonder and awe, which in the Maximian framework belongs to the level of sense perception that precedes discursive reasoning.[103]

Palamas was not prepared to let go of 'knowledge' altogether. While he rejected Barlaam's claim that the Fathers had used 'light' as a metaphor for knowledge, he at the same time claimed that this light was the purveyor of knowledge.[104] However, with this claim he ran into difficulties because hesychasts clearly did not possess knowledge in the way that Barlaam and other scholarly monks understood it. Therefore Palamas ended up extolling lack of knowledge as a positive quality: when he asks whether 'the knowledge of God that is present in Christians and the salvation resulting from it comes through knowledge of philosophy or through faith, which through ignorance abolishes this knowledge', he creates such a close link between faith and ignorance that the latter becomes a precondition for salvation.[105]

Palamas's response to Barlaam's model of monastic life is distinguished through its ruthlessness but it can hardly be called coherent: it is evident that he was less interested in presenting his own views on the role of reason than in effective polemic against his opponent.[106] Here is not the place for an in-depth analysis of Palamas's treatises, which pose great problems to the interpreter not only because of their length but also because of their nature: according to the rules of ancient rhetoric Palamas often seems to concede positions but he only does so in order to anticipate all possible objections.[107] Nevertheless, it seems safe to say that Palamas did not greatly advance the hesychastic argument in the debate with scholarly monks. Nor does his importance lie in

---

102 E.g. Palamas, *Défense*, I, 15.22–30 (triade 1.1.4). Cf. Maximos, *On love*, in *PG* 90, 985A; Elias Ekdikos, *Gnostic sentences*, in *PG* 90, 1158B. Palamas refutes an argument by Barlaam (based on Maximos, *On love* II.6) in the context of prayer where the question of graded ascent looms large: Palamas, *Défense*, I, 355.9–27 (triade II.2.16). Significantly, Palamas calls Maximos illuminated 'at the level of knowledge' and 'at the level beyond knowledge': Palamas, *Défense*, I, 201.3–5 (triade 1.3.41).

103 Ibid., I, 59.3–16 (triade 1.1.20). Cf. Maximos, *Ambigua*, in *PG* 91, 1113D–1116A. This distinction is not recognised by Sinkewicz, 'Gregory Palamas', 167.

104 Palamas, *Défense*, I, 131.8–14 (triade 1.3.10) and *passim*.

105 Ibid., II, 477.6–8 (triade II.3.43).

106 Meyendorff, *Introduction à l'étude*, 173–94, where his systematising presentation gives a misleading impression of the text.

107 E.g. Palamas, *Défense*, I, 311.23–313.1 (triade II.1.42). Lack of attention to this strategy can lead to serious misrepresentation.

the propagation of hesychasm as a monastic lifestyle: here Gregory of Sinai clearly played a much greater role.[108] Palamas's main achievement was to give the hesychastic vision a theological foundation and to have this foundation imposed on the Orthodox Church at large.

We have seen that Barlaam denied the central tenet of the hesychasts, namely that through visions it was possible for human beings to experience the divine. Accordingly he explained visions first as demonic illusions and later as figments of imagination.[109] When attempts to disabuse the hesychasts of their errors met with no success he accused them of reviving the late antique heresy of the Messalians, who had claimed that they could perceive God's being with their senses.[110] Such accusations posed a great danger to the practitioners of the hesychastic method because a similar position was attributed to the outlawed dualist sect of the Bogomils.[111] To counter Barlaam's attacks Palamas developed a conceptual framework that to his mind reconciled the hesychastic experience with traditional concepts of divine transcendence: he introduced a distinction between God's essence, which is beyond the reach of created being, and God's glory or operations, which are equally divine but which can be participated in.[112] In a second and final revision of his anti-hesychastic writings Barlaam not only denied the existence of such a distinction but also claimed that even the concept of a vision of divine glory was heretical.[113] His argument was based on a precedent: the heresy trial of the twelfth-century cleric Theodore of Blakhernai. Like Palamas, Theodore had proposed a distinction between God's being and his glory to justify mystical experiences but he had nevertheless been branded as a heretic.[114] However, this ingenious ploy failed to convince Barlaam's contemporaries, and in 1341 he found himself excommunicated first by a convention of Athonite monks and then by the patriarchal synod, which ordered his writings to be destroyed.[115] Barlaam's defeat did not translate into an immediate victory for Palamas. The distinction between essence and operations remained highly controversial and Palamas

---

108 Rigo, 'Gregorio il Sinaita', 83–4.
109 Palamas, *Défense*, I, 231.15–16 (triade II.1.3); I, 335.6–8 (triade II.2.9).
110 Cf. Schirò, *Barlaam Calabro*, 324.131.
111 A. Rigo, *Monaci esicasti e monaci bogomili. Le accuse di messalianismo e bogomilismo rivolte agli esicasti ed il problema dei rapporti tra esicasmo e bogomilismo* [Orientalia venetiana 2] (Florence: Leo S. Olschki Editore, 1989).
112 See Sinkewicz, 'Gregory Palamas', 161–4.
113 Palamas, *Défense*, II, 645–51 (triade III.2.3–4).
114 Ibid., II, 569.28–571.5 (triade III.1.7) makes clear that Theodore introduced this distinction during his trial expressly to ward off accusations of Messalianism. Cf. Gouillard, 'Quatre procès', 22–3.
115 Cf. *Reg.* no. 2211.

faced attacks from Gregory Akindynos, who had before remained neutral and had even disapproved of Barlaam's attacks on the hesychasts, and later also from the Constantinopolitan intellectual Nikephoros Gregoras.[116] However, Palamas and his followers overcame this opposition, too, and in the end achieved universal recognition for their doctrine.

Why were Palamas and his associates so successful? From contemporary accounts of their activities it is clear that they formed a close-knit group with a common agenda.[117] Moreover, several of them were former aristocrats with connections to the Constantinopolitan elite.[118] However, the different fate of Theodore of Blakhernai suggests a more fundamental change in the role of monks within Byzantine church and society. During the eleventh and twelfth centuries the deacons of St Sophia had staffed most major bishoprics and had monopolised the theological discourse whereas the monks were tightly controlled and largely marginalised.[119] However, this system did not survive the collapse of the empire in 1204 and from the later thirteenth century onwards we find monks not only in prominent positions in the church hierarchy but also at the forefront in the fight against a union with the Latins.[120] This helps to explain how the monks of Mount Athos could take the unprecedented step of issuing a doctrinal statement and of excommunicating adversaries even before the Constantinopolitan synod had taken up these matters, and how during the next decade they succeeded in prevailing over all opposition by clerics and laymen. Significantly, Gregory Palamas became archbishop of Thessalonike and his two allies Isidore Boukheiras and Philotheos Kokkinos (as well as Kallistos, a disciple of Gregory of Sinai) became patriarchs of Constantinople.

The success of the hesychastic method in the late Byzantine period is truly astonishing. Its proponents were able to subvert, appropriate or suppress well-established alternative models of spiritual life and to present themselves as the only true representatives of orthodox monasticism. However, this success resulted in a narrowing of the rich Byzantine spiritual tradition: Palamas's victory over Barlaam was ultimately also a rejection of Maximos the

---

116 See Hero, *Letters of Akindynos*, x–xxxiii, and H.-V. Beyer, 'Nikephoros Gregoras als Theologe und sein erstes Auftreten gegen die Hesychasten', *Jahrbuch der österreichischen Byzantinistik* 20 (1971), 171–88.

117 Cf. Meyendorff, *Introduction à l'étude*, 65–153.

118 Apart from Palamas one can mention Ioseph Kalothetos and David Disypatos. See Tsames, Καλοθέτου συγγράμματα, 21–34, and M. Candal, 'Origen ideológico del palamismo en un documento de David Disipato', *OCP* 15 (1949), 85–125.

119 P. Magdalino, *The empire of Manuel Komnenos, 1143–1180* (Cambridge: Cambridge University Press, 1993), 318–19.

120 D. M. Nicol, *Church and society in the last centuries of Byzantium, 1261–1453* (Cambridge: Cambridge University Press, 1979).

Confessor and his concept of a graded ascent in which deification is preceded by the recovery of man's lost rationality. With the disparagement of reason and its exclusion from Christian life eastern monasticism assumed a distinctly fundamentalist character. Like modern fundamentalisms this development may well be explained through the political instability of the late Byzantine period: at a time when their society and culture was attacked from all sides the Byzantines turned inward and strove to preserve the 'pure' inner core.

5

Art and liturgy in the later
Byzantine Empire

NANCY P. ŠEVČENKO

It is generally assumed that by the eleventh century the text of the Byzantine liturgy was well established and was performed in a consistent manner
throughout much of the Greek-speaking world. For the Eucharist, this assumption is essentially true, though some evolution was still to take place with the
widespread adoption of the Eucharistic liturgy of John Chrysostom in preference to that of St Basil and with the expansion of the *prothesis* rite, that is,
the prefatory rite before the beginning of the Eucharist. For the feasts of the
church year, however, this is less true, as new poetic pieces were still being
composed for, and saints being added to, the basic calendar of commemorations even after the end of the empire. Of most importance for the history of
the liturgy in this period was the merging of the liturgy of the Great Church
of Constantinople with Palestinian monastic rites: a process which started in
the ninth century and was only completed in the twelfth. The pomp and circumstance of the former was enriched by the poetic hymnody of the latter.
However, even as late as the fifteenth century, the church of Thessalonike
continued to preserve elements of the *Asmatike akolouthia*, as the liturgy of
the Great Church was known. Its elaborate ceremonies had some influence
on the art of the Balkans in the fourteenth century.[1]

Defining the relation of middle and late Byzantine art to this liturgy is
a challenge, in that so much of Byzantine art surviving from this period is

1 For a succinct survey of the developments, see R. F. Taft, *The Byzantine rite: a short history* (Collegeville, MN: Liturgical Press, 1992) and his articles collected in his *Liturgy in
Byzantium and beyond* (Aldershot: Variorum, 1995). See also T. Pott, *La réforme liturgique
byzantine: étude du phénomène de l'évolution non-spontanée de la liturgie byzantine* (Rome:
CLV – Edizioni liturgiche, 2000); S. Janeras, *Le Vendredi-saint dans la tradition liturgique
byzantine: structure et histoire de ses offices* [Analecta liturgica 13; Studia Anselmiana 99]
(Rome: Pontificio Ateneo S. Anselmo, 1988); H.-J. Schulz, *The Byzantine liturgy: symbolic
structure and faith expression* (New York: Pueblo Publishing, 1986); G. Bertonière, *The
historical development of the Easter Vigil and related services in the Greek church* [OCA 193]
(Rome: Pontificium institutum orientalium studiorum, 1972); A. Schmemann, *Introduction to liturgical theology* (London: Faith Press, and Bangor, Maine: American Orthodox
Press, 1966).

dominated and even fundamentally determined by church practices in their wider form. The liturgy affects the art on many levels: the very choice of subjects to be represented; their placement; the details of iconography within a composition; the overall conception of the scene, and the style in which it is presented. Prior scholarship has taken various approaches to this vast body of material. Stefanescu's fundamental work, *L'illustration des liturgies*, focuses on the Eucharist, seeing the themes present in a church setting as being all of them on some level illustrations of the Eucharist.[2] Walter's book, *Art and ritual*, is particularly concerned with the representation of various liturgical ceremonies in Byzantine art.[3] The study of Pallas, *Die Passion und Bestattung*, deals in part with the impact in the twelfth century of the 'new' monastic services and reveals that the relationship of art and liturgy was by no means static but can be said to have its own history.[4] The theme of art and liturgy is addressed in numerous individual studies by André Grabar and Gordana Babić.[5]

This chapter will proceed by dividing the Byzantine rite into two main components: the Eucharistic rite and those rites connected with the cycle of the church year. It will then turn to the primarily monastic Divine Office, that is, the Hours of the day, and to the hymnography that accompanies them. The first two components, those of the Eucharist and the calendar, roughly correspond to the spatial division of a Byzantine church of this period into the *naos*, or nave, which is the space of the laity (including monks), and the sanctuary, the space reserved for the ordained clergy. They also correspond to two conceptions of time: the Eucharist aiming to transcend time, while for the church calendar time is its fundamental organising principle.[6] In all

---

2 J. D. Stefanescu, *L'illustration des liturgies dans l'art de Byzance et de l'Orient* (Brussels: Institut de philologie et d'histoire orientales, 1936). See also Schulz, *Byzantine liturgy*, esp. 79–80.

3 C. Walter, *Art and ritual of the Byzantine church* (London: Variorum, 1982). See also N. K. Moran, *Singers in late Byzantine and Slavonic painting* [Byzantina Neerlandica 9] (Leiden: Brill, 1986) for images of ceremonies involving singers.

4 D. I. Pallas, *Die Passion und Bestattung Christi in Byzanz: der Ritus – das Bild* [Miscellanea Byzantina Monacensia 2] (Munich: Institut für byzantinistik und neugriechische Philologie der Universität München, 1965).

5 See A. Grabar, 'Une source d'inspiration de l'iconographie byzantine tardive: les cérémonies du culte de la Vierge', *CA* 25 (1976), 143–62; Grabar, 'Les peintures dans le chœur de Sainte-Sophie d'Ochrid', *CA* 15 (1965), 257–65; G. Babić, *Les chapelles annexes des églises byzantines: Fonction liturgique et programmes iconographiques* [Bibliothèque des cahiers archéologiques 3] (Paris: Klincksieck, 1969); Babić, 'Les discussions christologiques et le décor des églises byzantines au XII siècle', *Frühmittelalterliche Studien* 2 (1968), 368–86. See also *Vostochnochristjanskij chram: liturgija i iskusstvo*, ed. A. M. Lidov (St Petersburg: Dmitrii Bulanin, 1994).

6 Schmemann, *Liturgical theology*, 20, uses for the latter the phrase 'liturgy of time'. Cf. ibid., 38, n. 6, and 139–40.

sections, the analysis will deal first with illustrations of the relevant liturgical manuscripts, although it will soon become clear that Byzantine liturgical art is in no way a text-based art.

The Eucharist

Text and image in manuscripts of the Eucharistic liturgies

The 'ordinary', the fixed or invariable part of the liturgy, is found in the *eucholo-gion*, which survives in manuscripts from the eighth century onwards. These generally include the text of the Eucharistic liturgies of St John Chrysostom and of St Basil the Great, as well as various other services and texts for the use of a priest.[7] Though full *euchologion* manuscripts were never illustrated, certain prayers from the *euchologion* were accompanied by miniatures as early as the eleventh century: these were the so-called 'secret' prayers, the prayers spoken almost inaudibly by the officiating priest or bishop, assembled and copied in the order of the service onto parchment rolls. These 'liturgical' rolls (εἰλητάρια) contain the prayers of the three Byzantine liturgies, those of Chrysostom, Basil and the pre-sanctified; they may also include the words of the deacon, and the order of service for clerical ordinations. Where the liturgical rolls have any form of illustration, decoration is generally restricted to a headpiece at the beginning of the roll and figured initials.[8] The headpieces depict the author of the liturgy; the initials may relate loosely to the meaning or language of the prayer, although they are very often secular in character. A roll from Patmos (dating probably to the twelfth century) contains the liturgy of Basil the Great, who is shown celebrating at an altar under an extraordinary collection of domes and marble revetments familiar from contemporary Comnenian church architecture and miniatures. Basil is holding a roll, presumably one with the very prayers he wrote that follow in the parchment roll itself.[9]

Only rarely is the illustration of much intellectual sophistication, but that of a liturgical roll in Jerusalem (Greek Patriarchate, Stavrou 109), a product of Constantinople of the later eleventh century, is a remarkable attempt at

7 S. Parenti, *L'eucologio Barberini gr. 336* [Biblioteca ephemerides liturgicae 80] (Rome: CLV – Edizioni liturgiche, 1995).
8 B. V. Farmakovskij, 'Vizantijskij pergamennyi rukopisnyi svitok s miniaturami', *Izvestija Russkogo Arkhaeologicheskogo Instituta v Konstantinopole* 6 (1900), 253–359; V. Kepetzis, 'Les rouleaux liturgiques illustrés, 11e–14e siècles', unpublished thesis, Université de Paris IV (1979); S. E. J. Gerstel, 'Liturgical scrolls in the Byzantine sanctuary', *Greek, Roman and Byzantine Studies* 35 (1994), 195–204.
9 Patmos, Monastery of St John, Ms. gr. 707. See A. Kominis, *Patmos: the treasures of the monastery* (Athens: Ekdotike Athenon, 1988), 289–91; figs. 25–34.

interpreting visually the theology embedded in each of the various prayers. Marginal figures and initials at the beginning of each prayer mean that Gospel feasts are being attached to specific Eucharist prayers. Some of the themes, such as an incipient Heavenly Liturgy for the *Proskomide* prayer, were to be developed in monumental painting only considerably later, in the Palaiologan period.[10]

Eucharistic themes on objects used in or associated with the celebration of the Eucharist

The Eucharistic rite was reflected particularly closely in liturgical implements, though in the middle and late Byzantine periods these were generally fashioned from less precious materials than they had been in the early Christian period.[11] Patens may be inscribed with Christ's words at the Last Supper ('Take, eat, this is my body . . .'), the words spoken by the priest at the consecration of the host. A form of paten known as the *panagiarion*, used for transporting to the sanctuary the bread dedicated to the Virgin in the *prothesis*, receives an ever-expanding multi-figured decoration in the late Byzantine period: a fourteenth-century steatite example in the Xeropotamou monastery on Mount Athos bears representations both of the Heavenly Liturgy and of the Communion of the Apostles, themes by now common in sanctuary decoration.[12] The *aer*, a cloth to cover the chalice or the paten, was already being decorated with this communion scene in the twelfth century.[13] Bread stamps for the consecrated loaves exhibit a range of themes directly related to their liturgical purpose.[14] Large metal processional crosses often bore an image of the *Deesis* (Christ flanked by the Virgin and John the Baptist who petition Him), or of the Crucifixion, which was an appropriate choice.[15] By the early fourteenth century the Great *Aer*, a cloth to cover both chalice and paten, had become the

10 P. Vokotopoulos, *Byzantine illuminated manuscripts of the Patriarchate of Jerusalem* (Athens and Jerusalem: Greek Orthodox Patriarchate of Jerusalem, 2002), no. 19, figs. 43–58; A. Grabar, 'Un rouleau constantinopolitain et ses peintures', *DOP* 8 (1954), 163–99; Schulz, *Byzantine liturgy*, 80–9.

11 S. A. Boyd, 'Art in the service of the Liturgy: Byzantine silver plate', in *Heaven on earth: art and the church in Byzantium*, ed. L. Safran (University Park: Pennsylvania State University Press, 1998), 152–85, esp. 180–3; A. Ballian, 'Liturgical implements', in *Byzantium: faith and power (1261–1557)*, ed. H. C. Evans (New York, New Haven and London: Yale University Press (for the Metropolitan Museum of Art), 2004), 117–24.

12 I. Kalavrezou-Maxeiner, *Byzantine icons in steatite* [Byzantina vindobonensia 15] (Vienna: Verlag ÖAW, 1985), no. 131.

13 W. Woodfin, 'Liturgical textiles', in *Faith and power*, 295–8, and figs. 10.2 and 10.3.

14 G. Galavaris, *Bread and the liturgy: the symbolism of early Christian and Byzantine bread stamps* (Madison and London: University of Wisconsin Press, 1970).

15 J. A. Cotsonis, *Byzantine figural processional crosses* [Dumbarton Oaks Collection Publications 10] (Washington, DC: Dumbarton Oaks Research Library and Collection, 1994).

inspiration behind the *epitaphios* (fig. 5.1), a far larger textile which, following ancient interpretations of the Great Entrance as the procession bringing Christ to his tomb, was embroidered with the image of the dead Christ stretched out on a slab on his way to burial. Perhaps because of its decoration, the *epitaphios* was introduced, surely by the mid-fourteenth century, into a quite different liturgical context, that of the Good Friday and Holy Saturday ceremonies. By the fifteenth century, however, its Eucharistic meaning was receding and the stark image of the sacrificed Christ attended by angels was often replaced by a multi-figured depiction of the Lamentation.[16]

The various clerical vestments worn during the liturgy grew increasingly elaborate in the late Byzantine period, enveloping the celebrant in garments embroidered with Gospel scenes, with holy portraits, and even with the words of the liturgy itself. So the *orarion* of a deacon may display the words Glory Glory Glory, from the *Epinikios* Hymn, while the words of the creed adorn the minor *sakkos* of the metropolitan of Russia, Photios (1408–31).[17] Narrowly liturgical subjects, however, are relatively rare on vestments. In any case, a liturgical interpretation of their Gospel iconography presupposes a particular historicising approach to the interpretation of the liturgy, one that views the Eucharist as a re-enactment of the entire life of Christ. It was familar above all from the eleventh-century commentary of Nicholas of Andida and underlay the illustration of the Jerusalem roll mentioned above.[18]

Icons are often thought to have constituted an integral part of the celebration of the liturgy. The words of the Eucharistic liturgies make no reference to icons, which is not at all surprising, given the early date of their composition. Icons were never to serve as liturgical implements. Still, their very existence connects them to the Eucharist in that they confirm, as does the image of the Virgin in the apse, the message of the Incarnation and the possibility of the sanctification of the material into the divine that is at the heart of the Eucharist. Icons are mentioned in rubrics to the liturgies from the fourteenth century on, though

---

16 Woodfin, 'Liturgical textiles', 296–7; H. Belting, 'An image and its function in the liturgy: the Man of Sorrows in Byzantium', *DOP* 34–35 (1980–81), 1–16; S. Ćurčić, 'Late Byzantine *loca sancta*? Some questions regarding the form and function of *Epitaphioi*', in *The twilight of Byzantium: aspects of cultural and religious history in the late Byzantine Empire*, ed. S. Ćurčić and D. Mouriki (Princeton: Princeton University Press, 1991), 251–61; Robert F. Taft, *The Great Entrance: a history of the transfer of gifts and other preanaphoral rites of the liturgy of St. John Chrysostom* [OCA 200] (Rome: Pontificium institutum orientalium studiorum, 1978), 217–19.

17 Woodfin, 'Liturgical textiles'; P. Johnstone, *The Byzantine tradition in church embroidery* (Chicago: Argonaut, 1967).

18 R. Bornert, *Les commentaires byzantins de la Divine Liturgie du VIIe au XVe siècle* [Archives de l'orient chrétien 9] (Paris: Institut français d'études byzantines, 1966), esp. 180–206.

Figure 5.1 Epitaphios textile. Christ on a slab with angels with fans. Victoria and Albert Museum, London.

in connection with various preliminary rites taking place in the *naos*, not with the Eucharist itself.

By this time, icons had already taken their place in the *templon* or *iconostasis*, the barrier separating the *naos* from the apse and *bema* (i.e. sanctuary), and they faced the congregation directly. Earlier, in the eleventh century, the usual *templon* screen was closed at floor level by chancel slabs, but was still open above, with widely spaced columns supporting an epistyle. Originally curtains closed the spaces between the columns, to be replaced in the course of the twelfth century by large icon panels, so as to form an icon wall that blocked any view from the nave into the sanctuary.[19] These *iconostasis* icons were of Christ, and the Virgin, and, frequently, the person or event to whom or to which the church was dedicated. The epistyle either was painted or carried a row of icons above it. On these epistyle icons the three figures of the *Deesis* might be joined by angels and apostles in what is known as the 'Great *Deesis*', or flanked by a row of feast icons depicting the primary events in the life of Christ and of his mother from the Annunciation to the Dormition (*Koimesis*) of the Virgin, repeating, on a smaller scale, and in a more concentrated form, feast images found elsewhere in the church. The functional difference between these *iconostasis* images and those of the main feast cycle is still not entirely clear. Entrance from the nave into the sanctuary was made through doors in the centre of the *iconostasis*, doors which often bore an image of the Annunciation (the closed door of Ezekiel 46:1–2 being interpreted as a reference to the Virgin and the mystery of the Incarnation).

It has been proposed that certain of the large two-sided icons that have survived shorn of their original context came originally from *iconostaseis*, and bore a two-sided message, one addressed to the congregation, the other (on the side facing the sanctuary) to the clergy.[20] The themes painted on the sanctuary side of these icons may have been consciously integrated into the overall painted programme of that space, something that is not true of their *naos* side, which, as noted above, tends to repeat elements present in the *naos* programme. The large images of Christ and the Virgin facing the nave from

19 See most recently S. E. J. Gerstel, *Beholding the sacred mysteries: programs of the Byzantine sanctuary* [Monographs on the Fine Arts 56] (Seattle and London: University of Washington Press, 1999), 5–14 (although Patmos roll #719, cited ibid., 9 and dated by Dmitrievskij to the thirteenth century, is actually of the sixteenth or seventeenth century), and J.-M. Spieser, 'Le développement du templon et les images des Douze Fêtes', *Bulletin de l'Institut Historique Belge de Rome* 69 (1999), 131–64.

20 S. E. J. Gerstel, 'An alternate view of the late Byzantine sanctuary screen', in *Thresholds of the sacred: architectural, art historical, liturgical and theological perspectives on religious screens, east and west*, ed. S. E. J. Gerstel (Washington, DC: Dumbarton Oaks Center for Byzantine Studies, 2006).

their place on the *iconostasis* had a significant role to play in lay piety, if not in the actual liturgy.

Eucharistic subjects are rare on *iconostasis* icons, indeed on icons of any kind.[21] Sacrificial motifs, however, do make their way into later Byzantine iconography, for example, the Virgin and Child with instruments of the Passion and the Man of Sorrows (*Akra Tapeinosis*), as do a number of typological themes, which will be discussed below.[22]

Decoration of the sanctuary space

By the turn of the eleventh century the decoration of the sanctuary area – the lower walls of the apse and the *bema* – was being almost exclusively devoted to Eucharistic themes.[23] This development is unquestionably attached to the ritual that takes place in that space and is not unrelated to the closing of the *iconostasis*. On the walls of the apse were standing figures of bishops, among them the authors of the two main liturgies, John Chrysostom and Basil the Great, placed nearest to the centre. The bishops hold Gospel books, and wear the *omophorion*, the *insignium* that they acquired upon their ordination to episcopal rank.

Above the bishops was painted the Communion of the Apostles, with Christ offering from a painted altar bread and wine to the twelve apostles who approach him from left and right (fig. 5.2). This theme replaced the 'historical' Last Supper; the words of institution spoken by Christ at that time and reiterated by the celebrant ('Take, eat, this is my body . . .') are frequently inscribed onto the background of the scene. The composition, which was popular from the eleventh century on, depicted with some care the details of a contemporary Eucharist, complete with vessels, ciborium and proper liturgical gestures. Angel deacons stand by the altar holding *rhipidia* (liturgical fans).[24] The figure of Christ (or figures, as he is often represented twice, once offering the bread, once offering the wine) is shown wearing the *sakkos*, the vestment of the patriarch of Constantinople, first in the fourteenth century.

While the Communion of the Apostles composition remained remarkably stable, in the twelfth century the line of bishops took on a new aspect, depicted

21 One exception to prove the rule is an icon depicting the Communion of the Apostles: Χαριστήριον εἰς Ἀναστάσιον Κ. Ὀρλάνδον (Athens: Bibliotheke tes en Athenais Archaiologikes Hetaireias, 1967), III, 395.

22 J. Albani, 'Icons and the Divine Liturgy. A reciprocal relationship', in *Ceremony and faith: Byzantine art and the Divine Liturgy* (Athens: Hellenic Ministry of Culture – Directorate of Byzantine and Post-Byzantine Monuments, 1999), 57–62.

23 Gerstel, *Sacred mysteries*, 5–67.

24 Ibid., 48–67.

Figure 5.2 The Communion of the Apostles, and officiating bishops carrying liturgical scrolls. Staro Nagoričino, south half of the apse.

now not as standing frontal figures but as celebrants who bend towards the altar and hold out scrolls inscribed with the opening words of the 'secret' prayers, chosen from among the very texts assembled in the parchment 'liturgical' rolls described above.[25] Their number was constantly being increased over the centuries: celebrants line the *bema* walls as well as the apse, and above them, rows of busts in medallions were added, as though all the bishops in the history of the church were imagined as present, concelebrating in a single sanctuary.

The bishops move towards a painted altar at the centre of the apse wall, or towards an image there of Christ's sacrifice that took a variety of forms: one such was the *Hetoimasia* or prepared throne, on or near which rest the instruments of the Passion (crown of thorns, lance, sponge) flanked by angels clad as deacons; another was the startling image of the Christ child lying on a paten or altar, covered with an *aer* as though He were the bread about to be divided.[26] The first dated example of this graphic image is at the church of Kurbinovo of 1199.[27] The image there is labelled the *Amnos* (lamb); from the thirteenth century on, it was also called the *Melismos* (meaning partitioning or fraction).[28] With the growth of the *prothesis* rite and with the consecration of the host now thought to take place in the *prothesis* before the Great Entrance procession, rather than in the sanctuary, the image of the child Christ on the paten in the apse or in the *prothesis* gave way to that of the dead adult Christ stretched out on a tomb slab that evokes his tomb, an image, which, as we have seen, was to migrate to the *epitaphios*.[29]

The strongly Eucharistic thrust of the apse programme meant that other images spatially associated with it acquired Eucharistic overtones. The *Mandylion*, for example, the cloth relic bearing the imprint of Christ's face, became a sign of the Incarnation and as such was often found in connection with the Annunciation. It assumed Eucharistic significance, however, when placed in the apse in place of the *Amnos*.[30]

25 Ibid., 15–36.
26 E.g. the *Hetoimasia* (with dove as well) at Nerezi: I. Sinkević, *The church of St. Panteleimon at Nerezi: architecture, programme, patronage* (Wiesbaden: Reichert Verlag, 2000), 35–6; Gerstel, *Sacred mysteries*, 37–47; A. L. Townsley, 'Eucharistic doctrine and the liturgy in late Byzantine painting', *Oriens Christianus*, ser. iv. 22 (1974), 138–53.
27 L. Hadermann-Misguich, *Kurbinovo: les fresques de Saint-Georges et la peinture byzantine du XIIe siècle* [Bibliothèque de Byzantion 6] (Brussels: Éditions de Byzantion, 1975), 67–78.
28 R. F. Taft, 'Melismos and comminution: the fraction and its symbolism in the Byzantine tradition', *Studia Anselmiana* 95 (1988), 531–52.
29 Pott, *Réforme*, 169–94; Schulz, *Byzantine liturgy*, 64–7.
30 Gerstel, *Sacred mysteries*, 68–77.

The Heavenly Liturgy and other Eucharist images

In the late Byzantine period a dramatic form of Eucharist image was developed, that of the Heavenly Liturgy, the liturgy performed in perpetuity before the throne of God by the most exalted residents of heaven, the angels.[31] Hints of this had appeared earlier, in the Jerusalem roll.[32] In fresco painting, for example in the church of the Peribleptos at Mistra, these angels assume the roles and robes of deacons and priests, and are shown bearing in procession the liturgical implements such as chalice, paten, *asterikos* and *aer* from the *prothesis* to the sanctuary, in a vivid re-creation of the Great Entrance. The procession was depicted circling Christ in the dome, or in the *prothesis*, whence the angels emerge to make the Great Entrance, or even in the apse itself.

Other images are more purely typological in character. Often located in the vicinity of the *bema* or apse are certain Old Testament prefigurations of sacrifice: the Sacrifice of Isaac, Abraham offering food to the visiting Trinity, Elijah fed by the raven or the Three Hebrews in the Fiery Furnace; many of these have origins far back in monumental painting of the early Christian period. Eucharistic imagery drawn from hagiography included that of the desert hermit Mary of Egypt receiving communion from Zosimas,[33] and the Vision of Peter of Alexandria, which started as anti-Arian theology and became a liturgical statement once the figure of Christ was made to stand atop an altar.[34]

Cycle of the church year

Text and image in the Gospel lectionary and praxapostolos

Gospel readings proper to each day of the year were excerpted from the Bible and rearranged according to the demands of the church calendar in a manuscript called the Gospel lectionary. The usual lectionary starts with readings for the movable feasts, those dependent upon the date of Easter, from Easter Sunday to the end of Holy Week the following year. The readings for Lent are drawn roughly from each of the four Evangelists in turn (John, Matthew, Luke and, for Lent, Mark). Following these Gospel readings for the movable feasts comes a long calendar of fixed feasts, those celebrated on the same date every year, with reference to their assigned readings. Most of the fixed feasts commemorate saints, but also include important events in the

31 It was also known as the Divine Liturgy or the Celestial Liturgy.
32 V. Kepetzis, 'Tradition iconographique et création dans une scène de communion', *Jahrbuch der Österreichischen Byzantinistik* 32/5 (1982), 443–51.
33 Gerstel, *Sacred mysteries*, 57.
34 Walter, *Art and ritual*, 213–14.

Gospel story such as the Birth and the Presentation of the Virgin, the Nativity, the Baptism, the Presentation of Christ, the Annunciation, the Transfiguration, and eventually the Dormition of the Virgin. These are not arranged in the order in which they took place in historical time but in the order in which they are celebrated in the course of a single church year. This calendar section of a Gospel lectionary (entitled in some manuscripts a *menologion*, in some a *synaxarion*) starts with 1 September and ends with 31 August. The Gospel passage that is to be read on that day may be written out in full, or there is merely a cross-reference if it has already been written out in full earlier in the manuscript. There is a great range of types of illustration of the Gospel lectionary, from full-page feast images in one manuscript to little more than a couple of figured initials in another. One Gospel lectionary (Vaticanus graecus 1156) undertook to represent each saint and event celebrated, within the text and in the margins of the relevant notice; in others the illustration was limited to Evangelist portraits, some miniatures of the major feasts and portraits only of the more notable saints.[35]

The Gospel lectionary removed the events in the life of Christ from their historical sequence and arranged them into a sequence based on the church calendar instead. This liturgical reordering retroactively influenced the illustration of certain Gospel books, which have a miniature of an event in the life of Christ preceding each Gospel, but the subject chosen reflects the feast at which the Gospel passage was read.[36]

The two other books of scripture readings were the *praxapostolos* (readings from the Acts and Epistles) and the *prophetologion* (Old Testament readings). The latter was never illustrated; the former was illustrated primarily with portraits of the authors of this section of the New Testament.

Kurt Weitzmann argued that the illustrated Gospel lectionary was the source for the images of the Gospel feasts encountered on the walls of Byzantine churches of this period.[37] If one assumes that every image had

35 *Oriente cristiano e santità* (Milan: Centro Tibaldi; Rome: Ministero per i beni culturali e ambientali, 1998), no. 18. The miniatures go as far as December 31. On illustrated gospel lectionaries, see J. C. Anderson, *The New York Cruciform Lectionary* (University Park: University of Pennsylvania Press, 1992); M.-L. Dolezal, 'Illuminating the liturgical word: text and image in a decorated lectionary (Mount Athos, Dionysiou Monastery, cod. 587)', *Word & Image* 12 (1996), 23–60. On liturgical manuscripts in general, see N. P. Ševčenko, 'Illuminating the Liturgy: illustrated service books in Byzantium', in *Heaven on earth*, 186–228.

36 C. Meredith, 'The illustrations of Codex Ebnerianus. A study in liturgical illustration of the Comnenian period', *Journal of the Warburg and Courtauld Institutes* 29 (1966), 419–24.

37 Many of his studies on the subject have been reprinted in K. Weitzmann, *Byzantine liturgical psalters and gospels* (London: Variorum, 1980).

its origins in a book, that it was created specifically to accompany a written text from which it migrated into other media, then the Gospel lectionary is certainly the most likely source. Unfortunately, there are not nearly as many Gospel lectionaries adorned with feast scenes as one would like for this theory to be convincing (the decoration of the great majority of the illustrated lectionaries is restricted to portraits of the Four Evangelists). Furthermore, given the independent nature of Byzantine iconography, which is rarely a literal illustration of any single text, it is more likely that things worked the other way around and that the iconography of the feast cycle was developed first in monumental painting or on icons, and only then made its way into illustrated manuscripts and other media.

Text and image in homiletic and hagiographic collections

The concept of the church calendar is intrinsic to many other kinds of liturgical books.[38] Collections of homilies to be delivered on certain feast days were, from the eleventh century on, being arranged in manuscripts according to the date of the feast at which they were to be read.[39] This is true primarily for manuscripts of the Homilies of Gregory of Nazianzos (fig. 5.3), which, as would any Gospel lectionary, open with an Easter reading; in this case, with one of Gregory's homilies on Easter. While their illustrations, usually restricted to headpieces and initials, do tend to reflect the content of the homily, they also make reference to the feast at which the homily is read.[40] Though also read in services throughout the church year and often illustrated, the homilies of John Chrysostom were not organised according to the church calendar as were those of Gregory.[41] Homilies by other authors, such as George of Nikomedeia, which were read out at specific feasts, had a tremendous influence on the depiction of that feast, either directly or through hymnography based on these homilies.[42]

---

38 Walter, *Art and ritual*, 67–72.
39 A. Ehrhard, *Überlieferung und Bestand der hagiographischen und homiletischen Literatur der griechischen Kirche von den Anfängen bis zum Ende des 16. Jahrhunderts* [Texte und Untersuchungen zur Geschichte der altchristlicher Literatur 50–52] (Leipzig: J. C. Hinrichs Verlag, 1937–52), 3 vols. in 4.
40 G. Galavaris, *The illustrations of the Homilies of Gregory of Nazianzenus* [Studies in Manuscript Illumination 6] (Princeton: Princeton University Press, 1969); Ševčenko, 'Illuminating the liturgy', 219–20.
41 K. Krause, *Die illustrierte Homilien des Johannes Chrysostomos in Byzanz* (Wiesbaden: Reichert Verlag, 2004). His homilies are commentaries on the various books of the Bible (esp. Matthew, John and Genesis), and are collected therefore according to the book, not the calendar year.
42 H. Maguire, *Art and eloquence in Byzantium* (Princeton: Princeton University Press, 1981), 91–108; M. Vassilaki and N. Tsironis, 'Representations of the Virgin and their association with the Passion of Christ', in *Mother of God: representations of the Virgin in Byzantine art*, ed. M. Vassilaki (Milan: Skira, 2000), 453–63.

Figure 5.3 Gregory of Nazianzos writing his homilies. Mount Sinai, Ms. Gr. 339, fol. 4v.

The concept of the revolving church calendar was intrinsic to hagiographic manuscripts, those devoted to recording the saint or event to be commemorated each day of the year. The *Menologion* of Emperor Basil II (Vaticanus graecus 1613), a manuscript of around the year 1000 (the text is actually that of a *synaxarion* in that the notices for each saint are very brief), is fully illustrated with 430 separate miniatures; it contains at least one commemoration per day for the first six months of the year, September through February. Holy portraits and scenes of martyrdom predominate, and there are Gospel feasts as well as commemorations of interest to Constantinople, such as translations of relics into the city, and natural disasters it suffered. Each image shares a page with a sixteen-line summary of the saint's exploits. In several cases, especially for the catastrophes such as earthquakes, the representation of the event is replaced by an image of its liturgical celebration.[43] Only the first volume of this enormous undertaking survives; it is unknown whether a second one was ever executed.

There exists one later equivalent to the Basil *Menologion*, a fourteenth-century manuscript in Oxford containing in a single volume images of the commemorations for every day of the year. It has no text at all other than a closing poem and verse captions to the miniatures. Its iconographic roots seem to lie in the calendar cycles in monumental painting rather than in any manuscript tradition traceable back to the *Menologion* of Basil II.[44]

Longer hagiographic texts were also being assembled in calendar order.[45] The *Lives* of the saints composed by Symeon Metaphrastes in the late tenth century were arranged in the eleventh in a series of ten volumes, starting with one for the saints of September in volume i, and ending with the saints from May to August in volume x. The *Lives* were intended for reading at monastic *orthros* (matins). Despite the rich narrative character of the saints' lives, extensive miniature cycles illustrating these works of Metaphrastes are

---

43 Facsimile: *Il Menologio di Basilio II. Cod. Vaticano greco 1613* [Codices e Vaticani selecti . . . 8], 2 vols. (Turin: Fratelli Bocca, 1907). The Vatican is due to issue a new facsimile shortly. J. Baldovin, 'A note on the liturgical processions in the Menologion of Basil II (ms. Vat. gr. 1613)', Εὐλόγημα: *studies in honor of Robert Taft, S.J.*, ed. E. Carr *et al.* (Rome: Centro Studi S. Anselmo, 1993), 25–39. The interesting representation of the rain of ashes caused by the eruption of Vesuvius shown on *Il Menologio*, 164 is an exception.

44 Oxford. Bodl. Gr.th.f.1: I. Hutter, *Corpus der byzantinischen Miniaturenhandschriften: Oxford, Bodleian Library*, 3 vols. (Stuttgart: Hiersemann, 1982), III, no. 1.

45 Ehrhard, *Überlieferung.*

Figure 5.4 Calendar icon for the month of May. Mount Sinai, monastery of St Catherine.

scarce.[46] The usual system was to place a portrait of the saint in, or in place of, a painted headpiece at the beginning of his or her *Life*. In one set of volumes dated 1063, images of all the saints whose *Lives* were contained in a particular volume were assembled together on one folio to serve as its frontispiece. This kind of group portrait had its exact counterpart in contemporary calendar icons (fig. 5.4) and was paralleled by the poems of Christopher of Mytilene and others writing mnemonic calendar verses in the eleventh century and later.[47]

The church year in church decoration

Representations of the events and saints that together make up the church year filled the *naos* of a Byzantine church. The astonishing coordination of architecture and decoration characteristic of the interior of a domed Byzantine church transformed these commemorations into a system in which each component had a particular place relative both to the image of Christ in the central dome or vault, and to each other.[48] Surrounding Christ are angels or prophets; the major New Testament events unfold, in the form of twelve – more or less – feast scenes arranged in the vaults or along upper walls, while at a lower level the walls, together with subsidiary areas such as corner chapels, are lined with images of the saints. The system was not codified until post-Byzantine times,[49] but the positions of the various elements relative to Christ and to each other in a church programme were repeated fairly consistently in most Byzantine churches, whether cathedral, parish or monastic.

What is interesting here is how little influence the church calendar exerted on the articulation of the programme. The saints, for example, are not arranged at all according to the dates of their commemorations, but according to their profession, whether apostle, warrior, monk, female saint, hermit or stylite,

46 N. P. Ševčenko, *Illustrated manuscripts of the Metaphrastian Menologion* (Chicago and London: University of Chicago Press, 1990). Only occasionally was the elaborate textual narrative accompanied by a comparable illuminated narrative: a *panegyrikon*: Athos Esphigmenou 14, has longer cycles, though the texts are still a selection of Metaphrastian lives, here combined with other types of text: S. M. Pelekanides *et al.*, *The treasures of Mount Athos: illuminated manuscripts*, 4 vols. (Athens: Ekdotike Athenon (for the Patriarchal Institute for Patristic Studies), 1974–91), II, figs. 327–408, esp. 327–36.

47 N. P. Ševčenko, 'Marking holy time: the Byzantine calendar icons', in *Byzantine icons: art, technique and technology*, ed. M. Vassilaki (Heraklion: University of Crete Press, 2002), 51–62; E. Follieri, *I calendari in metro innografico di Cristoforo Mitileneo* [Subsidia hagiographica 63] (Brussels: Société des Bollandistes, 1980), 2 vols. All the calendar icons from the Byzantine period that survive today are located in the monastery of Mount Sinai.

48 The classic study is O. Demus, *Byzantine mosaic decoration* (London: Kegan Paul, 1948; reprinted New Rochelle: Caratzas Brothers, 1976). See also J.-M. Spieser, 'Liturgie et programmes iconographiques', *TM* 11 (1991), 575–90.

49 The *'Painter's Manual' of Dionysius of Fourna*, trans. P. Hetherington (London: Sagittarius Press, 1974).

with the various groups relegated to specific areas of the church. As there was not enough space to represent all the saints in the history of the church, those depicted were the leaders, the best-known figures of each 'choir' or category of saint. In this respect, they approach Christ as courtiers would approach the emperor, in well-defined groups. This ordering of saints is in striking contrast to the calendar cycles usually placed somewhere outside the *naos*, especially in the narthex, that show, month by month, the church commemorations for the whole year, in the tradition of the *Menologion* of Basil II.[50] In the *naos*, the saints have been liberated from earthly time and from the rotation of calendar time.

Within the feast compositions, the situation is a little different. They rotate around the central figure of Christ as if in the cyclical revolution of the church year. However, the cycle of feasts in a Byzantine church does not follow the liturgical sequence of the calendar, but maintains elements of historical time. For the events are displayed in roughly the order of the life of Christ (starting with the Annunciation, located in the eastern part of the *naos*). The maintenance of some aspect of historical time made it easier to incorporate into later Byzantine church programmes cycles of the Passion of Christ or of the Life of the Virgin, with their very strict narrative sequence. The placement of the individual feasts will vary with the architecture of each church, but there is always a recognisable chronological sequence. The conceptions of time are in constant dialogue. The ceremony of the *Pedilavum*, or the washing of feet on Maundy Thursday, sometimes took place under an image of Christ washing the feet of the twelve apostles.[51] The correspondence here of Gospel event, image of the event and liturgical commemoration resonates richly with these layers of time.

Earthly time was pushed further and further away from the sanctuary, away even from the *naos*, into the narthex at the western end of the church. The themes of the decoration of the narthex were more fluid and stressed its role as preparatory space. It has been suggested that the main liturgical themes relate to the penitential and preparatory character of the Lenten weeks leading to Christmas and Holy Week.[52] In the middle Byzantine period the lives of

50 P. Mijović, *Menolog* (Belgrade: Arheoloshki Institut, 1973).
51 W. Tronzo, 'Mimesis in Byzantium. Notes toward a history of the function of the image', *Res* 25 (1994), 61–76.
52 B. Todić, 'L'influence de la liturgie sur la décoration peinte du narthex de Sopoćani', in *Drevnerusskoe iskusstvo. Rus', Balkani XIII vek*, ed. A. L. Batalov *et al.* (St Petersburg: Dmitrii Bulanin, 1997), 43–58. See also S. Tomeković, 'Contribution à l'étude du programme du narthex des églises monastiques (XIe–première moitié du XIIIe siècle)', *B* 58 (1988), 140–54.

individual saints began to be painted, sometimes in as many as ten or twelve different episodes, in the narthex or side chapel. These cycles are often found in conjunction with tombs, in which case their purpose seems to have been to recount the saint's deeds that earned him or her the ear of God, and made him or her an effective intercessor for the deceased. Yet the visiting faithful could also come to address the portrait of the saint at any time, outside the strict hierarchy of the church interior, and outside the constraints of the church calendar.

Other ecclesiastical rites

There were of course many other services that took place only at irregular intervals: clerical ordinations, baptisms, weddings and funerals, as well as consecrations of churches, the blessing of houses, the purification of wells, and even, for the patriarch at least, coronations. Each of these occasions had its own rite, though few have left any significant trace in art.[53] Images of these services are found for the most part embedded in painted hagiographic cycles or chronicles: the three ordinations, to deacon, priest and bishop, for example, are a regular part of the *Vita* cycles of St Nicholas.[54] Burial scenes, originally showing a saint being laid in a stone sarcophagus in the presence of a censing bishop, become more elaborate over time, and there are fine fourteenth-century depictions of funeral ceremonies, complete with singers, that illustrate the death of St Nicholas and others.[55] The deaths of hermits such as St Ephrem or St Sabas are set instead into an expansive landscape of mountainsides and caves from which other hermits are emerging to attend the open-air rites for their dead colleague.[56]

Memorial services (μνημόσυνα) were held on the anniversary of an individual's death. The emperor John Komnenos stipulated in his *Typikon* of 1136 for the monastery of the Pantokrator in Constantinople, that on the anniversaries of his death and those of his wife and son, the famous icon of the Virgin Hodegetria was to be carried from its sanctuary across town to the monastery and set up by his tomb, where it was to remain overnight. On the next day, 'the divine liturgy should be celebrated while the holy icon is present'.[57]

---

53 Walter, *Art and ritual*, *passim*.
54 N. P. Ševčenko, *The life of St. Nicholas in Byzantine art* (Turin: Bottega d'Erasmo, 1983), 76–85.
55 Ibid., 134–42; Moran, *Singers*, 72–85.
56 *Faith and power*, no. 80. This fifteenth-century icon shows a large icon of the Hodegetria present at the funeral of Ephrem.
57 Thomas and Hero, II, 756; Ševčenko, 'Icons in the liturgy', *DOP* 45 (1991), 52.

John's brother Isaac Komnenos was buried in Thrace at the monastery of the Virgin Kosmosoteira which he had founded in 1152; icons of the Virgin and of Christ were to be set up permanently alongside his tomb, and the monks of the monastery were to pass by the tomb daily, and 'in front of the holy icons standing there' say prayers for his soul.[58] The icons in these cases had no specific liturgical function, but they provided a focus for the intercessory prayers at the tomb, whether these were yearly or daily. This documentary evidence for the Comnenian period is intriguing, in that it implies a relation of icon to actual liturgical rite at an earlier time than we would suspect if relying on the visual or liturgical sources alone.

The architectural setting of tombs such as these, mainly *arcosolia* (wall niches) over the grave, bore painted and/or sculpted decoration, but the themes depicted are generally concerned with salvation, not with the funeral rite itself.[59]

The liturgy of the Hours

Text and image in manuscripts of the Divine Office

The greatest contribution of monasticism to the development of the Byzantine liturgy is its hymnody, which reached Constantinople in the early ninth century, with the Palestinian monastic *cursus*. The *horologion*, the Byzantine Book of Hours, is attested in manuscripts from the ninth century on; it provides texts for each of the main Hours of the day (prime, terce, sext, none), together with those for *orthros*, vespers and *apodeipnon* (compline). It is rarely illustrated: only two extant *horologia* have any sort of extended programme of illustration: one of the late twelfth century now on Lesbos, with an office for each hour of the day, and another dating to the fifteenth century, of Cretan origin, but now in Baltimore.[60] In both these cases the illustration is essentially borrowed from other types of manuscripts: the biblical canticles for *orthros*, for example, are illustrated with traditional ode compositions well known from Psalter manuscripts. In the Baltimore *horologion*, the Hours of terce, sext and none are illustrated with scenes of Pentecost, Crucifixion and Lamentation respectively,

---

58 Thomas and Hero, II, 839.
59 S. Brooks, 'Sculpture of the late Byzantine tomb', in *Faith and power*, 95–103; E. Velkovska, 'Funeral rites according to Byzantine liturgical sources', *DOP* 55 (2001), 21–45.
60 Lesbos, Leimonos 295. See P. Vokotopoulos, "Η εικονογράφηση τοῦ κανόνος εἰς ψυχορραγοῦντα στὸ 'Ορολόγιον 295 τῆς μονῆς Λειμῶνος', Σύμμεικτα 9 (1994), 95–114. One image in the Lesbos Horologion (p. 222) shows what appear to be monks assembling for a service at the doors of a church. Baltimore, Walters w534. See N. P. Ševčenko, 'The Walters' Horologion', *Journal of the Walters Art Museum* 62 (2004), 7–21.

because the hour at which the original events took place (third, sixth and ninth) is specified in the Bible, and the corresponding monastic hour became a sort of memorial of the biblical event. It thus allowed the celebration of the three events on a daily basis and not just yearly.

The Psalter, a basic component of both cathedral and monastic rites, is one of the most frequently illustrated liturgical texts of all. Some Psalter manuscripts received significant visual commentary in the margins of their pages, commentary which tends to stress the typological and theological meanings of the passage more than its liturgical use.[61] The Old Testament canticles were consistently included in Psalter manuscripts; they once formed an essential part of *orthros* and were often the primary focus of decoration. A consistent iconography was developed for each of the nine biblical canticles: either the event that prompted the canticle was pictured (e.g. the Three Hebrews, the Crossing of the Red Sea, Moses receiving the Law, Jonah and the whale, etc.), or the individual involved (most of them prophets) was shown addressing a song of praise to God, arms upraised.[62] Unlike the others, the image accompanying the final canticle, the Magnificat – the only canticle drawn from the New Testament (Luke 1:46–54) – continued to develop in late Byzantine art, so that the image of the Virgin praising God after the Visitation begins to resemble icons of herself bearing Christ in her arms. This led in turn to a refashioning of the image of the Magnificat, such as we find in a Psalter in Jerusalem (Greek Patriarchate Taphou 55), where a patron approaches the standing Virgin and child: the Virgin has become a figure to whom prayers are addressed, not a figure addressing God herself.[63]

The liturgical manuscripts based on the yearly cycle – the *menaion* for the fixed feasts, the *triodion* for Lent and the *pentekostarion* for the period from Easter Sunday through Pentecost – developed late as individual books (twelfth, tenth and fourteenth century respectively), but together they recorded the hymns and prayers and readings for every day of the year. Some collections of specific types of hymns (the *octoechos* with hymns for each day of the week in

61 K. Corrigan, *Visual polemics in ninth century Byzantine psalters* (New York: Cambridge University Press, 1992); S. Der Nersessian, *L'illustration des psautiers grecs du Moyen Âge*, II, *Londres, Add. 19.352* [Bibliothèque des cahiers archéologiques 5] (Paris: Editions Klincksieck, 1970); A. Cutler, 'Liturgical strata in the marginal psalters', *DOP* 34–5 (1980–81), 17–30.
62 A. Cutler, *The aristocratic psalters in Byzantium* [Bibliothèque des cahiers archéologiques 13] (Paris: Picard, 1984); Weitzmann, *Liturgical psalters*.
63 N. P. Ševčenko, 'The Mother of God in illuminated manuscripts', in *Mother of God*, ed. M. Vassilaki, 155–65, esp. 158; Vokotopoulos, *Illuminated manuscripts*, no. 16. (fol. 260r). The figure of the Virgin is framed like an icon, even with a ring at the top for its suspension.

eight-week cycles; the *sticherarion* or collection of short poetic pieces arranged chronologically by feast day) very occasionally have some form of illustration. In an *octoechos* in Messina, the *stichera anastasima* are prefaced by unusual images of the presumed author of the *octoechos*, John of Damascus. This imagery has no roots in other manuscript illustration and is certainly a free and unusual improvisation on the monastic text.[64]

Monastic services were made up of hymns of varying lengths, above all the canon, a musical composition of nine verses or odes which, by the eleventh century, had come to replace the nine biblical canticles sung at *orthros*; several canons might be interwoven, ode by ode. An older hymn type, the *kontakion*, had been displaced by the canon, and survived in the Divine Office only in abbreviated form: its *proimion* and first *oikos* (or set of verses of a *kontakion*) might be inserted after the sixth ode of the canon. But one *kontakion*, the *Akathistos*, a hymn in twenty-four stanzas to the Virgin attributed to the sixth-century poet Romanos Melodos, continued to be sung in full at least once a year: on Saturday of the fifth week of Lent. The text of the *Akathistos* is sometimes included in Psalter manuscripts from the fourteenth century on.[65] The first half of the text conveys the Infancy story from the Annunciation to the Presentation in the Temple, while the second half focuses on elaborate praise to the Virgin. One splendid Byzantine manuscript is devoted almost entirely to this one poetic text.[66] The illustrations to the narrative section are fairly conventional, but when it comes to the verses of pure praise, interesting images are created of the Virgin surrounded by the faithful, in which the Virgin's poses begin to echo some of the Virgin icon types developed by the fourteenth century. Veneration of the Virgin in this ancient hymn is being conceived more and more often as the veneration of an icon of the Virgin. In the final stanza, the twenty-fourth, the faithful are shown quite literally venerating a specific icon, that of the Virgin Hodegetria placed on a wooden stand covered with a textile.[67]

---

64 Messina, San Salvatore 51. See A. Weyl Carr, 'Illuminated musical manuscripts in Byzantium. A note on the late twelfth century', *Gesta* 28 (1989), 41–52. In the fourteenth-century *sticherarion* (Athos Kutlumus 412) the decoration consists of a sequence of holy portraits: Pelekanides, *Treasures of Mount Athos*, I, figs. 377–84.

65 The earliest surviving *Akathistos* miniatures are in fact in a Bulgarian psalter of *c.*1360, the Tomić Psalter, Moscow (Historical Museum, muz, 2752). See A. Dzhurova, *Tomichov psaltir* [Monumenta slavico-byzantina et mediaevalia europensia I] (Sofia: Universitetsko izd-vo 'Kliment Okhridski', 1990). This manuscript illustrates Ps. 134, the *Polyeleos*, with a similar image of singers before an icon (fol. 226r): Moran, *Singers*, pl. VII.

66 Moscow, Historical Museum gr. 429, *c.*1360. See Ševčenko, 'Icons in the liturgy', 50, note 35 with bibliography.

67 On the *Akathistos* in both manuscripts and fresco, see Moran, *Singers*, 93–114.

Figure 5.5 *Akathistos* hymn, stanza 24. Markov Manastir, church of St Demetrios, north wall of the bema.

There is nothing equivalent to the elegant *Akathistos* illustration (fig. 5.5) when it comes to the illustration of the canons. A sequence of mediocre miniatures accompanies the canon for the separation of soul and body; these miniatures are attached to, and contemporary with, the late twelfth-century *horologion* manuscript on Lesbos mentioned above. The images track the course of the soul from its escape from the body of a dying monk, to its judgement and preliminary ascent to Paradise. Each ode of this canon has its own image, all closely related to the content of the verses. A comparable, but unrelated, set of images prefaces a twelfth-century Psalter (Athos Dionysiou 65); here they are attached not to a canon but to a rarely used alphabetical set of prayers designed for private not communal use, in a monastic cell.[68] The format of the Lesbos illustrations, one miniature per ode, occurs in illustrations to yet another canon, the 'Penitential' canon included in manuscripts of the *Heavenly Ladder* of John Klimax; they preface each ode of the canon and so

68 Pelekanides, *Treasures of Mount Athos*, I, figs. 118, 121–2; G. Parpulov, 'Text and miniatures from Codex Dionysiou 65', *Twenty-fifth Annual Byzantine Studies Conference. Abstracts* (College Park: Pennsylvania State University Press, 1999), 124–6.

recur at predictable intervals.[69] Of these illustrations, only the canon for the separation of soul and body is ever illustrated in monumental painting.

Hymnography in monumental painting

Portraits of hymnographers on the walls of Byzantine churches from the twelfth century on provide an indication of the importance of hymnography to monumental painting.[70] At the church of Nerezi (1164), for example, the entire lower section of the north wall is devoted to the representation of five of these poets, including Theodore of Stoudios and Joseph the Hymnographer, both of whom lived into the ninth century. The hymnographers here occupy a position more prominent than that awarded to the warrior saints to the west, and equal to the highly revered monastic saints of the early church painted opposite, on the south wall.[71]

Yet the impact of hymnography on monumental painting is not always easy to assess. To be sure, certain specific hymns are illustrated on the walls of churches, as with the *Akathistos* hymn, which is included fairly frequently in church programmes after the early fourteenth century (the earliest cycle in any medium being that painted in the church of the Olympiotissa at Elasson *c.* 1300).[72] The Nativity *sticheron* of John of Damascus was illustrated in some fourteenth-century Balkan churches: here a traditional Nativity composition was isolated from the feast sequence and expanded to include figures of the faithful, among them even actual historical personages, shown celebrating the feast by singing the hymn.[73] There is a sequence of scenes illustrating the canon for the separation of soul and body painted in a tower of the Chilandar monastery on Mount Athos.[74]

69 J. R. Martin, *The illustration of the Heavenly Ladder of John Climacus* [Studies in Manuscript Illumination 5] (Princeton: Princeton University Press, 1954), 128–49.

70 G. Babić, 'Les moines poètes dans l'église de la Mère de Dieu à Studenica', in *Studenica i vizantijska umetnosti oko 1200* (Belgrade: Srpska akademija nauka i umetnosti, 1988), 205–19; A. Grabar, 'Les images des poètes et des illustrations dans leurs œuvres et dans la peinture byzantine tardive', *Zograf* 10 (1979), 13–16.

71 Sinkević, *Nerezi*, 60–66; N. P. Ševčenko, 'The five hymnographers at Nerezi', *Palaeoslavica* 10 (2002), 55–68.

72 A. Paetzold, *Der Akathistos-Hymnos: die Bilderzyklen in der byzantinischen Wandmalerei des 14. Jahrhunderts* [Forschungen zur Kunstgeschichte und christlichen Archäologie 16] (Stuttgart: Franz Steiner Verlag, 1989); E. C. Constantinides, *The wall paintings of the Panagia Olympiotissa at Elasson in Northern Thessaly* (Athens: Canadian Archaeological Institute at Athens, 1992), 134–77.

73 Moran, *Singers*, 115–25.

74 B. Todić, 'Freske XIII veka u paraklisu na pirgu sv. Georgija u Hilandaru', *Hilandarski Zbornik* 9 (1997), 35–70 (English summary, 71–3), esp. 55–70, figs. 12–17 and sketch 11.

Sometimes the author of a canon sung at a particular feast is painted along-side or even within the representation of that feast. In the refectory at Patmos, for example, the hymnographers Kosmas and John of Damascus, like a pair of prophets, let down their scrolls into a Crucifixion scene.[75] They also flank depictions of the Dormition of the Virgin, holding scrolls with words from their Dormition canons. The two saints may even on occasion enter the frame of the composition and stand, if on a slightly enlarged scale, near the mourning apos-tles. The hymnographers in these compositions, like the singers mentioned above, serve to link a past event to its present celebration.

The effect of hymnography on the feast cycle is more elusive: it is not always easy to trace a particular motif back to a specific hymn, especially when the hymns are based on earlier prose texts. But it is clear that Romanos's Crucifixion *kontakion* influenced an eleventh-century ivory and a fourteenth-century fresco of the Crucifixion where the words of the *kontakion* are inscribed on the fresco.[76] Hymnography is thought to have had a significant influence on the development of new and more affective versions of the Passion events from the twelfth century on: Pallas and Belting have argued that readings and hymns involving the laments of the Virgin were introduced during the twelfth century into newly fashioned Good Friday services and led to the icon type of the Man of Sorrows (*Akra Tapeinosis*). If correct – and perhaps too much has been made of the newness of the service in question – these developments represent the clearest and closest ties between liturgy and art to be found outside the sanctuary area.[77]

Hymnography in other media

Icon painting follows much the same course as monumental painting in this regard. There are icons on which the twenty-four stanzas of the *Akathistos* Hymn surround the Virgin; there are icons of the Dormition which include the hymnographers Kosmas and John of Damascus. The Man of Sorrows, some-times on a diptych paired with a bust icon of the mourning Virgin, became a

---

75 They were apparently already present in the late twelfth-century Crucifixion at Bojana: E. Bakalova, 'Liturgična poezia i crkovna stenopis (Tekst ot oktoexa v Bojanskata c'rkvata)', *Starob'lgarska Literatura* 28–9 (1994), 143–52.

76 M. E. Frazer, 'Hades stabbed by the cross of Christ', *Metropolitan Museum Journal* 9 (1974), 153–61; G. Babić, 'Quelques observations sur le cycle des fêtes de l'église de Pološko (Macédoine)', *CA* 27 (1978), 163–78, esp. 172–4.

77 Pallas, *Passion*, 29–38; Belting, 'Image and its function', 5, 7. The service Pallas and Belting single out and call the *presbeia* is in structure actually nothing new for a Friday evening, nor does the crucial text they cite, the *typikon* of the Evergetis monastery, refer to it as a *presbeia*. See Ševčenko, 'Icons in the liturgy', 50–4; Janeras, *Vendredi-saint*, 427–28.

familiar icon type, postulated to be an actual participant in the Good Friday liturgy. More surely an actual participant in these liturgical ceremonies was the *epitaphios*, the large tomb-size covering that bore the image of the dead Christ (fig. 5.1). It was unquestionably to play a part in the burial processions of Good Friday and Holy Saturday, which are attested by the fourteenth century.

Icons of the Virgin, whatever their iconographic type, often acquired epithets that derive from those given to her in liturgical poetry (the *zoodochos pege*, the *platytera*, the *pammakaristos*, etc.).[78] Just occasionally the influence runs the other way: with the proliferation of miracle-working icons in late Byzantium, for example, poetic canons began to be composed not just to the Virgin but to individual icons of the Virgin. These canons to icons seem to belong to the post-Byzantine period, but some may prove to be earlier.[79]

Conclusions

The Byzantine liturgy and its commentators have continually wrestled with notions of earthly and heavenly time. The Eucharist was said to commemorate Christ's sacrifice and the events leading up to it, but it was at the same time an image, a figure of the fulfilment of these events in the eternal realm of God.[80] It evoked both a historical sequence of events and the timelessness of the heavenly kingdom. The writers who commented on the Eucharist went back and forth between two approaches, the Antiochene and Alexandrian, between Ἱστορία and Θεωρία.[81] Because the liturgical performance of an event served to link past and future, this art could dispense with other kinds of linkage such as extensive symbolism or allegory, and so it remains firmly and unwaveringly representational.

And it remains polyvalent: the drawing of strict one-to-one relationships usually failed. The various liturgical cycles and services – the movable feasts, the fixed feasts, the Hours, the Eucharist – jostle and overlap in the course of a day, and as a result the variable elements of the liturgy constantly give new tonalities and meaning to the fixed and unchanging ones. The same is

---

78 S. Eustratiades, Ἡ Θεοτόκος ἐν τῇ ὑμνογραφία [Ἁγιορετικὴ Βιβλιοθήκη 6] (Paris: Librairie ancienne; Chennevières-sur-Marne: L'Hermitage, 1930).

79 Ševčenko, 'Icons in the liturgy', 55.

80 Schmemann, *Liturgical theology*, 34–6, 57–64; Bornert, *Commentaires*, 36, 168–76.

81 R. F. Taft, 'The liturgy of the Great Church: an initial synthesis of structure and interpretation on the eve of Iconoclasm', *DOP* 34–5 (1980–81), 45–75; Bornert, *Commentaires*, esp. 52–82.

true of the art. In a church, one image resonates with the other, and the meaning of both is affected. The same image on a vestment or on the church wall may look identical if reproduced in a book, but on location it takes on a different colouring in each different context. Along with all the rich imagery and profound theological ideas that Byzantine art derived from the liturgy, it also learned how to move in and out of time, and how to play with context so as to enrich itself constantly with new levels of meaning.

6

Mount Athos and the Ottomans *c.*1350–1550

ELIZABETH A. ZACHARIADOU

Byzantine monasteries were located both in the countryside and in the cities, pre-eminently in Constantinople, and constituted centres of religious, cultural, philanthropic and economic life. They consisted of a complex of buildings, which apart from the monks' cells included the *katholikon* or main church, chapels, a refectory, a fountain, a bakery, storerooms and stables. Some of them also had hostels for pilgrims and travellers and hospitals and almshouses for the old. Quite often they had libraries and scriptoria, in which manuscripts were copied and in special cases beautifully illuminated. They were usually contained within strong defensive walls. Most of them possessed agricultural lands, which besides providing foodstuffs for the monks were a source of revenues, to be used for the benefit of the monastery – often to maintain or enhance its buildings. Their landed estates were largely acquired through imperial donations and grants of privileges – often in the shape of exemptions from state taxes. Private individuals also made donations to monasteries, usually in exchange for posthumous commemoration and prayers for the salvation of their soul. Donations in general were not just limited to landed property, for there were also gifts of cash and precious objects. Exemption from taxes and a stream of donations enabled monasteries to acquire additional properties through purchase. From the tenth century onwards their landed properties increased substantially thanks to the inclusion not only of fields and vineyards but also of mills, livestock and fishponds. Furthermore, they began to acquire urban rental properties, workshops and boats.

Certain general principles regulated monastic life. Cenobitic monasticism meant a community following an egalitarian way of life, with all the monks following the same routine and sharing the same food at a common table. There was also idiorrhythmic monasticism, which allowed for an individualised style of existence, in which monks were permitted to possess personal property. This form of monastic life, for reasons to be analysed, became more common in the last centuries of Byzantium and continued to be popular under the Ottomans.

Holy mountains were a characteristic feature of Byzantine monasticism. The great majority were situated in Asia Minor. One thinks of Mount Olympos (Ulus Dağ) in Bithynia, Mount Latros in the region of ancient Miletus, and Mount Galesion near Ephesos. However, these monastic centres went into terminal decline in the wake of the Turkish advance into Asia Minor following the victory of the Seljuq Sultan Alp Arslan over the Byzantines at the battle of Mantzikert in 1071. The Turkish nomads were recently and only superficially islamicised. Ignoring laws and rules, they marched into the country with their families and their flocks, plundering and destroying as they went. They created havoc, which lasted for at least thirty years. The monasteries stood little chance of survival. Their treasures attracted the rapacity of the nomads, who pillaged them and either enslaved or expelled the monks. Christodoulos, later to found the monastery of St John the Theologian on the island of Patmos, has left a vivid description of the barbarity of the Turkish occupation, which forced him to abandon his monastery of Stylos on Mount Latros.[1] The decline of the monasteries of Asia Minor worked to the advantage of Mount Athos. Its monasteries were to emerge from the period of Latin rule after 1204 with an enhanced reputation for a pious way of life.[2] They have preserved their unique character ever since. It served them well during the Ottoman conquest of Macedonia in the late fourteenth century, for the early Ottoman rulers were impressed by their spiritual authority and were anxious to fulfil the responsibilities expected of pious Muslim rulers. They began to apply the koranic principle of religious tolerance, which presupposes respect for the institutions of the Christians and the Jews. According to an old Islamic tradition (*hadith*) the Prophet Muhammad himself granted protection to the monastery of Sinai, while it was understood that during the holy war (*jihad*) monks were to be left unmolested and, once hostilities ended, were to enjoy temporary freedom from taxation.[3] The early Ottoman rulers applied these principles and, more to the point, exploited them to win over to their side the Greek Orthodox populations, who at that time considered their real enemies to be the Latins.[4] The monasteries of the region of Trebizond, which was conquered

---

1 N. Oikonomides, 'The monastery of Patmos in the eleventh and twelfth centuries and its economic functions', in N. Oikonomides, *Social and economic life in Byzantium* (Aldershot: Ashgate, 2004), VII, 4–7.

2 N. Oikonomides, 'Mount Athos: levels of literacy', *DOP* 42 (1988), 174.

3 F. Løkkegaard, 'The concepts of war and peace in Islam', in *War and peace in the middle ages*, ed. B. P. Maguire (Copenhagen: C. A. Reitzels Forlag, 1987), 270, 273.

4 See above, pp. 53ff.

by the Ottomans in 1461, survived under circumstances similar to those that prevailed in the Balkans.

Under Ottoman rule the monasteries of Mount Athos continued their life fairly undisturbed. If they received no more imperial donations, at least the Ottoman sultans confirmed them in possession of most of their landed properties and granted them privileges ensuring favourable taxation. Private individuals continued to make donations to the various monasteries, which took the form both of landed property and of cash and precious objects. Among them were distinguished personalities such as the *voevody* of Wallachia.[5] The fascination exercised by this most venerated of religious centres extended to those of humbler origin, who made donations of some importance. A case worth mentioning is that of the monastery of Kavallarea, situated in Venetian Crete, which was bequeathed by its abbot to the Athonite monastery of Dionysiou in 1555.[6] Donations to the monasteries of Athos multiplied during the period of the Ottoman expansion in the Balkans, because, as we shall see, they were favoured by prevailing circumstances. Therefore, Mount Athos continued to flourish economically under its new masters and remained a centre of education, culture and spiritual life.

It benefited from the understanding it developed with the early Ottoman rulers. This was apparently in place even before their conquest of Macedonia, if we are to believe an Athonite tradition which has the support of scattered pieces of historical evidence. This claims that in the days of Sultan Orkhan (1326–62) monks living on Mount Athos, disheartened by the destructive civil wars taking place in Byzantium, came to the conclusion that Constantinople would soon fall to the Ottomans. They therefore sent envoys to the Ottoman capital of Bursa (Prousa), seeking the sultan's protection. Orkhan, in return, graciously complied, confirmed them in possession of their landed properties, and granted them further privileges. When under Murad I (1362–89) the Ottomans moved their capital from Bursa to Edirne (Adrianople), the monks of Mount Athos again sent envoys in order to obtain a new confirmation. Although no surviving Ottoman documents corroborate this tradition, it preserves the interesting detail that the original documents issued by Orkhan in Bursa were stored in the chancery and the monks were later able to obtain

5 P. S. Năsturel, 'Le Mont Athos et ses premiers contacts avec la Principauté de Valachie', *Bulletin, Association Internationale d'Études du Sud-Est Européen* 1 (1963), 31–8; Năsturel, 'Aperçu critique des rapports de la Valachie et du Mont Athos des origines au début du XVIe siècle', *Revue des Études Sud-Est Européennes* 2 (1964), 93–126.
6 P. Nikolopoulos and N. Oikonomides, ''Ιερὰ Μονὴ Διονυσίου, κατάλογος τοῦ 'αρχείου', Σύμμεικτα 1 (1966), 291, no. 97.

copies of them.[7] Even if no such copies have been found, it points to continuing contacts between Mount Athos and the Ottoman court.

The motif of this story appears in more than one narrative dealing with the early relations between the Ottoman Sultans and Orthodox monks in the Balkans. It is found, for example, in the chronicle of Yazicioğlu Ali, written in the early fifteenth century. There it is connected not with the monks of Athos, but with those of the Prodromos monastery, near Serres. They were even more perspicacious than the monks of Athos, for they had foreseen the Ottoman conquest as far back as the days of Orkhan's father Osman, the eponymous founder of the Ottoman state! They travelled to his court and begged for his protection, which they obtained in the shape of a decree from him.[8] But this is pure legend, for in the days of Osman Ottoman power was limited to the frontiers of Bithynia and the likelihood of contacts with a monastery near Serres is so remote as to be impossible. By the reign of his grandson, Sultan Murad I, it was quite another matter. By then the Ottomans were established in Thrace, which became their base for raids against Macedonia. It was in these circumstances that the monks of the Prodromos monastery first established relations with the Ottomans, as is shown by a document of the year 1372–73 granted to them by Murad I. This document seems to be the first one issued by a sultan for the Prodromos monastery because there is no mention in it that Murad I was following the example of his father or grandfather in favouring the monastery, which was the normal practice of the Ottoman chancery. When, for example, Murad's grandsons, Musa Çelebi and Mehmed Çelebi, made grants to the monastery, they made it clear that they were confirming the privileges granted by their grandfather to the monastery.[9]

We have another example of this practice in the confirmation of the grant of a *timar* near Thessalonike made in 1386 by Murad I. It specified that the original grant had been made by Murad's father Orkhan to the present holder's father. The man in question came from a noble Serbian family, which had close connections with the Athonite monastery of St Paul.[10] This in itself offers additional support for the belief that already in the days of Orhkan relations

---

7 G. Smyrnakes, *Tὸ Ἅγιον Ὄρος* (Athens: Hetaireia 'Hellenismos', 1903), 109.

8 P. Wittek, 'Zu einigen frühosmanischen Urkunden (vi)', *Wiener Zeitschrift für die Kunde des Morgenlandes* 58 (1962), 197. The story of Yazicioğlu Ali is repeated by the seventeenth-century Ottoman historian, Müneccimbashi.

9 E. A. Zachariadou, 'Early Ottoman documents of the Prodromos Monastery', *Südost-Forschungen* 28 (1969), 1–12.

10 H.-G. Majer, 'Some remarks on the document of Murad I from the monastery of St Paul on Mount Athos (1386)', in *Mount Athos in the 14th–16th Centuries* [Ἀθωνικὰ Σύμμεικτα 4] (Athens: Institute for Byzantine Research, 1997), 33–9.

were being established between the monasteries of Athos and the Ottoman court.

This becomes all the more probable if we recall the situation in the Aegean during the first half of the fourteenth century. Mount Athos repeatedly suffered from naval raids by Turks, who were not necessarily Ottomans but were more likely to come from the various maritime Aegean emirates, which, unlike the Ottomans, had flotillas at their disposal. Some monasteries were pillaged, badly damaged or deserted; some were in danger of disappearing for good. Large numbers of monks were taken prisoner, while others searched for new places in which to continue their spiritual life. After one devastating Turkish attack, the distinguished Athonite theologian Gregory Palamas planned to flee to Jerusalem, but he finally moved to Thessalonike, which was well fortified. Another distinguished monk, Athanasios, left Athos for good and founded the monasteries of the Meteora in the inner region of Thessaly, which was still considered to be beyond the striking range of the Turks.[11]

A change occurred around 1350, after which there was a marked decrease in the number of Turkish raids on Mount Athos. This coincided with a period of revival and prosperity for Mount Athos during which new monasteries were erected and old ones, which had been deserted or destroyed, were restored and repopulated, for example the monasteries of Simonopetra and of St Paul. The monastery of Dionysiou was founded between 1356 and 1362, while at the same time the monasteries of Koutloumousiou and Kastamonitou were rebuilt.[12] Athonite monasteries were now able to acquire dependencies in Constantinople. For example, the monastery of Psychosostria in the capital passed under the control of the monastery of Vatopedi. The reason behind this transaction is revealing: a prosperous Athonite monastery was rescuing an impoverished metropolitan monastery.[13]

This reflects a change for the good in the fortunes of Mount Athos, but what was the explanation? The balance of probability suggests that it was the result of an agreement between the monks of Mount Athos and the Ottoman ruler Orkhan, which offered a degree of protection for their monasteries. This hypothesis receives indirect confirmation from the patriarch Philotheos. In a homily written no later than 1360 he states that even the infidels who ignore

---

11 D. M. Nicol, *Meteora: the rock monasteries of Thessaly* (London: Chapman and Hall, 1963; revised edn London: Variorum, 1975).

12 N. Oikonomides, 'Patronage in Palaiologan Mt Athos', in *Mount Athos and Byzantine monasticism*, ed. A. Bryer and M. Cunningham (Aldershot: Variorum, 1996), 100–2.

13 Angeliki Laiou, 'Economic activities of Vatopedi in the fourteenth century', in *The Monastery of Vatopedi: history and art* [Ἀθωνικὰ Σύμμεικτα 7] (Athens: Institute for Byzantine Research, 1999), 56.

Jesus Christ (obviously the Turks are meant) respect and admire the splendour of the virtues of the holy monks. One reason for this was the kindly way in which the monks received all those, whether they were Greeks, barbarians or infidels, who sought asylum on Mount Athos or were washed up on its shores after shipwreck. The patriarch describes what the monks unstintingly offered to their enforced visitors: food and clothes and shelter; they also helped them with repairs to their ships, or, if their ships were lost, the monks put at their disposal their own ships, full of provisions.[14] The inclusion of Turks among those succoured by the monks of Athos points once again to the existence of friendly relations between Mount Athos and the Ottomans in the days of Sultan Orkhan. A likely mediator between the monks and the Ottoman ruler was the emperor John VI Kantakouzenos (1347–54). Not only did he have very close ties with Mount Athos; he was also to become Orkhan's father-in-law.[15]

Another factor was the triumph of hesychasm, confirmed in 1351 under the auspices of John Kantakouzenos at the council of Blakhernai. It reinforced the spiritual ascendancy of Mount Athos both in Byzantium and among the different Orthodox peoples. One consequence was a spate of new foundations, which attracted monks from all over the Orthodox world. Though the motives behind these new foundations were largely spiritual, material considerations also entered into the reckoning. Mount Athos's comparative safety from Turkish raiding became increasingly attractive to donors. Mount Athos's spiritual eminence equally appealed to Ottoman rulers. As we have seen, protection of holy men and monasteries was part of their Islamic duty, but it cannot have escaped them that it might also be a way of reconciling their Christian subjects to their new masters. The quietism of the hesychasts meant that monasticism never became a focus for Orthodox resistance to the Ottoman advance into the southern Balkans. The tone was set by the hesychast leader Gregory Palamas, who fell into Ottoman hands in 1354. His courteous treatment at the Ottoman court left an excellent impression, even if Palamas never advocated collaboration, as his enemies insinuated.[16]

It has been important to establish how early close relations were established between the monasteries of Mount Athos and the Ottomans because these guaranteed the continued existence of this revered religious centre. At a time

14 Philotheos Kokkinos, Δογματικά Ἔργα, ed. D. Kaimakes (Thessalonike: Centre of Byzantine Studies, 1983), part 1, 482.104–12, 484.160–78.
15 A. Bryer, 'Greek historians on the Turks: the case of the first Byzantine–Ottoman marriage', in The writing of history in the middle ages: essays presented to Richard William Southern, ed. R. H. C. Davis and J. M. Wallace-Hadrill (Oxford: Clarendon Press, 1981), 471–93.
16 A. Philippidis-Braat, 'La captivité de Palamas chez les Turcs: dossier et commentaire', TM 7 (1979), 109–222.

when the Byzantine state was struggling for its very existence, the monasteries of Mount Athos prospered thanks to the *modus vivendi* established with the Ottomans. If anything, donations of property to the monasteries increased. They were often not so much acts of devotion, as a means of safeguarding property by placing it under the protection of a monastic foundation, which had a special relation with the prospective conqueror. This need was especially great after the battle of Maritsa in 1371, when the whole of Macedonia and the southern Balkans was continuously overrun by bands of Turkish warriors.[17] Instructive is the family history of Radoslav Hlapen, the Serbian lord of Edessa (Vodena) and Berroia, who was related to Tsar Stefan Dušan (1331–55).[18] His estates did not go directly to the monasteries of Athos, but his heirs ensured that the religious foundations situated within his territories passed under Athonite control, on the understanding that their properties would now be safe from Turkish raiding. In 1375, one of his daughters and her husband, Thomas Prealymbos, later to become despot of Ioannina, gifted to the Great Lavra the church of the Virgin Gabaliotissa at Edessa, together with its villages, fields, gardens, shops and mills, and movable property in the shape of manuscripts, icons and church plate, in the hope that transfer to an Athonite monastery would prevent it from falling prey to the Turks. Having recognised Sultan Murad I's overlordship, another of Hlapen's sons-in-law, the Caesar Alexios Angelos, the ruler of Thessaly, granted the small Salonican monastery of St Photis in 1389 to Nea Moni, a much grander monastery of the same city. But Nea Moni together with St Photis soon became possessions of the Great Lavra,[19] which neatly illustrates how property gravitated to the monasteries of Mount Athos under the conditions created by the Ottoman conquest.

Radoslav Hlapen and his family had another connection with Mount Athos. At some date between 1356 and 1366 a relative of theirs, Antonios Pagases, retreated to the Holy Mountain, where he bought and restored the monastery of St Paul, which was in ruins, eventually becoming its abbot after having been tonsured and having taken the monastic name of Arsenios. In 1385 his brother Nicholas Baldouin Pagases donated the monastery of Mesonesiotissa, situated

---

17 Cf. the case of the grand domestikos Demetrios Palaiologos and of his wife: A. Laiou, Ἡ διαμόρφωση τῆς τιμῆς τῆς γῆς στὸ Βυζάντιο', in *Βυζάντιο: Κράτος καὶ κοινωνία. Μνήμη Νίκου Οἰκονομίδη*, ed. A. Avramea, A. Laiou and A. Chrysos (Athens: Institute for Byzantine Research, 2003), 346–7.

18 On Hlapen, see H. Matanov, 'Radoslav Hlapen – souverain féodale en Macédoine méridional durant le troisième quart du XIVe siècle', *Études Balkaniques* 19 (1983), 68–87.

19 On these donations, cf. Elizabeth A. Zachariadou, 'Some remarks about dedications to monasteries in the late 14th century', in *Mount Athos in the 14th–16th centuries*, 29–31.

near Edessa, together with its villages, churches and other properties, to the monastery of St Paul. Fear of the Turks had a part to play because Edessa was to fall in that year to Sultan Murad I. This will explain why Baldouin expressed the wish that future lords, be they Christians or Muslims, respect his act of donation, while at the same time revealing his state of uncertainty. It is obvious that he was surrendering Mesonesiotissa and its properties to his brother on Mount Athos in a desperate bid to protect the monastery against present circumstances. The same strategy can be seen at a lower social level, where some of the few surviving peasant freeholders sold or donated their property to the Athonite houses.

Some individuals donated properties or sums of money – often of around one hundred *hyperpyra* – to the Athonite monasteries, on condition that they would receive an annual income in exchange. Such an arrangement involved the long-established institution of *adelphata*, which acquired new features in this period. For example, it became an investment, which could be made for a third party, be it a sister or a son.[20] The monasteries were offering what we would call nowadays an annuity. Often being paid in kind, it was even more advantageous to the monastery, because it provided a lucrative way of disposing of its agricultural surplus.

The number of the monks increased in Mount Athos as many settled there to save themselves from the tribulations of continual warfare. The father of St Nektarios took his two sons and retreated to a monastery after a devastating Turkish raid; St Philotheos and his brother, recruited as janissaries but then miraculously liberated, took refuge in a monastery.[21] Monks came to Mount Athos from all parts of the Balkans under threat from Ottoman conquest; they spoke different languages, but mostly a variant of Slavonic. This reinforced Athos's popular and cosmopolitan character.[22] With Stefan Dušan the Serbian presence on the Holy Mountain became more marked and challenged the Greek dominance. Between 1356 and 1371 Mount Athos was administered by Serbians, known as *Servoprotoi*.[23] However, Serbian influence declined

---

20 N. Oikonomides, 'Monastères et moines lors de la conquête ottomane', *Südost-Forschungen* 35 (1976), 6–8; Laiou, 'Economic activities of Vatopedi in the fourteenth century', 66–9.

21 E. A. Zachariadou, 'A safe and holy mountain: early Ottoman Athos', in *Mount Athos and Byzantine monasticism*, 128–9; B. Papoulia, 'Die Vita des Heiligen Philotheos vom Athos', *Südost-Forschungen* 22 (1963), 274–80.

22 Oikonomides, 'Monastères et moines lors de la conquête ottomane', 8–10.

23 C. Pavlikianof, Σλάβοι μοναχοί στό Ἅγιον Ὄρος ἀπό τόν Ι' ὡς τόν ΙΖ' αἰώνα (Thessalonike: University Studio Press, 2002), 141–50; R. Radić, "Η Μονὴ Βατοπεδίου καὶ ἡ Σερβία στὸν ΙΕ' αἰώνα', in *Monastery of Vatopedi*, 87–96.

following the defeat in 1371 by the Turks of the Serbian leaders John Uglješa, the founder of Simonopetra, and his brother Vukašin at the battle of the Maritsa.

During the years 1420–22, when the Italian humanist Cristoforo Buondelmonti visited the Holy Mountain, its monastic life was very well organised, to judge from the warm praises he lavished on it. The Florentine clergyman noted the sheer numbers of monks settled in the various Athonite monasteries and admired their way of life. Some followed the communal life in peace and tranquillity, while others pursued the eremitical life in complete solitude, praying day and night.[24] Shortly afterwards in 1423 Mount Athos passed officially under Ottoman lordship. The occasion was the cession of Thessalonike and its region by the Despot Andronikos Palaiologos to the Venetians; the Athonite monks refused to accept Latin masters and preferred to place themselves under the rule of Sultan Murad II (1421–51).[25] But this change of rulers did nothing to disturb the prosperity of the Holy Mountain, if we are to believe the antiquarian Ciriaco of Ancona, who paid it a short visit in November 1444. He was immensely impressed by the magnificence of the churches and monastic buildings at Vatopedi, the Lavra and Iveron and amazed by the rich holdings of the monastic libraries, which excited his collector's cupidity. He congratulated himself on the way he managed to acquire a copy of Plutarch's *Moralia* from a worthy monk of Iveron, while the abbot was away, incidentally on a mission to the Ottoman court.[26]

Even after 1453 the monasteries of Mount Athos provided members of the Byzantine aristocracy with a good place to finish their days.[27] But not all those who joined the Athonite monks were looking for the aura of sanctity. There were those who saw it as a means of salting away their money. Their activities sometimes came to the attention of the Ottoman tribunals. A notorious example is provided by Radić, the great *čelnik* or general-in-chief of the Serbian Despot Stefan Lazarević and, after the latter's death in 1427, of his son-in-law and successor George Branković.[28] Radić did not remain in the latter's service for long. Shortly after 1433, he decided to retreat to Mount Athos, where the *pax ottomanica* guaranteed order and stability, at a time when Serbia was

24 A. Pertusi, 'Monasteri e monaci italiani all'Athos nell'alto medioevo', *Le Millénaire du Mont Athos, 963–1963, études et mélanges* (Chevetogne: Éditions de Chevetogne, 1963), I, 243–50.

25 P. Schreiner, *Die byzantinischen Kleinchroniken* (Vienna: Verlag ÖAW, 1975), I, 473.

26 Cyriac of Ancona, *Later travels*, ed. E. W. Bodnar [The I Tatti Renaissance Library] (Cambridge, MA: Harvard University Press, 2003), 121–35.

27 E.g. Dionysios Iagaris, see *PLP*, no. 92053.

28 On this personage see E. A. Zachariadou, 'The worrisome wealth of the Čelnik Radić', in *Studies in Ottoman history in honour of Professor V. L. Ménage*, ed. C. Heywood and C. Imber (Istanbul: Isis Press, 1994), 383–97.

experiencing a turbulent period following the death in 1427 of Stefan Lazarević, which brought succession problems and the intervention of the Hungarians. Radić became a monk in the monastery of Kastamonitou, which he found destroyed by fire and almost deserted. Thanks to his generous benefactions it was restored and reorganised. Among his other bequests was a share in the revenues of a Serbian silver-mine. He also made donations to the monasteries of Vatopedi and St Paul. His case reveals that a prominent monk could defend his worldly interests from the safety of Mount Athos, now that he had become one of the Ottoman sultan's non-Muslim subjects (*dhimmîs*).

Apparently Radić was able to transfer his liquid assets to Mount Athos. Some idea of their size and composition emerges from the details of a lawsuit, which he brought against the brothers Yakub and Dimitri Yeremiaoğulları. They had deposited with him the huge sum of 35,000 silver coins and 6,000 golden coins, together with several objects of gold and silver. In due course, he restored these to the brothers, who allegedly extorted a further 1000 florins from him, which is why he went to the Ottoman courts. Radić was using the safety of Athos as a cover for his banking activities. The monastery of Kastamonitou was well defended and furthermore came under the protection of the Ottoman sultan.[29] It made a good depository for very substantial sums of money.

Thanks to his retreat to Mount Athos Radić was able to preserve his large fortune. It was the ideal place from which to cultivate high-ranking acquaintances among the Ottomans, such as the military commander-in-chief (*beğlerbeği*) of Rumelia Şihabeddin Paşa, whom he contacted to protect his interests at Novo Brdo, where he had a house and silver-mines. Şihabeddin Paşa was the commander of the Ottoman armies which conquered Novo Brdo in 1441. Radić argued that, since he himself was by virtue of his residence on Mount Athos a non-Muslim subject of the sultan, neither his property nor his revenues from his silver-mines should be affected by the Ottoman conquest. The paşa gave him assurances about his revenues and promised to bring the case of his house property before the *divan*. The presence of individuals such as Radić helps to explain why idiorrhythmic monasticism, which permitted the monks to possess personal property, prospered at the expense of the cenobitic way of life on Mount Athos during the last centuries of Byzantium and under the Ottomans.

Another case sheds light on the banking activities of the Athonite monasteries. It concerns Maria-Helena, daughter of the last Serbian Despot Lazar Branković. She was the granddaughter of Thomas Palaiologos, despot of the

---

29 Oikonomides, 'Patronage in Palaiologan Mt Athos', 107. Cf. Laiou, 'Economic activities of Vatopedi in the fourteenth century', 61–5.

Morea, and the widow of the last king of Bosnia, Stefan Tomasević, who was executed by the Ottomans after the conquest of his country in 1463. Maria-Helena was then only seventeen years old. She finally settled in the Ottoman territories with her two paternal aunts, Mara Branković, the widow of Sultan Murad II, and Katerina Kantakouzena, the countess of Cilli. When they died, Maria-Helena inherited their fortune, which, however, was difficult to trace because of the bequests they had made to various monasteries of Mount Athos, with which Mara maintained particularly good relations. To recover what she considered rightfully hers Maria-Helena went before an Islamic tribunal accusing the monks of Xeropotamou of holding the sum of 30,000 golden coins, which had allegedly been taken for safekeeping from the countess of Cilli by the latter's trusted servant Anastas, who became a monk of Xeropotamou. Maria-Helena accused the monks of holding on to the money after Anastas's death, even though it should have gone to her. She proved completely unable to substantiate her accusation.[30] Nevertheless, the incident shows what extraordinarily large sums of money were to be found in one Athonite monastery. Well before the middle of the sixteenth century it was common knowledge that they functioned as deposit banks. In 1545 Sultan Süleyman dismissed the *voevoda* of Wallachia Radul, but rumours were soon circulating that the latter had sent a huge treasure to Mount Athos. The sultan immediately sent orders to the *sancak-beğ* and the *kadi* of Thessalonike instructing them to find it and return it to the treasury.[31]

Under the Ottomans the monasteries of Mount Athos were able to increase their landed property thanks to continuing donations from the faithful. They exchanged their agricultural surpluses for cash within the framework of the institution of *adelphata* and functioned as places of deposit. Another side to their business activities was an active interest in shipping. This is reflected in old engravings of the monasteries of Mount Athos, which often depict their ships approaching the monastic dockyard – a feature of some monasteries.[32] In the Byzantine period several monasteries possessed commercial vessels, which were actually engaged in selling off their surplus agricultural produce, but were nominally used to bring foodstuffs for the monks, which justified the

---

30 V. Demetriades and E. A. Zachariadou, 'Serbian ladies and Athonite monks', *Wiener Zeitschrift für die Kunde des Morgenlandes* 84 (1994), 35–55.

31 M. Berindei and G. Veinstein, *L'Empire ottoman et les pays roumains, 1544–1545* (Paris: Éditions de l'École des hautes études en sciences sociales; and Cambridge, MA: Harvard Ukrainian Research Institute, 1987), 181–2, 183.

32 P. Mylonas, *Athos and its monastic institutions through old engravings and other works of art* (Athens: National Academy of Fine Arts, 1963), 32, 46, 172.

grant of fiscal exemptions on the part of the Byzantine emperors.[33] Included in the *Proskynetarion* of the monastery of Docheiariou is a miracle story, which probably goes back to the eleventh century.[34] It reveals the lengths to which the monks would go in order to present trade as an occupation blessed by God. According to the story, a boat of Docheiariou loaded with cereals produced on their estates was on a return journey to Mount Athos when violent winds drove it to Carthage in north Africa, which was suffering a devastating famine. The monks sold off some of their freight and exchanged the remainder for spices. On the way back contrary winds brought them to Constantinople, where they sold the spices and bought bread, which another miracle ensured was still warm when it reached the monastery. Under the Ottomans it was no longer necessary to invent stories of this kind, because the monasteries were quite open about the trade carried on in their ships, for which they received partial exemption from the payment of customs duties.[35]

The maritime and commercial activities of the Athonite monasteries had been important since the Byzantine period. Possession of commercial vessels presented their owners with practical problems, such as the need for safe harbours to take on water or to shelter from storms. Already in the tenth century the Great Lavra had taken the precaution of obtaining the grant of two strategically located islands from the Byzantine emperors of the day: St Eustratios near Lemnos and Gymnopelagesion or Kaloyeros near Euboea.

Under the Ottomans the monasteries of Athos seem to have become more interested in river traffic, which is perhaps a reflection of the development of their Balkan interests. As early as the middle of the fourteenth century, at a time when the Turks were devastating Macedonia with their raids, the Great Lavra had boats plying the River Strymon.[36] This must be yet another indication of friendly relations with the Ottomans, because without their compliance trade along the Strymon would not have been possible.

Radić, the Serbian benefactor of the monastery of Kastamonitou, endowed it with a boat, which worked the River Morava in Serbia. It was the

---

33 G. Pitsakis, 'Un cas particulier d'activité commerciale dans la Méditerranée byzantine: les monastères armateurs', *Méditerranées* 32 (2002), 63–87; M. Nystazopoulou-Pelekidou, 'Les couvents de l'espace égéen et leur activité maritime (Xe–XIIIe s.)', *Σύμμεικτα* 15 (2002), 109–30; C. Smyrlis, 'The management of the monastic estates: the evidence of the typika', *DOP* 56 (2002), 254.

34 N. Oikonomides, *Actes de Docheiariou* [AA 13] (Paris: P. Lethielleux, 1984), 14.

35 The monastery of St John the Theologian on the island of Patmos is the monastery with the best-documented maritime activity under the Ottomans: E. A. Zachariadou, 'Monks and sailors under the Ottoman sultans', *Oriente Moderno* 20 (2001), 143–7.

36 G. Makris, *Studien zur spätbyzantinischen Schiffart* (Genoa: Istituto di Medievistica, 1988), 233.

indispensable accompaniment of the share in a near-by silver-mine which he also donated to the monastery.[37] It seems unlikely, but not impossible, that the boat made the long journey along the Danube and into the Black Sea and eventually via the Straits to Mount Athos. It is, after all, difficult to imagine that the monks would have hoarded much of the raw silver produced by their Serbian mine in the monastery's vaults. Their boat is much more likely to have been trading somewhere closer to hand. We know that Venetians obtained Balkan silver from Dubrovnik,[38] while Belgrade was another outlet. The Athonite monasteries apparently preferred to deal with the Turks.

Although deeply anti-Latin, Mount Athos managed to obtain some protection from the representatives of the papacy in the Aegean waters, the Knights Hospitallers of Rhodes. Added to the earliest known licence issued by the Master of the Rhodian Hospital for *corso* against the boats of the infidel Turks and their subjects was the stipulation that an exception should be made for those of the Orthodox monks of *Mons Sanctus*.[39]

The economic development of Mount Athos and the concomitant increase of its prestige was reflected in the new programmes of decoration that several Athonite monasteries undertook in the mid-years of the sixteenth century. From 1535 onwards and during the next thirty years, wall painting flourished, with several painters invited to decorate churches, chapels and refectories with frescos. The Cretan Theophanes Strelitzas and his two sons painted excellent frescos in the church and the refectory of Lavra (1535) and also in those of the newly founded monastery of Stavroniketa (1546); another Cretan painter, *Kyr* Tzortzis, decorated with frescos the church of Dionysiou; the *katholikon* of Xenophon was also painted (1544); a painter from Thebes, Frangos Katelanos, left beautiful frescos on the walls of a chapel of Lavra (1560).[40]

This came to an abrupt end in 1568–69 when Sultan Selim II confiscated the landed properties of all the monasteries situated in his empire, including, of course, those of Mount Athos. The sultan was following the advice of Ebu's-su'ud, who since 1545 had occupied the highest post in the legal hierarchy of his empire, namely that of *sheikhu'l-islam*. This personage, who held office for more than sixty years under four sultans beginning as a very young man with Bayezid II (1481–1512), is considered one of the greatest Ottoman jurists. He

---

37 N. Oikonomides, *Actes de Kastamonitou* [AA 9] (Paris: P. Lethielleux, 1978), 6.
38 D. Kovacevic, 'Dans la Serbie et la Bosnie médiévales: les mines d'or et d'argent', *Annales (E.S.C.)* 15 (1960), 248–58.
39 A. Luttrell, 'The earliest documents on the Hospitaller *corso* at Rhodes: 1413 and 1416', *Mediterranean Historical Review* 10 (1995), 177–88.
40 M. Chatzidakis, Θησαυροί τοῦ Ἁγίου Ὄρους (Thessalonike: Politistike Proteuousa tes Europes, 1997), 24–5, 36.

made serious efforts to systematise and reformulate the Ottoman legislation in greater conformity with the Islamic tradition. His efforts were mainly concentrated in the reign of Selim II's father, Süleyman the Lawgiver (1520–66), when the empire was in its prime and required a clear solution to pressing legal problems.[41] Some of these related to the life of the non-Muslim subjects of the sultan and Ebu's-su'ud pointed out that Christian monasteries had no legal right to their estates because rural land belonged to the ruler and, as such, it should not be exploited for the benefit of churches and monasteries. Selim II had his own reasons for applying the theological interpretations of his *sheikhu'l-islam*. By confiscating the monastic properties he could satisfy the budgetary demands being made by his administration. These came at a time when he was preparing an expedition against Venetian-held Cyprus, which necessitated additional financial resources.[42]

The confiscation was a severe blow to both monastic and ecclesiastical authorities. However, a loophole remained open to them. They were able to redeem their buildings, flocks and any other property that Islamic law deemed suitable for private ownership. The problem of landed property was more delicate because properly it belonged to the sultan; the monks were allowed to keep and exploit it, but on condition of paying a special tax together with various land taxes. They were also permitted to retain their other possessions, but on the understanding that they would use them for charitable purposes and for the support of the destitute and travellers.

As a partial justification of his confiscation of the Athonite estates Selim II adduced the subterfuges employed by the monks both to evade the payment of taxes and to increase their landed property at the expense of the peasantry. In other words, there was a degree of uncertainty about their title to some of their estates. Following the redemption of their estates the monks found themselves unsurprisingly involved in a series of property disputes. These became a major concern of the patriarch Jeremias II (1572–95), who sent the patriarch Sylvester of Alexandria to Mount Athos to restore order. On the basis of this mission he issued a *typikon* for the monasteries of Mount Athos in the form of a patriarchal *sigillion*. It amounted to a programme for the reform of monastic life on the Holy Mountain. It recommended that the leading monastery of the Great Lavra return to the cenobitic life. The patriarch hoped

---

41 On Ebu's-su'ud see C. Imber, *Ebu's-su'ud: the Islamic legal tradition* (Edinburgh: Edinburgh University Press, 1997), 8–20, 159–62.

42 J. C. Alexander (Alexandropoulos), 'The Lord giveth and the Lord taketh away: Athos and the confiscation affair of 1568–1569', in *Mount Athos in the 14th–16th centuries*, 149–200. Cf. A. Fotic, 'The official explanation for the confiscation and sale of the monasteries (churches) and their estates at the time of Selim II', *Turcica* 26 (1994), 33–54.

that other houses would follow its example. The patriarch's initiative had only limited success.[43]

Selim II's confiscation of the Athonite estates marks a watershed in the history of the Holy Mountain. It brought to an end the prosperity and prestige that it had enjoyed for more than two centuries. There were to be no more major foundations after Stavroniketa in 1541. Thereafter the monks of Mount Athos owed much to the generosity of the Orthodox *voevody* of Moldavia and Wallachia, who had supplied most of the money needed to redeem the properties of the monasteries from the Ottoman state. Another important patron of the Holy Mountain was the tsar of Moscow. Closer cultural relations developed in the early sixteenth century, which intensified with the establishment of the Russian patriarchate in 1589.[44] This support from Orthodox rulers represented an enduring legacy of the 'Byzantine Commonwealth', of which Mount Athos had been so vital a focus.

---

43 J. P. Mamalakes, Τὸ Ἅγιον Ὄρος (Ἄθως) διὰ μέσου τῶν αἰώνων [Μακεδονικὴ Βιβλιοθήκη 33] (Thessalonike: Hetaireia Makedonikon Spoudon, 1971), 254–5.

44 I. Smolitsch, 'Le Mont Athos et la Russie', *Le Millénaire du Mont Athos*, I, 285–8. Cf. O. Alexandropoulou, Ὁ Διονύσιος Ἰβηρίτης καὶ τὸ ἔργο του Ἱστορία τῆς Ρωσίας (Heraklion: Bikelaia Demotike Bibliotheke, 1994).

7

The Great Church in captivity 1453–1586

ELIZABETH A. ZACHARIADOU

According to Byzantine juridical thought the state had two poles:[1] the emperor (*basileus*) and the patriarch, the former exercising political power (*potestas*) and the latter ecclesiastical authority (*auctoritas*). The capture of Constantinople on 29 May 1453 by the Ottomans meant the end of the Byzantine state. But if the Byzantine emperor was no more, the ecumenical patriarchate survived, though only because the religion of the conqueror permitted its existence.

Byzantium had existed under the shadow of the Ottomans for more than half a century before its final fall. This produced a series of problems for the ecumenical patriarch, now that the majority of the metropolitan and episcopal sees in Thrace and the southern Balkans, which constituted the core of the patriarchate of Constantinople, came under Turkish domination, leaving Constantinople as an island in the middle of Ottoman territories. Nevertheless, representatives of the Greek Orthodox Church were present and active in these territories. This situation had its roots in the aftermath of the battle of Mantzikert (1071), when much of Asia Minor passed under the control of the Seljuq Turks. By the end of the fourteenth century the Seljuqs were a distant memory and the dominant Anatolian power was now the Ottomans, who had already conquered Thrace and much of the Balkans. Both Seljuqs and Ottomans applied the principles of the Koran, which recognises the Peoples of the Book, that is, the Jews and the Christians.[2] The Orthodox Church survived under the Seljuq sultans with metropolitans and bishops established in several Anatolian towns. The Ottoman sultans equally took Orthodox communities under their protection, well aware that this increased

---

1 J. and P. Zepos, *Jus Graecoromanum* (Athens, 1931), I, 242: τὰ μέγιστα καὶ ἀναγκαιότατα μέρη.
2 E. A. Zachariadou, Δέκα τουρκικὰ ἔγγραφα γιὰ τὴ Μεγάλη Ἐκκλησία *(1483–1567)* [Sources 2] (Athens: Institute for Byzantine Research, 1966), 51–61.

their prestige in Christian circles. It was characteristic of their policy that, in those cases where they acquired former Byzantine territories, which had passed under Latin rule, one of their first actions was to re-establish the Orthodox ecclesiastical authorities. In similar fashion the sultans provided protection for monasteries and granted tax exemptions to monastic and ecclesiastical landed property. In some cases they guaranteed revenues to metropolitans and bishops through the grant of *timars*.[3] The patriarch of Constantinople together with the holy synod nominated metropolitans and bishops in the various towns of Asia Minor and the Balkans; but the latter were then obliged to obtain permission from the sultan before settling among their flock.[4] If not quite collaboration, this meant recognition of Ottoman authority by the Greek clergy. With the final fall of Constantinople the Orthodox Church acquired greater unity: not only was it officially recognised by the sultan; it was also administratively under the same political regime.

Constantinople was a city that carried symbolic meaning for both the Christian and the Muslim world. When Mehmed II entered it as a conqueror and declared that it was now the capital of his empire, he was realising an old Muslim dream. However, the city was devoid of inhabitants, because the victorious troops had enslaved its population. The sultan immediately took measures for its repopulation and the restoration of its buildings.[5] It needed a number of years before this decision took concrete shape. In the meantime, Adrianople remained the effective capital. The conqueror did not move his palace and the administration of the empire from the old to the new capital until 1460 at the earliest. By way of contrast, he had appointed Gennadios Scholarios[6] to the vacant patriarchal throne as early as January 1454. Since the other religious communities of Constantinople, the Jewish and the Armenian, were not officially organised until several years later,[7] it immediately becomes apparent that the restoration of the patriarchate was a priority for the sultan.

3 H. Inalcik, *Fatih devri üzerinde tetkikler ve vesikalar* (Ankara: Türk Tarih Kurumu XI, 1954), I, 151, 159. Cf. H. Inalcik, 'Ottoman archival materials on millets', in *Christians and Jews in the Ottoman empire*, ed. B. Braude and B. Lewis (London and New York: Holmes and Meier, 1982), I, 448–9.
4 Zachariadou, Δέκα τουρκικά ἔγγραφα, 149.
5 H. Inalcik, 'The policy of Mehmed II toward the Greek population of Istanbul and the Byzantine buildings of the city', *DOP* 23/24 (1969), 231–49.
6 C. J. G. Turner, 'The carrier of George-Gennadius Scholarius', *B* 39 (1969), 420–55; M. Cacouros, 'Un patriarche à Rome, un *katholikos didaskalos* au patriarcat et deux donations tardives de reliques du seigneur: Grégoire III Mamas et Georges Scholarios, le synode et la synaxis', in *Βυζάντιο: κράτος καὶ κοινωνία*, ed. A. Avramea, A. Laiou and E. Chrysos (Athens: Institute for Byzantine Studies, 2003), 106–22.
7 B. Braude, 'Foundation myths in the millet system', in *Christians and Jews*, I, 69–88.

The three eastern patriarchates of Alexandria, Antioch and Jerusalem, which had been under Islamic rule since the seventh century, provided the necessary precedents that allowed the conqueror to take decisions according to the principles of his religion.[8] But sheer expediency also played its part in the restoration of the patriarchate. The sultan reckoned correctly that the presence in Constantinople of the ecumenical patriarch would encourage Greek settlement.[9] Mehmed was well aware that his new capital needed inhabitants with experience of urban life and that he would find them among the Greek population. To this end he made repeated use of the well-tried Ottoman measure of compulsory resettlement (sürgün). Most of the immigrants came from Greek localities, such as Phokaia, Athens, Argos or Lesbos.[10] Mehmed II also saw the appointment of a patriarch with strong anti-Latin feelings, such as Gennadios, as a way of ingratiating himself with his Orthodox subjects.

The circumstances of Gennadios's appointment to the ecumenical throne remain unclear for two reasons. In the first place, fact was soon distorted by a mythology which aimed at showing that even the unbelievers had unlimited respect for the Orthodox faith; in the second, there is just so little contemporary evidence. Only three contemporaries, Kritoboulos, a Greek notable from Imbros, who wrote a biography of Mehmed II, the ecclesiastical official Theodoros Agallianos,[11] and Gennadios himself, have left any information about this important event, but even they failed to go into details. They described the restoration of the patriarchate as a quite unexpected event, which they attributed to the sultan's magnanimity, philanthropy and good will, while stressing his respect for the office and the person of the patriarch. All three belonged to the anti-unionist milieu and, consciously or unconsciously, wished to contrast the sultan's generous attitude towards Orthodoxy with Roman Catholic condescension. Since they also wished to influence Greek opinion in favour of the sultan, they chose to ignore the fact that his decisions conformed in large measure to Islamic political tradition.[12]

---

8 C. E. Bosworth, 'Christians and Jewish religious dignitaries in Mamlûk Egypt and Syria: Qalqashandi's information on their hierarchy, titulature and appointment', *International Journal of Middle East Studies* 3 (1972), 66–74, 199–216.

9 Zachariadou, Δέκα τουρκικὰ ἔγγραφα, 59–60.

10 Inalcik, 'Policy of Mehmed II', 235; H. Inalcik, 'Istanbul', in *Encyclopaedia of Islam*, second edition (Leiden: Brill, 1978), IV, 224–7.

11 C. G. Patrineles, Ὁ Θεόδωρος Ἀγαλλιανὸς ταυτιζόμενος πρὸς τὸν Θεοφάνην Μηδείας καὶ οἱ ἀνέκδοτοι λόγοι του (Athens: Academy of Athens, 1966).

12 Zachariadou, Δέκα τουρκικὰ ἔγγραφα, 41–2.

When describing the restoration of the patriarchate the sixteenth-century sources fall back on 'foundation myths', which were then reproduced by later sources. These were composed in order to extol the sultan's deep respect for the patriarchal institution and his affection for Gennadios personally. The historical context in which these traditions place Gennadios's appointment to the patriarchate is imaginary. They report that the event took place immediately after the capture of Constantinople, but Gennadios was then marching together with many other prisoners from Constantinople towards Adrianople, as he himself testifies. A further embellishment has the appointment taking place in the sultan's palace, after which several courtiers escorted the patriarch back to his residence. The 'myth' insisted that the whole procedure accorded with the old religious tradition which dictated that first the holy synod elect the patriarch and then the monarch accept and confirm its decision, but contemporary evidence shows that it happened exactly the other way round: the sultan appointed Gennadios as patriarch and then synod accepted and confirmed his will.[13]

Gennadios endured several months' captivity in the Ottoman capital of Adrianople before the intervention of rich and influential Byzantines employed in the palace or the Ottoman financial administration secured his release. If they were not personally acquainted with Gennadios, they had certainly heard about him, as he was the leader of the anti-unionist party in Constantinople. Among these personages were Demetrios Apokaukos and Thomas Katavolenos, secretaries to the sultan, both of whom had also served as his envoys to foreign states. It seems more than probable that it was they who suggested to the sultan that Gennadios might be the right person to fill the vacant patriarchal see.[14]

As was the rule with all appointees, whether entrusted with a religious, military or administrative post, Gennadios will have received from the sultan a special document, called a *berat*,[15] which set out his duties and prerogatives. The *berat* given to Gennadios has not been preserved; the earliest surviving patriarchal *berats* date to the years 1483 and 1525.[16] These nevertheless provide

---

13 Braude, 'Foundation myths in the millet system', 77–9. On the sources, see Zachariadou, Δέκα τουρκικὰ ἔγγραφα, 42–7.
14 Patrineles, Θεόδωρος Ἀγαλλιανός, 72–8.
15 H. Inalcik, 'The status of the Greek Orthodox Patriarch under the Ottomans', *Turcica*: (*Mélanges offerts à Irène Mélikoff par ses collègues, disciples et amis*), 21–23 (1991), 415–18. Cf. Inalcik, 'Ottoman archival materials on millets', I, 447; P. Konortas, Ὀθωμανικὲς θεωρήσεις γιὰ τὸ Οἰκουμενικὸ Πατριαρχεῖο, 1705-ἀρχὲς 20ου αἰώνα (Athens: Alexandreia, 1998), 53–5.
16 Zachariadou, Δέκα τουρκικὰ ἔγγραφα, 157–62, 174–8.

some guide to the contents of Gennadios's *berat*, as long as we keep in mind that they were issued in a period of relative stability, while Gennadios's appointment was made in a confused period of transition, which involved the creation of a new Ottoman capital. They do not support the tradition that the *berat* issued to Gennadios was the result of negotiations and conferred extensive privileges on the ecumenical patriarchate and the Greek Orthodox Church.[17] They suggest instead that any privileges were granted not to the ecumenical patriarchate but to the patriarch in person, for the Islamic law did not recognise a 'juristic person' at that time.[18] Nor did it acknowledge the Orthodox Church, as such, but identified it with the Greek community, or *millet*, as it came to be known by the nineteenth century.[19]

The patriarch's privileges comprised authority over the religious hierarchy as well as the management of ecclesiastical and monastic property; the application of Roman family law to the Greek Orthodox flock with respect to matrimony, divorce and inheritance; the right to collect taxes from among the Greek Orthodox population, about which more will be said; and, finally, some exemption from taxes. The last concession formed part of the general measures taken by the sultan to encourage the repopulation of his capital.[20]

Gennadios's reorganisation of the patriarchate was part of the transformation of the derelict Byzantine city into Ottoman Istanbul. The patriarch had to confront a series of problems created by new social and political conditions. The most mundane, but unquestionably important, was the question of security. Gennadios was unable to retain the glorious church of the Holy Apostles, which the sultan had originally granted him as the new seat of the patriarchate, because of the crime-infested character of its neighbourhood, which had been left deserted after the fall of the City. In its place the patriarch obtained the church of the Pammakaristos. This was in a safer neighbourhood, one already being repopulated by Greeks.[21]

If not re-established immediately after the fall of the Byzantine capital, as tradition has it, the patriarchal synod was reconstituted soon after Gennadios's appointment to the patriarchal see.[22] It continued to comprise, as it had in

---

17 Braude, 'Foundation myths in the millet system', 79.
18 A. Cohen, 'Communal legal entities', *Islamic Law and Society* 3 (1996), 75–90.
19 The term used in the fifteenth and sixteenth centuries was *taife*.
20 Inalcik, 'Policy of Mehmed II', 241–5.
21 *Ecthesis Chronica et Chronicon Athenarum*, ed. S. Lambros (London: Methuen, 1902), 19.
22 T. H. Papadopoullos, *Studies and documents relating to the history of the Greek church and people under Turkish domination* [Bibliotheca graeca aevi posterioris 1] (Brussels: s.n., 1952; second revised edition Aldershot: Variorum, 1990), 39–60; Konortas, Ὀθωμανικές θεωρήσεις, 124–5, 141–3.

the Byzantine epoch, the chief officers of the patriarchal administration and those metropolitans either residing within easy reach of the capital or visiting it for other reasons. With the help of this body Gennadios tried to solve the problems resulting from the sufferings of his flock. Thanks to the sultan's measures Constantinople acquired a considerable population of Greek Orthodox inhabitants who, however, formed an amorphous and unconnected society. Those who were forcibly transferred from various Greek territories to the capital settled together, forming neighbourhoods with some cohesion.[23] It was different, however, for the old Constantinopolitans who returned to their city in increasing numbers after 1459–60, when the sultan issued an order commanding those who had not returned to return immediately irrespective of whether they had left Constantinople before or after the fall of the City.[24] The sultan gave houses to those who returned but these were not their old houses, which in the meantime had been occupied either by Turks, by other Greeks, or by people of other ethnic origin. The situation was made more complicated by the return of other Constantinopolitans, who had been able by various means to ransom themselves. It was a long-drawn-out process, with individuals arriving separately rather than as part of a family group, since families tended to break up with different family members going to different masters and different places. This caused severe disruption to family life. Assuming that their spouses had not survived, many men and women married again, but, where their assumptions proved wrong, they found themselves accused of bigamy.[25]

Gennadios and his immediate successors confronted the problems caused by such marriages with human understanding and tolerance, using the legal principle «κατ᾽ οἰκονομίαν».[26] Apart from the social confusion, the Christian faith itself seemed to be in danger, as there were frequent conversions to Islam, which would only have increased in numbers if the church had rigorously enforced marriage law.

The difficulties encountered over marriages were only symptomatic of deeper tensions within the patriarchal administration. These were the stuff

23 S. Yerasimos, "Ἕλληνες τῆς Κωνσταντινούπολης στὰ μέσα τοῦ ιϛ´ αἰώνα᾽, Ἡ καθ᾽ἡμᾶς Ἀνατολή 2 (1994), 117–38.

24 Elizabeth A. Zachariadou, ʻConstantinople se repeupleʼ, in Ἡ ἅλωση τῆς Κωνσταντινούπολης καὶ ἡ μετάβαση ἀπὸ τοὺς μεσαιωνικοὺς στοὺς νεώτερους χρόνους (Heraklion: Panepistimiakes Ekdoseis Kretes, 2005), 47–59.

25 Patrineles, Θεόδωρος Ἀγαλλιανός, 133–9, 145–6.

26 G. Dagron, ʻLa règle et l᾽exception: analyse de la notion d᾽économieʼ, in Religiöse Devianz, ed. D. Simon (Frankfurt am Main: Vittorio Klostermann, 1990), 1–18.

of Theodore Agallianos's autobiographical writings, which provide a vivid insight into ecclesiastical politics under Gennadios. Agallianos had long been a confidant of the new patriarch, who promoted him to the important position of grand *chartophylax*. Among other things this post gave him responsibility for the supervision of the marriages of the Orthodox community. It was also one of the most lucrative in the patriarch's gift. Agallianos soon found himself under attack from other members of the patriarchal administration, who had support from leading members of the Greek community with access to the sultan's palace. Unable to master the situation Gennadios preferred to resign in 1456. This set a pattern, which persisted into the nineteenth century, of resignation followed by reinstatement. Gennadios himself resigned on three separate occasions, in 1456, 1463 and 1465.[27] Behind this pattern lay competition for office and for the benefits of office between competing groups of patriarchal officials, who had a vested interest in promoting their candidate to the patriarchal office.

The situation took a turn for the worse in the 1470s, when the patriarch incurred financial obligations towards the Ottoman state. The contradictions of the contemporary sources make it difficult to establish when and how these originated. It is clear, however, that, as part of the measures taken by Mehmed II for the repopulation of Constantinople, Gennadios and his immediate successors were exempt from any kind of taxation. But once Constantinople began to fill up, these exemptions were gradually modified and around 1471–72 abolished.[28]

These years roughly coincide with the first mention of taxes paid by the patriarch to the sultan's treasury, but it remains unclear exactly which patriarch was responsible. The initiative seems not to have come from the sultan. It is much more likely that it was first proposed by one of the parties jockeying for position around the patriarchal throne. Amid the welter of accusation and counter-accusation the most plausible conclusion is that the culprits came from the Trapezuntine community, which, established in Constantinople after the fall of their empire in 1461, wished to promote their own candidate, Symeon. According to an anonymous chronicler the Trapezuntines offered Mehmed II 1000 florins to dismiss Markos Xylokarabes, patriarch since 1466, and replace him by Symeon. The situation prompted the intervention of the Serbian princess Mara Branković, the sultan's stepmother and widow of Murad II, who also

27 V. Laurent, 'Les premiers patriarches de Constantinople sous domination turque', *REB* 26 (1968), 243–5, 249–50, 251–2.
28 Inalcik, 'Policy of Mehmed II', 242–5.

had her own candidate, the metropolitan of Philippoupolis, Dionysios. She appeared in person before the sultan and offered 2000 florins, thus persuading him to dismiss Symeon and replace him by Dionysios, who remained patriarch for four years, before being once again replaced by Symeon. This sum of 2000 florins became an annual tribute paid by the patriarch to the sultan for many decades to come. It is the sum stipulated in the *berat* granted to Symeon in 1483, when he ascended the patriarchal throne for the third time. By the accession of Patriarch Jeremias I (1522–46) it had risen to 3500 florins.[29] It was called *maktu* or lump sum, in the Ottoman documents, while the Greeks referred to it by the general term *kharadj*. Contemporaries make clear that the increasing rate at which it was levied was the result of higher bids made for the patriarchal throne by interested parties. Around 1500 a new Greek term, ἐπανέβασις, was coined for this bidding process.[30]

Apart from the annual tribute, the patriarchs started to present the sultans with a *pişkeş*, that is, a customary present given by anyone receiving a *berat* from the sultan: in the case of the patriarch, it amounted to 500 florins. This tax also had its origins in the 1470s. It was normally paid once – on ascent to the patriarchal throne – but if a new sultan succeeded to the throne, it had to be paid again, as the patriarch needed a new *berat*. Metropolitans and bishops, when appointed, also gave a *pişkeş*, with the amount varying according to the importance of their see.[31]

The financial obligations of the patriarchs towards the Ottoman state did much to damage their good reputation, as did the interference in ecclesiastical affairs of the *archontes*, as they were called. These were influential members of the Orthodox community. We have already seen how in the aftermath of the fall of the City *archontes* from Adrianople had a part to play in the restoration of the patriarchate. Once the patriarchate had been re-established in Constantinople and had developed into a minor centre of power within the framework of the Ottoman state, it increasingly attracted prominent Greeks. This was partly for reasons of social prestige, but management of the patriarchal revenues offered more tangible rewards. Demetrios Apokaukos, Mehmed II's Greek secretary, moved from Adrianople to Constantinople to undertake the financial administration of the patriarchal church on behalf

29 Zachariadou, Δέκα τουρκικά ἔγγραφα, 157, 159, 175–6.
30 *Historia politica et patriarchica Constantinopoleos*, ed. I. Bekker (Bonn: Ed. Weber, 1849), 136; Konortas, Ὀθωμανικὲς θεωρήσεις, 345–6.
31 *Ecthesis Chronica et Chronicon Athenarum*, 28–9; cf. Zachariadou, Δέκα τουρκικά ἔγγραφα, 82–9.

of the patriarch Dionysios I. The patriarch was beholden to Apokaukos, because the latter had arranged his redemption from slavery in the aftermath of the fall of the City. Contemporaries were confident that, while Dionysios was patriarch, the patriarchal finances would remain in Apokaukos's hands.[32]

Archontes, like Apokaukos, usually had connections with the Ottoman financial administration. They disposed of important capital assets and might be involved in tax farming and state monopolies, such as customs and salt production. They often had relatives, who having converted to Islam obtained high position in the Ottoman state. The *archontes* were therefore able to mediate on behalf of the Greek Orthodox clergy; sometimes with beneficial results. However, this role allowed them to intervene directly in the activities and business of the patriarchate, to the extent that they were able to participate unofficially in meetings of synod. When the patriarchs began to pay an annual tribute to the sultan, they became more and more dependent upon these notables, who could lend them money, but could also, as a *quid pro quo*, exercise pressure upon them in order to promote their own interests, which were often incompatible with the ideals of the church. The patriarchate owed 7000 florins to Mara Branković, whom we have already seen offering 2000 florins to the sultan in the hope of securing the elevation of her candidate to the patriarchal throne.[33] As the years passed and the taxes claimed by the Ottoman state increased, so the influence of the *archontes* grew to the detriment of the standing and prestige of the patriarchate.[34]

On the positive side these *archontes* remained attached to the traditions of Orthodoxy and contributed to the survival of Greek culture. They offered support to scholars and teachers; they maintained Greek schools and founded churches. Some of them were well educated. Their taste is reflected in the Greek manuscripts preserved at Topkapı, which are dated to the reign of Mehmed II. Though rather later, the case of the notorious Greek banker and businessman Michael Kantakouzenos is instructive. Despite his nickname – *Şeitanoğlu* (the Devil's son) – he was deeply involved in the affairs of the patriarchate. After his execution in 1575 on the orders of Sultan Murad III he left behind a remarkable collection of classical and theological manuscripts.[35]

---

32 E. A. Zachariadou, 'Les notables laïques et le patriarcat oecuménique après la chute de Constantinople', *Turcica* 30 (1998), 132.
33 Laurent, 'Premiers patriarches', 234, 256–7.
34 Zachariadou, 'Notables laïques', 119–34.
35 J. Raby, 'Mehmed the Conqueror's Greek scriptorium', *DOP* 37 (1983), 15–34; Zachariadou, 'Notables laïques', 124, 127–8.

This continuing stress on Greek culture explains why most of the fifteenth- and sixteenth-century patriarchs came from Greek-speaking territories, most often from Constantinople, the Peloponnese or Trebizond. One can also understand the odd case of the Serbian Patriarch Raphael I (1475–76), who managed to obtain the patriarchal throne without the support of the Greek community. Contemporaries were at pains to stress his ethnic origin, labelling him as Serbian, Bulgarian, Scythian or just plain 'barbarian'. They condemned him both for his drunkenness and for his lack of Greek, which meant that he had to use an interpreter. Without any support from the Greek *archontes* Raphael found it impossible to pay the sultan his annual tribute and was thrown into prison. It was a cautionary tale, which showed that far from being ecumenical the patriarchate was decidedly Greek: an outcome due in large measure to the influence of the *archontes*.[36]

According to the *berat*, which the patriarch received from the sultan, the former's authority extended over all the Orthodox inhabitants of the territories subject to the ecumenical patriarchate before 1453. It goes without saying that also included were all members of the ecclesiastical and monastic hierarchy, the structure of which survived unchanged, that is, metropolitans, archbishops and bishops, patriarchal and episcopal dignitaries and functionaries, and priests, together with abbots of monasteries, monks and nuns. The metropolitans, archbishops and bishops chosen by the patriarch and synod constituted the religious authorities recognised by the Ottomans and when appointed were in receipt of *berats*. The Ottoman administration ignored the lower clergy, the *papades*, who were dependent on the metropolitans and bishops, from whom they farmed their parish church; some priests, who possessed larger capital, were able to take on more than one parish church. The profession of priest was quite often hereditary under Ottoman domination.[37] Metropolitans, bishops and parish priests constituted the traditional network of ecclesiastical administration. There were, in addition, the patriarchal exarchs, who were directly appointed by the patriarch to administer certain villages, islands or small towns, which lay scattered within the jurisdiction of the ecumenical patriarchate and came under the patriarch's

36 Zachariadou, 'Notables laïques', 130–1.Cf. S. Runciman, *The Great Church in captivity: a study of the patriarchate of Constantinople from the eve of the Turkish conquest to the Greek War of Independence* (Cambridge: Cambridge University Press, 1968), 409.

37 P. Odorico (with S. Asdrachas, T. Karanastassis, K. Kostis and S. Petmézas), *Conseils et mémoires de Synadinos prêtre de Serrès en Macédoine (XVIIe siècle)* (Paris: Association Pierre Belon, 1996), 86–8, 90, 528–9.

direct administration. The office of exarch was already in existence during the Byzantine period, but became more prominent from the sixteenth century onwards.[38]

During the Byzantine period the state provided a regular income for the clergy, including the lower clergy,[39] but under Ottoman domination their income derived directly from taxes paid by the faithful. The collection of these taxes was a privilege granted by the sultans, who apparently continued the Byzantine tax, known as the *kanonikon*, levied on the inhabitants, the priests and the monasteries of a region in order to cover the expenses of their metropolitan or their bishop. Under the Ottomans the mechanism of taxation was pyramid-shaped: at the base were the rank and file of churchgoers and at the summit there was the ecumenical patriarch. The revenue from these taxes went not only to support the clergy, but also to meet their financial obligations to the Ottoman state, that is, the *pişkeş* paid by metropolitans, bishops and the patriarch himself for their *berat*, together with the annual tribute due from the patriarch to the sultan. These obligations were repeatedly mentioned to the faithful to justify the collection of taxes and are also mentioned in the sultans' *berats*, where it was stressed that they were optional and that nobody should be forced to pay against their will. Nevertheless, all ecclesiastical taxes became regular and compulsory, while new ones were introduced, such as the *embatikion*, that is, a sum paid by a clergyman to his bishop when he was ordained, and the *philotimon*, which was a special present. In addition the church levied taxes on fairs.[40]

Sometimes the collection of patriarchal taxes provoked an adverse reaction on the part of metropolitans and bishops. In these cases the patriarch sought the intervention of the sultan, who provided the necessary support, as long as he considered the taxes legal. If the financial state of the patriarchate became too difficult, the patriarch organised special tours with the aim of collecting the taxes in person. On such occasions he had to obtain a special document from the sultan commanding the Ottoman authorities to help the patriarch collect in full any back payments as well as the taxes of the current year and to ignore any excuses made by the debtors. During such tours the patriarch

---

38 M. Païzi-Apostolopoulou, Ὁ θεσμὸς τῆς πατριαρχικῆς ἐξαρχίας, 1405–1905 αἰώνας (Athens: Centre of Neohellenic Studies, 1995), 51–66.
39 E. S. Papagianni, Τὰ οἰκονομικὰ τοῦ ἔγγαμου κλήρου στὸ Βυζάντιο (Athens: A. N. Sakkoulas, 1986), 78–128.
40 E. Herman, 'Das bischöfliche Abgabenwesen im Patriarchat von Konstantinopel von XI. bis zur Mitte des XIX. Jahrhunderts', OCP 5 (1939), 437–67, 489–99. Cf. Zachariadou, Δέκα τουρκικὰ ἔγγραφα, 99–101.

was accompanied and helped by *archontes*.[41] Furthermore, in order to tap new sources of revenue, the patriarchs began to organise more extensive tours to territories situated outside the borders of the Ottoman Empire, but containing an Orthodox population, such as the Danubian principalities.[42] The scattered pieces of information that have been preserved are unfortunately a quite inadequate guide to the exact sums received in taxes by the patriarch from the clergy. Furthermore, decisions taken by synod on these matters were often modified or rescinded, making it still more difficult to reach any conclusion with the remotest statistical validity.[43] It is only certain that the sums collected varied from place to place depending on the prosperity of the different sees.

Apart from taxation – regular and extraordinary – the patriarchs had other sources of revenue. By the terms of his *berat* the patriarch was responsible for supervising the management of the financial affairs of metropolitans, bishops, abbots and even priests, including such general activities as the fairs organised on the feast day of the dedicatee of the local church. Also within the patriarch's remit came the properties administered by the clergy, such as vineyards, mills, fields and gardens, and even holy springs (*hagiasmata*). The monasteries still possessed fairly important landed estates, sometimes in full property (*mülk*), but more often only in usage (*tasarruf*). In normal circumstances, the manager of a monastery's properties was the abbot, who, however, came under the patriarch's direct jurisdiction. Metropolitan and episcopal sees as well as parish churches also possessed landed properties. It seems that the patriarch received a tithe from their agricultural production. He might also inherit the property of priests and monks who died without leaving heirs or a will.[44] Another source of income for the patriarch and all clergymen came in the form of the presents which they received after the performance of a religious ceremony, such as a christening or a wedding.

Given that metropolitans and bishops relied for their revenue on the Greek Orthodox population of the Ottoman Empire, they could only be established

---

41 Inalcik, 'The status of the Greek Orthodox Patriarch under the Ottomans', 428–31. Cf. Zachariadou, Δέκα τουρκικά ἔγγραφα, 102–3.

42 P. Konortas, 'Les contributions ecclésiastiques: *patriarchikè zèteia* et *basilikon charatzion*, Contribution à l'histoire économique du patriarcat oecuménique aux XVe et XVIe siècles', *Actes du IIe Colloque international d'histoire, économies méditerranéennes: équilibres et intercommunications, XIIIe–XIXe siècles* (Athens: Centre of Neohellenic Studies, 1986), III, 219–55.

43 D. G. Apostolopoulos, Ὁ Ἱερὸς Κῶδιξ τοῦ Πατριαρχείου Κωνσταντινουπόλεως στο Β΄ μισὸ τοῦ ΙΕ΄ αἰώνα: τὰ μόνα γνωστὰ σπαράγματα (Athens: Centre of Neohellenic Studies, 1992), 157–8, 161–2, 167–8.

44 Zachariadou, Δέκα τουρκικά ἔγγραφα, 92–3, 105, 172.

in towns, where the Greek Orthodox community was large enough to bear the expenses of their see. In theory, the number of these sees was fairly high because the ecumenical patriarchate continued to use the titles of some unoccupied metropolitan sees for honorific purposes. To take just one example, in the sixteenth century the church of the Greek Orthodox community of Venice enjoyed the status and title of the metropolitan see of Philadelphia, which had long ceased to function. More trustworthy when it comes to enumerating ecclesiastical sees are the Ottoman documents because their main purpose was pre-eminently practical, namely the registration of the clergy's financial obligations. The oldest Ottoman document enumerating sees dates to the year 1483 and lists fifty-seven of them; in the next one (from the year 1525) their number has decreased to fifty. But only forty are recorded in a list of metropolitan and episcopal sees dating to the period 1641–51, which itemises the amount of *pişkeş* paid to the sultan's treasury.[45] This may give an exaggerated impression of decline, because of the greater use made at that time of the institution of patriarchal exarchs, who seem not to have paid *pişkeş* to the sultan. Even if the Ottoman documents are neither accurate nor complete, we should not ignore the decrease in the number of episcopal sees they record. At first sight, it would appear to indicate a significant fall in the Greek Orthodox population. If so, this occurred after the impressive demographic increase which took place in the Ottoman Empire between 1530 and 1580, but which was then followed by a general decline. This hit the Greek Orthodox population particularly hard, because it was reinforced by conversions to Islam, which were a consequence of the economic crisis at the end of the sixteenth century. It left Christians so impoverished that they were unable to pay the special taxes burdening non-Muslims. Mass conversion was one solution.[46]

The Orthodox clergy had few means to counter the material attractions of conversion to Islam, which offered exemption from the taxes paid by non-Muslims, promised liberation from the humiliations of *dhimmî* status, and opened up opportunities of achieving higher social rank; even the possibility of entering the ruling class. The Orthodox clergy could only insist in the face of these temptations that standing firm in the old faith was the sole guarantee of salvation; nor did they omit to back up this message by publicising that the

---

45 Inalcik, 'Ottoman archival materials on millets', I, 440–3; Zachariadou, Δέκα τουρκικὰ ἔγγραφα, 114–17.

46 H. Inalcik, 'Impact of the *Annales* school on Ottoman studies and new findings', *Review* I (1978), 73–90; H. Inalcik, 'Islam in the Ottoman Empire', *Cultura Turcica* 5–7 (1968–70), 28–9.

penalty for apostasy from Islam was death. A favourite motif of the Orthodox hagiography of the *Tourkokratia* was that of the Christian convert to Islam, who, repenting of his action and returning to his faith, suffers martyrdom at the hands of the Muslims. This was an old theme, which can be traced back to the early centuries of the Arab conquest, that is, when conversion was becoming a menace to the Orthodox Churches in the east. The *vita* of the Christian Arab 'Abd al-Masîh, who suffered martyrdom in 860 in Ramla of Palestine, is one very early example. Born a Christian, he had joined the Arab army and fought against the Byzantines; but later he regretted what he had done, confessed his sins to a priest, and took refuge first in the monastery of St Sabas outside Jerusalem and later in St Catherine's monastery on Mount Sinai, where he became abbot. His reversion to Christianity was eventually discovered and he was tortured and executed.[47] This pattern reappeared under Turkish rule, when once again there were increased numbers of conversions to Islam. The persons, the time and the place changed but the plot remained the same. One finds it in the *vita* of St Michael the Younger, composed in the early fourteenth century by the Byzantine aristocrat and scholar Theodore Metochites. Michael was captured as a young boy and taken to Egypt where he converted and joined the Mamluk army, only to return in a fit of remorse to Christianity, which led to martyrdom. The story of St Theodore the Younger is very similar, but reflects conditions during the Ottoman conquest of the southern Balkans, when the Turks were rounding up young Christian boys for military service. Still a child, Theodore was captured in Thrace by the Turks and taken to Asia Minor, where, like so many other young Greeks, he converted to Islam. He later realised his mistake and was burnt as a martyr in Melagina. But such martyrdoms continued long after the Ottoman conquest was complete. There is the seventeenth-century example of the Cretan St Mark the Younger: a convert to Islam who apostasised and was burnt as a martyr in Izmir in May 1643.[48] The Orthodox Church used these martyrdoms to warn believers of the dangers of conversion to Islam. It was an act that inevitably brought feelings of remorse, which could only be assuaged through martyrdom.

47 M. N. Swanson, 'The martyrdom of Abd al-Masih, superior of Mount Sinai (Qays al-Ghassani)', in *Syrian Christians under Islam: the first thousand years*, ed. D. R. Thomas (Leiden: Brill, 2001), 106–29.

48 E. A. Zachariadou, 'The neomartyr's message', *Bulletin of the Centre for Asia Minor Studies* 8 (1990–91), 55–61; Zachariadou, Βίοι νεοτέρων ἁγίων: ἡ ἐπαγρύπνηση γιὰ τὸ ποίμνιο, in *The heroes of the Orthodox Church: the new saints, 8th–16th c.*, ed. E. Kountoura-Galake [International Symposium 15] (Athens: Institute for Byzantine Research, 2004), 215–25.

Another threat to the position of the Orthodox Church came from the increasingly powerful Ottoman religious establishment (*'ulema*). This came to a head at the beginning of the reign of Süleyman the Magnificent (1520–66). Ottoman theologians contended that, because Constantinople had not surrendered peacefully, but had resisted and had been conquered by force, its Orthodox inhabitants were not entitled, under Islamic holy law, to the rights that they enjoyed. Properly speaking, they and their children should have been reduced to slavery and their churches turned into mosques.[49]

A high official passed on details of the theologians' decisions and plans to the patriarch Theoleptos I, who immediately appealed to the grand vizier, whom he knew fairly well, imploring him to intervene in favour of the Orthodox community. News of the affair spread, causing consternation among the Greek community of the capital. The patriarch and the grand vizier met in secret to coordinate their efforts. Having distributed lavish presents to many high officials of the Ottoman administration, the patriarch appeared in person before the *divan*, accompanied by two *archontes*. Following the advice of the grand vizier he explained that the Byzantine capital had surrendered on terms to Sultan Mehmed, who for this reason granted special privileges to its inhabitants. Then he was asked to present witnesses who would confirm his words. The patriarch invited two witnesses living in Adrianople, who volunteered to join him in Istanbul and testify. They were supposed to be two janissaries, both 102 years old, who had served in the sultan's army besieging the Byzantine capital. The patriarch again appeared before the *divan*, this time accompanied by the two venerable old men, who promptly confirmed that the Byzantine capital had peacefully capitulated. Hearing this, the sultan refused to countenance the proposals of his theologians and proceeded to renew the old privileges enjoyed by the Orthodox Church and community.[50]

This account may not be the whole truth, but it includes a kernel of truth. It was natural for Muslim theologians to re-examine the question of why the Ottoman capital, taken by force seventy years ago, now included a prosperous Greek population, which had at its disposal a number of churches. This

---

49 *Historia politica et patriarcha*, 158–69.
50 C. G. Patrineles, 'The exact time of the first attempt of the Turks to seize the churches and convert the Christian people of Constantinople to Islam', in *Actes du Ier Congrès international des études balkaniques et sud-est européennes* (Sofia: Éditions de l'Academie bulgare des sciences, 1969), III, 567–72; E. A. Zachariadou, 'La chute de Constantinople et la mythologie postérieure', in *Turcica et Islamica: studi in memoria di Aldo Gallotta*, ed. U. Marazzi (Naples: Università degli studi di Napoli 'L'Orientale', 2003), II, 1022–31.

incident also reveals the confident spirit which then prevailed in the patriarchate. The patriarch is described as a personality able to bring the most difficult situations to a successful conclusion, thanks to his diplomatic skills, his use of bribery, and his network of acquaintances in palace circles – a personality absolutely deserving the community's warmest support. At the same time, it seems that a legend was forming according to which Constantinople, or at least part of it, was not taken by force of arms but surrendered to the Turks after capitulation. This legend aimed at providing the patriarchate and the Greek community with a greater degree of legitimation within the Ottoman system of government. It was known to the famous Ottoman traveller of the seventeenth century, Evliya Çelebi, who wrote that the Greek fishermen of the Golden Horn enjoyed privileges granted to them by Sultan Mehmed because they had surrendered their quarter between Aya Kapu and Fener Kapu to him.[51]

The failure of the *'ulema* to deprive the Greek community of its privileged status underlined how much a part of the Ottoman system the ecumenical patriarchate had become. This emerges very strongly from the *berat* which Süleyman I issued in 1525 to Theoleptos's successor as patriarch, Jeremias I (1522–46). In the *narratio*, which places special emphasis on the glories of Istanbul, the sultan explained that the appointment of the patriarch was necessary not only for the supervision of Christians with respect to their religious customs, but also for the appointment of metropolitans and bishops to territories outside the Ottoman Empire, as was the case with Chios, Crete, Wallachia, Moldavia and Russia, for when the Orthodox Christians of those parts needed a metropolitan or a bishop they turned to the ecumenical patriarch established in the Ottoman capital, which was protected by God.[52] In a sense, the patriarch exercised an authority which ran parallel to that of the sultan. This was furthered by the Ottoman conquest in 1517 of Syria and Egypt, which brought the three eastern patriarchates of Antioch, Jerusalem and Alexandria under Ottoman rule. In spiritual and dogmatic matters they had always been nominally subject to the authority of the ecumenical patriarchate, but now they came under its more effective control. In this the ecumenical patriarchs had the backing of the Ottoman sultans, because a growth in the geographical scope of patriarchal authority served to increase the prestige of the Ottoman capital. It may be no coincidence that, just as Sultan Süleyman I was known to western

51 *Narrative of travels in Europe, Asia and Africa in the seventeenth century by Evliya Efendi, translated from the Turkish by the Ritter J.v. Hammer* (London: Oriental Translation Fund, 1834), 159.
52 Zachariadou, Δέκα τουρκικά έγγραφα, 152.

Europeans as the Magnificent, so the Greeks gave the same appellation to one of his patriarchs, Joasaph II (1554–65).[53]

All the time, the patriarchate of Constantinople remained at odds with Rome. In the year 1483–84 the patriarch Symeon I presided over an 'ecumenical' council which abolished the union of churches signed in Florence in 1439.[54] In the middle of the sixteenth century the patriarch Dionysios II (1546–56) allegedly approved a visit of the titular metropolitan of Caesarea, Metrophanes, to the Vatican, which earned the patriarch a severe rebuke from synod and he was lucky to retain his throne.[55] In 1582 Pope Gregory XIII sent as his representative to Constantinople the Venetian Livius Cellini, who, among other tasks, visited the patriarch Jeremias II in order to explain the reform of the calendar, which the pope had recently carried out and which remains associated with his name. The patriarch responded evasively, displaying both religious conservatism and traditional suspicion towards Rome.[56]

On the other hand, the patriarchs established contacts with the Protestants. Stephan Gerlach, a Lutheran chaplain to the Austrian embassy, who spent five years in Constantinople (1573–78), served as an intermediary between the Lutherans and the patriarch Jeremias II. Although nothing positive on the theological level resulted from these contacts, they did produce Martin Crusius's *Turcograecia*, which made known to western Europeans the problems of the Great Church in captivity.[57]

The personality of Jeremias II dominates the history of the patriarchate during the second half of the sixteenth century.[58] Although his term of office was often troubled – he was twice removed from the patriarchal throne – he was active on the international scene and was the first ecumenical patriarch to visit north-eastern Europe. He travelled as far as Poland and Muscovy with a view to mediating among the peoples of the region, who were then divided on religious matters. His journey culminated in the foundation of a new Orthodox patriarchate, that of Russia, with its seat at Moscow, where Jeremias

53 Ibid., 24.
54 Apostolopoulos, Ἱερὸς Κῶδιξ, 123–33. Cf. Zachariadou, Δέκα τουρκικὰ ἔγγραφα, 39–40.
55 M. Manoussacas, *Lettere Patriarcali inedite (1547–1806)* (Venice: Istituto éllenico di studi bizantini e postbizantini, 1968), 5–10.
56 O. Halecki, *From Florence to Brest (1439–1596)* [Sacrum Poloniae millennium 5] (Rome and New York: Fordham University Press, 1958), 214–15.
57 E. Legrand, 'Notice biographique sur Jean et Théodose Zygomalas', *Recueil de textes et de traductions publié par les Professeurs de l'École des langues orientales vivantes à l'occasion du VIIIe Congrès international des orientalistes tenu à Stockholm en 1889* (Paris: Imprimerie nationale, 1889), 67–264, esp. 78–86. Cf. G. de Gregorio, 'Costantinopoli – Tubinga – Roma, ovvero la "duplice conversione" di un manuscritto bizantino (vat.gr.738)', *BZ* 93 (2000), 37–107, esp. 78–88.
58 C. Hannick and K. P. Todt, 'Jeremy II', in *Théologie byzantine et sa tradition*, 551–615.

sojourned in 1588 on his return journey. In the following year, the patriarchal synod in Constantinople, together with Patriarch Joachim of Antioch and Patriarch Sophronios V of Jerusalem, gave its approval to this momentous event, which meant official recognition by the religious authorities of a huge and populous country of the spiritual leadership of the ecumenical patriarchate.[59]

59 Halecki, *Florence to Brest*, 223–35; F. v. Lilienfeld and E. Bryner, 'Die autokephale Metropolie von Moskau und ganz Russland (1448–1589)', in *Die orthodoxe Kirche in Russland, Documente ihrer Geschichte (860–1980)*, ed. P. Hauptmann and G. Stricken (Göttingen: Vandenhoek and Ruprecht, 1988), 289–302.

8

Orthodoxy and the west: Reformation to Enlightenment

PASCHALIS M. KITROMILIDES

The dramatic milestone of 1453 put an end to theological and philosophical contacts between eastern and western Christianity. The intellectual ties and exchanges of the fourteenth and the early fifteenth century had introduced scholastic philosophy to Byzantium and had revived – to a limited degree to be sure – the knowledge of Latin in the east. The Greek-speaking regions of European culture with focal points at Constantinople, Mistras, and Trebizond, together with the Venetian-held territories of Crete and Cyprus, all experienced their own version of the Quattrocento Renaissance. After 1453 the survivors of this culture found refuge in the west and made their own distinctive contribution to the Renaissance in the west. In the east, under Ottoman rule, ecclesiastical, cultural and spiritual life took a radically different turn. The conquest sealed off Greek-speaking Orthodoxy for almost a century and a half and interrupted all interchange with western culture. Those who left almost never came back to share the benefits of their experience with the Orthodox world. Contacts between Orthodoxy and the west were largely in the hands of Latin missionaries, such as the Jesuits, whose activities – religious, educational and political – the Orthodox condemned as an unwarranted western intrusion. A particularly acute act of this confrontation was unfolding in Palestine over the guardianship of the holy places: the antagonism between the Franciscans and the Orthodox brotherhood of the Holy Sepulchre became so sharp in the seventeenth century that it escalated into an issue of European diplomacy, with France championing the Catholic cause while the Orthodox patriarchs of Jerusalem appealed to the Russian tsars and other Orthodox princes in Wallachia and Moldavia and elsewhere for support and protection.[1]

---

1 Archbishop of Athens Chrysostomos Papadopoulos, Ἱστορία τῆς Ἐκκλησίας Ἱεροσολύμων, second edition (Athens, 1970), 501–866; C. A. Frazee, Catholics and sultans: the Church and the Ottoman Empire 1453–1923 (Cambridge: Cambridge University Press, 1983), 59–60, 62–3, 145–8.

Another source of Catholic pressure on the Orthodox took the form of the foundation by Pope Gregory XIII in 1581 of the Greek College of St Athanasius in Rome. The official purpose of the Greek College was to train young men from the Orthodox East as clergymen and teachers, who would then return to minister in their places of origin. Integral to their training was their conversion to Catholicism and their transformation into agents of eventual union of the eastern churches with Rome. To facilitate the process, the Greek College and its alumni became closely connected with the development of Uniate churches in the Orthodox regions of Europe. The Greek College in Rome contributed greatly to the development of learning and nurtured two great authors who left their mark on Greek scholarship and literature: Leo Allatios (1587–1668) and Neophytos Rodinos (1576/77–1659). On account of the involvement of scholars, such as these, in propaganda activities on behalf of the western church either through their writings or through missionary work (or in the case of Rodinos both), the Greek College was perceived as a hostile institution by the Orthodox and its operation led to further estrangement between Orthodoxy and Catholicism.[2]

Orthodox–Protestant dialogue

This was the broader background to the curiosity and to a certain openness shown by the Orthodox at the turn of the sixteenth century towards the Protestant churches of central Europe. A shared hostility towards Catholicism was among the major factors which favoured Orthodox and Protestants drawing closer together in an attempt at mutual understanding. The first such initiative recorded in the sources was the despatch in 1558 by the patriarch of Constantinople Joasaph II the 'Magnificent' of his deacon Demetrios Mysos the Thessalonian to Wittenberg with the task of collecting information on the teachings of the Protestants. Deacon Demetrios's mission gave one of the Reformation's leading lights, the hellenist Philip Melanchthon, the opportunity to address a letter to the patriarch in 1559, outlining the basic beliefs of the Reformed Christians. For the patriarch's fuller information Melanchthon attached to his letter a Greek translation of the Augsburg Confession. In his letter he first gave thanks to God for saving the Christian Church in the east amid so many misfortunes and assured the patriarch that the Reformed Christians piously followed the holy scriptures, the canons of the ecumenical councils

---

2 Z. N. Tsirpanlis, *Τὸ ἑλληνικὸ κολλέγιο τῆς Ρώμης καὶ οἱ μαθητές του 1576–1700* (Thessalonike: Patriarchal Institute for Patristic Studies, 1980).

and the teaching of the Greek Fathers of the church. He also stated that they rejected the superstitions of illiterate Latin monks and begged the patriarch of the Orthodox to pay no attention to the calumnies of the enemies of truth against the Protestant Christians.[3]

Melanchthon's letter and the translation of the Augsburg Confession were duly delivered by Demetrios Mysos in Constantinople, but the patriarch and the synod were presumably not impressed by the claim to 'orthodoxy' on the part of the Protestants and avoided replying to them. After Melanchthon's death in 1560 direct contacts between Protestants and the patriarchate of Constantinople were suspended for more than ten years. Protestant influences upon the Orthodox world began to be felt, nevertheless. Via Transylvania and the principalities of Wallachia and Moldavia, Protestant ideas about the teaching of the scriptures found their way into the Orthodox world. Of special interest and importance was the influence of German religious art upon post-Byzantine painting in the sixteenth century, as witnessed by the impact of the engravings of Dürer and of Lukas Cranach the Elder upon the famous Apocalypse cycle on the exterior of the refectory of Dionysiou monastery on Mount Athos.[4]

The abortive contacts with Protestantism under Joasaph the 'Magnificent' found a more substantial sequel during the first patriarchate of Jeremias II Tranos (1572–79). This time the initiative emanated not from Wittenberg but from Tübingen. The occasion was the appointment in 1573 of Stephen Gerlach, an eminent Lutheran scholar, as chaplain to the Austrian embassy in Istanbul. Gerlach brought two letters addressed to Patriarch Jeremias from the eminent professors of the University of Tübingen, the great hellenist Martin Crusius and the theologian Jacob Andreae. This initiated a correspondence between the patriarch and the Tübingen professors, which extended until 1581: that is, it outlasted the patriarch's first term of office. In all, the Tübingen professors wrote eight letters and the patriarch wrote five in reply. Besides their own letters the Protestant professors sent six copies of the Augsburg Confession, addressed to the patriarch, to the metropolitan of Berroia Metrophanes, a future ecumenical patriarch, to the head of the patriarchal academy Theodosios Zygomalas, and to Gabriel Severos, another senior scholar and future titular metropolitan of Philadelphia, but resident in Venice. One final copy

---

3 Philaretos Vapheidis, Ἐκκλησιαστικὴ Ἱστορία, III-A', 1453–1700 (Constantinople: Gerardos 1912), 43–5; G. Hering, 'Orthodoxie und Protestantismus', *Jahrbuch der Österreichischen Byzantinistik* 31/32 (1981), 823–74, esp. 828–31.
4 P. Huber, *Apokalypse: Bilderzyklen zur Johannes-Offenbarung in Trier, auf dem Athos und von Caillaud d'Angers* (Düsseldorf: Patmos Verlag, 1989), 98–231.

was sent to Michael Kantakouzenos, a wealthy lay patron of the church. It was obvious that the Tübingen professors were canvassing Orthodox public opinion for their views. The Tübingen professors and the patriarch corresponded in Greek and the surviving letters supply an excellent record of the level of theological thinking at which the doctrinal exchanges between them went on. In outlining the principles of Protestant doctrine the professors stressed the points of agreement between the two churches, their shared belief in one saviour, Jesus Christ, and the acceptance of the holy scriptures as the basis of their faith. They added that the points of disagreement between the Orthodox and the Reformed churches were of secondary significance, while in his response the patriarch stressed the points of disagreement between Orthodoxy and Protestantism and accused the Protestants of introducing novelties. He stressed that the Orthodox faith was founded not only on the holy scriptures, but also on the ecumenical councils and the Fathers of the Church; he warned that faith based on the scriptures alone could lead to errors. In 1575 the patriarch sent to the Protestant theologians a refutation of the Augsburg Confession composed by himself with the help of Ioannes Zygomalas and other Orthodox theologians. The correspondence continued in Jeremias's second patriarchate (1580–84), but by 1581 the patriarch asked the Tübingen professors to cease annoying him with doctrinal issues since they did not show any willingness to conform to the true teachings of the church, especially in regard to the Fathers for whom they expressed their respect in words but not in deeds. The patriarch concluded the correspondence by suggesting to the Protestant professors that they write to him out of friendship if they so desired, but not to bother him with doctrine.[5]

These early attempts at reconnaissance and mutual discovery between Orthodoxy and Protestantism did not leave any serious mark on the Orthodox Church. The greatest product of the exchange between the two churches at this early stage in the Reformation's history was Martin Crusius's monumental work *Turcograecia*, published in Basel in 1584. This is the most important source on the condition of the Orthodox Church and of Greek culture and language produced in the sixteenth century and remains an inexhaustible mine of information on these subjects to the present day. The early contacts under Patriarch Jeremias II suggest suspicion towards the Protestants, rather than

---

5 See *Turcograeciae libri octo a Martino Crusio* (Basel: Leonardus Ostensius, 1584; reprinted Modena: Memor, 1972), 410–83. For an English translation see G. Mastrantonis, *Augsburg and Constantinople: the correspondence between the Tübingen theologians and Patriarch Jeremiah II of Constantinople on the Augsburg Confession* (Brookline, MA: Holy Cross Orthodox Press, 1982). See also I. N. Karmiris, Ὀρθοδοξία καὶ προτεσταντισμός (Athens, 1937), I, 31–7, 79–135.

the insecurity or even hostility which often characterised Orthodox dealings with the Catholics. Attitudes towards Protestantism were to change later on, after the highly dramatic experiences of the Orthodox Church under Patriarch Cyril I Loukaris in the early seventeenth century. Before turning to that controversial and ultimately tragic story, however, it would be useful to situate the relations of the Orthodox Church with the west within the evolving history of its experience of Ottoman rule in the century and a half after the fall of Constantinople.

The Orthodox Church after 1453

The conquest of 1453 destroyed the Orthodox Church as an institution of the Christian empire inaugurated by Constantine. The church no longer conferred legitimacy through anointing and coronation upon the wielder of the temporal sword; it no longer sanctified through its spiritual guidance the earthly order of things. It now attempted to adapt to an Islamic order by accepting the sovereignty of the House of Osman and by loyally submitting to the prevailing non-Christian powers. In return, the leaders of the church, patriarchs and prelates alike, were recognised by the Islamic state; not, however, as an institution of the subjected Christian population but in their personal capacity, as administrative agents of the Ottoman state charged with the task of supervising the 'erroneous religious customs of the infidels'.[6] It was in this capacity that the Orthodox religious leadership had to carry out its tasks, which as far as the state was concerned included ensuring the loyal submission of the Christian subjects of the sultan and the regular collection and delivery of their taxes. Within this overall set-up of political submission and ambiguous institutional status the ecclesiastical hierarchy with the ecumenical patriarch at its head strove to preserve within the Christian community the organisation, religious practices and spiritual traditions of the church. To keep the community of the faithful together and to survive amid the vicissitudes of centuries-long non-Christian rule – until finally recognised by the Ottoman reforms of the mid-nineteenth century as a collective institution representing Orthodox society – were no small accomplishments. They reflected not only the strength of collective memory and the effectiveness of socialising mechanisms within the church, but also the enduring power of the symbolic legacies of the

---

6 P. Konortas, Ὀθωμανικὲς θεωρήσεις γιὰ τὸ Οἰκουμενικὸ Πατριαρχεῖο (Athens: Alexandreia Publishing House, 1998), 315. On the status of the Orthodox Church under Ottoman rule see E. A. Zachariadou, Δέκα τουρκικὰ ἔγγραφα γιὰ τὴ Μεγάλη Ἐκκλησία (1483–1567) (Athens: Institute for Byzantine Research, 1996).

erstwhile Christian empire of New Rome. To ensure this survival the church had to carry out its tasks in the fields of pastoral work, philanthropy and education as best it could.

It is not without significance that one of Gennadios II Scholarios's first actions after being appointed patriarch by Mehmed the Conqueror was to re-establish a school of higher learning in Constantinople. In this patriarchal school Christian learning, the cultivation of the Greek language and some form of training in humane letters were enlisted in the effort to reproduce the cultural tradition that might ensure survival and continuity within the church, regardless of the ambiguities of its institutional standing in the political order.[7] The toll, however, of its anomalous position was heavy. The position of 'supervisor of the erroneous religious customs of the infidels' was an administrative office open to the highest bidder, and this introduced a source of constant turmoil and upheaval into the upper ranks of the hierarchy. Simony and corruption were the inescapable consequences. Between 1454 and 1600 the patriarchal throne saw at least thirty-six changes of occupant, involving twenty-four separate individuals. Very often tenure lasted for just a few months, even a few weeks. This created further problems: dissension and backstabbing did not so much scandalise the faithful as feed the rapacity of the state to the detriment of the church. The most dramatic reflection of this was the continuing confiscation of churches and their transformation into mosques – a practice that became a constant source of anguish for both the clergy and the faithful. The climax of this practice came in 1586 when the patriarchate was expelled from the monastery of the Pammakaristos, where the patriarch had had his seat since 1456. Patriarch Jeremias II, who had been exiled to Rhodes, returned to Istanbul in 1586 to find the patriarchal church, which he had lovingly embellished, transformed into a mosque: 'and he wept bitterly', the chronographer records.[8] The widespread desperation and low morale of the Orthodox community at the end of the sixteenth century was also reflected in the condition of the patriarchal academy, where instruction was practically abandoned in this period.[9] This condition of crisis and decline provides the broader background to the condition of the church when Cyril I Loukaris emerged on the scene. Cyril's six terms on the throne of John Chrysostom inaugurated a stormy period for the church, especially during Cyril's second to sixth tenures of the throne, which span the years 1620 to 1638. Cyril was one of the four great

7 The best source on the Patriarchal School still remains Manuel Gedeon, Χρονικά τῆς Πατριαρχικῆς Ἀκαδημίας (Constantinople: Patriarchal Press 1883).
8 [Pseudo-]Dorotheos, Βιβλίον Ἱστορικόν (Venice: Nikolaos Glykys, 1743), 454.
9 Gedeon, Χρονικά, 73–4.

patriarchs of the Ottoman period – along with Gennadios II, Jeremias II and Joacheim III. A gifted and charismatic visionary, he came to the throne with a strategy for the renewal of the church and for the reinvigoration of the faith.

Cyril Loukaris: a Protestant patriarch?

Cyril was born Constantine Loukaris in Candia (Iraklion), Crete in 1572.[10] He was exposed to the humanist culture of his island in the late Venetian period, but the strong devotion of his family to Orthodoxy led him in the direction of celibate monasticism. He probably began a novitiate in the foremost Orthodox religious house on Crete, the monastery of Angarathos, where his brother Maximos later became abbot (1619–41). Young Loukaris was a restless man – and was to remain so throughout his life. He pursued his studies in Venice, where he received instruction from Maximos Margounios, the bishop of Kythera, who was a staunch defender of Orthodoxy against Catholicism in his theological teaching. Young Constantine Loukaris also enrolled in the University of Padua, where Cesare Cremonini taught him neoaristotelian philosophy. He graduated in 1595 and towards the end of that year he was ordained deacon and priest in Constantinople by his cousin Meletios Pigas, patriarch of Alexandria, who was also a former member of the brotherhood at Angarathos. Shortly after his ordination Cyril Loukaris followed his patriarch to a synod convoked in 1596 in Constantinople by Jeremias II. The synod condemned the pseudo-union of the Orthodox and Catholic churches voted at Brest-Litovsk by a local synod in 1595. The 1596 synod despatched two exarchs to Poland to inform King Sigismund III of Poland of the decisions taken by the patriarchates of Constantinople and Alexandria and to participate in a second synod at Brest-Litovsk. One of the exarchs, representing Alexandria, was Loukaris. This trip prepared him for his life-long battle against the Jesuits. He made common cause with the Protestants, who were equally persecuted in Poland and Lithuania. This laid the groundwork for his rapprochement with the Protestants. Up to 1600 Loukaris undertook at least two long missions to Poland, Ukraine and Lithuania, working for the Orthodox cause in those regions. He reorganised the Orthodox school at Vilna and founded another one in L'viv. During the fierce persecution of the Orthodox in the year 1600 he barely escaped with his

---

10 From the voluminous literature see G. A. Hadjiantoniou, *Protestant Patriarch: the life of Cyril Lukaris (1572–1638) Patriarch of Constantinople* (London: The Epworth Press, 1961); Steven Runciman, *The Great Church in captivity* (Cambridge: Cambridge University Press, 1968), 259–88 and Karmiris, Ὀρθοδοξία, 177–232; G. Podskalsky, *Griechische Theologie in der Zeit der Türkenherrschaft 1453–1821* (Munich: C. H. Beck, 2000), 162–80.

life, while the exarch of the church of Constantinople, Nikephoros, lost his. In 1601, following Meletios Pigas's death, Cyril Loukaris, barely thirty years of age, was elected patriarch of Alexandria. In this capacity, occupying the second senior throne in the Orthodox Church, he continued his battle against Latin propaganda in Orthodox lands. In 1612 he left on another trip to south-western Russia. On the way he stopped in Istanbul, where following the expulsion of Patriarch Neophytos II the synod of the ecumenical patriarchate asked Cyril to serve as 'caretaker' of the throne of Constantinople. Cyril agreed and served for a month, but he found the financial obligations contingent upon his eventual election to the ecumenical throne so onerous that he resigned and continued on his trip to Russia.

After his return to Alexandria in 1614 Loukaris remained obsessed with the relentless proselytising activities of the Catholics in the east. He devised a grand strategy for the defence of Orthodoxy by courting the Protestant powers of Europe in order to develop a common front against Rome. At this early stage he turned to England. He was in correspondence with two successive archbish-ops of Canterbury, George Abbot and William Laud. The major result of these contacts was the offer by the Anglicans of a scholarship to a clergyman of the Alexandrine Church for theological training in Oxford. In 1617 this initiative brought Metrophanes Kritopoulos to England for five years, with the secret agenda of working for a possible union between Orthodox and Anglicans. Kri-topoulos's subsequent peregrinations elsewhere in Protestant Europe seem to have been dictated by this motive.[11] While Kritopoulos was travelling in Europe, his patriarch back in Alexandria was busy corresponding with promi-nent Protestant scholars and prelates, including the Dutch theologian and statesman David de Wilhelm and the archbishop of Spalato Marcantonio de Dominis, who had converted to Protestantism while residing in London. This correspondence is important because it shows Loukaris deeply troubled by the practices of his church, which he perceived as obsolete and superstitious and far removed from authentic Christian faith. He expressed a yearning for a return to 'evangelical simplicity', based on the authority of the scriptures and the Holy Spirit. He was critical of the behaviour of the Orthodox faithful, which he witnessed during a visit to Jerusalem. In his opinion it bordered on idolatry. He also expressed misgivings about the excessive authority ascribed to the Fathers in the Greek and Latin churches and confessed that he found

---

11 C. Davey, *Pioneer for unity: Metrophanes Kritopoulos (1589–1639) and relations between the Orthodox, Roman Catholic and reformed churches* (London: The British Council of Churches, 1987).

the doctrines of the Reformation truer to the spirit of the scriptures than those of the Orthodox and Catholic churches.[12]

These concerns reflect Loukaris's deeper spiritual and ecclesiastical anxieties, which derived from the dictates of his Christian conscience and from his sense of responsibility as a successor of the apostles for the condition of the faith among the masses of his flock. This strong sense of pastoral duty accompanied Cyril to Constantinople, where he was elevated to the ecumenical throne on 4 November 1620 by a vote of the synod. Thus began the patriarchate of Cyril I, 'famous for his virtue and wisdom' in the synod's judgement.[13] His tenure of the throne of Constantinople lasted, with brief interruptions, until 1638. This was a relatively long patriarchate and was marked not only by the scope of his pastoral and administrative work, but also by his pursuit on a truly pan-European scale of his grand strategy against the unrelenting pressure of the Catholic Church on the Orthodox world.[14]

Retrospective considerations and appraisals of Cyril Loukaris's presence in the history of the Greek East and of the Orthodox Church have stressed almost exclusively the politics of his grand strategy against Rome, a strategy that was premised on an Orthodox–Protestant alliance, which, however, eventually turned the patriarch into a prisoner of the Protestant powers. This is a rather limited and certainly a partial appraisal, which betrays the western origin of those who propound it and their primary interest in the patriarch as a political rather than as an ecclesiastical figure. A fuller perspective will also include the patriarch's frenetic work within the church, which aimed at infusing new life into all spheres of ecclesiastical activity. International politics were not Cyril's only or even his primary concern, and his Protestant alliances against Rome were rather a component of his policy for the protection and revival of the Orthodox Church after the crisis and decline experienced in the closing years of the sixteenth century. This was the patriarch's primary target. The Protestant alliance was conceived as a major weapon in the defence of Orthodoxy, not as an end in itself.

The deeper Orthodox motivation in Cyril's policies is clearly reflected in the record of his patriarchate. Few patriarchs have issued so many synodical edicts and other types of patriarchal documents. These were the product of his reforming energies, which were directed towards reforming or re-establishing

---

12 Vapheidis, Ἐκκλησιαστικὴ Ἱστορία III-Aʹ, 57–58. The letters in extenso in E. Legrand, *Bibliographie hellénique XVII siècle* (Paris: Picard, 1896), IV, 313–40.

13 Legrand, *Bibliographie hellénique*, 340–2.

14 G. Hering, *Ökumenisches Patriarchat und europäische Politik 1620–1638* (Wiesbaden: F. Steiner Verlag, 1968), 30–59, 207–47.

monasteries, canonising saints, settling questions of episcopal jurisdiction, and taking charge of the publication of religious books.[15] These activities formed the substance of the traditional pastoral work of the church. Cyril also took two other major initiatives. First, he reorganised and upgraded the moribund patriarchal academy by bringing in his former classmate at Padua, Theophilos Korydalleus.[16] This leading neoaristotelian took his patriarch's command seriously: starting in 1624 he redesigned the school's curriculum by introducing alongside sacred and Greek letters Latin and philosophy. He initiated a tradition of neoaristotelianism that was transplanted by his pupils to other major schools in the Greek East and formed a shared philosophical education for the Christian peoples of the Balkans until the coming of the Enlightenment a century and a half later. Korydalleus inevitably ran into trouble with the conservative educational establishment of the time and shared in his patriarch's adventures and downfall.

Cyril's second major initiative, truly revolutionary in character, was the introduction, for the first time, of a printing press to Istanbul to publish religious works for the needs of the faithful. In 1627 he invited Nikodemos Metaxas, a Cephalonian, who had been trained in the art of printing in London, to set up a printing press in Constantinople. With the help of the British Ambassador Sir Thomas Roe the press was introduced into Turkey and set up in the city close to the British Embassy for protection. It was the first printing press in the Greek world. Under the patriarch's supervision it began printing religious books, mostly anti-Catholic tracts. A few months later, however, the Jesuits with the help of the French Ambassador to the Porte, the Comte de Cési, managed to incite a sack of the printing house by the janissaries, who, failing to arrest Metaxas, destroyed his press.[17]

For the next ten years it was all-out war between the patriarch of Constantinople and the Roman Church. The *Propaganda Fide* at a meeting in July 1628, presided over by Pope Urban VIII himself, resolved to fight relentlessly against the patriarch until his elimination.[18] In order to find support in this battle Cyril had to rely on the Protestant ambassadors in Istanbul: the British, the Austrian and the Dutch. The Protestant ambassadors to the Sublime Porte,

---

15 M. Gedeon, Πατριαρχικοὶ πίνακες, ed. N. L. Phoropoulos (Athens: Syllogos pros diadosin ophelimon vivlion, 1996), 430–1, 433–4, 436–7, 439–40.

16 Gedeon, Χρονικά, 74–86; G. P. Henderson, *The revival of Greek thought 1620–1821* (Albany, NY: State University of New York Press, 1970), 12–19.

17 Evro Layton, 'Nikodemos Metaxas, the first Greek printer in the Eastern world', *Harvard Library Bulletin* 15 (1967), 140–68 and in greater detail L. Augliera, *Libri, politica, religione nel Levante del Seicento: la tipografia di Nicodemo Metaxas, primo editore di testi greci nell' oriente ortodosso* (Venice: Istituto Veneto, 1996), 9–91.

18 Hering, *Ökumenisches Patriarchat*, 110–13.

especially the British Sir Thomas Roe and his successor Sir Peter Wych, and the Dutch Cornelius Haga, supported Cyril in his efforts to face the machinations of the Jesuits and subsequently the Capuchins against him. The enemies of the patriarch attempted to turn the Ottoman authorities against him by accusing him of disloyalty and by ascribing political motives to his pastoral work. In the hope of dethroning the patriarch they also encouraged dissension in the synod by accusing him of heresy and by exaggerating his Protestant sympathies. More effective than the religious arguments were the large sums of money, which helped his namesake Cyril Kontaris, metropolitan of Berroia, to create a faction against him in synod.

Sir Thomas Roe retired from Constantinople in late 1627. Cyril gave him a truly royal departing gift for his sovereign Charles I: a manuscript of the Bible known as the *codex Alexandrinus*. Meanwhile the Austrian Ambassador Kuefstein, who was a Protestant, gave way to a Catholic. Thus Cyril's main support remained Cornelius Haga, the Dutch ambassador. Soon, however, the patriarch became his backer's prisoner. In exchange for their support Cornelius Haga and the chaplain of the Dutch Embassy Antoine Léger, both of them deeply committed Calvinists, pressured the patriarch to introduce Protestant measures and teachings in his church. The price of their support took the specific form of issuing a confession of Christian faith by the patriarch. It has been suggested that the text was drafted by Calvinist pastors in Geneva and revised by Léger to make it appear closer to some Orthodox dogmatic requirements and presented to the patriarch for his signature. Cyril apparently made some further revisions and signed the confession in 1629. Published that same year in Geneva was a Latin translation under the title of a 'Confession of Christian faith by Cyril, Patriarch of Constantinople'. Translations in English and French followed. In the title it was specified that the confession had the agreement of the other patriarchs of the eastern church. In 1633 a Greek version of the confession also appeared.[19]

The confession is a relatively short text of eighteen articles followed by four questions and answers on the basic tenets of the Christian faith.[20] Of the

19 On the circumstances of drafting the 'confession' Karmiris, Ὀρθοδοξία, I, 212–21; Hering *Ökumenisches Patriarchat*, 187–202. Hadjiantoniou, *Protestant Patriarch*, 99–109, strongly supports Cyril's authorship of the confession.

20 The text and commentary in I. Karmiris (ed.), Τὰ δογματικὰ καὶ συμβολικὰ μνημεῖα τῆς Ὀρθοδόξου Καθολικῆς Ἐκκλησίας (Athens, 1953), II, 562–71. An English translation in Hadjiantoniou, *Protestant Patriarch*, 141–5. See also C. Davey, 'Cyril Loukaris and his Orthodox confession of faith', *Sobornost* 22 (2000), 19–29. I. N. Karmiris, 'Περὶ τὸ πρόβλημα τῆς λεγομένης "Λουκαρείου" Ὁμολογίας', *Θεολογία* 56 (1985), 675–93, esp. 668–79, points out that the confession is fundamentally Calvinist in its theological content.

eighteen articles or chapters of the main text three (I, VI and VII) are entirely Orthodox on fundamental doctrinal principles (Trinity, Incarnation, original sin and its transmission). However, many others (II, III, IX, XVII) are entirely Protestant in outlook on issues of the authority of scripture and of the tradition of the Fathers and councils, ecclesiology, predestination, justification by grace alone, number of sacraments, the Eucharist, etc. Of these Protestant articles, II and XVII (on the authority of the scripture and the Eucharist) are entirely Calvinist in inspiration. Some other articles (especially IV, V, VIII, XVI and XVIII) are more conciliatory to Orthodox tradition, using phraseology that might accommodate Orthodox sensibility on issues of the divine inspiration of the scripture, creation, providence, the saints and their icons, baptism and life after death. The same is true of questions I, II and IV on reading the scriptures and on icons. Question III on the canonical books of the scriptures is radically Calvinist, reducing their number to twenty-two in the Old Testament but accepting the New Testament in its entirety.

The publication of the confession caused fury in Roman Catholic circles and considerable concern among the Orthodox. The patriarch himself never explicitly admitted authorship of the text, but to the end of his life neither by synodal act nor in writing did he officially either disown or condemn the confession published under his name. The question of the authorship of the so-called 'Loukaris Confession' has remained open and controversial to this date. The prevailing view among the Orthodox at the time and subsequently has been that when publishing the confession the Calvinists usurped the patriarch's name. This is borne out by the reactions of contemporaries. Cyril continued to enjoy the loyal support of the patriarch of Alexandria Gerasimos (Spartaliotis), despite the latter's refusal to entertain the feelers put out in 1628 by the Calvinists for a union of churches. Patriarch Theophanes of Jerusalem was equally convinced of Cyril's orthodoxy and wrote a letter from Jassy in 1630 to the Russian Orthodox reassuring them on this point. Of course, the Protestants, especially the Calvinists around Cornelius Haga and the pastors in Geneva, thought that the Reformation was finally on its way in the eastern church, but their enthusiasm was misplaced.

Although expelled from Istanbul the Jesuits managed in 1634 with the support of the French ambassador Marcheville to persuade Cyril Kontaris, metropolitan of Berroia – a personal enemy of Loukaris – to stage a revolt in the synod, which temporarily unseated the patriarch. He was almost immediately reinstated by the synod only to be evicted once again thanks to Kontaris in May 1635. Cyril went into exile in Chios and Rhodes. In April 1637, however, he was back on the ecumenical throne for his last patriarchate. Between 1630 and

1637 Cyril was dethroned and re-elected by the synod of Constantinople three times. The eminent historian of the church of Constantinople Manuel Gedeon interprets the persistence of the synod in reinstating Loukaris for a total of five (or six if the temporary tenure of 1612 is also counted) patriarchates as a decisive confirmation of his Orthodoxy and of the recognition of his devotion to the doctrines and the traditions of his church by the body most competent to judge, the hierarchy of the patriarchate of Constantinople.[21] The church was, however, in deep crisis. On 17 August 1637 Cyril wrote to the pastors, senators and governors of the Republic and Church of Geneva thanking them for their support of Orthodoxy but lamenting the condition of his church, which was under siege by the Jesuits and by his enemy Kontaris, who had paid 20,000 thalers to the Turks in order to unseat him. But the patriarch put his faith in Christ: 'if the Lord is my light and saviour, whom am I afraid of? The Lord is my life's defender.'[22]

Despite the patriarch's devotion and lively fighting spirit, the odds against him proved insurmountable. A year later, in June 1638, he was arrested on the charge that he was in secret communication with the Russians, who had just wrested Azov from the Ottomans. He was summarily tried for high treason and executed on 27 June 1638. According to the English consul in Smyrna, Paul Rycaut, this tragic dénouement of Loukaris's dramatic life had cost the papal curia 50,000 crowns.[23] At long last, Kontaris succeeded to the ecumenical throne as Cyril II, but only for a few months in 1638–39. Much to the satisfaction of his old teachers at the Jesuit school in Galata he had enough time to convoke a synod and have Loukaris condemned as the author of the heretical confession. However, subsequent synods of the Orthodox Church convened in Constantinople in 1638, 1642, 1672 and 1691, in Jassy in 1642, and in Jerusalem in 1672 condemned the confession as heretical but not Cyril I either as its author or as a Calvinist.[24] Although in the absence of conclusive evidence the question of authorship has remained open to this day, the confession itself has been unanimously condemned by the Orthodox. A long polemic against the confession lingered on in the Catholic tradition, and Roman Catholic theologians accused the Orthodox of being receptive to Protestantism because

---

21 Gedeon, Πίνακες, 433.
22 Legrand, Bibliographie hellénique, IV, 457–60, esp. 459.
23 Paul Rycaut, The history of the Turkish Empire from the year 1623 to the year 1677 (London: John Starkey, 1680), 71.
24 Vapheidis, Ἐκκλησιαστικὴ Ἱστορία, III-A', 76–81. An English version of pertinent source material in J. J. Overbeck (ed.), The Orthodox Confession of the Catholic and Apostolic Eastern Church (London: Thomas Baker, 1898) and J. N. W. B. Robertson (ed.), The Acts and Decrees of the Synod of Jerusalem (London: Thomas Baker, 1899).

of their failure to condemn Loukaris himself. To counter these strictures the metropolitan of Kiev Peter Moghila composed and published in Amsterdam in 1667 another confession of Orthodox faith, with the approval of the four patriarchs of the Orthodox Church.

Despite the voluminous source material and an extensive scholarly debate, definitive judgement of Loukaris's position remains an open challenge for historians. There is no doubt that his western contacts, his critical perception of the condition of his church and, in the final analysis, his Christian faith itself motivated his genuine desire to revive Orthodoxy through a renewal of the faith. In this quest – apparently on an entirely personal level – Loukaris flirted with Protestant ideas. But it seems unlikely that Loukaris as patriarch even considered the possibility of deviating from strict Orthodoxy by imposing Protestant views on the Orthodox Church. In this, modern academic theologians and historians concur with the judgement of earlier chronographers who expressed the authentic attitude of the Orthodox Church.[25] So what did the Reformation mean for Loukaris, how did it influence his pastoral attitude and ecclesiastical strategy, and how did it shape his vision of the Orthodox Church? It seems that at a time of crisis and decline and of relentless Catholic pressure Loukaris glimpsed in the Reformation not only an ally against Catholicism but also a model and a challenge for the reconstruction of Orthodoxy. Loukaris never conceded the Reformation's claims to Orthodoxy, not even in its Calvinist version, but recognised that it had opened up a path to Christian renewal. He was accordingly prepared in some areas of Christian practice to follow the Protestant lead, as his blessing for the translation of the New Testament into modern Greek suggests.

The translation was probably the patriarch's most important pastoral initiative. The task was entrusted in 1629 to the learned hieromonk Maximos Rodios from Gallipoli (hence known as Kallioupolitis), a former student of Korydalleus at the patriarchal academy and a devoted follower of Loukaris. While working on the translation Maximos resided in the Dutch Embassy and collaborated closely with Léger. As a model for his translation he used Diodati's modern Italian version of the New Testament. By 1632 the Dutch ambassador informed his government that the translation had been completed, but it still needed revisions against the original. The translator Maximos, however, died unexpectedly on 24 September 1633 without putting the finishing touches to his work. These were left to Léger and to Loukaris himself but publication in

---

25 V. Stephanidis, Ἐκκλησιαστικὴ Ἱστορία, fourth edition (Athens: Astir, 1978), 707.

Geneva was delayed until 1638; tragically just a few months after Cyril's own death.[26]

In his other pastoral and administrative work the patriarch remained true to the traditions of Orthodoxy and did not attempt to change them in any way that might distance them from Orthodox principles. He himself and the church militant which he led were victims of the same tragedy: in order to carry out his strategy for the defence and renewal of Orthodoxy Cyril, 'possibly the most brilliant man to have held office as patriarch since the days of St Photios', found himself implicated in political intrigue, but in such a way that not only did he become the prisoner of his Protestant protectors, but he was also left defenceless before the ferocity of an oriental despotism.[27] Thus his strategy of Orthodox renewal fell victim to the ruthless logic of power politics introduced by the Thirty Years War.

The long-term consequence of the high drama of Loukaris's patriarchate was the prevalence for the rest of the seventeenth century of a militant anti-Protestant spirit in the Orthodox Church. Several local councils condemned Calvinism and the 1629 confession ascribed to Loukaris. Even the church of Cyprus held a synod in 1668 presided over by Archbishop Nikephoros, which condemned Calvinism. After Peter Moghila's 1640 confession, which, on account of its Latin sources, verged dangerously on Catholicism, the patriarch of Jerusalem Dositheos (1669–1707) produced another confession answering Cyril's confession point by point. But to do this Dositheos drew heavily on Latin sources and went a long way in the direction of a Catholic theology on fundamental doctrinal questions. This anti-Protestant spirit in the Greek East will explain the otherwise surprising rapprochement between the Catholic and Orthodox churches in the closing decades of the seventeenth century, which was especially marked at the local level. Sharing places of worship and partaking of each other's traditions if not sacraments became a relatively common practice in areas, like several of the Aegean islands, with religiously mixed populations.[28] This rapprochement soon faltered, as a result of the forceful practices of the Catholic Church in those areas, such as the Peloponnese,

---

26 For a detailed and critical account see M. I. Manousakas, 'Νέα στοιχεῖα γιὰ τὴν πρώτη μετάφραση τῆς Καινῆς Διαθήκης στὴ δημοτικὴ γλώσσα ἀπὸ τὸν Μάξιμο Καλλιουπολίτη', *Μεσαιωνικὰ καὶ Νέα Ἑλληνικὰ* 2 (1986), 7–70.

27 T. Ware, *The Orthodox Church*, revised edition (Harmondsworth: Penguin, 1993), 96.

28 T. Ware, *Eustratios Argenti: a study of the Greek Church under Turkish rule* (Oxford: Clarendon Press, 1964), 16–42; Ware, 'Orthodox and Catholics in the seventeenth century: schism or intercommunion?' *Schism, heresy and religious protest*, ed. D. Baker (Cambridge: Cambridge University Press, 1972), 259–76.

conquered at the end of the seventeenth century by the Venetians from the Ottomans.

Orthodoxy and the Enlightenment

The eighteenth century dawned in the Greek East with Orthodoxy estranged from both branches of western Christianity. While it remained impervious to any spiritual dialogue with western Christianity until the nineteenth century, it nevertheless grappled with new intellectual challenges emanating from the west in the form of secular learning. These presented the Orthodox world both with opportunities and with dangers. The conventional view assumes that the Orthodox Church was *ab initio* and *ex principio* inimical to the varieties of secular learning originating in the West and devoted itself exclusively to the tradition of sacred letters transmitted in the culture of the Greek East. This is an overstatement, which is in need of considerable modification and refinement, if we are to provide an accurate description of the attitudes and practices which emerge from the historical record. Let us take, for example, the evidence supplied by the history of the patriarchal academy. It boasted scholars, such as Korydalleus, who was an exponent *par excellence* of western secular learning. If he owed his appointment to the patriarch Cyril Loukaris and did not long survive his patron's downfall, the Orthodox Church continued to look to western-trained scholars. In 1665, for instance, Alexander Mavrokordatos was appointed head of the patriarchal academy. He it was who introduced the first elements of modern scientific teaching into its curriculum.[29]

In the course of the eighteenth century the church showed a noteworthy openness to western learning by enlisting the services of western-trained scholars, representatives of a variety of shades of Enlightenment culture, whenever it planned the reform and upgrading of major institutions of ecclesiastical education. The most remarkable such occasion presented itself in 1753 when the patriarch Cyril V and the synod issued an edict placing under the aegis of the patriarchate of Constantinople an institute of higher education founded in 1748 on Mount Athos by Abbot Meletios of Vatopedi monastery. The purpose of the action was to create a college to train clergymen and scholars for the needs of the church. This project was entrusted to the foremost exponent of Enlightenment culture in the Greek world at the time, Eugenios Voulgaris (1716–1806). The story of the Athonite Academy under Voulgaris in the 1750s was the classic

---

29 A. Maurocordato, *Pneumaticum instrumentum circulandi sanguinis sive de motu et usu pulmonum*, ed. by Lorenzo Guerrieri (Florence: L. S. Olschki, 1965), 7–21.

test case of the possibilities and limits of the encounter of Orthodoxy with the Enlightenment.[30] Voulgaris was a devout man, a clergyman with impeccable Orthodox credentials. During his residence on Athos in the 1750s he was even the subject of miraculous healing by one of the most venerated icons on the Holy Mountain, the Virgin of the Akathistos at Dionysiou monastery. But he was also a rationalist, a scholar of modern philosophy and science. After his studies in Venice and Padua he returned to Greece and taught in schools in Ioannina and Kozani where he was embroiled in conflicts, personal and ideological, with conservative scholars, defenders of traditional learning, who accused him of heresy on account of his rationalism and scientific outlook. The official church seems not to have shared this distrust and saw these quarrels for what they really were: professional confrontations and generational conflicts among scholars. Patriarch and synod entrusted Voulgaris with the renewal of ecclesiastical education because they considered that he possessed the best available talents.

At the school on the hill standing above Vatopedi monastery, Voulgaris attempted to introduce a western model of higher education into an Orthodox cultural environment. In the early stages, so long as he enjoyed the support of Cyril V, things seemed promising. In a letter written in early 1756 to a former pupil, Kyprianos the Cypriot, whom he had taught in Ioannina, Voulgaris offered a very evocative lyrical description of the natural environment of the school, extolling its natural beauty, and proceeded with a rather surprising account of the curriculum of the Athonite Academy:

> There Demosthenes struggles, encouraging the Athenians against the Mace-
> donians; there Homer in his rhapsodies sings the heroic deeds around Ilion;
> there Thucydides narrates in sublime style the civil strife of the Greeks; there
> the father of history in Ionic style narrates earlier history and victories against
> the barbarians; here Plato expounds theology and Aristotle in multiple ways
> unravels the mysteries of nature; and the French, the Germans, and the English
> teach their novel philosophical systems.[31]

As it appears from this profile of his teaching at the Athonite Academy, Voulgaris's model for the revival and upgrading of learning within the Ortho-dox Church envisaged a substantial training in the classics combined with an exposure to modern European philosophy. The 'French, German, and English' philosophers whom Voulgaris taught on Mount Athos were Descartes, Leibniz

---

30 P. M. Kitromilides, 'Athos and the Enlightenment', in *Mount Athos and Byzantine monas-ticism*, ed. A. Bryer and M. Cunningham (Aldershot: Variorum, 1996), 257–72.
31 The text in *Παράλληλον φιλοσοφίας καὶ χριστιανισμοῦ* (Constantinople, 1830), 82–91; quotation at 91.

and Wolff, and John Locke. This curriculum could only be taught in a monastic environment for as long as Voulgaris enjoyed the full and unswerving support of the highest powers in the church. When Cyril V fell from the ecumenical throne, he retired to Mount Athos, where he began meddling in the affairs of the school. This encouraged other factions to come out openly against the modernist programme pioneered by Voulgaris, who feeling abandoned and betrayed resigned from the directorship in 1759.

This, however, was not the end of the openness of the church to western learning in the age of the Enlightenment. Voulgaris was replaced at the head of the Athonite Academy by Nikolaos Zerzoulis, known as one of the earliest proponents of Newtonian science in Greek culture. Voulgaris himself was called to Constantinople by Patriarch Seraphim II soon after his resignation in 1759 and charged with the reform of the patriarchal academy. His tenure there was too short to allow him to bring about major changes but he did introduce mathematics and modern science into the curriculum. His stay in Constantinople nevertheless had one major political consequence: he contributed to the rapprochement between the Great Church and the Russian Empire, ending a period of cold relations going back to the reforms imposed on the church in Russia by Peter the Great. This initiative was to cost Patriarch Seraphim II his throne in March 1761 and with his deposition came the end of Voulgaris's career at the patriarchal academy. There too Nikolaos Zerzoulis replaced him for a short period.

Other eighteenth-century patriarchs, notably Samuel I (1763–68, 1773–74), one of the towering figures in the ecclesiastical politics of the time, were inimical to western learning and modern philosophy. They may have preferred the more familiar and conventional Aristotelian philosophy but they never attempted to stop the teaching of modern philosophy. Furthermore, up to 1789 the church, as an institution, never adopted through synodical resolutions any policies hostile to western secular learning. The eighteenth century witnessed intense ideological conflicts between traditional and modernising scholars, as they struggled for control of major educational establishments. Yet remarkably before 1789 the church only once proceeded to the condemnation of a scholar for his philosophical views. This happened in 1723 and was directed against Methodios Anthrakitis, who had provoked the hostility of other scholars in Kastoria for teaching the philosophy of Malebranche and Descartes rather than that of Aristotle. But despite the agitation engineered against him by his local rivals, he was only called to appear before the synod of Constantinople when he was accused of adopting the heretical religious views of the Spanish mystic Miguel de Molinos. When he failed to appear, the synod issued an anathema against his presumed religious deviations, not his philosophical views. When Anthrakitis appeared repentant before it, the synod rescinded the anathema but ordered him from then on to teach only the views of Aristotle.[32] Many other important intellectual figures after Anthrakitis escaped the censure of the church despite their advanced views. This applies notably to Eugenios Voulgaris himself, but also to Nikephoros Theotokis, who openly taught Newtonian physics, and especially to Iosipos Moisiodax, who was embroiled in countless conflicts with the traditionalists on account of his militant espousal of the philosophical and scientific principles of the Enlightenment.[33] This vindicates the judgement made by Manuel Gedeon, who pointed out that, regardless of the conflicts between 'old' and 'new' philosophers, official ecclesiastical policy was never actively hostile to modern secular learning and to Enlightenment ideas, even if it remained vigilant and uncompromising where questions of doctrine and faith were concerned.[34]

Things were to change radically after 1789. The French Revolution proved a catalyst for profound ideological changes in the Greek East as in the rest of Europe. The critical moment came in 1793 with the regicide in France. The apocalyptic vision of the end of civilisation voiced in the arguments of the Counter-Revolution in the west was readily adopted in conservative environments in the Orthodox East. The first expression of this new polemical attitude of Orthodoxy against western liberal ideas came in a pamphlet entitled 'The misery of conceited sages', which was published anonymously in Trieste in 1793. It was probably the work of Athanasios Parios, the most militant counter-Enlightenment scholar writing from within the ranks of the church.[35]

The new approach of the church towards the Enlightenment and the ideologies of modernity manifested itself in 1793 with the excommunication of Christodoulos Pamblekis. This was the first case of excommunication of a scholar for his philosophical and religious views since the time of Anthrakitis, exactly sixty years earlier. Pamblekis studied at the Athonite Academy under Voulgaris in the 1750s and later on taught in Greek schools in central Europe. In 1786 he had published a book on the nature of philosophy, drawing on and paraphrasing from the *Encyclopédie*. Six years later the views expressed in this

---

32 Henderson, *Revival of Greek thought*, 33–40; P. M. Kitromilides, Νεοελληνικός Διαφωτισμός, third edition (Athens: Cultural Foundation of the National Bank of Greece, 2000), 43–8.

33 P. M. Kitromilides, *The Enlightenment as social criticism: Iosipos Moisiodax and Greek culture in the eighteenth century* (Princeton: Princeton University Press, 1992), 46–9, 80–2.

34 Manuel Gedeon, ' Ἐκκλησία καὶ ἐπιστήμη κατὰ τὸν ΙΗ' αἰῶνα', in Ἡ πνευματικὴ κίνησις τοῦ γένους, ed. A. Angelou-P. Iliou (Athens: Ermis, 1976), 97–113.

35 For a survey of 'counter-revolutionary' reactions, Kitromilides, Διαφωτισμός, 271–6, 428–31.

book provoked an attack in the form of a parody of a religious service by the bishop of Platamon Dionysios, who was an old enemy of Pamblekis since their days at the Athonite Academy. Pamblekis responded in the same year with an extensive treatise, which he subtitled 'Of theocracy'. In this text he declared himself proud to be called a new Rousseau or Voltaire by his enemies and launched an all out attack on the church, monasticism and the fundamentals of Orthodox faith, eventually adopting a pantheistic position. This was the first and only open systematic attack on the fundamentals of Christian faith to emerge in the literature of the Enlightenment in Greek. Pamplekis's enemies were quick to bring this to the attention of the church and in November 1793 Patriarch Neophytos VII and the synod of Constantinople issued an edict excommunicating Pamblekis and anathematising his views. Meanwhile the author had died in Leipzig in August 1793 while his controversial work was still in press. Thus he had no chance to rescind his views and the anathema of the church against him was never lifted.[36]

Anxieties and worries in the Orthodox East over what was happening in the world climaxed in a major crisis in 1798. During that year French revolutionary troops had literally crossed the threshold of the Ottoman world by landing in Egypt under General Bonaparte, who had meanwhile abolished the Republic of Venice in 1797 and brought its possessions, including the seven Ionian islands, under French revolutionary occupation. In exactly the same year a Jacobin-inspired conspiracy to overthrow Ottoman despotism and to establish a free 'Hellenic Republic' in the Balkans and Asia Minor was unravelled by the Austrian authorities, which arrested the protagonists, Rhigas Velestinlis and seven companions, in Trieste and Vienna.[37] The Sublime Porte was alarmed over the security of the empire and the alarm was transmitted and deeply imprinted upon the new patriarch Gregory V, who had already distinguished himself by his dynamism, pastoral work and piety as metropolitan of the great city of Smyrna. During his three patriarchates (1797–98, 1806–8, 1818–21) Gregory V was to inspire and lead the campaign of the church against the Enlightenment. His pastoral zeal, great learning, dedication to the traditions of the church and unbending will power were mobilised with remarkable tenacity in this cause. One of his first actions upon ascending the ecumenical throne was to reconstitute the patriarchate's printing press, thus reviving Cyril Loukaris's original,

36 The edict in M. Gedeon (ed.), Κανονικαὶ Διατάξεις (Constantinople: The Patriarchal Press, 1888), I, 279–91. For a discussion of the Pamblekis case see Kitromilides, Διαφωτισμός, 368–72.

37 P. M. Kitromilides, 'An Enlightenment perspective on Balkan cultural pluralism. The republican vision of Rhigas Velestinlis', History of Political Thought 24 (2003), 465–79.

if abortive, initiative. In the next quarter of a century the patriarchal press proved an effective instrument of Gregory V's attack on Enlightenment ideas. In August or September 1797, that is very shortly after the French occupation, Gregory addressed a pastoral encyclical to the Orthodox islanders of the Ionian islands warning them of the machinations of the 'primeval snake' against the true faith, machinations disguised as promises of liberty and equality. In 1798 the patriarch and the synod condemned the revolutionary pamphlet issued by Rhigas Velestinlis in Vienna 'because it is full of rottenness' and instructed the hierarchy to be vigilant and to collect all copies that might appear in their dioceses and forward them to Istanbul to be burnt. Encyclicals warning against the 'recently emergent disease' of French revolutionary ideas were sent to the hierarchy, clergy and laity of dioceses in Epiros, Crete and the Aegean islands, as well as to Smyrna.[38]

The most significant expression of Orthodox reaction to the Enlightenment and to French revolutionary ideas appeared in 1798 in the form of two pamphlets issued by the patriarchal press. One entitled *Paternal Instruction* was attributed to the patriarch of Jerusalem Anthimos. The text voiced a strong exhortation against the newly appearing 'systems of liberty', which represented the latest contrivances of the devil designed to lead the pious astray. Against the godless talk of liberty the author counselled submission to the powerful monarchy of the Ottomans, which had been raised by God above all other monarchies in the world in order to serve as a bridle on Latin heresy and as an agent for the salvation of the Orthodox. These arguments provoked strong reactions in liberal circles. In response the foremost Enlightenment thinker Adamantios Korais immediately published an anonymous tract entitled *Fraternal Instruction*. In it he questioned the attribution of *Paternal Instruction* to the pious patriarch of Jerusalem and answered point by point the servile arguments of the 'Byzantine dogmatist of 1798'.[39]

The other counter-revolutionary pamphlet issued by the patriarchal press was entitled *Christian Apology*, which was the work of Athanasios Parios. In it he warned the faithful against the illusory claims of liberty and equality as a sure recipe for atheism and damnation. It seems that the authorities of the patriarchal press had tampered with Parios's text, damping down his arguments. He accordingly proceeded with two fuller editions of his pamphlet,

38 N. Zakharopoulos, *Γρηγόριος V. Σαφὴς ἔκφρασις τῆς ἐκκλησιαστικῆς πολιτικῆς ἐπὶ Τουρκοκρατίας* (Thessalonike: [privately printed], 1974).
39 D. Thereianos, *Ἀδαμάντιος Κοραῆς* (Trieste: Austrohungarian Lloyd, 1889), I, 312. Cf. R. Clogg, 'The Dhidhaskalia Patriki (1798): an Orthodox Reaction to French Revolutionary Propaganda', *Middle Eastern Studies* 5 (1969), 87–115.

which gave him scope for more extreme views. They appeared in 1800 and 1805 respectively and were published at Leipzig at a safe distance from patriarchal censorship.

These measures taken during Gregory V's first patriarchate represented a clear strategy against the feared political effects of the Enlightenment. On a broader cultural level the 1790s were marked by proliferating Orthodox apologetics against the religious consequences of secular philosophy. This literature of Christian apologetics included works by Antonios Manuel (1791) and Prokopios Peloponnesios (1792). They were joined by Eugenios Voulgaris and Nikephoros Theotokis, once exponents of Enlightenment learning but now senior prelates in the Russian Church. Most of these apologetic works were translations or adaptations of western sources against Voltaire and the Enlightenment critique of religion. They supplied ammunition for further polemics like the anti-Voltairean work produced in 1802 by Makarios Kavvadias.[40] The ideological controversy provoked by the reverberation of the debate on the French Revolution in Greek culture provided the broader context for attacks on the Enlightenment that went beyond Christian apologetics. Against the challenges of the critical ideologies of modernity, the ecclesiastical intelligentsia attached to the patriarchate of Constantinople attempted to articulate an alternative perspective defending the traditional worldview.[41] The confrontation between modernising and traditionalist scholars took many directions and included the articulation of a vivid and occasionally excessive anticlericalism.[42]

Despite the ideological controversies of the 1790s, when a new project for the reform of the patriarchal academy was undertaken under Patriarch Kallinikos V in 1804 the open-mindedness towards the Enlightenment that had been exemplified half a century earlier under Cyril V and Seraphim II surfaced again in the blueprint for the new school which was transferred from the Phanar to Kuruçeşme on the Bosporus. Some important scholars who had made their mark on Greek Enlightenment culture were invited to collaborate, including Benjamin Lesvios, who had been embroiled in serious controversies with the anti-Copernicans at the academy of Ayvalik. The direction of the school was entrusted to a moderate clergyman, Dorotheos Proios, known for

---

40 For a survey Kitromilides, Διαφωτισμός, 434–43.

41 V. Makridis, *Die religiöse Kritik am Kopernikanischen Weltbild in Griechenland zwischen 1794 und 1821* (Frankfurt am Mein: Peter Lang, 1995).

42 R. Clogg, 'Anticlericalism in pre-Independence Greece', in *The Orthodox Churches and the West*, ed. Derek Baker (Oxford: Blackwell, 1976), 257–76; A. Tabaki, 'Lumières et critique des églises au XVIIIe siècle: le cas grec', in *Les Lumières et leur combat: la critique de la religion et des églises à l'époque des Lumières*, ed. J. Mondot (Berlin: BWV, 2004), 245–58.

his friendship with Korais. The curriculum included experimental physics, advanced mathematics and modern philosophy, besides an extensive pro-gramme of classical studies and religious education. Proios retired to become metropolitan of Philadelphia. His successors were other well-known Enlight-enment scholars such as Stephanos Doungas and Constantinos Koumas.[43]

The intensity of ideological conflict in Greek society in the decade leading up to the outbreak of the Greek revolution in 1821 eventually sealed the attitude of the church. This became evident during Gregory V's third patriarchate (1818–21). The patriarch returned to the throne from his exile on Mount Athos full of zeal for the defence of the faith. The patriarch and the synod implemented a series of pastoral measures in an attempt to stem the tide of ideological change. An encyclical in 1819 warned the faithful about the detrimental effects that the teaching of modern science and mathematics could have for the true faith and the salvation of the soul. A pamphlet entitled *Crito's Reflections*, which criticised the construction of a sumptuous mansion for one of the prelates of the church and suggested that the expense could be better used on the endowment of a school, was ceremoniously burnt in the courtyard of the patriarchate at the suggestion of the chief censor of the patriarchal press. Finally in March 1821, in a climate of alarm over the storm which was brewing, the patriarch convoked a synod whose task was to condemn outright 'philosophical teaching' and its major living exponents.[44]

This was the conclusion of three decades of confrontation between the church and the ideologies of modernity, a confrontation triggered by reactions to the French Revolution, which brought to an end a long-standing tradition in the Orthodox Church whereby the moderate versions of the Enlightenment were readily enlisted by the church in discharging her pastoral work and in promoting her educational initiatives.

---

43 Gedeon, Χρονικά, 179–89. C. Koumas gives his own account in Ἱστορίαι τῶν ἀνθρω-πίνων πράξεων (Vienna: Anton von Haykul, 1832), XII, 591–5.
44 For details see Kitromilides, Διαφωτισμός, 447–57.

9

Bars'kyj and the Orthodox community

ALEXANDER GRISHIN

Vasyl Hryhorovyc-Bars'kyj was a Slav mendicant pilgrim whose travels lasted twenty-four years between 1723 and 1747. They took him from his native Kiev through eastern Europe to Italy, where he worshipped at Christian shrines in Bari, Rome and Venice. He then travelled to the Holy Land, *en route* spending time in the Greek islands; he also spent two extended periods living on Mount Athos, visited Cyprus on three occasions, and travelled extensively throughout Greece and Asia Minor. He spent some time in Constantinople from where he returned home to Kiev.[1] While pilgrimages were common in this period, both by religious zealots and by curious travellers, Bars'kyj's pilgrimage was unusual in both its duration and its scope, as well as for the detailed written and illustrated record that he kept.[2] It was also unusual in that he wrote as an Orthodox traveller, who throughout his journeys sought out Orthodox communities and recorded their customs, churches, liturgies and traditions of worship from the perspective of a passionate insider, rather than as a curious outsider.

Although our knowledge of Bars'kyj's biography is relatively extensive, and extant sources for its study are rich and varied, basic questions such as the exact date of his birth, his precise name and details of his education remain unresolved. He appears to have been born in Kiev towards the end of 1701 in the region of the Monastery of the Caves; the third in a family of ten children, the son of a semi-literate merchant. In 1715 or 1716 he entered the

---

1 See T. G. Stavrou and P. R. Weisensel, *Russian travelers to the Christian East from the twelfth to the twentieth century* (Columbus, OH: Slavica, 1986), 70–3.

2 His untitled travel journal, usually referred to as 'The travels of Vasyl' Hryhorovyc-Bars'kyj in the holy lands of the East', survives in the autograph manuscript of over 500 folios, or about 240,000 words, and is accompanied by scores of painstakingly accurate archaeological drawings mainly of churches and monasteries. The autograph manuscript is in Kiev at the Akademiia Nauk Archive, Kiev v, No. 1062. The most accurate published edition is N. Barsukov, *Stranstvovaniia Vasil'ia Grigorovicha-Barskago po sviatym mestam vostoka s 1723 po 1747 g.*, 4 vols. (St Petersburg: Pravoslavnoe palestinskoe obshchestvo, 1885–87). References will be given below to the manuscript and not to the printed edition.

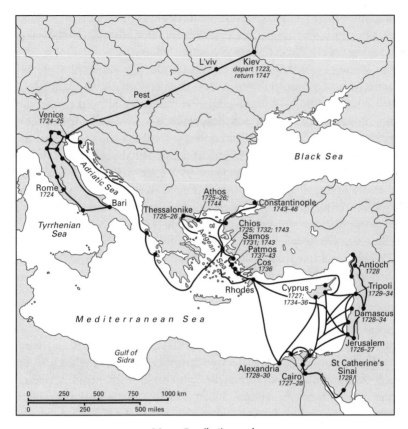

Map 3 Bars'kyj's travels

Kiev theological academy, but was unable to complete the eight-year course of study before illness in the form of a huge ulcer on his leg forced him to abandon his studies, and in July 1723 he went to L'viv to seek medical treatment. When he left Kiev, he possessed a very rudimentary education, which included a knowledge of the Slav languages, a working knowledge of Latin and a basic grounding in Orthodox theology. It was in L'viv that he found what he interpreted as a miraculous cure for his ailment and made a vow to go on a pilgrimage of thanksgiving to the shrine of St Nicholas at Bari. Also in L'viv, when attempting to gain admission to study at the local Jesuit academy, he experienced at first hand the persecution of Orthodox believers by the Uniate Roman Catholic authorities. It is within the context of a divided Ukraine – split between the Orthodox Russian Empire and the Roman Catholic

Polish–Lithuanian Commonwealth – that Bars'kyj's travel journal needs to be read. The author was a partisan Orthodox believer, whose pilgrimage was part of a journey of self-discovery and continuing education.

On leaving L'viv, Bars'kyj set out on foot for the shrine of St Nicholas at Bari, going on from there to Naples, Rome, Florence and Venice.[3] The first section of Bars'kyj's travel journal is characterised by the exceptional richness of autobiographical and topographical information. The novelty of the experience is reflected in the attention paid to the details of the pilgrimage. At the start of his journey Bars'kyj felt at home with the languages spoken in the Ruthenian lands of the Polish Commonwealth and noted with precision the names of the villages that he passed through and the distances between them; he commented on the surrounding countryside and on such details as whether the water in the streams that he crossed was clear or murky. He was also preoccupied with human relationships, both with his travelling companions and with the people whom they encountered, such as the Catholic bishop who chased them away from the monastery of the Holy Saviour near Sambor.[4]

At this early stage it is difficult to determine the exact purpose Bars'kyj had in mind in keeping this detailed diary of events and observations. The fact that most of the observations were made and recorded directly on the spot, rather than being put together later from memory, is attested by the inclusion of numerous incidental details such as the daily changes in the weather, reference to the days of the week, descriptions of casual encounters with people, and precise epigraphic records. Also, from time to time, he noted how he wrote his account, recalling how on one occasion he had 'sat until evening writing about my journey'.[5]

Until the winter of 1724–25, when Bars'kyj commenced his study of Greek in Venice, he was forced to rely exclusively on his knowledge of the Slav languages and Latin. During his early travels he constantly lamented his lack of knowledge of other languages, particularly of German, Italian and Greek. It meant that he frequently found monasteries and towns barred to him until he could find someone who knew Latin, usually a priest or a student, who could communicate his wishes to the guards on duty. The first thing Bars'kyj did on reaching a new town or village was to seek out fellow Slavs and he often recorded the number of Ruthenian, Russian, Polish or Serbian families

---

3 A. Grishin, 'Vasyl' Hryhorovyc Bars'kyj: an eighteenth-century Ukrainian pilgrim in Italy', *Harvard Ukrainian Studies* 17 (1993), 7–26.
4 Bars'kyj Ms., fol. 7v.
5 Bars'kyj Ms., fol. 12v.

that were resident in a particular place. It also appears that these people were often his primary source of information for his descriptions of the places he visited.

In the early part of his travel journal we encounter a number of Bars'kyj's expressed attitudes to various nationalities, in part reflecting his personal experiences, but also in part determined by their attitudes to the Orthodox religion. Having failed to gain admission either to Buda or to Pest, Bars'kyj found a Serbian community living outside their city walls. The Serbs were initially hostile to Bars'kyj, concluding from his appearance that he was a Catholic pilgrim on the way to Rome. On learning that he was Orthodox, he was embraced and invited to the Serbian church to celebrate the feast of the Descent of the Holy Spirit and a considerable sum of money was gathered to help him on his way.[6] Bars'kyj praises the Serbs for their warmth and hospitality, as he does the Greeks. He stayed twice with the Greek community at the church of St George in Venice, first in June 1724 and again from October 1724 until the end of February 1725. During his first stay he knew no Greek but was accepted as an Orthodox traveller. He noted that, although he could not understand the language, the church liturgy was similar to the one back home, except that here the Gospel was read not from the centre of the church but from the pulpit high up on the left-hand side.[7]

During his first two years of travelling Bars'kyj appeared to be constantly overwhelmed by the novelty of the experience, intimidated by his lack of knowledge of local languages and, for much of the time, preoccupied with the search for fellow Slavs, as much for companionship and support as for material sustenance. The next five years saw fundamental changes in his outlook, which are documented in the second part of Bars'kyj's travel journal. This deals with the events that took place between his second departure from Venice on 28 February 1725 and the end of 1729, by which time he had settled in Tripoli to further his studies as a guest of the patriarch of Antioch, Sylvester the Cypriot.

After his period of study in Venice he gained a degree of fluency in Greek and his travel journal entries are frequently punctuated with transcriptions of Greek inscriptions, discussion of Greek words and comments about various Greek manuscripts that he found in monastic libraries. He also became proficient in Arabic, sufficient for purposes of conversation, noting on one occasion that, as he could not find a Greek priest to hear his confession before the Christmas celebrations, 'I had to say my confession in Arabic.'[8] While the extent of his

---

6 Bars'kyj Ms., fols. 13v.–14v.
7 Bars'kyj Ms., fol. 26r.
8 Bars'kyj Ms., fol. 236r.

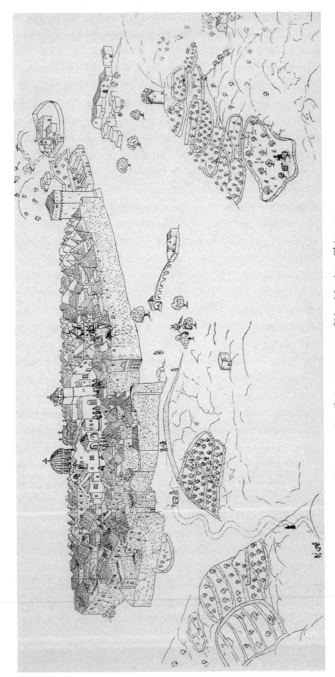

Figure 9.1 Bars'kyj, monastery of Nea Moni on Chios, 1732.

knowledge of Turkish at this stage of his travels is unclear, he does frequently explain Turkish words and was sufficiently at home in the language to swear abuse in Turkish at thieves who were preparing to attack him. While in the first part of his journal Bars'kyj emerges as the pilgrim who stands outside the city gates, waiting for someone who understands Latin or a Slavonic language, in the second part he appears as the accomplished polyglot, scornful of those who know but a single language.

Although poverty continued to stalk Bars'kyj, the second part of his journal is far less preoccupied with begging for alms as the sole means of financial support. Increasingly patriarchs, archbishops and abbots received him with honour, as a distinguished visitor rather than as a mendicant pilgrim. Greek monks and clerics more readily accepted him as belonging to their number and there were fewer instances of him being rejected as the suspect outsider. The pace of travel also slowed down somewhat, with Bars'kyj prepared to spend months in a particular town or weeks at a sacred site instead of a few rushed days or a couple of hours, as was previously the case.

More significantly, the second part of Bars'kyj's journal displayed fundamental changes in form and format. Most notable is his use of pen and ink line drawings to illustrate his observations: a practice which he started shortly after his arrival in Jerusalem on 30 September 1726. Frequently there is a close correlation between the drawings and the text, with Bars'kyj on occasion stating that a particular icon appeared the way in which he had shown it in the illustration, or that the structure of Joseph's Well or a topographical description could be more clearly understood by consulting the accompanying drawings, which were both detailed and carefully labelled.[9] At this stage of the journal, drawings play the role of explanatory footnotes or decorative vignettes. Bars'kyj was a naive but authentic recorder of what he saw. He was probably aware of the schematic formulae of architectural drawings found in Greek travel books of the time, but he appears to have adapted their conventions to the monuments before him rather than copying existing illustrations. What his drawings lack in the professionalism of their execution they gain in their precision of observation. His drawings have none of the baroque trappings and allegorical personifications that are such a common feature in the eighteenth century of western European travel books.

---

9 In Bars'kyj's text the many references that allude to his drawings include those concerning the miraculous icon at the Kykkos monastery on Cyprus, Joseph's Well and the overall appearance of Nazareth. See Bars'kyj Ms., fols. 180r, 190r, 237r.

The form of descriptions also starts to change gradually, as Bars'kyj moves away from his previously adopted form of listing general impressions interspersed with descriptions of towns and holy sites, to a much more analytical approach. The change is not purely one of the amount of detail included, or of the length of the entry. While exceptionally long and detailed descriptions of the monasteries of Nea Moni on Chios, St Sabas, outside Jerusalem, and St Catherine on Mount Sinai do appear in this section, there is a gradual change in Bars'kyj's method of presentation of his material. In the earlier part he listed conflicting pieces of evidence with contradictions not explained but treated as part of the greater wisdom of the Lord. In the second part a more rationalist approach is evident, even if scriptural authority remains of paramount significance. Since the Gospels mention that the Holy Family fled to Egypt, Bars'kyj had no difficulty in accepting a small dwelling in Cairo as being the house in which they stayed, when it was identified as such by the local Christian community.[10] However, when a contradiction arose, like two houses purporting to be the very house in which the Archangel Gabriel approached the Virgin Mary to deliver the Lord's message, then Bars'kyj adopted an analytical approach. The first candidate for this site was the shrine in Loreto, which Bars'kyj accepted as genuine when he visited it in 1724 and related the miracle of how the angels had transported the house there from Palestine.[11] He encountered the second candidate five years later in Nazareth itself. What is interesting is not so much that he declared the house in Loreto to be a fake, but the reasons he gave for his conclusion. While not doubting the ability of angels to carry houses, if they so desired, he found it impossible to accept that a whole house could disappear from Nazareth without the local inhabitants noticing it and without the event being recorded in local oral tradition. For Bars'kyj, the most important piece of evidence for discounting the Loreto building's identification as the authentic dwelling was, as he notes, 'that the house in Loreto is assembled out of red bricks, fired in ovens, but in Nazareth there have never been houses made out of bricks, nor are there now, but they are all made out of natural white stone cut out of the surrounding hills and in no way can bricks be found there, neither new nor ancient ones'.[12] Bars'kyj's boldness in rejecting an accepted tradition can be explained in part by the fact that here he was confronted by two contradictory traditions, one advanced by the Catholic Church and the other by the Orthodox Church, and in this instance the truth clearly lay on

10 Bars'kyj Ms., fol. 191r.
11 Bars'kyj Ms., fols. 32r–34r.
12 Bars'kyj Ms., fol. 293r.

the side of the Orthodox. In his subsequent writings, the same penetrating questioning of convention is applied to purely Orthodox traditions.

In the second part of his travel journal, Bars'kyj started to rely less on oral sources and to lean more heavily on literary sources. In one instance there is a lacuna in Bars'kyj's manuscript, with a note in the margin reminding the author to consult a book and to insert a short account of the saint's life.[13] Elsewhere, events to which Bars'kyj claims to be an eye witness, and in all probability was, are paraphrased from another literary source. This is the case with his detailed discussion of the Holy Fire, the miracle that was part of the Easter ritual for Orthodox Christians in the Church of the Holy Sepulchre. Despite his being present at the ceremony in April 1727, the prologue to his description betrays its dependence on much earlier writings in Church Slavonic. It contains the information that many pilgrims falsely say that the fire is carried from heaven by the Holy Spirit in the form of a dove while others see it like lightning, details which first appeared in early twelfth-century accounts. Bars'kyj was consciously reverting to the conventions of the *khozhdeniia* account, as found in the writings of the twelfth-century traveller from Rus, Igumen Daniil.[14] In this he was following Arsenii Sukhanov, who had come to the Holy Land half a century before Bars'kyj, but whose writings gained popularity in the 1720s,[15] during Bars'kyj's formative years in Kiev.[16] Bars'kyj would have had access to copies of the Daniil manuscript at both the Kiev Academy and the L'viv Academy[17] and he appears to be recalling the text from memory.

In terms of travel and distances, the second part of Bars'kyj's pilgrimage is one of great sea voyages. Despite his stated intention of returning home from Venice in the early spring of 1725, the chance meeting in the Piazza San Marco with the hieromonk Ruvym Gur'skyj led to a dramatic change in plans. Ruvym was a priest who had fallen from grace at the court of Tsar Peter the Great and fled St Petersburg because of a campaign of malicious gossip directed at him. He decided to join Bars'kyj on a pilgrimage to the holy shrines of Greece and they set out together by boat for Corfu on 28 February 1725, reaching the island on 9 April. Bars'kyj provides a detailed description of how they worshipped the relics of St Spyridon. From Corfu they sailed to Kephallenia (Cephalonia),

---

13 Bars'kyj Ms., fols. 131r–132v.

14 See A. Grishin, 'Vasylijy Bars'kyj and the xozhenija tradition', *Australian Slavonic and East European Studies Journal* 11 (1988), 29–42.

15 N. I. Ivanovskii, 'Proskinitarii Arseniia Sukhanova', *Pravoslavnii Palestinskii Sbornik* 7 (St Petersburg, 1889), pt 3.

16 For Bars'kyj's account of the Holy Fire, see Bars'kyj Ms., fols. 173r–176v.

17 The Kiev manuscript is a late sixteenth- or seventeenth-century copy held at the Kiev Academy Library, Cat. no. 157, while the one at L'viv is dated 1701 and is catalogue no. 132(105).

Zakynthos (Zante) and Mykonos, and finally arrived at Chios on 4 August 1725. This was the first of Bars'kyj's six visits to the island and produced his most detailed description of the Nea Moni monastery.

Bars'kyj set off from Chios on 9 September 1725 for Thessalonike, and thence to Athos where he spent the winter at the Russian monastery of St Panteleimon. Apart from St Panteleimon, where he felt at home, he appears to have received a somewhat hostile reception at the other monasteries when the monks learnt that he was a pilgrim travelling from Rome. He even had to have his Orthodoxy established before he was admitted to the Eucharist.[18] He left Athos on 1 February 1726, and spent the next seven months in Thessalonike, where he perfected his spoken Greek and developed a degree of fluency in Turkish.

On 1 September 1726, Bars'kyj set off by boat for the Holy Land, visiting along the way Rhodes and Cyprus. On 23 September he arrived at Jaffa, from where he travelled on foot as part of an escorted caravan to Jerusalem, but becoming separated from the caravan he was robbed and beaten. Undeterred he urged all Slavs to make the pilgrimage to the Holy Sepulchre, as 'there is no country from which so few pilgrims come as from the Russian countries'.[19] Bars'kyj's first stay in the Holy Land lasted about seven months, from September 1726 to April 1727. He travelled extensively, mostly residing in monasteries and frequently revisiting holy sites. He drew from oral sources much of the information that he provides concerning the Holy Land although he spent his four-week stay at the monastery of St Sabas reading books in the monastic library. Apart from visits to the Dead Sea and the Jordan River, and a trip to Bethlehem for Christmas, Bars'kyj passed most of his time in Jerusalem.

On 17 April 1727, Bars'kyj left by boat to visit Sinai, but was blown off course and fetched up at Limassol on Cyprus.[20] Seeing the hand of God in this, he stayed on the island for three months and visited and described a number of monasteries. By 31 July he managed to reach Cairo, from where he planned to travel to St Catherine's on Mount Sinai, but he was told that the monastery was inaccessible to visitors because of hostile Arabs. After a stay in Cairo that lasted some eight months, he set off for Sinai disguised as a sailor. First crossing the Gulf of Suez to al-Ṭûr he set out across the desert until he finally arrived at the monastery's locked gate on 31 March 1728. After

---

18 Bars'kyj Ms., fol. 116r.
19 Bars'kyj Ms., fol. 139v.
20 For a translation of Bars'kyj's account of Cyprus see *A Pilgrim's Account of Cyprus: Bars'kyj's Travels in Cyprus*, ed. A. D. Grishin [Sources for the History of Cyprus 3] (Altamont, NY: Greece and Cyprus Research Center, 1996).

many anxious hours he was smuggled into the monastery and he spent a week visiting the sacred sites and examining the library. His detailed discussion of the monastery displays considerable erudition over such things as the form of the liturgy celebrated on Sinai and parallels that could be discovered in monastic *typika*.[21] With an eye to the reform of the liturgy back home, Bars'kyj was becoming increasingly preoccupied with establishing the form of the earliest and authentic Orthodox liturgy. From Sinai he returned via Suez to Cairo, where he settled in the patriarchal palace. The exact sequence of writing of the second part of the travel journal is difficult to determine in view of the five-year time span. Internal evidence suggests that it was written in the form of diary-like entries arranged in their present order. It is also apparent that Bars'kyj intended to revise the manuscript, because he left certain lacunae in the text for things that he felt he needed to look up and insert. This task was never completed and the manuscript remains unedited.

The third and final part of Bars'kyj's travel journal deals with events that took place between 1730 and late 1744. The final three years of the pilgrim's travels between 1744 and his return to Kiev in September 1747 can only be reconstructed from letters, drawings and miscellaneous documents, as no written account survives. The detailed annotations made on the drawings executed in these last three years indicate that Bars'kyj intended to write up this section, but alas, his premature death, barely a month after his return to Kiev, robbed him of the opportunity to fulfil this task. Any fieldwork notes he may have assembled for this section have been lost, except for a small extract of notes dealing for the most part with Constantinople. The drawings which have survived, mainly dealing with the churches and monasteries of mainland Greece and Crete, are among the most valuable extant documents from the first half of the eighteenth century for art historians working on the Byzantine heritage of Greece.

The fact that the final section was never written indicates the extent to which Bars'kyj's working method had changed. Whereas earlier sections of his travel journal retained the sequence of a diary-like chronicle, studded with specific events from everyday life, rich in local colour and autobiographical detail, and precious for its immediacy, the method and presentation of the third section is quite different, for it required plenty of time to organise the material, plus access to a reasonably good library. It speaks for itself that Bars'kyj employed for the surviving fragment dealing with Constantinople at least eight secondary sources. In this final section, specific dates occur rarely and

---

21 Bars'kyj Ms., fols. 194r–205v.

circumstances of travel are largely incidental to the account. Bars'kyj initially assembled this material in the form of researched fieldwork notes full of epigraphic data, transcriptions from manuscripts and documents, measurements of buildings, and a record of the oral traditions associated with a monument. At a considerably later stage he reorganised his material within a rational structure, checking it and supplementing it with material from other literary sources.

The best illustration of Bars'kyj's working method in this period is his treatment of the material he gathered on Athos. He arrived on Athos for his second visit on 12 May 1744 and apparently stayed there until November of that year. His collection of material from each monastery followed a systematic pattern, which inhospitable monks might on occasion disrupt, as happened at the monastery of Koutloumousiou, where he was not allowed enough time to venerate the relics, measure the churches, research the history of the founders of the monastery, and investigate the library, the chrysobulls and other documents, as well as draw the monastery.[22] In fact, this list was the bare minimum for Bars'kyj. In his account of each of the twenty major monasteries we have what approaches an encyclopaedic survey of the physical, administrative and socio-economic structure of the monastery, as well as a detailed catalogue of its spiritual treasures. We are informed about the physical structure and setting of the monastery, which is illustrated by at least one carefully labelled drawing.[23] In most instances Bars'kyj carried out a detailed investigation into the history of the monastery, and presented an analysis of its possessions in terms of gardens, stock, beehives and vineyards, as well as dependent *sketes* and *kellia*. He also noted the administrative hierarchy of the monastery, the number and nationality of monks, and details of the church services and ecclesiastical procedures. The *katholikon* itself is described in great detail, usually accompanied with measurements and, in the case of the Lavra, Pantokrator, Dionysiou and St Paul monasteries, with a complete ground plan. Bars'kyj also describes the decorations within the churches, transcribes the inscriptions and notes the location of significant icons, wall paintings and mosaics, and relates some of the legends associated with them. He also provides lengthy lists of the contents of the monastic treasures, listing the relics (at times questioning their authenticity),[24] chrysobulls and charters.

22 Bars'kyj Ms., fol. 387v.
23 Of the Athos drawings, twenty-three separate full plate illustrations and nine drawings inserted in the text of the manuscript survive. Several of the major drawings associated with the monasteries of Vatopedi, Chilandar and the Protaton are lost.
24 For example, at the Dionysiou monastery he was shown a thin metal chain that allegedly was the one with which St Peter was bound. Bars'kyj soberly comments that it appeared

With the chrysobulls, he generally catalogued their Greek, Slavonic and Latin titles, but where he considered the text to be of critical significance to the foundation of the monastery, its endowment or its acquisition of an important relic, the entire text is transcribed in the original language and provided with a Church Slavonic translation.[25] The treatment of monastic libraries varies, reflecting both Bars'kyj's evaluation of their importance and the access that he gained to them. Sometimes he simply estimates the number of books and manuscripts in a library's holding, usually noting the number written on parchment and listing authors' names preserved in handwritten manuscripts. At other times he discusses specific manuscripts, disputed attributions and transcribed colophons. Apart from the main church and its treasures, Bars'kyj frequently goes on to list the chapels, both inside and outside the monastery, sometimes describing their decorations and miracle-working icons as well as the history of the important *sketes*. He usually concludes his account by relating a number of legends associated with the monastery.

Bars'kyj left the actual compilation of this material from Athos until 1745 or 1746, when back in Constantinople he had access to the library of the Russian Resident, Aleksei Andreevich Vishniakov, and his successor Nepliuev.[26] The material is arranged systematically, both within and between entries. The monasteries are discussed one by one in order of their location, first those on the eastern side of the Athos peninsula and then those on the western side. The monastery of Lavra is selected for the key entry, which is so massive that it takes up about a quarter of the entire volume dealing with Athos.[27] About a third of this entry deals with a detailed liturgical investigation and an account of church procedures and monastic rites. Many of the subsequent entries refer back to the Lavra entry, indicating the extent to which church buildings, economic management, monastic administration and liturgical rites followed or departed from the Lavra model. Bars'kyj occasionally makes reference to recent editions of books to which he had access in Constantinople and which

---

to him unlike other chains of the period that he had seen in Rome and, therefore, he doubted the authenticity of this relic: Bars'kyj Ms., fol. 471v.

25 For example, the entry on the Xeropotamou monastery contains a detailed transcription of the Greek text of the chrysobulls housed there: Bars'kyj Ms., fols. 449v–463r.

26 A. A. Vishniakov arrived in Constantinople in 1729 and replaced I. I. Nepliuev as the Russian resident in late 1734. He remained in this post until 1745, when he was succeeded by A. I. Nepliuev, his predecessor's son. The exact date of Bars'kyj's return to Constantinople is unknown. He was there in 1746, as attested in correspondence, but may well have arrived in 1745. See his letter of October 31, 1746, Barsukov, *Stranstvovaniia*, IV, 67–8.

27 The entry on the Lavra runs to over sixty-three folios, while his account of this monastery during the 1725 visit to Athos occupies merely a folio and a half, see Bars'kyj Ms., fols. 332v.–395v., cf. fols 110v.–111r.

he used to check the facts assembled in his field notes.[28] On other occasions he makes reference to events that occurred in Constantinople in 1746 that were of relevance to the monasteries he is describing.[29] If in the earlier parts of the journal Bars'kyj repeatedly made the point that he was presenting his reader with a fresh eye-witness account of something that had just happened, in the third part the emphasis is on the way he is offering the reader a considered and well-researched opinion, an opinion which would benefit and enlighten those at home.

The earlier dependence on oral sources for factual information almost totally vanished as Bars'kyj increasingly turned to documents and to archaeological evidence for his primary material. In the section on Athos, much of the material that he provides on the history of the monasteries is taken directly from the chrysobulls, which he had read and translated. On occasion he tries to relate the surviving buildings, icons and relics to those mentioned in the literary sources and to use the archaeological evidence as a method of checking the accuracy and reliability of those literary sources. This approach is particularly evident in his discussion of the monastery of Xeropotamou, where he tries to match the evidence of the surviving relics, icons and buildings to the inscriptions and to the information provided in the chrysobulls.[30] To judge from the letters of Isaiah the *hegoumenos* of Lavra and Bessarion the *skeuophylax* of Iveron, Bars'kyj's reputation as a scholar and a man of letters was very high on the Holy Mountain. They describe him as more learned than any other traveller.[31]

In the final section of the journal, drawings start to play an increasingly important role, not primarily as props and decorations for the text, but as supporting evidence. Bars'kyj is constantly calling the reader's attention to the drawings, pointing out the precise angle from which a drawing was made and the time of day at which the monument was recorded. This is to suggest not that the earlier drawings were generally fanciful studies, but rather that Bars'kyj's technical precision and powers of observation had increased with time. If one compares the finest and largest of his drawings from the early thirties, that of the monastery of Nea Moni on Chios of 1732 (fig. 9.1),[32] with any of his Athos

---

28 For example, at one stage he refers to a *Proskynetarion* published in Venice in 1745, to check the claims being made by the monks of the Chilandar monastery concerning a relic, see Bars'kyj Ms., fol. 400r.
29 Bars'kyj Ms., fol. 426v.
30 Bars'kyj Ms., fols. 444r.–463r.
31 Barsukov, *Stranstvovaniia*, IV, 64–7.
32 Ibid., II, 204: plate 26. For a discussion of this drawing and the literature devoted to it, see C. Bouras, *Nea Moni on Chios: history and architecture* (Athens: Commercial Bank of Greece, 1982), 50, esp. fn. 4.

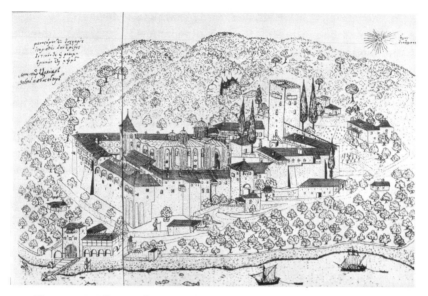

Figure 9.2 Bars'kyj, Docheiariou monastery viewed from the south-west, 1744.

drawings of a dozen years later, such as that of the monastery of Docheiariou of 1744 (fig. 9.2),[33] this development is evident. The first is a lavish drawing, but undated and largely without annotation, the only inscriptions being those that identify the garden of a local Russian monk and the chapel of St Anthony, and these inscriptions can only be understood when read within the general context of the description in the accompanying text. While scholars today may find it 'an invaluable source'[34] for the reconstruction of the monastery's appearance before the destruction of the dome in the 1881 earthquake, they are justified in noting some of the inaccuracies.[35] In the Docheiariou drawing the inscription informs us that it was drawn from the south-west in 1744, and another inscription identifies the rising sun to indicate the precise angle of view, while the text mentions that it was depicted as it appeared at midday.[36] Modern scholars have commented on how the *katholikon*, monastic walls, chapels and towers, as well as the shore line and the general topography, have been precisely observed, and Bars'kyj's accuracy is apparent when his drawing is compared with the monument, both as it exists today and as it appears in

33 Barsukov, *Stranstvovaniia*, III, 274: plate 21.
34 Bouras, *Nea Moni*, 50.
35 Ibid., 107.
36 Bars'kyj Ms., fol. 432r.

early photographs.[37] Frequent fires, earthquakes and wilful destruction have either demolished or totally transformed monuments on Mount Athos, in Cyprus and in Greece, making Bars'kyj's drawings an invaluable and unique record of otherwise vanished monuments.

Bars'kyj took pride in being a self-taught artist, as one passage in his journal makes explicit.[38] To the modern eye his technique in pen and ink looks simple and 'so uninfluenced, genuine and pure that it is at once able to express the artist's vision and his psychological approach to his subject',[39] but this did not prevent his approach from being that of a scholar, rather than of a dilettante. The precision with which Bars'kyj set out to tackle his task can be seen in the manner in which he copied 'Cleopatra's Needle', an obelisk, which he had seen in Alexandria in 1730. Having measured its width and estimated the height, and finding nobody to explain to him the meaning of the hieroglyphs, he proceeded to copy one side of the obelisk, as he says, 'to the amazement of onlookers'.[40] The resulting drawing is one of the earliest accurate transcriptions of hieroglyphs to be made in the eighteenth century.[41]

Further education may be the best explanation for the changes encountered in the final section of Bars'kyj's journal. With the support of the patriarch of Antioch, Sylvester the Cypriot, Bars'kyj spent the years between 1729 and 1734 studying under the distinguished scholar, the hieromonk Jacob.[42] Then from 1737 to 1743 Bars'kyj was on Patmos, at least part of the time studying at the Patmos School, initially under Makarios,[43] with whom he had spent some time on an earlier visit, and then with his successor Gerasimos. However, most of the time he studied independently, taught local children and wrote a textbook for the study of Latin by Greek speakers.[44] Bars'kyj appears to have placed

---

37 Peter Burridge writes concerning Bars'kyj's Docheiariou drawing, 'Every major element in Bars'kyj's illustration can be identified today.' P. J. Burridge, 'The development of monastic architecture on Mount Athos with special reference to the monasteries of Pantocrator and Chilandari', PhD dissertation, University of York (UK), 1976, 253.

38 Bars'kyj Ms., fol. 292r.

39 P. M. Mylonas, *Athos and its monastic institutions through old engravings and other works of art* (Athens: National Academy of Fine Arts, 1963), 21.

40 Barsukov, *Stranstvovaniia*, II, 163; the reproduction is plate 18. For a description of his process of work, Bars'kyj Ms., fol. 245r.

41 See E. Iversen, *Obelisks in exile* (Copenhagen: G. E. C. Gad Publishers, 1972), II, 90–147. I express my gratitude to Miss C. Andrews of the Department of Egyptian Antiquities at the British Museum in London for observations that she made to me concerning Bars'kyj's transcription of hieroglyphs.

42 On the hieromonk Jacob, see Bars'kyj Ms., fols. 240v.–241v., 247r., 264v.

43 On Makarios of Patmos, see Bars'kyj Ms., fols. 256v., 316v.–320v.

44 Bars'kyj's Latin grammar does not appear to have survived. For his discussion of it, see Bars'kyj Ms., fol. 320v.

considerable importance on the advice he received from Makarios of Patmos, as he lay on his deathbed in January 1737, that he should abandon his travels and should dedicate himself to the study of Greek, to benefit himself and his homeland.[45] While still at Patmos, it led him to inquire about the possibility of teaching Greek back in Kiev. Many years later, as we shall see, he received a positive response from the Kiev Academy.

While the exact impact of the Greek schools of learning on Bars'kyj is difficult to establish, there are a number of significant shifts in method and approach apparent in his journal. There is a growing critical awareness in his assessment of his sources. While the authority of scripture remains paramount, other literary and oral sources are rigorously assessed for their reliability. The authenticity of a chrysobull had to be established before the information that it contained could be accepted. An oral tradition needed to be tested against the written sources before it could be proclaimed as valid, and the fact that something was accepted by the Orthodox tradition as being authentic could not of itself be accepted as a validation. This critical attitude is apparent not only in a new interest in antiquarian and ethnographic detail, but also, more concretely, in his discussion both of the Kykkos icon and of Noah's stone at the monastery of the Archangels following his third visit to Cyprus.[46] While curiosity and the desire to experience different lands and customs were features of Bars'kyj's journal from the outset, new experiences were at first recorded within a fairly tight framework of a didactic religious interpretation. But by the third section of the journal Bars'kyj was examining, drawing and researching non-Christian buildings and monuments with the same care and precision that he had previously reserved for purely Christian monuments. For example, when he visited the island of Samos in 1731, he may have condemned Hera as a pagan goddess, but he proceeded to give a careful description of her sanctuary, which provided measurements and praised its beauty.[47] There is a similar fascination with the appearance, dress and customs of foreign peoples. Whereas in earlier sections of the travel journal, races were largely condemned because of their religion and were then dismissed as evil and hence not worthy of comment, later in the journal there is a whole wealth of closely observed detail concerning folk dress, headgear, jewellery and local customs. There are lengthy descriptions of folk costumes on Simi,[48] local pottery on Kos,[49]

45 Bars'kyj Ms., fol. 318r.
46 Bars'kyj Ms., fols. 285r., 285v., 295r., 295v.
47 Bars'kyj Ms., fol. 258r.
48 Bars'kyj Ms., fol. 248r.
49 Bars'kyj Ms., fol. 251v.

and the pattern of life in a village square with its coffee and tobacco, and the harmonious intermingling of Greeks and Turks.[50]

Changes to the model that Bars'kyj employed for his text will reflect his exposure to Greek education. If the first sections were influenced by the Slavonic *khozhdenie* tradition, then the final section owed much to the Greek *proskynetaria*. An eighteenth-century *proskynetarion* by Ioannis Komnenos was the single most important item of secondary literature used by Bars'kyj for his description of Athos.[51] He consulted both the 1701 and 1745 editions.[52] In some ways his account provides an improved, expanded and corrected version of Komnenos's illustrated guide to worship on Athos.

The emphasis of his journal gradually moved away from being a guidebook, diary and autobiography, to being a scholarly and polemical treatise designed to defend the truth, expose falsehood and benefit his homeland. The text is constantly punctuated with attacks on the Turkish oppressors and on papism, and sparkles with pious sermons concerning those who were prepared to suffer martyrdom for the sake of the Holy Orthodox Church. Providing a unifying thread to his account of his friendship with Patriarch Sylvester is the continuous struggle to preserve the independence of the Orthodox Church from the encroachments of Roman Catholicism.[53] In similar fashion, his very lengthy section on Mount Athos culminates in an attack on the treacherous policies of Michael VIII Palaiologos and the patriarch John XI Bekkos. Their persecution of anti-unionist monks in 1276[54] resonated with events occurring in Bars'kyj's native Ukraine, where the Orthodox faithful were under attack from Roman Catholic Uniates. On a different tack, Bars'kyj's precise record of the liturgical procedures, arrangement of church furnishings and church organisation of the Greek Orthodox Church was a contribution to the purification and preservation of the Orthodox tradition, both in Ukraine and in Russia. His journal increasingly became a guide to the ancient – and by implication, pure – traditions of Orthodoxy as they survived in the Holy Land, in the Greek lands and on the Holy Mountain.

---

50 Bars'kyj Ms., fol. 249v.

51 Ioannis Komnenos, Προσκυνητάριον τοῦ Ἁγιοῦ Ὄρους τοῦ Ἄθωνος (Venice: N. Glykys, 1745). For a discussion of some of the conventions of this tradition see K.-D. Seemann, *Die altrussische Wallfahrtsliteratur. Theorie und Geschichte eines literarischen Genres* (Munich: W. Fink, 1976); G. D. Lenhoff Vroon, 'The making of the medieval Russian journey', PhD dissertation, University of Michigan, 1978.

52 Bars'kyj mentions that he consulted the 1745 Venice edition of this Προσκυνητάριον in Constantinople, to check if there had been any changes made to a particular entry from the earlier 1701 edition, Bars'kyj Ms., fol. 400r.

53 Bars'kyj Ms., fol. 407r.

54 Bars'kyj Ms., fols. 487r.– 488v.

In terms of physical travel and the distances travelled, the third section of Bars'kyj's journal, between 1730 and 1744, is the least adventurous. For most of this period he was resident, studying or teaching in one of three centres, from where he travelled largely as a fare-paying passenger to specific destinations, for which he had letters of introduction as well as the necessary funding. The three centres were the patriarchal court of Sylvester the Cypriot in Tripoli and Damascus, the monastery of St John on Patmos, and the Russian Residence in Constantinople. When Bars'kyj travelled, it was more as a distinguished guest than as a mendicant pilgrim. In September 1743 he sailed to Ephesos and then on to Chios, where the monks of Nea Moni invited him to come and inspect their monastery. He put them to shame, accusing them of hypocrisy for looking down on him when he visited as a pauper pilgrim and, now that he was a distinguished and recognised scholar, trying to win his favour. When Bars'kyj finally did come to the monastery, he promptly condemned the monks for not looking after the books in the library, describing them as lacking the will for learning or enlightenment.[55] His new prosperity did not blunt his sense of the Orthodox as a persecuted people, never more vividly expressed than in his description of a meeting in 1735 with the patriarch Sylvester the Cypriot, and his old teacher Jacob, who had been forced to take refuge on the island of Cyprus:

> By chance in November my spiritual father and benefactor, the Patriarch of Antioch, Sylvester, with my first teacher Jacob visited Cyprus, having left their see. They were being persecuted by the Christian hating papists, who are of a different faith and who wanted to convert all of the Orthodox Arabs to their heresy.[56]

Bars'kyj saw similarities between the papists and the Muslims, who by imposing the *kharadj* tax on all non-Muslims in Cyprus had found a way of persecuting Christians. 'As I write this here, tears pour from my eyes as I remember how I saw many poor men, who could no longer endure the taxation and Turkish oppression, deny their faith in Christ.'[57] Bars'kyj, who himself had difficulties in paying the *kharadj*, identified himself with the oppressed Orthodox community.

The circumstances surrounding his departure from Constantinople remain confused. On 29 July 1745, his friend and benefactor the Russian Resident Vishniakov died, and Bars'kyj apparently quarrelled with his successor, Adrian

---

55 Bars'kyj Ms., fol. 325v.
56 Bars'kyj Ms., fol. 307r., fol. 307v.
57 Bars'kyj Ms., fol. 306v.

Ivanovich Nepliuev. From Bars'kyj's correspondence with Patriarch Sylvester[58] it appears that heated words were exchanged (possibly over Nepliuev's secret negotiations with the church of Rome on behalf of the Russian Empire), and Bars'kyj was threatened with arrest and prompt deportation by sea to St Petersburg. It was at this stage that he fled Constantinople and in October 1746 arrived in Bucharest on his way back home to Kiev. From here he complained in a letter to his mother how 'I could not fulfil my intention of staying in Constantinople for the completion of my task.'[59] He had two ends in view. He aimed to complete the manuscript containing the section on Constantinople, which survives only in note form, but he also needed to edit it for publication, when he hoped that it would serve both as an account of a pilgrimage and as a guide to the ancient traditions of Orthodox worship, which could be used in the reform of the church back in his homeland. He was never to complete these tasks.

While in Bucharest, Bars'kyj received from the prefect of the Kievo-Podol'sk School Varlaam Lashchevskyj an invitation to take up the position of teacher of Greek at the Kiev Academy.[60] He was delayed by illness in Bucharest until July 1747, when he left for Kiev where he arrived on 5 September 1747, after twenty-four years of travel. Shortly after his arrival, he lamented in a letter to Patriarch Sylvester 'neither dead, nor alive, I lie worn out, like a piteous corpse'.[61] About a month after his arrival in Kiev, on 7 October 1747, Bars'kyj died, and he was buried with great honour at the Kiev-Bratsk monastery, near the altar of the main church.[62]

---

58 Barsukov, *Stranstvovaniia*, IV, 69–74.
59 Ibid., IV, 68.
60 Ibid., IV, 72.
61 Ibid., IV, 72.
62 Bars'kyj's manuscript was first published in a highly abridged and corrupted edition by V. G. Ruban, *Peshekhnodtsa Vasiliia Grigorovicha Barskago* . . . (St Petersburg: Imperatorskaja akademiia nauk, 1778) with later editions in 1785, 1793, 1800 and 1819.

10

The legacy of the French Revolution: Orthodoxy and nationalism

PASCHALIS M. KITROMILIDES

The militancy of the Orthodox Church's response to western ideological influences on Orthodox society during the first and third patriarchates of Gregory V (1797–99, 1818–21) has created among many observers the false impression of a consistent and clear-cut opposition between the Orthodox Church and the Enlightenment. This has obscured the long tradition of fashioning its ecclesiastical, pastoral and educational strategy in a way that accommodated the Enlightenment. What is in fact indicated by the reactions of the Orthodox Church to the French Revolution in the late 1790s and to the Greek Revolution in the 1820s is the conflict between Orthodoxy and nationalism. While the Enlightenment confronted the church with a secular universalist ideology, which, questions of doctrine aside, could in some instances complement and even sustain its own ecumenical values, nationalism gave rise to a conflict, where the issues not only were on the level of secular versus transcendental values but also set the ecumenicity of Christian ideals against the parochialism of nationalism. The history of this conflict turned out to be identical with the history of the Orthodox Church in the nineteenth century.

Balkan nationalism

Nationalism became a real, as opposed to a theoretical problem for Orthodoxy, once the peoples of the Balkans rose up in arms against Ottoman rule in the early nineteenth century. The protracted revolts in the Balkans – first the Serb uprising, begun in 1804 and fought out intermittently until 1830, and then the Greek, from 1821 to 1832 – provided the crucible for the transformation of the Orthodox religious communities of the Balkans into modern nations. Part of the transformation involved the radical reshaping of local ecclesiastical communities from branches of ecumenical Orthodoxy into components of new nations. If the long-term ecclesiastical consequences of emerging Balkan nationalism were not immediately apparent in the case of the Serbs, they were in that of the Greeks. The Greek Revolution of 1821 had important effects on the condition of the church and on canonical order. The revolution was disowned and condemned by the patriarch of Constantinople Gregory V, but this action, which proved so controversial subsequently, did not save the patriarch, who was executed for high treason on Easter Sunday, 10 April 1821. He was hanged in front of the central gate of the patriarchate – a gate that has remained closed ever since. The patriarch did not march alone on the road to martyrdom. A host of other senior prelates were executed in Istanbul, including Dionysios of Ephesos, Athanasios of Nikomedeia, Gregory of Derkoi and Eugenios of Anchialos, while at Edirne (Adrianople) an ex-patriarch, Cyril VI, was also hanged. In Cyprus the head of the local autocephalous church, Archbishop Kyprianos, and other senior prelates together with many prominent laymen were executed *en masse* on 9 July 1821. Crete suffered in a similar way. The head of the local church, Metropolitan Gerasimos, seven bishops and many abbots were executed. Members of the hierarchy were also executed in Thessalonike and Larissa, while of the eight prelates of the Peloponnese who were incarcerated by the Ottoman governor in Tripolis in March 1821, five died in prison before the fall of that city to the Greeks on 23 September 1821. In other words, the revolutionary events in Greece created a host of new martyrs of the faith, martyrs who would eventually be co-opted into the nationalist pantheon as 'ethnomartyrs', thus contributing to the transformation of Orthodoxy's own philosophy and values.

The real and, as it turned out, lasting effects of the rising upon the church came in the form of the canonical consequences involved in the loosening of the administrative control exercised by the ecclesiastical centre in Constantinople upon the hierarchy and clergy in the provinces which had risen in revolt. The revolutionary conditions empowered the lower clergy by virtue of their intimate involvement in the life of their communities: once the community was up in arms, the local priest, regardless of the canonical edicts emanating from Constantinople, was *ipso facto* one of the leaders of the revolt. There were many instances of priests or deacons taking up arms themselves and participating in the fighting, some of them rising to pre-eminence among the military leadership of the revolution, gaining renown for their heroism, and eventually joining the pantheon of martyrs of the liberation of Greece, as in the legendary cases of the heroic deacon Athanasios (martyred in 1821) and the fiery archimandrite Gregorios Dikaios Papaflessas, who fell in 1825.

The position of the hierarchy was more complex and more delicate. In one way or another, those bishops who survived the fury of the Turks supported the revolution in the areas that came under the control of revolutionary forces. Some of them rose to prominence among the civilian leadership of the revolution and played important roles in the national assemblies that were convened at Epidauros in 1822, at Astros in 1823 and at Troezen in 1827. Caught up in the crucible of revolution, individual members of the higher and lower clergy of the Orthodox Church, in their differing ways, made common cause with the emergent national community. Although the clergy were thus crossing the Rubicon of nationalism, leaving behind the ecumenical teaching of Orthodox Christianity, they could salve their consciences by remembering that liberty and free will were also among the values taught in the Gospels: 'know the truth and it will set you free'.

Despite these seminal changes, at no stage did the hierarchy in revolutionary Greece question their canonical dependence on the ecumenical patriarchate. Throughout the period of the revolutionary struggle in Greece, the prelates and other members of the clergy who played an active role in revolutionary politics followed a consistent line of respect for the faith, upholding Orthodox canonicity and preserving the Christian morals of the people. Three of the bishops, Joseph of Androusa, Neophytos of Talantion and Theodoretos of Vresthena, played particularly active roles in the politics of the revolutionary assemblies: Joseph in particular, as minister of religion between 1822 and 1825. The assemblies paid special attention to questions of religious and ecclesiastical order. The constitutional charters voted by each of these assemblies recognised by their very first article Orthodox Christianity as the 'dominant religion' (ἐπικρατοῦσα θρησκεία) in the new free Greek state, but adding in the same article that the state tolerated the existence and free practice of all other religions and forms of worship. It is interesting to note that the first article of the 'Political Constitution of Greece' – drawn up at Troezen in 1827 – reversed the order and announced first the principle of freedom of religion and worship, adding to this that the religion of the 'Eastern Orthodox Church of Christ is the religion of the state'.

Beyond these provisos, however, the constitutional order of revolutionary Greece did not go. The specific ecclesiastical status of the Orthodox Church in the liberated territories was neither raised nor discussed in revolutionary Greece and although administrative communication with the patriarchate of Constantinople was interrupted, the spiritual authority of the patriarch was not questioned. The hierarchy in Greece continued the canonical commemoration of the patriarch's name in religious services, and as a sign of respect of the patriarch's canonical rights no ordinations of either bishops or even lower clergy were carried out until ecclesiastical affairs were regularised.[1] Through-out the revolutionary period (1821–27) and the subsequent short period of the government of Ioannis Kapodistrias two overall trends could be discerned in ecclesiastical affairs. One trend reflected the attitude of the Orthodox episco-pate, which had remained active in Greece in this period: they consistently and invariably insisted that the regulation of ecclesiastical affairs should be transacted exclusively on the basis of the canons of the church. In a remark-able document drafted in March 1827, in response to an invitation by the chairman of the Third National Assembly, a committee of five bishops put forward twenty-four proposals for the restoration of ecclesiastical order in Greece. Two of these, the first and the last, stand out. They started by sug-gesting that the National Assembly set up a synod of prelates, charged with the task of the governance of the church in Greece until the overall political situation was normalised. This, the five bishops insisted, was just a tempo-rary and interim measure. They ended by making their long-term view of ecclesiastical order crystal clear: under no circumstances could the church and clergy of Greece contemplate any form of separation from the one and only canonical authority they knew and recognised: the Great Church of Christ in Constantinople.[2]

If such was the prevailing attitude of the ecclesiastical body, the other gen-eral trend of the period consisted in a continuous stream of decisions, measures and expressions of concern for the orderly regulation of ecclesiastical affairs emanating from the National Assemblies and the civil authorities instituted by them. All this represented a radical change in the position of the church, which found itself an object of respect, interest and affection on the part of the civil authority for the first time in many centuries. The many measures and regulations intended to help the church fulfil its proper mission in soci-ety, including measures of financial assistance and support, were gradually, imperceptibly but irreversibly bringing the church under the aegis of civil authority and turning it into an instrument of the state. All this was entirely well intentioned and was carried out in a genuine belief that these measures would create the preconditions for the blossoming of the Christian spirit and Christian values in a regenerated Greece. In fact, this process led to the trans-formation of the Orthodox Church from an agent of canonical conscience so clearly expressed by its episcopacy in the 1820s into a nationalist institution, which would eventually substitute for its inherited faith in Christ the new

---

1 E. I. Konstantinides, Ἡ ἐν Ἑλλάδι ἐκκλησία κατὰ τὴν ἐπανάστασιν καὶ τὴν μέχρι τῆς ἀφίξεως τοῦ Ὄθωνος μεταβατικὴν ἐποχὴν (1821–1833) (Athens: [s.n.], 1970), 16–41.
2 Ibid., 44–52.

faith in the nation and in the values of nationalism. But this is looking ahead. The radical inner transformation of the Orthodox Church was a protracted process with many twists and turns, which in the course of the nineteenth and twentieth centuries confronted the Orthodox in south-eastern Europe with many crises of conscience.

The Greek ecclesiastical settlement

Greece's first head of state, Ioannis Kapodistrias, was a devout Orthodox, deeply concerned with the restoration of religious order and Christian morals in the fledgling state emerging from the war of independence. This was reflected in the pertinent initiatives of his administration. One of his main concerns had to do with the preservation of the administrative links between the Orthodox Church in the new Greek state and the ecumenical patriarchate, because Kapodistrias was convinced that the doctrinal communion between the two branches of Greek Orthodoxy might be upset if the administrative links were severed. The president's good intentions, however, were not much helped when in May 1828 Patriarch Agathangelos despatched a mission of four very senior prelates from the patriarchal synod to Greece bringing letters addressed to 'the clergy and notables of the Peloponnese and the Aegean Islands', whereby they were asked to resubmit to the Sublime Porte.[3] In a respectful and entirely conciliatory letter, Kapodistrias rejected the patriarch's admonition, pointing out that it was totally impossible for the people of Greece to give up the freedom they had won with so many sacrifices. In contrast to Agathangelos, his successor Konstantios I sent his good wishes and his blessings to the Greek state in August 1830 but expressed his concern about news of Calvinist infiltration among the Orthodox of Greece. Kapodistrias reassured the patriarch about Greece's devotion to Orthodoxy and to the Great Church. This in turn gave Konstantios the opportunity to insist on the complete re-establishment of administrative unity between the church in the territories of the Greek state and the Great Church of Constantinople.[4]

Things were left at that. Kapodistrias's murder in September 1831 was not only a great tragedy for the Greek state but also a tragedy for the future of relations between the church in Greece and the church of Constantinople. His approach to the ecclesiastical question was probably the only guarantee

3 Manuel Gedeon, Πατριαρχικοὶ Πίνακες, ed. N. L. Phoropoulos (Athens: Syllogos pros Diadosin Ophelimon Biblion, 1996), 607.
4 E. I. Konstantinides, Ἰωάννης Καποδίστριας καὶ ἡ ἐκκλησιαστική του πολιτική, fifth edition (Athens: A. Papanikolaou, 2001), 73–84.

for a smooth settlement of the ecclesiastical question between Greece and Constantinople. But while the Orthodox establishment was agonising over the issues posed by the challenges of modern politics and nationalism, Adamantios Korais, the foremost Greek political theorist of the Enlightenment, had already provided a categorical answer to all these dilemmas and questionings. This was set out in the *prolegomena* to his edition of Aristotle's *Politics*, which came out in 1821, the very first year of the Greek war of independence. Korais used it to instruct his embattled compatriots in the duties of a free citizen. He was the first writer to frame an unequivocally nationalist position on the ecclesiastical question:

> The clergy of the part of Greece that has so far been liberated . . . has no longer any obligation to acknowledge as its ecclesiastical head the patriarch of Constantinople, for as long as Constantinople remains contaminated by the seat of the lawless tyrant, they should instead be governed by a hieratic synod, freely elected by clergy and laymen, as was the practice in the ancient church, and as to some degree occurs nowadays in the church of our Russian coreligionists. It is entirely untoward for the clergy of the free and autonomous Greeks to obey the orders of a patriarch elected by a tyrant and forced to pay homage to a tyrant.[5]

This is a remarkable statement. It formed the first of eight articles on the status of the church in the free and well-ordered republic, which Korais visualised as the future of Greece. His proposal for the regulation of ecclesiastical affairs reflected faithfully the blueprint of Enlightenment views on the shape the church might be expected to take under a political order of freedom and of the rule of law. In doing this, however, Korais subjected the church to the requirements and priorities of the secular order, and although his sincere belief and hope was to see the church restored to evangelical purity, practising and teaching genuine Christian values, in fact he delivered her to the dictates of nationalism that formed the predominant content of the new political culture associated with the modern state.

Korais's counsels remained unheeded by Greek lay and ecclesiastical leaders in the 1820s. Somewhat paradoxically they were to be put into practice – partially and not necessarily with identical purposes in mind – not by liberal and republican thinkers and politicians like himself, but by the bureaucratic officials who took over the administration of the Greek Kingdom under the regency of Greece's first king, Otto. One of the regency's earliest actions, and

---

5 Adamantios Korais, Ἀριστοτέλους Πολιτικῶν τὰ σωζόμενα [Hellenike Bibliotheke 13] (Paris: F. Didot, 1821), p. cxx.

a distinctive mark of the statecraft connected with the establishment of the new state, was a unilateral declaration of the autocephaly of the Orthodox Church in Greece. That action was part of a political programme aimed at affirming the national independence and sovereignty of the new kingdom. Sovereignty was connected with absolutism on the legitimist model of Restoration Europe. This in turn entailed a policy of administrative centralisation, which not only involved breaking the power of local oligarchies and sectional interests and imposing military discipline on the chieftains of revolutionary armies, but also required bringing the church under control. In an act of 4 August 1833 the regency imposed an ecclesiastical settlement that declared the Orthodox Church in Greece independent of the mother-church in Constantinople. The head of the new autocephalous church was to be the Roman Catholic sovereign of the new kingdom, and its governance was delivered to clerical officials appointed by the crown. This was extreme caesaropapism, which was quite foreign to the traditions of the Orthodox Church and to the holy canons.[6] The regime thus imposed on the church in Greece was dictated by considerations of a political nature, which aimed to strengthen both national independence and royal absolutism. But these aims were promoted by subjecting the church to an Erastian settlement of Protestant inspiration, which meant transferring to Greece the model of church–state relations prevailing in German Protestant states and in the Scandinavian kingdoms.

There was widespread resistance to the ecclesiastical settlement, which was later completed by decrees abolishing most monasteries and practically all nunneries in Greece. It was only under considerable pressure that Orthodox bishops resident in the kingdom, numbering some fifty-two prelates, gave their assent to the proposed settlement, on 27 July 1833, insisting only that respect for the holy canons should be explicitly added to all relevant decrees. Resistance to the settlement, nevertheless, came from the monks and from a wide cross-section of society, especially in the countryside, where there was a real fear that the faith might be adulterated. On the level of theological argument Constantine Oikonomos led the resistance to unilateral autocephaly. This towering intellectual leader was deeply devoted to the canonical order represented by the patriarchate of Constantinople.[7] The most distinguished theological proponent of autocephaly was Theokletos Pharmakidis, a theologian trained in

6 J. A. Petropulos, *Politics and statecraft in the kingdom of Greece 1833–1843* (Princeton: Princeton University Press, 1968), 180–92.

7 On Oikonomos's contribution see G. D. Metallinos, Ἑλλαδικοῦ αὐτοκεφάλου παραλειπόμενα (Athens: Domos, 1989), 123–58.

Göttingen and a follower of Korais's views. He was to play the key role in the implementation of the ecclesiastical settlement.[8]

The ecumenical patriarchate under successive patriarchs rejected the settlement as uncanonical and broke off communion with the church of Greece, which it considered schismatic. The patriarchate's disagreement was primarily with the procedures followed in proclaiming autocephaly, not with autocephaly *per se*, to which Greece as a sovereign independent state was entitled according to the canons and the traditions of the church. But it took a long time to find the appropriate procedure for the accession of the church in Greece to autocephaly. In 1831 Patriarch Konstantios I and Prince Miloš Obrenović may have been able, without serious difficulty, to agree on the canonical procedures for the establishment of an autonomous church in the principality of Serbia,[9] but a similar agreement with Greece took seventeen years to reach. Eventually in July 1850, during the second patriarchate of Anthimos IV (1848–52), an agreement on Greek autocephaly was reached, once the Greek state and the church in Greece accepted unconditionally terms that in the patriarchate's judgement satisfied the requirements of the holy canons. On 29 June 1850, in response to formal applications by the Greek government on behalf of the church in Greece, the ecumenical patriarchate issued a 'Synodal Tome', granting autocephaly to the church of Greece, under a synod of bishops to be presided over by the metropolitan of Athens.[10]

The canonical aspect of the final resolution of the problem of Greek autocephaly is important in that it set a precedent for handling similar situations in the life of Orthodoxy later on in the nineteenth and in the twentieth century. More importantly, however, from the point of view of the history of Christianity itself, the issue of Greek autocephaly set up a model and supplied the canonical basis for sanctioning the piecemeal transformation of the universal Orthodox Church into national churches. Paradoxically, what had originally been an Erastian church settlement on the Protestant model underlay this transformation, while the ecumenical patriarchate, once its own formal requirements were satisfied, supplied the canonical sanction for turning regional churches into instruments of secular authority. The latter in turn used the churches for the enhancement of its own power by enlisting them in a leading role in nationalist projects.

8 C. Frazee, *The Orthodox Church and independent Greece 1821–1852* (Cambridge: Cambridge University Press, 1969), 103–5, 125–70.
9 Gedeon, Πίνακες, 610.
10 Ibid., 618. Cf. Metallinos, Ἑλλαδικοῦ, 123–277.

The Great Church's rejection of unilateral autocephaly remained a firm and uncompromising position. This rejection epitomised the conflict and the fundamental opposition between Orthodoxy and nationalism: the church remained adamant that it was not prepared to accept the logic of nationalism, because it involves a total indifference to the means so long as the 'higher' purposes of the nation are served and promoted.

The Serbian experience

In contrast to Greece, Serbia followed an alternative route in integrating the Orthodox Church into the national community associated with the modern state that emerged from the recurring revolts of the first three decades of the nineteenth century. In the case of Serbia, as in the case of Greece, the experience of revolt, ethnic conflict and fighting supplied a crucible for the transformation of a fragmented traditional society into the basis of a modern national community. The workings of the transformation are registered in sources such as the *Memoirs* of Prota Matija Nenadović, who in the account of his life, travels and involvement in Karageorge's revolt shows how the inherited Orthodox mentality of Christian Serbs provided the substratum upon which modern ideas of national assertion and political liberation were grafted.[11] It may explain why the enlistment of Serbian Orthodoxy in the nexus of national assertion was carried out in an entirely canonical manner, which invariably met the formal requirements of the Great Church and gained the approbation and praise of the foremost ecclesiastical historian in the jurisdiction of Constantinople, Philaretos Vapheidis, who remarked in connection with the church of Serbia: 'That Church stands out among Slavic Churches for its devotion and respect for the patriarchate of Constantinople, referring to it as occasion demanded and never severing its ties with the latter.'[12]

Accordingly the principality of Serbia applied on behalf of the church in its territories and received autonomy from Constantinople in 1831. When in 1878 the treaty of Berlin recognised Serbia as a fully independent kingdom, King Milan Obrenović and Metropolitan Michael of Belgrade wrote on 27 April and 4 May 1879 respectively to Constantinople requesting autocephaly, which a synodal tome issued by Patriarch Joachim III and the synod of Constantinople duly

11 *The memoirs of Prota Matija Nenadović*, trans. L. F. Edwards (Oxford: Clarendon Press, 1969). For commentary cf. P. M. Kitromilides, 'Balkan mentality. History, legend, imagination', *Nations and nationalism* 2 (1996), 163–91, esp. 182–6.
12 Metropolitan of Didymoteichon Philaretos Vapheidis, Ἐκκλησιαστικὴ Ἱστορία, ΙΙΙ-β´ (Alexandria: Patriarchal Press, 1928), 570.

granted. In 1919 the emergence of the unified Kingdom of Yugoslavia brought together within the borders of one state the different ecclesiastical jurisdictions governing Serbian Orthodox populations. Besides the Serbian church there were now the archbishoprics of Carlowitz, Dalmatia and Cattaro, and Montenegro. As part of the assertion of the new Kingdom of Serbs, Croats and Slovenes, the government of the kingdom wrote to Constantinople requesting the unification of all these different jurisdictions into one patriarchate of the Serbs. The agreement was reached on 18 March 1919, and on 12 September 1920, on the feast day of all Serbian Saints, the church of Serbia was proclaimed a patriarchate. Significantly, in an act symbolically reclaiming the entire Serbian ecclesiastical past, the new patriarch of the Serbs, Metropolitan Dimitrje of Belgrade, was enthroned at the old patriarchate of Peć on 28 August 1924.

This was a remarkable process, which combined respect for canonical formalities, thus guaranteeing ecclesiastical peace and at the same time achieving in the most effective way the national integration of the Serbian Church. The consistency with which the Serbian Church exemplified its respect for canonical order in the process of accession to autocephaly and patriarchal status stands in contrast to claims repeatedly advanced in Serbian nationalist historiography in the late nineteenth and throughout the twentieth century alleging ecclesiastical repression and attempts at 'hellenisation' by the ecumenical patriarchate at the expense of the Serbs. Obviously such claims were the product of retrospective reinterpretations of the historical record based mostly on distorted accounts by western observers who ignored or failed to understand the nature of Orthodox ecclesiastical politics in south-eastern Europe.[13] Such misunderstandings and distortions nevertheless served the needs of nationalist psychology, which explains the prominence they have received in the mainstream of Serbian and Yugoslav historiography.[14]

The Romanian experience

In an age of nationalist assertion, when Balkan politics was building up its modern rather sombre and unflattering reputation, the Serbian model of ecclesiastical transition found no followers in the Orthodox world. In contrast the Greek model of unilateralism found ready imitators among the Romanians and the Bulgarians, leading to serious conflicts and fractures in the body of Orthodoxy.

13 E.g. Jean Mousset, *La Serbie et son église 1830–1904* (Paris: Droz, 1938), 40–53; Albert Mousset, *Le royaume des Serbes, Croates et Slovènes* (Paris: Éditions Bossard, 1921), 89–101.
14 C. Jelavich, 'Some aspects of Serbian religious development in the eighteenth century', *Church History* 23 (1954), 144–52.

The 1859 union of the two autonomous principalities of Wallachia and Moldavia – by votes of their respective parliaments – under Prince Alexander Cuza opened up new prospects of ecclesiastical conflict in the Balkans. Cuza proceeded to the confiscation of monastic lands and other properties belonging to Orthodox ecclesiastical institutions (including the Holy Sepulchre and Mount Sinai), which provoked an outcry in ecclesiastical circles. In 1865 a bill for the proclamation of the independence of the church of Romania 'according to the requirements of the political and intellectual progress of nations' was introduced.[15] It set in motion a repetition of the story of Greek autocephaly. The new regime imposed on the church in Romania, in imitation of the Greek settlement of 1833, subordinated the church to the state with all appointments and decisions made subject to state approval.

The Great Church under Patriarch Sophronios III had already in 1863 protested – to no avail – against the confiscation of monastic properties in Romania, but in 1865 it reacted strongly to the proposed new ecclesiastical regime, pronouncing it contrary to the holy canons and doctrinally dubious.[16] The requirements of secular state building and the forces of nationalism in Romania, nevertheless, proved stronger than the canonical conscience of the church. Despite the overthrow of Cuza and the election in his place of a new prince, Carol Hohenzollern-Sigmaringen, the ecclesiastical question between Romania and Constantinople dragged on for another twenty years, until its final settlement in 1885. Intermediate attempts and proposals at settlement of the ecclesiastical question in 1867, 1870 and 1872–73 were rejected by Constantinople on the grounds that they were designed to serve secular interests and that they were consequently incompatible with the holy canons. When Romania was recognised as an independent kingdom in 1881, the Romanian hierarchy proceeded to a ceremonial act of great symbolic significance, which affirmed their assent to ecclesiastical independence. On 25 March 1882 they performed the solemn ceremony of blessing the holy oil used in the sacrament of chrism, a privilege that the ecumenical patriarchate had through the centuries reserved for itself. With this act the Romanian hierarchy sacralised their nation's aspirations to independence in the most effective way imaginable and integrated into an Orthodox religious framework the secular ambitions of Romanian nationalism. The patriarch Joachim III reacted sharply to this initiative, and in a letter of 10 July 1882 pointed out that in usurping this ancient privilege of the patriarchate the Romanian bishops were not only violating

---

15 Vapheidis, Ἐκκλησιαστικὴ, ΙΙΙ-B', 587.
16 Gedeon, Πίνακες, 623.

ancient canons but were moved by 'a desire for novelty', putting in serious jeopardy proper ecclesiastical order.[17] The crisis of the holy chrism delayed for three years the canonical recognition of autocephaly to which Romania, as a sovereign kingdom, was now entitled. This was only granted after the head of the Romanian Church, Kallinikos of Hungro-Wallachia, in agreement with the Romanian government, wrote to the patriarch Joachim IV, who on 25 April 1885 duly acceded to their request for autocephalous status with yet another synodal tome.[18]

The nationalist drive in the Romanian Church continued unabated, as scholarship attempted to re-create a distinct Romanian ecclesiastical past.[19] During the period 1892–1905 new conflicts arose between the churches of Romania and Constantinople over ecclesiastical jurisdiction in the regions of Epiros and Macedonia. The Romanians raised claims over Vlach-speaking communities, which they wanted to bring under the control of Romanian authorities on account of linguistic affinities.[20] In 1925 the assumption of patriarchal status by the autocephalous Romanian Church came about after consultations, which secured the ready agreement of Constantinople. The elevation of the autocephalous church of Romania to patriarchal status was the last symbolic act in the articulation and assertion of the national community of the Greater Romania produced by World War I.

The Bulgarian exarchate

The most serious of the conflicts that dramatised the incompatibility between the Orthodox canonical order and the aspirations of nationalism in the Orthodox Church arose over the question of the Bulgarian Church. Although the problem came to a head in the third quarter of the nineteenth century and led to a painful schism that took a long time to heal, the conflict was long in the making as a by-product of the growth of the Bulgarian national movement. The intensity of the confrontation, especially after the schism was finalised in 1872, was such that it coloured the whole understanding of the past and projected backwards confrontations, antagonisms and sensitivities that essentially wiped out the very meaning of Christian history in south-eastern Europe.

17 Vapheidis, Ἐκκλησιαστική, III-β', 595.
18 For a general survey M. Păcurariu, *Istoria Bisericii Ortodoxe Române* (Bucharest, 1994), III, 126–42.
19 See especially N. Iorga, *Istoria Bisericii Româneşti şi a vieţii religioase a Românilor*, second edition (Bucharest: Ministry of Religions, 1928), I–II.
20 Vapheidis, Ἐκκλησιαστική, III-β', 194–205.

Although the whole conflict was fought over questions of ecclesiastical jurisdiction and order, it was much more a conflict motivated by secular ambitions
and concerns over power, which left very little space for the Christian values
of solidarity, charity and peace to influence the attitudes of the parties.

In contrast to Greece, Serbia and Romania, the Bulgarian struggle for ecclesiastical independence preceded the emergence of a modern state. While in
the three other cases of Balkan Orthodoxy ecclesiastical emancipation was felt
to be a completion of national independence, for the Bulgarian nationalists the
struggle for their own church was seen as the prelude to national recognition
and emancipation. It was precisely for this reason that their claims did not
possess a canonical basis and were difficult to satisfy within the framework of
the holy canons. The Bulgarian struggle for ecclesiastical emancipation was
a substitute for a political liberation movement, which explains its intensity
and the extremes to which it went. All along the way it was a struggle guided
by a political, not by an ecclesiastical logic, with the inevitable result that the
two main parties to it, the Bulgarian nationalist hierarchy and the ecumenical
patriarchate, were unable to communicate, let alone understand each other's
position.

Bulgarian nationalists first voiced claims to some form of ecclesiastical
autonomy after the Crimean War (1854–56). To these demands the ecumenical patriarchate remained neither indifferent nor unresponsive. In 1861 and
again in 1867 the ecumenical patriarchs Joachim II and Gregory VI respectively put forward plans for the resolution of the problem. The second plan was
essentially a blueprint for the creation of an autonomous Bulgarian Church,
with jurisdiction over predominantly Bulgarian regions.[21] These proposals
were judged unsatisfactory by the Bulgarians, who, with the active encouragement of the Russian ambassador to the Sublime Porte Count Ignatiev,[22]
managed in February 1870 to obtain a firman from the Ottoman government,
which set up the Bulgarian exarchate, an autonomous church administration comprising thirteen Bulgarian dioceses, with nominal dependence on
Constantinople.[23]

The Bulgarians hailed the Ottoman decision as a harbinger of their future
independence but the ecumenical patriarchate rejected it and proceeded to

---

21 Ibid., III-B', 160–78.
22 See T. A. Meininger, *Ignatiev and the establishment of the Bulgarian Exarchate (1864–1872):
a study in personal diplomacy* (Madison: University of Wisconsin Press, 1970).
23 For general surveys see V. Stephanidis, Ἐκκλησιαστικὴ Ἱστορία, fourth edition (Athens:
Astir, 1978), 720–41; Z. Markova, *Le mouvement ecclésiastique national jusqu'à la guerre de
Crimée* (Sofia: Académie bulgare des sciences, 1976) and Markova, *The Bulgarian Exarchate*
(Sofia: Bulgarian Academy of Sciences, 1989).

convoke a major synod of Orthodox patriarchs in order to consider the question. The synod met in Constantinople and its proceedings lasted from 29 August to 17 September 1872. It was presided over by the ecumenical patriarch Anthimos VI, with the patriarchs Sophronios of Alexandria and Hierotheos of Antioch and Archbishop Sophronios of Cyprus and twenty-four prelates of the church of Constantinople participating. The synod pronounced the Bulgarian exarchate schismatic and it defrocked the leaders of the movement among Bulgarian bishops. The Bulgarian claims were rejected as lacking a canonical basis, in that they demanded an independent church of their own not on account of political independence (Bulgaria still being an Ottoman province) but on account of ethnic and national particularity. This the synod described as 'ethnophyletism' and condemned as a heresy.[24]

Despite repeated attempts to resolve the problem the Bulgarian schism survived until 1945.[25] Although Bulgaria became an autonomous principality in 1878 and an independent kingdom in 1908, its church remained outside the communion of Orthodox churches because nationalist passions had run so high that no one was prepared to go through the procedural formalities required for the accession to autocephaly. Passions between proponents of the patriarchate or the exarchate, between Greeks and Bulgarians, led to serious conflicts in Macedonia and Thrace, in Eastern Rumelia, and in Constantinople itself. In the early twentieth century, with the flare-up of the 'Macedonian Question' (1903–08), blood was spilt over the control both of shrines of Orthodox worship and of the consciences of the faithful. All this gained Orthodoxy its identification with nationalism; and Balkan politics its grim reputation. What was at stake in the struggle was power and territory, not religion, and the stakes were set by the modern states that were using the churches to fight out their own conflicts.[26]

The schism was revoked in just over a month, once the newly elected Exarch Stephen wrote on 21 January 1945 to Constantinople asking Patriarch Benjamin to forgive and rescind the schismatic status imposed on the Bulgarian Church. On 25 February 1945 Bulgaria was welcomed back into the

---

24 Metropolitan of Sardis Maximos Christopoulos, *The oecumenical patriarchate in the Ortho-dox Church* (Thessalonike: Patriarchal Institute for Patristic Studies, 1976), 303–9. The pertinent official documents are collected by M. Gedeon (ed.), Ἔγγραφα πατριαρ-χικὰ καὶ συνοδικὰ περὶ τοῦ Βουλγαρικοῦ ζητήματος (1852–1873) (Constantinople: Patriarchal Press, 1908).

25 E. Kophos, 'Attempts at mending the Greek–Bulgarian ecclesiastical schism (1875–1902)', *Balkan Studies* 25 (1984), 1–29.

26 P. M. Kitromilides, 'Imagined communities and the origins of the national question in the Balkans', *European History Quarterly* 19 (1989), esp. 177–85.

Orthodox communion.[27] It took the carnage of the two World Wars and their bloody impact on the Balkans to establish the full significance of the 1872 edict condemning 'ethnophyletism' as an un-Christian ideology, incompatible with the teachings and ideals of Orthodoxy.

The broader significance of the Bulgarian ecclesiastical question consisted in showing the extremes to which the conflict between Orthodoxy and nationalism could lead. Although in Macedonia, Eastern Rumelia and Thrace the ecclesiastical conflict interlocked with the lethal antagonism between Greek and Bulgarian nationalism that ravaged the lives of ordinary people in those regions, the confrontation between the ecumenical patriarchate and the exarchate was not, as some historians have suggested, identical with the conflict between two rival nationalisms, Greek and Bulgarian. The ecumenical patriarchate was not acting as an agent of Greek nationalism, which it had resisted with the same determination that it was to show in dealing with the manifestations of nationalism in the Romanian and Bulgarian churches. It is true that in the Greek and Romanian cases no major synod was convoked to condemn their unilateralism as an uncanonical path to autocephaly. This can be explained by the fact that neither of these churches nor the respective governments went to the same extremes as the protagonists of the exarchate in challenging canonicity and violating the formalities that expressed it in the life of the Orthodox Church. The fact that the Bulgarian hierarchy and the exarchate in its early stages were acting free of any checks that a responsible national government might impose on their behaviour will explain the extremities to which nationalist zeal led them and which made their solemn condemnation inevitable. The canonical conscience of the Orthodox Church as articulated in the condemnation of 'ethnophyletism' derived from a long tradition of Christian reflection on ecclesiastical order and was determined by a corpus of ecclesiastical law that could not be disregarded without risking a serious deviation from fundamental requirements of the faith. This is what secular historians often fail to grasp, when they charge the Orthodox Church with disguising its own peculiar nationalist motivations behind appeals to canonicity. This line of criticism is only possible if one disregards the Christian principles presupposed by ecclesiastical law, principles that are indeed ecumenical in outlook, transcendental in content and orientated towards the production of a universal community of faith and atonement. The condemnation of 'ethnophyletism' reminded the world of two things: that it was precisely these principles that were incompatible with nationalism and that the Orthodox Church, as a Christian institution,

---

27 See K. Ware and G. Ivanov, 'An historic reconciliation: the role of Exarch Stefan', *Sobornost* 1 (1979), 70–6.

was committed to uphold them, regardless of the human failings of its individual members and representatives, which had made the inroads of nationalism and phyletism possible in the first place.

Andreiu Saguna

The conflict between Orthodoxy and nationalism was not limited to the dramatic confrontations between aspiring national churches and the ecumenical patriarchate but also disturbed intra-church affairs at a local level. It was here that the conflict between Orthodoxy and nationalism produced crises of conscience of the greatest intensity. To illustrate this aspect of the problem, which was inherent in Orthodoxy's transition to the modern era, we shall take two examples drawn from the borderlands of the Orthodox world. The first is provided by the actions and the writings of Andreiu Saguna, head of the Romanian Orthodox Church in Transylvania (1846–73). Andreiu Saguna rose to the leadership of the Orthodox Church and more generally of the Romanian nation in Transylvania through the struggle for the restoration of a Romanian diocese in the region, thus cutting it off from the jurisdiction of the Serb archbishop of Carlowitz, head of all Orthodox in the Habsburg domains. That movement was a clear instance of the workings of nationalism in the church, and Archbishop Andreiu was fully conscious of the contradictions in which his activities involved him. On the one hand, his pastoral commitments, and his concern for his flock, together with the need to confirm its members in their allegiance to Orthodoxy from the pressures and lures of the Greek Catholic Church in Transylvania, all led in the direction of asserting the identity of the Orthodox community through an ecclesiastical establishment of their own – a project that led to conflict with the Orthodox Serb ecclesiastical authority. On the other hand, he knew that in the Christian tradition no necessary canonical link attached the church to a particular nation.[28]

However, true to the spirit of his age, Saguna became convinced that the Orthodox Church was by its very nature a national church and therefore its pastoral tasks included concern for the national identity and cultural tradition of its flock. At the same time he did not want the church to exercise a kind of secular political leadership but saw its role as a sanctifying mission in the world, which provided national churches with their justification. To fulfil this mission the church needed to preserve its autonomy, its moral traditions and

---

28 K. Hitchins, *Orthodoxy and nationality: Andreiu Saguna and the Rumanians of Transylvania, 1846–1873* (Cambridge, MA: Harvard University Press, 1977), 173–98.

its transcendental values, because only thus, Saguna believed, could a national church fulfil its mission effectively.[29]

Orthodoxy and Arab nationalism

A much more painful drama reflecting the consequences of nationalism in the Orthodox Church was acted out on the eastern frontier of Orthodoxy in Syria over the control of the ancient patriarchate of Antioch. In this case, the external manifestation of the conflict took the form of a confrontation over the language of church and hierarchy. In the Arab world the winds of nationalism were first felt in the middle decades of the nineteenth century among Christian Arabs who had been exposed to western education, primarily in schools set up by missionaries or in Greek schools operating under the aegis of Orthodox ecclesiastical authorities. It was in these circles that claims were first voiced on behalf of Arabic in the church and in support of native Arabic-speaking candidates for episcopal and patriarchal thrones. In this, Orthodox Arab nationalists, like the Bulgarians before them, were strongly encouraged by Russian diplomacy, whose imperial designs on the Balkans and the Near East counted on the use of the Orthodox Church as a most effective weapon. When in 1891 a Greek was once again elected to the patriarchal throne of Antioch, Arab resentment reached boiling point. With Russian encouragement and aided by protracted ecclesiastical crises in Constantinople and Jerusalem and by the Greek defeat in the 1897 war with Turkey, Arab nationalists finally managed to force the resignation of their Cypriot-born patriarch Spyridon in January 1898.[30] A native Arab Orthodox, Meletios of Lattakia (Laodikeia), was elected patriarch of Antioch in 1899. This was described as 'the first victory of Arab nationalism'.[31]

Similar attempts by Arab Orthodox to gain control of the patriarchate of Jerusalem were thwarted on a number of occasions in the twentieth century. These incidents demonstrate the extent to which nationalism has become a major motive in the life of the Orthodox Church as a consequence of broader changes initiated in the nineteenth century. The deeper significance of the transition from Orthodoxy to nationalism as a worldview and as an attitude to life is brought out – perhaps better than anywhere else in the Orthodox

29 K. Hitchins, *The identity of Romania* (Bucharest: The Encyclopedic Publishing House, 2003), 87–100.
30 B. Englezakis, *Studies on the history of the Church of Cyprus 4th–20th centuries* (Aldershot: Variorum, 1995), 323–420.
31 D. Hopwood, *The Russian presence in Syria and Palestine 1843–1914: church and politics in the Near East* (Oxford: Oxford University Press, 1969), 159–79.

experience – by the agonising dilemmas faced by two Orthodox Arab intellectuals in the early twentieth century, Khalîl Sakâkînî and Iskandar Qûbûrisî. In their different ways both of them found in nationalism and in the passionate commitments it generated an outlet from the embittered frustration associated with their social position as members of a vulnerable minority that had lost its prominence with the decline and disappearance of Ottoman rule in the Arab world. But the new, liberating commitment to nationalism proved to be incompatible with their Orthodox Christian identity. Although Arab nationalism had originated among Orthodox Christian communities, it turned out that, if an Arab was to commit his life to the nationalist cause, he had to leave his Christianity behind.[32] This is what both of these remarkable thinkers opted to do, leaving a powerful existential testimony on the incompatibility between Orthodox Christianity and nationalism.

The dilemma of the ecumenical patriarchate

The supranational centre of Orthodoxy, the ecumenical patriarchate, did not remain immune to the challenge of nationalism. Despite the long tradition of opposition to nationalism that extended back to Patriarch Gregory V and despite the condemnation of ethnophyletism in 1872, the lethal struggle against the exarchate in Macedonia dragged the patriarchate into the vortex of nationalism. At the turn of the nineteenth century a younger generation of dynamic prelates, with Chrysostom of Drama (and then of Smyrna) and Germanos of Kastoria (and then of Amasya) at their head, guided the Great Church towards an alliance with Greek nationalism, in order to defend the rights of the patriarchate. The alliance with nationalism brought them into conflict with the strategy of the patriarch Joachim III (1878–84, 1901–12), who was a firm believer in the supranational character of the Orthodox Church and resisted all initiatives to identify the patriarchate with the policies of any particular national state, even Greece.[33] Patriarch Joachim III believed that safeguarding the traditional privileges of the Orthodox community would provide the basis for the survival of the Christian people in a multicultural Ottoman state and therefore insisted on loyalty to the empire. He regarded with deep scepticism the inherent adventurism he perceived in nationalism. After the death of Joachim III in 1912, however, the patriarchate of Constantinople gave in to

---

32 Elie Kedourie, *The Chatham House version and other Middle-Eastern Studies*, new edition (Hanover and London: University Press of New England, 1984), 317–50, 450–7.
33 For a discussion in English see E. Kophos, 'Patriarch Joachim III (1878–1884) and the irredentist policy of the Greek state', *Journal of Modern Greek Studies* 4 (1986), 107–20.

the temptations of nationalism. The nationalist upsurge in Ottoman politics following the Young Turk revolt in 1908, the Balkan Wars (1912–13) and the outbreak of World War I in 1914 carried the Christian nationalities and their churches in the Ottoman Empire further down the precarious road of nationalism. In the immediate aftermath of the War, during the allied occupation of Istanbul, Patriarch Meletios IV (1921–23) openly championed the cause of Greek nationalism.

The Orthodox Church discovered, as the Armenian Church had already done, that succumbing to the temptations of nationalism came at a terrible price: in the shape of martyrdom and exile for their communities. The exodus of the Orthodox from Asia Minor and eastern Thrace, imposed by the treaty of Lausanne in 1923, was an incalculable tragedy for Christianity: it annihilated by fire and axe two thousand years of Christian history whose origins went back to the preaching of St Paul, the seven churches of Asia, and the pastoral miracle performed by the Greek Fathers of the fourth century. It was also a great tragedy for Turkish society: it deprived it of a rich heritage of pluralism and religious symbiosis, which might have made modern Turkey more amenable to the lessons of tolerance and respect for otherness. The only remnant of Orthodox Christianity in Turkey, left behind by this catastrophe, other than the great monuments of the past, has been the ecumenical patriarchate itself and its flock in Greater Istanbul and in the Aegean islands of Imbros and Tenedos. Some Orthodox Arab populations in south-eastern Turkey also remained under the jurisdiction of the patriarchate of Antioch. The Turkish-speaking Orthodox of the interior of Asia Minor, especially in the region of Cappadocia with its exquisite heritage of Christian art, were sacrificed to the Cronus of nationalism and expelled to Greece. Following this tragic interlude a succession of remarkable patriarchs has ensured that the patriarchate of Constantinople has returned to its genuine traditions of ecumenicity and faithful devotion to the canons, supplying the leadership which the Orthodox world needs to meet the challenges of the twenty-first century.

Nationalism has remained a problem for the Orthodox Church throughout the twentieth century. In the course of that century the vast majority of Orthodox believers lived under the jurisdiction of national churches, which in turn passed under the tight control of secular states. For the most part the states used the churches in order to promote their own political and nationalist agendas. The local national churches became effective instruments in achieving national cohesion and ideological integration in new states ruling over Orthodox populations in the Balkans and elsewhere. The symbolic and psychological power associated with the Christian religion in those regions and the earlier history of the church as an organising structure in the life of local communities provided the most effective supports to the nationalist projects of modern states, once the churches were enlisted among their administrative instruments: paradoxically by means of autocephaly, which emancipated national churches from Constantinople only to deliver them up to the control of secular states.

Secular control had two obvious consequences for both local and regional churches: there was, in the first place, the inevitable sacrifice of some of their Christian values and, in the second, entanglement in nationalist hatreds and passions. The real meaning of subjection to the state transpired once the states became communist and atheist, in Russia after 1917, in the Balkans and eastern Europe from 1945 to 1990. This sometimes meant martyrdom, which eventually worked to the advantage of both the faith and the moral stature of the Orthodox Church; it also meant the subversion of Christian values through the infiltration of the hierarchy by state agents. This was a destructive process, which was covered up by an escalation of nationalist zeal and by the reduction through blackmail of churches and patriarchates into pawns used for unholy purposes: propaganda, suppression, war, as the tragedies in the Balkans in the 1990s bear witness. The exploitation of the national Orthodox churches by the state was also exported to the wide-ranging Orthodox diaspora, which instead of becoming a field of inter-Orthodox encounter and solidarity, very often became an arena of nationalist confrontations in western Europe, North America and Oceania.

Most of these phenomena were connected with the higher reaches of church politics. At the grass roots another Orthodoxy survived, focused on parish worship and the observance of the lifecycle of the Christian tradition and on monasticism and its spiritual witness. This fragmented story has not been systematically written and some of its component parts are better known than others: for example, the Philokalic revival in Russia centred on the Optina monastery, and its impact on other Orthodox churches of eastern Europe is well known and is connected with the efflorescence of theological thought in the Orthodox diaspora. A less well known chapter of the story of the survival of Orthodox ethos and tradition in the age of the nationalisation of local churches is provided by the case of the greatest Greek prose writer in the second half of the nineteenth century, Alexandros Papadiamantis (1851–1911). Although the Orthodox inspiration of the work of the great nineteenth-century Russian novelists Gogol, Dostoevsky and Tolstoy is well known in the cultural history of Europe, outside Greece Papadiamantis's achievement is much less familiar and much less appreciated. Papadiamantis did not write epic novels like his Russian counterparts but he spent his inexhaustible talent in writing numerous short stories, which record, in an immediate and unassuming way and with genuine human feeling unsurpassed in its simplicity and its descriptive power, the daily round of the Orthodox experience, as a source of meaning, consolation, hope and beauty. No other writer in Greek or Balkan literature has written with more tenderness and affection about personal expressions of piety, about congregations worshipping, and about the emotional impact of Orthodox ritual set against the poetry of the Greek landscape. Papadiamantis shared with his famous Russian contemporaries the inspiration coming from the heritage of the *Philokalia*, which had lingered on in the Aegean insular world where he had grown up and which provided the primary material for his stories. But the Philokalic inspiration in Papadiamantis's prose was a source of solace and redemption for human suffering, not a force tearing apart the human personality by means of the dilemmas it posed. The renewed interest in Papadiamantis in the late twentieth century and the attraction exercised by his work on major Greek thinkers, such as Zisimos Lorenzatos, is a sign that amidst all the vicissitudes endured by Orthodoxy because of its association with nationalism, an inner spiritual core remains strong and viable as a life choice in the twenty-first century.[34]

---

34 *The drama of quality: selected essays by Zisimos Lorenzatos*, trans. L. Sherrard (Limni, Euboia: Denise Harvey Publications, 2000), 7–28.

PART II

*

THE RUSSIAN CHURCH

Russian piety and Orthodox culture
1380–1589

STELLA ROCK

Introduction

The chronological span of this chapter begins with the victory of Grand Prince Dmitrii of Moscow over a Tatar army at Kulikovo Field, a battle supposedly blessed by St Sergii of Radonezh and recognised as a defining spiritual, as well as political, moment in the life of the nation: as many disparate responses over the intervening centuries bear witness, from the near-contemporary versions of the Kulikovo Tale (*Zadonshchina*)[1] to Aleksandr Blok's classic poetic cycle *On Kulikovo Field* and the canonisation in 1988 of Dmitrii (honoured with the title Donskoi, 'of the Don'). Our period ends with the creation of the Russian patriarchate, formal recognition of the autocephalous status of the Russian Orthodox Church, shortly to be followed by the extinction of the first Russian royal dynasty and the 'Time of Troubles'. The interim period represents the gradual formation of what is generally called 'national consciousness': the spiritual, cultural and political transformation of a disparate collection of warring principalities forming mobile alliances with their Catholic, pagan and Muslim neighbours and overlords for economic or political gain, into an Orthodox nation, unified under tsar and patriarch and self-consciously promoting both a national faith and an ideology of a faithful nation.

This is the traditional, simplified, even mythologised, overview of a crucial period in Russian history and the history of the Russian Orthodox Church. Transformation from disparate principalities to centralised Muscovite state indeed took place, but the process was less linear and the details were less definite than is generally allowed. It is by no means certain, for example, that

---

1 R. Jakobson and D. S. Worth (eds.), *Sofonija's tale of the Russian–Tatar battle on the Kulikovo field* [Slavistic Printings and Reprintings 51] (The Hague: Mouton, 1963). I am most grateful for the guidance and collaborative support of Professor Robin Milner-Gulland and to Professor Eve Levin for many informative suggestions.

Map 4 Muscovy (c.1460)

St Sergii blessed Dmitrii's 1380 venture,[2] nor was the battle a decisive victory – the Tatars continued to exact tribute from the Russian lands until the late fifteenth century. The society and culture that emerged under Ivan IV 'the Terrible'[3] (1530–84) in the later sixteenth century was formed by the complex interactions of various groups and ideological influences. The special status accorded the Russian Church by the pagan and subsequently Islamic Golden Horde; the spiritual currents of bogomilism and hesychasm flowing from the Balkans and Byzantium; the trading relationship with the German Hansa; these

2 See for example John Fennell, *A history of the Russian church to 1448* (London: Longman, 1995), 238–9.
3 *Groznyi*, more accurately 'the Awesome'.

all impacted upon the Muscovite state. Integral parts of pre-Tatar Rus – russo-phone, Orthodox territories in the west and south which will eventually form the modern Belarus and Ukraine – came under the rule of the Grand Duchy of Lithuania (in alliance with Catholic Poland), fracturing the nascent Rus nation into two communities (often in rivalry) with very different political and religious experiences. In the fifteenth century the western Russians (to the Byzantines, 'Little Russians') managed to acquire their own metropolitan. Regional identities remained of paramount importance in Tver, Riazan, Iaroslav, Rostov, Viatka, Novgorod and Pskov, until the Muscovite grand princes swallowed these autonomous territories in their 'gathering-in of the Russian lands'.

Modern historiography no longer regards piety and culture as the preserve of elites, and the body of this chapter is concerned with the variegated material fabric of Russian life and the rich spectrums of belief and ritual shared by Russian society. Historians continue to grapple with dichotomies such as 'high' and 'low' culture, 'elite' and 'popular' belief, and seek to portray the diversity of a religious experience both male and female, clerical and lay, monastic and parish, urban and rural. To a certain extent, these historiographical dichotomies have been modified by the recognition of the fundamentally shared or common (if complex) nature of medieval and early modern Christian belief. By the sixteenth century, at least in the christianised communities of Russia (there were pagan 'subject peoples' and fluctuating Muslim and Jewish minorities throughout this period), peasant and prince alike regulated their lives according to the church calendar of fasts and feasts, generally used Christian names and marked the transitions of birth, marriage and death with Orthodox sacrament and ritual.[4] In supplication or thanksgiving they turned to pilgrimage, saints' cults and miraculous icons. They spoke a common language of devotion, and, if literature was primarily a medium of the educated, the culture of church architecture, liturgy, music, painting was accessible to all the faithful. Nor were proscribed forms of belief and practice confined to particular social classes or estates – local clergy as well as peasant women were reprimanded for practising charms and curses, and heretics were to be found in the entourage of the grand prince as well as amongst the urban poor.

'Lived Orthodoxy' and heterodoxy

One of the difficulties faced by those who seek to reconstruct Orthodoxy as it was actually practised during this period – 'lived' Orthodoxy – is that most

---

4 See D. H. Kaiser, 'Quotidian Orthodoxy. Domestic life in early modern Russia', in *Orthodox Russia: belief and practice under the Tsars*, ed. V. A. Kivelson and R. H. Greene (Philadelphia: Pennsylvania State University Press, 2003), 179–92.

sources are prescriptive or proscriptive, written by clerics to tell us what should and should not be done, and historians must decipher by inference what actually was done during the period in question. The *Domostroi*, a sixteenth-century work associated with the archpriest Sil'vestr of the Annunciation Cathedral in the Kremlin, offers spiritual, moral and practical guidance on managing a (wealthy) household. Instructions on issues such as curing sickness by prayer and pilgrimage, when and how to pray at home, what food to prepare on religious fast days, project a fairly detailed picture of the author's ideal of Christian family life.[5] The *Stoglav*, or *One Hundred Chapters*, which records the rulings made by the Church Council of 1551 on 'correct' or prohibited forms of piety and culture, is one of the most interesting sources of this type. Practices condemned by the church as unacceptable (mostly listed in chapters 41, 92 and 93) include amusements such as dancing, drunkenness, and the activities of itinerant minstrels (*skomorokhi*) who accompanied weddings and led people astray with 'devilish games'; graveside rituals on Trinity Sunday involving excessive lamenting followed by excessive merry-making; sorcery and various superstitions such as leaving cauls, salt and soap on the altar (apparently with the connivance of the parish priest); and lewd or unruly behaviour on the eve of church festivals, especially St John's Day, Christmas and Epiphany, described as 'foul pagan and Hellene customs and games'.[6] It is difficult to interpret these passages as accurately reflecting Muscovite piety in the sixteenth century, however, since the *Stoglav* cites canon law liberally, while various commentators have identified textual antecedents such as the *Izmaragd*, *Kormchaia kniga* (*Nomocanon*, or *Book of the Helmsman*, one of the earliest prescriptive texts inherited from Byzantium), *Statute of Vladimir*, and the Bible. Distinguishing 'eye-witness' testimony from literary borrowing is a complex and risky task, and observations of popular practices were no doubt made through the prism of this literary heritage. While this text offers glimpses of the lay public's piety, it tells us perhaps more about the preoccupations of the clerical hierarchy.

Studies of 'popular religion' or 'folk belief' have tended to focus on the problematic but highly influential concept of *dvoeverie* or 'double-belief', a term used by scholars since the mid-nineteenth century to describe the conscious or unconscious preservation of pagan beliefs and / or rituals by Russian Orthodox

---

5 Carolyn Johnston Pouncy (ed. and trans.), *The Domostroi: rules for Russian households in the time of Ivan the Terrible* (Ithaca, NY: Cornell University Press, 1994). The question of authorship and readership is dealt with by Pouncy, 37–49, and P. Bushkovitch, *Religion and society in Russia: the sixteenth and seventeenth centuries* (New York and Oxford: Oxford University Press, 1992), 47–9.

6 E. V. Emchenko, *Stoglav: issledovanie i tekst* (Moscow: Indrik, 2000), 402.

communities.[7] This concept has coloured academic perception of Russian medieval (and often modern) spirituality, leading to a preoccupation with identifying latent paganism in piety and culture. 'Double-belief' has often been considered a specifically Russian phenomenon, with the medieval origins of the term cited as evidence. The texts themselves suggest that the term was not originally understood in this way, however,[8] and that the preoccupations of Russian clerics were similar to those of their western European counterparts.

Limited sources that allow us to enter the non-clerical, 'common' mind do exist – primarily the multitude of birchbark letters preserved in Novgorod and some other Russian cities. However, the majority of these fragmentary testimonies to ordinary lives make no reference to religion, but are concerned with such material matters as commerce, legal disputes and family breakdown. They do, however, demonstrate that by the late fourteenth century peasants called themselves Christians, confirming a self-conscious Christian identity among the 'common people'.[9] Miracle stories, which proliferate from the sixteenth century, also offer some insight into lay piety, although usually mediated by their clerical recorders. Healing cults appear to have attracted, according to the records of those healed, predominantly local support from the lower gentry, merchants, artisans, well-to-do peasants and clerics, but even cults which eventually gain national significance, such as the miracle-working icon of the Mother of God of Kazan (discovered by the young daughter of a soldier in 1579), might be initiated by low-status individuals.[10]

Foreign travellers give another perspective on the externals of religious life: Sigismund von Herberstein (1486–1566),[11] Richard Chancellor (d.1556),[12] Anthony Jenkinson (1530–1611),[13] Antonio Possevino (1533–1611),[14] Giles Fletcher

---

7 See E. Levin, 'Dvoeverie and popular religion', in *Seeking God: the recovery of religious identity in Orthodox Russia, Ukraine, and Georgia*, ed. S. K. Batalden (DeKalb: Northern Illinois University Press, 1993), 31–52 for a brief summary of the historiography.

8 S. Rock, 'What's in a word? A historical study of the concept *dvoeverie*', *Canadian-American Slavic Studies* 35, no. 1 (2001), 19–28.

9 E. Levin, 'Lay religious identity in medieval Russia: the evidence of Novgorod birchbark documents', *General Linguistics* 35 (1997), 131–55.

10 Bushkovitch, *Religion and society*, 102–11.

11 Sigismund von Herberstein, *Moscovia der Haupstadt* (Vienna: Michael Zimmerman, 1557) [reprinted in, *Early exploration of Russia*, ed. Marshall Poe (New York: Routledge, 2003), 11].

12 'The voyage of Richard Chanceller Pilote major, the first discoverer by sea of the kingdome of Moscovia, Anno 1553', in Richard Hakluyt, *The principal navigations, voyages, traffiques and discoveries of the English nation* (London: J. M. Dent and Sons, 1927), 1, esp. 264–6.

13 Hakluyt, *Principal navigations*, 1, esp. 424–7, 430–7.

14 Antonio Possevino, *The Moscovia of Antonio Possevino, S.J.*, trans. Hugh F. Graham [UCIS Russian and East European Studies 1] (Pittsburgh, PA: University of Pittsburgh, 1977).

(d.1611)[15] and Jerome Horsey (d.1626)[16] (for example) recorded details of sixteenth-century Russian piety, some more reliably than others.[17] Foreign observers often contrasted the fervent devotion they witnessed (strict fasting four times a year, interminably long liturgies, the prolific use of icons and candles) with the incongruous tendencies of drunkenness and brutish behaviour, contributing to the creation of national stereotypes still current today.

One facet of what is generally called 'popular' piety is the prevalence of holy fools during this period. The most famous, St Basil the Blessed (d.1552), was canonised in 1588 and was so widely revered that he was buried alongside the Pokrov (or Protecting Veil of the Mother of God) Cathedral in Red Square, which eventually acquired the name St Basil's in his honour. *Iurodivye Khrista radi*, 'fools for Christ's sake' (from 1 Corinthians 4:10), are not solely a Russian phenomenon, but between the fourteenth and seventeenth centuries Russian society nurtured 'fools for Christ's sake' to a unique degree.[18] Feigning madness, holy fools wandered naked in the snow, inviting mockery and abuse by unconventional appearance and behaviour. Some spouted apparent nonsense, which subsequent events revealed as prophecy, and they are credited with having special verbal licence in a violent and increasingly autocratic society, as the legends surrounding St Basil and the Pskovian fool St Nikolai reveal.[19] Anachronistically, Basil is recorded as symbolically reproaching Ivan IV for the 1570 sack of Novgorod by offering him fresh meat. St Nikolai did the same when Ivan threatened Pskov, answering Ivan's declaration of Lenten abstinence with the rebuke that he drinks Christian blood without scruples.[20]

---

15 Giles Fletcher, *Of the Russe Common Wealth* (London: Thomas Charde, 1591) [reprinted in *Early exploration*, ed. Poe, 1].

16 'A Relacion or memoriall abstracted owt of Sir Jerome Horsey his travells, imploiments, services and negociacions, observed and written with his owne hand; wherein he spent the most part of eighteen years tyme', in *Russia at the close of the sixteenth century*, ed. E. A. Bond (London: Hakluyt Society, 1856; reprinted New York: Burt Franklin, 1963).

17 See Marshall Poe, *A people born to slavery: Russia in early modern European ethnography, 1476–1748* (Ithaca, NY: Cornell University Press, 2000); L. E. Berry and R. O. Crummey (eds.), *Rude and barbarous kingdom: Russia in the accounts of sixteenth-century English voyagers* (Madison: University of Wisconsin Press, 1968).

18 See G. P. Fedotov, *The Russian religious mind*, II, *The Middle Ages; the thirteenth to the fifteenth centuries* (Cambridge, MA: Harvard University Press, 1966), 316–43 for a good summary of Russian foolishness. See also S. Ivanov, *Holy Fools* (Oxford: Oxford University Press, 2006).

19 See for example Jerome Horsey on St Nikolai, in *Russia at the close of the sixteenth century*, 161.

20 Michael Petrovich, 'The social and political role of the Muscovite Fools-in-Christ: reality and image', *Forschungen zur Osteuropäischen Geschichte* 25 (1978), 283–96.

It has been argued that the city-stronghold of 'Lord Great' Novgorod 'expressed the stamp of Russian popular life and mind',[21] preserving 'true' Russianness because it largely escaped the devastation wreaked elsewhere by the Tatars. While paying tribute to Tatar overlords, the city continued intellectual and economic commerce with both east and west, which may explain why those heresies significant enough to be recorded during this period appear in Novgorod and its fellow trading centre Pskov. The late fourteenth-century *strigol'niki* or 'Shearers' criticised simony and the lax priesthood, and seem to have rejected the sacraments offered by a clergy they perceived as flawed and illegitimate. They also seem to have advocated confession to the earth,[22] an act interpreted by some as evidence of obdurate paganism and loyalty to 'Moist Mother Earth'.[23] Little more is known about this heresy, but it troubled the hierarchy for some time. In 1427, Metropolitan Photios wrote complaining about *strigol'niki* in Pskov, half a century after the chronicles record the drowning of certain *strigol'niki* in Novgorod, and during the later 'Judaiser' heresy Archbishop Gennadii accused one leader of being a *strigol'nik*.[24]

This so-called 'Judaiser' heresy of the late fifteenth century impacted upon both the elite and the lower clergy. 'Judaiser' was not a contemporary term but appeared in much later historiography, and the 'Jewishness' of the heresy is now seriously disputed.[25] The chief persecutors (Iosif of Volokolamsk and Archbishop Gennadii of Novgorod) are – as usual – the main recorders of the heresy, so any attempt to understand the true nature of the unorthodox beliefs circulating at this time will be only partially successful. Iosif declares that the heresy began when 'a Jew by the name of Skhariia' from Kiev converted two Novgorodian priests and, with the help of two more Jews from Lithuania, began to proselytise.[26] The heresy was apparently anti-Trinitarian, critical of the clergy and iconoclastic, and as such resembled early Protestant movements.

---

21 Fedotov, *Russian religious mind*, II, 333.
22 N. A. Kazakova and Ia. S. Lur'e, *Antifeodal'nye ereticheskie dvizheniia na Rusi XIV–nachala XVI veka* (Moscow: AN SSSR, 1955), 241.
23 See Fedotov, *Russian religious mind*, II, 135–9.
24 R. G. Skrynnikov, 'Ecclesiastical thought in Russia and the Church Councils of 1503 and 1504', *Oxford Slavonic Papers* 25 (1992), 37.
25 The most comprehensive work on this movement is Kazakova and Lur'e, *Antifeodal'nye*. Cf. Jakov S. Lur'e, 'Unresolved issues in the history of the ideological movements of the late fifteenth century', in *Medieval Russian culture*, ed. H. Birnbaum and M. S. Flier [California Slavic Studies 12] (Berkeley: University of California Press, 1984), 150–71. See also J. D. Klier, 'Judaizing without Jews? Moscow–Novgorod, 1470–1504', in *Culture and identity in Muscovy, 1359–1584* , ed. A. M. Kleimola and G. D. Lenhoff (Moscow: ITZ-Garant, 1997), 336–49.
26 Iosif Volotskii, *Prosvetitel', ili, Oblichenie eresi zhidovstvuiushchikh*, fourth edition (Kazan: Imperatorskii Universitet, 1903; reprinted Farnborough: Gregg International, 1972).

It spread to the Moscow court when the grand prince engaged the two clerical converts to serve in Kremlin churches – possibly as sympathisers of his plan for the secularisation of church lands.[27] Elena of Moldavia, Ivan III's daughter-in-law, and state secretary Fedor Kuritsyn were the highest-ranking 'heretics', and for some years the grand prince refused to root out the heresy with violence, despite an inquisitorial campaign launched against these heretics in 1487 by Archbishop Gennadii.

The fate of the heretics was intimately tied to the politics of the day: the conflict over church landholdings and the struggle for succession between Ivan III's grandson Dmitrii (son of Elena of Moldavia) and his son Vasilii, born to Ivan's second wife Sophia Palaiologina, niece of the last Byzantine emperor. The synod of 1490 dealt leniently with the heretics, and this first trial, which accused the heretics of refusing to venerate Moscow and Rostov saints, has been seen as having a distinctly anti-Novgorodian bias.[28] A later trial led by Vasilii in 1504 sentenced the heretics to death or life banishment, with Elena conveniently dying in prison in 1505.

Pious culture and creative piety

In broad terms Muscovite culture remained, culturally and to a large extent politically, a medieval society throughout the period under discussion and, as one might expect, its cultural monuments of written literature, visual art, architecture and notated music are intimately bound up with the purposes and expressions of religion. The historiography, personal and diplomatic correspondence, and legal-administrative texts that remain to us are also coloured by Orthodox Christianity. Nevertheless, it would be a mistake to imagine that all cultural production was of a pious nature. A vast quantity of oral literature (epic *byliny*, historical songs, lyrics, spells, riddles, etc.) was developed and circulated by the *skomorokhi*,[29] sometimes enjoying court favour (under Ivan IV for example), but always frowned upon by the church.

Relatively few western theological influences penetrated pious culture during this period, and for the most part the Russian elite remained suspicious of both Protestantism and Catholicism. There were exceptions: the Novgorodian Archbishop Gennadii, in addition to his interest in inquisitorial methods of controlling heresy, employed a Dominican monk for several years and used

---

27 J. L. I. Fennell, *Ivan the Great of Moscow* (London: Macmillan, 1961), 327.
28 Skrynnikov, 'Ecclesiastical thought', 36.
29 See Z. I. Vlasova, *Skomorokhi i fol'klor* (St Petersburg: Aleteiia, 2001); R. Zguta, *Russian minstrels: a history of the Skomorokhi* (Oxford: Clarendon Press, 1978).

Latin sources during the translation of the entire Bible into Slavonic (completed in 1499 but not disseminated in print until 1580–81).[30]

Medieval Russian culture has been described as 'intellectually silent', producing no great theological or scientific works, impoverished or stunted by limited access to classical education and secular knowledge and an excess of irrational religiosity, but this is to judge it unfairly.[31] The arts of book creation, painting, embroidery, the construction of churches and the decoration of palaces celebrated cultural qualities alien to us – originality was not valued, while loyalty to Orthodox tradition and established forms was; and slow, meditative devotion rather than quick flashes of genius created the cultural works that survive from this period. The creative reworking of existing spiritual material was valued above original theological composition, and the manner of book creation in medieval Russia has been compared to the workings of a kaleidoscope – new spiritual insights were gained by reshuffling the limited number of extant devotional texts into new patterns.[32]

G. P. Fedotov has fruitfully explored the *Izmaragd* (the *Emerald*), a devotional reader apparently compiled for both laypeople and clerics, as offering access to the piety of the literate community in the fourteenth and fifteenth centuries.[33] It begins with a glorification of books that belongs equally to the Kievan period of Russian piety and an exposition of the proper manner of reading all spiritual writings, whether scripture or didactic works. Reading, as well as writing, was considered an act of devotion, to be approached with diligence, absorbing and contemplating each word.

The clerical elite (monastic or 'black' clergy, from which bishops were chosen) and the great monastic houses have particular significance as the principal creators, reproducers and repositories of written culture during this period.

---

30 V. A. Romodanovskaia, 'O tseliakh sozdaniia Gennadievskoi Biblii ka pervogo polnogo russkogo Bibleiskogo kodeksa', in *Knizhnye tsentry Drevnei Rusi: Severnorusskie monastyri*, ed. S. A. Semiachko (St Petersburg: Dmitrii Bulanin, 2001), 278–305; H. R. Cooper, *Slavic Scriptures: the formation of the Church Slavonic version of the Holy Bible* (London, Ontario: Cranbury, 2003).

31 See Georges Florovsky, 'The problem of Old Russian culture', *Slavic Review* 21 (1962), 1–15; J. H. Billington, 'Images of Muscovy', *Slavic Review* 21 (1962), 24–34; D. S. Likhachev, 'Further remarks on the problem of Old Russian culture', *Slavic Review* 22 (1963), 115–20; F. J. Thomson, 'The corpus of Slavonic translations available in Muscovy: the cause of Old Russia's intellectual silence and a contributory factor in Muscovite cultural autarky', in *Christianity and the Eastern Slavs*, I, *Slavic cultures in the Middle Ages*, ed. B. Gasparov and O. Raevsky-Hughes [California Slavic Studies 16] (Berkeley: University of California Press, 1993), 179–214.

32 W. R. Veder, 'Old Russia's "intellectual silence" reconsidered', in *Medieval Russian culture*, ed. M. S. Flier and D. Rowland [California Slavic Studies 19] (Berkeley: University of California Press, 1994), II, 18–28.

33 Fedotov, *Russian religious mind*, II, 37–112.

They produced historiography in the shape of chronicles (the pinnacle of which is the sixteenth-century *Illustrated Chronicle Compendium* or *Litsevoi letopisnyi svod*, over 10,000 manuscript pages compiled under the guidance of Metropolitan Makarii) and hagiography recording the lives of significant individuals. In the late fourteenth and early fifteenth centuries, this creative activity was accelerated and shaped by a cultural movement that began in the Balkans as an attempt to reform the orthography and language of religious texts according to canonical norms, and developed into a drive for cultural renewal across Orthodox Europe as a whole. New saints' lives were written, new models of sanctity were promoted which highlighted the importance of the individual personality and experience, and a complex and rhetorical literary style known as 'word weaving' (*pletenie sloves*) developed. The new style reached Russia in part through the agency of Bulgarian and Serbian émigrés such as Metropolitan Kiprian. Among its early manifestations were the hagiographical writings of Epifanii 'The Wise' (*premudryi*), the 'word-weaving' author of the *Life of St Sergii* and the *Life of St Stefan of Perm*.[34] Scholars have termed this movement the 'Second South Slavonic Influence' (the first having occurred at the time of the conversion of Rus), but it does not do justice either to the native input or to the role played by renewed contacts with Byzantium and, most importantly, with Mount Athos (whence came the important hagiographer 'Pakhomii the Serb' in 1438).

Scholars agree that the mystical current of hesychasm was part of this pan-Slavic renewal process, but exactly how remains elusive. Part of the problem resides in the several definitions and uses of the term. Derived from the Greek ἡσυχασμός, 'being quiet', 'hesychasm' primarily describes the monastic practice of interior silence and continual prayer first established by the Desert Fathers and was not used to indicate a distinct spiritual movement until the fourteenth-century Byzantine revival of meditative prayer techniques, most characteristically the 'prayer of the heart' or Jesus Prayer and the striving towards the 'Divine and Uncreated Light' of Mount Tabor.[35] This revival was linked to Gregory of Sinai and Gregory Palamas, the former having a far greater impact on the Slavs. It was a movement that can be viewed more broadly as a revival of monastic spirituality, while there are scholars who have

---

34 V. G. Druzhinin (ed.), *Zhitie sviatogo Stefana, episkopa Permskogo napissanoe Epifaniem Premudrym* [Apophoreta slavica 2] (The Hague: Mouton, 1959), reprint of 1897 edition. An extract in English can be found in S. A. Zenkovsky, *Medieval Russia's epics, chronicles and tales* (New York: E. P. Dutton, 1964), 206–8.

35 See J. Meyendorff, *St Gregory Palamas and Orthodox spirituality* (Crestwood, NY: St Vladimir's Seminary Press, 1998) for a clear exposition of Palamas's hesychasm within the historical tradition of eastern monastic spirituality. See above chapter 4.

sought to identify a 'political hesychasm', which had varying degrees of impact on Byzantine and Slavic society.[36]

The extent to which hesychasm influenced Russian piety is debated,[37] as is its impact on Russian culture (specifically on the techniques of icon painting and 'word weaving').[38] It seems clear that the fourteenth-century Byzantine hesychast revival promoted international monastic contacts within the Orthodox world, and the translation and recopying of many Byzantine monastic works and their transmission to Slavic lands, and was in part responsible for the spectacular flourishing of monasticism that we see in late fourteenth- and early fifteenth-century Russia. The library of the Trinity-St Sergii monastery, for example, then contained a number of what Meyendorff calls 'the classics of hesychastic spirituality', as did that of the St Kirill-Belozerskii monastery.[39] Direct evidence of Byzantine hesychast influence in the shape of mystical visions and Palamite theology is hard to find in the hagiography of the period. However, in so far that it encouraged a more personal religion, which stressed the possibility of direct contact with the Divine and the supremacy of the spiritual over the secular, hesychasm appears to have impacted significantly upon the generations of monks who chose contemplative prayer in the forest 'deserts' of the Russian north and east over socially active life in the large urban or suburban cenobitic centres. As one might expect, the figurehead of these 'trans-Volgan elders', Nil Sorskii, makes clear references to hesychast practices in his monastic rule,[40] but it should be recalled that even the practical Iosif of Volokolamsk, who epitomises socially and politically active cenobiticism, recommends periods of silence and tearful recollection to his monks.[41]

Monastic humility, and the fear of inadvertently committing a heresy to paper by misrepresenting the sacred original, was an incentive to reproduce any spiritual treatise as exactly as possible, including accrued mistakes, but by the sixteenth century a new critical spirit had reached the clerical hierarchy. The

36 G. M. Prokhorov, 'Isikhazm i obshchestvennaia mysl' v Vostochnoi Evrope v XIV v.', in *Literaturnye sviazi drevnikh slavian*, ed. D. S. Likhachev [Trudy otdela devnerusskoi literatury 23] (Leningrad: Nauka, 1968), 86–108; P. Bushkovitch, 'The limits of hesychasm: some notes on monastic spirituality in Russia 1350–1500', *Forschungen zur Osteuropäischen Geschichte* 38 (1986), 97–109, esp. 109.

37 See Bushkovitch, 'Limits of hesychasm'.

38 See J. Meyendorff, 'Is "hesychasm" the right word?' in *Okeanos: essays presented to Ihor Ševčenko on his sixtieth birthday by his colleagues and students* [Harvard Ukrainian Studies 7] (Cambridge, MA: Harvard University Press, 1983), 447–57. See above 38–41.

39 J. Meyendorff, *Byzantium and the rise of Russia*, 124–5.

40 See G. A. Maloney, *Russian hesychasm: the spirituality of Nil Sorskii* (The Hague: Mouton, 1973) for the fullest English-language exposition of this.

41 D. M. Goldfrank, *The monastic rule of Iosif Volotsky* [Cistercian Studies Series 36] (Kalamazoo, MI: Cistercian Publications, 1983), 105.

Athonite monk Maksim Grek arrived in Moscow in 1518 to translate the Psalter and commentaries from Greek, and was detained there (probably against his will), continuing to translate and correct essential spiritual works. Maksim's life in Muscovy became sadly tangled in the politics of the day – his arrest in 1525 was in part a result of his vocal objections to Vasilii III's uncanonical divorce and remarriage in that year.[42] Imprisoned in Volokolamsk monastery, Maksim was retried six years later by Metropolitan Daniil for sins including 'Hellenic and heretical sorcery' and blasphemous translations, and imprisoned again in a Tver monastery. He was finally released to live freely in the Trinity-St Sergii monastery in 1551, five years before his death.[43] His translations of the Psalter, Gospels and Triodion were among the first books printed in the 1560s, and the church recognised his contribution to Russian Orthodoxy by canonising him in 1988. The 1551 Church Council, in addition to freeing Maksim, acknowledged the pressing need for systematic correction of church texts and for improved clerical education, but little was achieved before the country slid into the turmoil of the *Oprichnina* and, later, the 'Time of Troubles' (1598–1613), Ivan IV's legacy of political chaos.

The blossoming of icon painting during this period is explored below,[44] but while the work of Rublev and Dionisii is understandably celebrated as the pinnacle of medieval Russia's cultural achievement, the devotional art of women has often been overlooked. Workshops headed by royal women such as Solomoniia Saburova, the first wife of Vasilii III (d.1542), Irina Godunova (d.1603) and Evfrosiniia Staritskaia (d.1569) embroidered shrouds, altar cloths and liturgical vestments of complex symbolism and beauty, a form of icon painting in thread, or prayers in textile. These works were created within convents or presented to monasteries by wealthy women, in memory of deceased relatives, in thanksgiving or in supplication. One of the most poignant testimonies of Solomoniia's sorrow is a tapestry donated to the Trinity-St Sergii monastery in 1525, shortly before she was divorced and tonsured for failing to produce an heir. It records her hopes with illustrations of the miraculous fecundity of Anna, the aging mother of Mary; Elizabeth, the mother of John the Baptist; and the Mother of God herself.[45] The memoirs of a

---

42 J. Martin, *Medieval Russia 980–1584* (Cambridge: Cambridge University Press, 1995), 292.

43 J. V. Haney, *From Italy to Muscovy: the life and works of Maxim the Greek* (Munich: Wilhelm Fink Verlag, 1973).

44 See below chapter 12.

45 I. Thyrêt, *Between God and Tsar: religious symbolism and the royal women of Muscovite Russia* (DeKalb: Northern Illinois University Press, 2001), 25–7; D. B. Miller, 'Motives for donations to the Trinity-Sergius monastery, 1392–1605: gender matters', *Essays in Medieval Studies* 14 (1997), 91–106.

fifteenth-century nun from the Novgorodian nobility, Mariia Odoevskaia, record that she was especially valued by the abbess for her writing skills, copying 'books and chronicles'.[46] Wealthy women also, like men, commissioned the construction and decoration of churches,[47] and lay patronage supported the revival of masonry church construction, first in Novgorod where in the mid-fourteenth century boyars and wealthy merchants were frequent patrons.[48]

Church architecture is an indicative and important aspect of pious culture during this period, and the plain, monumental style of early Novgorod building gives way to a more variegated manner. The most interesting innovations, such as *kokoshniki*, decorative tiers of gables named after peasant women's headdresses, and the strange 'tent' churches that appear from the 1530s, are associated with Moscow. A conscious seeking of inspiration in the pre-Tatar past is observable in the fifteenth century: major restoration work was carried out on old buildings, and when Ivan III commissioned an Italian to build a suitably grand cathedral for the Moscow Kremlin, he ordered him to study early Russian architecture. By the end of the century, the Moscow Kremlin had been refashioned as a huge fortress, symbolic of Moscow's increased significance as the political centre of Russia.[49]

Of all the architectural landmarks that arose in this period, perhaps the most dramatic is the massive, astonishing edifice built to commemorate the capture of Kazan in 1552. St Basil's, as it is now known, consists of nine individual chapels grouped around a great spire. Several of the chapels are dedicated to feast days marking events in the siege of Kazan, and the central church to the Pokrov or 'Protecting Veil of the Mother of God'. One chapel is dedicated to the Trinity, symbolising national reconciliation, and another to the Entry into Jerusalem. The whole ensemble was often referred to as 'the Jerusalem', and there is clear evidence that it was perceived as an icon of the Holy City.[50] The characteristic Russian 'onion domes', although represented much earlier in manuscript illustrations and *siony* (miniature replicas of the Jerusalem Church

46 S. Bolshakoff, *Russian mystics* [Cistercian Studies Series 26] (Kalamazoo, MI: Cistercian Publications, 1980), 45.
47 N. Pushkareva, *Women in Russian history from the tenth to the twentieth century*, trans. and ed. Eve Levin (Armonk, NY: M. E. Sharpe, 1997), esp. 22–3.
48 D. B. Miller, 'Monumental building as an indicator of economic trends in northern Rus' in the late Kievan and Mongol periods, 1138–1462', *American Historical Review* 94 (1989), 360–90, esp. 383–5.
49 See R. Milner-Gulland, 'Art and architecture of Old Russia, 988–1700', in *An introduction to Russian art and architecture*, ed. R. Auty and D. Obolensky (Cambridge: Cambridge University Press, 1980), 28–56.
50 R. Milner-Gulland, *The Russians* (Oxford: Blackwell, 1997), 212–18. See below, pp. 299–300.

of the Resurrection or Holy Sepulchre), first appear in church architecture at the end of the sixteenth century. They have been described as iconographical motifs of the ancient shrine of the Holy Sepulchre, evidence of the importance of the Jerusalem motif in Russian piety and culture of this period.[51]

Monasticism

As the cultural traces of this period bear witness, the dominant form of piety was monasticism, in part the spiritual legacy of St Sergii of Radonezh (d.1392). While estimates of the numbers of monasteries vary, evidence suggests that around 150 new monasteries were founded in the fourteenth century, 250 or more in the fifteenth century and over 330 in the sixteenth century. While some of these will have failed to flourish or been destroyed by fire or plague, one may assume that by the end of the sixteenth century well over 500 monastic establishments were functioning on Muscovite territory.[52] There were over 700 monks at the Trinity-St Sergii monastery by the end of this period, but most major monasteries housed between 80 and 200 monks or nuns.[53] Many of these new monasteries were founded in remote rural areas, in contrast to earlier urban constructions. Hermitages and *sketes* (where generally two to six monks lived together in the wilderness) often developed into significant monasteries, contributing to the integration of new territories and the christianisation of indigenous peoples.

This flourishing of monasticism is hardly surprising – these were violent and uncertain times. The population was ravaged by wars with Lithuania, Livonia, Crimea and Kazan; by bloody power struggles between princes and noble factions; by continuing harassment from the Tatar horde, outbreaks of plague, and later the tyranny, pillage and executions of Ivan IV's reign. The belief, widespread at least within literate society, that the world was to end in 1492 (7000 years after its creation in 5508 BC) cannot but have encouraged this 'flight from the world'. The Orthodox Church was so assured that the world

51 A. M. Lidov, 'Ierusalimskii kuvuklii. O proiskhozhdenii lukovichnykh glav', in *Ikono-grafiia arkhitektury*, ed. A. L. Batalov (Moscow: Akademiia khudozhestv, 1990), 57–68.

52 See E. I. Kolycheva, 'Pravoslavnye monastyri vtoroi poloviny XV–XVI veka', in *Monash-estvo i monastyri v Rossii XI–XX veka*, ed. N. V. Sinitsyna (Moscow: Nauka, 2002), 81–115, for a recent overview of statistical data. The reprinted nineteenth-century multivolume *Istoriia Russkoi Tserkvi* by Metropolitan Makarii (Bulgakov) includes detailed surveys of monasticism during this period: see *Istoriia Russkoi Tserkvi v period postepennogo perekhoda ee k samostoiatel'nosti (1240–1589)* (Moscow: Izd. Spaso-Preobrazhenskogo Valaamskogo Monastyria, 1995–96), III, ch. 3; IV, pt I, ch. 4, and the updated appendices in each volume listing monastic establishments and the dates they were founded.

53 E. I. Kolycheva, 'Pravoslavnye monastyri vtoroi poloviny XV–XVI veka', 89.

would end that there were no liturgical calendars ready for the years following 1492, and they had to be prepared that year by Metropolitan Zosima.[54]

The impact of St Sergii on Russian culture was huge, and not just in terms of his ubiquitous symbolic value as the 'Builder of Russia'.[55] His immense reputation ensured that he was canonised soon after his death; his relics were uncovered in 1422 and the first church built in his honour was constructed in Novgorod in 1460. The decades around 1400 have been termed the 'Sergievan' period,[56] so great was his impact on society of the time, and the centre of intellectual and cultural life for much of this period was the monastery he founded, now called the Trinity-St Sergii, 70 kilometres north-east of Moscow. Sergii revitalised both the cenobitic tradition of Russian monasticism (a truly common life, with shared possessions and communal living in contrast to the more prevalent idiorrhythmic regime where monks lived separately and simply worshipped together) and the eremitic tradition, the practice of a solitary monastic life.

This eremitic tradition, through the example of St Sergii, impacted upon the social and geographical fabric of Russia in the colonisation of the northern territories. The Life of St Sergii of Radonezh portrays the manner in which the numerous monastic houses were founded during this period. An individual monk searching for silence and solitude sets up a hermitage.[57] He is joined by a small group of brothers seeking his spiritual guidance, and a new monastery develops which attracts more visitors, from which monks leave to seek a quieter place of prayer. This cycle was repeated over and over again by Sergii's disciples. Reputed to have established ten monasteries himself before his death, Sergii prepared a generation of monks who, together with their spiritual sons, subsequently founded the spectacular monasteries of the northern territories such as the Holy Dormition monastery of Kirill-Belozerskii (founded in 1397 by St Kirill, a monk of the Simonov monastery, where St Sergii of Radonezh's nephew was abbot), the Nativity of the Mother of God monastery of Ferapontov (founded in 1398) and the Saviour-Transfiguration monastery at Solovki.

54 M. S. Flier, 'Till the end of time: the Apocalypse in Russian historical experience before 1500', in Orthodox Russia, ed. Kivelson and Greene, 127–58.

55 N. Zernov, St Sergius, builder of Russia, with the life, acts and miracles of the holy abbot Sergius of Radonezh (London: SPCK, 1939).

56 R. Milner-Gulland, 'Russia's lost Renaissance', in Literature and western civilization, ed. D. Daiches and A. K. Thorlby (London: Aldus, 1973), III, 435–68.

57 Zhitie Sergiia Radonezhskogo, in Biblioteka Literatury Drevnei Rusi, IV, XIV–seredina XV veka, ed. D. S. Likhachev et al. (St Petersburg: Nauka, 1999), 256–411; M. Klimenko, The 'Vita' of St Sergii of Radonezh (Houston, TX: Nordland, 1980).

The development of this latter monastery on the Solovki islands in the White Sea illustrates this process. The monk Savvatii was tonsured in Kirill-Belozerskii monastery but, seeking a more peaceful place to pray, went first to the monastery of Varlaam and then, in 1429, to the absolute wilderness of the uninhabited Solovki islands, with German, another hermit who eventually left the islands. After Savvatii's death, German returned to Solovki with the monk Zosima in 1436, and together they gradually established a monastery. The monastery flourished materially and spiritually under the leadership of St Filipp, future metropolitan of Moscow, whose creative and organisational skills were honed as he oversaw the development of a system of canals, stone buildings including the cathedral, gardens, a bakery, mills, dams and reindeer herding. By the end of the sixteenth century, this island hermitage had become a massive White Sea fortress, emblematic of the changes the Russian Orthodox Church had undergone.[58]

Some historians have firmly linked the spread of monasteries with colonisation or an increasingly indentured peasantry,[59] and while these were certainly not articulated goals of the monks who spread northwards, they were in some areas by-products of monastic success. In the *Life of St Stefan* composed by Epifanii shortly after Stefan's death in 1396, we meet the unusual case of a monk who dedicated himself to missionary work, but rather than imposing on his neophyte Permians (Finnish tribes, the modern day Komi) the Church Slavonic used in all liturgical and spiritual texts, Stefan created instead an alphabet for them and translated the essential Christian works into their language. The Permian lands, formerly associated with Novgorod, were taken under the 'protection' of the Muscovite Grand Prince Dmitrii. Ironically, one of the objections to Christianity voiced by the Permians in Epifanii's *Life* is to rule from Moscow, with the burdens and taxes it entails. Epifanii credits St Stefan with interceding for the Permians in both Moscow and Novgorod. His experiment in linguistic accommodation was not to survive, however. In the sixteenth century Church Slavonic replaced the Permian liturgy, and the Permian people became russified, at least on an official level.

Lest the monastic revival appear entirely male, it should be recalled that not only wandering monks founded cloisters. Princess Evfrosiniia Staritskaia, for example, founded the convent of the Resurrection in Goritsy in 1544, but noble women seem to have been as much prisoners of convents as founders during

---

58 See R. R. Robson, *Solovki: the story of Russia told through its remarkable islands* (New Haven and London: Yale University Press, 2004) for the long view of Solovki's development.

59 I. U. Budovnits, *Monastyri na Rusi i bor'ba s nimi krest'ian v 14–16 vekakh (po 'zhitiiam sviatykh')* (Moscow: Nauka, 1966), 357–8.

this period, and Evfrosiniia was no exception. Tonsured (probably forcibly) after accusations of treason levelled by Ivan IV and subsequently murdered by the *oprichniki*, her convent also housed the widow of Ivan IV, Mariia Fedorovna (Nagaia), banished there by Boris Godunov,[60] Ivan's fourth wife Anna Alekseevna, and his daughter-in-law Pelageia Mikhailovna. Forcible tonsure was not only a convenient (if unreliable) way of silencing political rivals, both male and female. It was also a method of divorce.

Those who were unable or unwilling to join a monastery could contribute to its development by donation, and the expansion of monasticism was greatly aided by financial investment of princes, wealthy nobles, merchants and senior clerics. Popular donations included food, stone churches and villages – in return donors (and their relatives) could expect prayers and eternal remembrance in death. Bequests were popular, and the huge increase in landowning by the church as a result of nobles leaving family lands to monasteries rather than to their kin provoked one of the great debates of the day, between the 'Possessors' – those who supported church landowning – and the 'Non-Possessors', who argued that it was inappropriate for monasteries to own lands and to live from the labour of the peasants who farmed them.[61]

Two towering figures in the historiography of this period, Nil Sorskii (1433–1508) and Iosif of Volokolamsk (1439–1515), are usually portrayed as representatives of these two factions and of the two facets of monasticism – silent eremiticism and socially active cenobiticism – embraced as St Sergii's heritage. The difference was rather one of emphasis: in guiding others towards spiritual perfection, Nil stressed the inner life of the spirit; Iosif, outer practice.

The details of Nil's life are sketchy, since he left a small literary heritage: a few letters to 'spiritual sons', plus his *Ustav* or *Monastic Rule* (more a treatise on the interior life than regulations) and the short *Predanie* or *Tradition*. We know that he spent time on Mount Athos and in Kirill-Belozerskii monastery, before seeking undisturbed peace in the northern forests of the White Lake area. He favoured the *skete*, several brothers living together in the wilderness, rather than the complete solitude of eremiticism, and his followers are often referred to as the 'Trans-Volga Elders' because of their retreat into the northern wilds.

Nil is upheld as an example of Russian kenoticism, a self-emptying humility that led him, unlike Iosif, to avoid public life and political influence. Another

---

60 Jerome Horsey suggests she voluntarily entered, after being poisoned. See *Russia at the close of the sixteenth century*, 255.

61 See D. Ostrowski, 'Church polemics and monastic land acquisition in sixteenth-century Muscovy', *Slavonic and East European Review* 64 (1986), 355–79.

feature of this gentle spirituality traditionally attributed to Nil but vocalised rather by his followers, mercy towards heretics, distinguished him sharply from Iosif, who was an enthusiastic persecutor of the Judaisers. Nil was, however, equally keen to preserve the true faith, and the *Predanie* begins with a declaration of his orthodoxy and loyalty to the Orthodox Church. Nil is careful to cite the Fathers to support his declarations, and none of his spiritual writing can be deemed original. In brief, he advocated a flexible system of poverty, physical labour, abstinence (according to one's age and strength) and perpetual interior prayer.[62] A more unusual trait was his belief that not all religious texts are of equal worth; that one should read critically, and that erroneous texts should be corrected.

Iosif was born near the town of Volokolamsk into a devoutly religious family: one grandfather and both parents took monastic orders, as did two cousins and two brothers, one of whom became archimandrite of the Simonov monastery and archbishop of Rostov. Tonsured in the monastery of Pafnutii of Borovsk, he founded his own strictly cenobitic monastery near his birthplace. Donations from nobles and clerics such as Archbishop Gennadii of Novgorod (1484–1504) ensured that the monastery prospered materially. While Iosif is notorious for his political machinations, enthusiastic pursuit of heretics and support for monastic landownership, his ambitious programme of philanthropy included famine relief and the creation of services such as hospitals and orphanages – a programme which was followed by many of the large monasteries. Iosif was not amassing wealth for wealth's sake.

The most famous monastic dispute between those who aligned themselves with Nil Sorskii (and who came to be known as the Non-Possessors or Trans-Volga Elders) and those who fell into Iosif's camp was over church landholdings. This division was provoked by the activities of Ivan III, who was increasingly attracted by the large landholdings of monasteries and bishoprics. He was encouraged in this by the recently conquered Novgorodian nobility (subjugated by Ivan III in 1471), who urged him to take the lands of the church rather than their estates.[63] Iosif argued that monasteries could and should own lands and villages, using surplus wealth created for charitable ends; Nil argued that monks should live by the labour of their own hands and that wealth in a monastery was a temptation. Both positions had precedents.[64]

---

62 *Nil Sorsky: the complete writings*, ed. and trans. G. A. Maloney (New York: Paulist Press, 2003), 40.
63 Skrynnikov, 'Ecclesiastical thought', 34.
64 S. Hackel, 'Late medieval Russia: the possessors and non-possessors', in *Christian spirituality: high middle ages and Reformation*, ed. J. Raitt (London: SCM Press, 1989), 223–35.

Much has been made of the contrast between the two currents of monasticism represented by Nil and Iosif, but if there was acrimonious division over landholdings, this did not prevent Iosif from purchasing the writings of Nil for his monastery.[65] For all his harnessing of secular power when curbing heretics, Iosif was firmly committed to protecting church power and wealth from secular interference. There is also some evidence to suggest that Iosif and Nil collaborated in the condemnation of heretics, and even in writing the *Enlightener*.[66] However, Nil's followers, most notably the (forcibly) tonsured prince Vassian Patrikeev, stressed the need to forgive repentant heretics and be merciful to the obdurate, while Iosif advocated the punishment of the repentant and the death penalty for those who would not recant.[67] In the early sixteenth century the 'Josephites' triumphed: Vassian was put on trial (1531) and his followers were hounded into the forests beyond the Volga, where they remained a source of 'dissidence' and the possible inspiration for later heterodox movements. This victory of the 'Josephite mentality' – the belief that secular power should be utilised by the church, and the conviction that the church should be active in worldly affairs – is often credited with the entanglement of church and state, to the detriment of all, for the next four centuries.[68]

National ideologies / mythologies

This whole period can be characterised by a political, territorial and spiritual consolidation, culminating in the creation of an autocephalous, national church. A distinct but gradual parallel drift away from the mother-church in Byzantium mirrors this 'nationalisation' of Russian piety. In the 1390s, Patriarch Anthony IV of Constantinople had to write to Grand Prince Vasilii I to chastise him for omitting the name of the emperor from prayers and asserting that, while Russia had the church, it did not have the emperor.[69] Relations were not to improve in the following century, and the 1438–39 Council of Florence, which united the western and eastern churches under the papacy, speeded up the drive to autocephalous status. When Metropolitan Isidore returned to Moscow in 1441 to propagate this Florentine Union, Vasilii II swiftly imprisoned

65 D. M. Goldfrank, *The monastic rule of Iosif Volotsky* [Cistercian Studies Series 36] (Kalamazoo, MI: Cistercian Publications, 1983), 31.

66 Lur'e, 'Unresolved issues', 163–71.

67 See J. L. I. Fennell, 'The attitude of the Josephians and the Trans-Volga Elders to the heresy of the Judaisers', *Slavonic Review* 29 (1950–51), 486–509.

68 See D. Pospielovsky, *The Orthodox Church in the history of Russia* (Crestwood, NY: St Vladimir's Seminary Press, 1998), ch. 4.

69 Miklosich and Müller, ii, 191. See above pp. 31–2.

him for his perfidious behaviour and the Russian Church refused to recognise the legitimacy of the union. Seven years later, a council of Russian bishops elected Iona of Riazan as metropolitan without reference to Constantinople, an implicit declaration of autocephaly, however respectful their subsequent explanations.[70]

The fall of Constantinople in 1453, perceived by the Russians as divine punishment for apostasy, confirmed this nascent independence. With the rest of Orthodox Europe and the holy city itself under Muslim rule, the Russian clerical hierarchy envisaged themselves as the last guardians of the true faith, and it is in this context that the notorious concept of the 'Third Rome' appears, first articulated in several early sixteenth-century letters commonly attributed to the Pskov monk Filofei.[71] 'Moscow the Third Rome' has proved particularly popular in modern historiography as an explanation for Russian political behaviours, but rather than articulating a Muscovite ideological agenda of expansionism and autocracy, Filofei was stressing the duty of the grand prince to care for the purity of the Orthodox faith – specifically with regard to issues such as the protection of church lands, the correct way of making the sign of the cross, and the need to eradicate sodomy. Rome's and Constantinople's failure to preserve Orthodoxy led to their downfall, and since a fourth Rome there will not be, the failure of Moscow to do so will herald the apocalypse. While some historians have convincingly argued that the symbolic concept of the 'Third Rome' was less widespread than that of Moscow as a 'New Jerusalem', or Russia as a 'New Israel',[72] its unique appearance in an official document is significant – in the decree establishing the Moscow patriarchate in 1589, the whole of the 'great Russian Tsarstvo' is called a third Rome.[73]

The degree to which religiously inspired concepts such as 'Holy Russia', the 'Third Rome', the 'New Jerusalem' and their architectural, textual and

70 D. Obolensky, *Byzantium and the Slavs* (Crestwood, NY: St Vladimir's Seminary Press, 1994), 185.
71 For a discussion of authorship and dating, see *Slovar' knizhnikov i knizhnosti Drevnei Rusi*, ed. D. S. Likhachev (Leningrad: Nauka, 1989), II, 471–3; N. Andreyev, 'Filofey and his Epistle to Ivan Vasil'yevich', *Slavonic and East European Review* 38 (1959), 1–31. The letters are published in V. N. Malinin's *Starets' Eleazarova monastyria Filofei i ego poslaniia* (Kiev: Tipografiia Kievo-Pecherskoi Uspenskoi Lavry, 1901). An English translation of an extract from his letter to Vasilii III can be found in G. Vernadsky, *A source book for Russian history from early times to 1917*, I, *Early times to the late seventeenth century* (New Haven and London: Yale University Press, 1972), 155–6.
72 See for example J. Raba, 'Moscow – the Third Rome or the New Jerusalem?', *Forschungen zur Osteuropäischen Geschichte* 50 (1995), 297–307; D. B. Rowland, 'Moscow–the Third Rome or the New Israel?' *RR* 55 (1996), 591–614.
73 D. Ostrowski, *Muscovy and the Mongols: cross-cultural influences on the steppe frontier, 1304–1589* (Cambridge: Cambridge University Press, 1998), 239.

ceremonial representations are manifestations of a conscious political ideology is debated, and some concepts (such as the Third Rome) are certainly more significant in historiography and modern nationalist mythologising than they were in the sixteenth century.[74] However, the symbolic and practical contribution of the Russian Orthodox Church to the process of national consolidation and the development of a self-conscious national identity is clear. Religious rituals such as the Palm Sunday processions in Moscow, in which the tsar led the patriarch's horse in a pageant that replicated Christ's triumphal entry into Jerusalem, were public reminders of the ruler's role as guardian and guide of Orthodoxy,[75] and Metropolitan Makarii's formal coronation of Ivan IV as tsar and autocrat reflected both the mantle of religious authority the Muscovite rulers felt they had inherited from the fallen Constantinople, and their desire for divine sanction.

Rulers also found public pilgrimage and religious ritual an effective means of stamping their authority on newly acquired territories,[76] and Orthodox symbol and rhetoric bolstered both domestic and foreign conquest. The metropolitan of Moscow became a public supporter of the unifying activities of the grand prince – the chroniclers record that Metropolitan Filipp, on Grand Prince Ivan III's command, wrote to the rebellious Novgorodians ordering them to submit 'to him under whose strong arm God has placed you and the God-serving land of Russia', rather than their chosen leader, the Lithuanian Prince Mikhail Aleksandrovich of Kiev, who would lead them into the darkness of 'Latinism'.[77] The chroniclers present Ivan III's subjugation of Novgorod as a painful duty undertaken by a pious sovereign in defence of Orthodoxy, supported by the prayers of saints and God's favour. Ivan III's struggle with Lithuania was justified as a response to his Catholic son-in-law Alexander's refusal to allow his daughter Elena a Greek church and clergy, the efforts being made to convert her, the building of Catholic churches in formerly Russian towns such as Polotsk, and the persecution of Orthodox citizens of Lithuanian lands. Ivan IV followed his grandfather in his use of religious rhetoric to justify battles against Lithuania and other enemies, irrespective

---

74 See ibid., 219–43; P. Bushkovitch, 'The formation of a national consciousness in early modern Russia', *Harvard Ukrainian Studies* 10 (1986), 355–76; Andreyev, 'Filofey and his Epistle to Ivan Vasil'yevich', 1–31.

75 M. S. Flier, 'Breaking the code: the image of the Tsar in the Muscovite Palm Sunday ritual', in *Medieval Russian Culture*, ed. Flier and Rowland, II, 213–42.

76 N. S. Kollmann, 'Pilgrimage, procession and symbolic space in sixteenth-century Russian politics', in *Medieval Russian Culture*, ed. Flier and Rowland, II, 163–81.

77 R. Michell and N. Forbes, *The Chronicle of Novgorod: 1016–1471* [Camden Society, ser. iii, 25] (London: Camden Society, 1914), 210.

of the political realities: the 1552 'crusade' against Kazan, for example, was nevertheless supported by the (Muslim) Tatar Nogai.[78]

The political and territorial consolidation of the Russian land was mirrored by a unification and standardisation of Orthodoxy. This began with a consolidation of the liturgical calendar in the first half of the fifteenth century, which emphasised the continuity between 'Kievan' Rus and Muscovy by the revival or institution of various feasts such as that of St Olga, the first baptised ruler of Rus. The patron saints of the northern towns and monasteries were included later in the fifteenth century, and this process culminated in Metropolitan Makarii's *Great Menologion* (*Velikaia mineia chet'ia*), with spiritual readings for every day of the year.[79] The *Great Menologion*, which appeared in three editions dedicated to Ivan IV during the metropolitan's rule (1542–63), was Makarii's attempt to compile a definitive compendium of the spiritual heritage and Orthodox culture of Russia, reflecting a unified nation and church. Many of the texts integrated in this work, including some commissioned by Makarii, stress the duties of the divinely appointed tsar to protect the Orthodox faith and support the institution of the church, and develop a historiography of the world that places Moscow at the centre of Orthodox history.

Metropolitan Makarii also oversaw the creation of the *Book of Degrees of Imperial Genealogy* (*Stepennaia kniga tsarskogo rodosloviia*), a selective history of rulers and metropolitans which begins with a panegyric to the first baptised ruler of Rus, St Olga, and proceeds to connect 'autocrats of Russia' from the tenth-century Kievan saint-prince Vladimir I to Ivan IV in a continuous, sanctified dynasty descended from Caesar Augustus. Most of the ideas and texts incorporated in Makarii's *Great Menologion* and the *Book of Degrees* were unoriginal – the motif of the ruler as a 'second Constantine' and the myth of descent from Augustus appeared in the fifteenth century, for example. Their presentation in systematic fashion was, however, original, and signified the birth of a self-consciously Orthodox and autocratic state of 'Great Russia', wearing the inherited mantle of Byzantium with pride.

If the *Great Menologion* sought to establish the definitive spiritual library, the *Stoglav* Council of 1551 sought to standardise piety by confirming the 'rightness' of Moscow practices, ignoring regional differences and canonical correctness

78 See for example S. Bogatyrev, 'Battle for divine wisdom: the rhetoric of Ivan IV's campaign against Polotsk', in *The military and society in Russia, 1450–1917*, ed. E. Lohr and M. Poe (Leiden: Brill, 2002), 325–63.
79 R. D. Bosley, 'The changing profile of the liturgical calendar in Muscovy's formative years', in *Culture and identity in Muscovy, 1359–1584*, ed. A. M. Kleimola and G. D. Lenhoff (Moscow: ITZ-Garant, 1997), 26–38.

in some instances. The *Domostroi* offered a similar service to Russian households, as a manual on how to live correctly according to Orthodox morality.[80] These literary compendiums, the canonisations of regionally revered figures as national saints and the regulatory church councils of 1547, 1549 and 1551 can be viewed as a concerted effort to regulate or 'nationalise' the faith and to create a Russian national consciousness built on the interconnectedness of dynasty, territory and the Orthodox faith.[81] This constructed 'trinity' would soon be shattered by the death of the childless Tsar Fedor (1584–98), but before the dynastic crisis and turmoil of the 'Time of Troubles', the first Russian Patriarch Iov was installed in 1589 by the patriarch of Constantinople, Jeremias II, who had travelled to Moscow in 1588 to beg alms for his church and found himself effectively a prisoner until he agreed to Iov's consecration. The Russian nation and the Russian Orthodox Church had finally arrived.

---

80 Pouncy, *Domostroi*. See above p. 256.
81 D. B. Miller, 'The Velikie Minei Chetii and Stepennaia Kniga of Metropolitan Makarii and the origins of Russian national consciousness', *Forschungen zur Osteuropäischen Geschichte* 26 (1979), 263–373; Wil van den Bercken, *Holy Russia and Christian Europe: East and West in the religious ideology of Russia* (London: SCM Press, 1999), 140–60.

12

Art and liturgy in Russia: Rublev and his successors

LINDSEY HUGHES

In the thirteenth century large parts of Russia fell to the Mongol invaders.[1] The initial impact on religious life and art was devastating. Priests and monks were slain, churches and icons were burned, cult objects made of precious metals and gems were looted. The anonymous author of *The Tale of the Destruction of Riazan*, the first city to be attacked in 1237, recounted:

> They burnt the whole city of Riazan with all its renowned beauty and wealth and seized the relatives of the princes of Kiev and Chernigov. They destroyed God's churches and spilt much blood on the sacred altars. Not one person was left alive in the city, all had died and supped from the same cup of death. And all this came about for our sins.[2]

Even if we make allowances for the rhetorical insistence upon complete annihilation, the losses were devastating. The sheer number of Orthodox Christians who perished at the hands of pagans, together with the belief that God had inflicted ruin on Russia as a punishment 'for our sins', left the survivors and their descendants with the imperative of praying for the souls of the dead and the salvation of the living. In this disaster lay the seeds of a religious revival that has been described as 'the flowering of Russian holiness'.[3]

Russia's relationship with its new overlords was complex. Even after they adopted Islam in the fourteenth century, the Mongols, or Tatars as they were generally called in Russian sources, respected the local religions of their empire in return for political obedience and compliance in delivering up tribute in money and kind. They ruled from afar. In Russia there was no campaign of forced conversions, no tampering with the conventions of Orthodox ritual

---

1 I refer to Russia and Russian(s) throughout this chapter in the awareness that contemporary documents used the term Rus and variants.

2 D. S. Likhachev, *Pamiatniki literatury drevnei Rusi. XIII vek* (Moscow: Khudozhestvennaia literatura, 1981), 190–1.

3 Leonid Uspenskii, *Theology of the icon* (Crestwood, NY: St Vladimir's Seminary Press, 1992), II, 257.

or iconography, still less a ban on human images. A new church hierarchy eventually established itself. What is more, the Mongols exempted church lands from taxation and levies of recruits. That Russia was 'a conquered land whose conquerors were often not in evidence' allowed the maintenance in written sources of 'an ideology of silence' about the very fact of conquest.[4] At the same time, the threat of punitive raids was ever present – there were at least forty between 1247 and 1460 – and the requirement that priests pray for the khans kept alive the consciousness of occupation by an 'infidel' power. There was a population shift away from old urban centres. Refugees built wooden chapels and shrines in forests or on lakes, which attracted more settlers. In the same period over a hundred new monasteries were founded, with a further impetus given to prayerful retreat by the Black Death, which hit Russia in 1352–53.[5]

The Mongol impact on Russian culture was not uniform. The north-western cities of Novgorod and Pskov escaped devastation and their economies, based on trade, revived comparatively quickly. Their art and architecture flourished. Regions in the south-west that initially fell under Mongol control, including Kiev itself, later found themselves incorporated into Catholic Poland-Lithuania, where Orthodoxy had to accommodate itself to alien artistic conventions. In the Russian heartland local princes and primates who co-operated could prosper within a pecking order regulated by the Mongols. Competitiveness between princes manifested itself in support for cults of local saints, donations to monasteries, and commissions for churches, icons, manuscripts, church plate, vestments and other artefacts. The fourteenth and fifteenth centuries witnessed what has been described as a 'renaissance' or a 'golden age' in Russian Orthodox art,[6] against the background of the ever-present threat of raids from the east, the encroachment of Catholicism from the west, and internecine conflict as princes competed for supremacy.

This 'renaissance' had few direct links with the contemporaneous Italian Renaissance and was not focused on the rediscovery of Greek and Roman classical antiquity. It did not produce secular art. It was more a revitalising of the Byzantine roots of Orthodox art, which had endowed Russia with elements

---

4 See C. J. Halperin, *Russia and the Golden Horde: the Mongol impact on Russian history* (London: I. B. Tauris, 1985).

5 On the historical background, see R. O. Crummey, *The formation of Muscovy, 1304–1613* (London and New York: Longman, 1987).

6 M. A. Alpatov, *Drevnerusskaia ikonopis'* (Moscow: Iskusstvo, 1974), 12. The 1960s–1970s saw an officially approved revival of the study of Russia's early cultural heritage, which produced invaluable scholarly studies, as well as the more ideologically tendentious. See, for example, D. S. Likhachev, *Kul'tura Rusi vremeni Andreia Rubleva i Epifaniia Premudrogo (konets XIV–nachala XV v.)* (Moscow and Leningrad: Nauka, 1962).

of the classical heritage. At the same time, from the first centuries of Russian Christianity local artists put their own stamp on religious art. They created images of Russian saints and religious festivals, employed wood for building churches and local pigments for painting icons. The flattened Byzantine dome eventually developed into the distinctive Russian 'onion' cupola.[7] Regional variations in religious art were intensified by political fragmentation. New schools of icon-painting arose, although the term 'school' can be used only in a loose, geographical sense, since in most cases it is impossible to put names to artists or masters of workshops.[8]

Novgorod

In Novgorod a number of striking local features developed. From the late thirteenth century many small singled-domed, four-piered churches, with sloping or trefoil gables, were commissioned by communities of traders and urban districts, and dedicated to saints with local associations. The stuccoed façades were decorated with niches, windows and bands of brick, the interiors with fresco cycles. Among the best surviving examples are St Nicholas at Lipna (1293), St Theodore Stratelates (1361–62), and the Transfiguration on Il'in Street (1372).[9] The icon-painters of Novgorod favoured simple forms harmoniously arranged, blocks of bright colour – reds, whites and golds were particularly vivid – and black outlines.[10] One of the most famous examples is the late fifteenth-century icon of St George and the Dragon, in which the linked figures of saint, steed and dragon fill the picture space against a bright red background.[11] St George was venerated in princely cults. Many princes bore the name Iurii or Georgii and Novgorod's oldest monastery was dedicated to him. In popular culture he was associated with the protection of cattle and agriculture and was invoked to ward off unclean spirits. His feast day on 26 November marked the end of the agricultural year. This icon of St George and others like it could communicate

---

7 See A. M. Lidov, 'Ierusalimskii kuvuklii. O proiskhozhdenii lukovichnykh glav', in *Ikono-grafiia arkhitektury: sbornik nauchnykh trudov*, ed. A. L. Batalov (Moscow: Akademiia khudozhestv, 1990), 57–68.

8 For general introductions to Russian icon-painting, see M. V. Alpatov, *Early Russian icon painting* (Moscow: Iskusstvo, 1978); V. N. Lazarev, *Russian icon: from its origins to the sixteenth century*, ed. G. I. Vzdornov (Collegeville, MN: Liturgical Press, 1997).

9 See William C. Brumfield, *A history of Russian architecture* (Cambridge: Cambridge University Press, 1993), 64–70.

10 See V. Laurina (ed.), *Novgorod icons, 12th–17th century* (Oxford and Leningrad: Aurora, 1980).

11 For an illustration and discussion, including dating, see R. Grierson, *Gates of mystery: the art of Holy Russia* (Fort Worth, TX: InterCultura, [1992]), 180–2.

with viewers of differing levels of sophistication. A rhythmic combination of shapes and colours attracts the eye. The gleaming white of the saint's prancing horse contrasts with the dull colours of the fallen dragon. A dramatic folk narrative – the warrior-saint saves the maiden (not shown in this particular icon) by slaying the dragon – is underpinned by a theological discourse about the struggle between good and evil on earth, with the threatening cave of hell below and God's hand directing all the affairs of humankind pointing from heaven above.

There was no secular art, no freestanding portraits, landscapes or history paintings. Even when an icon illustrates recorded historical events, as for example in *The Battle of the Novgorodians with the Suzdalians* (mid–late fifteenth century) (fig. 12.1), which refers to a campaign against the city in 1170, at the heart of its message is divine grace.[12] The icon of Our Lady of the Sign, the palladium of Novgorod, miraculously intervenes to protect the city, summoning the warrior-saints George, Boris and Gleb to smite the enemy. Painted at a time when Novgorod's independence was under threat, the icon draws inspiration from the past in the firm belief that the actions and decisions of men were ever subject to the divine will. Force of arms was useless without the assistance of prayer and the intervention of saints.

Novgorodians prayed to icons for all aspects of their lives. For example, the iconography of the Byzantine saints Florus and Laurus, patrons of horses, evolved there in the fifteenth century. At the foot of the icon horses drink from a holy well near the saints' relics: at the top the Archangel Michael, another protector of livestock, gives a blessing.[13] Elijah protected against fires and brought rain. A famous early fifteenth-century icon shows a frontal view of the stern prophet against a bright red background. In other compositions he ascends in his fiery chariot into a red circle, the symbol of heaven.[14] St Paraskeva Piatnitsa was a patron of women's work and traditions. In her icon she wears a red cloak and holds a martyr's cross in her right hand and a spindle in her left.[15] One of the most universally venerated saints was St Nicholas, whose protective powers encompassed the health of humans and livestock, crops, bees and cities.[16]

The painters of Pskov used a distinctive palette of dark green and orange with white highlights and often incorporated elements of folk decoration into

---

12 See Alpatov, *Early Russian icon painting*, plate 114.
13 Ibid., plate 120.
14 Ibid., plates 24, 25, 57.
15 Grierson, *Gates of mystery*, 175–7.
16 See ibid., 165–9, for an early fourteenth-century example.

Figure 12.1 Battle of the Novgorodians with the Suzdalians, Novgorod School, mid-fifteenth century (tempera and gold on panel). Tretyakov Gallery, Moscow.

their works. The characteristic 'emerald' green can be seen in the mountains in the icon of the Syntaxis of the Mother of God (late fourteenth century), a composition based on a hymn glorifying the Nativity of Our Lord. The familiar shepherds, angels and Magi above are joined by a cantor and choir of deacons below, an image of the liturgy itself, which draws in the congregation who will praise God and bring their own gifts to Christ through worship.[17] Other regional centres of high-quality icon painting were Vladimir, Suzdal, Rostov and Tver, whose princes in the fourteenth century were contenders for political leadership.[18] One of the most celebrated Tver icons is the so-called Blue Dormition (late fifteenth century), one of countless examples of a popular subject.[19] What scholars dub a 'Northern' school of naive or 'primitive' art also emerged, distinguished by crude but bold draughtsmanship and the incorporation of folk motifs.

In all these centres the workshops of princes, archbishops and monasteries produced manuscript books. Various skills were required to make the ceremonial liturgical volumes – the Gospels, Acts of the Apostles and Psalter – which were used during services, borne in processions by priests and displayed before the altar. Many were richly bound in covers (*oklady*) of precious metals, engraved and embellished with gems. Manuscript illumination developed relatively late in Russia and remained very reliant upon icons and frescos as models. Images were used not as illustrations, but as embellishments of texts that the artists themselves may have been unable to read. The most frequent motifs were the four Evangelists, transmitters of the holy books. Major examples were the Siisk (1339–40) and Khitrovo Gospels (*c.* 1415), both of which were produced in Moscow.[20]

Moscow

From the fourteenth century political and religious power increasingly focused on the city and principality of Moscow, whose ambitious rulers of the line

17 Illustrated in I. Kozlova, *Masterpieces of the Tretyakov Gallery* (Moscow: Acropolis, 1994), 18.
18 See N. V. Rozanova, *Rostovo-suzdal'skaia zhivopis' XII–XVI vekov* (Moscow: Izobrazitel'noe iskusstvo, 1970); V. L. Vakhrina, *Ikony Rostova Velikogo* (Moscow: Severnyi palomnik, 2003); A. Rybakov, *Vologodskaia ikona: tsentry khudozhestvennoi kul'tury zemli Vologodskoi XIII– XVIII vekov* (Moscow: Galart, 1995).
19 Illustrated in *Masterpieces of the Tretyakov Gallery*, 31. See below on churches of the Dormition.
20 J. Cracraft, *The Petrine revolution in Russian imagery* (Chicago: University of Chicago Press, 1997), 64; O. S. Popova, *Russian illuminated manuscripts* (London and New York: Thames and Hudson, 1984).

of Daniil Aleksandrovich (1263–1303) annexed the lands of their kinfolk and rivals alike and secured Mongol approval for passing on the senior title of grand prince to their successors. In 1325 the head of the Russian Orthodox Church, Metropolitan Peter, established his residence in Moscow at the court of Prince Ivan I (1325–40), which gave a major boost to the arts. In 1327 Peter and Ivan laid the foundations of the first stone-built Dormition cathedral in the Moscow Kremlin. Churches dedicated to the Dormition (*Uspenie*) of the Mother of God were credited with miraculous properties, based on the apocryphal stories of the assumption of Mary's body and soul into heaven from Jerusalem in the presence of the Apostles. In Constantinople what were alleged to be her coffin and shroud became associated with the protection of the city against enemy raids and with the victory of Orthodox Christians over non-Christians. In Kiev the eleventh-century church of the Dormition in the Caves monastery was inspired by the miraculous vision of Mary vouchsafed to a converted pagan. Mary is also said to have burned a plan in the ground with fire from heaven. Thus churches supposedly designed by Mary herself became models for later Dormition cathedrals, of which the grandest was built in Vladimir in the twelfth century.[21] The construction of Moscow's Dormition cathedral expressed a belief in the transfer of God's grace to Moscow by way of Jerusalem, Constantinople, Kiev and Vladimir. The building's meaning was rooted in universal history and linked with sacred landscapes. It and other major cathedrals became key locations for the celebration of the liturgy in times of national victory and danger, as well as centres for the collection of the holiest icons and other cult objects.

Monasteries provided further protection for Moscow, both practical and spiritual. In about 1354 the future St Sergii of Radonezh (c. 1314–92) founded the Holy Trinity monastery (*lavra*) 40 kilometres to the north of the city. In Moscow itself in the 1360s–1370s the Saviour-Andronikov, Chudov (Miracles) and Simonov monasteries were established. Further north Kirill of Beloozero (d.1447) built a monastery on a lake, which attracted the settlement of many hermits in the area, and in the 1420s Saints Zosima and Savatii founded the Solovetskii monastery on the White Sea. Painters developed the iconography of these and other monastic saints, the earliest surviving examples of which may suggest the inward gaze of hesychasm. The doctrine and practice of hesychasm (Greek ἡσυχασμός, quietude) took form on Mount Athos in the fourteenth century and reached Russia from Constantinople and the Balkans.

---

21 D. S. Likhachev, 'Gradozashchitnaia semantika Uspenskikh khramov na Rusi', in *Uspenskii sobor Moskovskogo Kremlia*, ed. E. S. Smirnova (Moscow: Nauka, 1985), 17–23.

The belief that silent, prayerful exercises could put an individual in touch with the divine 'uncreated' light that appeared on Mount Tabor when Christ was transfigured was a monastic ideal, but some scholars suggest that leading icon-painters, too, were 'hesychasts themselves or were somehow associated with them'.[22] Lack of evidence makes it impossible to substantiate this claim, although in general contacts between Russian and foreign Orthodox artists increased during this period. Under the Greek metropolitan, Theognostos (1328–54), for example, many artists from Constantinople came to Moscow. By the end of the century a Greek colony and church were established in the city.

The Trinity cathedral (1422–23) of the Trinity-St Sergii monastery offers a good example of how art and liturgy worked in a monastic setting associated with hesychasm. St Sergii's biographer Epifanii the Wise recorded that the saint consecrated his cathedral 'so that contemplation of the Holy Trinity might conquer the fear of this world's detestable discord'.[23] Sergii was buried there. The church is a simple, single-domed structure, with decorative ogee-shaped gables known as *kokoshniki* beneath the dome, which create a pyramidal effect, one of the hallmarks of early Moscow architecture. It attracted pilgrims, who could participate in round-the-clock prayers over the saint's relics. It was for this church that Andrei Rublev is said to have painted his icon of the Old Testament Trinity, to hang on the iconostasis (fig. 12.2).[24]

Iconostasis

The *iconostasis* (or icon screen) remains integral to Russian Orthodox worship in church.[25] In Byzantine churches columns with curtains or a low openwork rail known as the *templon* separated the nave from the sanctuary. In time this feature developed into a two-storey screen, which in Russia from the late fourteenth to the early fifteenth century evolved into an even higher frame hung with icons. In the seventeenth century the framework would acquire distinctive architectural features, such as gilded, twisted and vine-entwined columns, cornices, and variously shaped apertures to house the icons. In large cathedrals the *iconostasis* had five horizontal tiers. At the top was a row of icons representing the Patriarchs of the Old Testament (from Adam to Moses), often with an icon of the Old Testament Trinity at the centre. Below them

22 Uspenskii, *Theology*, II, 261.
23 Ibid., 256; Likhachev, *Kul'tura Rusi vremeni Andreia Rubleva*.
24 See below, pp. 289–91.
25 N. Markina, 'The iconostasis', in *The art of Holy Russia: icons from Moscow 1400–1660* (London: Royal Academy of Arts, 1998), 69–75; N. Labrecque-Pervouchine, *L'iconostase: une évolution historique en Russie* (Montreal: Bellarmin, 1982).

Figure 12.2 The Holy Trinity (1420s) by Andrei Rublev (c.1370–1430) (tempera on panel). Tretyakov Gallery, Moscow.

came the Prophets, with Our Lady of the Sign (i.e. of Christ's incarnation) at the centre. Below that was a row of smaller icons of the major festivals of the New Testament. Next came the most impressive tier, the *Deesis* or prayer row, with a central image of Christ Enthroned in Glory. The *Deesis* celebrates the coming of Christ and his Kingdom, which is the central fact of the liturgy. The Mother of God stands to Christ's right, John the Baptist or Forerunner to his left, and to either side of them are saints (Peter and Paul are the most usual) and archangels, their heads bowed and bodies inclined towards Christ. The *Deesis* emphasised the role of the church building, itself an icon of God's house, as the location for the intercession of saints and angels on behalf of humankind. Their representations participate in the liturgy along with the congregation. As John Meyendorff writes, 'The religious art of Orthodoxy is inseparable from the awareness that man was created in the image of God and that the saintly figures on the icons are manifesting a holiness which, in the mind of God, is accessible to all in the liturgy.'[26]

At ground level is the *iconostasis*'s 'local' tier. This is pierced in the centre by the Royal or Holy Doors, which bear images (from top to bottom) of the Annunciation, the Communion of the Apostles and the four Evangelists to signify the entrance to the kingdom of God through which Christ is carried in the Eucharist.[27] To the right of the Doors hangs an icon of Christ in Majesty and the 'house' icon of the festival to which the church is dedicated (in the case of the Trinity cathedral, the icon of the Old Testament Trinity), to the left an icon of the Mother of God. Various icons complete the row.

The *iconostasis* was and is integral to the liturgy, both as an architectural setting for exits and entrances of priests with crosses at key moments in the service and as a microcosm of the universal history of Christianity and the annual cycle of the liturgical year. Scanning from top to bottom, worshippers could read the history of salvation as revealed in scripture and see the promise of the kingdom of Heaven, which made itself manifest through the images. The screen was construed not as a barrier between the symbolic space of the congregation in the nave (earth, the temporal) and the divine mysteries of the sanctuary (heaven, the eternal), but as a window that gave worshippers a glimpse of the presence of the heavenly. Believers received Holy Communion at this 'border' between heaven and earth in sight of the Royal Doors. The church's central function was to celebrate the Eucharist, which had both a commemorative aspect (recalling the Last Supper) and an anticipatory one (awaiting the Second Coming).[28]

The church building was itself an icon of heaven and earth, in both the arrangement of its interior (nave and sanctuary, domes) and the exterior space (the cupolas, tripartite division of the façades). Murals and icons throughout the church, set in liturgical space, played a supporting role to the *iconostasis*. In large churches, chapels and altars with their own small *iconostaseis* or

26 In Grierson, *Gates of mystery*, 41.
27 For an example, see ibid., 97.
28 Ibid., 37–44.

free-standing icons served individual worshippers, while cycles of frescos on the walls told the story of salvation as revealed in scripture. Christ Pantokrator looked down from the central dome, supported by seraphim. The Last Judgement was often depicted over the western door. Even the columns accommodated saintly figures. The forms of all images were regarded not as human invention, but as rooted in the historical reality of the prototype. They could be painted from life (e.g. the image of the Mother of God painted by St Luke), or created by a miracle (e.g. the Mandylion image of Christ, which was imprinted on a cloth), or based on the memory – passed down through the generations – of a saint's features and the shape of his beard, or, finally, sent by God through visions.

The icon of the Vladimir Mother of God (Our Lady of Tenderness) provides an interesting case study of the role of miraculous icons in local and national life and their impact on contemporary artists during our period. The twelfth-century Byzantine original, which legend attributed to St Luke, was first brought to Kiev, and then taken to Vladimir. In 1395 Tamerlane threatened Moscow and Prince Dmitrii of Moscow had the icon collected from Vladimir to help to 'save the Russian land'.[29] Legend has it that the Mother of God duly appeared to Tamerlane in a vision and commanded him to depart, which he did. The day the icon reached Moscow, 26 August, was celebrated as the feast of its reception or meeting (*sretenie*) and became a new icon subject. The Sretenskii monastery was founded on the spot where the Muscovites first greeted it.[30]

Once the icon was permanently transferred to Moscow it was placed to the right of the Royal Doors in the Kremlin cathedral of the Dormition.[31] Copies were made, including the so-called 'spare' (*zapasnaia*), in which Mary no longer gazed sorrowfully at the viewer but assumed a milder and more tender expression, her eyes turned towards her child. Some scholars believe that Andrei Rublev may have been involved in making at least one of the copies, on both stylistic and circumstantial grounds.[32] The icon was associated with

29 *Moskva, eia sviatyni i pamiatniki* [Izbrannye stat'i po opisaniiu Moskvy] (St Petersburg: Iablonskii, 1898), 38.
30 *Istoricheskoe opisanie moskovskogo Uspenskogo sobora i ego sviatyni* (Moscow: Efimov, 1880), 27–9; *Moskva, eia sviatyni*, 70–1.
31 O. E. Etingof, 'K rannei istorii ikony "Vladimirskaia Bogomater'" i traditsiia Vlakhernskogo Bogorodichnogo kul'ta na Rusi v XI–XII vv.', in *Drevnerusskoe iskusstvo: vizantiia i drevniaia Rus'. K 100-letiiu Andreia Nikolaevicha Grabara (1896–1990)*, ed. E. S. Smirnova (St Petersburg: Nauka, 1999), 296, 298–300.
32 E. K. Guseva, 'Ikony "Donskaia" i "Vladimirskaia" v kopiiakh kontsa XIV–nachala XIV v., in *Drevnerusskoe iskusstvo. XIV–XV vv* (Moscow: Nauka, 1984), 56.

other incidents of miraculous deliverance, including the Tatar retreat from Ugra river after a confrontation with Ivan III's army in 1480 and the decision on 23 June 1521 of the Crimean, Nogai and Kazan Tatars not to attack Moscow after they received a vision of many troops defending the city.[33] The icon was one of several holy objects associated with the notion of *translatio imperii*: in this case the migration of a twelfth-century icon from Constantinople signifying the transfer of the protection of the Mother of God to Moscow.[34]

Feofan Grek and Andrei Rublev

The earliest surviving examples of Moscow icon-painting date from the years following Toktamysh's raid of 1382, when Russian and foreign painters carried out commissions for Metropolitan Kiprian (1390–1406) and others to replace lost works. Common features in Moscow icons of the 'golden age' include elongated bodies, small hands and feet, calm, static poses, and a harmonious interplay of pure colours.[35] Among the artists attracted to Moscow in the late fourteenth century was Feofan Grek (Theophanes the Greek, c. 1340– c. 1410) from Constantinople.[36] His early art bore the mark of the so-called Palaiologan Renaissance in the Byzantine Empire. Feofan's most famous works were painted in Novgorod in 1378 for the church of the Transfiguration on Il'in Street. The frescos, which include an Old Testament Trinity, are highly stylised, 'expressionistic' and dynamic, created with free brush strokes, muted colours and white highlights. In the Moscow Kremlin Feofan is thought to have worked in the churches of the Nativity of the Mother of God (1395), the Archangel Michael (1399) and the Annunciation (1405), which was the princes' chapel royal. Icons from the *Deesis* row of the latter have been attributed to him, including the Saviour, the Mother of God and John the Baptist.[37] Also credited to his workshop are the famous icon of the Mother of God of the Don with the Dormition on the reverse and the Transfiguration from Pereislavl', in which bluish light emanates from Christ and falls on the disciples' clothing.[38]

---

33 *Moskva, eia sviatyni*, 76.

34 See J. Billington, *The icon and the axe* (London: Weidenfeld and Nicolson, 1966), 32.

35 *The art of Holy Russia*, 45.

36 The most detailed account of Feofan's career is a letter (c.1410) by Epifanii the Wise. On Feofan, see V. N. Lazarev, *Feofan Grek i ego shkola* (Moscow: Iskusstvo, 1961); M. V. Alpatov, *Feofan Grek* (Moscow: Iskusstvo, 1979); G. I. Vzdornov, *Feofan Grek, Tvorcheskoe nasledie* (Moscow: Iskusstvo, 1983).

37 See Engelina Smirnova, *Moscow icons, 14th–17th centuries* (Oxford: Phaidon, 1989), 263–4, for a discussion of these disputed attributions.

38 Alpatov, *Early Russian icon painting*, plates 59–66.

Specialists disagree about the extent of Feofan's influence on Russian painters. Indeed, it has been argued that the Greek's later works bore evidence of the influence of Russian artists, notably Andrei Rublev.[39] We still know little for certain about Rublev, the only medieval icon-painter whose name is familiar outside Russia. The serious study of his life and work began only in the first decade of the twentieth century with the cleaning of his Trinity icon, which was a landmark in the 'rediscovery' of icons as works of art.[40] Scholars disagree about Rublev's date and place of birth, his parentage and social status, and when and where he became a monk. The designation of 1960 as the six-hundredth anniversary of his birth had more to do with the Soviet promotion of Russian cultural heritage during the Cold War than with historical accuracy. Soviet historians labelled Rublev as a 'humanist', who succeeded 'in spite of' the canons of the church' in producing painting that 'shines like a priceless gem in the treasure house of Russian and world art'.[41] A copy of an inscription recording his death on 29 January 1430 was found among the papers of the eighteenth-century scholar G. F. Müller, but the original is lost.[42] More recently, V. G. Briusova has located Rublev's death 'around 1427'.[43]

Scholars rely on fragmentary references in chronicles and saints' lives, some contemporary, others not, to chart Rublev's activities, along with those of fellow painters such as Daniil Chernyi. A chronicle entry for 1395 mentions certain pupils (*uchenitsy*) of Feofan Grek working in the Moscow Kremlin, one of whom may have been Andrei.[44] Rublev's earliest surviving work may well be frescos in the Dormition cathedral 'na Gorodke' in Zvenigorod (1401 to 1405).[45] He is linked more reliably to Feofan in the year 1405, when it was recorded (probably after 1484) that the old Annunciation cathedral in the Moscow Kremlin was painted 'by Feofan the Greek icon-painter, the senior monk (*starets*) Prokhor from Gorodets and the monk (*chernets*) Andrei Rublev'.[46] Icons from

---

39 Uspenskii, *Theology*, II, 273–4, n. 48.
40 Early studies include N. P. Likhachev, *Manera pis'ma Andreia Rubleva* (St Petersburg: Tip. M. A. Aleksandrova, 1907) and N. I. Punin, *Andrei Rublev* (Petrograd: Apollon, 1916), 23.
41 See Lindsey Hughes, 'Inventing Andrei: Soviet and post-Soviet views of Andrei Rublev and his Trinity icon', *Slavonica* 9 (2003), no. 2, 83–90. Quotation from P. Sokolov-Skalia, 'Andrei Rublev', *Nauka i Religiia* 9 (1960), 85–7. See also N. Kuz'min, 'Zhivopis' pereshagnivshaia veka', *Literaturnaia Gazeta*, 15 Sept. 1960, 3.
42 G. I. Vzdornov, *Troitsa Andreia Rubleva. Antologiia* (Moscow: Iskusstvo, 1981), 7.
43 V. G. Briusova, *Andrei Rublev i moskovskaia shkola zhivopisi* (Moscow: Veche, 1998), 130.
44 For a summary of sources, see M. N. Tikhomirov, 'Andrei Rublev i ego epokha', *Voprosy istorii* 1 (1961), 3–15.
45 V. A. Plugin, *Master Sviatoi Troitsy: trudy i dni Andreia Rubleva* (Moscow: 'Mosgorarkhiv', 2001), 508.
46 Tikhomirov, 'Andrei Rublev i ego epokha', 6.

the left side of the Festival row of the iconostasis of the Annunciation cathedral attributed to Rublev include the Entry into Jerusalem, the Nativity of Christ, the Raising of Lazarus and the Transfiguration.[47]

The earliest contemporary reference to Rublev appears under the year 1408: 'On 25 May they began to paint the great stone cathedral church of [the Dormition of] the Holy Mother of God, which is in Vladimir, by the order of the great prince, and the artists were the icon-painter (*ikonnik*) Daniil [Chernyi] and Andrei Rublev.'[48] The subjects that survive include the Transfiguration, Entry into the Temple, and Joachim, Anna and Zacharius. In the 1420s Andrei and Daniil painted frescos for the Trinity cathedral in the Trinity-St Sergii monastery at the invitation of Abbot Nikon, in accounts of whose life it is related that the icon-painters 'decorated that church with wall paintings at the end of their God-pleasing and blessed lives, then departed to the Lord God, in closeness to one another, in spiritual union, just as they lived here, and this last painting they left as a memorial to themselves for all to see'.[49] Other sources, however, state that Andrei's last work was in the Andronikov monastery in Moscow, where 'the beautiful church was decorated in marvellous painting by his own hands'.[50] Sadly, neither these nor the Trinity frescos have survived, although the seventeenth-century over-painting of the latter may follow Rublev's outlines.[51]

Not one of Rublev's icons is dated (medieval icons rarely were) or mentioned in contemporary chronicles. Tradition alone suggested their provenance, supplemented later by stylistic and scientific analysis. This applies also to the Old Testament Trinity, 'the quintessential Russian icon' (fig. 12.2).[52] Many studies give its dates as 1422–27, on the grounds that Rublev completed his masterpiece for the new Trinity cathedral shortly before his death. The *Life of Nikon of Radonezh* recounts how the abbot asked Andrei to paint a house icon for the local tier of the iconostasis (completed by 1427) 'in praise of his [spiritual] father

---

47 Alpatov, *Early Russian icon painting*, plates 74, 76, 77, 79; Plugin, *Master Sviatoi Troitsy*, 21–43.

48 M. D. Priselkov, *Troitskaia letopis': rekonstruktsiia teksta* (Moscow and Leningrad: Nauka, 1950), 466; *Polnoe sobranie russkikh letopisei* (hereafter *PSRL*), xxv, 237; Tikhomirov, 'Andrei Rublev i ego epokha', 5–6.

49 *PSRL*, vi, 138.

50 *Kniga o Sergii* (Moscow, 1646), quoted in Tikhomirov, 'Andrei Rublev i ego epokha', 13.

51 Plugin, *Master Sviatoi Troitsy*, 509.

52 R. Milner-Gulland, *The Russians* (Oxford: Blackwell, 1997), 199. See also 'Andrei Rublev. (Sviatye zemli russkoi)', *Nauka i Religiia* 4 (1998), 32–3; A. Nikitin, 'Kto napisal "Troitsu Rubleva"?', *Nauka i Religiia* 8 (1988), 44–8.

Sergii the Miracle Worker'.[53] The icon hung to the right of the Royal Doors from the fifteenth century until the 1920s, when it was brought to Moscow and exhibited in the Tret'iakov Gallery, where it remains. An alternative version is that the icon was in fact made for St Sergii's tomb, and only later, by the time of the first description of the monastery in the 1640s, placed on the iconostasis.[54] However, some scholars have proposed a much earlier date, suggesting that Andrei painted a different version of the subject for the Trinity cathedral.[55] A radical theory claims that the icon was originally painted in Zvenigorod and donated to the Trinity monastery in the 1550s by Tsar Ivan IV, who had been baptised there.[56] It was only in Ivan IV's time that Rublev began to gain in reputation.

These perhaps irreconcilable discrepancies do not detract from the importance of the image, which is an expression of the essence of Christianity in pictorial form. The three figures seated around a table appear in Genesis 18:1–16 in an episode sometimes referred to as the 'Hospitality of Abraham'. Three men (angels) appear to Abraham under the oak of Mamre to foretell the miraculous birth of a son to his wife, Sarah, who is past childbearing age. The joyful couple have a servant slaughter a fatted calf to entertain the messengers. (Some versions of the icon show Abraham and Sarah with a servant killing a calf in the lower portion.[57]) Christian theologians interpret this passage as one of many examples of a prototype or prefiguration of the New Testament in the Old. The angels represent Father, Son and Holy Spirit, probably seated in that order from left to right.[58] The chalice represents the Eucharist, which is the pledge of eternal life (another cup is formed by the contours of the figures); the tree (the Tree of Life) prefigures the Cross, the building to the left is divine wisdom,

53 A. A. Saltykova, 'Ikonografiia "Troitsy" Andreia Rubleva', in *Drevnerusskoe iskusstvo. XIV–XV vv.*, ed. O. I. Podobedova (Moscow: Nauka, 1984), 81. The famous reference to Rublev painting the icon 'in praise of Sergii' was based on a seventeenth-century compilation, 'The narrative of the holy icon painters' (*Skazanie o sviatykh ikonopistsakh*).

54 V. Antonova, 'O pervonachal'nom meste "Troitsy" Andreia Rubleva', *Gos. Tret'iakovskaia Galereia: Materialy i issledovaniia* 1 (1956), 21–43.

55 See Briusova, *Andrei Rublev i moskovskaia shkola zhivopisi*, 20, who dates it about 1400 on stylistic grounds. For a summary of developments in Rublev studies, see V. G. Briusova, *Andrei Rublev* (Moscow: Izobrazitel'noe iskusstvo, 1995), 40–4.

56 Plugin, *Master Sviatoi Troitsy*, 509; V. A. Plugin, 'O proiskhozhdenii "Troitsy" Rubleva', *Istoriia SSR* 2 (1987), 64–79; Plugin, 'Andrei Rublev i Ivan Groznyi. O sud'be "Troitsy"', *Nauka i Religiia* 7 (1989), 55–8. This view has entered textbooks: e.g. V. D. Chernyi, *Iskusstvo srednevekovoi Rusi* (Moscow: Vlasos, 1997), 189.

57 See, for example, a mid-sixteenth-century Novgorod icon in Grierson, *Gates of mystery*, 114–17. On the iconography, N. Malitskii, 'K istorii kompozitsii vetkhozavetnoi Troitsy', *Seminarium Kondakovianum* 2 (1928), 33–46; Saltykova, 'Ikonografiia "Troitsy" Andreia Rubleva', 81; Uspensky, *Theology*, ii, 294–6, 398–402 and *passim*. See below p. 297.

58 No inscriptions identify the three. Opinion is divided over whether the central angel or the angel to the left represents Christ. See Vzdornov, *Troitsa Andreia Rubleva*, 12–13.

or perhaps the Church, and the mountain to the right spiritual strength. The 'otherworldly' geometry of the composition – the use of reverse perspective in the table and the intersecting triangle, the octagon and, most important, the circle encompassing the angels and chalice – create an aesthetic balance and harmony, as well as adding symbolic dimensions. The icon embodies the idea of sacrifice, the sacrifice of the calf (even where no calf is represented, a calf's head may be seen in the chalice) prefiguring the sacrifice of Christ the Lamb of God for mankind.[59]

A less complex but equally haunting image attributed to Rublev is the monumental Saviour thought to come from the *Deesis* of the cathedral of the Dormition 'na Gorodke' in Zvenigorod and tentatively dated to the first decade of the fifteenth century.[60] Christ's face is both awe-inspiring and compassionate, with 'an affinity with the Russian ideal of beauty'.[61] The image is made poignant by the damage to the panel and the story of how in 1918 the restorer G. O. Chirikov discovered it in a shed under a pile of firewood with two similarly sized images of St Paul and the Archangel Michael, salvaged from what is presumed to be a seven- or a nine-figure *Deesis*.[62] The three are now displayed in the Tretyakov Gallery.

Modern eulogies to Rublev that emphasise his prominence as an artist and craftsman of world stature or his credentials as a 'humanist' distort the medieval Russian view of an icon-painter, which is summed up in words attributed to Abbot Iosif of Volokolamsk (1439–1515), one of Rublev's earliest 'biographers'.

> These marvellous, famous iconographers, Daniil, Andrei, his disciple, and many others who were like them, had such virtuous zeal for fasting and the monastic life that they were able to receive divine grace. They constantly raised their mind and thought to the divine immaterial light and their bodily eye toward the images of Christ, of his All-pure Mother and of all the saints painted with material colours.[63]

In Rublev's work spirituality (beauty of spirit) and aesthetics (beauty of form) were inextricably linked.

---

59 See A. V. Voloshinov, *Troitsa Andreia Rubleva: geometriia i filosofiia* (Saratov: Nash Dom, 1997), 25, 27, 28–9, 32.
60 Plugin, *Master Sviatoi Troitsy*, 509.
61 Kozlova, *Masterpieces of the Tretyakov Gallery*, 20.
62 E. Konchin, 'Rublev: novye otkrytiia i starye legendy', *Znanie-sila* 10 (1974), 55–6.
63 Iosif of Volokolamsk, 'Answer to the curious and brief study of the Holy Fathers who lived in the monasteries of the Russian lands', quoted in Uspenskii, *Theology*, ii, 261. See above, pp. 269–71.

Kremlin[64]

Rublev's attainments were all associated with the Moscow region. Art, architecture and liturgy combined at their most impressive in the Moscow Kremlin, where local cults gave way to a national expression of the supreme role of Moscow's princes, supported by the hierarchs of the church. The Muscovite church and state presented themselves as defenders of Orthodoxy not only in Russia but also throughout the Orthodox world, an aspiration which historians often distil into the shorthand expression 'Moscow the Third Rome'. In 1480 Ivan III (1462–1505) formally renounced the payment of tribute to the Mongols. His adoption of the Byzantine (and Habsburg) double-headed eagle, his marriage to the niece of the last Byzantine emperor, and the sporadic addition of the title 'Tsar' (Caesar) to his other titles indicated imperial aspirations that also found visual expression in the reconstruction and refurbishment of the Kremlin towards the end of the fifteenth century. These were not simply 'prestige' projects for outward show. The Kremlin cathedrals lay at Moscow's sacred epicentre and its buildings and their contents formed a sacred landscape. The familiar cycle of the liturgical year was celebrated there with particular pomp and ceremony, reaching a height of splendour during Easter week, with the tsar, his male relatives, the boyars and church hierarchs in attendance. There were also special services to mark national victories and dynastic rites of passage: name days, baptisms and weddings (usually held in the Annunciation cathedral), coronations and funerals (later held in the Dormition and Archangel cathedrals respectively). In addition, the tsar's residence contained private chapels, including those for the use of wives and daughters, the tsaritsy and tsarevny, who were major commissioners of cult objects. The Kremlin icons were painted by the best masters or collected from elsewhere for their miraculous properties or special associations.

In 1475 Ivan III invited the Italian architect Aristotile Fioravanti to build a new Dormition cathedral after a replacement erected by Russian masters collapsed. Fioravanti was instructed to take the thirteenth-century Dormition cathedral in Vladimir as his model, not, as modern historians sometimes anachronistically assume, to ensure that the new church was 'national' in spirit or to avoid 'heretical' Catholic motifs, but to adhere to a mystical, miraculous tradition allegedly initiated by the Mother of God herself.[65] Completed in 1479, the five-domed cathedral combined Russo-Byzantine forms with Renaissance

---

64 See N. Abramowa *et al.* (eds.), *Der Kreml: Gottesruhm und Zarenpracht* (Munich: Hirmer, 2004).

65 S. Eliseev, 'Rozhdenie sobora', *Vstrechi s istoriei* 2 (Moscow, 1988), 90.

proportions and engineering. In 1484 Russian builders constructed the new chapel royal of the Annunciation. Tsar Vasilii III (1505–33) completed the trio of major Kremlin cathedrals with the cathedral of the Archangel Michael, designed in 1505–9 by another Italian, Alevisio Novi. The Venetian shell motifs in the gables were much imitated in later buildings. All three cathedrals were fitted with magnificent *iconostaseis* and painted throughout with fresco cycles. Even the new Palace of Facets (by Marco and Piero Antonio Solari, begun in 1487) was decorated inside with religious murals.[66]

This major building programme created work for painters, including Dionisii (*c.* 1440 to *c.* 1507) and his sons, who ran a highly successful network of workshops.[67] His first recorded works are the frescos of the church of the Nativity of the Virgin in the Pafnutiev-Borovskii monastery (1467–77). In 1481 he was commissioned to paint the frescos for the new Kremlin cathedral of the Dormition. Some fragments of his originals may survive, including the Adoration of the Magi, but most have been painted over.[68] The surviving *Deesis* tier is attributed in part to him, as are a pair of icons of Metropolitans Peter and Aleksii. His work has also been identified in the Kremlin Ascension monastery, the Volokolamsk monastery, the St Paul monastery at Obnorsk near Vologda (Trinity cathedral), and the St Ferapont monastery at Beloozero, where the blue, white and gold frescos of the cathedral of the Nativity of the Mother of God (1502–3?) are among his most complete surviving works. Dionisii and his team also painted the icons for the *Deesis* row (*c.* 1502). The elegantly proportioned, elongated figures occupy panels some 155 cm high and 60 cm wide, with subtly highlighted, variegated colours against gold backgrounds representing divine light.[69]

Dionisii's hallmarks were stylised, elongated, almost incorporeal figures, rhythmically organised against gold or white backgrounds. He used a minimum of detail. Even suffering is stylised and made harmonious, for example in the Crucifixion (*c.* 1500), in which Christ's body is contorted with just a slight curve and, in the Orthodox manner, devoid of all naturalistic renditions of injury. Dionisii and his school used colours full of radiance, achieving translucence without the use of much highlighting.[70] The favourite colours were ochre, cinnabar, red, purple, blue and emerald green.

---

66 On architecture, see Brumfield, *History*.
67 D. Chugunov, *Dionisii* (Leningrad: Izobrazitel'noe iskusstvo, 1979).
68 I. L. Buseva-Davydova, *Khramy Moskovskogo Kremlia: sviatyni i drevnosti* (Moscow: Nauka, 1997), 43–4.
69 V. A. Gusev, *Dionisii v Russkom muzee: k 500-letiiu rospisi Rozhdestvenskogo sobora Ferapontova* (St Petersburg: Palace Editions, [2002]).
70 Alpatov, *Early Russian icon painting*, 251.

Dionisii's career coincided with the rivalry between the followers of the ascetic teachings of St Nil Sorskii (1433–1508) and the more worldly views of St Iosif of Volokolamsk (1439–1515), known respectively as the Non-Possessors and the Possessors. His art was 'an unusual compromise, an attempt to combine two elements, which cannot be combined: an internal purity and an external ritualism'.[71] He has been described as medieval Russia's 'last great painter', a view compatible with the belief that the victory of the more worldly views of Iosif and the increasing 'triumphalism' of the state coincided with a decline in the spirituality of icon-painting in Russia. In the same period the Russian Orthodox Church battled to stamp out iconoclastic tendencies in the heresies of the dissident *strigol'niki* and the Judaisers. A church council pronouncement against the Judaisers issued in 1490 condemned those who 'mocked the images of Christ and the All Pure represented on the icons . . . Others have destroyed holy icons and burned them in the fire. You have reviled the holy image of those who are painted on the icons.'[72] A polemic with such heretics is inherent in the 'Message to an iconographer' (1480s/90s), variously attributed to either Iosif or Nil and perhaps written in response to Dionisii's appeal for guidance.[73]

Orthodox theology was expressed both in individual icons and in the relationships between images, time (the church year) and space (the church interior). In our period the majority of the Russian laity was illiterate, but this does not mean, as is sometimes assumed, that icons were some sort of pictorial teaching aid, which served *faute de mieux* as an alternative to texts. They themselves constituted the texts of Christian doctrine as much as the written word. It is true that many icons had to be seen from a distance and in dim light, hence the preference for bold, simple outlines and blocks of colour, allowing major subjects to be recognised easily, but the impulse behind 'paring down' images in this manner was as much spiritual as pedagogical. 'In its essence the icon is not a sermon, not an exhortation in colour. Its moral and educational power is exerted when people, as they gaze at it, give themselves over to artistic contemplation.'[74]

The few artists whose careers scholars are able to study to any degree worked mainly in major cathedrals and monasteries where records were preserved, but Orthodox devotions were not confined to the church or cloister, nor were icons restricted to officially consecrated spaces. Anywhere could serve as a

---

71 Grierson, *Gates of mystery*, 59.
72 Uspenskii, *Theology*, II, 263.
73 Ibid., 264.
74 M. Alpatov, 'The icons of Russia', in *The Icon*, ed. K. Weitzmann *et al.* (London: Studio Editions, 1982), 241.

house of God, from the peasant hut, with one or two icons in the corner forming a 'window to heaven' or a 'High Jerusalem', to the private chapel in a prince's palace.[75] Portable folding *iconostaseis* or single boards divided into tiers allowed the faithful to unfold a spiritual world anywhere. Icons were carried with armies in portable chapels and in processions of the cross on the street.

Ivan IV[76]

Developments during the reign of Ivan IV 'the Terrible' (1533–84) illustrate the complex links between art and architecture, liturgy, statehood and rulership, with reference both to Russia's perceived place in world history and to the enhanced role of its monarchs as protectors of the true faith. The notion of Moscow's rulers as God's elect imposed certain obligations upon them and required constant checks on the 'purity' of Russian spiritual life and practice. In 1547 there was a great fire in Moscow, which churchmen interpreted as a signal for repentance and purification. Icon painters from Novgorod were transferred to Moscow. With the help of Metropolitan Makarii, formerly archbishop of Novgorod, and himself an icon-painter, Ivan actively sponsored the production and collection of holy objects. Just as his predecessors had 'gathered in' the Russian lands under Moscow's leadership, now Ivan brought old icons or copies, saints' relics and other objects to Moscow from other cities. Makarii himself made many personal commissions, for example the so-called Borovskii Gospels in a silver gilt cover studded with jewels and mother-of-pearl (1530–33).

In the sixteenth century many new iconographic compositions were created to express complicated ideas that would 'appeal to the mind rather than the soul', as one historian has expressed it.[77] Highly complex subjects illustrated biblical texts, hymns and prayers. A famous example is the icon from the Dormition cathedral known as 'Blessed is the Host of the Heavenly Tsar' or the Church Militant, based upon texts from Daniel 12 and Revelation 19. In it the Archangel Michael leads another horseman identified as Ivan IV and his troops from Kazan to Moscow (from Sodom to the heavenly city of Jerusalem), escorted by angels bearing martyrs' crowns. Unidentified figures may include the saintly princes Vladimir and Boris and Gleb. Earthly battles

---

75 See O. Tarasov, *Icon and devotion: sacred spaces in imperial Russia*, trans. R. Milner-Gulland (London: Reaktion, 2002), 38–9.

76 On Ivan IV, see A. P. Pavlov and M. Perrie, *Ivan the Terrible* (London: Pearson / Longman, 2003).

77 Engelina Smirnova, 'Moscow icon painting from the 14th to the 16th century', in *The art of Holy Russia*, 34.

are thus represented in terms of cosmic struggle against the forces of evil, with the Muscovite military elite 'cast in the role of God's own warriors'. The composition has precedents in the Balkans.[78] A smaller version exists, dating from the third quarter of the sixteenth century, in which historical and biblical figures are identified by inscriptions.[79] To dismiss such icons as 'political' is misleading, for court life itself was construed on sacred models and parallels. In icons of saints, too, emphasis switched from the solitary transfigured image of the saint as a guide to contemplative prayer to a narrative of his deeds arranged around the edges of the panel, as an inspiration to others on how to live.

Many of the new 'theological' icons were packed with small details, which some historians have blamed on the influence of decorative 'oriental arabesques'[80] from Persia and Turkey, with a consequent loss of spirituality, and a 'disintegration of the Byzantine vision of liturgical art'.[81] Certainly, in the sixteenth century, and even more in the seventeenth, Russia's growing contacts with the outside world through diplomacy and trade, to and from both east and west, were bound to leave traces in art. There was also an upsurge in demand for icons for private prayer, usually of modest dimensions, but richly detailed to satisfy close scrutiny. The proliferation of miracle cults in the sixteenth century prompted the production of new iconographic subjects featuring miracles, as well as copies of older wonder-working icons.[82] Many examples of *menaion* or monthly calendar icons were made, comprising series of panels each containing rows of miniaturised images of saints and feasts for a single month of the church calendar.[83] Iconographic conventions were applied to images for liturgical purposes created in other media, for example in precious metals on chalices, and processional and reliquary crosses. Fabric palls or shrouds were made for the tombs of saints, bearing their full-length portraits, created with patchwork, embroidered inscriptions and embroidery of gold and silver threads and pearls. The palls for St Kirill of Beloozero in the Russian Museum are fine examples. Some of the best were made in the workshops of the tsaritsy, for example the pall of Metropolitan Filipp (1590s).[84]

78　See D. Rowland, 'Biblical military imagery in the political culture of early modern Russia. The Blessed Host of the Heavenly Tsar', in *Medieval Russian culture*, ed. M. S. Flier and D. Rowland (Berkeley: University of California Press, 1994), II, 197.

79　See *Art of Holy Russia*, 180–1, plate 33.

80　G. H. Hamilton, *The art and architecture of Russia* (London: Thames and Hudson, 1983), 159.

81　Grierson, *Gates of mystery*, 40.

82　On cults, see P. Bushkovitch, *Religion and society in Russia: the sixteenth and seventeenth centuries* (Oxford: Oxford University Press, 1992).

83　For examples, Grierson, *Gates of mystery*, 91–3: *Menaion* for December, Moscow, 1569.

84　Ibid., 146–7, 148–9, 160–1.

New subjects without prototypes were a temptation to deviation. The Church Council of a Hundred Chapters (*Stoglav*, 1551), which attempted to curb abuses and indiscipline in all areas of religious life, included among its pronouncements what has been called 'the first extended, public and authoritative commentary on visual art to be found in a Russian source'.[85] It reaffirmed strict rules on icon-painting, acknowledging the desirability of God-given talent, but deeming a painter's spiritual and moral qualities more important than mere technical skills. Chapter 43 stated that a painter must be irreproachably virtuous, humble, meek, pious and chaste and must always obey his spiritual father. Another requirement was to paint the holy images according to 'consecrated types'. Artists who painted not in accordance with the images, but 'out of their own invention and by guesswork', would be punished. Church hierarchs were responsible for organising inspections. The Council set great store by the example of the 'ancient painters', instructing artists to 'paint [the Trinity] from ancient models, such as the Greek icon painters, and as Andrei Rublev painted'.[86] Guidance was provided in pattern books or *podlinniki* containing outlines of standard icon types.

These rules were not enough to reassure the state secretary I. M. Viskovatyi, who objected at a church tribunal in 1553–54 that artists, especially those working in the Kremlin churches, were painting 'according to their own understanding', deviating from tradition, failing to include proper inscriptions and inserting 'profane' elements, including naturalistic features. Some figures were represented 'as though they were alive', in the 'Latin' manner. Others, such as God the Father depicted as an elderly man, were inadmissible.[87] The church rejected Viskovatyi's complaints.

In the sixteenth century more masonry churches were constructed in Russia than in all previous centuries put together. Most, like icons, followed traditional Byzantine designs, with the incorporation of Russian features such as the now developed onion dome and tiers of decorative *kokoshnik* gables. But there were also striking innovations, notably in the appearance of the *shater* or tent-shaped roof, built over an octagonal tower. Some architectural historians maintain that these octagonal pillars were inspired by wooden church architecture, although it is impossible to verify specific paths of diffusion. With restricted interior space, they were built to be viewed from outside. A remarkable trio of

---

85 Cracraft, *The Petrine revolution*, 51, contains a useful discussion.
86 *Rossiiskoe zakonodatel'stvo X–XX vekov* (Moscow: Iuridicheskaia literatura, 1985), II, 303.
87 Cracraft, *The Petrine revolution*, 54–5. For a fuller account, see D. B. Miller, 'The Viskovatyi affair of 1553–54. Official art, the emergence of autocracy, and the disintegration of medieval Russian culture', *RH/HR* 8 (1981), 293–332.

Figure 12.3 St Basil's Cathedral, Moscow.

such churches marked key dates in Ivan IV's life. His father Vasilii III built the church of the Ascension at Kolomenskoe in 1532 to celebrate his son's birth. The second, the church of John the Baptist at nearby D'iakovo, commemorated Ivan's coronation in 1547. The third was the church on Red Square popularly known as St Basil's cathedral (1555–61) (fig. 12.3).

Many key ideas about Russia's place in divine history, as well as its contemporary geopolitical role, were embodied in the architecture of St Basil's, which originally comprised nine chapels, each with its own *iconostasis*. It is more accurately named from the central chapel dedicated to the Protective Veil or Intercession (*Pokrov*) of the Mother of God. The festival falls on 1 October, which was the day before the Russians captured the Tatar stronghold of Kazan in 1552. The dedication therefore bears witness to Ivan IV's trust in the power of prayer on the eve of victory.[88] It has also been linked to the tsar's visit to the Intercession (Pokrovskii) monastery in Suzdal after the capture of Kazan, as well as to Ivan's dynastic links with the twelfth-century princes of Vladimir-Suzdal, who adopted the festival from Constantinople. The icon features a vision of the Virgin casting her protective mantle over the congregation in the church of St Blasios at Constantinople, a protection which was to be transferred to the Russian land.[89]

Surrounding the central chapel of the Intercession are four octagonal chapels, whose dedications can be linked to Ivan IV's triumphs and pious concerns. To the west is the chapel of Christ's Entry into Jerusalem, which was always associated with the theme of imperial triumph. To the north lies one dedicated to Sts Kiprian and Ustin'ia, whose festival fell on 2 October, the day of the capture of Kazan. To the east is the chapel of the Holy Trinity, which reflected Ivan's reverence for the Trinity-St Sergii monastery and for the icon of the Trinity.[90] To the south lies another dedicated to St Nicholas of Velikoretsk, which honoured a miracle-working icon brought to Moscow in 1555 for restoration and which was processed past the construction site. There are in addition four smaller rectangular chapels: to the north-west one dedicated to St Gregory of Armenia, whose feast day on 30 September coincided with Ivan's victory at Arskaia Pole in 1552; to the south-west another dedicated to St Varlaam Khutynskii, on whose festival on 6 November Ivan almost certainly made his triumphal entry into Moscow in 1552 after the conquest of Kazan; and to the

88 F. Kampfer, 'Über die Konzeption der Vasilij-Blazennyj-Kathedrale in Moskau', *Jahrbücher für Geschichte Osteuropas* 24 (1976), 485.

89 See discussion in Milner-Gulland, *The Russians*, 213–15. For an example, Grierson, *Gates of mystery*, 187.

90 M. Kudriavstev and T. Kudriavtseva, 'Krasnaia ploshchad' – khram pod otkrytym nebom', *Mera* 3 (1995), 29.

south-east and the north-east others dedicated to saints whose feast days fell on 30 August, the day of another Russian victory over the Tatars in 1552. The cathedral is thus a collection of shrines for offering votive thanks to the Mother of God, the Holy Trinity, and saints associated with the siege and conquest of Kazan. It is also construed as an icon of the heavenly kingdom of Jerusalem, which one symbolically enters through its western chapel. Later in Ivan's reign a Palm Sunday procession went from the inner sanctum of the Kremlin to the more public space of Red Square and then to this chapel.[91] The cathedral had counterparts in other art forms. There is a striking similarity, for example, between the central tower of St Basil's and the so-called Tsar's Seat (*tsarskoe mesto*) of Ivan IV in the Dormition cathedral, made in 1551. Both are decorated with *kokoshniki*, pediments and small columns, suggesting an ideological kinship in the idea of divine protection, a link between the place where the tsar celebrated the liturgy and the memorial to royal victory.[92]

The popular name for the cathedral derives from its associations with Basil the Blessed or Vasilii Blazhenny (1489–1552), a 'fool for Christ's sake'.[93] Basil roamed around Moscow in rags and heavy chains and was famed for his prophecies, including predicting the Moscow fire of 1547. He died shortly after prophesying that Ivan would kill his first-born son (which he did, in 1581).[94] It was another son, Tsar Fedor Ivanovich, who in 1588 added St Basil's chapel, next to the Trinity chapel. Prayers to St Basil were sung daily at his shrine, which has its own entrance at ground level. The chapel also contained the relics of Ioanna Khrista-rad (died 1599), a holy fool from Vologda.

Tsar Fedor Ivanovich (1584–98) has sometimes been depicted as a sort of royal holy fool. His death without issue ended the royal line that traced its origins back through the Moscow Daniilovichi to the semi-legendary Riurik. The rivalries engendered by its extinction were a root cause of the period of dynastic, social and national collapse known as the Time of Troubles (1598–1613) that occurred after the death of Fedor's successor, the boyar Boris Godunov (1598–1605).[95] The belief was that the Troubles, no less than the Mongol invasion almost four centuries earlier, were a punishment for Russia's 'sins'. In

---

91 See M. S. Flier, 'Breaking the code: the image of the tsar in the Muscovite Palm Sunday ritual', in *Medieval Russian Culture*, II, 213–42.

92 N. I. Brunov, *Khram Vasiliia Blazhennogo v Moskve* (Moscow: Iskusstvo, 1988), 97. J. Cracraft and D. Rowland, *Architectures of Russian identity, 1500 to the present* (Ithaca and London: Cornell University Press, 2003), 34–50.

93 A. Beliankin, *Skazanie o zhizni i chudesakh Sviatogo Blazhennago Vasiliia Khrista Radi Iurodivago Moskovskago chudotvortsa* (Moscow, 1884).

94 H. Boldyreff Semler, *Moscow: the complete companion guide* (London: Equator, 1989), 78.

95 On Godunov, see Cracraft and Rowland, *Architectures of Russian identity*, 34–51.

the seventeenth century, churches, monasteries, icons and holy objects would be needed as much as ever, but Russian culture would increasingly be subjected to currents from the west, a trend that culminated in Peter the Great's programme of westernisation and the appearance of new conventions in the design of religious art and architecture.

13

Eastern Orthodoxy in Russia and Ukraine in the age of the Counter-Reformation

ROBERT O. CRUMMEY

The age of the Counter-Reformation was a time of bitter conflict in the eastern Orthodox churches in Ukraine and Russia. Rooted in societies with radically different political systems, cultural heritages and confessional traditions, Orthodox leaders and faithful in the two countries responded to the inspiration and pressure of reformed Roman Catholicism in apparently contradictory ways. At the same time, over the course of the seventeenth century, they discovered that their fates were inextricably linked for better or worse. Moreover, they constituted two points in a triangular relationship: in spite of its vulnerable position, the ecumenical patriarchate continued to enjoy much of its traditional prestige and considerable practical influence in both.

Both of the East Slavic Orthodox Churches reflected the political, social and spiritual issues of the society of which they were integral parts. In Russia the Orthodox Church was the only legal Christian confession. Following the Byzantine model, the hierarchy had close ties to the tsars' government and the territorial jurisdictions of church and state were identical. The Muscovite church preserved the local variant of the Slavic Orthodox culture of earlier centuries and showed few signs of recent contact with other parts of Christian Europe.

In the Polish–Lithuanian Commonwealth, the eastern Orthodox Church faced radically different conditions. The kingdom was home to all of the major branches of Christendom – Roman Catholicism, eastern Orthodoxy, Protestantism and the Socinians – and a substantial Jewish population. This remarkable confessional diversity stemmed primarily from the power of the nobility and the concomitant weakness of the royal government. In a sense, the formula *cuius regio, eius religio* described the situation in the fiefdoms of the most powerful magnates, not in the commonwealth as a whole. The educated members of all confessions shared to some degree the Latin and vernacular culture of Renaissance Europe. Under King Sigismund III (1587–1632), a militant Roman Catholic, the policy of *de facto* toleration began to change. The royal government was committed to the Counter-Reformation policy of reuniting all Christians within the Roman church through missions to non-Catholics, both Protestant and Orthodox.

The relation of the eastern Orthodox churches to the Catholic Reformation was ambivalent and complex. On the one hand, like their Roman Catholic counterparts, their leaders struggled to strengthen and purify the practice of the faith. In particular, in both Ukraine and Russia, the members of the hierarchy strove to increase their authority over the lower clergy and laity; to improve the educational standards of the clergy; to standardise and purify liturgical books and their use; and to discipline the devotional practices and behaviour of their flocks.

On the other, adoption of these parts of the Catholic programme of reform meant defending Orthodoxy against the missionary pressure of the Roman Church with the enemy's own weapons. All of the East Slavic Orthodox churches insisted on maintaining the Slavonic liturgy. And, for the most part, they rejected papal hegemony, the cornerstone of Catholic reform. In Russia, the rejection was unequivocal. In the Polish–Lithuanian Commonwealth, the policy of recognising the pope as the leader of Christendom initially appealed to some prominent clergy and laity, but, over time, those who rejected papal authority became as militant as their Muscovite coreligionists.

Several central themes in the history of Orthodoxy in the age of the Counter-Reformation can be traced to pivotal events at the very end of the sixteenth century. Within the Polish–Lithuanian Commonwealth, many eastern Orthodox believers, both clergy and laymen, felt the stirrings of renewal that the Protestant and Catholic Reformations had aroused in Europe. Members of the hierarchy and leading laymen began to address the organisational weaknesses and low level of education within their communion and to respond to the pressure of the Catholic hierarchy and missionary orders. Laymen led the way. At the turn of the 1560s and 1570s, prominent Orthodox magnates promoted the publication of biblical and liturgical texts. Kostiatyn Ostrozsky, in particular, made his estate a centre of Orthodox publishing and founded a school. The Ostrih Bible of 1581, the first printed translation of the Old and New Testaments into Church Slavonic, is the best-known result of his initiatives. A few years later, starting in L'viv, Orthodox burghers began to found confraternities with precisely the same programme of defending their faith through education and publishing. The movement then spread to other urban centres of Orthodoxy in the commonwealth, including Vilnius and eventually Kiev.

For their part, Ipatii Potii, Kyryl Terletsky and other members of the Ortho-dox hierarchy looked to a reunion of Roman Catholic and Orthodox churches as the best way to defend their tradition. The ideal of reunifying the Body of Christ had wide appeal in the fifteenth and sixteenth centuries, especially after the ill-fated union of Florence of 1439, under which the eastern Orthodox churches would have retained their own liturgy in return for recognition of papal primacy. In Poland-Lithuania in the late sixteenth century, the lay leaders of Orthodoxy shared with the bishops the vision of a unified Christendom. The devil, however, lay in the details. For the laity, only union of all branches of Orthodoxy with Rome was acceptable. Potii and his colleagues, however, were open to a more limited union under which the Orthodox in the com-monwealth would unilaterally recognise the primacy of Rome. In addition to the ideal of a reunited Christendom, the bishops had a more practical reason for promoting the union: it held out the prospect of strengthening episcopal authority over parish priests and the laity, a central tenet of the Catholic Refor-mation. In 1596, after complex negotiations and under pressure from the king's government, all but two members of the hierarchy accepted the union of Brest, recognising the supremacy of the pope while retaining the Orthodox liturgy in Slavonic.

From the outset, many Orthodox believers, particularly the brotherhoods, the nobles and the monasteries, rejected the union. The opposition began to coalesce in Brest itself where two councils of the Orthodox met simultaneou-sly – one to ratify the union, the other to denounce it. The two groups soon became competing churches – the eastern Orthodox, loyal to the patriarch of Constantinople, and the Uniate Church. In the seventeenth century, their fortunes waxed and waned. At first, the Uniates seem to have held the stronger position. Most of the hierarchy accepted the union, as did their parish priests: within a few years, the anti-union Orthodox hierarchy had been reduced to a single bishop. Moreover, the most distinguished early leader of the Uniate Church, Metropolitan Iosyf Veliamyn Rutsky (1613–37), thoroughly reformed the monasteries under his jurisdiction and established the Basilian order to staff a system of schools housed in them. At the same time, the Uniates faced resistance from all sides. The Roman Catholic hierarchy treated its leaders with contempt and unsuccessfully pressed the Holy See to abolish it to clear the way for Catholic missionary activity.[1] And, in the early decades of the

1 S. Plokhy, *The Cossacks and religion in early modern Ukraine* (Oxford and New York: Oxford University Press, 2001), 65–93; B. A. Gudziak, *Crisis and reform: the Kyivan metropolitanate, the patriarchate of Constantinople, and the genesis of the Union of Brest* (Cambridge, MA: Harvard University Press, 1998).

seventeenth century, the opponents of the union led a remarkable recovery of Orthodoxy in Ukraine.

At the end of the sixteenth century, the status of the Orthodox Church in Russia also changed significantly. In 1589, while visiting the Russian capital in search of alms, Patriarch Jeremias II of Constantinople agreed, under extreme pressure, to the creation of the patriarchate of Moscow, and in 1590 and 1593 the other Orthodox patriarchs accepted the fait accompli. This symbolic act epitomised the changing relationship between the Greek and Russian branches of Orthodoxy. The Muscovite church had, in practice, been autocephalous since the election of Metropolitan Iona in 1448. Yet, even after 1589, the Greeks who came to Moscow for alms remained convinced that the Greek 'mother-church' was still the ultimate arbiter of eastern Orthodox belief and practice. For their part, the leaders of the Muscovite government and church were acutely aware of the fact that, after the fall of Byzantium in 1453, the tsardom was the only major Orthodox state left on earth and thus primary guardian of true Christianity.

Shortly thereafter, Muscovite Russia endured the Time of Troubles (1598–1613), a devastating political and social crisis made worse by the invasion of Polish and Swedish armies. These experiences shaped the later history of the Muscovite church in two important ways. First, Russia's sufferings undermined the conviction that, as the last Orthodox realm on earth, Muscovy enjoyed God's special blessing. Second, the Troubles emphasised the potential role of the Russian patriarch as leader in revitalising the community. However accurately, tradition holds that Patriarch Hermogen (1606–12) sent out pastoral appeals urging Russians to hold fast to the native tradition of Orthodoxy, reject all compromise with foreigners, and give their lives to restore the tsardom. Hermogen's three most powerful seventeenth-century successors – Filaret (1619–34), Nikon (1652 to 1658/66) and Ioakim (1674–90) – all followed his lead in using their office to impose their convictions and agendas on the church.

While Muscovy suffered, the fortunes of the Orthodox in Ukraine steadily improved, thanks in large measure to the emergence of the Zaporozhian Cossacks as a powerful military and political force. In the confessional struggles in the commonwealth, the Cossacks consistently defended Orthodoxy against all comers. The first important breakthrough took place in 1620. Taking advantage of the arrival in Ukraine of Patriarch Theophanes of Jerusalem, the Cossack leader, Hetman Petro Sahaidachny, and representatives of the Orthodox clergy proposed the re-establishment of an Orthodox hierarchy, a step made necessary by the fact that virtually all episcopal sees that had once been Orthodox were now occupied by Uniates. Accordingly, the Patriarch consecrated a new

Orthodox metropolitan of Kiev, Iov Boretsky, and other bishops. In its first years, the new hierarchy functioned illegally, but its leadership encouraged the Orthodox in Ukraine and Belarus to resist the Uniates' campaign to expropriate their churches. The resulting struggle took its most extreme form in the assassination of Uniate Archbishop Iosafat Kuntsevych in 1623.

In 1632, the Orthodox Church took another step towards confessional equality within the commonwealth. Sigismund III's death in that year set in motion the process of electing his successor. To gain the Orthodox magnates' allegiance, the successful candidate, Władysław IV, recognised the right of the Orthodox to their own metropolitan and bishops (but not the existing illegal hierarchy) but limited their authority to only half of the previously Orthodox dioceses of the realm.

The Romanov regime

The Orthodox church in Russia dealt with entirely different issues. After the Time of Troubles, the most obvious was the need to re-establish a functioning government and ecclesiastical administration. The Romanov family, a powerful boyar clan related by marriage to the old dynasty, played a crucial role in both. As a first step, the teenage Mikhail Romanov was crowned tsar in 1613. The new tsar's father, Filaret, would have been a far stronger candidate for the throne but for the fact that, in 1600, he had, against his will, taken monastic vows that were irrevocable by eastern Orthodox tradition even though made under duress. Thereafter, although by origin a lay politician and courtier, he could hold only ecclesiastical office. In 1619, on his return to Moscow after years of imprisonment in Poland, Filaret ascended the vacant patriarchal throne and, in practice, also acted as effective head of his son's government. Historians have usually characterised him as a forceful but unimaginative conservative and a staunch defender of Muscovite Orthodoxy against Roman Catholic influence.

After being consecrated by Patriarch Theophanes of Jerusalem, Filaret systematically built up the power and prestige of the Moscow patriarchate. He adopted the title *Velikii Gosudar* (Great Sovereign), normally applied only to tsars, and often used it in decrees issued jointly with his son. In light of Filaret's position as head of the ruling family, this practice made sense, but set a dangerous precedent. As patriarch he also made himself virtually ruler of a separate principality within the realm. He acquired estates in all parts of Russia in which he had judicial authority over all but the most serious crimes. To administer these territories and collect fees from the clergy, Filaret created separate patriarchal chanceries for administration, finances and judicial affairs, parallel to the offices of the state bureaucracy, and a corps of servitors – laymen as well as clergy – to manage them and serve as his retinue.

He adopted practical and symbolic measures to preserve the purity of Muscovite Orthodoxy. Fearing the corrupting influence of the Uniate movement, he insisted that only Orthodox baptism by triple immersion was valid and therefore that all foreigners – even Orthodox believers from the Polish-Lithuanian Commonwealth – had to be rebaptised in order to be received into the Russian Church. In 1620, a church council in Moscow adopted his policy.[2]

Finally, the 'Gutenberg revolution' belatedly took root in Muscovite Russia in the early seventeenth century, long after the Polish–Lithuanian Commonwealth had experienced its impact. Printing presented the church with an opportunity and a challenge. Well aware of the dangers of public discussion in print, tsars and patriarchs maintained a virtual monopoly over this revolutionary technology: the official Printing Office (*Pechatnyi Dvor*) published the overwhelming majority of books that appeared in Russia during the seventeenth century. Printing made it possible to provide parishes and monasteries with reliable copies of the service books that the Orthodox liturgy requires. Even so, there were perils, for publishing uniform editions of liturgical books requires the editors to establish authoritative texts. Given centuries of evolving liturgical practice within the Orthodox commonwealth, leading to different usages in different churches, and the inevitable variations in hand-copied manuscripts, how were editors in Russia – or, for that matter, Ukraine – to decide which variant was truly Orthodox?

As soon as he returned to Moscow, Filaret faced a crisis over this issue. In his absence, Tsar Michael had commissioned Abbot Dionisii of the Trinity-St Sergii monastery, the only important centre of learning in a devastated cultural landscape, to prepare new editions of fundamental liturgical texts beginning with the *Sluzhebnik* (Missal). He and his collaborators, Arsenii Glukhoi and Ivan Nasedka, compared recent Muscovite editions with a selection of earlier Slavonic and Greek texts and found a number of passages that, in their eyes, were illogical or tinged with heresy. Their work elicited a violent reaction. In 1618, a local ecclesiastical council attacked their editions, condemned Dionisii and the others as heretics, and defrocked them.

---

2 Metropolitan Makarii, *Istoriia russkoi tserkvi* (Düsseldorf: Brücken-Verlag, 1968–69), xi, 3–8, 23–33; A. V. Kartashev, *Ocherki po istorii russkoi tserkvi* (Moscow: Nauka, 1991), ii, 96–9; P. Pascal, *Avvakum et les débuts du raskol* (Paris and The Hague: Mouton, 1969), 25–7; S. A. Zenkovsky, *Russkoe staroobriadchestvo; dukhovnye dvizheniia semnadtsatogo veka* [Forum Slavicum xxi] (Munich: W. Fink, 1970), 70–4; P. Bushkovitch, *Religion and society in Russia: the sixteenth and seventeenth centuries* (New York: Oxford University Press, 1992), 52–3.

Filaret immediately made clear that the Printing House would continue to publish new editions of the liturgical books prepared by the best native scholars. Accordingly, at the urging of Patriarch Theophanes, he pardoned the disgraced editors and sent them back to work. Filaret remained vigilant for signs of heretical Latin influence. He refused to publish the catechism of the militant defender of Orthodoxy in Ukraine, Lavrentii Zyzanii; condemned the *Evangelie uchitel'noe* (Gospels with commentary) of Kyryl Tranquillon Stavrovetsky – a work also condemned by the metropolitan of Kiev – and attempted to prohibit the importation of all books from the commonwealth. The patriarch's caution meant that the *Pechatnyi Dvor* published a very modest number of books in his lifetime. But, by setting the programme in motion and assembling the scholars, he laid the groundwork for the flowering of ecclesiastical publishing under his unimposing successors, Ioasaf I (1634–40) and Iosif (1642–52).[3] From the late 1630s to the early 1650s, the *Pechatnyi Dvor* published new editions of the most important service books, a number of saints' lives and uncontroversial classics of eastern Christian spirituality such as writings of St John Chrysostom, St Ephraim the Syrian and St John Klimax.

Peter Mohyla

The revitalisation of Orthodoxy in Ukraine reached its culmination under Peter Mohyla, metropolitan of Kiev (1632–47). Of Moldavian princely origin, Mohyla saw himself both as a member of the nobility and ecclesiastical elite of the entire Polish–Lithuanian Commonwealth and as an ardent defender of eastern Orthodoxy. His consecration immediately followed Władysław IV's decision to recognise the right of the Orthodox Church to its own hierarchy. Mohyla, the archimandrite of the monastery of the Caves in Kiev, had the support of the nobility in Ukraine and the king. From the moment of his consecration in 1633, he showed his determination to put the church's house in order: he moved quickly, for example, to neutralise his predecessor, Isaia Kopynsky, a favourite of the Cossacks, whom the royal government had never recognised.

Mohyla reshaped the Orthodox Church in Ukraine. For models he had only to look to the recent successes of Roman Catholicism and Metropolitan Rutsky's reforms of the Uniate Church. Mohyla waged his reform campaign on many fronts. He worked hard to strengthen his authority over the bishops,

---

3 Pascal, *Avvakum*, 8–14, 21–4; Zenkovsky, *Russkoe staroobriadchestvo*, 91–6; Kartashev, *Ocherki*, II, 85–94; K. V. Kharlampovich, *Malorossiiskoe vliianie na velikorusskuiu tserkovnuiu zhizn'* (The Hague and Paris: Mouton, 1968), 103–12.

the parish clergy and the lay confraternities. To provide the metropolitan see with adequate revenue, he retained control of the Caves monastery and took over the administration of two other monasteries in Kiev. Re-establishing the authority of the metropolitan also meant rebuilding the traditional centre of Orthodoxy in Rus, Kiev. Mohyla oversaw the restoration of the cathedral of St Sophia and several other churches. Moreover, his statements and the panegyrics of his school repeatedly emphasised his and his city's direct lineage from St Vladimir, the first Christian ruler of Rus.

Education lay at the heart of Mohyla's programme. While archimandrite, he had founded a school in the Caves monastery whose purpose was to introduce the highest contemporary standards of study and instruction, epitomised by Jesuit schools, into a thoroughly Orthodox setting. In Mohyla's world, those were the standards of Roman Catholic and Uniate elite culture, which placed special emphasis on mastery of Latin, Polish and Ukrainian-flavoured Slavonic. Although initially controversial for this reason, the monastery school, which was soon united with the school of the Kiev lay confraternity, won the support of the patriarch of Constantinople and of the Cossack leadership. The royal government soon followed suit. In 1635, King Władysław's charter, however, did not fulfil Mohyla's aspirations since it gave approval for a 'school', not an academy, equal in standing to the Jesuit academies of the commonwealth.

The goal of the school was to prepare its graduates to defend Orthodoxy with the scholarly weapons of its rivals. Its curriculum closely followed established Catholic models. Instruction initially focused on languages – Latin, Polish, Greek and Slavonic – and proceeded to more complex verbal skills such as poetics and rhetoric. Advanced students were expected to master the most important literary genres of Latin-Polish culture. Under its charter, the school taught philosophy along Aristotelian models, but was not allowed to teach theology. Whether its curriculum depended too much on Roman Catholic models to be genuinely Orthodox, as some critics have argued, is beside the point: Mohyla and his collaborators used the only resources available in their time and place to train effective spokesmen for Orthodoxy.

Education and publishing went hand in hand. In strengthening his authority as metropolitan, Mohyla strove to make the Caves monastery the primary centre of Orthodox publishing in the commonwealth. Under his leadership, its press produced many editions, most importantly liturgical texts. Aware of the inconsistencies in existing editions, Mohyla's team of editors prepared new versions of the *Sluzhebnik* (Missal) in 1639 and the *Trebnik* (Sacramentary) in 1646, both ostensibly based on Greek and ancient Slavonic texts. In these publications, the editors achieved their goals of consistency, clarity and thoroughness. At the same time, as detailed studies of the texts have shown, Mohyla adopted Catholic sacramental theology in the explanatory passages and added some rites and practices of secondary importance that had Roman, but not Orthodox, roots. Nevertheless, the Orthodox in Ukraine adopted his editions without significant opposition.

The climax of Mohyla's work as a systematiser was the publication of his *Orthodox Confession of Faith*. Although, in this case as well, modern scholars have noted Roman Catholic influence on the formulations he used to state the central truths of the faith, the *Confession* won the approval of the eastern patriarchs and became the standard formulation of the church's teaching throughout the Orthodox world until the nineteenth century.

It is difficult to overstate Mohyla's accomplishments and impact on Orthodoxy as a whole. The Greek Church, whether under Ottoman rule or in exile, was impoverished, financially and culturally, and vulnerable to strong Roman Catholic and Protestant influence. For its part, the Russian Church was barely beginning to realise its potential as the leading force within eastern Christendom. In 1650, culturally at least, Kiev was the centre of the Orthodox world.[4]

Muscovite reforms

In the mid-seventeenth century, the Muscovite Church began to feel pressure for change. Like their counterparts elsewhere in Europe, would-be reformers among the clergy strove for consistency and good order in the celebration of the liturgy and attempted to raise the moral tone of parish life. Many of their complaints were not new. In 1636, for example, Ivan Neronov and other parish priests in Nizhnii Novgorod sent a petition to Patriarch Ioasaf, asking for his support in restoring order and dignity to services of worship. The petitioners recited a litany of long-standing abuses – *mnogoglasie* (the practice of chanting up to 'five or six' different parts of the service simultaneously) and other liturgical short cuts. They also complained at length about rowdy behaviour during services.[5] In a series of pastoral instructions, Patriarch Ioasaf strongly supported their demands for pious behaviour during the liturgy. The Nizhnii Novgorod petitioners also attacked the laity's boisterous celebration of non- or

---

4 I. Ševčenko, 'The many worlds of Peter Mohyla', *Harvard Ukrainian Studies* 8 (1984), 9–41; S. T. Golubev, *Kievskii mitropolit Petr Mogila i ego spodvizhniki* [Opyt tserkovno-istoricheskogo issledovaniia] (Kiev: Tip. G. T. Korchak-Novitskago, 1883–98); P. Meyendorff, 'The liturgical reforms of Peter Moghila: a new look', *St. Vladimir's Theological Quarterly* 29 (1985), 101–14; Plokhy, *Cossacks and religion*, 95–9, 236–46.
5 N. V. Rozhdestvenskii, 'K istorii bor'by s tserkovnymi bezporiadkami, otgoloskami iazychestva i porokami v russkom bytu XVII v.', *ChOIDR* 201 (1902, book ii), 19–23.

pre-Christian festivals such as Rusalii and Koliada at the most solemn times of the liturgical year. Folk minstrels (*skomorokhi*) drew their particular ire. On this issue too, the hierarchy agreed but could see no way to uproot these ancient practices.[6]

Attacking *mnogoglasie* was more controversial. Liturgical short cuts had crept into Russian Orthodoxy for good reason. Over the centuries, monastic services had become the norm in parishes, putting severe demands on the patience and stamina of even the most devout laypeople.[7] When the first attempts to set some limits to this traditional practice encountered vigorous opposition, Patriarch Iosif retreated, and in 1649, to the reformers' chagrin, a local ecclesiastical council chose to maintain the status quo.[8]

Paradoxically, the reformers' desire for an orderly and consistent liturgy opened the Muscovite church to books, scholars and school curricula from Ukraine – precisely what Filaret had feared. In the 1640s, the *Pechatnyi Dvor* published a number of works from Ukraine including the *Nomokanon* of Zaxarija Kopystens'kyi and the pioneering Slavonic grammar of Meletij Smotryc'skii. Moreover, since the Printing Office desperately needed more editors who knew Greek and Latin, Epifanii Slavynetsky and two other scholars from Ukraine joined its staff in 1649. Finally, from Ukraine came the *Book of Faith*, an Orthodox compilation of apocalyptic writings interpreting the union of Brest as a prelude to the Last Days, which, along with a Muscovite miscellany, the *Kirillova kniga*, and the writings of St Ephraim, stimulated apocalyptic reflection among the cultural elite of Moscow.[9]

The impact of Khmelnytsky's revolt

Between 1648 and 1654 dramatic changes in international politics and upheaval within the commonwealth presented the Orthodox churches with new opportunities and challenges. As the Cossack revolt led by Bohdan Khmelnytsky swept across Ukraine in 1648, Roman Catholics, Uniates and Jews all felt the rebels' wrath to varying degrees. Even though the rebels fought, among other things, for the rights of Orthodoxy, the leaders of the church found the consequences of the uprising to be distinctly ambivalent. Mohyla's immediate

---

6 *AAE*, IV, 481–2 (no. 321).
7 Pascal, *Avvakum*, 58–9.
8 'Deianiia Moskovskago tserkovnogo sobora 1649 goda', ed. S. A. Belokurov, *ChOIDR* 171 (1894, book iv), 1–52.
9 A. S. Zernova, *Knigi kirillovskoi pechati izdannye v Moskve v XVI–XVII vekakh* (Moscow: Gosudarstvennaia Ordena Lenina biblioteka SSSR imeni V. I. Lenina, 1958), 46–77; Pascal, *Avvakum*, 65–71, 128–32; Zenkovsky, *Russkoe staroobriadchestvo*, 91–101.

successor, Sylvester Kosov (1647–57), feared that the revolt would undercut the church's hard-won status within the commonwealth. On one level, his fears proved unjustified: through the initial victories and ultimate failure of the Khmelnytsky revolt, the Kiev school and Orthodox publishing ventures continued to thrive.

In other areas, he had every reason for uneasiness. When the tide of battle turned and Khmelnytsky saw no hope of winning equal rights for Ukraine and the Cossacks within the commonwealth without outside support, he turned to Orthodox Moscow. Under the terms of the Pereiaslav Agreement of 1654, the tsar agreed to extend his protection to Ukraine. From the beginning, Muscovites and Ukrainians had very different understandings of what the agreement meant. For Kosov and his successors, however, one implication was clear: the metropolitans of Kiev could expect strong pressure to shift their allegiance from the patriarch of Constantinople to Moscow, a change they were determined to resist.

The Orthodox churches in Ukraine and Russia now faced radically new conditions. Muscovite Russia increasingly dominated eastern Europe politically. In the ebb and flow of the Thirteen Years War (1654–67) with Poland, its forces gained control of Ukraine east of the Dnieper. Muscovite troops and officials first appeared there in 1654 long before the truce of Andrusovo of 1667 recognised the partition of Ukraine into Left and Right Banks, under Russian and Polish rule respectively. In the same years, Ukraine fell into 'the Ruin', a period of military weakness and political instability. One *hetman* followed another in rapid succession, each attempting to strengthen his power and protect his community by allying with an outside power, the Polish crown (itself in crisis), Muscovite Russia or the Ottoman Empire. The Orthodox metropolitanate of Kiev was also divided in practice although not in theory. When Kosov's successor as metropolitan, Dmitrii Balaban, left Kiev for Polish-controlled territory to avoid the pressure of the tsar's officials, the Russian government and the hierarchy in Moscow chose to deal with Orthodox on the Left Bank through a local member of the hierarchy, most often Bishop Lazar Baranovych of Chernihiv. Moreover, when the Russian army occupied Belarus, the patriarch of Moscow immediately took control of the Orthodox dioceses that had been under Kiev's jurisdiction.[10] Dmitrii Balaban's nightmare – Russian domination of the Orthodox Church in Ukraine – was only a step away.

---

10 F. E. Sysyn, 'The formation of modern Ukrainian religious culture: the sixteenth and seventeenth centuries', in *Church, nation and state in Russia and Ukraine*, ed. Geoffrey A. Hosking (London: Macmillan, 1991), 1–22, provides an excellent summary.

Nikon and reform

Although Muscovite Russia experienced serious political crises and social upheavals in the mid-seventeenth century, the Orthodox Church carried out its ministry in far more predictable circumstances than its counterpart in Ukraine, in part because of its very close ties with the tsars' government. Indeed, the decisive role of the new tsar, Aleksei Mikhailovich (1645–76), in the stormy events in the second half of the century illustrates the extent to which, long before Peter I, the decisions of the secular ruler ultimately determined the fate of the Russian Orthodox Church. Strong supporters of reform, the young ruler and his confessor, Stefan Vonifatiev, gathered like-minded men, traditionally known as the Zealots of Piety, including parish priests such as Neronov and his protégé, Avvakum, and in time the future patriarch Nikon. Everyone in this diverse group agreed that parish life must be revitalised through effective preaching, the full and orderly celebration of the liturgy, and strict enforcement of the church's moral teachings – all objectives they shared with the Catholic Reformation.

Before long, Aleksei and his allies made several of the reformers' demands official policy. Beginning in December 1648, the tsar issued a series of decrees, ordering local governors to ban *skomorokhi* and suppress the folk customs associated with them in every village and hamlet in their jurisdictions.[11] Issuing decrees, however, was much easier than changing deep-rooted patterns of behaviour: scattered evidence suggests that the *skomorokhi* continued to practise their ancient trade in the remote countryside into the eighteenth century and many of the agrarian rites and folk festivals survived long enough for modern ethnographers to record them.[12]

The reformers also won their battle for *edinoglasie* (celebrating the liturgy with no overlapping or short cuts). Reversing the decision of 1649, another ecclesiastical council, in February 1651, made the practice obligatory in parish churches as well as in monasteries.[13]

The implementation of the Zealots' programme of reform from above aroused violent opposition among the laity. Avvakum's hagiographic autobiography, written roughly twenty years after the events, describes his clashes

---

11 N. Kharuzin, 'K voprosu o bor'be moskovskago pravitel'stva s narodnymi iazycheskimi obriadami i sueveriiami v polovine XVII v.', *Etnograficheskoe Obozrenie*, 1 (1879), 143–51; *AI*, IV, 124–6.

12 R. Zguta, *Russian minstrels: a history of the Skomorokhi* (Philadelphia: University of Pennsylvania Press, 1978), 63–5; M. M. Gromyko, *Mir russkoi derevni* (Moscow: Molodaia Gvardiia, 1991), 325–9, 345–60.

13 Pascal, *Avvakum*, 156–8.

with his parishioners while parish priest of Lopatitsy. Twice, in 1648 and 1652, in fear for his life, he fled his parish for the safety of Moscow. As he recalled them, Avvakum's methods of enforcing liturgical and moral order and rebuking sinners were hardly subtle.[14] Other reformist priests suffered through similar tribulations, taking the brunt of laypeople's anger at demands from above that they abruptly change their traditional way of life.

Legal and economic issues also threatened the reformers' campaign. The Law Code of 1649 significantly changed the legal relationship of church and state by creating a monastery chancery (*Monastyrskii Prikaz*) and by giving it authority to try criminal and civil cases involving both clergymen and the inhabitants of all church lands except the patriarchal domain.[15] Moreover, under pressure from urban taxpayers, the government confiscated the tax-exempt urban settlements in which the church's dependants conducted trade. Although neither the judgement of churchmen by the secular government nor the confiscation of ecclesiastical property was unprecedented, the sweeping provisions of the Code made clear that neither the church's judicial privileges nor its lands were sacrosanct.

When Nikon became patriarch in 1652, many of the latent tensions within the Russian church erupted into open conflict. Nikon aroused enormous controversy in his own day and still fascinates and perplexes us. Born into a peasant family in the Nizhnii Novgorod area, he served briefly as a parish priest before taking monastic vows in the Anzerskii Skit on an island in the White Sea where he followed a severely ascetic rule of life. He also displayed great energy and administrative talent, qualities that ultimately brought him to the position of abbot of the Kozheozerskii monastery. In this capacity, he travelled to Moscow in 1646 and met Tsar Aleksei.

From that moment, Nikon became a favourite of the tsar and an ally of the church reformers at his court. With Aleksei's unconditional support, he quickly rose to the patriarchal throne. The tsar immediately appointed him archimandrite of the Novospasskii monastery in Moscow, a favourite foundation of the Romanov family. In 1649, he was consecrated metropolitan of

---

14 Archpriest Avvakum, *Zhitie Protopopa Avvakuma im samim napisannoe i drugie ego sochineniia*, ed. N. K. Gudzii (Moscow: Goslitizdat, 1960), 61–4; Archpriest Avvakum, *The Life written by himself: with the study of V. V. Vinogradov*, trans. and ed. Kenneth N. Brostrom (Michigan Slavic Translations 4) (Ann Arbor: University of Michigan Press, 1979), 45–50.

15 *Sobornoe ulozhenie 1649 goda: tekst, kommentarii*, ed. L. I. Ivina, G. V. Abramovich *et al.* (Leningrad: Nauka, Leningradskoe otdelenie, 1987), 69–70, 242–6; M. I. Gorchakov, *Monastyrskii prikaz, 1649–1725 g. opyt istoriko-iuridicheskago izsliedovaniia* (St Petersburg: A. Transhel', 1868), 40–90.

Novgorod, the second most powerful position in the hierarchy. In both of these capacities, he carried out the programme of the reformers with characteristic determination.

During his tenure in Novgorod Nikon made it clear that, in his opinion, the ultimate responsibility for the spiritual wellbeing of Russia lay with the church's leaders, not the secular ruler. For example, in 1652, as part of a campaign to canonise martyred leaders of the Russian Church, he brought the relics of Metropolitan Filipp, already widely recognised as a saint, from the Solovetskii monastery to Moscow. While in Solovki, he publicly read Tsar Aleksei's statement of contrition for the sin of his predecessor, Ivan IV, in ordering Filipp's murder.

Once enthroned as patriarch with the enthusiastic support of the tsar and the rest of the reformers, Nikon acted as though he personified the church. He strove to transform its organisational structure into an effective hierarchical administration with the patriarch at the top and reacted ruthlessly to any sign of opposition from other members of the hierarchy. Like Filaret, he added extensive lands to the patriarch's own domain and, in addition to building or repairing other churches, maintained three important monasteries – the Iverskii, the Krestnyi and the Voskresenskii or New Jerusalem – as his own foundations. A man of imposing appearance, he impressed visiting clergymen with his magnificent vestments, his long sermons and his dramatic manner of celebrating the liturgy. Moreover, beginning in 1653, with the tsar's consent, he began to use the epithet *Velikii Gosudar*, previously used by only one patriarch – Filaret, father of a tsar and effective head of state.

The long-standing campaign to publish accurate liturgical books and distribute them throughout Russia, however, quickly took a fateful turn. The tsar, the new patriarch and some of their collaborators decided that the best way to revitalise Russian Orthodoxy was to forge closer ties with eastern Orthodoxy, especially the ecumenical patriarchate. In 1649, the latest of a long line of Greek visitors, Patriarch Paisios of Jerusalem and Arsenios the Greek, a scholar of dubious background including a Roman Catholic education, appeared in Moscow and tried to convince the tsar and Nikon that, in so far as they differed, Greek liturgical practices were authentically Orthodox while Russian usages were erroneous local innovations. To test this claim, a Russian monk, Arsenii Sukhanov, made two journeys in 1649–50 and 1651–53 to investigate the condition of the Greek Church. His findings included a report that monks on Mount Athos had burned Russian liturgical books as heretical and his experiences led him to conduct a bitter debate with visiting Greeks in Moscow in 1650 on the

Orthodoxy of Russian practices.[16] Following the advice of the Greeks took the tsar and Nikon down a dangerous path, for, as many Russians firmly believed, it was the Greeks' apostasy at the council of Florence that had thrust Orthodox Russia into the centre of world history. Moreover, it was well known that the main centres of contemporary Greek Orthodox learning and publishing were in Roman Catholic countries.

Against this background, on 11 February 1653 the Printing Office published a new edition of the Psalter, which omitted the customary article instructing worshippers on the correct way to cross themselves. Then, within days, Nikon filled the gap with an instruction (*pamiat'*) to the faithful to use the so-called three-finger sign of the cross, holding their thumb, index and middle fingers together. Muscovite tradition, embodied in the protocols of the *Stoglav* council of 1551, held to the two-finger sign with only the index and middle fingers extended. Then, in early 1654, a local church council approved the principle of revising Russian liturgical books 'according to ancient parchment and Greek texts (*po starym kharateinym i grecheskim knigam*)'. As Nikon's contemporary opponents and the best modern scholars have argued, the new editions of the service books were based, not on ancient manuscripts, but on very recent Greek editions and mandated the substitution of contemporary Greek practices for traditional Russian usages.[17]

New editions followed one another in rapid succession – *Sluzhebniki* (Missals) in 1654 and 1655, and in 1654 the *Skrizhal*, a treatise on the nature of liturgy, together with Nikon's justification of his reforms. In addition to the sign of the cross, the most controversial changes in the details of the liturgy included the four-pointed instead of eight-pointed cross on the sacred wafer and on church buildings; the triple rather than double Alleluia after the Psalms and the Cherubic hymn; the number of prostrations and bows in Lent; a new transliteration of 'Jesus' into Slavonic (*Iisus* instead of *Isus*); and small but significant alterations in the wording of the Nicene Creed.

Nikon's liturgical reforms fit into two broader contexts. The standardisation of Russian and Greek liturgies arose from the aspiration to bring Orthodox Christians together under Russian leadership. Yet the churches and societies that formed that commonwealth were distinctly different. In Russia, where universal adherence to Orthodoxy was a given, defining authentic Russian

---

16 Kartashev, *Ocherki*, II, 126–31.

17 On the reforms, N. F. Kapterev, *Patriarkh Nikon i Tsar' Aleksei Mikhailovich*, 2 vols. (Sergiev Posad: Tipografiia Sviato-Troitskoi Sergievoi Lavry, 1909–12); Paul Meyendorff, *Russia, ritual, and reform: the liturgical reforms of Nikon in the 17th century* (Crestwood, NY: St Vladimir's Seminary Press, 1991). S. V. Lobachev, *Patriarkh Nikon* (St Petersburg: Iskusstvo–SPB, 2003), 123–5, argues that Nikon issued his instruction in 1654, not 1653.

Orthodox belief and practice was the primary agenda. For the Orthodox in Ukraine, the central fact of life was struggle against Roman Catholicism and the Uniate Church. Thus similar changes in liturgical texts aroused no opposition in Ukraine, but stirred up bitter controversy in Russia. Moreover, scholars have recently argued that Nikon's liturgical reforms arose from a new understanding – widespread elsewhere in European Christendom – of liturgy as a commemoration of Christ's life, death and resurrection in which words, gestures and ritual objects may legitimately have several different levels of meaning simultaneously.[18]

Whatever their broader implications, the new service books altered some of the most frequently repeated words, gestures and visible symbols in the liturgy. Even more jarring was the autocratic manner in which Nikon introduced the new editions: against the advice of the ecumenical patriarch and the tsar, he insisted that only the reformed usage was acceptable. In 1656, he repeatedly branded the two-finger sign of the cross and other traditional Russian practices as heretical.[19]

The reforms and the patriarch's intransigence in enforcing them split the reform coalition. In a series of increasingly agitated letters written in late 1653 and early 1654 to the tsar and Vonifat'ev, Ivan Neronov severely criticised Nikon's abandonment of Russia's heritage and the arrogance with which he was treating his former friends. The three-finger sign of the cross and the altered number of deep bows (*poklony*) in services were specific examples of these destructive policies. In one letter to Vonifat'ev, he told of hearing a voice from an icon urging him to resist Nikon's reforms, a story later retold in his friend Avvakum's autobiography.[20] For their outspoken protests, the authorities excommunicated Neronov and imprisoned him in a remote northern monastery and exiled Avvakum to Siberia. According to tradition, the one bishop who in 1654 openly questioned the reforms, Pavel of Kolomna, lost his see and his life for his stand.[21]

As these examples indicate, resistance to the liturgical reforms began with individuals and small, scattered groups. Beginning with Spiridon Potemkin in

18 K. C. Felmy, *Die Deutung der Göttlichen Liturgie in der russischen Theologie: Wege und Wandlungen russischer Liturgie-Auslegung* [Arbeiten zur Kirchengeschichte 54] (Berlin, New York: Walter de Gruyter, 1984), 80–111; B. A. Uspensky, 'The schism and cultural conflict in the seventeenth century', *Seeking God: the recovery of religious identity in Orthodox Russia, Ukraine, and Georgia*, ed. S. K. Batalden (DeKalb: Northern Illinois University Press, 1993), 106–43.

19 Kapterev, *Patriarkh Nikon*, I, 192–8; Meyendorff, *Russia*, 61–2.

20 *Materialy dlia istorii raskola za pervoe vremia ego sushchestvovaniia*, ed. N. Subbotin (Moscow: Redaktsiia 'Bratskoe slovo', 1874–90), I, 51–78, 99–100; Avvakum, *Zhitie*, 65.

21 Subbotin, *Materialy*, I, 100–2.

1658, a few prominent clergymen, members of the ecclesiastical elite, wrote detailed critiques of Nikon's reforms. They received valuable support from Bishop Aleksandr of Viatka who, although he did not write any polemics of his own, encouraged those who did and collected a library of texts to support the antireform position. Despite some differences in details, the works of Potemkin, Nikita Dobrynin *Pustosviat*, the priest Lazar and others all attacked the internal inconsistencies in the new service books and raised fundamental questions about the legitimacy of Russian Orthodoxy. For if traditional Russian usages were heretical, were all previous generations of Russian Christians – saints and sinners alike – damned as heretics? Although these manuscripts had very limited circulation, they served as a valuable resource for later generations of polemicists against the reformed church.

Their opponents, the defenders of Nikon's policies, had far more powerful weapons at their disposal – the resources of the Printing Office and the support of the hierarchy and government. In 1668, for example, the Ukrainian-trained court poet and royal tutor Simeon Polotsky published *Zhezl pravleniia*, the first in a long series of attacks on the conservative opposition.[22]

The opposition to Nikon

Small numbers of uneducated laypeople also expressed opposition to the reforms. In 1657, the ecclesiastical and governmental authorities imprisoned the Rostov weaver Sila Bogdanov and two companions for publicly condemning the new service books.[23]

More radical still were the small groups that made up the Kapiton movement. Beginning in the 1620s or 1630s, Kapiton and his followers rejected the Orthodox Church and its clergy as corrupt and practised extreme forms of asceticism, such as rigorous fasting in all seasons; if official accusations can be believed, some even starved themselves to death. In 1665 and 1666, the authorities investigated several informal monastic communities that followed his fundamental teachings. And although not their central concern, these later followers of Kapiton included the new liturgical books in their list of grievances against the church.

In the short run, isolated objections to the new liturgical texts did nothing to shake Nikon's overwhelming power over the church and influence at court.

---

22 G. B. Michels, *At war with the church: religious dissent in seventeenth-century Russia* (Stanford: Stanford University Press, 1999), 112–15.

23 Ibid., 33–8; *Dokumenty Razriadnogo, Posol'skogo, Novgorodskogo i Tainogo Prikazov o raskol'nikakh v gorodakh Rossii, 1654–1684 gg.*, ed. V. S. Rumiantseva (Moscow: Akademiia nauk SSSR, Institut istorii SSSR, 1990), 29–58.

The only threat to his position lay in his dependence on his royal patron. Suddenly, however, Aleksei and Nikon parted ways in 1658. After the tsar refused to settle several seemingly trifling conflicts to Nikon's satisfaction, the patriarch withdrew from Moscow to the New Jerusalem monastery and left the day-to-day business of the church in the hands of a *locum tenens*, the metropolitan of Krutitsy. At the same time, Nikon still thought of himself as the patriarch. For example, in 1659, he attempted to anathematise his replacement for playing the role of Christ in the annual Palm Sunday procession.

Nikon's self-imposed exile without abdicating the patriarchal office created an extremely awkward situation. As messages and emissaries shuttled back and forth between Moscow and New Jerusalem, it became clear that there was no hope of reconciliation, for, in addition to intense personal animosity, Nikon and Aleksei's government had radically different ideas about the relations of church and state in a Christian monarchy. In his lengthy *Refutation* of 1664 Nikon insisted in the strongest possible terms on the superiority of the spiritual power to the secular arm.[24] Therefore, in matters of principle such as, for example, the complete judicial independence of the church from lay justice, the church and its primate should prevail. Was Nikon, as he claimed, simply restating fundamental Orthodox principles? Many of his arguments and examples do indeed come from classic Orthodox texts. Nevertheless, the vehemence with which he made his case stretched the elastic Orthodox notion of the 'symphony' of church and state beyond breaking point. And, as many scholars have noted, Nikon borrowed some of his most telling images – for example, likening the church to the sun and secular government to the moon – from papal polemics of the high Middle Ages.[25] Finally, Nikon's attitudes ran counter to the tendency of governments and ecclesiastical leaders all across sixteenth- and seventeenth-century Europe to collaborate in making the church a force for maintaining political cohesion and social order, a process some historians call 'confessionalisation'.

In this situation, Aleksei had no choice but to replace Nikon. But with what procedures and on what grounds could a patriarch be deposed? It is a measure of the tsar's desperation that his most valuable agent in arranging Nikon's deposition was Paisios Ligarides, a former apostate to Roman Catholicism

---

24 W. Palmer, *The Patriarch and the Tsar* (London: Trübner and Co., 1871–76), I; Patriarch Nikon, *Patriarch Nikon on church and state – Nikon's 'Refutation' (Vozrazhenie ili razorenie smirennago Nikona, bozhieiu milostiiu Patriarkha, protiv voprosov boiarina Simeona Streshneva)*, ed. V. A. Tumins and G. Vernadsky (Berlin, New York and Amsterdam: Mouton, 1982).

25 Contrast M. V. Zyzykin, *Patriarkh Nikon: ego gosudarstvennyia i kanonicheskiia idei*, 3 vols. (Warsaw: Sinodal'naia Tipografiia, 1931–38), with Kapterev, *Patriarkh Nikon*.

who styled himself metropolitan of Gaza, an office from which he had been deposed. After a local ecclesiastical council in 1666 had been unable to reach a compromise whereby Nikon would abdicate the patriarchate, but maintain his episcopal dignity and administrative control of his favourite monasteries, the government chose a more radical solution, an 'ecumenical' council of eastern Orthodoxy with the participation of the other patriarchs, only two of whom actually appeared. Its decisions were a foregone conclusion. On 12 December 1666 the council deposed Nikon for dereliction of duty, insulting the tsar and mistreating the clergy, reduced him to the rank of an ordinary monk, and imprisoned him in the remote Ferapontov monastery.

The government and its ecclesiastical allies dealt with the critics of the reformed liturgy in a similar fashion. Taking a reconciliatory position, the local council of 1666 had proclaimed that the new rites were correct, but avoided condemning traditional Russian practices. Several of the leaders of the opposition, particularly Ivan Neronov and Aleksandr of Viatka, reconciled themselves with the new dispensation in order not to divide the body of Christ. Others resisted to the bitter end.

The ecumenical council of 1666–67 settled the issue simply and radically. It declared that only the reformed liturgy was true Orthodox usage and condemned traditional Russian practices and the *Stoglav*, which sanctioned them, as heretical. Simultaneously, its representatives exerted intense pressure on the recalcitrant critics of the new liturgy to recant. One, Nikita Dobrynin, yielded – temporarily as it turned out. Five others – Avvakum, Lazar, Epifanii, Nikifor and deacon Fedor – held out. All were defrocked, two had their tongues cut out for insulting the tsar, and all were sent to prison in Pustozersk on the Arctic coast.

The councils of 1666–67 had far-reaching implications for the future of the Russian Church. They made clear that Tsar Aleksei and his advisers – the secular government and its ecclesiastical allies – had decisive power over the church. Thereafter any religious dissenters understood correctly that the state was also their enemy.

Moreover, for better or worse, Aleksei's government chose to make scholars from Ukraine and the Greek world and their local disciples the intellectual leaders of the Russian Church. New understandings of the uses of language and new educational methods and artistic styles, based ultimately on Roman Catholic models, became norms for the cultural elite of the court and much of the church's leadership.

The decisions of 1666–67 appeared to have restored peace and uniformity to the Russian Church. The enforcement of the reformed liturgy seemed to proceed successfully. As Michels has shown, the Printing Office quickly sold each printing of the new service books and, by 1700, the new liturgical texts had spread to even the most remote parts of the realm.[26]

Matters were not so simple, however. Even in disgrace and prison, Nikon retained the allegiance of many of the faithful who revered him as the true patriarch and turned to him for spiritual counsel. He remained intransigent in his belief that the state – the agent of the Antichrist – had trampled on the rights of the church. Nevertheless, in 1681, Aleksei's son, Fedor, gave him permission to return to his beloved New Jerusalem, although he died before reaching it.

The origins of the Old Believers

On the other side, the determined defenders of traditional Russian practices – the Old Believers – understood full well that, after 1667, there could be no compromise with the official church or the state. Avvakum and his fellow prisoners smuggled virulent attacks on the new order to small groups of supporters in Moscow and elsewhere. Their execution at the stake in 1681 only added the authority of martyrdom to their teachings. Ironically, they agreed with Nikon, their old enemy, that the reign of the Antichrist, precursor of the Last Days, had begun.

Ultimately the decisions of 1666–67 had brought not peace but the sword. Outbursts of violent resistance to the state and the church became a regular feature of the Russian landscape in the last decades of the seventeenth century. Local grievances fuelled each uprising: opposition to the reformed church also played a prominent part in the rebels' demands. In the most dramatic instance, the Solovetskii monastery, long a law unto itself, rebelled against the imposition of the new liturgy and held out against besieging government troops from 1668 until 1676. Even though its surviving defenders were massacred, its example strengthened the determination of other opponents of the new order in state and church.

The bloody uprising in Moscow in 1682, in which Old Believers led by Nikita Dobrynin joined forces with the mutinous garrison, made the explosive mixture of political and religious opposition unmistakably clear. When Sophia emerged from the crisis as regent for her two brothers, her government issued the decree of December 1684, which mandated death at the stake for

26 Michels, *War*, 28–30, 143–4.

all unrepentant Old Believers and severe penalties for anyone who sheltered them, and enforced it even in the most remote areas of the country.[27]

The government's intransigence elicited equally militant responses. Scattered groups of religious radicals had already demonstrated the ultimate form of protest against the powers of this world – suicide by fire. Following their lead, in the 1680s and 1690s groups of militants seized isolated monasteries and villages – notoriously the Paleostrovskii monastery in 1687 and 1689 and Pudozh in 1693 – and, when government forces attacked them, burned themselves alive rather than surrender. These episodes of mass suicide, which combined social banditry and religious fanaticism, profoundly shocked the government, the church and more moderate Old Believers, one of whom, Evfrosin, in 1691 wrote a denunciation of the practice as a violation of the traditional Christian prohibition of suicide.[28]

The second response of the opponents of the reformed church was less spectacular but ultimately more successful. Many fled to remote corners of the realm or beyond the borders of the empire, founded unofficial communities, and began to adapt Orthodox liturgical observances to their new circumstances. Some fugitive groups soon fell victim to governmental persecution; others, such as the Vyg community, managed to survive and became the principal centres of the Old Belief in the first decades of the eighteenth century.

In the last years of the century, Patriarch Ioakim (1674–90) set the agendas for the official church. By background a member of the service nobility, he proved to be a strong-willed leader who, like Nikon, saw the patriarch as the personification of the church. At the same time, he understood the necessity of collaboration with the secular government. Within the ecclesiastical administration, he strove for a disciplined, clearly organised hierarchy free from the routine interference of the state. On the recommendations of the councils of 1666–67 and a local council of 1675, Ioakim abolished the *Monastyrskii Prikaz* in 1677 and replaced it with a system under which committees of clergymen conducted trials of churchmen and administered church lands.

Ioakim's understanding of the church required that the hierarchy, under the patriarch's leadership, control devotional life and ecclesiastical culture. In dealing with popular religion, Ioakim suppressed unofficial and unverifiable saints' cults, notably the veneration of Anna of Kashin. He also continued

---

27 *PSZRI*, II, 647–50 (no. 1102).
28 R. O. Crummey, *The Old Believers and the world of Antichrist: the Vyg community and the Russian state, 1694–1855* (Madison: University of Wisconsin Press, 1970), 39–57; G. B. Michels, 'The violent Old Belief: an examination of religious dissent on the Karelian frontier', *RH/HR* 19 (1992), 203–29.

his predecessors' sporadic attempts to make sure that all candidates for the priesthood were literate and committed to the official policies of the church.[29] Since, in his view, an embattled church required educated priests, he tried to found a theological academy in Moscow. The first two attempts, however, collapsed because of the theological and political controversies between the so-called Latinophile and Grecophile parties within the ecclesiastical elite – both of which, in reality, adapted international Latin scholarship to Orthodox uses.

His greatest achievement, however, was the agreement, concluded with the support of *Hetman* Samoilovych in 1686, that the new metropolitan of Kiev, Gedeon, would transfer his allegiance from Constantinople to the patriarch of Moscow. This accord ended a long period of conflict and ambiguity. Since 1657, the metropolitan church of Kiev had been divided along secular political lines: the metropolitans of Kiev had resided in Polish-controlled territory while the Moscow government and hierarchy recognised a 'vicar' of the Orthodox church in Left-Bank Ukraine.

Gedeon's consecration in Moscow put an end to the impasse. He was a strong candidate for the office. As bishop of Lutsk on the Right Bank, he staunchly defended the Orthodox cause at much personal cost. Many leading members of the clergy, however, strongly opposed him and refused to participate in the electoral synod because of his well-known conviction that the best way to defend Orthodoxy was to accept Moscow's jurisdiction over the church in Ukraine. Nevertheless, Gedeon and Samoilovych pressed on and, in the end, under great political pressure, a new ecumenical patriarch reluctantly accepted the new relationship between Moscow and Kiev.

Although Gedeon had done his best to guarantee the preservation of the independent traditions of the metropolitan church of Kiev, the Russian hierarchy soon began to treat dioceses and parishes in Ukraine just like any others in the Russian Orthodox Church. And since then, the fates of the Orthodox churches in Ukraine and Russia have been inextricably linked, with profound consequences for both.[30]

The partition of Ukraine after 1654 also changed the fate of the Uniate Church. On the verge of extinction during the Khmelnytsky revolt, the Uniates began to rebuild in the territories still ruled from Warsaw and, by the end of the seventeenth century, all of the Orthodox dioceses in the areas of Ukraine under Polish rule had accepted the union.

---

29 Michels, *War*, 31–2, 163–70, 187.
30 Kharlampovich, *Malorossiiskoe vliianie*, 214–32.

By the end of the seventeenth century, the Orthodox churches in Russia and Ukraine had achieved some of the goals they shared with the Catholic Reformation. The hierarchy exercised tighter control over diocesan and parish life, enforced a revised standardised liturgy, and collaborated with the secular authorities in maintaining public order and moral discipline. The Orthodox in Ukraine and Belarus had created a system of education and scholarship designed specifically to meet the challenge of Catholicism and, in the second half of the century, introduced them into Russian church life. If, institutionally, the Russian government and hierarchy had absorbed the Ukrainian church, Ukrainians came to dominate ecclesiastical culture and education in Russia. Thus the united church appeared formidable and seemed to enjoy the advantages of both traditions. In some ways, however, the appearance of strength was deceiving. In both Russia and Ukraine, part of the Orthodox flock had left the church. By 1700, the Uniate Church controlled all of the once-Orthodox dioceses in Ukraine west of the Dnieper and, to the east, the Old Believers had withdrawn from the official church into their own refuges of conservative Russian Orthodoxy. Finally, the longstanding dependence of the Russian church on the secular government left it vulnerable to a wilful reforming autocrat. When Peter I abolished the patriarchate and in 1721 created the holy synod to govern the church, Russian and Ukrainian Orthodox believers had to face radically new challenges.

14

The Russian Orthodox Church in imperial Russia 1721–1917

SIMON DIXON

Under pressure of revolutionary upheaval, the system of Russian ecclesiastical government established by Peter I in 1721 was swiftly dismantled in 1917. On 5 August the Provisional Government abolished the holy synod. Ten days later, an all-Russian church council gathered in Moscow in the hope of securing strong leadership in troubled times. Having determined to restore the patriarchate before the Bolshevik seizure of power, the delegates drew lots on 5 November to appoint Metropolitan Tikhon (Bellavin) from an elected shortlist of three to an office last held in 1700. Though circumstances forced Tikhon into crisis management rather than strategic direction, there was plenty of practical significance for the council to discuss: the synod had not only retained jurisdiction over marriage and divorce, but also continued to manage its own consistory courts, ecclesiastical schools, and the censorship of religious books.[1] Yet few churchmen were satisfied by mere administrative autonomy.[2] Many believed that by forcibly separating the secular sphere from the sacred, Peter had perverted the very nature of the church, reducing it to what Florovskii later described as a period of 'Babylonian captivity', in which Russia's 'ecclesiastical consciousness' was forced to develop under 'the dual inhibition of administrative decree and inner fear'.[3]

Anxious to explain rather than condemn, recent historians have modified many traditional stereotypes on the basis of unprecedented archival access. But now that new evidence has shown how misleading it is to dismiss the

1 G. L. Freeze, 'Handmaiden of the state? The church in imperial Russia reconsidered', *JEcclH* 36 (1985), 89. On these issues at the council, E. V. Beliakova, *Tserkovnyi sud i problemy tserkovnoi zhizni* (Moscow: Dukhovnaia biblioteka, 2004).
2 J. P. LeDonne, *Absolutism and ruling class: the formation of the Russian political order, 1700–1825* (New York: Oxford University Press, 1991), 334, n. 8.
3 G. Florovskii, *Puti russkogo bogosloviia*, second edition (Paris: YMCA, 1981), 89. For criticism of Peter at the council, D. Pospielovsky, *The Russian Church under the Soviet regime 1917–1982* (Crestwood, NY: St Vladimir's Seminary Press, 1984), I, 30; C. Evtuhov, 'The church in the Russian revolution: arguments for and against restoring the patriarchate at the church council of 1917–1918', *Slavic Review* 50 (1991), 503–6.

Russian Church as 'static, corrupt and intellectually barren',[4] it is all the more important, and in some ways more difficult, to understand why a far from monolithic institution found it so hard to respond to the spiritual needs of its flock. Though developments such as the social formation of the clergy inevitably reflected changing patterns of secular reform and counter-reform,[5] this chapter will suggest that the main motor of ecclesiastical change lay in complex currents of religious rivalry, driven from within and beyond Russia's multinational empire. The church's response to these challenges created as many difficulties for its mission as the restrictive framework imposed by the state.

The first century of the synodal regime

Like his father before him, Peter I (1682–1725) sought to emasculate the church's political power and exploit its material wealth. More ambitious than Aleksei Mikhailovich (1645–76), he saw religion as a means of disciplining rational and industrious subjects. Yet if the tsar's strategy was never in doubt, his tactics varied. When Patriarch Adrian died on 16 October 1700 – shortly after the declaration of war against Sweden on 19 August and a month before the Russian defeat at Narva on 19 November – Peter took the opportunity to seize temporary control of monastic revenues and to appoint an inexperienced Ukrainian, Stefan (Iavorskii), as *locum tenens* of the patriarchal throne. Though it was nowhere suggested that the patriarchate should be abolished, Stefan was obviously intended to be Peter's man: since his return from the grand embassy, the tsar had promoted Ukrainians not only as western-educated scholars capable of dispelling Muscovite ignorance, but also as a way of destabilising a potentially disloyal native episcopate. Stefan, however, was no cipher: between 1708 and 1712, he wrote, and sometimes gave, sermons openly critical of the tsar. Preoccupied by war in these years, Peter paid little attention to ecclesiastical affairs. Though he returned to them in 1715, it was not until 1718 that the trial of the tsarevich crushed most of the opponents who expected the tsar's death to herald the restoration of the patriarchate. Peter now moved towards its formal abolition under the guidance of Feofan (Prokopovich), a Ukrainian who had reacted against his Jesuit education in Rome in favour of an exalted view of the monarch's role in the church, which had something in common with the Protestant arguments Peter first heard in England in 1698 in conversation with

4 E. Keenan, 'Muscovite political folkways', *RR* 45 (1986), 164.
5 G. L. Freeze, *The parish clergy in nineteenth-century Russia: crisis, reform, counter-reform* (Princeton: Princeton University Press, 1983).

Bishop Gilbert Burnet. The *Spiritual Regulation* (*Dukhovnyi reglament*), commissioned from Feofan late in 1718 and published on 25 January 1721, argued that a collegial regime suited Russian circumstances better than the patriarchate, since a patriarch risked being mistaken for 'a kind of second sovereign, equal to or even greater than the autocrat himself'. At its first meeting on 14 February, Peter's new spiritual college was renamed the Most Holy Governing Synod (*Sviateishii Pravitel'svuiushchii sinod*), a title designed to echo the former patriarch's spiritual aura and the juridical authority of the senate. Unconvinced, the new body's 'archbishop president', Stefan (Iavorskii), was among the first to question its canonical legitimacy by seeking in vain to retain liturgical references to the eastern patriarchs to whom the Russian Church had nominally owed allegiance since Adrian's death.[6]

Divided in its leadership, institutionally embryonic, and no better equipped to implement its policies at local level than the secular power, the synod took time to establish its authority. The influence of the lay over-procurator, an office created in 1722, fluctuated according to the ability of the incumbent. Not until the 1740s were punitive measures against 'superstition'[7] reshaped into a positive campaign of popular religious instruction, and it was only then that the synod began to tighten its grip on diocesan administration on the basis of increasingly standardised bureaucratic procedures.[8] Mid-century achievements offered a new generation of bishops a platform for development in the reign of Catherine II (1762–96). As in the secular sphere, provincial progress remained haphazard, and the energy required to improve clerical performance was sometimes so fierce that charges of episcopal despotism seem hard to deny.[9] Yet prelates such as Platon (Levshin) and Gavriil (Petrov), who initially impressed the empress as preachers, partly shared her commitment to enlightened reform and were willing to express it in similarly rational terms.[10] Platon's brief period in active charge of the diocese of Moscow in the late-1770s

6 V. Zhivov, *Iz tserkovnoi istorii vremen Petra Velikago* (Moscow: Novoe literaturnoe obozrenie, 2004), comments on an extensive historiography including J. Cracraft, *The church reform of Peter the Great* (London: Macmillan, 1971).

7 A. I. Lavrov, *Koldovstvo i religiia v Rossii 1700–1740 gg.* (Moscow: Drevlekhranilishche, 2000), esp. 347–75; E. B. Smilianskaia, *Volshebniki, bogokhul'niki, eretiki: narodnaia religioznost' i 'dukhovnaia prestupleniia' v Rossii XVIII veka* (Moscow: Indrik, 2003).

8 G. L. Freeze, 'Institutionalizing piety: the church and popular religion, 1750–1850', in *Imperial Russia: new histories for the empire*, ed. J. Burbank and D. L. Ransel (Bloomington: Indiana University Press, 1998), 211–20.

9 See, for example, Samuil (Mislavskii)'s intemperate letters to the bursar of Rostov's episcopal palace, 1777–79, in A. I. Videneeva, *Rostovskii arkhiereiskii dom i sistema eparkhial'nogo upravleniia v Rossii XVIII veka* (Moscow: Nauka, 2004), 270–341.

10 V. M. Zhivov, *Iazyk i kul'tura v Rossii XVIII veka* (Moscow: Iazyki russkoi kul'tury, 1996), 368–73.

not only rid the old capital of troublesome vagrant clergy, but introduced in the process a controversial office that survived until 1917: that of 'upholders of good order' (*blagochinnye*). These were appointed supervisors, who replaced elected clerical elders as the consistory's principal diocesan agents.[11] As supernumerary priests were purged, so the quality of the remaining clergy was improved. Platon's commitment to clerical education helped to transform underfunded grammar schools into specialist theological seminaries whose empire-wide enrolments rose from 4673 in 1766 to 29,000 in 1808. Though brutalised by their teachers, isolated from their flock by a curriculum steeped in Latinity, and impoverished by their lowly social status, Russia's parish priests were now more professionally prepared than ever before.[12]

The age of Enlightenment may have left the Russian Church stronger in administrative terms, but its legacy of religious toleration was more complex. The reign of Elizabeth (1741–61) saw a determined attempt to challenge the schismatic communities, which had formed in response to persecution in the reign of her father, Peter I. Church and state also embarked in tandem on a conversion campaign that brought some 430,000 people – the overwhelming majority of Mordvins, Chuvash, Cheremis and Votiaks in the central Volga region – into Orthodoxy between 1741 and 1755.[13] But the wisdom of such initiatives was questioned when it emerged that local zealots had achieved their aims only by resorting to violence that their superiors had never intended (a pattern that was to recur in the nineteenth century). Under Catherine II, *raison d'état* combined with enlightened conviction to produce a gentler approach to mission. Muslims were treated with kid gloves in newly annexed territories in the south. Exiled schismatics were permitted to return from Poland, and though sceptical churchmen sought to impede the impact of toleration,[14] Old Believers were relieved of the obligation to pay a double poll tax in 1782 and confirmed, three years later, in their right to elect (and be elected) to posts in urban government. Hopes were raised in the 1780s that a new 'unitary faith'

11 K. A. Papmehl, *Metropolitan Platon of Moscow (Petr Levshin, 1737–1812): the enlightened prelate, scholar and educator* (Newtonville, MA: Oriental Research Partners, 1983), 55–8. Cf. Platon, *Instruktsiia blagochinnym iereiam ili protoiereiam* (Moscow, 1775).

12 G. L. Freeze, *The Russian Levites: parish clergy in the eighteenth century* (Cambridge, MA: Harvard University Press, 1977), ch. 4; table 3, 88.

13 M. Khodarkovsky, 'The conversion of non-Christians in early modern Russia', in *Of religion and empire: missions, conversion and tolerance in tsarist Russia*, ed. R. P. Geraci and M. Khodarkovsky (Ithaca, NY: Cornell University Press, 2001), 115–43; P. W. Werth, 'Coercion and conversion: violence and the mass baptism of the Volga peoples, 1740–55', *Kritika* 4 (2003), 543–69.

14 See, for example, G. L. Bruess, *Religion, identity and empire: a Greek archbishop in the Russia of Catherine the Great* (Boulder, CO: East European Monographs, 1997), 135–76.

(*edinoverie*), permitting Old Believers to retain their own ritual provided they acknowledged the authority of the church, might draw them back into the fold. But by 1818 Filaret (Drozdov) was among those bishops who feared that the Old Believers had instead profited from a long period of relative quiescence to build in number and strength to the point where they threatened to 'seduce' Orthodox into the schism.[15]

Filaret was the leading representative of a new current of thought that sought to strengthen the church by recovering its apostolic roots and recasting its teachings in a distinctively Russian mode.[16] It had taken almost sixty years to bring about a critical approach to western learning. First to feel the pinch in the 1760s were the Ukrainian bishops, whose 'shameful' influence was blamed by Sumarokov for the 'incorrect and provincial dialect' allegedly adopted by the clergy as a whole.[17] Yet the Russian Metropolitan Platon still required Orthodox schools to teach in Latin as a way of preserving the church's scholarly respectability in the west: the vernacular was introduced only gradually after 1808. Not until 1820 was it typical for Evgenii (Bolkhovitinov) to condemn Feofilakt (Gorskii)'s theology, published in Latin in Leipzig in 1784, for 'disgracing not only himself but the whole Russian Church in front of foreigners' because 'whole pages of it were copied from Lutheran theologians!!!'[18] Antipathy towards foreign learning was matched by growing hostility towards the fashionable mysticism that blurred denominational distinctions under the umbrella of universal Christianity in the reign of Alexander I (1801–25): the symbol of Prince A. N. Golitsyn's cosmopolitan approach to religion, the Russian Bible Society founded in 1813, was abolished nine years later. By then, foreign influences had come under unprecedented Orthodox pressure. Banished from St Petersburg and Moscow in 1815, the Jesuits were forbidden the empire in 1820; freemasonry was suppressed along with other secret societies in 1822; later in the decade, British missions in Siberia attracted hostile surveillance

---

15 Though precise numbers are impossible to calculate, the sixfold increase recorded by the synod between 1764 and 1825 was probably an underestimate: Freeze, 'The rechristianization of Russia', 248, n. 136. See also, P. Pera, 'Despotismo illuminato e dissenso religioso: I vecchi credenti nell'età di Caterina II', *Rivista Storica Italiana* 97 (1985), 501–617; G. L. Freeze, 'The rechristianization of Russia: the church and popular religion, 1750–1850', *Studia Slavica Finlandensia* 7 (1990), 107–8.

16 R. L. Nichols, 'Orthodoxy and Russia's Enlightenment', in *Russian Orthodoxy under the old regime*, ed. R. L. Nichols and T. G. Stavrou (Minneapolis: University of Minnesota Press, 1978), 83–4.

17 A. P Sumarokov, 'O pravopisanie', in *Polnoe sobranie vsekh sochinenii*, second edition (Moscow: Universitetskaia tipografiia, 1787), x, 24.

18 I. K. Grot (ed.), 'Perepiska Evgeniia s grafom D. I. Khvostovym', in *Sbornik statei chitannykh v otdelenii russkago iazyka i slovesnosti Imperatorskoi Akademii Nauk* (St Petersburg: Tipografiia imperatorskoi akademii nauk, 1868), v: 1, 187, 20 May 1820.

from Orthodox diocesan authorities and most were closed down in the 1830s. No longer content to be first among equals in its own empire, the Russian Church wanted to dominate: but domination on its own terms proved an elusive goal.

Heterodox challenges

Superficially, the reign of Nicholas I (1825–55) was a period of militant Orthodox regeneration marked by diocesan expansion and state-sponsored conversion campaigns. The process began where the need seemed greatest: in the west, where the Uniate Church was formally 'reunited' with Orthodoxy in 1839 in the aftermath of the Polish revolt of 1830. A further burst of activity followed in the mid-1840s. Targeted in earnest from 1843, approximately half the 50,000 Jewish recruits under the age of eighteen were baptised in the army by 1855; some 800 pagan Maris in the Orenburg region were baptised in 1845; and in the diocese of Riga, established in 1836, at least 74,000 Latvians and Estonians were accepted into Orthodoxy between 1845 and 1847 during the episcopate of Filaret (Gumilevskii).[19] In the following decade, the theological academy established at Kazan in 1842 became the centre of professor N. I. Il'minskii's mission to teach Christianity in their native languages to Muslim children of the Volga and Urals regions.[20]

These campaigns cannot be lightly dismissed: though many Tatars understood little of their new faith at the time of their baptism, the Christian identity of their descendants remained sufficiently firm to create a problem for Soviet authorities in the 1920s.[21] However, since some 'conversions' were motivated by violence or the promise of elusive material incentives, many proved insincere: Russians were obliged to celebrate the 'end' of the Uniate Church on at least two further occasions, in 1875 and 1946, and it flourishes still today. No less alarming was a growing sense that, like the Old Believers, the church's heterodox rivals were sufficiently vigorous not only to maintain their own

---

19 J. D. Klier, 'State policies and the conversion of Jews in imperial Russia', in *Of religion and empire*, 102–4; P. W. Werth, 'Baptism, authority, and the problem of *zakonnost'* in Orenburg diocese: the induction of over 800 "pagans" into the Christian faith', *Slavic Review* 56 (1997), 456–80; W. Kahle, *Die Begegnung des baltischen Protestantismus mit der russisch-orthodoxen Kirche* (Leiden: E. J. Brill, 1959), esp. 104–23.

20 R. P. Geraci, *Window on the East: national and imperial identities in late tsarist Russia* (Ithaca, NY: Cornell University Press, 2001), chs. 2 and 4.

21 P. W. Werth, 'From "pagan" Muslims to "baptized" communists: religious conversion and ethnic particularity in Russia's eastern provinces', *Comparative Studies in Society and History* 42 (2000), 497–523.

confessional identity, but even to tempt ignorant Russians, if not into outright apostasy, then certainly into insidious error.

It was therefore disconcerting for the church to find state support for Orthodox proselytism withdrawn once excessive clerical zeal prompted civil unrest. Prince A. A. Suvorov, governor-general of the Baltic provinces from 1848 to 1861, was openly disrespectful to Orthodox clergy, surrounding the bishop's palace in Riga with troops to prevent Filaret (Gumilevskii) from attempting further conversions. Alexander II's secret decision to release Lutherans in mixed marriages from the obligation to baptise their children into Orthodoxy allowed between 30,000 and 40,000 Estonians and Latvians to revert to Lutheranism between 1865 and 1874.[22] Only in the Crimea – from where Innokentii (Borisov) complained in 1852 that 'the ruling religion is in many cases so only in name' because 'real rights' lay 'with foreign faiths and even those who are not Christians' – was it accepted that the Tatars were a security risk: rumours of a purge in 1856 accounted for the exodus, over the following decade, of at least half a million and perhaps 900,000 Muslims to the Ottoman Empire.[23] Bishops elsewhere discovered that provincial governors in the 1860s and 1870s were prepared to offer a measure of protection to the church's rivals, either in order to keep the peace, as in Zabaikal, or, as in the case of Turkestan's Mikhail von Kaufman, because they regarded religion as a matter belonging to the private sphere.[24] When even the schismatic Old Belief came to seem attractive to the tsarist regime as a repository of conservative values in unsettled times, the road to wider toleration was open.

Bishops were left to rue the consequences of institutional overstretch as men better suited to the scholarly life were thrust into the hostile environment of the borderlands or of dioceses 'infected' by the schism. 'Everything [in Riga] is alien', complained Filaret (Gumilevskii) in 1842, 'and everything that I call my own is far away'.[25] 'If it pleases God for me to be here', wrote Leontii

22 A. Chumikov, 'General-gubernatorstvo kniazia A. A. Suvorova v pribaltiiskom krae, 1848–1861', Russkii Arkhiv 28 (1890), III, 58–88; Russification in the Baltic Provinces and Finland, 1855–1914, ed. E. C. Thaden (Princeton: Princeton University Press, 1981), 44–6, 50, 55–6.
23 T. Butkevich, Innokentii Borisov, byvshii arkhiepiskop khersonskii (St Petersburg: I. L. Tuzov, 1887), 350–4; A. W. Fisher, 'Emigration of Muslims from the Russian empire in the years after the Crimean War', Jahrbücher für Geschichte Osteuropas 35 (1987), 356–71.
24 K. Kharlampovich, 'K biografii Veniamina, arkhiepiskopa irkutskago', Khristianskoe Chtenie (1906), II, 139–44; D. Brower, 'Russian roads to Mecca: religious tolerance and Muslim pilgrimage in the Russian empire', Slavic Review 55 (1996), 569–70.
25 S. Smirnov (ed.), Pis'ma Filareta, arkhiepiskopa chernigovskago k A. V. Gorskomu (Moscow: M. G. Volnaninov, 1885), 86, 28 August 1842. Savva (Tikhomirov), Rechi govorennyia v raznoe vremia (Tver': Gubernskoe pravlenie, 1892), 138, expresses similar sentiments about Polotsk in the late 1860s.

(Lebedinskii) from Podolia in 1865, 'then it is my duty to oppose evil', but he made no attempt to conceal the misery of his 'struggles' with the Poles.[26] Huge sums were raised to transform landmarks such as the Pochaev lavra in Volhynia, retaken from the Basilians in 1837, into recognisably Orthodox holy places. But most new dioceses offered their leaders distinctly inferior accommodation: 'the decrepitude of this most meagre and uncomfortable shelter', declared the renowned ascetic Ignatii (Brianchaninov) on arrival in Stavropol in 1858, 'has made it quite impossible for a bishop to live in'.[27] Were such complaints merely redolent of the episcopal pomposity ridiculed by Leskov in *The Little Things in a Bishop's Life*, they would scarcely be worthy of emphasis. But they signified something more important than that. Isolated, insecure and further depressed by pessimistic bulletins from Russian missions as far apart as Japan and the Holy Land, many leading churchmen were persuaded that Orthodoxy was endangered even in Russia itself.

Intellectual responses

In an attempt to strengthen the church, scholars intensified the quest begun by Filaret (Drozdov) for an authentic Russian Orthodoxy. By the 1880s, that search had crystallised into a sharply confessionalised sense of *tserkovnost'* (church-mindedness)[28] derived from research at the theological academies of Moscow, Kiev, St Petersburg and Kazan. Since the initial step was to purge Orthodox teachings of foreign impurities, students were encouraged to 'draw a clear line between that which is strictly ours and all that should be alien to us'.[29] Patristic texts, their principal primary resource, were translated on the basis of a programme adopted in 1843 and published, along with a mountain of theological scholarship, in the academies' learned journals. The fundamental discipline was history: an expedient antidote to biblical excess; a technically sophisticated subject thanks to contemporary German developments; and

26 'Pis'ma moskovskago mitropolita Leontiia (Lebedinskago)', *Chteniia v obshchestve istorii i drevnostei rossiiskikh pri Moskovskom universitete* (1908), II: IV, 26, to Prot N. I. Ogloblin, 22 August 1865.

27 Quoted in L. Sokolov, *Episkop Ignatii Brianchaninov: ego zhizn', lichnost' i moral'no asketicheskiia vozreniia* (Kiev: Tipografiia I-yi Kievskoi arteli pechatnago dela, 1915), I, 237.

28 The *exclusive*, confessional aspect of '*tserkovnost'*' is missing from the penetrating analysis of the concept's *inclusive*, communal meanings in V. Shevzov, 'Letting the people into church: reflections on Orthodoxy and community in late imperial Russia', in *Orthodox Russia: belief and practice under the tsars*, ed. V. A. Kivelson and R. H. Greene (University Park: Pennsylvania State University Press, 2003), 67–71.

29 I. A. Iakhontov, *Sobranie dukhovnykh literaturnykh trudov, 1844–1885* (St Petersburg: V. S. Balashov, 1885–90), II, 2: St Petersburg undergraduate dissertation, 1843.

an ideal tool for an enterprise designed to peel away layers of inauthentic accretions in search of apostolic origins. Though Lord Acton may not have realised it, here was a context where history did indeed go on 'invading other provinces, resolving system into process, and getting the better of philosophy – for a whole generation'.[30]

In some ways, however, the church's scholars became victims of their own success. In the face of rapidly accumulating evidence, the attempt to differentiate Orthodoxy lost its initial clarity of focus. Though cataloguing projects offered a safe retreat from philosophical speculation and a valuable preliminary to research – Savva (Tikhomirov)'s catalogue of the synodal library and vestry went through three editions in as many years[31] – the riches they revealed were overwhelming, and it was always possible that more remained to be discovered. No sooner had the liturgist A. A. Dmitrievskii completed his work on the manuscript holdings of Orthodox monasteries in Palestine than he began to contemplate work in western Europe.[32] Scholars who planned an edition of the Slavonic Bible's 'fundamental texts' in 1915 proposed to examine some 4300 Old Testament manuscripts.[33] As the prospects of further work stretched towards infinity, so the chances of definitive conclusions dwindled. Though most Orthodox scholars unwittingly illustrated Trevor-Roper's claim that specialists 'in any subject, by a kind of natural law, tend to bury themselves deeper and deeper in the *minutiae* of their own dogma', none would have shared his preference for 'fertile error' over 'sterile accuracy'.[34] No Russian theologian who sought to 'correct' the service books could escape the shadow of the schism, a product of some notoriously fertile errors in the seventeenth century.[35] So long as it seemed wiser to enumerate defects in current practice than to suggest improvements, hesitation and confusion were bound to prevail. The entire history of the translation of the Bible into Russian – contentious since the collapse of the Bible Society and further discredited by the discovery in 1841 of unauthorised translations by G. P. Pavskii – may be characterised as an

30 Quoted in H. Butterfield, *Man on his past* (Cambridge: Cambridge University Press, 1955), 98.
31 *Ukazatel' dlia obozreniia Moskovskoi Patriarshei nyne, Sinodal'noi, riznitsy i biblioteki*, third edition (Moscow: Universitetskaia tipografiia, 1858). See also *Opisanie Slavianskikh rukopisei Moskovskoi Sinodal'noi biblioteki*, ed. A. V. Gorskii and K. I. Nevostruev, 3 parts (Moscow: Sinodal'naia tipografiia, 1855–69).
32 B. I. Sove, 'Russkii Goar i ego shkola', *Bogoslovskie Trudy* 4 (1968), 39–89.
33 K. I. Logachev (ed.), 'Dokumenty Bibleiskoi Komissii, II: organizatsiia, printsipy raboty i deiatel'nost' komissii, 1915–1921', *Bogoslovskie Trudy* 14 (1975), 167–8.
34 H. R. Trevor-Roper, *History, professional and lay: an inaugural lecture delivered before the University of Oxford on 12 November 1957* (Oxford: Oxford University Press, 1957), 19, 22.
35 B. I. Sove, 'Problema ispravleniia bogosluzhebnykh knig v Rossii v XIX–XX vekakh', *Bogoslovskie Trudy* 5 (1970), 25–68.

obsession with error. Even the official version, completed in 1870 three years after the death of its principal sponsor, Filaret (Drozdov), was vulnerable to charges of inaccuracy.[36] On the central question of Orthodox attitudes to the west, a leading scholar admitted in 1885 that 'no definitive programme' had yet been worked out.[37] Nor was the position any clearer with regard to church music, which the composer Iurii Izvekov dismissed in 1913 as 'a jumble of contradictory viewpoints, irreconcilable ideas and unsystematised accretions'.[38]

Worse still, the church could find no way of resolving the sorts of debate that inevitably arose from theological research based on patristic sources that were themselves shot through with disagreement. Rivalry between orders had been a key strength of the Catholic Reformation. Not only did Orthodoxy lack such orders, but the very nature of its claim to a monopoly of truth also militated against diversity of opinion. As Meyendorff wrote of an earlier period, 'if there is a feature of "Russian" Orthodoxy which can be seen as a contrast to the Byzantine perception of Christianity, it is the nervous concern of the Russians in preserving the very letter of the tradition received from "the Greeks"'.[39] So the greatest stumbling block in what was essentially a creative enterprise was the supposed immutability of the tradition that Russian scholars sought to defend, and yet were paradoxically obliged at least in part to re-create.[40] No allowance was made for doctrinal development. As early as 1840 A. N. Murav'ev contrasted the position of the early church, when much was still 'indeterminate', with that of his own day, in which 'all things have been decided and classed and catalogued'. 'We must not "move the landmarks"', he insisted to the Oxford divine William Palmer: 'We do not live now in the age of the Councils when . . . things could be changed.'[41] In

36 I. A. Chistovich, *Istoriia perevoda Biblii na russkii iazyk*, second edition (St Petersburg: M. M. Stasiulevich, 1899); S. K. Batalden, 'Gerasim Pavskii's clandestine Old Testament: the politics of nineteenth-century Russian biblical translation', *Church History* 57 (1988), 486–98.

37 A. P. Lopukhin, 'Sovremennyi zapad v religiozno-nravstvennom otnoshenii', *Khristianskoe Chtenie* 2 (1885), 450.

38 Quoted by V. Morosan, 'Liturgical singing or sacred music? Understanding the aesthetic of the new Russian choral school', in *Christianity and the arts in Russia*, ed. W. C. Brumfield and M. M. Velimirović (Cambridge: Cambridge University Press, 1991), 128.

39 J. Meyendorff, *Byzantium and the rise of Russia: a study of Byzantino-Russian relations in the fourteenth century* (Cambridge: Cambridge University Press, 1981), 25.

40 This difficulty also complicated collaborations between secular and ecclesiastical scholars on the rediscovery of Byzantine notation and the restoration of medieval Russian icons: see *Russkaia dukhovnaia muzyka v dokumentakh i materialakh*, ed. S. Zvereva et al. (Moscow: Iazyk slavianskoi kul'tury, 1998–2002) and G. I. Vzdornov, *Istoriia otkrytiia i izucheniia russkoi srednevekovoi zhivopisi: XIX vek* (Moscow: Iskusstvo, 1986).

41 *Notes of a visit to the Russian church in the years 1840, 1841*, by the late William Palmer, MA, selected and arranged by Cardinal Newman (London: Kegan Paul Trench, 1882), 163, 225.

such a climate, it was not so much secular censors who inhibited theological discussion as churchmen themselves. 'Orthodoxy has no system, and should not have one', declared the Slavophile Iurii Samarin.[42] But it was hard for Russian scholars reliant on German systematic theology to navigate between the extremes of imitation and denigration. Too often, their 'denunciatory theology' (oblichitel'noe bogoslovie) was marked by a shrillness of tone that invited Vladimir Solov'ev to respond in kind:

> This pseudo-Orthodoxy of your theological school, which has nothing in common with the faith of the Universal Church or with the piety of the Russian people, contains not a single positive element, but only arbitrary denials, which are the product of a polemic nurtured by *parti-pris* . . . All your 'Orthodoxy' and the whole of your 'Russian Idea' are therefore at bottom only a national protest against the universal power of the pope. But in whose name? Here lie the origins of the true difficulty of your situation.[43]

Pastoral responses

Conscious of their scholarly imperfections, Orthodox nevertheless intended their research to underpin vigorous pastoral action. The need for such action was confirmed by a major synodal inquiry of 1818–21, which determined to increase the church's influence over a predominantly illiterate society by intensifying its teaching role (uchitel'stvo).[44] Improved preaching offered one obvious way forward. 'Nothing is better written than our sermons', declared the young liberal Nikolai Turgenev in 1815, complimenting Russian bishops on their 'native intelligence' and classical learning: 'Unfortunately, very few of us read sermons.'[45] So long as most remained elaborate works of literature rather than simple homilies, the problem seemed likely to persist. 'What sort of sermon covers seventy pages?' enquired the mordant Metropolitan Filaret in 1833. 'And who would hear it out?'[46] An effective revival of preaching required scholars to refine an authentically Orthodox homiletics, bishops to inspire

42 *Socheneniia Iu. F. Samarina*, 12 vols. (Moscow: Tipographiia A. I. Mamontova, 1878–1911), v, 163.
43 V. Soloviev, *La Russie et l'église universelle* (Paris: Nouvelle librairie parisienne, 1889), 18, 20.
44 Freeze, 'The rechristianization of Russia', 109–10.
45 E. I. Tarasov (ed.), *Dnevniki Nikolaia Ivanovicha Turgeneva za 1811–1816 gody* (St Petersburg: Tipografiia imperatorskoi akademii nauk, 1913), II, 299–300, 26 June 1815.
46 Savva (ed.), *Pis'ma Filareta, mitropolita moskovskago k kolomenskago k vysochaishim osobam i raznym drugim litsam* (Tver': Gubernskoe pravlenie, 1888), 67, Filaret to Gavriil (Rozanov), 21 October 1833.

clergy to master an unfamiliar activity, and priests to communicate well with their flock. None of these aims could be accomplished quickly, and there were obvious risks in exposing incompetent novices to the mockery of their parishioners or to forensic examination by experienced Old Believer *nachetchiki*. Yet the synod persisted in its efforts to stimulate pastoral commitment, gathering systematic information on clerical performance in the 1840s, and the church displayed an increasing interest in contemporary social problems exemplified in the writings of Archimandrite Fedor (Bukharev) and the Moscow journal, *The Orthodox Review (Pravoslavnoe Obozrenie)*. The most significant practical developments came in urban areas after 1880. Impatient with progress in the parishes, where it often proved difficult to persuade clergy to assume an extra burden, activist clerics in St Petersburg founded the 'Society for the Propagation of Religious and Moral Enlightenment in the Spirit of the Orthodox Church' in 1881 in order to provide teams of preachers to evangelise the city's population. From modest beginnings in the dockland, the society grew to build its own churches and to supply an active mission to the capital's factories and halls. In 1887–88, some 50,000 workers attended 161 lectures across the city; by 1904 the society claimed that its 6000 lectures had attracted a total audience of two million.[47]

Nor was it thought sufficient to preach. Antonii (Vadkovskii) urged students at the St Petersburg theological academy in 1888 to 'continue Christ's work on earth, show people the true meaning of life, help the destitute, heal grieving hearts, preach emancipation to prisoners, give sight to the blind, and liberate the tormented'. These, he pointed out, were tasks that demanded that churchmen 'say less and do more'.[48] Antonii was as good as his word, retaining a personal commitment to prison visiting throughout his episcopate. A much wider range of churchmen, long conscious of unfavourable western contrasts between the 'fecundity' of Roman philanthropy and the 'sterility' of Russian provision, had made serious attempts to offer systematic charity to the poor.[49] The monastic almsgiving at the core of eighteenth-century

---

47 P. Valliere, *Modern Russian theology – Bukharev, Soloviev, Bulgakov: Orthodox theology in a new key* (Edinburgh: T. & T. Clark, 2000), ch. 2; S. Dixon, 'The church's social role in St. Petersburg, 1880–1914', in *Church, nation and state in Russia and Ukraine*, ed. G. A. Hosking (London: Macmillan, 1991), 167–92; P. Herrlinger, 'Orthodoxy and the experience of factory life in St. Petersburg, 1881–1905', in *New labor history: worker identity and experience, 1840–1918*, ed. M. Melancon and A. K. Pate (Bloomington, IN: Slavica, 2002), 33–66, at 55.

48 *Slova i rechi Antoniia, episkopa Vyborskago, rektora S.-Peterburgskago dukhovnoi akademii* (St Petersburg: Sinodal'naia tipografiia, 1890), 115–16.

49 Père Theiner, *L'église schismatique russe, d'après les relations récentes du prétendu Saint-Synode*, trad. de l'italien par monseigneur Luquet (Paris: Gaume frères, 1846), lvii.

Russian philanthropy could no longer cope with the social consequences of urbanisation, and critics of begging thought it 'too idealistic for contemporary conditions'.[50] Just as they had turned to the west for theological expertise, so it was natural to compare Orthodox pastoral work with contemporary Protestant and Catholic practice. As Gladstone had demanded in a parallel inquiry: 'Why should not the sounder scheme have the advantage of that organisation, through which the more erroneous one has recovered from a state of extreme and nearly desperate exhaustion, and still maintains a fight against a portion at least of her adversaries on something like equal terms?'[51] The SPCK and the Salvation Army were among the models that attracted Orthodox attention. Ultimately, however, they settled for confraternities (*bratstva*), on the model of those formed to defend Orthodoxy against Latin proselytism in Lithuania and Ukraine in the sixteenth century, which offered a more fruitful way forward than the often lifeless parish trusteeships formed in the 1860s. In St Petersburg, Father Aleksandr Gumilevskii showed what could be done: having founded a journal, *The Spirit of a Christian* (*Dukh khristianina*) in 1861, he went on to establish a charitable society in one of the capital's poorest parishes – the Sands – where he achieved a popular and successful realisation of his vision of an Orthodox brotherhood as 'a living Christian union of Orthodox people, warmed by Christian love'.[52]

Monastic impulses

Though much remained to be done, the Orthodox response to the challenge of heterodoxy had made signal advances by the end of the nineteenth century. Yet pastoral initiatives founded on theological research had never lacked critics within the church. A monk whom Palmer encountered at Sergiev Pustyn in 1840 'kept repeating that prayer and holiness have more efficacy than learning' and, when Palmer suggested that the church needed both, gave the impression that 'the current had already set far too much in the direction of intellectual cultivation'.[53] For the rest of the imperial period, the monasteries offered an

---

50 G. P. Smirnov-Platonov in *Detskaia Pomoshch'* 1 (1885), 48–54. On the eighteenth century, see J. M. Hartley, 'Philanthropy in the reign of Catherine the Great: aims and realities', in *Russia in the age of the Enlightenment*, ed. R. Bartlett and J. M. Hartley (London: Macmillan, 1990), 167–202.

51 W. E. Gladstone, *Church principles considered in their results* (London: John Murray, 1840), 397–8.

52 A. Lindenmeyr, *Poverty is not a vice: charity, society and the state in imperial Russia* (Princeton: Princeton University Press, 1996), 129–36.

53 *Notes of a visit to the Russian church*, 201.

alternative form of piety, distinct from, and sometimes in competition with, the work of the secular clergy.

It scarcely seemed likely in the eighteenth century that a Russian religious revival would be carried on a monastic 'wave of holiness'. Monasticism was a prime target of the *Spiritual Regulation*, and since Peter's immediate successors did nothing to mitigate his hostility to 'useless' contemplation, the number of religious of both sexes almost halved from 25,207 in 1724 to 14,282 in 1738. Prompted by urgent fiscal need in the wake of the Seven Years War, Catherine II took the antimonastic trend to its logical conclusion by expropriating the monasteries' lands and peasantry in 1764. Some 496 Russian houses were abolished in the process, 136 of them convents.[54] Apart from the Trinity lavra at Sergiev Posad, the Alexander Nevsky lavra founded by Peter I in his new capital, and the Chudov monastery in the Moscow Kremlin, only 67 convents and 319 monasteries survived the empress's reform outside Ukraine, 161 of which were entitled to no official endowment under the new regulations. Yet the nadir was still to come. For the next thirty years, even the limited establishments of the remaining houses proved impossible to fill as aspirants were inhibited from taking their vows by a combination of explicit imperial disapproval and a covert attack on monastic values by archpriest Pëtr Alekseev of Moscow's Archangel Cathedral, a prominent member of the white clergy, who was anxious to discredit Metropolitan Platon.[55] Had Potemkin prevailed, the consequences might have been still more severe. In 1786, the theologically adept prince, who twelve years earlier had himself ostentatiously retreated to the Alexander Nevsky lavra during a period of personal crisis, argued that no more than three monasteries were required for 'straightforward monks' in the whole of Russia: the remainder should be either closed or converted to hospitals, schools and almshouses.[56]

This grim picture helps to explain why only three monks were resident at Optina pustyn by the turn of the century, one of whom was blind.[57] Yet it was from a hermitage attached to this monastery in Kaluga province that three

---

54 V. V. Zverinskii, *Materialy dlia istoriko-topograficheskago issledovaniia o pravoslavnykh monastyriakh v Rossiiskoi imperii* (St Petersburg: V. Bezobrazov, 1890–97), I, x–xii.

55 B. V. Titlinov, *Gavriil Petrov: Mitropolit novgorodskii i sanktpeterburgskii: ego zhizn' i deiatel'nost', v sviazi s tserkovnymi delami togo vremeni* (Petrograd: M. Merkushev, 1916), 681–714; O. A. Tsapina, 'Secularization and opposition in the time of Catherine the Great', in *Religion and politics in enlightenment Europe*, ed. J. E. Bradley and D. K. Van Kley (Notre Dame, IN: University of Notre Dame Press, 2001), 342–3, 350–71.

56 Quoted *in extenso* by N. N. Lisovoi, 'Vosemnadtsatyi vek v istorii russkogo monashestva', in *Monashestvo i monastyri v Rossii: XI–XX veka*, ed. N. V. Sinitsyna (Moscow: Nauka, 2002), 200–1.

57 J. B. Dunlop, *Staretz Amvrosy* (London: Mowbrays, 1975), 33.

spiritual elders (*startsy*) – Leonid (Nagolkin), Makarii (Ivanov) and Amvrosii (Grenkov), the model for Dostoevsky's Father Zosima in *The Brothers Karamazov* – were to achieve, from 1829, 'a kind of informal reintegration of Russian culture, in both its high and low variants, in a way which neither the imperial state nor the intellectuals were able to emulate'.[58] Their inspiration came from Mount Athos. Alienated by the scholasticism imparted to pupils at Kiev's Mogila academy – 'within their souls there is darkness and gloom, though upon their tongues there be all manner of wisdom'[59] – Paisii (Velychkovskii) travelled to Athos in search of spiritual enlightenment in 1746. Seventeen years later, he left to establish his own monastery at Neamț in Moldavia, attracting some 700 monks by the time of his death in 1794. It was from there that his disciples transmitted to Russia the hesychast tradition of spiritual direction that inspired so many prominent nineteenth-century intellectuals, from Ivan Kireevskii to Leo Tolstoy.[60]

The *startsy*'s care for female souls is only one reason for Russia's participation in the European feminisation of religion. While some women ultimately acquired a sufficient aura of holiness to dispense spiritual advice of their own,[61] most Russian nuns were humble in both origin and intent. Though individual motives are often obscure, economic need almost certainly added urgency to the spiritual conviction of many peasants who devoted their lives to God. The scale of the movement is not in doubt. Between 1850 and 1912, the total numbers of male religious, including novices, rose from 9997 to 21,201: but this represents relative stagnation alongside the growth in female numbers from 8533 to 70,453.[62] Responding to popular demand, Catherine II authorised the first autonomous women's communities almost immediately after the secularisation of 1764. Some 217 such communities had been formed by 1907, 86 of them after 1890. Of the 156 founded between 1764 and 1894, two-thirds ultimately became official convents, as the hierarchy, led by Filaret (Drozdov), belatedly recognised the opportunity to sponsor rather than to spurn exemplars of a disciplined, communal life.[63] Most such communities were small,

58 G. Hosking, *Russia: people and empire, 1552–1917* (London: HarperCollins, 1997), 241.
59 *The life of Paisij Velyčkovs'kyj*, trans. J. M. E. Featherstone (Cambridge, MA: Harvard University Press, 1989), 18.
60 R. L. Nichols, 'The Orthodox elders (*Startsy*) of imperial Russia', *Modern Greek Studies Yearbook* 1 (1985), 1–30.
61 B. Meehan-Waters, 'The authority of holiness: women ascetics and spiritual elders in nineteenth-century Russia', in *Church, nation and state in Russia and Ukraine*, 38–51.
62 I. Smolitsch, *Geschichte der russischen Kirche 1700–1917* (Leiden: E. J. Brill, 1964), 1, 713.
63 B. Meehan, 'Popular piety, local initiative, and the founding of women's religious communities in Russia, 1764–1907', in *Seeking God: the recovery of religious identity in Orthodox Russia, Ukraine, and Georgia*, ed. S. K. Batalden (DeKalb: Northern Illinois University

and their charitable activities modest. However, where a wealthy foundress offered the prospect of greater scope, the risks increased in proportion to the scale of the enterprise. The Vladychne-Pokrovskaia community of Sisters of Mercy, founded with the support of the Moscow hierarchy in 1869, collapsed in debt within five years and its foundress, Mother Mitrofaniia, born Baroness Praskov'ia Grigor'evna Rosen (1825–98), was placed under synodal investigation.[64] In the wake of such a scandal, one can understand why Metropolitan Isidor (Nikol'skii) deterred his own acolyte, Mother Evfaliia, from converting her Vvedenskaia community near Kiev into a convent and frustrated her ambition to become abbess of some 500 sisters in 1885 on the grounds that she would 'not be able to control such a big family'.[65] Consistently well-managed institutions such as the convent of the Exaltation of the Cross at Nizhnii Novgorod nevertheless proved highly successful, profiting from its position at the centre of Russia's trade routes in a period of rapid industrialisation.[66]

Though some monasteries were notorious centres of drunkenness and immorality, of the sort that prompted the tsar himself to instigate a synodal investigation in 1901, many remained vigorous centres of pilgrimage to the end of the old regime. Smaller monasteries proved vulnerable both to inflation and to conscription in the First World War. Those in the western battlegrounds were particularly badly affected. But many of the larger monasteries and convents actively participated in the war effort at a time when much of the rest of the church, as we shall now see, had been driven deep into crisis.[67]

The church in late imperial Russia

By 1900, no thinking churchman could be unaware of the intellectual, spiritual and pastoral energies competing for influence in Russian Orthodoxy. The challenge was to channel them into a productive synthesis capable of harmonising the interests of hierarchy, clergy and laity in a manner acceptable to the secular

Press, 1993), 84, 87; Meehan, 'Metropolitan Filaret (Drozdov) and the reform of women's monastic communities', RR 50 (1991), 310–23; E. B. Emchenko, 'Gosudarstvennoe zakonodatel'stvo i zhenskie monastyri v XVIII – nachale XX veka', in Tserkov' v istorii Rossii: Sbornik 5, ed. O. I. Vasil'eva et al. (Moscow: RAN, IRI, 2003), 171–221.

64 I. A. Kurliandskii, 'Mitropolit Innokentii (Veniaminov) i Igumeniia Mitrofaniia. (Po novym arkhivnym dokumentam)', in Tserkov' v istorii Rossii: Sbornik 3 (Moscow: RAN, IRI, 1999), 134–59.

65 R[ossiiskii] G[osudarstvennyi] I[storicheskii] A[rkhiv], f[ond] 834, op[is] 4, d[elo] 1193, l[ist] 89, Isidor to Evfaliia, 5 August 1882; ll. 36–7, same to same, 24 February 1885.

66 W. G. Wagner, 'Paradoxes of piety: the Nizhegorod convent of the Exaltation of the Cross, 1807–1935', in Orthodox Russia, 211–38.

67 S. M. Kenworthy, 'The mobilization of piety: monasticism and the Great War in Russia, 1914–1916', Jahrbücher für Geschichte Osteuropas 52 (2004), 388–401.

power. K. P. Pobedonostsev, synodal over-procurator between 1880 and 1905, sought the solution in stricter central control. But whereas bureaucratisation had arguably increased the church's efficiency in the eighteenth century, the opposite was now true. Even the most isolated parishes in the empire were suffocated by a rising demand for paperwork: by 1914 the Karelian priest Father Aleksandr Loginevskii was obliged to communicate five times as often with his diocesan consistory in Vyborg as his father had done in the late 1880s.[68] Pobedonostsev's revival of 'learned monasticism', a concept first borrowed from Catholicism in the seventeenth century, proved equally controversial. The over-procurator intended his phalanx of ascetic scholar-administrators to discipline unruly clergy and challenge contemporary moral decay. But the image of ambitious prelates 'dancing'[69] to his tune in the synod did nothing to enhance the church's reputation for holiness. And though resilient leaders such as Sergii (Stragorodskii) emerged in the last years of the old regime, so did hotheads such as Sergii's acolyte, Kiprian (Shnitnikov), and his anti-Semitic contemporary, Iliodor (Trufanov). While the former inflamed Orthodox relations with Lutherans in Finland after 1905, the latter even attacked the synod itself in 1907, which forced his mentor Archbishop Antonii (Khrapovitskii) to the conclusion that his protégé's 'entire literary output bore witness to his hysterical insanity'.[70]

By then, the synodal regime had few supporters. Though the Slavophile cleric A. M. Ivantsov-Platonov had called for the restoration of conciliar government as early as 1882, his cause gathered momentum only twenty years later when Nicholas II read an attack on Peter I's church reforms in the conservative newspaper *Moskovskie Vedomosti*.[71] Invited to comment, Metropolitan Antonii (Vadkovskii) told the tsar that he had 'always believed' that 'sooner or later' Russian 'public opinion would be obliged to declare it shameful and impossible for Holy Rus to live under such an abnormal system of ecclesiastical government'.[72] When even its own senior member questioned the synod's

---

68 The ratio of average annual communications from Suojärvi was 550 in 1914–16 to 109 in 1887–91: calculated from letterbooks at Mikkelin maakunta-arkisto, Suojärven ortodoksisen seurakunnen arkisto, II Ab2–5.

69 'Kniazia tserkvi: iz dnevniki A. N. L'vova', *Krasnyi Arkhiv* 39 (1930), 122, 17 Dec. 1892. See also, S. I. Alekseeva, *Sviateishii sinod v sisteme vysshikh i tsentral'nykh gosudarstvennykh uchrezhdenii poreformennoi Rossii, 1856–1904 gg.* (St Petersburg: Nauka, 2003), esp. 44–70.

70 RGIA, f. 796, op. 191, v otd., 2 stol, d. 143z, l. 68.

71 J. W Cunningham, *A vanquished hope: the movement for church renewal in Russia, 1905–1906* (Crestwood, NY: St Vladimir's Seminary Press, 1981), 66–78. The articles were by the terrorist-turned-monarchist L. A. Tikhomirov, who remained influential after 1905: L. A. Tikhomirov, *Tserkovnyi sobor, edinolichnaia vlast' i rabochii vopros* (Moscow: Moskva, 2003).

72 RGIA, f. 1579, op. 1, d. 36, l. 10b., Antonii to Pobedonostsev, 4 April 1905, quoting his report to Nicholas II of March 1903.

authority, reform was widely assumed to be imminent. Yet Nicholas, guided by Pobedonostsev, continued to regard a council as politically inopportune. Since laymen saw a council as a means of increasing their voice in parochial affairs, clergy as a way of gaining a foothold in diocesan management, and bishops as a means of undermining the entire synodal bureaucracy, it was far from irrational for the tsar to agonise about conciliarism's subversive potential. Yet his touch in ecclesiastical affairs was uncertain. Though Nicholas had intended the canonisation of Serafim of Sarov in 1903 as a symbol of national integration and divine legitimacy, embarrassment ensued when the popular demand for uncorrupted remains could not be satisfied.[73] In March 1906, after Pobedonostsev's retirement, the tsar once again inadvertently achieved the worst of all worlds by continuing to refuse a council, but authorising a pre-conciliar commission whose published record offered a tempting target to critics by revealing widespread Orthodox dissension on crucial matters of principle without providing a mechanism for their resolution.[74]

Lacking conciliar authority, the church was vulnerable to the revolutionary turmoil of 1905. On 9 January – 'Bloody Sunday' – Father Georgii Gapon's leadership of the St Petersburg assembly of Russian workers ended in tragedy when troops fired on a peaceful, but unauthorised, demonstration to the Winter Palace. On 17 April – Easter Sunday – the tsar issued a toleration edict in an attempt to prevent the spread of sedition, granting his subjects an unprecedented personal choice in matters of faith.[75] Shocked church leaders descended into mutual recrimination. When reformist clergy in St Petersburg met their metropolitan in February to condemn Orthodoxy's 'unnaturally powerless' position 'in this period of social upheaval', Pobedonostsev denounced them as 'agitators and troublemakers'.[76] When the prime minister declared his sympathy for conciliarism, Pobedonostsev dismissed his sources as 'idealists' and 'ideologues', 'unacquainted with reality'.[77] A recluse since Bloody Sunday, the over-procurator saw his world in ruins: 'Everyone – secular and clerical – has gone out of his mind.'[78] Metropolitan Antonii was indeed close to collapse. Outraged by unfounded charges of a conspiracy with Witte – 'one wants to

---

73 G. L. Freeze, 'Subversive piety: religion and the political crisis in late imperial Russia', *Journal of Modern History* 68 (1996), 312–29.
74 See, in particular, F. E. Mel'nikov, *Bluzhdaiushchee bogoslovie: obzor veroucheniia gospodstvuiushchei tserkvi* (Moscow: P. P. Riabushinskii, 1911). On the commission, Cunningham, *A vanquished hope*, 205–312.
75 *PSZRI* tret'e sobranie, xxv: 1, 26, 126.
76 RGIA, f. 797, op. 75, II otd., 3 stol, d. 439, l. 70b.
77 *Istoricheskaia perepiska sud'bakh pravoslavnoi tserkvi* (Moscow: I. D. Sytin, 1912), 10–11, 32–3.
78 L. Shokhin (ed.), '"Mat' moiu, rodimuiu Rossiiu, uroduiut": Pis'ma K. P. Pobedonostseva S. D. Sheremetevu', *Istochnik* 6 (1996), 6, 16 April 1905.

be the dictator of a republic', alleged a leading salon hostess, 'the other its patriarch'[79] – he confessed in June that his head had 'completely cracked'.[80] Antonii watched, bewildered, as colleagues sought to settle old scores. Eager for revenge on the lay professors who had helped to hound him out of the Moscow theological academy in 1895, Antonii (Khrapovitskii) branded their demands for curricular autonomy as a campaign for 'the right to deny the divinity of Jesus Christ in their lectures'; privately he recommended disbanding the academies and expelling their rebellious students.[81]

In such a poisoned atmosphere, the politicisation of Russian public life was bound to create further ecclesiastical divisions. In the aftermath of Gapon's abortive trade-union experience, many successful pastoral techniques seemed tantamount to socialism. Yet official disapproval did not prevent renovationist priests in St Petersburg and Moscow from matching their calls for ecclesiastical reform with a deeper commitment to workers' material needs.[82] Far from being confined to the two capitals, social and political radicalism flourished in provincial dioceses such as Viatka, Smolensk, Kazan and Vladimir. Even in Tambov, where Bishop Innokentii (Beliaev) was a prominent right-winger, a diocesan assembly of clergy in September 1906 found justice in 'the people's striving for a better future' and declared its sympathy with the liberation movement 'in so far as it goes by peaceful means and in accordance with Christian principles'.[83] But the pressure against such opinions was exemplified by the fate of the liberation movement's most prominent clerical figure. Father Grigorii Petrov, who campaigned against social injustice in his newspaper *Pravda Bozhii* (God's Truth), first published in January 1906, was imprisoned in a monastery to prevent him taking his seat as a Constitutional Democrat (Kadet) in the second Duma. In January 1908, under pressure from Metropolitan Vladimir (Bogoiavlenskii) of Moscow, who was the one prelate Pobedonostsev thought had kept his head in 1905, Petrov was defrocked for being 'as good a

79 A. Bogdanovich, *Tri poslednikh samoderzhtsa* (Moscow: Novosti, 1990), 343, 29 April 1905.
80 RGIA, f. 1574, op. 2, d. 133, l. 14, Antonii to Pobedonostev, 29 June 1905.
81 'V tserkovnykh krugakh pered revoliutsiei: iz pisem arkhiepiskopa Antoniia volynskago k mitropolitu kievskomu Flavianu', *Krasnyi Arkhiv* 31 (1928), 207, 8 October 1905. Antonii's main target was the reformist professor V. I. Myshtsyn, allegedly 'a blindly unquestioning nihilist and adulterer'.
82 S. Dixon, 'The Orthodox church and the workers of St Petersburg, 1880–1914', in *European religion in the age of great cities 1830–1930*, ed. H. McLeod (London: Routledge, 1995), 119–41; P. Herrlinger, 'Raising Lazarus: Orthodoxy and the factory *narod* in St Petersburg, 1905–14', *Jahrbücher für Geschichte Osteuropas* 52 (2004), 341–54.
83 G. L. Freeze, 'Church and politics in late imperial Russia: crisis and radicalisation of the clergy', in *Russia under the last tsar: opposition and subversion 1894–1917*, ed. A. Geifman (Oxford: Blackwell, 1999), 280–4; quote at 281.

revolutionary as Gapon'.[84] 'I believe in the one holy, conciliar, apostolic church', retorted the unrepentant preacher, 'but I reject with all my strength and understanding the servile, monkish Byzantinism and soulless *pobedonost-sevshchina* (triumphalism) that passes under the name of Orthodoxy.'[85]

Whereas clergy on the left tended to advocate shorter services and more accessible sermons, the right insisted on maintaining the full panoply of Orthodox liturgical practice: elaborate icon processions and lengthy masses celebrated with due episcopal pomp. Their greatest commitment to social Christianity lay in commandeering much of the church's long-standing temperance campaign, a natural enough cause for advocates of popular restraint.[86] Many of the right's actions, however, served to undermine rather than stabilise Nicholas II's pseudo-constitutional bureaucratic regime. Iliodor, whose hunger strike at his Tsaritsyn monastery in January 1911 threatened to bring down the prime minister, agitated for the release of the church from its Petrine straitjacket – 'not a single act of state, be it the publication of new laws, the declaration of war, or the participation of peasants and workers, should be managed without the preliminary advice and blessing of the church'[87] – and for the deliverance of the tsar from treacherous ministers. Whereas Stolypin distrusted the press, Iliodor mercilessly exploited it. Denouncing the October manifesto for 'inundating long-suffering Russia with blood', he demanded the death penalty for Witte and urged Russians to take the law into their own hands: 'I, the monk Iliodor, bless you in the great and holy work of emancipating the dear Motherland from atheists, robbers, blasphemers, bomb-throwers, firebrands, lying journalists and slanderers – all of them cursed by God and condemned by men.'[88] Comparing Stolypin to Pontius Pilate, Iliodor incited peasant delegates to the fourth monarchist congress in April 1907 to demand the compulsory alienation of private property, unnerving even Aleksandra Bogdanovich by his apparent determination to destroy 'not only the people sitting in the ministries, but the walls of the ministries themselves'.[89] Trading on the freebooting tradition of his native Don Cossack region, Iliodor heralded his mass Volga pilgrimage in

84 RGIA, f. 796, op. 187, d. 6668, ll. 230b. (Archbishop Nikolai's report); 55, Synod decision; S. P. Mel'gunov (ed.), 'K. P. Pobedonostsev v dni pervoi revoliutsii', in *Na chuzhoi storone*, ed. S. P. Mel'gunov (Berlin, 1924), VIII, 188, Pobedonostsev to S. D. Voit, 7 April 1905.
85 *Pis'mo sviashchennika Grigoriia Petrova Mitropolitu Antoniiu* (St Petersburg: Pravda, 1908), 16.
86 P. Herlihy, *The alcoholic empire: vodka and politics in late imperial Russia* (New York: Oxford University Press, 2002), ch. 5.
87 *Pravda ob ieromonakhe Iliodore* (Moscow: L. I. Ragozin, 1911), 5.
88 *Veche*, 1 February 1907.
89 *Rech'*, 28 April 1907; *Novoe vremia*, 28 April 1907; Bogdanovich, *Tri poslednikh samoderzhtsa*, 425–6, 4 May 1907.

summer 1911 as the first step towards a new popular movement in the manner of the seventeenth-century rebel Stenka Razin. 'The Don is the river of popular anger', his supporters proclaimed. 'If only it could speak, it would have much to say about the way that the guileless, simple people struggled for the truth, how they were enemies of "accursed Rus", and how, finally, they became autocracy's best support.'[90]

On visits to St Petersburg Iliodor took care to be seen at the convent founded in memory of John of Kronstadt, a fellow supporter of the Union of Russian People.[91] The church promoted the Kronstadt holy man as a rival to Tolstoy, whose excommunication in 1901 had merely served to stimulate his cult following, but their efforts backfired when Father John himself unexpectedly became an object of veneration.[92] Closely acquainted with John's followers, the moderate St Petersburg missionary D. I. Bogoliubov rallied to their defence: 'They are, it is true, people of little education, and therefore inclined to an exaggerated judgement of the people and the things they respect. However, their intentions are good and ascetically Orthodox, and the church has nothing to fear from their existence.'[93] But that was not how it seemed to the synod, which condemned the Ioannity as sectarians (khlysty) in 1912. Alarmed by the people's tendency to reject the church's authority in favour of spiritual guides of their own choosing, leading churchmen were equally critical of Ivan Churikov – 'Brother Ivanushka' – whose popular temperance movement, inspired by Father John, drew hundreds of thousands to the Gospel between 1894 and 1913 and survived Churikov's excommunication into the Soviet era.[94] Other charismatic individuals attracted smaller followings. And no amount of ecclesiastical vigilance could deter increasing numbers of Russians from abandoning the intricate form of Orthodoxy honed in the theological academies for the reassuring certainties of evangelical Protestantism. Pobedonostsev had warned Alexander II as early as 1880 that 'the masses' would be seduced by Colonel V. A. Pashkov's teachings into simplistic conclusions: 'indifference to sin, an empty and fantastic faith, and love of Christ that is both far-fetched and

90 *Pravda ob ieromonakhe Iliodore*, 77.
91 See the photograph in M. V. Shkarovskii, *Sviato-Ioannovskii stavropigial'nyi zhenskii monastyr': istoriia obiteli* (St Petersburg: Logos, 2001), 94–5.
92 N. Kizenko, *A prodigal saint: Father John of Kronstadt and the Russian people* (University Park: Pennsylvania State University Press, 2000), 197–232, 249–60, verges on the uncritical.
93 RGIA, f. 796, op. 442, d. 2290, l. 240.
94 Tsentral'nyi istoricheskii gosudarstvennyi arkhiv gorod S.-Peterburga, f. 19, op. 97, d. 54; RGIA, f. 796, op. 442, d. 2407, ll. 141–73; Herrlinger, 'Orthodoxy and the factory *narod*', 352–3; N. I. Iudin, *Churikovshchina (sekta 'trezvenikov')* (Leningrad: Obshchestvo 'Znanie' RSFSR, 1962).

arrogant'.[95] The evangelical movement did indeed become Orthodoxy's most vigorous rival. From 1907, the young Baptist preacher Wilhelm Fetler enjoyed a 'great reaping and gathering season' among the workers of St Petersburg so that there was 'never a Gospel service held without conversions resulting'. Fetler's Gospel Hall on Vasilevskii island seated 2000; in the empire as a whole, the movement could probably boast millions of adherents.[96]

The sectarian menace helps to explain why only a minority of churchmen saw the 1905 toleration edict as an opportunity for peaceful, unfettered mission. Most, like Sergii (Stragorodskii), instead felt betrayed: 'After a century of peaceful existence under the protection of the law, behind the strong wall of state security, our church now ventures out, defenceless and without shelter, directly onto the field of battle, to face the enemies' attack.'[97] Orthodox scholars had long drawn on patristic authority to justify state intervention on behalf of their church. Now they were reduced to an unedifying struggle to limit the scope of the toleration edict and to thwart its local impact.[98] Though accurate statistics are hard to determine, apostasy reached a peak in the western borderlands, where earlier attempts to impose an alien faith were exposed as a sham: a third of the 'Orthodox' population of the diocese of Kholm had converted to Catholicism by 1907.[99] More damaging than the exodus itself were the attitudes engendered by the threat: even in dioceses where the church's worst fears remained unrealised, the assumption persisted that disaster was imminent.[100] The alarmist tone of the majority at the Kiev missionary conference in July 1908 allowed the renegade archimandrite Mikhail (Semenov) to mock an increasingly defensive church, dependent on 'external' means of support, reduced to 'primitive' missionary work, and convinced that it faced a 'crisis' in which it would be 'vanquished' by rivals.[101] The conversion to the schism of

---

95 RGIA, f. 1574, op. 2, d. 63, l. 2.
96 R. S. Latimer, *With Christ in Russia* (London: Hodder and Stoughton, 1910), 26, 31; A. McCaig, *Wonders of grace in Russia* (Riga: Revival Press, 1926), 119–31.
97 Episkop Sergii, *Slova i rechi 1901–1905 gg.* (St Petersburg: M. Merkushev, 1905), 29–35. For press reactions, see *Reformy veroterpimosti na poroge XX veka i sostoianie gosudarstvennoi tservki v Rossii*, ed. G. M. Kalinin (Nizhnii Novgorod: Tipografiia O. R. Provorovoi, 1905).
98 On the pettifogging central campaign, P. Waldron, 'Religious reform after 1905: Old Believers and the Orthodox church', *Oxford Slavonic Papers*, n.s. 20 (1987), 110–39.
99 T. R. Weeks, *Nation and state in late imperial Russia: nationalism and russification on the western frontier, 1863–1914* (DeKalb: Northern Illinois University Press, 1996), 180–3.
100 S. Dixon, 'Sergii (Stragorodskii) in the Russian Orthodox diocese of Finland: apostasy and mixed marriages, 1905–1917', *Slavonic and East European Review* 82 (2004), 59–66.
101 Arkhimandrit Mikhail, 'Na s'ezde', *Tserkov'* 29 (1908), 1010–11; Mikhail, 'Moi vpechatleniia: s kievskago missionerskago s'ezda', *Tserkov'* 30 (1908) 1038–42; 34 (1908), 116; and more generally, H. J. Coleman, 'Defining heresy: the fourth missionary congress and the problem of cultural power after 1905 in Russia', *Jahrbücher für Geschichte Osteuropas* 52 (2004), 70–92.

such a prominent reformist as Mikhail in November 1907 added plausibility to the Old Believers' claims that they, long condemned as fanatical reactionaries, were in fact the most creative force in Russian religious life. Indeed, once the synod had been preserved from root-and-branch reform by the tsar's refusal to call a council, it was no longer the Old Believers who could be charged with stagnation but the Orthodox themselves.

Conclusion

Emerging from a period of relative toleration in the 1820s, a newly assertive Russian Orthodox Church was challenged by religious rivals. Unanticipated resistance to conversion campaigns under Nicholas I prompted churchmen to define their confessional position, the better to defend it, and to base an increasingly evangelist internal mission on authentic theological foundations. Yet an unavoidable reliance on western scholarship and pastoral methods made their attempt to differentiate Orthodoxy both complex and controversial. Neither monks nor bureaucrats trusted abstract learning. Statesmen who expected the church to reinforce the tsarist regime were alarmed to discover that its mission could create civil unrest, that its research subverted synodal authority, and that the clergy's growing pastoral commitment ultimately prompted calls for social and political reform. Threatened with collapse in 1905, the government ranked imperial security higher than ecclesiastical satisfaction. Most churchmen saw the toleration edict of 17 April as a betrayal of the confessional policies they had struggled for so long to refine. Prevented from channelling demands for *sobornost* through the authoritative mechanism of a council, the church's leaders were instead drawn into damaging, politicised disputes. Within an increasingly polarised church, debates moved ever further away from the spiritual needs of its flock. Though by the end of the old regime atheists and zealots were firmly entrenched at the extremes of the popular religious spectrum, the majority of Orthodox Russians continued, even after 1905, to seek the sorts of peaceful accommodation between folk-belief and Christian doctrine that had characterised Russian religious practice for centuries.[102] Since humble believers were often more tolerant, more patient and more adaptable than those responsible for their spiritual care, they proved better able to withstand the Bolshevik onslaught than did Patriarch Tikhon and his divided, inflexible church.

---

102 V. Shevzov, *Russian Orthodoxy on the eve of revolution* (New York: Oxford University Press, 2004); G. L. Freeze, 'A pious folk? Religious observance in Vladimir diocese, 1900–1914', *Jahrbücher für Geschichte Osteuropas* 52 (2004), 323–40.

15

Russian piety and culture from Peter the Great to 1917

CHRIS CHULOS

Paradigms and stereotypes

Peter the Great's desire to transform his empire through a broad array of modernising reforms helped to shape the course of Russian history for the next two centuries. Among the great leader's notable achievements, the construction of a European-style capital facing westwards, the creation of a standing army, the introduction of a regularised system of taxation and the reorganisation of higher education often overshadow the importance of Peter's reform of the Orthodox faith. Tension between secular and religious authority was not new to Russia. The destructive conclusion of the mid-seventeenth-century struggle between the overbearing Patriarch Nikon and Tsar Aleksei Mikhailovich ostensibly over reforms in ritual practice ended disastrously for the patriarch, who was unseated, and for the church, which was rent by schism. Those accepting reform were considered to be proper Orthodox Christians, while those defending the existing rituals were soon branded Old Believers, Old Ritualists or schismatics (*starovery, staroobriadtsy, raskol'niki*). Although the schism of 1666–67 produced some of Russia's most colourful religious figures, among them self-immolators and flagellants, any lingering doubts about ultimate secular authority were resolved between 1700, when the young Tsar Peter failed to replace the recently deceased Patriarch Adrian, and the enactment of the *Spiritual Regulation* in 1721 that replaced the patriarchate with the secular administrative apparatus of the holy synod.[1]

Peter's ecclesiastical reforms were left incomplete yet unchallenged at the time of his death. Throughout the eighteenth century, state policy sought to

---

1 Informative overviews of the Church Schism of 1666–67, the reign of Peter the Great and the Spiritual Regulation can be found in R. O. Crummey, *The Old Believers and the world of Antichrist: the Vyg community and the Russian State, 1694–1855* (Madison: University of Wisconsin Press, 1970); L. Hughes, *Russia in the age of Peter the Great* (New Haven and London: Yale University Press, 1998); *The spiritual regulation of Peter the Great*, ed. and trans. A. V. Muller (Seattle: University of Washington Press, 1972); J. Cracraft, *The church reform of Peter the Great* (Stanford: Stanford University Press, 1971).

define and contain the institutions and expressions of Orthodox Christianity in the secular terms of Enlightenment thought that reached its apogee during the reign of Catherine the Great. Comparing herself to her great predecessor, Catherine saw herself as completing Peter's institution building and, soon after gaining power, expropriated ecclesiastical lands. While the tsarina's actions were justified as a means of solving the state's growing fiscal problems, the confiscation of church property symbolised the diminished political and economic power of Russian Orthodoxy. In the course of a century, schism, abolition of the patriarchate, institution of a secular administrative apparatus and loss of property left weakened and disorientated church leaders searching for opportunities to reinstate the faith's lost public prestige and independence. The nineteenth century saw a gradual restoration of Orthodoxy's public authority, beginning with inclusion in the proto-nationalistic trinity that became the slogan of Tsar Nicholas I's reign – Orthodoxy, Autocracy and Nationality. This famed trinitarian maxim of spiritual, secular and ethnic qualities of Russian identity, coined in the early 1830s, represented administrative nostalgia and a response to liberal and revolutionary movements in continental Europe more than actual reality. At a time when Russians and ethnic minorities within the empire were becoming interested in their own linguistic, folkloric and religious heritages, this equation expressed a strong defence of monarchy and its two main pillars of support.[2]

The impact of Orthodox Christianity on Russian history and its place in the formation of an ethnic identity stood at the centre of the most controversial cultural and philosophical debates that remain unresolved to this day. One side can be organised under the general rubric of Slavophilism that included the original group of mid-nineteenth-century intellectuals whose pro-Orthodox and communalist and exceptionalist convictions were rooted in the fear of the non-Orthodox and ill-defined western individualistic, self-interested 'other'. Slavophiles and their ideological heirs have argued that Orthodoxy has bestowed upon the Russian people (narod) concern for the well-being of the group, which contrasts sharply with Catholic and Protestant individualism, competition and callousness that place low priority on the good of the

---

2 N. V. Riasanovsky, *Nicholas I and official nationality in Russia, 1825–1855* (Berkeley: University of California Press, 1959); J. Remy, *Higher education and national identity: Polish student activism in Russia, 1832–1863* [Bibliotheca historica 57] (Helsinki: Suomalaisen kirjallisuuden seura, 2000). Interest in national traits that included language, folklore and faith, among other things, emerged throughout post-Napoleonic Europe as eighteenth-century political borders were redrawn. See E. Gellner, *Nations and nationalism* (Oxford: Blackwell, 1983); and E. J. Hobsbawm, *Nations and nationalism: programme, myth, reality* (Cambridge: Cambridge University Press, 1992).

community. At the centre of Slavophile idealism were the family, the church and the village commune that brought people together in their common goals. Westernisers and their successors have taken up an opposing position, arguing at times that Russian peasants suffered as a result of the village commune and that Orthodoxy provided a ritualistic practice absent of religious understanding. At the heart of these debates lay fundamentally different interpretations of the western-inspired reforms of Peter the Great and whether or not they adhered to Russia's true character or betrayed it.[3]

By the mid-nineteenth century the political, social and cultural landscape of Russia was on the verge of radical transformation. The emancipation of the serfs in 1861 brought expectation and hope in the areas of economic development that were predicated upon the spread of primary schooling, basic literacy and improved communication (both transportation and information) under the rubric of the Great Reforms. Among the consequences of the enormous changes introduced under the Tsar Liberator, Alexander II, were, on the one hand, the diversification of society and culture and, on the other, the intensification of isolation among Russians, depending on their educational levels, their proximity to major urban centres and their political loyalties. Urban-educated teachers travelled in considerable numbers to every corner of the empire. They went equipped with textbooks and illustrations that supported the latest scientific paradigms of the natural world and of human civilisations, but they also took with them prevailing stereotypes about religion and superstition, which underlined the disadvantages of folk belief and practice. Many well-intended educators came from a clerical background and sought nothing less than to lift their fellow countrymen out of their eternal poverty and to lead them along the path to lasting prosperity through economic, and quite often political, self-sufficiency.[4]

Notions of self-sufficiency went hand in hand with church leaders' belief that emancipation should not be limited to the peasantry, but also applied to

3 A. Walicki, *The Slavophile controversy: history of a conservative utopia in nineteenth-century Russian thought* (Oxford: Oxford University Press, 1975); and Walicki, *A history of Russian thought* (Stanford: Stanford University Press, 1979).
4 A splendid overview of Russian history in the eighteenth and nineteenth centuries can be found in G. Hosking, *Russia: people and empire, 1552–1917* (London: HarperCollins, 1997). On the educational initiatives and changes in the church that followed the emancipation of the serfs, see B. Eklof, *Russian peasant schools: officialdom, village culture, and popular pedagogy, 1861–1914* (Berkeley: University of California Press, 1986); G. L. Freeze, *The parish clergy in nineteenth-century Russia: crisis, reform, counter-reform* (Princeton: Princeton University Press, 1983), chs. 5–10; A. Sinel, *The classroom and the chancellery: state educational reform in Russia under Count Dmitry Tolstoi* (Cambridge, MA: Harvard University Press, 1973).

the burdensome Petrine formula of church–state relations. By the beginning of the twentieth century the legal separation of church and state and the restoration of the defunct patriarchate became a centrepiece of the clerical and secular press and diocesan clergy assemblies. With a promise from Nicholas II in the turbulent year of 1905 to convoke the first national church council in more than two centuries, religious leaders and ordinary parish clergymen busied themselves with preparations for the seminal event. Crisis after crisis distracted the doomed tsar, so that only his abdication in February 1917 cleared the path for the council to be called by the provisional government. Although the new dynamics of the church–state relationship briefly augured well for Orthodoxy in Russia, the triumph of the Bolsheviks soon demonstrated the limits of organised religion's authority, as well as the resilience of piety among rank-and-file Russians who considered themselves believers.[5]

The paradigms and stereotypes about Orthodox piety and culture that evolved between 1700 and 1917 tended towards binary opposites – pagan or pious, backward or progressive, ignorant or informed.[6]

Church and state

Already weakened by the schism of 1666–67, the Orthodox Church never entirely recovered from Peter the Great's forceful subordination of church administration to secular power. The tsar's originally benign approach that led him to withhold nominating a successor to the deceased Patriarch Adrian ended with the formal reorganisation of the faith under a holy synod of elite bishops led by a secular administrator. Despite the over-procurator's control of the day-to-day affairs of the synod, its members still retained authority over ecclesiastical matters. By 1832, when Nicholas I's Minister of Education, Count Sergei Uvarov (1786–1855), coined the patriotic slogan of Orthodoxy, Autocracy and Nationality, the church was far less a servant of the state or imperial wishes than might be supposed. The popularity of certain bishops, the rise of widespread spirituality independent of formal church through devotion to favourite shrines and holy men (especially the famed elders, or *startsy*,

---

5 C. J. Chulos, 'Religion and grass-roots re-evaluations of Russian Orthodoxy, 1905–1907', in *Transforming peasants: society, state and peasants, 1861–1931*, ed. J. Pallot [Selected Papers from the Fifth World Conference of Central and Eastern European Studies, Warsaw, 1995] (Basingstoke: Macmillan, 1995), pp. 90–112. On the council, see D. Pospielovsky, *The Russian church under the Soviet regime, 1917–1982* (Crestwood, NY: St Vladimir's Seminary Press, 1984), I, ch. I.

6 See C. J. Chulos, 'Myths of the pious or pagan peasant in post-emancipation central Russia (Voronezh province)', *RH/HR* 22 (1995), 181–216.

of Optina monastery), and a current of thought among the episcopate that favoured greater independence from the state all serve to refute a widely held view among critics of Russian Orthodoxy that the church was little more than the handmaiden of the state.[7]

Another important factor that helped the church to maintain at least a semblance of independence from the state in the eighteenth century was an educational system for training future clergy. Introduced during the reign of Peter the Great, the number of seminaries and seminarians saw remarkable growth in the last half of the eighteenth century. In 1814, a four-tiered structure of clerical education culminating in the spiritual academy was established that served as the model for the rest of the century. At the bottom came the religious primary schools that attracted young men who aimed no higher than the office of psalmist. Those with strong enough talents and desires continued on to the seminary. Most of these young men were ordained either as deacons or as priests. A select few graduated to one of the four theological seminaries in the empire (St Petersburg, Moscow, Kiev and Kazan) and thus were assured prominent appointments as bishops. Although the religious schools were plagued by harsh conditions, brutal discipline and ill-trained instructors, clerical education had become by the 1860s a *sine qua non* for a parish assignment. The Great Reforms, which benefited the rest of Russian society indirectly, had the direct result of initiating a sweeping reform of church schools in 1867 and 1869. Its aim was to improve curricular and living experiences and to attract to religious service young men from outside the clerical estate. Much attention has been given to the failure of these reforms, the most obvious example being the student uprisings beginning in the 1880s, which rendered the seminary synonymous with revolutionary activism. More to the point, the cohorts of clergy trained in post-emancipation religious schools were likely to be more sensitive to the material needs of parishioners and to their demands for parish reform, a fact that often put them at odds with tsarist officials. Furthermore, the high sense of duty, which inspired this large cadre of parish clergymen, emerges from the extremely high quality of the diocesan clerical

---

7 See G. L. Freeze,'Handmaiden of the state? The Orthodox church in imperial Russia reconsidered', *JEcclH* 86 (1985), 82–102. On popular devotion to spiritual leaders as well as their appeal to cultural elites, see R. L. Nichols, 'The Orthodox elders (*startsy*) of imperial Russia', *Modern Greek Studies Yearbook* 1 (1985), 1–30; L. J. Stanton, *The Optina Pustin monastery in the Russian literary imagination: iconic vision in works by Dostoevsky, Gogol, Tolstoy and others* [Middlebury Studies in Russian Language and Literature 3] (New York: Peter Lang, 1995); *Philaret, Metropolitan of Moscow, 1782–1867: perspectives on the man, his works, and his times*, ed. V. Tsurikov (Jordanville, NY: Variable Press, 2003).

newspapers and from the complex debates carried on by many diocesan clerical assemblies.[8]

Nor should the efforts of rank-and-file believers be overlooked. By the sweat of their brows and through personal sacrifice, they provided financial support for their parish clergy, churches and charities that included care for the indigent. In an outpouring of devotion that increased markedly after the emancipation of the serfs and the subsequent improvement in land, sea and rail transportation, Orthodox faithful flocked to nearby and faraway shrines that were significant to their personal conceptions of the world, as well as to the legitimacy of the empire. The combined force of believers' spiritual expression and improved clerical training brought about a religious renaissance that restored the moral authority of Russian Orthodoxy. While not always united, believers and parish clergymen formed an important alternative approach to the faith that was propped up by suspicion of both religious and secular authority based in St Petersburg and Moscow. At the same time, church hierarchs began to demand a national council that would decide on a wide range of pressing issues, from the restoration of the patriarchate to the role of women in the parish. However, they failed to seek support from below, preferring to fall back on theology and historical precedent. When the provisional government convoked the first national church council months after the abdication of Nicholas II in February 1917, it provided symbolic closure to a wound begun by the imperial period's founder and grandmaster of ceremonies. Sadly, the restoration of the patriarchate and progressive rulings on parish life came at a time when the great mass of believers was so alienated from the church leaders that they were only too willing to support efforts to bring down the hierarchical institutions of Orthodoxy. These very same believers were not, however, willing to abandon their parishes or local religious life.[9]

Popular piety in the centres and peripheries

Quite unconnected to the schism of 1666–67 was the less formal division within the church created by Peter the Great. This was between the type of

---

8 Freeze, *Parish clergy*, 319–29, 354–63; B. V. Titlinov, *Dukhovnaia shkola v Rossii v XIX stoletii*, 2 vols. (Vil'na, 1908–9; reprinted Farnborough: Gregg International Publishers, 1970); C. J. Chulos, *Converging worlds: religion and community in peasant Russia, 1861–1917* (DeKalb: Northern Illinois University Press, 2003), 99–100.

9 See C. J. Chulos, 'Religious and secular aspects of pilgrimage in modern Russia', *Byzantium and the North/Acta Byzantina Fennica* 9 (1997–98), 21–58. The complexity of parish life has been described in Chulos, *Converging worlds*, chs. 4, 7; V. Shevzov, 'Chapels and the ecclesial world of pre-Revolutionary Russian peasants', *Slavic Review* 55 (1996), 585–613.

believer he sought to create – educated and loyal through their confession – and those against which this ideal would be measured, the benighted masses yet to benefit from the tsar's reforms. As Peter's reforms were disseminated from St Petersburg to the provincial capitals, popular piety became inseparable from location, educational level and political orientation. Social and physical mobility brought individuals from all levels of Russian society into greater, though not necessarily closer, contact beginning in the eighteenth century, a phenomenon that accelerated in the last decades of the nineteenth century as a result of improved transportation and communication.

Behind the new religious categorisation lay the notion of *dvoeverie*, a term first used in medieval sermons, which gradually became the descrip- tor favoured by Russia's educated elite. By the end of the nineteenth century, ethnographers imbued *dvoeverie* with an enlightened condescension towards their social inferiors who lacked more than a basic education. *Dvoeverie* became a symbol of all that was wrong with rural Russia. Mired in a mentality that gave credence to superstitions, dark forces, witches, sorcerers and the ubiqui- tous evil eye, peasants stood as formidable obstacles to the westernisation of Russia in the eighteenth century and to modernisation and industrialisation in the nineteenth and early twentieth centuries. What these critiques failed to appreciate were the varieties of Orthodox piety that enabled all Russians, peasants included, to make sense of often harsh and senseless conditions of life, whether at the imperial court or in the most remote village.[10]

Educated and uneducated Orthodox believers shared many things in com- mon. All Russians who considered themselves to be Orthodox Christians divided their world into sacred and profane spaces that aimed at resacralising imperfect earthly life as the Kingdom of Heaven.[11] Based in Orthodox theology, religious belief and practice took on a highly personal and local meaning that encompassed both the simple icon corner (*krasnyi ugol*) in the peasant hut and reliquaries in imperial palaces. If the peasantry sought to benefit from good relations with the spirits of the house (*domovoi*), forest (*leshii*), hills (*gornyi*)

---

10 E. Levin '*Dvoeverie* and popular religion', in *Seeking God: the recovery of religious identity in Orthodox Russia, Ukraine, and Georgia*, ed. S. K. Batalden (DeKalb: Northern Illinois University Press, 1993), 31–52; C. J. Chulos, 'The end of "cultural survivals" (*perezhitki*): remembering and forgetting Russian peasant religious traditions', *Studia Slavica Finlan- densia* 17 (2000), 190–207; L. Engelstein, 'Old and new, high and low: straw horsemen of Russian Orthodoxy', in *Orthodox Russia: belief and practice under the tsars*, ed. V. A. Kivelson and R. H. Greene (University Park: Pennsylvania State University Press, 2003), 23–32.

11 S. L. Baehr, *The paradise myth in eighteenth-century Russia: utopian patterns in early secular Russian literature and culture* (Stanford: Stanford University Press, 1991), 14–16.

and water (*vodianoi*), they also appealed to favoured saints to heal, protect and ensure a bountiful harvest. Moving easily between these folk traditions and established Orthodox teachings and holy people, peasants acted rationally by working within the norms of their belief system to increase their odds for good fortune and abundance. Peasant religious customs resembled those of educated Russians who sought the advice of famous and not-so-famous spiritual elders, curried favours from nationally and locally important saints during pilgrimages and retained a fascination with the wondrous powers of the invisible world.[12]

In a very basic way Orthodox piety provided a rhythm to the prosaic western calendar that Peter imported into Russia, as well as meaning to the stages of human life. Every believer was expected to mark the year by a constant procession of annual holidays that divided the year into two main fast and feast periods associated with Christmas and Easter. Additionally, Wednesdays and Fridays were set aside for fasting and contemplation. Under the rubric of 'little tradition' fell innumerable religious holidays observed in communities and by individuals that honoured parish churches, patron saints and wonder-working icons. The passage of human time was commemorated by three chief rituals that also registered major shifts in the life of communities. Baptism in the first few days following birth, as was customary in imperial Russia, recognised the addition of a new member of the community as well as the new responsibilities of both the parents and the baby once it reached maturity. Marriage called upon the discerning powers of parents and matchmakers to assure a match that would suit both families first, the community second and the individual last (although the concerns of the bride- and groom-to-be moved closer to the centre in the late nineteenth century). At all levels of society, youth was dominated by the importance of finding a good spouse.[13] For peasants, this required a combination of divination, proper behaviour and matchmaking expertise. For the growing bourgeoisie, a good union could provide a step up the precarious

---

12 V. Goretskii and V. Vil'k, *Russkii narodnyi lechebnyi travnik i tsvetnik*, second edition (Moscow: Universitetskaia tip., 1903); F. Wigzell, *Reading Russian fortunes: print culture, gender and divination in Russia from 1765* (Cambridge: Cambridge University Press, 1998).

13 M. M. Gromyko, *Traditsionnye normy povedeniia i formy obshcheniia russkikh krest'ian XIX v.* (Moscow: Nauka, 1986), 161–226; T. A. Bernshtam, *Molodezh' v obriadovoi zhizni russkoi obshchiny XIX–nachala XX v.: polovozrastnoi aspekt traditsionnoi kul'tury* (Leningrad: Nauka, 1988); T. A. Bernshtam, *Molodost' v simvolizme perekhodnykh obriadov vostochnykh slavian: uchenie i opyt Tserkvi v narodnom khristianstve* (St Petersburg: Peterburgskoe Vostokovedenie, 2000); C. Worobec, *Peasant Russia: family and community in the post-emancipation period* (Princeton: Princeton University Press, 1991; reissued DeKalb: Northern Illinois University Press, 1995), chs. 4–5.

and shifting social ladder and thus necessitated great care and, often, fastidious deal-making. For the elite, considerations of pedigree and wealth were never far beneath the surface. Regardless of one's position, marriage brought expectations for reproduction, baptism and the process of identifying suitable partners for the next generation. The once youthful couple eased into middle age when they gradually assumed the mantle of the elderly generation and began to await their ultimate fate. Equally valued by peasant and tsar alike, a proper death nevertheless had very different consequences for each. Peasants who met with untimely, violent or unnatural deaths were considered to cast a pall over the community they once inhabited. If death came naturally, however, deceased members of society acted as auxiliary spiritual members of the community who could bring good fortune and provide protection for their loved ones left behind. Concerns about a proper death among better-off Russians can be found everywhere from political assassination to reactions to suicide. When Alexander II was finally brought down by revolutionaries after numerous prior attempts on his life, the imperial propaganda machinery cranked out hagiographic literature, replete with iconographic images, which were designed both to demonstrate that the tsar was in full control of his mental and religious faculties until the very end and to conceal the extent of damage to the royal corpse.[14]

As peasants moved to towns and cities to take jobs in the nascent industries that sprouted up throughout Russia in the last decades of the nineteenth century, they took with them their traditions and customs. The church's ambivalence about its urban mission contributed to its failure to win over either the intelligentsia or the emerging working classes, yet the power of Orthodoxy continued to motivate individuals on a personal level.[15] Religion inspired workers to social engagement, artistic creation and revolutionary activism.[16]

14 Philippe Ariès's influential typology of attitudes towards death in western Europe has yet to be written for Russia. See his *Western attitudes toward death: from the middle ages to the present*, trans. Patricia M. Ranum (Baltimore: Johns Hopkins University Press, 1974).
15 G. L. Freeze, "'Going to the intelligentsia": the church and its urban mission in post-reform Russia', in *Between tsar and people: educated society and the quest for public identity in late imperial Russia*, ed. E. W. Clowes, S. D. Kassow and J. L. West (Princeton: Princeton University Press, 1991), 215–32; S. Dixon, 'The Orthodox church and the workers of St. Petersburg, 1880–1914', in *European religion in the age of great cities, 1830–1930*, ed. H. McLeod (New York: Routledge, 1995), 119–45; K. P. Herrlinger, 'Class, piety and politics: workers, Orthodoxy and the problem of religious identity in Russia, 1881–1914', PhD dissertation, University of California, Berkeley, 1996.
16 A. Lindenmeyr, *Poverty is not a vice: charity, society and the state in imperial Russia* (Princeton: Princeton University Press, 1996); B. G. Rosenthal, 'The search for a Russian Orthodox work ethic', in *Between tsar and people*, 57–74; M. D. Steinberg, 'Workers on the cross: religious imagination in the writings of Russian workers, 1910–1924', *RR* 53 (1994), 213–39;

As believers adapted Orthodox piety to the new dynamics of urban surroundings, its practice took on new forms that often led to a more privatised practice of the faith, a shift that may have eventually contributed to the church's rapid demise in the public sphere after 1917, as well as Orthodoxy's survival in clandestine form among secret communities of believers.

One of the great religious developments of the eighteenth and nineteenth centuries was the spread of disaffection among the educated with the Russian Orthodox Church and its teachings. Peter's assault on the church remained mostly a matter of government prerogative until the publication of the famous *First philosophical letter* of Pëtr Chaadaev (1794–1856), a precursor to the still unresolved debates between the Slavophiles and westernisers and their heirs. In one fell swoop, Chaadaev argued that Russia was a historical misfit, alienated from any western European heritage, disdained by its European cousins and debilitated by the Orthodox faith that held Russia back from educational enlightenment with the gravest of consequences. Quickly condemned as a raving lunatic by Tsar Nicholas, Chaadaev decided to make official amends by retracting his charges, yet he failed to issue an overwhelming argument to the contrary. Chaadaev's critique followed by his recantation inspired the key philosophical debates of the 1840s that spread to all branches of intellectual activity, artistic creativity and eventually political activism. Critic Vissarion Belinskii (1811–48) and writer and publisher Alexander Herzen (1812–70) became known as outspoken critics of Russia and proponents of a more European orientation in the manner of Peter the Great, while Ivan Kireevskii (1806–56), Konstantin (1817–60) and Ivan Aksakov (1823–86), and Alexei Khomiakov (1804–60) became champions of the 'Great Slavic Traditions'. The first group and their successors revelled in western-style education and institutions (economic, though not always political), while the latter favoured Orthodox communalism as formulated in the organic *sobornost* and reverence for strict adherence to religious and historical tradition.[17] Despite their apparent inability to come to a common ground, both camps had a deep appreciation for the building blocks of modernisation – education and literacy.

and R. E. Zelnik, 'To the unaccustomed eye: religion and irreligion in the experience of St. Petersburg workers in the 1870s', in *Christianity and the Eastern Slavs*, II, *Russian culture in modern times*, ed. R. P. Hughes and I. Paperno [California Slavic Studies 17] (Berkeley: University of California Press, 1994), 49–82.

17 A. Gleason, *European and Muscovite: Ivan Kireevskii and the origins of Slavophilism* (Cambridge, MA: Harvard University Press, 1972). *Sobornost* signifies both a spiritual communalism and a council of peers, who make decisions for the good of the community. Nineteenth-century philosophers and theologians presented *sobornost* as a Slavic ideal that eluded the nations and empires of central and western Europe.

Education, literacy and popular culture

More than anything else in post-Petrine Russia, the expansion of primary schooling and the spread of literacy in the last decades of the nineteenth century held great promise. Both religious and secular elites hoped that a basic education would disabuse the people (*narod*) of their ancient customs that had left them ignorant and poverty-stricken. To achieve spiritual and moral enlightenment and prosperity, the Education Statute of 1864 established the principles for what would eventually become a national secular primary school system that was soon paralleled by parish schools. According to this statute, the main purpose of primary education was to instill the people with religious and moral precepts while providing basic literacy and numeracy. Although the support of the political system was added to these goals after the 1866 attempt on the life of the tsar, the secular primary school retained a deeply religious component and satisfied a widespread demand of peasants for such a curriculum. So strong was the interest in religious instruction that in 1884 the holy synod established a parallel parish school system that challenged its secular counterparts for more than two decades. Despite this rapid expansion of primary schooling, parish communities were at a financial disadvantage. While they excelled in attracting pupils, they failed to attract financing for permanent buildings, well-trained instructors and basic instructional materials. New regulations introduced in 1907 by the Ministry of Education linked school funding to rigid standards of quality that few parishes could meet. The result was the precipitous decline in the number of parish schools and their enrollments in the decade preceding the overthrow of Tsar Nicholas II.[18]

Primary schooling brought a new interaction between the peasantry and the lower urban classes on the one hand, and their social and intellectual superiors on the other. Among the ranks of the burgeoning profession of schoolteacher were clergymen and their daughters (even in secular schools where religious education was required to be taught), who worked alongside secularly trained instructors. Teachers' different worldviews brought new perspectives to their pupils' limited experience and often these educators of the people inspired revolutionary activism aimed at reforming the social and political system as a means of ending poverty and deprivation. By the 1890s, *zemstvo* schoolteachers

---

18 Eklof, *Russian peasant schools*, chs. 2, 6; J. Brooks, 'The zemstvo and the education of the people', in *The zemstvo in Russia: an experiment in local self-government*, ed. T. Emmons and W. S. Vucinich (Cambridge: Cambridge University Press, 1982), 243–78; J. Brooks, *When Russia learned to read: literacy and popular literature, 1861–1917* (Princeton: Princeton University Press, 1985), ch. 2.

were closely watched by local authorities seeking to stem the growing tide of unrest and protest throughout the countryside and urban areas, yet parish schoolteachers, moved by their pupils' circumstances and social denigration, were just as likely to propagate radical means to change the existing order.[19] For parish schoolteachers, change began with the reform of parish life and often led to calls for the overthrow of the hierarchical structures of the Orthodox Church and for civil disobedience. Police records attest to the spread of activism among parish schoolteachers, to the collusion of members of the clerical estate (particularly the lower orders of psalmist and deacon), and to the utter devotion of parishioners to these cultural enlighteners.[20]

By the beginning of the twentieth century, despite the uneven development of primary schooling in Russia, basic education, often of just a few years, had succeeded in creating a substantial literate mass among the peasantry and lower urban working classes (amounting to more than 25 per cent of adults by 1917). No longer were Russia's literate to be found only among the upper echelons of society. The taste of new readers lay with religious tales, adventure stories, mysteries, biographies and current events (in the form of penny newspapers) – each representative of middle-brow literature that made cultural elites cringe. Entire industries related to mass publishing sprouted up, many with their own rags-to-riches owners whose peasant backgrounds suggested to Russia's lower classes the prospects that lay ahead for those possessing a measure of ingenuity and derring-do.[21] As peasants encountered new, secular ideas about the world and the history of Russia, they combined elements of folk and urban cultures. At the same time Orthodox piety became more diverse in its expression and less amenable to control by an increasingly anxious holy synod. As the synod's censorial prerogatives were diminished after 1865 and eventually abolished in 1905, the production of popular religious items from icons to saints' biographies became less stylised, though no less formulaic, and flirted with influences from Orthodoxy's rival Old Believers and sectarian movements. The free mixing of secular and sacred imagery could be seen everywhere, especially in the widely used almanacs or peasant calendars whose covers typically portrayed an agricultural scene with a church in the background. Beyond the inside cover the reader could find a list of dates important in the religious, secular

---

19 *Zemstvos* were semi-democratic district and provincial administrative organs responsible for a broad range of social and cultural initiatives in rural Russia beginning in 1864. By 1912 *zemstvos* had been opened in forty-three of Russia's fifty European provinces.

20 See C. A. Frierson, *Peasant icons: representations of rural people in late nineteenth-century Russia* (New York: Oxford University Press, 1993).

21 Brooks, *When Russia learned to read*, chs. 8–9; C. A. Ruud, *A Russian entrepreneur: publisher Ivan Sytin of Moscow, 1851–1934* (Montreal: McGill-Queen's University Press, 1990).

and agricultural year. With basic literary skills, a newly literate Russian could move smoothly from the traditional culture into which he or she was born to the rapidly changing and secularised civic culture of late imperial Russia. The transformation was neither unidirectional nor entirely complete for most individuals, but it was significant none the less.[22]

Even the Bible became a contested piece of literature in both its availability and its interpretation. Although a modern Russian translation of the entire holy book was not sanctioned by the holy synod until 1876, shortly after the appearance of the first translation of Karl Marx's *Capital*, the New Testament and non-approved versions of the Bible were already becoming widely available in the 1860s. Concerned that the Holy Scriptures in the hands of ordinary believers untrained in theology would lead to incorrect, personal interpretation and challenges to ecclesiastical authority reminiscent of the Lutheran revolution, church officials vigorously sought to control the distribution of the Bible. Groups such as the Society for the Dissemination of Holy Scripture in Russia (est. 1863) and the British and Foreign Bible Society developed an extensive colportage system that helped to distribute nearly 1 million bibles annually by the end of the nineteenth century. Old Believers and sectarian leaders were often blamed by ecclesiastical authorities for duping the peasantry through their biblical exegesis while ordinary believers merely expressed a logical curiosity in the basic texts of their faith. Religious renegade and erstwhile author Leo Tolstoy collaborated with Vladimir Grigor'evich Chertkov in the distribution of religious and secular tracts written at levels easily comprehended by individuals with basic literacy skills. Rather than view peasants' thirst for religious knowledge in a positive light, Orthodox leaders preferred to see challenges to their authority.[23]

As Russia was learning to read, folk culture provided familiar themes, artistic forms and storylines for theatre and, after 1908, cinema. Modern theatre was introduced into Russia in the mid-eighteenth century and developed rapidly during the reign of Catherine the Great. Influenced by Enlightenment thinkers, the Russian theatre of the eighteenth century was highly stylised and secular, and remained so with a few exceptions until the fall of the house of Romanov. As theatrical productions spread to the countryside in the last half of the nineteenth century, peasants experienced for the first time organised productions of unfamiliar themes. Often, these productions were staged

---

22 Chulos, *Converging worlds*, ch. 6.
23 S. K. Batalden, 'Colportage and the distribution of the Holy Scriptures in late imperial Russia', in *Christianity and the eastern Slavs*, II, *Russian culture*, 83–92; Chulos, *Converging worlds*, 85–6.

by acting troupes on the run from local authorities who condemned their works as a threat either to local moral sensibilities or to tsarist authority. The arrival of the People's House (*narodnyi dom*) via England and Germany in the 1880s combined traditional elements of peasant carnivals with the repertoires of travelling theatrical productions. People's Houses were about more than theatre, for they often included libraries and tearooms for more serious gatherings.[24]

The appearance of the cinema offered numerous opportunities and limitless possibilities for interaction between diverse social strata. Within four years of the first Russian film production in 1908, cinema reached all segments of the population, urban and rural, literate and illiterate, well off or indigent, who now had a common cultural form that could be shared instantaneously and simultaneously. Ready themes from folk tales, popular literature and the traditional *lubok* helped to idealise and exaggerate the role of religious faith in the life of Russia. Supporting a ban on representation of Orthodox clergymen and religious ritual on screen, church leaders were unable to utilise this new cultural medium to promote their own interests, to instruct the faithful or to probe important religious issues. Increasingly, both the higher and the parish clergy viewed cinema as a rival to religious services and as a hypnotic influence on the youth who were swept away by the exciting and often risqué themes of the movies. When folk tradition was portrayed cinematically, it was often cast in a negative light no better than the image of the upper classes and their hangers-on who favoured illicit love, excessive drinking, abundant luxury, and new morals that rejected traditional social norms – all implicitly subversive qualities that had little concern for Orthodox piety.[25] Keenly aware as the tsarist authorities were of the power of cinema, they never made systematic use of film for propaganda purposes until the outbreak of World War I. Instead, they followed the well-worn path of trying to return the genie to the bottle and, in much the same way as the church, refused to allow independent filmmakers to portray or to use images of the imperial household on the silver screen, except when royal image makers created their own propaganda. The chief examples were short clips of the coronation of Nicholas II in 1896, documentary

24 G. A. Khaichenko, *Russkii narodnyi teatr kontsa XIX–nachala XX veka* (Moscow: Nauka, 1975), 115–16.
25 N. M. Zorkaia, *Na rubezhe stoletii: u istokov massovogo iskusstva v Rossii, 1900–1910 godov* (Moscow: Nauka, 1976), ch. 1; Y. Tsivian, *Early cinema in Russia and its cultural reception* (Chicago: University of Chicago Press, 1998); J. Leyda, *Kino: a history of the Russian and Soviet film*, third edition (Princeton: Princeton University Press, 1983), chs. 1–7; R. Stites, *Russian popular culture: entertainment and society since 1900* (Cambridge: Cambridge University Press, 1992), 27–34.

footage and fictional portrayal of the royal family in connection with the tercentenary of the house of Romanov in 1913, and an officially sanctioned 'Imperial Chronicle' (*Tsarskaia khronika*) beginning in 1907.[26]

The concerns of Orthodox officials proved true with the release of several movies with strong religious themes beginning in October 1917. On the eve of the Bolshevik ascent to power, a two-part movie entitled *Satan triumphant* (*Satana likuiushchii*) successfully played to the general fascination with the occult and possession, as well as broad hostility towards religious extremism and anything German. The exaggerated asceticism of the main character, the Lutheran Pastor Talnox (and in part II, his son Sandro), is matched by his self-induced sexual suffering as he lusts after his late wife's beautiful sister, with whom he shares a house along with his brother-in-law, a hapless hunchbacked artist. Their uneasy family life is suddenly brought down by the visit one stormy night of none other than Satan himself who wreaks havoc on the household and prods Talnox into seducing his sister-in-law and fathering a child on her.[27] The following year, a different sort of religious suffering and destruction of pre-revolutionary social and cultural taboos was the subject of *Fr Sergii* (*Otets Sergii*), an adaptation of a Tolstoy tale. This film portrayed Orthodox religious ritual (sympathetically and accurately) in this fictional story about a former prince who takes monastic vows after his beloved becomes the mistress of the tsar. Eventually, the prince takes clerical vows and becomes known as Fr Sergii, a famous religious preacher with a growing stream of admirers, including women who swoon at the sight of his intense eyes and spiritual devotion. When Fr Sergii yields to carnal desires, he imposes a punishment in the form of a self-inflicted wound, leaves the priesthood and becomes a teacher in a peasant school in order to redeem his soul.[28]

The idealisation of folk culture in popular entertainment was supported by the scholarly disciplines that were emerging in late nineteenth-century Russia. Ethnography in particular placed the researcher's focus on the mundane customs and special traditions of peasant life in an attempt to discover and define the essence of the Russian soul. The resultant cataloguing of objects, behaviours and beliefs paid great attention to piety, especially when it took the

26 Tsivian, *Early cinema*, 127; R. Taylor, *The politics of the Soviet cinema, 1917–1929* (Cambridge: Cambridge University Press, 1979), 10. The Imperial Chronicles were intended both to inform the Russian public of the tsar's official activities and to create official images of the royal family.

27 P. Usai, L. Codelli, Carlo Monatanaro and D. Robinson, *Silent witnesses: Russian films, 1908–1919* (Pordenone: Biblioteca dell'immagine, 1989), 422–6.

28 Ibid., 484–8.

form of superstition, thus enshrining notions of the dual faith for generations to come.[29]

Modernisation and national identity

For the majority of Russia's Orthodox Christians, the faith's rich variety of symbols and rituals provided the foundation for a proto-national identity that began with the local parish or village and expanded to include the entire empire.[30] Ignorant of theological principles, most believers nevertheless placed the Eucharist and liturgy at the centre of religious tradition, imagining that they shared this sacrament with their coreligionists throughout the empire. The parish served as the most accessible manifestation of Russian Orthodox identity for all the faithful, but with improvements in transportation and the spread of literacy after 1861, pilgrimage and related literature provided new opportunities for mass creations of wider-ranging associations.[31]

The convergence of religious and secular identities among Russia's peasantry is found in village histories, which can usually be traced to a mythical event or an event that took on mythic proportions – a visit of a tsar, the spontaneous appearance of a wonder-working icon or an interaction with a holy person. By locating their villages within a greater historical context, peasants connected their small communities to larger and larger entities that included the entire cosmos.[32] Peter the Great's larger than life image dominated village tales from the eighteenth to the early twentieth century. Often, a visit by the rumbustious tsar was commemorated by the construction of a church or the acquisition of a special icon (occasionally a gift of the tsar himself).[33] Icons also played important roles in the historical development of communities by offering their protective powers against calamity. Disputes over ownership of and user rights to special icons sharpened communities' sense of identity as they argued their cases to the diocesan authorities and appealed local decisions

---

29 See B. M. Firsov and I. G. Kiseleva, *Byt velikorusskikh krest'ian-zemlepashtsev: opisanie materialov etnograficheskogo biuro kniazia V. N. Tenisheva (na primere Vladimirskoi gubernii)* (St Petersburg: Izd-vo Evropeiskogo Doma, 1993).

30 E. J. Hobsbawm and T. Ranger, *The invention of tradition*, Introduction, and 263–307.

31 V. and E. Turner, *Image and pilgrimage in Christian culture: anthropological perspectives* (Oxford: Basil Blackwell, 1978), 10–11; V. Turner, *Drama, fields and metaphors: symbolic action in human society* (Ithaca, NY: Cornell University Press, 1974), 201–7.

32 See M. Eliade, *Images and symbols: studies in religious symbolism* (Princeton: Princeton University Press, 1991), 40; R. Redfield, *The little community and peasant society and culture* (Chicago: University of Chicago Press, 1960).

33 N. V. Riasanovsky, *The image of Peter the Great in Russian history and thought* (New York: Oxford University Press, 1985), 83–4.

to the holy synod. When the originals of famous icons were unavailable or too far away to secure a temporary loan, reproductions were purchased and treated with great reverence, while at the same time creating symbolic links with distant parts of the Orthodox world.[34]

Holy people – living or dead – and religious shrines offered another concrete linkage between dispersed and disparate communities. With the spread of literacy, short biographies resembling abbreviated saints' lives (*zhitie*) were published about these exceptional individuals and attracted a growing audience for the popular series, *Troitskie listki*, which was published by the venerable Trinity-St Sergii monastery outside Moscow between 1884 and 1917. Holy fools (*iurodivye*), wanderers (*stranniki, podvizhniki*) and more sedentary spiritual athletes served as the heroes and heroines of these stories and created a human web connecting believers of all social backgrounds. Used by clergymen in their weekly sermons, distributed free during religious holidays and sold at many religious kiosks (especially at shrines), these biographies offered multiple paradigms for the religious life and reinforced religious and social traits that readers could recognise as Russian.

Many of these stories featured men and women who refused to accept their lot in life and ignored their social obligations, choosing instead to lead solitary and often strange lives such as Andrei the Holy Fool (1744–1812). The son of a small landowner in central Russia, Andrei decided at a young age to follow a different path in life and wandered the countryside naked (as holy fools were wont to do) with a knout and axe slung over his shoulder. An odd sight, Andrei was ridiculed by local children but eventually he gained a following of devoted believers who admired his spirituality and good works. After his death, Andrei's remains were interred at the Meshchovsk monastery in Kaluga, which became a pilgrimage destination for those seeking to benefit from his spiritual powers.[35] The stories of individuals like Andrei served two purposes: to publicise the shrines at which their remains could be venerated or at which their wondrous powers were commonly experienced, and to hold up as examples Russians from all walks of life who chose paths different from those inherited at birth.[36]

A cross-section of Russian society could be found at shrines throughout the year, but especially during annual festivals that attracted throngs of pilgrims.

---

34 Chulos, *Converging worlds*, 47–52; V. Shevzov, 'Miracle-working icons, laity and authority in the Russian Orthodox Church, 1861–1917', *RR* 58 (1999), 26–48.

35 'Andrei, iurodstvovavshii v gorode Meshchovske', *Troitskie Listki* 203 (1905). Cf. E. M. Thompson, *Understanding Russia: the holy fool in Russian culture* (Lanham, MD: University Press of America, 1987).

36 Chulos, *Converging worlds*, 68–72.

As pilgrimages gained in popularity, religious and secular publications offered eyewitness accounts, travel information and pricing for those interested in embarking on such a journey. Readers of the illustrated national religious newspaper *Russian Pilgrim* (*Russkii Palomnik*) who were interested in attending the annual feast day celebration of Anna of Kashin in Tver province learned how to travel from Moscow and St Petersburg, what train transfers were required, the duration of travel (which was 13 hours from each capital), and which lodgings offered reasonably priced and comfortable accommodations.[37] On the rare occasion of a canonisation, more than 100,000 pilgrims might flock to the ceremonies. Descriptions of the controversial canonisation of Serafim of Sarov in 1903, which created a very public divide between church leaders and members of the imperial family, who sought to use the event to demonstrate its divine favour, provided travel guidance to future pilgrims to the new holy site.[38] Exact kilometres travelled, class of tickets, ruble prices for a hotel in Arzamas and then details about the final coach ride to Sarov were included, as well as recommendations for less expensive trips that included a steam boat from Nizhnii Novgorod via the Oka river.[39] Together, icons and holy people united both literate and illiterate Russians in their shared Orthodox culture and reminded them of their membership in a larger community that encompassed all regions of the empire.

Personal faith did not always lead to an Orthodox conclusion as the steady growth in sectarianism and irreligiosity attests. The crucial turning point came with the publication of the Edict on Religious Tolerance in 1905 that diminished the restrictions on sectarian groups, thus permitting them to practise their faith in public without fear of reprisal.[40] Falling away from religion altogether occurred almost entirely among the better-educated urban population and was associated with opposition to prevailing social and political norms. Russia's great thinkers struggled with the symbols and values of Orthodox

37 Putnik (N. Lender), 'Nakanune kashinskikh torzhestv. (Vpechatleniia nashego spetsial'nogo korrespondenta)', *Russkii Palomnik* 25 (1909), 344; E. Poselianin, 'Kashinskie torzhestva', *Russkii Palomnik* 25 (1909), 392.

38 G. L. Freeze, 'Tserkov', religiia i politicheskaia kul'tura na zakate staroi Rossii', *Istoriia SSSR* 2 (1991), 107–19; Freeze, 'Subversive piety: religion and the political crisis in late imperial Russia', *Journal of Modern History* 68 (1996), 308–50.

39 S. A. Arkhangelov, *Starets Serafim i Sarovskaia pustyn'* (St Petersburg: Izd. P. P. Soikina, 1903), 194–7.

40 R. R. Robson, *Old Believers in modern Russia* (DeKalb: Northern Illinois University Press, 1995). Sergei Zhuk has argued that sectarianism blossomed in the southern provinces in the nineteenth century and by the early twentieth century had begun to influence provinces throughout European Russia. See S. Zhuk, *Russia's lost reformation: peasants, millennialism, and radical sects in Russia and Ukraine, 1830–1917* (Washington, DC: Woodrow Wilson Center Press, 2004).

Christianity even when they rejected them for more appealing secular alternatives. Russia's writers, artists and philosophers struggled with ways to reconcile their penchant for the essence of the Orthodox faith they considered to have redeeming qualities and their rejection of organised religion. This ambiguous stand on religion coloured the 'Russian Idea', whose essentialist definition of identity has been painted in religious as well as irreligious and secular tones, and is also present in the communism that dominated most of the Soviet period. At the beginning of the twentieth century, symbolists dominated the Russian art world. Their work betrays the influences of the magic, superstitions and otherworldliness that were inseparable from Orthodoxy. The cultural activity associated with the 'Silver Age' of the first decade of the twentieth century was deeply embedded in spiritual and psychological structures found in Orthodoxy.[41]

As Russia's peasantry began to migrate in large numbers to urban areas in search of work, traditional Orthodox piety remained a powerful force. While large urban cathedrals may not have been as welcoming as familiar village churches, workers sustained themselves spiritually by organising religious reading groups and choirs, by employing religious themes in their creative writing and by adhering to traditional Orthodox customs.[42] Rather than disappearing in the face of literacy and migration, Orthodox piety offered a means of easing the transition from traditional to modern life. This devotion to the faith did not, however, prevent the rapid and devastating demise of the Orthodox Church after 1917 because the gap that had long separated the upper clergy, parish priests and the faithful proved insurmountable in the years leading up to the Bolshevik Revolution. While faith remained strong among the vast majority of Russians, a lack of confidence in the church and its clerics favoured a decentralised, democratised and localised faith that became highly individualised and easily hidden during antireligious campaigns of the 1920s.[43]

As Russian society experienced tumultuous change, opportunities for women grew within the strict context imposed by the Orthodox Church. A majority of pilgrims were women travelling in groups, spending large periods of time away from family and domestic responsibilities. When they returned to their villages, they were often spiritually renewed and shared tales

41 L. Engelstein, 'Paradigms, pathologies and other clues to Russian spiritual culture: some post-Soviet thoughts', *Slavic Review* 57 (1998), 864–77.
42 Herrlinger, 'Class, piety and politics: workers, Orthodoxy and the problem of religious identity in Russia, 1881–1914'; Steinberg, 'Workers on the cross', 213–39.
43 Chulos, *Converging worlds*, 104–11.

of exotic places they had visited and strange people they had encountered. A smaller number of women from all strata of society chose a more radical path and formed lay nunneries or women's communities (*zhenskie obshchiny*) that remained beyond the formal supervision of monasteries. These lay communities of religious women provided leadership roles not available anywhere else. Within the more traditional realm of parish life, women were active in charitable activities and education, but also sought with increasing frustration to obtain official permission to serve as members of parish councils and in more important capacities in the various religious services. In a more prosaic way, women throughout Russia – regardless of their social standing – served as the guardians of tradition who took it upon themselves to instruct the next generation in the customs and beliefs they felt were essential to survival and prosperity. While their accomplishments were belittled by male-orientated restrictions, the efforts of pre-revolutionary women were rewarded during the national church council of 1917–18, which accorded them the right to be active members of parish councils and to engage in most administrative functions of the local religious community. As the Romanov dynasty's time on the political stage drew to a close, the varieties of popular piety challenged more traditional elements within Orthodoxy, but also turned out to be the strongest source of support for the faith once the antireligious movements unleashed their destructive forces in the countryside and cities alike.[44]

Russian Orthodoxy in the context of European Christianity

A comparative approach to the history of Christianity in Europe underscores the overwhelming commonalities in experiences of faithful individuals and communities throughout the centuries, but especially since the fateful eighteenth century, when the French Revolution helped to demystify the idea of divine mandate of royal families and public prominence of favoured churches. The secularisation of the church in France was part of the democratic values propounded by revolutionaries, but it was also a logical consequence of the Lutheran Reformation's brash insubordination to the Catholic Church. Just

---

44 B. Meehan, 'Popular piety, local initiative and the founding of women's religious communities in Russia, 1764–1907', in *Seeking God*, 83–105; B. Meehan-Waters, 'To save oneself: Russian peasant women and the development of women's religious communities in prerevolutionary Russia', in *Russian peasant women*, ed. B. Farnsworth and L. Viola (New York: Oxford University Press, 1992), 121–33; B. Meehan, *Holy women of Russia: the lives of five Orthodox women offer spiritual guidance for today* (Crestwood, NY: St Vladimir's Seminary Press, 1997).

as the latter was proven to be only one among many spiritual and religious options in the western sphere of Christianity after Luther's fateful act in 1517, churches throughout Europe and Russia after the events of 1789 faced the prospects of being politically and socially marginalised. Although Russia has been cast as coming late to the innovations of Europe, the reforms of Peter the Great and the confiscation of church lands by Catherine the Great preceded the events in Paris by several decades. The ultimate result in most countries was the separation of church and state and the replacement of the church's social functions with secular institutions of welfare and education. Chronology and extremism separates Russia from its European cousins, but essentially the effects of secularisation and modernisation on established Christian faiths were the same. Accordingly, one of the capstones of the modern era is the marginalisation of religion in society and culture, or the radical transformation of dominant faiths to accommodate public and personal disaffection with traditional forms of belief and practice. The leading schemes of this process emphasise the subordination of dominant churches to secular political authority and the consequent withdrawal of religion from the public sphere. Where religious institutions once served important social functions through philanthropic and educational efforts, they now faced increasing competition from nonsectarian social welfare activities of the government or private institutions and the well-trained and better-funded state primary and secondary schools.[45] At different times and in different ways, most of Europe struggled in the nineteenth century as traditional ways of life among elites and commoners reacted to the secularising by-products of industrialisation and modernisation. The Europe of 1800 was radically different politically, socially and culturally from Europe at the end of World War I, and nowhere was this more apparent than in Russia, which had begun its extreme attempt at departure from the past by legally separating church and state and by introducing increasingly restrictive measures against all forms of public religiosity.

As scholars began to question the usefulness of grand and generalising social and cultural theories in the 1960s and 1970s, secularisation as a concept fell under a cloud of suspicion. Studies of the people – peasants and workers alike – and their faith stood at the centre of these critiques as social historians shifted their attention from elites to the subordinated classes. Taking an interdisciplinary approach, Natalie Zemon Davis forged new paths towards the

45 B. Wilson, *Religion in secular society* (New York: Penguin Books, 1969); D. Martin, *A general theory of secularization* (New York: Harper and Row, 1978); K. Dobbelaere, 'Secularization: a multi-dimensional concept', *Current Sociology* 29 (Summer 1981), 1–216.

discovery of the so-called 'magical/superstitious' beliefs of commoners.[46] She posited that practices and beliefs of communities aimed at explaining how the uneducated and powerless members of society integrated the 'symbols and discourse of the Church Universal for local votive use', in just the same way as rational thinkers who mixed, matched and excluded elements of different types of Christian experience.[47] When these theoretical frameworks were applied to Russia in the late 1980s and 1990s, scholars found striking similarities in the way peasants in Russia and Europe conceptualised the world around them just prior to and during their transformation into modern industrial nations.[48] While much less attention has been given to religious change among the elites in the late nineteenth and early twentieth centuries, new research suggests that the Russian church hierarchy was anything but monolithic in its response to issues of the day such as urbanisation, mobility and revolutionary solutions to social and economic problems. Moreover, Russia's cultural elites and philosophers were equally diverse and together represented points across the religious and political spectra, from ultra-nationalist to atheist, from staunch monarchist to communist.

Nation-building and national identity, two ideas that set Europe on fire after the Congress of Vienna in 1815, did not bypass Russia despite certain peculiarities. Language, literature, religion and myth helped to unite the diverse ethnic populations of the European part of the Russian Empire, as they did in the west. As Geoffrey Hosking has seen, what distinguished Russia was the creation of a sense of state rather than a sense of nationhood. A political focal point for this identity was the imperial family, its histories and its ceremonies. As the nineteenth century drew to a close, public ceremonies and celebrations focused

---

46 N. Z. Davis, 'Some tasks and themes in the study of popular religion', in *The pursuit of holiness in late medieval and renaissance religion (Papers from the University of Michigan Conference)*, ed. C. Trinkaus and H. A. Oberman [Studies in Medieval and Reformational Thought 10] (Leiden: E. J. Brill, 1974), 307–36.

47 W. Christian, *Local religion in sixteenth-century Spain* (Princeton: Princeton University Press, 1981), 181. Cf. T. Kselman, *Belief in history: innovative approaches to European and American religion* (Notre Dame: University of Notre Dame Press, 1991), Introduction.

48 J. E. Clay, 'Russian peasant religion and its repression: the Christ-Faith (*khristovshchina*) and the origins of the 'Flagellant' myth, 1666–1837', PhD dissertation, University of Chicago, 1989; Chulos, 'Pious or pagan peasant', 181–216; C. J. Chulos, 'Peasant perspectives of clerical debauchery in post-empancipation Russia', *Studia Slavica Finlandensia* 12 (1995), 33–53; Chulos, *Converging worlds*; V. Shevzov, 'Popular Orthodox in late imperial Russia', PhD dissertation, Yale University, 1994; C. Worobec, *Possessed: women, witches and demons in imperial Russia* (DeKalb: Northern Illinois University Press, 2001); M. M. Gromyko, *Pravoslavie i russkaia narodnaia kul'tura*, 4 vols. (Moscow: Koordinatsionno-metodicheskii tsentr prikladnoi etnografii In-ta etnologii i antropologii RAN, 1993–1994). Cf. E. Weber, *Peasants into Frenchmen: the modernization of modern France, 1870–1914* (Stanford: Stanford University Press, 1976).

almost exclusively on the tsar as the symbolic father of subjects who often spoke different languages, belonged to different ethnic groups and practised different religions.[49] An independent public sphere able to promote alternative identities may have been more restrictive than elsewhere in Europe, but it allowed for new expressions of being Russian that relied less on the person of the tsar or on Orthodoxy than on the imperial model. The emerging literary markets for high-, low- and middle-brow readers posed the broadest challenges to tradition as they pondered the possibility of a unified identity in a multinational and multiethnic empire or presented secular notions of Russianness that emphasised the geographical expanse of the empire and its historical achievement.[50]

In the decade leading up to World War I, the Russian autocracy faced growing and seemingly irreversible social and political unrest without offering any viable alternatives to eventual revolution. Peter the Great had left his mark by creating a schizophrenic Russia that shifted uneasily between its older Slavic Orthodox and newer western selves as it created a new path for the empire. By way of contrast, Tsar Nicholas II preferred to lean on the Slavic Orthodox roots of his people in an attempt to revive an outdated Muscovite notion of tsar and people as united in history and destiny. In this, the doomed tsar deferred to what he considered to be the natural inclination of his subjects towards a new type of Orthodox piety, which longed for a distant past while taking advantage of the benefits of modern technologies.

49 This is a basic theme of Hosking, *Russia, people and empire*. Cf. R. Wortman, *Scenarios of power: myth and ceremony in Russian monarchy*, 2 vols. (Princeton: Princeton University Press, 1995–2000).
50 Brooks, *When Russia learned to read*, ch. 6.

PART III

*

EASTERN CHRISTIANITIES

16

Eastern Christianities (eleventh to fourteenth century): Copts, Melkites, Nestorians and Jacobites

FRANÇOISE MICHEAU

The Coptic, Melkite, Nestorian and Jacobite communities possessed distinctive features, which set them apart from the other Orthodox churches studied in this volume. The first – and not the least important – was their establishment in countries which were under Muslim – and not Christian – rule. This was in complete contrast to the situation existing in the Byzantine Empire and in the kingdoms of Armenia and Georgia to the north, or in Nubia and Ethiopia to the south. A consequence of this was their juridically inferior status, known in Arabic as *dhimma*. This guaranteed members of the community rights of protection for themselves and their property, but in other ways discriminated against them. Their place in society cannot, however, just be reduced to a matter of juridical status, since there were marked variations according to time, place, social setting and reigning dynasty. In the first centuries of Islam Christianity, originally the dominant faith in most of the lands conquered by the Arabs, remained a majority faith, but by the eleventh century this was no longer so. Its progressive decline produced a new cultural outlook characterised by a reaffirmation of identity, which might require, depending on circumstance, accommodation with Islam or alliance with foreign powers.[1]

Another distinctive feature of these Christian communities was their heterogeneity, which stemmed from the fact that there was no good reason for any Muslim power to impose on them one ecclesiastical obedience rather than

---

[1] R. W. Bulliet, 'Process and status in conversion and continuity', in *Conversion and continuity: indigenous Christian communities in Islamic lands (8th–18th centuries)*, ed. M. Gervers and R. J. Bikhazi [Papers in Mediaeval Studies 9] (Toronto: Pontifical Institute of Mediaeval Studies, 1990), 1–12, where he presents conversion as 'a process, which changed both Christian and Islamic communities' (p. 5), with the former remaining 'in many respects members of a single society' (p. 7) This 'Muslim–Christian matrix has displayed four "states"' (pp. 7–8): the first two correspond to a period when the Muslims were politically, but not numerically, dominant, while the last two were characterised by the divisions and rivalries among Muslim powers, the external threat from non-Islamic forces, and a 'greater social differentiation'.

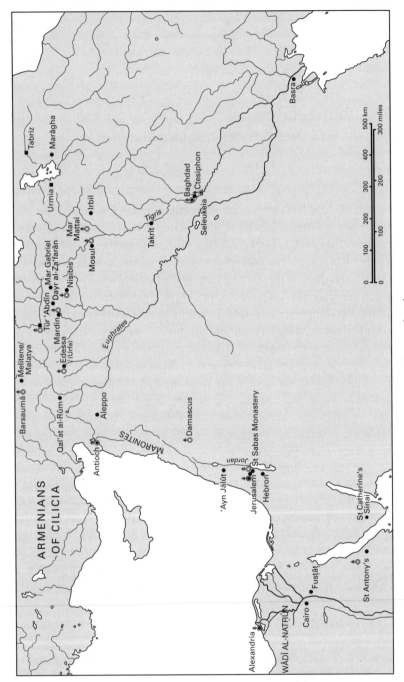

Map 5 Eastern churches

another. It was not uncommon for several communities to congregate in the same place, which tended to be a source of conflict and weakness rather than strength. These divisions went back to the christological controversies of the fifth century, which split the eastern churches into three separate allegiances, known for convenience's sake as Chalcedonian (those who accepted the council of Chalcedon (451)) and Monophysite and Nestorian (those who did not). The independent and rival hierarchies that emerged often had their centre of gravity within a particular region, but this did not mean that they were able to eliminate their rivals. The history of Christian communities in the lands of Islam normally focuses on these different churches.[2] In this chapter I shall begin with a short introduction on their history and geography. However, my main purpose will be to study their main features and developments as a single phenomenon, without, of course, neglecting what was distinctive about each denomination.

Ecclesiastical geography

A Monophysite church, currently known as the Coptic Church,[3] was the dominant force in Egyptian Christianity under Islam. Organised around the patriarchal see of Alexandria, the Coptic Church displayed a strongly Egyptian identity. From the eighth century onwards the patriarchs were frequently resident at Fusṭāṭ, the capital of Muslim Egypt. During the two centuries that followed they abandoned Alexandria, which now lacked both security and prestige. When not at Fusṭāṭ they preferred to stay in different towns of the Delta or in desert monasteries. The definitive transfer of the patriarchal residence from Alexandria to Cairo occurred during the patriarchate of Cyril II (1078–92), and not, as is usually said, during that of his predecessor Christodoulos (1047–77). This step was less a matter of the patriarchs wishing to be closer to the centre of power and much more a result of the vigorous centralising policy of the grand vizier Badr al-Jamālī, who insisted that the patriarch establish himself in the capital.[4] The patriarchs continued all the same to be ordained at both Alexandria and Fusṭāṭ.

---

2 A good synthesis of this approach can be found in *Histoire du christianisme des origines à nos jours*, ed. J.-M. Mayeur, C. Pietri, A. Vauchez and M. Venard, 13 vols. (Paris: Desclée, 1990–2000).

3 The terms Copt and Coptic derive from the Arabic *Qibṭ*, itself derived from the Greek Αἴγυπτος, which is a corruption of the Ancient Egyptian Ha-Ker-Ptah.

4 See J. Den Heijer, 'Le patriarcat copte d'Alexandrie à l'époque fatimide', in *Alexandrie médiévale*, ed. C. Décobert [Études alexandrines 8] (Cairo: Institut français d'archéologie orientale, 2002), II, 83–97.

In 969 Egypt passed under the rule of a new dynasty, the Fatimids, who claimed descent from 'Alî and Fâṭima. They based their legitimacy on the Ismailî variant of Shi'a doctrine, which meant rivalry with the Abbasids of Baghdad, who upheld the Sunni doctrine. They adopted a largely favourable attitude towards the Christians. This may have been a reaction to the position in which the Fatimids found themselves in Egypt: a minority among an overwhelmingly Sunni population. Another consideration was the need to maintain good relations with the Christian powers of Byzantium and western Europe. An exception to this favourable treatment of Christians was the persecution carried out by the Fatimid Caliph al-Ḥâkim during the years 1004–13,[5] which involved the implementation of clothing regulations, prohibition of the public celebration of Christian festivals, confiscation of the property belonging to churches and monasteries, destruction of the church of the Holy Sepulchre (1009), and dismissal of Christian and Jewish functionaries. But it is often forgotten that at the end of his reign al-Ḥâkim rescinded these measures: he restored the confiscated property, authorised the rebuilding of churches, and even allowed those converted to Islam under duress to revert to Christianity. This allowed the Copts to recover the privileged position which they had momentarily lost, particularly in the administration, where they held numerous posts and high office.

The integration of the Copts into an unmistakably Arab Egypt led inevitably to arabisation,[6] which had certainly been facilitated by the fact that the Coptic Church was a purely Egyptian church. A Coptic prelate proclaimed in the thirteenth century: 'May God – praised be He – make victorious their sultan, and he is our sultan, and their imam, and he is our shepherd.'[7] These words reveal the loyalty that existed – at least among the elite – to a community presided over by the sultan.

We now come to the Melkite Church. Melkite meaning royal or imperial was a term applied to those loyal to the Chalcedonian creed, which was

---

5 This policy was both an aberration and in breach of the obligations imposed by *dhimma*. Historians have long considered it as the product of the madness of a ruler struck down by 'melancholy', as the medieval medical handbooks described it. But a new interpretation suggests that al-Ḥâkim's motivation was a wish to impose Ismaili doctrines, to punish the pride of the Christians who occupied high administrative office, and to improve morals, within a millenniarist perspective connected to the year 400 of the hegira. In any case, it was not only Jews and Christians who were the sole objects of al-Ḥâkim's religious policy.

6 See A. S. Atiya, *A history of Eastern Christianity* (London: Methuen, 1968).

7 Sawîrus ibn al-Muqaffa', *History of the patriarchs of the Egyptian Church, known as the History of the Holy Church*, IV, 2: Cyril III, Ibn Laklak (1216–1243 A.D.), ed. A. Khater and O. H. E. Burmester (Cairo: Société d'archéologie copte, 1974), (text) 74; (trans.) 150.

adopted by the emperors of Constantinople. In Egypt it had its own patriarch of Alexandria, but it only ever had a few followers, limited in the main to Alexandria and the Delta. By way of contrast, in Syria[8] and particularly in Palestine it was a more formidable force. The Melkites held the patriarchate of Jerusalem, which was the only one where there was not a double hierarchy. In central and northern Syria the Byzantine reconquest of 969 reinforced their position. For more than a century Antioch and the surrounding region came under Byzantine rule. But confronting them were the Jacobites, as they have come to be called, their Monophysite rivals.

The Jacobite Church took its name from its founder, Jacob Baradaeus, a sixth-century bishop of Edessa. It established its own patriarchate of Antioch. It was especially strong in northern Syria, but in the tenth century it lost much of its flock to Islam and, following the Byzantine reconquest, to the Melkites. Its centre of gravity moved eastwards to the Jazira[9] or Upper Mesopotamia, where its main establishments were the monastery of Barṣaumâ near the city of Melitene / Malaṭya, that of Dayr al-Za'farân near Mârdîn, and that of Mar Mataï near Mosul. Although there continued to be a Jacobite 'patriarch of Antioch and Syria', from the ninth century the holder of this title preferred to reside in different monasteries of northern Syria. From the time of the Byzantine reconquest various places served as the patriarchal residence, notably the monastery of Barṣaumâ in the twelfth century and the town of Qal'at al-Rûm in the thirteenth.

Neither must we forget the Maronite Church. Very little is known about its early development, and it only enters history at the time of the crusades. According to local tradition it took its name from a monk John Maron, who became patriarch at the end of the seventh century. He was a follower of the Monothelite heresy,[10] even if from the sixteenth century onwards the Maronites have proclaimed their 'perpetual Orthodoxy'. Originally established at Apamea, the Maronite patriarch fled in the eleventh century to the mountains of Lebanon, which became the centre of the Maronite Church.

There is one final region that needs to be considered: Mesopotamia, where the Nestorians predominated. They followed the teaching of Nestorios, patriarch of Constantinople, who was condemned at the first council of Ephesus

---

8 This is the region running from Mount Sinai in the south to the passes of the Taurus in the north referred to in Arabic texts as al-Shâm.

9 This is an Arabic term meaning island used to designate the region between the Tigris and the Euphrates.

10 This was a doctrinal compromise put forward by the emperor Herakleios, which the Orthodox Church subsequently rejected.

(431) for privileging the human nature of Christ. Having embraced the Nestorian confession in 486 the church of Persia had established its independence under the authority of a patriarch, who resided at Seleukeia. In the face of Byzantine hostility most of the Syrian Nestorians settled in the Persian Empire. After the Arabic conquest the Nestorians experienced their hour of glory under the Abbasids, when a number of them held high administrative office or were employed as secretaries and doctors and were highly esteemed. In 780 their catholicos[11] Timothy I transferred his residence from Ctesiphon to Baghdad. The language and culture of this church is Syriac. Even in Baghdad, but especially in northern Mesopotamia, it was in competition with other Syrians in the shape of the Jacobites. Some modern writers, such as Père Fiey, distinguish the eastern Syrians (Nestorians) from the western Syrians (Jacobites). In the twelfth century the Jacobite metropolitan in charge of the Oriental territories (i.e. those formerly included in the Sassanian Empire) took the title of *maphrian* and established himself at Takrît, which provoked the pillaging and confiscation of churches.[12] In the middle of the twelfth century the *maphrian* moved to the monastery of Mar Mattaï, close to Mosul, which from 1127 was the capital of an autonomous principality. There the Jacobite and Nestorian communities enjoyed a period of stability and prosperity, of which the most notable evidence is their contribution to the development of the art of inlayed metal ware.[13]

The Nestorian Church was divided into 'interior' and 'exterior' provinces. The former covered Mesopotamia (Nisibis, Basra, Irbil, Mosul) and the confines of Iran, while the latter corresponded to the 'Orient' (eastern Iran, Arabia, central Asia, China, the coasts of India and Indonesia), where Nestorianism established itself as a result of intense missionary activity between the fifth and eighth centuries. If Christianity was in full retreat in Iran by the end of the eleventh century, the communities further to the east continued to exist and excited the interest of westerners, who discovered the 'Orient' in the thirteenth century, but their history lies outside the remit of this chapter.

Each of these churches was autonomous under the guidance of a patriarch – also called pope in the Coptic Church or catholicos in the Nestorian Church. Lists of these patriarchs were established long ago, even if more recent studies have made some slight additions and corrections. Designation of patriarch was by election. The future patriarch was chosen by an assembly, the composition

---

11 This is the term currently in use for the Nestorian patriarch.
12 The title is first mentioned in 1123.
13 See J.-M. Fiey, *Mossoul chrétienne* (Beirut: Imprimerie catholique, 1959); E. Baer, *Ayyubid metalwork with Christian images* (Leiden: E. J. Brill, 1988).

of which varied according to church and period, but included bishops and abbots, sometimes priests and monks; sometimes even influential members of the laity. It was also necessary to obtain confirmation from the Muslim ruling authorities.[14] Only then could the solemn ordination of the new patriarch take place. If you read the ecclesiastical chronicles of the different churches, it is clear that this process produced violent quarrels among the candidates, with recourse to simony, tribal feuds and political infighting, and to the good offices of a Muslim ruler. Leaving aside personal ambitions, the rivalry among candidates for office often reveals the underlying divisions within the different Christian communities. It equally reveals an ecclesiastical organisation grounded in personal ties and the influence of the 'powerful'.

By way of illustration I shall limit myself to two examples. The first concerns the Coptic Church, which experienced a vacancy lasting nearly twenty years following the death of John VI in 1216.[15] Christians in Egypt were effectively divided into two parties. The first supported the priest Dâ'ûd, a native of the Fayyûm, who eventually succeeded to the patriarchal throne in 1235 as Cyril III. He had a pragmatic view of the relationship of the church to power and wealth and enjoyed wide support among Christian functionaries. His opponents backed a series of candidates – notably, a monk renowned for his asceticism – who took a harder, more uncompromising line. The struggle crystallised around the two cities into which Cairo was divided. Dâ'ûd's partisans were most strongly represented in al-Qâhira, the urban centre established by the Fatimids, which housed the political elite. His opponents were concentrated in Fusṭâṭ, the old town, which housed the venerable old church known as al-Mu'allaqa. The numerous twists and turns of this episode reveal not only that both sides sought to obtain the precious diploma of investiture from al-Kâmil, the Ayyubid sultan of the day, but also that they had no hesitation in offering him considerable sums of money. Dâ'ûd's supporters eventually paid 2000 dinars for his investiture. For his part, al-Kâmil had no desire to designate a patriarch until he had the full support of the Christian community and he did his best to act as an honest broker. A modern historian cannot help but feel that such a crisis can only have contributed to the weakening and discrediting the Coptic Church, just at the moment when the soldiers of the Fifth Crusade had taken Damietta and were marching on Cairo.

---

14 See the charter granted to the catholicos 'Abdishô' III, edited by A. Mingana, 'A charter of protection granted to the Nestorian Church A.D. 1138 by Muktafi II, Caliph of Baghdad', *Bulletin of the John Rylands Library* 10 (1926), 127–33.
15 See *History of the patriarchs*, IV, 2.

The schism within the Jacobite Church during the years 1252–63 provides a second example of a conflict over a patriarchal throne.[16] It was a matter of the two rival patriarchs, who had been elected on the death of Ignatios II: Dionysios, metropolitan of Melitene/Malaṭya, and the *maphrian* Bar Ma'dânî. The former was elected in 1252 at the monastery of Barṣaumâ by a small assembly comprising the bishops of the 'western' provinces (i.e. west of the Upper Euphrates), while the latter was elected a little later at Aleppo by the bishops of the 'eastern' provinces (i.e. Ṭûr 'Abdîn and the upper valley of the Tigris). Over a period of several years the two patriarchs attempted to impose themselves on the church as a whole. With promises of large sums of money they sought the support of the Muslim authorities, be they the Seljuqs of Konya or the Ayyubids of Damascus. The appearance of the Mongols complicated the affair still further, though, paradoxically, allowing its dénouement. This schism was far from being the only one that divided the eastern and western poles of the Jacobite Church. Its history was one where local considerations often took precedence over any feeling of unity. But leaving these to one side, Dionysios's ignorance of Arabic makes him seem a figure emblematic of a church which lived off its religious and cultural traditions; which was not well attuned to current political realities; which was hostile to the policy of rapprochement with the Latins initiated by Patriarch Ignatios II, Dionysios's predecessor; and which saw in the Mongols an ally against Islam. Bar Ma'dânî, in contrast, had the support of the Christian elite, who welcomed integration, frequented the centres of power, acted as administrators and doctors, and preferred to flee before the Mongols.

The status and application of *dhimma*

The *dhimma* status, which applied to Christian communities in the lands of Islam, is well known. It went back to the time of the Arab conquests in the seventh and eighth centuries and, in its broad lines, was fixed in the treaties of *fiqh* in the eighth and ninth centuries.[17] It granted the 'peoples of the Book', Jews and Christians, the protection of the Muslim ruling authority, freedom of worship, and continuation of their ecclesiastical, communal and judicial organisation, together with property rights and freedom to trade. In return, the

---

16 See Bar Hebraeus, *Chronicon ecclesiasticum*, ed. J. B. Abelloos and T. J. Lamy (Paris and Louvain: C. Peeters, 1877), II, cols. 695–744.

17 *Fiqh* is a term used for Muslim law, in the sense of implementing the *sharî'a*. The first codification of the legal condition of *dhimmîs* was the work of Abû Yûsuf Ya'qûb, kadi of the Abbasid caliph Hârûn al-Rashîd, in the *Kitâb al-kharaj*, trans. E. Fagnan [Bibliothèque archéologique et historique 1] (Paris: P. Geuthner, 1921).

dhimmîs had to recognise the political sovereignty of Islam, to respect Muslims, to refrain from ostentatious religious celebrations, to wear distinctive clothing and, finally, to pay a poll-tax known as *jizya*. Some contemporary writers have seen these conditions as proof of the remarkable tolerance shown by the Muslims, while others have condemned it as an act of oppression inflicted on non-Muslims. There can, however, be no doubt that it provided security and autonomy on the one hand, and legal inferiority on the other, which was applied variously depending on region, period, rulers and social setting.

The general trend is quite clear. In the period under consideration, from the eleventh to the fourteenth century, *dhimma* status was imposed more severely and the material position of *dhimmîs* deteriorated. Behind this were general developments within Islam. Just as the schism of 1054 is of great symbolic significance for Orthodoxy, so the year 1055 marks an equally important rupture in the history of Islam, for in that year the Seljuq leader Tughril Beg entered Baghdad, putting an end to the dream of a pan-Islamic community united around its caliph. The Seljuqs of Iraq and Iran – and in their wake various military dynasties, first in Syria, and then with Saladin in Egypt – developed new models of legitimacy and of the exercise of power, for which the defence of Sunni Islam was central. At a time when the demographic, cultural and social influence of Christianity was on the wane, Islam set the social norm, which meant the strict application of Muslim law and of *dhimma* status. It is significant that the earliest version of the so-called pact of 'Umar should date precisely from the twelfth century, since it was taken as authoritative when it came to establishing *dhimma* status.[18]

Instructive are the policies pursued by the sultan Saladin (1171–93). He revived measures that had apparently fallen into disuse: for example, Christians were required to wear a yellow belt, were forbidden to ride horses or mules, and were expected to show due modesty in their religious ceremonies and buildings, which meant among others things the removal of crosses from the exterior of churches. Such a rigorist attitude on the part of the rulers might have encouraged further measures against Christians. It was to guard against this that Saladin reminded the inhabitants of Aleppo that in return for respect for Muslim law minorities could expect protection. He informed them: 'When we ordered the *dhimmîs* to wear the distinctive clothing which distinguishes them from Muslims . . . we heard that gangs of thugs inflamed by hatred attacked

---

18 See al-Turtushî, *Sirâj al-mulûk* (Cairo, 1289/1872), 135ff.; trans. M. Alarcón, *Lámparas de los príncipes por Abubéquer de Torotosa*, II (Madrid: Instituto de Valencia de Don Juan, 1931), 143ff. Cf. A. Fattal, *Le statut légal des non-musulmans en pays d'Islam* (Beirut: Imprimerie catholique, 1958), 60–3.

the *dhimmîs* with words and detestable actions in contravention of their rights under the *dhimma* pact. We strongly disapprove of this and we forbid either fomenting or executing such things.'[19]

Besides developments peculiar to the lands of Islam, two other factors, this time external, conspired to undermine the position of Christian communities: the crusades and the Mongol conquests.

The crusades and the position of eastern Christianities

In an *excitatorium* of November 1095 addressed to the Flemings Pope Urban II first sketched the conquest of Jerusalem by the Turks and the sufferings of the Christians before making his appeal in the following words: 'Being much distressed by the proper concern which we felt about the news of this disaster we have visited France, where we have implored most of the princes of the land and their subjects to liberate the Churches of the East.'[20] Apart from the destruction of the church of the Holy Sepulchre by al-Ḥâkim, Christian propaganda resorted to the grave consequences that the Turkish conquest had for the Christians. But, as Claude Cahen has magisterially demonstrated,[21] once masters of Syria the Turks quickly restored order, did not significantly modify the position of non-Muslims and did not impede pilgrimages to Jerusalem. This is borne out by an observation of a Coptic historian:

> The Ghuzz [i.e. Türkmen] had taken possession of the city of Jerusalem the protected and they had denied the descent of the light in the church of the Holy Resurrection over the Noble Sepulture, but, when they learned the verity of its descent every year, they had consideration for the Christians, who were living in it, and they employed for the administration of the country a Christian man, a Jacobite, a lover of Christ, known as Manṣûr al-Balbâyî, and he had a wife like himself, and he was of assistance to every one who arrived in Jerusalem from among the Christians of Egypt and of their countries besides it. He endeavoured to rebuild the church of the Jacobite Orthodox in Jerusalem.[22]

19 See A.-M. Eddé, *La principauté ayyoubide d'Alep (579/1183–658/1260)* [Freiburger Islam Studien 21] (Stuttgart: Franz Steiner Verlag, 1999), 465.
20 H. Hagenmeyer, *Die Kreuzzugsbriefe aus den Jahren 1088–1100* (Innsbruck: Verlag der Wagner'schen Universitäts-Buchhandlung, 1901), 136–7. Cf. B. Hamilton, *The Latin Church in the Crusader States: the secular church* (London: Variorum, 1980), 1.
21 C. Cahen, 'Notes sur l'histoire de l'Orient latin: 1 – En quoi la conquête turque appelait-elle la croisade?', *Bulletin de la Faculté des Lettres de Strasbourg* 21 (1950–51), 118–25 [= C. Cahen, *Turcobyzantina et Oriens christianus* (London: Variorum, 1974), c].
22 *History of the patriarchs*, II, part 3: (text) 299; (trans.) 364.

The arrival of the crusaders upset the political and religious balance of the Near East, which in time proved harmful to eastern Christians with the exception of the Maronites and possibly the Armenians. In the newly created crusader states the Franks – by definition Latins loyal to Rome – imposed their authority on native Christians, in the same way as on the Muslims. In point of fact, the position of Christians varied according to the community they belonged to. The Melkites had more to lose with the arrival of the crusaders, because they were not only the most numerous in the Latin states, but also recognised as close to the Byzantines. So, following the conquest of Antioch and Jerusalem, the crusaders instituted Latin patriarchs, driving out the existing Melkite patriarchs, who were forced to seek refuge at Constantinople. The same happened with the majority of bishops on the pretext that a single body cannot have two heads. The Melkites were now subject to a Latin hierarchy, which did not, however, insist on the Latin rite. As a result, James of Vitry, bishop of Acre (1216–29), was horrified to discover that the Greek Christians of his diocese had married priests, used leavened bread in the communion service, included the right of confirmation in infant baptism, and omitted the *filioque* from the Nicene creed.[23] Over the twelfth century relations between the Melkites and the Latins in the kingdom of Jerusalem improved somewhat. Relations were more strained in the principality of Antioch, where they were complicated by political conflict with a succession of Byzantine emperors, who had never given up their claim to Antioch and the Orontes valley. They refused to recognise the Latin patriarchs of Antioch, supporting instead a rival line of Orthodox patriarchs in exile at Constantinople.

In contrast, the other churches preserved their own hierarchies, since their patriarchal seats lay outside the Latin states, as did most of their members. Within the Latin states the Jacobites retained their religious autonomy and places of worship. The Jacobite patriarch of Antioch, Michael the Syrian (1166–99), wrote as follows:

> The Franks, who occupied Antioch and Jerusalem, had . . . bishops in their states. And the leaders of our Church lived among them, without being perse-cuted or harassed by them, for, even if the Franks agreed with the Greeks over the double nature, they still disagreed with them over several points of faith and their customs were quite different . . . [They] never made any difficulties over matters of faith, nor did they seek to impose a single observance on all

23 *Lettres de Jacques de Vitry*, ed. R. B. C. Huygens (Leiden: E. J. Brill, 1960), ii.136–49: 84–5. Cf. Hamilton, *The Latin Church*, 163–4.

Christians of whatever language. They were content without further enquiry or examination to consider Christian whoever venerated the cross.[24]

Generally speaking, the attitude of the Jacobites towards the crusaders varied according to circumstance: sometimes they displayed indifference, sometimes they were realistic and conciliatory, even favourably disposed because of a common hostility to the Melkites, but sometimes they were antagonistic, as was the case in 1148 when the crusaders sacked the great monastery of Barṣaumâ.

Being at a greater distance from the Latins, the Christian communities in Mesopotamia and Egypt were less directly affected by the creation of the Latin states. Nevertheless, the Copts were bitterly opposed to the First Crusade. The author of the *History of the Patriarchs of Alexandria*, as we have already seen, took pleasure in the restoration of peace and order to Jerusalem in the aftermath of the Turkish conquest, but a few pages on we find him writing as follows:

> They [the Franks] gained possession of the noble city of Jerusalem and its district in the month of Ramadan of the Lunar Year 492. We, the community of Christians, the Jacobites, the Copts, did not join in the pilgrimage to it, nor were we able to approach it, on account of what is known of their hatred of us, as also, their false belief concerning us and their charge against us of impiety.[25]

Thanks to the crusades the Latin Church came to have a better knowledge of these Oriental churches and sought to effect a union of churches by persuading their leaders, whether patriarch or catholicos, to accept Roman primacy and to subscribe to the same confession of faith, while respecting their individual rituals.[26] Initiated in the twelfth century, this strategy was fully developed in the thirteenth thanks to the missionary work of the Dominicans and the Franciscans. So in 1237 the Jacobite Patriarch Ignatios II visited Jerusalem, where after being well received by the Dominicans he solemnly swore obedience to the see of Rome and provided an Orthodox profession of faith drawn up in Arabic and Syriac. Those Coptic and Nestorian archbishops, who were also present in Jerusalem, followed suit. Pope Gregory IX sent them letters of congratulation. Patriarch Ignatios renewed his submission in 1246 during a visit from the papal envoy, Andrew of Longjumeau, while seeking assurances that Rome would respect the autonomy of his church. However, such declarations of obedience were considered to be purely personal actions and did not apply

---

24 *Chronique de Michel le Syrien, patriarche jacobite d'Antioche (1166–1199)*, trans. J.-B. Chabot (Paris: E. Leroux, 1905), III, 222.

25 *History of the patriarchs*, II, part 3: (text) 249; (trans.) 398–9.

26 J. Richard, *La papauté et les missions d'Orient au Moyen Âge (XIIIe–XVe siècles)* [Collection de l'École française de Rome 33], second edition (Rome: École française de Rome, 1998).

to the whole body of the church. The death of Ignatios II in 1252, the ensuing schism,[27] the Mongol whirlwind, and finally the fall of the crusader states in 1291 meant that this rapprochement would lead nowhere.

There were equally contacts between Rome and the Nestorians. The most important were those that took place under the catholicos Yahballâhâ III (1281–1317), as part of exchanges between the papacy and the Ilkhâns of Persia.[28] There were, however, no long-lasting consequences, for the Nestorians remained attached to their beliefs, traditions and ritual. Leaving aside the Armenians,[29] this unionist policy only obtained concrete results in the case of the Maronites, who entered the Roman obedience in 1182 and renounced the Monothelite heresy, despite strong internal opposition. This union was sealed by the papal bull *Quia divinae sapientiae*, which Pope Innocent III presented to the Maronite patriarch in 1215 on the occasion of the latter's visit to the Fourth Lateran Council. It guaranteed the continuing existence of the Maronite hierarchy and ritual.

The appearance of an aggressive form of Christianity in the Near East in the shape of crusades backed by the papacy led to a decisive change in Muslim attitudes towards Christians.[30] This did not affect the legal position, since the Muslim authorities, religious and political alike, made a clear distinction between the Christians living in the lands of Islam, known as *naṣrânî*, and the crusaders, denoted by the general term of Franks (*Ifranj*). While the former enjoyed *dhimma* status, the latter had come from abroad to seize Muslim territory and were therefore infidels against whom war was justified. However, the appeals for *jihad* against the Franks made by devout men and by the rulers of Syria and Egypt were couched in terms of the impiety of the Christian polytheists, who polluted Jerusalem with their presence. Such accusations rebounded on the native Christians, as Louis Pouzet has shown in his study of religious life in Damascus in the thirteenth century. He notes that the term *kuffâr* (infidels) was now applied to the Christians of the city, who were insulted as adorers of the cross.[31]

---

27 See above, p. 380.
28 In 1288 Barṣaumâ, a Nestorian monk, was sent to the west by the Ilkhân Arghun and received by Pope Nicholas IV, who according to Syriac sources recognised Yahballâhâ III as patriarch of the Church of the East. Thereafter the Dominican Ricoldo di Montecroce worked hard to persuade the catholicos and his flock to reject the doctrines of Nestorios.
29 See below, pp. 415–17.
30 See E. Sivan, 'Note sur la situation des chrétiens sous les Ayyûbides', *Revue d'Histoire des Religions* 172 (1967), 117–30.
31 L. Pouzet, *Damas au VIIe/XIIIe siècle: vie et structures religieuses dans une métropole islamique* [Recherches. Collection publiée sous la direction de la Faculté des Lettres et des Sciences Humaines de l'Université Saint-Joseph] (Beirut: al-Mashraq, 1988), cap. 7.

Even if exceptional, still more revealing of the climate of suspicion created by the crusades were the reprisals against Christians. When Jocelyn of Courtenay, prince of Edessa, laid siege to Aleppo in 1123 and pillaged the surrounding region, the *kadi* and the *ra'îs* – the leaders of the community – insisted that the Christians of the city repair at their own expense the Muslim cemeteries and places of worship desecrated by the Franks. The two bishops of the city, one a Melkite, the other a Jacobite, reluctant to be lumped together with the Franks, refused to make good the damage done. The *kadi* responded by transforming four of the city's six churches into mosques and by driving out the bishops.

The crusades of the thirteenth century were primarily directed against Egypt, with particularly severe consequences for the Copts. During the 1218–19 siege of Damietta by the armies of the Fifth Crusade the Muslim authorities imposed heavy additional taxation on the Copts of Egypt, who were also the objects of mob violence. They became the scapegoats of collective fears. At Alexandria the church of St Mark was destroyed on the pretext that it might serve as a landmark for the enemy. In the 1240s the *kadi* 'Uthmân al-Nâbulusî found the numbers of Copts in the administration offensive and composed a violent denunciation of their misdeeds.[32] But the appearance of the Mongols in the mid-thirteenth century was to aggravate still more this climate of suspicion, which the crusades had helped to create.

The consequences of the Mongol conquest

Following the *kuriltay* of 1206, where the Mongol chiefs recognised Genghis Khan as Great Khan or supreme leader, the Mongols embarked upon a series of conquests which made them masters of an immense empire extending from China to the gates of Europe. In the Near East their conquest of Iraq, the fall of Baghdad and the execution of the last Abbasid caliph in 1258, the invasion of Syria in 1260, and the creation of the Ilkhânate of Iran by Hülegü, one of Ghengis's grandsons, profoundly altered the religious and political situation. Eastern Christians were happy to ally with the invaders, who for their part favoured the Christians. A ruling of Genghis Khan insisted on the equal standing of all religions and established the principle of honouring all religious leaders. In addition, Nestorian Christianity had had a presence in inner Asia for centuries, notably among the Kereit, and its influence penetrated the Mongol court through the agency both of the Christian wives of the Great Khans and of

32 C. Cahen, 'Histoires coptes d'un cadi médiéval', *Bulletin de l'Institut Français d'Archéologie Orientale* 59 (1960), 133–50.

Nestorian dignitaries, such as the Symeon who served the Great Khan Ögodei and his successors as a doctor and a secretary.

The Mongol conquests were the occasion for spectacular massacres, but the Mongol armies often spared the Christians and their property. For example, the Nestorians escaped the sack of Baghdad. In Syria many Christians welcomed the Mongols, if there were others who preferred flight or resistance. In March 1260, when Kitbugha, Hülegü's great Nestorian general, entered Damascus in triumph, flanked by King Het'um of Armenia, and Prince Bohemond VI of Antioch, the Christian inhabitants of the city acclaimed him and then in August organised an anti-Muslim demonstration after receiving a *firman* from Hülegü, which granted each religious community the right to practise its religion publicly.[33] And shortly afterwards, in May 1260, a Syrian painter gave a new twist to the iconography of the Exaltation of the Cross by showing Constantine and Helena with the features of Hülegü and of his Nestorian wife Doquz-Khatun.[34] The undisguised delight shown by the Christians would soon bring savage reprisals following the victory of the Mamluks at 'Ayn Jâlût in September 1260 and their recovery of the Syrian cities. This time, any suspicion of complicity with the Mongol enemy was well founded.

The aftermath of the destruction of the Abbasid caliphate (1258) was an auspicious time for the Christian communities under Mongol rule in Iran and Mesopotamia. Churches were built and Christians were even exempted from the poll tax. In 1281 a monk from Inner Mongolia became Nestorian patriarch with the name Yahballâhâ III (1281–1317), despite his poor grasp of Syriac. At Marâgha, the Ilkhân capital, he set about the building of a large monastery. His patriarchate marks the high point of Nestorian Christianity, which profited from the unification of Asia under the Mongols to the extent that it comprised 30 provinces and 250 bishoprics. However, Christians were also the victims of anti-Mongol riots, such as those at Mosul in 1262 and at Baghdad in 1268. Their position deteriorated after the conversion in 1295 of the Ilkhân Ghazan to Islam. Once more the stipulations of *dhimma* came into force, while clothing regulations were reimposed and tax exemptions removed. Churches were destroyed at Tabriz in 1296 and at Irbil in 1310. In the fourteenth century Nestorian Christianity disappeared from Iran and from southern and

---

33 D. Sourdel, 'Bohémond et les chrétiens de Damas sous l'occupation mongole', in *Dei Gesta per Francos: études sur les croisades dédiées à Jean Richard*, ed. M. Balard, B. Z. Kedar and J. S. Riley-Smith (Aldershot: Ashgate, 2001), 295–9.
34 Bibl. Vatican cod. syr. 559. See J. M. Fiey, 'Iconographie syriaque. Hulagu, Doquz Khatun . . . et six ambons?', *Le Muséon* 88 (1975), 59–68.

central Iraq and took refuge in Upper Mesopotamia around Mosul, where having abandoned Baghdad the Nestorian catholicos now established his residence.

Egypt passed under the rule of Mamluk sultans in 1250 and Syria in 1260. The Mamluks based the legitimacy of their military regime on their ability to defend Islam against the crusaders and the Mongols, which took the form of a double *jihad*. The accusation of Christian collusion with these enemies of Islam became a refrain of the propaganda directed against the *dhimmîs*. For example, during Sultan Baybars's campaign against the crusader strong-points of Caesarea and Arsûf in 1265 a series of fires swept through Cairo. It was immediately assumed that these were an act of revenge on the part of local Christians. In Syria the conquest of Frankish territories produced popular attacks on Christians, such as the destruction in 1262 of the church of the Annunciation at Nazareth and the massacre of Christians that followed the fall of Antioch in 1268. Even in Egypt there was a growing number of popular attacks on Christians, which were encouraged by the bigotry of preachers, by the intransigence of the *ulemâ*, and by anxiety in the face of Mongol aggression. But behind this hostility lay Muslim opposition to the influence exercised in the administration by Christian secretaries – a stock charge of anti-Christian polemic.[35] It is this social aspect that deserves underlining.[36] So, in 1301 Sultan Qalâwûn re-enacted a decree which had already been applied on a number of occasions, but always rescinded, excluding Jews and Christians from public office and at the same time strictly enforcing the discriminatory measures associated with *dhimma* status. Furthermore, he closed down the churches of Cairo and had several of them destroyed, a fate also suffered by certain synagogues. It required the intervention of the Byzantine emperor and the king of Aragon to persuade the sultan to reopen the churches and to rescind the measures taken. It is not without significance that at this juncture only outside intervention allowed an improvement in the position of the local Christians. But it did not prevent similar crises reoccurring in 1320 and 1354. The number and violence of these anti-Christian outbreaks created a climate of fear, which was the direct cause of numerous conversions to Islam. These contributed to the growth of a new group which made its appearance in the fourteenth century. Its members were known as *musâlima*, or 'islamised', and were identified

---

35 See M. Perlmann, 'Notes on anti-Christian propaganda in the Mamlûk Empire', *Bulletin of the School of Oriental and African Studies* 10 (1939–42), 843–61.
36 L. S. Northrup, 'Muslim–Christian relations during the reign of the Mamluk Sultan al-Mansûr Qalâwûn (A.D. 1278–1290)', in *Conversion and continuity*, ed. Gervers and Bikhazi, 253–61.

as such in the biographical dictionaries of the time. They were often suspected of only being nominal Muslims, having converted under pressure.[37] Though much diminished and more introspective, the Coptic community still remained important in some areas and continued to play an active role in Egyptian society.

Arabisation and the emergence of an Arab Christianity

One general feature characterised the future development of Christian communities in the lands of Islam. This was arabisation, by which I mean the adoption of Arabic, not just as a vernacular, but as a literary and liturgical language, which in turn led to the emergence of a truly Arabic Christianity. When the Byzantines annexed Edessa in 1031, some Jacobites left the city along with the other 'Arabs', because, in the words of Michael the Syrian, 'in language and writing they were close to the Arabs'.[38] The ties linking Christianity to the Arabic language are ancient and complex. Christians contributed to the development of the Arabic script, language and culture.[39] From the turn of the eighth century there appeared the first translations of the Bible into Arabic. By our period Christian communities were largely, but not completely, arabised. It depended on a number of factors: original language, region, ecclesiastical tradition and social setting.

Coptic, the language written and spoken in Egypt at the time of the Arab conquest, gave ground to Arabic. The different Coptic dialects[40] were replaced by Arabic ones, so much so that the eleventh-century compiler of the *History of the Patriarchs of Alexandria* decided to translate the biographies of the patriarchs from Coptic into Arabic, giving as his reason that 'today Arabic is the language that the people of Egypt know . . . most of them being ignorant of Coptic and Greek'.[41] Coptic did not totally disappear, however, as a spoken language. There are some interesting pointers from the work of the twelfth-century Coptic author Abû Makârim, who writes of one village

---

37 D. P. Little, 'Coptic converts to Islam during the Baḥrî Mamluk Period', in ibid., 843–61.

38 *Chronique de Michel le Syrien*, III, 280.

39 It was in the Christian kingdom of the Lakhmids that the northern Arabic script was created. With the rise of Islam this eclipsed the southern Arabic script. The role of Christians as translators from the Greek and the Syriac, mainly at Baghdad in the ninth century, is very well known.

40 Coptic divides into two major dialects: Sahidic in Upper Egypt (from the Arabic *Sa'îd*) and Bohaïric in the Delta (from the Arabic for sea, *baḥarî*).

41 *History of the patriarchs of the Egyptian Church*, ed. B. Evetts (Paris: P. Fages, 1904), I, 115.

where both Muslims and Christians spoke Coptic. He also has the story of a Jewish convert to Christianity who assimilated to the extent of speaking Coptic.[42] As a literary language, Coptic became a dead language. There is nothing written in it after the eleventh century. The desire to preserve this heritage led in the thirteenth and fourteenth centuries to a renewed interest in the Coptic language. It resulted in twenty or more Coptic grammars, written in Arabic and making use of Arabic terminology, as well as Arabic–Coptic dictionaries, some of which were organised in the classic alphabetical order of Arabic lexicography. These works have been studied by A. Sidarus,[43] who has noted that in the thirteenth century they dealt mostly with Bohaïric dialects and in the fourteenth century Sahidic. This reflected the concentration of the Coptic population in Middle Egypt. The final triumph of Arabic affirmed the coming into being from the Fatimid period onwards of a truly Arab Egypt, with which the Copts strongly identified, while retaining their religious individuality.[44]

It was quite otherwise with Greek. At the time of the Arab conquest of Egypt and Syria it was a liturgical and literary language mostly used by the Melkites, who spoke various Coptic dialects in Egypt and Aramaic ones in Syria and Palestine. Greek would soon give place to Arabic, so that by the ninth century, at least in Muslim territories, Melkite scholars had practically ceased to write in Greek. Those parts of northern Syria reconquered by the Byzantines in 969 saw a renewal of literary activity in Greek. For example, the Melkite patriarchs of Antioch installed by Constantinople wrote in Greek. Paradoxically, it was under Byzantine auspices that Antioch became an important centre of translation of biblical, patristic and literary texts from Greek to Arabic. This favoured the arabisation of the Melkite liturgy, which had further consequences, for adapting the liturgical language to the needs of the vernacular was a characteristic trait of the Melkite Church.[45]

---

42 M. Martin, 'Chrétiens et musulmans à la fin du XIIe siècle', in *Valeur et distance: identités et sociétés en Égypte*, dir. C. Décobert (Paris: Maisonneuve et Larose, 2000), 86–7.

43 A. Sidarus, 'La philologie copte arabe au Moyen Âge', in *La signification du Bas Moyen Âge dans l'histoire et la culture du monde musulman* [Actes du 8e Congrès de l'Union européenne des Arabisants et Islamisants, Aix-en-Provence 1976] (Aix-en-Provence: Edisud, 1978), 267–81.

44 J.-C. Garcin, 'L'arabisation de l'Egypte', *Revue de l'Occident Musulman et Méditerranéen* 43 (1987), 130–7; U. Haarmann, 'Regional sentiment in medieval Islamic Egypt', *Bulletin of the School of Oriental and African Studies* 43 (1980), 55–66.

45 This will explain why a liturgy in Syriac continued to be used in the patriarchate of Antioch, as well as at the Melkite monastery of St Catherine of Sinai, where the liturgy was celebrated in Greek, no doubt for the benefit of pilgrims coming from the Byzantine Empire, in Arabic, and in Syriac in a chapel set aside for Syrians.

The history of the development of Syriac and of the various Aramaic dialects is still more complex and difficult to establish.[46] The populations of Syria and Mesopotamia, who spoke Aramaic, gradually adopted Arabic as their vernacular. In the twentieth century Aramaic only continued to be spoken in a few isolated areas: in the mountains of Kurdistan, in the Ṭûr ʿAbdîn, around Urmiya and in the plains of Mosul,[47] as well as in a few villages to the north of Damascus, notably Maʿlûlâ. But in the crusading period Syriac speakers, in other words those connected with the Jacobite and the Nestorian churches, were far more numerous. We have already noted that Dionysios, metropolitan of Melitene, who laid claim to the patriarchate in 1252, did not know any Arabic. When he went before the Ayyubid sultan of Damascus to plead his case, he had recourse to an interpreter.[48]

In contrast to Coptic and Greek, Syriac more than continued as a literary language. Traditionally, the thirteenth century is remembered as the golden age of Syriac literature.[49] It was only in the fourteenth century that it gave ground to Arabic. Its literary achievements are well known and are often studied for their own sake, without regard for the context of their time. It would be particularly valuable to know why one and the same author will by turns use both Arabic and Syriac. A good example is Bar Hebraeus (known in Arabic as Abû'l-Faraj ibn al-ʿIbrî), *maphrian* of the eastern Jacobite Church from 1264 to 1286, who left a large corpus of works – thirty-one according to the list drawn up by his brother – in the fields of history, theology, philosophy, medicine, astronomy, grammar and belles-lettres.[50] This literary activity corresponded to the preoccupations of a prelate: to bring comfort to the Syriac community, to enrich its intellectual heritage and to preserve its standing in the Near East. If Bar Hebraeus mostly wrote in Syriac or translated philosophical and medical treatises from Arabic to Syriac, he also made use of Arabic, either writing directly in the language or establishing Arabic versions of some of his Syriac works. For instance, his historical oeuvre comprises, on the one hand, a universal chronicle written in Syriac consisting of two separate parts, one devoted to secular history and the other to ecclesiastical history, and, on the other, an abridged universal chronicle, written in Arabic. Recent research has

---

46 Syriac is the Aramaic dialect of Edessa, which became in the fourth and fifth centuries the learned language of Syria and Mesopotamia.
47 For this reason Syriac was given official status in Iraq alongside Arabic and Kurdish, and in 1975 the Syriac Academy of Baghdad was established.
48 See above, p. 380.
49 P. Kawerau, *Die jakobitische Kirche im Zeitalter der syrischen Renaissance* (Berlin: Akademie-Verlag, 1955).
50 J.-M. Fiey, 'Esquisse d'une bibliographie de Bar Hébraeus (†1286)', *Parole de l'Orient* 13 (1986), 279–312.

shown that the two chronicles were independent of one another and based on different historiographical traditions: Christian and Syriac for the former; Arab for the latter. They were addressed to different audiences: the former to the prelates of the Jacobite Church, who were steeped in biblical culture; the latter to the Christian communities, who were linguistically and culturally arabised.[51]

Literary activities

Within the limits of this chapter it is not possible to provide an exhaustive survey of literary activity carried on in the Arabic and Syriac languages by Christian scholars, since both the genres and the works of literature are numerous and various. The reader can find much that is valuable in the reference books of Graf[52] for Arabic works and of Baumstark[53] for Syriac works, but these are limited properly speaking to religious literature, thus excluding the contribution of Christians to the growth of Arabic culture, notably in the areas of poetry, philosophy and the sciences. Turning to the field of Christian literature, Coptic, Melkite, Jacobite and Nestorian authors cultivated all the usual genres: theological *summa*, biblical commentaries, apologies, legal handbooks, collections of sermons, works of history.

Behind the compilation of large-scale theological handbooks lay an encyclopaedic inspiration, which meant that they offered a synthesis, rather than any new theological insights. A good example is the *summa* compiled in Arabic by the Nestorian Mârî ibn Sulaymân in the twelfth century with the pleasing title of the 'Book of the Tower', in which he presents his undertaking as comparable to the construction of a building. Each of his seven chapters is given an architectural heading: the foundations, the ground plan, the supporting columns, etc., ending with irrigation works and gardens. Another example is the *Kitâb Majmû' Uṣûl al-Dîn*, which was compiled around 1260 by Abû Isḥâq Ibn al-'Assâl. The Banû 'Assâl were a rich and famous Coptic family, which supplied the Egyptian administration with a number of secretaries. This *summa*

51 See L. I. Conrad, 'On the Arabic Chronicle of Bar Hebraeus: his aims and audience', *Parole de l'Orient* 19 (1994), 319–78; D. Aigle, 'Bar Hebraeus et son public, à travers ses chroniques en arabe et en syriaque', *Le Muséon* 118 (2005), 83–106; F. Micheau, 'Le *Kâmil* d'Ibn al-Athîr, source principale de l'histoire des Arabes dans le *Mukhtaṣar* de Bar Hébraeus', *Mélanges de l'Université St-Joseph* 58 (2005).
52 G. Graf, *Geschichte der christlichen arabischen Literatur*, II, *Die Schriftsteller bis zur Mitte des 15 Jhs.* [Studi e testi 133] (Vatican: Biblioteca apostolica vaticana, 1947). Cf. R. Coquin in *Christianismes orientaux: introduction à l'étude des langues et des littératures* (Paris: Éditions du Cerf, 1993).
53 A. Baumstark, *Geschichte der syrischen Literatur* (Bonn: De Gruyter, 1922).

provided a systematic presentation of Christian dogma, supported by long passages from the Church Fathers, but also from philosophers, both Christian and Muslim, particular use being made of the *Kitâb al-Arba'în* of al-Râzî.[54] The same combination of theology and philosophy reappears in the celebrated encyclopaedia which Abû'l-Barakât compiled in the following century under the title *Miṣbâḥ al-Ẓulma* ('Lamp of Darkness').

In our period there were a large number of apologetic works, but with features that distinguished them from those of earlier centuries.[55] Genres, such as polemic and disputation, were much less well developed than apologetics, where a Christian author explained, defended and justified Christian dogma against Muslim aspersions. He would defend the dogmas of the Trinity and the unity of the Godhead, of the Incarnation and the double nature of Christ, with the aid of arguments drawn from scripture and those based on reason. The Melkites boasted two great apologists: in the eleventh century they had 'Abdallâh ibn Faḍl, a native of Antioch, who was the author of numerous works in defence of Christianity, including a 'Demonstration of the Orthodox Faith', which criticises the errors of the Jacobites and the Nestorians. In the twelfth century Paul al-Râhib, a monk of Antioch, who became bishop of Sidon, compiled at least five treatises directed against pagan philosophers, Jews, Muslims and other Christian denominations. His contemporary, the Nestorian metropolitan Elie ibn Shinaya, was the author of a work, in which he defends the doctrine of the Trinity against the Muslims, the divinity of Christ against the Jews, and the Nestorian emphasis on the humanity of Christ against the Melkites and the Jacobites. It becomes apparent that some of these treatises were just as much designed to justify the doctrines of one church over another as they were to defend Christianity against outsiders. Something of an exception is a little tract entitled 'Treatise about the unanimity of the faith (*Kitâb ijtimâ' al-amâna*)': its eleventh-century author, an otherwise unknown Jacobite called 'Alî ibn Dâwud al-Arfâdî, is at pains to prove that despite divergences over the formulation of the mystery of Christ the different Christian confessions shared the same faith.[56]

The theological *summa*, along with the apologetical treatises, testify to the influence of theological and philosophical concepts that are properly Muslim. Unfortunately modern research – often too steeped in ecclesiastical

---

54 See G. C. Anawati, 'The Christian communities in Egypt in the Middle Ages', in *Conversion and continuity*, ed. M. Gervers and R. J. Bikhazi, 237–51.

55 See K. Samir, 'Bibliographie du dialogue islamo-chrétien. Auteurs chrétiens de langue arabe', *Islamochristiana* 2 (1979), 201–45, where he provides a brief analysis of each treatise.

56 G. Troupeau, 'Le livre de l'unanimité de la foi de 'Alî ibn Dâwud al-Arfâdî', in *Études sur le christianisme arabe au Moyen Âge* (Aldershot: Variorum, 1995), XIII.

history – has failed to bring out these instances of 'inculturation'[57] and has overlooked examples of Christian theologians presenting the doctrine of the Trinity according to categories of Muslim thought. The Nestorian 'Abdallâh ibn al-Ṭayyib (†1043)[58] explains that, while 'the essence of the Creator (dhât al-bâri') is one, His attributes (sifât) are multiple'. It was his opinion that the Christians 'say that this essence is a substance (jawhar) and they term the attributes properties (khawâṣṣ) . . . they also believe that God in His essence possesses the attribute of knowledge ('ilm), of knowing ('âlim), and of being known (ma'lûm) . . . They call the attribute of knowledge paternity, that of knowing filiation and that of being known procession'. He concluded by insisting that God 'is one in respect of His essence, but multiple in respect of His attributes'. It looks as though Christian authors did their best to resist the growing pressures from Islam by defending themselves against the charge of associationism, which left them open to the accusation of unbelief. They did this by demonstrating that the doctrine of the Trinity did not impugn divine unity, while at the same time displaying a degree of discretion in that they avoided any direct attacks on Islam and its prophet.

This was also a period of ambitious legal handbooks. The various churches had preserved their law and their institutions. As a result, the ecclesiastical authorities assumed judicial functions in all areas of private law. The legal compendia included not only the edicts of councils and synods dealing with doctrine, but also regulations concerning ecclesiastical organisation; the status of the clergy, monks and laity; liturgical order; the administration of the sacraments; institutions, such as schools, monasteries and hospitals; and stipulations relating to private and family law covering marriage, descent, adoption, wills, inheritance, property transactions and so on. Among these legal compilations the following stand out: the compendium written in Arabic by 'Abdallâh ibn al-Ṭayyib in the eleventh century for the Nestorian Church; the decrees of the same church compiled about the same time by Elias of Nisibis, but in Syriac; the two works of Abdisho written in 1318 – a collection of synodal canons and rules of ecclesiastical judgements, which have remained standard works for the Nestorian Church to the present day; and finally, turning to the Coptic Church, two Nomokanones: the first compiled in the twelfth century by Michael, bishop of Damietta, was among the first of these legal handbooks to

---

57 I prefer the term 'inculturation' (the slow and beneficial assimilation of the religious, ethical, cultural and social assumptions of one culture by another) to 'acculturation' (the adoption by a minority of a dominant culture).

58 G. Troupeau, 'Le traité sur l'Unité et la Trinité de 'Abd Allâh ibn al-Ṭayyib', in Études sur le christianisme arabe, vi.

arrange laws and rulings by subject matter instead of randomly; the second drawn up by Ibn al-'Assâl was published in 1238 and remains to the present the main legal code of the Coptic community in the sphere of private law.

Collections of sermons and of hymns, obviously with liturgical uses in mind, constituted another literary form cultivated in the period under review. Since the churches preferred sermons made famous by the early Fathers, homiletic literature in Arabic began in the form of translations. In the eleventh century the Melkite deacon of Antioch, 'Abdallâh ibn Faḍl, translated most of John Chrysostom's sermons into Arabic. But in the twelfth century there started to appear sermons written in the rhymed and rhythmic Arabic known as *saj'*, while hymns used the popular Arabic poetic metre of *rajaz*. The Nestorian catholicos Elias ibn al-Hadithî (1176–90) is usually regarded as the initiator of this genre. He wrote his sermons in a brilliantly rich Arabic characterised by the use of *saj'*. His employment of Arabic eloquence for Christian purposes found many imitators in the thirteenth century among the different Christian denominations. Can it have been sheer coincidence that at exactly this juncture Islam saw the development of the art of the sermon (*wa'z*) and the role of the preacher (*wu'âz*)? Leaving aside the doctrinal divisions separating Christianity and Islam, it has become a vital task to examine their shared religious sentiment, as revealed by the use of similar literary forms and themes.

The numerous historical works written by Christian authors equally take up a variety of positions in relation to the Arabic and Muslim cultural context. Syriac historiography, properly speaking, is dominated by the magisterial works of Michael the Syrian and of Bar Hebraeus.[59] Following a tradition going back to Eusebius of Caesarea, they set side by side two universal histories: the one secular and the other ecclesiastical. Their works reveal most of all the concerns of prelates intent on writing the history of their church: they wanted to bring comfort to the Jacobite community and to preserve its standing in the Near East. The Coptic and Nestorian communities equally produced their own works of history. In the twelfth century Mârî ibn Sulaymân inserted into the fifth chapter of his 'Book of the Tower' a veritable history of the Nestorian catholicate.

The Coptic Church has the monumental *History of the Patriarchs of Alexandria*.[60] The first part to 1046 is a compilation of older sources, traditionally

---

59 See above, pp. 391–2.
60 Sawîrus ibn al-Muqaffa', *History of the patriarchs of the Egyptian Church, known as the History of the Holy Church*, ed. and trans. Y. 'Abd al-Masîh, A. Khater, A. S. Atiya and O. H. E. Burmester, 4 vols. (Cairo: Société d'archéologie copte, 1943–74). See J. den Heijer, *Mawhûb ibn Manṣûr ibn Muffarigh et l'historiographie copto-arabe: étude sur la composition de l'* Histoire des Patriarches d'Alexandrie [CSCO 513, Subs. 83] (Louvain: E. Peeters, 1989).

attributed to Sawîrus ibn al-Muqaffa' (fl. 955–987), but actually the work of Mawhûb, who lived a century later. The second part, covering the period from 1047 to 1216, consists of contemporary lives of the individual patriarchs, which were very well documented. The third part from 1216 contains a series of brief notices with the exception of a detailed and original life of Patriarch Cyril III (1216–43).

In contrast to these thoroughly partisan histories it would be difficult to distinguish many of the Arab chronicles written by Christian authors from those written by Muslim authors, were it not for a special emphasis on events involving Christians. These were histories, which had assimilated the themes and methodology of Arabo-Muslim historiography. They were very largely the work of Copts, such as al-Makîn ibn al- 'Amîd[61] and Ibn al-Râhib,[62] both authors in the thirteenth century of universal histories. The former would find a continuator in the fourteenth century in the person of al-Mufaddal ibn Abî'l-Fadâ'il.[63] At the same time Ibn al-Suqâ'î[64] was compiling a biographical dictionary, the only Christian author to do so. These historians were members of the cultured urban elite of Egypt. Belonging to a minority religious community did not prevent them adopting the vocabulary, the thought patterns and the outlook of the ruling class.

The sciences – medicine in particular – belong to this common cultural sphere, where religious differences give way to the development and transmission of shared knowledge. Medicine was a profession largely dominated by Christians. At Baghdad the tradition of influential Christian doctors in the service of the caliphs still continued. So because of his influence at court the Nestorian doctor–priest Ibn al-Wâsiti was able to obtain the appointment of a patriarch in 1092 and then in 1105 the lifting of anti-Christian measures. A few days before he died in 1132 he was himself elected patriarch. Another Baghdad personality was Ibn al-Tilmîdh, a priest and a doctor who died in 1165. He was very popular with his contemporaries and enjoyed the favour of the caliphs. His main contribution was to the training of new doctors, many of whom then went to Syria and Egypt. Along with Jewish physicians there were numerous

61 Trans. A.-M. Eddé and F. Micheau, *Chronique des Ayyoubides (602–658=1205/6–1259/60)* [Documents relatifs à l'histoire des croisades 16] (Paris: Belles Lettres, 1994).

62 A. Sidarus, *Ibn ar-Râhibs Leben und Werk: ein koptisch-arabischer Encyclopädist des 7/13 Jahrhunderts* [Islamkundliche Untersuchungen 36] (Freiburg im Breisgau: Klaus Schwarz, 1975).

63 Al-Mufaddal ibn Abî'l-Fadâ'il, *Histoire des sultans mamlouks*, ed. and trans. E. Blochet (jusqu'en 716/1316) in *Patrologia Orientalis* 12 (1919), 345–550; 14 (1920), 375–672; 20 (1929), 3–270.

64 Ibn al-Suqâ'î, *Tâlî Kitâb Wafayât al-A'yân: un fonctionnaire chrétien dans l'administration mamelouke*, ed. and trans. J. Sublet (Damascus: Institut français, 1974).

Nestorian, Melkite and Jacobite doctors, though curiously few Copts. They were to all appearances extremely well integrated into Muslim society.[65] It was current practice for Christian physicians to have Muslim pupils and vice versa. Successful individual careers are easy to trace through biographical dictionaries, but they should not obscure the fact that the field of medicine, just like administration, was highly competitive. By practising an expertise that enjoyed social approval Christians – now that they were a minority – sought to preserve a privileged position in societies which were more likely to force them from the centres of power and positions of influence. From time to time there was Muslim criticism of Christian doctors, which should be seen as an attempt to deprive *dhimmîs* of this means of access to power. At the end of the eleventh century, for example, al-Ghazâlî encouraged his readers to study medicine, which to his way of thinking Muslims had rather neglected. He found it deplorable that in many small towns and cities Muslims were at the mercy of foreign practitioners, by whom he meant Christians or Jews.[66]

The role of monasteries

The central role of monasticism and of monasteries in the religious and intellectual life of eastern Christianities is well known. Monasteries were particularly numerous in Egypt, in Palestine, around Antioch, in the Ṭûr 'Abdîn massif in Upper Mesopotamia, and around Hîra in southern Iraq. After the Arab conquest of the seventh century these monasteries still retained their importance and dynamism. Their sphere of influence was not solely limited to the Christian communities. Witness to this is a particular genre of Arabic literature known as *Kitâb al-diyârât*, or Book of monasteries. Well known for the illustrations done at the end of the tenth century by al-Shabushtî,[67] these were anthologies of poems, written on the occasion of visits made to Christian monasteries by Muslim poets. They were an eloquent witness both to the attractions exercised by the monasteries on Christian and Muslim alike

65 See A.-M. Eddé, 'Les médecins dans la société syrienne du VIIe/XIIIe siècle', *Annales Islamologiques* 29 (1995), 91–109. F. Micheau, 'Les médecins orientaux au service des princes latins', in *Occident et Proche-Orient: contacts scientifiques au temps des croisades. Actes du Colloque de Louvain-la-Neuve, 24 et 25 mars 1997*, ed. I. Draelants, A. Tihon and B. van den Abeele (Louvain: Brepols, 2000), 95–115.

66 See H. Lazarus-Yafeh, *Studies in al-Ghazzali* (Jerusalem: Magnes Press, 1975), 444–5.

67 H. Kilpatrick, 'Monasteries through Muslim eyes: the *Diyârât* Books', in *Christians at the heart of Islamic life: church life and scholarship in 'Abbasid Iraq*, ed. D. Thomas [The History of Christian–Muslim Relations 1] (Leiden and Boston: Brill, 2003), 19–37; G. Troupeau, 'Les couvents chrétiens dans la littérature arabe', *Nouvelle Revue du Caire* 1 (1975), 265–79 [= G. Troupeau, *Études sur le christianisme arabe au Moyen Âge*, xx].

and to their place in tenth-century Arab culture. Later geographical works, such as those of Yâqût, Abû'l-Makârim, al-'Umarî and al-Maqrîzî, copied their descriptions of monasteries. Sometimes they would add that such and such a foundation was now a ruin, but this was never done systematically. The lack of proper archaeological data has meant that our present state of knowledge more or less precludes the establishment of a satisfactory list of monasteries existing in the period from the eleventh to the fourteenth centuries, let alone pronouncing on their fate.

However, there is little dispute over the general lines of development. This period saw the disappearance of a large number of monasteries, as a result of the combined effect of two factors: on the one hand, the contraction of the churches meant not only fewer monks but also fewer gifts with which to maintain the monastery fabric; on the other, it was a time of devastation in those regions suffering war, invasions and the extortions of the Bedouin. The history of individual monasteries is often a litany of destruction and pillage, all the more damaging because without sufficient resources the Christian communities struggled to reconstruct buildings and to restore economic life. There were of course regional variations, with monastic life surviving better in some areas than in others. A good example is Middle Egypt, about which we are well informed thanks to the remarkable studies of Père Martin. Ancient monasteries survived better on the right bank of the River Nile than on the left bank. Fourteen out of the sixteen ancient sites on the right bank have been identified. Of these, six are still active religious centres. On the left bank twenty-two of the thirty sites attested by papyri have completely disappeared. Only three have survived as village churches. The difference can be explained by the fact that the left bank boasts rich agricultural land, where the population is largely – totally in the case of the capital Ashmûnayn – islamised, whereas the precipitous right bank has few inhabitants and, to repeat the author's conclusion, 'served as a refuge for the minority against the pressures of the Muslim majority'.[68]

Generally speaking, monasteries sited in cities, or close by, seem to have disappeared more quickly and in greater numbers. So it was at Baghdad, where in the Seljuq period the sources mention five churches still functioning, but no monasteries. Under the Umayyads there were five monasteries situated in Damascus and its environs, but these had disappeared by the twelfth century. Another example is the famous 'Upper Monastery' (Dayr al-aʿla) at Mosul,

---

68 M. Martin, 'La province d'Ašmūnayn: historique de sa configuration religieuse', *Annales Islamologiques* 23 (1987), 1–28.

which in the ninth and tenth centuries had been at the centre of the Nestorian Church. By the thirteenth century, despite the continuing strength of the Christian community at Mosul, it had been turned into a simple church. Much the same happened with monasteries close to Cairo, such as that of Nahyâ, a few kilometres to the west of the capital, which served the Fatimids as a very agreeable summer retreat, but when Abû'l-Makârim visited it in 1173 it had only seven monks and was in the process of being deserted. In the fourteenth century al-Maqrîzî noted that it was now completely ruined.

These developments meant that monasteries were less and less important as centres of social interaction and education, becoming primarily places of refuge and of pilgrimage, which preserved the spiritual and cultural values of eastern Christianity. We shall use the examples of some celebrated monasteries to illustrate this, beginning with the monastery of Barṣaumâ,[69] which took its name from a fifth-century ascetic, Barṣaumâ, but only emerges in the light of history in the eighth century. It lies close to Melitene / Malatya, but in a remote region in the heart of the Taurus mountains. It numbered some hundreds of monks. The miracles attributed to the relics of Barṣaumâ attracted the crowds. In the twelfth century it became one of the principal patriarchal residences. It was probably here that Michael the Syrian compiled his chronicle, to be followed by the anonymous of 1232 and Bar Hebraeus. Pillaged in 1148 by Jocelyn of Courtenay, prince of Edessa, it was then destroyed by a spectacular fire in 1183. Its reconstruction was the work of Michael the Syrian, who reconsecrated it on 15 May 1194. It remained a centre of the Jacobite Church until its destruction in the closing years of the thirteenth century.

From the ninth century the monastery of St Catherine founded by the emperor Justinian at the foot of Mount Sinai became the resting place of the relics of St Catherine of Alexandria.[70] It became a popular destination for pilgrims, including westerners. It boasts an exceptionally rich library, with some 2300 Greek manuscripts, 600 Arabic, 270 Syriac, 85 Georgian and 45 Slavonic.[71] This is a reflection not only of the importance of its scriptorium, but also of its

69 E. Honigmann, *Le couvent de Barsauma et le patriarcat jacobite d'Antioche et de Syrie* [CSCO 146 (Subsidia 7)] (Louvain: L. Durbecq, 1954).

70 *Le Sinaï durant l'Antiquité et le Moyen Âge: 4000 ans d'histoire pour un désert* (Actes du colloque 'Sinaï', UNESCO, 19–21 septembre 1997), ed. D. Valbelle and C. Bonnet (Paris: Errance, 1998).

71 A. S. Atiya, *The Arabic manuscripts of Mount Sinai: a hand-list of the Arabic manuscripts and scrolls microfilmed at the Library of the Monastery of St Catherine* [Publications of the American Foundation for the Study of Man 1] (Baltimore: Johns Hopkins University Press, 1955); M. Kamil, *Catalogue of all manuscripts in the monastery of St Catherine on Mount Sinai* (Wiesbaden: Harrassowitz, 1970); P. Géhin, 'La bibliothèque de Sainte Catherine du Sinaï. Fonds ancien et nouvelles découvertes', in *Sinaï*, 157–64.

sphere of influence, since it acquired many of its manuscripts through dona-tions from abroad. To take the example of the one Latin manuscript held by the library: this is a Psalter of the ninth century almost certainly of north African provenance, which was brought to the monastery in the thirteenth century.

The monastery of St Sabas goes back to a saint of that name, who decided in 478 to shut himself away in a cave in the gorge of Kedron, some 15 kilometres from Jerusalem.[72] The monastic buildings are set on a narrow platform on the edge of the ravine and to the present day shelter a community of Melkite monks. This monastery quickly became an important centre of literary activity, dominated in the eighth century by the figure of John of Damascus. The tombs of St Sabas and of John of Damascus attracted pilgrims, at least until the thirteenth century when the relics of the former were transferred to Venice and those of the latter to Constantinople. The monastery suffered from the repressive policies of the Mamluk Sultan Baybars and thereafter had a less prominent role to play, even if its monks continued to produce literary works.[73] Some 250 years ago a large part of its rich library was destroyed in a fire, but nearly 800 manuscripts were saved and transferred in the nineteenth century to the patriarchate of Jerusalem.[74]

From the many Coptic monasteries established both in the desert regions of the Wâdî al-Naṭrûn (to the west of the western branch of the Nile delta) and close to the Red Sea we shall single out St Antony's monastery. This consisted of a vast complex of buildings and gardens protected by a wall 2 kilometres long. It experienced a particularly prosperous period in the twelfth and thirteenth centuries after its final emancipation from the Syrian monks of the Wâdî al-Naṭrûn. The large number of Coptic manuscripts produced by the monastery from 1231 to 1306 and preserved today in Cairo testifies to the existence of an excellent scriptorium and a well-stocked library, which will have underpinned the intellectual revival of the thirteenth century; this is best illustrated by the activities of the Banû 'Assâl, a leading Coptic family.

The work of the scriptorium sometimes went hand in hand with artis-tic activities. For example, a gospel book embellished with fifty-two mag-nificent miniatures (now in the Vatican Library), was copied around 1220 in the monastery of Mar Mattaï near Mosul, one of the most ancient Jacobite

---

72 D. Pringle, *The churches of the Crusader Kingdom of Jerusalem: a corpus*, II (Cambridge: Cambridge University Press, 1998), 258–68.

73 Y. Frenkel, 'Mar Saba during the Mamlouk and Ottoman periods', in *The Sabaite heritage in the Orthodox Church from the fifth century to the present*, ed. J. Patrich [Orientalia lovaniensia analecta 98] (Louvain: Peeters, 2001), 111–16.

74 A. Peristeris, 'Literary and scribal activities at the monastery of St Saba', in *Sabaite heritage*, 171–94.

monasteries of Upper Mesopotamia, where Bar Hebraeus was buried. In addition, the library of the monastery of Dayr al-Zaʿfaran in the Ṭûr ʿAbdîn – known as the Saffron monastery on account of its yellow walls – has preserved, among others, two magnificent gospel books of the thirteenth century, whose illustrations, even more than those of the Mar Mattaï gospel book, betray strong Byzantine influences. But Syriac and Coptic art would follow a quite different line of development.

Religious life

A sarcastic little work entitled the 'Priests' banquet', which we surely owe to the pen of the Christian physician Ibn Buṭlân (†1066),[75] sheds precious light on the life of the Syriac clergy in the Ṭûr ʿAbdîn. Modelled on the Arabic genre of *Maqâmât* or 'Séances', which relate the deeds and sayings of a hero in elegant and refined language, the narrator describes a banquet, which took place at Mârdîn in the house of the priest. This satire denounces the clergy for the following shortcomings: their ability to make money out of their ministry (especially over funerals and prayers for the dead); their ignorance of church music; and their incompetence as preachers, being content to rehash the works of John Chrysostom, rather than devise eloquent new sermons. But this satire also reveals a clergy who were relatively well-to-do, were on good terms with their Muslim neighbours, and had a perfect command of Arabic language and culture.

The celebration of the liturgy dominated religious life. It was regulated by the calendars of the different churches, but local festivals also had an important role to play. The latter combined a mixture of ancient agrarian traditions and local memories with a more strictly Christian content, but this did not prevent Muslims taking part, so much so that paradoxically knowledge of these festivals has often only come down to us through Muslim sources. This is the case for the feast of Holy Thursday, celebrated in Egypt and Syria under a variety of names: 'Lentil Thursday', 'Rice Thursday' or even 'Egg Thursday'.[76] It took

75 Ibn Buṭlân, *Le banquet des prêtres: une* maqâma *chrétienne du XIe siècle*, trans. J. Dagher and G. Troupeau (Paris: Geuthner, 2004).
76 Evidence is supplied by the following authors: for Alexandria al-Bakrî (eleventh century); for Cairo al-Maqrîzî (fourteenth century); for Syria Ibn-Shaddâd (thirteenth century), al-Dimashqî (fourteenth century) and Ibn Taymiyya (fourteenth century). The latter, a hanbalite thinker well known for his rigorism, castigated Muslims who participated in Christian festivals in a treatise entitled 'the necessity of following the right path, so as to separate yourself from the companions of Gehenna': see G. Troupeau, 'Les fêtes des chrétiens vues par un juriste musulman', in *Mélanges offerts à Jean Dauvillier* (Toulouse: Centre d'histoire juridique méridionale, 1979), 795–802 [=*Études sur le christianisme arabe au moyen âge*, XIX].

over the customs marking the rebirth of spring: coloured eggs, dishes of rice or lentils, the censing of houses and tombs, the branding of livestock, and the hanging out of clothes to air. In the fourteenth century the Muslim scholar al-Maqrîzî recorded that 'Lentil Thursday has remained to this day one of Cairo's grandest festivals.'

Our period nevertheless saw islamisation reinforced, which often meant that Muslims appropriated Christian festivals and holy places. Many places where Christians venerated the memory of some Old Testament prophet or local saint merged into a religious fabric that was properly speaking Muslim. To take but one example: the Christian sanctuary of Bahnasâ, which preserved the memory of the flight into Egypt. This was increasingly islamised from the early thirteenth century by the construction there of numerous tombs for Muslim holy men.[77] 'The guide to pilgrimage places'[78] compiled by al-Harawî (d.1215), an Aleppan ascetic, regarded as Muslim a whole series of Near Eastern sanctuaries which had formerly been Christian or Jewish. The 'twin noble *harams*' of Hebron and Jerusalem [79] provide the most striking examples of Muslim appropriation. The sanctuary at Hebron, where Jews and Christians venerated the tomb of Abraham, became over the centuries a popular Muslim shrine. In 1266, when, following his first victories over the Franks, the Mamluk sultan Baybars went on pilgrimage to Hebron, he promulgated an edict forbidding Christians and Jews from entering the sanctuary – a prohibition which remained in force until the Israelis occupied the city in 1967. From the eleventh to the fourteenth century the city of Jerusalem, a holy city common to Jews, Christians and Muslims, lived through troubled times: under Fatimid rule from 970, it passed under Seljuq domination in 1073, only to be seized by the crusaders on 15 July 1099, when for nearly a century it was the capital of the Latin kingdom of Jerusalem. Falling to Saladin on 2 October 1187, it returned to the emperor Frederick II in 1229; ravaged by the Khwarizmians in 1244, it finally passed to the Mamluks of Egypt. Each new regime brought profound religious and social changes, which were reflected in the topography of the city. The end result was the transformation of Jerusalem from the Mamluk period onwards into a mainly Muslim city,[80] even if there was still an

---

77 C. Décobert, 'Un lieu de mémoire religieuse', in *Valeur et distance*, 247–63.

78 al-Harawî, *Guide des lieux de pélerinage*, ed. and trans. J. Sourdel-Thomine, 2 vols. (Damascus: Institut français, 1953–57).

79 The Mamluks applied the expression al-*haramayn*, which traditionally designated Mecca and Medina, to the new religious topography that they were creating in Palestine and Syria.

80 See M. H. Burgoyne, *Mamluk Jerusalem: an architectural study* (London: Festival of Islam Trust (for the British School of Archaeology at Jerusalem), 1987). A fiscal survey from

important Jewish community; even if Christians, including Latins,[81] from the various denominations continued to live there; even if pilgrims continued to flock there from all over the Christian world.

Between the eleventh and fourteenth centuries the churches in Egypt, Syria and Iraq underwent a series of profound upheavals. The process of islamisation turned Islam into the majority religion; political life became dominated by militaristic regimes which were fervently Muslim, despite (or perhaps because of) their reliance on foreign recruits; *dhimma* status was applied with increasing rigour; the crusades and Latin settlement constituted a challenge to Islam, while the Mongol conquest created a new political order. The different Christian communities did not react in identical ways, but adopted different strategies depending on the time, the place and the setting. Broadly speaking, they attempted to balance the preservation of a distinct identity against the needs of accommodation. On the one hand, the continued use of their own language, or even their own script in the case of *karshûnî*,[82] provided a means of distinguishing themselves from the dominant culture, Arab in language and Muslim in faith, as did keeping alive particular customs and the memory of a rich past – the preservation, in other words, of a cultural heritage – but this sometimes meant withdrawing far from the centres of activity and power. On the other, accommodation required the blurring of cultural boundaries and the promotion of social integration, as quite clearly happened among the urban elite, best documented in the careers of Christian secretaries and physicians. It made possible the emergence of heavily arabised Christian communities, who had a role to play in the future development of the Near East, but it also favoured conversion to Islam, which, in some sense, was the final stage in the process of assimilation. There was a third solution. This was to seek outside support. The ties established with the papacy and Latin missionaries, the reception of Greek pilgrims and monks at the monastery of St Catherine on Mount Sinai, and the hopes placed in the Mongols when they first arrived on the scene, are all good examples of a strategy which allowed churches to strengthen their position with outside help, but which left them open to the accusation that they were alien to the lands of Islam.

the beginning of the Ottoman period gives 934 heads of families, of whom 616 were Muslim, 199 Jewish and 119 Christian.

81 In the 1330s the Franciscans were authorised to found a monastery on Mount Sion, with responsibilities for the reception of western pilgrims.

82 This is Arabic written in the Syriac script.

17

The Armenians in the era of the crusades
1050–1350

S. PETER COWE

The defining issue for Christendom in the period under discussion was undoubtedly one of ecclesiology. In the case of the Armenians this took the form of renewed debate with the other Christian traditions which had emerged in Byzantium, western Europe and the Near East in the course of late antiquity, when a common patristic matrix developed distinct constellations of doctrine, rite and order with characteristic emphases, forms and expressions.

The onset of the Arab period in Armenian history ushered in an era of consolidation inaugurated by the catholicate of Yovhan Ōjnecʻi (717–728).[1] Synods reaffirmed Armenia's one-nature Christology, not only clarifying the distinctive Armenian doctrine of the incorruptibility of Christ's flesh in an Orthodox fashion, but also linking this doctrinally both to the joint celebration of the Nativity and Baptism of Christ on 6 January and to the use of unleavened bread and unmixed wine in the Eucharist.[2] The structures of the institutional church, its sacraments and the legitimacy of its representational art were defended against the Paulicians, a widespread iconoclastic sect. Compilations on doctrine and canon law were drawn up and a greater sense of historical identity gradually emerged, which expressed itself in an expanded sanctorale, highlighting local saints, particularly martyrs, and celebrating their accomplishments in hymns, *vitae* and encomia.[3] Of particular significance in this connection was the signal devotion among Armenians of all theological

---

1 A. Mardirossian, *Le livre des canons arméniens (Kanonagirkʻ Hayocʻ) de Yovhannēs Awjnecʻi: église, droit et société en Arménie du IVe au VIIIe siècle* [CSCO 606] (Louvain: Peeters, 2005).
2 S. P. Cowe, 'Armenian Christology in the seventh and eighth centuries with particular reference to the contributions of Catholicos Yovhan Ōjnecʻi and Xosrovik Tʻargmaničʻ', *Journal of Theological Studies* 55 (2004), 30–54.
3 Mayis Avdalbegyan, *'Yaysmawurkʻ' žołovacunerǝ ev nrancʻ patmagrakan aržekʻǝ* ['Menologium' Compilations and their Historiographical Value] (Erevan: Armenian Academy of Sciences, 1982), 122–36. For a brief overview of the oeuvre of Vardan Arewelcʻi, the most prolific author in this field, see Norayr Połarean, *Haygrołner* [Armenian Writers] (Jerusalem: St James Press, 1971), 294–9.

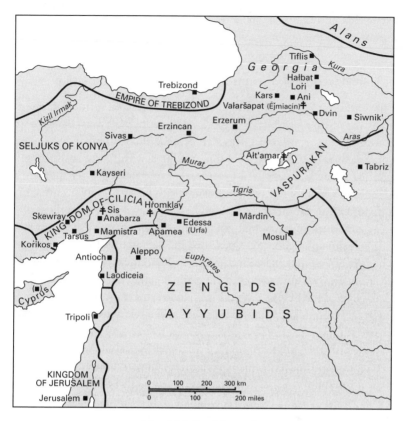

Map 6 Medieval Armenia

complexions to St Gregory the Illuminator, who had established Christianity as the religion of the Armenian court in the early fourth century.[4]

The historical course of the ecclesial dialogue mentioned above was determined in significant measure by the large-scale movements of peoples which punctuated the era: in the mid-eleventh century the Seljuq Turks came out of the east, to be followed by the Mongols in the thirteenth century and the Timurids in the 1380s, while the crusades ensured continuous waves of military, ecclesiastical and mercantile contacts with the west. Inevitably, these contacts underlined religious differences, which were a source of much friction.

---

4 S. P. Cowe, 'An Armenian Job fragment from Sinai and its implications', *Oriens Christianus* 72 (1992), 148–54.

Despite this, substantial interchange occurred, which left its imprint on the various ecclesiastical polities involved in the process.

A period of disruption and regrouping, 1050–1150

By the time our period opens the course of large-scale Armenian resettlement in the former marchlands of eastern Cappadocia between the Byzantine and Arab spheres of influence was already well into its third and final phase. Beginning as a means of repopulating the area with Christians during the Byzantine advance under Basil I in the 880s, it gained greater momentum under Nikephoros II Phokas after 963, at which point Armenians grew to be the majority population. It culminated in the gradual relocation there of the royalty and much of the nobility of the three main western successor states to the Armenian kingdom re-established in 884.[5] In 1022 King Sennek'erim-Yovhannēs of Vaspurakan bequeathed his realm to the empire, under pressure both from the Byzantines and from the initial Seljuq incursions, and Ašot IV of Ani followed suit in 1039. Armenians then became imperial vassals under an alien Byzantine bureaucratic structure, while their territories were reorganised as themes.[6]

A parallel process can also be detected in ecclesiastical affairs, which brought into renewed contact Greek, Armenian and Jacobite communities as well as the heretical Tondrakite sect, with varied results. One of these was the formation in the 980s on the initiative of Catholicos Xačik of Syrian and Armenian sees parallel to the Byzantine ones. Perhaps unforeseen by the court in Constantinople, this in turn provoked ethnic and religious polemic between the confessions over mutually unacceptable divergences in rite and doctrine. This resulted in the rebaptism of those faithful who altered their affiliation.[7] The integration and neutralisation of Armenian secular authority encouraged the patriarchs of Constantinople in their attempts to suppress the Armenian catholicate. Catholicos Petros was called to Constantinople in 1045 for theological discussions, and again two years later. To counter pressure from the Byzantines he

---

5 S. P. Cowe, 'Armenian immigration patterns to Sebastia, tenth–eleventh centuries', *UCLA International Conference on Armenia Minor–Sebastia/Sivas*, ed. R. G. Hovannisian (Costa Mesa, CA: Mazda Publishers, 2004), 115–24.

6 See Robert Hewsen, *Armenia: a historical atlas* (Chicago: University of Chicago Press, 2001), 125–6.

7 The religious polemic led to exchanges between the Armenian catholicos and the Greek metropolitans of Sebasteia and Melitene as well as a succession of Jacobite patriarchs. It produced anti-Chalcedonian refutations by Anania Narekac'i (d.c.985) and his namesake Anania Sanahnec'i (d.c.1070).

took the precaution – in contravention of accepted practice – of consecrating his nephew as his successor. The latter was summoned to the capital a year after assuming office in 1058 by the new emperor Constantine X Doukas, who required him to accept Chalcedonian Christology and the supremacy of the patriarch of Constantinople: in other words, to renounce his autocephaly. On refusing, he was held in captivity until 1062 and then confined to Sebasteia. On his death three years later the emperor at first prohibited a new election, but then relented against the cession of the Armenian kingdom of Kars.[8] The candidate subsequently cleared for election to the catholicate was Vahram, an avid philhellene, who had previously entered Byzantine service and had held the post of duke of Mesopotamia for ten years from 1048. In this capacity he destroyed the sectarian stronghold of T'ondrak and dispersed its adherents.[9] He belonged to the house of Pahlawuni, which claimed descent from the line of St Gregory the Illuminator. His consecration as Catholicos Grigor II inaugurated an unbroken series of hierarchs from that lineage over the next century and a half.

The second half of the eleventh century witnessed the consolidation of Seljuq power in Anatolia through the capture of Ani in 1064, reinforced in 1071 by the decisive victory over Byzantine forces at Mantzikert. The resulting power vacuum created the conditions which allowed Armenians to establish *de facto* autonomy in the hill country south of the Taurus range.[10] Its relative security led to a southward movement in the centre of gravity of the Armenian polity and the foundation of a series of small fiefdoms. These gradually evolved into a new kingdom in Cilicia (1198–1375), which was to play an important role in the political and religious history of the region over the rest of our period.[11]

The fragmentation and dispersion of the Armenian nation is dramatically etched in the constant travels of the catholicos Grigor II (1065–1105), as he sought to minister to his far-flung flock. With earlier precedents in mind, petty Armenian princes sought to persuade the catholicos to take up residence on their territories, as a means of strengthening their claims to legitimacy. Sheer expediency forced Grigor to raise others to the rank of catholicos, so that they would have the authority to take the necessary decisions on the

---

8 Cowe, 'Armenian immigration patterns', 125.

9 Avedis K. Sanjian, 'Gregory Magistros: an Armenian Hellenist', in Τὸ Ἑλληνικόν: *Studies in honor of Speros Vryonis, Jr.* (New Rochelle, NY: Caratzas, 1993), II, III–58.

10 This corresponded very roughly to the former themes of Lykandos, Melitene, Tarsos, Seleukeia, Antioch and Edessa.

11 For a convenient map of these territories, see C. Mutafian, *Le royaume arménien de Cilicie xiie–xive siècle* (Paris: Éditions du CNRS, 1993), 18.

ground.[12] Thus Gēorg Loṙecʻi resided with Apłłarip Arcruni in Tarsos from 1069; Sargis, nephew of Catholicos Petros, settled in the domain of Philaretos Brachamios (Vahram) at Honi in Lykandos in 1073; Grigor's nephew Barseł was consecrated bishop in Ani and then elevated to the rank of catholicos eight years later in Hałbat, one of the main monasteries of the small remaining Bagratid kingdom of Loṙi-Tašir; while there is evidence that Grigor visited Egypt and established another nephew, his namesake, as supreme ecclesiastical authority over the expanding Armenian community there. In other instances, separatist tendencies dictated such moves, as in the case of Vaspurakan, which desired to perpetuate its status as an independent kingdom at least in the ecclesiastical realm by declaring Altʻamar a separate catholicate in 1113. In doing so it instituted a schism that was only settled in 1441. Similarly, it seems that at the beginning of the twelfth century the Seljuqs of Rum briefly toyed with the strategy of segregating their Armenian population from the rest of the Armenian Church by installing Anania, bishop of Sebasteia, as an anti-catholicos.[13] Much later it appears that Mamluk opposition to the Latinophile orientation of the Cilician Armenian court was a factor in the creation of an Armenian patriarchate in Jerusalem (1311), with a view to exercising jurisdiction over the Christian Armenian community in the Mamluk lands.[14]

At the same time it corresponded to the spiritual needs of a community that was increasingly dispersed. The disruption to the regular rhythms of transit trade in the mid-eleventh century intensified the exodus of Armenian merchants and artisans, who now swelled the ranks of their countrymen further afield in the relative calm of the Crimea, Kievan Rus, Poland and the western Black Sea coast. They also settled in various Italian ports.[15] There were even trading connections with Iceland, where we hear of the arrival of three Armenian 'bishops', presumably at the invitation of the Norwegian king, Harald Sigurdson.[16] Other Armenian traders were deported eastwards first by the Seljuqs and then by the Mongols to form thriving colonies in north-eastern Iran.[17]

---

12 A. Kapoïan-Kouymjian, *L'Égypte vue par des Arméniens* (Paris: Fondation Singer-Polignac, 1988), 7–19.

13 Haïg Berbérian, 'Le patriarcat arménien du Sultanat de Roum', *Revue des Études Arméniennes* 3 (1966), 233–41.

14 Bezalel Narkiss (ed.), *Armenian art treasures of Jerusalem* (Jerusalem: Massada Press, 1979), 17.

15 G. Dédéyan, *Histoire des Arméniens* (Toulouse: Privat, 1982), 391–400.

16 Y. R. Dachkévytch, 'Les Arméniens en Islande (XIe siècle)', *Revue des Études Arméniennes* 20 (1986–87), 321–36.

17 A. G. Abrahamyan, *Hamaṙot urvagic hay gałtavayreri patmutʻyan* [Concise sketch of the history of Armenian colonies] (Erevan: Haypethrat, 1964), 240–1.

The Armenians were widely valued for their military prowess. In the aftermath of the Byzantine defeat some enterprising commanders moved to Egypt under the Fatimids where the Armenian Badr al-Jamâlî (1074–94) founded a dynasty of viziers lasting almost a century. Though most adopted Islam, they acted as patrons of the older Christian Armenian community established there, which underwent something of a renaissance. This is reflected in the building of some thirty churches and monasteries, of which the White Monastery near Sohag is the best preserved, featuring several frescos and inscriptions, the work of the artist T'ēodor of K'esun.[18]

Although Armenians were often wary of Byzantium's hegemonic ambitions, many in this era still looked to Constantinople as the primary representative of Christendom in the Near East. The capital possessed a growing Armenian population, which exploited its position as a conduit for renewed translation from Greek into Armenian. Their activities had great influence on the development in the eleventh and twelfth centuries of the Armenian *menologion* (*yaysmawurk'*) and of the liturgy of St Athanasius, which drew on elements from its Byzantine counterpart attributed to St John Chrysostom.[19] Moreover, the energetic catholicos Grigor II earned his epithet 'Martyrophile' (*Vkayasēr*) through commissioning a range of *vitae* and other texts from Greek and Syriac, an enterprise which several of his successors advanced into the late thirteenth century.[20] While the focus of these endeavours tended to be older patristic works not yet available in Armenian, Armenian Chalcedonian translators operating in areas under Byzantine and Georgian control placed their emphasis on post-Chalcedonian Fathers, for example St John Klimax and St John of Damascus.[21] Their monasteries, such as K'obayr, K'iranc' and Axt'ala (Płnjahank'), which flourished in the thirteenth century in the northern region of Loṙi, manifest the middle Byzantine penchant for fresco programmes

18 Kapoïan-Kouymjian, *Égypte*, 15–16; Seda B. Dadoyan, *The Fatimid Armenians* [Islamic History and Civilization Studies and Texts 18] (Leiden: Brill, 1997), 85–105.

19 Nersēs Akinean, 'Yovsēp' Kostandnupolsec'i, targmanič yaysmawurk'i (991)' [Yovsēp' Kostandnupolsec'i as translator of the menologium], *Handēs Amsōreay* 71 (1957), 1–12; H.-J. Feulner, *Die armenische Athanasius-Anaphora* [Anaphorae orientales 1] (Rome: Pontificio istituto orientale, 2001), 456–8.

20 Garegin Zarbhanalean, *Matenadaran haykakan t'argmanuteanc' naxneac' (dar D-ŽG)* [Library of Ancient Armenian Translations (Fourth–Thirteenth Centuries)] (Venice: St Lazar's Press, 1889), xxviii–xxxi; Levon Ter Petrossian, *Ancient Armenian translations* (New York: St Vartan's Press, 1992), 9–11.

21 S. P. Cowe, 'Medieval Armenian literary and cultural trends (twelfth–seventeenth centuries)', in *History of the Armenian people from ancient to modern times*, ed. R. G. Hovannisian (New York: St Martin's Press, 1997), I, 311.

enveloping the entire wall space of the church in contrast to the more modest embellishment typical of medieval Armenian churches.[22]

A novel feature of the late eleventh century was the opening of Armenian relations with the Latin church, which unfolded over the next four and a half centuries against the backdrop of the twelfth-century papal policy of drawing the various 'schismatic' Eastern churches into union under Roman primacy. The first overtures in 1080 were extended by Pope Gregory VII to Catholicos Grigor II, who, according to some, had paid a prior visit to Rome.[23] This contact inaugurated a rich and diverse range of ecclesiastical, theological, political and cultural interchange pursued in different parts of the Near East as well as via the Armenian communities in the west. As a result, it is probably true that westerners got to know the Armenians better than any of the other 'oriental' Christian confessions.

Direct contacts were established in the course of the First Crusade, during which Armenian princes like the Rubenid Kostandin I assisted the crusaders on their passage through Cilicia to Antioch, while T'oros, the Armenian Chalcedonian ruler of Edessa, welcomed Baldwin of Boulogne into his city in 1098, which was soon to be transformed into a crusader county. An early rapport developed with the Kingdom of Jerusalem (1099–1187), three of whose queens were of Armenian descent.[24] A number of high-ranking Armenians went on pilgrimage in those years, including Catholicos Grigor III and his brother Nersēs, who accompanied the papal legate Alberich to the synod of the cenacle in 1141/2 after participating in a similar gathering in Antioch. The same year also witnessed an amicable exchange of letters between Pope Eugenius III and the catholicos.[25]

This could not disguise the fact that the initiative in near eastern geopolitics had passed to Zangi, emir of Mosul, and his son Nûr al-Dîn. The former made himself master of Aleppo in 1128 and then of Edessa in 1144, which provoked the Second Crusade (1147–48). Its failure prepared the way for Nûr al-Dîn's annexation of Damascus in 1154 and then of Egypt in 1169. His success persuaded Armenians, such as Mleh, brother of Prince T'oros, of the advantages of entente, so much so that Mleh accepted Islam and allied with Nûr al-Dîn,

---

22 A. Lidov, *The mural paintings of Akhtala* (Moscow: Nauka, 1991).

23 Kapoïan-Kouymjian, *Égypte*, 11–13.

24 Baldwin I married Arta, daughter of the Rubenid prince T'oros I, and their daughter Melisende in turn married Fulk of Anjou, while Baldwin II married Morphia, daughter of Gabriël of Melitene.

25 A.-B. Schmidt and P. Halfter, 'Der Brief Papst Innozenz II an den armenischen katholikos Gregor III: ein wenig beachtetes Dokument zur Geschichte der Synode von Jerusalem (Ostern 1141)', *Annuarium Historiae Conciliorum* 31 (1999), 50–71.

who himself had married an Armenian princess. Returning from exile on his brother's death, he seized power with Zangid support and led a mercurial reign, first defeating the combined forces of Antioch and Jerusalem in 1172 and then regaining control of most of the Cilician seaboard from Byzantium in the following year. However, on Nûr al-Dîn's death in 1174 he fell victim to a palace coup. This tumultuous interlude underlines the unsettled tenor of Armenian life at the time, which is also reflected in the absence of any major work of art.

Monastic life

From the late ninth century the wealth of the Bagratid realm found expression in displays of piety through major donations by aristocrats and later by rich merchants. These fuelled a significant growth in Armenian monastic construction.[26] In fact, most churches at this time were built within large monastic complexes which appropriated the secular structure of the *gawit'* as an important space for the daily office, lectures, manuscript copying, burial, etc., and, as they expanded over the next four centuries, were gradually equipped with libraries, refectories and belfries, as well as oil and wine presses catering to their domestic needs.[27] Scale was a key differential from the early period, the new *cenobia* sometimes housing hundreds of monks, their daily round often governed by the norms of St Basil's rule under the oversight of the class of *vardapets* (doctors of theology licensed to preach and teach), who were now entering their most influential phase in both responsibilities and prestige.[28] Moreover, thanks to the generosity of their donors, these communities soon became powerful economic units rich in real estate, manpower and equipment (mills, etc.) in contrast to the caves or modest wooden structures of the past.[29] These monasteries also became institutes of higher learning to an unprecedented degree, with a structured curriculum which concentrated on the elucidation of the Bible, patristic authors and a corpus of textbooks from Greek antiquity.[30] Monastic scriptoria such as that of Skewṙay would rival the

26 Vrej Nersessian, *The Tondrakian movement* (London: Kahn and Averill, 1987), 74–5.
27 P. Donabédian, J.-M. Thierry and N. Thierry, *Armenian art* (New York: Harry N. Abrams, 1989), 195–200.
28 S. P. Cowe, 'Armenological paradigms and Yovhannēs Sarkawag's "discourse on wisdom" – philosophical underpinning for an Armenian renaissance?' *Revue des Études Arméniennes* 25 (1994–95), 137–43.
29 For the popular uprisings this wealth sometimes provoked, see Nersessian, *The Tondrakian movement*, 76–7.
30 Paroyr M. Mouradyan, 'Les principes de la classification des livres en Arménie médiévale', in *Armenian studies in memoriam Haïg Berbérian*, ed. Dickran Kouymjian (Lisbon: Calouste Gulbenkian Foundation, 1986), 591–600.

seat of the catholicos at Hṙomklay in the exquisite quality of their copying and illumination.[31] Outside the Armenian highlands and Cilicia, a series of Armenian monasteries was located on the Black Mountain near Antioch, which also sustained Greek, Georgian, Syrian and Latin communities in this period and hence encouraged international contacts. The most illustrious medieval Armenian monastic centre of higher learning at this time was founded at Glajor in the region of Siwnikʻ, whose activities spanned the years 1280–1340. It gained such a reputation under its director Esayi Nčecʻi that students came from all over the Armenian lands to study there.[32]

The patterns of spirituality practised in Armenian monasteries had significantly changed from the external asceticism of the earlier period to a more pronounced concern for interiority. In this it reflected a widespread preoccupation of the era also evidenced in Byzantium and in the developing sufi tradition of Islam, which in turn seems influenced by earlier Christian mystical writers like St Isaak of Nineveh.[33] The fundamental creed of the sect of Tondrakites, moulded out of a Paulician matrix, may be viewed as an extreme manifestation of this approach. Its threat to a proper understanding of the economy of the incarnation, crucifixion and resurrection provoked a multimedia response: from learned doctrinal treatises to the proliferation of a characteristically Armenian type of monument, the *xačkʻar*, a large rectangular block of stone elaborately carved with a representation of the cross in an infinite variety of motifs.[34] Persecution resulted in the sect going underground in inaccessible areas of the Armenian terrain and surfacing periodically as late as the nineteenth century.[35] Others fled or were deported to the Armenian centre at Philippopolis in Bulgaria. Transforming their belief system in the course of their geographical migration, they influenced the views of later sects like the Bogomils and the Albigensians.[36]

---

31 *Treasures in heaven: Armenian illuminated manuscripts*, ed. T. F. Mathews and R. S. Wieck (New York: The Pierpoint Morgan Library, 1994), 68–74.

32 G. M. Grigoryan, *Syunikʻɔ Ōrbelyanneri ōrokʻ (XIII–XV darer)* [Siwnikʻ in the days of the Ōrbēleans (thirteenth–fifteenth centuries)] (Erevan: Armenian Academy of Sciences, 1981), 241.

33 J. Baldick, *Mystical Islam* [New York University Studies in Near Eastern Civilization 13] (New York: New York University Press, 1989), 15–20.

34 *Armenian folk arts, culture, and identity*, ed. L. Abrahamian and N. Sweezy (Bloomington: Indiana University Press, 2001), 60–70; Donabédian and Thierry, *Armenian art*, 123–4, 205–7, figs. 67–8, 89, 105–7.

35 Nersessian, *The Tondrakian movement*, 89–96. A similar fate was met by the syncretistic sect of *arewordikʻ* [children of the sun], a part of which was reconciled to the church in the 1170s at Samosata by Nersēs Šnorhali.

36 Babken H. Harutʻyunyan, *Hayastani patmutʻyan atlas, I mas* [Historical Atlas of Armenia, Part I] (Erevan: Erevan State University, 2004), 60.

Discussions on church union with Byzantium

In 1165, around the time Mleh was furthering his Muslim contacts in exile, a chance discussion between bishop Nersēs Šnorhali and the imperial *protostrator* Alexios Axouch during a campaign in Cilicia began a desultory set of theological discussions over the possibility of ecclesiastical rapprochement with Byzantium, which lasted until the Emperor Manuel I Komnenos's death in 1180.[37] The emperor entrusted these negotiations with the Armenians to an experienced theologian-diplomat called Theorianos, who had the task of realising Manuel's goal of preserving Antioch's client-status as a basis for expanding his authority south towards Jerusalem and northwards over the sultanate of Konya. The nine points the emperor presented for acceptance in 1171 encompassed the ratification of the last four ecumenical councils, confession of the Chalcedonian definition and anathema of those denying it, omission of the phrase 'who was crucified for us' from the trisagion hymn, and a few ritual issues including the employment of leavened bread and wine mixed with water in the preparation of the eucharistic elements, as well as the canonical regulation that the emperor should confirm appointments to the catholicate.[38] Nersēs sought to call a synod to review the stipulations, but died before this could be done. After much further discussion under his successor Grigor Tłay (1173–93), a synod of thirty-three hierarchs and abbots, including Jacobite representatives and the catholicos of Albania, finally met at Hŕomklay in 1178 and offered a balanced and judicious response. In certain areas such as Christology they displayed a conciliatory disposition 'for the peace of the church', while in others they maintained that the *onus probandi* remained firmly on the Greek side, such as in demonstrating the final four councils did not contradict the first three and in remonstrating that the addition to the *trisagion* was of Greek not Armenian origin.[39] Significantly, their handling of the question of the standing of the catholicate and the problem of succession reveals the degree to which Antioch had become a focus of Armenian ecclesiastical ambition, as was also the case in the temporal sphere. The signatories approved of imperial sanction on condition that the Armenian catholicos henceforth be acknowledged as

---

37 L. B. Zekiyan, 'St. Nersēs Šnorhali en dialogue avec les Grecs: un prophète de l'oecuménisme au XIIe siècle', in *Armenian studies in memoriam Haïg Berbérian*, 861–83.
38 Zekiyan, 'St. Nersēs Šnorhali en dialogue avec les Grecs', 866–67.
39 See Clemens Galanus, *Conciliationis Ecclesiae Armenae cum Romana* (Rome: Urban Press, 1651), I, 331–44 (for the synodal acts); J. Meyendorff, *Christ in eastern Christian thought* (Crestwood, NY: St Vladimir's Seminary Press, 1987), 35 (for the theological point at issue).

patriarch of Antioch, thereby maintaining his autocephaly.[40] Neilos Doxopatres's near contemporary Greek treatise on the five patriarchal jurisdictions was translated into Armenian at this juncture and clearly played a part in discussions on the status of the Armenian see.[41]

Nevertheless, these synodal decrees were not representative of all shades of contemporary Armenian ecclesiastical opinion. Opposition came from a group of scholars and prelates collectively referred to as the 'northern *vardapets*'.[42] Their respect for tradition is well illustrated by a later issue arising from the service of Armenian troops on Georgian campaigns under the command of the brothers Zak῾arē and Ivanē Erkaynabazuk, who were dignitaries of the Georgian court. Whereas the Georgians had obtained dispensation to celebrate the liturgy on portable altars during manoeuvres, the Armenian forces had not received permission to introduce this practice. Although the synod of Sis gave its permission (1204), the rigorist party in the north refused to adhere to the ruling and blocked the measure at the local synods Zak῾arē summoned at Loṙi (1205) and at his capital in Ani (1207), compelling him to impose it within the context of military discipline.[43]

At the other end of the spectrum, a number of Armenian churchmen focused less on the historical precedents of the Armenian confessional tradition and matters of institutional advantage in inter-church negotiations, but appealed rather to the spiritual reality of the church as the body of Christ, affirming this as the basis for the underlying unity of Christendom. Their number included figures such as Mxit῾ar Goš (*c*. 1140–1213), and in the next generation Vardan Aygekc῾i (*c*. 1170–1235) from Greater Armenia.[44] In the thirteenth century the popular poet Frik gave voice to another point of view on Christian unity: he argued that its absence had been a major factor in Muslim advances and proceeded to list the key foibles of each communion, which had militated against greater cohesion and cooperation.[45]

---

40 Abēl Mxit῾areanc῾, *Patmut῾iwn žołovoc῾ hayastaneayc῾ ekełec῾woy* [History of the Synods of the Armenian Church] (Vałaršapat: Mother See Press, 1874), 116–17.

41 F. N. Finck, *Des Nilos Doxopatres taxis ton patriarchikon thronon armenisch und griechisch* (Ējmiacin and Marburg: Vagarshapad, 1902).

42 They came under the leadership of Grigor Tutēordi and Dawit῾ K῾obayrec῾I and were concentrated in territories then under Georgian control.

43 Mxit῾areanc῾, *Patmut῾iwn žołovoc῾ hayastaneayc῾ ekełec῾woy*, 118–22.

44 Paroyr Muradean, 'Dawanakan handuržołakanut῾ean ew azgamijean hamerašxut῾ean gałap῾arə ŽB–ŽG dareri Hayastanum' [The idea of confessional tolerance and internal national solidarity in twelfth–thirteenth century Armenia], *Ganjasar* 4 (1994), 95–108.

45 Frik, *Frik Diwan*, ed. Tirayr Melik῾ Muškambarean (New York: Melgonean Foundation, 1952), 274–80.

The Armenian churchman most actively engaged at this time in inter-confessional contacts at the highest level was the young archbishop of Tarsos, Nersēs Lambronac'i (1153–98). In his oft-quoted words, 'Spain and the East are limbs of the one Head, [as are] Greeks and barbarians, Armenians and Georgians, Syrians and Egyptians [Copts]. All are bound together in Him in spirit and have clothed themselves in Him through faith.'[46] He led the Armenian delegation which was sent in 1197 to the Byzantine Emperor Alexios III Angelos and to the patriarch George Xiphilinos, with the intention of clarifying the religious issues associated with the emperor's initial willingness to grant Prince Levon of Cilicia a crown, thereby elevating his lands to the rank of kingdom. Discussions were prolonged to Pentecost, but concluded without issue. Moreover, it appears that the stimulus for Alexios's gesture was intelligence that negotiations towards the same end were already far advanced with the German emperor. Nersēs was also involved in those talks, having been sent to greet Frederick Barbarossa in 1190 as he entered Cilician territory, only to learn of his untimely death.[47] However, he profited by the occasion to render into Armenian the Latin ritual book sent by Pope Lucius III, as well as the coronation *ordo*, and St Benedict's rule.[48] Around this time the Armenians also adopted the Latin episcopal mitre, ring and crosier, in the place of the Byzantine episcopal crown, which now devolved to regular priests.

Church union with the Latins

That Cilician civil and ecclesiastical interests were focused on the German Empire and the papacy in the final years of the twelfth century is to be set against the backdrop of Byzantine reverses in Bulgaria, Serbia and Cyprus, which had claimed independence in 1184 and fell to the crusaders seven years later. All these gained imperial recognition after a formal submission to papal supremacy in the course of the 1190s. Armenia followed their precedent, Prince Levon (1198–1219) being crowned king on 6 January 1198 in the once Greek church of St Sophia in Tarsos, the largest in the realm, with Conrad of

---

46 Nersēs Lambronac'i, *Atenabanut'iwn vasn miut'ean ekelec'woy ew čaṙk' i hambarjumn K'ristosi ew i galust Hogwoyn Srboy* [Synodal oration on church union and homilies on Christ's Ascension and Pentecost], ed. Mesrop Taliadean (Calcutta, 1851), 35.

47 Anoushavan Tanielian, 'Archbishop Nersēs Lambronac'i''s commentary on Wisdom of Solomon', unpublished PhD thesis, Columbia University (2003), 34–5.

48 Nersēs Akinean, *Nersēs Lambronac'i ark'episkopos Tarsoni keank'n ew grakan vastaknerə* [Nersēs Lambronac'i, archbishop of Tarsus: life and literary achievements] (Vienna: Mxitarist Press, 1956), 284–8, 302–16.

Wittelsbach, archbishop of Mainz, officiating.[49] The archbishop had arrived the previous year with instructions from Innocent III to obtain Armenian recognition of Roman primacy and to align Armenian with Roman practice on a number of matters. These included adopting a fixed calendar for regulating the celebration of saints' days rather than the traditional Armenian movable system determined by the Easter cycle, and breaking the Nativity and Lenten fasts with only fish and olive oil.[50] Levon summoned a synod in Tarsos to ratify the process. Only twelve bishops signed, but their voice prevailed.[51]

The growth of pro-western sentiment in various Armenian communities over the twelfth century can be gauged by a series of apocryphal writings such as the *Sermo de Antichristo*, which enshrined Armenian eschatological expectations associated with the Seljuq invasion. These culminated in the *Dašanc' t'ułt'* (Letter of Concord),[52] which purports to relate not only the meeting in Rome between the first Christian kings Constantine I and Trdat III but also – and more importantly – the instruction and consecration of the first Armenian catholicos Gregory the Illuminator by Pope Sylvester. It put forward the claim that the parties agreed to divide the exercise of ecclesiastical and secular authority between them.[53] The document's import is obviously that submission to the papacy and a western alliance will be of appreciable benefit in reinforcing the Armenian power base in the Near East. Appeal to its message was frequently made in exchanges with the papacy over the next few centuries.

As already indicated, a close but complex relationship had developed between Cilicia and Antioch. Common interests led them to unite against Byzantium, but internal rivalries occasioned harsh acts of duplicity and reprisal. Since the 1170s Armenian ecclesiastical ambitions had focused on the patriarchate of Antioch. Indeed, one advantage of church union under the pope was to free the Armenian catholicos from interference from the Latin patriarch, who continued to claim jurisdiction over the sees of Tarsos and Mamistra, which

49 S. P. Cowe, 'The inauguration of the Cilician coronation rite and royal ideology', *Armenian Review* 45 (1992), 51, 54–5.
50 The Armenians had traditionally supplemented these with dairy products.
51 Tanielian, 'Archbishop Nersēs Lambronac'i''s commentary on Wisdom of Solomon', 37–8.
52 K. V. Šahnazareanc', *Dašanc' tłt'oc' k'nnut'iwnn u herk'umǝ* [Investigation and Refutation of the Letter of Concord] (Paris, 1862).
53 Zaroui Pogossian, 'A revised-diplomatic edition, and a historical and textual investigation of "Letter of love and concordance between the Emperor Constantine the Great and Pope Sylvester and the King of the Armenians Trdat the Great and St. Gregory the Illuminator"', unpublished PhD thesis, Central European University, Budapest (2004).

had had Latin bishops at the time these cities came under Armenian control.[54] Another aspect of ecclesiastical interaction between the two states was Prince Levon's policy *vis-à-vis* the Jacobite community. In 1192 he appointed Theodore Bar Wahbun as anti-patriarch and attempted to have the Jacobite communities of the region submit to his jurisdiction.[55] Antioch's gradual decline marked by its reduction in territory and forced union with Tripoli after Saladin's attack in 1187 favoured Levon's efforts to gain ascendancy over it through an astute policy of intermarriage. However, the competing claims of members of the Antiochian princely house, coupled with the interests of the Italian merchant communities, conspired to thwart him to the end of his reign.

Papal missionary initiatives

The missionary ethos of the two mendicant orders of Dominicans and Franciscans founded in the first half of the thirteenth century, combined with their structural flexibility, discipline and institutional organisation, rendered them an unprecedented spiritual force for proselytising among the Armenians and other eastern Christians and for furthering papal diplomacy. The Franciscans established various centres in Cilicia and played an increasingly important role as the century progressed, in various spheres including that of religious art.[56] Het'um II (1289–1301), in particular, petitioned the pope for a personal retinue of six friars at court and later entered the brotherhood himself.[57] The Dominicans made a slower start in establishing contacts, but became more pivotal in the following century.

This was the time of Mongol domination, which after initial upheavals worked to the benefit of the Armenian Church. From 1255 it was exempted from the payment of tax to the Mongols.[58] Het'um I (1226–69) of Cilicia and several princes of Greater Armenia took the precaution of placing themselves under Mongol suzerainty, thus protecting their subjects from arbitrary

---

54 J. Richard, *La papauté et les missions d'Orient au Moyen Âge (XIIIe–XVe siècles)* [Collection de l'École française de Rome 33], second edition (Rome: École française de Rome, 1998), 43, 49–50.

55 P. Kawerau, *Die jakobitische Kirche im Zeitalter der syrischen Renaissance* (Berlin: Akademie Verlag, 1955), 68–9.

56 H. Evans, 'Manuscript illumination at the Armenian patriarchate in Hṙomkla and the west', unpublished PhD thesis, New York Institute of Fine Arts (1989), 153–4.

57 Richard, *Papauté*, 52.

58 R. Bedrosian, 'Armenia during the Seljuk and Mongol periods', in *History of the Armenian people*, ed. R. G. Hovannisian, I, 261.

exactions. As a result, both Armenian regions enjoyed a significant degree of stability and prosperity in the mid-thirteenth century, in marked contrast to the struggles of the crusader states to hold their own, while the Latin conquest of Constantinople in 1204 had dealt a nigh mortal blow to Byzantine power. This is the setting against which to view the Armenians' lack of interest in exploring more fully the implications of the union with Rome promulgated by Levon I.

In 1243 Catholicos Kostandin Barjrberdc'i (1221–67) responded positively to Innocent IV's query regarding recognition of the sacrament of extreme unction and other liturgical rites. However, the more substantive issues debated during his long term of office, the *filioque* and Petrine primacy, only exposed the extent of the differences separating the two sides. Among the messengers the pope dispatched to the east on 25 March 1245 in the run up to the first Council of Lyons was the Franciscan Dominic of Aragon, who was to secure an Armenian confession of faith. When King Het'um I discussed this with his mentor Vardan Arewelc'i, the latter responded by writing a brief compilation of fifteen Latin errors.[59] It may be that the creation in 1247 of a new archiepiscopal see at the monastery of St Thaddaeus was also part of this reaction to papal primacy. Not only was St Thaddaeus the traditional guarantor of the apostolicity of the Armenian Church,[60] but his monastery also lay close to the Mongol summer quarters, not far from Maku in north-western Iran.

Similarly, though the synod of Sis of 1251 accepted the *filioque* doctrine, it provoked a major reaction from the church in Greater Armenia, which threatened to create a schism by setting up an anti-catholicos. Both Vanakan Vardapet and Vardan Arewelc'i appear to have accepted the orthodoxy of the dual procession of the Spirit for the theologically sophisticated, if not for the general populace, but their language and images seem to suggest that they had in mind either the Spirit's activity in the economy or the patristic formula 'from the Father through the Son in the Spirit'. Latin polemicists found their formulations unsatisfactory.[61]

Moreover, the acerbity with which Mxit'ar Skewr̄ac'i and the legate Thomas Agni de Lentino clashed at Acre in 1262 over Petrine primacy caused the pope to send the Dominican William Freney to Cilicia to try to restore a more cordial

---

59 *Girk' t'łt'oc'* [Book of Letters], ed. Arch. Norayr Połarean (Jerusalem: St James Press, 1994), 657–65.
60 Levon Xačikyan, 'Artazi haykakan išxanut'yunə ev Corcori dproc'ə' [The Armenian principality of Artaz and the school of Corcor], *Banber Matenadarani* 11 (1973), 134.
61 J. N. D. Kelly, *Early Christian doctrines* (London: A. & C. Black, 1977), 256–63.

atmosphere.[62] In keeping with the Armenians' reservations about these earlier papal overtures was their absence from the Second Council of Lyons in 1274, to which even the Ilkhân sent a representative at Gregory X's invitation.[63]

Trade routes facilitate religious interchange

The favourable conditions attendant on the *pax mongolica* intensified the volume of trade linking China with Central Asia, Russia, southern Caucasia and Asia Minor via the new Ilkhânid centre of Tabrîz and on to the Cilician port of Ayas, whence Italian shipping transported Oriental commodities to western Europe. A more northerly land route through Erzurum, Erzincan and Sivas was also used.[64] Many Armenian merchants were engaged in this traffic, leading to the formation of communities in various entrepôts and to the construction of churches.[65] The Latin mendicant orders also profited from these circumstances. The Franciscans established centres in the following sites with a significant Armenian population: Erzurum, St Thaddaeus, Salmast, Karpi, Tiflis, Sulṭânîya and Tabrîz, while the Dominicans possessed houses in Tabrîz and Marâgha.[66] Complaints were soon being voiced that Roman doctrine was encroaching on Greater Armenia, having already infiltrated Cilicia, the main Byzantine cities and the old Bagratid capital of Ani.[67]

We are perhaps best informed about Erzincan, which boasted one of the most vibrant Armenian merchant and artisan communities of the thirteenth and fourteenth centuries. Türkmen dominated the surrounding countryside, while the local Mengüjakid court patronised Persian culture.[68] Literary and canonical references suggest a degree of interrelation between the communities, sometimes consolidated by ties of marriage or family alliance.[69] For instance, the rules of the confraternity of Armenian urban youth drawn up

62 Mxit'ar Skewṙac'i, *Patasxanik' Mxit'ar k'ahanayi Skewṙac'woy yaḷags hamapetut'ean erkotasan aṙak'eloc'* [On the equal rank of the twelve apostles] (Jerusalem: St James Press, 1865).

63 C. Dawson (ed.), *The Mongol mission: narratives and letters of the Franciscans in Mongolia and China in the thirteenth and fourteenth centuries* (London and New York: Sheed and Ward, 1955), xxi.

64 For a map of these routes, see Hewsen, *Historical atlas*, 135. For Armenian communities in China, see Dawson, *Mongol mission*, 232–3.

65 Dédéyan, *Histoire des Arméniens*, 395–400.

66 Richard, *Papauté*, 116.

67 Step'annos Örbēlean, *Hakačaṙut'iwn ənddēm erkabnakac'* [Refutation of the Dyophysites] (Constantinople, 1756), 43.

68 C. Cahen, *Pre-Ottoman Turkey* (London: Sidgwick and Jackson, 1968), 108–9.

69 Ē. Baḷdasaryan, *Hovhannes Erznkac'in ev nra xratakan arjak ə* [Yovhannēs Erznkac'i's paraenetic prose] (Erevan: Armenian Academy of Sciences, 1977), 120–8.

in 1280 reflect the impact of Caliph al-Naṣîr's earlier reforms of similar Muslim organisations,[70] while the christocentric allegorical poetry of Kostandin Erznkac'i from the late thirteenth century is the first to introduce the Persian love motif of the rose and the nightingale into Armenian literature, suggesting familiarity with sufi verse on mystical union with the divine beloved.[71] Nevertheless, undercurrents of tension were also present, which led the Seljuqs to coordinate a series of anti-Armenian attacks with the Mamluk Sultan Baybars's campaign against Cilicia in the mid-1270s.[72]

The previous decade had witnessed the consolidation of Mamluk power in the Near East. The Mamluks seized control of Syria in 1260 and then threw back the Mongol armies, which included Armenian contingents, at the battle of 'Ayn Jâlût. For more than a century thereafter – until the final demise of the Cilician kingdom in 1375 – support for the Mongols and alignment with the west made the Armenians the special object of Mamluk wrath. During this period the Mamluks became the Armenians' main foe, leaving their stamp on the oral epic *Daredevils of Sasun*, in which the prime antagonist is Msra Melik' (King of Egypt). In typical epic fashion the conflict appears 'writ small', featuring the historical nexus of exorbitant tax impositions on the Christian population, the destruction of monasteries, Christian–Muslim family relations, etc.[73]

At the end of the thirteenth century the political and military situation turned decisively against the Armenians of Cilicia. The Jochid Mongols of the Golden Horde centred in Sarai on the lower Volga accepted Islam and made common cause with the Mamluks. In 1291 the latter captured Acre, the last mainland crusader outpost. The following year they attacked Hŕomklay, seat of the Armenian catholicate, and took the incumbent Step'anos IV into captivity. His successor, Grigor Anavarzec'i (1293–1307), was thus compelled to take up residence in the Cilician capital of Sis, where he found himself confronted with the ecclesiastical implications of King Het'um II's diplomatic initiatives. The king's decision to betroth his two sisters, one into the Lusignan royal house of Cyprus and the other into the Palaiologan dynasty of Byzantium, raised questions of Christian unity.[74] Anavarzec'i's call 'in these debased times'

---

70 D. A. Breebaart, 'The development and structure of the Turkish futüwah guilds', unpublished PhD thesis, Princeton University (1961), 52–68.

71 S. P. Cowe, 'The politics of poetics: Islamic influence on Armenian verse', *Proceedings of the symposium redefining Christian identity: Christian cultural strategies since the rise of Islam* (Leuven: Peeters, 2006)

72 Richard, *Papauté*, 101.

73 Trans. L. Surmelian, *Daredevils of Sassoun* (Denver: A. Swallow, 1964), 142–8.

74 S. P. Cowe, 'Catholicos Grigor Anavarzetsi (1293–1307) and Metropolitan Step'anos Orpelian in dialogue', in *UCLA International Conference Series on Historic Armenian Cities and Provinces: Cilicia*, ed. R. G. Hovannisian (Costa Mesa, CA: Mazda Publishers, in press).

for Armenians to unite 'with the Greeks and all nations' was at least partly impelled by pragmatic concerns.[75] Nevertheless, his broad erudition is clear from his revision of the *Menologion*, in which he included commemorations from the Byzantine and Roman sanctorale: a testimony to his fluency in Greek and Latin.[76] Moreover, his famous letter to the king suggests that his stance was not determined by pragmatism alone. Issues of ecumenism weighed heavily upon him. He subscribed to the idea developed in Chalcedonian Armenian circles from the sixth century that to be a true follower of St Gregory meant sharing in communion with the universal church.[77] This explains his proposal that the Armenian church accept all the ecumenical councils and thereby the Chalcedonian christological definition. Though initially opposed to the practice of adding water to the eucharistic wine, the weight of patristic authority convinced him of its validity.[78] That Grigor remained true to his own traditions is underlined by his refusal to accept further demands by the papacy: he opposed a call for the celibacy of parish priests and saw no need to seek papal permission to eat fish and oil during Lent. Though acknowledging the primacy of the Roman see, he also recognised the dignity of the other four ancient patriarchates of the east.[79]

Opposition in Greater Armenia now centred in the south in Siwnik' under the Ōrbēlean house, whose fortunes had been rising since 1256 when they had received their lands as an *inju* directly under Mongol suzerainty.[80] Along with other nobility and upper clergy, members of the family met in conclave in the 1290s under the presidency of Archbishop Step'anos Ōrbēlean in order to protect the *status quo* from the compact with the papacy. They argued that the Armenian Church rested on a unitary ecclesial tradition founded by the apostles Thaddaeus and Bartholomew, developed by St Gregory the Illuminator, defined by the first three ecumenical councils, and maintained by

---

75 Step'annos Ōrbēlean, *Patmut'iwn nahangin Sisakan* [History of the province of Siwnik'] (Tiflis: Ałaneanc' Press, 1910), 448.

76 Grigor Anavarzec'i', 'T'ułt' tearn Grigori Hayoc' katołikosi zor greac' ar krōnawor tagaworn Het'om [*sic*], hayr ark'ayin Hayoc' Lewoni' [Letter of the Lord Grigor, catholicos of the Armenians, which he wrote to the cleric king Het'um, father of Lewon, King of the Armenians] in Galanus, *Conciliationis*, I, 444. The authenticity of this text has been queried because of the lack of corroborating manuscript evidence. Recently, however, the work has been identified in codices 2037 (AD 1421) and 7841 (AD 1688) of the Maštoc' Matenadaran Institute in Erevan according to an oral presentation by Nerses Ter-Vardanyan on 25 February 2005. Anavarzec'i' is known to have read the works of Jerome and Bede in the original.

77 Cowe, 'An Armenian Job fragment', 148–52.

78 Grigor Anavarzec'i', 'T'ułt' tearn Grigori Hayoc' katołikosi', 438. He compiled a dossier of patristic authorities on the subject for the synod of Sis (1307).

79 Ibid., 450.

80 Grigoryan, *Syunik'e Ōrbelyanneri ōrok'*, 75.

the whole apparatus of local synods from the fifth century which rejected the council of Chalcedon as crypto-Nestorian.[81] Consequently, they demanded that Grigor refrain from all Chalcedonian contacts and desist from celebrating the feast of the Nativity with them on 25 December, but that he keep those feast days as ordained by St James; in other words, according to the early Jerusalem lectionary, from which Armenian practice derives.[82] Here Ōrbēlean waxed eloquent in the face of his superior's possible appeal to military intervention by the king: 'We are ready for suffering, exile, prison, and death to preserve the traditions of the apostolic Fathers.'[83] He also made the appeal for the first time for the nobles who had gone to Cilicia to return to Greater Armenia and for the seat of the catholicate to return to its early site in the monastery of Ējmiacin.[84]

The new century witnessed a number of last ditch attempts to seal a grand Latin–Armenian–Mongol alliance against the Mamluks. In one of these the Ilkhân Ghazan initiated correspondence with the Christian powers in 1302, but to no avail. After an unsuccessful Mongol campaign in 1305 to stem Mamluk incursions, the Armenian noble Hetʿum of Koŕikos went west to pursue discussions, and in August 1307, while at Poitiers, he composed his Mongol history *La flor des estoires de la terre d'orient* at the request of Pope Clement V.[85] In the same year, at papal insistence, another synod of Sis was held to ratify Anavarzecʿiʾs theological and liturgical adjustments towards Roman orthodoxy.[86] However, it was unrepresentative of the church as a whole, with hierarchs from Greater Armenia conspicuous by their absence. The *vita* of the conservative prelate Gēorg Skewŕacʿi notes widespread popular protest, which precipitated a series of deportations to Cyprus.[87] The Mongol response can be gauged by the murder of King Levon III and his uncle Hetʿum II, now a Franciscan friar,

81 Ōrbēlean, *Hakačaŕutʿiwn ənddēm erkabnakacʿ*, 16.
82 Athanase Renoux, *Le codex arménien Jérusalem 121* [PO 36, fasc. 168] (Turnhout: Brepols, 1971), 166.
83 Ōrbēlean, *Hakačaŕutʿiwn ənddēm erkabnakacʿ*, 186.
84 Avedis K. Sanjian, 'Stepʿanos Orbelian's "Elegy on the holy cathedral of Etchmiadzin": critical text and translation', in *Armenian and biblical studies*, ed. M. E. Stone (Jerusalem: St James Press, 1976), 237–82.
85 D. Bundy, 'Hetʿum's la flor des estoires de la terre d'orient: a study in medieval Armenian historiography and propaganda', *Revue des Études Arméniennes* 20 (1986–87), 231–2. The final book sets out an abortive plan for cooperation with the Mongols.
86 A. Balgy, *Historia doctrinae catholicae inter Armenos unionisque eorum cum ecclesia romana in concilio florentino* (Vienna: Mxitʿarist Press, 1878), 301–12.
87 Ē. Bałdasaryan, 'Gevorg Skevŕacʿu ʿvarkʿ ʾə' [The life of Gēorg Skewŕacʿi], *Banber Matenadarani* 7 (1964), 399–435; D. Bundy, 'The anonymous life of Gēorg Skewŕacʿi in Erevan 8356: a study in medieval Armenian hagiography and history', *Revue des Études Arméniennes* 18 (1984), 491–502.

together with their entourage, when they visited the local Mongol ruler later that year.

Muslim–Christian hostilities

The Mongol authorities found it more difficult to maintain law and order and religious equilibrium, at a time when the conversion of the Ilkhân Ghazan to Islam in June 1295 meant that the religious landscape in Iran was changing rapidly.[88] The Ilkhân banned Buddhist clergy from Iran and his commander Nawruz attacked Christian churches in Naxčawan, Artaz and Marâgha, but was then punished for his excesses. This encouraged Het'um II to approach Ghazan in 1299 about easing the situation of non-Muslims who had been suffering unjustly.

Ghazan's brother and successor Öljeitu's religious transition is even more illustrative of the rapid pace of the changing balance of power. First he was baptised Nicholas in honour of the new pope, Nicholas IV. Then he accepted the Sunni creed, before finally adopting Shi'ite Islam.[89] During his reign (1304–16) discrimination against Christians increased, provoking increased Armenian emigration to Cilicia and the Crimea. Forced conversions to Islam ensued, and new taxes were levied and regulations enacted, which according to a colophon of 1307 required Christians to wear a blue cloth so as to distinguish them in public.[90] These measures gradually undermined the status of the *naxarars* or upper nobility, whose socio-political structure had provided Armenians with a form of regional cohesion since Parthian times. While some houses were compelled to leave their lands, others sought to maintain indirect control by transferring ownership to the bishop, who was normally a scion of the same house, since Islamic law protected a *waqf* or religious trust, which was not normally liable to tax impositions. In consequence, episcopal succession in several Armenian sees such as Erzkna (Erzincan) and Maku and the catholicates of Alt'amar and Caucasian Albania passed lineally within the same family for many generations through the institution of the prince-bishop (*parontēr*).[91] This

---

88 A salient factor in the Ilkhân Ghazan Khan's conversion was the need to maintain solidarity with elements within the Mongol army.

89 T. T. Allsen, *Culture and conquest in Mongol Eurasia* (Cambridge: Cambridge University Press, 2001), 36.

90 Levon Xačikyan (ed.), *ŽD dari hayeren jeřagreri hišatakaranner* [Colophons of fourteenth-century Armenian manuscripts] (Erevan: Armenian Academy of Sciences, 1950), 46.

91 R. H. Hewsen, 'The Artsrunid house of Sefedinian: survival of a princely dynasty in ecclesiastical guise', *Journal of the Society for Armenian Studies* 1 (1984), 123–38.

process inevitably paved the way for the gradual recognition of Armenians as an ethno-confessional entity in law.

Armeno-Latin interaction in Greater Armenia

In 1318, in keeping with the greater focus on mission characteristic of the Avignon papacy, John XXII created two vast dioceses in the Near and Far East entrusted to the Dominicans and Franciscans respectively. The former was centred on the Ilkhânid capital of Sulṭânîya, so that the incumbent might act as the pope's personal emissary. It was also furnished with six suffragan sees, of which three (Sivas, Tabrîz and Marâgha) had a sizeable Armenian population.[92] As the pontiff's correspondence indicates, he was quite involved in Armenian affairs and well informed on the subject.[93] He had recently pressed for the convocation of the synod of Adana in 1316 to reconfirm the acts of Sis of nine years earlier, and wanted to engage the prelates of Greater Armenia more systematically than had ever been attempted before.[94]

Zak'aria Artazec'i of the princely family of Maku and the catholicos's exarch in the east at St Thaddaeus monastery (1298–c. 1340) was a key figure in this task. A pro-Latin confederate of Grigor Anavarzec'i, he was one of the few eastern churchmen to attend the synod, after which he took the step of accepting Catholicism, as he discussed in his exchange of letters with Yohan Ōrbēli, metropolitan of Siwnik'.[95] He was the recipient of two personal letters from the pope in 1321, who commended him for drawing souls back to the 'church'.[96]

At the pope's behest his assistant, Yovhannēs Corcorec'i, with the help of Bishop Bartolomeo da Poggio, translated Thomas Aquinas's commentary on the fourth book of Peter Lombard's *Sentences*, the main western medieval primer on the sacraments.[97] At some point a Franciscan house was established at St Thaddaeus, which engaged in rendering into Armenian other Latin scholastic manuals and liturgical books during the 1320s–30s. Through this process Armenians were introduced to western developments in Aristotelian logic, ethics, natural philosophy (physics), metaphysics and aesthetics

---

92 Richard, *Papauté*, 169–73.
93 S. P. Cowe, 'The role of correspondence in elucidating the intensification of Latin–Armenian ecclesiastical interchange in the first quarter of the fourteenth century', *Journal of the Society for Armenian Studies* 13 (2003/4), 49–50.
94 Balgy, *Historia doctrinae catholicae*, 313–35.
95 Cowe, 'The role of correspondence', 53–4.
96 Ibid., 62–3.
97 Xačikyan, 'Artazi haykakan išxanut'yunə', 198–9.

(grammar and literary criticism), as well as practical manuals embodying a western perception of various Near Eastern communities and how to engage them in debate.[98] The results of this translation process are significant historically as one of the earliest attempts to render contemporary Latin thought into another language, antedating by a generation the first Greek renderings of the brothers Demetrios and Prochoros Kydones.[99]

Esayi Nčec'i, the director of the monastic academy of Glajor, was extremely widely read and possessed an excellent understanding of the development of doctrine and church history. Profoundly engaged with western ideas, he was initially open to involvement in dialogue with the Latins, while still preserving Armenian autocephaly intact. Indeed, in 1323 his close associate and successor, Tiratur Kilikec'i, commissioned one of our earliest extant copies of Aquinas's commentary on Peter Lombard in Armenian.[100] This balance is well illustrated by the illuminations in the Glajor Gospel from the turn of the fourteenth century, which include a number of typically western scenes, while in general reflecting Armenian theology and scriptural exegesis.[101] Like Šnorhali before him, Nčec'i also accepted the legitimacy of predicating either one or two natures in Christ, depending on how these were defined.[102] Of an eirenic disposition, he maintained that it was better to be slow to engage in disputation and quick to approach conciliation and peace. At the same time, he argued that in an unequal alliance the partner better endowed with material resources should not exploit his advantage to deprive the other of his rights.[103]

The fluidity of the theological situation is reflected in the vacillating positions taken up by Armenian scholars, such as Mxit'ar Sasnec'i, who broke with his former mentor Nčec'i in the 1320s in favour of Ōrbēlean's 'harder-line' position on divergence of liturgical rites.[104] One of the first Armenian thinkers to respond to the Latin position, he agreed that previously the Armenians

98 M. A. van den Oudenrijn, *Linguae haicanae scriptores ordinis praedicatorum congregationis fratrum unitorum et ff. Armenorum ordinis s. Basilii citra mare consistentium quodquod hucusque innotuerunt* (Berne and Munich: A. Francke, 1960), 19–295; S. P. Cowe, 'Catholic missionaries to Armenia and anti-catholic writings', in *Where the only-begotten descended: the church of Armenia through the ages*, ed. Kevork B. Bardakjian (Detroit, MI: Wayne State University Press, in press).

99 See pp. 66–67, 70–71.

100 Xačikyan, *ŽD dari hayeren jeṙagreri hišatakaranner*, 174.

101 T. Mathews and Avedis K. Sanjian, *Armenian gospel iconography: The tradition of the Glajor Gospel* [Dumbarton Oaks Studies 29] (Washington, DC: (Dumbarton Oaks Research Library and Collection, 1991).

102 Esayi Nčec'i, 'T'ult' Esayeay vardapeti aṙ tēr Matt'ēos' [Letter of the vardapet Esayi to the Lord Matt'ēos], *Č̣rak'al* (1860), 157–64; (1861), 205–11.

103 Nčec'i, 'T'ult' Esayeay vardapeti', 162.

104 Mxit'ar Sasnec'i, *Mxit'ar Sasnec'i's theological discourses*, ed. S. P. Cowe [CSCO 21 (Armenian text); 22 (English translation)] (Leuven: Peeters, 1993), 101–2 (trans.).

had accepted the Franks as brothers and rejoiced at their unity in Christ, but he detected a dichotomy between the Franks' 'Hellenic wisdom' and what he took to be their lax moral standards and their lack of discipline in matters of fasting.[105] The contention by his contemporary Yovhannēs Tarberuni that divine wisdom is communicated through illumination not logic and inference points up the contrast between the essentially neoplatonic cast of contemporary Armenian theology and the Aristotelian foundations of the Dominican tradition.[106]

For the mission to the central and eastern parts of Greater Armenia, where urban life and trade arteries were less of a fixture, the recently inaugurated see of Marâgha and its bishop Bartolomeo da Poggio proved to be of the greatest importance, for he aroused the curiosity of Armenian monks about Roman theological scholarship. In a remarkably short time this led to the unprecedented establishment of an Armenian congregation affiliated with the Dominican order, very different from the status of the Franciscans at St Thaddaeus and providing a model for the new wave of Uniate foundations associated with the Counter-Reformation. In 1330 the bishop moved to the monastery of K'řna in the Ernjak district of the Siwnik' region with a group of friars. Developments over the next years were also rapid: in 1331 the monastery was entrusted to the order and by 1337 it worshipped according to the Dominican breviary and missal, signalling a break with the traditional Armenian liturgy.[107] The Dominican version of St Augustine's rule became the arbiter of discipline, and the community's constitution was ratified by Innocent VI on 31 January 1356 as the *Fratres Unitores* of the congregation of St Gregory the Illuminator.[108] The new organisation then became the catalyst for bringing conformity to other Armenian Uniate groups, first to the monastery of St Nicholas in Caffa, and then to the Armenian Basilian communities in Italy, which were incorporated into the order.[109] The congregation's further integration into the Latin Church is signalled by their investment with the privileges of the Dominican *Societas Peregrinantium*, the order's missionary wing, by Urban V on 20 November

---

105 Ibid., xv–xvii (trans.).
106 Yovhannēs Tarberuni, 'Yovhannu vardapeti Tarberunwoy dawanut'iwn hawatoy' [The vardapet Yovhannēs Tarberuni's confession of faith], *Čřak'at* 2 (1861), 223.
107 M. A. van den Oudenrijn, 'L'évêque dominicain Fr. Barthélemy fondateur supposé d'un couvent dans le Tigré au 14e siècle', *Rassegna di Studi Etiopici* 4 (1946), 14.
108 M. A. van den Oudenrijn, 'The Monastery of Aparan and the Armenian writer Fra Mxit'aric', *Archivum Fratrum Praedicatorum* 1 (1930), 267.
109 J. Richard, 'La papauté en Avignon et l'Arménie', in *Arménie entre Orient et Occident*, ed. C. Mutafian (Paris: Bibliothèque nationale de France, 1996), 187.

1362. In its heyday in mid-century, the order is supposed to have claimed the affiliation of fifty monasteries and about 700 monks, though it was badly hit by the Black Death of 1347–48.[110] Clearly the *Fratres Unitores* went further than any other Armenian confession in identifying themselves as Latins, their Armenian heritage being preserved only in the matter of language. Consequently, it is not surprising that, though not a major feature of early lists of discrepancies between Latins and Armenians, the pivotal question of baptism, the rite of entry into the church, was raised most frequently and vociferously by their members, especially Nersēs Palienc', archbishop of Manazkert. On this count an Armenian delegation to Avignon for assistance against Mamluk attack on Cilicia in 1336 was detained on suspicion of heresy. Thereafter, at Benedict XII's behest, Palienc' instigated a minute investigation of the Armenian creed and practice that culminated in the compilation of 117 articles against the Armenian Church, which clouded Armeno–papal relations for about two decades.[111] Apart from the usual trinitarian and christological issues, it raised a large number of sacramental issues and questions of canon law,[112] which were debated at the synod of Sis of 1341/2. Significantly, the response, offering a point by point refutation of the charges, was brought to Avignon by the Armenian Franciscan Daniel of Tabrîz, previously a monk of St Thaddaeus.[113]

Aftermath

Such papal scrutiny draws attention once more to the religious complexity of the Armenian polity at the close of our period. Despite various attempts to resolve the schism at Alt'amar begun in 1113 by the elevation of a separate catholicate on the old Arcruni lands, it continued to defy a solution.[114] The catholicate at Sis still nominally in union with Rome vacillated in its religious orientation depending on which party was in the ascendant. Increasing disaffection with their Lusignan monarchs from Cyprus and internecine struggles

110 Van den Oudenrijn, 'The Monastery of Aparan', 294.
111 A. L. Tăutu, *Acta Benedicti XII (1334–1342)* [Fontes ser. iii, 8] (Rome: Typis polyglottis vaticanis, 1958), 119–55.
112 S. P. Cowe, 'Catholic missionaries to Armenia and anti-catholic writings'.
113 For the text of the rebuttal, see Tăutu, *Acta Benedicti XII*, 160–234, and, for the identity of the bearer, P. Pelliot, 'Zacharie de Saint-Thadée et Zacharie Séfêdinian', *Revue de l'Histoire des Religions* 126 (1943), 150–4.
114 After attempts to resolve the issue by King Het'um II in the late thirteenth century and by Grigor Tatewac'i in the mid-fourteenth, the dispute was finally settled as part of the reorganisation of the church following the return of the catholicate to Ējmiacin in 1441.

in the Cilician body politic weakened the social fabric of the realm. Repeated Mamluk attacks hastened the decline of the local economy and the renewed exodus of the merchant and artisan population.[115] Links with the Genoese trading posts on the Black Sea, for example, encouraged the growth of Armenian colonies in the Crimea and in the hinterlands to the north and west, leading to the expansion of colonies such as that of L'viv, whose growing importance was recognised by its elevation to the status of an episcopal see in mid-century.[116]

The situation of Greater Armenia became increasingly unstable with the decline of the Mongol Ilkhâns from the 1330s onward, opening up a power vacuum facilitating the disastrous Timurid invasions of the last two decades of the century. Despite this, a resurgence of the Armenian Apostolic Church is manifest there under the forceful monastic leadership of Małak'ia Lrimec'i. This, combined with the skill in argument of Yovhan Orotnec'i (d. 1387) and his pupil Grigor Tat'ewac'i, helped to regain the momentum from the *Fratres Unitores*.[117] Their works oppose doctrines such as purgatory and defend the traditional Armenian christological position. At the same time, Grigor's theological compendium, the *Book of Questions* of 1397, attests the impact of Aquinas's sacramental theology and Hugh Ripelin's angelology and demonology.[118] Moreover, his other main writings, two volumes of sermons and a *Oskep'orik*, or treasury, of 1407, similarly reveal his familiarity with the views of Augustine, Isidore and Ibn Rushd (Averroes), etc., presumably mediated by translations made by the *Fratres Unitores*.[119]

The logical conclusion of this phase of internal Armenian dialogue on union with Rome played itself out at the council of Florence at which the *Decretum pro Armenis* of 22 November 1439 was ratified by catholicos Kostandin VI Vahkac'i on behalf of the church.[120] However, this decisive *démarche* in turn provoked an equally swift, unequivocal retort from influential members of the

---

115 T. Sinclair, 'Cilicia after the kingdom: population, monasteries, etc. under the Mamluks', in *UCLA International Conference Series on historic Armenian cities and provinces: Cilicia*, in press.

116 Richard, *Papauté*, 92; Donabédian and Thierry, *Armenian art*, 270.

117 Van den Oudenrijn, 'The Monastery of Aparan', 284–96.

118 Sergio La Porta, 'Grigor Tat'ewac'i's Book of Questions: introduction, translation, and commentary – vol. 3: the theology of the Holy Dionysius', unpublished PhD thesis, Harvard University (2001), 117. See also Nona Manukyan, 'The role of Bartolomeo di Bologna's sermonary in medieval Armenian literature', *Le Muséon* 105 (1992), 321–5.

119 Grigor Tat'ewac'i, *Girk'* or *koči oskēp'orik* [Book called Miscellany] (Constantinople: Abraham Dpir, 1746), 9–143.

120 Richard, *Papauté*, 264–6.

Greater Armenian clergy, who decided that the time was ripe to implement their predecessors' frequently reiterated threats of schism. Thus in 1441 the cathedral of Ējmiacin in the ancient capital of Vałaršapat became the seat of an anti-catholicate, which soon established itself as the primary see of the whole church.[121] The medieval Cilician episode in Armenian history had now come to an end.

121 Tʿovma Mecopʿecʿi, *Tʿovma Mecopʿecʿi patmagrutʿyun* [Tʿovma Mecopʿecʿi historio-graphy], ed. Levon Xacikyan (Erevan: Magałatʿ, 1999).

Church and diaspora: the case
of the Armenians

S. PETER COWE

During the past four centuries of its existence the Armenian Church has min-
istered to an increasingly diversified society whose geographical dispersion
now embraces every continent apart from Antarctica. This time frame has
also witnessed its encounter with modernism and the major factors associated with the movement that has come to be known as globalisation. Whereas
at the beginning of the period the church was fundamentally the sole institution perpetuating Armenians' corporate identity after the fall of the Cilician
kingdom, it has since become one body among several others and has had
to contend against competing worldviews. In particular, it has had to come
to terms with religious plurality, as Armenians have been exposed to different ecclesial forms and confessional affiliation, and in more recent times to
various secular ideologies. Similarly, in the sphere of inter-faith relations, it
has experienced a complex interaction with Islam, the dominant force in the
surrounding region, ranging from peaceful coexistence to proselytism and
outbreaks of persecution.

Background

During the sixteenth century the Armenian plateau became a battleground
between the rival Ottoman and Safavid empires, with consequent destruction
of towns and disruption of communal life. The historian Grigor Daranałc'i
vividly documented the decline of monasticism,[1] reflected in the notable reduction in manuscript production in monastic scriptoria.[2] As a religious minority
in eastern Anatolia and southern Caucasia, Armenians had to maintain a low

---

1 Grigor Daranałc'i, *Žamanakagrut'iwn Grigor vardapeti Kamaxec'woy kam Daranałc'woy*
  [Chronicle of Grigor Kamaxec'i or Daranałc'i], ed. M. Nšanean (Jerusalem: St James
  Press, 1915).
2 Dickran Kouymjian, 'Dated Armenian manuscripts as a statistical tool for Armenian
  history', in *Medieval Armenian culture*, ed. T. J. Samuelian and M. E. Stone [University of
  Pennsylvania Armenian Texts and Studies 6] (Chico, CA: Scholars Press, 1984), 425–38.

public profile. Any new churches were unostentatious structures, while the *semantron* (a wooden board struck by a metal instrument) increasingly replaced more obtrusive bells.[3] In parts of the hinterland the community began to lose its language and started to employ the local variety of Turkish, the lingua franca of the region.[4] To meet this need the church published religious and devotional manuals in Turkish, but written in Armenian letters.

Paradoxically the supreme catholicos in Ējmiacin[5] enjoyed an enhanced status. Because Islamic jurisprudence distinguished minorities by religious confession, not ethnicity, the church became the only institution tolerated by the authorities. This did not prevent successive catholicoi – in the spirit of the crusading era – sending embassies to Rome to implore assistance in liberating Armenia from Muslim rule. A staple on these missions was the *Letter of Concord*, a medieval *apocryphon* describing the consecration of St Gregory the Illuminator by Pope Sylvester. In return for acknowledging papal supremacy St Gregory received primacy over the churches of the east and ownership of several of the key pilgrim sites in Jerusalem and the Holy Land. Later the work was translated into Italian and reprinted several times in the sixteenth and seventeenth centuries.[6]

The Counter-Reformation and mission to the Armenians

Beginning with Pope Gregory XIII (1572–85) the papacy sought to establish closer ties with the Armenians as part of a reassertion of its presence in the Near East. The process culminated in the creation of the *Congregatio de Propaganda Fide* in 1622 with a polyglot press to produce liturgical books and other tracts in all the languages of the area. This was complemented by the foundation in 1627 of the *Collegium Urbanum*, which trained priests for work among eastern Christians in the hope of reuniting these communities with

---

3 For conditions in the important Mesopotamian city of Amid, see Ēd. Xondkaryan, *Mkrtič Naĺaš* (Erevan: Armenian Academy of Sciences, 1965), 29–40. Other characteristic elements of their minority condition included payment of the poll tax, wearing clothes to distinguish them from the Muslim majority, and a prohibition on bearing arms and riding a horse.

4 For the wider Turkish cultural influence on Armenia from the seventeenth to nineteenth centuries, see S. P. Cowe, 'The politics of poetics: Islamic influence on Armenian verse', *Proceedings of the symposium redefining Christian identity: Christian cultural strategies since the rise of Islam* (Leuven: Peeters, 2006).

5 Incorporated in the Ottoman Empire in 1514.

6 Ninel Oskanyan *et al.*, *Hay girk'ə 1512–1800 t'vakannerin* [The Armenian Book between the dates 1512–1800] (Erevan: Myasnikyan Library, 1988).

Rome. Its creation inaugurated a prolific period of translation from Latin into Armenian. The Armenian Bible presented problems, which led to the setting up of a commission of theologians under the *Propaganda* to revise it to the standard of the Vulgate.[7]

Under Richelieu's enthusiastic prefect of missions Fr Joseph de Paris, the French largely dominated mission work among the Armenians. Between 1609 and 1628 Jesuit and Capuchin bridgeheads had been established in Istanbul, Izmir and Aleppo, as well as in the recently created Armenian community of New Julfa in Iran. Their task was eased by the existence of a highly complex network of Armenian mercantile communities extending from the main entrepôts of the Safavid and Ottoman empires to major cities of western Europe.

Thus, France financed most of these missionary operations with a view to cultivating its image as protector of near eastern Christians and to fostering a loyal francophile constituency as well as containing Habsburg ambitions in the east. This marriage of sacred and secular is well illustrated by Richelieu's acquisition of Armenian type from Jacques Sanlecques in 1633 in order to reprint the first Armeno–Latin dictionary and Armenian grammar of the Milanese philologist Francesco Rivola.[8]

The convergence of France's strategic interest in the Near East and Armenian aspirations to restore their state resulted in active Armenian participation in the diplomacy of the era. This was at its height while Yakob IV (1655–80) was catholicos of Ējmiacin. He entered into discussions with Louis XIV through his merchant envoy Shahmurat of Bitlis and agreed to support the French protégé to the Ottoman throne.[9] The complexity of Armenian involvement is highlighted by the case of Archbishop Aṙak'el Babik, who went on a mission in 1662 to Rome and Venice for the Armenian catholicos, returning to the east as Venetian ambassador to Iran to incite the Safavids to make common cause against the Ottomans, their longstanding foe.[10]

Armenian Catholic clergy were also involved in this round of diplomatic initiatives and tended to be somewhat more trusted because of their shared creed. The Dominican *Fratres Unitores* established in the 1330s continued to function,

---

7 *Arménie entre Orient et Occident*, ed. R. H. Kévorkian (Paris: Bibliothèque nationale, 1996), 89.
8 Oskanyan, *Hay girk'ə 1512–1800 t'vakannerin*, 20–1.
9 R.H. Kévorkian, 'La diplomatie arménienne entre l'Europe et la Perse au temps de Louis XIV', in *Arménie entre Orient et Occident*, 190. It seems that the project involved crowning Azaria Awag, a student of the *Propaganda*, as king of Armenia.
10 Kévorkian, 'La diplomatie arménienne', 190.

though much reduced in numbers and significance, from their mother house of Aparanner in Armenia's heartland.[11] Armenian Dominicans acted as ambassadors for both Persian shahs and European powers. Emblematic of their participation is that of Matt'ēos Awanik', archbishop of Naxǰewan, who undertook a mission to Shah Sulaymân in 1669 with letters from Louis XIV, Clement IX and the Venetian doge. Accompanying him on this assignment was Petros Petik, a graduate of the *Collegium Urbanum*, who earned the gratitude of the Habsburg emperor Leopold for his diplomatic skills, which deflected Ottoman ambitions away from Poland and the Habsburg Empire for the next two decades. In recognition of his services he received the title of Count of Patta.[12]

To strengthen Armenian participation in an alliance with western powers Catholicos Yakob IV set off on a journey to Rome in 1664 to make his submission to the papacy, but anti-Latin intrigues at Ējmiacin meant that he never got further than Istanbul. On his deathbed he is supposed to have left a Latin profession of faith. One of his more enduring legacies was the first printing of the Armenian Bible in 1666 by his compatriot Oskan Erevanc'i in Amsterdam, another striking manifestation of the role of the diaspora at this time.[13] While in Ējmiacin, Oskan encountered the missionary Paolo Piromalli, then engaged in the project of collating the Armenian scriptures with the Vulgate. Oskan studied Latin with him and on that basis translated various pseudepigraphic books outside the traditional Armenian canon as well as introducing significant Vulgate readings into the Gospels and other texts. He set off for Livorno and Rome in 1662, before moving to Amsterdam, where an Armenian press had recently been established, to produce his lavish edition featuring seven newly prepared typefaces and further embellished by the woodcuts of Christoffel van Sichem the Younger.[14]

---

11 Ani Pauline Atamian, 'The archdiocese of Naxǰewan in the seventeenth century', unpublished PhD thesis, Columbia University (1984), 44–7.

12 Kévorkian, 'La diplomatie arménienne', 194–5. For the case of Ełia Mušełean, a convert to Catholicism, involved in a Persian diplomatic mission to Russia, see B. L. Čugaszyan, *Ełia Mušełean Karnec'i, T'urk'eren–Hayeren baṙaran* [Turkish–Armenian Dictionary] (Erevan: Armenian Academy of Sciences, 1986). For the continuation of Armenian diplomatic activities into the nineteenth century, see G. A. Bournoutian, *The Khanate of Erevan under Qajar Rule 1795–1828* (Costa Mesa, CA: Mazda Publishers, 1992), 15.

13 Oskanyan, *Hay girk' ə 1512–1800 t'vakannerin*, 44–50.

14 On the development of Armenian publications of the Bible, see S. P. Cowe, 'An 18th century Armenian textual critic and his continuing significance', *Revue des Études Arméniennes*, n.s. 20 (1986–87), 527–41; *Treasures in Heaven: Armenian illuminated manuscripts*, ed. T. F. Mathews and R. S. Wieck (New York: The Pierpoint Morgan Library, 1994), 121–2.

L'viv

The Roman Church obtained its major success at L'viv, where an Armenian community first established in 1340 by Casimir the Great flourished under Polish rule. At first it benefited from the policy of granting internal autonomy to foreign merchant communities, domestic Armenian issues being adjudicated on the basis of their own law code. In keeping with this, religious freedom was granted in 1367, on which occasion the Armenian archiepiscopal see was moved there from the Crimea, exercising a wide jurisdiction over Armenians in Wallachia and Moldavia. Over the next three centuries the community's wealth increased from its role in international trade with the Ottoman Empire and Iran. Armenians also acted as bankers and diplomats[15] for the Polish crown. Gradually, however, as a result of greater pressure on minorities to assimilate, the religious affiliation of the Armenians of L'viv became an issue of some importance for both church and state.[16] From the fifteenth century various attempts were made to entice the community into union with Rome, a proposition favoured by a succession of Armenian bishops.

The irregular election of a twenty-two-year-old priest Nikołayos T'orosowicz as Armenian prelate in 1626 further advanced the cause of union.[17] Consecrated on the promise of relieving the Armenian catholicos of his debts to the Persian shah, he presented his creed to Rome and later appealed for support to the Catholic hierarchy when strife broke out within his flock. Nine years later he went to Rome to receive the pallium and was granted a status equal to the local Roman Catholic archbishop. However, delays over the next three decades in implementing liturgical and doctrinal modifications led in 1664 to the establishment of a papal academy (Collegium Pontificium Leopoliensis Armenorum) in L'viv, which continued to function for over a century.[18] Its first director was the elderly missionary savant Clemens Galanus, who had a long history of working with Armenians. About twenty years earlier he had founded a school in Constantinople, where he had instructed Armenian children and perfected his command of the language, which he subsequently taught at the Collegium Urbanum. In that capacity he produced an Armenian

---

15 In 1666 Bogdan Kourtei was Polish ambassador to Russia and Iran.

16 J. Richard, La papauté et les missions d'Orient au Moyen Âge (XIIIe–XVe siècles), second edition (Rome: École française de Rome, 1998), 267–70.

17 On this figure, see Aṙak'el Dawriẑec'i, Girk' patmut'eanc' [Book of Histories], ed. L. A. Xanlaryan (Erevan: Armenian Academy of Sciences, 1990), esp. 293–303, 305–10; G. A. Bournoutian, The history of Aṙak'el of Tabriz (Costa Mesa: Mazda Press, 2005), I, 265–83.

18 Anonymous, Bṙni miut'iwn hayoc' Lehastani ənd ekełec'woyn Hṙovmay: vamanakakic' yišatakarank' [The forcible union of the Armenians of Poland with the church of Rome: contemporary memoirs] (St Petersburg, 1884), xxix–xxxiv.

grammar for missionaries, but his magnum opus is a three-volume bilingual treatise *Conciliationis ecclesiae Armenae cum Romana* (1650–61), which for the first time provided the western public with a connected history of Armenian Christianity. Despite treating Armenian dogmatic 'errors' from a Roman perspective, he nevertheless defended the Armenian orthodoxy against the attacks of more unreasonable Latin critics.[19]

Galanus was accompanied by a French colleague Louis-Marie Pidou de Saint-Olon (1637–1717), who succeeded him as director in 1666 and introduced the students to Jesuit school drama, which was already well established in Poland, as in his native France.[20] His historical tragicomedy of 1668, *The Martyrdom of St Hṙip'simē*, relates the impact of the death in Armenia of a Roman martyr in the early fourth century as a catalyst for the country's conversion to Christianity. It directed an only slightly veiled message towards the local Armenian community.[21] In the epilogue Hṙip'simē, already sanctified, descends from the heavenly places to address the audience directly. She will continue to be their tutelary as long as they remain faithful to the church of her homeland, i.e. that of Rome, a point the author underlines in his dedication to Archbishop T'orosowicz, when he claims that the doctrine *extra ecclesiam nulla salus* applies only to the Catholic faith.[22] Thereafter developments were swift. In 1668 Pidou arranged the archbishop's dispatch to Rome, where he remained for seven years. In the meantime, Clement X assigned as coadjutor Bishop Vardan Yunanian, a former pupil of the L'viv college, who succeeded T'orosowicz on his death in 1681. There then ensued a gradual stabilisation of the union with Rome until the area passed under Russian control in 1772.

New Julfa

Towards the end of the protracted struggle between the Ottomans and the Safavids Shâh 'Abbâs (1587–1629) evacuated a swathe of Armenian border

---

19 Oskanyan, *Hay girk'ǝ 1512–1800 t'vakannerin*, 32–5, 37–8.

20 See F. Richard, 'Missionnaires français en Arménie au XVIIe siècle', in *Arménie entre Orient et Occident*, 200. And for school drama, see P. Lewin, 'The Ukrainian school theater in the seventeenth and eighteenth centuries: an expression of the baroque', *Harvard Ukrainian Studies* 5 (1981), 54–65.

21 So devoted were Latin missionaries serving among the Armenians to the memory of Hṙip'simē that they even attempted to steal her bones from the old capital of Vałaršapat. See M. A. van den Oudenrijn, 'Der heilige Gregor der Erleuchter und die Heiligen Hripsimeanz in Unitorien', *Handēs Amsōreay* 62 (1948), 588–96.

22 See S. P. Cowe, 'The play "martyrdom of St. Hṙip'simē": a novel variant on the theme of Armenia's Christianization', in *Hay grakanut'yune ev k'ristoneut'yune* [Armenian Literature and Christianity] (Erevan: Armenian Academy of Sciences, 2002), 96–110.

territory and resettled the population in various parts of his realm. Special treatment was accorded to the opulent merchant community of Julfa, which was relocated opposite his new capital at Isfahan. It enjoyed rights not afforded to other religious minorities, such as permission to elect their own mayor, employ bells and conduct religious processions in public.[23] These were granted because of the community's domination of the Iranian silk trade.[24] The new diocese quickly expanded, with some seventy churches founded within its first half-century. At one point the shah contemplated rebuilding the monastery of Ējmiacin in New Julfa in order to assure the community's continuing loyalty. However, he was finally satisfied with a token gesture of relocating fifteen stones, now incorporated into one of the churches there. The second bishop, Xacatur Kecarec'i (1620–46), was particularly active, creating an influential school where a host of Armenian luminaries studied, including several later catholicoi. Around 1636 he also established the first printing press in Iran, which issued an important series of service books, an initiative in which it appears he gained assistance in acquiring ink and paper from the recent French Capuchin mission in Isfahan under Fr Pacifique de Provins.[25]

Despite this, the Capuchins were forbidden to preach in Armenian churches, and tensions between the two communities grew with the arrival in 1650 of the Jesuits, who had French government support; to the extent that the next prelate, Dawit' (1652–83), threatened them with expulsion.[26] Nevertheless, some influential Armenians like Xoǰa Sarhat of the Šehrimanean family became converts and financed the construction of a chapel and a school. By the 1680s polemical tracts were distributed by both sides, and the theologian and artist Yovhannēs Mrk'uz often engaged in debates with the missionaries as well as with representatives of the Armenian Catholics like the poet Step'anos Daštec'i.[27]

23 For a contextualisation of this within the shah's overall treatment of Armenians, see Vazken S. Ghougassian, *The emergence of the Armenian diocese of New Julfa in the seventeenth century* (University of Pennsylvania Armenian Texts and Studies 14), (Atlanta, GA: Scholars Press, 1998), 56–76.

24 See Ina Baghdiantz McCabe, *The shah's silk for Europe's silver: the Eurasian trade of the Julfa Armenians in Safavid Iran and India (1530–1750)* [University of Pennsylvania Armenian Texts and Studies 15] (Atlanta, GA: Scholars Press, 1999).

25 Richard, 'Missionnaires français en Arménie', 197.

26 Ghougassian, *Armenian diocese of New Julfa*, 125–56.

27 This initiative included the first publication of Grigor Tatewac'i's *Book of Questions* of 1397, in which a number of Catholic doctrines are condemned, on which see Oskanyan, *Hay girk' ә 1512–1800 t'vakannerin*, 286–7.

The art of New Julfa represents a true synthesis of east and west.[28] An excellent example of this are Mrkʻuzʻs wall paintings in the All-Saviour cathedral, whose western models have recently been discovered. Subsequently, four generations of artists from the Hovnatʻanean family produced frescos with characteristic floral borders in the Persian style for the churches of Ējmiacin, Agulis, Šoṙot, Meghri and Varag.

However, by the close of the seventeenth century the climate of tolerance was disappearing in tandem with worsening economic conditions. In order to relieve the pressures on Armenians to convert to Islam, Mrkʻuz resorted to discussions on the shared beliefs of Christianity and Islam. These adverse conditions, exacerbated by the Afghan revolt of 1722 and the anarchy following the assassination of Nâdir Shah in 1747, provoked a wide-scale Armenian exodus to the benefit of several other colonies, but particularly those of south and south-east Asia.[29]

Greater Armenia

By the end of the sixteenth century the long struggle between the Ottomans and the Safavids was coming to an end. This allowed the inhabitants of the Armenian plateau a chance of recovery. One of the first indications of renewal was the movement to found the Mec Anapat (The Great Hermitage) near the major monastery of Tatʻew in 1611, which signalled a revival of monastic life. The founders Sargis of Saḷmosavankʻ and Kirakos of Trebizond had gone on pilgrimage to Jerusalem to study the traditional eremitic centres in the Judaean desert, as a later community member Nersēs Mokacʻi celebrates in verse.[30] Another important monastery undergoing a revival at this time was Amrdolu in Bitlis under its abbot Barseḷ Aḷbakecʻi (d.1615), who renovated its school and encouraged the study of grammar and theology.[31]

It was Pʻilipos Aḷbakecʻi (1632–55) who finally put the affairs of the monastery of Ējmiacin, the primatial see, in order. He re-established its economic

---

28 See John Carswell, *New Julfa: the Armenian churches and other buildings* (Oxford: Clarendon Press, 1968).

29 Ghougassian, *Armenian diocese of New Julfa*, 57–168. Armenians spread to a number of entrepôts including Rangoon, Singapore and Batavia (Jakarta), Hong Kong, etc., on which see M. J. Seth, *Armenians in India* (Calcutta: Armenian Holy Church of Nazareth, 1983), 614. For a convenient map of the South Asian diaspora, see R. H. Hewsen, *Armenia: a historical atlas* (Chicago: University of Chicago Press, 2001), 160.

30 A. G. Doluxanyan, *Nersēs Mokacʻi, Banastelcutʻyunner* [Nerses Mokacʻi, Poems] (Erevan: Armenian Academy of Sciences, 1975), 44–63.

31 On this important medieval monastery see Nersēs Akinean, *Baḷēši dprocʻə* [The School of Bitlis] (Vienna: Mxitʻarist Press, 1952).

stability and set about repairing the main cathedral, adding a bell tower in 1654. He profited from a visit to the Persian court to recover the relic of St Gregory the Illuminator with which bishops are consecrated. Of even greater moment was his journey to Jerusalem in 1651 in the course of which he eased strains between the church's other main sees. He convoked a synod in the Holy City to settle various jurisdictional issues, which had arisen between the Armenian patriarchate of Jerusalem and the catholicate of Sis. He then continued his journey to the Ottoman capital, where he resolved disputes within the Armenian patriarchate of Constantinople.[32]

These were in part associated with the mercurial career of the hierarch Eliazar Aynt'apc'i, who in short order became patriarch of Jerusalem (1649), then of Constantinople (1651), only to resign the following year and return to Jerusalem, where he was imprisoned, as he sought to protect the properties and privileges of the Armenian community from the Greek patriarchate.[33] Although the see of Jerusalem was subordinate to Constantinople at this time, he attempted to make it the centre of a pan-Ottoman jurisdiction independent of the authority of Ējmiacin. With this in mind he established the Ējmiacin chapel in the St James's monastery in Jerusalem and had himself consecrated catholicos of West Armenia in 1664 by the catholicos of Sis.[34] This opened a schism, which persisted all through the reign of Catholicos Yakob of Ējmiacin and only came to an end in 1681, when Eliazar was elected as the latter's successor. After his installation as catholicos he set about healing the even older dispute with the catholicate of Ałt'amar, which still controlled a few dioceses around the shores of Lake Van.

Russia

A permanent Armenian community existed in Moscow from the late fifteenth century, but without its own church. The Armenians in Russia had to wait until 1639 before they received permission from the tsar to establish a church. This was for their community at Astrakhan, a key point on the trade route along the

---

32 For the synodal acts, see Abēl Mxit'areanc', *Patmut'iwn žołovoc' hayastaneayc' ekełec'woy* [History of the synods of the Armenian church] (Vałaršapat: Mother See Press, 1874), 143–8.

33 S. P. Cowe, 'Pilgrimage to Jerusalem by the eastern churches', in *Wahlfahrt kennt keine Grenzen*, ed. L. Kriss-Rettenbeck and G. Möhler (Munich: Bayerisches Nationalmuseum, 1984), 316–30.

34 On this chapel, see Bezalel Narkiss, *Armenian art treasures of Jerusalem* (Jerusalem: Massada Press, 1979), 126–8, and on its tiles, J. Carswell and C. J. F. Dowsett, *Kütahya tiles and pottery from the Armenian cathedral of St James, Jerusalem* (Oxford: Clarendon Press, 1972), 6–23.

Volga which linked Iran and Russia. The commercial power of the Armenians led to a treaty being signed between the Armenian trading company of New Julfa and Russia in 1667. Among other things this treaty made provision for the establishment of an Armenian church in Moscow. Peter the Great (1682–1725) showed interest in plans for the re-establishment of Armenian statehood under Russian suzerainty presented to him by the young Armenian noble Israyēl Ōri, but these had to be shelved in 1706 with the onset of the Swedish War.

Once the war was over Peter could turn to his southern frontiers. In 1716 he approved the creation of an archbishop for the Armenians of Russia with his seat at Astrakhan. The archbishop was to have jurisdiction over the large number of Armenians who had moved to the north Caucasus. Connected with this was the edict promulgated the following January, granting religious freedom to Armenians who emigrated to Russia. Exploiting the turmoil of the Afghan invasion in Iran, Peter launched an offensive down the Caspian coast. The original intention was to coordinate this thrust with a revolt by local Armenians and Georgians, but the tsar pulled back, leaving the area open to Ottoman aggrandisement and occupation until 1735. This in turn led to further Armenian emigration to Russia. No restrictions were now placed on the construction of Armenian churches.

Armenians in the Ottoman Empire

The vast bulk of the Armenian population continued to live in the six eastern *vilayets* of the Ottoman Empire, which comprised much of their historic homeland.[35] There were also substantial Armenian communities in the major cities, the largest being in Istanbul, which by 1700 numbered some 60,000. The prestige of its bishop led to him assuming the patriarchal title in the mid-sixteenth century, but he only asserted his control over the sees of central Anatolia towards the end of the following century after a protracted struggle with the catholicoi of Sis.[36] In the same way as the ecumenical patriarchate, the Armenian patriarchate suffered from a rapid succession of candidates seeking to exploit its authority for personal gain, but periodically it was also able to produce the strong, principled figure, such as Yovhannēs Kolot (1715–41), who in 1726 was able to have the new catholicos of Ējmiacin elected and

---

35 For their location, see Hewsen, *Armenia: a historical atlas*, 188–212.
36 Soon the catholicate of Sis would enter a long tenure of office (1733–1865) by scions of the Ajapahean family known for their anti-Catholic stance.

consecrated at Constantinople. Thereafter the catholicoi acknowledged the patriarch's mediatory role in regulating relations with the Sublime Porte.[37]

To the mid-seventeenth century, Catholic missionaries were active in various cities of the empire, and found some of the Armenian patriarch of Constantinople[38] open to persuasion regarding union with Rome.[39] But this did not last: the religious orientation of the Armenian Church of Constantinople became more traditionalist as a result of the growing influence of a new class of financially influential çelebis and amiras, who mostly originated from provincial cities like Amasya and Sivas. Suspicion of Catholic missionaries became so intense that in 1714 Patriarch Awetikʿ Ewdokacʿi secured the closure of Jesuit operations in Istanbul.[40]

Western criticism of the poor quality of the education available to the Armenian clergy was not entirely justified. Under the direction of Vardan Bałišecʿi (d.1704) the monastery school at Amrdolu in Bitlis offered a very sound education. Bałišecʿi updated the curriculum to include the study of history, expanded the library holdings, and had many old texts copied and returned to circulation. Patriarch Kolot was a product of the monastery, which became the model for the monastery and seminary he founded in Üsküdar. Moreover, with the lifting of restrictions on printing, Istanbul became the main centre of the Armenian publishing trade. Taking advantage of the technology, Kolot issued a series of medieval anti-Latin treatises. Building on his legacy, his student and successor Yakob Nalean (1741–49; 1752–64) created a patriarchal academy in Kum Kapı and was the author of a series of theological works including the *Rock of Faith* (1733).

It is largely from this period that the Armenian community attained its classic form in Ottoman jurisprudence, as a *millet*, in the sense of a religious confessional minority, which enjoyed a high degree of internal autonomy under the leadership of the Armenian patriarch of Constantinople, who represented them before the sultan.[41] As such, the patriarch possessed both religious and temporal power, and until the Hattı Şerif (Noble Rescript) of 1839 he possessed penal authority over the people, with his own jail and small police force

---

37 See Kevork B. Bardakjian, 'The rise of the Armenian Patriarchate of Constantinople', in *Christians and Jews in the Ottoman Empire*, ed. B. Braude and B. Lewis (New York: Holmes and Meier Publishers, 1982), 94–5.
38 Patriarch Kirakos.
39 Richard, 'Missionnaires français en Arménie', 196–202.
40 Affairs reached such a pitch that Patriarch Awetikʿ was intercepted by French forces while travelling to Jerusalem in 1703 and abducted.
41 As a further reinforcement of the category's confessional, not ethnic, composition, from 6 August 1783 the Armenian *millet* also incorporated their co-religionists of the Jacobite Syrian church.

in the capital. He would superintend the appointment of tax collectors for his people, oversee their religious, charitable and educational institutions, and apply censorship of the press.

A new Uniate Armenian monastic order and patriarchate

As the European Catholic missions gradually lost their momentum in the early eighteenth century, a new Armenian community was formed in Constantinople on 8 September 1701 on the initiative of the zealous young monk Mxit'ar Sebastac'i (1676–1749), whose name the order subsequently adopted. After studying in the monasteries of Ējmiacin, Sevan and Erzurum, Mxit'ar made contact in 1693 with missionaries in Aleppo, where Jesuit, Capuchin and Carmelite missions existed until their suppression in 1774. Escaping the anti-Catholic atmosphere of the capital, the group settled temporarily at Methone in southern Greece, then under Venetian control, before setting sail for Venice itself in 1715. Two years later the brotherhood was given residence on the island of San Lazzaro, in the Venetian lagoon.

Adopting the Benedictine rule, the monks took an oath to 'religion and the homeland', thereby clearly severing the unitary Armenian ethno-confessional identity fostered by the *millet* structure. The order mobilised its body of strongly motivated manpower with technical training on a western model to achieve a series of goals, religious, educational and cultural. Mxit'ar became actively involved in publishing, issuing a second edition of the Bible in 1733, as well as commentaries, devotional material and scholarly studies. He also produced several reference books to improve instruction in Armenian (grammar, dictionary, etc.) and instituted an important network of schools which continues to function in various Armenian communities worldwide. The order produced a series of translations and systematic scholarly studies of high erudition, of which one of the most salient was Mik'ayēl Č'amč'ean's three-volume history of Armenia from earliest times to the present (1784–86) as well as various periodicals to keep Armenians abreast of the latest developments in diverse aspects of modern life, all of which impressed Napoleon on his visit to the island. The order split in 1772, with one faction leaving for Trieste before settling permanently in Vienna in 1811.[42]

Associated with the rise of the Mxit'arists was the foundation of a Uniate patriarchate in Aleppo on 26 November 1740 under the primacy of Abraham

---

42 Recently declining vocations and other factors have led to a reunification.

Arciwean, which received papal ratification two years later. Its existence was the cause of tensions and disruption within the Armenian community, because its members were still officially counted as part of the Armenian *millet* and hence under the jurisdiction of the patriarch of Constantinople.

India

The first stable Armenian community was founded on the subcontinent in the sixteenth century as merchant networks fanned out from Armenian centres, such as Julfa, around the same time as the Portuguese reached India. The first Armenian church in the Moghul capital of Agra dates from 1562, and other early communities were established in Delhi, Bombay, Surat and Calcutta, and along the Coromandel coast of Madras, where the first Armenian church was built in 1712.

The Armenian community in India grew as a result of the economic decline of New Julfa and maintained commercial contacts with such distant centres as Amsterdam. Most importantly, its members' knowledge of languages and familiarity with the local market rendered it a crucial intermediary for the East India Company. These international contacts prepared the groundwork for Madras to become the catalyst for major new advances in Armenian social thought in the 1770s and 1780s. There a group of likeminded thinkers formed, comprising the New Julfa pearl merchant Agha Šahamir Šahamirean, the tutor to his sons Movsēs Baḷramean, and the soldier adventurer Yovsēpʻ Ēmin. They offered a modernist explanation of the loss of Armenian statehood, explaining historical events not in terms of divine intervention by way of either miracle or punishment for communal sin, but through the autonomy of human agency.[43] Moreover, in their appeal to youth, they boldly reinterpreted the image of the religious martyr giving his/her life in defence of the faith in terms of zealous patriots actively engaged in building their country, relying on lay initiative rather than ecclesiastical diplomacy. Similarly, they argued that the church should lose its primacy in local community affairs. Poor relief was to be regulated by a set of byelaws providing for the election of an executive committee to administer a fund based on annual dues. It was to be outside the control of the clergy, whose involvement was limited to the purely spiritual realm.[44]

---

43 This view was expounded in the work *Nor Tetrak* (New Pamphlet) of 1776, on which see Oskanyan, *Hay girkʻə 1512–1800 tʻvakannerin*, 489–91.

44 These byelaws are contained in the pamphlet *Nšawak* (Target) of 1783, on which see ibid., 541–3.

Their deep commitment to a representative democratic form of government with popular participation characterised by a strict delimitation of duties, checks and balances, and transparency in operation, was also embedded in the group's draft constitution for a liberated Armenian state informed by the Enlightenment principles of the rule of law and the rights of man. There the division of church and state was rigorously maintained, and to that end the educational system was also set under state management and made mandatory for both boys and girls. No discriminatory tax was to be applied to minorities in the state as were levied on the Christian communities in Muslim states, yet a certain remnant of the *millet* consciousness remains in terms of land ownership and eligibility for holding public office. These were to be the sole preserve of members of the Armenian Apostolic Church and were therefore not even extended to Armenian Catholics.

This was the first articulation of a new voice: that of the merchant middle class over against the traditional elites of the clergy and aristocracy. It was inevitable that it would be strenuously opposed by the catholicos of the time, Simēon Erevanc'i (1710–80), whose conception of Armenian identity – with its focus on Holy Ējmiacin – was entirely traditional.[45] Nevertheless, some of the hierarchy, such as the abbot of the monastery of the Holy Precursor in Muš, the second most famous pilgrim site on the Armenian plateau, cooperated with the group around Šahamirean, who also maintained contact with Archbishop Yovsēp' Arłut'eanc' (1743–1801), prelate of the Armenians of Russia.

Catholic and Protestant *millets*

As we have observed, seventeenth-century Catholic missionary activity culminated in the establishment of two institutions in the following century, the Mxit'arist order and the Uniate patriarchate, both still incorporated within the single Armenian *millet*. At the same time, these maintained a rather different profile, the former accepting much of the heritage of Armenian Christianity while acknowledging papal supremacy, the latter much more directly Roman in outlook and orientation. Inevitably this produced friction, which manifested itself during talks with the patriarchate in 1810, 1817 and 1820 regarding the possibility of reintegration within the Apostolic Church. In view of the fact that

---

45 Simēon Erevanc'i also finalised the names of the saints to be commemorated in the liturgical diptychs. For a recent study, see Sebouh Aslanian, *Dispersion history and the polycentric nation: the role of Simeon Yerevants's Girk' or koči partavcar in the eighteenth-century nation revival* [Bibliothèque d'arménologie 'Bazmavep' 39] (Venice: St Lazar's Press, 2004).

some of the European powers, notably France, were supporting the Catholic separatist position, while also lending their aid to the Greeks currently in revolt against central authority, the sultan took reprisals on the Catholic Armenian community in 1827 and deported them from the capital to the hinterlands. However, Ottoman defeat in the war led in May 1831 to the allied insistence on the community's return and its full separate representation in a Catholic *millet*.[46] Three years later their ethnarch Yakobos was elevated to the rank of patriarch on a par with his Apostolic counterpart.

In 1810 eschatological concerns impelled the American Board of Commissioners for Foreign Missions to spread the faith in the Near East.[47] One of the first steps was to publish the Bible in classical Armenian and then, for the first time, in the modern vernacular. As their materials found a rapport among Armenians, it was decided to launch a more concentrated mission in 1830 under the experienced leadership of Eli Smith, H. Dwight and W. Goddell. Despite the protests of the patriarch, they set up schools in the capital, Izmir, and other centres. Requests made over the next few years for the creation of an Evangelical *millet* won the support of Prussia, Britain and the USA. Finally, on 1 July 1846 they announced the opening of the first Evangelical Armenian Church of Constantinople, and their separate status received the sultan's ratification the following November. Evangelical missionaries went on to found institutes of higher learning in the provinces, such as Euphrates College at Xarberd and Anatolia College in Marsovan, near Sivas, which gave Armenian youth a basic grounding in the arts and sciences, often acting as a conduit for graduates to continue their studies in the USA and make their fortune there. Later in the century, whole evangelical communities, such as those of Xarberd and Bitlis, emigrated to America to practise their religion free of interference.

Tanzimat and the Armenian constitution

Since the eighteenth century an increasing number of talented young Ottoman Armenians have gone abroad to complete their education, usually in medicine or agriculture, mostly in Italy and France. They were exposed there to a more liberal, progressive political philosophy emphasising broader participation in

---

46 Hagop Barsamian, 'The eastern question and the tanzimat era', in *The Armenian people from ancient to modern times*, ed. R. G. Hovannisian (New York: St Martin's Press, 1997), II, 186.

47 The same impulse led to the settling of representatives of the Basler Mission in the area of Šamax in southern Caucasia around the same time. Their converts were largely followers of a neo-Tondrakite sect, which had centred on the town of Xnus.

civil society and greater social mobility associated with technological skill. On their return, the graduates formed a new professional class, which sought wider scope for self-expression within the structures of the *millet*. This pressure became all the more insistent after 1848, the 'year of the revolutions'. It was primarily directed against the almost absolute control of *millet* affairs by the *amira* class, whose influence was now on the wane with the gradual introduction into the empire of European-style banks.[48] These developments internal to the *millet* paralleled the effect of the broader Ottoman reform movement (1839–78), which had the support of the western powers. It was also evidenced in the socio-cultural phenomenon known as *Zart'onk'* (Awakening). At its heart were self-financed voluntary organisations, which sought to expand the *millet's* limited provisions by raising standards of education and by promoting a higher secular culture inspired by Romantic nationalism. It involved the replacement of classical Armenian by a modern standardised literary medium, the diffusion of the periodical press, and the emancipation of women. It aimed at reuniting Armenians, divided by ecclesiastical politics.[49]

The Armenian constitution of 1863

The movement for modernisation and reform attained a significant victory with the ratification of a 'constitution', which made possible a critical transfer of power from the patriarch to a series of assemblies and councils, where the laity predominated. The key provision was the creation of a general assembly of 120 lay representatives and twenty clergy, which was to nominate the patriarch for the sultan's approval. Under it came a religious assembly of fourteen clergy, but far more important was a political assembly of twenty laymen responsible for education, the financial administration of the *millet*, and monasteries, which now acquired an educational and utilitarian function, maintaining libraries and printing presses, operating seminaries and hospitals, and so on. They were following the model set by Mkrtic Xrimean, abbot of Varag monastery near Lake Van, who furnished his monastery with a library, a museum and a press on which he published the periodical *Arciw Vaspurakani*

---

48 See Hagop Barsoumian, 'The dual role of the Armenian *amira* class within the Ottoman government and the Armenian *millet*', in *Christians and Jews*, I, 171–84.

49 The movement is characterised by the Armenian Catholic writer Mkrtič Pešiktašlean's poem *Ełbayr emk' menk'* [We are brothers], which emphasises the achievement of unity in nationalism, patriotism and an appeal to service of the homeland. All too often Armenians had been separated by circumstances beyond their control. Now they are to unite, as brothers and offspring of Mother Armenia, the personified homeland, and join in common action.

(Eagle of Vaspurakan). He also founded a school employing modern pedagogical methods and rejecting the application of corporal punishment. Though damaged in the massacres of 1895–96, it continued to function until 1915. The provisions of the constitution, with certain adaptations, still govern the Armenian patriarchate of Constantinople and catholicate of Cilicia.

Entry of southern Caucasía into the Russian Empire

The establishment of the Qâjâr dynasty in Iran in 1794 renewed strong central rule in the country and compelled the submission of the regional khans, including the king of Georgia, who attempted to counterbalance this by cultivating closer ties with Russia. In the course of the first Russo-Persian War (1804–13) all Georgia, including the important commercial city of Tiflis with a majority Armenian population, was annexed, while the second (1826–28), in which Armenian volunteers fought alongside the Russian army, led to the Russian annexation of the khanates of Erevan and Naxǰewan.[50] Moreover, by the treaty of Adrianople (1829) some 90,000 Armenians settled on Russian territory newly acquired from the Ottoman Empire, including a number of Catholic communities. As a result, Armenians once again constituted a majority in areas of the eastern part of their historic homeland.

These developments had a series of implications for ecclesiastical administration. Ējmiacin's incorporation into the Russian Empire meant the cession to the patriarch of Constantinople of any residual authority within Ottoman territory. In 1844 Ējmiacin accepted the patriarchate of Constantinople's complete internal autonomy and renounced the practice of dispatching its own representatives (*nuirak*) into the Ottoman sphere to distribute the holy chrism and to collect funds from the faithful.[51]

The *Polozhenie* (statute) of 1836 determined the Armenian Church's legal status in the Russian Empire. From now on the clergy and lay representatives were to put forward two names for the office of catholicos, leaving the final choice to the tsar, to whom the successful candidate was to swear an oath of allegiance. The catholicos of Ējmiacin obtained primacy over the catholicate of Caucasian Albania as well as over the other five Armenian dioceses of the empire (Erevan, Georgia, Širvan, Nor Naxǰewan-Bessarabia and Astrakhan). A

---

50 Bournoutian, *The Khanate of Erevan*, 13–26. For the situation of the Armenian population in Tiflis, see R. G. Suny, *The making of the Georgian nation* (Bloomington: Indiana University Press, 1988), 88.

51 Bardakjian, 'The rise of the Armenian Patriarchate of Constantinople', 96.

Russian procurator was to attend convocations of the holy synod in Ējmiacin, but, because the Armenian Church was not in communion with the Russian, it was granted autonomy in deciding its internal affairs, in contrast to its Georgian counterpart.[52] It also retained supervision of the network of church schools and the Armenian clergy were guaranteed tax-exempt status and security of property.

Modern education and secularism

Progressive clergy like Gabriēl Patkanean and Xačatur Abovean took the first steps towards the establishment of a modern east Armenian idiom. The former even employed it for his short-lived newspaper *Ararat*. Liberal clergy came under pressure from both the Armenian hierarchy and the Russian censors for what was perceived as their suspicious heterodox views and new-fangled methods. By the end of the decade the first virulently secular and anticlerical review appeared, the *Hiwsisap'ayl* (Northern Lights), published in Moscow by Mik'ayēl Nalbandean and Step'an Nazarean, who harshly criticised the Mxit'arist order's political conservatism from a socialist standpoint and insisted that the church must not dominate any national revival. Many writers in the modern idiom saw themselves as a new cultural force for national progress and hence in conflict with the church over the issue of leadership in society. The popular novelist Raffi (Yakob Melik'-Yakobean) also propagated a socialist creed in his utopian vision of a future Armenian state in his novel *Xent'e* (The Fool), in which he visualises an ergonomic Protestant-style building which does double duty as both church and school, and the priest similarly offers the children instruction in science. Men and women mingle freely, not segregated in traditional fashion in different sections of the nave or gallery, the laity participate directly in the service, improvising prayers and singing hymns, while the preacher selects as his text the verse 'in the sweat of thy face shalt thou eat bread' (Genesis 3:19), interpreting this not as punishment for original sin, but as an appeal to the community to transform their environment through empowered self-help rather than remaining passive in fatalistic quiescence.[53]

At the same time, perceiving Armenian nationalism as separatist and subversive, the reactionary tsar Alexander III (1881–94) instituted an aggressive

---

52 A. L. H. Rhinelander, 'Russia's imperial policy: the adminstration of the Caucasus in the first half of the nineteenth century', *Canadian Slavonic Papers* 17 (1975), 225–6.

53 Raffi, *The fool: events from the last Russo-Turkish War 1877–78*, trans. D. Abcarian (Princeton: Gomidas Institute, 2000). More conservative and pro-church writers supported newspapers like the *Melu Hayastani* [Bee of Armenia].

policy of russification. Various currents of free thinking circulated even in the Gevorgian Spiritual Academy at Ējmiacin, the highest Armenian educational establishment in Transcaucasia during the tsarist period; nor was the Armenian catholicos free from suspicion by the Russian authorities. In line with this, in 1885 the viceroy of Transcaucasia, Prince A. M. Dondukov-Korsakov, ordered the closure of the network of some 500 Armenian church schools in the region and their replacement by Russian institutions. However, Armenians undermined the measure by setting up 'secret' schools, forcing a reversal of policy and the reopening of the schools the following year, though the instructors were replaced and the curriculum more closely monitored.

A second attempt to abrogate the *Polozhenie* was made by Nicholas II on 2 January 1903 through his viceroy Prince Golitsyn, ordering him to confiscate church property and to transfer the Armenian schools to Russian jurisdiction in order to advance the cause of russification. Once again it had the opposite effect. Mkrtic Xrimean, now catholicos, resisted the measure; he instigated protest marches; violent clashes ensued, leading to the stabbing of the viceroy by political extremists. The resulting concessions included replacing the viceroy with a figure more amenable to Armenian culture and the repeal of the confiscation of church properties on 1 August 1905.

Nevertheless, an impressive array of Armenian intellectuals and artists left Russia to study in various German universities over this period, many enriching church life with new approaches, which sought to integrate east and west. Scholars and theologians like Karapet Tēr-Mkrtčean, Eruand Tēr-Minasean and Garegin Yovsēpʻeancʻ studied at the universities of Leipzig, Berlin, Halle and Tübingen. Their experiences promoted a movement for reform, which, however, was overtaken, as in Russia, by circumstances before it achieved its full potential. One of the main achievements was the introduction of the Gregorian calendar.[54] The multitalented musicologist Komitas Vardapet (Sołomon Sołomonean), originally from Istanbul, laid the foundation of his work on medieval notation and modern harmonisation in Berlin.[55] On his return, he established a polyphonic choir at Ējmiacin and produced three-part and four-part settings of the liturgy. Similarly, the four-part setting by Makar Ekmalean, which subsequently established itself in general usage, was published at Leipzig in 1896. After studying at the Munich Academy of Fine Arts in the 1880s, the artist Vardges Sureneancʻ produced a series of paintings on ecclesiastical

54 This change does not apply to the Armenian Patriarchate of Jerusalem, whose liturgical calendar is still governed by the status quo decree of 1857.
55 Komitas Vardapet, *Armenian sacred and folk music*, trans. D. Gulbenkian [Caucasus World] (Richmond: Curzon Press, 1998).

themes, including a depiction of the Virgin and Child which graces the altar in Ējmiacin. Subsequent developments in the church's liturgical life, such as the widespread adoption of the organ and the introduction of pews and kneeling pads in newer churches, arguably lend the Armenian Church more of a European ambience than any of the other eastern churches.

The turn of the century maelstrom

The natural development of cultural revival, of more active lay participation in society and of the growth of nationalist aspirations was the crystallisation of various political parties in the last two decades of the century. These included the Hnčakean Revolutionary Party founded in Geneva in 1887 and the Federation of Armenian Revolutionaries of 1890, which two years later became the Armenian Revolutionary Federation. Their appearance was marked by disputes on the ideological role of socialism, resulting in widespread polarisation of public opinion as the parties strove to win converts to their creed in the cities and provincial towns, thereby posing a challenge to the church's traditional authority in community affairs.[56] In 1890 Hnčakean demonstrators disrupted the liturgy in the patriarchal cathedral at Istanbul, compelling Patriarch Xorēn Ašəgean to deliver a petition to the sultan for the proper implementation of Article 61 of the Treaty of Berlin regarding injustices against the Armenians.[57] Another demonstration in the capital five years later led to the community taking refuge in their churches from harsh reprisals. Meanwhile, the Great Powers were reviewing the 'Armenian Question' and proposed several new provisions, including the right for Armenians forcibly converted to Islam to return to their original faith. However, the response proved even more extreme. In Urfa, for example, around 3000 Armenians were burned alive in their cathedral on 28 December 1895.[58]

The overthrow of the sultan and proclamation of the Ottoman constitution in 1908 ushered in a new period of expanded civil liberties, which began with positive aspirations, but was again overtaken by events. A speech in the following year by the Armenian bishop of Adana about his community learning self-defence excited the ire of reactionary elements, who massacred many local

---

56 M. Matossian, *The impact of Soviet policies in Armenia* (Leiden: Brill, 1962), 91. A small percentage of Armenians also joined the Russian Social Democratic Labour Party or became Armenian Marxists.

57 R. G. Hovannisian, 'The Armenian question in the Ottoman Empire 1876 to 1914,' in *The Armenian people from ancient to modern times*, I, 218.

58 Ibid., 223.

Christians, including Armenian Catholics and Protestants, Greeks and Nestorians, who were not directly involved in the nationalist project.[59] As usual, the Armenian patriarch's protestations at the Sublime Porte met with no redress.

Deeply concerned about the exodus of the Armenian population of the eastern *vilayets* to southern Caucasia, Europe and the USA, in 1912 Catholicos Gēorg Sureneanc' moved the tsar to exert pressure on the Ottoman government for reform. However, the proposals for enhanced autonomy that emerged are highly ironic, given the officially organised deportations that began within a matter of months.

Genocide and global diaspora

During the deportations, the able-bodied men were often killed, and atrocities marked the inhuman forced marches of the rest of the population into the Syrian desert. Among the 1.5 million victims who perished during the years 1915–23 were some 4000 clergy. In 1912 the Armenian patriarch of Constantinople had presented the government with a full accounting of the churches and monasteries under his jurisdiction, which, in Ōrmanean's tally, amounted to 2200 structures, most of which were destroyed.[60] A similar fate befell both the catholicate of Sis, which had presided over thirteen dioceses, of which only the see of Aleppo was to survive, and the Armenian Catholic church which previously administered nineteen sees and 156 churches. Meanwhile, the catholicate of Alt'amar was completely eliminated. Refugees heroically struggled to preserve some of their community's sacred objects from loss. The events left a deep psychological and spiritual scar on survivors, who strove amid the chaos and disorientation to come to terms with issues of theodicy and providence.

Hundreds of thousands of refugees, casualties of war and deportation, taxed the church's resources not only in Caucasia, but also in the Near East. The patriarch of Constantinople, Zawēn Eliayean, was exiled to Baghdad, then to Mosul, while the catholicos of Sis, Sahak II Xapayean, escaped with his flock after the French evacuation in 1921 to Bab near Aleppo, and then on to the Jerusalem patriarchate, the largest Armenian institution in the region. The church set up a network of orphanages and schools in Syria, Lebanon and Cyprus to provide relief to the children whose families had not survived.

---

59 Ibid., 231. By the time of the genocide there were four unions of evangelical congregations in the Ottoman Empire with a population of around 51,000, and two in the USA.
60 Currently there are about thirty active Armenian churches in Istanbul, and three in the provinces (Kayseri, Diyarbekir and Vakif Köy).

The catholicate of Sis – or Cilicia – was reorganised in 1929 with four sees, under a new primatial see at Antelias, north of Beirut. From 1931 the catholicate boasted a printing press and an official review called *Hask*. Its standing was further raised by the election of the illustrious scholar Garegin Yovsēpʿeancʿ (1945–52) to the see. Meanwhile, Armenian Catholic refugees fled to the monastery of Bzommar in Lebanon, to which their patriarchal see returned from Istanbul in 1931. In the interim a council of bishops was convoked in Rome to reorganise the church.

The church in the Soviet Republic of Armenia

With the establishment of Soviet rule in November 1920 came the official proclamation of atheism as state doctrine and the graded introduction of persecution against religion and the church. A state decree nationalised cultural institutions and removed schools from church supervision. The catholicate of Ējmiacin was seized and the seminary transformed into a public school, while religious instruction in schools was prohibited. In 1922 the *Polozhenie* governing the church's legal status was disbanded and a temporary constitution put in place, which permitted the creation of a supreme spiritual council two years later.

The ideological struggle reached its peak towards the end of the twenties, marked by the launch of the illustrated review *Anastuac* (Atheist) in January 1928 and the founding of the antireligious university in Erevan in November 1929. Collectivisation of agriculture led to a Siberian exile for many priests, condemned as 'kulaks'.[61] In such a climate it comes as no surprise that on the death of Catholicos Gevorg (9 May 1930) authorisation for a new election was not immediately forthcoming. This negative attitude towards the Armenian Church was always tempered by the existence of the diaspora.[62] Hence, after a hiatus of two years, pragmatic Kremlin policy makers altered their stance so as not to disrupt the entry of diaspora funds to the republic.[63] Accordingly, internal and international electors met and chose Xoren Muradbekyan (1932–38) for the supreme office, though his reign marked another grim nadir for the church before the twentieth century was half done. Stalin's antireligious persecution ushered in a new phase of destruction and desecration of churches

---

61 Matossian, *Impact of Soviet policies*, 148.
62 W. Kolarz, *Religion in the Soviet Union* (London: St Martin's Press, 1961).
63 Matossian, *Impact of Soviet policies*, 150. It is interesting that the electors discussed the possibility of removing the primatial see from Ējmiacin to Jerusalem.

and monasteries in Armenia.[64] The campaign reached its height in 1936–38 – the Years of Terror. More than seventy clergy were arrested in the first months of 1937 alone; many were shot or sent into exile. The unexpected death of the catholicos in April 1938 has usually been imputed to the authorities, angered by his encyclical of the previous year which called for church renewal.[65]

The onset of World War II dictated another abrupt policy change in order to maximise the war effort. As each republic fielded its own divisions, the infusion of a modicum of patriotic spirit was tolerated to rouse the men to martial ardour. During this period the *locum tenens* was Gevorg Čorekčyan, a representative of the generation who had studied in Leipzig. He skilfully exploited the opportunity to promote a partial reconciliation with the state. He mobilised the church as an instrument of state propaganda. Among other things he appealed to rich Armenians abroad to fund a tank column.[66] His efforts led to the reopening of churches and the recall of priests from Siberia, and on 14 November 1943 to the creation of a council for the affairs of the Armenian Church. On 19 April 1945 Čorekčyan was granted a rare audience with Stalin, which resulted in the appointment of ten new bishops, the election of a new catholicos, the publication of the periodical *Ējmiacin*, and the reopening of the printing press and seminary. On 31 May Čorekčyan received a medal 'for the Defence of Caucasia', while in the following month he was elected catholicos and accepted as *primus inter pares* by his counterpart of Cilicia, Garegin Yovsēp'eanc'.[67] Čorekčyan was also responsible for making the controversial appeal to the diverse Armenian communities of the diaspora to make their patriotic contribution by returning to the liberated homeland (21 November 1945). In response, around 100,000 Armenians from Europe, America and the Middle East relocated to the republic over the next four years, though many suffered great hardships there and some barely set foot on Armenian soil before they were condemned to exile.[68] As part of his accommodation with the state Čorekčyan cooperated in its Cold War policies. His encyclical of

---

64 There were 162 Armenian Catholic villages in different republics of the USSR.

65 Several sources suggest the catholicos was strangled, or poisoned. See Mesrob K. Krikorian, 'The Armenian church in the Soviet Union, 1917–1967', in *Aspects of religion in the Soviet Union 1917–1967*, ed. R. H. Marshall, Jr (Chicago: University of Chicago Press, 1971), 245. He was buried in the church of St Gayanē, but subsequently buried at the west door of the cathedral at Ējmiacin at the behest of Catholicos Garegin I.

66 Kolarz, *Religion in the Soviet Union*, 160.

67 Matossian, *Impact of Soviet policies*, 194. At that time there were only fifty-nine parishes in Armenia, down from a figure of 491 in 1914.

68 For the contrary position of Armenian Catholic Cardinal Ałajanean, who had been born in Transcaucasia, see Kolarz, *Religion in the Soviet Union*, 166. On 27 November 1945 Čorekčyan also appealed to the three great powers for the return of the Ottoman Armenian provinces.

1948 enjoining patriotic clergy abroad to fight all traitors encoded a particular political agenda. Similarly, his participation in the Stockholm Peace Appeal of the same year furthered Soviet objectives regarding the peace movement.[69]

Building on earlier internal tensions within the Armenian polity, the increased polarisation between capitalist and communist ideologies produced a growth of factionalism within the Armenian diaspora. Armenian immigration to the USA expanded enormously in the years leading up to and following the genocide, requiring its own hierarchical representation. One of the upper clergy, Archbishop Lēon Durean, was denounced as pro-Soviet by political opponents and murdered in the Holy Cross Church, New York, on Christmas Eve 1933. Despite attempts at conciliation, the rupture did not heal, but found expression in schism through the creation of parallel jurisdictions.

Similar political divisions among the Armenians of Lebanon, at the time the largest diaspora community, occasioned a delay of four years after the death of Garegin Yovsēp'eanc' before the election of a successor to the catholicate of Cilicia. Complicating the process was the intervention of the catholicate of Ējmiacin. Catholicos Vazgen Palyčan embarked on a visit to the Middle East in the early spring of 1956. Arriving in Lebanon a few days before the election of his counterpart, he sought to postpone the final choice.[70] Nevertheless, the election proceeded, with Bishop Zareh P'ayaslean of Aleppo approved by the majority vote. Tensions between the primatial sees spilled over into the dioceses under their supervision. Over the next few decades the see of Kuwait and the Arab Gulf together with those of Greece and Iran passed under Cilician jurisdiction, while the see of Damascus moved to the jurisdiction of Ējmiacin, and parallel jurisdictions developed in the three sees of North America.[71]

The Armenian Church and the ecumenical movement

In 1962 the World Council of Churches extended membership to both catholicates of the Armenian Church, which later sent spectators to Vatican II. Both Catholicos Garegin Sargisean of Cilicia and his current successor Aram K'ešišean (1995–) have assumed central executive roles in the WCC. From 1964 to 1971 membership of the WCC Faith and Order Commission encouraged representatives of the different Orthodox churches to hold a series of informal

69 Matossian, *Impact of Soviet policies*, 194–5.
70 Kolarz, *Religion in the Soviet Union*, 171–5.
71 For the background to Palyčan's 1960 visit to the west, see ibid., 175.

meetings to review the issues dividing them: Christology, recognition of councils and saints, imposition of anathemas, and so on. These were then followed from 1985 to 1993 by an Official Joint Commission, which arrived at an agreed statement on Christology now being reviewed by the individual churches.[72] The catholicates have since 1971 also entered into dialogue with the Roman Catholic Church. Catholicos Garegin I and his successor Catholicos Aram have both signed statements in the context of a series of joint communiqués issued by Pope John Paul II and the heads of the oriental churches. In addition, in 1965 on the fiftieth anniversary of the genocide there were talks directed towards a rapprochement between the Armenian Evangelical churches in the Near East and the Apostolic Church; in 1968 there was a merger of the Armenian Evangelical Union of the eastern USA with that of Canada, which was then extended the next year to California, to form the Armenian Evangelical Union of North America.

Vazgen Palyčan's long period of office (1955–94) provided the church in the Soviet Republic with an important measure of stability. He brought dignity and respect to the catholicate, and his intervention was crucial in cases of popular unrest.[73] He oversaw the re-creation of the synod of bishops and witnessed a significant change of the popular attitude towards the church during *perestroika*, when church attendance and participation in communion were viewed as a powerful form of political protest.[74] From 1987 to 1993 the church was an uneasy spectator, as mass meetings and protests in the Erevan Opera Square voiced increasing disaffection with the government's handling of affairs. The earthquake that struck Armenia on 7 December 1988 made deep demands on the church's charitable and spiritual resources, while at the same time breaking down the political barriers which had separated Armenia from large sections of the diaspora and inaugurating greater cooperation between the two catholicates.

The last decade and a half has been one of enormous activity as the church establishes its legal status and social and spiritual role within the new Republic of Armenia, which declared independence on 21 September 1991. There is increased scope for the church's social, charitable and educational activities.[75]

---

72 For the text of the four agreed statements (1989–93) see 'Appendix', *St Nersess Theological Review* 1 (1996), 99–110.
73 On two occasions he restrained popular emotions in the capital, first on the fiftieth anniversary commemoration of the Armenian Genocide (1965) and then during a demonstration against the Supreme Soviet Building in connection with the Karabagh Movement.
74 Kolarz, *Religion in the Soviet Union*, 173.
75 These normally take the traditional form of *diakoniai*.

Teachers trained at a theological faculty which opened in 1995 at the Erevan State University are responsible for religious instruction in the schools. The church is also more visible via mass media, with its own radio and television channels and periodical press. Training of priests has been augmented by the creation of two new seminaries. Catholicos Garegin I Sargisean (1995–99), a man of vision and a powerful orator, increased the number of internal dioceses to eight, coterminous with the civil administrative regions. Over 150 churches have been returned by the state for church use and a range of new shrines constructed, including the cathedral of St Gregory the Illuminator, consecrated in 2001 in the presence of Pope John Paul II by Catholicos Garegin II Nersisyan (1999–) on the 1700th anniversary of the conversion of Armenia.

The constitution ratified in 1995 maintains freedom of religion, conscience and expression, and, while recognising a special relation with the Apostolic Church historically, rejects an established church. In keeping with this more enlightened climate, the Armenian Catholic Church created a new diocese of Armenia, Georgia and eastern Europe in 1991, centred in Gyumri and supported by the Mxit'arist order. Similarly, the Evangelicals received official recognition on 1 July 1994 and the next year formed the Union of Evangelical Churches of Armenia with over thirty churches.

Contemporary concerns

Political and economic upheavals in the Middle East, such as the Lebanese War (1975) and the Iranian Revolution (1979), have led to further demographic dislocation in the diaspora communities, while Armenian pilgrimage to Jerusalem has declined along with the resident Armenian population of the Holy Land as a result of the Israeli–Palestinian conflict. Indian independence in 1947 effected a major relocation of the Armenian population to Australia, which is now the centre of the diocese encompassing the Indian subcontinent, once under the jurisdiction of New Julfa in Iran. The most recent wave of emigration, however, has been from the Armenian Republic, provoked by the destruction of the infrastructure, economic stagnation and unemployment. This has resulted in Moscow and Los Angeles currently having the largest concentrations of Armenians worldwide after the capital Erevan.

In ministering to a nation so widely scattered over the planet, the Armenian Church faces a series of complex issues: relations between homeland and diaspora, identity questions posed by the second and subsequent generations of immigrants, the impact of mixed marriages, and so on. Like other Orthodox churches, it faces decisions on liturgical reform, spiritual renewal and the role of women in the church, including female monasticism and the order of deaconesses.[76] Finally, as a Christian communion fully engaged with the modern world, the Armenian Church is occupied with secularism and the need to update its articulation of the theology of creation to address the demands of environmental ecology.[77]

[76] For the early, medieval and early modern history of the order of deaconess in the Armenian Church, see Abel Oghlukian, *The deaconess in the Armenian Church*, trans. S. P. Cowe (New Rochelle, NY: St Nersess Armenian Seminary, 1994).

[77] For a treatment of this subject, see Vigen Guroian, *Faith, church, mission: essays for a renewal in the Armenian church* (New York: Armenian Prelacy, 1995).

19

Church and nation: the Ethiopian Orthodox *Täwahedo* Church (from the thirteenth to the twentieth century)

DONALD CRUMMEY

Ethiopia claims one of the oldest national traditions in Christendom. In the second quarter of the fourth century, the Ethiopian king, Ezana, together with his court, converted to Christianity. At the request of Ezana, St Athanasios, bishop of Alexandria, appointed Ethiopia's first bishop. Royal initiative thus founded a national church episcopally dependent on Alexandria. We know little about the pace of popular conversion, but Christianity did become embedded in the farming communities of the Ethiopian highlands, where it remains a deeply popular religion.[1] Royal dominance and popular commitment were the two poles of historic Ethiopian Christianity. Performing the role of mediator between these were, on the one hand, the Egyptian-appointed bishops, and on the other – and more importantly – the monasteries, which dotted the landscape, both geographical and cultural.

Ethiopian history unfolded on a high tableland, much intersected by mountain ranges and deeply fissured river valleys, which, during the principal rains lasting from mid-June to mid-September, is extremely difficult to traverse. The Ethiopian plateau lies at the southern end of the Red Sea and at the headwaters of the Blue Nile, the source of Egypt's annual flood. Christianity came to Aksum, then the principal town on the northern plateau, as part of the Hellenistic culture of the traders who plied the Red Sea in the early centuries of the era.[2] The Aksumite kingdom was the most powerful state in the southern

---

1 For this, as for so many other issues, see the masterly work by Taddesse Tamrat, *Church and state in Ethiopia, 1270–1527* (Oxford: Clarendon Press, 1972). Also useful, but more problematic, is Sergew Hable Sellassie, *Ancient and medieval Ethiopian history to 1270* (Addis Ababa: United Printers, 1972).

2 Good accounts of Ethiopia's classical history are S. Munro-Hay, *Aksum: an African civilization of late antiquity* (Edinburgh: Edinburgh University Press, 1991); Munro-Hay, 'Aksum. History of the town and empire', in *Encyclopædia Æthiopica* (Wiesbaden: Harrassowitz Verlag, 2003), I, 173–9; and D. W. Phillipson, *Ancient Ethiopia: Aksum, its antecedents and successors* (London: British Museum Press, 1998).

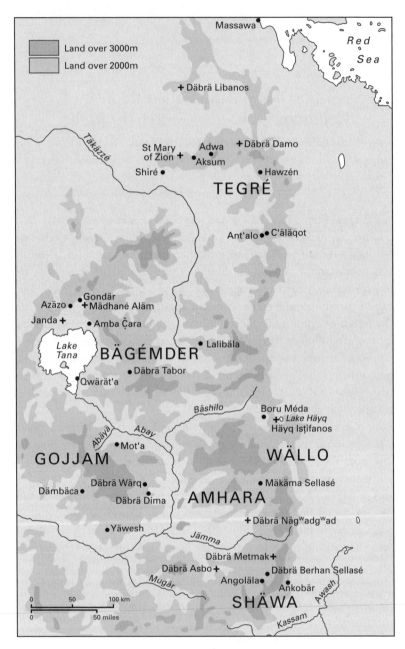

Map 7 Ethiopia

Red Sea, and the country remained sensitive to developments stemming from this direction. The highlands, which presented such a challenge to Ethiopia's rulers, presented an even greater challenge to external powers, and afforded the country a degree of autonomy *vis-à-vis* the millennial forces which swept the region. Of these forces, Islam was one of the most powerful. Its rise, in the seventh century of the era, ended Aksumite dominance in the Red Sea. Over time, Islam came to dominate the Hellenistic world into which the Aksumites had fitted so comfortably.

Ethiopians came to see themselves as an island of Christianity in a hostile sea of Islam and of paganism. The patriarchates – of Alexandria and of Antioch – to which they looked for guidance were subjected to Muslim rule in the first decades of the Islamic era and the adherents of the churches which they led soon became minorities. The Nubian Christian kingdoms of the middle Nile Valley were slower to succumb, the last of them passing out of the historical record in the fifteenth century.[3] Meanwhile, Islam was establishing itself on the western side of the Red Sea, on the coastlands below the Ethiopian highlands, from where it slowly spread inland along routes of trade. In the Ethiopian region, both Islam and Christianity were confronted with a multiplicity of religious beliefs and practices which both viewed as pagan. As we shall see, the struggle against pre-Christian belief and practice was waged not simply on the frontiers of the kingdom but even within the royal court itself.

Ethiopia's position as an outpost of Christendom allowed the development of beliefs and practices which, while unfairly viewed as exotic, were none the less distinctive. Ethiopians never lost the sense of being part of Christendom. Their sense of Orthodoxy came in their commitment to christological doctrine as they had received it from Alexandria. This doctrine they understand as *täwahedo*, or union, emphasising the union of the divine and human natures in Christ, whom they view as one person with one nature, which is uniquely divine *and* human. The common western designation of this position as 'Monophysite' sits uneasily with some of its adherents.[4]

---

3 W. Y. Adams, *Nubia: corridor to Africa* (Princeton: Princeton University Press, 1977), 525–46.
4 On the occasion of the meeting in Addis Ababa of the churches of the Syrian–Alexandrian connection, two authoritative publications were issued, one by the patriarchate, the other by 'The Ethiopian Orthodox Mission', a palace-supported organisation based at the Church of the Holy Trinity: *The Church of Ethiopia: a panorama of history and spiritual life* (Addis Ababa: Ethiopian Orthodox Church, 1970) [hereafter *Panorama*]; and Aymro Wondmagegnehu and Joachim Motovu (eds.), *The Ethiopian Orthodox Church* (Addis Ababa: The Ethiopian Orthodox Mission, 1970). Both retain their value as authoritative statements. For a more recent sympathetic account, by a member of the Greek Orthodox Church, see C. Chaillot, *The Ethiopian Orthodox Tewahedo Church tradition: a brief introduction to its life and spirituality* (Paris: Inter-Orthodox Dialogue, 2002). Older, sympathetic accounts

In many aspects of religious practice the Ethiopians were, and remain, conventionally Orthodox. Ordination to the priesthood and diaconate is the prerogative of a bishop standing in apostolic succession; their parish clergy are married; monasticism traces its roots to St Anthony; they share the religious calendar common throughout the Orthodox world; they recognise seven sacraments, of which Baptism and the Eucharist are held pre-eminent; they observe nine major festivals in honour of Christ: Nativity, Epiphany, Annunciation, Palm Sunday, Good Friday, Easter, Ascension, Pentecost and Transfiguration. However, as we will see, this was a Christianity deeply conscious of its Semitic roots, this consciousness reinforced by the fact that, since the centuries preceding the Christian era, Ethiopia has been culturally and politically dominated by Semitic speakers. Today, observance of the Sabbath as a feast day of equal status with Sunday is normative; circumcision is practised; Christian Ethiopians follow dietary prescriptions derived from the Torah; and they liken the altar (*tabot*) on which they celebrate the Eucharist to the Ark of the Covenant. Moreover, while marriage is *de rigueur* for the clergy, the church has not fully succeeded in imposing its views of marriage on the laity. Most Ethiopian Christians marry according to lay customs, and divorce is an accepted practice for the laity. However, church norms are recognised in that most Ethiopian Christians view their marriage practices as barring them from receiving the Eucharist, and instead channel their religious devotion into rigorous fasting.

Equally, the commitment to Alexandrian teaching as a touchstone of Orthodoxy did not lead to unanimity, but rather created a framework within which redefinition was constant. The monasteries constituted the restless frontiers of Ethiopian Christendom. They were organised into two broad orders, following the leadership of two saintly monks – Éwost'atéwos and Täklä Haymanot – of the thirteenth and early fourteenth centuries. Episcopal authority could do little to contain the orders, unless backed by the power of the state, which was comparatively weak. For virtually a millennium, following the seventh-century eclipse of Aksum, Ethiopia's kings ruled from roving capitals, seeking to dominate by their seasonal presence an agrarian society and the regional lay and clerical rulers who depended on the surpluses produced by that society. For most of its history, the Ethiopian Church had but one metropolitan bishop, and he a Copt. Only rarely did he have the support of suffragan bishops. Thus, in ecclesiastical affairs the monasteries played a role analogous to that played by regional princes in the polity at large. And, at base, there were the parishes, staffed by priests and deacons who were at the same time farmers – parishes in which agriculture and the liturgical calendar dominated life.

A historical synopsis[5]

The foundations of the Ethiopian Orthodox Church were laid in the three centuries following the conversion of the court. The Bible and the liturgy were translated into Ge'ez, the common language of Aksum, a Semitic language related to the languages of South Arabia. Ethiopian tradition attributes the introduction of monasticism to 'the Nine Saints', Syrians in origin, whose arrival is usually dated to the late fifth century in the aftermath of the council of Chalcedon, from which they were dissidents.[6] They are said to have founded an array of monasteries, still active, across what is now northern Ethiopia. Tradition also attributes the origins of church music, the practice of liturgical dance and the composition of numerous hymns to St Yaréd, who flourished in the first half of the sixth century. In this period also lie the origins of the practice of pilgrimage to the Holy Places of Palestine and Egypt. The period was brought to an end by the rise of Islam.

Not until the thirteenth century did the Christian kingdom re-emerge to the full light of history, with the seizure of the throne in 1270 by a dynasty claiming both the legitimate mantle of the Aksumite rulers and descent from the biblical King Solomon and the Queen of Sheba. The Zagwé, whom the Solomonics displaced, had made an enduring mark on Ethiopian Christianity through the creation of a remarkable set of eleven rock-hewn churches at a site later named after the dynasty's most distinguished member, Lalibäla. Solomonic renewal in the state was preceded by renewal in the church, which expressed itself in a vigorous monastic movement. Evangelising by monks led to one of the most notable periods in the expansion of the Ethiopian Church, into the heart of the central plateau, and beyond the Blue Nile to the south, staking out for the church the provinces of Bägémder and Gojjam, which it now views as its heartland.

For the first century of the new dynasty, conflict marked the relations between the royal court and the monks. However, charisma was slowly

---

5 A useful general account is to be found in S. Munro-Hay, 'Christianity. History of Christianity', in *Encyclopædia Æthiopica*, I, 717–23.

6 For a judicious statement of the standard interpretation, see Taddesse, *Church and state*, 23–5. More sceptical, pointing out that the hagiographies of the saints were all composed one thousand years after the period to which, ostensibly, they pertain, is Munro-Hay, 'Christianity'.

subverted by rich land grants and monastic energy was increasingly chan-
nelled into theological disputation rather than into political activity. Theological dispute reached a climax in the reign of King Zär'a Ya'qob (Seed of Jacob)
(r.1434–68), perhaps the most creative and authoritative voice in the history of
the Ethiopian Church. A council, presided over by the king himself, established
the Sabbath as a holy day equal in status to Sunday, made normative the veneration of the Virgin Mary, through an elaborate array of feast days supported
by religious tracts and painting,[7] and suppressed sectarian dissent and magical
practice. Zär'a Ya'qob led a movement of 'religious nationalism', that created
a model of church–state relations; this survived the turbulent century which
began during the reign of his great grandson, Lebnä Dengel (Incense of the
Virgin) (r.1508–40).[8]

Between 1527 and 1632 the Ethiopian church and state were battered by
invasion and civil war, which brought both to their extremity: 1527 saw the
launching of a great jihad led by Aḥmad ibn Ibrahim, popularly known as 'Grañ'
(the left handed). The development of a Christian state in the central highlands of Ethiopia had been paralleled by that of a chain of Muslim sultanates
reaching from the coast via the eastern highlands and the Great Rift Valley into
the highlands adjoining the Christian state. Relations were uneasy, balancing
mutual profit from trade with the quest for dominance. From the earlier fourteenth through to the earlier sixteenth century, the Christians held the upper
hand, thanks to their strategic position and greater cohesion. However, all this
was overthrown by Aḥmad's forces, which overran the Christian highlands,
destroyed and pillaged churches and monasteries, and made the Ethiopian
rulers refugees within their own kingdom. Aḥmad proclaimed a sultanate of
Habasha, and both Muslim and Christian sources agree that large-scale defec-
tions from the Christian faith occurred.[9] In the short run the conflict came to
an end with Aḥmad's death in battle in 1543. However, the jihad proved to have
a more lasting impact on both Christian and Muslim polities. Through weakening the frontier defences of the Christian state and distracting the attention

7 For an excellent introduction to the religious art of Ethiopia, see M. Heldman, African Zion:
the sacred art of Ethiopia (New Haven: Yale University Press, 1993). See also S. Chojnacki,
Major themes in Ethiopian painting: indigenous developments, the influence of foreign models,
and their adaptation from the thirteenth to the nineteenth century [Äthiopistische Forschungen
10] (Wiesbaden: Franz Steiner Verlag, 1983).
8 The phrase is Taddesse's: Church and state, ch. 6: 'Zar'a Ya'iqob and the growth of religious
nationalism (1380–1477)'.
9 The jihadist viewpoint is forwarded by Chihab ed-Din Ahmed Ben 'Abd el-Qader, Histoire
de la conquête de l'Abyssinie (XVIe siècle) (Paris: Ernest Leroux, 1897); for a Christian account,
see W. Conzelman (ed. and trans.), Chronique de Galâwdêwos (Claudius) roi d'Éthiopie (Paris:
É. Bouillon, 1895).

of both Muslim and Christian power away from the frontiers, it opened the way for the remarkable expansion of the Oromo people, speakers of a Kushitic language, and, at this stage, adherents of neither Christianity nor Islam.[10]

The migration of the Oromo reversed the two and a half centuries of southward expansion of Christian power and culture, hammered the Christian kingdom, making recurrent inroads which, in several key areas, turned into settlement, creating insecurity and draining resources, and forced the withdrawal of the kingdom northwestward into the great bend of the Blue Nile and the regions around Lake Tana, to its north. By the end of the sixteenth century many of the splendid churches built by the Solomonics had disappeared and significant areas, previously inhabited by Christians, now passed into the hands of the newcomers.[11] It was in these circumstances that two of Ethiopia's rulers at the beginning of the seventeenth century turned to the Catholic faith, represented by Jesuit missionaries behind whom stood the power of Portugal and Spain. A Portuguese expeditionary force had played a key role in the death of Aḥmad Grañ and its survivors settled in Ethiopia, marrying Ethiopian women. Their presence was a constant reminder of the efficacy of European arms.

The Jesuits had first arrived in Ethiopia in 1557 on the misunderstanding that the Ethiopian rulers were prepared to submit to Catholic belief and practice.[12] Quickly disabused they retreated to northern Ethiopia, where the mission atrophied. A Jesuit priest was sent out in 1603 to revive it, but found himself called to court by King ZäDengel (The Virgin's) (1603–4), who explored Jesuit teaching sympathetically. ZäDengel was soon to be succeeded by King Susenyos, who, in 1607, fought his way to the throne and quickly turned to the Jesuits. In 1622 he made an open, formal submission to Rome, establishing Catholicism as the religion of court and country. But Catholicism served this Solomonic ruler no better than Orthodoxy had in transforming his relations with the powerful forces which dominated in the provinces – the monasteries and the noble lineages. Rebellion mounted, and in 1632 Susenyos abdicated in favour of his son, Fasilädäs, who directly restored *Täwahedo* Orthodoxy, expelled the Jesuits, and cut ties to Portugal and Spain.

---

10 For a general account of the sixteenth and seventeenth centuries see Mordecai Abir, *Ethiopia and the Red Sea: the rise and decline of the Solomonic dynasty and Muslim–European rivalry in the region* (London: Cass, 1980).

11 See Mohammed Hassen, *The Oromo of Ethiopia: a history, 1570–1860* (Cambridge: Cambridge University Press, 1990).

12 For a nuanced and informative account of the Jesuit mission, see H. Pennec, *Des Jésuites au Royaume du Prêtre Jean (Éthiopie): stratégies, rencontres et tentatives d'implantation 1495–1633* (Paris: Fundação Calouste Gulbenkian, 2003).

Fasilädäs inherited the throne of an exhausted, dispirited country with no option other than a return to the Orthodoxy of Zär'a Ya'qob. He benefited from his reaffirmation of the value of tradition in church and polity and his rule ushered in three generations of comparative peace and cultural revival. At Gondär he established the first fixed capital since Aksum and built churches and palaces. His son Yohännes I (r.1667–82), and grandson Iyasu I, the Great (r.1682–1706), followed his example, presiding over a state from which the threat of external forces had receded. However, the rise of Jesuit influence early in the century had sparked vigorous and diverse responses from the Ethiopian Church, bringing Christology back to the centre of disputation among the Orthodox, responses which slowly hardened into sectarianism associated with the two rival monastic orders. Both Yohännes and Iyasu presided over a succession of councils devoted to Christology, but, unlike Zär'a Ya'qob, they were unable to impose unity. Iyasu was assassinated and the fifteen years following his death were violent and uncertain. In the christological controversies the sources suggest that the principal party of innovation was the Éwost'atians, whose slogan was *Qebat*, or Unction, which emphasised the role of the unction of the Holy Spirit in effecting the union of the divine and the human in Christ. From their own standpoint they were deeply committed to an anti-Chalcedonian position, in harmony with the theological tradition of Alexandria.[13] *Qebat* teaching was resisted by the followers of Täklä Haymanot, who themselves advocated a position which claimed that Jesus had become Son of God through the Grace (*Säga*) of the Holy Spirit. He is, they said, the Son of Grace, *YäŞäga Lej*. A third party, much the smallest, associated with the bishops of the nineteenth century, was known as *Karra* or Knife.

Qebat forces were probably behind the assassination of Iyasu I, and in the reign of his brother Téwoflos (r.1708–11) *Qebat* became established doctrine. It was to hold this position for almost sixty years. Establishment came at a price, however. In the reign of Iyasu's son Dawit (r.1716–21), perhaps one hundred monks of the order of Täklä Haymanot were slaughtered by palace troops. This was an early climax and the same level of violence was not again reached until the nineteenth century, and possibly not even then. Nevertheless, sectarian positions hardened, and within each sect new positions were

13 Getatchew Haile, 'Materials on the theology of Qebat or unction', in *Ethiopian studies: Proceedings of the Sixth International Conference, Tel-Aviv, 14–17 April 1980*, ed. G. Goldenberg (Rotterdam: A. A. Balkema, 1986), 205–50. See also Getatchew Haile, *The faith of the Unctionists in the Ethiopian Church (Haymanot Mäsihawit)* [CSCO, Scriptores Æthiopici 91] (Louvain: Peeters, 1990); Kindeneh Endeg Mihretie, 'The role of *Qebatoč* in the Christological controversy within the Ethiopian Orthodox Church (1620–1764)', unpublished MA thesis, Addis Ababa University, 2004.

forwarded. Sectarianism did not dampen other expressions of Orthodox religion. The great church foundations of Gondär, notably the churches of Däbrä Berhan Sellasé by Iyasu I in 1694 and of Däbrä Ṣähay Qʷesqʷam by Empress Mentewwab in the 1740s, set a standard, which was emulated throughout the country for almost 150 years.[14] Major churches continued to be founded in the town itself into the 1780s. Moreover, the Gondär period saw a recovery of the legacy so badly battered by the storms of the sixteenth and early seventeenth centuries. Manuscripts were copied. New manuscripts were written. And painting thrived, adorning manuscripts and church buildings alike.[15] The great foundations each supported several hundred clergy, who, in turn, made Gondär a centre of church education, a role it has played down to the present.

The Ethiopian state and church entered the nineteenth century in a state of disarray. At the end of the 1760s powerful regionally based nobles succeeded in toppling the throne and instituting a succession of puppet rulers, gaining effective power for themselves and their lineages. Ethiopia's clerical chroniclers likened the period to the biblical period preceding the foundation of the Jewish kingdom and dubbed it the *Zämänä Mäsafent*, 'Era of the Judges'. The fate of the church was most poignantly seen in the careers of the bishops, who attempted to lead the church, during the first half of the nineteenth century. They were abused, chased from Gondär and forced into internal exile, their doctrinal authority rejected. At this stage their particular enemies were the monks of Däbrä Libanos and the *Ṣäga* doctrine, which they professed. Ethiopia had experienced previous periods of weak central institutions, but by the 1830s there were clear signs that the outside world was unlikely to leave the country alone. Egypt was reviving and expanding, and in the 1830s its armies reached the borderlands which separated Ethiopian authority from the authority of states based in the upper Nile Valley. At the same time Europeans – missionaries, both Protestant and Catholic, and lay travellers – became a constant presence in the highlands, reviving memories both of the Jesuit conflicts and of the potential that Europe offered for military support.[16] Revival of the Ethiopian

---

14 For an account of the founding of Ethiopian churches in general and of Däbrä Berhan Sellasé and Däbrä Ṣähay Qʷesqʷam, in particular, see D. Crummey, *Land and society in the Christian Kingdom of Ethiopia: from the thirteenth to the twentieth century* (Urbana: University of Illinois Press, 2000). For an excellent account of a seventeenth-century foundation, see Anaïs Wion, '"Aux confins le feu, au centre le paradis": Qoma Fasilädäs, un monastère royal dans l'Éthiopie du 17ème siècle', unpublished PhD dissertation, 2 vols., Université de Paris – Panthéon Sorbonne, 2003.

15 Gondärine art is richly represented in Heldman, *African Zion*.

16 In general see, Mordechai Abir, *Ethiopia: the era of the princes. The challenge of Islam and the unification of the Christian Kingdom 1769–1855* (London: Longmans Green, 1968); D. Crummey, *Priests and politicians: Protestant and Catholic missionaries in Orthodox Ethiopia*,

state was an imperative, and the three rulers who effected that revival each saw the revival of a united church as an essential element in the revival of the state.

Political revival began in 1855 with the accession to the Solomonic throne of Kassa Haylu, who took the throne name of Téwodros II. He ruled until 1868. He fought his way to power, and in transforming himself from warrior to statesman he revived the authority of the bishops and tried to restore doctrinal unity to the church. The council of Amba Čara, in 1854, established the bishop *Abunä* Sälama as the arbiter of Alexandrian orthodoxy, and pronounced anathema on sectarianism. In 1855, Sälama crowned Téwodros as King of Kings of Ethiopia. While bishop and king soon came into conflict – over issues of land and authority – the king maintained a formal propriety in their relations and never resorted to sectarianism to undermine the bishop's authority.[17] Téwodros's eventual successor was Yoḥännes IV (1872–89), who by proclaiming himself 'King of Zion' laid claim to the legacy of Aksum, as shown by his choice of the church of St Mary of Zion in Aksum as his coronation church. Like Téwodros, he sought ecclesiastical revival and unification. To this end he pursued a policy of suppressing the *Qebat* and *Ṣäga* sectarians. At the council of Boru Méda in 1878, where he basked in the submission of Menilek, the last of the major provincial rulers to hold out, he proclaimed the faith of the church to be the *Karra* doctrine of Qérelos, Sälama and Atnatéwos, and vigorously enforced it. As for episcopal authority, in 1881 Yoḥännes persuaded the Coptic patriarch to appoint an unprecedented four bishops.

Yoḥännes set the agenda which, under his successor Menilek II (1889–1913), carried the Ethiopian Orthodox Church into the twentieth century. Sectarianism was marginalised and the doctrinal position forwarded at the council of Boru Méda has remained normative to the present. Expansion of the episcopacy pointed, obliquely to be sure, towards a new national organisation for the church. Menilek lacked the zeal of Téwodros or Yoḥännes, but his adoption of their policies set a final seal upon them.

Church and state entered the twentieth century in a condition far different from that of a century before. The monarchical state was restored; doctrinal

1830–1868 (Oxford: Clarendon Press, 1972); and S. Rubenson, *The survival of Ethiopian independence* (London: Heinemann Educational Books, 1976).

17 D. Crummey, 'Doctrine and authority: Abunä Sälama, 1841–1854,' in *IV Congresso Internazionale di Studi Etiopici* (Rome: Accademia Nazionale dei Lincei, 1972), I, 567–78; Crummey, 'Orthodoxy and imperial reconstruction in Ethiopia, 1854–1878', *JThSt* 29 (1978), 427–42; and D. Crummey and Getatchew Haile, '*Abunä* Sälama: Metropolitan of Ethiopia, 1841–1867. A new Ge'ez biography', *Journal of Ethiopian Studies* 37 (2004), 191–209.

unity prevailed in the church. In 1896, Menilek defeated an invading Italian army at the Battle of Adwa, firmly establishing his country's independence. In the decades preceding Adwa, Menilek's armies had carried the authority of the state far and wide, and with it the presence of the Orthodox Church. The century was to see momentous transformations. An episcopal hierarchy was established and then indigenised and expanded. Expansion was territorial as well as institutional, the church establishing a presence in far-flung corners of the new Ethiopian Empire and overseas in Jamaica and in North America. The church entered into regular conversations with other churches of the Alexandrian–Syrian connection and became a member of the World Council of Churches. But its central role in the construction of the modern Ethiopian state brought burdens and limitations, as well as privileges. Menilek's eventual successor, Haile Sellassie I (1930–74), retained the vision of church, state and nation which animated his predecessors, but the country over which he ruled was far more diverse than that vision allowed. Territorial expansion in the later nineteenth century had brought within the fold of the state large numbers of Muslims and peoples adherent to neither Christianity nor Islam. Moreover, the modernisation espoused by Menilek and pursued by Haile Sellassie eventually overwhelmed the monarchy, and, with the deposition of Haile Sellassie in 1974, ushered in an era of revolution, disestablishment of the church and the creation of a secular state.[18]

Monks and monarchs: the Ethiopian nation

In many ways the definitive Ethiopian state and nation were formed in the two centuries following the establishment of the Solomonic dynasty in 1270. This process climaxed in the reign of Zär'a Ya'qob (1434–68), who reconciled local practice with Alexandrian authority. The dominant forces that we can most readily see at work were the monks and the royal court. Conflict marked their early relations.

---

18 The literature on the Ethiopian Revolution is voluminous. Two accounts of outstanding value are Andargachew Tiruneh, *The Ethiopian revolution, 1974–1987: a transformation from an aristocratic to a totalitarian autocracy* (Cambridge: Cambridge University Press, 1993); and C. Clapham, *Transformation and continuity in revolutionary Ethiopia* (Cambridge: Cambridge University Press, 1988). For the fate of the church, see Haile Mariam Larebo, 'The Ethiopian Church and politics in the twentieth century: part 2', *Northeast African Studies* 10 (1988), 1–23; Haile Mariam Larebo, 'The Orthodox Church and state in Ethiopian revolution', *Religion in Communist Lands* 14 (1986), 148–59; J. Persoon, 'Monks and cadres in the land of Prester John: an interdisciplinary study of modern Ethiopian monasticism and its encounter with communism', unpublished PhD dissertation, London University, 2003.

Monastic revival preceded the Solomonic rise.[19] A formative figure in this revival was Iyäsus Mo'a (Jesus has prevailed), who, around 1248, founded the monastery of St Stephen on an island in Lake Häyq.[20] Iyäsus Mo'a had started his career at Däbrä Damo, one of the ancient monasteries of northern Ethiopia. Early traditions ascribe to him a pact with Yekunno Amlak, founder of the new dynasty, for whom his support seems, indeed, to have been important. From the community of Iyäsus Mo'a monks dispersed across the landscape of Amhara and the province of Shäwa, to its south, founding their own monasteries. The most famous of his disciples was Täklä Haymanot (Plant of Faith), who founded the monastery of Däbrä Asbo (later known as Däbrä Libanos) around 1284, and who came, in the memory of later generations, to overshadow his master.[21]

Thirteenth-century monasticism in central Ethiopia saw itself continuing a monastic tradition which reached back to Aksum. It was informal, charismatic and committed to poverty. Individual holy men settled in wild, unsettled areas, attracting followers and creating communities through the rigour of their practice. They survived by gathering wild fruits and hiring out their labour to nearby farm villages at harvest time.[22] From this position of independence some found themselves increasingly drawn to political involvement. Most prominent was Bäṣälotä Mika'él (By the Prayer of St Michael), a second-generation follower of Iyäsus Mo'a.[23] Meanwhile, the dynasty, having passed through a series of succession crises following the death of its founder, was now represented by the vigorous, expansionist Amdä Ṣeyon (Pillar of Zion) (1314–44), one of its greatest members.

In his first appearance at court Bäṣälotä Mika'él attacked the metropolitan of the church, Abunä Yoḥännes, for simony. For this he was exiled to Tegré.[24]

19 On medieval Ethiopian monasticism see Taddesse, Church and state. But see also S. Kaplan, The monastic holy man and the christianization of early Solomonic Ethiopia [Studien zur Kulturkunde 73] (Wiesbaden: Franz Steiner Verlag, 1984); M.-L. Derat, Le domaine des rois éthiopiens (1270–1527): espace, pouvoir et monachisme (Paris: Publications de la Sorbonne, 2003).

20 The two oldest extant Ethiopian manuscripts are copies of the four gospels from this monastery: Ethiopian Monastic Microfilm Library, St John's University, Collegeville, MN, MS. 1832, Gold Gospel, Häyq Estifanos; and Paulos Sadua, 'Un manoscritto etiopico degli Evangeli', Rassegna di Studi Etiopici 11 (1952), 9–28.

21 For a rich account of the careers of Iyäsus Mo'a and Täklä Haymanot, see Taddesse, Church and state, 158–73.

22 Ibid., 110, 172; Kaplan, Monastic holy man, 36–9, 54.

23 See S. Wolde Yohannes and D. Nosnitsin, 'Bäṣälotä Mika'él', in Encyclopædia Æthiopica, I, 493–4.

24 Taddesse's account rests heavily on the hagiographies, published and unpublished, of the principal monastic figures involved. The royal chronicles also reflect these events: R. Basset, Études sur l'histoire d'Éthiopie (Paris: Imprimerie nationale, 1882), 10–11 (text);

He shortly returned to court, where he attacked Amdä Seyon himself, for defying Christian sexual morality in having married more than one wife, in keeping concubines and in committing incest with one of the wives of his father.[25] New here were not the practices, which were deep-seated and were to persist for generations, but the fervour in attacking them. Bäṣälotä Mika'él was again exiled to northern Ethiopia, where he died. Around 1337 a new metropolitan, *Abunä* Ya'qob, reached Ethiopia and picked up the threads of Bäṣälotä Mika'él's mission. Relations between the metropolitans and the monasteries were often uneasy, mediated by the royal court, on which the metropolitans were dependent for imposition of their authority. Ya'qob allied himself with the monks and excommunicated the king, who then flogged and exiled Ya'qob's monastic allies. Tension carried over into the reign of Amdä Seyon's successor, Sayfä Rä'ad (1344–71), who imitated his father in marrying three wives. Continuing opposition from bishop and monks led to exile – the bishop back to Egypt and the monks beyond the frontiers of the kingdom. The kings prevailed in these clashes, but found the price of attack from the church to be high. The accession of Sayfä Rä'ad's son Dawit (1382–1411) brought a transition from confrontation to a new synthesis and integration in the fifteenth century.[26] This synthesis involved the absorption of the new monasticism into the mould of the old: in other words, the conversion of charisma into establishment, which was made possible through rich royal grants of land.[27]

While the monks of central Ethiopia consciously stood in the tradition of St Anthony and of the historic monasteries dating to Aksumite times, and honoured the discipline which they had inherited, they were also restlessly innovating, wary of their autonomy and prone to controversy over numerous points of doctrine, the Trinity included. Some of their beliefs and practices challenged a royal court increasingly concerned to impose a unity of belief and practice in the church.[28] In northern Ethiopia, a monk called Estifanos gathered a following with his preaching of austerity and his insistence that

---

99–100 (trans.); F. Béguinot, *La Cronaca Abbreviata d'Abissinia: nuovo versione dall'Etiopico* (Rome: Tipografia della casa edit. italiana, 1901), 7–10.

25 This follows the account in Crummey, *Land and society*, 25–6. Cf. Taddesse, *Church and state*, 98–118. For religious disputes within the Ethiopian Church at this time, see Getatchew Haile, 'Religious controversies and the growth of Ethiopic literature in the fourteenth and fifteenth centuries', *Oriens Christianus* 65 (1981), 102–36.

26 See Getatchew Haile, 'From strict observance to royal endowment: the case of the monastery of Däbrä Halle Luya, EMML 6343, fols. 177r–118v', *Le Muséon* 93 (1980), 163–4. Cf. Kaplan, *Monastic holy man*, 55.

27 See Crummey, *Land and society*, 17–49.

28 See Taddesse, *Church and state*, ch. 6.

reverence was due to God alone, not to the Blessed Virgin, nor to such physical representations as icons or crosses, nor to worldly figures such as the
king.[29] The Stephanites were readily suppressed, but more serious were the
followers of Éwosṭatéwos, who advocated observance of the Sabbath as a holy
day equally worthy as Sunday.[30] The followers of Täklä Haymanot and the
metropolitans both opposed the Éwosṭatian position on the Sabbath.

These conflicts were resolved at the council of Däbrä Meṭmaq in 1449,
over which King Zär'a Ya'qob (1434–68) presided.[31] He managed, at one and
the same time, to reimpose episcopal authority and to regularise belief and
practice according to Ethiopian, rather than Alexandrian, precedent. He had
obtained two bishops from Cairo, along with a suffragan, and persuaded them
to accept observation of the Sabbath.[32] This practice the council successfully
declared to be normative, along with adoration of the Blessed Virgin, whose
intercession, Zär'a Ya'qob proclaimed, effected salvation. He introduced a
host of monthly festivals whereby She would be honoured.[33] These actions
of the council proved lasting, and the common practices which it mandated
strengthened a 'religious nationalism' throughout Ethiopian Christendom. So
strong had this nationalism become, a rupture with Alexandria was openly
discussed at a council during the reign of Zär'a Ya'qob's successor. The king had
yet other concerns. He felt himself threatened by the practice of sorcery and
witchcraft within the royal court itself, and attempted, ruthlessly, to stamp
it out. Devout and learned as Zär'a Ya'qob was,[34] he followed the marital
practices of his predecessors. He had three official wives whose individual

29 See Taddesse Tamrat, 'Some notes on the fifteenth century Stephanite 'Heresy' in the
Ethiopian Church', *Rassegna di Studi Etiopici* 22 (1966), 103–15; and Getatchew Haile, 'The
cause of the Ǝst'ifanosites: a fundamentalist sect in the Church of Ethiopia', *Paideuma:
Mitteilungen zur Kulturkunde* 29 (1983), 93–119.

30 See G. Lusini, *Studi sul monachesimo eustaziano (secoli XIV–XV)* (Naples: Istituto universitario orientale, 1993).

31 For the date, I follow Derat, *Domaine des rois éthiopiens*, 170. Taddesse, *Church and state*,
230, gives 1450. In addition to the numerous writings of the king, an important primary
source is J. Perruchon, *Les Chroniques de Zar'a Yâ'qôb et de Ba'eda Mâryâm, rois d'Éthiopie
dès 1434 à 1478* (Paris: Émile Bouillon, 1893).

32 See Getatchew Haile, 'The Homily of As'e Zär'a Ya'eqob of Ethiopia in honour of
Saturday', *Orientalia Lovaniensia Periodica* 13 (1982), 185–231.

33 Getatchew Haile, 'Ethiopian Orthodox Täwahédo Church', in *Encyclopædia Æthiopica*, II,
414–21; and Getatchew Haile, *The Mariology of Emperor Zär'a Ya'eqob of Ethiopia* [Orientalia
christiana analecta 242] (Rome: Pontificium institutum studiorum orientalium,
1992).

34 He was a prolific author. See C. Conti Rossini and L. Ricci (ed. and trans.), *Il Libro della
Luce del Negus Zar'a Ya'qob (Mashafa Berhan)* [CSCO, Scriptores Æthiopici 47 (text), 48
(trans.); 51 (text), 52 (trans.)] (Louvain: Secrétariat du Corpus scriptorum christianorum
orientalium, 1964–1965); Getatchew Haile (ed. and trans.), *The Epistle of Humanity of
Emperor Zär'a Ya'eqob (Tomarä Tǝsbǝ't)* [CSCO, Scriptores Æthiopici 95 (text), 96 (trans.)]
(Louvain: Peeters, 1991).

courts featured prominently in the organisation of the royal camp. Finally, the king's rule was tyrannical and produced a strong reaction, especially in the years following his death, while the consensus on doctrine and the synthesis of episcopal authority and monasticism which he effected proved ephemeral, haunting future generations as an ideal too often beyond grasp. It was to be almost 400 years before Ethiopian rulers again achieved this integration.

The royal church

One institution of church and state, possibly born and certainly developed under the medieval Solomonics, which survived the upheavals and destructive violence of the years from 1527 to 1632 was the royal church.[35] To be sure, many of these churches were destroyed during the *jihad* of Aḥmad Grañ and others were lost to the Christian kingdom during the Oromo wars of the latter half of the sixteenth century. Nevertheless, the institution provides a bridge from the medieval to the Gondär period and beyond and played a role in the revival of the Solomonic monarchy in the later nineteenth century. It caught the attention of the Portuguese priest Francisco Alvares, who visited Ethiopia in the 1520s, and whose account has remained invaluable for its detailed insights into the Solomonic kingdom on the eve of the cataclysmic *jihad*.[36] Alvares believed that this institution was peculiarly characteristic of the (then) districts of Amhara and Shäwa, where the Solomonics were based. It emerges from the broader historical record in the course of the sixteenth century, during the reigns of Zär'a Ya'qob and his son Bä'edä Maryam (By the Hand of Mary) (1468–78). Bä'edä Maryam's foundation of Atronsä Maryam was famous for its wealth and for harbouring the remains of numerous earlier metropolitans and of three of the king's predecessors, most notably the dynasty's founder, Yekunno Amlak.[37]

---

35 See M.-L. Derat and H. Pennec, 'Les églises et monastères royaux d'Éthiopie (XVe–XVIe et XVIIe siècles): permanences et ruptures d'une stratégie royal', in *Ethiopia in broader perspective: Papers of the XIIIth International Conference of Ethiopian Studies*, ed. Katsuyoshi Fukui, Eisei Kurimoto and Masayoshi Shigeta (Kyoto: Shokado Book Sellers, 1997), I, 17–34; Derat, *Le domaine des rois éthiopiens*, ch. 6 and 7; and Crummey, *Land and society*, 29–35 and as indexed.

36 C. F. Beckingham and G. W. B. Huntingford, *The Prester John of the Indies*, 2 vols. (London: Cambridge University Press for the Hakluyt Society, 1961).

37 Getatchew Haile, 'A history of the *Tabot* of Atronəsä Maryam in Amhara (Ethiopia)', *Paideuma: Mitteilungen zur Kulturkunde* 34 (1988), 13–22. The church's wealth impressed both Alvares, for whom see Beckingham and Huntingford, *Prester John*, II, 332–3; and the chronicler of the jihadist Aḥmad Grañ, for whom see Chihab ed-Din, *Histoire de la conquête*, 311–13. See also, M.-L. Derat, 'Atronsä Maryam', in *Encyclopædia Æthiopica*, I, 394–5.

One function of the royal church was to serve as a dynastic burial site, and later kings would be buried in churches of their own foundation. But the royal church also served other functions. Founded by kings, not monks, these churches were beholden to the former, from whose favour they derived their wealth and from association with whom they derived their prestige. Reciprocally, in their magnificence they manifested monarchy to regional and local populations. Alvares saw them as quite distinct from monasteries, which characterised the landscape of northern Ethiopia, but, despite their similarities to the great 'collegiate' churches of medieval Europe, they retained their links to the monastic orders, and typically had the status of *gädam*, or sanctuary, a word often taken as synonymous with 'monastery'.[38] So they straddled the European divide between 'secular' as opposed to 'monastic' churches. Characteristic features were: the conceptualisation of their clergy as *däbtära*, a term which Alvares renders as 'canon';[39] royal initiative in their founding; richness of continuing royal patronage; and the church as royal tomb and shrine. The royal churches were supported primarily by grants of land, some lands providing revenues derived from tribute and rent, for support of the Mass and maintenance of the church fabric, other lands providing direct support for the clergy with which the churches were staffed. Some churches also enjoyed the right to tax local markets and benefited from the fees, which derived from their judicial rights over the lands under their control.

The royal churches also played useful roles within the diffuse structure of ecclesiastical organisation, which, in many respects, was minimal. The principal monastic orders had national visibility, but were held together by informal fraternal ties, rather than by any tighter governance. The metropolitan bishops had hierarchical prestige, but the hierarchy was extremely flat and prestige was

---

38 Beckingham and Huntingford, *Prester John*, I, 256. For the meaning of *gädam*, see *Käsaté Berhan* Täsamma, *Yä'Amareñña Mäzgäbä Qalät* (Addis Ababa: Artistic Printing Press, 1951 Eth. Cal.), 1192; I. Guidi, *Vocabolario Amarico-Italiano* (Rome: Istituto per l'Oriente, 1953; reprint of the edition of 1901), cc. 776–7; J. Baeteman, *Dictionnaire Amarigna–Français suivi d'un vocabulaire Français–Amarigna* (Dire Dawa: Imprimerie St Lazare, 1929), cc. 1009–10. For an example of a foundation in which the establishment of sanctuary is central, see D. Crummey, 'Theology and political conflict during the *Zämänä Mäsafent*: the cast of Esté in Bägémder', in *Proceedings of the Ninth International Congress of Ethiopian Studies, Moscow, 26–29 August 1986*, ed. A. Gromyko *et al.* (Moscow: Nauka, 1988), v, 201–11.

39 *Däbtära*, originally 'tabernacle' or 'tent': A. Dillmann, *Lexicon Linguae Æthiopicae cum Indice Latino* (Osnabrück: Biblio Verlag, 1970; reprint of the original edition of 1865), c. 1106. By derivation the term was originally applied to the clergy who served in the churches of the royal camp; by further derivation it acquired the meaning of 'cantor': Guidi, *Vocabolario*, cc. 671–2; Baeteman, *Dictionnaire*, 908; Täsamma, *Mäzgäbä Qalät*, 1098. Increasingly it also referred to specialists in various branches of church learning.

hard to translate into real power. Church property came under the control of local institutions, which in turn were the basis of local autonomy. The bishops had no substantive role in the process of royal land granting, although they often supported the grants with their formal sanction. The royal court provided such national organisation as the church possessed, but in cooperation with the bishops and prestigious monastic leaders – first the *Aqabé Sä'at*, prior of Häyq Estifanos, and later the *Ecägé*, or prior of Däbrä Libanos. This recognised, *de facto*, the power and autonomy of the monasteries, but did little to curb them. In this situation the royal church functioned as an alternative local node of authority and influence, one directly dependent on royal patronage, at least in origin.

The rulers, from Yeshaq (1413–30) onwards, were prolific founders of churches.[40] Yeshaq founded churches and endowed existing monasteries in the Lake Tana region. Zär'a Ya'qob founded numerous churches: Däbrä Näg^{w}ädg^{w}äd and Mäkanä Sellasé in Amhara; Däbrä Metmaq and Däbrä Berhan Sellasé in Shäwa. All these churches were magnificent, but Däbrä Berhan Sellasé may have been the most important to the king. This seems to have been how later generations saw the situation for, over 200 years later, his descendant, Iyasu I (1682–1706), revived the name for his own most favoured church.[41] Zär'a Ya'qob also endowed existing monasteries, and is probably responsible for the ascendancy which the monastery of Däbrä Libanos of Shäwa and its monastic followers of Täklä Haymanot were to enjoy down into the twentieth century. Bä'edä Maryam's son Na'od (1495–1508) founded Mäkanä Sälam and was buried there. For Alvares, Mäkanä Sälam was the paradigmatic royal church. Immediately following his departure from Ethiopia in 1526 the great *jihad* of Ahmad ibn Ibrahim Grañ broke out. It brought the plundering and destruction of the royal churches, Mäkanä Sellasé, Däbrä Näg^{w}ädg^{w}äd and Atronsä Maryam prominent among them. Yet the conqueror of Grañ, Gälawdéwos (1540–59), and his principal successor, Särsä Dengel (Sprout of the Virgin) (1593–97), both revived the tradition and founded churches whose splendour still resonates.[42]

40 See Crummey, *Land and society*, 30; R. E. Cheesman, *Lake Tana and the Blue Nile: an Abyssinian quest* (London: Macmillan, 1936), 168–71.
41 F. A. Dombrowski, *Tanasee 106: eine Chronik der Herrscher Äthiopiens* (Wiesbaden: Franz Steiner Verlag, 1983), I, 36 (text); II, 155 (trans.); Perruchon, *Chroniques*, 52–7, 67–8, 70–3, 86–7, 91–2 and 101; G. W. B. Huntingford, *The land charters of northern Ethiopia* (Addis Ababa: Institute of Ethiopian Studies and Faculty of Law, Haile Sellassie I University, 1965), 36–8, docs. 17, 18, 19 and 20. See Crummey, *Land and society*, 30–1, 88–9.
42 See Crummey, *Land and society*, 38–41, 55, 59 (table 4).

The royal church was a cornerstone of the Gondär kingdom, founded in the 1630s in reaction to Ethiopia's brief engagement with Roman Catholicism. A major act in Fasilädäs's founding of Gondär was the establishment and endowment of the church of Mädhané Aläm (Saviour of the World). In founding a new capital, he did not ignore an earlier capital and its major church. In Aksum he had the church of St Mary of Zion rebuilt and freshly endowed with land.[43] All of Fasilädäs's successors, for 150 years, without exception founded churches, in which many of them were buried. His grandson Iyasu was equally generous to Aksum.[44] His son and successor, Yohännes I, founded the church of Egziabhér Ab (God the Father), in which he was initially buried.[45] He refounded a church dedicated to St Mary at Azäzo, just outside the town. Azäzo Maryam was originally a Jesuit establishment, but Yohännes refounded it as the motherhouse of the monastic order of Täklä Haymanot, whose original motherhouse, Däbrä Libanos of Shäwa, had not survived the *jihad* and Oromo migrations.

Most notable among the Gondär establishments were Däbrä Berhan Sellasé and Däbrä Şähäy Q^{w}esq^{w}am.[46] All these churches were richly endowed with agricultural lands dedicated, as we have seen, to the support of the Mass as well as to maintenance of the fabric of the church, and for 'embers'. Rulers also gave lands for commemoration services and for direct support of the clergy. Clergy held their lands on an individual basis in return for service, and passed these lands to their descendants, always on condition that service was paid. These were sizeable establishments, Däbrä Berhan Sellasé being officially founded with 160 *däbtära*, while Däbrä Şähäy Q^{w}esq^{w}am was endowed with 260 *däbtära*. Däbrä Berhan Sellasé and Däbrä Şähäy Q^{w}esq^{w}am became models of the royal church, their precedent evoked by later foundations in Tegré, to the north, and in Gojjam, to the south. Although the Gondär kingdom collapsed in the

---

43 For the foundation document of Mädhané Aläm, see the manuscript of the *Gäbrä Hemamat* still held at the church, also available on microfilm at the Center for African Studies, University of Illinois, and the Institute of Ethiopian Studies, Addis Ababa University, reference number Illinois/IES, 84.I.7–8. For the Aksum church, see Stuart Munro-Hay, 'Aksum S'əyon', in *Encyclopædia Æthiopica*, I, 183–5; C. Conti Rossini, *Documenta ad Illustrandam Historiam*, I, *Liber Axumae* [CSCO 27] (Paris: E typographeo reipublicae, 1909), 76–7 (text); 92–9 (trans.).

44 Huntingford, *Land charters*, 61–2 (doc. 63). See also ibid. (doc. 64). This is primarily a collection of documents translated from Conti Rossini's *Liber Axumae*. The document numbers are the same in both works.

45 See Crummey, *Land and society*, 82–3.

46 See I. Guidi, *Annales Iohannis I, Iyyasu I, et Bakaffa* [CSCO, Scriptores Æthiopici ser. altera] (Paris: E typographeo reipublicae, 1903), v, 176–7; vi, 88–105/95–114. Cf. Crummey, *Land and society*, 88–9, 107–8. Mentewwab also munificently founded Narga Sellasé on one of the islands in Lake Ţana: M. Di Salvo, S. Chojnacki and O. Raineri, *Churches of Ethiopia: the monastery of Narga Sellase* (Milan and New York: Skira and Abbeville Pub. Group, 1999).

1770s, later generations saw the royal church as one of its essential legacies. The 'judges', who succeeded the Gondär kings, each found the establishment of a church an important act of legitimation for his reign.[47] So, too, did the rulers who aspired to resurrect the monarchy in the later nineteenth century, with one significant exception: Téwodros, who, from the 1850s onwards, did so much to set the model of restoration.

We have already noted how Téwodros restored the authority of the bishops and insisted on doctrinal unity and the suppression of sectarianism. However, he resented the landed wealth of the Gondär churches, and, for him, the *däbtära* associated with them epitomised the decadence into which the kingdom had fallen. During the second year of his reign, he and the Gondär clergy came into confrontation to which both authority and the control of land were central.[48] Ironically, this confrontation brought about a rapprochement between the clergy and the bishop, which reinforced the king's institutional reforms, while his detestation of Gondär and its clerical establishment intensified with each passing year. Téwodros founded no churches of consequence, and, towards the end of his reign, launched a root and branch assault against the Gondär churches. He plundered and burned the city and its churches in 1864 and in 1866, adding to the royal treasury 'everything of value' from the churches, 'bells, chalices, crosses of gold and silver, and almost one thousand manuscripts'.[49]

His successors, Täklä Giyorgis II (1868–71) and Yohännes IV, were as ostentatious in their restoration of the Gondär churches as Téwodros had been in their destruction. Yohännes proved attentive to an array of historical churches, first among them being Aksum Ṣeyon, where he was crowned. Following the precedents of Zär'a Ya'qob and Iyasu I, he founded the church of Däbrä Berhan Sellasé in Adwa, and under his tutelage one of his principal vassals, King Täklä Haymanot of Gojjam, made numerous foundations throughout the lands under his control.[50]

In 1889, following the death in battle of Yohännes, the throne passed to Menilek of Shäwa, a province associated with the earliest years of the Solomonic dynasty, but one which had been cut off from the rest of Christian

---

47 Examples of such establishments, each of which evoked one or more Gondär models, are: the churches of *Qeddus* Mika'él, Adwa; Däräsgé Maryam; Qäranyo Mädhané Aläm; and Mot'a Giyorgis; for which see Crummey, *Land and society*, 108, 111, 154, 157.

48 Ibid., 204–5.

49 S. Rubenson, *King of Kings: Tewodros of Ethiopia* (Addis Ababa: Haile Sellassie I University, 1966), 71–2. The bulk of these manuscripts, following a British military expedition to Ethiopia in 1868, ended up in the British Museum and are now in the British Library.

50 Crummey, *Land and society*, 205–7, 210–14. Also Habtamu Mengistie, 'Lord, Zéga and peasant in rural eastern Gojjam', unpublished MA thesis, Addis Ababa University, 2003.

Ethiopia by the Oromo migrations of the sixteenth and seventeenth centuries.[51] Following a pattern set by previous rulers of the province, Menilek moved southward, and, in 1874, settled at Enṭoṭṭo, on the hills above what is today Addis Ababa, founding a church dedicated to St Mary. It was here that he was crowned.[52] In 1886 he moved downhill to create Ethiopia's modern capital city, where he founded in the early 1890s two churches, one dedicated to the Trinity and one to St George. It was in the latter that two of his successors, Zäwditu (1916–30) and Haile Sellassie (Power of the Trinity) (1930–74), were to be crowned. The church of St George was, in Haile Sellassie's phrase, 'the royal church'.[53] Perhaps the final incarnation of the royal church was the Trinity Church, Addis Ababa.[54] Its rebuilding was one of the foundational acts of Haile Sellassie as emperor. He started the process in 1931, just after ascending the throne and assuming his regnal name, and completed it shortly after his restoration to power in 1941, following the Italian occupation which had begun with the invasion of 1935. It was here that, eventually, he was to be buried.

Christology and conflict[55]

Founding churches and granting land to existing foundations was one of the devices that Yoḥännes IV used in his attempt to unify the church after two and a half centuries of doctrinal, sectarian strife. Christological controversies internal to the Ethiopian Orthodox Church broke out at a council held in 1620, during the reign of Susenyos, and clearly had their origins in the ethos created by the Jesuits, who attacked the Ethiopian christological position as heretical.[56]

51 H. Marcus, *The life and times of Menelik II: Ethiopia 1844–1913* (Oxford: Clarendon Press, 1975).

52 See Haile Gabriel Dagne, 'The establishment of churches in Addis Ababa', in *Proceedings of the International Symposium on the Centenary of Addis Ababa, November 24–25, 1986*, ed. Taddese Beyene (Addis Ababa: Institute of Ethiopian Studies, Addis Ababa University, 1987), 57–78.

53 *The autobiography of Emperor Haile Sellassie I. 'My life and Ethiopia's progress' 1892–1937*, ed. and trans. Edward Ullendorff (London: Oxford University Press, 1976), 175.

54 Haile Gabriel, 'Churches of Addis Ababa', 62–3.

55 See U. Zanetti, 'Christianity in the Ethiopian society', in *Encyclopædia Æthiopica*, I, 723–8; J. L. Bandrés and U. Zanetti, 'Christology', in ibid., I, 728–32.

56 See A. Martínez, 'Paul and the other: the Portuguese debate on the circumcision of the Ethiopians', in *Ethiopia and the missions: historical and anthropological insights*, ed. V. Böll et al. [Afrikanische Studien 25] (Münster: LIT Verlag, 2005). On the origins of the controversy, see Kindeneh, 'The role of Qebatoč', 50–1; Merid W. Aregay, 'The legacy of Jesuit missionary activities in Ethiopia', in *The missionary factor in Ethiopia*, ed. Getatchew Haile, A. Lande and S. Rubenson (Frankfurt am Main: Peter Lang, 1998),

Jesuit missionaries arrived in Ethiopia in 1557, as part of larger movements which had brought both the Ottoman Turks and the Portuguese into the north-west Indian Ocean and the Red Sea. The Jesuit mission rested on a fundamental misconception that the Ethiopian court was prepared to embrace Catholic belief and practice.[57] The Jesuit mission comprised six members led by Bishop Andre de Oviedo. Its claims to the allegiance of Ethiopia's ruler were quickly disabused by Emperor Gälawdéwos, but out of his dialogue with the missionaries came a seminal statement of Ethiopian belief, the so-called *Confessio Claudii*.[58] The emperor eventually banished the Jesuits, who took up residence in the northern province of Tegré at a place called Fremona, not far from the modern Adwa. There they were a dwindling presence until the last Jesuit died in the 1590s.

Their mission was renewed with the arrival in Ethiopia in 1603 of Fr Pero Paes, who found an Ethiopia deeply shaken not only by decades of war against the Oromo but also by a prolonged succession struggle, which had broken out in 1597 on the death of Emperor Särṣä Dengel. One of the contenders, ZäDengel (1603–4), brought Paes to court and tentatively committed himself to the Catholic faith, thereby setting a precedent which influenced his immediate successor, Ya'qob (1604–7), and, more importantly, the eventual victor, Susenyos (1607–32).[59] In 1617 the latter's interest in, and commitment to, Catholicism provoked a major rebellion, which led with the active support of the Orthodox bishop *Abunä* Semon raised the banner of Orthodoxy. Susenyos crushed the rebellion and the bishop lost his life. Four years later the court led by Susenyos formally committed itself to Catholicism, an undertaking maintained in the face of mounting rebellion until 1632, when the intensity

31–56. A primary text is I. Guidi, 'Uno squarcio di storia ecclesiastica di Abissinia', *Bessarione* 8 (1900), 10–25. Texts, expressive of some of the views circulating in the early seventeenth century, are to be found in E. Cerulli, *Scritti teologici etiopici dei secoli XVI–XVII*, I, *Tre opuscoli dei Mikaeliti* (Vatican: Biblioteca apostolica vaticana, 1958).

57 Important sources are *Chronique de Galâwdêwos (Claudius) roi d'Éthiopie*, ed. W. E. Conzelman (Paris: É. Bouillon, 1895); *The Portuguese Expedition to Abyssinia in 1541–1543, as narrated by Castanhoso, with some contemporary letters, the short account of Bermudez and certain extracts from Correa*, ed. R. S. Whiteway (London: Hakluyt Society, 1902).

58 See L. Lozza, 'La confessione di Claudio re d'Etiopia', *Rassegna di Studi Etiopici* 5 (1946), 67–78.

59 Major sources for this period are *Chronica de Susenyos, rei de Ethiopia*, ed. F. M. Esteves Pereira (Lisbon: Imprensa Nacional, 1891–1900), 2 vols.; *Rerum Æthiopicarum scriptores occidentales inediti a sæculo XVI ad XIX* (Rome: C. de Luigi, 1903–1917), 15 vols. Still useful are Balthazar Tellez, *The travels of the Jesuits in Ethiopia* . . . (London: J. Knapton et al., 1710); Job Ludolf, *New history of Ethiopia* (London: Samuel Smith, 1682). See now Pennec, *Des Jésuites au royaume du Prêtre Jean*.

of resistance forced him to abdicate.[60] The 1610s must have been a decade of intense Jesuit preaching, which attacked Ethiopian orthodoxy on a very broad front and called into question virtually all points where the Ethiopian tradition deviated from Tridentine norms. Not least of these was the Ethiopian rejection of the council of Chalcedon, whose claims the Jesuits forcefully promoted at the council sponsored by Susenyos in 1620.

The first sect to emerge from these controversies was located among the monastic followers of Ewosṭatéwos and advocated the doctrine of *Qebat* or Unction. Subsequently, their rivals, the monastic followers of Täklä Haymanot, gave rise to the teaching of *YäṢäga Lej*, Son of Grace. Given their origins in the confrontation with the Chalcedonian Jesuits, it is not surprising that subsequent interpretation has read these sects in the light of their apparent proximity to a Chalcedonian position.[61] This is undoubtedly Eurocentric. The contending parties thought of themselves as defenders of the Alexandrian tradition against western teaching and they should be approached, in the first instance, on these terms.[62]

Nevertheless, as we have seen, doctrinal disagreements were divisive and rivalry was acrimonious, and at times violent. The official position of the Ethiopian Orthodox Church today is to interpret the parties and their positions in light of the decisions of the councils of Amba Čara (1854) and Boru Méda (1878). The background to these councils was shaped by the abuse suffered by the metropolitans of the earlier nineteenth century – *Abunä* Yosab (*c.* 1770–1803), *Abunä* Qérelos (1815–28?) and *Abunä* Sälama (1841–67).[63] They were rudely buffeted by the conflicts between Ethiopia's regionally based princes. At the political centre was a dynasty with Muslim Oromo origins ruling from Däbrä Tabor. Their leading opponents were the rulers of northern Ethiopia, generally drawn from noble lineages of the province of Tegré. On their southern flank were the princes of Gojjam province. Finally, separated from these contending parties, but of increasing importance through the century, was Shäwa province and its ruling house.

---

60 See Girmah Beshah and Merid W. Aregay, *The question of the union of the churches in Luso-Ethiopian relations (1500–1632)* (Lisbon: Junta de Investigaçoes do Ultramar, 1964), 97–104.
61 Crummey, *Priests and politicians*, ch. 2. Particularly controversial has been the interpretation of the Roman Catholic scholar Ayyala Takla Haymanot, whose dissertation was originally published as Mario da Abiy-Addi', *La dottrina della Chiesa etiopica dissidente sull'Unione Ipostatica* (Rome: Pontificium institutum studiorum orientalium, 1956) and later translated into Amharic.
62 Kindeneh, 'The role of *Qebatoč*', does this for the Ewost'atian party.
63 I. Guidi, 'Le liste dei metropoliti d'Abissinia', *Bessarione* 6 (1899), 13–14.

The century did not open propitiously. In 1803, on the death of *Abunä* Yosab, the Däbrä Tabor ruler, *Ras* Gugsa, plundered the episcopal property, and, in league with the *ečägé*, established the Three Births faith in his domains.[64] Qérelos, Yosab's eventual successor, came from Tegré, where he was already embroiled in doctrinal controversy. He was quickly dragged into the matrix of sectarian and regional rivalry, but the death of his sponsor, *Ras* Wäldä Sellasé, soon after his arrival in 1815 left him in a weak position. When a few years later he was called to Gondär for a doctrinal council, he found his authority rejected, and, according to some sources, was driven violently from town. He returned an isolated figure to Tegré, where his authority was largely disregarded.[65]

Qérelos's successor was *Abunä* Sälama,[66] who arrived in Ethiopia in 1841. His appointment, like that of his predecessor, was in response to a delegation sponsored by the ruler of northern Ethiopia. As had probably been the case in 1815, the metropolitan's presence was the ideological dimension of what was otherwise a military campaign to unseat the Däbrä Tabor rulers. The strategy failed, the battle was lost and Sälama took up residence in Gondär, where he soon came into conflict with *Yäṣäga Lej* partisans, who in 1841 had effected a coup in the province of Shäwa, ousting the established leaders of the province's principal churches.

There were now three clearly defined doctrinal groups. Still prominent were the *Qebat*, who in contemporary controversies advocated the position that it was appropriate to think of two births in Christ, one from the Father, from eternity, and one from the Blessed Virgin; the union of the divine and human natures being effected at the moment of conception. By contrast the *Yäṣäga Lej* partisans advocated three births, one from the Father, one from the Blessed Virgin and one through the subsequent action of the Holy Spirit. The party of the metropolitans was the smallest and known by the pejorative *Karra*, or 'Knife.' They, with the *Qebat*, recognised two births, but rejected *Qebat* emphasis on the unction of the Holy Spirit in effecting the union of the two natures in Christ. Their enemies held that they had cut off either the third birth or the unction of the Holy Spirit.

---

64 H. Weld Blundell, *The Royal Chronicle of Abyssinia 1769–1840* (Cambridge: Cambridge University Press, 1922), 190 (text); 474 (trans.).

65 Guidi, 'Metropoliti', 14; Weld Blundell, *Royal Chronicle*, 197 (text); 484 (trans.); C. Conti Rossini, 'La cronaca reale abissina dall'anno 1800 all'anno 1840', *Rendiconti della Reale Accademia dei Lincei* ser. v, 25 (1916), 32–8 (text); 890–3 (trans.); Conti Rossini, 'Nuovi documenti per la storia d'Abissinia nel secolo XIX', *Atti della Reale Accademia Nazionale dei Lincei* ser. vii, 2 (1947), 362–5; Crummey and Getatchew, '*Abunä* Sälama', first page of the translation.

66 See Crummey and Getatchew, '*Abunä* Sälama'.

Sälama's efforts to gain restitution for the ousted Shäwan clergy eventually resulted, in 1846, in his violent expulsion from Gondär, back to Tegré. Here, again like Qérelos before him, he found himself marginalised.[67] An uneasy deadlock lasted into the early 1850s, when it was broken with the rise to the throne of Téwodros II, whose ambition, soon realised, was to revive the Solomonic monarchy. Central to his vision of a revived monarchy and kingdom was a unified church, and central to that vision was the restoration of episcopal authority.

By 1853 Téwodros had established military supremacy in the central provinces and summoned Sälama to Gondär. The bishop re-entered the city in June 1854. In August, Téwodros joined the bishop and summoned leading authorities, including representatives of both the *Qebat* and the *Yäṣäga Lej* schools, to a council. It met at Amba Čara, near Gondär. Téwodros challenged the sectarians by evoking the authority of Alexandria and of the Alexandrian-appointed metropolitans. 'Has there', he asked the council, 'been any one of the archbishops of Alexandria who preached a third birth by grace or natural birth by the unction of the Holy Spirit?' In defence of these teachings, their adherents pleaded, 'But this is not in Alexandria, rather our fathers here have taught us.' Téwodros then proclaimed, 'Do not deviate from the faith of these our fathers archbishops and metropolitans.' Finally, the council condemned a variety of teachings, which the chronicler describes as 'the creed and ordinance of those who maintain, "The Son of God was born by Grace through a third birth".'[68]

The following month, Téwodros proclaimed himself *negus* (king) and married his wife in a church ceremony. In February 1855 Sälama crowned him with the title *negusä nägäst* (king of kings). Téwodros then reorganised his court, giving the bishop not only precedence over the *ečägé*, or prior of Däbrä Libanos, but also control of the office of the *liqä kahnat*, general supervisor of the clergy, one previously held by the *ečägé*. Through these actions Téwodros laid down the template for modern Ethiopian monarchs: a church unified around Alexandrian doctrine under episcopal authority, the kings themselves bound to a church-sanctified monogamy.[69] The latter was a radical departure from the practice of their Solomonic forerunners; the former an echo of Zär'a Ya'qob's vision that religious and secular nationalism were inseparable.

---

67 Crummey, *Priests and politicians*, ch. 4.
68 The words are those of the anonymous author of the Ge'ez chronicle of *Abunä* Sälama. See Crummey and Getatchew, '*Abunä* Sälama'.
69 D. Crummey, 'Imperial legitimacy and the creation of neo-Solomonic ideology in nineteenth-century Ethiopia', *Cahiers d'Études Africaines* 28, no. 109 (1988), 13–43.

The sectarian appeal, at the council of Amba Čara, to the authority of their Ethiopian forefathers, rather than to that of Alexandria, echoed fifteenth-century calls for an independent Ethiopian Church. With sectarian dissidence sidelined, Ethiopian religious nationalism would come in the twentieth century to focus on the new-found authority of the bishops and find expression in calls for the indigenisation of the episcopacy.

The template was followed by all of Téwodros's successors: the ephemeral Täklä Giyorgis II; Yohännes IV; Menilek II; and Haile Sellassie I. The reign of Yohännes was most important in reinforcing the precedents established by Téwodros and in returning to the church endowment practices of earlier Solomonics. His wife had died sometime in the late 1860s and he appears, thereafter, to have been celibate, following practice normative for the clergy. He suppressed the *Qebat* faith, adhered to by some of the monasteries in his domain.[70]

He put his lasting stamp on the church between 1878 and 1881. Political power in nineteenth-century Ethiopia expressed itself on the battlefield and Yohännes, like Téwodros, had fought his way to power. In the years following his coronation he pursued the subjugation of the historic territories, which he viewed as the patrimony of his royal predecessors. In the course of 1873–74 he secured the submission of Gojjam province, heartland of *Qebat* teaching. While he acted to suppress *Qebat* in Gojjam, he seems to have allowed its ruler, now a leading vassal, *Ras* Adal, some space for doctrinal toleration. Such was not the case with the province of Shäwa and its *Yäṣäga Lej* adherents. In 1878 he forced the submission of his last outstanding rival, Menilek, ruler of Shäwa, and, following Menilek's submission, he called a church council at Boru Méda in Wällo province, close to the ancient monastery of St Stephen of Hayq. At Boru Méda he established the precedence of Alexandria in questions of Christology and then produced a letter from the Coptic patriarch, which condemned sectarianism in general and the 'Son of Grace' teaching in particular.[71] It established, as had Amba Čara, the *Karra* doctrine of *Abunä* Sälama and his predecessors. The council was followed by an active suppression of the

---

70 Crummey, 'Orthodoxy and imperial reconstruction', 438–9.
71 Cf. ibid. Two chronicle sources are particularly useful: *Aläqa* Lämläm's Amharic history of As'é Täklä Giyorgis and As'é Yohännes, Bibliothèque Nationale (Paris), *Manuscrits éthiopiens*, 259, f. 24; and Gäbrä Sellasé, *Tarikä Zämän ZäDagmawi Menilek* (Addis Ababa, 1959 Eth. Cal.), ch. 27; also translated and annotated as M. de Coppet, *Chronique du règne de Ménélik II*: Maisonneuve frères (Paris, 1930), 2 vols. For accounts of the council from both 'Son of Grace' and *Karra* standpoints, together with a statement of 'Son of Grace' doctrine, see Yaqob Beyene (ed. and trans.), *Controversie Cristologiche in Etiopia: contributo alla storia delle correnti e della terminologia nel secolo XIX* [Supplemento n. 11 agli *Annali* 37 (1977), fasc. 2] (Naples: Istituto orientale di Napoli, 1977).

'Son of Grace' school. Three years later, Yoḥännes obtained from Alexandria four bishops, an unprecedented number.[72]

Following Boru Méda, christological controversy ceased to be a central issue for the Ethiopian Church, which affirmed its adherence to the faith as received from Alexandria. The 'Son of Grace' school was marginalised and lost all its positions of influence. *Qebat*, by contrast, has quietly remained influential within the churches of Gojjam province.[73] Development and indigenisation of the episcopacy, by contrast, became central concerns of the twentieth century.

An indigenous episcopal hierarchy

The four bishops – Péṭros, Mattéwos, Luqas and Yoḥännes – whom Yoḥännes IV received from the Coptic patriarch in 1881, were technically peers, equal in rank, but Péṭros, who resided at the court of the emperor, was recognised as metropolitan. They were also, in the strict sense, without dioceses. Three were assigned to major political figures, the fourth to Gondär. *Abunä* Mattéwos was assigned to Menilek of Shäwa; Yoḥännes, who was shortly to die, to Gondär; and Luqas to *Negus* Täklä Haymanot of Gojjam.[74] Precedence amongst the ecclesiastics reflected the secular precedence of their princely patrons. Péṭros enjoyed the status of metropolitan only during the life of Yoḥännes IV. Following the latter's death in 1889 and the ascent to the throne of Menilek, Mattéwos was recognised as metropolitan and retained this position of precedence, outliving his peers and his patron, until his death in 1926. As for the bishops' territorial jurisdiction, it was neither more nor less than the political sway of their patrons. Yoḥännes IV had been satisfied to see ecclesiastical authority divided, not simply among the four bishops, but also between the bishops and the *ečägé*, assigning to the latter within his court the office of *liqä kahnat*. Menilek, by contrast, returned to the precedent set by Téwodros and gave control of this influential and lucrative office to Mattéwos.[75] Mattéwos's ascendancy increasingly became an object of resentment to Ethiopian churchmen, who in the 1920s began a campaign to indigenise the episcopacy.

This campaign coincided with the rise of *Ras* Täfäri Mäkonnen, who, in 1930, was to be crowned *Negusä Nägäst* Haile Sellassie I, claiming, as did all

72 Zewde Gabre-Sellassie, *Yohannes IV of Ethiopia: a political biography* (Oxford: Clarendon Press, 1975), 108–9.
73 Kindeneh, 'Role of *Qebatoč*'.
74 Sergew H. Sellassie, 'The period of reorganisation', in *Panorama*, 31–41.
75 For Mattéwos, see the summary accounts by Getatchew Haile, 'Ethiopian Orthodox *Täwhédo* Church' and Sergew, 'The period of reorganisation'.

Solomonic monarchs, to be *seyumä Egzi'abehér*, 'Elect of God'.[76] His reign has been associated indelibly with Ethiopia's grappling with modernity, a process in which he sought to act as a leader.[77] Modernisation was a tool to transform Ethiopia, to overcome the weakness manifest by the country's inability effectively to resist Fascist invasion in 1935, and to make it truly a peer player in the international arena. Simultaneously, like his predecessors, he, too, held a vision of an Ethiopia in which Orthodox Christianity played a central role. He brought together modernisation, Orthodoxy and the Amharic language in the system of education, based on western models, which he put in place following his restoration in 1941.[78] Modernisation and Orthodoxy were equally tools to support autocracy, for the emperor's vision of political power was the product of his upbringing at the court of his uncle Menilek and was based on his understanding of the Ethiopian past Thus, transformation of the church, like transformation of the country at large, was a process always subordinated to the interests of imperial rule.[79]

Between 1926 and 1959 the Ethiopian Church underwent an unprecedented transformation, which indigenised its leadership and elaborated its institutional capacities, but which left it as subject to political interference from the state as it had been in the beginning. Agitation for change started well before

76 The epithet 'Lion of Judah', popularly applied to Haile Sellassie in foreign sources, rests on a fundamental misunderstanding of the slogan 'Mo'a anbässa zä'emNägädä Isra'el', 'The Lion of the Tribe of Judah has prevailed', a reference to Revelations 5:5, which, as Sven Rubenson has shown, is a national motto, not a royal title: S. Rubenson, 'The Lion of Judah, Christian symbol and / or imperial title', *Journal of Ethiopian Studies* 3 (1965), 75–85. For misuse of the epithet see L. O. Mosley, *Haile Selassie: the conquering lion* (London: Weidenfeld and Nicolson, 1964), and P. Schwab, *Haile Selassie I: Ethiopia's Lion of Judah* (Chicago: Nelson-Hall, 1979). The emperor did nothing to discourage this usage, which began to creep into official documents.

77 See Bahru Zewde, *A history of modern Ethiopia 1855–1991*, second edition (Oxford, Athens, OH and Addis Ababa: James Currey, Ohio University Press and Addis Ababa University Press, 2001). For a general account of Haile Sellassie and the church, see Haile Mariam Larebo, 'The Ethiopian Orthodox Church and politics in the twentieth century: part 1', *Northeast African Studies* 9, 3 (1987), 1–17. Haile Sellassie's autobiography is in two volumes: Haile Selassie I: 1, *My life and Ethiopia's progress 1892–1937*, ed. and trans. E. Ullendorff (London: Oxford University Press, 1976); 11, *My life and Ethiopia's progress*, ed. H. G. Marcus with Ezekiel Gebissa and Tibebe Eshete (East Lansing: Michigan State University Press, 1994).

78 Abebe Fissiha, 'Education and the formation of the modern state of Ethiopia, 1896–1974', unpublished PhD dissertation, University of Illinois at Urbana-Champaign, 2000. The emperor's concern with education may be seen in *Selected speeches of His Imperial Majesty Haile Selassie First 1918–1967* (Addis Ababa: Imperial Ethiopian Ministry of Information, 1967), of which Section 1 (pp. 1–87) is dedicated to the subject. See also, with reference to the pre-invasion years, H. G. Marcus, *Haile Sellassie I: the formative years, 1892–1936* (Berkeley: University of California Press, 1987), 99, 137.

79 Bahru Zewde, 'Economic origins of the absolutist state in Ethiopia (1916–1935)', *Journal of Ethiopian Studies* 17 (1984), 1–29.

the death of Mattéwos in 1926 and was directed against what critics saw as his overweening power and his practice of simony. This agitation, which arose from increasing nationalist feeling amongst Ethiopian Christians, led, slowly but inexorably, to a drive for autocephalous status, which culminated with the crowning of an Ethiopian patriarch as leader of the Ethiopian Orthodox Church in 1959.[80] But autocephaly meant only peer status *vis-à-vis* the Coptic Church and the churches under the Syrian patriarchate, not the power of the church to determine its own fate *vis-à-vis* state authority.

Development of the church's national structure started in September 1926 shortly before the death of Mattéwos, with the promulgation of a constitution for the church, which enlarged the authority of the *ečägé* and created a holy synod. Negotiations for the appointment of Mattéwos's successor were complicated by Ethiopian demands that the new metropolitan be empowered to consecrate bishops and then by the death of the Coptic patriarch himself. Finally, in 1929 agreement was reached on the consecration of a new metropolitan, a Copt who took the name Qérelos, and of five supporting bishops, all Ethiopians and all monks. At each stage of the process church assemblies made the major decisions, nominating the candidates for consecration, and then creating a diocesan structure within which they were to work.[81] It was a momentous development: 'For the first time in its history Ethiopia had a partially Ethiopianised hierarchy and a diocesan structure which had some relationship to the country's needs.'[82]

The road to full autonomy proved bumpy.[83] In 1935 the Italians invaded the country and absorbed Ethiopia into an Italian East Africa, which came to an end six short years later. However, the period of Italian domination both complicated and advanced the movement towards autonomy. In 1936 Haile Sellassie went into exile, taking with him the new *ečägé*, *Abba* Gäbrä Giyorgis, and leaving behind the metropolitan and four Ethiopian bishops (one of the original five had died). Initially, the Italians attacked the church, executing both *Abunä* Pétros and *Abunä* Mika'él for their refusal to cooperate. Following

---

80 Adugna Amanu, 'The Ethiopian Orthodox Church becomes autocephalous', unpublished BA thesis, Haile Sellassie I University, 1969. See also Sergew H. Sellassie in *Panorama*, 34–6; Aymro and Motavu, *The Ethiopian Orthodox Church*, 11–14; S. Chernetsov, 'Ethiopian Täwahedo Orthodox Church. From the time of Yohannes IV to 1959', in *Encyclopædia Æthiopica*, II, 421–4.

81 In addition to Adugna and Chernetsov, see also Gäbrä Egzi'abehér Élyas, *Prowess, piety, and politics: the chronicle of Abeto Iyasu and Empress Zewditu of Ethiopia (1909–1930) recorded by Aleqa Gebre-Igziabiher Elyas*, ed. and trans. R. K. Molvaer (Cologne: Rüdiger Köppe Verlag, 1994), chs. 81, 94–6.

82 Adugna, 'Autocephalous', 21–2.

83 Cf. ibid. and Chernetsov, 'Yohannes IV to 1959'.

an assassination attempt against the Italian governor, the occupying authority bombed a number of monasteries, most prominently Däbrä Libanos. Hundreds died in these attacks. The policy of terror was followed by a policy of accommodation and by attempts, eventually successful, in the short run, to break the ecclesiastical ties between Addis Ababa and Alexandria. Pressure to break with Alexandria pushed *Abunä* Qérelos, the metropolitan, beyond his willingness to cooperate with the Italians, and he left for Egypt. The Italians seized this opportunity to call an ecclesiastical assembly, which, at the end of 1937, formally elected *Abunä* Abreham (one of the original five Ethiopian bishops and designated acting archbishop by Qérelos on his departure) to the status of archbishop and metropolitan and sanctioned the breaking of relations with Alexandria. Abreham then consecrated five new bishops. Although their action met with excommunication from Alexandria and from the leading Ethiopian churchman in exile, *Ečägé* Gäbrä Giyorgis, the Italians had pressed the issue of independence to its logical end. But they did so in defiance of Alexandria, not with its acquiescence. Gaining that acquiescence was the task taken up by Haile Sellassie on his return to power in 1941, by which time Abreham, who died in 1939, and his successor had consecrated twelve bishops, who, in turn, had ordained numerous priests and deacons and blessed many *tabots*.

Qérelos returned to Ethiopia in 1942 and resumed his position as archbishop and metropolitan. The Copts lifted their excommunication from the entire Ethiopian Church, including those who had been consecrated bishop during the Italian occupation, provided that the latter return to the status which they had previously held. Nationalist feelings continued to run high, with an Ethiopian ecclesiastical council demanding immediate autonomy in November 1945. The emperor had scruples over the Apostolic Succession and shared with his nineteenth-century predecessors deference to Alexandrian authority. He therefore did not support the demand which challenged his control of the process. The Copts nevertheless felt threatened by the Ethiopian demand and finally agreed in 1948 to the consecration, in Alexandria, of four Ethiopians as bishops.[84] One of them was *Ečägé* Gäbrä Giyorgis, who took the episcopal name of Baselyos, another, who was eventually to succeed Baselyos in his high office, took the name Téwoflos. The understanding was that, on the death of Qérelos, his successor would be an Ethiopian. Qérelos died in October 1950. The following January Baselyos was elected by an Ethiopian assembly and consecrated as the first Ethiopian archbishop and metropolitan. Eight years later,

---

84 For the text of this agreement, see Aymro and Motavu, *Ethiopian Orthodox Church*, Appendix C.

a new Coptic patriarch, eager to overcome tensions between the two churches exacerbated by the circumstances of his own election, publicly informed the Ethiopians of his 'desire' to elevate the head of the Ethiopian Church to the status of patriarch with full authority 'to appoint bishops and archbishops on his own'.[85] On 28 June 1959, Archbishop Baselyos was anointed patriarch in a ceremony in Cairo attended by both the emperor and the Egyptian president Nasser. The Ethiopian Orthodox Church had become autocephalous. Since all the newly created bishops were drawn from the ranks of the monks, the process ended the tension between episcopal and monastic poles of authority in the church.

Now governed by a holy synod, consisting of six bishops, chaired by the patriarch, the church took on a new, more elaborate structure. By the mid-1960s it had fourteen dioceses, corresponding to the principal administrative divisions of the country, each headed by an archbishop, with an additional archbishop in Jerusalem. With the consecration of new bishops and archbishops, the episcopacy expanded, with archbishops resident in all the major provincial capitals, their courts and administrative structure modelled on the office of the patriarchate. Holy synod had authority over spiritual matters, while the material interests of the church were managed by an administrative board. One of the earliest acts of Haile Sellassie's restored government was a decree of 1942, establishing regulations for the administration of all church lands.[86] Exactly how these regulations functioned is not very well known. A good deal of church revenue was now collected by the government and maintained in a special account in the government treasury.[87] The government turned the bulk of these funds over to the patriarchate, where they became the responsibility of an administrator general, a secular official appointed by the emperor. At the same time, a good deal of church revenue continued to flow directly to the anciently endowed churches and monasteries, who thus retained a degree of material independence from the patriarch and provincial archbishops. The endowed churches also continued to exercise local administrative rights. The central administration of the church expanded, with offices for the oversight of such matters as education and development. In 1944 a theological college was established in Addis Ababa, where it eventually became affiliated to Haile Sellassie I University.

---

85 Adugna, 'Autocephalous', 48.
86 Crummey, *Land and society*, 237–40. For the text of this, and other fiscal decrees of the period, see Gäbrä Wäld Engeda Wärq, 'Ethiopia's traditional system of land tenure and taxation', *Ethiopia Observer* 5 (1962), 327–8, 331–2. See also Aymro and Motavu, *Ethiopian Orthodox Church*, Appendix A.
87 Aymro and Motavu, *Ethiopian Orthodox Church*, 20.

However, there were distinct limits to the extent to which the church was now free to govern itself. The revised Ethiopian constitution of 1955 recognised Orthodox Christianity as the state religion and made provision for the state financially to support the church.[88] The constitution also gave the emperor the right to promulgate edicts, decrees and regulations for the church and to approve the candidates nominated for election to the ranks of bishop and archbishop.[89] The management of the secular affairs of the patriarchate was in the hands of an official appointed by the emperor. Six months after Baselyos's elevation to the status of patriarch, the emperor opened a department of religion within his private cabinet, directing to it 20 per cent of general church revenues, and re-creating the division of ecclesiastical authority which had characterised the royal courts of old. To head the department he appointed *Liqä Sel̠ṭenat* Habtä Maryam, who was also head of the 'Holy Trinity Cathedral', Haile Sellassie's 'royal' church.

Within the framework of its own history and expectations the Ethiopian Orthodox Church had become autonomous. Intimate relations with the palace were part of those expectations. Haile Sellassie had realised the vision of Zär'a Ya'qob, Téwodros and Yoḥännes IV – a state and nation to which a church, embedded in local culture and internationally recognised, was central, a church in which episcopal and monastic authority were reconciled. It was a church with increasing numbers of adherents beyond its own borders, in the Caribbean and North America. However, the country which Haile Sellassie had inherited from Yoḥännes and Menilek was not the country of Gondär times, but a multiethnic state in which the language with the largest number of first-language speakers was not Amharic, but Oromo; one in which Muslims constituted a very significant proportion of the population.[90] Moreover it was a country whose government had unleashed forces of modernity, which, increasingly, proved beyond its control; one in which ethnic relations were complicated by class relations deriving from a system of land tenure that ensured inequality. It was a country on a continent and in a region of increasing volatility. It was a country on the verge of revolution.

---

88 For passages from the revised Constitution of 1955, of relevance to the church, see Aymro and Motavu, *Ethiopian Orthodox Church*, Appendix B.

89 Adugna, 'Autocephalous', 51–2.

90 In spite of several recent censuses the numbers surrounding ethnicity and religious adherence remain highly controversial.

20

Coptic Christianity in modern Egypt

ANTHONY O'MAHONY

Christian presence in modern Egypt

The word Copt derives from the Greek for an inhabitant of Egypt (Αἴγυπτος), arabised into 'Qibt' and thence into 'Copt', and has been used in modern times, especially since the sixteenth century, to designate the Christian inhabitants of Egypt and the language used by them in their liturgy.[1] According to the church historian Eusebius (*Ecclesiastical History* 2: 16, 24), reflecting the traditions of his day, the evangelist Mark first preached the Gospel in Alexandria, and the Coptic Church claims an unbroken succession of patriarchs from that time to the present.[2] Since the fourth century the church in Egypt has dated events from the accession of Diocletian as emperor in 284, heralding a period later referred to as the age of the martyrs because of the numerous victims of persecution, who included the patriarch Peter (d.311).[3] The Arab invasion and conquest of Egypt in the seventh century was marked by a series of Coptic revolts, which were suppressed with increasing severity and violence.[4]

By the twelfth century, the Christians had ceased to be a majority. Thereafter the Copts continued to decline as a proportion of the overall population, until stabilising in the early nineteenth century.[5] As a sign of their submission

---

1 Pierre du Bourguet, 'Copt', in *The Coptic encyclopaedia*, ed. Aziz Atiya (New York: Macmillan, 1991), II, 599–601.
2 U. Zanetti, 'Les chrétientés du Nil: Basse et Haute Égypte, Nubie, Éthiopie', in *The Christian East: its heritage, its institutions and its thought: a critical reflection*, ed. R. F. Taft [OCA 251] (Rome: Pontificio istituto orientale, 1996), 181–216.
3 Annick Martin, 'Aux origines de l'Église copte. L'implantation et le développement du christianisme en Égypte (Ier–IVe siècle)', *Revue des Études Anciennes* 83 (1981), 35–56.
4 O. Meinardus, 'The attitude of the Orthodox Copts towards the Islamic state from the 7th to the 12th century, *Ostkirchliche Studien* 13 (1963), 153–70; J. Tagher, *Christians in Muslim Egypt: an historical study of the relations between Copts and Muslims from 640 to 1922* [Arbeiten zum spätantiken und Koptischen Ägypten 10] (Altenberge: Oros, 1998).
5 The evidence from the papyri, for instance, suggests that much of the population was still Coptic during the twelfth century. See G. Frantz-Murphy, 'Conversion in early Islamic Egypt: the economic factor', in *Documents de l'Islam médiéval: nouvelles perspectives de*

to Islamic authority they were obliged to pay tribute and special taxes, in particular *jizya* and the *kharaj*. The doctors of Islamic law tended to draw quite distinct boundaries between Muslims and non-Muslims, and to interpret the subjection of *dhimmîs*[6] to Islamic authority as a justification for discriminatory and humiliating measures imposed upon them.[7] The Islamic polemical impulse, which tended to focus on the disloyal and devious character of non-Muslims, gained momentum in the thirteenth and fourteenth centuries. It differed from previous polemic, which tended to centre on doctrinal issues and aimed at conversion. In the new polemic Christians were condemned *en masse* as enemies who could not be redeemed by their conversion, which was invariably presented as opportunistic and fraudulent.[8] Paradoxically, large-scale conversions of Christians to Islam provided the context for this type of polemic; its characterisation of Christians still has a strong hold on modern Islamic discourse regarding the Coptic community in Egypt.

From 1798 to 1801 the French Expedition lifted the discriminatory measures imposed in the name of the 'Covenant of 'Umar'[9] and ended the payment of the *jizya*.[10] But these measures had little impact on traditional patterns of

recherche, ed. Yusuf Ragib [Textes arabes et études islamiques 29] (Cairo: Institut français d'archéologie orientale, 1991), 11–18. On conversion in the Mamluk period, see D. Little, 'Coptic converts to Islam during the Bahri Mamluk period', in *Conversion and continuity: indigenous Christian communities in Islamic lands: eighth to eighteenth centuries*, ed. M. Gervers and R. J. Bikhazi (Toronto: Pontifical Institute of Mediaeval Studies, 1990), 263–88; I. A. Lapidus, 'The conversion of Egypt to Islam', *Israel Oriental Studies* 2 (1972), 248–62; Y. Lev, 'Persecutions and conversion to Islam in eleventh-century Egypt', *Asian and African Studies* 22 (1988), 73–93.

6 *Dhimma* can indicate protection, obligation or responsibility. In this context it signifies the 'pact of protection' extended to non-Muslims who willingly submitted to Islamic authority and paid certain taxes, notably the *jizya* (or poll-tax) and the *kharadj*, a land tax. See above, pp. 380–2.

7 A. Noth, 'Möglichkeiten und Grenzen islamischer Toleranz', *Saeculum* 29 (1978), 190–204; 'Abgrenzungsprobleme zwischen Muslimen und Nicht-Muslimen: die Bedingungen 'Umars (*as-surut al-'umariyya*) unter anderem Aspekt gelesen', *Jerusalem Studies in Arabic and Islam* 9 (1987), 290–315.

8 See B. Catlos, 'To catch a spy: the case of Zayn al-Din and Ibn Dukhan', *Medieval Encounters* 2 (1996), 99–113, which deals with the dismissal and execution of Ibn Dukhân, an Egyptian Christian, who held high rank in the financial administration in the late twelfth century.

9 The 'historical' precedent most referred to by Muslim writers is the so-called Pact or Covenant of 'Umar, a spurious treaty ascribed to the Caliph 'Umar I (634–644), which is more probably a refinement of Abbasid jurists some two centuries later. Its terms are quite harsh and it contains proscriptions of dress and behaviour, which no doubt reflect the ideals of the jurists who formulated it rather than the actual conditions in which non-Muslims typically lived. See above, p. 381.

10 H. Motzki, *Dimma und Égalité: die nichtmuslimischen Minderheiten Ägyptens in der zwischen Hälfte des 18. Jahrhunderts und die Expedition Bonapartes (1798–1801)* [Studien zum Minderheitenproblem im Islam, 5; Bonner orientalistische Studien, n.s. 27] (Bonn: Selbstverlag des orientalistischen Seminars der Universität Bonn, 1979).

thought and behaviour, before the middle of the nineteenth century when the provisions of Islamic law were increasingly replaced by new ideas adopted from the man-made law, which was intended to free the protected non-Muslims, the *dhimmîs*, and to make them full citizens, *muwâtînûm*. The administrative and legal reforms of the Ottoman Empire, known as the Tanzimat, culminating in the edicts of 1839 and 1856, established equality before the law for all of the sultan's subjects, though it was the final abolition of the *jizya* in 1855 that is commonly considered to have formalised the full integration of the Copts into Egyptian society. They participated in the parliament of Khedive Ismâ'îl, were well represented in the administration, and generally supported the 'Urabi rebellion. Yet, the relations between Copts and Muslims, between Copts and the state, were not quite as harmonious as some writers have suggested. Muḥammad 'Alî did not send a single Copt on his student missions to Europe. In fact, some of his educational programmes were set up specifically to break the Coptic monopoly in the government departments of land survey and revenue collection. Although the Copts were pleased with the abolition of the *jizya*, they opposed being drafted to serve in the army; this was seen as an islamising measure.[11] Fifty years later, the 'Revolution of 1919' seemed to signal the victory of equality and national unity over religious separatism.

A survey of the long process of arabisation and islamisation of Egypt shows a regional distribution of Copts, who can be found in small pockets surrounded by areas where Christianity is almost non-existent or in predominantly Christian areas.[12] This distribution dates back to the early conquest when large areas were systematically cleared of Christians.[13] By the fifteenth century the islamisation movement had come to an end and the Coptic Church entered a long period of hibernation that was to last until the mid-nineteenth century.

From the mid-seventeenth century onwards there is a relative abundance of data on the numbers of Christians in Egypt. The various estimates are as follows: James of Verona in 1335 – some 30,000 tribute-paying Christians; Prosper Alpin in 1530 – 50,000 Christians; Dapper in 1668 – 100,000 Christians; Vansleb in 1673 – 10,000 or according to the patriarch at most 15,000 Copts paying tribute; Benoît de Maillet around 1700 – more than 30,000 Copts; the Jesuit Maucollet in 1710 – 40,000 Copts. There are three more figures for the

---

11 A. Schlicht, 'Les chrétiens en Égypte sous Mehemmet Ali', *Le Monde Copte* 6 (1979), 44–51.

12 M. Martin, 'Le Delta chrétien à la fin du XIIIe siècle', *OCP* 63 (1997), 181–99; Martin, 'La province d'Ašmūnayn: historique de sa configuration religieuse', *Annales Islamologiques* 23 (1987), 1–29.

13 M. Martin, 'Note sur la communauté copte entre 1650–1850', *Annales Islamologiques* 18 (1982), 194–202.

number of Christians in Cairo only. Correspondence from the French embassy in Constantinople in 1702 mentions 40,000 Copts in Cairo and 5000–6000 other Christians in Cairo. In 1702 also, Boucher de la Richardière estimated that out of the 500,000 inhabitants of Cairo 24,000 were Christians, while around 1720 Claude Sicard reckoned that the city had more than 20,000 Christians, mainly Copts.[14]

Two comments need to be made regarding these figures. The most reliable ones are those concerning estimates of the number of Christians 'paying tribute', which indicates either the *jizya* or the *kharaj*. The tribute was fixed by the region or by the village and was proportional to the number of Christian families and depended upon how wealthy they were. Whereas according to Vansleb there were 10,000 or at the most 15,000, this figure in reality corresponds to the 100,000 or 150,000 Christians given by Dapper. But it will be noticed then that the number of 'tributaries', that is to say the size of the Coptic community, had declined by half or two-thirds between the fourteenth and seventeenth centuries. The second comment is that the highest figures turn out to be closest to the actual reality in Egypt towards the end of the eighteenth century. The low figures are based upon an estimate for the number of Christians in Cairo and then for the whole of Egypt. Cairo would have seemed to travellers one of the greatest cities in the world and with just as many if not more inhabitants than Paris, and one of its immediately striking features was its overwhelmingly Islamic appearance and the weak position of the Christian minority, which consisted in part of Greeks, Armenians and Syrians, who were incomers. The Jesuit Sicard estimated the number of churches in Cairo at around twenty or twenty-five, which compared with 1140 large and small mosques.[15] Given that the route to Cairo was either by land or along the Nile through Lower Egypt where Christians were particularly thinly spread, it is not surprising that the figures derived from the capital and then applied to the whole of the country were so low.

Most of these estimates concern the late seventeenth and eighteenth centuries. However, between 1675 and c.1725 Vansleb and Sicard, two experts on Christian Egypt, allow us to gain a sufficiently detailed idea of the life of the Coptic community. The seven surviving monasteries which maintained some type of monastic life – St Paul's monastery was still abandoned – were sparsely inhabited in Vansleb's time. At St Antony he found nineteen religious who

14 Ibid., 202.
15 Claude Sicard, *Œuvres* [Bibliothèque d'étude 85] (Cairo: Institut français d'archéologie orientale du Caire, 1982), III, 116, 122.

were in poor shape,[16] while Sicard half a century later reckoned their numbers at only fifteen, in addition to about a dozen at St Paul's.[17] Again according to Sicard, at the Wâdî al-Naṭrûn, a main centre for Coptic monasticism, there were only two religious; there were two deacons at St Makarios and four religious at Anba Bishoi, whereas Deir al-Sûrianî and Deir al-Barâmûs had proper communities. At the end of the eighteenth century a hand-written note commemorating the visit of the Coptic Patriarch John XVIII in 1781 increased these figures considerably by putting the number of religious at al-Barâmûs at twelve and nine respectively, plus eighteen and twelve at Bishoi, and correspondingly twenty religious at St Makarios and eighteen at al-Sûrianî; one might nevertheless ask if the monks constituting part of these figures actually lived in their monasteries. Finally, Deir al-Muharraq seemed to have been populated largely by Ethiopian monks, to the extent that it was called the monastery of the Abyssinians.[18] The total number of Coptic monks during the seventeenth and eighteenth centuries thus fluctuated around about 100, and maybe even fewer.

Another indication of the state of the Coptic Church in Egypt is the distribution of Coptic bishoprics. At the beginning of the sixteenth century (1508), there were eighteen bishoprics, of which ten were in Upper Egypt and eight north of Cairo.[19] During the time of Vansleb and Sicard, the number of bishoprics was drastically reduced both in the Delta and even in Upper Egypt.[20] By contrast, the situation of the twelve bishoprics as described by Sicard at the beginning of the eighteenth century continued almost unchanged until the end of the nineteenth century.

A major achievement of the French Expedition to Egypt (1798–1801) was the *Description de l'Égypte*, where Jomard put the total population of Egypt at 2,500,000 on the basis of the number of villages and the consumption of grain; he estimated the Christian and Jewish population at 215,000–220,000. If the number of Jews is subtracted from this figure – according to Sicard, there were only about 7000–8000 of them in Cairo – and those for Levantine Christians, mainly Greeks and Armenians, the resulting number of Copts comes to just

---

16 J. M. Vansleb, *Nouvelle relation en forme de journal d'un voyage fait en Egypté* (Paris: Compagnie de libraires associés, 1678), 311.

17 Sicard, *Œuvres*, I, 24, 40.

18 S. Sauneron, 'La Thébaïde en 1668', *Bulletin de l'Institut Français d'Archéologie Orientale du Caire* 67 (1969), 141.

19 J. Muyser, 'Contribution à l'étude des listes épiscopales de l'Eglise copte', *Bulletin de la Societé d'Archéologie Copte* 10 (1944), 162–3.

20 J. M. Vansleb, *Histoire de l'Église d'Alexandrie* (Paris: Chez la veuve Clousier; Chez Pierre Promé, 1677), 26–7; Sicard, *Œuvres*, II, 72.

under 200,000. Jomard reckoned that there were 10,000 Copts in Cairo; this number is probably too low given our knowledge of the early eighteenth century.[21]

After the *Description de l'Égypte*, a whole series of new estimates is found in the years 1830–40; at 150,000–160,000 these figures are slightly lower than those of the beginning of the century. In 1827, Renoüard de Bussière put the number of Copts at 160,000. In 1835 E. Lane counted 150,000 Copts, of whom 10,000 were in Cairo; he put the total population at 4 million. In 1836 Jomard – once again in Egypt – counted 160,000 Copts and attributed the decline compared to the beginning of the century to the depopulation of the countryside and the heavy losses of life during the wars of Muḥammad ʿAlī. This figure is corroborated by St John, who visited Egypt in the same year. He also put the number of Copts in Cairo at 10,000; in 1838 Michaud and Poujoulat give 150,000, while in 1840 Clot bey also has 150,000 out of a total population of 3 million. Writing at the same time, Cadalvène reduces the figure for the number of Copts to 145,000. After 1840, the estimates rise at the same time as Egypt's population. In 1854, Vimercati puts the figure for Copts again at 160,000, whereas the next year, on the basis of information supplied by the patriarchate, Butcher gives an estimate of 217,000 Copts out of a total population of 5 million. The sharp rise may have something to do with the abolition of the *jizya* that same year. Dalfi in 1861 provides the figure of 382,438 Christians in a total population of 4,606,160. At the end of the century, before the first official survey in 1897, the figures rise to 700,000–800,000 Copts in a total Egyptian population of 9 to 10 million.[22]

The census of 1907 found that 7.9 per cent of the population of Egypt was Christian. The four decennial censuses carried out between 1917 and 1947 reported 8 per cent. A slight decline was found in 1960 at 7.4 per cent, which at 6.6 per cent was even more pronounced in 1966 and can be explained by the departure of many Syrian-Lebanese, Armenian and Greek Christian communities during Nasser's regime.

It is difficult to establish anything hard and fast about the present number of Christians in Egypt, especially the actual size of the community. The Egyptian government census, conducted in November 1976, reported a total of 2,315,560 Copts or 6.31 per cent of the total population. This figure met with incredulity and protests from the Copts themselves, who threatened to launch their own head count. The government dissuaded them, but Coptic sources continue to speak of a much higher figure. Coptic groups outside

21 Martin, 'Note sur la communauté copte entre 1650–1850', 211.
22 Ibid., 211–12.

Egypt speak of 8 to 10 million, or roughly 20 per cent of the total population, a figure that has gained wide currency, although it remains untested. According to the central bureau of statistics in 1990, Egypt had a population of 56 million, of which 94.12 per cent were Muslims and only 5.87 per cent were Christians, amounting to some 3,287,200.[23]

A recent phenomenon in the Coptic Orthodox Church is the establishment of new Coptic communities outside Egypt. Emigration of the Copts in sizeable numbers started some three decades ago. Emigration from Egypt by Coptic Christians needs to be seen in the context of general Egyptian patterns. Broadly two periods of emigration can be discerned. The first belongs to the era of Nasser (1952–70), during which a limited number of young Egyptians were encouraged to study abroad and schoolteachers were sent out to work in neighbouring states. Migration was politically controlled principally through visa requirements. Nasser's nationalisation policies in the economy also led to a number of well-to-do families leaving Egypt to settle in the west. Amongst these were Coptic families. The presence abroad of economically resourceful individuals from this early phase of emigration has been important in the establishment of Coptic churches in the west that followed at a later stage. The majority of the emigrants were professionals and intellectuals, thus forming part of the Egyptian 'brain-drain'. Today, the Coptic Church has numerous churches and a growing monastic presence in western Europe, the USA, Canada and Australia, with approximately some 450,000 (10 per cent of the Coptic Church members) abroad today. In response to this situation the Coptic Church has sent many of its best priests, monks and scholars to serve the communities in the diaspora.[24] Since the Second World War, and particularly since 1960, the Coptic Church has established itself in other parts of Africa, partially as a reaction to the independence movements which according to Coptic ecclesiology favoured the implantation of the Coptic Church, seen as the most ancient African Christian church.[25]

23 al-Ahram, 8 November 1990. M. Martin, 'The renewal in context: 1960–1990', in Between the desert and the city: the Coptic Orthodox Church today, ed. N. van Doorn-Harder and K. Vogt (Oslo: Novus Forlag, 1997), 15–21, where he suggests that the size of the Coptic community has declined from about 7 per cent in the 1960s, when the renewer Kyrillos VI became pope, to about 6 per cent today. The most recent censuses suggest the absolute number of Copts to be about 3,600,000. Y. Courage and P. Fargues, Chrétiens et Juifs dans l'Islam arabe et turc (Paris: Fayard, 1992), 283–6, observe that the decrease in the proportion of Copts to Muslims over the space of twenty years is in part connected to a lower birth-rate, owing to a higher social status and to recent emigration.
24 N. Stene, 'Into the lands of immigration', in Between the desert and the city, 254–64.
25 C. Chaillot, 'Activités missionnaires de l'Église copte en Afrique', Le Monde Copte 20 (1992), 99–103.

Religious reform and renewal of the Coptic Church

The present Coptic revival is a result of a long internal development, tending to reinforce both the religious link, which binds the religious community together, and the position of the community in relation to the Muslim majority. To understand the nature of the current Coptic renewal, it is necessary to go back some decades, for in certain aspects this renewal is an internal reaction to developments within the community itself. In fact, renewal was carried out in two phases, very different in nature if not opposed, one 'lay' and the other 'monastic'. Most observers of the Coptic scene divide the recent history of the community into several distinct phases within the overall renewal of the Coptic Church: a period of lay reform and in particular the formation of the *Majilis al-Millî* (community council) in 1874, which emerged from within the Coptic elite; the monastic revival and the 'Sunday' School Movement – 1930–50; the time of Patriarch Kyrillos VI (1959–71) and the election of Anba Shenûda in 1971, as patriarch of the Coptic Church until the present.

In the first period, about the end of the reign of Khedive Ismâ'îl (1863–79), the Copts not only participated in, but were also sometimes in the forefront of Egypt's modernisation, which allowed them to regroup as a structured community. In 1874, a number of lay Copts formed a society to press for communal reform and for a better supervision of communal affairs, financial as well as juridical. The formation of the *Majilis al-Millî*, the lay council of the community, was to have a profound and long-lasting influence. In 1875, the council's scheme to form a theological college, the first attempt at a systematic religious training of the (mostly hereditary) clergy, was approved by the patriarch. The *Majilis al-Millî* consolidated and fostered the emergence of the great Coptic families, many of whom had been formed in the missionary schools and especially the Protestant school at Asiût.

They fostered a liberal spirit among the laity and were prone to mild anticlericalism towards a still culturally 'backward clergy'; they were nearly always in conflict with the patriarch. Most of those supporting reform were drawn from the educated middle and landed class. They had been exposed to a certain type of western thinking and a few had even abandoned Egyptian ways in favour of European culture. Their aim seemed to be to redesign the church as some kind of western parliamentary system with all decisions and offices subject to the will of the people. This reveals the influence of American Presbyterian missionaries whose own church functioned along similar lines, but it was an odd model to choose for a church whose very survival says something about the aptness of its ways. The clergy, of course, had once controlled practically all areas of life in the community: religion, justice, charity and education among them. Their role was not only being increasingly questioned but had also been substantially diminished. They understandably felt threatened by the better educated and often articulate laymen. The clergy were not, whatever the reformers liked to believe, all corrupt unthinking reactionaries. They were, of course, interested in protecting their power, but many also hoped, by maintaining the church's ancient arrangements, to preserve the community's cohesion and religious character, for therein lay safety.

In 1881, several leading lay Copts formed a Coptic charitable society. This society equally played an important role in promoting reform. The end of the nineteenth century is characterised by the emergence of a variety of Coptic reform societies with branches in all major cities. The period after 1882 has been called the golden age of Coptic history: a dwindling minority in the mid-eighteenth century had swelled into an entrenched one of about a million by 1914. This striking advance of confidence and education manifested itself in an intense cultural activity. About a dozen Coptic journals and periodicals were founded, some of which still exist. Several literary clubs were established, also contributing to strengthen communal solidarity.[26] These varied activities were possible only because they were founded on a solid economic basis. From the late nineteenth century until the land reform and nationalisation following the revolution of 1952, the Copts owned much good arable land and controlled an estimated three-fifths of all Egyptian commerce.[27]

These societies and journals not only aroused a new sense of awareness among the Copts of their distinctiveness as an ethnic-religious community, but also created – because Egyptian society was modernising – a perception of the economic and political interests which the community possessed in the nation. But because the Copts were a minority, their attempts to vindicate their rights only brought discrimination. The result was the first confessional crisis, when the Copt lay congress of Asiût of 1911, which expressed the claims of the community, was opposed by the counter-congress of Muslims in Heliopolis.[28]

26 B. L. Carter, *The Copts in Egyptian politics, 1918–1952* (London: Croom Helm, 1984), 43–9.
27 T. Philip, 'Copts and other minorities in the development of the Egyptian nation-state', in *Egypt from monarchy to republic: a reassessment of revolution and change*, ed. S. Shamir (Boulder, CO: Westview Press, 1995), 131–50.
28 Subhi Labib, 'The Copts in Egyptian society and politics, 1882–1919', in *Islam, nationalism and radicalism in Egypt and the Sudan*, ed. G. Warburg and U. M. Kupferschmidt (New York: Praeger, 1983), 301–20; D. Behrens-Abouseif, *Die Kopten der ägyptischen Gesellschaft von der mitte des XIX Jahrhunderts bis 1923* (Freiburg im Breisgau: Klaus Schwarz Verlag, 1972); D. Behrens-Abouseif, 'The political situation of the Copts, 1798–1923', in *Christians*

The Copts maintained an ambivalent position towards the British. On the one hand, they looked upon them as their protectors, but on the other, they felt that the British were not doing enough for them. As the number of Syrian, Armenian, British and even Muslim employees in the upper ranks of the administration rose at the cost of positions held by the Copts, the Copts' resentment of the Muslims, the other minorities and the British increased. The enthusiasm particularly of British churchmen and missionaries for Coptic Church reform led the Coptic clergy to suspect that all British interference was ultimately designed to win converts to Anglicanism.[29] This disappointment and the economic difficulties during the war led many Copts, but by no means the community as a whole, to join the nationalist movement after the war. The *Wafd* was particularly attractive, for it based its programme on secular national unity, on equality for all Egyptians, and on participation of all in the political process.

Another sensitive issue was the question of religious education in government schools. This especially concerned the Copts, who attended government schools in large numbers. In 1937 some 80 per cent of all Coptic students attended government schools. The issue was not whether religion should be taught in government schools; Muslims supported the idea and Copts certainly did not oppose it, with such unrepresentative exceptions as Salâma Mûsâ, who demanded full separation of state and 'church', that is, rejection of any religious instruction in government schools.[30]

The issue of religion as it presented itself to the Copts was, rather, whether in addition to the teaching of Islam the state should provide Christian students with instruction in Christianity. Here the contradiction in the two principles anchored in the Egyptian constitution of 1923 came to the fore: equal rights and freedom of faith for all citizens versus Islam as the religion of the state.

---

and Jews in the Ottoman empire: the functioning of a plural society, ed. B. Braude and B. Lewis (New York and London: Holmes and Meier, 1982), II, 185–205.

29 The British either considered playing or played a greater role in Coptic Church affairs in the Sudan and Ethiopia. In the late 1920s, they refused to let the metropolitan of Khartoum return to the Sudan because his behaviour had been scandalous, and they wanted his deputy (*wakîl*), the reformist Hanna Salâma, left in charge. In 1926–27 they were as opposed as the Egyptians to the investiture of an Ethiopian as metropolitan to Ethiopia. The Foreign Office in London even wondered if the appointment of an 'anglophile' metropolitan could not somehow be discreetly engineered: Carter, *The Copts in Egyptian politics*, 54–5. The head of the Ethiopian church had been a Copt for many centuries until 1952: Ayele Takhahaymanot, 'The Egyptian Metropolitan of the Ethiopian Church: a study on a chapter of history of the Ethiopian Church', *OCP* 56 (1988), 175–222.

30 For the Salâma Mûsâ 'lay' Coptic vision see Vernon Egger, *A Fabian in Egypt: Salmah Musa and the rise of professional classes in Egypt, 1909–1939* (Lanham, MD: University Press of America, 1986).

The Copts demanded equal treatment for their students, that is, government-paid instruction in the Christian religion. The government argued, sometimes explicitly, that a state whose official religion was Islam could not finance the propagation of Christianity. In all events, the government had to expect heavy Muslim opposition to any step in this direction. Often the Copts were put on the defensive over an even more sensitive issue: whether Coptic students should be excused from instruction in Islam and whether they should be obliged to take exams in Islamic studies.

After the First World War, the national *Wafd* movement brought about a sacrosanct union in which community tensions tended to become obliterated; but soon afterwards, the decline of the *Wafd* and the rise of the Muslim Brothers only accentuated the Coptic dilemma. Even before 1940, this cropped up in criticism of the official population statistics: Christians alleged that there was a deliberate underrepresentation of the Coptic population to cover up confessional discrimination against them in the distribution of government and civil service posts and political representation. Copts and Muslims accused one another of holding some economic and administrative citadels to which the other had virtually no access. The Muslims thought the Coptic community profited economically from the western and 'Christian' occupation of the country, while the Copts maintained that the British 'Residency' practised a pro-Muslim policy.[31]

The *Majilis al-Millî* was organised with the permission of the government, which registered its constitution. This constitution, however, underwent many changes. The original constitution, which was accepted on 14 May 1883, was changed on 31 December 1908, 12 February 1912 and 22 July 1927. The constitution set out the organisation and functions of the *Majilis al-Millî* and also sought to settle the relationship between it and the Coptic patriarchate. It claimed (1) that the *Majilis* should deal with matters concerning 'personal status', such as marriage, divorce and adoption; (2) that it should supervise the *waqfs*, religious endowments, and have a record of their budget; (3) that it should appoint a director of the patriarchate and a director of *waqfs*; (4) that it should supervise all Coptic schools and the theological seminary; (5) that it should look after all benevolent associations and look after the affairs of the poor and underprivileged; (6) that it should keep a record of the number of churches, convents and monasteries; (7) that it should work for the 'spiritual' improvement of the clergy and train and prepare them for their task; and

---

31 L. Bowie, 'The Copts, the *Wafd* and religious issues in Egyptian politics', *The Muslim World* 67 (1971), 106–26.

finally (8) that it should elect with the assistance of the patriarch four clergy who would apply canon law to those matters dealing with 'personal status' questions.

These new responsibilities of the *Majilis al-Millî* restricted in some measure the power of the patriarch as well as that of the clergy by giving power to the laity. However, several changes occurred in the constitution of the *Majilis al-Millî* as a consequence of disputes between the patriarchate, the clergy and the laity. On 31 December 1908, the original constitution, which was passed on 14 May 1883, was amended: (1) the patriarch was given the right to appoint an acting president of the *Majilis al-Millî* in his absence; (2) the supervision over the *waqfs* was given to the patriarch, who was to be assisted by four members of the clergy, appointed by himself. On 12 February 1912, the constitution was changed once more: (1) the number of the members of the *Majilis al-Millî* should be twelve, four to be appointed by the patriarch and eight to be elected by the community; (2) the supervision over the *waqfs*, schools, monasteries and convents reverted to the patriarch, who was to be assisted in their supervision by four bishops. These changes, however, were not readily accepted by the Coptic community, because of the power which was now concentrated in the members of the clergy. Thereupon, the members of the *Majilis al-Millî* spent a great deal of effort until they obtained an order from the government on 22 July 1927 which returned to the laity the rights and responsibilities it had under the constitution of 1883. This explicitly stated that the *Majilis al-Millî* was to consist of twelve lay members and twelve sub-members, to be elected by church suffrage, in other words by the general community. It was also to supervise the *waqfs*, churches, monasteries, convents, the press and any 'personnel status' issues under the chairmanship of the patriarch. The latter, for his part, was to have the right to elect four clergy to apply canon law in those matters which the *Majilis al-Millî* had decided upon.

Generally, the relationship between the *Majilis al-Millî* and successive patriarchs was rather cool, for the patriarchs always looked on the *Majilis al-Millî* as an organisation which restricted their authority. The *Majilis al-Millî*'s success in gaining control of the community was, in fact, somewhat limited. It spent much of its energy in trying to gain what it saw as its rights, rather than exercising the ones it had. Following his election, Kyrillos VI (1959–71) declared in his message to the Coptic Church that he had decided to cooperate with the *Majilis al-Millî* for the good of the people and the clergy. By this time, however, the *Majilis al-Millî* no longer enjoyed its initial rights and responsibilities. The final blow came in 1962, with Nasser's abolition of the Coptic *Majilis al-Millî*, returning communal authority and leadership, such as was left, to the clergy.

In 1960, a law passed by the Egyptian government stated that all Coptic *waqfs* were to be placed under the supervision of a special committee of Coptic *waqfs*.[32] From 1968 on, the ministry of *waqfs*, which was responsible for Islamic endowments, acquired rights over certain Christian *waqfs* on the grounds that some of the beneficiaries might be Muslims. This was possible, for example, if the endowment made general provision for helping the poor. Some 150 to 200 *waqfs* were expropriated in this way. The Coptic Church's continued call for the restoration of these *waqfs* from the ministry has become a particularly sensitive issue in church–state relations.[33]

But to pass to the situation today, a profound change has been perceptible in the Coptic community, the only community of importance in Egypt after the disappearance of practically all the other Christian minorities. The Coptic leaders are no longer the same: the notables among the laity, who came from the great Coptic families or had risen to official posts in the administration, have given way to a group of bishops and monks. Because this change places the relationship between Coptic Christianity, the Muslim community, and the Egyptian society and state on an altogether different footing, its impact must be carefully weighed.

Among the conditions and the social consequences of the Coptic renewal, the following should be noted: the dismantling of the influence of the great landed 'Wafdist' families, which beginning in 1952 led to a diminution of the influence of the Coptic notables on their community. From which follows the decline of the *Majilis al-Millî*, a decline hastened by the government's determination to strengthen the 'unity of the nation' by playing down community differences and above all differences with Christians, for example over reform of the 'personal status' laws.[34] Under Nasser we see the abolition of political parties, and the militarisation of the upper ranks of the administration and political positions, a situation exacerbated by the fact that no high-ranking Coptic officers participated in the revolution. Symptomatic too was the fact that no Copt was elected to the *Majilis al-Umma* (parliament) in the elections of 1964, 1968, 1971, 1976 or 1979. Copts were still represented, however, because a new law empowered the government to appoint up to ten members of parliament, but this meant that Coptic representation in parliament now depended

---

32 O. Meinardus, 'The emergence of the laymen's movement in the Coptic Church: the *Majilis al- Milli'*, *Publications de l'Institut d'Études Orientales de la Bibliothèque Patriarcale (Alexandrie)* 12 (1963), 75–82.

33 J. D. Pennington, 'The Copts in modern Egypt', *Middle Eastern Studies* 18 (1982), 170.

34 For a historical overview of questions of 'personal status' within the context of Islam for the Christian communities in Egypt see Ernest Semaan Freig, 'Statut personnel et autonomie des chrétiens en Égypte', *Proche-Orient Chrétien* 24 (1974), 251–95.

exclusively on the goodwill of the ruler. The Copts had once again become more of a traditional minority.

The emergence of a new university-educated Coptic middle class, which is more conscious of its own values, has seen the growth of the Sunday School Movement, where the young people of this middle class have taken a lead in Christian religious instruction, which was weak or non-existent in the public schools. The importance of the Sunday School Movement, which cannot be exaggerated, is due not so much to the number of people who receive instruction, although substantial, as to the fact that the group of catechists responsible for the movement became a sort of personification of the 'identity' of the new Coptic middle class.

It is from this milieu – from the youth of the new Coptic middle class who have put life into the Sunday School Movement – that the influential priests and monks come and it is upon this milieu that they first exercised their influence through a multitude of small publications, sessions, retreats and other means of contact. While the older Coptic notables were concerned with integrating their community into the nation as it was being formed and were searching for a lay way of life that was 'liberal' and some would say 'secular' in the name of democratic principles universally recognised, this new group-awareness, by contrast, is concerned first with the life of the Coptic community. 'All authentic service begins and ends with the Church . . . [and] has for its aim to link Christ and the community' (Matta al-Miskin).[35] It could be argued that Arab nationalism, which has continued to root itself in Islam, has not been without influence on the style adopted by the Coptic renewal. The return to the Arab-Muslim heritage has a strict parallel in the return of the Christian to his Coptic monastic heritage.[36]

The Coptic monastic revival in modern Egypt

Egypt is the land not only where Christian monasticism originated, but also where the modern monastic revival began. For more than four decades large numbers of young Copts have retreated into the desert, reviving the ancient monasteries once founded in the fourth and fifth centuries. The monasteries

35 M. Martin, 'The Coptic–Muslim conflict in Egypt: modernisation of society and religious transformation', *Cemam Reports* 1 (1973), 31–54.
36 Dina El-Khawaga, 'L'affirmation d'une identité chrétienne copte: saisir un processus en cours', in *Itinéraires d'Égypte: mélanges offerts au père Maurice Martin, SJ*, ed. C. Décobert [Bibliothèque d'étude 107] (Cairo: Institut français d'archéologie orientale du Caire, 1992), 345–65.

have been enlarged and modernised, and provision made for a monastic life suited to women.[37] The number of monastic vocations has increased at the same pace as the quality of recruits: the monks of the new generation are in the majority young university graduates, especially engineers and technicians, and as their religious zeal has restored the image of monasteries as centres of spirituality, their technical competence has turned the monasteries into prosperous economic units. Coptic monasticism today reminds one of the Cistercian monastic and agricultural pioneers of medieval Europe. The modernisation of the church is essentially their work. They have adopted quite a strict version of the Pachomian rule, which involves isolation within their cells outside the office and manual work.[38] At the same time the old traditions are upheld, while the spiritual writings of the early centuries, preserved in numerous manuscripts in the monastic libraries, have become standard reading. Tradition is the heart of this renewal. For the first time in their long history, the desert monasteries are woven into the fabric of the parish churches of the cities, the towns and the villages. Many of the monastic clergy no longer remain for most of their active life in the desert, but have linked themselves into the spiritual life of the Coptic community as a whole. To join a monastery for many young Coptic men means the total identification of the person with the church. This is an important witness in a situation where the church represents the faith of a religious minority. Others embrace the monastic life as a sign of protest against the laxity and the worldliness of church and society. Moreover, it should not be forgotten that the higher ranks of the Coptic clergy are selected, as already mentioned, from the ranks of the monks. This means that there may be cases where a man joins the monastic life out of a desire for an eventual leadership role within the community.[39]

Although the monasteries are located in the desert, they are today easily accessible and large numbers of visitors from all areas and levels of the church pass through the gates. Many of the young bishops of the Coptic Orthodox Church are themselves products of this monastic revival. Through books and pamphlets as well as magazines, they help to make the monastic tradition

37 N. van Doorn-Harder, *Contemporary Coptic nuns* (Columbia, SC: University of South Carolina Press, 1995); Doorn-Harder, 'Following the holy call: women in the Coptic Church', *Parole de l'Orient* 25 (2000), 733–50.
38 See the work of Armand Veilleux OCSO, *La liturgie dans le cénobitisme pachômien au quatrième siècle* [Studia Anselmiana 57] (Rome: IBC – Libreria Herder, 1968); Veilleux, *Instructions, letters, and other writings of St Pachomius and his disciples* [Pachomian Koinonia 3; Cistercian Studies 47] 3 vols. (Kalamazoo, MI: Cistercian Publications, 1981).
39 J. H. Watson, 'The Desert Fathers today: contemporary Coptic monasticism', in *Eastern Christianity: studies in modern history, religion and politics*, ed. A. O'Mahony (London: Melisende, 2004), 112–39.

accessible. Their influence manifests itself in youth work and among Coptic students at the universities. There can be no doubt that the monastic revival has affected and does affect the Coptic Church at large.

At the same time, theology in the Coptic Orthodox Church is taught at the Coptic theological seminaries, primarily the Coptic theological seminary at al-Abbasîya and the higher institute for Coptic studies, both attached to the patriarchate in Cairo. But while the renewal in the monasteries is nourished by patristic literature, especially the writings of the monastic fathers, the seminaries rely on textbooks shaped by contact with western academic theology, even if their content is still heavily dependent upon a theological tradition deeply rooted in medieval Arabic theological literature.[40] Although there is a long history of co-existence between the two traditions and forms of theological literature, there are today signs of growing tension, largely caused by the increasing contact with western patristic and ecumenical theology.[41]

Following a golden age in the fourteenth century, Coptic theological writing almost ceased until the beginning of the nineteenth century. With Muhammad 'Alî, Egypt was suddenly opened up to the west. In addition to explorers, merchants, technical experts and secular teachers, missionaries of various Protestant and Catholic affiliations settled in the country in growing numbers. Many of them soon engaged in teaching activities aimed at the Coptic Orthodox. This was especially true of the British missionaries from the Church Missionary Society who hoped to influence the Coptic Church in the direction of the Reformation and its theology. Instead of establishing an Anglican Church in Egypt, which did in fact come later, they tried to work with the Orthodox. Numerous Copts who later became prominent in the church were educated in their schools. With the enthronement of Patriarch Kyrillos IV (1854–61) – 'Abû al-'Islâh', the father of reform as he has been called by some – their influence was at its peak. For a short time they even managed the first Coptic Orthodox theological school.[42]

The latter part of the century saw a Coptic Orthodox reaction against western Christian influence. Partly it was in opposition to some of the more radical reforms of Kyrillos IV, but mainly it was part of the growth of Egyptian national consciousness strengthened by the British occupation in 1882. The church had by then accepted many of the methods of the new missionaries

40 S. Rubenson, 'Arabic sources for the theology of the early monastic movement in Egypt', *Parole de l'Orient* 16 (1990–91), 33–47.
41 S. Rubenson, 'Tradition and renewal in Coptic theology', in *Between the desert and the city*, 35–51.
42 Samir Sekaly, 'Coptic communal reform, 1860–1914', *Middle Eastern Studies* 6 (1970), 247–75.

in areas like education and the distribution of literature. Now Copts educated in modern schools used these against the missionaries. In this way, the late nineteenth century gave rise to a renewal of Coptic theological literature, though largely in a polemical form, but it was their opponents, Catholic and Protestant rather than Muslim, who decided the themes, thus making the role of the Coptic theologians largely apologetic. Exposure to missionary activity had, however, made a deep impact. It was within a western – mainly Catholic – theological framework that the Copts chose to defend their position on controversial issues. Unfortunately the ecclesiastical conflicts between the reformers in the *Majilis al-Millî* and the hierarchy long prevented effective reforms of theological education.

An outgrowth of this defence of the Coptic Orthodox tradition against the proselytism of the missionaries, and one of the most important factors behind the revival that started in the 1940s, was the Sunday School Movement. Based on ideas largely taken from Protestant missions, it was the work of some of the great Copts of the early twentieth century, such as Ḥabib Girgis, and became the major form of Coptic religious instruction in the growing cities, especially Cairo. Through these schools young Copts received a thorough religious training under enthusiastic young teachers. In them a new generation of lay leaders with modern secular education became devoted to the church. A large number of them later entered the desert monasteries, contributing to their revival. But the schools were still dependent on the old 'scholastic' tradition, to which western methods of religious instruction, in particular Bible reading and a systematic exposition of liturgy and the sacraments, were added.

A very different impetus came out of the desert tradition itself, which gained strength from the general disenchantment among young Egyptians, Muslim and Copt alike, with the Egyptian kingdom and its dependence on the British. From before the Second World War radical hermits retreated to the desert and began to attract disciples. In the monasteries they found not only spiritual leaders, but also libraries with manuscripts containing their spiritual heritage, the writings of the radical monastic leaders of the first Christian centuries, like St Antony, St Makarios and St Isaac of Nineveh. But some, such as the uneducated Ethiopian monk 'Abd al-Masîḥ al-Ḥabashî, did not find the life in the monasteries sufficiently exacting and retreated further into the desert so that they might live the life of the Desert Fathers of the fourth century.

In 1959 the monastic revival received powerful support with the election of Kyrillos VI as patriarch of Alexandria. He was a well-known hermit and preacher, who had studied the early spiritual fathers and had for some time been the disciple of 'Abd al-Masîh al-Habashî. As a strong spiritual leader without any bonds to the pre-revolution Coptic elite, Patriarch Kyrillos VI could cooperate well with Nasser and strengthen the position of the church in general and Coptic monasticism in particular. With his support, hermits and young enthusiastic monks undertook to rebuild and revive the old monasteries, which then attracted young men from Cairo and elsewhere.

In the monasteries the teachings from the Sunday Schools were supplemented by readings of the Church Fathers and especially the monastic fathers. This necessitated modern Arabic translations of key patristic texts; numerous works, especially those of St Athanasios and St Cyril but also the homilies of St Makarios, have been translated. Also required was a training of a more patristic and less scholastic type. Thus, the monastic revival has laid a basis for a patristic revival as well as a modern Coptic Orthodox theological literature grounded in early monastic theology, its most prominent and prolific representative being the abbot of the monastery of St Makarios, Father Matta al-Miskin.

Father Matta was born and grew up in Alexandria, where he became a successful pharmacist before he turned monk in 1948. He fully engaged himself in the reading of the early monastic Fathers and soon began to write extensively on spiritual life, quoting the Fathers, especially St Isaak of Nineveh. In the 1960s Matta al-Miskin refused to be enrolled in a monastery and decided to live with his disciples as hermits in Wâdî Râyan. Here they established an ascetic life according to the tradition of the first monastic movement and continued to study the writings of the Fathers. In 1969 he and his disciples were asked to take over the almost ruined monastery of St Makarios. Under his leadership the monastery was enlarged and completely renovated, and soon attracted numerous young monks.[43]

An important feature characteristic of Matta al-Miskin's writings is their concentration on the incarnation, prayer and communion. In the tradition of so many of the early Fathers, especially St Athanasios and St Cyril of Alexandria, two of Matta al-Miskin's favourite Fathers, the incarnation is central to his theology. The incarnation reconciles heaven and earth. Through the incarnation man is given the capacity to transform transience of life into a history of salvation. Another important aspect of this emphasis on the incarnation is Matta al-Miskin's view on the historical character of Christian faith. Especially

---

43 S. Tyvaert, 'Matta el Maskine et le renouveau du monastère de saint Macaire', *Istina* 48 (2003), 160–79.

in his ecumenical appeals, Matta al-Miskin stresses the historical character of doctrine, which he maintains is part of the inculturation that is central to Christian faith as faith in the incarnate Son of God. The church is called not only to manifest Christian unity but also to unite the world. This task presupposes a Christian unity, which can only be achieved through a communion of saints, that is, communion based on repentance, humility, love and mercy.[44]

Despite its spectacular renaissance, Egyptian monasticism still suffers from the latent antagonism within its ranks – and has done so for years. It reflects essential differences between the two key figures who have come to personify monastic renewal: the patriarch Shenûda III, himself a former monk, and Fr Matta al-Miskin. The abbot of St Makarios subscribes to the traditional monastic ideal of a society withdrawn within itself, which is immovable and acts on its environment only by witness and prayer, which, in turn, requires a renunciation of the world. By contrast, the model followed by Shenûda, as represented in the monasteries of Deir Anba Bishoi, has a direct impact on the outside world: just as they have played a driving role in the renovation of the church, the monks act as a ferment within the Coptic community by putting their own knowledge and the monasteries' infrastructure at the service of the community.

The Coptic Church since the election of Shenûda III as patriarch

The election of Shenûda III as patriarch also coincided with the change in political regime which followed the death of Nasser and the election of Sadat. Shenûda has attempted to provide the Coptic community not only with a church that is capable of defending the interests of the community within Egyptian political life and society, but also with a church which will support and nourish the spiritual needs of the community and by extension the religious culture and civil society of Egypt.

The Coptic Church possesses a strongly popular character, which manifested itself in the election procedure.[45] The first step was to publish a list of nine candidates: this was drawn up in June 1971 by a special electoral commission of nine bishops and nine laymen under the chairmanship of the *locum tenens*.

---

44 Nevine Mounir Tawfiq, 'Le chrétien et la société dans la pensée du père Matta al-Maskin', *Proche-Orient Chrétien* 50 (2000), 80–104.

45 O. Meinardus, 'Election procedures for the patriarchal throne of Alexandria', *Ostkirchliche Studien* 16 (1967), 132–49, 304–24.

The list was printed in the daily press and fixed to the door of all cathedrals, so that the faithful could take note and, if they wished, raise objections. The list consisted of six bishops and three priest-monks. Another commission was responsible for drawing up the list of electors. There were 700 of these, forty of them representatives of the Ethiopian Church, reflecting the strong historical and doctrinal ties between the two churches. On 29 October the electors chose by ballot three out of the remaining five candidates: Anba Samuel, Anba Shenûda and Fr Timotheos. On 31 October they made their final choice by lot. Before the beginning of the liturgy the three names were placed in a casket, which was then sealed and deposited on the altar. Before the distribution of communion the deacons selected one of the young boys present in the congregation, who was given communion and had a special prayer recited over him. At the end of the service he was blindfolded and drew one of the lots from the casket. This bore the name of Anba Shenûda. On 31 October 1971 Anba Shenûda was elected head of the Coptic Orthodox Church of Egypt, in succession to Patriarch Kyrillos VI who had died on 9 March 1971. He is the one hundred and seventeenth patriarch in the Coptic line of succession to the throne of St Mark.

Anba Shenûda was born in 1923, in a village in the region of Asiût in Upper Egypt. He received a degree in English from the University of Cairo in 1947 and continued with advanced studies at the Egyptian Institute of Archaeology. In 1948 he took part in the Palestinian war as an infantry officer. In 1949 he received the theological diploma from the Coptic seminary in Cairo and was then appointed to teach there. He withdrew in 1954 to the monastery of Deir al-Sûrianî in the Wâdî al-Natrûn and was ordained priest there in the following year, where he came under the influence of an Ethiopian ascetic who had come to live in the Egyptian desert. Since 1935 the Ethiopian Abuna 'Abd al-Masîḥ al-Ḥabashî had inhabited a cave some 3 miles south of the monastery of Deir al-Barâmûs in the Wâdî al-Natrûn, where he practised an extreme asceticism. His consistent fasting and long vigils, in some ways even surpassing the austerity of his fourth-century models, left a lasting impact on many monks in the Coptic Church, and in particular on Shenûda. Shenûda's predecessor as patriarch, Kyrillos VI (1959–71), called him from the monastery in 1959 to become one of his secretaries, and in 1962 he was consecrated bishop, with special responsibility for religious education and the direction of the seminary. Shenûda was part of that generation of Coptic monastic clergy who would profoundly associate itself with the need for internal spiritual and structural reform. He has pointed out on a number of occasions that he would like to see the church today as strong as in the days of the fifth and sixth centuries.

This goal explains many of the structural developments that are so evident in recent years within the Coptic Church.

During his time as patriarch, Shenûda has developed the episcopate of the church. In 1971 there were twenty-three bishoprics in Egypt; by 2001 this had risen to forty-nine. For the diaspora there were three bishops in 1971 and there are now nineteen. References to the monastic origin of the hierarchs explain the degree of importance and the significance that the respective monasteries have had at a given time. Thus, for example, from the seventh to the thirteenth century twenty-five out of thirty-six patriarchs used to be monks of St Makarios in the Wâdî al-Naṭrûn. From the seventeenth to the nineteenth century, ten of the twelve patriarchs came from St Antony monastery. In the middle of the twentieth century, sixteen bishops have served as monks in the Deir al-Sûrianî. Under Shenûda, his home monastery Deir Anba Bishoi has provided numerous monks for the episcopate.

In 1971 there were approximately 200 monks; in 2001 there are some 1200, as reported in the official organ of the patriarchate, *Al-Kiraza*. They are located in the eleven historic monasteries: Deir Anba Antuni (St Antony); Deir Anba Bula (St Paul); Deir al-Barâmûs (Romans); St Makarios; Deir Anba Bishoi; Deir al-Sûrianî (The Syrians); St Samuel *al-Qalamûn*; Deir al-Muharraq; St Menas; Deir Anba Bakhum; Deir Anba Girgis *al-Riziqât*; and twelve new monasteries that have reoccupied ancient monastic sites abandoned many centuries ago.[46]

A major characteristic of the Coptic revival is a renewed emphasis on the monastic and ecclesial traditions.[47] This is realised in more frequent celebrations of the Eucharist, stress on the church's identity as an Apostolic church, renewed emphasis on the study of the Coptic language, commemoration of the glorious past, on Egypt as the homeland of monasticism, reading of the Church Fathers, and upholding martyrdom, even in the present day. At the same time, the church has attempted to restore the practice of certain sacraments which were beginning to fall into oblivion, such as the sacrament of reconciliation, or fasting, particularly honoured in the Coptic religious tradition. This practice lends itself to be used as an instrument of political protest; at the instigation of the patriarch the entire community may thus give a silent but spectacular sign of protest. Shenûda made use of this device on several occasions during disagreements with the political authorities. By emphasising public prayer and fasting, the religious authorities not only intended to strengthen the faith but also wanted to provide the Christian community with

46 J. Masson, 'Trente ans de règne de Shenûda III, Pape d'Alexandrie et de toute l'Afrique', *Proche-Orient Chrétien* 51 (2001), 317–32.
47 F. Sidarous, 'Église copte et monde moderne', *Proche-Orient Chrétien* 30 (1980), 211–65.

modes of expression and of action close to those used by the Muslim community. Furthermore, the Coptic Church stresses family life and strives to draw groups from different social strata, age and education into the church system. Hence there are groups for women, children of different ages, youth, university students, young couples and so on. Service to the church and a social life that rallies around the church have become central for most Copts.[48]

The controversial question of building churches is traditionally one that divides the hawks and the doves in the Coptic community. Owing to the influx of peasants to the cities and the general problem of population growth, the need to construct churches is strongly felt. It is current practice that a set number of new churches are permitted to be built within Egypt each year and that each new building requires a presidential decree of authorisation. The regulations concerning church buildings are strict: before qualifying for a presidential permit the church site is required not to be situated beside a mosque, a major square or any government building. The congregation for which the church is to be built should also have the permission of local sheikhs and Muslim leaders. Obviously, several of these conditions are difficult to fulfil, especially if the Muslim population object and build a mosque beside the area designated as a church site. In 1972, Muslims set fire to an 'illegal' church in Khanka. A committee set up in the aftermath of the incident concluded that of 1442 Coptic churches only 500 had permits. For this reason some of the major clashes between Coptic and Muslim groups during recent decades have been centred on the question of legal and illegal churches.[49]

To these efforts at reviving Christianity inside Egypt corresponded initiatives to increase its worldwide influence. After showing its evangelising dynamism during the first centuries, the patriarchate of Alexandria withdrew into itself after the Muslim conquest. Shenûda has not really turned things upside down but has nevertheless imparted to Egyptian Christianity a certain missionary impetus in the only direction allowed, given the restrictions imposed by Islam, that is, Africa. Aware of the fact that the patriarchate of Alexandria has been the first and largest Christian church on the continent, Shenûda as early as 1976 appointed a bishop for African affairs. He was also the first head of the Coptic Church to undertake trips abroad, visiting Ethiopia, Sudan, Zaire and Kenya. In return, he entertained representatives of the African churches in Cairo. The

---

48 D. El-Khawaga, 'Les services sociaux dispensés par l'Église copte: de l'autonomisation socio-économique à l'affirmation politique', in *Exils et royaumes: les appartenances au monde arabo-musulman aujourd'hui*, ed. Gilles Kepel (Paris: Éditions FNSP, 1993).
49 Sami Awad Albeeb Abu-Sahlieh, *Non-musulmans en pays d'Islam: cas de l'Égypte* (Fribourg, CH: Éditions Universitaires, 1979).

Coptic Church has been involved in creating an independent ecclesiastical structure in Eritrea, in opposition to the Ethiopian Church which no longer has a Copt at its head.[50]

Conclusion

The Coptic Church in Egypt has experienced a profound change during the modern era. From a church seeking only to survive, it now experiences something which echoes its past revival, renewal and evangelisation. However, because in Egypt Islam dominates the public sphere, it has often been forced to internalise this renewal within monastic space, which is, however, accessible to the entire community. But owing to emigration the Coptic community now also has an existence as a diaspora church. And more than this, as an ancient church of Africa it is attempting to be part of the continent's future beyond the influence of Islam, not only in its most recent sphere of ecclesial influence in Ethiopia and now Eritrea, but also as a dynamic and evangelising church across east, west and southern Africa.

50 E. C. Suttner, 'Eritreas Eigenstaatlichkeit und die Kirchen', *Una Sancta* 49 (1994), 106–24; R. Voigt, 'Die erythräisch orthodoxe Kirche', *Oriens Christianus* 88 (1999), 187–92. See above p. 486.

21

Syriac Christianity in the modern Middle East

ANTHONY O'MAHONY

The term Syriac Christianity refers to the various Middle Eastern and Indian churches which belong to the Syriac tradition. Since late antiquity they have divided liturgically and doctrinally into three main groups: the Syrian Orthodox Church[1] sometimes known erroneonsly as the Jacobite Church, which has rejected the doctrinal definition of the council of Chalcedon (451) and insists on the oneness of humanity and divinity in the incarnate Christ; the Church of the East,[2] sometimes known wrongly as the Nestorian or Assyrian Church, which has on different grounds rejected the council of Chalcedon, essentially because it did not distinguish strictly enough between the two natures in Christ; and finally the Maronites of the Lebanon, who have come to accept the definitions of Chalcedon. Cutting across this scheme has been the creation of eastern rite Catholic churches.[3] The term 'Syrian' used here to designate individual churches is thus much broader than the geographical area of modern Syria. There have long been Syrian churches in India, but they now spread over all five continents, with sizeable diaspora communities in western Europe, the Caucasian states, North and South America and Australasia.[4]

---

1 B. Dupuy, 'L'Église syrienne d'Antioche des origins à aujourd'hui', *Istina* 35 (1990), 171–88; Dupuy, 'Aux origines de l'Église syrienne-orthodoxe de l'Inde', *Istina* 36 (1991), 53–61. A classic description of the Syrian Church can be found in I. Zaide, 'L'Église syrienne', in *DTC* 14, col. 3018–88.

2 B. Dupuy, 'Essai d'histoire de l'Église "assyrienne" ', *Istina* 34 (1990), 159–76; J. F. Coakley, 'The Church of the East since 1914', *Bulletin of the John Rylands University Library of Manchester* 78 (1996), 179–98. The term 'Assyrian' was made current by the Anglican missionary and writer W. A. Wigram. It is, of course, inexact, as is the term 'Nestorian'. See S. P. Brock, 'The "Nestorian" Church: a lamentable misnomer', *Bulletin of the John Rylands University Library of Manchester* 78 (1996), 23–36.

3 The Syrian Catholic Church, with its Indian offshoot known as the Syro-Malankara Church, has separated from the Syrian Orthodox Church, while the Chaldaean Church, with its Indian offshoot known as the Syro-Malabar Church, has separated from the Church of the East.

4 H. Teule, 'Middle Eastern Christians and migration: some reflections', *Journal of Eastern Christian Studies* 54 (2002), 1–23.

The Syrian Orthodox Church[5]

From the seventeenth century onwards the history of the Syrian Orthodox Church has seen a struggle between a romanising party and one opposed to all union.[6] For most of the nineteenth century the anti-unionists were in the ascendant, but at the turn of the century there was a shift towards Rome. The bitterness of these disputes was soon overshadowed by the catastrophe which overtook the Syrian churches in the declining years of the Ottoman Empire. The first intimations came with the bloody repression of the Armenians in 1894–96. The massacres were not, however, limited to the Armenians, and the Syrian Christians of the region also suffered terrible losses. Figures vary, but one contemporary account puts the number of Syrian dead at 25,000, including 3000 burnt alive in the cathedral of Edessa (Urfa), in which they had taken shelter. Even more dire were the massacres perpetrated under the cover of the First World War in 1915. Once again, alongside the Armenian genocide, Christians of the Syrian churches perished in large numbers. In the oral tradition of the Syrian Orthodox, 1915 is known as *sayfo*, '(the year of) the sword' or *firmano*, '(the year of) the *firman*' (i.e. of the warrant to kill the Christian population). The figures given by Bishop (later Patriarch) Ephrem Barsaum in 1919 put the figure for Syrian Orthodox losses alone at over 90,000, more than a third of its population in the Middle East. Eight out of the twenty dioceses in the Middle East were either totally, or very largely, wiped out, and whole areas which had formerly had a sizeable Syrian Orthodox population were now left with none, since those who had escaped the massacres had fled elsewhere.[7]

Far from bringing an end to their sufferings, peace only created new difficulties for Syrian Christians. The Treaty of Lausanne did not include them among the minorities which the fledgling Turkish state undertook to protect. Aware of a total lack of external support, and confronted by a state which made no secret of its antipathy for Christians, many of them took advantage of the exchange of populations following the treaty to leave the modern

---

5 C. Sélis, 'L'Église syrienne orthodoxe', *Contacts* 187 (1999), 214–24. S. Brock, 'The Syrian Orthodox Church in the twentieth century', in *Christianity in the Middle East: studies in modern history, theology and politics*, ed. A. O'Mahony (London: Melisende, 2005). Of great value is C. Sélis, *Les Syriens orthodoxes et catholiques* (Tournai: Brepols, 1988).

6 Iskandar Bcheiry, 'A list of the Syrian Orthodox patriarchs between 16th and 18th century', *Parole de l'Orient* 29 (2004), 211–61.

7 See 'Documents sur les événements de Mardine, 1915–1920', *Collectanea: Studia Orientalia Christiana* 29/30 (1996/97), 5–220. For an eyewitness account of the French Dominican Jacques Rhétoré, see *Les chrétiens aux bêtes: souvenirs de la guerre sainte proclamée par les Turcs contre les chrétiens en 1915*, ed. Joseph Alichoran (Paris: Éditions du Cerf, 2004).

Turkish Republic. The patriarchal see, which had been located at the monastery of Dayr al-Zaʿfarân since 1293, transferred in 1924 to Homs in French mandatory territory.[8]

But even this did not bring an end to the troubles of Syrian Christians. Syrian Orthodox villages in parts of Ṭûr ʿAbdîn fell victim to the Kurdish uprising of 1925/26. The survivors fled south *en masse*, settling in the Lebanon, northern Iraq, and especially Syria, where they revitalised isolated Christian communities living there since the Middle Ages. In addition to settling in Lebanon and Syria, a significant number of refugees fled to the west, and particularly North America, where an archdiocese for North America was created in 1957, and is currently responsible for the care of some 35,000 Syrian Orthodox, while others went to Brazil and Argentina. The Arab–Israeli conflict in 1948, the June War of 1967 and the Palestinian *intifada* provided further impetus for the emigration of the Syrian Orthodox community from the Holy Land, led by Mar Athanasius Samuel, bishop of Jerusalem, who then did much for the development of the Syrian Orthodox community in America. The Syrian Orthodox in Iraq suffered from the war between the Kurds[9] and the government of Baghdad, the long Iran–Iraq war, and the period of sanctions which followed the Gulf wars. There was also a second wave of emigration in the 1970s from eastern Turkey, where, trapped in the fighting between the Turkish army and the Kurdish PKK insurgents, whole families followed the young Syrian Orthodox men who had left the region to work in Germany or increasingly in Sweden.[10]

Through this time of troubles monastic life has come to play an increasingly vital cultural and spiritual role within the Syrian Orthodox Church. From a low point in the mid-twentieth century it has seen an impressive revival over the last half-century. The monastery of Mar Gabriel in Ṭûr ʿAbdîn, seat of the metropolitan Mar Timotheos Samuel Aktash, has played a significant role in this revival. The monastery has a school which provides training in liturgical services and classical Syriac. Many of the young men now teaching Syriac in Europe received their training at this school. Further examples of the Syrian Orthodox monastic revival in the Middle East can be seen in the monastery and seminary of St Ephrem in Saîdnâyâ, north of Damascus, consecrated in 1996, and in the monastery of Mary, Bearer of God, situated at

---

8 Then in 1959 to Damascus.
9 Ray Jabre Mouawad, 'The Kurds and their Christian neighbours: the case of the Syrian Orthodox', *Parole de l'Orient* 17 (1992), 127–42.
10 K. Merten, *Die syrisch-orthodoxen Christen in der Türkei und in Deutschland* [Studien zur orientalischen Kirchengeschichte 3] (Hamburg: LIT Verlag, 1997).

Tel Wardiyat, to the west of al-Haseke in eastern Syria, consecrated in 2000. While no Syrian Orthodox monasteries have yet been founded in America, the situation in Europe, under Metropolitan Mar Julius Cicek, is very different. In 1981 the opportunity arose to purchase a former Catholic monastery outside the village of Glane on the German/Dutch border. The building was converted into the monastery of St Ephrem, serving not only as the seat of the metropolitan, but also as a cultural and religious focus for the entire émigré community. Two other Catholic monasteries have also been acquired and converted, becoming the monastery of Mar Agwen at Art in Switzerland and the monastery of Mar Ya'qûb at Warburg in Germany. The European diaspora now has some sixty churches and is served by 125 priests. There are currently some 150,000 Syrian Orthodox in Europe, perhaps half of the total church membership.

The offshoots of the Syrian Orthodox Church on the Malabar coast in southwest India form an even older diaspora. From the late nineteenth century the patriarchs of the Syrian Orthodox Church found themselves increasingly involved in the affairs of the Indian Malankara Church. In 1912 there was a split in the community when a significant section declared itself an autocephalous church and announced the re-establishment of the ancient catholicosate of the east in India. In 1930, a schism produced the Syro-Malankar Church, which followed the Syrian Catholic rite. In an attempt to restore some kind of order the Syrian Patriarch Mar Ignatius XXXVI (Elias II) made a visit to the Malabar coast in 1932, which only hastened his death. The two sides were at last reconciled in 1958 when the Indian Supreme Court declared that only the autocephalous catholicos and bishops in communion with him had legal standing. But in 1975 the Syrian patriarch excommunicated and deposed the catholicos and appointed a rival, an action that resulted in the community splitting yet again. In June 1996 the Supreme Court of India rendered a decision that (a) upheld the constitution of the church that had been adopted in 1934 and made it binding on both factions, (b) stated that there is only one Orthodox church in India, currently divided into two factions, and (c) recognised the Syrian Orthodox patriarch of Antioch as the spiritual head of the universal Syrian Church, while affirming that the autocephalous catholicos has legal standing as the head of the entire church, and that he is custodian of its parishes and properties.[11]

---

11 The precise size of these two communities is difficult to determine. The autocephalous Malankara Orthodox Syrian Church has in the region of 2,500,000 members, while the autonomous church under the supervision of the Syrian Orthodox patriarchate had about 1,200,000 faithful.

The Syrian Catholic Church

During the seventeenth century individual Syrian Orthodox bishops, under the guidance of Roman Catholic missionaries, recognised the supremacy of Rome. These unions were of a local and temporary nature. As the number of Roman Catholic missionaries increased, the logistical framework and ecclesiastical context for a wider and more comprehensive union with the Syrian Orthodox emerged. A second factor contributing to union was the political situation of Syrian Orthodox Christians in the Ottoman Empire, in which each minority, whether of a religious or a national character, normally became a self-governing *millet* or 'nation'. Each of these Christian *millets* was ruled by a patriarch or the equivalent, and the bishops and clergy assumed civil duties, the most important of which was the collection of taxes and the administration of justice both in ecclesiastical and to a limited extent in civil law. The Syrian Orthodox Church was not, to its misfortune, granted the status of an independent *millet* until 1882 but was considered part of the Armenian *millet*.[12] Hence, the Syrian Orthodox Church was dependent on the decisions of the Armenian patriarch of Constantinople. This arrangement was not in the best interest of the Syrian Orthodox Church, which under the Ottomans suffered precipitous decline.[13]

The combination of a Latin missionary presence, the example of the Maronites and the difficult position of the Syrian Orthodox Church in the Ottoman Empire made union with Rome attractive. So it was that in 1656, Abdul-Ghal Akhijan, a Syrian from Mârdîn, converted to Catholicism and under the name Andreas was consecrated as the first Syrian Catholic bishop by the Maronite patriarch. In 1662, he was officially recognised as patriarch by the Ottoman authorities, although it was only in 1677 that he received his investiture from Rome. The fledgling church sought French protection in 1663, which its detractors pounced upon.[14] On the death of Akhijan in 1677, the French imposed a candidate of their own, but this line of 'French patriarchs', as they were disparagingly called, ended in 1721. Remnants of the Syrian Catholic Church found refuge in the mountains of Lebanon, where they received support from the French, the Maronite Church and the Druze Emirs. Towards

---

12 Though this was not formalised until 1783.

13 Olivier Raquez, 'L'Église syrienne catholique', in *Sacrae Congregationis de Propaganda Fide: memoria rerum 1622–1972*, ed. J. Metzler (Rome, Freiburg and Vienna: Herder, 1973), III, pt 2, 19–28.

14 See J. Metzler, 'Die syrisch-katholische Kirche von Antiochen', in *Sacrae Congregationis de Propaganda Fide*, II, 368–78; and for the Ottoman background J. Hajjar, 'La question religieuse en Orient au déclin de l'Empire ottoman (1683–1814)', *Istina* 13 (1968), 153–236.

the end of the eighteenth century the climate of opinion within the Syrian Orthodox Church began to shift, thanks to the efforts of Roman missionaries who won over a number of dignitaries and monasteries. Their major success was the conversion of the archbishop of Aleppo, Michael Jarweh, who with four other bishops declared union with Rome. He took advantage of the lengthy vacancy that followed the death of Patriarch George IV (1768–81) to have himself elected patriarch. Pope Pius VI (1775–99) sent Jarweh formal acceptance of the union in 1783. However, the Syrian Orthodox Church had already elected Patriarch Matthew (1782–1817), who was in control of the patriarchate in Mârdîn when Jarweh and his party arrived. Hounded by both the Ottoman authorities and the Syrian Orthodox hierarchy, he fled to Baghdad and later to Mount Lebanon, where he died in 1800.[15] The pro-union succession was preserved owing to the four other bishops who also joined the union with Rome, and continues to the present Catholic patriarch of Antioch of the Syrians.

With the help of missionaries, the Syrian Catholic Church gained adherents. The French, whose interests lay in Lebanon and Syria, pressured the Ottoman sultan into recognising the Syrian Catholic Church as a distinct *millet* in 1830. This move further disadvantaged the Syrian Orthodox Church, since it was still dependent on the Armenian patriarchate in Constantinople. Catholic missionary activity continued among the Syrian Orthodox. In 1882 an indigenous Catholic missionary order – the missionaries of St Ephrem – was founded at Mârdîn. By the turn of the nineteenth century many Syrian Orthodox had become Catholic; estimates place the number between 60,000 and 65,000. The expansion of the Syrian Catholic Church came to an abrupt halt in 1915, 'the year of the sword'.

In the course of the nineteenth century the Syrian Catholic Church experienced a period of latinisation of its liturgy, governance and customs, a phenomenon that did not spare the other Near Eastern Catholic churches. For example, the Roman Church imposed celibacy on Syrian Catholic priests at the synod of Sharfeh (1888). A mixed clergy of married and celibate priests had been the norm in ancient Christianity and continues to be the case in the Orthodox churches, whereas the discipline of only celibate priests is peculiar to the Latin Church.

During the period of Ottoman massacres the Syrian Catholic Church possessed in the person of Patriarch Ignatius Ephrem Raḥmânî (1898–1929) one of

---

15 Pierre Chalfoun, 'L'Église syrienne catholique et son patriarche Michel Giavré sous la gouvernement ottoman au 18ème siècle', *Parole de l'Orient* 9 (1979–80), 205–38.

its brightest lights. He published a number of works, particularly in the fields of history, liturgy and translation, from the printing press he had established at Sharfeh. The patriarchate of Raḥmânî was a generally propitious time for the Syrian Catholic Church, with a considerable increase in members, particularly from the Syrian Orthodox Church. In 1902 he created a seminary for Syrian Catholic clergy on the Mount of Olives in Jerusalem, entrusting its management to the Benedictines.[16] In the previous year he had founded the congregation of Ephremite Sisters of the Mother of Mercy at Mârdîn and at Ḥârisa-Darûn.[17] In 1913 several Syrian Orthodox bishops converted to Catholicism. Raḥmânî oversaw the transfer of the patriarchate to Beirut from Mârdîn in order to protect his church from the Ottomans and from clashes with the Syrian Orthodox. After the 1915 massacres many Syrian Catholics took refuge in the Lebanon, particularly after the end of the Great War, when the Lebanon became a French protectorate. The period of the French mandate was, for the Syrian Catholics, a period of socio-cultural advancement and ecclesial renewal. Encouraged by Pope Benedict XV and protected by the French mandate, the Syrian Catholics launched a new round of missionary work. Many Orthodox from the Syrian community in Iraq converted to Catholicism.

Ignatius Gabriel Tappuni, who became patriarch on Raḥmânî's death in 1929, was made a cardinal in 1935, thereby recognising, at least implicitly, this Roman office as superior to his position as Syrian Catholic patriarch. With strong personal ties to France, to whom he owed his cardinal's hat, Tappuni continued to pursue, until his death in 1968, the ideal of an Eastern Christianity drawing from the wellsprings of both western and Arab cultures. A seasoned Vatican hand, he had the ear of the curia and was adept at handling the rivalries between Roman institutions. During the Second Vatican Council, he was the only eastern church dignitary with a seat on the presidential council. The council's decision that the eastern Catholic churches should eliminate Latin practices and return to their native traditions owed much to his influence. Thanks to his efforts, his church enjoyed an influence out of all proportion to its small membership.

Ignatius Antony II Hayek proved a worthy successor to Gabriel Tappuni. Born in Aleppo, he undertook lengthy studies in Rome, ending with a degree in canon law. Returning as a parish priest, his involvement with charitable organisations brought him into close contact with the impoverished workers

---

16 See D. Trimbur, 'Vie et mort d'un séminaire syrien-catholique: l'établissement bénédictin de Jérusalem', *Proche-Orient Chrétien* 52 (2002), 303–52.
17 The Order would disappear in the turmoil of the First World War, but was refounded at Ḥarîsa in 1958.

and refugees of Aleppo's *bidonvilles*. He was elected archbishop of Aleppo in 1959, and took part in all the sessions of the Second Vatican Council before succeeding to the patriarchate in 1968. In addition to revising all the liturgical books used in the Syrian Catholic rite, he was the moving force behind the construction of a new cathedral in Aleppo and, despite the war, both of the cathedral of the Annunciation and of the church of St Behnam in Beirut. During Hayek's patriarchate, the monastery of Our Lady of Deliverance at Sharfeh underwent major restoration, without losing any of its traditional character. He also had the foresight to establish Syrian Catholic missions in the USA, Canada, Australia, Venezuela and Sweden, as well as renewing the mission in Paris and restoring the procuratorship in Rome. Having served his church for thirty years, he resigned in 1998 at the age of eighty-eight, and was succeeded by Ignatius Mûsâ I Dâ'ûd, who was elected patriarch of the Syrian Catholic Church in 1998 and enthroned in the cathedral of Our Lady of the Annunciation in Beirut. During Dâ'ûd's visit to Rome shortly afterwards, the pope chose to renew an old tradition. Rather than presenting a pallium to the newly appointed patriarch, John Paul II said that in order to 'recognise the dignity of the patriarchal duty' there would be a eucharistic concelebration, on the grounds that 'the Eucharist is by nature the symbol which best expresses full communion, of which it is, at the same time, the inexhaustible source'. The pope went on to say that 'this gesture, which will remain engraved in the memory of the faithful, will be repeated' whenever a new eastern patriarch visits the Vatican.[18] On being appointed, in 2000, prefect for the congregation for Oriental churches,[19] he resigned the patriarchal throne in 2001, but received the patriarchal title *ad personam* and was created cardinal-bishop.

The current holder of the title of patriarch of Antioch and all the East of the Syrians is Ignatius Buṭrus VIII. Born in 1930, at Aleppo, he was forced, like his predecessor, to leave Jerusalem and continue his studies at Sharfeh as a consequence of the Arab–Israeli conflict. His election to the see of Jerusalem and the Holy Land in 1996 was quickly followed by his election as patriarch by the synod meeting at Sharfeh in mid-February 2001. Concelebration of the liturgy with the pope in the Vatican the following June sealed his elevation to

---

18 See 'The Syrian Catholic Church', *Eastern Churches Journal* 6 (1999), 289–90.

19 The congregation for the Oriental churches, one of the offices of the Roman curia, was established in 1862 as part of the sacred congregation for the Propagation of the Faith and became an autonomous institution during the pontificate of Benedict XV (1914–22). It has the same role with regard to bishops, clergy, religious and faithful in the eastern Catholic churches that other curial offices have in relation to the Latin Church. The congregation for the Oriental churches also oversees the Jesuit-directed Pontifical Oriental Institute in Rome, an important centre for eastern Christian studies.

the patriarchal throne.[20] There are at present some 130,000 Syrian Catholics worldwide, with many communities in Lebanon, Iraq and Syria. There is a Syrian Catholic diocese for the USA and Canada, which was established in 1996, and a chaplain for Syrian Catholics in Australia.

The Maronite Church[21]

The origins of the Maronite Church are shrouded in mystery. At some point in the twelfth century this church of mountain-dwelling monks entered into a formal union with Rome,[22] but with the fall of the crusader states contact with Latin Christendom became intermittent, until the Maronites were 'rediscovered' in the fifteenth and sixteenth centuries by Franciscan friars residing in Palestine.[23] From this period onwards, several legates were sent to Mount Lebanon to restore relations with the Maronites. In 1470 the first Maronite priest was sent to Rome for theological and scholarly training. The priest, Gabriel Ibn al-Qila'l, had been recruited by the Franciscan Order in Palestine, and after his stay in Rome and a short intermezzo in Mount Lebanon in 1493 he settled in Cyprus as the prior of the Franciscan convent until his death in 1516. He becomes an important figure in the creation of a Maronite historiography.[24]

There were recurring accusations that the Maronite Church was deliberately obscuring its, presumed, heretical origins. These were refuted in the seventeenth century thanks to a scholarly campaign led by Patriarch Iṣṭifan al-Duwayhî (1670–1704), who also played an important role in consolidating ties with Rome and France and who acquired high esteem among the Maronites as a spiritual leader and a scholar.[25] He laid the groundwork for the synod of

---

20 The liturgy and the later meeting of the pope and Syrian Catholic bishops is described briefly in *Eastern Churches Journal* 8 (2001), 306–7.

21 See H. Suermann, *Die Gründungsgeschichte der maronitischen Kirche* [Orientalia biblica et christiana 10] (Wiesbaden: Harrassowitz, 1998); Suermann, 'Die Lage des Klosters Mar Maron', *Parole de l'Orient* 13 (1986), 197–223.

22 See Charles Frazee, 'The Maronite middle ages', *Eastern Churches Review* 10 (1978), 88–100; Kamel Salibi, 'The Maronite Church in the middle ages and its union with Rome', *Oriens Christianus* 42 (1958), 92–104; R. Hiestand, 'Die Integration der Maroniten in die römische Kirche, zum ältesten Zeugnis der päpstlichen Kanzlei (12 Jahrhundert)', *OCP* 54 (1988), 119–52.

23 M. Roncaglia, 'Le relazioni della Terra Santa con i Maroniti del Monte Libano e di Cipro dal 1564 al 1569', *Archivum Franciscanum Historicum* 46 (1953), 417–47.

24 H. Douaihy, *Un théologien maronite: Ibn Al-Qila'i, évêque et moine franciscain* (Kaslik: Bibliothèque de l'Université Saint-Esprit de Kaslik, 1993).

25 R. van Leeuwen, 'The crusades and Maronite historiography', in *East and West in the Crusader States*, ed. K. Ciggaar, A. Davis and H. Teule (Leuven: Peeters, 1996), 51–62; Sarkis Tabor, 'Les relations de l'église maronite avec Rome au XVIIe siècle', *Parole de l'Orient* 9 (1978–80), 255–75.

Lebanon (30 September to 2 October 1736), which marked a major turning point in the reform of the Maronite Church.[26] For the first time, definitive diocesan boundaries were established, creating eight dioceses: six in Lebanon, one for Cyprus and one for Aleppo.[27] Many significant Latin practices were either introduced or formally accepted, including the prohibition of chrismation and Eucharist as part of the rite of Christian initiation for children and the prohibition against the laity receiving the eucharistic wine at the liturgy, two practices that offended the Roman liturgical tradition. Also, the powers and privileges of the Maronite patriarch over and against the other Maronite bishops were greatly extended. In 1741 the decisions of this council received formal papal approval and acquired the force of pontifical law.

It was at this time that two Maronites, members of the Assemani (as-Sim'ânî) family, Joseph Simon (1687–1768) and Stephen Evodius (1709–82), came to prominence in both church affairs and Syriac scholarship.[28] Pope Clement XII (1730–40) appointed Joseph Assemani apostolic *visitator* to the synod of Lebanon. He took this opportunity to collect the oriental manuscripts which form the nucleus of the Vatican Library's oriental manuscript collection. The contents of these Syriac manuscripts he set forth in his *Bibliotheca orientalis Clemento-Vaticana*, which remains a point of reference for modern Syriac scholarship. Succeeding Joseph as prefect of the Vatican Library was his nephew Stephen, who continued his work and published an edition of its Persian, Turkish and Arabic manuscripts. Other members of this industrious and gifted family held various positions of importance in the Vatican.

The *Propaganda Fide* at Rome sought the rigorous implementation of all the decrees of the Mount Lebanon synod and was especially insistent on the observance of regulations about the residence of bishops and on the abolition of mixed monasteries. However, the various synods held after 1736 at the request of the *Propaganda* failed to meet its demands. The Maronites did not see things in the same light as the curia, largely because they followed the Arabic text of the decrees of the Mount Lebanon synod, supposing it to be identical with the Latin. It turned out that the Arabic version was substantially different from the Latin text printed in Rome in 1820. There was a long-drawn-out dispute that lasted from 1830 until 1833, when Patriarch Joseph Hobaîs (1823–45), a firm

---

26 P. Rouhana, 'Histoire du synode libanais de 1736', *Parole de l'Orient* 13 (1986), 111–64; Rouhana, 'Identité ecclésiale maronite dès origines à la veille du Synode libanais', *Parole de l'Orient* 15 (1988–89), 215–60.

27 W. de Vries, 'Note sur la date de la fondation du siège archiépiscopal des Maronites à Alep', *L'Orient Syrien* 5 (1960), 351–8.

28 P. Raphael, *Le rôle du collège maronite romain dans l'orientalisme aux XVIIe et XVIIIe siècles* (Beirut: Université Saint Joseph de Beyrouth, 1950).

defender of the 1736 reform, finally accepted the Latin text of the synod[29] and in 1835 set about their implementation.

During the sixteenth and seventeenth centuries we see a significant growth in the Maronite population, together with a southward movement of Maronite communities from their traditional northern mountain domain. This was accompanied by both the construction of new monasteries[30] and the conversion of several important Druze chiefs to the Maronite Church,[31] culminating in that of Amîr Bashîr II al-Shehâbî (1788–1840), which greatly strengthened the position of the Maronites. It was Bashîr II who waged the first struggle for the independence of Lebanon from the Ottomans. Despite this, the mid-eighteenth century ushered in a period of turmoil both for Lebanon and for the Maronite Church, which was to last until the end of the nineteenth century. The Hindiyya affair, which pitted three patriarchs and the emirs of Lebanon against the Jesuits and the pope, delayed implementation of the reforms of the synod of Mount Lebanon.[32] Stabilisation only came during the long patriarchate of Paul Mubârak Mas'ad (1854–90), who definitively established the Maronite Church within the Roman framework while retaining many of its distinctive elements. The reopening in 1893 on papal instructions of the Maronite College in Rome provided posthumous confirmation.[33]

Bashîr's desire to see the benefits of western civilisation come to Lebanon, as well as his military alliance with Muḥammad 'Alî of Egypt against the Ottomans, introduced the western powers into Lebanon. The relationship between Druze and Christian Maronites deteriorated after Bashîr's death, degenerating into the destruction of Druze and Christian villages, which climaxed in the massacres of April–July 1860. In response to these atrocities French troops occupied Lebanon, which brought the massacres to an end and led in 1861 to Ottoman recognition of the autonomy of Lebanon under a Christian

29 It was carefully translated into Arabic and published in 1900. See the recent critical edition, Elias Atallah, *Le Synode libanais de 1736*: I, *Son influence sur la restructuration de l'Église maronite*; II, *Traduction du texte original arabe* (Antelias and Paris: Centre d'études et de recherches orientales, 2002).

30 R. van Leeuwen, *Notables & clergy in Mount Lebanon: the Khazin Sheikhs and the Maronite Church (1736–1840)* (Leiden: Brill, 1994).

31 See R. J. Mouawad, 'Muslim Christians? The strange case of the white Maronites', *Theological Studies* (Beirut) 24 (2003), 3–18.

32 Avril M. Makhlouf, 'Hindiyye Anne 'Ajeymi in her ecclesiastical and political situation', *Parole de L'Orient* 16 (1990–91), 279–87; Makhlouf, 'Spirituality between East and West Christendom: the Maronite mystic Hindiyya Anne 'Ajaymi', in *Eastern Christianity*, 269–95.

33 It had been closed in 1808. In May 1917 Benedict XV created the 'Sacred Congregation for the Oriental Churches'; to this congregation were entrusted the relations between Rome and the Maronite Church: see G. M. Croce, 'Alle origini della Congregazione Orientale e del Pontificio Istituto Orientale', *OCP* 53 (1987), 257–333.

governor. This was at a time when only the Maronite clergy offered credible leadership.[34] It therefore assumed full civil responsibilities for the Maronites, in addition to spiritual ones.

This did not protect the Christian communities of the Lebanon from persecution. To the estimated 100,000 murdered between 1900 and 1914 must be added the countless victims of the atrocities committed under the aegis of the Young Turks, which only came to an end with the arrival in September 1918 of General Allenby and the forces under his command. The Maronite Patriarch Buṭrus Elias Hoyek (1898–1931) travelled to the peace conference at Versailles to fight for an independent Lebanon, which had become part of the French mandate at the end of the war. Patriarch Hoyek was instrumental in ending France's direct administration of Lebanon. The Republic of Lebanon, under the French mandate, was declared on 23 May 1926. Following the occupation of Lebanon by British and Free French armies, Lebanon was granted full independence on 26 November 1941.

Lebanon's precarious balance of nations and religions has been tested throughout the twentieth century. At the forefront of the struggle to maintain an independent and unified Lebanon were the Maronite patriarchs, Anṭun 'Arîḍah and his successor Bolos al-Ma'ûshî, who played pivotal roles in the first decades of independence.[35] Survival during the civil war of 1975–90 consumed the Maronite Church. Some 670,000 Christians became displaced by the conflict as compared to 158,000 Muslims; the social and economic consequences for all Christian communities were immense and led to widespread emigration. The failure of the state and of political institutions increased the importance and leadership role of the Maronite patriarch.[36] Following this, Patriarch Peter Nasrallah (1986 to the present) has, with the permission of Pope John Paul II, led the Maronite Church along the path of a series of reforms which seek to eliminate some of the Latin practices of the Maronite liturgy, as well as to reorientate the church's pastoral and social ministries after fifteen years of civil war.[37] A significant aspect of this programme was concern for the Maronites who had emigrated to swell the ranks of established communities in Europe,

---

34 R. van Leeuwen, 'The control of space and communal leadership: Maronite monasteries in Mount Lebanon', *Revue des Mondes Musulmans et de la Méditerranée* 79–80 (1996), 183–99.

35 Including establishing close relations with the state of Israel, see L. Zittrain Eisenberg, 'Desperate diplomacy: the Zionist–Maronite Treaty of 1946', *Studies in Zionism* 13 (1992), 147–63.

36 Boutros Labaki, 'The Christian communities and the economic and social situation in Lebanon', in *Christian communities in the Arab Middle East: the challenge of the future*, ed. A. Pacini (Oxford: Clarendon Press, 1998), 222–58.

37 Mounir Khairallah, 'Le synode patriarchal maronite', *Proche-Orient Chrétien* 53 (2003), 51–63, 289–305.

Australia and the Americas.[38] There has also been a renewal in the eremitical tradition of the Maronite Church, bringing about a repopulation of the Qadisha valley by Maronites and other Christians.[39] Even if its influence has diminished, the Maronite Church will continue to play an important role in the new political landscape, because the Lebanon remains the spiritual home of the Maronite people.

The Church of the East[40]

At the beginning of the twentieth century, the area settled by the Church of the East had been reduced essentially to the rough, mountainous land of Hakkâri along the present-day border between Turkey and Iraq.[41] By then the church, which had once embraced all of East Syrian Christianity, numbered no more than some 150,000 and comprised a few Christian tribes.[42] Behind this decline lay a combination of western missionary work[43] and Kurdish attacks. However debatable the benefits brought by the missionaries may be, they at least made the Church of the East look outwards to the major churches for protection against its enemies.[44] Since 1914 their story has been one of displacement, then

---

38 There is also a growing Maronite diaspora in the Middle East. See L. Wehbé, 'The Maronites of the Holy Land: a historical overview', in *Eastern Christianity*, 431–51.

39 Guita G. Hourani and A. B. Habchi, 'The Maronite eremitical tradition: a contemporary revival', *Heythrop Journal* 45 (2004), 451–65.

40 R. Le Coz, *Histoire de l'Église d'Orient: chrétiens d'Irak, d'Iran et de Turquie* (Paris: Éditions du Cerf, 1995); J. Yacoub, *Babylone chrétienne: géopolitique de l'Église de Mésopotamie* (Paris: Desclée de Brouwer, 1996); W. Baum and D. W. Winkler, *The Church of the East: a concise history* (London: RoutledgeCurzon, 2003). See also the classic work of J. Joseph, *The Nestorians and their Muslim neighbours* (Princeton: Princeton University Press, 1961); revised as *The modern Assyrians of the Middle East: encounters with Western Christian missions, archaeologists and colonial powers* (Leiden: Brill, 2000).

41 M. Chevalier, *Les Montagnards chrétiens du Hakkari et du Kurdistan septentrional* [Publications du département de géographie de l'Université Paris-Sorbonne 13] (Paris: Université Paris-Sorbonne, 1985). Besides this mountain region, Urmia and Van were the only other areas with significant numbers of East Syriac Christians.

42 Baum and Winkler, *The Church of the East*, 135.

43 J. F. Coakley, *The Church of the East and the Church of England* (Oxford: Clarendon Press, 1992); Coakley, 'The Archbishop of Canterbury's Assyrian Mission Press: a bibliography', *Journal of Semitic Studies* 30 (1985), 35–73; M. Tamcke, 'Luther Pera's contribution to the restoration of the Church of the East in Urmia', *Harp* 8/9 (1995–96), 251–61; H. L. Murre van den Berg, 'The American Board and the eastern Church: the "Nestorian Mission" (1844–1846)', *OCP* 65 (1999), 117–38; E. C. Suttner, 'Die Union der sogenannten Nestorianer aus der Gegend von Urmia (Persien) mit der russischen orthodoxen Kirche', *Ostkirchliche Studien* 44 (1995), 33–40.

44 See Coakley, 'The Church of the East since 1914', 180, where he argues that the missionary endeavour weakened the church in the longer term by the way it unwittingly fostered dependency and enabled graduates of mission schools to emigrate rather than to take up the calling of parish priest. For the counterarguments see H. L. Murre van den Berg,

of frustration when their resettlement as a single community repeatedly failed, then of settling down as a minority in Iraq and in very small communities in other countries.[45]

On the eve of World War I, the British, French and Russians deliberately used the politics of nationalism to win allies and weaken the Ottoman Empire. The Assyrian region of settlement lay on the line dividing the interests of Turkey and Russia. As late as 1914 Patriarch Mar Shim'ûn XIX (Benjamin) (1903–18) approached the Turkish provincial governor to negotiate for the security of his East Syrian tribes. The governor offered two separate guarantees, but Kurdish–Turkish attacks on Christians soon followed, because the Christians were seen as allies of Russia. On 10 May 1915 news of the massacres of Christians and hopes of support from the Russians induced Patriarch Mar Shim'ûn XIX to declare war on Turkey in the name of his nation (*millet*). Shortly thereafter the strategic situation changed. The Russians had to withdraw from Van; the Kurds attacked the Assyrians and forced them higher into the mountains. Many East Syrian villages and churches were destroyed. These desperate straits led to the Assyrians' decision to evacuate all of their tribes from the Hakkâri mountain region. Under the skilful leadership of their *malik*, 50,000 men, women and children gathered together and reluctantly advanced towards Urmia, where they hoped to secure aid from Russian troops.[46] On the plains they joined with the Assyrians they met. The 'Mountain Nestorians' had left their homeland behind, and few would ever see it again.[47]

Mar Shim'ûn XIX was assassinated in Iran in 1918, to be succeeded in quick succession by first one nephew and then another, who was consecrated in Iraq as Mar Shim'ûn XXI.[48] Still young, he was dispatched to England for his education, while the government of the 'nation' rested in the hands of an aunt, Lady Surma, who with her English upbringing was the virtual regent. Back from England Mar Shim'ûn was regarded by the Iraqi government as the civil leader of the Nestorians in their country; he was also the religious head of all those in Russia and India. Disregarding the petition he presented to the Lausanne Conference seeking the return of his people to their homeland, the

---

'Migration of Middle Eastern Christians to western countries and Protestant missionary activities in the Middle East: a preliminary investigation' *Journal of Eastern Christian Studies* 54 (2002), 39–49.

45 Coakley, 'The Church of the East since 1914', 179–98.
46 D. Méthy, 'L'action des Grandes Puissances dans la région d'Ourmia (Iran) et les Assyro-Chaldéens 1917–1918', *Studia Kurdica* 1–5 (1988), 77–100.
47 Baum and Winkler, *The Church of the East*, 137–8.
48 He later changed this to Mar Shim'ûn XXIII.

League of Nations assigned the Hakkâri region in 1925 to Turkey.[49] With the withdrawal of the British administration from Iraq in 1931 Mar Shimʿûn lost his only ally. Suspicious of the guarantees made by Iraq to its minorities, he protested about the treatment of his people to the government in Baghdad, only to find himself under arrest, deprived of his Iraqi nationality and, in August 1933, deported to Cyprus. Meanwhile the governor of Mosul ordered the Assyrians to lay down their arms. Some refused and sought refuge in Syria, but were ordered back by the French military. Under attack from regular and irregular forces, they and other groups of Assyrians underwent severe and bloody repression in July–August 1933. Their case was submitted to the League of Nations.[50]

Mar Shimʿûn left for the United States in 1940, where he spent most of the remainder of his life, which ended in assassination at San José on 6 November 1975. With his death, hereditary succession to the patriarchate came to an end. On 17 October 1976 five Assyrian bishops, two Italian bishops who had been consecrated by Mar Shimʿûn, and representatives of the church in Iraq gathered at Alton Abbey in Hampshire[51] to elect Mar Dinkha Khnanaya as the new patriarch and 120th successor to the seat of Seleukeia-Ctesiphon. At the age of thirty-three, Mar Dinkha had been appointed metropolitan of Teheran and Iran by Mar Shimʿûn – thus becoming the nineteenth bishop in his family. Until the Iran–Iraq war (1980–88), Mar Dinkha had his see in Teheran; thereafter he transferred it to Chicago. The two wars in the Persian Gulf region brought renewed hardship to the Christian minority. In Iraq Saddam Hussein sought to institute a plan of arabisation, affecting in particular the Kurds and the Christians of northern Iraq, who were violently expelled. In 1988, as part of his policy of repression, Saddam Hussein had many Christian villages, churches and monasteries in northern Iraq destroyed, and a wave of Kurdish and Christian refugees fled to Turkey, Iran, Jordan and Syria.[52]

Patriarch Mar Dinkha IV sought to lead the Assyrians out of their isolation and neglect by focusing on ecumenical engagement; and by consolidating the

---

49 J. Yacoub, 'La question assyro-chaldéenne, les puissances européennes et la Société des Nations', *Guerres Mondiales et Conflits Contemporains* 38 (1988), 104–20.

50 Khaldun S. Husry, 'The Assyrian affair of 1933', *International Journal of Middle East Studies* 5 (1974), 161–76, 344–60, but his version of events has been challenged by J. Joseph, 'The Assyrian affair: a historical perspective', ibid. 6 (1975), 115–17. Large numbers of Assyrians joined the British military and became a feared fighting force, see David Omissi, 'Britain, Assyrians and the Iraq levies, 1919–32', *Journal of Imperial and Commonwealth History* 27 (1989), 301–22.

51 Also present were three Anglican bishops.

52 A. O'Mahony, 'Eastern Christianity in modern Iraq', in *Eastern Christianity*, 11–43; O'Mahony, 'Christianity in modern Iraq', *International Journal for the Study of the Christian Church* 4 (2004), 121–42.

links of the Church of the East with its offshoots in India, where individual congregations and priests have returned to the jurisdiction of Mar Dinkha.[53] In November 1995 a former opponent, Metropolitan Mar Aprem, made his peace along with all his congregations. In January 2000 Mar Dinkha visited India to celebrate the reunification of the Indian church with the Church of the East.

Since 1972 the Church of the East has been split into two. By far the larger is the Holy Apostolic and Catholic Church of the East, which is subdivided into four metropolitanates, namely Baghdad, Malabar, Trichur (Kerala) and Beirut, together with other dioceses in the United States, Canada, Australia and Europe. This group is recognised as a church by, amongst others, the Vatican, the WCC (World Council of Churches) and the Anglicans. The other is the Old Apostolic and Catholic Church of the East – sometimes known as the 'Old Calendarists' – which broke away from the main church in 1968 in protest at Mar Shim'ûn's adoption of the Gregorian calendar. Under Mar Addai II it has its patriarchate in Baghdad, with its seat divided between Kirkuk, Mosul and Trichur (Kerala), as well as a bishopric in al-Haseke (Syria). It also has dioceses in North America, Australasia and Europe. There are no accurate statistics about the number of Christians in the Middle East. However, the following figures may give at least an idea of the size and spread of the Church of the East. At the beginning of the twenty-first century, the Church of the East has approximately 385,000 members, and the 'Old Calendarists' perhaps 70,000 at most.

The Chaldean Church[54]

The origins of the Chaldean Church go back many centuries. In the thirteenth century, Catholic missionaries, Dominicans and Franciscans, were active among the faithful of the Church of the East. In 1445 those settled on the island of Cyprus accepted the Roman confession of faith. Their leader Timothy, archbishop of Tarsus, was granted permission to attend the closing sessions of the council of Florence, where he was referred to as the archbishop

53 Notably the Indian metropolitan church of Trichur.
54 R. Sbardella, 'L'unione della chiesa caldea nell'opera del P. Tommaso Obicini da Novara', *Collectanea: Studia Orientalia Christiana* 5 (1960), 373–452; Giuseppe Beltami, *La chiesa nel secolo dell'unione* [OCA 83] (Rome: Pontificium institutum orientalium studiorum, 1933); S. Bello, *La congrégation de S. Hormisdas et l'Église chaldéenne dans la première moitié du XIXe siècle* [OCA 122] (Rome: Pontificium institutum orientalium studiorum, 1933); A. Lampart, *Ein Märtyrer der Union mit Rom: Joseph I (1681–1696), Patriarch der Chaldäer* (Einsiedeln: Benziger Verlag, 1966); G. Sorge, 'Giovanni Simone Sullaqa: primo patriarca dell' "Unione formale" della chiesa caldea', *Annuarium Historiae Conciliorum* 12 (1980), 427–40.

of the 'Chaldeans'.[55] Since then the term 'Chaldean' has come to be used for those East Syrians in union with Rome.

Though this union did not last, in 1552 a group of Syrian bishops elected the abbot of the monastery of Rabban Hurmizd, Yûhannâ Sulâka, patriarch in protest against the tradition of hereditary succession to the patriarchate of the Church of the East, with nephew following uncle, which meant not only that one family dominated the church, but also that an untrained minor might ascend the patriarchal throne. To strengthen the position of their candidate the bishops sent him to Rome to negotiate a new union. Early in 1553 Pope Julius III proclaimed him Patriarch Shim'ûn VIII 'of the Chaldeans' and ordained him a bishop in St Peter's Basilica on 9 April 1553. The new patriarch returned to his homeland and began to initiate a series of reforms. But opposition, led by the rival patriarch, was strong. Sulâka was quickly captured by the Ottoman governor of Amâdîya, and was tortured and executed in January 1555.[56] Over the next two hundred years, there was much turmoil and changing of sides as the pro- and anti-Catholic parties struggled with one another.

The Catholic Patriarch Shim'ûn XIII returned to the Church of the East in 1692 and moved his see from Urmia to the more remote location of Kochanes in the Hakkâri Mountains of Kurdistan.[57] In 1772 his successor, Shim'ûn XV, made overtures to Rome about the restoration of union, but to no avail because by this time the papacy recognised a different line of Catholic patriarchs, beginning with Joseph, bishop of Amida, whose declaration of union received papal approval in 1681.[58] Confirmation came in the form of the title 'patriarch of Babylon of the Chaldeans', which Rome then conferred on his successor, Yûsuf (Joseph) II.[59]

---

55 I.e. *archiepiscopus Chaldaeorum, qui in Cypro sunt.* Before 1445 there are only three instances in western sources of 'Chaldean' referring to oriental Christians, but with the meaning of 'Syriac speaker' rather than in union with Rome: see J.-M. Fiey, 'Comment l'occident en vint à parler de "Chaldéens"?', *Bulletin of the John Rylands University Library of Manchester* 78 (1996), 163–70.

56 J. Habbi, 'Signification de l'union chaldéenne de Mar Sulaqa avec Rome en 1553', *L'Orient Syrien* 9 (1966), 99–132, 199–230; J. M. Vosté, 'Mar Johanan Soulaqa: premier patriarche des Chaldéens', *Angelicum* 8 (1931), 187–234. Sulaqa is seen as a martyr for the unity of the church under a Catholic banner: see J.-M. Fiey, 'Martyrs sous les Ottomans', *Analecta Bollandiana* 101 (1983), 387–406.

57 This is the line that began with Sulâka in 1553 and constitutes the present line of patriarchs of the Church of the East.

58 Lampart, *Ein Märtyrer der Union mit Rome.*

59 Joseph II was an accomplished defender of the Catholic cause and union with Rome within the eastern Christian community, H. Teule, 'Joseph II, Patriarch of the Chaldeans (1696–1734), and the "Book of the Magnet": first soundings', in *Studies on the Christian Arabic Heritage,* ed. H. G. B. Teule and R. Y. Ebied (Leuven: Peeters, 2004), 221–41.

A new Chaldean line appeared in the early nineteenth century, when Bishop Yuhanna Hormizd, a cousin of the catholicos of the Church of the East, converted to Catholicism and obtained the see of Mosul. Hormizd was in competition for the title of patriarch of Babylon of the Chaldeans with the Josephite line, which opportunely came to an end in 1830. On 5 July 1830 Pope Pius VIII (1829–30) then conferred the patriarchal title on Hormizd, creating a single line of Chaldean patriarchs that continues to the present.[60]

The seat of the patriarchate was fixed at Mosul; and in 1846 the Ottoman Porte recognised the Chaldeans as a *millet* in their own right. This was followed by the election of Joseph Audo (1847–78) as patriarch. His long reign witnessed renewed conflict between the Chaldean Church and Rome.[61] Confronted by growing anticlericalism in Europe, the papacy was in no position to adjust its polemic to the particular needs of a remote constituency such as the Chaldean Catholics of a distant Ottoman province. It insisted on extending pontifical prerogatives into the administration of the Chaldean Church. Relations of Audo with the *Propaganda* focused at first on the relationship of the Chaldean Church with its sister church in India. The traditional dependence of the latter on the former (solemnly approved by Pius IV in 1562) had lapsed. Requests made to the *Propaganda* by Malabar Christians for permission to restore their old relationship with the Chaldean Church met with refusal. They therefore turned from 1849 onwards to Patriarch Audo, who in the face of papal displeasure consecrated Thomas Rokkos in 1860 as bishop for India. The apostolic delegate to Mesopotamia thundered excommunication. Pius IX tacitly denied the excommunication but in 1861 summoned Audo to Rome, where the latter reluctantly agreed to stop interfering in the affairs of the Malabar Church. This was not the only issue on which Audo was at loggerheads with Pius IX. In 1869, after initial hesitations, Audo opposed the pope's decision to appropriate to the Holy See the appointment of bishops of eastern rite churches. Like other opponents of this measure, he received an invitation to attend the first Vatican Council of 1869–70, where he once again gave in to papal pressure. His discomfort and resentment is evident in a long and rather ponderous speech he made to the council, in which he defended the legitimacy of oriental disciplinary traditions. On the question of papal infallibility he voted with the minority. So it comes as no surprise that in 1876 he dispatched another bishop to India, thus producing a schism in the Malabar Church. Pius IX reacted vigorously

60 J. Habbi, 'L'unification de la hiérarchie chaldéenne dans la première moitié du XIX siècle', *Parole de l'Orient* 2 (1971), 121–43, 305–27.

61 C. Korolevskij, 'Audo (Joseph)', in *Dictionnaire d'histoire et de géographie ecclésiastique* v (Paris: Letouzey et Ané, 1931), 317–56.

with the issue of the encyclical *Quae in Patriarchatu*, which demanded unconditional submission. The aging patriarch submitted in 1877.[62] At least he had the satisfaction, just before he died, of knowing that the papacy had made concessions on the appointment of bishops.[63]

For the Chaldean Church the twentieth century has brought destruction and renewal. The Chaldeans lost many of their clergy among the tens of thousands of those massacred in the Turkish persecutions of 1915–17. Among those Chaldeans who were murdered were such luminaries as bishop Addai Shir,[64] who made contributions to the study of Syriac literature through providing catalogues of manuscript collections in the possession of the Chaldean Church as well as editions of Syriac texts.

The renewal of Chaldean Catholic institutions began after the Second World War under the leadership of Patriarch Paul II Cheikho (1958–89) and was carried through by his successor, Patriarch Mar Raphael I Bidawid (1989–2003). In times of conflict and political upheaval these two Chaldean patriarchs navigated the community through the difficult and challenging seas now charted by the Christians of the Middle East: between minority and majority, between Christianity and Islam. Elected patriarch of the Chaldeans in December 1958, Paul Cheikho had to nurse his community through some very difficult times in modern Iraqi history. His near thirty-year tenure saw three revolutions (1958, 1963, 1968), three regimes, the emergence of an oil-driven economy, the Kurdish revolt, and the long Iran–Iraq war. Cheikho did all he could to adapt the organisation of his church to difficult and changing times. The Kurdish uprising brought new travails to the Christians in Iraq. Over the course of the fighting between the Iraqi army and the Kurds, many Christian villages and churches were destroyed or plundered, including in June 1969 the monastery of Rabban Hurmidz near Alqosh – a major spiritual centre of the Chaldean Church.[65] These events led to the traumatic displacement of Christians from the north of Iraq, where they had formed prosperous farming communities. Between 1961 and 1995 the Christians living in the north dwindled from the million mark to around 150,000. They moved southwards into the large cities of Iraq. Paul Cheikho met the challenge, constructing some twenty-five churches in Baghdad to serve the needs of his Chaldean Catholic community.[66]

---

62 J. Habbi, 'Les Chaldéens et les Malabares au XIXe siècle', *Oriens Christianus* 64 (1980), 82–108.
63 To be extended still further in 1889.
64 Assad Sauma Assad, 'Addai Shir, 1867–1915', *Harp* 8/9 (1995–96), 209–20.
65 Baum and Winkler, *The Church of the East*, 146.
66 See sub 'Iraq', in *Proche-Orient Chrétien* 39 (1989), 346.

Other challenges came in the shape of government demands for seminary reform and the extension of military service to priests and religious; to be followed in 1975 by the nationalisation of the school system which had a direct impact upon Catholic schools. In 1984, during the Iran–Iraq war, Cheikho led an ecumenical and interfaith delegation to the Vatican in witness to the suffering of Iraqi society in general, and of Christian communities in particular. While remaining loyal to the Iraqi government, he stood up for the rights of the church. For example, he opposed the government when it sought to impose the study of the Qur'an in Christian schools.

As bishop of Amâdîya in Kurdistan from 1957 to 1965 Cheikho's successor Mar Raphael Bidawid dealt with the opening stages of the Christian exodus from northern Iraq. He was then transferred to the Chaldean diocese of Beirut (Lebanon) until his election as patriarch of the Chaldean Catholic Church in 1989. His death in Beirut on 7 July 2003, shortly after the collapse of the Ba'athist regime in Baghdad, complicated the election of a successor, which required the intervention of the Vatican. Pope John Paul II called the Chaldean bishops to Rome for deliberations, which ended in the election on 3 December 2003 of the 76-year-old Emmanuel-Karim Delly as patriarch of Babylon of the Chaldeans, taking the name Emmanuel III.[67] In accordance with the pope's preference for a concelebrated liturgy as an affirmation of unity, the Cardinal Prefect Ignatius Mûsâ I Dâ'ûd and the new patriarch concelebrated the Divine Liturgy using the Chaldean rite at the altar of the 'Chair' in the basilica of St Peter.[68]

The Chaldean Church, with over 70 per cent of all Christians, is the largest church in modern Iraq. In Baghdad alone, which is one of the largest Christian centres in the Middle East, there are some thirty parishes with a total of 200,000–250,000 faithful. There are other Iraqi dioceses at Kirkuk, Irbil, Basra, Mosul, Alqosh, Amâdîya and al-Sulaymâniyya, 'Aqra and Zakho. The Chaldean diaspora represents a significant element of the church, with bishops and dioceses in Lebanon, Syria, Turkey, Armenia and Georgia, Israel and Jordan, Egypt, Iran, Australasia, Europe and North America. The church has also had to develop a flexible response to the number of Christian refugees in the region; for example, Bidawid appointed a patriarchal vicar in 2002 to care for the Chaldean refugees in Jordan living in difficult circumstances. In America a new eparchy was established in 2002 for some 35,000 new Chaldean arrivals.

67 *La Croix*, 5 September 2003.
68 *L'Osservatore Romano*, 16 December 2003.

This now supports the older Chaldean eparchy, which looks after some 80,000 Chaldean Catholics.[69]

Ecumenical dialogue among the Syriac churches

The greatest challenge and the most important achievement of the bilateral and multilateral ecumenical theological dialogues that have taken place among Syrian churches has been the opportunity for each church to express its theological tradition and understanding of its theology, history, role in christological disputes, sacraments, liturgy and modern contribution to Christendom. Three main factors can be identified as being responsible for these developments: the ecumenical movement and the establishment (in 1948) of the WCC; the Second Vatican Council; and the large-scale emigration from the Middle East to Europe, the Americas and Australia of Christians from the non-Chalcedonian churches. Large-scale emigration started with the widespread massacres in eastern Turkey, above all in 1915, 'the year of the sword', when huge numbers were either killed or displaced. In recent decades the political instability of the Middle East has led to further waves of emigration. Although emigration has in general been disastrous from the point of view of the life of the indigenous churches in the Middle East, there have at least been other consequences: it has provided the possibility of publication without censorship, and it has made western churches more aware of the existence of these non-Chalcedonian churches, which in turn has provided an opportunity and an incentive for theological dialogue.

Sebastian Brock has identified three strands to this modern dialogue: the first is that between the Chalcedonian eastern Orthodox churches and the non-Chalcedonian oriental Orthodox churches, which began in 1964 and continues to the present; the second is that between the Roman Catholic Church and the non-Chalcedonian oriental Orthodox churches which began in 1971. The third is the multilateral dialogue among all churches of the Syriac tradition initiated and facilitated by the PRO ORIENTE Foundation in Vienna in 1994.[70]

The first unofficial meeting at the PRO ORIENTE Foundation in 1971 resulted in a joint declaration between the Chalcedonian and non-Chalcedonian churches known as the Vienna Formula, the text of which has been received officially

---

69 A. O'Mahony, 'The Chaldean Catholic Church: the politics of church–state relations in modern Iraq', *Heythrop Journal* 45 (2004), 435–50.

70 S. Brock, 'The Syriac churches in ecumenical dialogue on Christology', in *Eastern Christianity*, 46–7.

and is fundamental to all subsequent dialogue. The agreement on Christology states that Jesus Christ is

> perfect in His divinity and perfect in His humanity. His divinity was not separated from his humanity for a single moment, not for the twinkling of an eye; His humanity is one with His divinity without commixtion, without confusion, without division, without separation. We . . . regard His mystery as inexhaustible and ineffable and for the human mind never fully comprehensible or expressible.[71]

Following the Vienna Formula, the next major breakthrough took place in 1984, with the joint declaration of Pope John Paul II and Syrian Orthodox Patriarch of Antioch and All the East Ignatius Zakka Iwas.[72] Their declaration includes the statement that the schisms that arose in the fifth century 'in no way affect or touch the substance of their faith, since these arose only because of differences in terminology and culture and in the various formulae adopted by different theological schools to express the same matter'. The part of the declaration concerning Christology closely follows the language of the Vienna Formula. It is recognition that the disagreement in Christology is one of terminology only and does not touch the substance of Christian doctrine.

Though starting rather later, bilateral discussions between the Church of the East on the one hand and the Syrian Orthodox and Catholic eastern rite churches on the other have achieved significant breakthroughs in consultations held throughout the 1990s.[73] However, the Coptic Orthodox Church has asserted its authority over the other oriental Orthodox churches, preventing the Church of the East from participating either in further official consultations with the Syrian Orthodox Church or in the MECC (Middle East Council of Churches), despite the advocacy of the Roman Catholic Church.[74]

In 1984 an official meeting took place between the catholicos of the Church of the East, Mar Denkha IV and Pope John Paul II. They set up the Joint Commission for Theological Dialogue between the Roman Catholic Church

---

71 The full text of the Vienna Formula is available in PRO ORIENTE, *Syriac Dialogue 1* (Vienna: PRO ORIENTE, 1994), 27–8.

72 See Brock, 'The Syriac churches in ecumenical dialogue', 51–2. The declaration was originally printed in *L'Osservatore Romano*, 24 June 1984.

73 D. W. Winkler, 'The current theological dialogue with the Assyrian Church of the East', in *Symposium Syriacum VII* [OCA 256] (Rome: Pontificium institutum orientalium studiorum, 1998), 158–73.

74 See O. Meinardus, 'About heresies and the Syllabus Errorum of Pope Shenuda III', *Coptic Church Review* 22 (2001), 98–105 and the response by S. Brock, '"About heresies and the Syllabus Errorum of Pope Shenuda III": some comments on the recent article by Professor Meinardus', ibid. 23 (2002), 98–102.

and the Assyrian Church of the East, which has provided a basis for the subsequent bilateral dialogue.[75] In 1985 the Church of the East applied to join the MECC, only to be blocked by the Coptic Orthodox Church. However, the matter of the Church of the East remained on the agenda of the MECC in 1992 and 1994. At a regional symposium of Pro Oriente held at the Deir Anba Bishoi monastery in the Wâdî al-Naṭrûn in Egypt in 1991, a fierce debate erupted concerning the participation of the Church of the East in Pro Oriente consultations, with the Copts refusing to discuss the finer points of theological and terminological questions surrounding the council of Ephesus (431).[76] Nevertheless, the Pro Oriente Foundation continued to discuss the involvement of the Church of the East in its activities.

In 1994 Pro Oriente initiated a dialogue between the Church of the East, the Syrian Orthodox Church and the eastern Catholic churches of the Syriac tradition, including church officials and theologians representing sister churches in India. The event itself was of great significance even without a substantial christological agreement.[77] A common declaration of faith promulgated by Mar Denkha IV and Pope John Paul II in the same year stated that the two churches had the same understanding concerning Christology and the Virgin Mary.[78] Following this declaration, the MECC decided to move forward with the inclusion of the Church of the East.

Despite the staunch opposition of the Coptic Orthodox Church to any dialogue with or to any participation of the Church of the East in ecumenical affairs, the two churches produced a draft common declaration on Christology in 1995. This document, which drew heavily on the Vienna Formula which the Coptic Church had formally accepted, as well as from the common declaration of faith, was quickly ratified by the synod of bishops of the Church of the East.[79] The Coptic Church synod has subsequently rejected this document. The result of these developments has been to halt any further official consultation between the Church of the East and the Syrian Orthodox Church.

75 D. W. Winkler, *Ostsyrisches Christentum: Untersuchungen zu Christologie, Ekklesiologie, und zu den ökumenischen Beziehungen der assyrischen Kirche des Ostens* [Studien zur orientalischen Kirchengeschichte 26] (Münster: LIT Verlag, 2003), 146. The Chaldean Church is also represented on the joint commission.

76 Brock, 'The Syriac churches in ecumenical dialogue', 53. The paper that set off the debate at this conference was by André de Halleux, 'Nestorius, histoire et doctrine', *Irénikon* 66 (1993), 38–51, 163–77; trans. without notes in Pro Oriente, *Syriac Dialogue 1*, 200–15.

77 G. O'Collins and D. Kendall, 'Overcoming christological differences', *Heythrop Journal* 37 (1996), 382–90.

78 The key passage of this text is quoted in Brock, 'The Syriac churches in ecumenical dialogue', 54–5.

79 For a lengthy citation from this text, see Brock, 'The Syriac churches in ecumenical dialogue', 55–8.

A more hopeful outcome from the PRO ORIENTE Syriac Dialogues has been the opening of bilateral dialogue between the Syrian Orthodox and Syrian Catholic churches. The first meeting between the patriarchs Ignatius Zakka Iwas and Ignatius Mûsâ Cardinal Dâ'ûd, presently the head of the Congregation for the Oriental Churches, took place in November 1999. Both the Syrian Catholic and the Maronite churches have regularly participated in the PRO ORIENTE consultations since 1994. Representatives of delegations from these churches have not only contributed papers on Christology, but have also begun to discuss the liturgy and sacraments.[80]

In 1996, the Church of the East and the Roman Catholic Church met to outline the course of the discussion for future meetings. The productivity of these future meetings rested in part on the clear goal that the participants set out: the restoration of full ecclesial unity of the Church of the East. In pursuit of this goal the two patriarchs stipulated that the entire common theological, patristic, liturgical, linguistic, cultural and historical inheritance of both churches should be the objects of study and reflection.[81] A 'Commission for Unity' was established with the task of creating a common catechism and a common institute for training priests, deacons and catechists in the Detroit metropolitan area (a region that has large concentrations of members of both churches), as well as other important cultural and ecclesiastical joint projects.

In October 2001, Rome issued a document entitled 'Guidelines for Admission to the Eucharist between the Chaldean Church and the Church of the East'. This two-page document covered the conditions under which Chaldean Catholics of the diaspora are permitted to receive communion within the Church of the East. These revolve around the question of the validity of the eucharistic prayer of Addai and Mari, employed in the Church of the East. This is a eucharistic prayer which does *not* contain Jesus's so-called 'words of institution': 'This is my body . . . This is my blood.' Roman Catholic liturgics requires the presence of these two formulae for there to be a Eucharist. These words of institution were therefore added to the eucharistic prayer employed in the Chaldean Catholic Church. However, scholars of the Roman Church have now established that the eucharistic prayer of Addai and Mari is ancient, and that this prayer without Jesus's words is consequently a valid eucharistic

---

80 S. Brock, 'The Syriac churches and dialogue with the Catholic Church', *Heythrop Journal* 45 (2004), 435–50.
81 Ibid., 155.

prayer.[82] Pope John Paul II approved this determination early in 2001. This is a major step for the Roman Catholic Church, since for centuries it has taught that without these words in the eucharistic prayer there is no eucharistic sacrament.[83] It shows a proper respect for the traditions of the eastern churches.

82 Guy Vanhoomissen, 'Une messe sans paroles de consécration? À propos de la validité de l'anaphore d'Addaï et Mari', *Nouvelle Revue Théologique* 127 (2005), 36–46; M. Smyth, 'Une avancée œcuménique et liturgique. La note romaine concernat l'Anaphore d'Addaï et Mari', *La Maison-Dieu* 233 (2003), 137–54.
83 Winkler, *Ostsyrisches Christentum*, 158.

PART IV

*

THE MODERN WORLD

22

Diaspora problems of the Russian emigration

SERGEI HACKEL

Diaspora

The question of diaspora is proposed for the agenda of the long-delayed 'great and holy' council of the Orthodox Church. Indeed, since 1976 it has been given pride of place in that agenda: it is a question that needs to be resolved 'as quickly as possible'.[1] In the absence of any such resolution there is a wide range of factors, ecclesiological as well as pastoral, which will continue to frustrate the Orthodox at large.

The Old Testament concept of diaspora provides insufficient guidance. It assumes not only a single faith for all concerned – a reasonable assumption for Orthodox Christians of modern times – but also a single sacred centre. Any substitute was necessarily of limited duration, no matter how long it might last: reversion to the primal centre will always be desired, as the yearning for Jerusalem expressed in Psalm 137 emphasises.

Despite its post-Constantinian attractions as a pilgrim destination, Jerusalem was hardly to play so prominent a role in Christian thought. In any case, it was not deemed to be the 'home' from which the faithful were dispersed. Other apostolic centres such as Rome, Antioch or Alexandria came to be treated as equally, if otherwise, important. In due course the foundation of Constantinople (330) was to give the eastern capital ever greater prominence. In 381 the second ecumenical council advanced it to second place in order of major Christian sees, and an apostolic pedigree was eventually invented to confirm its role.[2] Its early claim to the title 'ecumenical' (470s–480s) suggested claims to widespread, if not universal, status. At the very least it claimed 'the

---

1 'La Diaspora orthodoxe': adopted text of the inter-Orthodox preparatory commission (1990), *Épiskepsis* 22: 452 (1991), 21–2.
2 See F. Dvornik, *The idea of apostolicity in Byzantium and the legend of the Apostle Andrew* (Cambridge, MA: Harvard University Press, 1958).

privilege of investigating and of answering pressing ecclesiastical questions arising in the churches throughout the *oikoumene*'.[3]

Constantinople

Historical developments were to give this title added prominence, especially those which involved ever greater separation from Rome. Even when Constantinople ceased to be the centre of a Christian empire (1453), its self-esteem and aspirations were not abandoned. The patriarchate's subject status in the Ottoman dispensation required some adaptation of the terms employed. Nevertheless, the Muslim rulers of the former empire authorised the patriarch of Constantinople to take precedence in church affairs throughout their lands, even though this might involve other ancient patriarchates. Earlier in 1370 the Byzantine patriarch Philotheos had felt able to speak of himself as 'the leader of all Christians found anywhere in the inhabited earth'. In his words, 'all of them depend on me'.[4] These were concepts which retained some moral force in centuries to come.

However, even in the Christian east, Constantinople needed to accommodate a variety of other centres of importance, often outside the boundaries of the Byzantine or Ottoman empires. Many resulted from a missionary outreach of the Byzantine patriarchate, to which they were subject for a time. But some were to mature into separate jurisdictions, each with individual myths of independence. So, the establishment of a patriarchal church in the Bulgarian capital of T'rnovo enhanced its imperial claims, so much so that it was called a third Rome.[5] The image of a third Rome was to pass into Russian thought after the fall of Constantinople. It was at first related to the city of Novgorod,[6] but Moscow was soon to claim full possession of the myth.[7] This may have helped to justify its claims to found a separate patriarchate, one for which the patriarch of Constantinople was required in 1589 to give his blessing. In due course Moscow was to become one of several jurisdictions with distinct

3 Neilos, patriarch of Constantinople (1380–88), quoted in Maximos of Sardes, *The oecumenical patriarchate in the Orthodox Church*, trans. Gamon McLellan (Thessalonike: Patriarchal Institute for Patristic Studies, 1976), 276.

4 F. Miklosich and J. Müller, *Acta et diplomata graeca mediiaevi sacra et profana* (Vienna, 1860), I, 521.

5 D. Obolensky, *The Byzantine Commonwealth: eastern Europe, 500–1453* (London: Weidenfeld and Nicolson, 1971), 246–7.

6 'Povest' o Novgorodskom belom klobuke', in *Pamiatniki Literatury Drevnei Rusi*, ed. L. Dmitriev and D. S. Likhachev (Moscow: Khudozhestvennaia literatura, 1988–94), VII, 228.

7 V. Malinin, *Starets Eleazarova monastyria Filofei i ego poslaniia: istoriko-literaturnoe izsledovanie* (Kiev: Tipografiiia Kievo-Pecherskoi Lavry, 1901), prilozheniia vii.45.

diasporas, each with a different ethnic and ecclesiological basis from anything that had previously prevailed.

Phyletism

Migrations of Orthodox populations to one part of the world or another occurred for a variety of reasons. These no longer formed a unified and well-defined diaspora, which was loyal to some single mother-church. Determining the character of each was rather a combination of disparate origins and prospects with the evolution *in situ* of separate church administrations. Even where the loyalties of formerly dependent churches seemed secure, or at least formally maintained, the very passage of time might prompt a revision of the situation.

Thus, many Russians in America claimed some vague affiliation with their mother-church, even when the circumstances of the Soviet period favoured no such thing. They might go further, as they did in 1924 when they claimed effective independence, while yet remaining 'Russian' in their ways. Only much later, in 1970, did the Russian archdiocese (*metropolia*) in the New World negotiate its formal independence from the Moscow patriarchate[8] – regardless of protests from Constantinople.[9]

Such independence may be one form in which diaspora situations find their resolution. The diaspora takes on a new identity and ceases to be a mere extension of its parent body. At the same time it seeks to be 'independent of nationalisms'.[10] The Russian diaspora in America was initially the result of migration in search of income, which, as in Alaska, could also take the form of colonial expansion. But a different reason for diasporas was the disruption of empires which had previously ensured the ecclesial coexistence of disparate subject nations.

Liberation from the Turks led to the emergence of several independent churches in the Balkans. Thus, Constantinople accepted the autonomy of the Serbian Orthodox Church in 1832 and its autocephaly in 1879. Greece established its own national church in 1852 after the successful conclusion of the national uprising against Ottoman rule thirty years before. The Romanian provinces had asserted their ecclesial independence by 1885. The patriarchate

---

8 S. Surrency, *The quest for Orthodox unity in America* (New York: Saints Boris and Gleb Press, 1973), 155–62.
9 Correspondence between Athenagoras Spyrou, patriarch of Constantinople, and the *locum tenens* of the patriarch of Moscow, metropolitan Pimen Izvekov in *Zhurnal Moskovskoi Patriarkhii* 9 (1970), 6–15.
10 J. Meyendorff in *Contacts* 77 (1970), 310.

of Constantinople had little choice but to accept these innovations. However, there was one exception, and it provoked an important riposte. When in 1870 the newly re-established Bulgarian Orthodox Church sought to confirm its rights over its own diaspora in Constantinople and its vicinity, the patriarchate saw this as an untoward intrusion. Was Bulgarian ethnicity to override canonical norms? It was a matter of principle, and in 1872 the patriarch of Constantinople convened a local council in order to define and defend it. In the process it declared 'phyletism' to be 'contrary to the teaching of the Gospel and holy canons of our blessed fathers'. Such phyletism involved the parallel existence of 'nationally defined' churches, and these were firmly condemned. In any case, there should never be rival jurisdictions in any one place.[11] The continued existence of such churches seemed to ridicule the decisions of 1872. Yet their diasporas were to multiply throughout the succeeding years.

When in 1922 the Turks forcibly dispersed the Greek population of Asia Minor beyond its ancient borders, Constantinople itself was faced with new diaspora problems of its own. Some of the uprooted faithful were assimilated into neighbouring churches, like the Greek. Others formed diaspora communities, with affiliation to the patriarchate as of old. Hence exarchates of Constantinople were set up in 1922 for both America and Europe. In the process the diaspora situation became the norm. Meanwhile, in terms of resident population, the actual diocese of Constantinople was reduced to a flimsy remnant of its former self. But its understanding of pre-eminence survived.

The Russian diaspora

The Russian revolutions of 1917 produced changes along the western frontiers of the former Russian Empire which prompted the establishment of national Orthodox churches in Poland, Latvia, Estonia and Finland during the succeeding decades. Some of these were to generate their own diasporas as the result of the Second World War. But more important numerically was the dispersal of more than a million Russians into different parts of the world in the aftermath of civil war (1918–22). This resulted from the imposition of Soviet rule, with its attendant assault on religion. The Russian diaspora was seen to have pastoral concern for the refugees in its midst. But it also had the task of supporting its distant and afflicted mother-church.

---

11 Text of the council's preparatory commission (1872), quoted in Maximos, *Oecumenical patriarchate*, 251–2.

Different attitudes to the homeland made for long-lasting divisions within the diaspora. Equally divisive was another problem: how should émigré church people relate to western Christians in the context of an embryonic ecumenical movement?

Since there was no precedent for such problems, they had to be addressed ad hoc. The patriarchate of Moscow and all Russia re-established in 1917 had no time to discuss them at its wide-ranging council of 1917–18. It was left to the patriarch, his synod and his counsellors to formulate a policy in the emergency conditions which confronted them all. The resulting decree of 1920 urged bishops who were cut off from the Moscow patriarchate to set up independent bodies of their own, preferably in conjunction with their neighbouring hierarchs. It was assumed that this would occur within the patriarchate's former bounds.[12] In accordance with precedents in canon law, those Russian churchmen who found themselves within the patriarchate of Constantinople sought its blessing for their sojourn there. Their leader had anticipated a rebuff, expecting to be treated in the same way as the Bulgarians of half a century before, but times had changed and in 1920 they were duly granted recognition as associates of the local church, regardless of their language and their ways. As it was, the Russians hardly paused to count their blessings. The Serbian patriarchate seemed to offer prospects of greater independence, and the following year many Russian émigrés transferred to the kingdom of the Serbs, Croats and Slovenes, which produced another change in their ecclesiastical allegiance.

It was the beginning of the Russian diaspora's various realignments. In the following decade, some of the émigrés sought to maintain or re-establish links with their mother-church in Moscow, though this, because of Soviet interference, became more difficult as time went by. Others obeyed the instructions given by their mother-church in 1920 and created an autonomous organisation, which initially called itself the 'temporary higher Russian Orthodox Church administration abroad'. In due course its one-time validation from the Constantinopolitan and Serbian patriarchates ceased to be effective. Nevertheless, it saw no good reason to renew it. By contrast, there were others who believed such validation to be a *sine qua non*. When in 1931 Metropolitan Evlogii Georgievskii at the head of his diocese of western Europe broke with Moscow, he immediately submitted to Constantinople. By this time the Russian diaspora was hopelessly divided, however irrelevant their differences may now seem.

---

12 Bishop Gregory Afonsky, *A history of the Orthodox Church in America 1917–1982* (Kodiak, AK: St Herman's Theological Seminary Press, 1984), 128–9.

A United diaspora?

Initial hopes had been for a unified archdiocese abroad. The 'temporary higher Russian Orthodox church administration abroad' which took shape in Serbia at Sremski Karlovci, and which at first was accorded the right to proceed with its affairs within the confines of the Serbian patriarchate, also hoped to reach out to other parts of the world. When Metropolitan Evlogii Georgievskii came in 1922 to consider the strategy required, he proposed a federal structure for the temporary church administration which had meanwhile been renamed 'the temporary holy episcopal synod of the Russian Orthodox Church outside Russia'.[13] At this stage Evlogii had gained the singular advantage of sponsorship from 'home' as well as from the church abroad. At his patriarch's behest he had become the Moscow patriarchate's ruling bishop in western Europe, while he was yet unchallenged as a senior member of the Karlovci synod. This caused no more than a tremor at the time. But it was the kind of arrangement which was not to be repeated. Up to a point, the Evlogii plan outlasted this short-lived unity in the diaspora milieu. But it survived only in the context of a distinct and separate Russian Church Abroad. The opportunity was lost too early for Russian émigrés to manifest their faith and order in a coherent fashion and throughout the world. As envisaged by Evlogii, the plan postulated semi-independent church provinces in western Europe, the Balkans, the far east and north America, with conciliar consultations between them once a year. But it hardly advanced beyond the drafting stage. Meanwhile, Evlogii's own status was questioned by the synod of the Church Abroad, from which he was to part company in 1926. Platon, metropolitan of the Russian archdiocese in North America, broke with the Karlovci synod at the same time and for similar reasons. Separate diasporas were now the order of the day.[14]

By this time the synod of the Church Abroad had already clashed with Moscow. It had involved itself in the monarchist cause and was thought to have prepared an appeal for the Genoa conference of 1922 to restore the Romanov dynasty by force. This was an impression that gained currency as the result of right-wing manipulation of the media in the shape of a press release on the need for a 'crusade' against the Soviets. It was, however, not based on any consensus, let alone any decision of an émigré conference held

13 Georgii Mitrofanov, *Istoriia Russkoi Pravoslavnoi Tserkvi 1900–1927* (St Petersburg: Satis, 2002), 419.
14 *Put' moei zhizni: Vospominaniia Mitropolita Evlogiia, izlozhennye po ego rasskazam T. Manukhinoi* (Paris: YMCA-Press, 1947), 606–7, 610–11. Evlogii was to repeat his proposals in 1935, but to no effect (ibid., 633–4).

the previous year. It was immediately interpreted as church intervention in secular affairs. The Soviet authorities responded by putting new pressures on the church 'at home'.[15] Not surprisingly, the patriarch of Moscow and his council distanced themselves from the synod of the Church Abroad. A patriarchal decree of 5 May 1922 went so far as to 'liquidate' its structures.[16] Not that Evlogii himself was to retain his patriarchate's favour for much longer. He had accepted his appointment to western Europe as the patriarch's representative. But increasing persecution of his mother-church had resulted in the patriarch's acting successor, Metropolitan Sergii Stragorodskii, submitting in 1927 to the state's demands. Hence his requirement that clergy in the Russian emigration should formally declare their loyalty to the USSR. In Sergii's words, 'We have demanded from our clergy abroad that they commit themselves in writing to be completely loyal to the Soviet government in regard to all its endeavours in the social field'.[17] This put diaspora clergy into an impossible position. Evlogii proposed an alternative to suit them, which involved agreement simply not to use the pulpit for political ends. It was as much as the Moscow patriarchate could expect, and Sergii agreed.[18] But he was not the master of his situation, and worse was to come.

When Evlogii participated in a day of prayer for persecuted Russian Christians which had been organised by the archbishop of Canterbury in the spring of 1930, Sergii accused Evlogii of campaigning against the USSR. At the peak of Stalin's assault on religion, Sergii could no longer modify any of his earlier demands. Evlogii was dismissed that summer. More than that, he was suspended as a cleric.

Since his diocese refused to accept this ruling of a subjugated Moscow patriarchate, Evlogii looked elsewhere for canonical support. Precedent argued for an appeal to Constantinople. In 1931 the ecumenical patriarch Photios II issued a *tomos* to his Russian petitioners. This took into account the émigrés' 'abnormal and baleful position', and promulgated 'a temporary rectification of the church situation in the Russian Orthodox congregations of western Europe'. These were now to form a new exarchate of the patriarchate of Constantinople, while still remaining 'independent as a peculiarly Russian Orthodox church

15 Interrogation of Patriarch Tikhon (1922) in V. Vorob'ev, *Sledstvennoe delo patriarkha Tikhona: sbornik dokumentov* (Moscow: Pravoslavnyi Sviato-Tikhonovskii Bogoslovskii Institut, 2000), 154.
16 M. E. Gubonin, *Akty sviateishego Tikhona, patriarkha Moskovskogo i vseia Rusi* [Pozdneishie dokumenty i perepiska o kanonicheskom preemstve vysshei tserkovnoi vlasti 1917–43] (Moscow: Pravoslavnyi Sviato-Tikhonovskii Bogoslovskii Institut, 1994), 193.
17 Quoted in Lev Regel'son, *Tragediia Russkoi Tserkvi 1917–1945* (Paris: YMCA-Press, 1977), 433.
18 Evlogii, *Put' moei zhizni*, 619.

organization, which freely orders its own affairs'. Earlier attempts to follow such a path had no success. Consequently, this one was cautiously labelled 'temporary', but it was to last for many decades.[19] Another solution was tried by two of Evlogii's parishes – one in Paris and the other in Berlin – which proclaimed their loyalty to Moscow, but it involved only a few dozen people.

The role of the state

The starting point of the post-revolutionary diaspora was a common home-land, but access to its persecuted church was precluded in the pre-war years. Indeed, the Soviet authorities seemed minded to destroy not only its buildings, but also its structure and its personnel. Many of the faithful suffered deten-tion, and some execution. Only at a distance could the diaspora seek to build reserves against the day when these might be of use to their compatriots in the Soviet Union. There was no one way in which the task was undertaken. Some worked towards the faithful conservation of the past, while the aspirations and achievements of a 'Holy Russia' in the years before the revolution continued to provide inspiration. There was therefore no call for any major renovation in church life. Such, largely, was the position of the Church Abroad. By con-trast, Evlogii's exarchate tended to foster creative reconsideration of inherited positions. But this also involved concern for the Russia of the days to come. In the words which Mother Maria Skobtsova wrote in 1937:

> Our Church [in western Europe] was never so free.
> Such freedom that it makes your head spin. Our mission is to show that a free Church can work miracles. And if we bring back to Russia our new spirit – free, creative, daring – our mission will be accomplished. If not, we shall perish ignominiously.[20]

Hitler's invasion of the USSR in 1941 prevented any such mission. In the pre-war years Hitler had made some moves to unite the diaspora by diplomacy and diktat. When a Nazi civil servant talked to a leading figure in Evlogii's diocese in 1938, he insisted that 'we do not want to have two [émigré] churches, nor will we tolerate any such thing'. Recognition of the Church Abroad by Hitler's Germany was reckoned 'a fact beyond dispute' to the extent that the authorities considered taking 'police measures' against any competition.[21] A

---

19 Ibid., 625–7.
20 Konstantin Mochul'skii, 'Monakhinia Maria Skobtsova', *Tretii Chas* 1 (1946), 65.
21 Minutes of the meeting between W. Haugg and Fr Ioann Shakhovskoi, quoted in M. V. Shkarovskii, *Natsistskaia Germaniia i Pravoslavnaia Tserkov'* (Moscow: Izdatel'stvo Kru-titskogo Patriarshego Podvor'ia, 2002), 99.

symbol of Nazi approval was the building of a handsome Russian cathedral for the Church Abroad in Berlin (1936–38), entirely at the state's expense. The Church Abroad found it expedient to promote a German convert to Orthodoxy, Serafim Lade, as ruling bishop of the Church Abroad in Berlin, and in Germany at large. Not that he was minded to become the equivalent of the Lutheran Reichsbischof Ludwig Müller with his Nazi-dominated 'Deutsche Christen'. Serafim was never brought into play by the Nazi establishment to rally the Orthodox of the German-occupied territories, nor was he allowed to visit former Soviet territories. He was not part of the abortive Nazi plans to enthrone a compliant patriarch of Moscow, being passed over in favour of Dionisii Valedinskii, metropolitan of Warsaw.[22] The most that Serafim could do was minister to a wretched new diaspora, the Russians in the Nazi work battalions and camps.[23]

The spontaneous revival of Orthodox life in areas of German occupation was often tolerated by Wehrmacht personnel; even, at the outset of the Russian war in 1941, by individual Nazi leaders. But Hitler had his own plans for the eventual liquidation of the Orthodox Church on Russian soil. He intended to replace it with a pagan cult. No matter that in 1941 he had favoured preparations for Russian diaspora clergy to re-enter a 'liberated' homeland for the propagation of their faith,[24] no such plans were promoted in the war.

Meanwhile the war had helped to modify the antireligious policy of another dictator. In dire need of patriotic support from the Soviet population, Stalin had in 1943 permitted a carefully controlled revival of Orthodox church life. The revival was to provide an important ingredient in his dealings with the western powers. It was sufficiently convincing for the Moscow patriarchate's plenipotentiary, Metropolitan Nikolai Iarushevich, to be received by King George VI in 1945. The British establishment did not stop to question how a Russian cleric could represent an erstwhile ally with its atheism still in place.

But if the revival was authentic, did this not affect the status of the Russian diaspora itself? Soviet propaganda of the day sought to allay the exiles' anti-Soviet suspicions with a picture of countless alienated Russians returning to the bosom of their mother-church. It was imperative to act quickly, while émigrés were still convinced that the war had proved to be a beneficial catalyst for Soviet society at large; so much so that Evlogii could think of an immediate return

22 Ibid., 136–7.

23 M. V. Shkarovskii, *Politika Tret'ego reikha po otnosheniiu k Russkoi Pravoslavnoi Tserkvi v svete arkhivnykh materialov 1935–1945 godov (Sbornik dokumentov)* (Moscow: Izdatel'stvo Krutitskogo Patriarshego Podvor'ia, 2003), 130–44.

24 D. Pospielovsky, *The Orthodox Church in the history of Russia* (Crestwood, NY: St Vladimir's Seminary Press, 1998), 224.

to Moscow since 'it is time to go home'. Not only had 'one's soul suffered enough through exile in foreign parts', but 'the supreme church authorities [in Moscow] promise us the calm evolution of church life'.[25] The metropolitan could thus envisage himself returning to Russia at the head of his entire flock.[26] It was almost a biblical image of a diaspora coming to an end. Fortunately, it was not to be.

For the present, the Soviet authorities were anxious to expedite Evlogii's application to revert to his pre-1931 status as pastor of the patriarchate of Moscow. In writing to Aleksii Simanskii, the newly installed patriarch of Moscow, Evlogii insisted on an important caveat: 'In advance of my appeal to your holiness, we must still elicit the blessing of the ecumenical patriarch for this reunion with [our] mother-church.'[27]

Metropolitan Nikolai was quick to give him false assurances to the effect that Constantinople had already agreed the necessary changes. This was in September 1945. Later that month the agreement between Moscow and Evlogii was signed and sealed. But Constantinople did not hear from Moscow until November. The new arrangements left much to be desired.

With Evlogii's death in 1946 the situation was still unresolved. His successor as archbishop of the diocese of western Europe was Vladimir Tikhonitskii, who had no wish to accept the degree of subordination claimed by the patriarchate of Moscow. Nor did he intend to resuscitate the old émigré divisions. In the hope of healing them, the new archbishop turned to Metropolitan Anastasii Gribanovskii, the ruling bishop of the Church Abroad, and proposed that the latter should be united with the diocese of western Europe, but with one important rider: the Church Abroad was to revert to dependence on the patriarchate of Constantinople, which had briefly been the position in 1920. For his part, Vladimir was willing to yield his place as ruling bishop to Anastasii.[28] It was a rare opportunity to restore the fragile unity of earlier years. But Anastasii refused to surrender his church's independence.

Although Evlogii's reversion to Moscow was mismanaged, it was nonetheless Moscow that managed to gain ground from the affair. Evlogii's people were of two minds. There were those (the majority) who resolved to reassert their links with Constantinople. There were also those who, in deference to Evlogii, preferred to keep the patriarch of Moscow as their head. In the

25 Metropolitan Evlogii Georgievskii, address of 18 February 1945, quoted in Evlogii, *Put' moei zhizni*, 669.
26 Evlogii's conversation with Tatiana Manukhina (1946) in ibid., 672.
27 Letter of 3 April 1945, quoted in ibid., 671.
28 *Mitropolit Vladimir, sviatitel'-molitvennik* (Paris: privately published, 1965), 152.

process, a modest number of parishes was added to the Moscow loyalists of 1931. In consolidated form, this now formed a western European exarchate of its own. For good measure, another exarchate was added for the central parts of Europe. Each was an outpost of the Russian Church. Each also helped to further the foreign policies of the Moscow patriarchate. These policies were necessarily determined by the Soviet government's council for religious affairs. Émigrés were not usually themselves their prime promoters. Even so, independent churchmen were welcome to the Soviet state since these could veil or even validate such policies by means of the credibility which they had earned abroad. At the behest of Stalin, the council for religious affairs ensured that a gathering of the world's Orthodox churches should take place at Moscow in 1948, the fifth centenary of Russia's self-proclaimed independence from Constantinople.[29] It seemed a good moment for the Russian church authorities to seize the initiative and transform the jubilee into an ecumenical council, no less. In the process, the Constantinople patriarchate would be put in the shade, and the old dream of Moscow the third Rome would be realised at long last.[30]

In the event, the project was reduced to a conference, and no such council was ever to take place. But the idea that Moscow should take precedence in the Orthodox world was long to outlive the Stalin period. This was no longer 1931 or even 1948. Russian church affairs were proceeding on what appeared to be an even keel, the more so since the Khrushchev persecutions (1959–64) were carefully concealed. Was it reasonable for Constantinople still to be charged with the protection of émigré Russians? As the result of pressures from the Moscow patriarchate, Constantinople suddenly suspended its Russian exarchate in 1965 and urged its members to return 'home'. It made little difference. The exarchate retired for some years into a self-authenticating independence as an Orthodox archdiocese of France and western Europe, but was then in 1971 received back by the patriarchate of Constantinople. Had independence lasted longer, there might have been the need to reconsider the importance of validation from a parent church. Not that the problem was new. It had been posed in the distant 1920s by the Russian Church in exile, but it remained unresolved until 1970 when, as we have seen, the Russian archdiocese (*metropolia*) in the New World negotiated its formal independence from the patriarchate of Moscow, but its earlier experience had been one of 'temporary' independence.[31]

29 M. V. Shkarovskii, *Russkaia pravoslavnaia tserkov' pri Staline i Khrushcheve (gosudarstvenno-tserkovnye otnosheniia v SSSR v 1939–1964 godakh)* (Moscow: Izdatel'stvo Krutitskogo Patriarshego Podvor'ia, 1999), 301–3.
30 Quoted with approval in *Zhurnal Moskovskoi Patriarkhii* 9 (1946), 56.
31 *Iubileinyi sbornik v pamiat' 150-letiia Russkoi Pravoslavnoi Tserkvi v Severnoi Amerike* (New York: Izdanie izdatel'skoi iubileinoi komissii, 1945), II, 29.

Soviet rule prompted and perpetuated the divisions of the Russian emigration. But the divisions still remained in place when the Soviet Union ended. Initially, a reinvigoration of the Moscow patriarchate was not enough to stimulate
moves towards a merger. Yet the patriarchate had not forgotten its imperialist
dreams of years gone by. Proposals of 1975 and 1976 were in 2003 reformulated
in beguiling terms. The patriarch of Moscow signed the newly refurbished text
as his own.[32] It was comprehensive in its outreach and addressed the greater
part of Europe. Even so, it ignored the patriarchate of Constantinople, including its exarchates, and thereby sought to diminish its status. It also ignored
other diasporas, such as the Romanian, Serbian and Antiochean. The text
addressed itself only to a Russian audience, or at least to those who belonged
to 'the Russian tradition'. All Russian-origin jurisdictions were encouraged to
ponder the prospect of a unified metropolitan province of western Europe,
which might ultimately form an independent church. Meanwhile, so it was
implied, the Moscow patriarchate could be its sponsor during the gestation
process.

The proposals provoked some debate. Many European supporters of the
Moscow patriarchate thought them to be reasonable and even selfless. There
were also Russian members of the Constantinople jurisdiction who raised
their voices in support. Yet most of those who had been addressed were left
nonplussed. The project seemed burdened by a *Wunschzettel* which could be
seen as Muscovite and even phyletistic to a fault. Was a future church of western Europe necessarily to be concerned only with Russians or, more loosely,
with Orthodox Christians 'of Russian background'? There were at the same
time other matters which engaged the patriarchate of Moscow. After decades
of estrangement, it found itself in dialogue with the Church Abroad. Earlier
the patriarchate had repeatedly doubted the latter's canonicity. The Church
Abroad, for its part, went further in its rejection of the Moscow patriarchate.
It considered it to be a church 'devoid of grace'. All this had to be set aside.
By 2004 it was possible for courteous meetings to take place between the
leaders of the two churches in Moscow. The president of Russia, Vladimir
Putin, who helped to bring about their meeting, suggested that, even in the
present situation, it would be false to speak of them as separate churches: 'In
the awareness of our people, the Russian Church is one.'[33] His was a populist,
not to say phyletistic approach. The church leaders were more cautious on the
subject: the burdens of the past could hardly be so lightly shed. Meanwhile, the

---

32 'Poslanie Aleksiia II, Patriarkha Moskovskogo i vseia Rusi', *Russkaia Mysl'* 14 (4451), 10–16
April 2003, 13.
33 *Russkaia Mysl'* 22 (4507), 3–9 June 2004, 11.

Russian Orthodox Church Abroad sought to have its existing autonomy recognised by the Moscow patriarchate: 'recognised', not 'granted', since the latter would involve some recognition of the Moscow patriarchate as its 'mother-church'.[34]

The diaspora and the Christian west

There was another issue that the Church Abroad wished to discuss with the Moscow patriarchate. This revolved around relations with non-Orthodox communities and with inter-confessional organisations. It was agreed at the outset that such relations should correspond to the traditions of the church.[35] However, the Church Abroad had always taken a negative view of such relations: it regarded ecumenism as a betrayal of Orthodoxy and its presuppositions as heretical.[36] It profoundly disapproved of the participation of the Moscow patriarchate in the ecumenical movement. This the Soviet authorities encouraged for reasons of their own. Only with the end of Soviet rule and the consequent scaling down of Moscow's ecumenical commitments could the question of relations with other Christian communities be properly addressed.

By contrast, Evlogii's diocese had maintained a positive stance from the start. At the consecration in 1924 of the church which was to serve as the diaspora's theological institute in Paris, he expressed his aspirations in no uncertain terms. Not only did he hope that this church would serve as a meeting place for Russians in their hour of need: 'I would also wish that our foreign friends, who represent western Christianity, should find their way to this community . . . May this church be a place where everyone may grow closer together, [a place] where all Christians may share fraternal love.'[37] This involved more than taking part in ecumenical debates, important though this was in decades when the diaspora was able to provide the west with unprecedented contact with the Christian east. Field work, in the sense of sharing in the worship of the other, vouchsafed insights to participants in either family of churches. Fr Sergii Bulgakov introduced such worship in the context of the Faith and Order movement from the 1920s. Others in Evlogii's jurisdiction, such as Nicolas Zernov, argued for its central role in the ecumenical gatherings of such newly founded bodies as the fellowship of St Alban and St Sergius

---

34 Archbishop Mark Arndt, quoted in *Russkaia Mysl'* 21 (4506), 27 May to 2 June 2004, 11.
35 Agenda of the joint commission of the two churches (2003), summarised in *Russkaia Mysl'* 21 (4506), 27 May to 2 June 2004, 11.
36 Anathema by the bishops of the Church Abroad (1983) in *The struggle against ecumenism* (Boston: The Holy Orthodox Church in North America, 1998), 132–3.
37 Evlogii, *Put' moei zhizni*, 444.

(1928). The Orthodox in gatherings like these encouraged western Christians to engage in 'retraditioning', that is, the discovery of a once common, but forgotten, path. Such was the conviction of Fr Georges Florovsky, one of Evlogii's most prominent priests. Since no representatives from the USSR could then participate in any of the consultations of the ecumenical movement, it fell to the diaspora to represent Russian interests in this and in other spheres. Florovsky was to become a leading figure in the early years of the WCC (World Council of Churches). Two graduates of the Paris theological institute, Fr John Meyendorff and Fr Alexander Schmemann, were later to continue such work in the context of the American diaspora. Meyendorff was to become the chairman of the Faith and Order commission of the WCC.

Scholarship

The Russian Orthodox Church in the USSR had no institutes of higher education from 1928 to 1945. Nor was it likely that any of its theological works would see the light of day. The diaspora was faced with the task of making good these defects; hence the foundation in 1925 of the Institut Saint-Serge.[38] Its first dean was Sergii Bulgakov. Metropolitan Evlogii's diocese of western Europe was thus able to train many generations of its theological students for service in the wider church. Some of their number went on to become important scholars in their various fields. More productive still was the dedicated staff who taught them. Their writings were usually produced in Russian. But many were translated at the time or since into the major European languages. Thus they also made their contribution to the Christian west. Most of their Russian works appeared in a publishing house which the Christian west itself provided and maintained. In 1920 western friends of the Russian emigration, such as Paul Anderson, John Mott, Donald Lowrie and Gustav Kullmann, secured support from the American YMCA. This body was to sponsor its Russian clients for over sixty years. The enterprise still bears its name.

The fact that western Christians were involved in this sponsorship caused dismay among the members of the Church Abroad. Ecumenism was a problem in itself. In this case there were additional suspicions that freemasons were involved. At times the bishops of the Church Abroad convinced themselves that this was so. Hence their declaration of 1932: 'The Russian emigration is

---

38 Alexis Kniazeff, *L'Institut Saint-Serge: de l'Académie d'autrefois au rayonnement d'aujourd' hui* (Paris: Éditions Beauchesne, 1974).

thoroughly poisoned by masonry.'[39] But their attitudes to the YMCA were to mellow with the years.[40] In any case, it was not just a question of having a publishing house at one's beck and call. More important was the orthodoxy of its authors. The liberalism of the church historian George Fedotov might pass the critics' muster. It was quite another matter when theologians put about fresh formulations of dogmatic truths. When Bulgakov's work of the émigré period came to be assessed, each of the diaspora's jurisdictions used the controversial nature of his teachings as a peg on which to hang their disparate views.

The Church Abroad, in the person of its leader Metropolitan Antonii Khrapovitskii, had been expressing discontent with some of Bulgakov's teachings since the 1920s. Such feelings came to a head in 1936 with the submission of a detailed work on Bulgakov's 'heresies' to the council of the Church Abroad. Nobody could have expected the beleaguered Moscow patriarchate to busy itself with such things. But Metropolitan Sergii Stragorodskii promptly heeded a denunciation of Bulgakov by a member of the patriarchate's isolated base in Paris. The metropolitan also made use of depositions from another source, his representative in Lithuania, Metropolitan Elevferii Bogoiavlenskii. Although it is obvious that Sergii himself had no access to the works in question, he issued a condemnation of Bulgakov's teachings in so far as they 'often distort the dogmas of the Orthodox faith and in some respects directly echo false teachings which have already been condemned by the councils [of the church] . . . They are alien to the Holy Orthodox Church of Christ.'[41]

Metropolitan Evlogii had more than Bulgakov to defend. The whole question of freedom was at stake. 'To ignore church freedom is to be deprived of church life as well as good pastoral concern', he wrote. 'We have to safeguard inner spiritual freedom, according to the teaching of apostle Paul (Galatians 5:3), while sheltering it from political assaults and from constraints resulting from a formal apprehension of God's Truth.'[42] In the process Bulgakov gained Evlogii's formal approbation. At his side were other innovative thinkers, who helped to shape the Orthodoxy of the time and place. Some, like Fr Nikolai

39 Quoted in Archbishop Nikon (N. P. Rklitskii), *Zhizneopisanie blazhennieshago Antoniia, mitropolita Kievskago i Galitskago*, 10 vols. (New York: Izd. Sievero-Amerikanskoi i Kanadskoi eparkhii, 1956–63), VII, 290–1.
40 Mikhail Nazarov, *Missiia russkoi emigratsii*, second edition (Moscow: Rodnik, 1994), I, 210–11.
41 Metropolitan Sergii Stragorodskii (1935), quoted in Monakhinia Elena [Kazimirchak-Polonskaia], *Professor protoierei Sergii Bulgakov 1871–1944* (Moscow: Izdatel'stvo Pravoslavnogo universiteta imeni o Aleksandra Menia, 2003), 327.
42 Metropolitan Evlogii, quoted in ibid., 295.

Afanas'ev, may have influenced churches other than their own.[43] The diaspora encouraged more than mere mimesis of the past. Be that as it may, the Bulgakov affair was yet one more reminder of different diaspora concerns. The Church Abroad had its own publishing outlets, whose output hardly overlapped with that of the YMCA press. Thus, in 1922 a press was set up in Slovakia which was named after St Iov of Pochaev. But its principal concern was pastoral. It produced prayer books and pocket editions of the gospels. It also published church periodicals of interest to the general reader.

When the Nazis invaded Slovakia in 1938, they demonstrated the importance of this press by checking the circulation of its publications in Germany itself. However, the press was not alone. Several German-based initiatives also made their mark in the succeeding years. Some of this was due to a follower of Archbishop Evlogii, the priest Ioann Shakhovskoi. After the Nazi invasion of the Soviet Union, however, there was a prohibition on export to the newly occupied lands of church literature or goods. The monastic publishers at the Slovakian press were bitterly disappointed. Earlier, they had dreamed of vindicating their émigré vocation by transferring their energies to their native soil. As they put it: 'We continue urgently to prepare missionary literature for the Russian Church as its liberation proceeds, and incidentally prepare ourselves for missionary work out there.'[44]

The war years brought Russians nearer in a different way. After 1945 vast numbers of prisoners and forced labourers were to find themselves under the supervision of the western allies. The newcomers had no sympathy for the Moscow patriarchate, and many of them merged gratefully with the Church Abroad, the more so since, under Nazi pressure, few of the parishes in western Germany, loyal to Archbishop Evlogii, survived the war.

It was the emigration of numerous displaced persons to the New World that prompted the translation of the headquarters of the Church Abroad to the USA in 1946. It also reinvigorated the church's monastery-cum-seminary, which had been established at Jordanville in 1928. This was to become the most prolific publisher of the jurisdiction. Like the Pochaev press, which it now absorbed, Jordanville sought to meet pastoral and liturgical needs. But it was not minded to emulate the YMCA press with its fresh examination of received truths. The Orthodox Church in America was foremost in this field,

---

43 See Aidan Nichols, *Theology in the Russian diaspora: church, fathers, eucharist in Nikolai Afanas'ev, 1893–1966* (Cambridge: Cambridge University Press, 1989), 60, 253 n.70.

44 Munich archive of the German diocese of the Russian Church Abroad, [1941], quoted in Shkarovskii, *Natsistskaia Germaniia*, 262 and n.269.

with its St Vladimir's Seminary press founded in 1968. The seminary, with its Russian orientation, had been founded thirty years previously. It was to grow into an inter-cultural institution with an outreach that went beyond its original diaspora framework. By contrast, Jordanville was built 'dans le plus pur style russe'[45] in order to reflect a single nation's vision of its idyllic past.

Those who chose the Moscow jurisdiction included several scholars of importance. A number of them taught in the post-war years at a Parisian centre for francophone and western-orientated Orthodox studies, the Institut Saint-Denys, which was set up in 1944. But its eventual deviation from Orthodox practice and belief caused most of these scholars to leave. Its founder Fr Evgraf Kovalevskii was in 1953 to set up a separate Église Catholique-Orthodoxe de France. It was an unusual way for the diaspora to develop. Acculturation was the prime requirement in the new foundation, though this, in the view of its critics, might challenge the very 'pillar and ground of the truth' (I Timothy 3:15). Several centres of the Orthodox western rite offered no such challenge, 'different' though they were. But most of them did not outlive their dedicated founding fathers.[46] This was in the period from the late 1930s to the 1960s. Of more modest profile than the Institut Saint-Denys was the seminary established in 1953 at Villemoison near Paris by the patriarchate of Moscow. Vladimir Lossky was pre-eminent among its teachers.[47]

Culture

The Russian diaspora in Europe made its impact on the western world by means of scholarship. It also contributed its art and music. A fresh perception of the medieval icon was to fertilise the painters of the emigration. Not that all the churches of the emigration were willing to sponsor a revival of the rediscovered norms. But the second half of the century saw the production of distinguished revivalist work by iconographers such as Grigorii Krug[48] and Leonid Uspenskii. Uspenskii organised a school for icon-painters in Paris, and

---

45 Nikita Struve, *Soixante-dix ans d'émigration russe 1919–1989* (Paris: Fayard, 1996), 75.
46 For example, Alexis van der Mensbrugghe, *Missel, ou livre de la synaxe liturgique approuvé et autorisé pour les églises orthodoxes de rite occidental relevant du Patriarcat de Moscou* (Paris: Éditions Setor, 1962).
47 Vladimir Lossky, *Essai sur la théologie mystique de l'Église d'Orient* (Paris: Aubier, 1944); trans. as *The mystical theology of the eastern Church* (Cambridge and London: J. Clarke & Co. Ltd, 1957).
48 Higoumène Barsanuphe, *Icônes et fresques du Père Grégoire* (Marcenat: Monastère orthodoxe Znaménié, 1999).

published penetrating studies of the art.[49] Both painters were members of the Moscow exarchate in Paris. Ivan Gardner, one-time bishop of the Church Abroad, studied and performed the choral music of the Russian past. He, too, produced a panoramic survey of his field.[50]

Among the emigration's numerous choirs, few were as influential as that of the Institut Saint-Serge. Under the guidance of I. K. Denissoff and the Ossorguines, father and son, Saint-Serge revived the Russian tradition of the monastic male-voice choir. The singers shared the icon-painters' aim, which was to play a vital role in worship. But their work also made its impact on a wider public through the choir's recordings and its tours. Whether it was choral singing or icon painting, the diaspora sought to preserve and enhance a tradition which was effectively eclipsed at home.

Worship

Ultimately, it was something less evident that helped to reveal the emigration's worth not only to the outside world but also to itself. None of its structures would have mattered, nor any other way in which it sought to make its contribution to the public good, had not its life been based on fundamentals in the eucharistic sphere. Without the worshipping community, so many of its theologians felt, all the rest was merely décor. This décor might be justified by reference to a complex of inherited traditions, but no more than that. By contrast, it was the vitality with which the faithful worshipped that showed how 'Holy Russia' might be treated as a prospect and a programme, rather than as a pious myth. Their readiness to reshape simple sitting rooms and shabby barracks into churches transformed such settings into 'Thresholds of the Kingdom'. Many were convinced that it was worship that undergirded the diaspora's life and bound its members firmly to each other. At this level, reminders of 'the one thing needful' (Luke 10:42) took precedence over the question of 'jurisdictions'. For such worship could involve a more authentic revelation of the church than any patriarchal edict. 'Where the Eucharist is,

49 L. Ouspensky and V. Lossky, *The meaning of icons*, trans. G. E. H. Palmer and E. Kadloubovsky, third English edition (Crestwood, NY: St Vladimir's Seminary Press, 1982); also L. Ouspensky, *Theology of the icon*, trans. A. Gythiel, 2 vols. (Crestwood, NY: St Vladimir's Seminary Press, 1992).
50 Johann von Gardner, *Russian church singing*, trans. V. Morosan, 2 vols. (Crestwood, NY: St Vladimir's Seminary Press, 1997–2000).

there is the fullness of the church', noted Afanas'ev in the Paris emigration.[51]
These words point out the diaspora's truest validation.

Prospects for the future

Not that diasporas as such required perpetual validation. After all those years
'abroad', there were exiles who were ready to consider whether the diaspora
mentality should continue to remind them of what was once and therefore
ought to be. Would not a diaspora situation bring diminishing returns in years
to come?

Already in 1970 the patriarchate of Moscow had formally recognised the
independence of the 'Russian' archdiocese in the New World. Several decades
later, in 2004, the patriarch of Antioch conceded effective autonomy to his
own American diaspora.[52] Meanwhile, there were members of the American
diaspora under Constantinople who voiced their hope for greater separation
from their mother-church. They argued that continued dependence on Constantinople linked them too much with their forebears' distant past. Be that as
it may, the separate origins of these diasporas, and their former ethnic aspirations, offer little promise of their integration into a single church, 'one, holy,
catholic and apostolic' though that is what it seeks to be.

When the 'great and holy council' meets, there is certainly one question
which will demand a well-considered answer: might not partisan commitment
to a church administration of the relevant ancestral people prejudice devotion
to the one who is the Lord of all (Romans 10:12)?

---

51 Nicolas Afanassieff, 'The church which presides in love', in J. Meyendorff *et al.*, *The
primacy of Peter* (London: The Faith Press, 1963), 76.
52 *The Word* 49 (7) (2004), 6–9.

23

The Orthodox Church and communism

MICHAEL BOURDEAUX AND ALEXANDRU POPESCU

The two Russian revolutions of 1917 (March and October) found the Russian Orthodox Church poised to embark on its own programme of reform. It was always the policy of Lenin (Vladimir Il'ich Ulianov) and the Bolsheviks to portray the state religion as benighted, clinging to the past, upholding outmoded values. Because of believers' lack of contact with the outside world, the totality of censorship and the cessation of objective historical research in the Soviet Union, this view tended towards acceptance in the world at large.

The Russian Orthodox Church stands alone

The truth was very different, as recent research has begun to uncover since the partial opening of archives in Russia. The late nineteenth and early twentieth centuries were, in fact, one of the most dynamic and creative periods in the history of the Orthodox Church.[1] Debates on the role of the parish and the laity were widespread and, even if inconclusive, were not always comfortable for the hierarchy.

The abdication of Tsar Nicholas II in March 1917 led to the summoning of a *pomestny sobor*,[2] which met on 16 August 1917 for its first public session in the cathedral of Christ the Saviour, which was later to be destroyed. The agenda was huge, but the early sessions indicated that the approach to church reform would be balanced and unemotional. The debate on the restoration of the patriarchate was just getting underway on 28 October when the bombardment of the Kremlin, a mere stone's throw away, interrupted it. In an atmosphere of extreme tension, Metropolitan Tikhon (Bellavin) of Moscow was elected patriarch, the first time the office had been held since Peter the Great had

---

1 See the magisterial study by Vera Shevzov, *Russian Orthodoxy on the eve of the Revolution* (New York: Oxford University Press, 2004).
2 I.e. a 'local [church] council', with 'local' signifying in one country, as opposed to *vselenskii sobor* or 'ecumenical council'.

abolished the patriarchate in 1721 and replaced it by a lay administration under an over-procurator.

Had this *sobor* been able to run its course, doubtless reforms would have followed in rapid succession. As it was, the success of the October Revolution cut off the work of the *sobor* in its early stages. The church lost its voice almost before it had found it. Lenin demonstrated his hostility to the church at once, passing a law on 4 December confiscating all church property and following this on 23 January 1918 by the *Decree on the Separation of the Church from the State and the School from the Church*.

At a stroke the church lost its heritage and its wellbeing, despite the theoretical guarantee contained in the 1918 Constitution, which gave the right to 'religious and anti-religious propaganda . . . for all citizens'.[3] The destruction which followed was systematic and universal. Stalin's *Law on Religious Associations* of April 1929 did little other than legalise the resulting status quo. Stalin's constitution removed the right to religious propaganda, but believers had never enjoyed this in practice. The all-embracing demand that 'religious associations' (parishes) should be registered placed their control in the hands of the state that, far from registering parishes, closed them down systematically. The church had no administration, no dioceses, no schools, no training for the ministry, no monasteries, no publications. In the countryside – except in secret – the church virtually ceased to exist. All this happened in a country that proclaimed the separation of church and state.

In the major cities scattered churches remained open, but the clergy who served in them could remain only by servile subjugation to the state. Beginning with Patriarch Tikhon, the authorities began to force compliance to the new regime by imprisonment, torture and – in many cases – execution.[4] Tikhon was forced to withdraw his anathema against the Bolsheviks. His statement of loyalty to the regime appeared in the government newspaper, *Izvestiia*, in June 1923. He died less than two years later in obscure circumstances, almost certainly a victim of Stalin's henchmen. No further patriarch could be elected until World War II. His acting successor, Metropolitan Sergii Stragorodskii, published a declaration which became the official policy of the Russian Orthodox Church throughout the rest of the communist period. The statement proclaimed: 'We want to be Orthodox and at the same time to recognise the

---

3 For a full discussion of this little-understood point, see Michael Bourdeaux, *Religious ferment in Russia: Protestant opposition to Soviet religious policy* (London: Macmillan, 1968), 108–10.

4 For an account of these years, see Nikita Struve, *Christians in contemporary Russia* (London: Harvill Press, 1967), 34–58.

Soviet Union as our fatherland, whose joys and successes are our joys and successes and whose setbacks are our setbacks.'[5]

During the 1920s there was an abortive attempt by a group called the *Obnovlentsy* (Renovators) to seek an ideological accommodation with the Soviet state.[6] This movement, inspired by the communist authorities, sought to force clergy to take an oath of loyalty to the regime. Those who refused suffered the fate of Metropolitan Veniamin of Petrograd (St Petersburg), who was summarily tried and then shot on 12 August 1922. The movement lingered on for a few years, but never found popular favour and had effectively died out by the beginning of World War II.

The Orthodox Church and World War II

While the Soviet Union contained the overwhelming majority of the world's population of Orthodox believers, there were countries which, at the time of the upheaval of the Second World War, still considered themselves to be 'Orthodox': Greece, Bulgaria, Romania. Most other countries of the Near and Middle East contained a significant minority of Orthodox believers, not to mention a diaspora which by this time had spread into many countries. All of these countries, in one way or another, were deeply affected by World War II.

Yet the catastrophe for billions of people, not least for the vast numbers in the Soviet Union who perished as a result of the war, did have some beneficial effects for those who had somehow preserved their religious faith against the communist onslaught, for Stalin halted and eventually reversed his antireligious policies. The Nazi invasion of 1941 caught the country so totally unprepared that it caused immediate demoralisation. One way of re-establishing shattered morale was to persuade the church to bolster patriotic sentiment. It was considered capable of doing this even after virtual annihilation over the previous two decades, but to achieve this, prison doors had to open to allow those clergy who had survived and were prepared to take an oath of loyalty to return to their churches. Now they were metaphorically wearing martyrs' crowns, with all that meant for their influence and personal relations.

In 1943 Stalin invited Metropolitan Sergii and a handful of other surviving church leaders to a meeting in the Kremlin, at which he promised rewards for the war effort. These included restoration of the patriarchate (which seemed to Sergii a vindication of his 1927 compromise), the re-establishment of a

---

5 Quoted in Michael Bourdeaux, *Opium of the people: the Christian religion in the USSR* (London: Faber and Faber, 1965), 56.
6 Struve, *Christians in contemporary Russia*, 35–40.

diocesan structure, the opening of monasteries and seminaries, and even the right to a publication, *Zhurnal Moskovskoi Patriarkhii* (Journal of the Moscow Patriarchate). The next ten years to Stalin's death in 1953 and the five years thereafter were, by comparison with the immediate past, almost a golden age, during which the church re-established some semblance of normality.

In addition, there was a significant revival of church life in those territories conquered by the Germans thanks to the activities of Dmitrii Voskresenkii, better known as Metropolitan Sergii. He was originally installed as metropolitan of Vilnius and All Lithuania, Latvia and Estonia by the Soviets, when they occupied Riga in 1940. He subsequently threw in his lot with the Nazis. As the latter pushed eastwards, so, in his capacity as exarch of 'Ostland', Metropolitan Sergii claimed jurisdiction over the conquered territories. He had no canonical authority for his action, nor, in the circumstances, was it possible for him to achieve it. The church in these ex-Soviet territories was in a deplorable state and Sergii set about putting this right. He called this enterprise the Pskov Spiritual Mission, and it was the ancient city of Pskov, where scarcely a single church had been left active and intact, that witnessed the greatest revival. By 1943 some eighty-five priests were celebrating the liturgy in over 220 parishes.[7] Sergii's murder, after the repossession of Pskov by the Red Army, remains a crime for which the Germans blamed the Soviets and vice versa.

The rest of the Orthodox world

Greece was caught up in a conflict with communist guerrillas and the late 1940s saw the murder of some sixty Orthodox priests, some following torture and even crucifixion, but the attempt to turn the country into yet another client state of Moscow in the Balkans, alongside contiguous Bulgaria and Albania, failed. After the shaking of the foundations of European civilisation, the Orthodox churches in Bulgaria and Romania found themselves in states now subservient to the Kremlin.

Bulgaria achieved independence in 1908.[8] But the first Balkan war (1912), followed soon afterwards by the First World War, saw the country entangled in a succession of disadvantageous alliances, which entailed the loss of territory and led in 1935 to King Boris's authoritarian regime. Bulgaria then entered World War II on the side of the Nazis. Inevitably, this led to subjugation by the Red Army and the conversion of the country into the Soviet Union's closest political

---

7 Ibid., 68–73.
8 For a succinct account of Bulgaria's convoluted church history, see T. Beeson, *Discretion and valour*, revised edition (London: Collins Fount Paperbacks, 1982), 329–31.

ally. An almost identical religious heritage had long given Russia and Bulgaria a feeling of brotherhood. There were many, too, who felt truly indebted to the Russians for the part they had played in breaking Bulgaria's subservience to the Turkish yoke in 1878 and were not hostile to their new masters.

The creation in 1870 of the Bulgarian exarchate played a key role in the establishment of a Bulgarian identity. The Soviets were astute enough to maintain it in existence, even when they abolished the monarchy in 1946. They facilitated its promotion to patriarchal status in 1953, reckoning that this would provide them with an instrument of foreign policy. Thus the Kremlin could exploit the Bulgarian Orthodox Church in its aim of sovietising the Bulgarian people.

This did not save the Bulgarian Church from repression, however. There was the inevitable law decreeing the separation of church and state, but evidently the church had not become subservient enough to suit the Soviet overlords and a period of antireligious repression followed (1948–52). The head of the church, Exarch Stefan, was exiled to a remote village. In 1952 he smuggled a message to his people, reminding them of their religious heritage and condemning other church leaders still in power for failing to defend him. He died in 1957, and this did indeed lead to a period where the church leadership did the bidding of the Communist Party.

The Romanian Orthodox Church
under communism[9]

Repression of the church was an essential element in the imposition of a Soviet model on Romania. In 1948 the adoption of the Law on Religious Confessions enabled the Communist Party to take control of the largest Orthodox community outside the Soviet Union. This law established state control over episcopal appointments, ensured strong Communist Party representation in the holy synod, and imposed a new statute on the Romanian Orthodox Church, centralising its administration under its patriarch. All church property was nationalised and the Uniate Church was forcibly united with the Orthodox Church by Decree no. 358/1948. The spiritual leaders of the Jewish community and of various Protestant churches were imprisoned or exiled, while Orthodox and Uniate priests and bishops who refused to collaborate became one of the largest groups of political prisoners.

Following the Hungarian uprising in 1956, a new period of terror began when the Decree no. 318/1958, defining new crimes punishable by death, was

9 This section (to p. 567) is the work of Dr Alex Popescu.

passed to prevent any similar uprising in Romania. By Decree no. 410/1959, Orthodox monasteries and monastic seminaries were closed and most monks and nuns aged fifty-six or younger were forced to leave their monasteries and to find secular jobs.

In 1965, Nicolae Ceauşescu emerged as the leader of the Romanian Communist Party. At first, there were signs of liberalisation in domestic policy. Ceauşescu soon gained international respect when he recognised the state of Israel and refused to support the Soviet invasion of Czechoslovakia in 1968. Rather than affirming Romanian identity, Ceauşescu's anti-Soviet nationalism fed a self-glorifying ideology that in later years developed into a neo-Stalinist personality cult and a new brand of nepotistic despotism. While tolerating the majority Romanian Orthodox Church as the 'national' church, Ceauşescu ensured that it was systematically infiltrated, to serve his anti-Russian programme.

Provided that they were loyal to the regime, Orthodox church leaders avoided the worst of the persecution and they created an impressive 'show' in ecumenical forums, presenting government policies as more liberal than they in fact were. This entailed a degree of basic compromise, which was hidden from the large number of foreign church leaders with whom the Romanians came into contact. The Romanian Orthodox Church joined the WCC (World Council of Churches) in 1961 and soon became by far the most ecumenically minded of all the Orthodox churches. Behind the scenes, however, there was persecution of believers, brutal at times. Petre Ţuţea, for example, spent thirteen years as a prisoner of conscience and a further twenty-eight years under house arrest at the hands of the secret police, the *Securitate*. None of this hidden history found its way into the ecumenical forums where Romanian church leaders played leading roles.[10] It was only after the fall of the Berlin Wall and the overthrow in 1989 of Ceauşescu that the true experience of Romanian Orthodox under communism began to emerge.

Under communism, all forms of religion were rejected programmatically as philosophically incompatible with Marx's dialectical materialism. Lenin and Stalin put into practice the classic Marxist formula, which derives religious alienation from the more basic economic and social alienation and, consequently, transforms the struggle against religion into a struggle against the inequitable social system. One important phenomenon was that of so-called re-education, or 'brainwashing' as it was called in the west.

---

10 Alexandru Popescu, *Petre Ţuţea: between sacrifice and suicide* (Aldershot: Ashgate, 2004).

In Romania the architects of re-education aimed to eliminate religion, particularly the majority Christian faith, and traditional Romanian culture, especially amongst the younger generation. National consciousness was to be subordinated to communist ideology. The psychological engineering was intended to change human nature by obliterating what Christianity, along with Judaism and Islam, designates as God's image within the human person and by replacing this image with the Marxist-Leninist ideal of an atomised, isolated individual, who energetically subscribes to the totalitarian 'party'.

How was this to be done? The Soviet educationalist Anton Makarenko in his *Pedagogical Poem, The Road to Life*, finished in 1935, designed a method of re-education through violence and intimidation for homeless children and juvenile offenders. His goal was to impose a new personality based on the values of dialectical materialism, which regarded material existence as the determinant of human consciousness. A phrase used by prisoners of conscience to describe this ideal of a communist individual was *homo sovieticus*; by which they understood a stultified, spiritually dead humanity, in which personality had been destroyed in favour of collective identity.

Makarenko's method was also used in Soviet labour camps on prisoners of war, who later formed the vanguard of the Red Army as it invaded eastern Europe from 1944. Among these were Romanians, who were repatriated at the end of the war and were then used within the Romanian prison system to inflict sustained physical and psychological torture on their fellow prisoners. Torture and terror were used to 'unmask' the person and reveal 'the beast within' – the person's alleged real identity – leading eventually to enforced rejection of God and country, denunciation of family and friends, and confession of crimes that had never been committed. This process of extorting false confessions was later extended, when re-educated victims were used as ideological contaminants within society. People had also to accept the assertion of Soviet 'superiority' over western capitalism, and the idea that every member of the Soviet working class could and should become a model of Soviet humanity and culture.

This Soviet-inspired programme of 're-education and unmasking' was undertaken between 1949 and 1952 (beginning at Suceava, then in prisons at Pitești, Ocnele Mari, Târgșor, Gherla and Târgu Ocna), and between 1960 and 1964 (at Aiud, Gherla and Botoșani). The experiment was carried out also on the canal built by political prisoners, linking the Danube with the Black Sea, and in the sanatorium of Târgu Ocna where gravely ill prisoners were held. Almost entirely ignored by the western media, this programme was supervised from Moscow by Beria and Stalin himself.

The experiment of re-education in Romania took place in two phases: the first, between 1949 and 1952, when tens of thousands of young people who refused to submit to the Soviet occupation and ideology were imprisoned; the second, between 1960 and 1964, when a general amnesty was granted to political dissidents, following the Red Army's withdrawal in 1958. These two phases differed in at least two respects. The first aimed to re-educate the younger generation (mainly students and school pupils accused either of belonging to anticommunist and promonarchist organisations, or of being 'enemies of the working class') and to bring them into the communist fold. The second was aimed at mature people, who had usually experienced at least a decade of political imprisonment. Victims of the second stage were no longer to be brainwashed (unlike the young people subjected to the first), but 'persuaded' by more subtle methods to cooperate with the now firmly established communist state. These methods, however, still involved confinement in filthy conditions and deprivation of the basic necessities of life, together with reportedly deliberate poisoning and infection with TB.

The programme of re-education and unmasking was a system carefully designed to depersonalise what the Romanian Christian dissident Petre Ţuţea described as the 'primordial mask' of humanity, which cannot be obliterated, only damaged, and the 'divine mask' which can be reclaimed only by literally 'dis-covering' individual vocation. Contrary to Makarenko's theories, some prisoners experienced the divine presence in a way that transfigured them. Some discovered their mission through embodying Christ's narrative in their own lives. Their individual stories, illustrated in works of art, personal relationships or prayerful silence, were understood by them as a witness to the incarnation. These little-known accounts are part of a vast twentieth-century martyrology.

The story of resistance in the Soviet bloc varies from country to country. In Romania, individual Christians kept up armed partisan resistance until after the death of Stalin in 1953. Other forms of resistance, which continued throughout the communist period, were non-cooperation (e.g. through a solidarity of silence, and resistance to agricultural collectivisation) and implicit subversion of communist principles.

A significant example of subversion was the practice of the 'prayer of the heart' by political prisoners. This tradition of unceasing prayer, known in the Balkans as hesychasm, or the attainment of inner stillness through prayer (specifically the Jesus Prayer), flourished in Romanian prisons like Aiud, Ocnele Mari and Gherla, where copies of the first two volumes of Dumitru Stăniloae's translation of the Greek *Philokalia* (an anthology of ascetical and mystical texts on hesychast spirituality dating from the third to the fifteenth century) had been smuggled in. Stăniloae is an example of an intellectual who, while appearing to make concessions to the status quo, in fact through his writing undermined the very principles on which the political structure was based.[11]

Under communism the hesychast tradition enjoyed an astonishingly vigorous revival among Orthodox believers. Spiritual fathers such as Hieromonk Arsenie Boca (1910–89) at Brâncoveanu monastery, Sâmbăta de Sus in Transylvania and Archimandrite Ilie Cleopa (1912–98)[12] at Sihăstria monastery in Moldavia inspired powerful spiritual movements and attracted large numbers of Christians deprived both of the church sacraments and of the liberty to confess their faith.

Between 1945 and 1958, the Romanian hesychast tradition was further revitalised by the 'Burning Bush' movement at the monastery of St Antim Ivireanul in Bucharest, where monks and lay intellectuals sought a deeper apprehension of the Jesus Prayer under the guidance of the remarkable scholar and *staretz* Vasile Vasilachi (1909–2003). Along with many of his fellow neo-hesychasts he was to be imprisoned for discussing patristic works, which were held to be 'inimical to the régime'.

Celebration of the Eucharist was also a fundamental act of resistance. Though deprived of formal church ritual, inmates of political prisons became a Eucharistic community focused on and sustained by the communion of their faith. The following description (corroborated by many other prisoners' accounts) conveys a sense of the extraordinary power of religious experience which, celebrated in countless different ways, in the most ingenious and courageous forms, contributed to the witness of the church against state-directed atheism:

> On Easter Eve in May 1951, the priests celebrated a Liturgy attended by all the political prisoners working as forced labour in the mine of Baia Sprie, in the north of Transylvania. A few minutes before midnight all the working prisoners of the shift gathered in a lateral gallery where an altar was arranged with the face of Jesus figured on it by means of the smoke of the calcium carbide cap lamps. Gimlets and drills of various lengths were suspended on the ceiling in the form of a huge xylophone. In order to mark the moment of the Resurrection we shot with cannons improvised from pipes in which we put calcium carbide and water.

11 *Filocalia, sau, Culegere din scrierile sfinţilor părinţi care arată cum se poate omul curăţi, lumina şi desăvârşi,* trans. D. Stăniloae, 12 vols. (Sibiu: Dacia Traiana, 1947–79); D. Stăniloae, *Din Istoria Isihasmului în Ortodoxia Română* (Bucharest: Scripta, 1992).
12 A. Popescu, 'Archimandrite Cleopa Ilie – the good Shepherd', *The Guardian*, 8 December 1998, 18.

These pipes were stopped up at one end and had a wooden plug in the other. The pipe had a small hole in which we could put the flame of the cap lamps. Explosions were powerful and added to the sound produced by the bells and the xylophone improvised from drills. Shortly before midnight there was silence, as in a tomb. All cap lamps were switched off. There was complete darkness. Father Antal, an ex-assistant bishop to the patriarch, lit his cap lamp and his voice could be heard: 'Come and take light.' Then prisoners one by one went to take light from the priest. Then the priest addressed us three times with the Christian greeting: 'Christ is Risen!' We all responded: 'He is Risen indeed!' Then after the Gospel reading we all sang: 'Christ is risen from the dead, trampling down death by death . . .'

The drill bits sounded like an organ and one of us improvised a veritable oratorio on them. The warders went and reported the situation to the administration. The Commandant, Colonel Szabo, was furious. His first step was to lock up all the priests, who had celebrated the Easter Eucharist underground. But when the other prisoners had to begin work they went on strike in solidarity with the priests. Not long after this the forced labour colony at Baia Sprie was closed down.[13]

There were more Christian martyrs in the twentieth century than at any other time. Under communism the martyrs demonstrated the power of faith to resist atheist ideology and indoctrination. Of the new Russian martyrs, only those of the Stalinist period (not those of later periods) have been canonised by the Moscow patriarchate. In post-communist Romania no martyrs of the communist period have been acknowledged: crimes against humanity perpetrated by the communist state have still to be officially acknowledged. Such facts are symptomatic of the problems facing the churches in the aftermath of communism.[14]

Political subservience and resistance: spirituality preserved

Conventionally, the keynote of Orthodox life in the second half of the twentieth century has often seemed to be its subservience to political authority. This is a

---

13 A. Ciolte and V. Achim (eds.), *Triunghiul Morţii, Baia Sprie 1950–1954* (Baia Mare: Gutinul, 2000). I acknowledge Father Nicolae Grebenea's permission to use my English translation from an unpublished interview about his imprisonment at Baia Sprie, 1 September 2000, Piatra Neamţ, Romania.

14 Alexandru Popescu, 'Mission as martyrdom in post-marxist societies', in *Together in mission: Orthodox churches consult with the Church Mission Society* (Moscow: CMS, 2001), 32–3. I am indebted to James Ramsay, formerly Anglican Chaplain in Bucharest, for making available to me his unpublished 'Reflections on religion and spiritual life in modern Romania'.

superficial view. The most remarkable feature of the Orthodox Church over all the countries where it was subjugated to communism was the survival – and eventually the revival – of spirituality, especially in Russia, but also to a certain extent in Romania. If one is to look for the root of that revival, it will be found deep in the period of physical persecution of the Lenin–Stalin period. By 1941 (the year of the Nazi invasion) the wasteland that was the Christian face of Russia contained pockets of underground resistance which state pressure had been powerless to eliminate.

There was scarcely anywhere for these cells to maintain their underground existence save in the prison camps themselves. The most remarkable ecclesiastical document to survive from the inter-war years is a letter of 1926 addressed by a group of bishops imprisoned in the former monastery of Solovki in the European Arctic, which was converted into a prison camp.[15] They write in moderate tones, yet present a condemnation of atheist polices and the lack of any willingness on the part of the authorities to establish a dialogue with the church:

> The government, both in the laws it passes and in the exercise of its functions, does not remain neutral in relation to belief and disbelief, but quite clearly takes up a position on the side of atheism, using all the means of state at its disposal for its establishment, development and spread as a counterweight to all religions.[16]

Other notable literature has emerged from the prison camps. This began to circulate in deepest secrecy in the 1970s, but then gradually found its way abroad, making the world public aware of the existence of *samizdat*.[17] The Christian origin of so much of this writing has yet, however, to gain the recognition it deserves. This would contribute significantly to the changing face of Russia at the end of the century and insert a factor in the countdown to the end of the Soviet regime.

A work which should occupy a place in Russian literary history, but does not yet do so, is *Otchizna neizvestnaia* (The Unknown Homeland), an anonymous biography of a priest, a certain Fr Pavel.[18] The country of the title is Siberia, to which the priest was exiled in the 1930s, following his arrest in Petrograd (Leningrad) after the Revolution. It was after he had lost all – his parish, his wife, his home – that the truly effective part of his ministry began, a story of

---

15 Reproduced in full in Struve, *Christians in contemporary Russia*, 351–61.
16 Ibid., 353.
17 Literally 'self-published', but in fact not published at all: 'privately circulated' is a better description.
18 *The unknown homeland*, trans. Marite Sapiets (Oxford: A. R. Mowbray, 1978).

pain and suffering, but bringing to life the essence of religious experience. The author appears to be a young man, writing in the third person, who became a convert and gave up a life of crime and degradation to become a disciple. The prison authorities released Fr Pavel simply in order for him to die (presumably not wanting to create a martyr within the barbed wire of the camp's confines). The account of Fr Pavel's ministry on his deathbed and the sanctity of the spot marking his grave take us to the heart of the power of the Russian Orthodox Church to survive:

> The same evening, when Fr Pavel's death became known, half the collective farm came to the Zakharovs' house. The priest had lived there for about four months, but for many people he had become their 'adviser', 'benefactor' and 'dear father' . . . So the story of the exiled pastor came to an end. But though the storm blows over the new and old grave mounds, covering them with snow, though the storm whirls over the distant cemetery, wrapping it in a mantle of snow, though time goes by and the years disappear . . . still the cherry tree will go on arraying itself anew in its wedding colours every spring, and the path of remembrance, prayer and veneration, which leads to such graves, will never be overgrown.[19]

The opposition to Soviet control of the Orthodox Church and the perceived compromise of the Moscow patriarchate took on a more organised form in the middle of the 1960s. Two Moscow priests, Frs Nikolai Eshliman and Gleb Yakunin (who was only thirty at the time), circulated two appeals, one to Nikolai Podgorny (chairman of the Presidium of the Supreme Soviet of the USSR), the other, in a different tone, to Patriarch Aleksii, but containing roughly the same set of evidence about the interference of the secular authorities in the life of the church and begging for a more robust defence on the part of the church.[20] Church matters were officially in the hands of the government's Council for Religious Affairs, which Stalin had established at the end of the Second World War as part of the new set of relations between church and state. Both of these documents adopted an objective and even legal tone. They were the first comprehensive attempt on the part of any churchman to set out the overall situation of the Russian Orthodox Church since the Revolution.

The only reply to either appeal came from the patriarch, who, instead of answering the charges, removed the priests from their parishes (though he stopped short of defrocking them). Fr Eshliman soon withdrew from the fray, but Fr Yakunin has continued to be active into the twenty-first century. There

---

19 Ibid., 242, 247.
20 M. Bourdeaux, *Patriarch and prophets: persecution of the Russian Orthodox Church today* (London: Macmillan, 1969), 189–223.

was no widespread open support for the two priests. However, one senior figure, Archbishop Ermogen of Kaluga, did take up the issues, for which intervention he was forced to retire to the Zhirovitsy monastery. He claimed in particular that the only way to solve these questions was to convene a *sobor*, which had not happened since the election of Patriarch Aleksii in 1945. The government's control of church affairs had produced an intolerable situation, or as the archbishop put it:

> Here lies the basic disaster. The discretion of the government officials completely controls all questions concerned with granting priests their requests for registration legally to conduct services . . . This paralyses the internal church activity of the diocesan bishop and makes him completely dependent on the government official.[21]

There was not a single bishop at that time whose pastoral administration could proceed unaffected by secular interference. Yet collectively they averted their gaze. There was no tradition of protest and they hoped that, by not becoming involved in the dispute, they would be able to carry on their work, using the limited freedom available to them. This varied considerably from area to area, depending on the antireligious motivation of the local representative of the Council for Religious Affairs.

Yet without question there were from the second half of the 1960s growing numbers of protest documents, but also a more profound expression of spiritual concerns. One such topic was the revival of monasticism. At this time there were still monasteries in existence, which had reopened during or after World War II. Nikita Khrushchev decided, as part of his antireligious campaign (1959–64), to close these down, possibly intending to leave one or two behind as showplaces for the benefit of foreign visitors. One of the key targets was the flourishing monastery at Pochaev in western Ukraine. The monks themselves, continually harassed by the local atheist authorities, found support in the persons of local village women, relatives and friends of the victims. Between them, over a period of several months, they amassed the facts, wrote them up in simple but accurate form, and smuggled the resulting documents to the west. The texts focused world attention on a specific issue, a community and a building, which had never happened before.[22]

It is almost certain that the resulting publicity in the world press saved the monastery. The *Zhurnal Moskovskoi Patriarkhii* itself began to report on activities at Pochaev: for example, the celebration of the anniversary of the

21 Bourdeaux, *Patriarch and prophets*, 251–2.
22 Ibid., 74–84, 97–116.

acquisition of the relics of St Iov on 28 August 1966.[23] Before long there was a report on a visit by a group of Americans – a sure sign that the Soviets had relented.[24] The west acquired documents, such as those defending the Pochaev monastery in various ways, but by the end of the 1960s the reading of *samizdat* became an essential feature for the study of the USSR.[25]

Monasticism was beginning to emerge as an enduring feature of Orthodox spiritual life. This cause was taken up by a remarkable publicist for the Russian Orthodox Church, Anatolii Levitin, a layman who had formerly been a deacon in the Living Church. Among many themes in his work, the defence of monasticism as a spiritual reality in the developing life of the Orthodox Church stands out. His essay, *Monasticism in the Modern World*, is a prelude to the revival during the last decade of the twentieth century, when hundreds of new monasteries and convents opened in all parts of Russia and Ukraine. Levitin wrote:

> Monasticism is not an institution, foundation or a historical phenomenon, but an element, just as love, art and religion are elements . . . It is a miracle, a direct act of God's grace, which changes human nature itself . . . We firmly believe in the coming of a new wave of monasticism in the Russian Church. The future of Russia is with the ardent and zealous young people of our country who, despite opposition, are every day attaining to the faith. New monks will come from among them – zealous warriors for Christ's cause. They will renew and transform the Church of Christ and the Russian land with their purity, self-sacrifice and spiritual ardour.[26]

The old order overturned

Despite scattered (though convincing) evidence that the spiritual life of the Russian Orthodox Church had survived during the 1960s and 1970s and may even have begun to revive, there was a grey and static quality about the Soviet Union during the years in office of Leonid Brezhnev as general secretary of the Communist Party. Mikhail Gorbachev was elected on 11 March 1985, following a period of over two years of gerontocracy, when two consecutive leaders, Iuri Andropov and Konstantin Chernenko, had proved themselves barely able to

---

23 *Zhurnal Moskovskoi Patriarkhii* 12 (December 1966), 38.
24 Ibid., 11 (November 1967), 12.
25 See, for example, Michael Bourdeaux, *Risen indeed: lessons in faith from the USSR* (London: Darton, Longman and Todd, 1983), 5–9. See especially in the religious field the work of Keston College, a research institute from 1969 located near Bromley in Kent, England (later in Oxford).
26 Bourdeaux, *Patriarch and prophets*, 87, 89–90.

walk, let alone lead a superpower towards solving the economic and political difficulties which were increasingly besetting it. Gorbachev memorably referred to the previous two decades as a period of *zastoi* (stagnation).

During this time the church had visibly raised its international profile through its active membership of the WCC, which it had joined in 1961. Scarcely an international meeting took place without the significant presence of Russian church leaders. There was also a permanent office in the WCC headquarters in Geneva, staffed by a stream of men eager for foreign experience at a time when international travel was still an impossible dream for the vast majority. The authorities expected them to uphold Soviet policies, deny the facts of persecution, and faithfully report back on any useful contacts. It is now widely believed that the brief of the office at Geneva went further: to control the agenda of the WCC on international affairs.[27]

Meanwhile, at home in the Soviet Union, the KGB rooted out any attempt to build up a local Orthodox community. Such was the fate of the 'Christian Seminar' which Vladimir Poresh and Aleksandr Ogorodnikov founded as students in Moscow in 1973. A group of not more than twenty would meet from time to time in an atmosphere of common enquiry and in a spirit of friendship, bereft of study materials or trained leadership. They founded their own *samizdat* journal, *Obshchina* (Community). For this they were sentenced on 1 August 1979 to eight years of imprisonment and exile.[28] Fr Gleb Yakunin received an even longer sentence (ten years: 1977–88) for a direct ecumenical initiative, the founding in 1976 of the 'Christian Committee for the Defence of Believers' Rights'. Through their prodigious activity, this group collected no fewer than 423 documents, comprising nearly 3000 pages, and covering the activity and suppression of almost all religious groups in the Soviet Union.[29]

A stasis prevailed in the general area of church–state relations during the 1970s and early 1980s, which was no less immobile than the stagnation to which Gorbachev would shortly refer. In 1971 Metropolitan Pimen was elected patriarch, on the death of Aleksii I. Pimen was, if anything, more passive in his relations with the state than Aleksii had been, and he remained in office during the whole of this period, up to his death in May 1990, when Aleksii II was elected to follow him.

---

27 Jane Ellis, *The Russian Orthodox Church: a contemporary history* (London and Sydney: Croom Helm, 1986), 270.
28 For a short account of the activity of the Christian Seminar, see P. Walters and J. Balengarth, *Light through the curtain* (Tring: Lion Publishing, 1985), 92–5, 104–8.
29 Michael Bourdeaux, *Gorbachev, Glasnost and the Gospel* (Sevenoaks: Hodder and Stoughton, 1990), 6–10.

When Gorbachev came to power, it took him a full year to assess the order in which he should tackle the myriad problems besetting the Soviet Union. Religious liberty was a subject which probably did not cross his desk in these early days. The more general issue of human rights did not, however, escape his notice and it offended his dignity when he travelled abroad to be confronted by Jewish activists and their sympathisers calling for freedom for Anatolii Shcharanskii, the imprisoned activist.[30] Shcharanskii's release on 11 February 1986 was the first step in a major change of policy, but the Chernobyl disaster two months later undoubtedly accelerated the pace of change and after this Gorbachev began to proclaim the upholding of human values as something essential for his administration, as it sought to reform the Soviet Union under the slogans of *glasnost* (openness) and *perestroika* (restructuring).

The pressure on the churches began to lift. Gradually they received some of their property back and the first stage commenced of rebuilding the desecrated churches and monasteries. In Moscow, most notably, the church undertook the huge project of restoring the Danilov monastery as its administrative centre (which, curiously enough, had been given back by Andropov in 1983, after doing duty as a boys' reformatory). It was only gradually that Gorbachev began to see that the Orthodox Church could be an ally in his quest for reform. In one of the coincidences of history, Gorbachev's short time in office fortuitously reached its heyday at the same time as the Orthodox Church was due to celebrate its millennium (St Vladimir had been baptised in 988). He readily, therefore, granted the Moscow patriarchate permission to put on an international 'show', the like of which Russia had never seen before.

With the anniversary due in early June 1988, Gorbachev received the leading clergy of the patriarchate in the Kremlin on 29 April, when he promised a new law and complete religious liberty in return for the church's support in promoting *perestroika*. 'Believers are Soviet people, workers, patriots', he stated, 'and they have the full right to express their convictions with dignity. *Perestroika*, democratisation and *glasnost* concern them as well – in full measure and without any restrictions. This is especially true of ethics and morals, a domain where universal norms and customs are so helpful for our common cause.'[31]

Virtually overnight the church achieved a high profile in the Soviet media. Every newspaper ran front-page articles extolling it and reporting specifically on its new relationship with the state. By the time June arrived and foreign

30 Ibid., 26–7.
31 Quoted in ibid., 44.

guests, hastily summoned, began to pour in, Moscow's two TV channels were sometimes simultaneously transmitting information about the day's events and, for example, documentary information about the life of the church.[32] The culmination of these events was twofold. A great ceremonial celebration took place in the Bolshoi Theatre, a kind of pageant of Russian history, narrated by the great actor Sergei Bondarchuk, attended by the highest dignitaries of church and state, stopping short only of Gorbachev himself, although his wife was there. The choir of the Bolshoi sang the traditional Russian paean *Mnogoie leto* (Long life) to the church, and the choir of the Moscow Theological Academy responded. The event was televised throughout the Soviet Union. Although some more conservative church opinion felt that the event was vulgar, church–state relations would never be the same again.[33]

Gorbachev promised a new law guaranteeing religious liberty to replace Stalin's *Law on Religious Associations*, which had remained in place over a period of almost sixty years and was appropriate only to a time that had vanished by the end of the Second World War. After a period of consultation, the new law came into force in October 1990. It removed virtually all restrictions on religion, including those on foreign missionaries, and permitted the teaching of religion in schools. As the Russian Orthodox Church emerged from the period of communist domination, it found itself confronted by a huge agenda, affecting every area of its life. The election of the metropolitan of Leningrad, Aleksii (Ridiger), as Patriarch Aleksii II in June 1990 put a new and vigorous man in charge of the church at this time of unprecedented opportunity. He was an Estonian by birth, but with a Russian mother, and was brought up bilingually. He had also had a great deal of international experience, resulting from his work with the Conference of European Churches, eventually as its president. He was also a person who had grown up under the most severe restrictions. As a schoolboy, he had seen his country Estonia, before the Second World War an independent democracy, overrun by the Soviets, by the Nazis and then by the Red Army again. This time the Soviet Union imposed a steel grip on his country. His rise to power as bishop of Tallinn in 1961 can be explained only by his willingness to work within the system. His eventual election as patriarch ensured that a steady hand would be at the helm, but also one richly experienced in dealing with the secular authorities. Those who elected him cannot have imagined that just over a year later he would find himself in a

32 Ibid., 42–64.
33 Ibid., 61–3.

country which had lost all the component parts of its empire. His own country of Estonia won its independence and the church under his jurisdiction was now scattered over fourteen newly independent countries.

Patriarch Aleksii's innate conservatism ensured that under his administration the Moscow patriarchate became arguably the most 'Soviet' of all institutions that remained after the collapse of the Soviet system. He turned his back on the ecumenism which had formed such a prominent part of his earlier life.[34] He encouraged new legislation (passed in 1997), which gave the Russian Orthodox Church pride of place among Christian denominations (Islam, Buddhism and Judaism were also designated 'traditional' – and therefore favoured – religions in Russia), to the detriment of Catholicism, Protestantism and all other Christian minorities.

As the Orthodox Church began to experience full – and indeed privileged – freedom in Russian society, it undertook a vigorous programme of rebuilding and restoring churches and monasteries which had been destroyed or allowed to fall into ruin, thus transforming the look of ancient town centres everywhere. New dioceses were created, and seminaries founded in all areas for the training of future priests. There was a new publishing programme to start to make good the gap of seventy years. There was notable new social activity – work in hospitals, old-people's homes and prisons, and military chaplains. In every single one of these areas of enterprise, the conservatism which had helped the church to survive the years of persecution was evident and new episcopal appointments did not seem likely to start breaking the mould. Sociological surveys in Russia indicate that the majority of Russians claim allegiance to the traditional faith, but churchgoing as such has failed to keep pace with the expansion of the church's activities. Nevertheless, after the collapse of the communist system and at the beginning of the third millennium, Russia presented the image to the world of being an Orthodox country.

Bulgaria and Romania after communism

The same could be said of Bulgaria and Romania, though their situations are as different from each other as they are from Russia's. The Bulgarian Orthodox Church is riven by a schism which has its origins in communist times. It is believed that some 85 per cent of Bulgarians still claim allegiance to the Orthodox Church, so the persistence of this schism is a national scandal, but

---

34 For a study of ecumenism in Russia, see John Witte Jr. and Michael Bourdeaux, *Proselytism and Orthodoxy in Russia: the new war for souls* (Maryknoll, NY: Orbis Books, 1999).

lay people are powerless to do anything about it. This originated in 1992, when the United Democratic Forces (UDF) government interfered in the church's affairs. Their basic contention was that the election of Patriarch Maxim in communist times was rigged and therefore invalid and that consequently the holy synod, the ruling body, was illegitimate. The Board for Religious Affairs (itself a dubious survival from the days when communism controlled the church) replaced Maxim by Metropolitan Pimen of Nevrokop. The opposition Bulgarian Socialist Party (BSP), a reformed and modernised descendant of the Communist Party, backed Maxim.

In 1998 Patriarch Bartholomaios of Constantinople, the nominal leader of world Orthodoxy but lacking executive jurisdiction over individual national churches, visited the country in the company of a host of other senior figures, but the outcome brought no progress. It will take some time yet for the legacy of communism to disappear.[35]

The Romanian Orthodox Church, too, has had problems in coming to terms with its past. Patriarch Teoktist presided over a church which saw its freedom visibly diminish in President Ceauşescu's later days. This affected the church especially in many rural areas, where the authorities were trying to reduce the independent spirit manifested almost universally in the countryside. One means of doing this was to pull down individual housing and replace it by communal blocks built of concrete. However much priests were involved in defending the integrity of their communities at local level, the patriarch continued to pay fulsome tribute to Ceauşescu. The last of these messages, a Christmas greeting in 1989, reached many of its recipients after the summary execution of the disgraced leader on 25 December. The next issue of *Romanian Orthodox Church News* (a journal published in Bucharest in English) opened with the words:

> After several decades of slavery under communist dictatorship and a lot of suffering from Ceauşescu's cruel dictatorship, we rejoice that God has turned His face to our people and, having seen the multitude of innocent children and youth killed by the repressive forces of the dictator, saved us from the shadow of death and set us at liberty.[36]

Patriarch Teoktist offered to resign, but the holy synod requested him to stay on after he had given the lead in repenting, a step followed by several other hierarchs who admitted to having collaborated with the communist regime.

---

35 See J. Broun, 'Schism in Bulgaria and the new law on confessions', *Frontier* (Keston Institute) 3 (Winter 2004), 4–9.
36 *Romanian Orthodox Church News* 6 (1989), 3.

The Romanian Orthodox Church was therefore able to embark on a period of quiet reform without secular interference and remains unquestionably the most potent symbol of the nation.

The Serbian Orthodox Church

In Serbia, too, now an independent nation, the Orthodox Church has emerged strongly. Here, as everywhere, the collapse of communism has enhanced both the symbolic and actual power of the Orthodox Church. However, in order to understand the history of the Serbian Orthodox Church during the period of almost half a century when it coexisted with a communist government, it is necessary to appreciate the state in which it was left at the end of the Second World War. During the pre-war decades the kingdom of Yugoslavia, as it was then called, united Serbs, Croats and Slovenes. In it the Serbs enjoyed a position of special privilege, with the Serbian Orthodox Church supporting the monarchy and vice versa. During the war the church continued to support the monarchy, as well as the anti-Tito partisans, but at the same time a split occurred with Croatia, which was mainly Catholic. Here the Ustaše emerged, a fascist mob in league with the Nazis. Among much else the Ustaše took up arms against the Serbian minority in Croatia, murdering three leading hierarchs and over 200 clergy. A puppet 'Croatian Orthodox Church' came into being. The Ustaše destroyed or badly damaged many hundreds of Serbian Orthodox churches and monasteries.

The establishment of a communist regime in what now became Tito's Yugoslavia saw the Serbian Orthodox Church at first attempting to re-establish its pre-war position, but in this it first faced the virulent atheism of the Stalin period. The state confiscated church lands, thus depriving it of its basic income, and abolished the right of the Orthodox Church to organise religious education in schools (teaching on church premises was never outlawed, but restrictions often made it impossible to conduct). The patriarchate and clergy sought accommodation with the new regime, but for a decade made little headway.

As in other communist countries, the regime forced clergy to join politically loyal 'priests' associations', causing widespread concern among the hierarchy, which was attempting to rebuild church life. A new decree on the *Legal Status of Religious Communities* of 1953 defined the rights of all churches, but for years the very people who passed this law failed to respect it.

Throughout this period there had been show trials of recalcitrant clergy, culminating in the case against Bishop Arsenije of the Montenegrin Littoral in 1954. Before this, four priests were tried in Cetinje (Montenegro) and the court extracted 'confessions' implicating the bishop in antistate activities. They had allegedly discussed the return of the monarchy and even the possibility of assassinating President Tito. On the testimony of the priests Bishop Arsenije received a sentence of eleven and a half years, even though he was already over seventy. He had certainly opposed the priests' associations and Patriarch Vikentije's attempts to reach an accommodation with the regime, but the sentence was out of proportion to any possible offence. On appeal, the sentence was reduced to five and a half years, but Arsenije was released, a sick man, in August 1956, while still being barred from any public duty. He retired from his bishopric, and after the official expiry of his sentence in 1960 he accepted the titular see of Budim.

Patriarch Vikentije died in 1958, having achieved more than a little success in keeping the church alive in difficult circumstances. Most notably, he had managed to keep open a seminary in Belgrade for the training of future priests. President Tito sent a wreath to his funeral, which was attended by government representatives, as well as many delegations from foreign churches. His successor was Patriarch German, elected by a substantial majority. He outlived Tito by many years, remaining in office until his death, aged ninety-two, in 1991, just when Yugoslavia was on the verge of disintegration. His achievement was to steer his church into better times and ensure that it became the most unrestricted of all the Orthodox Churches existing under communist regimes. In this he was, of course, aided by the expulsion of Yugoslavia from the Soviet bloc and by its subsequent inclusion in the 'Third World' group of nations.

German had been a married parish priest in the inter-war years, having studied law at the Sorbonne. He was transferred to the office of the synod in 1938 (aged thirty-nine). His wife died in 1951, so he took monastic vows and was soon consecrated bishop, spending a short period in the United States from 1956. He was a tireless traveller and knew personally church leaders all over the world.

On his election as patriarch, German did not renounce any of his predecessor's policies, dealing firmly with the priests' associations, rather than abolishing them. He had a great impact in ecumenical circles, but faced many problems at home, not all arising from the communist dictatorship. By far the most serious of these was the secession of the Macedonians, who formed their own independent church in 1967. Macedonia has, since time immemorial, been a territory disputed between Serbia, Bulgaria and Greece, but had never been an independent territory (that is, until the disintegration of Yugoslavia in the 1990s). The Bulgarians occupied it during the Second World War, but the Soviets decreed that it should become a constituent state of Yugoslavia.

Nationalism was always strong in the area and the Orthodox clergy lost no time in claiming a right to independence from the Serbian Orthodox Church. After twenty years of dispute, even the diplomatic skills of Patriarch German were insufficient to prevent the Macedonian Orthodox declaring their church autocephalous, which the Yugoslav government welcomed. To this day, neither the Serbian nor any other Orthodox Church has recognised the Macedonian claims, but with the advent of independence for the 'Former Yugoslav Republic of Macedonia' (the country's official name) the prospect of a quick resolution to this problem is more distant than ever.

The Serbian Orthodox Church embodies the spirit of the nation, but to an exaggerated degree. This did not put it in a strong position, under German's successor Patriarch Pavle, to mediate between warring ethnic factions in the post-communist débâcle. The Orthodox churches were deeply scarred by the experience of communism, yet survived with remarkable resilience. The period since the collapse of communism has seen their strong revival everywhere.

24

Modern spirituality and the Orthodox Church

JOHN BINNS

The study of Christian spirituality investigates the self-understanding, the identity and the mode of operation of the church. It is founded on the church's formation narratives, which identify its foundation with the gift of the Holy Spirit. This is clear from the fourth gospel, which tells how, on the day of the Resurrection, Christ breathed on his disciples with the words 'receive the Holy Spirit' (John 20:22), while St Luke recounts how, on the day of Pentecost, the mission of the church began with the coming of the Spirit on the disciples in the form of wind and fire (Acts 2:1–4). So we are shown that the work of the Spirit guides this newly formed community in a variety of ways, such as the proclaiming of the word, mighty works of healing and power, and the formation of a disciplined and ordered community. Spirituality is the discipline which describes and examines the process of how the church subsists, how it understands and defines itself, how it structures and shapes its life, how it engages with other religious communities and the society around, and from where it draws its vitality and resources. It is concerned with the church in its concrete and specific existence as opposed to its eternal and unchanging message. The study of spirituality is located at the intersection of theology, history and sociology, seeking to give a clear account of how the church functions in history but viewed from its own perspective of theology. Contributors to a recent history of Christian spirituality were asked to bear in mind that 'Christian spirituality is the lived experience of Christian belief in both its more general and specialised forms. It is possible to distinguish spirituality from doctrine in that it concentrates not on faith itself but on the reaction faith arouses in religious consciousness and practice.'[1]

The Orthodox Church, like any modern religious community, is varied and diverse. In historic Orthodox regions, traditional forms of religious expression

---

1 See *Christian spirituality: origins to the twelfth century*, ed. B. McGinn and J. Meyendorff (London: Routledge and Kegan Paul, 1986), xv.

persist in the villages, with monasteries and other holy places providing a focus for popular devotion. In Islamic countries of the Middle East, a minority church is struggling to adapt and protect itself in an often hostile and intolerant environment. In the west – and increasingly in other parts of the Orthodox world – a culture of secularism, of liberal democracy and of a market economy is challenging the church to find new ways of expressing its life. In this rich and confusing variety of forms of church life, it may seem an impossible task to identify either a single modern spirituality or a single Orthodox spirituality. However, it is precisely the teaching of the Orthodox Church that there is a single unified spiritual tradition, handed down through generations, which creates the church. From this tenaciously held conviction comes its common life shared by a widespread and varied community of believers.

This unified stream of tradition, which is Orthodoxy, comes out of two sources. These are the two distinct and different types of experience which the Orthodox communities have experienced over the 2000-year history of the church. The spiritualities which derive from them can be called Christendom and Martyrdom.[2]

The beginning of the Christian Byzantine Empire – or Christendom – in the east can be conveniently, although crudely, dated to the year 312, when Christianity came under the protection of the Emperor Constantine (312–337). This not only brought about a new relationship between church and state, but was also the start of the Byzantine Empire, which continued until 1453 when the city of Constantinople fell to the Turks. During this great sweep of over a millennium of history a Christian emperor and a Christian patriarch saw themselves as working together to create and direct a universal Christian society. Under this Byzantine regime a Christian culture was formed – with its own distinctive architecture, literature, philosophy, theology, liturgy, monastic life, iconography, hymnography and legal code. The Orthodox Church as we know it, at least in its Chalcedonian form, is the product of this cultural development. The liturgy of St John Chrystostom, for example, reached the form in which it is now celebrated in the fourteenth century under the influence of architecture, court ceremonial and monastic worship.[3] Some have expressed dissatisfaction with this ever-present Byzantinism, fearing that its influence will lead to a conservative clinging to a specific cultural form rather than the fresh presentation

2 B. Jackson, *Hope for the Church: contemporary strategies for growth* (London: Church House, 2002), 56, succinctly defines Christendom as 'society organised around an alliance of church and state, where the Christian faith is the official glue, the guiding principle of its laws and culture'.

3 See H. Wybrew, *The Orthodox Liturgy* (London: SPCK, 1989).

of the gospel to a new generation. Others find in Byzantine culture a creative synthesis of Greek philosophical searching and Hebrew religious awe, which stands against western individualism.[4] The continuing creativity of the Byzantine tradition is shown in many ways, but a good example is the rejection by modern iconographers of nineteenth-century westernised styles of painting in favour of the austere, hieratic forms of Byzantine models. Although the Byzantine Empire was in decline after 1204 when the crusaders captured the city, the imperial dream remained seductive and influential in late medieval Serbia and Bulgaria, and especially in Russia where the idea of Moscow as the Third Rome, succeeding to Rome and Constantinople, encouraged Russian imperial ambitions. The ancient Christian kingdoms of Armenia and Ethiopia, both established in the fourth century, were also Christian kingdoms which shared the ideals of the Byzantine project. The Christian empire of Ethiopia persisted until the military coup of 1973.

Alongside this confident and even triumphalist culture, Orthodox have undergone harsher and more negative experiences. In 1453, after a long decline, Constantinople finally fell to the Ottoman armies and before long a Muslim caliph took the place of the Christian ruler as the head of the eastern empire. Orthodox lands were still part of an empire, but one in which they were the ruled rather than the rulers. For the Orthodox patriarchates of the Middle East, Antioch, Alexandria and Jerusalem, this process had begun several centuries earlier, with the Arab military conquests of the mid-seventh century. More recently, periods of violent persecution have devastated the churches: in Turkey from 1895 to 1925; in Russia from 1918 to 1990; and in Serbia and surrounding areas from 1940 to 1945. These last examples justify us in referring to the twentieth century as that in which more Christians have died for their faith than any other. Thus throughout the Orthodox lands the church has suffered prolonged and destructive oppression. This has included periods of tolerance, as well as discrimination and outright persecution, but throughout all these forms of oppression, a new spirituality developed in which the exemplars were the martyrs, and Christian life became the enduring of suffering. The church had the calling to maintain the purity of the Orthodox faith undiminished. For this the qualities needed were strictness, fortitude and an unbending willpower. This style of spirituality interacted with that of monasticism in which the ascetic life was seen as a form of martyrdom. The impact

---

4 For a negative view of Byzantium, see A. Schmemann, *The journals of Father Alexander Schmemann 1978–1983* (Crestwood, NY: St Vladimir's Seminary Press, 2000). For a more positive assessment, see C. Yannaras, *Philosophie sans rupture* (Geneva: Labor et Fides, 1986), 7.

of a martyrdom spirituality can be seen both in the unbending rigour of many monasteries, such as the monastery of Esphigmenou on Mount Athos, where a banner is hung proclaiming 'Orthodoxy or Death', and also in the depth of compassion hinted at in the response given by Metropolitan Antony Bloom of the Russian Orthodox cathedral in London, when asked whether the church in Russia was free under communism. 'The freedom of the church is to love until death' was his reply.

With a spirituality shaped by these two huge communal experiences, the Orthodox Church is now entering upon a new stage of its life. In the final decade of the twentieth century the communist governments, which had ruled much of the Orthodox Church, disappeared with extraordinary rapidity. The church had a new freedom and self-determination forced upon it, and alongside this has come the need to function in a modern society, where democracy, secularism, a market economy and individualism are cultural norms. A church formed in an autocratic, religious, traditional and corporate setting has to define itself anew and assert its identity and self-understanding. This has been a massive shock. Western churches became used to this modern world over centuries, and helped to create it, but for the east this new world culture arrived with suddenness. Of course some countries such as Greece became independent over a century earlier, and in others, mainly in the Middle East, Christians remain a beleaguered minority. But the church as a whole was precipitated into a new and uncertain world.[5] The questions asked of the Orthodox Church in the modern world are how it will reaffirm its identity in the new climate of freedom, how it will relate to this new culture which surrounds it, and whether it can develop a new spirituality to equip itself to survive, to witness and to grow in this modern world.

One church which has adapted successfully to the demands of a modern society is the Coptic Church of Egypt, even allowing for the fact that the modernity of a Middle Eastern society is different from that in the west. Here the church has responded to life in a modern society in three different ways. All three came out of the Sunday School Movement in Cairo and are identified with three of the leaders of the modern Coptic Church. The first is Abbot Matthew the Poor, or Matta el-Miskin, who established his monastic community at the monastery of St Makarios in the desert of Wâdî el-Naṭrûn as a centre of traditional monastic ascetic life, but combined with enterprising economic development in the desert. Next comes Bishop Samuel, who worked in

---

5 The Church of Greece became independent in 1833 and was recognised as autonomous by the ecumenical patriarch in 1850.

collaboration with western agencies and churches, in order to advance Coptic aspirations. Finally, Pope Shenûda III helped his church to become aware of its identity and vitality, and so gave a new confidence and political awareness to the Coptic community. These approaches were at first in competition, but then worked in harmony to produce a dramatic revival of the Coptic Church. This triple movement shows that successful modernisation is not the uncritical adoption of new ideas but rather a revitalisation of the tradition within a new form of society, in other words a 'revolutionary traditionalism'. This example of church revival in Egypt shows how the Orthodox Church can become a vibrant mission community, engaged with a modern society yet drawing life from its tradition.[6] Here then is the dual task of a modern Orthodox spirituality – first the revival of the tradition and second the setting up of structures to enable the church to adapt and to function effectively in a modern society.

The process of reviving the church begins with trying to understand what the church is. One of the main subjects exercising Orthodox theologians has been ecclesiology, which they have addressed as an urgent and problematic task. For the early Christians the church was a community of those called out by God, formed into the body of Christ on earth, and empowered by the Holy Spirit. In the second century Ignatius of Antioch wrote of the church as a community, with the bishop at its centre, surrounded by the priests and deacons, celebrating the Eucharist, making Christ present in the forms of bread and wine and so making the people into the church, the Body of Christ. Each community thus created into the church is complete and whole, with nothing lacking.[7] The simplicity of this understanding became obscured in the centuries which followed. In the Byzantine Empire the boundaries of the church were synonymous with those of the empire, and so the church became an institution instead of a distinct community. It came to perform a ritual function creative of culture rather than being a prophetic challenge to that culture. As Alexander Schmemann commented, 'In order to evangelise the empire, the Church had to turn itself into a religion.'[8] This development is most clearly seen in Russia after Peter the Great, when the church was governed by a synod presided over by the state-appointed over-procurator, who was often not a Christian. The church was structured along the lines of a department of state, with clergy resembling government officials. As well as this

---

6 See S. S. Hassan, *Christians versus Muslims in modern Egypt* (Oxford: Oxford University Press, 2003), esp. 5–10, 85–99.

7 Ignatius of Antioch, *Epistles to the Smyrnaeans 8 and Romans 2*.

8 A. Schmemann, *An introduction to liturgical theology* (London and Bangor, ME: American Orthodox Press, 1966).

distortion of church life, the experience of oppression produced different and more tangible dangers to the church: as Christian education was restricted, so financial penalties for church membership were imposed, while elections to ecclesiastical office were influenced by the state. In communist Russia the church as an institution was systematically dismantled. By the year 1940 there were only three bishops remaining out of the 150 or so existing before the Revolution: the patriarchal *locum tenens* Sergii, Metropolitan Aleksii, and the liaison between church and state, Nikolai Kruititskii.

It is hardly surprising then that Orthodox theologians have given so much attention to ecclesiology, and have reaffirmed the clarity and simplicity of the Ignatian understanding of the nature of the church as communion. Aleksei Khomiakov (1804–60) saw the basis of church life in the local community gathered together in faith, forming a unity in plurality, moving together in love towards union with God. His understanding is expressed by the Russian *sobornost*, which is sometimes translated as community.[9] This rich theological tradition was developed and articulated by Nikolai Afanas'ev (1893–1966), Alexander Schmemann (1921–83) and John Zizioulas (Metropolitan Ioannes of Pergamon) (1931–). The church comes into being at the Eucharist, when the bishop, or his representative, presides and where the community gathers together, the sacrament of bread and wine is transformed by the Spirit into the Body and Blood of Christ, and the church becomes a spirit-led community. This is a powerful and creative way of conceiving the church which provides continuity with the past, emphasises the importance of the liturgy, and can bring into being and sustain the church community in a variety of settings, and provide a clear foundation for its life. The recovery of the centrality of the liturgy not only has parallels with the parish communion movement in the western church, but also has influenced the ecumenical movement. While for the western parish communion movement renewal meant returning to primitive models, for the Orthodox it meant entering into the riches of Byzantine liturgy, and thus renewing local communities. Also, the west encouraged regular receiving of communion, while in the east this often remains infrequent although the regular, even weekly, receiving of Holy Communion is increasingly encouraged. The Orthodox liturgy is also an effective agent of mission, and many first are attracted by and then become committed to the Orthodox Church through the richness, power and sheer beauty of the worship. The

---

9 Khomiakov never actually used the word *sobornost*, although he did write extensively of its derivatives – *sobirat*: to gather together; *sobor*: council; and *sobornyi*: catholic. See V. Shevzov, *Russian Orthodoxy on the eve of the Revolution* (Oxford: Oxford University Press, 2004), 30.

liturgy was the great product of Byzantine culture and sustained the church through dark days of oppression when other forms of expression were denied, and it is now enabling new life to spring up. Modern spirituality begins with meditation on the church and its worship.

If the liturgy is the action which creates the church, then the monastery is the place where the church is sustained. Monasteries are far more than centres set apart for prayer. They are places where the rich and intricate liturgical tradition is maintained and prayed; they are centres for local devotion and often pilgrimage; they have provided education and training, especially of church leaders since bishops are drawn from the monastic body, and are often centres of local economic and social life. In many and varied ways they provide the resources and vitality of church life. So the church needs strong monasteries. The centre of monasticism is Mount Athos in Greece, the Holy Mountain. Here, for over a thousand years, monks have been attracted by the spectacular landscape, by the isolation from the world, and above all by the strength of monastic tradition, which has led to a concentration of ecclesiastical life in a small enclave. Its uniqueness is emphasised by the restrictions preventing the presence of women on the mountain. Through most of the twentieth century monastic life on Mount Athos has declined steadily and inexorably. From the high figure of 7432 monks in 1903 the numbers had sunk to a nadir of 1145 monks in 1971. Its demise was widely predicted. Huge buildings were decaying and emptying. One visitor reported on a visit to the monastery of Zographou when he was told there were no monks present. 'Athos is dying fast. The disease is incurable. There is no hope', wrote John Julius Norwich.[10] Extraordinarily, in the years which followed, there has been a revival. It began in the hermitages and small settlements, called *sketes*, where young monks were attracted by the teaching and example of some of the well-known spiritual fathers. These groups grew into new communities and gradually moved into the monasteries, which were progressively repopulated, rebuilt and renewed. The previous style of life, known as idiorrhythmic, by which each monk retained his own possessions and decided on his own life style, was replaced by the cenobitic life, in which monks lived in common under the direction of the abbot. Other groups of monks came from the Meteora in Thessaly and from Euboea, while novices began to arrive from other Orthodox countries as well as Greece. The number of monks on the mountain had grown to 1642 by 2000. Spiritual renewal had taken place alongside numerical growth, with younger and well-educated monks enabling the monasteries to develop as centres of church life

10 J. J. Norwich and R. Sitwell, *Mount Athos* (London: Hutchinson, 1966), 14.

as well as nurturing a disciplined ascetic life. Monastic renewal has spread from Mount Athos. One elder, Father Ephraim, became abbot of the monastery of Philotheou. As his community grew he was able to send monks to three other monasteries on Athos and also founded at least sixteen monasteries in the USA and Canada.[11]

Renewal in monastic life has also taken place in other parts of the Orthodox world – in Russia, Romania and Egypt. In the Syrian mountainous region of the Ṭûr Abdîn, now located in south-eastern Turkey, the extinction of monastic life seemed likely with the decline in numbers of the Christian population of the region owing to political pressure. It now seems as though this may be averted, and recent reports suggest a slight but measurable growth in the number of Christians in the region.

A strand of the tradition of modern Orthodox theology developed in nineteenth-century Russia, where intellectual and social ferment gave rise not only to the communist revolution but also to a quieter revolution in Orthodox theological thought. Nicolas Zernov referred to this as the 'Russian Religious Renaissance', which is the title of the book in which he set out the thinking of some of these writers. A remarkable body of writing came from theologians from within this Russian tradition – such writers as Sergii Bulgakov, Pavel Florensky, Nikolai Berdyaev and Georges Florovsky, and later Vladimir Lossky, Alexander Schmemann and John Meyendorff.[12] Florovsky used the slogan 'forward to the Fathers' to sum up a theological programme which studied the Fathers, and found in them a basis for a theology which was faithful to the patristic inheritance but also engaged with a modern society. Some Fathers, previously little studied, became known. As a result of their researches and publishing, Dionysios the Areopagite, Maximos the Confessor, Symeon the New Theologian and Gregory Palamas have come to be read and known to the Christian world. The work of translating, commenting and reflecting on the writing of the Fathers has continued, with a growing volume of published material, especially through the St Vladimir's Seminary Press in

---

11 See R. Gothóni, *Paradise within reach: monasticism and pilgrimage on Mt Athos* (Helsinki: Helsinki University Press, 1993); Gothóni, *Tales and truth: pilgrimage on Mount Athos past and present* (Helsinki: Helsinki University Press, 1994); G. Speake, *Mount Athos: renewal in paradise* (New Haven and London: Yale University Press, 2002).

12 See, among others, J. Pain and N. Zernov (eds.), *A Bulgakov anthology* (London: SPCK, 1976); G. Florovsky, *The collected works*, 14 vols. (Belmont: Nordland Publishing Co., 1972–87); V. Lossky, *The mystical theology of the eastern Church* (London: J. Clarke, 1957); A. Schmemann, *For the life of the world: sacraments and orthodoxy* (Crestwood, NY: St Vladimir's Seminary Press, 1973). For a full bibliography, see N. Zernov, *Russkie pisateli emigratsii: biograficheskie svedeniia i bibliografia ikh knig po bogosloviiu, religioznoi filosofii, tserkovnoi istorii i pravoslavnoi kulture* (Boston: G. K. Hall, 1973).

New York. This rediscovery of the Fathers is the result of the interaction of east and west, as many of these writers left Russia after the communist revolution and settled in the west, especially in Paris and New York. They experienced for themselves the two worlds of Orthodox patristic theology and western critical academic research. This meeting of two cultures has helped Zernov's Russian Renaissance to become an Orthodox Renaissance. The example of Timothy Ware, an Anglican Oxford don who became Orthodox and now writes as Bishop Kallistos of Diokleia, is instructive. His writings are much read and valued.[13] They help to integrate a western academic environment and a rigorous Orthodox theology, so suggesting the pivotal role of western Orthodoxy in modern spirituality.

Renewal in theology has remained faithful to its monastic roots, where the encounter with God takes place in a liturgical and ascetical context. This theological tradition is hesychasm, from the Greek ἡσυχασμός, a term which can be translated as surrendering to silence and which describes the state of leaving behind the fantasies of fallen human existence to enter into the presence of God. The method of achieving this is through ascetic discipline and also the practice of the Jesus Prayer. This prayer takes several forms, based on New Testament sentences such as Luke 18:13, and is usually 'Lord Jesus Christ Son of the Living God, have mercy on me, a sinner.' Continued repetition of this can lead to access to the contemplative state. The origins of hesychasm lie in the early desert monasteries, and its formulation in the writing of Byzantine Fathers, especially Gregory Palamas (1296–1359). The practice was maintained in the monasteries, and especially on Mount Athos. A significant moment in the modern revival of hesychasm was the publication of the *Philokalia* in 1782. The *Philokalia*, or love of the beautiful, is a voluminous and disparate anthology of writings of various Fathers on the life of prayer, written between the third and fifteenth centuries, assembled by members of the Kollyvades renewal movement.[14] In its – enlarged – Romanian edition, translated by Dumitru Stăniloae, it runs to 4650 pages in twelve volumes.[15] Paisii Velichkovsky translated the *Philokalia* into Slavonic in 1793, and Feofan the Recluse into Russian in the following century. There is an English translation

---

13 The first volume of his collected works is published: K. Ware, *The inner kingdom* (Crestwood, NY: St Vladimir's Seminary Press, 2001).

14 Kollyvades is derived from the Greek *kollyva*, the sweetened boiled wheat used at memorial services. The group protested against the practice of holding these services on Sundays as well as the traditional Saturdays. The compilers of the *Philokalia* were Makarios of Corinth (1731–1805) and Nikodemos the Hagiorite (1749–1809).

15 *Filocalia, sau, Culegere din scrierile sfinţilor părinţi care arată cum se poate omul curăţi, lumina şi desăvârşi*, trans. D. Stăniloae, 12 vols. (Sibiu: Dacia Traiana, 1947–79).

in progress.[16] It presents a comprehensive summary of patristic theological teaching, prepared for use by those seeking to live and practise disciplines of prayer. So the hesychastic tradition, which brings together theological reflection and monastic practice, is encapsulated in a single simple prayer and a single book. The adaptability of these two formulations of the tradition is shown in the popular work *The Way of a Pilgrim*, which describes the discovery of hesychasm by an anonymous Russian peasant.[17] The *Philokalia* and the Jesus Prayer have enabled the Orthodox Church as a whole to reappropriate the theological tradition developed in the Byzantine period, which has provided a theoretical basis for the growing monastic life within a materialistic and work-dominated modern society. The practice of the Jesus Prayer is spreading among both eastern and western Christians, as a simple form of prayer which can be used at several levels, from that of a quick 'arrow' prayer to a lifelong method of contemplative living. However, one should not overestimate its use, for it is the celebration of liturgical prayer that remains the basis of monastic devotion.

Theological renewal has not only taken place in the research, writing and teaching of university professors but has become a popular movement among the laity. Christian education was often restricted under Arab and Ottoman rule, and was even more tightly controlled under communist governments. Once these restrictions were removed there was a widespread thirst for learning and study. Often on the initiative of clergy or laity rather than on that of the hierarchy, the churches have set up various forms of educational institutions, which consequently have a popular base. In 1907 Father Eusebios Matthopoulos founded the 'Brotherhood of Theologians', or Zoë movement, in Greece. The members, many of them graduates of theology, travelled around Greece preaching and teaching and were especially effective in assisting the church in the struggle against communism after the Second World War. More recently, in Russia, two priests, Father Vsevolod Schpiller, who died in 1992, and Father Vladimir Vorobiev, have done much to encourage education. After the fall of communism, their teaching enterprise has grown dramatically. It has grown into the St Tikhon's Orthodox Theological Institute, now designated as a Humanities University and accredited by the state education department. It has over 4000 students, of whom 1442 are full-time. There are thirteen regional centres, including one specifically for men in the army. Full-time students must be less than thirty-five years old and there are similar numbers of men and

---

16 *The Philokalia*, trans. G. E. H. Palmer, P. Sherrard and K. Ware, 4 vols. (London: Faber and Faber, 1979–95). The fifth and final volume is eagerly awaited.
17 *The way of a pilgrim*, trans. R. M. French (London: SPCK, 1954).

women. Graduates of St Tikhon's become priests, icon-restorers, teachers, workers in social institutions such as orphanages, choir directors and Sunday School directors – and some become teachers in the Institute. This vibrant and burgeoning institution demonstrates the growth of educational demand and provision among Orthodox Christians and provides a pool of recruits for service within the church.[18] Similar initiatives have sprung up in other Orthodox countries, such as the Sunday School Movement in Egypt and Ethiopia. All Orthodox churches value education and the empowerment of lay members of the church and are equipping a growing number of articulate and committed church members to carry out the mission and teaching work of the church.

An essential component of any account of modern Orthodox spirituality is the revival in the devotion to icons. Following a period in the nineteenth century when icons were often painted in a westernised naturalistic style, modern icon-painters have sought to recover the styles and forms of Byzantine painting. Painters such as Gregory Krug and Leonid Uspensky in the Russian diaspora, Photis Kontoglou in Greece, Father Zinon in Russia and Pavel Aksentejevic in Serbia are among those who have demonstrated the possibility of a vibrant contemporary expression within traditional Byzantine forms. Icons belong within an ecclesiastical system, and form part of Orthodox worship. But they have also become popular in many parts of the Christian world, and images such as that of the Vladimir Mother of God are widely reproduced. This growth of interest in icons suggests that Orthodox spirituality and devotion have contributed to modern Christianity far beyond traditional Orthodox lands. Traditionalists may regret the removal of icons from their proper liturgical setting, but their wide diffusion has led to a deeper appreciation of Orthodoxy, which has in turn helped to integrate it into modern religious society.

The Orthodox Church has responded to the challenges and opportunities offered by new political freedom with dramatic results. In 1990 there were in Russia eighteen monasteries, three theological schools and forty churches in Moscow. Ten years later these institutions had grown so that there were 500 monasteries, over fifty theological schools and 300 churches in Moscow. The numbers have continued to rise. The totality of church tradition developed in the Byzantine period provided a coherent and varied system of spirituality, which could be easily appropriated. Its concrete expression in architectural

---

18 I am grateful to Julia Klushina and Natalia Koulkova, teachers at St Tikhon's, for introducing me to their institute.

forms, icons and liturgy enabled the flowering to be swift, apparent and persuasive.

Orthodox often refer to autonomous national churches as local churches to emphasise that they are rooted in a *locus* or place. The strength of Orthodox spirituality is shown by its ability to locate itself in varying cultures and settings, including traditional Orthodox areas and new mission fields. It also gives new insights and vitality to the spiritual traditions of non-Orthodox churches. The different historical experiences, which have been noted, have prevented the development of a clear unified administrative structure. The Orthodox churches have tended to adapt themselves to the prevailing political order under which they have lived. Under the early Byzantine Empire, the five dioceses in the major administrative urban centres had a recognised priority – Rome, Constantinople, Antioch, Alexandria and Jerusalem – known as the pentarchy. Then under the Ottomans, the patriarch of Constantinople was the head of the Christian *millet* or nation. As new nations gained independence, so new churches became autonomous, as opposed to autocephalous: that is to say, while the former enjoyed independence in the management of their internal affairs, they continued to recognise the ultimate authority of a mother-church. The latter, in contrast, were bound by no such constraints. However, the tempestuous political changes of the twentieth century have left this system of a family of autonomous churches ill equipped to respond to the needs of new Orthodox communities and of new Orthodox countries.

For many Orthodox the most urgent challenge is the organisation of the church in the west.[19] Looked at from an eastern perspective, this is the problem of the diaspora. Diaspora, a Greek word meaning scattering, describes here the migration from east to west which has been taking place for centuries. So, for example, the first Greek church in London was founded in 1677, in what is still called Greek Street, in Soho. The process has accelerated in the last hundred years as people have fled from communist regimes, from the devastation of world wars, from Cyprus following invasion by Turkish troops in 1974, from an increasingly fundamentalist Islamic Middle East, and then from eastern Europe and Russia with the relaxation of boundary controls since 1990. There are now well over 25 million Orthodox in the west, and in many places it is one of the few religious groups that is growing. Many Orthodox churches have established dioceses in the west to care for their displaced members and as a result there is a confusing plurality of jurisdictions, which not only contradicts the

---

19 For a good summary, see A. Kyrlezhev, 'Problems of church order in contemporary Orthodoxy', *Sourozh* 95 (February 2004), 1–21.

ecclesiological principle that there should be only one bishop in each place, but also intrudes into what is historically the territory of the patriarchate of Rome, the papacy. Many members of Orthodox churches in the west are often second- or third-generation western nationals and so identify more with the land in which they now live. Others are western converts who find the ethnic character of churches unnatural. There is a growing sense among many Orthodox in the west that they are western Christians not eastern Christians, and they hope that a local western Orthodox Church will be formed to give a common identity to the growing western Orthodox churches and to encourage their mission. The rapid growth of these western Orthodox churches suggests that the title of *eastern* Orthodox Church will become increasingly anachronistic.

The longings for an indigenous church are felt most keenly and expressed most strongly in the USA, where the openness to immigrants has led to the growth of Orthodox parishes of varied ethnic composition. In 1872 a Russian diocese was established in San Francisco, which quickly developed into a multi-ethnic church. Tikhon Bellavin, consecrated as bishop in 1898 at the age of thirty-three, formed new dioceses to include Arabs, Greeks, Serbs, Romanians and Albanians. In 1907 the dioceses held the first All-American Council, with decisions taken on a democratic basis.[20] This unity disintegrated, in part because of the need of individual parishes to establish independence from a Russian church increasingly controlled by the Russian communist government. In 1950, Leonty Turkevich, who had served with Bishop Tikhon at the start of the century, became bishop and encouraged decentralisation, lay initiatives, the use of English in the liturgy and the admission of women into the seminaries. His example encouraged a sense of a distinctive American Orthodox Church life, and in 1967 the Orthodox Church of America (OCA) was formed – as the result of a name change away from the more cumbersome Russian Orthodox Greek Catholic Church of America. The Moscow patriarchate granted it autocephaly three years later in 1970. Unfortunately, other patriarchates did not follow Moscow's example, and the OCA remains unrecognised by most Orthodox. In spite of this, it is influential through its seminary, St Vladimir's, and its extensive publishing programme, together with its English-speaking church life. This expresses a strong tradition of indigenous American Orthodoxy which looks to the early Orthodox missionaries in Alaska, especially St Herman of Alaska, as well as to a full participation in modern American Christian life. In other parts of the west,

20 Bishop Tikhon became patriarch of Moscow in 1917 and died under house arrest in 1929.

Orthodox churches are more recently established and local traditions less well developed.

The reaction of the patriarchs to the infant OCA shows the difficulties involved in setting up ecclesiastical structures for the west. The churches value and need their diaspora communities. Orthodox communities in the west often consist of those who have been displaced or forced to leave their homeland. Even if they left willingly, they value the links with their homelands and need to maintain their cultural and national identity. The dioceses in the west are now large, and wealthy, and so form an influential part of the national church in the east. They are especially valuable to smaller churches in the Middle East, such as the Syrian Orthodox Church or the churches of Israel and Palestine where large-scale recent migration has left the church in the homeland diminished and weakened, and relying on the support and membership of the communities in exile. The ecumenical patriarch has a particular interest, since the council of Chalcedon (451) gave him jurisdiction over Orthodox Christians in 'barbarian lands', which is taken as being anywhere outside the territory of national Orthodox churches. So, not only do the big Greek dioceses of the diaspora form the major part of his community, but also the patriarchate claims responsibility for directing the process of setting up new churches. While ecclesiological principles require the establishment of unified local western churches, there are many factors standing in the way of this development.

Political changes also present problems of organisation and identity in the historic Orthodox lands. Here the boundaries of the national church have usually coincided with those of the state. As a result the churches have identified themselves with national aspirations. When the new nations of the Balkans were struggling for freedom from Ottoman rule this was a creative relationship and the churches encouraged the development of national language, culture and institutions. They became the focus of the new state shaping and identifying itself in the nationalist struggle against Ottoman imperial authority. But once the nation was established the same identification could easily change into a narrow, exclusive and intolerant nationalism. The dangers of this were recognised by a council which met in Constantinople in 1870 and condemned the 'new and destructive principle of nationality'. It identified a new heresy called phyletism. Its error was to exaggerate the ethnic dimension to church life, in the sense that it becomes restricted to those of one race, rather than to those of one locality, meaning those of all races in a given territory. It therefore offends against the catholicity of the

church, which includes people of all races within it.[21] The destructive potential of ethnic nationalism has been seen in many countries in the years since
1990, most tragically in the Balkans, although it must be acknowledged that
here the churches have also provided a courageous witness for peace and
reconciliation.

New nations also pose a challenge to church organisation and force the
question of whether a new nation necessarily requires a new church. In the
new republic of the Ukraine, the second largest country in Europe, there
are at present four churches – the Moscow patriarchate with its strength in
the east, a new patriarchate in Kiev, an alternative autocephalous Orthodox
Church in the west, and a Greek Catholic Church also in the west. A good
example of a fully local church is provided by Albania, a small country with only
3.5 million inhabitants, in which the church suffered extreme persecution under
a communist government between 1944 and 1990. There were, for example,
no public liturgies in the country for twenty-three years. Following the fall
of communism, Anastasios Yannoulatos, Greek by birth and a professor of
theology in Athens, archbishop in East Africa and an ecumenist, was in 1992
consecrated archbishop. He has been careful to select both ethnic Greek and
Albanian bishops, has always insisted on speaking Albanian on ecclesiastical
occasions, and has provided service and care for all regardless of ethnicity or
faith. The result is a vibrant Christian community, with many new local clergy
and a local leadership. The archbishop's concern to ensure a fully local church
has contributed to the renewal of the Orthodox Church in this poorest of
European nations.

Participation in the international world order requires the Orthodox to
define not only their internal ecclesiastical relations but also their external relations with other churches and faiths. Generally these have not been good. The
Orthodox historical memory includes the day in 1204 when the Latin crusaders
captured Constantinople, which resulted in a weakened Byzantine Empire,
much less able to resist the Turks; the formation of Greek Catholic churches
in communion with the pope in place of previously Orthodox communities;
and more recently the arrival from the west of well-funded and aggressive
evangelising Christian missions in former communist countries. These have
combined to make relations between Orthodox and other churches difficult.

---

21 The 1870 Council's statement was somewhat lacking in moral authority, since it was
issued in the context of a struggle between the new Bulgarian exarchate and the ecumenical patriarchate. Both competed for the allegiance of Bulgarians. As a result of the
disagreement a Bulgarian patriarch was not elected until 1953 and not recognised by
Constantinople until 1961.

There are signs that the frostiness of many ecumenical relationships is relaxing. Actions such as the return, in 2004, of the relics of St John Chrysostom from Rome to Constantinople, from where they were plundered by crusaders in 1204, are significant signs of reconciliation and hope.

Orthodox have been involved in the ecumenical movement from its beginnings. At the first meeting of the World Council of Churches (WCC) in 1948 there were representatives of the ecumenical patriarchate and of the Greek Orthodox Church, and these were to be joined by the Russian and other Orthodox churches. All benefited from this collaboration, with western Christians providing much-needed support for the Russians against communist persecution. But the Orthodox often found their colleagues difficult to work with. Since Roman Catholics were not members, the WCC had a predominantly Protestant membership; social and political action was preferred to doctrinal discussion; intercommunion was seen as a way a testifying to a shared commitment rather than as the end of a process of negotiation and discussion; and some talked as though the WCC was a kind of super-church transcending denominational divisions. These tensions resulted in a decision by Orthodox churches to attend the meeting of the WCC at Harare in 1998 but not to worship with others and not to vote. As a result a commission was set up to discuss how Orthodox might in future participate, and it is due to report in 2008. For many Orthodox, other churches are suspect and ecumenism is a grave and modern heresy, threatening the integrity of the Orthodox faith, but Orthodox have remained faithful participants in the ecumenical movement and have contributed a corrective to some of the western assumptions of the ecumenical movement.

Alongside the formal WCC involvement there have been a number of bilateral and multilateral conversations with other churches, which have been carried on in an atmosphere that has ranged from warm and cordial to chilly and suspicious. The most dramatic result has been the official decision to strive to overcome one of the oldest divisions, that between Chalcedonian and non-Chalcedonian Orthodox churches which has split the eastern Christian world since 451. After a series of discussions, which took place between 1964 and 1991, the delegates were able to say that 'we on both sides have preserved the same faith in our Lord Jesus Christ'.[22] Full communion has yet to be restored but in practice there is close cooperation and even intercommunion in many places, especially in Syria.

---

22 See C. Chaillot and A. Belopopsky, *Towards unity: the theological dialogue between the Orthodox Church and the Oriental churches* (Geneva: Inter-Orthodox Dialogue, 1998), 36.

Contribution to inter-faith dialogue is more potential than actual, but here too the Orthodox Church has an important contribution to make, especially in the difficult area of Christian and Muslim relationships. The two faiths grew up in the same Middle Eastern environment and have been involved in a 'living dialogue' ever since. Relations have gone through various stages, including violent conflict and damaging legal discrimination in which the Orthodox have until recently usually been the victims. But the Orthodox occupy a potentially creative and reconciling space between western Christians and Muslims. Like the Muslims, they were the victims of the violence of crusaders between the eleventh and thirteenth centuries, and then later suffered with Muslims at the hands of colonising powers in the nineteenth and twentieth centuries. Orthodox can also remind westerners that they have neglected the needs of Middle Eastern Christian communities which have been in sharp decline owing to emigration to the west and to the attacks of a militant fundamentalist Islam, while western states and churches have shown relatively little interest in their plight.

The Orthodox Church is confronted with organisational problems. These affect its spirituality; they raise the question whether the church as an institution has the adaptability and the internal resources required to develop an international spirituality capable of accommodating the needs of western Orthodox. This will require not only an inclusive local spirituality, which will contribute to the emergence of new nation states, but also an ecumenical spirituality, which can engage with other churches, and indeed faith communities, in a way which contributes to the ecumenical dialogue without compromising the distinctively Orthodox witness.

Lying behind these problems of organisation is the question of how the church adjusts, develops and changes. Its emphasis on local church life, brought into being through the liturgy, and its rejection of any form of centralised authority, such as is seen in the Roman papacy, raises the question of how the church might change – if it wanted to. It is difficult to see how an issue such as the ordination of women to the priesthood could be debated and decided on, and what body could do this. While it is true that most Orthodox would strongly argue against this, there needs to be at least the possibility of such changes. In the Byzantine Empire, the development of the tradition was facilitated and enabled by the ecumenical councils, convened by the emperor and attended by bishops. These pronounced not only on doctrine but also on disciplinary and legal matters. In the contemporary Orthodox Church, local synods of bishops in the various national churches meet regularly, and deal with disciplinary and other matters. But larger questions need the authority of a general council. Although there have been hopes that a 'Great and Holy Pan-Orthodox Council' may in due course meet and there have been a series of preparatory meetings from the 1930s up to 1990, this has been interrupted as a result of the fall of communist governments. There seems now little prospect that it will meet in the foreseeable future.

Corresponding to the absence of a universal decision-making body is the erosion of the power of the ecumenical patriarch. Once the bishop of the capital of a vast, wealthy and powerful empire, today the senior Orthodox bishop presides in a city with less than 2000 Orthodox inhabitants, whose movements are restricted by a nationalist but anti-Christian Turkish government. A serious restriction to the freedom of the patriarchate is the requirement of the government that the patriarch should be a Turkish citizen, which results in a diminishing pool of possible candidates for this high office. There is speculation that the patriarchate may be forced to move out of the traditional capital either to a place nearby such as the island of Rhodes or more radically to Geneva or New York, so establishing himself as a leader of world Orthodoxy rather than a local bishop. A change of this nature would only take place if it became impossible to sustain the institution in modern Istanbul. There are various consequences of this power vacuum at the centre. It enables the patriarch to wield a distinct spiritual authority. The present patriarch, Bartholomaios I, said at his enthronement that he was 'a loyal citizen subject to the laws of his country', with a power 'which remains purely spiritual, a symbol of reconciliation, a force without weapons, which rejects all political goals and maintains a distance from the deceiving arrogance of secular power'. This has not, however, prevented some quarrels with other parts of the church, culminating in 1996 in a break in communion between Constantinople and Moscow as a result of a dispute concerning the jurisdiction over the church in Estonia. The ecumenical patriarch's preoccupation with preserving his position in a politically insecure situation impedes the exercise of a unifying role in world Orthodoxy.

All churches have to struggle with new ethical, social and economic questions, raised by scientific discovery and technological advances. The freedom from political repression for the majority of Orthodox has exposed them to this variety of questions and problems. The basis of the Orthodox approach to ethics is a reliance on the tradition of the church. Ethics as a discipline has not been a usual category of thought in Orthodox theology, but is seen as belonging within a holistic understanding of the spiritual life. The resources for Christian living and ethical decision-making lie within the liturgical and theological traditions, which come from the Fathers of the Church. This is no retrogressive looking back to the thinking of a former age but rather a belief that the same Holy Spirit who has guided the church in previous generations will continue to do so, speaking in a way which is both fresh and contemporary but also consistent with the past. The Fathers who witnessed to this tradition are the main source for these modern questions.

There are signs that this approach will provide a distinctive contribution. Almost as soon as the Russian communist government fell, the Russian Orthodox Church entered into a process of discussion and research by bishops, theologians and practitioners in various disciplines. In 2000, after six years of reflection, the Russian bishops' council issued a lengthy document on social policy. The stance adopted was conservative but it also demonstrated flexibility in dealing with new questions. So homosexuality was condemned as a sinful tendency; but divorce was sanctioned in certain circumstances, and contraception was not ruled out. Abortion and euthanasia were condemned. Thus Orthodox were shown that, while traditional teaching is to be upheld, they can and should engage creatively in difficult pastoral situations. Another area of involvement has been ecology. In 1989 the ecumenical patriarch Demetrios declared that the first day of the ecclesiastical year, 1 September, was to be a day of prayer for the protection of the natural environment. A major international conference on the environment was held on the island of Crete in 2001. The patristic emphasis not only on the responsibility of man to offer the creation in thanks to God but also on the involvement of the natural order in the final salvation brought by Christ has provided a spiritual and doctrinal basis for engaging in such questions. It points to the fruitful possibilities of the creative use of the teaching of the Fathers.

For the Orthodox Church, modern spirituality has a clear identity. The sudden political changes which have taken place since 1990 in eastern Europe have placed the churches firmly in a new modern age, with a set of opportunities and challenges to express and live the traditional faith. This Orthodox faith, as lived in the liturgy, the ascetical tradition and the teaching of the Fathers, is a living and creative faith, which provides both stability in a changing world and also the resources to engage with it. The success of Orthodox mission in the west and the attraction of many features of Orthodox spirituality to non-Orthodox and Orthodox alike testify to its relevance to the modern world. Structural problems remain acute and there seems little prospect of immediate resolution. This will hamper the development of the Orthodox Church into a truly international and ecumenical body. The temptation to become inward looking, reactionary and intolerant is ever present in all religious bodies, and especially in the Orthodox Church with its rich historical tradition.

It must be resisted as foreign to the spirit of the New Testament. A more hopeful prospect is an Orthodox Church with a revitalised patristic, liturgical and monastic tradition; firmly established throughout the world; engaging in a positive yet authentically Orthodox dialogue with the various institutions of the modern world. This, we dare to say, is modern Orthodox spirituality, which we hope will increasingly prevail in the actual communities of the Orthodox Christians.

Spirituality, we began by reminding ourselves, is a study in discernment as to how the Spirit of God is guiding the church which it has called into being. New life comes in unexpected ways and in unforeseen places. 'The wind blows where it chooses and you hear the sound of it, but you do not know where it comes from or where it goes. So it is with everyone who is born of the Spirit' (John 3:8). The re-emergence of the church after communism, the flourishing of monasticism, the supply of ascetics and martyrs – such gifts to the church cannot be predicted or their continuing supply relied on. In noting the presence of the signs of life in the church, we realise that its life depends on the presence of God in its midst and also that we can be confident that future movements of the Spirit may be unpredictable in their nature but can be trusted to be given generously.

Select bibliography

General bibliography to Part I: The ecumenical patriarchate (chapters 1–10)

1 Collections of sources, calendars, prosopographies

Blackwell dictionary of Eastern Christianity, ed. K. Parry, D. J. Melling, D. Brady, S. H. Griffith and J. F. Healey (Oxford: Blackwell, 1999)

Delehaye, Hippolyte, *Propylaeum ad Acta Sanctorum Novembris: Synaxarium ecclesiae Constantinopolitanae* (Brussels: Société des Bollandistes, 1902)

Dictionnaire de spiritualité ascétique et mystique, doctrine et histoire, 17 vols. (Paris: Beauchesne, 1932–95)

Dmitrievskij, A. A., *Opisanie liturgiceskich rukopisej*, 3 vols. (Kiev and St Petersburg: Kievskaja dukhovnaja Akademia, 1895–1917; reprinted Hildesheim: G. Olms, 1965)

Goar, Jacques, *Εὐχολόγιον seu Rituale Graecorum* (Venice: Bartholomaei Javarina, 1730; reprinted Graz: Akademische Druck- und Verlagsanstalt, 1960)

Legrand, Émile, *Bibliographie hellénique ou Description raisonnée des ouvrages publiées en grec par des Grecs*, 4 vols. (Paris: E. Leroux, 1885–1906; reprinted Paris: Maisonneuve et Larose, 1962)

Majeska, G., *Russian travelers to Constantinople in the fourteenth and fifteenth centuries* [DOT 19] (Washington, DC: Dumbarton Oaks Research Library and Collection, 1984)

Miklosich, F. and Müller, J., *Acta et diplomata graeca medii aevi sacra et profana*, 6 vols. (Vienna: C. Gerold, 1860–90)

Notitiae episcopatuum ecclesiae Constantinopolitanae, ed. J. Darrouzès [Géographie ecclésiastique de l'Empire byzantin 1] (Paris: Institut français d'études byzantines, 1981)

Nystazopoulou-Pelekidou, M., *Βυζαντινὰ ἔγγραφα τῆς Μονῆς Πάτμου*, 2 vols. (Athens: Ethnikon Idryma Ereunon, 1980)

Oxford dictionary of Byzantium, ed. A. P. Khazdan, 3 vols. (New York: Oxford University Press, 1991)

Prosopographisches Lexikon der Palaiologenzeit [Veröffentlichungen der Kommission für Byzantinistik 1], 13 fasc. (Vienna: Verlag ÖAW, 1976–96)

Les regestes des actes du Patriarcat de Constantinople, ed. V. Grumel, V. Laurent and J. Darrouzès, 7 vols. (Paris: Institut français d'études byzantines, 1932–91)

Das Register des Patriarchats von Konstantinopel: I, *Edition und Übersetzungen der Urkunden aus den Jahren, 1315–1331*, ed. H. Hunger and O. Kresten; II, *1337–1350*, ed. C. Cupane and E. Schiffer; III, *1350–1363*, ed. J. Koder, M. Hinterberger and O. Kresten [CFHB 19, 1–3] (Vienna: Verlag ÖAW, 1981–2001)

Tăutu, A. L., *Acta Honorii III (1216–1227) et Gregorii IX (1227–1241)* [Pontificia Commissio ad redigendum codicem iuris canonici orientalis. Fontes: ser. iii, III] (Rome: Typis polyglottis vaticanis, 1950)

Thomas, J. and Hero, A., *Byzantine monastic foundation documents*, 5 vols. (Washington, DC: Dumbarton Oaks Research Library and Collection, 2000)

2   Sources

Athanasios I

Talbot, Alice-Mary Maffry, *The correspondence of Athanasius I, Patriarch of Constantinople: letters to the Emperor Andronicus II, members of the imperial family, and officials* [CFHB 7; DOT 3] (Washington, DC: Dumbarton Oaks Center for Byzantine Studies, Trustees for Harvard University, 1975)

Talbot, Alice-Mary Maffry, *Faith healing in late Byzantium: the posthumuous miracles of the Patriarch Athanasios I of Constantinople by Theoktistos the Stoudite* [The Archbishop Iakovos Library of Ecclesiastical and Historical sources 8] (Brookline, MA: Hellenic College Press, 1983)

Athos

Actes de Chilandar: I, *Des Origines à 1319*, ed. M. Živojinović, V. Kravari and C. Giros [AA 20] (Paris: CNRS, 1998)

Actes de Dionysiou, ed. N. Oikonomidès [AA 4] (Paris: P. Lethielleux, 1968)

Actes de Docheiariou, ed. N. Oikonomidès [AA 13] (Paris: P. Lethielleux, 1984)

Actes de Kastamonitou, ed. N. Oikonomidès [AA 9] (Paris: P. Lethielleux, 1978)

Actes de Kutlumus, ed. P. Lemerle [AA 2], second edition (Paris: P. Lethielleux, 1988)

Actes d'Iviron: I, *Des Origines au milieu du XIe siècle*; II, *Du milieu du XIe siècle à 1204*; III, *De 1204 à 1328*; IV, *De 1328 au début du XVIe siècle*, ed. J. Lefort, N. Oikonomidès and D. Papachryssanthou (with H. Métrévéli) [AA 14, 16, 18, 19] (Paris: P. Lethielleux, 1985–95)

Actes de Saint-Pantéléèmôn, ed. P. Lemerle, G. Dagron and S. Ćirković [AA 12] (Paris: P. Lethielleux, 1982)

Chomatianos, Demetrios

Demetrii Chomateni Ponemata diaphora, ed. Günter Prinzing [CFHB (Series Berolinensis), 38] (Berlin: Walter de Gruyter, 2002]

Chronicles

Die byzantinischen Kleinchroniken, ed. P. Schreiner [CFHB 12], 3 vols. (Vienna: ÖAW, 1975)

Select bibliography

Doukas, Michael

Grecu, V., *Ducas: istoria Turco-Bizantina (1341–1462)* ([Bucharest]: Editura Academiei Republicii Populaire Romîne, 1958)

Eustathios of Thessalonike

Eustathios of Thessalonike, *The capture of Thessaloniki*, trans. J. R. Melville Jones (Canberra: Australian Association for Byzantine Studies, 1988)

Gregory of Sinai

Kallistos, Patriarch of Constantinople, Βίος καὶ πολιτεία τοῦ ἐν ἁγίοις πατρὸς ἡμῶν Γρηγορίου τοῦ Σιναΐτου, ed. I. Pomialovskii, in *Zhitie izhe vo svatykh otca nashego Grigorija Sinaita* [Zapiski istoriko-filologicheskago fakulteta imperatorskago S.-Peterburgskago Universiteta 35] (St Petersburg, 1896), 1–46

Komnene, Anna

Annae Comnenae Alexias, ed. Diether R. Reinsch and Athanasios Kambylis [CFHB (Series Berolinensis) 40] (Berlin: Walter de Gruyter, 2001)

Manuel II Palaiologos

The letters of Manuel II Palaeologus: text, translation, and notes, ed. G. T. Dennis [CFHB 8; DOT 4] (Washington, DC: Dumbarton Oaks Center for Byzantine Studies, Trustees for Harvard University, 1977)

Manuel II Palaiologos, *Dialoge mit einem 'Perser'*, ed. E. Trapp [Wiener byzantinistische Studien 2] (Vienna: Böhlau, 1966]

Manuel II Palaiologos, *Entretiens avec un Musulman: 7e controverse*, ed. Théodore Khoury [Sources chrétiennes 115] (Paris: Éditions du Cerf, 1966)

Pachymeres, George

Pachymeres, George, *Relations historiques*, ed. A. Failler; trans. V. Laurent [CFHB 24 (Series Parisiensis)], 5 vols. (vols. I–II, Paris: Belles Lettres, 1984; vols. III–V, Paris: Institut français d'études byzantines, 1999–2001)

Psellos, Michael

Michel Psellos, *Chronographie*, ed. É. Renauld, 2 vols. (Paris: Belles Lettres, 1926; reprinted Paris: Belles Lettres, 1967)

Michele Psello. Imperatori di Bisanzio (Cronografia), ed. S. Impellizzeri; trans. S. Ronchey, 2 vols. (Milan: Fondazione L. Valla/A. Mondadori, 1984).

Michele Psellos, *Autobiografia: encomio per la madre*, ed. U. Criscuolo (Naples: M. D'Auria editore, 1989)

Select bibliography

Sphrantzes, George

Georgios Sphrantzes, *Memorii 1401–1477*, ed. V. Grecu [Scriptores Byzantini V] (Bucharest: Editura Academiei Republicii Socialiste România, 1966)

Symeon the New Theologian

Hausherr, I. and Horn, G., *Un grand mystique byzantin: Vie de Syméon le Nouveau Théologien par Nicétas Stéthatos* [OCA 14] (Rome: Pontificium institutum orientalium studiorum, 1928)

Symeon of Thessalonike

Politico-historical works of Symeon, Archbishop of Thessalonica (1416/17 to 1429): critical Greek text with introduction and commentary, ed. D. Balfour [Wiener byzantinistische Studien 13] (Vienna: Verlag ÖAW, 1979)

Syropoulos, Sylvester

Les mémoires du grand ecclésiarque de l'Église de Constantinople Sylvestre Syropoulos sur le concile de Florence (1438–1439), ed. V. Laurent [Concilium Florentinum. Documenta et scriptores, ser. B, vol. 9] (Paris: Éditions CNRS, 1971)

3   General works

Angold, Michael, *Church and society in Byzantium under the Comneni 1081–1261* (Cambridge: Cambridge University Press, 1995)

Barker, John W., *Manuel II Palaeologus (1391–1425); a study in late Byzantine statesmanship* (New Brunswick, NJ: Rutgers University Press, 1969)

Beck, Hans-Georg, *Kirche und theologische Literatur im byzantinischen Reich* [Handbuch der Altertumswissenschaft 12. Abt.: Byzantinisches Handbuch 2. T., 1. Bd.] (Munich: C. H. Beck, 1959)

Bryner, Erich, *Die orthodoxen Kirchen von 1274 bis 1700* [Kirchengeschichte in Einzeldarstellungen II/9] (Leipzig: Evangelische Verlagsanstalt, 2004)

Byzantine diplomacy, ed. J. Shepard and S. Franklin (Aldershot: Variorum, 1992)

Βυζάντιο: Κράτος καὶ κοινωνία. Μνήμη Νίκου Οἰκονομίδη, ed. A. Avramea, A. Laiou and A. Chrysos (Athens: Institute of Byzantine Studies, 2003)

Byzantium and Serbia in the 14th century, ed. E. Papadopoulou and D. Dialete [International Symposia 3] (Athens: National Hellenic Research Foundation, 1996)

Byzantium: faith and power (1261–1557), ed. H. C. Evans (New York: Metropolitan Museum of Art, 2004)

Cambridge history of the Byzantine Empire, ed. J. Shepard (Cambridge: Cambridge University Press: 2006)

Chadwick, Henry, *East and West: the making of a rift in the church from apostolic times until the Council of Florence* [Oxford History of the Church] (Oxford: Oxford University Press, 2003)

Christians and Jews in the Ottoman Empire, ed. B. Braude and B. Lewis, 2 vols. (London and New York: Holmes and Meier, 1982)

Cutler, Anthony and Spieser, Jean-Michel, *Byzance médiévale 700–1204* [Univers des formes 41] (Paris: Gallimard, 1996)

Dagron, Gilbert, *Emperor and priest: the imperial office in Byzantium* (Cambridge: Cambridge University Press, 2003)

Dimaras, C. T., *A history of modern Greek literature* (London: University of London Press; Albany: State University of New York Press, 1972)

Dix, Gregory, *The shape of the Liturgy*, second edition (London: Dacre Press; A. & C. Black, 1945)

Ehrhard, Albert, *Überlieferung und Bestand der hagiographischen und homiletischen Literatur der griechischen Kirche von den Anfängen bis zum Ende des 16. Jahrhunderts*, 3 vols. [Texte und Untersuchungen zur Geschichte der altchristlicher Literatur 50–52] (Leipzig: Hinrich, 1936–52)

L'empereur hagiographe: culte des saints et monarchie byzantine et post-byzantine, ed. P. Guran and B. Flusin (Bucharest: Colegiul Noua Europa, 2001)

Fine, J. V. A., *The early medieval Balkans* (Ann Arbor: University of Michigan Press, 1983)

  The late medieval Balkans (Ann Arbor: University of Michigan Press, 1987)

Geanakoplos, Deno J., *Byzantine East and Latin West: two worlds of Christendom in Middle Ages and Renaissance. Studies in ecclesiastical and cultural history* (Oxford: Basil Blackwell, 1966)

  Interaction of the 'sibling' Byzantine and Western cultures in the Middle Ages and Italian Renaissance (330–1600) (New Haven and London: Yale University Press, 1976)

Gedeon, Manuel, Πατριαρχικοὶ Πίνακες, ed. N. L. Phoropoulos (Athens: Syllogos pros Diadosin Ophelimon Biblion, 1996)

Gill, Joseph, *Byzantium and the papacy, 1198–1400* (New Brunswick, NJ: Rutgers University Press, 1979)

Halecki, Oscar, *Un empereur de Byzance à Rome: vingt ans de travail pour l'union et pour la défense de l'Empire d'Orient 1355–1375* [Travaux historiques de la société des sciences et des lettres de Varsovie 8] (Warsaw: Towarzystwo Naukowe Warszawskie, 1930; reprinted London: Variorum, 1972)

  From Florence to Brest (1439–1596) [Sacrum Poloniae millennium 5] (Rome and New York: Fordham University Press, 1958)

Histoire du christianisme des origines à nos jours, dir. J.-M. Mayeur, 14 vols. (Paris: Desclée, 1990–2001)

Hunger, H. and Kresten, O., *Studien zum Patriarchatsregister von Konstantinopel II* (Vienna: Verlag ÖAW, 1997)

Hussey, Joan Mervyn, *The Orthodox Church in the Byzantine Empire* [Oxford History of the Christian Church] (Oxford: Clarendon Press, 1986)

Krautheimer, Richard (with Slobodan Ćurčić), *Early Christian and Byzantine architecture* [Pelican History of Art], fourth revised edition (Harmondsworth: Penguin, 1986)

Lemerle, Paul, *Cinq études sur le XIe siècle byzantin* (Paris: CNRS, 1977)

Magdalino, Paul, *The Empire of Manuel Komnenos, 1143–1180* (Cambridge: Cambridge University Press, 1993)

Medieval Christian Europe: east and west, tradition, values, communications, ed. V. Giuzelev and A. Miltenova (Sofia: IK 'Gutenberg', 2002)

Meyendorff, John, *Introduction à l'étude de Grégoire Palamas* [Patristica Sorbonensia 3] (Paris: Seuil, 1959); trans. G. Lawrence, *A study of Gregory Palamas* (London: Faith Press, 1964)
> 'Spiritual trends in Byzantium in the late thirteenth and early fourteenth centuries', in *The Kariye Djami*, ed. P. Underwood (Princeton, NJ: Princeton University Press, 1975), IV, 93–106
> *Byzantium and the rise of Russia: a study of Byzantino-Russian relations in the fourteenth century* (Cambridge: Cambridge University Press, 1981)
> 'Mount Athos in the fourteenth century: spiritual and intellectual legacy', *DOP* 42 (1988), 157–65
Le Millénaire du Mont Athos, 963–1963, études et mélanges, 2 vols. (Chevetogne: Editions de Chevetogne, 1963)
Morris, Rosemary, *Church and people in Byzantium* (Birmingham: Centre for Byzantine, Ottoman and Modern Greek Studies, University of Birmingham, 1990)
> *Monks and laymen in Byzantium, 843–1118* (Cambridge: Cambridge University Press, 1995)
Mother of God: representations of the Virgin in Byzantine art, ed. M. Vassilaki (Milan: Skira, 2000)
Mount Athos and Byzantine monasticism, Papers from the twenty-eighth Spring Symposium of Byzantine Studies, Birmingham, March 1994, ed A. A. M. Bryer and M. Cunningham (Aldershot: Variorum, 1996)
Nicol, Donald MacGillivray, *Church and society in the last centuries of Byzantium* [The Birkbeck Lectures 1977] (Cambridge: Cambridge University Press, 1979)
> *The last centuries of Byzantium 1261–1453*, second edition (Cambridge: Cambridge University Press, 1993)
> *The reluctant emperor: a biography of John Cantacuzene, Byzantine emperor and monk, c. 1295– 1383* (Cambridge: Cambridge University Press, 1996)
Obolensky, D., *The Byzantine commonwealth: eastern Europe 500–1453* (London: Weidenfeld and Nicolson, 1971)
> *Six Byzantine portraits* (Oxford: Clarendon Press, 1988)
Papadakis, Aristeides (with Meyendorff, John), *The Christian East and the rise of the papacy: the Church 1071–1453* [The Church in History 4] (Crestwood, NY: St Vladimir's Seminary Press, 1994)
Papadopoullos, T. H., *Studies and documents relating to the history of the Greek church and people under Turkish domination* (Brussels: *s. n.*, 1952; second edition, London: Variorum, 1990)
Perceptions of Byzantium and its neighbors (843–1261), ed. O. Z. Pevny (New York: Metropolitan Museum of Art, 2000)
Podskalsky, Gerhard, *Theologie und Philosophie in Byzanz: der Streit um die theologische Methodik in der spätbyzantinischen Geistesgeschichte (14/15. Jh.), seine systematischen Grundlagen und seine historische Entwicklung* [Byzantinisches Archiv 15] (Munich: C. H. Beck, 1977)
> *Christentum und theologische Literatur in der Kiever Rus' (988–1237)* (Munich: C. H. Beck, 1982)
> *Griechische Theologie in der Zeit der Türkenherrschaft 1453–1821* (Munich: C. H. Beck, 1988)
> *Theologische Literatur des Mittelalters in Bulgarien und Serbien 865–1459* (Munich: C. H. Beck, 2000)
> *Von Photios zu Bessarion: der Vorrang humanistisch geprägter Theologie in Byzanz und deren bleibende Bedeutung* (Wiesbaden: Harrassowitz, 2003)

Runciman, S., *The Great Church in captivity: a study of the Patriarchate of Constantinople from the eve of the Turkish conquest to the Greek war of independence* (Cambridge: Cambridge University Press, 1968)

Setton, Kenneth M., *The Papacy and the Levant (1204–1571)* [Memoirs of the American Philosophical Society 114, 127, 161, 162], 4 vols. (Philadelphia: American Philosophical Society, 1976–84)

Speake, Graham, *Mount Athos: renewal in paradise* (New Haven and London: Yale University Press, 2002)

Stephanidis, Vasilios, Ἐκκλησιαστικὴ Ἱστορία, fourth edition (Athens: Astir, 1978)

Théologie byzantine et sa tradition, ed. G. and V. Conticello [Corpus Christianorum], 2 vols. (Turnhout: Brepols, 2002)

Thomas, John Philip, *Private religious foundations in the Byzantine Empire* [DOS 24] (Washington, DC: Dumbarton Oaks Research Library and Collection, 1987)

Vapheidis, Philaretos, Ἐκκλησιαστικὴ Ἱστορία, III-A', 1453–1700 (Constantinople: Gerardos, 1912)

Ware, Timothy, *The Orthodox Church*, second edition (Harmondsworth: Penguin, 1993)

1   Shepard: The Byzantine Commonwealth

1   Sources

Corpus poeticum boreale: the poetry of the old northern tongue from the earliest times to the thirteenth century, ed. and trans. G. Vigfusson and F. York Powell, 2 vols. (Oxford: Clarendon Press, 1883)

Danilo II, *Žitije kralja Milutina*, in Archbishop Danilo et al., *Životi kraljeva i arhiepiskopa srpskih*, ed. D. Daničić (Zagreb: US. Galca, 1866; reprinted London: Variorum, 1972), 102–61

Darrouzès, J., 'Le traité des transferts. Édition critique et commentaire', *REB* 42 (1984), 147–214

Epifanii Premudryi, *Zhitie sviatogo Stefana episkopa Permskogo*, ed. V. G. Druzhinin (St Petersburg: Arkheograficheskaia kommissia, 1897)

Fletcher, Giles, *Of the Russe Commonwealth* (London: Thomas Charde, 1591; reprinted Cambridge, MA: Harvard University Press, 1966)

'Gramota mitropolita Kipriana pskovskomu dukhovenstvu s nastavleniami o sovershenii razlichnyk sviashchennodeistvii', in *RIB* VI (St Petersburg, 1880), cols. 239–42

Grčke povelje srpskih vladara, ed. A. Solovjev and V. A. Mošin (Belgrade: Srpska kraljevska akademija, 1936; reprinted London: Variorum, 1974)

Jagić, V., *Rassuzhdeniia iuzhnoslavianskoi i russkoi stariny o tserkovnom-slavianskom iazyke* (St Petersburg: Imperatorskaia akademiia nauk, 1896)

Kievo-Pecherskii paterik, ed. L. A. Ol'shevskaia in *Biblioteka literatury drevnei Rusi*, ed. D. S. Likhachev (St Petersburg: Nauka, 1997), IV; trans. M. Heppell, *The Paterik of the Kievan Caves Monastery* (Cambridge, MA: Ukrainian Research Institute of Harvard University, 1989)

Maksim Grek, *Tvoreniia* (in Russian trans.), 3 vols. (Moscow: Sviato-Troitskaia Lavra, 1996)

Metochites, Theodore, Πρεσβευτικός, in K. N. Sathas, Μεσαιωνικὴ Βιβλιοθήκη, I (Venice: Typois tou Chronou, 1872; reprinted Athens: B. N. Gregoriades, 1972), 154–93

'Mitropolita Zosimy izveshchenie o paskhalii na os'muiu tysiachu let', in RIB VI (St Petersburg, 1880), cols. 795–802

Nestor Iskander, The tale of Constantinople: of its origin and capture by the Turks in the year 1453, ed. and trans. W. K. Hanak and M. Philippides (New Rochelle, NY: Aristide D. Caratzas Publisher, 1998)

Novgorodskaia pervaia letopis' starshego i mladshego izvodov, ed. A. N. Nasonov (Moscow and Leningrad: Akademia nauk SSSR, 1950; reprinted [Polnoe Sobranie Russkikh Letopisei 3] (St Petersburg: Iazyki russkoi kul'tury, 2000)

'Otvety konstantinopol'skogo patriarshogo sobora na voprosy saraiskogo episkopa (Feognosta)', in RIB VI, prilozheniia I (St Petersburg, 1880), cols. 5–12

Pamiatniki literatury Drevnei Rusi, IV, XIV–seredina XV veka, ed. L. A. Dmitriev and D. S. Likhachev (Moscow: Khudozhestvennaia literatura, 1981)

'Poslanie konstantinopol'skogo patriarkha k russkomu igumenu ob inocheskoi zhizni', in RIB VI (St Petersburg, 1880), cols. 187–90

Povest' Vremennykh Let, ed. V. P. Adrianova-Peretts and D. S. Likhachev, second edition (St Petersburg: Nauka, 1996)

Speransky, M. N., Serbskoe zhitie litovskikh muchenikov [Chteniia v imperatorskom obshchestve istorii i drevnostei rossiiskikh pri Moskovskom universitete] (Moscow: Universitetskaia tipografiia, 1909), I

Tsamblak, Gregory, Pokhvalno slovo za Evtimii, ed. P. Rusev et al. (Sofia: Izdatelstvo na Bulgarskata akademiia na naukite, 1971)

Slovo za mitropolit Kiprian, ed. N. Doncheva-Panaiotova (Veliko T'rnovo: Izdatelstvo PIK, 1995)

Typikon of St Sava, ed. V. Ćorović, Spisi sv. Save, in Zbornik za Istoriju, Jezik i Kniževnost Srpskog Naroda 17 (1928), 5–13

Zakonik tsara Stefana Dušana, ed. M. Begović et al., 3 vols. (Belgrade: Srpska akademija nauka i umetnosti, 1975–97)

Zhitie Andreia Iurodivogo v slavianskoi pis'mennosti, ed. A. M. Moldovan (Moscow: Azbukovnik, 2000)

2   Secondary works

Alekseev, A. I., Pod znakom kontsa vremen: ocherki russkoi religioznosti kontsa XIV–nachala XVI vv. (St Petersburg: Aleteiia, 2002)

Allsen, T. T., 'Saray', in Encyclopedia of Islam, IX, second edition (Leiden: Brill, 1995), 41–4

Andreescu, S., 'Alliances dynastiques des princes de Valachie (XIVe–XVIe siècles)', Revue des Études Sud-Est Européennes 23 (1985), 359–68

Andreev, J., 'Ivan Alexandăr et ses fils sur la dernière miniature de la chronique de Manasses', Etudes Balkaniques 4 (1985), 39–47

Angelov, D., 'The eschatological views of medieval Bulgaria as reflected in the canonical and apocryphal literature', Bulgarian Historical Review 18 (1990), 21–47

Angusheva-Tihanova, A., 'The mount reflecting heaven: the sermon on the Transfiguration by Gregory Camblak in the context of Byzantine and medieval Slavic literature', Bsl 62 (2004), 217–38

Arranz, M., 'L'aspect rituel de l'onction des empereurs de Constantinople et de Moscou', in *Roma, Costantinopoli, Mosca* [Da Roma alla terza Roma, documenti e studi 1] (Naples: Edizioni scientifiche italiane, 1983), 407–15

'Couronnement royal et autres promotions de cour. Les sacrements de l'institution de l'ancien Euchologe constantinopolitain', *OCP* 56 (1990), 83–133

Arzhantseva, I., 'The Christianization of North Caucasus (religious dualism among the Alans)', in *Die Christianisierung des Kaukasus. The Christianization of Caucasus (Armenia, Georgia, Albania)*, ed. W. Seibt (ÖAW: Philosophisch-historische Klasse Denkschriften 296) (Vienna: Verlag ÖAW, 2002), 17–36

Bakalova, E., 'The earliest surviving icons from Bulgaria', in *Perceptions of Byzantium and its neighbors* [see general bibliography], 118–35

Balfour, D., 'Was St Gregory Palamas St Gregory the Sinaite's pupil?', *St Vladimir's Theological Quarterly* 28 (1984), 115–30

Baronas, D., *Trys Vilniaus kankiniai: Gvenimas ir istorija: istorine studija ir šaltiniai* (Vilnius: Aidai, 2000)

'The three martyrs of Vilnius: a fourteenth-century martyrdom and its documentary sources', *Analecta Bollandiana* 122 (2004), 83–134

Baronas, D. et al., *Christianity in Lithuania* (Vilnius: Aidai, 2002)

Baun, J., 'Middle Byzantine "tours of hell": outsider theodicy?', in *Strangers to themselves: the Byzantine outsider*, ed. D. Smythe (Aldershot: Ashgate, 2000), 47–60

Tales from another Byzantium (Cambridge: Cambridge University Press, 2006)

'Last things', in *Cambridge History of Christianity*, III, ed. T. F. X. Noble and J. M. H. Smith (Cambridge: Cambridge University Press, 2007)

Bibikov, M. B., 'Russko-vizantiiskie otnosheniia: tsentry peresecheniia kul'tur', in *Vostochnaia Evropa v drevnosti i srednevekov'e: kontakty, zony kontaktov i kontaktnye zony*, ed. E. A. Mel'nikova (Moscow: IVI RAN, 1999), 47–54

Biliarsky, I., 'Le rite du couronnement des tsars dans les pays slaves et promotion d'autres *axiai*', *OCP* 59 (1993), 91–139

Hierarchia: l'ordre sacré. Études de l'esprit romanique [Veröffentlichungen aus dem Gebiete von Kirche und Staat 51] (Freiburg: Éditions universitaires Fribourg, 1997)

Institutsiite na srednovekovna B'lgariia (Sofia: Universitetsko izdatelstvo 'Sv Kliment Okhridski', 1998)

'Some observations on the administrative terminology of the second Bulgarian empire (13th–14th centuries)', *BMGS* 25 (2001), 69–89

Bojović, B. I., *L'idéologie monarchique dans les hagio-biographies dynastiques du Moyen Âge serbe* [OCA 248] (Rome: Pontificio istituto orientale, 1995)

'Une monarchie hagiographique. La théologie du pouvoir dans la Serbie médiévale (XII–XV siècles)', in *L'empereur hagiographe* [see general bibliography], 61–72

Børtnes, J., *Visions of glory: studies in early Russian hagiography* [Slavica Norvegica 5] (Oslo: Solum, 1988)

Challis, N. and Dewey, H. W., 'The blessed fools of Old Russia', *Jahrbücher für Geschichte Osteuropas* 22 (1974), 1–11

Ćirković, S. M., 'Between kingdom and empire: Dušan's state 1346–1355 reconsidered', in *Byzantium and Serbia in the 14th century* [see general bibliography], 110–20

The Serbs (Oxford: Blackwell, 2004)

Ćorović, V., *Sveta gora i Khilandar do šesnaestog veka* (Belgrade: Manastir Khilandar na svetoj gore, 1985)

Ćurčić, S., 'The Nemanjić family tree in the light of the ancestral cult in the church of Joachim and Anna at Studenica', *Zbornik Radova Vizantološkog Instituta* 14–15 (1973), 191–5

   Gračanica: King Milutin's church and its place in late Byzantine architecture (University Park: Pennsylvania State University Press, 1979)

   'Religious settings of the late Byzantine sphere', in *Byzantium: faith and power* [see general bibliography], 65–77

Ćurčić, S. and Hadjitryphonos, E., *Secular medieval architecture in the Balkans 1300–1500 and its preservation* (Thessalonike: Aimos, Society for the Study of the Medieval Architecture in the Balkans and Its Preservation, 1997)

Deér, J., *Die heilige Krone Ungarns* (ÖAW: Philosoph.-hist. Klasse, Denkschriften 91) (Vienna: Böhlau Verlag, 1966)

Djurić, I., 'Titles of the rulers of the Second Bulgarian Empire in the eyes of the Byzantines', in *Charanis studies: essays in honor of Peter Charanis*, ed. A. E. Laiou-Thomadakis (New Brunswick, NJ: Rutgers University Press, 1980), 31–50

Drevnerusskoe iskusstvo: Sergii Radonezhskii i khudozhestvennaia kul'tura Moskvy XIV–XV vv., ed. M. A. Orlova *et al.* (St Petersburg: D. I. Bulanin, 1998)

Eastmond, A., *Royal imagery in medieval Georgia* (University Park: Pennsylvania State University Press, 1998)

   '"Local" saints, art, and regional identity in the Orthodox world after the fourth crusade', *Sp* 78 (2003), 707–49

Entsiklopediia russkogo igumena XIV–XVvv. Sbornik prepodobnogo Kirilla Beloozerskogo, ed. G. M. Prokhorov (St Petersburg: Oleg Abyshko, 2003)

Fedotov, G. P., *The Russian religious mind*, 2 vols. (Cambridge, MA: Harvard University Press, 1946–66)

Flier, M. S., 'The throne of Monomakh. Ivan the Terrible and the architectonics of destiny', in *Architectures of Russian identity, 1500 to the present*, ed. J. Cracraft and D. Rowland (Ithaca and London: Cornell University Press, 2003), 21–33

   'Till the end of time. The apocalypse in Russian historical experience before 1500', in *Orthodox Russia* (q.v. below), 127–58

François, V., 'Elaborate incised ware: une preuve du rayonnement de la culture byzantine à l'époque paléologue', *Bsl* 61 (2003), 151–68

Franklin, S., 'The empire of the *Rhomaioi* as viewed from Kievan Russia: aspects of Byzantino-Russian cultural relations', *B* 53 (1983), 507–37

   Byzantium–Rus–Russia (Aldershot: Ashgate, 2002)

   Writing, society and culture in early Rus, c. 950–1300 (Cambridge: Cambridge University Press, 2002)

Franklin, S. and Shepard, J., *The emergence of Rus, 750–1200* (London: Longman, 1996)

Garidis, M., 'Icônes du XIIIe siècle dans l'aire du patriarchat de Jerusalem', in *Εὐψυχία: mélanges offerts à Hélène Ahrweiler*, ed. M. Balard *et al.* [Byzantina sorbonensia 16] (Paris: Publications de la Sorbonne, 1998), I, 225–38

Gavrilović, Z., *Studies in Byzantine and Serbian medieval art* (London: Pindar Press, 2001)

Guran, P., 'Jean VI Cantacuzène, l'hésychasme et l'empire. Les miniatures du codex Parisinus graecus 1242', in *L'empereur hagiographe* [see general bibliography], 73–121

'Patriarche hésychaste et empereur latinophrone. L'accord de 1380 sur les droits impériaux en matière ecclésiastique', *Revue des Études Sud-Est Européennes* 39 (2001), 53–62

Hanak, W. K., 'One source, two renditions: *The tale of Constantinople* and its fall in 1453', *Bsl* 62 (2004), 239–50

Hannick, C., 'Byzantinische Rhetorik in der Lobrede des Grigorij Camblak auf Evtimij von Tŭrnovo', *Anzeiger für Slavische Philologie* 22 (1993), 81–5

Helms, M. W., *Craft and the kingly ideal: art, trade and power* (Austin: University of Texas Press, 1993)

Hetherington, P., 'The jewels from the crown: symbol and substance in the later Byzantine imperial regalia', *BZ* 96 (2003), 157–68

Horníčková, K., 'The power of the word and the power of the image. Towards an anthropological interpretation of Byzantine magical amulets', *Bsl* 59 (1998), 239–46

'The Byzantine reliquary pectoral crosses in central Europe', *Bsl* 60 (1999), 213–50

Images of the Mother of God: perceptions of the Theotokos in Byzantium, ed. M. Vassilaki (Aldershot: Ashgate, 2005)

Ivanov, S. *Vizantiiskoe missionerstvo* (Moscow: Iazyki slavianskoi kul'tury, 2003)

Holy Fools (Oxford: Oxford University Press, 2006)

Kaimakamova, M., 'Istoriografskata stoinost na "B'lgarski Apokrifei Letopis"', in *Civitas divino-humana: in honorem annorum LX Georgii Bakalov*, ed. T. Stepanov and V. Vachkova (Sofia: Tangra TanNakRa, 2004), 417–41

Kaiser, D. H., *The growth of the law in medieval Russia* (Princeton: Princeton University Press, 1980)

Kiss, E., 'The state of research on the Monomachos crown and some further thoughts', in *Perceptions of Byzantium and its neighbors* [see general bibliography], 60–83

Kivelson, V. A., 'Merciful father, impersonal state. Russian autocracy in comparative perspective', *Modern Asian Studies* 31 (1997), 635–63

Korać, D., 'Sveta Gora pod srpskom vlašću (1345–1371)', *Zbornik Radova Vizantološkog Instituta* 31 (1992), 1–199

Korobeinikov, D. A., 'Diplomatic correspondence between Byzantium and the Mamluk Sultanate in the fourteenth century', *Al-Masaq* 16 (2004), 53–74

Kresten, O., *Die Beziehungen zwischen den Patriarchaten von Konstantinopel and Antiocheia unter Kallistos I. und Philotheos Kokkinos im Spiegel des Patriarchatsregisters von Konstantinopel* [Abhandlungen der geistes- und sozialwissenschaftlichen Klasse 6] (Mainz: Akademie der Wissenschaften und der Literatur, 2000)

'Die Affäre des Metropoliten Symeon von Alania im Spiegel des Patriarchatsregisters von Konstantinopel', *Österreichische Akademie der Wissenschaften – Anzeiger der philosophisch-historischen Klasse* 137 (2002), 5–40

Kuchkin, V. A., 'Sergii Radonezhskii i "Filoveevskii krest"', in *Drevnerusskoe iskusstvo: Sergii Radonezhskii i khudozhestvennaia kul'tura Moskvy XIV–XV vv.*, ed. M. A. Orlova *et al.* (St Petersburg: D. I. Bulanin, 1998), 16–22

Lozanova, R., 'Apocalyptic ideas after the fall of the Byzantine empire. Word and image', in *Medieval Christian Europe* [see general bibliography], 305–14

Magdalino, P., 'The history of the future and its uses: prophecy, policy and propaganda', in *The making of Byzantine history: studies dedicated to Donald M. Nicol*, ed. R. Beaton and C. Roueché (Aldershot: Variorum, 1993), 3–34

Majeska, G. P., 'Russo-Byzantine relations 1240–1453: a traffic report', *XVIIIth International Congress of Byzantine Studies, major papers* (Moscow: Institut Slavianovedeniia i Balkanistiki AN SSSR i Institut Vseobshchei Istorii AN SSSR, 1991), 27–51

Makarov, N. A., 'Rus' v XIII veke: kharakter kul'turnykh izmenenii', in *Rus' v XIII veke: drevnosti temnogo vremeni*, ed. N. A. Makarov *et al.* (Moscow: Nauka, 2003), 5–11

Maksimović, L., 'Byzantinische Herrscherideologie und Regierungsmethoden im Falle Serbien. Ein Beitrag zum Verständnis des byzantinischen Commonwealth', in *Polypleuros Nous: Miscellanea für Peter Schreiner zu seinem 60. Geburtstag*, ed. C. Scholz and G. Makris (Munich and Leipzig: K. G. Saur Verlag, 2000), 174–92

'L'empire de Stefan Dušan: genèse et caractère', *TM* 14 (2002), 414–28

Malamut, E., 'Les reines de Milutin', *BZ* 93 (2000), 490–507

'La circulation des manuscrits grecs en Europe milieu XIVe–milieu XVe siècle', in *Medieval Christian Europe* [see general bibliography], 85–113

Marjanović-Dušanić, S., *Vladarske insignije i državna simbolika u Srbiji od XIII do XV veka* (Belgrade: Srpska akademija nauka i umetnosti, 1994)

Mavromatis, L., *La fondation de l'empire serbe: le kralj Milutin* [Βυζαντινὰ κείμενα καὶ μελέται 16] (Thessalonike: National Hellenic Research Foundation, 1978)

'La formation du deuxième royaume bulgare vue par les intellectuels byzantins', *Etudes Balkaniques* 4 (1985), 30–8

Methodios und Kyrillos in ihrer europäischen Dimension, ed. E. Konstantinou (Frankfurt am Main: Peter Lang, 2005)

Miller, D. B., 'The coronation of Ivan IV of Moscow', *Jahrbücher für Geschichte Osteuropas* 15 (1967), 559–74

Morris, R., 'The political saint of the eleventh century', in *The Byzantine saint*, ed. S. Hackel [Studies supplementary to *Sobornost* 5] (London: Fellowship of St Alban and St Sergius, 1981), 43–50

'The origins of Athos', in *Mount Athos and Byzantine monasticism* [see general bibliography], 37–46

Musin, A. A., *Khristianizatsiia novgorodskoi zemli v IX–XIV vekakh: pogrebal'nyi obriad i khristianskie drevnosti* [Archaeologica Petropolitana Trudy 5] (St Petersburg: Institut istorii material'noi kul'tury, 2002)

Nastase, D., 'Le mont Athos et la politique du patriarcat de Constantinople, de 1355 à 1375', *Σύμμεικτα* 3 (1979), 121–77

'Le mont Athos pendant l'occupation latine de Constantinople: quelques considérations', *Byzantinisch-neugrichischen Jahrbücher* 22 (1985), 126–30

'Les débuts de la communauté oecuménique du mont Athos', *Σύμμεικτα* 6 (1985), 251–314

'Les débuts de l'église moldave et le siège de Constantinople par Bajazet Ier', *Σύμμεικτα* 7 (1987), 205–13

'Le monastère athonite des Ibères et l'Espagne', in *L'empereur hagiographe* [see general bibliography], 55–60

Năsturel, P. Ş., 'Les fastes épiscopaux de la métropole de Vicina', *Byzantinisch-neugrichischen Jahrbücher* 21 (1971–74) [1976], 33–42

Le mont Athos et les roumains: recherches sur leurs relations du milieu du XIVe siècle à 1654
  [OCA 227] (Rome: Pontificium institutum studiorum orientalium, 1986)
'Mais où donc localiser Vicina?', *BF* 12 (1987), 145–71
Nikolaeva, T. V., *Proizvedeniia russkogo prikladnogo iskusstva s nadpisiami XV – pervoi chetverti*
  XVI v. (Moscow: Arkheologiia SSSR svod arkheologicheskikh istochnikov EI–49, 1971)
Nikolov, A., 'Starob'lgarskiat prevod na "Izlozhenie na pouchitetelni glavi k'm imperator
  Iustinian" ot diakon Agapit i razvitie na ideiata za dostoinstvoto na b'lgarskiia vladitel
  v kraiia na IX-nachaloto na X v.', *Paleobulgarica* 24 (2000), 76–105
'"A useful tale about the Latins": an Old Bulgarian translation of a lost Byzantine anti-
  Latin text of the end of 11th–early 12th century', *Scripta & E-scripta* 1 (2003), 99–119
Obolensky, D., 'Nationalism in eastern Europe in the middle ages', *Transactions of the Royal
  Historical Society*, ser. v, 22 (1972), 1–16
'Some notes concerning a Byzantine portrait of John VIII Palaeologus', *Eastern Churches
  Review* 4 (1972), 141–6
'Late Byzantine culture and the Slavs: a study in acculturation', in *XVe Congrès interna-
  tional d'études byzantines. Rapports et co-rapports* [Athens, 1976] (Athens: Association
  internationale des études byzantines, 1981), 3–26
'A *Philorhomaios anthropos*: Metropolitan Cyprian of Kiev and all Russia', *DOP* 32 (1978),
  79–98
The Byzantine inheritance of Eastern Europe (London: Variorum, 1982)
Oikonomides, N., 'Byzantine diplomacy, AD. 1204–1453: means and ends', in *Byzantine diplo-
  macy* [see general bibliography], 73–88
'Emperor of the Romans – emperor of Romania', in *Byzantium and Serbia in the 14th
  century* [see general bibliography], 121–8
Orchard, G. E., 'Dissent and monastic reform in fifteenth-century Russia', in *Orthodoxy and
  heresy in religious movements: discipline and dissent*, ed. M. R. Greenshields and T. A.
  Robinson (Lewiston, Maine: Edwin Mellen Press, 1992), 36–59
Orthodox Russia: belief and practice under the tsars, ed. V. A. Kivelson and R. H. Greene
  (University Park: Pennsylvania State University Press, 2003)
Patriarkh Evtimii t'rnovski i negovoto vrema, ed. G. Danchev *et al.* (Veliko T'rnovo: Univer-
  sitetsko izdatelstvo 'Sv. Sv. Kiril i Metodii', 1998)
Pavlikanov, C., 'The Athonite monastery of Zographou and its property in Hierissos in the
  late 13th and the early 14th century', *BZ* 97 (2003), 559–65
Pentcheva, B. V., 'The "activated" icons: the Hodogetria and Mary's *Eisodos*', in *Images of
  the Mother of God* [q.v. above], 195–207
Polyviannyi, D. I., 'Vizantiisko-slavianskaia obshchnost' v predstavleniiakh bolgar X–XIV
  vv.', in *Sbornik statei k 70-letiiu akademika Gennadiia Grigorevicha Litavrina* [=Slaviane i
  ikh sosedi 6] (Moscow: Izdatel'stvo Indrik, 1996), 100–8
*Kul'turnoe svoeobrazie srednevekovoi Bolgarii v kontektse vizantiisko-slavianskoi obshchnosti
  IX–XV vekov* (Ivanovo: Ivanovskii gosudarstvenii universitet, 2000)
Popescu, E., 'Quelques données sur les relations de l'église de Dobroudja et de Moldavie
  avec l'église russe aux XIIe–XIVe siècles', in *The legacy of Saints Cyril and Methodius
  to Kiev and Moscow*, ed. A.-E. Tachiaos (Thessalonike: Hellenic Association for Slavic
  Studies, 1992), 143–55
Christianitas Daco-Romana: Florilegium Studiorum (Bucharest: Editura Academiei Române,
  1994)

Popov, G., 'Novootkrito svedenie za prevodacheska deinost na b'lgarskite knizhovnitsi v Sveta Gora prez p'rvata polovina na XIV v.', *B'lgarski Ezik* 28 (1978), 402–10

Price, R. M., 'The holy man and Christianisation from the apocryphal apostles to St Stephen of Perm', in *The cult of saints in late antiquity and the early middle ages: essays on the contribution of Peter Brown*, ed. P. A. Hayward and J. Howard-Johnston (Oxford: Oxford University Press, 1999), 215–38

Primov, B., 'Spread and influence of Bogomilism in Europe', *Byzantinobulgarica* 6 (1980), 317–37

Prinzing, G., *Die Bedeutung Bulgariens und Serbiens in den Jahren 1204–1219* (Munich: Institut für Byzantinistik und neugriechische Philologie der Universität, 1972)

'Das Papsttum und der orthodox geprägte Südosten Europas 1180–1216', in *Das Papsttum in der Welt des 12. Jahrhunderts*, ed. D.-E. Hehl *et al.* (Stuttgart: Thorbecke, 2002), 137–84

'A quasi-patriarch in the state of Epiros: the autocephalous archbishop of "Boulgaria" (Ohrid) Demetrios Chomatenos', *Zbornik Radova Vizantološkog Instituta* 41 (2004), 165–82

'Zum Austausch diplomatischer Geschenke zwischen Byzanz und seinen Nachbarn in Ostmittel- und Südosteuropa', *Mitteilungen zur Spätantiken Archäologie und Byzantinischen Kunstgeschichte* 4 (2005), 139–73

Raffensperger, C., 'Revisiting the idea of the Byzantine Commonwealth', *BF* 28 (2004), 159–74

Rowell, S. C., *Lithuania ascending: a pagan empire within east-central Europe, 1295–1345* (Cambridge: Cambridge University Press, 1994)

Rowland, D., 'Two cultures, one throne room. Secular courtiers and orthodox culture in the Golden Hall of the Moscow Kremlin', in *Orthodox Russia* [q.v. above], 33–58

'Moscow – the Third Rome or the New Israel?', *Russian Review* 55 (1996), 591–614

Rybakov, B. A., *Strigol'niki: Russkie gumanisty XIV stoletiia* (Moscow: Nauka, 1993)

Rydén, L., 'The vision of the Virgin at Blachernae and the feast of Pokrov', *Analecta Bollandiana* 94 (1976), 63–82

Schreiner, P., 'Byzanz und die Mamluken in der 2. Hälfte des 14. Jahrhunderts', *Der Islam* 56 (1979), 296–304

'Klosterbibliotheken in Ost und West. Unterschiede und Gemeinsamkeitens', in *Medieval Christian Europe* [see general bibliography], 19–29

Ševčenko, I., 'A neglected Byzantine source of Muscovite political ideology', *Harvard Slavic Studies* 2 (1954), 141–79

'Russo-Byzantine relations after the eleventh century', *Proceedings of the XIIIth International Congress of Byzantine Studies* [Oxford, 1966], ed. J. M. Hussey *et al.* (London, 1967), 93–104

'Religious missions seen from Byzantium', *Harvard Ukrainian Studies* 12–13 (1988–89), 7–27

Byzantium and the Slavs in letters and culture (Cambridge, MA and Naples: Harvard Ukrainian Research Institute and Istituto universitario orientale Napoli, 1991)

'Nekotorye zamechaniia o politike Konstantinopol'skogo patriarkhata po otnosheniiu k Vostochnoi Evrope v XIV v.', *Sbornik statei k 70-letiiu akademika Gennadiia Grigorevicha Litavrina* [=Slaviane i ikh sosedi 6] (Moscow: Izdatel'stvo Indrik, 1996), 133–9

Shalina, I. A., 'Bogomater' efesskaia-polotskaia-korsunskaia-toropetskaia', in *Chudotvornaia ikona v Vizantii i Drevnei Rusi*, ed. A. M. Lidov (Moscow: Martis, 1996), 200–51

Shchapov, I. N., *Vizantiiskoe i iuzhnoslavianskoe pravovoe nasledie na Rusi v XI–XIII vv.* (Moscow: Nauka, 1978)

　　State and church in early Russia, 10th–13th centuries (New Rochelle, NY: A. D. Caratzas, 1993)

Shepard, J., 'Byzantium and the steppe-nomads: the Hungarian dimension', in *Byzanz und Ostmitteleuropa 950–1453*, ed. G. Prinzing and M. Salamon (Wiesbaden: Harrassowitz, 1999), 55–83

　　'Slavic Christianities, 800–1100', in *Cambridge history of Christianity*, III, ed. T. F. X. Noble and J. M. H. Smith (Cambridge: Cambridge University Press, 2007)

　　'Manners maketh Romans? Young barbarians at the emperor's court', in *Byzantine style and civilisation: studies in memory of Steven Runciman*, ed. E. Jeffreys (Cambridge: Cambridge University Press, forthcoming)

Shevzov, V., 'Letting the people into church. Reflections on Orthodoxy and community in late imperial Russia', in *Orthodox Russia* [q.v. above], 59–77

Soulis, G. C., *The Serbs and Byzantium during the reign of Tsar Stephen Dušan (1331–1355) and his successors* (Washington, DC: Dumbarton Oaks Library and Collection, 1984)

Spinei, V., *Moldavia in the 11th–14th centuries* (Bucharest: Editura Academiei Republicii Socialiste Române, 1986)

Srednevekovoe rasselenie na Belom ozere, ed. N. A. Makarov et al. (Moscow: Iazyki russkoi kul'tury, 2001)

Stănescu, E., 'Byzance et les pays roumains IIe–15e siècles', *Actes du XIV Congrès international des études byzantines, Bucarest, 6–12 septembre 1971* (Bucharest: Editura Academiei Republicii Socialiste România, 1974), I, 393–431

Stephenson, P. A., *Byzantium's Balkan frontier: a political study of the northern Balkans, 900–1204* (Cambridge: Cambridge University Press, 2000)

　　The legend of Basil the Bulgar-Slayer (Cambridge: Cambridge University Press, 2003)

Tachiaos, A.-E. N., 'Gregory Sinaites' legacy to the Slavs: preliminary remarks', *Cyrillomethodianum* 7 (1983), 113–65

　　'The testament of Photius Monembasiotes, metropolitan of Russia (1408–31): Byzantine ideology in XVth-century Muscovy', *Cyrillomethodianum* 8–9 (1984–85), 77–109

Tăpkova-Zaïmova, V. and Miltenova, A., 'Political ideology and eschatology. The image of the "king-saviour" and concrete historical personages', in *Relations et influences réciproques entre grecs et bulgares, XVIIIe–XXe siècle* (Thessalonike: Institute for Balkan Studies, 1991), 441–51

　　Istoriko-apokaliptichnata knizhnina v'v Vizantiia i v srednovekovna B'lgariia (Sofia: Universitetsko izdatelstvo 'Sv. Kliment Okhridski', 1996)

Teteriatnikov, N., 'The image of the Virgin Zoodochos Pege: two questions concerning its origin', in *Images of the Mother of God* [q.v. above], 225–38

Thomson, F. J., 'The Bulgarian contribution of the reception of Byzantine culture in Kievan Rus': the myths and the enigma', *Harvard Ukrainian Studies* 12–13 (1988–89), 214–61

　　'"Made in Russia": a survey of the translations allegedly made in Kievan Russia', in *Millennium Russiae Christianae: Tausend Jahre christliches Russland 988–1988*, ed. G. Birkfellner (Cologne: Böhlau Verlag, 1993), 295–354

'Gregory Tsamblak. The man and the myths', *Slavica Gandensia* 25.2 (1998), 5–149

The reception of Byzantine culture in mediaeval Russia (Aldershot: Ashgate, 1999)

Timberlake, A., 'Older and younger recensions of the First Novgorod Chronicle', *Oxford Slavonic Papers* n.s. 33 (2000), 1–35

Todorova, E., 'More about *Vicina* and the west Black Sea coast', *Etudes Balkaniques* 2 (1978), 124–38

Turilov, A. A. and Floria, B. N., 'Khristianskaia literatura u slavian v seredine X–seredine XI v. i mezhslavianskie kul'turnye sviazi', in *Khristianstvo v strankakh vostochnoi, iugo-vostochnoi i tsentral'noi Evropy na poroge vtorogo tysiacheletiia*, ed. B. N. Floria (Moscow: Iazyki slavianskoi kul'tury, 2002), 398–458

Uspensky, B. A., *Tsar' i patriarkh: kharisma vlasti v Rossii (Vizantiiskaia model' i ee russkoe pereosmyslenie)* (Moscow: Iazyki russkoi kul'tury, 1998)

Vodoff, V., 'L'idée impériale et la vision de Rome à Tver', XIVe–XVe siècles', in *Roma, Costantinopoli, Mosca*, ed. P. Catalano *et al.* [Da Roma alla terza Roma. Documenti e studi 1] (Naples: Edizioni scientifiche italiane, 1983), 475–93

Princes et principautés russes X–XVII siècles (Northampton: Variorum, 1989)

'Le culte du *znamenie* à Novgorod. Tradition et réalité historique', *Oxford Slavonic Papers* 28 (1995), 1–19

Autour du mythe de la Sainte Russie: christianisme, pouvoir et société chez les Slaves orientaux (X–XVIIe siècles) (Paris: Institut d'études slaves, Centre d'études slaves, 2003)

Walter, C., 'The iconographical sources for the coronation of Milutin and Simonida at Gračanica', in *L'art byzantin au début du XIVe siècle*, ed. S. Petković (Belgrade: Filozofski fakultet, Odeljenje za istoriju umetnosti, 1978), 183–200

'Marriage crowns in Byzantine iconography', *Zograf* 10 (1979), 83–91

Art and ritual of the Byzantine church (London: Variorum, 1982)

Prayer and power in Byzantine and papal imagery (Aldershot: Variorum, 1993)

Woodfin, W. T., 'The dissemination of Byzantine embroidered vestments in the Slavic world to A.D. 1500', in *Medieval Christian Europe* [see general bibliography], 688–92

Wortman, R. 'The Russian coronation: rite and representation', *The Court Historian* 9.1 (2004), 15–31

Zhilina, N. V., *Shapka Monomakha: istoriko-kul'turnoe i tekhnologicheskoe issledovanie* (Moscow: Nauka, 2001)

2   Angold: Byzantium and the west

1   Sources

Argyriou, Asterios, *Macaire Makrès et la polémique contre l'Islam: édition princeps de l'éloge de Macaire Makrès et de ses deux œuvres anti-islamiques* [Studi e testi 314] (Vatican: Biblioteca apostolica vaticana, 1986)

Canart, Paul, 'Nicéphore Blemmyde et le mémoire adressé aux envoyés de Grégoire IX (Nicée, 1234)', *OCP* 25 (1959), 310–25

Fyrigos, Antonis, *Barlaam Calabro Opere contro i Latini* [Studi e testi 347–8], 2 vols. (Vatican: Biblioteca apostolica vaticana, 1998)

Gill, Joseph, *Quae supersunt Actorum Concilii Florentini* [Concilium Florentinum. Documenta et scriptores, ser. B, vol. 5, fasc. 1 and 2] (Rome: Pontificium institutum studiorum orientalium, 1953)

 Orationes Georgii Scholarii in Concilio Florentino habitae [Concilium Florentinum. Documenta et scriptores, ser. B, vol. 8, fasc. 1] (Rome: Pontificium institutum studiorum orientalium, 1964)

Golubovich, H., 'Disputatio Latinorum et Graecorum seu Relatio apocrisariorum Gregorii IX de gestis Nicaeae in Bithynia et Nymphaeae in Lydia 1234', *Archivum Franciscanum Historicum* 12 (1919), 418–70

Gregoras, Nikephoros, *Fiorenzo o intorno alla sapienza*, ed. P. A. M. Leone [Byzantina e neohellenica napolitana 4] (Naples: Università di Napoli, 1975)

Hoeck, Johannes and Loenertz, Raymond-J., *Nikolaos-Nektarios von Otranto, Abt von Casole: Beiträge zur Geschichte der ost-westlichen Beziehungen unter Innozenz III. und Friedrich II.* [Studia patristica et Byzantina 11] (Ettal: Buch-Kunstverlag, 1965)

Hofmann, Georg, *Acta Latina Concilii Florentini* [Concilium Florentinum. Documenta et scriptores, ser. B vol. 6] (Rome: Pontificium institutum studiorum orientalium, 1955)

Kolbaba, Tia M., 'Barlaam the Calabrian. Three treatises on Papal Primacy', *REB* 53 (1995), 41–115

Laurent, Vitalien and Darrouzès, Jean, *Dossier grec de l'union de Lyon (1273–1277)* [Archives de l'orient chrétien 16] (Paris: Institut français d'études byzantines, 1976)

Loenertz, Raymond-J., *Correspondance de Manuel Calécas* [Studi e testi 152] (Vatican: Biblioteca apostolica vaticana, 1950)

Mercati, Giovanni, *Notizie di Procoro e Demetrio Cidone, Manuele Caleca e Teodoro Meliteniota: ed altri appunti per la storia della teologia e della letteratura bizantina del secolo XIV* [Studi e testi 56] (Vatican: Biblioteca apostolica vaticana, 1931)

Palamas, Gregory, *Défense des saints hésychastes*, ed. J. Meyendorff [Spicilegium sacrum Lovaniense, études et documents 30–31], 2 vols. (Louvain: Spicilegium sacrum Lovaniense, 1959)

 The one hundred and fifty chapters, ed. and trans. R. E. Sinkewicz [Studies and Texts 83] (Toronto: Pontifical Institute of Mediaeval Studies, 1988)

2   Secondary works

1054–1954, L'église et les églises: neuf siècles de douloureuse séparation entre l'Orient et l'Occident, 2 vols. (Chevetogne: Éditions de Chevetogne, 1954–55)

1274, année charnière: mutations et continuités; Actes du colloque international, Lyon–Paris, 30 septembre–5 octobre 1974 [Colloques internationaux du Centre national de la recherche scientifique 558] (Paris: CNRS, 1977 [i.e. 1978])

Alexakis, Alexander, *Codex Parisinus Graecus 1115 and its archetype* [DOS 34] (Washington, DC: Dumbarton Oaks Library and Collections, 1996)

 'The Greek Patristic *testimonia* presented at the council of Florence (1439) in support of the *filioque* reconsidered', *REB* 58 (2000), 149–65

Avvakumov, Georgij, *Die Entstehung des Unionsgedankens: die lateinische Theologie des Hochmittelalters in der Auseinandersetzung mit dem Ritus der Ostkirche* [Veröffentlichungen des Grabmann-Institutes 47] (Berlin: Akademie Verlag, 2002)

Bazini, Hélène, 'Une première *édition* des œuvres de Joseph Bryennios: les *Traités adressés aux Crétois*', *REB* 62 (2004), 83–132

Blanchet, Marie-Hélène, 'La question de l'union des églises (13e–15e siècles). Historiographie et perspectives', *REB* 61 (2003), 5–48

Blanchet, Marie-Hélène and Ganchou, T., 'Les fréquentations byzantines de Lodisio de Tabriz, Dominicain de Péra (1453): Géôrgios Scholarios, Iôannès Chrysolôras et Théodôros Kalékas', *B* 75 (2005), 70–103

Boojamra, John Lawrence, *The Church and social reform: the policies of Patriarch Athanasios of Constantinople* (New York: Fordham University Press, 1993)

Cacouros, Michel, 'Un patriarche à Rome, un *katholikos didaskalos* au patriarcat et deux donations trop tardives de reliques du seigneur: Grégoire III Mamas et Georges Scholarios, le synode et la *synaxis*', in *Βυζάντιο* (see general bibliography), 71–124

Cammelli, Giuseppe, *I dotti bizantini e le origini dell' umanesimo*, I, *Manuele Crisolora* (Florence: Centro nazionale di studi sul Rinascimento, 1941)

Delacroix-Besnier, Claudine, 'Conversions constantinopolitaines au XIVe siècle', *Mélanges de l'École Française de Rome* 105 (1993), 715–61

Les Dominicains et la chrétienté grecque aux XIVe et XVe siècles [Collection de l'École française de Rome 237] (Rome: École française de Rome, 1997)

Dondaine, A., '"Contra Graecos". Premiers écrits polémiques des Dominicains d'Orient', *Archivum Fratrum Praedicatorum* 21 (1951), 320–446

Eszer, Ambrosius K., *Das abenteuerliche Leben des Johannes Laskaris Kalopheros: Forschungen zur Geschichte der ost-westlichen Beziehungen im 14. Jahrhundert* [Schriften zur Geistesgeschichte des ostlichen Europa 3] (Wiesbaden: O. Harrassowitz, 1969)

Franchi, Antonino, *Il concilio II di Lione (1274) secondo la 'Ordinatio Concilii Generalis Lugdunensis'* [Studi e testi francescani 33] (Rome: Edizione fransescane, 1965)

La svolta politico-ecclesiastica tra Roma e Bisanzio (1249–1254): la legazione di Giovanni da Parma; il ruolo di Federico II [Spicilegium pontificii Athenaei Antoniani 21] (Rome: Ponticifium Athenaeum Antonianum, 1981)

Gill, Joseph, *The Council of Florence* (Cambridge: Cambridge University Press, 1959)

Personalities of the Council of Florence: and other essays (Oxford: Basil Blackwell, 1964)

Kolbaba, Tia M., 'Meletios Homologetes *On the Customs of the Italians*', *REB* 55 (1997), 137–68

The Byzantine lists: errors of the Latins (Urbana and Chicago: University of Illinois Press, 2000)

Laurent, Vitalien, 'Les préliminaires du concile de Florence: les Neuf Articles du Pape Martin V et la réponse inédite du patriarche de Constantinople Joseph II (Octobre 1422)', *REB* 20 (1962), 5–60

Loenertz, Raymond, 'Autour du traité de Fr. Barthélemy de Constantinople contre les Grecs', *Archivum Fratrum Praedicatorum* 6 (1936), 361–71

'Mémoire d'Ogier, protonotaire, pour Marco et Marchetto nonces de Michel VIII Paléologue auprès du Pape Nicholas III, 1278 printemps–été', *OCP* 31 (1965), 374–408

Masai, François, *Pléthon et le platonisme de Mistra* (Paris: Belles Lettres, 1956)

Meyendorff, John, 'Projets de concile oecuménique en 1367: un dialogue inédit entre Jean Cantacuzène et le légat Paul', *DOP* 14 (1967), 147–77

Munitiz, Joseph, 'A reappraisal of Blemmydes' first discussion with the Latins', *Bsl* 51 (1990), 20–6

Papadakis, Aristeides, *Crisis in Byzantium: the filioque controversy in the patriarchate of Gregory II of Cyprus (1283–1289)* (New York: Fordham University Press, 1983)

Papadopoulos, Stylianos G., 'Thomas im Byzanz: Thomas Rezeption und Thomas Kritik im Byzanz zwischen 1354 und 1435', *Theologie und Philosophie* 49 (1974), 274–305

Roberg, Burkhard, *Die Union zwischen der griechischen und der lateinischen Kirche auf dem II. Konzil von Lyon (1274)* [Bonner historische Forschungen 24] (Bonn: Ludwig Röhrscheid, 1964)

Das zweite Konzil von Lyon [1274] [Konziliengeschichte. Reihe A, Darstellungen] (Paderborn: Schöningh, 1990)

Roncaglia, P. M., *Les frères mineurs et l'église grecque orthodoxe au XIIIe siècle (1231–1274)* [Biblioteca bio-bibliographica della terra santa e dell'oriente francescano, ser. ii, Studi ii] (Cairo: Centre d'études orientales de la custodie franciscaine de Terre-Sainte, 1954)

Ševčenko, Ihor, 'Intellectual repercussions of the Council of Florence', *Church History* 24 (1955), 291–323

Wilson, N. G., *From Byzantium to Italy: Greek studies in the Italian Renaissance* (London: Duckworth, 1992)

Woodhouse, C. M., *Gemistos Plethon: the last of the Hellenes* (Oxford: Clarendon Press, 1986)

3   Gerstel and Talbot: The culture of lay piety in medieval Byzantium

1   Sources

Bees-Seferlis, H., 'Unedierte Schriftstücke aus der Kanzlei des Johannes Apokaukos des Metropolitan von Naupaktos (in Aetolien)', *Byzantinische-Neugriechische Jahrbücher* 21 (1971–74), 55–160

Ioannis Tzetzae Epistulae, ed. P. A. M. Leone (Leipzig: B. G. Teubner, 1972)

Kurtz, E., *Die Gedichte des Christophoros Mitylenaios* (Leipzig: Neumann, 1903)

Manuelis Philae Carmina. Ex codicibus Escurialensibus, Florentinis, Parisinis et Vaticanis, ed. Emmanuel Miller (Paris: Excusum in Typographeo Imperiali, 1855)

Mazaris' Journey to Hades or Interviews with Dead Men about Certain Officials of the Imperial Court (trans.) [Seminar Classics 609] (Buffalo: State University of New York at Buffalo, 1975)

Papadopoulos-Kerameus, A., 'Zhitija dvukh' Vselenskikh' patriarkhov' XIV v., svv. Afanasiia I i Isidora I', *Zapiski Istoriko-Filologicheskago Fakul'teta Imperatorskago S.-Peterburgskago Universiteta* 76 (1905), 1–51

Petit, L., 'Typikon du monastère de la Kosmosotira près d'Aenos (1152)', *Izvestiia Russkago Archeologicheskago Instituta v Konstantinopole* 13 (1908), 17–75

Pignani, A., *Matteo di Efeso: racconto di una festa popolare* (Naples: M. D'Auria, 1984)

Rosenqvist, J. O., *The hagiographic dossier of St. Eugenios of Trebizond in Codex Athous Dionysiou 154* (Uppsala: Uppsala Universitet, 1996)

Sargologos, É., *La vie de Saint Cyrille le Philéote moine byzantin (1110)* (Brussels: Société des Bollandistes, 1964)

Trempelas, P., Μικρὸν Εὐχολόγιον, ι, Αἱ ἀκολουθίαι καὶ τάξεις μνήστρων καὶ γάμου, εὐχελαίου, χειροτονιῶν καὶ βαπτίσματος (Athens: [s.n.], 1950)

Tsames, D. G., Φιλοθέου Κωνσταντινουπόλεως τοῦ Κοκκίνου Ἁγιολογικὰ Ἔργα, I, Θεσσαλονικεῖς Ἅγιοι (Thessalonike: Aristoteleio Panepistemio Thessalonikes, 1985)

Tsougarakis, D., *The Life of Leontios, Patriarch of Jerusalem* [The Medieval Mediterranean 2] (Leiden: E. J. Brill, 1993).

Veselovskij, A. N., 'Razyskanija v oblasti russkogo duchovnogo sticha', *Sbornik Otdelenija Russkago Jazyka i Slovesnosti Imperatorskoj Akademii Nauk* 53 (1891–92), suppl. 3–174

2   Secondary works

Dagron, G., 'Jamais le dimanche', in *Εὐψυχία: mélanges offerts à Hélène Ahrweiler*, ed. M. Balard *et al.* (Paris: Publications de la Sorbonne, 1998), 165–75

Drandakes, N. B., "Ὁ Ταξιάρχης τῆς Χαρούδης καὶ ἡ κτιτορικὴ ἐπιγραφή του', *Λακωνικαὶ Σπουδαί* I (1972), 275–91

Foss, C., *Nicaea: a Byzantine capital and its praises* (Brookline, MA: Hellenic College Press, 1996)

Kalopissi-Verti, S., *Dedicatory inscriptions and donor portraits in thirteenth-century churches of Greece* (Vienna: Verlag ÖAW, 1992)

Karpov, S. P., 'Chto i kak prazdnovali v Kaffe v XV veke', *Srednie Veka* 56 (1993), 226–32

Kyriakis, M. J., 'Medieval European society as seen in two eleventh-century texts of Michael Psellos', *Byzantine Studies/Études Byzantines* 3 (1976), 77–100

Laiou, A., 'The festival of "Agathe": comments on the life of Constantinopolitan women', in *Byzantium: tribute to Andreas N. Stratos*, ed. N. A. Stratos (Athens: [N. A. Stratos], 1986), I, 111–22

Macrides, R., 'Justice under Manuel I Komnenos', *Fontes Minores* 6 (1984), 140–55

Manoussacas, M., 'Un acte de donation à l'église Sainte-Kyriakè de Mouchli (1457)', *TM* 8 (1981), 315–19

Moutsopoulos, N., 'Ἀπὸ τὴν Βυζαντινὴ Καρύταινα', *Πελοποννησιακά* 16 (1985–86), 129–202

Rautman, M., 'Ignatios of Smolensk and the late Byzantine monasteries of Thessaloniki', *REB* 49 (1991), 143–69

Taft, R., 'The frequency of the eucharist in Byzantine usage: history and practice', *Studi sull' Oriente Cristiano* 4 (2000), 103–32

Tourta, A., 'Fortifications of Gynaikokastro, Greece', in *Secular medieval architecture in the Balkans, 1300–1500, and its preservation*, ed. S. Ćurčić and E. Hadjitryphonos (Thessalonike: Aimos, Society for the Study of the Medieval Architecture in the Balkans and Its Preservation, 1997), 110–13

4   Krausmüller: The rise of hesychasm

1   Sources

Corpus Dionysiacum, II, *De coelesti hierarchia, De ecclesiastica hierarchia, De mystica theologia, Epistolae*, ed. G. Heil and A. M. Ritter (Berlin and New York: Walter de Gruyter, 1991)

Elias Ekdikos, *Chapters*, in *PG* 90, 1401–61

Évagre le Pontique, *Traité pratique ou Le moine*, ed. A. and C. Guillaumont, 2 vols. (Paris: Éditions du Cerf, 1971)

Gregory of Sinai, *Opera*, in PG 150, 1240–1345

Halkin, François, 'Deux vies de S. Maxime le Kausokalybe, ermite au Mont Athos (XIVe s.)', *Analecta Bollandiana* 54 (1936), 38–109

Hausherr, Irénée, *La méthode d'oraison hésychaste* [OCA 9.2] (Rome: Pontificium institutum studiorum orientalium, 1928)

Hero, Angela C., *Letters of Gregory Akindynos: Greek text and English translation* [DOT 7; CFHB 21] (Washington, DC: Dumbarton Oaks Research Library and Collection, 1983)

Hesychius of Sinai, *Chapters on sobriety*, in PG 93, 1480–1544

Ἰωσὴφ Καλοθέτου Συγγράμματα, ed. D. G. Tsames [Θεσσαλονικεῖς Βυζαντινοὶ Συγγραφεῖς 1] (Thessalonike: Centre of Byzantine Studies, 1980)

Latyshev, V. V., *Methodii Patriarchae Constantinopolitani Vita S. Theophanis Confessoris* [Zapiski Rossiiskoi akademii nauk (po istoriko-filologicheskomu otdeleniju), ser. viii, 13.4] (Petrograd: Rossiiskaia akademiia nauk, 1918)

Maximos the Confessor, *Ambigua*, in PG 91, 1031–1417

Nicephorus the Monk, *On sobriety and the guarding of the heart*, in PG 147, 945–66

Nicetas Stethatos, *Chapters*, in PG 120, 851–952

Schirò, Giuseppe, *Barlaam Calabro. Epistole greche. I primordi episodici e dottrinari delle lotte esicaste* [Testi 1] (Palermo: Istituto siciliano di studi bizantini e neogreci, 1954)

Syméon le Nouveau Théologien, *Catéchèses*, ed. B. Krivochéine, 3 vols. (Paris: Éditions du Cerf, 1963–4)

Theoleptos of Philadelphia, *The monastic discourses: a critical edition, translation and study*, ed. R. E. Sinewicz [Studies and Texts 111] (Toronto: Pontifical Institute of Mediaeval Studies, 1992)

2 Secondary works

Beyer, Hans-Veit, 'Nikephoros Gregoras als Theologe und sein erstes Auftreten gegen die Hesychasten', *Jahrbuch der Österreichischen Byzantinistik* 20 (1971), 171–88

Candal, Manuel, 'Origen ideológico del palamismo en un documento de David Disipato', *OCP* 15 (1949), 85–125

Dagron, Gilbert, 'Rêver de Dieu et parler de soi. Le rêve et son interprétation d'après les sources byzantines', in *I sogni nel Medioevo* (Seminario internazionale Roma 2–4 ottobre 1983, ed. T. Gregori [Lessico intellettuale europeo 35] (Rome, 1985), 37–55

Gouillard, Jean, 'Quatre procès de mystiques à Byzance (vers 960–1143). Inspiration et autorité', *REB* 36 (1978), 5–81

Hausherr, Irénée, 'L'hésychasme: étude de spiritualité', *OCP* 22 (1956), 5–40, 247–85

Hisamatsu, E., *Gregorios Sinaites als Lehrer des Gebets* [Münsteraner theologische Abhandlungen 34] (Altenberge: Oros, 1994)

Kirchmeyer, J., 'Hésychius le Sinaïte', in *Dictionnaire de spiritualité* [see general bibliography], VII (1971), 408–10

Lossky, Vladimir, *Théologie mystique de l'Église d'Orient* (Paris: Aubier Montaigne, 1944)

Meyendorff, John, *St Grégoire Palamas et la mystique orthodoxe* (Paris: Éditions du Seuil, 1959)

Rigo, Antonio, *Monaci esicasti e monaci bogomili: le accuse di messalianismo e bogomilismo rivolte agli esicasti ed il problema dei rapporti tra esicasmo e bogomilismo* (Orientalia venetiana 2] (Florence: Leo S. Olschki Editore, 1989)

'Niceforo l'esicasta (XIII sec.): alcune considerazioni sulla vita e sull'opera', in *Amore del bello, studi sulla Filocalia. Atti del Simposio Internazionale sulla Filocalia* (Magnano: Edizioni Qiqajon, 1991), 79–119

L'amore della quiete: ho tes hesychias eros: l'esicasmo Bizantino tra il 13 e il 15 secolo (Magnano: Edizioni Qiqajon, 1993)

'Gregorio il Sinaita', in *Théologie byzantine et sa tradition* [see general bibliography], II, 30–130

Sinkewicz, Robert E., 'A new interpretation for the First Episode in the controversy between Barlaam the Calabrian and Gregory Palamas', *JThSt* n.s. 31 (1980), 489–500

'The solutions addressed to George Lapithes by Barlaam the Calabrian and their philosophical context', *Mediaeval Studies* 43 (1981), 151–217

'The doctrine of the knowledge of God in the early writings of Barlaam the Calabrian', *Mediaeval Studies* 44 (1982), 196–222

'Gregory Palamas', in *Théologie byzantine et sa tradition* [see general bibliography], II, 131–88

5   Ševčenko: Art and liturgy in the later Byzantine Empire

1   Sources

Ajjoub, Maxime (Leila) (with Paramelle, Joseph), *Livre d'heures du Sinaï (Sinaiticus Graecus 864)* [Sources chrétiennes 486] (Paris: Éditions du Cerf, 2004)

Arranz, Miguel, *Le typicon du monastère du Saint-Sauveur à Messine* (Rome: Pontificium institutum orientalium studiorum, 1969)

L'Eucologio Costantinopolitano agli inizi del secolo XI: Hagiasmaterion e Archieratikon (Rituale e Pontificale) con l'aggiunta del Leitourgikon (Messale) (Rome: Pontificia università gregoriana, 1996)

Jordan, Robert H., *The Synaxarion of the monastery of the Theotokos Evergetis: September to February* [Belfast Texts and Translations 6.5] (Belfast: Belfast Byzantine Enterprises, 2000)

Mateos, Juan, *Le Typicon de la Grande Église* [OCA 165], 2 vols. (Rome: Pontificium institutum studiorum orientalium, 1962–63)

Monumenta Musicae Byzantinae. Lectionaria, I, *Prophetologium*, ed. C. Hoeg, G. Zuntz and G. Engberg (Copenhagen: Munksgaard, 1970)

Mother Mary and Ware, Kallistos, *The Festal Menaion* (London: Faber and Faber, 1969)

The Lenten Triodion (London: Faber and Faber, 1978)

2   Secondary works: liturgy

Arranz, Miguel, 'Les grandes étapes de la liturgie byzantine: Palestine – Byzance – Russie. Essai d'aperçu historique', in *Liturgie de l'église particulière et liturgie de l'église universelle* [Bibliotheca ephemerides liturgicae subs. 7] (Rome: Edizioni liturgiche, 1976), 43–72

Baldovin, John F., *The urban character of Christian worship: the origins, development and meaning of stational liturgy* [OCA 228] (Rome: Pontificium institutum studiorum orientalium, 1987)

Bertonière, Gabriel, *The historical development of the Easter Vigil and related services in the Greek church* [OCA 193] (Rome: Pontificium institutum studiorum orientalium, 1972)

Bornert, René, *Les commentaires byzantins de la Divine Liturgie du VIIe au XVe siècle* [Archives de l'orient chrétien 9] (Paris: Institut français d'études byzantines, 1966)

Follieri, Enrica, *I calendari in metro innografico di Cristoforo Mitileneo* [Subsidia hagiographica 63] 2 vols. (Brussels: Société des Bollandistes, 1980)

Janeras, Sebastià, *Le Vendredi-saint dans la tradition liturgique byzantine: structure et histoire de ses offices* [Studia Anselmiana 99] (Rome: Pontificio Ateneo S. Anselmo, 1988)

Kucharek, Casimir A., *The Byzantine-Slav Liturgy of St. John Chrysostom: its origin and evolution* (Allendale, NJ: Alleluia Press, 1971)

Mateos, Juan, 'Quelques problèmes de l'orthros byzantin', *Proche-Orient Chrétien* 11 (1961), 17–35, 201–20

Pott, Thomas, *La réforme liturgique byzantine: étude du phénomène de l'évolution non-spontanée de la liturgie byzantine* [Bibliotheca ephemerides liturgicae subs. 104] (Rome: CLV – Edizioni liturgiche, 2000)

Schmemann, Alexander, *Introduction to liturgical theology* [Library of Orthodox Theology 4] (London: Faith Press; Bangor, MA: American Orthodox Press, 1966)

Schulz, Hans-Joachim, *The Byzantine liturgy: symbolic structure and faith expression* (New York: Pueblo Publishing Co., 1986)

Taft, Robert F., *The Byzantine rite: a short history* (Collegeville, MN: Liturgical Press, 1992)

Liturgy in Byzantium and beyond (Aldershot: Variorum, 1995)

Velkovska, Elena, 'Funeral rites according to Byzantine liturgical sources', *DOP* 55 (2001), 21–45

3 Secondary works: history of art

Anderson, Jeffrey C., *The New York Cruciform Lectionary* (University Park: University of Pennsylvania Press, 1992)

Babić, Gordana, 'Les discussions christologiques et le décor des églises byzantines au XII siècle: les évêques officiant devant l'Hétoimasie et devant l'Amnos', *Frühmittelalterliche Studien* 2 (1968), 368–86

Les chapelles annexes des églises byzantines: fonction liturgique et programmes iconographiques [Bibliothèque des cahiers archéologiques 3] (Paris: Klincksieck, 1969)

Bakalova, Elka, 'Liturgicna poezia i crkovna stenopis (Tekst ot oktoexa v Bojanskata c'rkvata)', *Starobulgarska Literatura* 28–9 (1994), 143–52

Belting, Hans, 'An image and its function in the liturgy: the Man of Sorrows in Byzantium', *DOP* 34–35 (1980–81), 1–16

Das Bild und sein Publikum im Mittelalter: Form und Funktion früher Bildtafeln der Passion (Berlin: Mann, 1981); trans. as *The image and its public in the Middle Ages: form and function of early paintings of the Passion* (New Rochelle, NY: A. D. Caratzas, 1990)

Carr, Annemarie Weyl, 'Illuminated musical manuscripts in Byzantium. A note on the late twelfth century', *Gesta* 28 (1989), 41–52

Ceremony and faith: Byzantine art and the Divine Liturgy, ed. G. Livieratou (Athens: Hellenic Ministry of Culture, 1999)

Der Nersessian, Sirarpie, *L'illustration des psautiers grecs du moyen âge*, II, Londres, Add. 19.352 [Bibliothèque des cahiers archéologiques 5] (Paris: Klincksieck, 1970)

Dolezal, Mary-Lyon, 'Illuminating the liturgical word: text and image in a decorated lectionary (Mount Athos, Dionysiou Monastery, cod. 587)', *Word and Image* 12 (1996), 23–60

Dufrenne, Suzy, 'L'enrichissement du programme iconographique dans les églises byzantines du XIIIème siècle', in *L'art byzantin du XIIIe siècle: Symposium de Sopoćani 1965*, ed. V. J. Djurić (Belgrade: Faculté de philosophie, Dépt de l'histoire de l'art, 1967), 35–46

Dzhurova, Aksiniia, *Tomichov psaltir* [Monumenta Slavico-Byzantina et Mediaevalia Europensia 1], 2 vols. (Sofia: Universitetsko izd-vo 'Kliment Okhridski', 1990)

Galavaris, George, *The illustrations of the Homilies of Gregory of Nazianzenus* [Studies in Manuscript Illumination 6] (Princeton: Princeton University Press, 1969)

The illustrations of the Prefaces in Byzantine Gospels [Byzantina Vindobonensia 11] (Vienna: Verlag ÖAW, 1979)

Gerstel, Sharon E. J., 'Liturgical scrolls in the Byzantine sanctuary', *Greek, Roman and Byzantine Studies* 35 (1994), 195–204

Beholding the sacred mysteries: programs of the Byzantine sanctuary [Monographs on the Fine Arts 56] (Seattle and London: University of Washington Press, 1999)

Grabar, André, 'Un rouleau constantinopolitain et ses peintures', *DOP* 8 (1954), 163–99

Jolivet-Lévy, Catherine, *Les églises byzantines de Cappadoce: le programme iconographique de l'apside et de ses abords* (Paris: Presses du CNRS, 1991)

Krause, Karin, *Die illustrierte Homilien des Johannes Chrysostomos in Byzanz* (Wiesbaden: Reichert Verlag, 2004)

Il menologio di Basilio II. (Cod. Vaticano greco 1613) [Codices e Vaticanis selecti. . . 8], 2 vols. (Turin: Fratelli Bocca, 1907)

Meredith, Cecilia, 'The illustrations of *Codex Ebnerianus*. A study in liturgical illustration of the Comnenian period', *Journal of the Warburg and Courtauld Institutes* 29 (1966), 419–24

Mijović, Pavle, *Menolog: istorijsko-umetnicka istrazivanja* [Posebna Izdanja 10] (Belgrade: Arheoloski Institut, 1973)

Moran, Neil K., *Singers in late Byzantine and Slavonic painting* [Byzantina Neerlandica 9] (Leiden: E. J. Brill, 1986)

Nelson, Robert S., *The iconography of preface and miniature in the Byzantine gospel book* [Monographs on Architecture and the Fine Arts 36] (New York: New York University Press, 1980)

Pallas, Demetrios I., *Die Passion und Bestattung Christi in Byzanz: Der Ritus – das Bild* [Miscellanea Byzantina Monacensia 2] (Munich: Institut für byzantinistik und neugriechische Philologie, 1965)

Pätzold, Alexandra, *Der Akathistos-Hymnos: Die Bilderzyklen in der byzantinischen Wandmalerei des 14. Jahrhunderts* [Forschungen zur Kunstgeschichte und christliche Archäologie 16] (Stuttgart: F. Steiner Verlag, 1989)

Ševčenko, Nancy Patterson, *Illustrated manuscripts of the Metaphrastian Menologion* [Studies in Medieval Manuscript Illumination 54] (Chicago and London: University of Chicago Press, 1990)

'Icons in the Liturgy', *DOP* 45 (1991), 45–57

'The Five Hymnographers at Nerezi', *Palaeoslavica* 10 (2002), 55–68

'The Walters' Horologion', *Journal of the Walters Art Museum* 62 (2004), 7–21

Spieser, Jean-Michel, 'Liturgie et programmes iconographiques', *TM* 11 (1991), 575–90

'Le développement du templon et les images des Douze Fêtes', in *Les images dans les sociétés médiévales: pour une histoire comparée*, ed. J.-M. Sansterre et J.-C. Schmitt (Turnhout: Brepols, 1999) [= *Bulletin de l'Institut Historique Belge de Rome* 69 (1999), 131–64]

Stefanescu, J. D., 'L'illustration des liturgies dans l'art de Byzance et de l'Orient', *Annuaire de l'Institut de Philologie et d'Histoire Orientales* 1 (1932), 21–77; 3 (1935), 403–510; also printed separately (Brussels: Institut de philologie et d'histoire orientale, 1936)

Todić, Branislav, 'L'influence de la liturgie sur la décoration peinte du narthex de Sopoćani', in *Drevnerusskoe iskusstvo. Rus', Vizantiia, Balkany: XIII vek*, ed. A. L. Batalov *et al.* (St Petersburg: Dmitrii Bulanin, 1997), 43–58

Tomeković, Svetlana, 'Contribution à l'étude du programme du narthex des églises monastiques (XIe–première moitié du XIIIe siècle)', *B* 58 (1988), 140–54

Tronzo, William, 'Mimesis in Byzantium. Notes toward a history of the function of the image', *Res* 25 (1994), 61–76

Velmans, Tania, 'Une illustration inédite de l'Acathiste et l'iconographie des hymnes liturgiques à Byzance', *CA* 22 (1972), 131–65

Vokotopoulos, Panagiotes, Ἡ εἰκονογραφήση τοῦ κανόνος εἰς ψυχορραγοῦντα στὸ Ὁρολόγιον 295 τῆς μονῆς Λειμῶνος', *Σύμμεικτα* 9 (1994), 95–114

Walter, Christopher, *Art and ritual of the Byzantine church* (London: Variorum, 1982)

Weitzmann, Kurt, *Byzantine liturgical psalters and gospels* (London: Variorum, 1980)

6 Zachariadou: Mount Athos and the Ottomans

1 Sources

Cyriac of Ancona, *Later travels*, ed. E. W. Bodnar (with C. Foss) [I Tatti Renaissance Library] (Cambridge, MA: Harvard University Press, 2003)

Nikopoulos, P. and Oikonomides, N., "Ιερά Μονή Διονυσίου, κατάλογος του ἀρχείου', *Σύμμεικτα* 1 (1966), 257–326

Philotheos Kokkinos, *Δογματικὰ Ἔργα*, ed. D. Kaimakes (Thessalonike: Centre of Byzantine Studies, 1983)

2 Secondary works

Alexander (Alexandropoulos), J. C., 'The Lord giveth and the Lord taketh away: Athos and the confiscation affair of 1568–1569', in *Mount Athos in the 14th–16th centuries* [Ἀθωνικὰ Σύμμεικτα 4] (Athens: Institute for Byzantine Research, 1997), 149–200

Alexandropoulou, Olga, Ὁ Διονύσιος Ἰβηρίτης καὶ τὸ ἔργο του Ἱστορία τῆς Ρωσίας (Heraklion: Bikelaia Demotike Bibliotheke, 1994)

Berindei, M. and Veinstein, G., *L'Empire ottoman et les pays roumains, 1544–1545* (Paris: Éditions de l'École des hautes études en sciences sociales; Cambridge, MA: Harvard Ukrainian Research Institute 1987)

Demetriades, V. and Zachariadou, Elizabeth A., 'Serbian ladies and Athonite monks', *Wiener Zeitschrift für die Kunde des Morgenlandes* 84 (1994), 35–55

Select bibliography

Fotic, A., 'The official explanation for the confiscation and sale of the monasteries (churches) and their estates at the time of Selim II', *Turcica* 26 (1994), 33–54

Imber, C., *Ebu's-su'ud: the Islamic legal tradition* [Jurists: Profiles in Legal Theory] (Edinburgh: Edinburgh University Press, 1997)

Laiou, Angeliki, 'Economic activities of Vatopedi in the fourteenth century', in *The Monastery of Vatopedi: history and art* [Ἀθωνικὰ Σύμμεικτα 7] (Athens: Institute for Byzantine Research, 1999), 55–72

'Ἡ διαμόρφωση τῆς τιμῆς τῆς γῆς στὸ Βυζάντιο', in *Βυζάντιο* (see general bibliography), 339–48

Løkkegaard, L., 'The concepts of war and peace in Islam', in *War and peace in the Middle Ages*, ed. B. P. Maguire (Copenhagen: C. A. Reitzels Forlag, 1987), 263–81

Luttrell, A., 'The earliest documents on the Hospitaller *corso* at Rhodes: 1413 and 1416', *Mediterranean Historical Review* 10 (1995), 177–88

Majer, H. G., 'Some remarks on the document of Murad I from the monastery of St Paul on Mount Athos', in *Mount Athos in the 14th–16th centuries* [Ἀθωνικὰ Σύμμεικτα 4] (Athens: Institute for Byzantine Research, 1997), 33–9

Makris, G., *Studien zur spätbyzantinischen Schiffart* [Collana storica di fonti e studi 52] (Genoa: Istituto di Medievistica, 1988)

Mamalakes, Ioannes P., *Τὸ Ἅγιον Ὄρος (Ἄθως) διὰ μέσου τῶν αἰώνων* [Μακεδονικὴ Βιβλιοθήκη 33] (Thessalonike: Hetaireia Makedonikon Spoudon, 1971)

Matanov, H., 'Radoslav Hlapen – souverain féodale en Macédoine méridional durant le troisième quart du XIVe siècle', *Études Balkaniques* 19 (1983), 68–87

Mylonas, P., *Athos and its monastic institutions through old engravings and other works of art* (Athens: National Academy of Fine Arts, 1963)

Năsturel, P. Ş., 'Le Mont Athos et ses premiers contacts avec la Principauté de Valachie', *Bulletin, Association Internationale d'Études du Sud-Est Européen* 1 (1963), 31–8

'Aperçu critique des rapports de la Valachie et du Mont Athos des origines au début du XVIe siècle', *Revue des Études Sud-Est Européennes* 2 (1964), 93–126

Nystazopoulou-Pelekidou, Marie, 'Les couvents de l'espace égéen et leur activité maritime (Xe–XIIIe s.)', *Σύμμεικτα* 15 (2002), 109–30

Oikonomidès, N., 'Monastères et moines lors de la conquête ottomane', *Südost-Forschungen* 35 (1976), 1–10

"Οι δύο σερβικές κατακτήσεις τῆς Χαλκιδικῆς τὸν ΙΔ᾽ αἰώνα', *Δίπτυχα* 2 (1980–81), 294–9

'Byzantium between East and West (XIII–XV cent.)', in *Byzantium and the West c.850–1200*, ed. J. D. Howard-Johnston (Amsterdam: Adolf M. Hakkert Publisher, 1988), 319–32

'Mount Athos: levels of literacy', *DOP* 42 (1988), 167–78

'Patronage in Palaiologan Mount Athos', in *Mount Athos and Byzantine monasticism* [see general bibliography], 99–111

'The monastery of Patmos in the eleventh and twelfth centuries and its economic functions', in *Social and economic life in Byzantium* (Aldershot: Ashgate, 2004), VII, 1–17

Papoulia, Basilike, 'Die Vita des Heiligen Philotheos vom Athos', *Südost-Forschungen* 22 (1963), 274–80

Pavlikianof, Kiril, *Σλάβοι μοναχοί στὸ Ἅγιον Ὄρος ἀπὸ τὸν Ι᾽ ᾽ως τὸν ΙZ᾽ αἰώνα* (Thessalonike: University Studio Press, 2002)

Pertusi, A., 'Monasteri e monaci italiani all'Athos nell'alto medioevo', in *Millénaire du Mont Athos* [see general bibliography], I, 217–51

Pitsakis, G., 'Un cas particulier d'activité commerciale dans la Méditerranée byzantine: les monastères armateurs', *Méditerranées* 32 (2002), 63–87

Radić, R., 'Ἡ Μονὴ Βατοπεδίου καὶ ἡ Σερβία στὸν IE' αἰώνα', in *The Monastery of Vatopedi: history and art* [Ἀθωνικὰ Σύμμεικτα 7] (Athens: Institute for Byzantine Research, 1999), 87–96

Sklavenites, T. E., 'Ἡ βιβλιοθήκη τῶν ἐντύπων τῆς Μονῆς Μεγίστης Λαύρας τοῦ Ἄθω', *Μνήμων* II (1987), 83–121

Smolitsch, I., 'Le Mont Athos et la Russie', *Millénaire du Mont Athos* (see general bibliography), I, 279–318

Smyrlis, C., 'The management of the monastic estates: the evidence of the typika', *DOP* 56 (2002), 245–61

Smyrnakes, G., Τὸ Ἅγιον Ὄρος (Athens: Hetaireia 'Hellenismos', 1903)

Wittek, Paul, 'Zu einigen frühosmanischen Urkunden (VI)', *Wiener Zeitschrift für die Kunde des Morgenlandes* 58 (1962), 165–97

Zachariadou, E. A., 'Early Ottoman documents of the Prodromos Monastery', *Südost-Forschungen* 28 (1969), 1–12

'The worrisome wealth of the Čelnik Radić', in *Studies in Ottoman history in honour of Professor V. L. Ménage*, ed. C. Heywood and C. Imber (Istanbul: Isis Press, 1994), 383–97

'A safe and holy mountain: early Ottoman Athos', in *Mount Athos and Byzantine monasticism* [see general bibliography], 127–32

'Some remarks about dedications to monasteries in the late 14th century', in *Mount Athos in the 14th–16th centuries* [Ἀθωνικὰ Σύμμεικτα 4] (Athens: Institute for Byzantine Research, 1997), 27–31

'Monks and sailors under the Ottoman sultans', in *The Ottomans and the sea*, ed. Kate Fleet [= *Oriente Moderno* 20 (2001), 140–7]

Živojinović, M., 'The trade of Mount Athos monasteries', *Zbornik Radova Vizantološkog Instituta* 29–30 (1991), 101–16

7 Zachariadou: The Great Church in captivity

I Sources

Apostolopoulos, D. G., Ὁ Ἱερὸς κώδιξ τοῦ Πατριαρχείου Κωνσταντινουπόλεως στὸ Β' μισὸ τοῦ IE' αἰώνα, τὰ μόνα γνωστὰ σπαράγματα (Athens: Centre of Neohellenic Studies, 1992)

Conseils et mémoires de Synadinos prêtre de Serrès en Macédoine (XVIIe siècle), ed. P. Odorico avec la collaboration de S. Asdrachas, T. Karanastassis, K. Kostis and S. Petmézas (Paris: Association Pierre Belon, 1996)

Ecthesis Chronica et Chronicon Athenarum, ed. S. Lampros (London: Methuen, 1902)

Historia Politica et Patriarchica Constantinopoleos, ed. I. Bekker (Bonn: Ed. Weber, 1849)

Manoussacas, M., *Lettere Patriarcali inedite (1547–1806)* (Venice: Istituto ellenico di studi bizantini e postbizantini, 1968)

Patrineles, C. G., Ὁ Θεόδωρος Ἀγαλλιανὸς ταυτιζόμενος πρὸς τὸν Θεοφάνην Μηδείας καὶ οἱ ἀνέκδοτοι λόγοι του (Athens: Academy of Athens, 1966)

Zachariadou, Elizabeth A., Δέκα τουρκικά ἔγγραφα γιά τή Μεγάλη Ἐκκλησία
(1483–1567) [Sources 2] (Athens: Institute for Byzantine Research, 1966; reissued
1996)

2 Secondary works

Bosworth, C. E., 'Christians and Jewish religious dignitaries in Mamlûk Egypt and Syria:
Qalqashandi's information on their hierarchy, titulature and appointment', *Interna-
tional Journal of Middle East Studies* 3 (1972), 59–74, 199–216
Braude, B., 'Foundation myths in the millet system', in *Christians and Jews in the Ottoman
Empire* (see general bibliography), I, 69–88
Cacouros, M., 'Un Patriarche à Rome, un *katholikos didaskalos* au Patriarcat et deux dona-
tions très tardives de reliques du seigneur: Grégoire III Mamas et Georges Scholarios,
le synode et la synaxis', in Βυζάντιο (see general bibliography), 71–124
De Gregorio, G., 'Costantinopoli – Tubinga – Roma, ovvero la "duplice conversione" di un
manoscritto bizantino (vat.gr.738)', *BZ* 93 (2000), 37–107
Hannick, C. and Todt, K. P., 'Jeremy II', in *Théologie byzantine et sa tradition* (see general
bibliography), II, 551–615
Herman, E., 'Das bischöfliche Abgabenwesen im Patriarchat von Konstantinopel von XI.
bis zur Mitte des XIX. Jahrhunderts', *OCP* 5 (1939), 434–513
Inalcik, Halil, 'Islam in the Ottoman Empire', *Cultura Turcica* 5–7 (1968–70), 19–29
    'The policy of Mehmed II toward the Greek population of Istanbul and the Byzantine
    buildings of the city', *DOP* 23/24 (1969), 231–49
    'Impact of the *Annales* school on Ottoman studies and new findings', *Review* 1 (1978),
    69–99
    'Ottoman archival materials on millets', in *Christians and Jews in the Ottoman Empire* (see
    general bibliography), I, 437–49
    'The status of the Greek Orthodox Patriarch under the Ottomans', *Turcica (Mélanges
    offerts à Irène Mélikoff par ses collègues, disciples et amis)* 21–23 (1991), 407–36
Konortas, P., 'Les contributions ecclésiastiques: Patriarchikè Zèteia et Basilikon Charatzion,
    contribution à l'histoire économique du patriarcat oecuménique aux XVe et XVIe
    siècles', *Actes du IIe Colloque international d'histoire, économies méditerranéennes: équilibres
    et intercommunications, XIIIe–XIXe siècles* (Athens: Centre of Neohellenic Studies, 1986),
    III, 219–55
    Ὀθωμανικές θεωρήσεις γιά τό Οἰκουμενικό Πατριαρχεῖο, 1705 – ἀρχές 20ου αἰώνα
    (Athens: Alexandreia, 1998)
Laurent, Vitalien, 'Les premiers patriarches de Constantinople sous domination turque',
    REB 26 (1968), 229–63
Legrand, E., 'Notice biographique sur Jean et Théodose Zygomalas', *Recueil de textes et de
    traductions publié par les Professeurs de l'École des langues orientales vivantes à l'occasion du
    VIIIe Congrès international des orientalistes tenu à Stockholm en 1889* (Paris: Imprimerie
    nationale, 1889), 67–264
Lilienfeld, F. von and Bryner, E., 'Die autokephale Metropolie von Moskau und ganz
    Russland (1448–1589)', in *Die orthodoxe Kirche in Russland: Dokumente ihrer Geschichte
    (860–1980)*, ed. P. Hauptmann and G. Stricker (Göttingen: Vandenhoeck und Ruprecht,
    1988), 225–369

Païzi-Apostolopoulou, Machi, Ὁ θεσμὸς τῆς πατριαρχικῆς ἐξαρχίας, 1405–1905 αἰώνας (Athens: Centre of Neohellenic Studies, 1995)

Papagianni, Eleutheria S., Τὰ οἰκονομικὰ τοῦ ἔγγαμου κλήρου στὸ Βυζάντιο (Athens: A. N. Sakkoulas, 1986)

Patrineles, C. G., 'The exact time of the first attempt of the Turks to seize the churches and convert the Christian people of Constantinople to Islam', in Actes du 1er Congrès international des études balkaniques et sud-est européennes (Sofia: Academie bulgare des sciences, 1969), III, 567–72

Stathi, Penelope, Ἀλλαξοπατριαρχείες στὸν θρόνο τῆς Κωνσταντινούπολης (1705–1805 αἰ.)', Μεσαιωνικὰ καὶ Νέα Ἑλληνικά 7 (2004), 37–66

Swanson, Mark N., 'The martyrdom of Abd al-Masih, superior of Mount Sinai (Qays al-Ghassani)', in Syrian Christians under Islam: the first thousand years, ed. D. Thomas (Leiden: Brill, 2001), 106–29

Turner, C. J. G., 'The career of George-Gennadius Scholarius', B 39 (1969), 420–55

Yerasimos, S., ''Ελληνες τῆς Κωνσταντινούπολης στὰ μέσα τοῦ IΣΤ' αἰώνα', Ἡ καθ' ἡμᾶς Ἀνατολή 2 (1994), 117–38

Zachariadou, Elizabeth A., 'The Neomartyr's message', Bulletin of the Centre for Asia Minor Studies 8 (1990–91), 51–63

'Τὰ λόγια καὶ ὁ θάνατος τοῦ Λουκὰ Νοταρά', in Ροδωνιά, Τιμή στὸν Μ. Ι. Μανούσακα (Rethymno: University of Crete, 1994), I, 135–46

'Les notables laïques et le patriarcat oecuménique après la chute de Constantinople', Turcica 30 (1998), 119–34

'La chute de Constantinople et la mythologie postérieure', in Turcica et Islamica: studi in memoria di Aldo Gallotta, ed. U. Marazzi (Naples: Università degli studi di Napoli 'L'Orientale', 2003), II, 1013–31

'Βίοι νεοτέρων ἁγίων: ἡ ἐπαγρύπνηση γιὰ τὸ ποίμνιο', in The heroes of the Orthodox Church: the new saints, 8th–16th centuries, ed. E. Kountoura-Galake [International Symposium 15] (Athens: Institute for Byzantine Research, 2004), 215–25

'Constantinople se repeuple', in 1453. Ἡ ἅλωση τῆς Κωνσταντινούπολης καὶ ἡ μετάβαση ἀπὸ τοὺς μεσαιωνικοὺς στοὺς νεώτερους χρόνους (Heraklion: Panepistimiakes Ekdoseis Kretes, 2005), 47–59

8 Kitromilides: Orthodoxy and the west: Reformation to Enlightenment

1 Sources

Acts and Decrees of the Synod of Jerusalem, ed. J. N. W. B. Robertson (London: Thomas Baker, 1899)

Crusius, Martinus, Turcograeciae libri octo (Basel: Per L. Ostenium, S. Henricpetri impensis, 1584; repr. Modena: Memor, 1972)

[Pseudo] Dorotheos of Monemvasia, Βιβλίον Ἱστορικόν (Venice: Nikolaos Glykys, 1743)

Gedeon, Manuel, Κανονικαὶ Διατάξεις (Constantinople: The Patriarchal Press, 1888)

Kallioupolitis, Maximos, Ἡ Καινὴ Διαθήκη τοῦ Κυρίου ἡμῶν Ἰησοῦ Χριστοῦ, ed. E. C. Kasdaglis, 3 vols. (Athens: Cultural Foundation of the National Bank of Greece, 1995–99)

Karmiris, Ioannis, Τὰ δογματικὰ καί συμβολικὰ μνημεῖα τῆς Ὀρθόδοξου Καθολικῆς Ἐκκλησίας, 2 vols. (Athens: [s. n.], 1953)

Mastrantonis, George, *Augsburg and Constantinople: the correspondence between the Tübingen theologians and Patriarch Jeremiah II of Constantinople on the Augsburg Confession* (Brookline, MA: Holy Cross Orthodox Press, 1982)

Maurocordato, A., *Pneumaticum instrumentum circulandi sanguinis sive de motu et usu pulmonum*, ed. Lorenzo Guerrieri (Florence: L. S. Olschki, 1965)

Overbeck, J. J. *The Orthodox Confession of the Catholic and Apostolic Eastern Church* (London: Thomas Baker, 1898)

Παράλληλον Φιλοσοφίας και χριστιανισμοῦ (Constantinople, 1830)

Rycaut, Paul, *The history of the Turkish Empire from the year 1623 to the year 1677* (London: Thos. Basset, R. Clavell, J. Robinson and A. Churchill, 1687)

2   Secondary works

Augliera, Letterio, *Libri, politica, religione nel Levante del Seicento: la tipografia di Nicodemo Metaxas, primo editore di testi greci nell' oriente ortodosso* (Venice: Istituto Veneto, 1996)

Clogg, Richard, 'The Dhidhaskalia Patriki (1798): an Orthodox reaction to French revolutionary propaganda', *Middle Eastern Studies* 5 (1969), 87–115

'Anticlericalism in pre-Independence Greece', in *The Orthodox Churches and the West*, ed. D. Baker (Oxford: Blackwell, 1976), 257–76

Davey, Colin, *Pioneer for unity: Metrophanes Kritopoulos (1589–1639) and relations between the Orthodox, Roman Catholic and reformed churches* (London: The British Council of Churches, 1987)

'Cyril Loukaris and his Orthodox confession of faith', *Sobornost* 22 (2000), 19–29

Frazee, Charles A., *Catholics and sultans: the Church and the Ottoman Empire 1453–1923* (Cambridge: Cambridge University Press, 1983)

Gedeon, Manuel, Χρονικὰ τῆς Πατριαρχικῆς Ἀκαδημίας (Constantinople: Patriarchal Press, 1883)

Ἡ πνευματικὴ κίνησις τοῦ γένους, ed. A. Angelou and P. Iliou (Athens: Ermis, 1976)

Hadjiantoniou, George A., *Protestant Patriarch: the life of Cyril Lucaris (1572–1638) Patriarch of Constantinople* (London: Epworth Press, 1961)

Henderson, George P., *The revival of Greek thought 1620–1821* (Albany, NY: State University of New York Press, 1970)

Hering, Gunnar, *Ökumenisches Patriarchat und europäische Politik 1620–1638* (Wiesbaden: F. Steiner Verlag, 1968)

'Orthodoxie und Protestantismus', *Jahrbuch der Österreichischen Byzantinistik* 31/32 (1981), 823–74

Huber, Paul, *Apokalypse: Bilderzyklen zur Johannes-Offenbarung in Trier, auf dem Athos und von Caillaud d'Angers* (Düsseldorf: Patmos Verlag, 1989)

Karmiris, Ioannis N., Ὀρθοδοξία καί Προτεσταντισμός (Athens: A. Z. Dialismas, 1937)

Περί τὸ πρόβλημα τῆς λεγόμενης "Λουκαρείου" Ὁμολογίας', Θεολογία 56 (1985), 675–93

Kitromilides, Paschalis M., 'Athos and the Enlightenment', in *Mount Athos and Byzantine monasticism* (see general bibliography), 257–72

The Enlightenment as social criticism: Iosipos Moisiodax and Greek culture in the eighteenth century (Princeton: Princeton University Press, 1992)

Νεοελληνικὸς Διαφωτισμός, third edition (Athens: Cultural Foundation of the National Bank of Greece, 2000)

Κυπριακὴ Λογιοσύνη, 1571–1878: προσωπογραφικὴ θεώρηση [Texts and Studies of the History of Cyprus 43] (Nicosia: Kentro Epistemonikon Ereunon, 2002)

'An Enlightenment perspective on Balkan cultural pluralism. The republican vision of Rhigas Velestinlis', *History of Political Thought* 24 (2003), 465–79

Layton, Evro, 'Nikodemos Metaxas, the first Greek printer in the Eastern world', *Harvard Library Bulletin* 15 (1967), 140–68

Legrand, Émile, *Bibliographie hellénique [. . .] dix-septième siècle*, IV (1896) (see general bibliography)

Makridis, V., *Die religiöse Kritik am Kopernikanischen Weltbild in Griechenland zwischen 1794 und 1821* (Frankfurt am Main: Peter Lang, 1995)

Manousakas, M. I. 'Νέα στοιχεῖα γιὰ τὴν πρώτη μετάφραση τῆς Καινῆς Διαθήκης στὴ δημοτικὴ γλώσσα ἀπὸ τὸν Μάξιμο Καλλιουπολίτη', *Μεσαιωνικὰ καὶ Νέα Ἑλληνικά* 2 (1986), 7–70

Papadopoulos, Chrysostomos, *Ἱστορία τῆς Ἐκκλησίας Ἱεροσολυμῶν*, second edition (Athens: [s.n.], 1970)

Ἱστορία τῆς Ἐκκλησίας Ἀλεξανδρείας (62–1934), second edition (Athens: Patriarchate of Alexandria, 1985)

Tabaki, Anna, 'Lumières et critique des églises au XVIIIe siècle: le cas grec', in *Les Lumières et leur combat: la critique de la religion et des églises à l'époque des Lumières*, ed. by J. Mondot (Berlin: BWV, 2004), 245–58

Therianos, D., *Ἀδαμαντίος Κοραῆς*, 3 vols. (Trieste: Austrohungarian Lloyd, 1889–90)

Tsirpanlis, Z. N., *Τὸ ἑλληνικὸ κολλέγιο τῆς Ρώμης καὶ οἱ μαθητές του 1576–1700* (Thessalonike: Patriarchal Institute for Patristic Studies, 1980)

Ware, Timothy, *Eustratios Argenti: a study of the Greek Church under Turkish rule* (Oxford: Clarendon Press, 1964)

'Orthodox and Catholics in the seventeenth century: schism or intercommunion?', in *Schism, heresy and religious protest*, ed. D. Baker (Cambridge: Cambridge University Press, 1972), 259–76

Zaharopoulos, N. G., *Γρηγόριος Ε′. Σαφὴς ἔκφρασις τῆς ἐκκλησιαστικῆς πολιτικῆς ἐπὶ Τουρκοκρατίας* (Thessalonike: privately printed, 1974)

10   Kitromilides: The legacy of the French Revolution

1   Sources

Drama of quality: selected essays by Zisimos Lorenzatos, trans. L. Sherrard (Limni, Euboia: Denise Harvey, 2000)

Gedeon, Manuel, *Ἔγγραφα πατριαρχικὰ καὶ συνοδικὰ περὶ τοῦ Βουλγαρικοῦ ζητήματος (1852–1873)* (Constantinople: Patriarchal Press, 1908)

Korais, Adamantios, *Ἀριστοτέλους Πολιτικῶν τὰ σωζόμενα* [Hellenike Bibliotheke 13] (Paris: F. Didot, 1821)

Memoirs of Prota Matija Nenadović, trans. L. F. Edwards (Oxford: Clarendon Press, 1969)

2   Secondary works

Christopoulos, Maximos (Metropolitan of Sardis), *The oecumenical patriarchate in the Orthodox Church* (Thessalonike: Patriarchal Institute for Patristic Studies, 1976)

Englezakis, Benedict, *Studies on the history of the Church of Cyprus 4th–20th centuries* (Aldershot: Variorum, 1995)

Frazee, Charles A., *The Orthodox Church and independent Greece 1821–1852* (Cambridge: Cambridge University Press, 1969)

Hitchins, Keith, *Orthodoxy and nationality: Andreiu Saguna and the Rumanians of Transylvania, 1846–1873* (Cambridge, MA: Harvard University Press, 1977)

The identity of Romania (Bucharest: The Encyclopedic Publishing House, 2003)

Hopwood, Derek, *The Russian presence in Syria and Palestine 1843–1914: church and politics in the Near East* (Oxford: Oxford University Press, 1969)

Iorga, Nicolae, *Istoria Bisericii Românești și a vieții religioase a Românilor*, 2 vols., second edition (Bucharest: Ministry of Religions, 1928)

Jelavich, Charles, 'Some aspects of Serbian religious development in the eighteenth century', *Church History* 23 (1954), 144–52

Kedourie, Elie, *The Chatham House version and other Middle-Eastern studies*, new edition (Hanover and London: University Press of New England, 1984)

Kiril, Patriarch of the Bulgarians, *Bulgarskata Ekzarchija v Odrinsko i Makedonija sled osvoboditelnata vojna*, 2 vols. (Sofia: Sinodalno izd-vo, 1969–70)

Bulgarskoto naselenie v Makedonija i borbata za suzdavane na ekzarchijata (Sofia: Sinodalno izd-vo, 1971)

Kitromilides, Paschalis M., 'Imagined communities and the origins of the national question in the Balkans', *European History Quarterly* 19 (1989), 149–92

Enlightenment, nationalism, Orthodoxy: studies in the culture and political thought of southeastern Europe (Aldershot: Variorum, 1994)

'Balkan mentality. History, legend, imagination', *Nations and nationalism* 2 (1996), 163–91

Konstantinides, Emmanuel I., *Ἡ ἐν Ἑλλάδι Ἐκκλησία κατὰ τὴν ἐπανάστασιν καὶ τὴν μέχρι τῆς ἀφίξεως τοῦ Ὄθονος μεταβατικὴν ἐποχήν (1821–1833)* (Athens: [s.n.], 1970)

Ἰωάννης Καποδίστριας καὶ ἡ ἐκκλησιαστικὴ τοῦ πολιτική, fifth edition (Athens: A. Papanikolaou, 2001)

Kophos, Evangelos, 'Attempts at mending the Greek–Bulgarian ecclesiastical schism (1875–1902)', *Balkan Studies* 25 (1984), 1–29

'Patriarch Joachim III (1878–1884) and the irredentist policy of the Greek state', *Journal of Modern Greek Studies* 4 (1986), 107–20

Markova, Zina, *Le mouvement ecclésiastique national jusqu'à la guerre de Crimée* (Sofia: Académie bulgare des sciences, 1976)

Bulgarian Exarchate 1870–1879 (Sofia: Bulgarian Academy of Sciences, 1989)

Meininger, Thomas A., *Ignatiev and the establishment of the Bulgarian Exarchate (1864–1872): a study in personal diplomacy* (Madison: University of Wisconsin Press, 1970)

Metallinos, G. D., *Ἑλλαδικοῦ αὐτοκεφάλου παραλοιπόμενα* (Athens: Domos, 1989)

Mousset, Albert, *Le royaume des Serbes, Croates et Slovènes* (Paris: Éditions Bossard, 1921)

Mousset, Jean, *La Serbie et son église 1830–1904* (Paris: Droz, 1938)

Nicolaïdou, Eleftheria, *Ἡ Ρουμανικὴ προπαγάνδα στὸ βιλαέτι τῶν Ἰωαννίνων καὶ στὰ βλαχόφωνα χωριὰ τῆς Πίνδου* (Ioannina: Society for Epirot Studies, 1995)

Pacurariu, Mircea, *Istoria Bisericii Ortodoxe Române*, III (Bucharest: [s.n.], 1994); trans. as *Geschichte der rumänischen orthodoxen Kirche* [Oikonomia 33] (Erlangen: Lehrstuhl für Geschichte und Theologie des christlichen Ostens, 1994)

Pavlowitch, Stevan K., *Serbia: the history behind the name* (London: C. Hurst, 2002)

Petropulos, John A., *Politics and statecraft in the kingdom of Greece 1833–1843* (Princeton: Princeton University Press, 1968)

Ware, Kallistos and Ivanov, Gregorii, 'An historic reconciliation: the role of Exarch Stefan', *Sobornost* I (1979), 70–6

General bibliography to Part II: The Russian Church (chapters 11–16)

I Collections of sources, calendars, prosopographies

Early exploration of Russia, ed. M. Poe, 12 vols. (London: Routledge Curzon, 2003)

Fedotov, G. P., *A treasury of Russian spirituality* (London: Sheed and Ward, 1952)

Likhachev, D. S., *Pamiatniki literatury drevnei Rusi. XIII vek* (Moscow: Khudozhestvennaia literatura, 1981)

Polnoe sobranie russkikh letopisei, 25 vols. (St Petersburg: Academiia nauk. Institut istorii, 1841–)

Rossiiskoe zakonodatel'stvo X–XX vekov, ed. O. I. Chistiakova, 9 vols. (Moscow: Iuridicheskaia literatura, 1984–85)

Vernadsky, George, *A source book for Russian history from early times to 1917*, I, *Early times to the late seventeenth century* (New Haven: Yale University Press, 1972)

Zenkovsky, Serge A. (ed. and trans.), *Medieval Russia's epics, chronicles and tales* (New York: E. P. Dutton, 1964)

2 General works

Architectures of Russian identity, 1500 to the present, ed. J. Cracraft and D. Rowland (Ithaca, NY and London: Cornell University Press, 2003)

Art of Holy Russia: icons from Moscow 1400–1660 (London: Royal Academy of Arts, 1998)

Bercken, Wil van den, *Holy Russia and Christian Europe: East and West in the religious ideology of Russia* (London: SCM Press, 1999)

Between tsar and people: educated society and the quest for public identity in late imperial Russia, ed. Edith W. Clowes, Samuel D. Kassow and James L. West (Princeton: Princeton University Press, 1991)

Billington, James, *The icon and the axe* (London: Weidenfeld and Nicolson, 1966)

Brumfield, William C., *A history of Russian architecture* (Cambridge: Cambridge University Press, 1993)

Brumfield, William C. and Velimirović, Milos M., *Christianity and the arts in Russia* (Cambridge: Cambridge University Press, 1991)

Bushkovitch, Paul, *Religion and society in Russia: the sixteenth and seventeenth centuries* (Oxford: Oxford University Press, 1992)

Christianity and the Eastern Slavs, I, *Slavic cultures in the Middle Ages*, ed. B. Gasparov and O. Ravevsky-Hughes [California Slavic Studies 16] (Berkeley: University of California Press, 1993)

Christianity and the Eastern Slavs, II, *Russian culture in modern times*, ed. Robert P. Hughes and Irina Paperno [California Slavic Studies 17] (Berkeley: University of California Press, 1994)

Chulos, C. J., *Converging worlds: religion and community in peasant Russia, 1861–1917* (DeKalb: Northern Illinois University Press, 2003)

Church, nation and state in Russia and Ukraine, ed. Geoffrey Hosking (New York: St Martin's Press, 1991)

Cracraft, James, *The church reform of Peter the Great* (Stanford: Stanford University Press, 1971)

The Petrine revolution in Russian imagery (Chicago: University of Chicago Press, 1997)

Crummey, Robert O., *The Old Believers & the world of Antichrist: the Vyg community and the Russian state, 1694–1855* (Madison: University of Wisconsin Press, 1970)

The formation of Muscovy, 1304–1613 (London and New York: Longman, 1987)

Culture and identity in Muscovy, 1359–1584, ed. A. M. Kleimola and G. D. Lenhoff (Moscow: ITZ-Garant, 1997)

Dixon, Simon, 'The Orthodox church and the workers of St. Petersburg, 1880–1914', in *European religion in the age of great cities, 1830–1930*, ed. Hugh McLeod (New York: Routledge, 1995), 19–45

Drevnerusskoe iskusstvo. XIV–XVI vv., ed. O. I. Podobedova (Moscow: Nauka, 1984)

Fedotov, George P., *The Russian religious mind*, II, *The Middle Ages; the thirteenth to the fifteenth centuries* (Cambridge, MA: Harvard University Press, 1966)

Fennell, J. L. I., *Ivan the Great of Moscow* (London: Macmillan, 1961)

A history of the Russian Church to 1448 (London: Longman, 1995)

Firsov, S. L., *Pravoslavnaia tserkov' i gosudarstvo v poslednee desiatiletie sushchestvovaniia samoderzhaviia v Rossii* (St Petersburg: Izd-vo russkogo khristianskogo gumanitarnogo instituta, 1996)

Russkaia tserkov' nakanune peremen (konets 1890-kh–1918 gg.) (Moscow: Dukhovnaia literatura, 2002)

Flier, Michael S., 'Breaking the code: the image of the tsar in the Muscovite Palm Sunday ritual', in *Medieval Russian culture*, II (q.v. below), 213–42

Freeze, Gregory L., *The Russian Levites: parish clergy in the eighteenth-century* (Cambridge, MA: Harvard University Press, 1977)

The parish clergy in nineteenth-century Russia: crisis, reform, counter-reform (Princeton: Princeton University Press, 1983)

'Handmaiden of the state? The Orthodox church in imperial Russia reconsidered', *JEcclH* 86 (1985), 82–102

'Subversive piety: religion and the political crisis in late imperial Russia', *Journal of Modern History* 68 (1996), 308–50

Gates of mystery: the art of Holy Russia, ed. R. Grierson (Fort Worth, TX: InterCultura, 1992)

Golubinskii, E., *Istoriia russkoi tserkvi: period vtoroi, Moskovskii*, II, parts 1 and 2 [Slavistic Printings and Reprintings 117/3 and 4] (The Hague: Mouton, 1969); reprint of Moscow, 1900 edition

Halperin, Charles J., *Russia and the Golden Horde: the Mongol impact on medieval Russian history* (Bloomington: Indiana University Press, 1987)

Hamilton, George H., *The art and architecture of Russia* (London: Thames and Hudson, 1983)

Hosking, Geoffrey: *Russia, people and empire, 1552–1917* (London: HarperCollins, 1997)

Hughes, Lindsey, *Russia in the age of Peter the Great* (New Haven and London: Yale University Press, 1998)

Introduction to Russian art and architecture, ed. R. Auty and D. Obolensky [Companion to Russian Studies 3] (Cambridge: Cambridge University Press, 1980)

Kizenko, Nadieszda, *A prodigal saint: Father John of Kronstadt and the Russian people* (University Park: Pennsylvania State University Press, 2000)

Likhachev, D. S., *Kul'tura Rusi vremeni Andreia Rubleva i Epifaniia Premudrogo* (Moscow: AN SSSR, 1962)

Makarii (Bulgakov), Metropolitan, *Istoriia russkoi tserkvi v period postepennogo perekhoda ee k samostoiatel'nosti (1240–1448)* [Istoriia russkoi tserkvi 3] (Moscow: Izd. Spaso-Preobrazhenskogo Valaamskogo Monastyria, 1995)

Istoriia russkoi tserkvi v period postepennogo perekhoda ee k samostoiatel'nosti (1240–1589) [Istoriia russkoi tserkvi 4] (Moscow: Izd. Spaso-Preobrazhenskogo Valaamskogo Monastyria, 1996)

Martin, Janet, *Medieval Russia 980–1584* (Cambridge: Cambridge University Press, 1995)

Medieval Russian culture, [I], ed. H. Birnbaum and M. S. Flier [California Slavic Studies 12] (Berkeley: University of California Press, 1984)

Medieval Russian culture, II, ed. M. S. Flier and D. Rowland [California Slavic Studies 19] (Berkeley: University of California Press, 1994)

Milner-Gulland, Robin, *The Russians* (Oxford: Blackwell, 1997)

Nikol'skii, N. M., *Istorii russkoi tserkvi* (Moscow: Izd. Polit. Literatury, 1983)

Obolensky, Dimitri, *The Byzantine Commonwealth: Eastern Europe, 500–1453* (London: Weidenfeld and Nicolson, 1971)

Byzantium and the Slavs (London: Variorum, 1971)

The Byzantine inheritance of Eastern Europe (London: Variorum, 1982)

Of religion and empire: missions, conversion, and tolerance in tsarist Russia, ed. R. P. Geraci and M. Khodarkovsky (Ithaca and London: Cornell University Press, 2001)

Orthodoxe Kirche in Russland: Dokumente ihrer Geschichte (860–1980), ed. P. Hauptmann and G. Stricker (Göttingen: Vandenhoeck and Ruprecht, 1988)

Orthodox Russia: belief and practice under the tsars, ed. V. A. Kivelson and R. H. Greene (University Park: Pennsylvania State University Press, 2003)

Pavlov, A. P. and Perrie, Maureen, *Ivan the Terrible* (London: Pearson/Longman, 2003)

Poe, Marshall, *A people born to slavery: Russia in early modern European ethnography, 1476–1748* (Ithaca, NY: Cornell University Press, 2000)

Pospielovsky, Dimitry, *The Orthodox Church in the history of Russia* (Crestwood, NY: St Vladimir's Seminary Press, 1998)

Pravoslavie i russkaia narodnaia kul'tura, ed. M. M. Gromyko, 4 vols. (Moscow: Koordinatsionno-metodicheskii tsentr prikladnoi etnografii In-ta etnologii i antropologii RAN, 1993–94)

Pushkareva, Natalia, *Women in Russian history from the tenth to the twentieth century* (Armonk, NY: M. E. Sharpe, 1997)

Riasanovsky, Nicholas V., *Nicholas I and official nationality in Russia, 1825–1855* (Berkeley: University of California Press, 1959)

The image of Peter the Great in Russian history and thought (New York: Oxford University Press, 1985)

Russian Orthodoxy under the old regime, ed. R. L. Nichols and T. G. Stavrou (Minneapolis: University of Minnesota Press, 1978)

Seeking God: the recovery of religious identity in Orthodox Russia, Ukraine and Georgia, ed. S. K. Batalden (DeKalb: Northern Illinois University Press, 1993)

Shevzov, Vera, *Russian Orthodoxy on the eve of revolution* (New York: Oxford University Press, 2004)

Slovar' knizhnikov i knizhnosti Drevnei Rusi: Vyp. 2 (vtoraia polovina XIV–XVI v.), ed. D. S. Likhachev (Leningrad: Nauka, 1989)

Smolitsch, Igor, *Russisches Mönchtum: Entstehung, Entwicklung und Wesen, 988–1917* [Das östliche Christentum, n.F., Heft 10/11] (Würzburg: Augustinus-Verlag, 1953)

Die Geschichte der russischen Kirche, 1700–1917 [I Studien zur Geschichte Osteuropas 9; II Forschungen zur osteuropäischen Geschichte 45], 2 vols. (Leiden: E. J. Brill, 1964–91)

Stavrou, T. G. and Weisensel, P. R., *Russian travelers to the Christian East from the twelfth to the twentieth century* (Columbus, OH: Slavica, 1986)

Walicki, Andrzej, *A history of Russian thought* (Stanford: Stanford University Press, 1979)

Wortman, Richard, *Scenarios of power: myth and ceremony in Russian monarchy*, 2 vols. (Princeton: Princeton University Press, 1995–2000)

Zguta, Russell, *Russian minstrels: a history of the Skomorokhi* (Philadelphia: University of Pennsylvania Press, 1978)

Zinkewych, Osyp and Sorokowski, Andrew, *A thousand years of Christianity in Ukraine: an encyclopedic chronology* (New York: Smoloskyp Publishers, 1988)

11   Rock: Russian piety and Orthodox culture

1   Sources

Berry, L. E. and Crummey, R. O., *Rude and barbarous kingdom: Russia in the accounts of sixteenth-century English voyagers* (Madison: University of Wisconsin Press, 1968)

The Chronicle of Novgorod: 1016–1471, trans. R. Michell and N. Forbes [Camden Society, ser. iii., 25] (London: Offices of the Society, 1914)

Domostroi: rules for Russian households in the time of Ivan the Terrible, ed. and trans. Carolyn Johnston Pouncy (Ithaca, NY: Cornell University Press, 1994)

Emchenko, E. V., *Stoglav: issledovanie i tekst* (Moscow: Indrik, 2000)

Fletcher, Giles, *Of the Russe Common Wealth* (London: Thomas Charde, 1591), reprinted in *Early exploration of Russia*, I (see general bibliography)

Goldfrank, David M., *The monastic rule of Iosif Volotsky* [Cistercian Studies Series 36] (Kalamazoo, MI: Cistercian Publications, 1983)

Herberstein, Sigismund von, *Moscovia der Haupstadt* (Vienna: Michael Zimmerman, 1557), reprinted in *Early exploration of Russia*, II (see general bibliography)

Jakobson, Roman and Worth, Dean S. (eds.), *Sofonija's tale of the Russian–Tatar battle on the Kulikovo Field* [Slavistic Printings and Reprintings 51] (The Hague: Mouton, 1963)

Kazakova, N. A. and Lur'e, I. S., *Antifeodal'nye ereticheskie dvizheniia na Rusi XIV–nachala XVI veka* (Moscow: AN SSSR, 1955)

Klimenko, Michael, *The 'Vita' of St Sergii of Radonezh* (Houston, TX: Nordland, 1980)

Makarii, Saint, Metropolitan of Moscow and All Russia, *Velikiia Minei Chetii*, 19 vols. (St Petersburg: Tip. Imp. akademii nauk, 1868–1915)

Malinin, V. N., *Starets' Eleazarova monastyria Filofei i ego poslaniia* (Kiev: Tipografiia Kievo-Pecherskoi Uspenskoi Lavry, 1901)

Nil Sorsky: the complete writings, ed. and trans. George A. Maloney (New York: Paulist Press, 2003)

Possevino, Antonio, *The Moscovia of Antonio Possevino, S.J.*, trans. Hugh F. Graham [UCIS Series in Russian and East European Studies 1] (Pittsburgh, PA: University of Pittsburgh, 1977)

Russia at the close of the sixteenth century. Comprising the Treatise 'Of the Russe Common Wealth' by Dr Giles Fletcher; and 'A Relacion or memoriall abstracted owt of Sir Jerome Horsey his travells, imploiments, services and negociacions, observed and written with his owne hand; wherein he spent the most part of eighteen years tyme', ed. Edward A. Bond [Hakluyt Society 20] (London: Hakluyt Society, 1856; reprinted, New York: Burt Franklin, 1963)

Volotskii, Iosif, *Prosvetitel', ili, Oblichenie eresi zhidovstvuiushchikh*, fourth edition (Kazan: Imperatorskii Universitet, 1903; reprinted Farnborough: Gregg, 1972)

'The voyage of Richard Chanceller Pilote major, the first discoverer by sea of the kingdome of Moscovia, Anno 1553', in Richard Hakluyt, *The principal navigations, voyages, traffiques and discoveries of the English nation*, 8 vols. (London: J. M. Dent and Sons, 1927), 1

Weiher, Eckhard, Shmidt, S. O. and Shkurko, A. I., *Die grossen Lesemenäen des Metropoliten Makarij: Uspenskij spisok. Velikie Minei Chet'i mitropolita Makariia: Uspenskii spisok* [Monumenta linguae Slavicae dialecti veteris 39, 41 and 45] (Freiburg im Breisgau: Weiher, 1997–2001) (published text for the month of March only)

Zernov, Nicholas, *St Sergius, builder of Russia, with the life, acts, and miracles of the holy abbot Sergius of Radonezh* (London: SPCK, 1939)

Zhitie sviatogo Stefana episkopa Permskogo, napissanoe Epifaniem Premudrym, ed. V. G. Druzhinin (St Petersburg: Arkheograficheskaia Kommissia, 1897; reprinted The Hague: Mouton, 1959)

2   Secondary works

Andreyev, N., 'Filofey and his Epistle to Ivan Vasil'yevich', *Slavonic and East European Review* 38 (1959), 1–31

Billington, James H., 'Images of Muscovy', *Slavic Review* 21 (1962), 24–34

Birnbaum, Henrik, 'On the significance of the second South Slavic influence for the evolution of the Russian literary language', *International Journal of Slavic Linguistics and Poetics* 21 (1975), 23–50

Bogatyrev, Sergei, 'Battle for divine wisdom: the rhetoric of Ivan IV's campaign against Polotsk', in *The military and society in Russia, 1450–1917*, ed. E. Lohr and M. Poe (Leiden: Brill, 2002), 325–63

Bolshakoff, Sergius, *Russian mystics* [Cistercian Studies Series 26] (Kalamazoo, MI: Cistercian Publications, 1980)

Bosley, Richard D., 'The changing profile of the liturgical calendar in Muscovy's formative years', in *Culture and identity in Muscovy, 1359–1584* (see general bibliography), 26–38

Budovnits, I. U., *Monastyri na Rusi i bor'ba s nimi krest'ian v 14–16 vekakh (po 'zhitiiam sviatykh')* (Moscow: Nauka, 1966)

Bushkovitch, Paul, 'The formation of a national consciousness in early modern Russia', *Harvard Ukrainian Studies* 10.3/4 (1986), 355–76

'The limits of hesychasm: some notes on monastic spirituality in Russia 1350–1500', *Forschungen zur Osteuropäischen Geschichte* 38 (1986), 97–109

Fennell, J. L. I., 'The attitude of the Josephians and the Trans-Volga Elders to the heresy of the Judaisers', *Slavonic Review* 29 (1950–51), 486–509

Flier, Michael S., 'Till the end of time: the Apocalypse in Russian historical experience before 1500', in *Orthodox Russia: belief and practice under the tsars* (see general bibliography), 127–58

Florovsky, Georges, 'The problem of Old Russian culture', *Slavic Review* 21 (1962), 1–15

Hackel, Sergei, 'Late medieval Russia: the possessors and non-possessors', in *Christian spirituality: high middle ages and Reformation*, ed. J. Raitt (London: SCM Press, 1989), 223–35

Haney, Jack V., *From Italy to Muscovy: the life and works of Maxim the Greek* (Munich: Wilhelm Fink Verlag, 1973)

Hébert, Maurice LaBauve, *Hesychasm, word-weaving, and Slavic hagiography: the literary school of Patriarch Euthymius* (Munich: Verlag Otto Sagner, 1992)

Hunt, Priscilla, 'Ivan IV's personal mythology of kingship', *Slavic Review* 52 (1993), 769–809

Huttenbach, Henry R., 'The Judaizer heresy and the origins of Muscovite anti-semitism', *Studies in Medieval Culture* 4 (1970–71), 496–506

Klier, John D., 'Judaizing without Jews? Moscow–Novgorod, 1470–1504', in *Culture and identity in Muscovy, 1359–1584* (see general bibliography), 336–49

Kolycheva, E. I., 'Pravoslavnye monastyri vtoroi poloviny XV–XVI veka', in *Monashestvo i monastyri v Rossii XI–XX veka*, ed. N. V. Sinitsyna (Moscow: Nauka, 2002), 81–115

Levin, Eve, 'Dvoeverie and popular religion', in *Seeking God: the recovery of religious identity in Orthodox Russia, Ukraine, and Georgia* (see general bibliography), 31–52

'Lay religious identity in medieval Russia: the evidence of Novgorod birchbark documents', *General Linguistics* 35 (1997), 131–55

Likhachev, D. S., *Nekotorye zadachi izucheniia vtorogo iuzhnoslavianskogo vliianiia v Rossii* (Moscow: AN SSSR, 1958)

'Further remarks on the problem of Old Russian culture', *Slavic Review* 22 (1963), 115–20

Luria, Jakov S., 'Unresolved issues in the history of the ideological movements of the late fifteenth century', in *Medieval Russian culture*, [1] (see general bibliography), 150–71

Maloney, George A., *Russian hesychasm: the spirituality of Nil Sorskii* (The Hague: Mouton, 1973)

Meyendorff, John, *Byzantium and the rise of Russia: a study of Byzantino–Russian relations in the fourteenth century* (Cambridge: Cambridge University Press, 1981)

'Is "hesychasm" the right word?', in *Okeanos: essays presented to Ihor Ševčenko on his sixtieth birthday by his colleagues and students* [=*Harvard Ukrainian Studies* 7 (1983)], 447–57

Miller, David B., 'Monumental building as an indicator of economic trends in northern Rus' in the late Kievan and Mongol periods, 1138–1462', *The American Historical Review* 94 (1989), 360–90

'Motives for donations to the Trinity-Sergius monastery, 1392–1605: gender matters', *Essays in Medieval Studies* 14 (1997), 91–106

Milner-Gulland, Robin, 'Russia's lost Renaissance', in *Literature and western civilization*, ed. D. Daiches and A. K. Thorlby (London: Aldus, 1973), III, 435–68

'Art and architecture of Old Russia, 988–1700', *Introduction to Russian art and architecture* (see general bibliography), 1–70

Ostrowski, Donald, 'Church polemics and monastic land acquisition in sixteenth-century Muscovy', *Slavonic and East European Review* 64 (1986), 355–79

Muscovy and the Mongols: cross-cultural influences on the steppe frontier, 1304–1589 (Cambridge: Cambridge University Press, 1998)

Petrovich, Michael, 'The social and political role of the Muscovite Fools-in-Christ: reality and image', *Forschungen zur Osteuropäischen Geschichte* 25 (1978), 283–96

Raba, Joel, 'Moscow – the Third Rome or the New Jerusalem?', *Forschungen zur Osteuropäischen Geschichte* 50 (1995), 297–307

Robson, Roy R., *Solovki: the story of Russia told through its most remarkable islands* (New Haven and London: Yale University Press, 2004)

Rock, Stella, 'What's in a word? A historical study of the concept *Dvoeverie*', *Canadian-American Slavic Studies* 35, no. 1 (2001), 19–28

Romodanovskaia, V. A., 'O tseliakh sozdaniia Gennadievskoi Biblii kak pervogo polnogo russkogo Bibleiskogo kodeksa', in *Knizhnye tsentry Drevnei Rusi: Severnorusskie Monastyri*, ed. S. A. Semiachko (St Petersburg: Dmitrii Bulanin, 2001), 278–305

Rowland, Daniel B., 'Moscow – the Third Rome or the New Israel?', *RR* 55 (1996), 591–614

Skrynnikov, R. G., 'Ecclesiastical thought in Russia and the Church Councils of 1503 and 1504', *Oxford Slavonic Papers* 25 (1992), 34–60

Stremooukhoff, Dimitri, 'Moscow the Third Rome: sources of the doctrine', *Speculum* 28 (1953), 84–101

Thomson, Francis, 'The corpus of Slavonic translations available in Muscovy: the cause of Old Russia's intellectual silence and a contributory factor to Muscovite cultural autarky', in *Christianity and the Eastern Slavs*, I, *Slavic cultures in the Middle Ages* (see general bibliography), 179–214

Thyrêt, Isolde, *Between God and tsar: religious symbolism and the royal women of Muscovite Russia* (De Kalb: Northern Illinois University Press, 2001)

Vlasova, Z. I., *Skomorokhi i fol'klor* (St Petersburg: Aleteiia, 2001)

12   Hughes: Art and liturgy: Rublev and his successors

Secondary works

Abramowa, N., *et al.* (eds.), *Der Kreml: Gottesruhm und Zarenpracht* (Munich: Hirmer, 2004)

Alpatov, M. A., *Drevnerusskaia ikonopis'* (Moscow: Iskusstvo, 1974)

Early Russian icon painting (Moscow: Iskusstvo, 1978)

Feofan Grek (Moscow: Iskusstvo, 1979)

'The icons of Russia', in *The Icon*, ed. K. Weitzmann *et al.* (London: Studio Editions, 1982), 237–52

Antonova, V., 'O pervonachal'nom meste "Troitsy" Andreia Rubleva', *Gos. Tret'iakovskaia Galereia: Materialy i Issledovaniia* 1 (1956), 21–43

Beliankin, A., *Skazanie o zhizni i chudesakh Sviatogo Blazhennago Vasiliia Khrista Radi Iurodivago Moskovskago chudotvortsa* (Moscow, 1884)

Boldyreff Semler, Helen, *Moscow: the complete companion guide* (London: Equator, 1989)

Briusova, V. G., *Andrei Rublev* (Moscow: Izobrazitel'noe iskusstvo, 1995)

Andrei Rublev i moskovskaia shkola zhivopisi (Moscow: Veche, 1998)

Brunov, N. I., *Khram Vasiliia Blazhennogo v Moskve* (Moscow: Iskusstvo, 1988)

Buseva-Davydova, I. L., *Khramy Moskovskogo Kremlia: sviatyni i drevnosti* (Moscow: Nauka, 1997)

Chernyi, V. D., *Iskusstvo srednevekovoi Rusi* (Moscow: Vlasos, 1997)

Chugunov, D., *Dionisii* (Leningrad: Izobrazitel'noe iskusstvo, 1979)

Eliseev, S., 'Rozhdenie sobora', *Vstrechi s istoriei* 2 (1988), 75–91

Etingof, O. E., 'K rannei istorii ikony "Vladimirskaia Bogomater"' i traditsiia Vlakhernskogo Bogorodichnogo kul'ta na Rusi v XI–XII vv.', in *Drevnerusskoe iskusstvo. Vizantiia i drevniaia Rus'. K 100-letiiu Andreia Nikolaevicha Grabara (1896–1990)*, ed. E. S. Smirnova (St Petersburg: Nauka, 1999), 290–305

Gusev, V. A., *Dionisii v Russkom muzee: k 500-letiiu rospisi Rozhdestvenskogo sobora Ferapontova* (St Petersburg: Palace Editions, [2002])

Guseva, E. K., 'Ikony "Donskaia" i "Vladimirskaia" v kopiiakh kontsa XIV-nachala XV v.', in *Drevnerusskoe iskusstvo. XIV–XV vv* (see general bibliography), 46–58

Hughes, Lindsey, 'Inventing Andrei: Soviet and post-Soviet views of Andrei Rublev and his Trinity Icon', *Slavonica* 9 (2003), 83–90

Istoricheskoe opisanie moskovskogo Uspenskogo sobora i ego sviatyni (Moscow: Efimov, 1880)

Kämpfer, Frank, 'Über die Konzeption der Vasilij-Blazennyj-Kathedrale in Moskau', *Jahrbücher für Geschichte Osteuropas* 24 (1976), 481–98

Konchin, E., 'Rublev: novye otkrytiia i starye legendy', *Znanie-sila* 10 (1974), 55–6

Kozlova, I., *Masterpieces of the Tretyakov Gallery* (Moscow: Acropolis, 1994)

Kudriavtsev, M. and Kudriavtseva, T., 'Krasnaia ploshchad' – khram pod otkrytym nebom', *Mera* 3 (1995), 29–39

Kuz'min, N., 'Zhivopis' pereshagnivshaia veka', *Literaturnaia Gazeta*, 15 Sept. 1960, 3

Labrecque-Pervouchine, Nathalie, *L'iconostase: une évolution historique en Russie* (Montreal: Bellarmin, 1982)

Laurina, V., *Novgorod icons, 12th–17th century* (Oxford and Leningrad: Aurora, 1980)

Lazarev, V. N., *Feofan Grek i ego shkola* (Moscow: Iskusstvo, 1961)

  Russian icon: from its origins to the sixteenth century (Collegeville, MN: Liturgical Press, 1997)

Lidov, A. M., 'Ierusalimskii kuvuklii. O proiskhozhdenii lukovichnykh glav', in *Ikonografiia arkhitektury: sbornik nauchnykh trudov*, ed. A. L. Batalov (Moscow: Akademiia khudozhestv, 1990), 57–68

Likhachev, D. S., 'Gradozashchitnaia semantika Uspenskikh khramov na Rusi', in *Uspenskii sobor Moskovskogo Kremlia*, ed. E. S. Smirnova (Moscow: Nauka, 1985), 17–23

Likhachev, N. P., *Manera pis'ma Andreia Rubleva* (St Petersburg: Tip. M. A. Alexandrovna, 1907)

Malitskii, N., 'K istorii kompozitsii vetkhozavetnoi Troitsy', *Seminarium Kondakovianum* 2 (1928), 33–46

Markina, Natalia, 'The iconostasis', in *The art of Holy Russia* (see general bibliography), 69–75

Meyendorff, John, 'The legacy of beauty; liturgy, art, and spirituality in Russia', in *Gates of mystery* (see general bibliography), 37–44

Miller, David, 'The Viskovatyi affair of 1553–54. Official art, the emergence of autocracy, and the disintegration of medieval Russian culture', *RH/HR* 8 (1981), 293–332

Moskva, eia sviatyni i pamiatniki. (Izbrannye stat'i po opisaniiu Moskvy) (St Petersburg: Iablonskii, 1898)

Nikitin, A., 'Kto napisal "Troitsu Rubleva"?', *Nauka i Religiia* 8 (1988), 44–8

Plugin, V. A., 'O proizkhozhdenii "Troitsy" Rubleva', *Istoriia SSSR* 2 (1987), 64–79

   'Andrei Rublev i Ivan Groznyi. O sud'be "Troitsy"', *Nauka i Religiia* 7 (1989), 55–8

   Master Sviatoi Troitsy: trudy i dni Andreia Rubleva (Moscow: 'Mosgorarkhiv', 2001)

Popova, Olga, *Russian illuminated manuscripts* (London and New York: Thames and Hudson, 1984)

   'Medieval Russian painting and Byzantium', in *Gates of mystery* (see general bibliography), 44–59

Priselkov, M. D., *Troitskaia letopis': rekonstruktsiia teksta* (Moscow and Leningrad: Nauka, 1950)

Punin, N. I., *Andrei Rublev* (Petrograd: Apollon, 1916)

Rowland, Daniel, 'Biblical military imagery in the political culture of early modern Russia. The Blessed Host of the Heavenly Tsar', in *Medieval Russian culture*, II (see general bibliography), 182–212

   'Architecture and dynasty: Boris Godunov's uses of architecture, 1584–1606', in *Architectures of Russian identity* (see general bibliography), 34–51

Rozanova, N. V., *Rostovo-suzdal'skaia zhivopis' XII–XVI vekov* (Moscow: Izobrazitel'noe iskusstvo, 1970)

Rybakov, A., *Vologodskaia ikona: tsentry khudozhestvennoi kul'tury zemli Vologodskoi XIII–XVIII vekov* (Moscow: Galart, 1995)

Saltykova, A. A., 'Ikonografiia "Troitsy" Andreia Rubleva', in *Drevnerusskoe iskusstvo. XIV–XV vv* (see general bibliography), 77–85

Smirnova, Engelina, 'Moscow icon painting from the 14th to the 16th century', in *The art of Holy Russia* (see general bibliography), 45–58

   Moscow icons, 14th–17th centuries (Oxford: Phaidon, 1989)

Sokolov-Skalia, P., 'Andrei Rublev', *Nauka i Religiia* 9 (1960), 85–7

Tarasov, Oleg, *Icon and devotion: sacred spaces in imperial Russia* (London: Reaktion, 2002)

Tikhomirov, M. N., 'Andrei Rublev i ego epokha,' *Voprosy Istorii* 1 (1961), 3–15

Uspenskii, Leonid, *Theology of the icon*, 2 vols. (Crestwood, NY: St Vladmir's Seminary Press, 1992)

Vakhrina, V. L., *Ikony Rostova Velikogo* (Moscow: Severnyi palomnik, 2003)

Voloshinov, A. V., *Troitsa Andreia Rubleva: geometriia i filosofiia* (Saratov: Nash Dom, 1997)

Vzdornov, G. I., *Troitsa Andreia Rubleva: antologiia* (Moscow: Iskusstvo, 1981)

   Feofan Grek, Tvorcheskoe nasledie (Moscow: Iskusstvo, 1983)

13   Crummey: Eastern Orthodoxy in Russia and Ukraine in the age of Counter-Reformation

1   Sources

Avvakum, Archpriest, *Archpriest Avvakum, the Life written by himself: with the study of V. V. Vinogradov*, trans. and ed. Kenneth N. Brostrom [Michigan Slavic Translations 4] (Ann Arbor: University of Michigan Press, 1979)

Zhitie protopopa Avvakuma, im samim napisannoe, i drugie ego sochineniia, ed. N. K. Gudzii (Moscow: Goslitizdat, 1960)

'Deianiia Moskovskago tserkovnogo sobora 1649 goda', ed. S. A. Belokurov, *ChOIDR* 171 (1894, book IV), 1–52

Dokumenty Razriadnogo, Posol'skogo, Novgorodskogo i Tainogo Prikazov o raskol'nikakh v gorodakh Rossii, 1654–1684 gg., ed. V. S. Rumiantseva (Moscow: Akademiia nauk SSSR, Institut istorii SSSR, 1990)

Kharuzin, N., 'K voprosu o bor'be moskovskago pravitel'stva s narodnymi iazycheskimi obriadami i sueveriiami v polovine XVII v.', *Etnograficheskoe Obozrenie* 1 (1879), 143–51

Materialy dlia istorii raskola za pervoe vremia ego sushchestvovaniia, ed. N. Subbotin, 9 vols. (Moscow, Redaktsiia 'Bratskago Slova', 1874–90)

Nikon, Patriarch, *Patriarch Nikon on church and state – Nikon's 'Refutation' (Vozrazhenie ili razorenie smirennago Nikona, Bozhieiu milostiiu Patriarkha, protiv voprosov boiarina Simeona Streshneva)*, ed. Valerie A. Tumins and George Vernadsky (Berlin, New York and Amsterdam: Mouton, 1982)

Novosel'skii, A. A., 'Rospis' krest'ianskikh dvorov, nakhodivshikhsia vo vladenii vyshego dukhovenstva, monastyrei i dumnykh liudei po perepisnym knigam 1678 g.', *Istoricheskii Arkhiv* 4 (1949), 88–149

Palmer, William, *The Patriarch and the Tsar*, 6 vols. (London: Trübner and Co., 1871–76)

Rozhdestvenskii, N. V., 'K istorii bor'by s tserkovnymi bezporiadkami, otgoloskami iazychestva i porokami v russkom bytu XVII v.', *ChOIDR* 201 (1902, book II), 1–31

Sobornoe ulozhenie 1649 goda: tekst, kommentarii, ed. L. I. Ivina, G. V. Abramovich *et al.* (Leningrad: Nauka, Leningradskoe otdelenie, 1987)

2   Secondary works

Bogdanov, A. P., *Russkie patriarkhi, 1589–1700*, 2 vols. (Moscow: 'Terra', Izdatel'stvo 'Respublika', 1999)

Dunning, Chester S. L., *Russia's first civil war: the time of troubles and the founding of the Romanov dynasty* (University Park: Pennsylvania State University Press, 2001)

Felmy, Karl Christian, *Die Deutung der Göttlichen Liturgie in der russischen Theologie: Wege und Wandlungen russischer Liturgie-Auslegung* [Arbeiten zur Kirchengeschichte 54] (Berlin and New York: de Gruyter, 1984)

Flier, Michael S., 'Court ceremony in an age of reform. Patriarch Nikon and the Palm Sunday ritual', in *Religion and culture in early modern Russia and Ukraine*, ed. Samuel H. Baron and Nancy Shields Kollmann (DeKalb: Northern Illinois University Press, 1997), 74–95

Golubev, S. T., *Kievskii mitropolit Petr Mogila i ego spodvizhniki* [Opyt tserkovno-istoricheskogo issledovaniia], 2 vols. (Kiev: Tip. G. T. Korchak-Novitskago, 1883–98)

Gorchakov, M. I., *Monastyrskii prikaz, 1649–1725 g. opyt istoriko-iuridicheskago izsliedovaniia* (St Petersburg: A. Transhel', 1868)

Got'e, I. V., *Zamoskovnyi krai v XVII veke* (Moscow: Gosudarstvennoe sotsial'no-ekonomicheskoe izdatel'stvo, 1937)

Gromyko, M. M., *Mir russkoi derevni* (Moscow: Molodaia Gvardiia, 1991)

Gudziak, Borys A., *Crisis and reform: the Kyivan metropolitanate, the patriarchate of Constantinople, and the genesis of the Union of Brest* (Cambridge, MA: Harvard University Press, 1998)

Kapterev, N. F., *Patriarkh Nikon i Tsar' Aleksei Mikhailovich*, 2 vols. (Sergiev Posad: Tipografiia Sviato-Troitskoi Sergievoi Lavry, 1909–12)

Kharakter otnoshenii Rossii k pravoslavnomu vostoku v XVI i XVII stoletiiakh (Sergiev Posad: Izdanie knizhnago magazina M. S. Elova, 1914)

Kartashev, A. V., *Ocherki po istorii russkoi tserkvi*, 2 vols. (Moscow: Nauka, 1991)

Keep, J. L. H., 'The régime of Filaret, 1619–1633', *Slavonic and East European Review* 38 (1960), 334–60

Kharlampovich, K. V., *Malorossiiskoe vliianie na velikorusskuiu tserkovnuiu zhizn'*, 1 (Kazan: Izdanie knizhnago magazina M. A. Golubeva, 1914; repr. The Hague: Mouton, 1968)

Lobachev, S. V., *Patriarkh Nikon* (St Petersburg: Iskusstvo – SPB, 2003)

Luzhnyts'kyi, Hryhor, *Ukrains'ka tserkva mizh Skhodom i Zakhodom: narys istorii ukrains'koi tserkvy* (Philadelphia: Provydinnia, 1954)

Makarii, Metropolitan of Moscow, *Istoriia russkoi tserkvi*, 12 vols. (Düsseldorf: Brücken-Verlag, 1968–69)

Meyendorff, Paul, 'The liturgical reforms of Peter Moghila: a new look', *St Vladimir's Theological Quarterly* 29 (1985), 101–14

Russia, ritual, and reform: the liturgical reforms of Nikon in the 17th century (Crestwood, NY: St Vladimir's Seminary Press, 1991)

Michels, Georg B., 'The violent Old Belief: an examination of religious dissent on the Karelian frontier', *RH/HR* 19 (1992), 203–29

At war with the church: religious dissent in seventeenth-century Russia (Stanford: Stanford University Press, 1999)

Mironowicz, Antoni, *Prawoslawie i unia za panowania Jana Kazimierza* [Dissertationes universitatis Varsoviensis 443] (Bialystok: Dzial Wydawnictw Filii UWW Bialymstoku, 1996)

Pascal, Pierre, *Avvakum et les débuts du raskol*, second edition (Paris and The Hague: Mouton, 1969)

Plokhy, Serhii, *The Cossacks and religion in early modern Ukraine* (Oxford and New York: Oxford University Press, 2001)

Rumiantseva, V. S., 'The Russian church and state in the 17th century', in *The Russian Orthodox Church: 10th to 20th centuries* (Moscow: Progress, 1988), 81–103

Ševčenko, Ihor, 'The many worlds of Peter Mohyla', *Harvard Ukrainian Studies* 8 (1984), 9–41

Skrynnikov, R. G., *Sviatiteli i vlasti* (Leningrad: Lenizdat, 1990)

Stefanovich, P. S., *Prikhod i prikhodskoe dukhovenstvo v Rossii v XVI–XVII vekakh* (Moscow: Indrik, 2002)

Stroev, P. M., *Spiski ierarkhov i nastoiatelei monastyrei rossiiskiia tserkvi* (St Petersburg: Tipografiia V. S. Balasheva, 1877)

Sysyn, Frank E., 'The formation of modern Ukrainian religious culture: the sixteenth and seventeenth centuries', in *Church, nation and state in Russia and Ukraine* (see general bibliography), 1–22

Uspensky, Boris A., 'The schism and cultural conflict in the seventeenth century', in *Seeking God* (see general bibliography), 106–43

Zenkovsky, Serge A., *Russkoe staroobriadchestvo; dukhovnye dvizheniia semnadtsatogo veka* [Forum Slavicum 21] (Munich: W. Fink, 1970)

Zernova, A. S., *Knigi kirillovskoi pechati izdannye v Moskve v XVI–XVII vekakh* (Moscow: Gosudarstvennaia Ordena Lenina biblioteka SSSR imeni V. I. Lenina, 1958)

Zhukovskyi, Arkadii, *Petro Mohyla i pytannia iednosty tserkov* (Paris: Ukrains'kyi vil'nyi universytet, 1969)

Zyzykin, M. V., *Patriarkh Nikon: ego gosudarstvennye i kanonicheskie idei*, 3 vols. (Warsaw: Sinodal'naia Tipografiia, 1931–38)

14   Dixon: The Orthodox Church in imperial Russia

Secondary works

Alekseeva, S. I., *Sviateishii Sinod v sisteme vysshikh i tsentral'nykh gosudarstvennykh uchrezhdenii poreformennoi Rossii 1856–1904 gg.* (St Petersburg: Nauka, 2003)

Coleman, H. J., 'Defining heresy: the fourth missionary congress and the problem of cultural power after 1905 in Russia', *Jahrbücher für Geschichte Osteuropas* 52 (2004), 70–92

    Russian Baptists and spiritual revolution, 1905–1929 (Bloomington: Indiana University Press, 2005)

Cracraft, J., *The church reform of Peter the Great* (London: Macmillan, 1971)

Dixon, Simon M., 'The church's social role in St Petersburg, 1880–1914', in *Church, nation and state in Russia and Ukraine* (see general bibliography), 167–92

    'How holy was Holy Russia? Rediscovering Russian religion', in *Reinterpreting Russia*, ed. G. Hosking and R. Service (London: Arnold, 1998), 21–39

    'Sergii (Stragorodskii) in the Russian Orthodox diocese of Finland: apostasy and mixed marriages, 1905–1917', *Slavonic and East European Review* 82 (2004), 50–73

    'Religious ritual at the eighteenth-century Russian court', in *Monarchy and religion*, ed. Michael Schaich (Oxford: Oxford University Press, forthcoming)

Engelstein, L., 'Holy Russia in modern times: an essay on Orthodoxy and cultural change', *Past and Present* 173 (2001), 129–56

Etkind, A., *Khlyst: sekty, literatura i revoliutsiia* (Moscow: Novoe literaturnoe obozrenie, 1998)

Florovskii, G., *Puti russkogo bogosloviia*, second edition (Paris: YMCA, 1981)

Freeze, G. L., 'Institutionalizing piety: the church and popular religion, 1750–1850', in *Imperial Russia: new histories for the empire*, ed. J. Burbank and D. L. Ransel (Bloomington: Indiana University Press, 1998), 210–49

    'Church and politics in late imperial Russia: crisis and radicalisation of the clergy', in *Russia under the last tsar: opposition and subversion 1894–1917*, ed. A. Geifman (Oxford: Blackwell, 1999), 269–97

    'A pious folk? Religious observance in Vladimir diocese, 1900–1914', *Jahrbücher für Geschichte Osteuropas* 52 (2004), 323–40

Kahle, W., *Die Begegnung des baltischen Protestantismus mit der russisch-orthodoxen Kirche* (Leiden: E. J. Brill, 1959)

Köhler-Bauer, M., *Die geistlichen Akademien in Russland im 19. Jahrhunderts* [Veröffentlichungen des Osteuropa-Instituts München, Reihe Geschichte 64] (Wiesbaden: Harrassowitz, 1997)

Kondakov, I. E., *Gosudarstvo i pravoslavnaia tserkov' v Rossii: evoliutsiia otnoshenii v pervoi polovine XIX veke* (St Petersburg: Rossiiskaia Natsional'naia Biblioteka, 2003)

Kurliandskii, I. A., *Innokentii (Veniaminov), mitropolit moskovskii i kolomenskii* (Moscow: Rossiiskaia akademiia nauk, Institut rossiiskoi istorii, 2002)

Lavrov, A. I., *Koldovstvo i religiia v Rossii 1700–1740 gg.* (Moscow: Drevlekhranilishche, 2000)

Papmehl, K. A., *Metropolitan Platon of Moscow (Petr Levshin, 1737–1812): the enlightened prelate, scholar and educator* (Newtonville, MA: Oriental Research Partners, 1983)

Polunov, A.Iu., *Pod vlast'iu ober-prokurora: Gosudarstvo i tserkov' v epokhu Aleksandra III* (Moscow: AIRO-XX, 1996)

Smilianskaia, E. B., *Volshebniki, bogokhul'niki, eretiki: narodnaia religioznost' i 'dukhovnaia prestupnost'' v Rossii XVIII veka* (Moscow: Indrik, 2003)

Titlinov, B. V., *Gavriil Petrov: Mitropolit novgorodskii i sanktpeterburgskii: ego zhizn' i deiatel'nost', v sviazi s tserkovnymi delami togo vremeni* (Petrograd: Tipografiia M. Merkusheva, 1916)

Tsapina, O. A., 'Secularization and opposition in the time of Catherine the Great', in *Religion and politics in enlightenment Europe*, ed. J. E. Bradley and D. K. Van Kley (Notre Dame: University of Notre Dame Press, 2001), 334–99

Videneeva, A. I., *Rostovskii arkhiereiskii dom i sistema eparkhial'nogo upravleniia v Rossii XVIII veka* (Moscow: Nauka, 2004)

Waldron, P., 'Religious reform after 1905: Old Believers and the Orthodox church', *Oxford Slavonic Papers* n.s. 20 (1987), 110–39

'Religious toleration in late imperial Russia', in *Civil rights in imperial Russia*, ed. O. Crisp and L. Edmondson (Oxford: Clarendon Press, 1989), 103–19

Werth, P. W., *At the margins of Orthodoxy: mission, governance, and confessional politics in Russia's Volga-Kama region, 1827–1905* (Ithaca, NY: Cornell University Press, 2002)

Zhivov, V., *Iz tserkovnoi istorii vremen Petra Velikogo* (Moscow: Novoe literaturnoe obozrenie, 2004)

Zvereva, S., *Aleksandr Kastal'skii: Idei, tvorchestvo, sud'ba* (Moscow: Vuzovskaia kniga, 1999)

15   Chulos: Russian piety and culture from Peter the Great to 1917

1   Sources

'Andrei, iurodstvovavshii v gorode Meshchovske', *Troitskie Listki* 203 (1905)

Arkhangelov, S. A., *Starets Serafim i Sarovskaia pustyn'* (St Petersburg: Izd. P. P. Soikina, 1903)

Belliustin, I. S., *Description of the clergy in rural Russia: the memoir of a nineteenth-century parish priest*, trans. with an interpretative essay by Gregory L. Freeze (Ithaca, NY: Cornell University Press, 1985)

Firsov, B. M. and Kiseleva, I. G., *Byt velikorusskikh krest'ian-zemlepashtsev: opisanie materialov etnograficheskogo biuro kniazia V. N. Tenisheva (na primere Vladimirskoi gubernii)* (St Petersburg: Izd-vo Evropeiskogo Doma, 1993)

Goretskii, V. and Vil'k, V., *Russkii narodnyi lechebnyi travnik i tsvetnik*, second edition (Moscow: Universitetskaia tip., 1903)

Maksimov, S. V., *Nechistaia, nevedomaia i krestnaia sila* [Etnograficheskoe biuro kniazia V. N. Tenisheva] (St Petersburg: R. Golike and A. Vil'borg, 1903; reprinted St Petersburg: 'POLISET', 1994)

Popov, G., *Russkaia narodno-bytovaia meditsina* [Etnograficheskii biuro kniazia V. N. Tenisheva] (St Petersburg: Tip. A. S. Suvorina, 1903)

Poselianin, E., 'Kashinskie torzhestva', *Russkii Palomnik* 25 (1909), 392

Putnik (N. Lender), 'Nakanune kashinskikh torzhestv. (Vpechatleniia nashego spetsial'nogo korrespondenta)', *Russkii Palomnik* 25 (1909), 344

Snegirev, I. M., *Russkie prostonarodnye prazdniki i suevernye obriady*, 2 vols. (Moscow: Universitetskaia tip., 1837–39)

The spiritual regulation of Peter the Great, ed. and trans. Alexander V. Muller (Seattle: University of Washington Press, 1972)

Titlinov, B. V., *Dukhovnaia shkola v Rossii v XIX stoletii*, 2 vols. (Vil'na, 1908–9; repr. Farnborough: Gregg International Publishers, 1970)

2   Secondary works

Baehr, Stephen Lessing, *The paradise myth in eighteenth-century Russia: utopian patterns in early secular Russian literature and culture* (Stanford: Stanford University Press, 1991)

Batalden, Stephen K., 'Colportage and the distribution of the Holy Scriptures in late imperial Russia', in *Christianity and the Eastern Slavs*, II (see general bibliography), 83–92

Bernshtam, T. A., *Molodezh' v obriadovoi zhizni russkoi obshchiny XIX–nachala XX v.: polovozrastnoi aspekt traditsionnoi kul'tury* (Leningrad: Nauka, 1988)

Molodost' v simvolizme perekhodnykh obriadov vostochnykh slavian: uchenie i opyt tserkvi v narodnom khristianstve (St Petersburg: Peterburgskoe Vostokovedenie, 2000)

Brooks, Jeffrey, 'The zemstvo and the education of the people', in *The zemstvo in Russia: an experiment in local self-government*, ed. Terence Emmons and Wayne S. Vucinich (Cambridge: Cambridge University Press, 1982), 243–78

When Russia learned to read: literacy and popular literature, 1861–1917 (Princeton: Princeton University Press, 1985)

Buganov, A. V., *Russkaia istoriia v pamiati krest'ian XIX veka i natsional'noe samosoznanie* (Moscow: Institut etnologii i antropologii Akademii nauk, 1992)

Chulos, Chris J., 'Myths of the pious or pagan peasant in post-emancipation central Russia (Voronezh province)', *RH/HR* 22 (1995), 181–216

'Peasant perspectives of clerical debauchery in post-emancipation Russia', *Studia Slavica Finlandensia* 12 (1995), 33–53

'Religious and secular aspects of pilgrimage in modern Russia', in *Byzantium and the North* [=*Acta Byzantina Fennica* 9 (1997–98)], 21–58

'Religion and grass-roots re-evaluations of Russian Orthodoxy, 1905–1907', in *Transforming peasants: society, state and peasants, 1861–1931*, ed. Judith Pallot [Selected Proceedings of the V ICCEES Conferences, Warsaw, 1995, ed. Ron Hill] (London: Macmillan, 1998), 90–112

'"A place without taverns": village space in the afterlife', in *Beyond the limits: the concept of space in Russian history and culture*, ed. Jeremy Smith [Studia Historica 62] (Helsinki: Finnish Historical Society, 1999), 191–9

'The end of "cultural survivals" (*perezhitki*): remembering and forgetting Russian peasant religious traditions', *Studia Slavica Finlandensia* 17 (2000), 190–207

'Orthodox identity at Russian holy places', in *National identity in contemporary Russia*, ed. Chris J. Chulos and Timo Piirainen (Aldershot: Ashgate, 2000), 28–50

Davis, Natalie Zemon, 'Some tasks and themes in the study of popular religion', in *The pursuit of holiness in late medieval and renaissance religion (Papers from the University of Michigan Conference)*, ed. Charles Trinkaus and Heiko A. Oberman [Studies in Medieval and Reformational Thought 10] (Leiden: Brill, 1974), 307–36

Eklof, Ben, *Russian peasant schools: officialdom, village culture, and popular pedagogy, 1861–1914* (Berkeley: University of California Press, 1986)

Engelstein, Laura, 'Paradigms, pathologies and other clues to Russian spiritual culture: some post-Soviet thoughts', *Slavic Review* 57 (1998), 864–77

'Old and new, high and low: straw horsemen of Russian Orthodoxy', in *Orthodox Russia: belief and practice under the tsars* (see general bibliography), 23–32.

Evtuhov, Catherine, *The cross and the sickle: Sergei Bulgakov and the fate of Russian religious philosophy, 1890–1920* (Ithaca, NY: Cornell University Press, 1997)

Freeze, Gregory L., 'The rechristianization of Russia: the church and popular religion 1750–1850', *Studia Slavica Finlandensia* 7 (1990), 101–36

'"Going to the intelligentsia": the church and its urban mission in post-reform Russia', in *Between tsar and people* (see general bibliography), 215–32

'Tserkov', religiia i politicheskaia kul'tura na zakate staroi Rossii', *Istoriia SSSR* 2 (1991), 107–19

Frierson, Cathy A., *Peasant icons: representations of rural people in late nineteenth-century Russia* (New York: Oxford University Press, 1993)

Gleason, Abbott, *European and Muscovite: Ivan Kireevsky and the origins of Slavophilism* (Cambridge, MA: Harvard University Press, 1972)

Gromyko, M. M., *Traditsionnye normy povedeniia i formy obshcheniia russkikh krest'ian XIX v.* (Moscow: Nauka, 1986)

Khaichenko, G. A., *Russkii narodnyi teatr kontsa XIX–nachala XX veka* (Moscow: Nauka, 1975)

Klibanov, A. I., *Istoriia religioznogo sektantstva v Rossii (60–e gody XIX v.–1917 g.)* (Moscow: Nauka, 1965)

Levin, Eve, '*Dvoeverie* and popular religion', in *Seeking God* (see general bibliography), 31–52

Leyda, Jay, *Kino: a history of the Russian and Soviet film*, third edition (Princeton: Princeton University Press, 1983)

Lindenmeyr, Adele, *Poverty is not a vice: charity, society and the state in imperial Russia* (Princeton: Princeton University Press, 1996)

Meehan, Brenda, 'Popular piety, local initiative and the founding of women's religious communities in Russia, 1764–1907', in *Seeking God* (see general bibliography), 83–105

Meehan-Waters, Brenda, 'To save oneself: Russian peasant women and the development of women's religious communities in pre-revolutionary Russia', in *Russian peasant women*, ed. Beatrice Farnsworth and Lynne Viola (New York: Oxford University Press, 1992), 121–33

'The authority of holiness: women ascetics and spiritual elders in nineteenth-century Russia', in *Church, nation and state in Russia and Ukraine* (see general bibliography), 38–51

Holy women of Russia: the lives of five Orthodox women offer spiritual guidance for today (Crestwood, NY: St Vladimir's Seminary Press, 1997)

Minenko, N. A., *Kul'tura russkikh krest'ian Zaural'ia XVIII – pervaia polovina XIX v.* (Moscow: Nauka, 1991)

Nichols, Robert L., 'The Orthodox elders (*startsy*) of imperial Russia', *Modern Greek Studies Yearbook* 1 (1985), 1–30

Remy, Johannes, *Higher education and national identity: Polish student activism in Russia, 1832–1863* [Bibliotheca historica 57] (Helsinki: Suomalaisen kirjallisuuden seura, 2000)

Robson, Roy R., *Old Believers in modern Russia* (DeKalb: Northern Illinois University Press, 1995)

Rosenthal, Bernice Glatzer, 'The search for a Russian Orthodox work ethic', in *Between tsar and people* (see general bibliography), 57–74

Ruud, Charles A., *A Russian entrepreneur: publisher Ivan Sytin of Moscow, 1851–1934* (Montreal: McGill–Queen's University Press, 1990)

Shevzov, Vera, 'Chapels and the ecclesial world of pre-Revolutionary Russian peasants', *Slavic Review* 55 (1996), 585–613

'Miracle-working icons, laity and authority in the Russian Orthodox Church, 1861–1917', *RR* 58 (1999), 26–48

Sinel, Allen, *The classroom and the chancellery: state educational reform in Russia under Count Dmitry Tolstoi* (Cambridge, MA: Harvard University Press, 1973)

Stanton, Leonard J., *The Optina Pustin monastery in the Russian literary imagination: iconic vision in works by Dostoevsky, Gogol, Tolstoy and others*, ed. Thomas R. Beyer, Jr. [Middlebury Studies in Russian Language and Literature 3] (New York: Peter Lang, 1995)

Steinberg, Mark D., 'Workers on the cross: religious imagination in the writings of Russian workers, 1910–1924', *RR* 53 (1994), 213–39

Stites, Richard, *Russian popular culture: entertainment and society since 1900* (Cambridge: Cambridge University Press, 1992)

Taylor, Richard, *The politics of the Soviet cinema, 1917–1929* (Cambridge: Cambridge University Press, 1979)

Thompson, Ewa M., *Understanding Russia: the holy fool in Russian culture* (Lanham, MD: University Press of America, 1987)

Tokarev, S. A., *Religioznye verovaniia vostochnoslavianskikh narodov XIX – nachala XX v.* (Moscow: Izd. AN SSSR, 1957)

Tsivian, Yuri, *Early cinema in Russia and its cultural reception*, trans. Alan Bodger; ed. Richard Taylor (Chicago: University of Chicago Press, 1998)

Tsurikov, Vladimir, *Philaret, Metropolitan of Moscow, 1782–1867: perspectives on the man, his works, and his times* (Jordanville, NY: Variable Press, 2003)

Usai, Paolo, Codelli, Lorenzo, Monatanaro, Carlo and Robinson, David, *Silent witnesses: Russian films, 1908–1919* (Pordenone: Biblioteca dell'immagine, 1989)

Walicki, Andrzej, *The Slavophile controversy: history of a conservative utopia in nineteenth-century Russian thought* (Oxford: Oxford University Press, 1975)

Wigzell, Faith, *Reading Russian fortunes: print culture, gender and divination in Russia from 1765* (Cambridge: Cambridge University Press, 1998)

Worobec, Christine, *Peasant Russia: family and community in the post-emancipation period* (Princeton: Princeton University Press, 1991; reprinted DeKalb: Northern Illinois University Press, 1995)

Possessed: women, witches and demons in Imperial Russia (DeKalb: Northern Illinois University Press, 2001)

Zelnik, Reginald E., 'To the unaccustomed eye: religion and irreligion in the experience of St. Petersburg workers in the 1870s', in *Christianity and the Eastern Slavs*, II (see general bibliography), 49–82

Zhuk, Sergei, *Russia's lost reformation: peasants, millennialism, and radical sects in Russia and Ukraine, 1830–1917* (Washington, DC: Woodrow Wilson Center Press, 2004)

Zol'nikova, N. D., *Sibirskaia prikhodskaia obshchina v XVIII veke* (Novosibirsk: Nauka Sibirskoe otdelenie, 1990)

Zorkaia, N. M., *Na rubezhe stoletii: u istokov massovogo iskusstva v Rossii, 1900–1910 godov* (Moscow: Nauka, 1976)

Zyrianov, P. N., *Pravoslavnaia tserkov' v bor'be s revoliutsiei 1905–1907 gg.* (Moscow: Nauka, 1984)

General bibliography to Part III: Eastern Christianities
(chapters 16–21)

1 Collections of sources

Corpus Scriptorum Christianorum Orientalium (Paris: ex Typographeo Reipublicae, 1903–40; Louvain: L. Durbecq; Secrétariat CSCO; Peeters, 1949–)

Patrologia Orientalis (Paris: Firmin-Didot, 1903–78; Turnhout: Brepols, 1979–)

Receuil des historiens des croisades: documents arméniens, ed. E. Dulaurier, 2 vols. (Paris: Belles Lettres, 1869, 1906)

2 Sources

Bar Hebraeus, *Chronicon ecclesiasticum*, ed. and trans. J. B. Abelloos and T. J. Lamy, 3 vols. (Paris and Louvain: C. Peeters, 1872–77)

Chronique de Michel le Syrien, patriarche jacobite d'Antioche (1166–1199), ed. A. J. Butler, trans. J.-B. Chabot, 4 vols. (Paris: E. Leroux, 1905; reprinted Brussels: Culture et Civilisation, 1963)

3 General works

Allsen, Thomas T., *Culture and conquest in Mongol Eurasia* (Cambridge: Cambridge University Press, 2001)

Arménie entre Orient et Occident, ed. R. H. Kévorkian (Paris: Bibliothèque nationale, 1996)

Arpee, Leon, *History of Armenian Christianity from the beginning to our time* (New York: Armenian Missionary Association of America, 1946)

Assfalg, J. and Krüger, P., *Petit dictionnaire de l'Orient chrétien* [Petits dictionnaires bleus] (Turnhout: Brepols, 1991)

Atiya, A. S., *A history of Eastern Christianity* (London: Methuen, 1968)

Baldick, Julian, *Mystical Islam* [New York University Studies in Near Eastern Civilization 13] (New York: New York University Press, 1989)

Bat Ye'or, *Les chrétientés d'Orient entre jihâd et dhimmitude (VIIe–XXe siècle)* (Paris: Éditions du Cerf, 1991); trans. M. Kochan and D. Littman, *The decline of eastern Christianity under Islam* (Madison, NJ: Fairleigh Dickinson University Press, 1996)

Between the desert and the city: the Coptic Orthodox Church today, ed. Nelly van Doorn-Harder and Kari Vogt (Oslo: Novus forlag, 1997)

Billioud, J.-M., *Histoire des chrétiens d'Orient* (Paris: L'Harmattan, 1995)

Brissaud, A., *Islam et chrétienté: Treize siècles de cohabitation* (Paris: R. Laffont, 1991)

Browne, L. E., *The eclipse of Christianity in Asia from the time of Muhammad till the fourteenth century* (Cambridge: Cambridge University Press, 1933; reprinted New York: Fertig, 1967)

Bulliet, R. W., *Conversion to Islam in the medieval period: an essay in quantitative history* (Cambridge, MA and London: Harvard University Press, 1979).

Cahen, Claude, *Pre-Ottoman Turkey: a general survey of the material and spiritual culture c.1071–1330* (London: Sidgwick and Jackson; New York: Taplinger, 1968)

Chrétiens du monde arabe: un archipel en terre d'Islam, ed. B. Heyberger [Collection mémoires 94] (Paris: Éditions Autrement, 2003)

Christianismes orientaux: introduction à l'étude des langues et des littératures, ed. M. Albert *et al.* [Initiations au christianisme ancien] (Paris: Éditions du Cerf, 1993)

Christians and Jews in the Ottoman Empire, ed. B. Braude and B. Lewis, 2 vols. (New York: Holmes and Meier, 1982)

Conversion and continuity: indigenous Christian communities in Islamic lands. Eighth to eighteenth centuries, ed. M. Gervers and R. J. Bikhazi [Papers in Mediaeval Studies 9] (Toronto: Pontifical Institute of Mediaeval Studies, 1990)

Conversion to Islam, ed. N. Levtzion (New York and London: Holmes and Meier, 1979)

Courbage, Y. and Fargues, P., *Chrétiens et Juifs dans l'Islam arabe et turc* (Paris: Fayard, 1992; new edition [Petite bibliothèque Payot 310], Paris: Payot et Rivages, 1996); trans. J. Marbo, *Christians and Jews under Islam* (London and New York: Tauris, 1997)

Dawson, Christopher, *The Mongol mission: narratives and letters of the Franciscans in Mongolia and China in the thirteenth and fourteenth centuries* (New York: AMS Press, 1955)

Ducellier, A., *Chrétiens d'Orient et Islam au Moyen Âge. VIIe–XVe siècle* [Collection universitaire histoire 335] (Paris: A. Colin, 1996)

Eastern Christianity: studies in modern history, religion and politics, ed. A. O'Mahony (London: Melisende, 2004)

Eddé, A.-M., *La principauté ayyoubide d'Alep (579/1183–658/1260)* [Freiburger Islam Studien 21] (Stuttgart: Franz Steiner Verlag, 1999)

Eddé, A.-M., Micheau, F. and Picard, C., *Communautés chrétiennes en pays d'Islam du début du VIIe siècle au début du XIe siècle* [Regards sur l'histoire. Histoire médiévale 118] (Paris: Sedes, 1997)

Hajjar, J., *Les chrétiens uniates du Proche-Orient* (Paris: Éditions du Seuil, 1962)

Hewsen, Robert H., *Armenia: a historical atlas* (Chicago: University of Chicago Press, 2001)

Heyberger, B., 'Les chrétiens', in *États, sociétés et cultures du monde musulman médiéval, Xe–XVe siècle*, ed. J.-C. Garcin [Nouvelle Clio. L'histoire et ses problèmes] (Paris: PUF, 2000), III, 145–63

Histoire des Arméniens, ed. G. Dédéyan (Toulouse: Privat, 1982)

History of the Armenian people from ancient to modern times, ed. R. G. Hovannisian, 2 vols. (Basingstoke: Macmillan; New York: St Martin's Press, 1997)

Janin, R., *Les églises orientales et les rites orientaux* (first edition, Paris: Maison de la bonne presse, 1914; fifth edition, Paris: Letouzey and Ané, 1997)

Kawerau, P., *Das Christentum des Ostens* (Stuttgart: Kohlhammer, 1972)
   Ostkirchengeschichte, 4 vols. [CSCO 441, 442, 451, 456. Subs. 64, 65, 70, 71] (Louvain: E. Peeters, 1982–84)

Kelly, J. N. D., *Early Christian doctrines* (London: Black, 1977)

Khawam, R., *L'univers culturel des chrétiens d'Orient* (Paris: Éditions du Cerf, 1987)

Leipoldt, J., *Religionsgeschichte des Orients* [*Handbuch der Orientalistik*, ed. B. Spuler, I, VIII, 2] (Leiden: Brill, 1961)

Meyendorff, John, *Christ in eastern Christian thought* (Crestwood, NY: St Vladimir's Seminary Press, 1987)

Moffett, S. H., *A history of Christianity in Asia*, I, *Beginnings to 1500* (San Francisco: Harper, 1992; second edition, Maryknoll, NY: Orbis, 1998)

Müller, C. and Detlef, G., *Geschichte der orientalischen Nationalkirchen* [Die Kirche in ihrer Geschichte] (Göttingen: Vandenhoeck and Ruprecht, 1981)

Musset, H., *Histoire du christianisme spécialement en Orient*, 3 vols. (Harissa (Lebanon): Impr. St Paul; Jerusalem: Impr. des PP. Franciscains, 1948–49)

Pouzet, L., *Damas au VIIe/XIIIe siècle: vie et structures religieuses dans une métropole islamique* [Recherches. Collection publiée sous la direction de la Faculté des Lettres et des Sciences Humaines de l'Université Saint-Joseph] (Beirut: al-Mashraq, 1988)

Religion in the Middle East: three religions in concord and conflict, ed. A. J. Arberry, 2 vols. (Cambridge: Cambridge University Press, 1969)

Richard, J., *La papauté et les missions d'Orient au Moyen Âge (XIIIe–XVe siècles)* [Collection de l'École française de Rome 33], second edition (Rome: École française de Rome, 1998)

Roma-Armenia, ed. C. Mutafian (Rome: Edizioni de Luca, 1999)

Sivan, E., 'Note sur la situation des chrétiens sous les Ayyûbides', *Revue d'Histoire des Religions* 172 (1967), 117–30

Tritton, A. S., *The Caliphs and their non-Muslim subjects: a critical study of the Covenant of 'Umar* (Oxford: Oxford University Press, 1930; reprinted London: F. Cass, 1970)

Turan, O., 'Les souverains seldjukides et leurs sujets non-musulmans', *Studia Islamica* I (1953), 65–100

Valognes, J.-P., *Vie et mort des chrétiens d'Orient des origines à nos jours* (Paris: Fayard, 1994)

16 Micheau: Eastern Christianities: Copts, Melkites, Nestorians and Jacobites

1 Sources

Abû Yûsuf Ya'kûb, *Kitâb al-kharâdj*, trans. E. Fagnan, *Le livre de l'impôt foncier* [Bibliothèque archéologique et historique 1] (Paris: P. Geuthner, 1921)

Cahen, C., 'Histoires coptes d'un cadi médiéval', *Bulletin de l'Institut Français d'Archéologie Orientale* 59 (1960), 133–50

Evetts, B. T. A., *The churches and monasteries of Egypt and some neighbouring countries, attributed to Abû Sâlih the Armenian* [Anecdota oxoniensis. Semitic series 7] (Oxford: Clarendon Press, 1895; reprinted [Islamic Geography 44], Frankfurt am Main: Institute for the History of Arabic Science, 1992)

al-Harawî, *Kitâb al-ishârât ilâ ma'rifat al-ziyârât*, ed. and trans. J. Sourdel-Thomine, *Guide des lieux de pèlerinage*, 2 vols. (Damascus: Institut Français, 1953–57)

Ibn Butlân, *Le banquet des prêtres: une maqâma chrétienne du XIe siècle*, trans. J. Dagher and G. Troupeau (Paris: Geuthner, 2004)

Ibn al-Ṣuqâ'î, *Tâlî kitâb wafayât al-A'y'ân*, ed. and trans. J. Sublet, *Un fonctionnaire chrétien dans l'administration mamelouke* (Damascus: Institut Français, 1974)

al-Makîn ibn al-'Amîd, trans. A.-M. Eddé and F. Micheau, *Chronique des Ayyoubides (602–658 = 1205/6–1259/60)* [Documents relatifs à l'histoire des croisades 16] Paris: Belles Lettres, 1994)

al-Mufaḍḍal ibn Abî 'l-Faḍâ'il, *Histoire des sultans mamlouks*, ed. and trans. E. Blochet in *Patrologia Orientalis* 12 (1919), 345–550; 14 (1929), 375–672; 20 (1929), 3–270

Sawîrus ibn al-Muqaffa, *History of the patriarchs of the Egyptian Church*, ed. and trans. A. Khater, A. S. Atiya and O. H. E. Burmester, 4 vols. (Cairo: Société d'archéologie copte, 1943–74)

2 Secondary works

i. The Melkite churches

Dauvillier, J., 'Byzantins d'Asie centrale et d'Extrême-Orient', *Revue des Études Byzantines* 11 (1953), 62–87 [= Dauvillier, J., *Histoire et institutions des églises orientales au Moyen Âge* (London: Variorum, 1983), XVI]

Grumel, V., 'Le patriarcat et les patriarches d'Antioche sous la seconde domination byzantine (969–1084)', *Échos d'Orient* 33 (1934), 129–47

Nasrallah, J., 'L'église melchite en Irak, en Perse et dans l'Asie centrale', *Proche-Orient Chrétien* 25 (1975), 135–73; 26 (1976), 16–33

'Les historiens musulmans, source de l'histoire de l'Église melchite', *Bulletin d'Études Orientales* 30 (1978), 101–17.

ii. The Coptic Church

Amélineau, E., *La géographie de l'Égypte à l'époque copte* (Paris: Imprimerie nationale, 1893)

Bourguet, P. du, *Les Coptes* [Que-Sais-Je? 2398] (second edition, Paris: Presses universitaires de France, 1992)

Butler, A. J., *The ancient Coptic churches of Egypt*, 2 vols. (Oxford: Clarendon Press, 1884)

Cannuyer, C., *Les Coptes* [Coll. Fils d'Abraham] (Turnhout: Brepols, 1996)

Coptic Egypt: the Christians of the Nile [New Horizons] (London: Thames and Hudson, 2000)

Chauleur, S., *Histoire des Coptes d'Égypte* (Paris: La Colombe, 1960)

The Coptic encyclopedia, ed. A. S. Atiya, 8 vols. (New York: Macmillan, 1991)

Den Heijer, J., 'Considérations sur les communautés chrétiennes en Égypte fatimide: l'état et l'église sous le vizirat de Badr al-Jamâlî (1074–1094)', in *L'Égypte fatimide, son art et son histoire*, ed. M. Barrucand (Paris: Presses de l'Université de Paris-Sorbonne, 1999), 569–78

'Le patriarcat copte d'Alexandrie à l'époque fatimide', in *Alexandrie médiévale*, ed. C. Décobert [Études alexandrines 8] (Cairo: Institut français d'archéologie orientale, 2002), II, 83–97

Fiey, J.-M., 'Coptes et Syriaques, contacts et échanges', *Studia Orientalia Christiana Collectanea* 15 (1972–73), 295–366

Gril, D., 'Une émeute anti-chrétienne à Qûs au début du VIII/XIVe siècle', *Annales Islamologiques* 16 (1980), 241–74

Kammerer, W., *A Coptic bibliography* (Ann Arbor: University of Michigan Press, 1950; reprinted New York: Kraus, 1969)

Labib, S. J., 'Ein köptischer Martyrer des XIII. Jhdts.: al-Habîs Bûlus ar-Râhîb al-Qibtî', *Der Islam* 58 (1981), 321–6

Martin, M., 'La province d'Ašmûnayn: historique de sa configuration religieuse', *Annales Islamologiques* 23 (1987), 1–28

'Chrétiens et musulmans à la fin du XIIe siècle', in *Valeur et distance: identités et sociétés en Égypte*, ed. C. Décobert (Paris: Maisonneuve et Larose, 2000), 83–91

Meinardus, O., *Christian Egypt, ancient and modern* [Cahiers d'histoire égyptienne] (Cairo: French Institute of Oriental Archaeology, 1965; second edition Cairo: American University in Cairo Press, 1977)

Munier, H., *Recueil des listes épiscopales de l'Église copte* [Publications de la Société d'archéologie copte. Textes et documents] (Cairo: Société d'archéologie copte, 1943)

Partrick, T. H., *Traditional Egyptian Christianity: a history of the Coptic Orthodox Church* (Greensboro, NC: Fisher Park Press, 1996)

Richards, D., 'The Coptic bureaucracy under the Mamluks', in *Colloque international sur l'histoire du Caire* (Cairo: Ministry of Culture of the Arab Republic of Egypt, 1969), 373–81

Rondot, P., 'L'évolution historique des Coptes', *Cahiers de l'Orient Contemporain* 22 (1950), 129–55

Viaud, G., *La liturgie des Coptes d'Égypte* (Paris: Maisonneuve, 1978)

Les pèlerinages coptes en Égypte (Cairo: Institut français d'archéologie orientale, 1979)

Zaborowski, J. R., *The Coptic martyrdom of John of Phanijœit: assimilation and conversion to Islam in thirteenth-century Egypt* [The History of Christian–Muslim Relations 3] (Leiden and Boston: Brill, 2005)

Zaki, M. S., *Histoire des Coptes d'Égypte* (Versailles: Éditions de Paris, 2005)

iii. The Syriac churches: Jacobite and Nestorian

Abuna, Albir, *Taʾrīkh al-kanīsa al-sūryaniyya al-sharqiyya*, 3 vols. (Beirut: al-Mashraq, 1992–93)

Allard, M., 'Les chrétiens à Bagdad', *Arabica* 9 (1962), 375–88

Chabot, J.-B., 'Les évêques jacobites du VIIIe au XIIIe siècle d'après la chronique de Michel le Syrien', *Revue de l'Orient Chrétien* 4 (1899), 444–52, 512–42; 5 (1900), 605–36; 6 (1901), 189–220

Dauvillier, J., 'Les provinces chaldéennes "de l'extérieur" au Moyen Âge', in *Mélanges F. Cavallera* (Toulouse: Bibliothèque de l'Institut catholique, 1948), 261–316 [= Dauvillier, J., *Histoire et institutions des églises orientales au Moyen Âge* (London: Variorum, 1983), I]

'L'expansion de l'Église syrienne en Asie centrale et en Extrême-Orient au Moyen Âge', *L'Orient Syrien* 1 (1956), 76–87 [= Dauvillier, *Histoire et institutions des églises orientales au Moyen Âge*, XIII]

'L'archéologie des anciennes églises de rite chaldéen', *Parole de l'Orient (Mélanges François Graffin)* 6–7 (1975–76), 357–86 [= Dauvillier, J., *Histoire et institutions des églises orientales au Moyen Âge*, XI]

Fiey, J.-M., *Mossoul chrétienne: essai sur l'histoire, l'archéologie et l'état actuel des monuments chrétiens de la ville de Mossoul* [Recherches publiées sous la direction de l'Institut des lettres orientales de Beyrouth 12] (Beirut: Imprimerie catholique, 1959)

Assyrie chrétienne: contribution à l'étude de l'histoire et de la géographie ecclésiastiques et monastiques du nord de l'Iraq [Recherches publiées sous la direction de l'Institut des lettres orientales de Beyrouth 22, 23, 42], 3 vols. (Beirut: Imprimerie catholique, 1965–68)

Jalons pour une histoire de l'Église en Iraq [CSCO 310. Subs. 36] (Louvain: Secrétariat du CSCO, 1970)

'Les diocèses du maphrianat syrien. 629–1860', *Parole de l'Orient* 5 (1974), 133–64, 331–94; 8 (1976–78), 347–78

Chrétiens syriaques sous les Mongols (Il-Khanat de Perse, XIIIe–XIVe siècles) [CSCO 362. Subs. 44] (Louvain: Secrétariat du CSCO, 1975)

Nisibe, métropole syriaque orientale et ses suffragants des origines à nos jours [CSCO 388. Subs. 54] (Louvain: Secrétariat du CSCO, 1977)

Communautés syriaques en Iran et en Irak des origines à 1552 (London: Variorum, 1979)

Chrétiens syriaques sous les Abbassides surtout à Bagdad (749–1258) [CSCO 420. Subs. 59] (Louvain: Secrétariat du CSCO, 1980)

'Les insaisissables nestoriens de Damas', in *After Chalcedon: studies in theology and church history offered to Prof. A. van Roey for his seventieth birthday* [Orientalia lovaniensa analecta 18] (Leuven: Peeters, 1985), 167–80

Pour un Oriens christianus novus: répertoire des diocèses syriaques orientaux et occidentaux [Beiruter Texte und Studien 49] (Beirut: in Kommission bei F. Steiner, Stuttgart, 1993)

Haddad, R. M., *Syrian Christians in Muslim society* (Princeton: Princeton University Press, 1970)

Hage, W., *Die syrisch-jakobitische Kirche in frühislamischer Zeit* (Wiesbaden: O. Harrassowitz, 1966)

Honigmann, E., *Le couvent de Barṣaumâ et le patriarcat jacobite d'Antioche et de Syrie* [CSCO 146. Subs. 7] (Louvain: L. Durbecq, 1954)

Kawerau, P., *Die jakobitische Kirche im Zeitalter der syrischen Renaissance* (Berlin: Akademie-Verlag, 1955)

Le Coz, R., *Histoire de l'Église d'Orient: Chrétiens d'Irak, d'Iran et de Turquie* (Paris: Éditions du Cerf, 1995)

Meinardus, O., 'The Nestorians in Egypt', *Oriens Christianus* 51 (1967), 112–22

Mingana, A., 'A charter of protection granted to the Nestorian Church in A.D. 1138, by Muktafi II, Caliph of Baghdad', *Bulletin of the John Rylands Library* 10 (1926), 127–33

Segal, J. B., *Edessa: the 'Blessed City'* (Oxford: Clarendon Press, 1970)

Vries, W. de, 'Die Patriarchen der nichtkatholischen syrischen Kirchen', *Ostkirchliche Studien* 33 (1984), 2–45

iv. The Maronite Church

Daou, B., 'Le site du couvent principal de Saint-Maroun en Syrie', *Parole de l'Orient* 3 (1972), 145–52

Dib, P., *L'Église maronite*, 1, *L'Église maronite jusqu'à la fin du Moyen Âge* (Paris: Letouzey and Ané, 1930; new edition, Beirut: Librairie orientale, 2001)

Frazee, Charles, 'The Maronite middle ages', *Eastern Churches Review* 10 (1978), 88–100

Gribomont, J., 'Documents sur les origines de l'Église maronite', *Parole de l'Orient* 5 (1974), 95–132

Moosa, M., *The Maronites in history* (Syracuse, NY: Syracuse University Press, 1986)

Rajji, M., 'Le monothélisme chez les Maronites et les Melkites', *JEcclH* 2 (1951), 38–42

Salibi, K. S., 'The Maronites of Lebanon under Frankish and Mamluk rule, 1099–1516', *Arabica* 4 (1957), 288–303

'The Maronite church in the middle ages and its union with Rome', *Oriens Christianus* 42 (1958), 92–104

Maronite historians of mediaeval Lebanon [American University of Beirut. Publication of the Faculty of Arts and Sciences. Oriental Series 34] (Beirut: American University of Beirut, 1959; reprinted New York: AMS Press, 1980)

v. Dhimma status, conversion and taxation

Abel, A., 'La djizya: tribut ou rançon?', *Studia Islamica* 32 (1970), 5–19

Anawati, G. C., 'Factors and effects of arabization and islamization in medieval Egypt and Syria', in *Islam and cultural change in the Middle Ages*, ed. S. Vryonis (Wiesbaden: O. Harrassowitz, 1975), 17–41

Ashtor, E., 'The social isolation of Ahl al-dhimma', in *P. Hirschler Memorial Book*, 1949 [= Ashtor, E., *The medieval Near East* (London: Variorum, 1978), VII]

Ayyoub, M. M., 'Dhimmah in the Qur'ân and ḥadîth', *Arab Studies Quarterly* 5 (1983), 172–82

Bat Ye'or, *Le dhimmi: profil de l'opprimé en Orient et en Afrique du Nord depuis la conquête arabe* (Paris: Anthropos, 1980); trans. D. Maisel, P. Fenton and D. Littman, *The dhimmi: Jews and Christians under Islam* (Rutherford, N J: Fairleigh Dickinson University Press, 1984)

Behrens-Abouseif, D., 'Locations of non-Muslim quarters in medieval Cairo', *Annales Islamologiques* 22 (1986), 117–32

Bosworth, C. E., 'Christian and Jewish religious dignitaries in Mamluk Egypt and Syria', *International Journal of Middle-East Studies* 3 (1972), 59–74, 199–216

'The "Protected People" (Christians and Jews) in medieval Egypt and Syria', *Bulletin of the John Rylands Library* 62 (1979), 11–36

Brett, M., 'The spread of Islam in Egypt and North Africa', in *Northern Africa: Islam and modernization*, ed. M. Brett (London: Frank Cass, 1974), 1–12

Cahen, C., 'L'Islam et les minorités confessionnelles au cours de l'histoire', *La Table Ronde* 126 (1958), 61–72

'Histoire économico-sociale et islamologie. Le problème préjudiciel de l'adaptation entre les autochtones et l'islam', in *Actes du Colloque sur la sociologie musulmane 1961* [Correspondance d'Orient 5] (Brussels: Centre pour l'étude des problèmes du monde musulman contemporain [1962]), 197–215 [= Cahen, C., *Les peuples musulmans dans l'histoire médiévale* (Damas: Institut français, 1977), 169–88]

Cheïkho, L., *Les vizirs et secrétaires arabes chrétiens en Islam (622–1517)*, ed. C. Hecheïmé (Joûnié: al-Maktabah al-Bulusiyah, 1987) (in Arabic)

Décobert, C., 'Sur l'arabisation et l'islamisation de l'Égypte médiévale', in *Itinéraires d'Égypte: mélanges offerts à Père Maurice Martin S.J.*, ed. C. Décobert (Cairo: Institut français d'archéologie orientale, 1992), 273–300

Dennett, D. C., *Conversion and the Poll Tax in early Islam* [Harvard Historical Monographs 24] (Cambridge, MA: Harvard University Press, 1950; reprinted New York: Arno, 1973)

Fattal, A., 'Comment les dhimmi étaient jugés en terre d'Islam?', *Cahiers d'Histoire Égyptienne* 3 (1951), 321–41

Le statut légal des non-musulmans en pays d'Islam [Recherches publiées sous la direction de l'Institut des lettres orientales de Beyrouth 10] (Beirut: Imprimerie catholique, 1958; reprinted Beirut: al-Mashraq, 1995)

Fiey, J.-M., 'Conversions à l'islam de juifs et de chrétiens sous les Abbassides d'après les sources arabes et syriaques', in *17e Congrès international des sciences historiques*, II, *Section chronologique. Méthodologie: la biographie historique* (Madrid: Comité Español de Ciencias Históricas, 1992), 585–94

Lapidus, I. M., 'The conversion of Egypt to Islam', *Israel Oriental Studies* 2 (1972), 248–62

Lev, Y., 'Persecution and conversion to Islam in eleventh-century Egypt', *Asian and African Studies* 22 (1988), 73–91

Levitzion, N., 'Conversion under Muslim domination: a comparative study', in *Religious change and cultural domination (XXX International Congress of Human Sciences in Asia and North Africa)*, ed. D. Lorenzen (Mexico City: Colegio de México, 1981), 19–38

Little, D. P., 'Coptic conversion to Islam during the Baḥrî Mamlûks', *Bulletin of the School of Oriental and African Studies* 39 (1976), 552–69

Løkkegaard, F., *Islamic taxation in the classic period* (Copenhagen: Branner and Korch, 1950; reprinted New York: Arno, 1973; Philadelphia: Porcupine Press, 1978)

Mansouri, T., 'Les dhimmis en Égypte mamluke, statut légal et perceptions populaires', *Ibla* 164 (1989), 255–70

Perlmann, M., 'Notes on anti-Christian propaganda in the Mamlûk Empire', *Bulletin of the School of Oriental and African Studies* 10 (1939–42), 843–61

Samir, K., 'Le commentaire de Tabarî sur Coran 2, 62 et la question du salut des non-musulmans', *Annali dell Istituto Orientale di Napoli* 40 (1980), 556–617

'The role of Christians in the Fâṭimid government services of Egypt to the reign of al-Ḥâfiẓ', in *Second Woodbrooke–Mingana Symposium on Arab Christianity and Islam. 19–22 September 1994*, ed. D. Thomas [=*Medieval Encounters* 2 (1996), 177–92]

Vermeulen, U., 'The rescript of al-Malik aṣ-Ṣâliḥ against the dhimmîs (755 A.H. / 1354 A.D.)', *Orientalia Lovaniensia Periodica* 9 (1978), 175–84

vi. The Latin Church and the crusades

Brincken, A. D. von den, *Die 'Nationes Christianorum Orientalium' im Verständnis der lateinischen Historiographie von der Mitte des 12. bis in die zweite Hälfte des 14. Jahrhunderts* [Kölner historische Abhandlungen 22] (Cologne: Böhlau, 1973)

Cahen, C., 'Notes sur l'histoire de l'Orient latin: I – En quoi la conquête turque appelait-elle la croisade?', *Bulletin de la Faculté des Lettres de Strasbourg* 21 (1950–51), 118–25 [= Cahen, C., *Turcobyzantina et Oriens Christianus* (London: Variorum, 1974), c]

Fiey, J.-M., 'Chrétiens syriaques entre croisés et Mongols', in *Symposium Syriacum [I] 1972* [OCA 197] (Rome: Pontificium Institutum orientalium studiorum 1974), 327–41

Hamilton, B., *The Latin Church in the Crusader States: the secular church* (London: Variorum, 1980)

Hiestand, Rudolf, 'Die Integration der Maroniten in die römische Kirche, zum ältesten Zeugnis der päpstlichen Kanzlei (12 Jahrhundert)', *OCP* 54 (1988), 119–52

Hitti, P.K., 'The impact of the crusades on eastern Christianity', in *Medieval and Middle Eastern studies in honor of Aziz Suryal Atiya*, ed. S. A. Hanna (Leiden: Brill, 1972), 211–17

Mansouri, T., 'Les dhimmis et la croisade', *Mésogeios* 12 (2002), 101–15

Martin, J. P., 'Les premiers princes croisés et les Syriens jacobites de Jérusalem', *Journal Asiatique* 12 (1888), 471–90; 13 (1889), 33–80

Micheau, F., 'Croisades et croisés vus par les historiens arabes chrétiens d'Égypte', in *Itinéraires d'Orient: hommages à Claude Cahen* [=Res Orientales 6 (1994)], 169–85

'Les médecins orientaux au service des princes latins', in *Occident et Proche-Orient: contacts scientifiques au temps des croisades. Actes du Colloque de Louvain-la-Neuve, 24 et 25 mars 1997*, ed. I. Draelants, A. Tihon and B. van den Abeele (Louvain: Brepols, 2000), 95–115

'Les croisades dans la Chronique universelle de Bar Hébraeus', in *Chemins d'outre-mer: études d'histoire sur la Méditerranée médiévale offertes à Michel Balard*, ed. D. Coulon, C. Otten, P. Pagès and D. Valérian [Byzantina Sorbonensia] (Paris: Publications de la Sorbonne, 2004), II, 553–72

Pahlitzsch, J., *Graeci und Suriani im Palästina der Kreuzfahrerzeit: Beiträge zur Geschichte des griechisch-orthodoxen Patriarchats von Jerusalem* [Berliner historische Studien 33. Ordenstudien 15] (Berlin: Duncker und Humbolt, 2001)

Sourdel, D., 'Bohémond et les chrétiens de Damas sous l'occupation mongole', in *Dei Gesta per Francos: études sur les croisades dédiées à Jean Richard*, ed. M. Balard, B. Z. Kedar and J. S. Riley-Smith (Aldershot: Ashgate, 2001), 295–9

vii. Art, literature and intellectual life

Aigle, D., 'Bar Hébraeus et son public, à travers ses chroniques en arabe et en syriaque', *Le Muséon* 118 (2005), 83–106

Atiya, A. S., *The Arabic manuscripts of Mount Sinaï: a hand-list of the Arabic manuscripts and scrolls microfilmed at the Library of the Monastery of St Catherine* [Publications of the American Foundation for the Study of Man 1] (Baltimore: Johns Hopkins University Press, 1955)

Baumstark, A., *Die christlichen Literaturen des Orients*, 3 vols. (Leipzig: G. J. Göschen, 1911)
    Geschichte der syrischen Literatur (Bonn: De Gruyter, 1922)
Blau, J., *A grammar of Christian Arabic, based mainly on South-Palestinian texts from the first millennium*, 3 vols. [CSCO 267, 276, 279. Subs. 27, 28, 29] (Louvain: Secrétariat du CSCO, 1966–67)
Brock, S., *Syriac studies: a classified bibliography (1960–1990)* (Kaslik: Université St Ésprit, 1996). Completed in *Parole de l'Orient* 21 (1998), 241–350; 29 (2004), 263–410
Brockelmann, C., Finck, F. N., Leipoldt, J., and Littmann, E., *Geschichte der christlichen Literaturen des Orients* (Leipzig: C. F. Amelang, 1907)
Cheïkho, L., *Les savants arabes chrétiens en Islam (622–1300)*, ed. C. Hechaïmé (Joûnié: al-Maktabah al-Bulusiyah, 1983) (in Arabic)
Conrad, L. I., 'On the Arabic Chronicle of Bar Hebraeus: his aims and audience', *Parole de l'Orient* 19 (1994), 319–78
Den Heijer, J., 'Quelques remarques sur la deuxième partie de l'Histoire des Patriarches d'Alexandrie', *Bulletin de la Société d'Archéologie Copte* 25 (1983), 107–24
    'Sawîrus ibn al-Muqaffa', Mawhûb Ibn Manṣûr Ibn Mufarrigh et la genèse de "l'Histoire des Patriarches d'Alexandrie"', *Bibliotheca Orientalis* 41 (1984), cols. 336–47
    Mawhûb Ibn Manṣûr Ibn Mufarrigh et l'historiographie copto-arabe: étude sur la composition de l'Histoire des Patriarches d'Alexandrie [CSCO 513. Subs. 83] (Louvain: E. Peeters, 1989)
Eddé, A.-M., 'Les médecins dans la société syrienne du VIIe/XIIIe siècle', *Annales Islamologiques* 29 (1995), 91–109
Fiey, J.-M., 'Esquisse d'une bibliographie de Bar Hébraeus (†1286)', *Parole de l'Orient* 13 (1986), 279–312
Graf, G., *Geschichte der christlichen arabischen Literatur*, II, *Die Schriftsteller bis zur Mitte des 15 Jhs.* [Studi e testi 133] (Vatican: Biblioteca apostolica vaticana, 1947)
Kamil, M., *Catalogue of all manuscripts in the Monastery of St Catherine on Mount Sinaï* (Wiesbaden: Harrassowitz, 1970)
Le Coz, R., *Les médecins nestoriens au Moyen Âge: les maîtres des Arabes* [Comprendre le Moyen-Orient] (Paris: L'Harmattan, 2004)
Leroy, J., *Les manuscrits syriaques à peintures conservés dans les bibliothèques d'Europe et d'Orient*, 2 vols. [Institut français d'archéologie de Beyrouth. Bibliothèque archéologique et historique 77] (Paris: P. Geuthner, 1964)
Micheau, F., 'Le *Kâmil* d'Ibn al-Athîr, source principale de l'Histoire des Arabes dans le *Mukhtaṣar* de Bar Hébraeus', *Mélanges de l'Université St-Joseph* 58 (2005)
    'Biographies de savants dans le *Mukhtaṣar* de Bar Hébraeus', in *L'Orient chrétien dans l'empire musulman (Mélanges en l'honneur de G. Troupeau)* [Studia Arabia] (Paris and Versailles: Éditions de Paris, 2005)
Nasrallah, J., *Histoire du mouvement littéraire dans l'église melchite du Ve au XXe siècle: contribution à l'étude de la littérature arabe chrétienne*: II, 1 (634–750) (Damascus: Institut français, 1996); II, 2 (750-10e siècle) (Louvain: Peeters, 1988); III 1 (969–1250) (Louvain: Peeters, 1973); III, 2 (1250–1516) (Louvain: Peeters, 1981)
Rescher, N., *The development of Arabic logic* (Pittsburgh, PA: University of Pittsburgh Press, 1964)
Samir, K., 'Bibliographie du dialogue islamo-chrétien. Auteurs chrétiens de langue arabe', *Islamochristiana* 2 (1979), 201–45

Sidarus, A., *Ibn ar-Râhibs Leben und Werk: ein koptisch-arabischer Encyclopädist des 7/13 Jahrhunderts* [Islamkundliche Untersuchungen 36] (Freiburg im Breisgau: Klaus Schwarz, 1975)
'La philologie copte arabe au Moyen Âge', in *La signification du Bas Moyen Âge dans l'histoire et la culture du monde musulman* [Actes du 8e Congrès de l'Union européenne des Arabisants et Islamisants, Aix-en-Provence 1976] (Aix-en-Provence: Edisud, 1978), 267–81
'Essai sur l'âge d'or de la littérature copte arabe (XIIIe–XIVe siècles)', in *Acts of the Fifth International Congress of Coptic Studies (Washington 1992)*, ed. D. Johnson (Rome: CIM, 1993), II, 443–62
Todt, S. R., 'Die syrische und die arabische Weltgeschichte des Bar Hebraeus – ein Vergleich', *Der Islam* 65 (1988), 60–80
Troupeau, G., *Études sur le christianisme arabe au moyen âge* (Aldershot: Variorum, 1995)
Vööbus, A., *History of asceticism in the Syrian Orient: a contribution to the history of culture in the Near East*, 3 vols. [CSCO 184, 197, 500. Subs. 14, 17, 81] (Louvain: Peeters, 1958, 1960, 1988)
History of the School of Nisibis [CSCO 266. Subs. 26] (Louvain: Secrétariat du CSCO, 1965)

viii. Monasteries

Burmester, O. H. E., *A guide to the monasteries of the Wadi'n-Natrun* (Cairo: Société d'archéologie copte, 1954)
Farag, F. R., *Sociological and moral studies in the field of Coptic monasticism* (Leiden: Brill, 1984)
Kilpatrick, H., 'Monasteries through Muslim eyes: the *Diyârât* books', in *Christians at the heart of Islamic rule: church life and scholarship in 'Abbasid Iraq*, ed. D. Thomas [The History of Christian–Muslim Relations 1] (Leiden and Boston: Brill, 2003), 19–37
Krüger, P., 'Das syrische-monophysitische Mönchtum im Ṭûr-'Abdîn von seinen Anfängen bis zur Mitte des 12. Jahrhunderts', *OCP* 4 (1938), 5–46
Leroy, J., *Moines et monastères du Proche-Orient* (Paris: Horizons de France, 1958)
Mouton, J.-M., 'La présence chrétienne au Sinaï à l'époque fatimide', in *L'Égypte fatimide, son art et son histoire*, ed. M. Barrucand (Paris: Presses de l'Université de Paris-Sorbonne, 1999), 613–24
Le Sinaï médiéval, un espace stratégique de l'Islam (Paris: PUF, 2000)
Nasrallah, J., 'Le couvent de Saint-Siméon l'Alépin', *Parole de l'Orient* 1 (1970), 327–56
'Couvents de la Syrie du Nord portant le nom de Siméon', *Syria* 49 (1972), 127–59
Nau, F., 'Notice historique sur le couvent de Qartamin', in *Actes du 14e Congrès international des orientalistes (Alger 1905)* (Paris: E. Leroux, 1907), IIe partie, section 2, 37–111
Sabaite heritage in the Orthodox Church from the fifth century to the present, ed. J. Patrich [Orientalia lovaniensia analecta 98] (Leuven: Peeters, 2001)
Sinaï de la conquête arabe à nos jours, ed. J.-M. Mouton (Cairo: Institut français d'archéologie orientale, 2001)
Sinaï durant l'Antiquité et le Moyen Âge: 4000 ans d'histoire pour un désert [Actes du colloque 'Sinaï', UNESCO, 19–21 septembre 1997], ed. D. Valbelle and C. Bonnet (Paris: Errance, 1998)
Troupeau, G., 'Les couvents chrétiens dans la littérature arabe', *La Nouvelle Revue du Caire* 1 (1975), 265–79 [= Troupeau, G., *Études sur le christianisme arabe au Moyen Âge* (Aldershot: Variorum, 1995), XX]

Zakharia, K., 'Le moine et l'échanson, ou le *Kitâb al-diyârât* d'al-Shabushtî et ses lecteurs', *Bulletin d'Études Orientales* 53–54 (2001–2), 59–74

Zayyât, H., *al-Diyârât al-naṣrâniyya fî l-islâm* (Beirut: al-Mashraq, 1938; reprinted Beirut: al-Mashraq, 1999)

viii. Religious life

Baumstark, A., *Liturgie comparée: principes et méthodes pour l'étude historique des liturgies chrétiennes*, revised Dom B. Botte (Chevetogne and Paris: Éditions de Chevetogne, 1953)

Canard, M., 'La destruction de l'église de la Résurrection par le calife Ḥâkim et l'histoire de la descente du feu sacré', *B* 35 (1955), 16–43 [= Canard, M., *Byzance et les musulmans du Proche Orient* (London, Variorum, 1973), xx]

Dalmais, I. H., *Les Liturgies d'Orient* [Je sais, je crois iii. Partie 10] (Paris: A. Fayard, 1959; reprinted [Rites et symboles 10], Paris: Éditions du Cerf, 1980)

Décobert, C., 'Un lieu de mémoire religieuse', in *Valeur et distance: identités et sociétés en Égypte*, ed. C. Décobert (Paris: Maisonneuve et Larose, 2000), 247–63

Fiey, J.-M., 'Le pèlerinage des Nestoriens et Jacobites à Jérusalem', *Cahiers de Civilisation Médiévale* 12 (1969), 113–26

Halm, H., 'Der Treuhänder Gottes. Die Edikte des al-Ḥâkim', *Der Islam* 63 (1986), 11–72

Salaville, S., *Liturgies orientales*, 3 vols. (Paris: Bloud and Gay, 1932–42)

Sauget, J.-M., *Bibliographie des liturgies orientales (1900–1960)* (Rome: Pontificio istituto orientale, 1962)

Troupeau, G., 'Les fêtes des chrétiens vues par un juriste musulman', in *Mélanges offerts à Jean Dauvillier* (Toulouse: Centre d'histoire juridique méridionale, 1979), 795–802 [= Troupeau, G., *Études sur le christianisme arabe au Moyen Âge*, xix]

Valensi, L., *La fuite en Égypte: histoires d'Orient et d'Occident* (Paris: Éditions du Seuil, 2002)

17   Cowe: The Armenians in the era of the Crusades

1   Primary sources

Č'amč'ean, Mik'ayēl, *Hayoc'patmut'iwn* [History of the Armenians], 3 vols. (Venice, 1784–86; reprinted Erevan: Erevani hamalsarani hrataraṭut'yun, 1984)

Conciliationis ecclesiae Armenae cum Romana, ed. Clemens Galanus (Rome: Urban Press, 1650)

Esayi Nč'ec'i, 'T'ult' Esayeay vardapeti aṙ tēr Matt'ēos' [Letter of the vardapet Esayi to the Lord Matt'ēos] *Č'ṙak'al* (1860), 157–64; (1861), 205–11

Frik, *Frik Diwan*, ed. Tirayr Melik' Muškambarean (New York: Melgonean Foundation, 1952)

Girk' or koč'i oskēp'orik [Book called pot pourri] (Constantinople: Abraham Dpir, 1746)

Girk' t'łt'oc' [Book of Letters], ed. Arch. Norayr Połarean (Jerusalem: St James Press, 1994)

Grigor Anavarzeci, 'T'ult' teaṙn Grigori Hayoc' katołikosi zor greac' aṙ krōnawor tagaworn Het'om [*sic*], hayr ark'ayin Hayoc' Lewoni' [Letter of the Lord Grigor, Catholicos of the Armenians, which he wrote to the cleric king Het'um, father of Lewon, king of the Armenians] in *Conciliationis ecclesiae Armenae cum Romana*, ed. Clemens Galanus (Rome: Urban Press, 1650), 435–51

Grigor Tat'ewac'i, *Girk' harc'manc'* [Book of questions] (Constantinople: Astuacatur Kostandnupolsec'i, 1729)

Grigor Tłay, *Grigor katołikosi tłay kočec'eloy namakani* [Correspondence of Catholicos Grigor called youth] (Venice: St Lazar's Press, 1865)

Het'um of Koṙikos, *La flor des estoires de la terre d'orient* in *Recueil des historiens des croisades: documents arméniens*, ii, ed. Edouard Dulaurier (Paris: Belles Lettres, 1906), 111–253

Kirakos Ganjakec'i, *Patmut'iwn* [History], ed. K. Melik'-Ōhanjanyan (Erevan: Armenian Academy of Sciences, 1961)

Linguae haicanae scriptores ordinis praedicatorum congregationis fratrum unitorum et ff. Armenorum ordinis s. Basilii citra mare consistentium quodquod hucusque innotuerunt (Berne and Munich: A. Francke, 1960)

Matt'ēos Uṙhayec'i, *Žamanakagrut'iwn* [Chronicle], ed. M. Melik'-Adamyan and N. Ter-Mik'ayelyan (Erevan: Erevan State University Press, 1991)

Mxit'ar Sasnec'i, *Mxit'ar Sasnec'i's theological discourses*, ed. and trans. S. P. Cowe [CSCO 21 (Armenian text); 22 (English translation)] (Leuven: Peeters, 1993)

Mxit'ar Skewṙac'i, *Patasxanik' Mxit'ar k'ahanayi Skewṙac'woy yałags hamapetut'ean erkotasan aṙak'eloc'* [On the equal rank of the twelve apostles] (Jerusalem: St James Press, 1865)

Mxit'areanc', Abēl, *Patmut'iwn žołovoc' hayastaneayc' ekełec'woy* [History of the synods of the Armenian Church] (Vałarṣapat: Mother See Press, 1874)

Nersēs Lambronac'i, *Atenabanut'iwn vasn miut'ean ekełec'woy ew čaṙk' i hambarjumn K'ristosi ew i galust Hogwoyn Srboy* [Synodal oration on church union and homilies on Christ's Ascension and Pentecost], ed. Mesrop Tałiadean (Calcutta, 1851)

Nersēs Šnorhali, *Əndhanrakan t'ułt'k'* [General epistles] (Jerusalem: St James Press, 1871)

Des Nilos Doxapatres τάξις τῶν πατριαρχικῶν θρόνων: armenisch und griechisch, ed. F. Finck (Ējmiacin and Marburg: Vagarshapad, 1902)

Smbat Sparapet, *Taregirk'* [Chronicle], ed. S. Agelean (Venice: St Lazar's Press, 1956)

Step'anos Ōrbēlean, *Hakačaṙut'iwn ənddēm erkabnakac'* [Refutation of the Dyophysites] (Constantinople, 1756)

Step'anos Ōrbēlean, *Patmut'iwn nahangin Sisakan* [History of the province of Siwnik'] (Tiflis: Ałaneanc' Press, 1910)

T'ovma Mecop'ec'i, *T'ovma Mecop'ec'i patmagrut'yun* [T'ovma Mecop'ec'i historiography], ed. Levon Xačikyan (Erevan: Magałat', 1999)

Vardan Arewelc'i, *Hawak'umn patmut'ean Hayoc'* [Compendium of Armenian history], ed. Łewond Ališan (Venice: St Lazar's Press, 1862)

Yovhannēs Tarberuni, 'Yovhannu vardapeti Tarberunwoy dawanut'iwn hawatoy' [The vardapet Yovhannēs Tarberuni's confession of faith], *Č'ṙak'ał* 2 (1861), 221–7

2 Secondary works

Abrahamyan, A. G., *Hamaṙot urvagic hay gałtavayreri patmut'yan* [Concise sketch of the history of Armenian colonies] (Erevan: Haypethrat, 1964)

Akinean, Nersēs, *Nersēs Lambronac'i ark'episkopos Tarsoni keank'n ew grakan vastaknerə* [Nersēs Lambronac'i, archbishop of Tarsus: life and literary achievements] (Vienna: Mxitarist Press, 1956)

'Yovsēp' Kostandnupolsec'i, targmanič yaysmawurk'i (991)' [Yovsēp' Kostandnupolsec'i as translator of the menologium], *Handēs Amsōreay* 71 (1957), 1–12

Armenian folk arts, culture, and identity, ed. L. Abrahamian and N. Sweezy (Bloomington: Indiana University Press, 2001)

Avdalbegyan, Mayis, *'Yaysmawurk' 'žołovacunerə ev nranc' patmagrakan aržek'ə* ['Menologium' compilations and their historical and literary value] (Erevan: Armenian Academy of Sciences, 1982)

Bałdasaryan, H., 'Gevorg Skevŕac'u 'vark'ə' [The life of Gēorg Skewŕac'i], *Banber Matenadarani* 7 (1964), 399–435

  Hovhannes Erznkac'in ev nra xratakan arjakə [Yovhannēs Erznkac'i's paraenetic prose] (Erevan: Armenian Academy of Sciences, 1977)

Berbérian, Haïg, 'Le patriarcat arménien du Sultanat de Roum', *Revue des Études Arméniennes* 3 (1966), 233–44

Boase, T. S. R., *The Cilician Kingdom of Armenia* (Edinburgh and London: Scottish Academic Press, 1978)

Bozoyan, Azat A., *Byuzandiayi arevelyan kałakakanut'yunə ev kilikyan Hayastanə žb dari 30-70-akan t'vakannerin* [Byzantium's eastern policy and Cilician Armenia in the 1130s–70s] (Erevan: Armenian Academy of Sciences, 1988)

Bundy, David, 'The anonymous life of Gēorg Skewŕac'i in Erevan 8356: a study in medieval Armenian hagiography and history', *Revue des Études Arméniennes* 18 (1984), 491–502

  'The council of Sis', in *After Chalcedon: studies in theology and church history offered to Albert van Roey for his seventieth birthday* [Orientalia lovaniensia analecta 18] (Leuven: Peeters, 1985), 42–56

  'Het'um's la flor des estoires de la terre d'orient: a study in medieval Armenian historiography and propaganda', *Revue des Études Arméniennes* 20 (1986–87), 223–35

  'The trajectory of Roman Catholic influence in Cilician Armenia: an analysis of the councils of Sis and Adana', *Armenian Review* (winter 1992), 73–89

Collenberg, W. H. Rudt de, *The Rupenides, Hethumides and Lusignans: the structure of the Armeno-Cilician dynasties* (Paris: Klincksieck, 1963)

Coureas, Nicolas, 'The papacy's relations with the kings and the nobility of Armenia in the period 1300–1350', in *Actes du Colloque: 'Les Lusignans et L'Outre Mer'*, ed. C. Mutafian (Poitiers: Presses universitaires de Poitiers, 1993), 106ff

Cowe, S. Peter, 'An Armenian Job fragment from Sinai and its implications', *Oriens Christianus* 72 (1992), 123–57

  'The inauguration of the Cilician coronation rite and royal ideology', *Armenian Review* 45 (1992), 49–59

  'Armenological paradigms and Yovhannēs Sarkawag's "discourse on wisdom" – philosophical underpinning for an Armenian renaissance?' *Revue des Études Arméniennes* 25 (1994–95), 125–55

  'Generic and methodological developments in theology in Caucasia from the fourth to eleventh centuries within an east Christian context', in *Il Caucaso: cerniera fra culture dal Mediterraneo alla Persia (secoli IV–XI)* [Settimane di studio del Centro italiano di studi sull'alto medioevo 43] (Spoleto: Centro italiano di studi sull' alto medioevo, 1996), 647–83

  'The role of correspondence in elucidating the intensification of Latin–Armenian ecclesiastical interchange in the first quarter of the fourteenth century', *Journal of the Society for Armenian Studies* 13 (2003/4), 47–68

'Armenian Christology in the seventh and eighth centuries with particular reference to the contributions of Catholicos Yovhan Ōjnecʻi and Xosrovik Tʻargmaničʻ', *JThSt* 55 (2004), 30–54

'Armenian immigration patterns to Sebastia, tenth–eleventh centuries', in *UCLA International Conference on Armenia Minor – Sebastia / Sivas*, ed. R. G. Hovannisian (Costa Mesa, CA: Mazda Publishers, 2004), 111–36

'Catholic missionaries to Armenia and anti-catholic writings', in *Where the only-begotten descended: the church of Armenia through the ages*, ed. Kevork B. Bardakjian (Detroit, MI: Wayne State University Press, in press)

'Catholicos Grigor Anavarzetsi (1293–1307) and Metropolitan Stepʻanos Orpelian in dialogue', in *UCLA International Conference Series on Historic Armenian Cities and Provinces: Cilicia*, ed. R. G. Hovannisian (Costa Mesa, CA: Mazda Publishers, in press)

'The politics of poetics: Islamic influence on Armenian verse', in *Proceedings of the symposium redefining Christian identity: Christian cultural strategies since the rise of Islam* (Leuven: Peeters, in press)

Dachkévytch, Yaroslav R., 'Les Arméniens en Islande (XIe siècle)', *Revue des Études Arméniennes* 20 (1986–87), 321–36

Dadoyan, Seda B., *The Fatimid Armenians* [Islamic History and Civilization Studies and Texts 18] (Leiden: Brill, 1997)

Donabédian, Patrick, Thierry, Jean-Michel and Thierry, Nicole, *Armenian art* (New York: Harry N. Abrams, 1989)

L'Eglise arménienne et le grand schisme d'Orient [CSCO 574] (Louvain: Peeters, 1999)

Feulner, Hans-Jürgen, *Die armenische Athanasius-Anaphora* [Anaphorae orientales 1] (Rome: Pontificio istituto orientale, 2001)

Garsoïan, Nina G., *The Paulician heresy: a study of the origin and development of Paulicianism in Armenia and the eastern provinces of the Byzantine Empire* [Columbia University Publications in Near and Middle East Studies. Series A, 6] (The Hague and Paris: Mouton, 1967)

Grigoryan, G. M., *Syunikʻɘ Ōrbelyanneri ōrokʻ (XIII–XV darer)* [Siwnikʻ in the days of the Ōrbēleans (thirteenth–fifteenth centuries)] (Erevan: Armenian Academy of Sciences, 1981)

Halfter, Peter, *Das Papsttum und die Armenier im frühen und hohen Mittelalter: von den ersten Kontakten bis zur Fixierung der Kirchenunion im Jahre 1198* (Cologne: Böhlau, 1996)

Hamilton, Bernard, 'The Armenian church and the papacy at the time of the crusades', *Eastern Churches Review* 10 (1978), 61–87

Harutʻyunyan, Babken H., *Hayastani patmutʻyan atlas, I mas* [Historical atlas of Armenia, part 1] (Erevan: Erevan State University, 2004)

Hewsen, Robert H., 'The Artsrunid house of Sefedinian: survival of a princely dynasty in ecclesiastical guise', *Journal of the Society for Armenian Studies* 1 (1984), 123–38

Kapoïan-Kouymjian, Angèle, *L'Égypte vue par des Arméniens* (Paris: Fondation Singer-Polignac, 1988)

Kazhdan, Alexander, 'The Armenians in the Byzantine ruling class predominantly in the ninth through twelfth centuries', in *Medieval Armenian Culture* (Chico, CA: Scholars Press, 1983), 439–51

Select bibliography

Kogean, L. S., *Hayoc' ekelec'in minčew Florentean žolov* [The Armenian Church up to the Council of Florence] (Beirut: [s.n.], 1961)

Lidov, Alexei, *The mural paintings of Akhtala* (Moscow: Nauka, 1991)

Manukyan, Nona, 'The role of Bartolomeo di Bologna's sermonary in medieval Armenian literature', *Le Muséon* 105 (1992), 321–5

Mardirossian, A., *Le livre des canons arméniens (Kanonagirk' Hayoc') de Yovhannēs Awjnec'i: église, droit et société en Arménie du IVe au VIIIe siècle* [CSCO 606] (Louvain: Peeters, 2005)

Mathews, Thomas and Sanjian, Avedis K., *Armenian Gospel iconography: the tradition of the Glajor Gospel* [DOS 29] (Washington, DC: Dumbarton Oaks Research Library and Collection, 1991)

Mathews, Thomas F. and Wieck, R. S., *Treasures in Heaven: Armenian illuminated manuscripts* (New York: The Pierpoint Morgan Library, 1994)

Muradean, Paroyr, 'Les principes de la classification des livres en Arménie médiévale', in *Armenian studies in Memoriam Haïg Berbérian*, ed. Dickran Kouymjian (Lisbon: Calouste Gulbenkian Foundation, 1986), 591–600

'Dawanakan handuržołakanut'ean ew azgamijean hamerašxut'ean gałap'arɔ ŽB–ŽG dareri Hayastanum' [The idea of confessional tolerance and internal national solidarity in twelfth–thirteenth century Armenia] *Ganjasar* 4 (1994), 95–108

Mutafian, Claude, *Le royaume arménien de Cilicie XIIe–XIVe siècle* (Paris: Éditions du CNRS, 1993)

Narkiss, Bezalel (ed.), *Armenian art treasures of Jerusalem* (Jerusalem: Massada Press, 1979)

Nersessian, Vrej, *The Tondrakian movement* (London: Kahn and Averill, 1987)

Oudenrijn, M. A. van den, 'The monastery of Aparan and the Armenian writer Fra Mxit'aric', *Archivum Fratrum Praedicatorum* 1 (1930), 265–308

'L'évêque dominicain Fr. Barthélemy fondateur supposé d'un couvent dans le Tigré au 14e siècle', *Rassegna di Studi Etiopici* 4 (1946), 7–16

Pelliot, Paul, 'Zacharie de Saint-Thadée et Zacharie Séfêdinian', *Revue de l'Histoire des Religions* 126 (1943), 150–4

Połarean, Norayr, *Hay grołner* [Armenian writers] (Jerusalem: St James Press, 1971)

Renoux, Athanase, *Le codex arménien Jérusalem 121* [PO 36, fasc. 168] (Turnhout: Brepols, 1971)

Sanjian, Avedis K., 'Step'anos Orbelian's "Elegy on the holy cathedral of Etchmiadzin": critical text and translation', in *Armenian and biblical studies*, ed. M. E. Stone (Jerusalem: St James Press, 1976), 237–82

'Gregory Magistros: an Armenian Hellenist', in *TO 'EΛΛHNIKON: Studies in honor of Speros Vryonis, Jr.* (New Rochelle, NY: Caratzas, 1993), II, 111–58

Schmidt, Andrea-Barbara and Halfter, Peter, 'Der Brief Papst Innozenz II an den armenischen katholikos Gregor III: ein wenig beachtetes Dokument zur Geschichte der Synode von Jerusalem (Ostern 1141)', *Annuarium Historiae Conciliorum* 31 (1999), 50–71

Sinclair, Tom, 'Cilicia after the kingdom: population, monasteries, etc. under the Mamluks', in *UCLA International Conference Series on Historic Armenian Cities and Provinces: Cilicia*, ed. R. G. Hovannisian (Costa Mesa, CA: Mazda Publishers, in press)

Stewart, Angus D., *The Armenian kingdom and the Mamluks: war and diplomacy during the reigns of Het'um II (1289–1307)* [Medieval Mediterranean 34] (Leiden: Brill, 2001)

Surmelian, Leon, *Daredevils of Sassoun* (Denver, CO: A. Swallow, 1964)

T'amrazyan, Hrač'ya, *Grigor Narekac'in ev norplatonut'yunə* [Grigor Narekac'i and neoplatonism] (Erevan: Nairi, 2004)

Tekéyan, Pascal, *Controverses christologiques en Arméno-Cilicie* [OCA 124] (Rome: Pontificium institutum orientalium studiorum, 1939)

Ter Petrossian, Levon, *Ancient Armenian translations* (New York: St Vartan's Press, 1992)

Xač'ikyan, Levon, *ŽD dari hayeren jeṙagreri hišatakaranner* [Colophons of fourteenth-century Armenian manuscripts] (Erevan: Armenian Academy of Sciences, 1950)

'Artazi haykakan išxanut'yunə ev Corcori dproc'ə' [The Armenian principality of Artaz and the school of Corcor], *Banber Matenadarani* 11 (1973), 125–210

Esayi Nč'ec'in ev Glajori hamalsaranə (1280–1340 t'.t'.) [Esayi Nč'ec'i and the university of Glajor (1280–1340)] (Los Angeles: L. K. Khacheryan, 1988)

Yuzbashian, Karen N., 'L'administration byzantine en Arménie aux Xe–XIe siècles', *Revue des Études Arméniennes* 10 (1973–74), 139–83

Zekiyan, Levon B., 'Le colonie armene del medioevo in Italia e le relazioni culturali italo-armene (Materiale per la storia degli Armeni in Italia)', in *Atti del primo simposio internazionale di arte armena (Bergamo, 28–30 giugno, 1975)*, ed. G. Ieni and L. B. Zekiyan (Venice: San Lazzaro, 1975), 803ff

'St Nersēs Šnorhali en dialogue avec les Grecs: un prophète de l'oecuménisme au XIIe siècle', in *Armenian Studies in Memoriam Haïg Berbérian*, ed. Dickran Kouymjian (Lisbon: Calouste Gulbenkian Foundation, 1986), 861–83

18 Cowe: Church and diaspora: the case of the Armenians

1 Primary sources

Bṙni miut'iwn hayoc' Lehastani ənd ekełec'woyn Hṙovmay: žamanakakic' yišatakarank' [The forcible union of the Armenians of Poland with the church of Rome: contemporary memoirs] (St Petersburg, 1884)

Daranałc'i, Grigor, *Žamanakagrut'iwn Grigor vardapeti Kamaxec'woy kam Daranałc'woy* [Chronicle by Grigor Kamaxec'i or Daranałc'i], ed. M. Nşanean (Jerusalem: St James Press, 1915)

Dawrižec'i, Aṙak'el, *Girk' patmut'eanc'* [Book of histories], ed. L. A. Xanlaryan (Erevan: Armenian Academy of Sciences, 1990)

Doluxanyan, A. G., *Nersēs Mokac'i, Banastełcut'yunner* [Nerses Mokac'i, Poems] (Erevan: Armenian Academy of Sciences, 1975)

2 Secondary studies

Abrahamyan, A. G., *Hamaṙot urvagic hay gałtavayreri patmut'yan* [Concise sketch of the history of Armenian colonies] (Erevan: Haypethrat, 1964)

Akinean, Nersēs, *Baɫēši dproc'ə* [The School of Bitlis] (Vienna: Mxit'arist Press, 1952)

Anasean, Y. A., 'Turk'akan futuvvate ew hayere (Ōsmanean kaysrut'ean juloɫakan k'aɫak'akanut'ean Patmut'iwnic')' [The Turkish fütüvvet and the Armenians (an episode from the history of the Ottoman Empire's assimilationist policy)] *Handēs Amsōreay 93* (1979), 21–69

Ashjian, Mesrop, 'The millet system', in *Armenian church patristic and other essays* (New York: Armenian Prelacy, 1994), 227–51

The Armenian Church in America (New York: Armenian Prelacy, 1995)

Arpee, Leon, *A century of Armenian Protestantism, 1846–1946* (New York: The Armenian Missionary Association of America, 1946)

Arzumanean, Zavhn, *Azgapatum (1910–1930)* [National history] (New York: St Vartan's Press, 1995) [= vol. IV of Ōrmanean, Maɫakia, *Azgapatum* [National history], 3 vols. (Istanbul, 1914)]

Aslanian, Sebouh, *Dispersion history and the polycentric nation: the role of Simeon Yerevants's Girk' or koči partavcar in the 18th century nation revival* [Bibliothèque d'arménologie 'Bazmavep' 39] (Venice: St Lazar's Press, 2004)

Azarya, Victor, *The Armenian quarter of Jerusalem* (Berkeley: University of California Press, 1984)

Bampuk'yean, Gēorg, *Yovhannēs patriark' Kolot* [Patriarch Yovhannēs Kolot] (Istanbul: Murad Ofset, 1984)

Bardakjian, Kevork B., *The Mekhitarist contributions to Armenian culture and scholarship* (Cambridge, MA: Middle East Department, Harvard College Library, 1976)

'The rise of the Armenian patriarchate of Constantinople', in *Christians and Jews in the Ottoman Empire* [see general bibliography], I, 89–97

Barsamian, Hagop, 'The eastern question and the Tanzimat era', in *A history of the Armenian people from ancient to modern times* [see general bibliography], II, 175–202

Bournoutian, George A., *The Khanate of Erevan under Qajar rule 1795–1828* (Costa Mesa, CA: Mazda Press, 1992)

The history of Aṛak'el of Tabriz, I (Costa Mesa, CA: Mazda Press, 2005)

Carswell, John, *New Julfa: the Armenian churches and other buildings* (Oxford: Clarendon Press, 1968)

Carswell, John and Dowsett, C. J. F., *Kütahya tiles and pottery from the Armenian cathedral of St James, Jerusalem* (Oxford: Clarendon Press, 1972)

Cowe, S. Peter, 'Pilgrimage to Jerusalem by the eastern churches', in *Wahlfahrt kennt keine Grenzen*, ed. L. Kriss-Rettenbeck and G. Möhler (Munich: Bayerisches Nationalmuseum, 1984), 316–30

'An 18th-century Armenian textual critic and his continuing significance', *Revue des Études Arméniennes*, n.s. 20 (1986–7), 527–41

'The play "martyrdom of St. Hṛip'simē": a novel variant on the theme of Armenia's Christianization', in *Hay grakanut'yune ev k'ristoneut'yune* [Armenian literature and Christianity], ed. A. Eɫiazaryan *et al.* (Erevan: Armenian Academy of Sciences, 2002), 96–110 [Eastern Armenian]

Čugaszyan, B. L., *Eɫia Muşeɫean Karnec'i, T'urk'eren–Hayeren baṛaran* [Turkish–Armenian dictionary] (Erevan: Armenian Academy of Sciences, 1986)

Ervine, Roberta R., 'Changes in Armenian pilgrim attitudes between 1600 and 1857: the witness of three documents', in *The Armenians in Jerusalem and the Holy Land*, ed. M. E. Stone, R. R. Ervine and Nira Stone [Hebrew University Armenian Studies 4] (Leuven: Peeters, 2002), 81–96

Gazer, Haçik Rafi, *Die Reformbestrebungen in der armenisch-apostolischen Kirche im ausgehenden 19. und im ersten Drittel des 20. Jahrhunderts* (Göttingen: Vandenhoeck and Ruprecht, 1996)

Ghougassian, Vazken S., *The emergence of the Armenian diocese of New Julfa in the seventeenth century* [University of Pennsylvania Armenian Texts and Studies 14] (Atlanta, GA: Scholars Press, 1998)

'The quest for enlightenment and liberation: the case of the Armenian community of India in the late eighteenth century', in *Enlightenment and diaspora: the Armenian and Jewish cases*, ed. R. G. Hovannisian (Atlanta, GA: Scholars Press, 1999), 241–64

Guroian, Vigen, *Faith, church, mission: essays for a renewal in the Armenian church* (New York: Armenian Prelacy, 1995)

Heyer, Franz, *Die Kirche Armeniens* [Kirchen der Welt 18] (Stuttgart: Evangelisches Verlagswerk, 1978)

Hovannisian, Richard G., 'The Armenian question in the Ottoman Empire 1876 to 1914', in *A history of the Armenian people from ancient to modern times* [see general bibliography], II, 203–38

'Armenia's road to independence', in *A history of the Armenian people from ancient to modern times* [see general bibliography], II, 275–302

Keshishian, Aram, *The catholicosate of Cilicia, her place and status in the Armenian church* (Antelias: Catholicate of Cilicia Press, 1962)

The witness of the Armenian church in a diaspora situation (Beirut: Armenian Prelacy of Lebanon, 1978)

Kévorkian, Raymond H., 'Livre missionnaire et enseignement catholique chez les Arméniens 1583–1700', *Revue des Études Arméniennes* 17 (1983), 589–99

'La diplomatie arménienne entre l'Europe et la Perse au temps de Louis XIV', in *Arménie entre Orient et Occident* [see general bibliography], 188–95

'Le négoce international des Arméniens au XVIIe siècle', in *Arménie entre Orient et Occident* [see general bibliography], 142–51

'Les Arméniens et la France (1600–1914)', in *Arménie entre Orient et Occident* [see general bibliography], 211–14

Kévorkian, Raymond H. and Mahé, J.-P., *Le livre arménien à travers les âges: catalogue de l'exposition tenue au Musée de la Marine, 2–21 octobre, 1985* (Marseilles: La Maison arménienne de la jeunesse et de la culture, 1985)

Kouymjian, Dickran, 'Dated Armenian manuscripts as a statistical tool for Armenian history', in *Medieval Armenian culture*, ed. T. J. Samuelian and M. E. Stone [University of Pennsylvania Armenian Texts and Studies 6] (Chico, CA: Scholars Press, 1984), 425–38

Krikorian, Mesrob K., 'The Armenian church in the Soviet Union, 1917–1967', in *Aspects of religion in the Soviet Union 1917–1967*, ed. Richard H. Marshall (Chicago: University of Chicago Press, 1971), 239–56

K'ristonya Hayastan hanragitaran [Christian Armenia: encyclopaedia], ed. Artaşes Lazaryan (Erevan: Haykakan hanragitarani glxavor xmbagrut'yun, 2002)

Lewin, Paulina, 'The Ukrainian school theater in the seventeenth and eighteenth centuries: an expression of the baroque', *Harvard Ukrainian Studies* 5 (1981), 54–65

McCabe, Ina Baghdiantz, *The shah's silk for Europe's silver: the Eurasian trade of the Julfa Armenians in Safavid Iran and India (1530–1750)* [University of Pennsylvania Armenian Texts and Studies 15] (Atlanta, GA: Scholars Press, 1999)

Maksoudian, Krikor, *Chosen of God: the election of the catholicos of all Armenians* (New York: St Vartan Press, 1995)

Matossian, Mary, *The impact of Soviet policies in Armenia* (Leiden: Brill, 1962)

Mouradian, Claire, *De Staline à Gorbachev, histoire d'une république soviétique: l'Arménie* (Paris: Éditions Ramsay, 1990)

Oghlukian, Abel, *The deaconess in the Armenian Church*, trans. S. P. Cowe (New Rochelle, NY: St Nersess Armenian Seminary, 1994)

Oskanyan, Ninel *et al.*, *Hay girk'ə 1512–1800 t'vakannerin* [The Armenian book between the dates 1512–1800] (Erevan: Myasnikyan Library, 1988)

Oudenrijn, M. A. van den, 'Der heilige Gregor der Erleuchter und die Heiligen Hripsimeanz in Unitorien', *Handēs Amsōreay* 62 (1948), 588–96

Raffi (Yakob Melik'-Yakobean), *The fool: events from the last Russo-Turkish War 1877–78*, trans. D. Abcarian (Princeton: Gomidas Institute, 2000)

Rhinelander, A. L. Hamilton, 'Russia's imperial policy: the administration of the Caucasus in the first half of the nineteenth century', *Canadian Slavonic Papers* 17 (1975), 218–35

Richard, Francis, 'Missionnaires français en Arménie au XVIIe siècle', in *Arménie entre Orient et Occident* [see general bibliography], 196–202

Sanjian, Avedis K., *The Armenian communities in Syria under Ottoman dominion* (Cambridge, MA: Harvard University Press, 1965)

Sarkissian, Karekin, 'The Armenian church', in *Religion in the Middle East* [see general bibliography], I, 482–520

Seth, M. J., *Armenians in India* (Calcutta: Armenian Holy Church of Nazareth, 1983)

Step'anyanc', Step'an, *Hay aṙak'elakan ekełec'in stalinyan blnapetut'yan ōrok'* [The Armenian Apostolic Church during the Stalinist dictatorship] (Erevan: Apolon, 1994)

Suny, Ronald G., *The making of the Georgian nation* (Bloomington: Indiana University Press, 1988)

Ter-Minassian, Anahide, *Nation et religion* (Milan: ICOM, 1980)

Xondkaryan, H., *Mkrtic Nałaš* (Erevan: Armenian Academy of Sciences, 1965)

19   Crummey: Church and nation: the Ethiopian Orthodox *Täwahedo* Church

I   Manuscripts

Ethiopian Monastic Microfilm Library, St John's University, Collegeville, MN, MS. 1832, Gold Gospel, Häyq Estifanos

Illinois/IES, 84.I.7–8, manuscript of the *Gäbrä Hemamat*, Mädhané Aläm Church, Gondär; microfilm copy at the Center for African Studies, University of Illinois, and the Institute of Ethiopian Studies, Addis Ababa University

Lämläm, *Aläqa*, Amharic history of Aṣé Täklä Giyorgis and Aṣé Yohännes, Bibliothèque nationale (Paris), *Manuscrits éthiopiens*, 259

2 Sources

Basset, René, *Études sur l'histoire d'Éthiopie* (Paris: Imprimerie nationale, 1882)

Béguinot, Francesco, *La Cronaca Abbreviata d'Abissinia: nuovo versione dall'Etiopico* (Rome: Tipografia della casa edit. italiana, 1901)

Cerulli, Enrico, *Scritti teologici etiopici dei secoli XVI–XVII*, 1, *Tre opuscoli dei Mikaeliti* (Vatican: Biblioteca apostolica vaticana, 1958)

Chihab ed-Din Ahmed Ben 'Abd el-Qader, *Histoire de la conquête de l'Abyssinie (XVIe siècle)*, ed. and trans. René Basset [Publications de l'école supérieure des lettres d'Alger 19–20], 2 vols. (Paris: Ernest Leroux, 1897–1909)

Conti Rossini, Carlo, *Documenta ad Illustrandam Historiam*, 1, *Liber Axumae* [CSCO 54; Scriptores Æthiopici, ser. ii, 2] (Paris: E typographeo reipublicae, 1909)

'La cronaca reale abissina dall'anno 1800 all'anno 1840', *Rendiconti della Reale Accademia dei Lincei* ser. v, 25 (1916), 779–923

'Nuovi documenti per la storia d'Abissinia nel secolo XIX', *Atti della Reale Accademia Nazionale dei Lincei*, ser. vii, 2 (1947), 357–416

Conzelman, William (ed. and trans.), *Chronique de Galâwdêwos (Claudius) roi d'Éthiopie* [Bibliothèque de l'École des hautes études. Sciences historiques et philosophiques 104] (Paris: É. Bouillon, 1895)

Gäbrä Egzi'abehér Élyas, *Prowess, piety and politics: the Chronicle of Abeto Iyasu and Empress Zewditu of Ethiopia (1909–1930) recorded by Aleqa Gebre-Igziabiher Elyas*, ed. and trans. R. K. Molvaer (Cologne: Rüdiger Köppe Verlag, 1994)

Gäbrä Sellasé, *Tarikä Zämän ZäDagmawi Menilek* (Addis Ababa, 1959 Eth. Cal.); trans. M. de Coppet, *Chronique du règne de Ménélik II*, 2 vols. (Paris: Maisonneuve frères, 1930)

Getatchew Haile, 'Materials on the theology of Qebat or unction', in *Ethiopian Studies: Proceedings of the Sixth International Conference, Tel-Aviv, 14–17 April 1980*, ed. G. Goldenberg (Rotterdam: A. A. Balkema, 1986), 205–50

The faith of the Unctionists in the Ethiopian Church (Haymanot Mäsihawit) [CSCO, Scriptores Æthiopici 91] (Leuven: Peeters, 1990)

The Mariology of Emperor Zär'a Ya'eqob of Ethiopia [OCA 242] (Rome: Pontificio istituto orientale, 1992)

Guidi, Ignazio, 'Le liste dei metropoliti d'Abissinia', *Bessarione* 6 (1899), 1–16

'Uno squarcio di storia ecclesiastica di Abissinia', *Bessarione* 8 (1900), 10–25

Annales Iohannis I, Iyasu I, et Bakaffa [CSCO 24; Scriptores Æthiopici ser. ii, 5] (Paris: E typographeo reipublicae, 1903)

Annales Regum Iyasu II et Iyo'as [CSCO 61; Scriptores Æthiopici ser. ii, 6] (Paris: E typographeo reipublicae, 1910)

Haile Sellassie I, *The autobiography of Emperor Haile Sellassie:* 1, *'My life and Ethiopia's progress' 1892–1937*, ed. and trans. Edward Ullendorff (London: Oxford University Press, 1976); ii, *My life and Ethiopia's progress*, ed. and annotated Harold G. Marcus with Ezekiel Gebissa and Tibebe Eshete; trans. Ezekiel Gebissa with Guluma Gemeda (East Lansing: Michigan State University Press, 1994)

Huntingford, G. W. B., *The land charters of northern Ethiopia* (Addis Ababa: Institute of Ethiopian Studies and Faculty of Law, Haile Sellassie I University, 1965)

Imperial Ethiopian Ministry of Information, *Selected speeches of His Imperial Majesty Haile Selassie First 1918–1967* (Addis Ababa: Publications and Foreign Languages Press Department, 1967)

Paulos Sadua, 'Un manoscritto etiopico degli Evangeli', *Rassegna di Studi Etiopici* 11 (1952), 9–28

Perruchon, Jules, *Les Chroniques de Zar'a Yâ'eqôb et de Ba'eda Mâryâm, rois d'Éthiopie dès 1434 à 1478* [Bibliothèque de l'École des hautes études 93] (Paris: É. Bouillon, 1893)

Weld Blundell, H., *The Royal Chronicle of Abyssinia 1769–1840* (Cambridge: Cambridge University Press, 1922)

Yaqob Beyene, *Controversie Cristologiche in Etiopia: contributo alla storia delle correnti e della terminologia nel secolo XIX* [Annali dell' Istituto Orientale di Napoli suppl. 11] (Naples: Istituto Orientale di Napoli, 1977)

3 Secondary works

Abir, Mordechai, *Ethiopia: the era of the princes. The challenge of Islam and the unification of the Christian Kingdom 1769–1855* (London: Longmans Green, 1968)

Ethiopia and the Red Sea: the rise and decline of the Solomonic dynasty and Muslim–European rivalry in the region (London: Cass, 1980)

Adams, William Y., *Nubia: corridor to Africa* (Princeton: Princeton University Press, 1977)

Andargachew Tiruneh, *The Ethiopian revolution, 1974–1987: a transformation from an aristocratic to a totalitarian autocracy* (Cambridge: Cambridge University Press, 1993)

Ayyala Takla Haymanot, see Mario da Abiy-Addi'

Bahru Zewde, 'Economic origins of the absolutist state in Ethiopia (1916–1935)', *Journal of Ethiopian Studies* 17 (1984), 1–29

A history of modern Ethiopia 1855–1991, second edition (Oxford, Athens, OH and Addis Ababa: James Currey, Ohio University Press and Addis Ababa University Press, 2001)

Bandrés, José L. and Zanetti, Ugo, 'Christology', in *Encyclopaedia Æthiopica* [q.v.], 1, 728–32

Chaillot, Christine, *The Ethiopian Orthodox Tewahedo Church tradition: a brief introduction to its life and spirituality* (Paris: Inter-Orthodox Dialogue, 2002)

Chernetsov, Sevir, 'Ethiopian Täwahedo Orthodox Church. From the time of Yohannes IV to 1959', in *Encyclopædia Æthiopica* [q.v.], II, 421–4

Chojnacki, Stanislaw, *Major themes in Ethiopian painting: indigenous developments, the influence of foreign models, and their adaptation from the 13th to the 19th century* [Äthiopistische Forschungen 10] (Wiesbaden: Franz Steiner Verlag, 1983)

Clapham, Christopher, *Transformation and continuity in revolutionary Ethiopia* (Cambridge: Cambridge University Press, 1988)

Crummey, Donald, 'Doctrine and authority: Abunä Sälama, 1841–1854', in *IV Congresso Internazionale di Studi Etiopici* (Rome: Accademia nazionale dei lincei, 1972), 1, 567–78

Priests and politicians: Protestant and Catholic missionaries in Orthodox Ethiopia, 1830–1868 (Oxford: Clarendon Press, 1972)

'Orthodoxy and imperial reconstruction in Ethiopia, 1854–1878', *JThSt* 29 (1978), 427–42

'Imperial legitimacy and the creation of neo-Solomonic ideology in 19th-century Ethiopia', *Cahiers d'Études Africaines* no. 28–1, 109 (1988), 13–43

Land and society in the Christian Kingdom of Ethiopia: from the thirteenth to the twentieth century (Urbana: University of Illinois Press, 2000)

Crummey, Donald and Getatchew Haile, 'Abunä Sälama, metropolitan of Ethiopia, 1841–1867: a new Ge'ez biography', *Journal of Ethiopian Studies* 37 (2004), 5–40

Derat, Marie-Laure, *Le domaine des rois éthiopiens (1270–1527): espace, pouvoir et monachisme* (Paris: Publications de la Sorbonne, 2003)

Di Salvo, Mario, Chojnacki, Stanislaw and Raineri, Osvaldo, *Churches of Ethiopia: the monastery of Narga Sellase* (Milan and New York: Skira and Abbeville Pub. Group, 1999)

Encyclopædia Æthiopica, ed. S. Uhlig (Wiesbaden, Harrassowitz Verlag, 2003–)

Ethiopia and the missions: historical and anthropological insights, ed. V. Böll et al. [Afrikanische Studien 25] (Münster: LIT Verlag, 2005)

Ethiopian Orthodox Church, ed. Aymro Wondmagegnehu and Joachim Motovu (Addis Ababa: The Ethiopian Orthodox Mission, 1970)

Getatchew Haile, 'From strict observance to royal endowment: the case of the monastery of Däbrä Halle Luya, EMML 6343, fols. 177r–118v', *Le Muséon* 93 (1980), 163–4

'Religious controversies and the growth of Ethiopic literature in the fourteenth and fifteenth centuries', *Oriens Christianus* 65 (1981), 102–36

'The cause of the Ǝsṭifanosites: a fundamentalist sect in the Church of Ethiopia', *Paideuma. Mitteilungen zur Kulturkunde* 29 (1983), 93–119

Haile Gabriel Dagne, 'The establishment of churches in Addis Ababa', in *Proceedings of the International Symposium on the Centenary of Addis Ababa, November 24–25, 1986*, ed. Taddese Beyene (Addis Ababa: Institute of Ethiopian Studies, Addis Ababa University, 1987), 57–78

Haile Mariam Larebo, 'The Orthodox Church and state in Ethiopian revolution', *Religion in Communist Lands* 14, 2 (1986), 148–59

'The Ethiopian Orthodox Church and politics in the twentieth century: parts 1 and 2', *Northeast African Studies* 9, 3 (1987), 1–17; 10, 1 (1988), 1–23

Hammerschmidt, Ernst, *Äthiopien: christliches Reich zwischen Gestern und Morgen* (Wiesbaden: Harrassowitz, 1967)

Heldman, Marilyn, *African Zion: the sacred art of Ethiopia* (New Haven: Yale University Press, 1993)

Heyer, Friedrich, *Die Kirche Äthiopiens: eine Bestandsaufnahme* (Berlin: Walter de Gruyter, 1971)

Kaplan, Steven, *The monastic holy man and the christianization of early Solomonic Ethiopia* [Studien zur Kulturkunde 73] (Wiesbaden: Franz Steiner Verlag, 1984)

Lusini, Gianfrancesco, *Studi sul monachesimo eustaziano (secoli XIV–XV)* (Naples: Istituto universitario orientale, 1993)

Marcus, Harold, *The life and times of Menelik II: Ethiopia 1844–1913* (Oxford: Clarendon Press, 1975)

Haile Sellassie I: the formative years, 1892–1936 (Berkeley: University of California Press, 1987)

Mario da Abiy-Addi', *La dottrina della chiesa etiopica dissidente sull'Unione Ipostatica* [OCA 147] (Rome: Pontificio istituto orientale, 1956)

Martínez, Andreu, 'Paul and the other: the Portuguese debate on the circumcision of the Ethiopians', in *Ethiopia and the missions* [q.v. above]

Merid W. Aregay, 'The legacy of Jesuit missionary activities in Ethiopia', in *Missionary factor in Ethiopia*, ed. Getatchew Haile, A. Lande and S. Rubenson [Studien zur interkulturellen Geschichte des Christentums 110] (Frankfurt-am-Main and New York: P. Lang, 1998), 31–56

Mohammed Hassen, *The Oromo of Ethiopia: a history, 1570–1860* (Cambridge: Cambridge University Press, 1990)

Mosley, Leonard, *Haile Selassie: the conquering lion* (London: Weidenfeld and Nicolson, 1964)

Munro-Hay, Stuart, *Aksum: an African civilization of late antiquity* (Edinburgh: Edinburgh University Press, 1991)

'Christianity. History of Christianity', in *Encyclopædia Æthiopica* [q.v.], I, 717–23

'Aksum. History of the town and empire', in *Encyclopædia Æthiopica* [q.v.], I, 173–9

Pennec, Hervé, *Des Jésuites au Royaume du Prêtre Jean (Éthiopie): stratégies, rencontres et tentatives d'implantation 1495–1633* (Paris: Fundação Calouste Gulbenkian, 2003)

Phillipson, D. W., *Ancient Ethiopia: Aksum, its antecedents and successors* (London: British Museum Press, 1998)

Rubenson, Sven, 'The Lion of Judah, Christian symbol and/or imperial title', *Journal of Ethiopian Studies* 3 (1965), 75–85

King of Kings: Tewodros of Ethiopia [Historical Studies 2] (Addis Ababa: Haile Sellassie I University, 1966)

The survival of Ethiopian independence (London: Heinemann Educational Books, 1976)

Samuel Wolde Yohannes and Denis Nosnitsin, 'Bäṣälotä Mika'él', in *Encyclopædia Æthiopica* [q.v.], I, 493–4

Schwab, Peter, *Haile Selassie I: Ethiopia's Lion of Judah* (Chicago: Nelson-Hall, 1979)

Sergew H. Sellassie, 'The period of reorganization', in *The Church of Ethiopia: a panorama of history and spiritual life* (Addis Ababa: Ethiopian Orthodox Church, 1970), 31–41

Ancient and medieval Ethiopian history to 1270 (Addis Ababa: United Printers, 1972)

Taddesse Tamrat, 'Some notes on the fifteenth century Stephanite 'Heresy' in the Ethiopian Church', *Rassegna di Studi Etiopici* 22 (1966), 103–15

Church and state in Ethiopia, 1270–1527 (Oxford: Clarendon Press, 1972)

Zanetti, Ugo, 'Christianity in the Ethiopian society', in *Encyclopædia Æthiopica* [q.v.], I, 723–8

Zewde Gabre-Sellassie, *Yohannes IV of Ethiopia: a political biography* (Oxford: Clarendon Press, 1975)

20 O'Mahony: Coptic Christianity in modern Egypt

Secondary works

Abu-Sahlieh, Sami Awad Albeeb, *Non-musulmans en pays d'Islam: cas de l'Égypte* (Fribourg CH: Éditions universitaires, 1979)

Behrens-Abouseif, Doris, *Die Kopten der ägyptischen Gesellschaft von der mitte des XIX Jahrhunderts bis 1923* (Freiburg im Breisgau: Klaus Schwarz Verlag, 1972)

'The political situation of the Copts, 1798–1923', in *Christians and Jews in the Ottoman Empire* [see general bibliography], II, 185–205

Bowie, Leland, 'The Copts, the *Wafd* and religious issues in Egyptian politics', *The Muslim World* 67 (1971), 106–26

Carter, Belinda L., *The Copts in Egyptian politics, 1918–1952* (London: Croom Helm, 1984)

Chaillot, Christine, 'Activités missionnaires de l'Église copte en Afrique', *Le Monde Copte* 20 (1992), 99–103

Doorn-Harder, Nelly van, *Contemporary Coptic nuns* (Columbus: University of South Carolina Press, 1995)

'Following the holy call: women in the Coptic Church', *Parole de l'Orient* 25 (2000), 733–50

Egger, Vernon, *A Fabian in Egypt: Salmah Musa and the rise of professional classes in Egypt, 1909–1939* (Lanham, MD: University Press of America, 1986)

Freig, Ernest Semaan, 'Statut personnel et autonomie des chrétiens en Égypte', *Proche-Orient Chrétien* 24 (1974), 251–95

El-Khawaga, Dina, 'L'affirmation d'une identité chrétienne copte: saisir un processus en cours', in *Itinéraires d'Égypte: mélanges offerts au père Maurice Martin, S. J.*, ed. C. Décobert (Cairo: Institut français d'archéologie orientale, 1992), 345–65

'Les services sociaux dispensés par l'Église copte: de l'autonomisation socio-économique à l'affirmation politique', in *Exiles et royaumes: les appartenances au monde arabo-musulman aujourd'hui*, ed. Gilles Kepel (Paris: Éditions FNSP, 1993)

Labib, Subhi, 'The Copts in Egyptian society and politics, 1882–1919', in *Islam, nationalism and radicalism in Egypt and the Sudan*, ed. G. Warburg and U. M. Kupferschmidt (New York: Praeger, 1983), 301–20

Lapidus, Ira A., 'The conversion of Egypt to Islam', *Israel Oriental Studies*, 2 (1972), 248–62

Little, Donald, 'Coptic converts to Islam during the Bahri Mamluks period', in *Conversion and continuity* [see general bibliography], 263–88

Martin, Annick, 'Aux origines de l'Église copte. L'implantation et le développement du christianisme en Égypte (Ier–IVe siècle)', *Revue des Études Anciennes* 83 (1981), 35–56

Martin, Maurice, 'The Coptic–Muslim conflict in Egypt: modernisation of society and religious transformation', *Ceman Reports* 1 (1972–73), 31–54

'Note sur la communauté copte entre 1650–1850', *Annales Islamologiques* 18 (1982), 194–202

'Le Delta chrétien à la fin du XIIIe siècle', *OCP* 63 (1997), 181–99

'The renewal in context: 1960–1990', in *Between the desert and the city* [see general bibliography], 15–27

Masson, Jacques, 'Trente ans de règne de Shenouda III, pape d'Alexandrie et de toute l'Afrique', *Proche-Orient Chrétien* 51 (2001), 317–32

Meinardus, Otto, 'The attitude of the Orthodox Copts towards the Islamic state from the 7th to the 12th century', *Ostkirchliche Studien* 13 (1963), 153–70

'The emergence of the laymen's movement in the Coptic Church: the *Majilis al- Milli*', *Publications de l'Institut d'Études Orientales de la Bibliothèque Patriarcale d'Alexandrie* 12 (1963), 75–82

'Election procedures for the patriarchal throne of Alexandria', *Ostkirchliche Studien* 16 (1967), 132–49, 304–24

Motzki, Harald, *Dimma und Égalité: die nichtmuslimischen Minderheiten Ägyptens in der zwischen Hälfte des 18. Jahrhunderts und die Expedition Bonapartes (1798–1801)* [Studien zum Minderheitenproblem im Islam 5; Bonner orientalistische Studien, n.s. 27] (Bonn: Selbstverlag des orientalistischen Seminars der Universität Bonn, 1979)

Pennington, J. D., 'The Copts in modern Egypt', *Middle Eastern Studies* 18 (1982), 131–57

Philip, Thomas, 'Copts and other minorities in the development of the Egyptian nation-state', in *Egypt from monarchy to republic: a reassessment of revolution and change*, ed. Shimon Shamir (Boulder, CO: Westview Press, 1995), 131–50

Rubenson, Samuel, 'Arabic sources for the theology of the early monastic movement in Egypt', *Parole de l'Orient* 16 (1990–91), 33–47

'Tradition and renewal in Coptic theology', in *Between the desert and the city* [see general bibliography], 35–51

Schlicht, Alfred, 'Les chrétiens en Égypte sous Mehemmet Ali', *Le Monde Copte* 6 (1979), 44–51

Sekaly, Samir, 'Coptic communal reform, 1860–1914', *Middle Eastern Studies* 6 (1970), 247–75

Sidarous, Fidel, 'Église copte et monde moderne', *Proche-Orient Chrétien* 30 (1980), 211–65

Stene, Nora, 'Into the lands of immigration', in *Between the desert and the city* [see general bibliography], 254–64

Suttner, Ernst C., 'Eritreas Eigenstaatlichkeit und die Kirchen', *Una Sancta* 49 (1994), 106–24

Tagher, Jacques, *Christians in Muslim Egypt: an historical study of the relations between Copts and Muslims from 640 to 1922* [Arbeiten zum spätantiken und koptischen Ägypten 10] (Altenberge: Oros, 1998)

Takhahaymanot, Ayele, 'The Egyptian metropolitan of the Ethiopian Church: a study on a chapter of history of the Ethiopian Church', *OCP* 56 (1988), 175–222

Tawfiq, Nevine Mounir, 'Le chrétien et la société dans la pensée du père Matta al-Maskin', *Proche-Orient Chrétien* 50 (2000), 80–104

Tyvaert, Serge, 'Matta el Maskine et le renouveau du monastère de saint Macaire', *Istina* 48 (2003), 160–79

Veilleux, Armand, *La liturgie dans le cénobitisme pachômien au quatrième siècle* [Studia Anselmiana 57] (Rome: IBC – Libreria Herder, 1968)

Instructions, letters, and other writings of St Pachomius and his disciples [Pachomian Koinonia 3; Cistercian Studies 47], 3 vols. (Kalamazoo, MI: Cistercian Publications, 1981)

Voigt, Rainer, 'Die erythräisch orthodoxe Kirche', *Oriens Christianus* 88 (1999), 187–92

Watson, John H., 'The Desert Fathers today: contemporary Coptic monasticism', in *Eastern Christianity* [see general bibliography], 112–39

Zanetti, U., 'Les chrétientés du Nil: basse et haute Égypte, Nubie, Éthiopie', in *The Christian East: its heritage, its institutions and its thought: a critical reflection*, ed. R. F. Taft [OCA 251] (Rome: Pontificio istituto orientale, 1996), 181–216

21   O'Mahony: Syriac Christianity in the modern Middle East

Secondary works

Atallah, Elias, *Le Synode libanais de 1736*: I, *Son influence sur la réstructuration de l'Église maronite*; II, *Traduction du texte original arabe* (Antelias and Paris: Centre d'études et de recherches orientales, 2002)

Baum, Wilhelm and Winkler, Dietmar W., *The Church of the East: a concise history* (London: RoutledgeCurzon, 2003)

Bcheiry, Iskandar, 'A list of the Syrian Orthodox patriarchs between 16th and 18th century', *Parole de l'Orient* 29 (2004), 211–61

Bello, P. S., *La congrégation de S. Hormidas et l'Église chaldéenne dans la première moitié du XIXe siècle* [OCA 122] (Rome: Pontificium institutum orientalium studiorum, 1939)

Brock, Sebastian, 'The "Nestorian" Church: a lamentable misnomer', *Bulletin of the John Rylands University Library of Manchester* 78 (1996), 23–36

'The Syriac churches and dialogue with the Catholic Church', *Heythrop Journal* 45 (2004), 435–50

'The Syriac churches in ecumenical dialogue on Christology,' in *Eastern Christianity* [see general bibliography], 44–65

'The Syrian Orthodox Church in the twentieth century', in *Christianity in the Middle East: studies in modern history, theology and politics*, ed. A. O'Mahony (London: Melisende, 2005)

Chalfoun, Pierre, 'L'Église syrienne catholique et son patriarche Michel Giavré sous le gouvernement ottoman au XVIIIe siècle', *Parole de l'Orient* 9 (1979–80), 205–38

'L'Église syrienne catholique en Syrie au XVIIIe siècle', *Parole de l'Orient* 13 (1986), 165–82

Chevalier, Michel, *Les Montagnards chrétiens du Hakkari et du Kurdistan septentrional* [Publications du département de géographie de l'Université Paris-Sorbonne 13] (Paris: Université Paris-Sorbonne, 1985)

Coakley, J. F., 'The Archbishop of Canterbury's Assyrian Mission Press: a bibliography', *Journal of Semitic Studies* 30 (1985), 35–73

The Church of the East and the Church of England (Oxford: Clarendon Press, 1992)

'The Church of the East since 1914', *Bulletin of the John Rylands University Library of Manchester* 78 (1996), 179–98

'The patriarchal list of the Church of the East', in *After Bardaisan: studies on continuity and change in Syriac Christianity in honour of Professor Han J. W. Drijvers*, ed. G. J. Reinink and A. C. Klugkist [Orientalia lovaniensia analecta 89] (Leuven: Peeters, 1999), 65–83

'Mar Elia Aboona and the history of the East Syriac patriarchate', *Oriens Christianus* 85 (2001), 119–38

'Bishops of the Church of the East, 1861–1918', *Harp* 15 (2002), 197–204

Douaihy, H., *Un théologien maronite: Ibn Al-Qila'i, évêque et moine franciscain* (Kaslik: Bibliothèque de l'Université Saint-Esprit de Kaslik, 1993)

Dupuy, Bernard, 'L'Église syrienne d'Antioche des origines à aujourd'hui', *Istina* 35 (1990), 171–88

'Essai d'histoire de l'Église "assyrienne"', *Istina* 34 (1990), 159–76

'Aux origines de l'Église syrienne-orthodoxe de l'Inde', *Istina* 36 (1991), 53–61

Habbi, Joseph, 'Signification de l'Union chaldéenne de Mar Sulaqa avec Rome en 1553', *L'Orient Syrien* 9 (1966), 99–132, 199–230

'L'unification de la hiérarchie chaldéenne dans la première moitié du XIX siècle', *Parole de l'Orient* 2 (1971), 121–43, 305–27

'Les Chaldéens et les Malabares au XIXe siècle', *Oriens Christianus* 64 (1980), 82–108

Hourani, Guita G. and Habchi, Antoine B., 'The Maronite eremitical tradition: a contemporary revival', *Heythrop Journal* 45 (2004), 451–65

Joseph, John, *The modern Assyrians of the Middle East: encounters with western Christian missions, archaeologists and colonial powers* (Leiden: Brill, 2000)

Lampart, Albert, *Ein Märtyrer der Union mit Rom: Joseph I (1681–1696), Patriarch der Chaldäer* (Einsiedeln: Benziger Verlag, 1966)

Le Coz, Raymond, *Histoire de l'Église d'Orient: chrétiens d'Irak, d'Iran et de Turquie* (Paris: Éditions du Cerf, 1995)

Leeuwen, Richard van, *Notables and clergy in Mount Lebanon: the Khazin Sheikhs and the Maronite Church (1736–1840)* (Leiden: Brill, 1994)

'The control of space and communal leadership: Maronite monasteries in Mount Lebanon', *Revue des Mondes Musulmans et de la Méditerranée* 79–80 (1996), 183–99

'The crusades and Maronite historiography', in *East and West in the Crusader States*, ed. K. Ciggaar, A. Davis and H. Teule (Louvain: Peeters, 1996), 51–62

Levi della Vida, Giorgio, *Documenti intorno alle relazioni delle chiese orientali con la S. Sede durante il pontificato di Gregorio XIII* [Studi e testi 143] (Vatican: Biblioteca apostolica vaticana, 1948)

Makhlouf, Avril M., 'Hindiyye Anne 'Ajeymi in her ecclesiastical and political situation', *Parole de l'Orient* 16 (1990–91), 279–87

'Spirituality between East and West Christendom: the Maronite mystic Hindiyya Anne 'Ajaymi', in *Eastern Christianity* [see general bibliography], 269–95

Merten, K., *Die syrisch-orthodoxen Christen in der Türkei und in Deutschland* [Studien zur orientalische Kirchengeschichte 3] (Hamburg: LIT, 1997)

Mouawad, Ray Jabre, 'The Kurds and their Christian neighbours: the case of the Syrian Orthodox', *Parole de l'Orient* 17 (1992), 127–42

O'Mahony, Anthony, 'Christianity in modern Iraq', *International Journal for the Study of the Christian Church* 4 (2004), 121–42

'The Chaldean Catholic Church: the politics of church–state relations in modern Iraq', *Heythrop Journal* 45 (2004), 435–50

'Eastern Christianity in modern Iraq', in *Eastern Christianity* [see general bibliography], 11–43

Raphael, Pierre, *Le rôle du Collège maronite romain dans l'orientalisme aux XVIIe et XVIIIe siècles* (Beirut: Université St-Joseph de Beyrouth, 1950)

Rhétoré, Jacques, *Les chrétiens aux bêtes: souvenirs de la guerre sainte proclamée par les Turcs contre les chrétiens en 1915*, ed. Joseph Alichoran (Paris: Éditions du Cerf, 2004)

Rouhana, Paul, 'Histoire du synode libanais de 1736', *Parole de l'Orient* 13 (1986), 111–64

'Identité ecclésiale maronite dès origines à la veille du Synode libanais', *Parole de l'Orient* 15 (1988–89), 215–60

Tabor, Sarkis, 'Les relations de l'Église maronite avec Rome au XVIIe siècle', *Parole de l'Orient* 9 (1978–80), 255–75

Taylor, William, 'Antioch and Canterbury: the Syrian Orthodox Church and the Church of England – a study in ecumenical relations in the early twentieth century', in *Christianity in the Middle East: studies in modern history, theology and politics*, ed. A. O'Mahony (London: Melisende, 2005)

Yacoub, Joseph, 'La question assyro-chaldéenne, les puissances européennes et la Société des Nations', *Guerres Mondiales et Conflits Contemporains* 38 (1988), 104–20

Babylone chrétienne: géopolitique de l'Église de Mésopotamie (Paris: Desclée de Brouwer, 1996)

Smyth, M., 'Une avancée œcuménique et liturgique. La note romaine concernat l'Anaphore d'Addaï et Mari', *La Maison-Dieu* 233 (2003), 137–54

Vanhoomissen, Guy, 'Une messe sans paroles de consecration? À propos de la validité de l'anaphore d'Addaï et Mari', *Nouvelle Revue Théologique* 127 (2005), 36–46

Wehbé, Louis, 'The Maronites of the Holy Land: a historical overview', in *Eastern Christianity* [see general bibliography], 431–51

Winkler, Dietmar W., 'Miaphysitism: a new term for use in the history of dogma and ecumenical theology', *Harp* 10 (1997), 33–40

   'The current theological dialogue with the Assyrian Church of the East', in *Symposium Syriacum VII* [OCA 256] (Rome: Pontificio istituto orientale, 1998), 158–73

   Ostsyrisches Christentum: Untersuchungen zu Christologie, Ekklesiologie, und zu den ökumenischen Beziehungen der assyrischen Kirche des Ostens [Studien zur orientalischen Kirchengeschichte 26] (Münster: LIT Verlag, 2003)

Zaide, Ignace, 'L'Église syrienne', *DTC* 14, cols. 3018–88

General bibliography to Part IV: The modern world (chapters 22–24)

Afonsky, Bishop Gregory, *A history of the Orthodox Church in America 1917–1982* (Kodiak, AK: St Herman's Theological Seminary Press, 1984)

Alexander, Stella, *Church and state in Yugoslavia since 1945* (Cambridge: Cambridge University Press, 1979)

Anastasios (Yannoulatos), archbishop of Tirana and all Albania, *Facing the world: Orthodox Christian essays on global concerns* (Crestwood, NY: St Vladimir's Seminary Press, 2003)

Beeson, Trevor, *Discretion and valour*, revised edition (London: Collins, 1982)

Behr-Sigel, E. and Ware, K. *The ordination of women in the Orthodox Church* [Risk Books Series 92] (Geneva: WCC Publications, 2000)

Binns, J., *An introduction to the Christian Orthodox churches* (Cambridge: Cambridge University Press, 2002)

Bourdeaux, Michael, *Opium of the people: the Christian religion in the USSR* (London: Faber and Faber, 1965)

   Religious ferment in Russia: Protestant opposition to Soviet religious policy (London: Macmillan, 1968)

   Patriarch and prophets: persecution of the Russian Orthodox Church today (London: Macmillan, 1969)

   Risen indeed: lessons in faith from the USSR (London: Darton, Longman and Todd, 1983)

   Gorbachev, Glasnost and the Gospel (Sevenoaks: Hodder and Stoughton, 1990)

Bourdeaux, M. and Filatov, S., *Sovremennaia religioznaia zhizn' Rossii*, 4 vols. (Moscow: Logos, 2002–2006)

A Bulgakov anthology, ed. J. Pain and N. Zernov (London: SPCK, 1976)

Chaillot, C. and Belopopsky, A., *Towards unity: the theological dialogue between the Orthodox church and the Oriental churches* (Geneva: Inter-Orthodox Dialogue, 1998)

Clement, O., *Conversations with Ecumenical Patriarch Bartholomew I* (Crestwood, NY: St Vladimir's Seminary Press, 1997)

Ellis, Jane, *The Russian Orthodox Church: a contemporary history* (London and Sydney: Croom Helm, 1986)

Fletcher, W. C., *A study in survival: the Church in Russia 1927–1943* (London: SPCK, 1965)

Florovsky, G., *The collected works*, 14 vols. (Belmont: Nordland Publishing Co., 1972–87)

Forest, Jim, *The resurrection of the Church in Albania: voices of Orthodox Christians* (Geneva: WCC Publications, 2002)

Hackel, Sergei, *A pearl of great price: the life of Mother Maria Skobstova, 1891–1945*, revised edition (London: Darton, Longman and Todd, 1982)

    The Orthodox Church, revised edition (Witney: St Stephen's Press, 1994)

Hassan, S. S., *Christians versus Muslims in modern Egypt: the century-long struggle for Coptic equality* (Oxford: Oxford University Press, 2003)

Kniazeff, Alexis, *L'Institut Saint-Serge: de l'Académie d'autrefois au rayonnement d'aujourd'hui* (Paris: Éditions Beauchesne, 1974)

Kolarz, Walter, *Religion in the Soviet Union* (London: St Martin's Press, 1961)

Kyrlezhev, A., 'Problems of church order in contemporary Orthodoxy', *Sourozh* 95 (Feb. 2004), 1–21

Light through the curtain, ed. Philip Walters and Jane Balengarth (Tring: Lion Publishing, 1985)

Lossky, Vladimir, *The mystical theology of the Eastern Church* (Cambridge and London: J. Clarke & Co. Ltd, 1957)

Mitrofanov, Georgii, *Istoriia russkoi pravoslavnoi tserkvi 1900–1927* (St Petersburg: Satis, 2002)

Nichols, Aidan, *Theology in the Russian diaspora: church, fathers, eucharist in Nikolai Afanas'ev, 1893–1966* (Cambridge: Cambridge University Press, 1989)

Philokalia, trans. G. E. H. Palmer, P. Sherrard and K. Ware, 4 vols. (London: Faber and Faber, 1979–95)

Popescu, Alexandru, *Petre Țuțea: between sacrifice and suicide* (Aldershot: Ashgate, 2004)

Pospielovsky, Dimitry, *The Russian Church under the Soviet regime, 1917–1982* (Crestwood, NY: St Vladimir's Seminary Press, 1984)

Proselytism and Orthodoxy in Russia: the new war for souls, ed. John Witte Jr. and Michael Bourdeaux (Maryknoll, NY: Orbis Books, 1999)

Put' moei zhizni: vospominaniia Mitropolita Evlogiia, izlozhennye po ego rasskazam T. Manukhinoi (Paris: YMCA-Press, 1947)

Schmemann, Alexander, *An introduction to liturgical theology* (London and Bangor, Maine: American Orthodox Press, 1966)

    For the life of the world: sacraments and orthodoxy (Crestwood, NY: St Vladimir's Seminary Press, 1973)

    The Journals of Father Alexander Schmemann 1978–1983 (Crestwood, NY: St Vladimir's Seminary Press, 2000)

Shevzov, V., *Russian Orthodoxy on the eve of the Revolution* (Oxford: Oxford University Press, 2004)

Shkarovskii, M. V., *Russkaia pravoslavnaia tserkov' pri Staline i Khrushcheve (gosudarstvenno-tserkovnye otnosheniia v SSSR v 1939–1964 godakh)* (Moscow: Izdatel'stvo krutitskogo patriarshego podvor'ia, 1999)

    Politika Tret'ego reikha po otnosheniiu k russkoi pravoslavnoi tserkvi v svete arkhivnykh materialov 1935–1945 godov (Sbornik dokumentov) (Moscow: Izdatel'stvo krutitskogo patriarshego podvor'ia, 2003)

Speake, G., *Mount Athos, renewal in Paradise* (New Haven and London: Yale University Press, 2002)

Struve, Nikita, *Christians in contemporary Russia* (London: Harvill Press, 1967)

    Soixante-dix ans d'émigration russe 1919–1989 (Paris: Fayard, 1996)

Surrency, S., *The quest for Orthodox unity in America* (New York: Saints Boris and Gleb Press, 1973)

The Unknown Homeland, trans. Marite Sapiets (Oxford: A. R. Mowbray, 1978)

Walker, A. and Carras, C., *Living Orthodoxy in the modern world* (London: SPCK, 1996)

Ware, K. *Collected Works*, 1 *The inner kingdom*, (Crestwood, NY: St Vladimir's Seminary Press, 2001)

    'Orthodox theology in the new millennium: what is the most important question?' *Sobornost* 26.2 (2004), 7–23

The Way of a Pilgrim, trans. R. M. French (London: SPCK, 1954)

Wybrew, H., *The Orthodox Liturgy* (London: SPCK, 1989)

Yannaras, C., *Philosophie sans rupture* (Geneva: Labor et Fides, 1986)

Zernov, N., *Russkie pisateli emigratsii: biograficheskie svedeniia i bibliografiia ikh knig po bogosloviiu, religioznoi filosofii, tserkovnoi istorii i pravoslavnoi kulture* (Boston, MA: G. K. Hall, 1973)

    The Russian religious renaissance of the twentieth century (London: Darton, Longman and Todd, 1963)

Index